THE LITERATURE
OF RENAISSANCE ENGLAND

THE OXFORD ANTHOLOGY OF ENGLISH LITERATURE
General Editors: Frank Kermode and John Hollander

Medieval English Literature
J. B. TRAPP, Librarian, Warburg Institute, London

The Literature of Renaissance England
JOHN HOLLANDER, Hunter College;
and FRANK KERMODE, University College London

The Restoration and the Eighteenth Century
MARTIN PRICE, Yale University

Romantic Poetry and Prose
HAROLD BLOOM, Yale University;
and LIONEL TRILLING, Columbia University

Victorian Prose and Poetry
LIONEL TRILLING and HAROLD BLOOM

Modern British Literature
FRANK KERMODE and JOHN HOLLANDER

The Literature of Renaissance England

JOHN HOLLANDER
Hunter College

FRANK KERMODE
University College London

New York OXFORD UNIVERSITY PRESS
London Toronto

Selections from the following works were made possible by the kind permission of their respective publishers and representatives:

An Anthology of Old English Poetry, translated by Charles W. Kennedy, copyright © 1960 by Oxford University Press, Inc.; reprinted by permission.

Beowulf: The Oldest English Epic, translated by Charles W. Kennedy, copyright 1940 by Oxford University Press, Inc.; renewed 1968 by Charles W. Kennedy; reprinted by permission.

Sir Gawain and the Green Knight, translated by Brian Stone, copyright © 1959, 1964, 1973 by Brian Stone; reprinted by permission of Penguin Books Ltd.

The Oxford Book of Ballads, edited by James Kinsley, copyright © 1969 by Oxford University Press; reprinted by permission of The Clarendon Press, Oxford.

The Romance of the Rose, translated by F. S. Ellis, reprinted by permission of J. M. Dent & Sons Ltd.

General Editors' Preface

The purpose of the Oxford Anthology is to provide students with a selective canon of the entire range of English Literature from the beginnings to recent times, with introductory matter and authoritative annotation. Its method is historical, in the broadest sense, and its arrangement, commentary, and notes, both analytic and contextual, have benefited not only from the teaching experience of the several editors, but from a study of the virtues and shortcomings of comparable works. A primary aim has been to avoid the insulation of any one section from the influence of others, and more. positively, to allow both student and instructor to come to terms with the manner in which English literature has generated its own history. This aim has been accomplished in several ways.

First, a reorganization of chronological phases has allowed the Tudor and Stuart periods to be unified under the broad heading of the English Renaissance, with two editors collaborating over the whole extended period. Similarly, the nineteenth century has two editors, one for the poetry of the whole period, and one for the prose. This arrangement seemed appropriate in every way, especially since neither of these scholars could be called a narrow specialist in "Romantic" or "Victorian," as these terms are used in semester- or course-labels.

Every contributing editor has worked and taught in at least one period or field outside the one for which he is, in this anthology, principally responsible, and none has ever allowed specialization to reduce his broader commitment to humane studies more largely considered. Thus we were able to plan a work which called for an unusual degree of cross reference and collaboration. During a crucial phase in the preparation of the text, the editors held daily discussions of their work for a period of months. By selection, allusion, comparison, by direction and indirection, we contrived to preserve continuity between epochs, and to illuminate its character. At the same time, the close co-operation of the various editors has precluded the possibility of common surrender to any single dominating literary theory; and the teacher need have no fear that he must prepare to do battle with some critical Hydra showing a head on every page.

The method of selecting text was consistent with these principles. In the eighteenth- and nineteenth-century sections it was our general policy to exclude the novel, for obvious reasons of length; but in the twentieth, where short fiction becomes more prominent and more central, we have included entire works of fiction, or clearly defined parts of them—for example, *Heart of Darkness,* "The Dead," the "Nausicaa" episode of *Ulysses,* and *St. Mawr.* On the other hand we were persuaded, after much reflection, that a different principle must apply in the cases of Spenser and Milton, where we waived the requirement of completeness. To have given the whole of one book—say, the First of *The Faerie Queene*—would have been a solution as easy as it is, no doubt, defensible; but it is asking a great deal of students to see that portion of the poem as an epitome of the rest, which is often so delightfully different; and we decided that we must provide selections from the whole poem, with linking commentary. We did the same for *Paradise Lost* though without abandoning the practice of providing complete texts when this was both possible and desirable; for example, *Comus* is reprinted entire, and so is a lesser-known but still very important masque, Jonson's *Pleasure Reconciled to Virtue,* which is interesting not only in relation to *Comus* but as an illustration of the part poetry can play in political spectacle and—more generally—in the focusing of the moral vision. Minor texts have been chosen for their exemplary force and their beauty, as well as to embody thematic concerns. If the teacher wishes, he or she may work, both within and across periods, with recurrent patterns as large as the conception of the Earthly Paradise, or with sub-genres as small but as fascinating as the Mad Song. It will also be evident from certain patterns of selection—*The Tempest* as the Shakesperean play, the very large amount of Blake, the emphasis given to D. H. Lawrence's poems as well as his fiction—that a genuinely modern taste, rather than an eager modishness, has helped to shape our presentation of the historical canon. It is also hoped that the unusually generous sampling of material in certain sections—notably the Renaissance, eighteenth century, and the Romantics—will allow the teacher to use secondary or minor works, if he so chooses, to highlight these newer concerns or to fill in contextual background.

As for the annotations, the editors have never been afraid to be lively or even speculative. They have consistently tried to avoid usurping the teacher's role, as providing standard or definitive readings might do. On the other hand, the commentary goes beyond merely providing a lowest common denominator of information by suggesting interpretive directions and levels along which the teacher is free to move or not; and of course he always has the freedom to disagree. The editors have been neither prudish nor portentous in their tone, nor have they sought—in the interests of some superficial consistency, but with leaden effect—to efface their personal styles.

Texts have all been based on the best modern editions, which happen quite often to be published by the Oxford University Press. Spelling and punctuation have been modernized throughout, save in three instances: portions of the medieval period, and the texts of Spenser and Blake, two poets whose spelling and punctuation are so far from idiosyncrasies to be silently normalized that they constitute attempts to refashion poetic language. In the medieval section, modern verse translations of *Beowulf* (by C. W. Kennedy) and of *Gawain* (by Brian Stone) have been adopted. Glossaries of literary and historical terms in all periods have been provided, sometimes keyed to the annotations, sometimes supplementing the larger headnotes. These, it will be noticed, seek to illuminate the immediate contexts of the literature of a period rather than to provide a dense précis of its social, political, and economic history. Similarly, the reading lists at the end of each volume are not exhaustive bibliographies; in the happy instance where a teacher finds an extensive bibliography advisable, he or she will want to supply one.

A word about the pictures. They are not to be thought of simply as illustrations, and certainly not as mere decorations, but rather as part of the anthologized material, like the musical examples and the special sections (such as the one on Ovidian mythology in the Renaissance and on the Urban Scene in the eighteenth century). Throughout, the reader is introduced to the relations between poem as speaking picture, and picture as mute poem. Aside from contextual and anecdotal illustration, of which there is indeed a good deal, the pictorial examples allow teachers, or students on their own, to explore some of the interrelations of texts and the visual arts in all periods, whether exemplified in Renaissance emblems or in contemporary illustrations of Victorian poems.

Finally, an inevitable inadequate word of acknowledgment. To the English Department of Dartmouth College the editors are deeply indebted for having so generously and hospitably provided a place in which to work together for a sustained period. The staff of the Dartmouth College Library was extraordinarily helpful and attentive.

All of the editors would like to extend a note of gratitude to the many academics throughout the United States who willingly made suggestions as to what should be included as well as excluded. A special note of thanks to Jim Cox of Dartmouth College and Paul Dolan of the State University of New York at Stony Brook for their challenging and always helpful comments.

And finally to the entire staff of the New York branch of the Oxford University Press who have done more than could be humanly expected in connection with the planning and execution of this book. We would especially like to thank our editor John Wright, as well as Leona Capeless and her staff, Mary Ellen Evans, Patricia Cristol, Joyce Berry, Deborah Zwecher, and Jean Shapiro. An unusual but very deserved note of thanks to the Production people, especially Gerard S. Case and Leslie Phillips and to the designer, Frederick Schneider, whose excellent work speaks for itself.

New York   Frank Kermode
September 1972   John Hollander

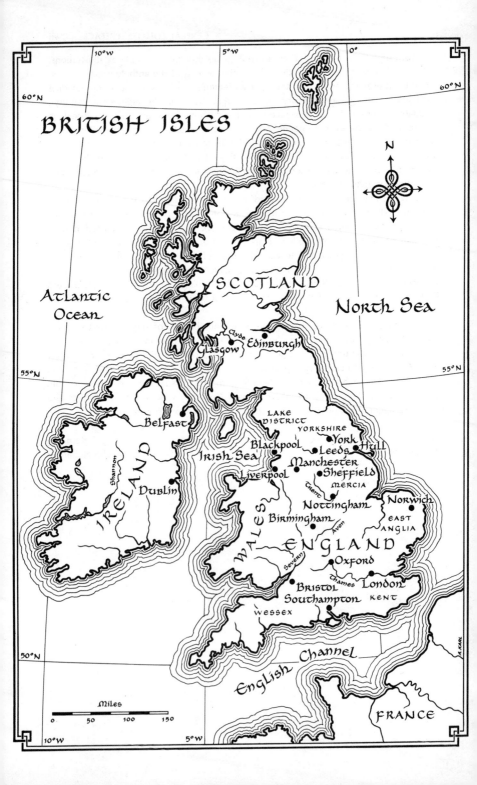

Contents

* An asterisk indicates that a work does not appear in its entirety.

The Development of Prose

THE LITERATURE
OF RENAISSANCE ENGLAND

The Renaissance

RENAISSANCE AND RENASCENCES

As a historical term, the "Renaissance" can mean a good many things, most of them having to do with what was happening to Europe half a millennium ago. Used purely to refer to a rebirth of interest in, and knowledge of, some of the ideas and discursive forms of classical antiquity which had been lost for a thousand years, it could, of course, be pushed back even farther. Some scholars have found in the design of some of the great Gothic architecture of the twelfth century the operation of principles of proportion and numerical order which we usually associate with the kind of neo-classical architecture called "humanist." An economic historian might be far more excited about what was happening to the production of woolen cloth in the fourteenth century than about some of the changes two centuries later in the ritualized behavior —religious, political, and linguistic—of the people who used and were enriched by that cloth.

The invention (1454) of movable-block printing (for texts, as distinguished from carved woodcuts for pictures, which had come earlier) and the discovery (1492) of the New World across the western oceans were both crucial events in the history of the shaking-loose of European culture from the political and conceptual structures in which it had lived for so long. And yet, artists and thinkers in fourteenth- and early fifteenth-century Italy were taking leaps of the eye, hand, and mind which would remain unexcelled in other realms of human activity for nearly a hundred years. The relation between discovery and invention is always a complex one, rather like a matter of deciding on the precedence of chicken over egg: the discovery of certain properties of the ground lens leads to the invention of a telescope which leads to the discovery of Jupiter's moons, but the chain has no beginning and never ends. It is even harder to trace the links between the social and technological events during the period from 1450 to 1650, say, and the aspects of the human imagination which, if they are being born again, are appearing in a new form. Wherever one tries to pin down the life-span of the period—in Italy, earlier; in Northern Europe, later—whether in painting, sculpture, and architecture, or in music, or in the technologies of exploration and economic expansion, it will begin and end differently. But there is a trace of common self-awareness in the name itself, for the general rebirth which, by consensus, all historians of all fields continue, when talking generally, to use.

The word "Renaissance" was probably employed in this context for the first time by Giorgio Vasari (1511–74), the Italian painter and architect who is today best known for his *Lives of the Most Excellent Painters, Sculptors and Architects* (1568), in a passage in which he was arguing for the modern view, which was not necessarily that of the early Renaissance, that an artist is not a mere handicraftsman, but a learned and imaginative figure—a "creator" in our sense, rather than a "maker." The community of artists could feel this sense of itself, and its recent history (Vasari saw the predecessor of the painting of his age in Giotto, as the Elizabethan writers in England would, as we shall see, look back to Chaucer). A general sense, of newness and freshness, all over Europe and in every sphere of activity, however, is the literary dream of the nineteenth century. The unique problem of England's Renaissance with respect to the Continent is a result of her twofold alienation from sources of influence during the fifteenth century: she was Northern and she was insular. England had no "quattrocento" like Italy's, and no local traditions in the arts like those of the very great painters of Flanders in the fifteenth century, or like the Flemish musicians who were so to influence the Italian Renaissance composers. John Dunstable, who died in 1453, was the last English practitioner of the arts to have much of an impact on the Continent for more than a century and a half. Scotland, which in the fifteenth century had a much more exciting literary culture than England, maintained very close ties with France—Mary, Queen of Scots (1542–87) was half-French, and married to the Dauphin of France—and in a particular way was thereby less insular. Scotland's intellectual traditions, as manifested, for example, in its approach to the Reformation, and in its subsequent educational system, were quite different from England's.

The literary and intellectual culture of England, during a period which overlapped only at the beginning what is called the Renaissance in Italy, was a complex product of the energies and talents of individual men and of the institutions, conventions, and styles which were open to them as instruments for those energies. To try to understand Shakespeare's genius as a function of a historical moment seems hopeless; to try to understand why, from 1590 to around 1610, the genius of a middle-class, self-educated man from Warwickshire might have flowered in the theater, to such a degree that some of the greatest wisdom of his age might be embodied in popular plays, is not. More than in any other period in recent history, the sixteenth and seventeenth centuries represent the use of what would look to us like imprisoning conventions—linguistic and intellectual patterns—in order to escape from other conventions which had preceded their use, and for so long a time that they resembled Nature, that they were all there was. The radical, humanistic notion of *originality* involved going back to true sources, to origins (today we would call this being "derivative," but our view reflects an intervening cultural phase of Romantic elevation of the notion of the self). In contemplating this long historical moment, then, we must try to understand the ways in which these new conventions—of everything from verse forms and rhyme schemes to ways of making sense out of something shown one—are used and transformed by major talents, and are beautifully exemplified by minor ones. (It is always instructive to learn how something which one truly admires in a great writer is merely a phrase, a turn, a strategy, an element of style, which he shares with even his tedious contemporaries, and that what we have admired is simply what defines our distance from his historical period.) All these conventions would themselves have arisen by adaptation or outright borrowing of ancient, or contemporary European, ones. It may seem strange that in the evolution of a great literary culture an important part might be played by the struggle, not totally successful, of a courtier and diplomat to translate and paraphrase some Italian love poems written two hundred years before. But Sir Thomas Wyatt's getting Petrarch's *Rime* (or sonnets) into English was just the kind of act which, unlike the action of vast, impersonal forces massively taking place over decades, has observable, and traceable, consequences for the individual human imagination.

By the English Renaissance, historians of literature and culture mean the period from about 1509 to 1660, the reign of the Tudor Henry VIII and his children and the first two Stuarts, and the revolutionary government of the Commonwealth which was brought about by troubles boiling up in the reigns of the Stuarts. Culturally speaking, there is a great deal of continuity in English life after the restoration of Charles II to the throne until the end of the century, though the lives and careers of individual writers and thinkers stretch across its chronological boundaries. Literary history is always concerned with self-consciousness, or at least with self-awareness; what an age thinks of itself defines it as an age, and the Restoration, with its Frenchified court fashions, its irreversibly altered Parliament, its Royal Society, and its integration of the lives of Court and Town (London) is really a part of the Europe of the Enlightenment. But there are other continuities, like the one between the convictions of the earliest Tudor humanists, Bacon's visions of the Institution of Reason in the middle of that period, and Milton's final and total presentation of the humanist program in the broadest sense. (This might be called attempting to transform the future of man by refocusing the light of his past.) It is such traditions, too, which help to shape this century and a half of both evolution and violent change.

HUMANISM

One of the important things to remember about the sixteenth century in England is that the New Learning, the interest in and access to classical culture, did not become fully associated with courtly life and patronage until late in the period of Elizabeth's reign. In Italy there were not only many local princes and wealthy families, as in Florence, or corporate municipalities, like Venice, but also the princes of the church in Rome to encourage the arts of splendor and, for a long while, of enlightenment. In England there was a court intent on its international and religious politics, for some time involved in a kind of cold war with Spain; and although it did support some humanistic scholarship, it was unable to bring together the arts and learning in anything like European fashion until the last years of Elizabeth's reign. The great Italian families had subsidized scholarship as well as pageantry; in England the early classical learning was the work and dream of the universities and of schoolmasters.

The rise of humanism can itself certainly be pushed back farther into history. Petrarch's Laureate Oration in 1341 was a dramatic instance in the career of that great precursor not only of Renaissance lyric poetry and its personal muses but also of classical scholarship. (Petrarch himself discovered texts of Cicero and Quintilian, the Roman rhetorician who became so important for the shape of written style later on.) But when the Dutch scholar Desiderius Erasmus (1466–1536), as he called himself—in a made-up Greek-Latin name both halves of which meant "lovable"—came to England, first to Oxford and then, later, to Cambridge in 1509, the new approach to classical learning that had emerged in Europe was only beginning to take hold. The use of Cicero's Latin rather than that of the medieval church, the study of Greek and even of Hebrew, the publication, editing, commentary upon, and appreciation of texts by classical authors became part of a vast institution for shifting the grounds of authority in human affairs. In the intellectual sphere this consisted of a turning from the rigid logical and rhetorical systems of scholasticism (see Glossary), in their day instruments of light, but by the fifteenth century more like walls. The use of classical models for prose style and for kinds of verse was far more than merely a stylistic change. They were assertions of the learned mind's unchallengeable right to make its own contract with classical learning, unmediated by the systems of medieval scholasticism.

THE REFORMATION

If some humanist scholars like Erasmus and, in England, Sir Thomas More, could remain in the church, there were others who could not. All across sixteenth-century Europe, we can observe a parallel to the humanist program in the various movements to substitute for the authority of the Roman Catholic Church a previously unthinkable notion of Christianity, of civilization, as something not necessarily embodied therein. In 1517, Martin Luther tacked his ninety-five theses to the door of his church in Wittenberg. In 1532, John Calvin's *Institutes of the Christian Religion* was published in Switzerland. In 1535, Henry VIII was able to designate himself the Supreme Head of the Church of England. In 1558, the Scottish reformer John Knox returned to his native country from Geneva, and the Calvinist character of the church in Scotland was firmly established; in the North, the Highlanders remained Roman Catholic, but else-where the "kirk" (as it is called in Scots) was Presbyterian. The Church of England itself, it must be remembered, was still by no means truly reformed. By confiscating the wealth of the monasteries Henry VIII dotted the English countryside with ruins, but it was only at the end of his reign that he began to build upon them, and over the bones of men like Sir Thomas More, who, as Lord Chancellor, refused to acknowledge, in place of the papal authority, a king who had broken with it over a divorce refused. In 1539 the Great Bible was in use in churches, but it was not until the brief reign of his son Edward VI (from 1547 to 1553) that the famous English Prayer Book, over which so much fighting would be done in less than a hundred years, was made available for a purely English liturgy. The Book of Common Prayer was published in 1549; four years later the Articles of Faith made the English church a Protestant one beyond doubt. Mass had become a communion service, and worship and Scripture had been brought over into the vernacular.

Thomas Cranmer, the Archbishop of Canterbury under whom all this was happening, and who had allowed the burning of various sorts of deviationists—too papal in out-look, or too Protestant—was himself one of the victims of the next monarch's reign. Mary Tudor, Henry's daughter by Catharine of Aragon and wife of Philip II, was Roman Catholic, and until her sister Elizabeth's accession in 1558, a compensatory reaction raged. Catholicism and the influence of Spanish power were two fears that plagued England until the succeeding reign of James. Despite its own mode of ref-ormation, the English church still thought of itself as Catholic, and it was groups of reformers within it, whom we loosely designate as Puritan, who sought continuously to make it less so. They ranged from those who wanted to do away with bishops altogether, to those who merely wanted to stem the drift toward re-alliance with Rome which seemed to them to be a natural movement toward decay. Some of the more extreme of them fled en masse to Holland, which, since it had become independent of Spain, was a haven for religious refugees of all sorts. Others stayed behind, suffering various changes of fortune in the early decades of the seventeenth century. In general, it should be remembered that the English church was seeking throughout this period to maintain a kind of balance between two strong forces, Rome and the more thoroughgoing consequences of Geneva, home of Calvinism.

In 1603, James VI of Scotland became king of England (he was the great-grandson of Henry VII's daughter, Margaret). He had already planted some of the seeds of later discontent by introducing (in 1600) bishops into Scotland, much to the hatred of the Presbyterians there. Almost forty years later, his son Charles allowed his Puritan-persecuting Archbishop of Canterbury, William Laud, to try again to Anglicize the Scottish church, and precipitated the fighting known as the "Bishops' War" (1639). Charles's attempts to raise more money for its continuance led to the calling of the Long Parliament, which eventually beheaded both Archbishop Laud (1645) and the King (1649). Throughout the reigns of the first two Stuarts, the dangers of Rome and Spain were not a matter of universal national consciousness as they had been under Elizabeth, but when the Catholicism of Charles I's French wife, Henrietta Maria, helped to jeopardize national trust in him as Defender of the (English) Faith, Puritan factions in Parliament and Presbyterian ones in Scotland and England united for a while in maintaining the course and safety of the Reformation. For an absolutely committed mid-seventeenth-century Protestant like John Milton, the Reformation continued through the course of the Commonweath, and through the eventual conflicts between the powerful, official Presbyterian party (which had become for him the abrogator of freedom) and the more liberal congregationalist faction called the Independents. The Reformation must be seen as an institutional process which, after it had succeeded in establishing Protestant churches, continued, like a kind of permanent revolution, to unfold in the individual positions and visions of particular religious thinkers. Its primary movement, from the time of its beginning in the sixteenth century, was toward the *internalization* of institutions: individual conscience, rather than the structure of a church hierarchy to mediate between God and Man; an identification of Christ as the Light of the World with an inner light within men, and so forth. It was a process which continued later in the seventeenth and eighteenth centuries, in such manifestations as millenarian sects, the Quakers, and, later on, in the religious revival among a rising middle class, which eventually gave rise to Methodism within the Church of England itself.

It should also be briefly observed that the Roman church's own reaction to the rise of Protestantism, the Counter Reformation as it is called, produced a new approach to what Protestantism had isolated from other parts of life as *religion* (rather than the totality of spiritual life in its infusion of the material life, which marked the organic quality of medieval Christianity). The Council of Trent, which met sporadically between 1545 and 1563 to reformulate the doctrine of the Roman church, initiated this trend toward reform of some of the material abuses attacked by the early Protestants, as well as toward new modes of religiousness, including missionary work and more practical popular religious instruction—the Jesuits were instrumental in this. But English hopes that the Council would see the way to some kind of *via media* (or "middle way"), not unlike Richard Hooker's "Anglicanism," were disappointed, and in the end the Council sharpened the differences between the Roman and the Reformed churches. There was an English interest (because a Protestant one) in the Thirty Years' War in Germany (ended 1648), and at times an almost paranoid fear of the Jesuits; aside from these the Counter Reformation remained a curiosity of Continental faith.

A NEW IMAGE OF THE WORLD

Another revision of authority previously vested in an older order occurred in connection with the mixture of invention and discovery mentioned earlier. The explorations of the New World for purposes of economic development and, particularly in England's case, the undermining of Spanish colonial power in the West Indies by naval strength brought with them one kind of opening up. Another was in the exploration of the conceptual new world of the cosmos. The Ptolemaic cosmology which had prevailed since classic times was being gradually undermined, during the sixteenth and seventeenth centuries, by new discoveries which could not be accommodated to it as they previously had been (see Glossary: Astronomy and Astrology). Without cataloguing the scientific developments of the period under discussion, we may observe in one sequence of revisions of the older world picture some of the sorts of change which might affect the life of the mind for all men of thought. The Ptolemaic model of the universe corresponded to observed phenomena by positing transparent spheres of huge magnitude, moving concentrically about the earth, each carrying a heavenly body, or, the last but outside one, all the fixed stars which do not move in relation to each other. Circles and spheres were traditional symbols of perfection, and in order to maintain both the idea of a perfectly constructed universe and the actuality of what happened in the sky night after night, astronomers since classical times had been forced to adapt and change the model slightly; for example, they built so-called "epicycles," or circular reroutings, onto the circular path of the planets. But the basic idea of planned and patterned circularity was there. In the year of his death, the Polish astronomer Nicolaus Copernicus (1473–1543) published his treatise *On the Revolution of the Spheres,* which put the sun, not the earth, at the center of the model, but left the notion of circular paths of motion about it. This meant asserting that what "really" happened in the sky was not what "apparently" happened, but that a picture of reality with concentric circles on it, no matter how disturbing in its decentralization of the earth—and, by implication, of humanity—in the divine scheme, could still look orderly.

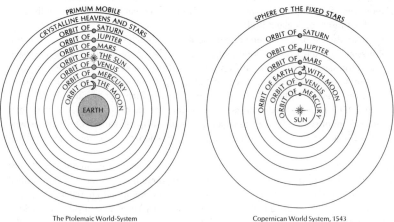

The Ptolemaic World-System   Copernican World System, 1543

Johannes Kepler (1571–1630) wrecked that order when he formulated his laws of planetary motion, published in 1609: the planets, he showed, moved in elliptical orbits, not circular ones, with the sun at one of the foci of the ellipse. But he showed a kind of beautiful regularity in their motion which to us, today, looks as mysteriously contrived as any nest of circles. The planets move more quickly when nearer the sun, more slowly when far away; but these changes in speed are so orderly that the planets, as he put it, sweep out "equal areas in equal times." That means merely this: if we take two points on the elliptical path that are, say, one planetary month apart, and then take two more at the other end of the orbit, at the "fast end" they will be farther apart than at the distant one. Now, if we draw lines from those points toward the sun, at one of the foci of the ellipse, we will get two pie-shaped wedges, one long and thinnish, the other shorter and fatter. But their areas will always be equal. Moreover, Kepler showed, the square of its periodic time at any point around its ellipse will be proportional to the cube of its mean distance from the sun.

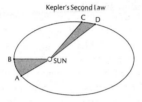

Kepler's Second Law

If the time taken to travel A-B and C-D is the same, then the two shaded bits, different in shape, will always be equal in area.

These are elegances of order which it takes a bit more than simple arithmetic to comprehend as orderly at all. But one more shift or dislocation of the idea of orderliness occurs during the seventeenth century which we might glance at. For Kepler, these were "laws," but if one could not show *why* they were true, then, no matter how carefully formulated, they might recede into the status of phenomena again. This is what finally happened. Galileo Galilei (1564–1642) discovered that the earth's gravitational pull on all objects could be mathematically described as an accelerating force (this is aside from the astronomical observations for which he was so famous—his perfecting of the refracting telescope led him to conclude that the moon shone by reflected light, that Jupiter had four satellites, that the Milky Way was the massed effect of countless stars, etc.). Sir Isaac Newton (1642–1727) would finally take a huge conceptual leap, and argue that the gravity which Galileo had described was *not* just a local peculiarity of the surface of the earth, but applied as a force acting between any two or more bodies, anywhere. Kepler's Second Law, then, could be shown to be an effect which would have to be true, given the gravitational situation of the sun and the planet in question. With such a notion, any connection between simple observation of what were called the "appearances," obvious to any reasonable man, and the proper explanation or mathematical model, was gone. By the end of the English Renaissance, science (or "natural philosophy" as it was called) had become a special sort of explanation, given in totally different sorts of language from moral, or metaphysical, or even psychological accounts.

Cosmology, banishing the older astrology, was, of course, not the only kind of

revision of the older picture of the world. Alchemy, with its highly symbolic interpretation of the realities behind natural processes, gave way to chemistry, whose
concerns had been mostly a by-product of the true, religious alchemical quest. The
inner structure of the human totality, with its humors and spirits which reflected in
their composition the basic, four-part grouping of elements in the universe, gave way
to specific biological answers to clearly defined questions. The whole program sketched
out in Francis Bacon's dream of methods for reaching truth (see Headnote to Bacon)
began to be, with the establishment of the Royal Society in 1660, an actuality.

THE INSTRUMENT OF PROSE

Just as the new science would need mathematical languages in which to express
complicated relationships, the far more general problem of human discourse required
a new sort of language as well. The humanist program had started with Latin, and the
Classics generally; it soon moved to a rebuilding of the vernacular. There are really
two phases to this development in the sixteenth century: the first established the
authority of antiquity, the second insisted that it could be fulfilled in the vernacular.
Schoolmasters like Richard Mulcaster (head of the Merchant Taylors' School and
teacher of Spenser) might have their boys play ball in Latin, and by the 1590's there
were still debates going on among literary critics about whether English poetry should
be written in classical meters or not, although Sir Philip Sidney had argued persuasively
in his *Defence of Poesie* that the only way for English poets to be truly like the
classical ones they so admired was by being themselves. The modes of eloquence
were, of course, prose and verse. It is hard for a twentieth-century reader, with his
built-in notion that prose is plain, universal, and ordinary and that verse is special,
ornate, and idiosyncratic, to understand how this was not true, really, until the end of
the seventeenth century. An ordinarily competent sonnet, for example, written as a
dedicatory poem to some friend's book on anything from logic to gardening, would
be truly anonymous in character—unless a considerable poet with a marked style
were to put it to such a purpose, those verses would constitute the equivalent of a
formal, common prose in our day and before. Any literate person might have learned
in school to compose verses in Latin and, later on, in Greek. To do so in English was
no indication of special poetic gifts.

The prose styles of the sixteenth and seventeenth centuries were in a state of
flux just because of the phases of the humanist learning mentioned above. The first
style taught for English prose was modeled on Cicero—elaborate, balanced, ornate,
with many dependent clauses and rounded periods. In one of its more affected and
personal styles, it developed into the so-called Euphuistic prose (see Headnote to
John Lyly) of the last decades of the sixteenth century. But in sermons, treatises, tracts,
and even translations of foreign authors, the so-called Senecan prose favored by Bacon,
a livelier, jumpier style involving short sentences and sudden turns and variations of
pace, began to replace it. The spoken language could not enter the written one to
shape and extend its resources as easily as one might think. There was no prose fiction
in our sense of the word, and even a picaresque romance of great brilliance and
linguistic power like Thomas Nashe's *The Unfortunate Traveller* (1594) is written in a
prose more highly patterned than most contemporary verse today. It is, indeed,
through the verse and occasional prose of the theater on the one hand, and in certain
kinds of song texts which contain more of the music of speech than they allow for

the addition of melody on the other, that the spoken word begins to inform the written one.

TRANSLATIONS; THE EXAMPLE OF MONTAIGNE

One of the ways in which the resources of the language could be augmented was a natural concomitant of decreasing insularity through translation of the classical and contemporary European authors who both might and might not be read in the original. The English Bible was a matter of necessity to the reform not only of liturgy but of the relation of even the simplest of men to God's word. Translations of secular authors served two purposes: in the case of, say, Sir Thomas North's very important translation of Plutarch's *Parallel Lives* (1579) from the Greek, to which fewer people would have access than to Latin. The fragments of the *Aeneid* done into verse by the Earl of Surrey (1517–47) were more than merely toying with a new verse form (the blank verse which he borrowed from the Italian), but a kind of act of commitment to a literary tradition that he and the other earlier Tudor writers were trying to join. Getting the great works of other languages into English meant also creating a canon, a basic body of almost *scriptural* secular works, which would have the same power and general reference as biblical texts. Arthur Golding's Ovid of 1567 (see *The Renaissance Ovid*) and George Chapman's Homer (*Iliad,* 1611; *Odyssey,* 1616) were verse translations of the first importance. But perhaps the most important piece of Elizabethan translation as far as the subsequent history of English prose was concerned, was the version by the linguistic scholar John Florio (c. 1553–1625) of the *Essays* of Montaigne.

Michel Eyquem de Montaigne (1533–92) was a scholar, lawyer, and skeptical philosopher who retired to his tower near Bordeaux to meditate and put together those commonplace books or scraps of quotations with an added commentary which eventually outgrew the quotations, and became his meditational trials, or essays into thought. His is the final blow struck against dogmatism, and he is the predecessor, writing from his book-lined study, not only of French philosophers of subsequent centuries but, in Florio's translation, of many English writers as well. Bacon knew him, and so did Burton, Shakespeare, Donne, Ralegh, Ben Jonson, and many others. His vision of the contemplative life, vastly different from that of medieval Christianity, saw a new kind of relation between man's mind and the thoughts of others, and he defined solitude in a new way:

> A man that is able may have wives, children, goods, and chiefly health, but not so tie himself unto them that his felicity depend on them. We should reserve a storehouse for ourselves, what need soever chance, altogether ours and wholly free, wherein we may hoard up and establish true liberty and principal retreat and solitariness, wherein we must go alone to ourselves to take our ordinary entertainment, and so privately that no acquaintance or communication of any strange thing may therein find place; there to discourse, to meditate and laugh, as without wife, without children and goods, without train or servants, that if by any occasion they be lost it seem not strange to us to pass it over. We have a mind moving and turning in itself; it may keep itself company; it hath wherewith to offend and defend, wherewith to receive and wherewith to give. . . . [*Of Solitude*]

This "storehouse" (*arrière-boutique*—"back of the shop," Montaigne calls it) becomes for humanist meditative writers more than merely a locale, a room, a place, but rather a whole region of the mind, a condition of relation to thought and nature. But perhaps one of the most famous and resonant examples of Montaigne's concept of what was in his phrase "the human condition" and its dignity is to be found in his famous essay "Of Cannibals," in which he broods over the meaning of civilization itself. In 1562 at Rouen he had met some natives of the New World, and in his essay of about 1580 he describes the condition of some of these inhabitants of the tropical Americas, and goes on to remark that "there is nothing in that nation that is either barbarous or savage, unless men call that barbarism which is not common to them." The whole following passage is of great interest and merit:

As indeed we have no other aim of truth and reason than the example and *Idea* of the opinions and customs of the country we live in. There is ever perfect religion, perfect policy,[1] perfect and complete use of all things. They are even savage, as we call those fruits wild which nature of herself and of her ordinary progress hath produced; whereas indeed they are those which ourselves have altered by our artificial devices and diverted from their common order, we should rather term savage. In those are the true and most profitable virtues and natural properties most lively and vigourous, which in these we have bastardised, applying them to the pleasure of our corrupted taste. And if, notwithstanding, in diverse fruits of those countries that were never tilled we shall find that in respect of ours they are most excellent and as delicate unto our taste, there is no reason art should gain the point of honour of our great and puissant[2] mother nature. We have so much by our inventions surcharged the beauties and riches of her works that we have altogether overchoked her. Yet, wherever her purity shineth she makes our vain and frivolous enterprises wonderfully ashamed.

> Ivies spring better of their own accord,
> Unhaunted plots much fairer trees afford.
> Birds by no art much sweeter notes record.
> Propertius[3] I *Elegies* ii 10.

All our endeavour or wit cannot so much as reach to represent the nest of the least birdlet, its contexture,[4] beauty, profit and use, no nor the web of a silly[5] spider. *All things,* saith *Plato, are produced either by nature, by fortune. or by art: the greatest and fairest by one or other of the two first, the least and imperfect by the last.* Those nations seem, therefore, so barbarous unto me, because they have received very little fashion from human wit and are yet near their original naturality. The laws of nature do yet command them, which are but little bastardised by ours; and that with such purity as I am sometimes grieved the knowledge of it came no sooner to light, at what time there were men that better than we could have judged of it. I am sorry *Lycurgus*[6] and *Plato* had it not, for meseemeth that what in those nations we see by experience doth not only exceed all the pictures wherewith licentious Poesy had proudly embellished the golden age, and all her quaint inventions to feign a happy condition of man, but also the conception and desire of Philosophy. They could not imagine a genuity[7] so pure and simple as we see it by experience, nor ever believe our society might be maintained with so little art and human combination. It is a nation, would I answer *Plato*, that hath no kind of traffic, no knowledge of Letters, no intelligence of numbers, no name of

1. Government.
2. Capable.
3. Sextus Propertius, Roman elegiac poet (*c.* 54 B.C.–*c.* 2 B.C.).
4. Structure.
5. Simple.
6. As framer of the constitution of Sparta; Plato, as propounder of a Utopian republic (in *Laws* X).
7. Nature.

magistrate nor of politic superiority; no use of service, of riches or of poverty; no contracts, no successions, no partitions, no occupation but idleness; no respect of kindred but common, no apparel but natural, no manuring [8] of lands, no use of wine, corn, or metal. The very words that import lying, falsehood, treason, dissimulations, covetousness, envy, detraction, and pardon, were never heard of amongst them. How dissonant would he find his imaginary commonwealth from this perfection! [9]

COMMONPLACES

Montaigne's meditative prose was a great instrument for both the transmission of knowledge and the discovery of the self. It arose from commentary on texts of other authors, and it should be observed that this process of taking off from a text, obviously basic to scriptural commentaries and those of classical scholars, and the fundamental method of homiletic prose, the sermons of both Anglican and Puritan divines throughout this period, was an intellectual operation of a much more general character. In a way, there remained an unbroken tradition going back to medieval times of beginning all exposition with a text from tradition; if there was not a particular passage from biblical or classical sources, there might be one of a number of received ideas, set themes or topics, the response to which on the part of the writer would generate copy (from copia or "plenty"). Thus, the notion of the "theatrum mundi," that "all the world's a stage" was one topic; the concept of the locus amoenus or "lovely place," the garden associated with pastoral ideal realms, Eden, and various classical gardens was another. And in a peculiar way, the presence of classical mythology, whether embodied in particular formulations or quotations from Ovid or Virgil, or passed through a filter of received tradition and interpretive commentary (see The Renaissance Ovid) was always available. It is only the philosophical tradition of the seventeenth century which begins, as a counterpart to the raising of scientific questions based only on observed phenomena, to produce discourse based only upon the topic questions posed by self-awareness. Montaigne had, while still surrounded by his books, allowed their light to strike a spark of questioning ("Who am I? What do I know? What is what I know good for?") in him. His French follower, René Descartes (1596–1650), would carry this even farther by wondering what, if anything, it was possible to be absolutely certain of. Thomas Hobbes (1588–1679), although his view of the lives of Montaigne's noble savages was vastly different, also stems from him in a different way. (See the Glossary: Rhetoric.)

LANGUAGE AND THE THEATER

The theater in the sixteenth century blended a native, vernacular popular tradition with a learned one. Latin plays based on the tragedies of Seneca were written and acted in schools; it was not until an English drama with recognizable links to that classical tradition developed that any truly public theater was able to emerge. In 1561, an English blank-verse tragedy called Gorboduc, by Thomas Norton and Thomas Sackville, was played first at the Inner Temple and then before the Queen, as a kind

---

8. Cultivation.
9. The foregoing passage seems to be imitated in Shakespeare's The Tempest, II.i.54 ff. It is interesting that Florio's Protestant reticence leads him not to translate the quotation which follows: "Men sprung from the Gods" (from Seneca's Epistles XC).

of warning to her to beget an heir, so that the English throne would be safe from the disasters of division portrayed in the play. The Inns of Court—the Middle Temple, Inner Temple, Gray's Inn, and Lincoln's Inn—were the London law schools whose students and fellows contributed so much to the intellectual and cultural life of the city of London. The two universities were producing students who, after classical studies and training in rhetoric, might often read law before going into government service. Younger sons of noble families and older ones of the merchant classes and yeomanry shared a background in classical learning and a sense of sophistication that made the dining halls of the Inns of Court a breeding ground for the theater that would later come outdoors. An outdoor theater was built in London in 1576, and from then until 1642, in the more generally public theaters built south of the Thames, and in the more private coteries of the Inns of Court, a great theatrical tradition arose and flourished. Traveling companies of actors, writing and producing their own plays, attached to the household of some nobleman for protection against ordinances hostile to strolling players, moved about the country; but the theaters bred their own companies and audiences with their own expectations and, consequently, styles produced to meet them. There were also intimate, learned court plays which, in the early years of James's reign, developed into the court masque, a unique and totally unreconstructable lost theatrical realm. During this period of almost seventy years, the English stage developed a complex literary and political history of its own, and at this point it will only be remarked again how that history was the function of contributions as various as those of song-and-dance clowns on the one hand, and learned poets like Christopher Marlowe, who brought to blank-verse tragedy a kind of poetic style nurtured on non-dramatic (epic and elegiac) classical verse in English, on the other. The stage remained, despite the Puritan attacks upon it, a public institution which attracted the interests and energies of men as diverse as the highly learned, ideologically neoclassical Ben Jonson and the prosaic, popularly entertaining Thomas Dekker (c. 1570–c. 1641), who attacked Jonson (his erstwhile collaborator) in a broad satiric onslaught. It reflected the rest of the literary culture of the nation which surrounded it in all of its phases (the Jacobean tragedies of John Webster and Cyril Tourneur will be recognized even by the beginning student of the period as having more to do with the world of John Donne's later poems and sermons, and with Burton's *Anatomy of Melancholy,* than with the literary conventions of the 1590's). When the theaters finally closed, by order of the Puritan Parliament in 1642, a whole chapter in the development of English imaginative language came to an end.

THE FORMS OF VERSE

In some periods of change, the question of forms of activity can seem to matter more than content. In the practical history of the Reformation in England, the form of a prayer book could be defended with force of arms; in the literary history of the 1580's and 90's, arguments about verse forms could conceal debates about larger issues. One such argument was about how literally classical English verse should be. Upholders of quantitative scansion tried to establish Latin and Greek traditions in the actual structure of English poetry; their opponents maintained that analogues of classical forms were the only appropriate ones. But the two sides agreed that there were ways of working from classical models of form, as well as of reference and allusion. The case of the English heroic couplet is a good instance of this. During the later decades of the sixteenth century, the rhymed pairs of iambic pentameter lines in English served various purposes: closing scenes in blank-verse drama, closing the English form of the sonnet, translating (as with Marlowe's *Hero and Leander*) classical heroic verse, which in Greek or Latin was in unrhymed hexameters. After Wyatt and Surrey the so-called "fourteener,"

> *A line that rumbles on like this for just a bit too long*

when used in couplets, had a classical ring to it, for it was "long" like the hexameter. Golding's Ovid (see *The Renaissance Ovid*) is in this meter. But the pentameter couplet began to eclipse the longer ones, both for translating and, even more important, *standing for,* heroic verse. Then, too, there were the forms of epigram and satire. In classical verse, these are written in unrhymed "elegiac" couplets, a longer hexameter followed by a shorter pentameter. The English heroic couplet served for this as well. By the beginning of the seventeenth century the form was doing both jobs—so much so, that Ben Jonson, careful neoclassicist that he was, indented the second line of his couplets when used in epigrams, to stand for the classical couplets, but had them printed flush left when they stood for heroic hexameters. By the mid-century, the heroic couplets were so entrenched as the verse mode of both heroic and elegiac that Milton had to apologize, in a second printing, for the blank verse which he had used for the epic meter of *Paradise Lost.*

The later sixteenth century and the early seventeenth century saw a proliferation of lyric forms for verse, and with them, an ever varying set of relations between what the forms stood for, or suggested, about the poet's intention, and what the forms did in the way of affecting the language of the poem. Sir Philip Sidney's great experiments in the songs from the *Arcadia* developed in two directions the possibilities of using the formal structures of verse to control tone of voice and the structure of poetic discourse. One of these moved toward a patterning of surface, a decorative draping of grammatical parallelisms and mirrorings over the basic shape of a line. The other involved the opposition between line structure, its fixed number of stressed and unstressed syllables, and the ways in which the sound of a speaking voice would push against those patterns. From one of these directions the Spenserian diction branches off; from the other, the sonnets of Shakespeare and the lyrics of Donne. It should be remembered that there was, up through the turn of the seventeenth century, a strong general sense of formal discovery and invention, and that between the pre-1590's verse of the kind which C. S. Lewis has called "drab" and the carefully controlled and measured "plain style" of some of Ben Jonson's verse and that of his followers, there are not only a few decades of literary development, but changing assumptions about the relation of imagery, density of thought, and allusion to the verse forms in which they were set out.

While the Elizabethan literary debates frequently centered on the ways in which style should mirror intention, Jacobean and Caroline poets moved in one of three directions. Either they helped to make a tradition of the strong lines of John Donne—the so-called Metaphysical school, or they took the course that ran, through what Alexander Pope would call in the next century "Denham's strength and Waller's sweetness"—the contrived elegance in the way in which tone of voice is submerged in the formality of verse, and the tact with which imagery is introduced and led away from in poetry of statement or praise—to the Augustan style of John Dryden. There was also a third tradition (and it must be understood that individual poets often drew upon more than one stream) which had a curious fate—Spenser's followers in the early seventeenth century, Michael Drayton, William Browne, Giles and Phineas Fletcher, all interested in extended mythological poems, found themselves running against a tide. They were more admired in the nineteenth century than in our day, which is still influenced by the reinterpretation of the seventeenth century brought about by the influence of T. S. Eliot in his poetry and criticism. The only poem attributed to John Donne in Palgrave's *Golden Treasury of Songs and Lyrics,* a major Victorian anthology, is not by Donne at all. The minor Spenserians, poets of great skill and more than charm, will one day again be read with interest.

Some of the literary history of the last forty years may lead the beginning student of seventeenth-century poetry to believe that "lines" meant factions. This was not true, although occasionally the rhetoric of criticism might make it seem so. The cavalier poets, for example, while united in their loyalty to the king and the church, differed widely in how much Donne's wit and energy (Thomas Carew, for example, pledges himself to these), and how much Jonson's elegance and firm tactfulness characterized their verse. The Spenserian tradition ends up in Milton, a very great poet of the Puritan faction, and perhaps rightly so, Spenser's vision being radical and Protestant. But Andrew Marvell, a major talent and a devoted political servant of the Commonwealth, extends the styles of cavalier verse in developing his own. Many of the seventeenth-century lyric poets were clergymen, and the student cannot help but notice how many poets in the line of Donne were, like him, in holy orders; when they were, they were Anglican and, when the fighting started, Royalist.

THE CIVIL WAR

The Revolution was the second major center of upheaval in the period we have been calling the English Renaissance, the first being the turbulent fluctuations of Catholic and Anglican power in the mid-sixteenth century and the ensuing uneasiness about Rome and Spain which lasted well into Elizabeth's reign. Even after the defeat of the Armada (1588), the Elizabethan court was marked by uncertainty, rapid changes in the wind of favor, and the lack of norms of approach to preferment and finding appropriate governmental posts; thus a well-connected and useful man like Francis Bacon could get nowhere in the court of Elizabeth, and it was only with the accession of James that, particularly for men of letters, there was more of an official openness.

James's tutor, as a boy, had been the Great Scotch humanist George Buchanan (another of whose pupils, earlier on, had been Montaigne). James, however, did not respond with any sympathy to the teachings of his former tutor's tract *De Jure Regni* (On the Law of the Realm), in which the rule of kings is subjected to popular will and welfare. Instead, he formulated a doctrine of the divine right of kings. Intellectual, learned, and contentious, James was impractically given to the elevation of his favorites; men like Robert Carr (who became involved in a major scandal when he arranged for the murder of Sir Thomas Overbury), and, after him, the Duke of Buckingham, whom James ennobled as he did many others, engendered some mistrust.

The court of his son Charles was marked by a certain royal grandeur without the intellectual cast of his father's: Charles was a great patron of painters (Van Dyck and Rubens) and a collector of pictures—many of which Cromwell subsequently sold; and he preferred the pure spectacle and stage effects of Inigo Jones, the great stage designer, in his masques, or court entertainments, to the allegorical visions of Ben Jonson for which that spectacle had been originally employed. Despite his almost spiritual sense of the condition of kingship, he agreed, three years after ascending the throne in 1628, to Parliament's Petition of Right, in order to secure its vote on funds he needed. The Petition, although aimed at specific grievances such as the king's ability to declare martial law, and certain taxing privileges, in fact established the supremacy of parliamentary law over regal power. Charles largely ignored its provisions, and from 1629 until 1640 he ruled without calling any Parliament at all. A war with France made him unpopular, as did an attempt to extend to inland counties with no use for ships a tax known as *ship-money* (traditionally a levy only on certain port cities to help finance the royal support of shipping). But Charles needed money, and called what turned out to be a short, querulous session of Parliament lasting for three weeks in 1640. Several months later the so-called Long Parliament, under whom Charles was eventually beheaded, was called into session.

The Long Parliament drafted a Grand Remonstance against Charles, in his absence, in 1641; his attempt, early in 1642, to arrest five members of Parliament brought on war that year. After four years of fighting, Charles surrendered, was imprisoned, escaped and was recaptured, and finally, after trial at Westminster as "the tyrant, traitor and murderer, Charles Stuart," was executed in 1649. The parliamentary government which succeeded him had split into two factions, a Presbyterian one and an Independent one, under Oliver Cromwell (1599–1658). For a while Parliament had been dominated by the first, while Cromwell had control of the army; but fearful that the Presbyterian faction might finally return power to the crown, Cromwell took virtual control of the nation. An Instrument of Government in 1653 named him Lord Protector and formally established a Commonwealth.

During all this, Royalist refugees, aristocratic and clerical, and those who were neither but were ideologically committed to established power, like Thomas Hobbes, had fled to France, and a circle of English émigrés remained there for various lengths of time. Charles II, who had himself crowned in 1651 in Scotland, attempted to lead an attacking force into England that year, was defeated, and joined the rest of the exiles in France after a dramatic forty days of escape through England. Following nine years of exile, the wave of political confusion after Cromwell's death and during the tenure of Richard Cromwell, his son, allowed Charles to return to England. He landed at Dover on May 29, 1660, his thirtieth birthday.

The continuities of English town and country life had been far less disturbed by the events of the past two decades—the closing of the theaters being a notable exception —than had institutions of power and patronage. Strongly Anglican clergyman and fellows of Oxford and Cambridge colleges had lost their posts. But largely, the Restoration signaled the donning of new styles, new fashions or, as the fashionably French word went, "modes." The tight lacing of Elizabethan corsets had given way, after lasting through the Jacobean reign, to a loosening of line of dress and of hair; this had been associated with Cavalier rather than with "Roundhead" or Puritan factions in the time of the Civil War, and came back to Restoration fashion with a vengeance. But traces of the world view which such styles of costume reflect are evident in the literature, primarily in the poetry, of the 1630's and after; for the imagination, outward styles can be seen as the objectification of states of mind. The peculiar paradoxes of English cultural styles during this whole period—particularly with respect to Continental ones—remain fascinating. King's College Chapel, in Cambridge, finished in 1539, remains a triumph of late English gothic architecture; when it was dedicated, the high-

Renaissance triumph of St. Peter's in Rome was already under construction. The peculiar blending of the gothic and the baroque temperaments which we find in John Donne, those strange remnants of medievalism in Shakespeare, are reflected in the seventeenth-century façade of the chapel of Peterhouse, Cambridge, whose gothic arched long window is surmounted, on the outside, by a typically seventeenth-century baroque broken pediment. These co-existing and contrasting strands of tradition, the pulls and tensions of orthodoxy and Protestantism, royalism and republicanism, insularlity and cosmopolitanism, make for a complex and often slightly awkward picture. But perhaps by virtue of this very awkwardness, this being out of phase with so many normative developments of European cultural history, the magnificent aspects of the earliest humanist programs continued to flower and bear fruit in a visionary mid-century literature well after it should have. The massive geniuses of Shakespeare, Spenser, and Milton, concentrated in this brief time, are enough for any culture's life history.

THE RENAISSANCE OVID

Along with Virgil and eventually, through him, Homer, the greatest repository of narrative aside from the Bible upon which Renaissance poetry depended was Ovid's *Metamorphoses*. The Roman poet's epic of transformations ("Change is my subject," he starts out) was not merely a brilliant collection of much of the classical mythology which involved changes of state of being—people into animals, plants, rocks, and fountains, even stars. It provided a kind of form or template for poetic realization of a whole world view. In the sixteenth and seventeenth centuries, that view still embraced a vision of cosmic order reflected in smaller orders and structures; of the signatures of a transcendent world being legible in the appearances of the immediate one; of theories of the relation of eternal patterns to changeable substances; of the objectification of human feelings and thoughts in ways more fluid than those provided by surviving medieval personifications and allegories. Ovid's book was not merely a handbook of stories, for his own sensuous, artful, witty, and often very dramatic poetic style provided many rhetorical and figurative models for English poets of the Tudor and Stuart eras.

Modern readers think of ancient myths primarily as stories. Some more sophisticated readers, particularly those with some experience of modern anthropology or with the history of science, will understand them as early kinds of explanations about natural phenomena and processes. For poetry, however, the importance of mythology has always resided in the relation of stories to the meanings that were to be extracted from them by imaginative readings. The notion of a "moralized" story goes back to early Greek philosophical commentators on Homer, and, in a sense, the whole allegorical tradition can be said to stem from ways of reading traditional stories. With Ovid, this process began with the tedious homily and sometimes farfetched moralizings of the fourteenth-century French *Ovide Moralisé*, but Renaissance writers and painters began building up a massive body of Ovidian interpretation. These readings of the classical stories occurred in special handbooks of mythology and in poems, plays, and masques which derived from them, and continued the interpretation further. This is not to speak of paintings and prints, which from this point of view are silent texts, what Ben Jonson called "a mute poesy."

Arthur Golding (1536?–1605?) published in 1567 his great translation of the *Metamorphoses* in rhyming fourteener couplets, which was known by Shakespeare and his contemporaries along with the Latin original; and although its own virtues are those of capturing some of Ovid's poetic art to a remarkable degree, it makes a bow toward interpretation in an appended "Epistle" which Golding wrote in the manner of some earlier mythographers. Two passages from Golding's version appear below. The first is Ovid's description of the Golden Age, one of the four phases, as originally given by the Greek poet Hesiod, of human history, and an important parallel to the Judaeo-Christian story of the Fall from Paradise. The Golden Age, presided over by Saturn before any of the final structures of Olympian gods, men, animals, underworld, and so forth had arisen, was followed by a declining series of silver, bronze, and iron epochs, the last of which all human history seems to have occupied. It is a concept central to English Renaissance notions of pleasure and virtue, and Ovid's vision of it influences countless verbal and visual pictures of lovely places, from Eden through the backgrounds for pastoral poetry to imagined worlds in which there is no gap between what is good, what gives pleasure, and what is for both of those reasons beautiful.

The other passage from Golding's Ovid is a small part of the well-known story of the sculptor Pygmalion and his statue, with which he falls in love. Ovid tells it in his famous tenth book, of which Golding says in his "Epistle":

> The tenth book chiefly doth contain one kind of argument
> Reproving most prodigious lusts of such as have been bent
> To incest most unnatural . . . Moreover, it doth show
> That beauty (will they, nill they) aye doth men in danger throw,
> And that it is a foolishness to strive against the thing
> Which God before determineth to pass in time to bring.
> And last of all, Adonis' death doth show that manhood strives
> Against forewarning, though men see the peril of their lives.

(Had Shakespeare believed this last to be a good reading, he could have written no poem on it.) The Pygmalion story is cited by Ovid as part of the legendary material surrounding the background of the Venus story, for the eventual child of the union of Pygmalion and his quickened creation was named Paphos, and Paphos became the poetic name for Cyprus, the island of the goddess's birth. The tale is best known to modern readers through George Bernard Shaw's play, which ingeniously transforms substance into language, converting the sculptural act into the skill of a professor of linguistics in making a cockney street-girl talk like a lady of high degree, and the enlivening of the statue into her spiritual awakening to a sense of her own freedom. Golding's version of Ovid is followed by two brief commentaries, and finally by a longer passage from the great translation of George Sandys in 1626, with a full and detailed commentary added in 1632. The various mythographers move from the crudest readings, which try to account for the myth on the basis of distorted fact or else to glue a moral onto it, to far more imaginative and symbolic views. Caxton's early reading is of the first type; aimed primarily at artists is that of the Dutch poet, painter, and writer on art Carel van Mander, who commented on the meanings in Ovid as part of an artist's handbook (*Het Schilderbouck*) in 1604. A German emblem book from the late sixteenth century shows a picture of the sculptor and his statue with a motto stating that the best marriages are made in heaven ("Der best heürath kompt den gott schüpt").

Also given are two different examples of the ways in which Ovidian materials, known through their interpreted versions, work their way into minor literary forms. Aside from the massive use of mythography by Spenser and Milton, who not only drew upon Renaissance writers on myth in many languages but also derived further mythologies of their own from them, Ovidian story could be used anecdotally, as in the concluding section of a poem from Tottel's Miscellany of 1557, and as part of an erotic epyllion by John Marston, *The Metamorphoses of Pygmalion's Image* (see Headnote to *Hero and Leander*), although, in this instance, a not very good one.

A mid-seventeenth-century critical work devoted to the continuing life of ancient myth in its contemporary interpretation was Henry Reynolds's *Mythomystes* (1632), "wherein a short survey is taken of the nature and value of true poesy, and depth of the ancients above our modern poets." A passage from it concludes this section. Reynolds was arguing for the poetic importance of mythological themes at a time when a fashionable poet could speak of "the goodly exiled train / Of gods and goddesses" and of "The silenced tales of the Metamorphoses" as having lost imaginative relevance, at least to erotic poetry.

Throughout all these mythographic ingenuities, distortions, and homilies lay such

Renaissance convictions as the one that held classical mythology to be at worst a distorted, slightly crippled but reconstructible model of biblical truth. The act of reconstruction could itself be thought of as one of the nobler activities of the mind or, at very least, as exemplifying that twofold source of pleasure and profit which poetry and art were felt to be:

> If poets then with leesings° and with fables shadowed° so
> The certain truth, what letteth° us to pluck these visors fro
> Their doings, and to bring again the darkened truth to light,
> That all men may behold thereof the clearness shining bright?
> The readers therefore earnestly admonished are to be
> To seek a further meaning than the letter gives to see.
> The travail tane in that behalf although it have some pain,
> Yet makes it double recompense with pleasure and with gain. . . .
>
> (Golding, "Epistle" XV. 537–44)

From Arthur Golding's Ovid's Metamorphoses

[The Golden Age°]

Then sprang up first the golden age, which of itself maintained
The truth and right of everything, unforced and unconstrained.
There was no fear of punishment, there was no threatening law
In brazen tables nailèd up to keep the folk in awe.
There was no man would crouch or creep to Judge, with cap in hand:
They livèd safe without a Judge in every realm and land.
The lofty pine tree was not hewn from mountains where it stood,
110   In seeking strange and foreign lands, to rove upon the flood.°
Men knew no other countries yet than where themselves did keep;
There was no town enclosèd yet, with walls and ditches deep.
No horn nor trumpet was in use, no sword or helmet worn:
The world was such that soldiers' help might easily be forborn.
The fertile earth as yet was free, untouched of spade or plough,
And yet it yielded of itself of every thing enough.
And men themselves, contented well with plain and simple food,
That on the earth of nature's gift, without their travail stood,
Did live by raspis,° hips and haws,° by cornels,° plums and cherries,
120   By sloes and apples, nuts and pears, and loathsome bramble berries,
And by the acorns dropped on ground from Jove's broad tree in field.
The springtime lasted all the year, and Zephyr with his mild
And gentle blast did cherish things that grew of own accord,

---

leesings lies
fables shadowed "Shadow" means "image," and the stories are thought of as being "imaged" or conceived so as to be pregnant with meanings.
letteth prevents

The Golden Age from I. 89–150
rove upon the flood that is, as the mast of a ship—the point being that there was no technology, no rearrangement of the natural into the artificial, nor was there need of it

raspis berries
hips and haws rose hips and hawthorne berries
cornels cherries

The ground untilled, all kinds of fruit did plenteously afford.
No muck nor tillage was disposed on lean and barren land,
To make the crops of better head, and ranker for to stand.
Then streams ran milk, then streams ran wine, and yellow honey flowed
From each green tree whereon the rays of fiery Phoebus glowed.

1567

[Pygmalion's Statue Comes to Life°]

As soon as he came home,° straightway Pygmalion did repair
Unto the image of his wench, and leaning on the bed
Did kiss her. In her body straight a warmness seemed to spread;
He put his mouth again to hers, and on her breast did lay
His hand. The ivory waxèd° soft, and putting quite away
All hardness, yielded underneath his fingers, as we see
310   A piece of wax made soft against the sun, or drawn to be
In divers shapes by chafing it between one's hands, and so
To serve to uses. He amazed stood wavering to and fro
Tween joy and fear to be beguiled again he burnt in love,
Again with feeling he began his wishèd hope to prove.
He felt it very flesh indeed. By laying on his thumb,
He felt her pulse's beating. Then he stood no longer dumb
But thankèd Venus with his heart, and at the length he laid
His mouth to hers, who was as then become a perfect maid.
She felt the kiss and blushed thereat, and lifting fearfully
320   Her eyelids up, her lover and the light at once did spy.

1567

From William Caxton's Ovid, His Book of Metamorphose

This is to say that some great lord might have a maid or a servant in his house,
which [1] was poor, naked and coude [2] no good; but [3] she was gentle and of fair
form; but she was dry and lean as an image. This rich man that saw the fair
clothed, nourished and taught her so much, that she was well endoctrined. [4]
And that it pleased him to espouse her and take her to [5] his wife, of whom
he had after a fair son, prudent, wise and of great renomee. [6]

1480

Pygmalion's . . . Life from X. 243–97
came home from a festival of Venus, at which

1. Who.
2. Knew.
3. Except that.

he had prayed for his beautiful statue of a girl
to come to life
waxèd grew

4. Educated.
5. For.
6. Renown.

From Carel van Mander's Painter's Manual

Pygmalion in love with his own handiwork is to be compared with those who, too much in love with their own good works, trust in themselves, wherein no life is to be found, until they emerge from themselves, and turn toward the true *Venus,* which is to be explained as true love of God and of one's neighbour, through which the virtues become alive and fruitful.

1604

From George Sandys's Ovid's Metamorphosis°

Pygmalion seeing these to spend their times
So beast-like, frighted with the many crimes
That rule in women, chose a single life,
And long forbore the pleasure of a wife.
Meanwhile, in ivory with happy art
A statue carves, so graceful in each part
120 As women never equalled it, and stands
Affected to the fabric of his hands.
It seemed a virgin, full of living flame,
That would have moved if not withheld by shame.
Such art his art concealed, which he admires,
And from it draws imaginary fires;
Then often feels it with his hands, to try
If 'twere a body, or cold ivory.
Nor could resolve: who, kissing, thought it kissed;
Oft courts, embraces, wrings it by the wrist,
130 The flesh impressing (his conceit was such)
And fears to hurt it with too rude a touch.
Now flatters her, now sparkling stones presents
And orient pearl (love's witching instruments),
Soft-singing birds, each several-coloured flower,
First lilies, painted balls, and tears that pour
From weeping trees.° Rich robes her person deck;
Her fingers, rings; reflecting gems, her neck;
Pendants her ears; glittering zone,° her breast.
In all, showed well, but showed, when naked, best.
140 Now lays he her upon a gorgeous bed,
With carpets of Sidonian purple spread,
Now calls her wife. Her head a pillow pressed,
Of plumy down, as if of sense possessed.
Now came the day of *Venus*' festival,

Ovid's Metamorphosis George Sandys (1578–1644) was famous for his work as a colonial administrator in the first Virginia colony, and the earlier books of his translation may have been the first literary poetry (balladry aside) produced in the English colonies in America. His translation, it will be noticed, makes frequent use of a dramatic shift of verb tense in the narration; it was also highly influential in in the history of the heroic couplet in English verse.

tears . . . trees amber
glittering zone sparkling band

23

Through wealthy *Cyprus* solemnized by all.
White heifers decked with golden horns° by strokes
Of axes fall; ascending incense smokes.
He, with his gift, before the altar stands:
'You Gods, if all we crave be in your hands,
150   Give me the wife I wish, one like—' he said,
But durst not say, 'Give me my ivory maid.'°
The golden *Venus*, present at her feast,
Conceives his wish, and friendly signs expressed;
The fire thrice blazing, thrice in flames aspires.
To his admired image he retires,
Lies down beside her, raised her with his arm,
Then kissed her tempting lips, and found them warm.
That lesson oft repeats, her bosom oft
With amorous touches feels, and felt it soft.
160   The ivory dimpled with his fingers lacks
Accustomed hardness; as Hymettian wax°
Relents with heat, which chafing thumbs reduce
To pliant forms, by handling framed for use.
Amazed with doubtful joy and hope that reels,
Again the lover, what he wishes, feels.
The veins beneath his thumbs impression beat:
A perfect virgin, full of juice and heat.
The Cyprian prince with joy expressing words
To pleasure-giving *Venus* thanks affords.
170   His lips to hers he joins, which seem to melt;
The blushing virgin now his kisses felt,
And fearfully erecting her fair eyes,
Together with the light, her lover spies.
Venus the marriage blessed which she had made.

                                        1626

[Commentary]
Pygmalion . . . deterred by . . . the many vices which reigned in women, resolved to live a single life; who, carving the image of a virgin in ivory surpassing the perfection of nature, fell in love with his own workmanship. Nor is it extraordinary for excellent artisans to admire their own skill, which adds to industry as industry to perfection. And perhaps the life which was given it by the Goddess was no other than the grace and beauty of the figure which Apelles,[1] in his pictures, called the *Venus*, which made it live in the estimation of those times and the admiration of posterity, as his son by her might be taken for the honour acquired by his admirable art, the Grecian and the Roman statues, after so many hundreds of years, affording as long a life to the fame of the artificer.

golden horns gilded, for the festival
ivory maid Sandys later calls her Eburnia, "ivory."

Hymettian wax from a mountain in Attica famed for its honey

1. Fabled painter of antiquity.

But taken historically, this statue may be some virgin on whom Pygmalion was enamoured, who long as obdurate as the matter whereof she was made, was mollified [2] at length by his obsequiousness, the ivory expressing the beauty of her body, and her blushes the modesty of her mind. . . . Blushing is a resort of the blood to the face, which in the passion of shame labours most in that part, and is seen in the breast as it ascendeth, but most apparent in those that are young, in regard of their greater heat and tender complexions. Which proceeds not from an infirmity of the mind, but the novelty of the thing, nor can be either put on or restrained: the ensign [3] of native modesty and the colour of virtue. A beautiful and modest wife is therefore here said to be given him by the Goddess in reward of his devotion, as the greatest temporal happiness.

Neither may Pygmalion's being in love with an image be altogether fictitious: since both Pliny and Lucian make mention of a youth of no ignoble family (his name suppressed for the foulness of the fact) who grew so desperately enamoured on that celebrated statue of naked Venus carved in Parian marble by Praxiteles, and enshrined in her temple at Knidos, that all the day long he would gaze thereon, moving his lips as if he sued for acceptance, sigh, change colour, and expressing all the distemperatures of a lover, offering at her altar whatsoever his means would afford. And so far his fury increased, that hiding himself one evening in the temple, and being locked in by the sexton, he ran to the statue, embraced it strictly [4] in his arms, warming the cold marble with his burning kisses, and so contaminated it with his lust, [5] that the stains ever after remained as a monument of his impiety. Who either struck with the horror of the deed, or that it was not in nature to satisfy his desires, threw himself from a rock and so perished. Beautiful women, though metamorphosized into stone, would not want [6] their lovers.

1632

From Tottel's Miscellany

[The Tale of Pygmalion
with Conclusion upon the Beauty of His Love]

Twixt nature and Pygmalion there might appear great strife,
20   So seemly was this image wrought, it lacked nothing but life.
His curious eye beheld his own devisèd work,
And, gazing oft thereon, he found much venom there to lurk;
  For all the featured shape so did his fancy move,
That with his idol whom he made Pygmalion fell in love.
  To whom he honour gave, and decked with garlands sweet,

2. Literally, "softened"; usually used figuratively to apply to the emotions, obdurate reserve or "hard-heartedness" being, as it were, melted; notice how Sandys uses in his explication the very image of melting drawn from the myth.
3. Emblem, insignia; but here, more like a flag, in the modern sense.
4. Tightly.
5. He ejaculated on it.
6. Lack.

And did adorn with jewels rich, as is for lovers meet.
 Sometimes on it he swooned, sometime in rage would cry:
It was a wonder to behold how fancy bleared his eye.
 Since that this image dumb inflamed so wise a man,
30 My dear, alas, since I you love, what wonder is it then?
 In whom hath nature set the glory of her name,
And brake her mould in great dispraise your like she could not frame.

1557

From John Marston's The Metamorphosis of Pygmalion's Image

'O gracious Gods, take compassion,
140 Instill into her some celestial fire
That she may equalise affection
And have a mutual love, and love's desire.
 Thou knowest the force of love: then pity me,
 Compassionate° my true love's ardency.'

Thus having said, he riseth from the floor
As if his soul divinèd him good fortune,
Hoping his prayers to pity moved some power;
For all his thoughts did all good luck importune,
 And therefore straight he strips him naked quite,
150 That in the bed he might have more delight.

Then thus, 'Sweet sheets,' he says, 'which now do cover
The idol of my soul, the fairest one
That ever loved, or had an amorous lover,
Earth's only model of perfection,
 Sweet happy sheets, deign for to take me in,
 That I my hopes and longing thoughts may win.

With that his nimble limbs do kiss the sheets,
And now he bows him for to lay him down,
And now each part, with her fair parts do meet,
160 Now doth he hope for to enjoy love's crown:
 Now do they dally, kiss, embrace together,
 Like Leda's twins at sight of fairest weather.°

Yet all's conceit—but shadow of that bliss
Which now my Muse strives sweetly to display
In this my wondrous metamorphosis.

Compassionate sympathize with
Like . . . weather Leda was raped by Zeus in the form of a swan; she produced two eggs, from which emerged Castor and Pollux, and Helen. Helen and her half-sister Clytemnestra (the offspring of Leda and her husband Tyndareus, king of Sparta) are central to the stories of the Trojan War and the House of Atreus; the brothers, known as the Dioscuri, became the constellation of Gemini, the twins, which when visible ahead in a storm, was an omen of good weather to come, according to Horace in one of his poems.

Deign to believe me, now I sadly say:
   The stony substance of his Image feature
   Was straight transformed into a living creature.

For when his hands her fair-formed limbs had felt,
170 And that his arms her naked waist embraced,
   Each part like wax before the sun did melt,
   And now, O now, he finds how he is graced
     By his own work. Tut! Women will relent
   When as they find such moving blandishment.

1598

From Henry Reynolds's Mythomystes [1]

. . . who can make that rape of Proserpine—whom her mother Ceres (that under the species of corn might include as well the whole genus of the vegetable nature [2]) sought so long for in the earth—to mean other than the putrefaction and succeeding generation of the seeds we commit to Pluto, or the earth, whom they make the god of wealth, calling him also *Dis quasi dives* (the same in Latin that *Pluto* is in Greek), rich or wealthy, because all things have their original [3] from the earth, and return to the earth again? Or what can Jupiter's blasting of his beloved Semele, after his having deflowered her, and the wrapping of his son he got on her (Bacchus or wine) in his thigh after his production, mean other than the necessity of the air's heat to his birth in generation, and (after a violent pressure and dilaceration [4] of his mother the grape) the like close imprisoning of him also, in a fit vessel, till he gain his full maturity and come to be fit aliment? . . . the adultery of Mars and Venus, by which the chemists [5] will have meant the inseparability of those two metals that carry their names (witness that exuberance of Venus, or copper, which we call Vitriol, [6] that is seldom or never found without some mixture more or less of Mars, or iron, in it, as her husband Vulcan, or material fire, finds and shows the practitioners in chemistry). And . . . Hebe's stumbling and falling with the nectar-bowl in her hand, and thereby discovering her hidden parts to the gods as she served them at their board, meaning the nakedness of the trees and plants in autumn, when all their leaves are fallen from them by the downfall or departure of the spring, which their Hebe (or goddess of youth, as the ancients called her, because the spring renews and makes young all things) means.

1633

1. This strange treatise of mystical, neoplatonist interpretation, based heavily on the thought of Pico della Mirandola (1463–94), contains strong arguments for mythopoetic treatments of the old stories, in many ways opposed to the spirit of its age (except for Milton). It is a good example of how the Greek myths had penetrated alchemical thinking, and of the later sort of general, rather than specifically moral, interpretation.
2. Vegetable kingdom.
3. Origin.
4. Tearing apart.
5. The alchemists, whose own conceptual language was full of sexual metaphors, and whose very names for metals and minerals and processes were mythological.
6. Copper sulphate.

THE ENGLISH BIBLE

The men who translated the Bible into English had to face the problem of all translators, in its most concentrated form. Their version had to be faithful to a divinely inspired, incorruptible original, preserved by the authority of the church.

The first real biblical translation, made in Alexandria about the third century B.C., was the Greek Old Testament, known as the Septuagint (Greek: seventy, because completed by, the story goes, seventy-two translators in seventy-two days), which became the Old Testament of the Greek-speaking world. From this version of the original Hebrew and from the original Greek of the New Testament were made the Old Latin translations. These were superseded, from the fifth century A.D. onward, by the Vulgate (Latin: made public or common), prepared by St. Jerome, between 383 and 405. Jerome used the Greek and Hebrew to check his Latin. His Vulgate became and remained the Bible of the West: on it the medieval church based itself. Even its mistranslations became hallowed by use and tradition.

Bible translation in England begins in the late seventh century, when Cædmon, a monk of Whitby (see Vol. I), is said to have made a metrical paraphrase of parts of Scripture. Other Old English paraphrases exist, dating from the ninth century onward (Genesis, Exodus, and Daniel), and there is much poetry on biblical themes, such as Cynewulf's *Christ*. There is a metrical paraphrase of the story of Judith and Holofernes (tenth century) and, in the eleventh, Ælfric's paraphrase of the Heptateuch (the first seven books of the Bible). The Psalter, used in public worship and private devotion, was given Old English glosses in the ninth century and fully translated in the tenth. There is a metrical version of the late thirteenth and two prose renderings of the fourteenth, one by Richard Rolle, the hermit and mystic.

Of the New Testament, partial prose and verse translations were made during the fourteenth century, but none of these—nor any of those that had gone before—were intended to give the very words of Scripture to ordinary people. The notion of translating the whole Bible into English belongs to John Wyclif (c. 1330–84), the famous Oxford theologian and religious reformer, to whom the law of faith and morals was the Bible, rather than the authority of a pope and church whose example had been weakened by dissension and corruption. To obey the Bible's precepts meant that the words of the Bible must be available to all men. This was to become the characteristic Protestant position.

Though Wyclif probably did not translate himself, his ideas fired his followers to produce two English translations of the entire Bible. The first, made during Wyclif's lifetime, probably between 1380 and 1384, was literal; the second (of the 1390's), more free, in a vigorous native English. It is not the work of a "simple creature" as its Prologue says, but fully answers the translator's aim "to translate as clearly as he could to the sentence" (that is, according to the sense). There must have been "many good fellows [companions] and cunning [knowledgeable] at the correcting of the translation."

"A translator hath great need," says the author of the Prologue (probably John Purvey), "to study well the sense both before and after, and then also he hath need to live a clean life and be full devout in prayers, and have not his wit occupied about worldly things, that the Holy Spirit, author of all wisdom, knowledge and truth, dress him for his work and suffer him not to err."

The translation of the Bible was associated, in the official mind, with the more inflammatory social precepts and practices of the Lollards, as Wyclif's followers were called. In 1408, translation of the Scriptures into English, or even reading such translations, without the permission of the church authorities, was forbidden. (This was the prohibition which must have hindered William Caxton from printing the Bible in English, as he had done for so many other books.)

With the Renaissance, there came a renewed interest in the text of the Scriptures. Erasmus published an edition of the Greek New Testament in 1516, with his own new Latin translation; and the renewed study of Greek and Hebrew gave scholars a deeper insight into the meaning of the Bible. With the Reformation, a new interest in having the Bible in the vernacular was added: in 1522, Martin Luther published his translation into German. Luther's example inspired William Tyndale (c. 1494–1536), an exile in Germany for his Protestant opinions. In 1526, complete printed copies of the New Testament in English were smuggled into England. This translation by Tyndale, printed in Germany, had a profound influence on all subsequent Protestant versions. Its circulation was still illegal, since it had been made without sanction of the authorities and contained unacceptable turns of phrase (often adopted by translators today): "washing" for "baptism," "love" for "charity," "congregation" for "church," "elder" for "priest"—simple words, from which the filth of centuries of corrupt practice and insincerity and institutionalism—as Tyndale saw it—had been cleansed.

Tyndale was burned for his beliefs and his practice of them, with the approval of Henry VIII. Henry later sanctioned the use of the Bible prepared by Miles Coverdale (1488–1569), published abroad in 1535; and of another version in 1537. Both are greatly indebted to Tyndale's New Testament (revised 1534) and to his partial translations, published and unpublished, of the Old. Work on the Great Bible, Coverdale's revision of the 1537 version, began in 1538, on the King's command to provide "one book of the whole Bible of the largest volume in England"; and to "expressly provoke, stir and exhort every person to read the same, as that which is the very lively word of God, that every Christian person is bound to embrace, believe and follow, if he look to be saved."

This was the Bible that was prescribed for use in churches until the end of the reign of Edward VI. During that reign other translations were made, including an experimental partial Gospel translation by Sir John Cheke, who was attempting to replace the Greek words of the original by exact native English copies: "crossed" for "crucified," "mooned" for "lunatic." In 1557, when the Catholic Queen Mary was on the throne, a group of Puritan exiles began an independent version (the Geneva Bible), which they finally dedicated in 1560 to Queen Elizabeth, the Protestant sovereign who was to build up again "the ruins of God's house" in England, and war against the Roman church, the "Whore of Babylon." The Geneva translation, though the most accurate so far, was not acceptable to the leaders of the church in England, who set about revising the Great Bible to produce the Bishops' Bible (1568–69), which became the official Bible of the Elizabethan church.

The Roman church's reply was the translation prepared from the Latin Vulgate—not from the Hebrew and Greek, as were the Protestant versions, following the dictates of the New Learning. It was the work of English Catholic exiles, but chiefly of Gregory Martin, during Elizabeth's reign. Known now as the Douay-Rheims version (1582–1610), it aimed to counter the "false translations" of the Protestants, corrupting, "adding, detracting, altering, transposing, pointing and [using] all other guileful means: specially where it serveth for the advantage of their private opinions."

After Elizabeth's death in 1603, King James I and his bishops decreed "that a translation be made of the whole Bible, as consonant as can be to the original Hebrew and Greek," for exclusive use in the English church. Six panels of translators, forty-seven scholars in all, divided the work, which was published in 1611 as

> The Holy Bible, Conteyning the Old Testament and the New: Newly Translated out of the Originall tongues, with the former Translations diligently compared and revised, by his Majesties speciall commandement. Appointed to be read in Churches.

This is the Authorized Version. The translators disclaim any intention of making a new translation; their purpose was to revise old ones. (How true this is can be seen from the way in which they echo Tyndale's translation throughout.) They were not puffed up with their own knowledge; they "prayed to the Lord, the Father of our Lord," to the effect that St. Augustine did: " 'O let thy Scriptures be my pure delight; let me not be deceived in them, neither let me deceive by them.' " They set themselves to translate the Hebrew of the Old Testament and the Greek of the New—thus going back to the original texts and avoiding, as had Tyndale, the suspicion of "Popery." But they use "charity" and "church" and "priest." They give alternative translations in the margins when they are in doubt. They make deliberate use of the richness of English in synonyms;

> we have not tied ourselves to an uniformity of phrasing, or to an identity of words . . . For is the Kingdom of God become words and syllables? Why should we be in bondage to them, if we may be free? . . . We have on the one side avoided the scrupulosity of the Puritans, who leave the old Ecclesiastical words . . . as when they put *washing* for *baptism,* and *congregation* instead of *church;* as also on the other side we have shunned the obscurity of the Papists, in their *azymes*,[1] *tunike, rational, holocausts*,[2] *prepuce*,[3] *pasche*[4] and a number of such like, whereof their late translation [the Douay-Rheims] is full, and that of purpose to darken the sense, that since they must needs translate the Bible, yet by the language thereof it may be kept from being understood. But we desire that the Scripture may speak like itself, as in the language of Canaan,[5] that it may be understood even of the very vulgar.[6]

The Authorized Version sums up in itself all the aspects of English Bible translation: its strong conservatism and traditionalism; its determination to present the very words of Scripture in a form as simple and as near the language in which they were originally written, so that their sanctity, not any hallowing and mystery conferred on them by the church, will carry them direct to the minds and souls of the readers.

The particular passage, I Corinthians 13, chosen to display these various versions is not only a magnificent and widely quoted one, but its most famous image has suffered a curious fate, in the Authorized Version, because of changes in meaning since the seventeenth century. Verse 12 represents, in the Greek, the state of mediation of reality that the earthly life entails; in an image from Plato, St. Paul says that it is like the difference between seeing in a mirror and seeing what the mirror reflects. "Glass" no longer means mirror primarily, particularly with an article; the words "dark" and

---

1. Passover cakes, unleavened bread.
2. Burnt offerings.
3. Foreskin.
4. Easter.
5. Hebrew (Isaiah 19:18), the language common to more lands than Israel.
6. True common people, ordinary folk.

"obscure" have switched some of their tones of meaning (Spenser talks of his allegory as a "darke conceit," meaning a puzzling or difficult one). Modern students tend to read verse 12 as if it meant: "Now we see things as if through smoked or dark glasses; then, they will be removed"—a good image of mediation (suggesting having to stare at solar eclipses through dark glasses, etc.) but not St. Paul's. (See John Donne's sermon on this text, below.)

J. B. Trapp prepared the Headnote to this section and I Corinthians 13; John Hollander edited The Psalms in English Verse.

From The Second Wycliffite Version

If I speke with tungis of men and of aungels, and I have not charite, I am maad as bras sownynge, or a cymbal tynklynge.[2] And if I have prophecie, and knowe alle mysteries, and al kunnynge, and if I have al feith, so that I meve hillis fro her place, and I have not charite, I am nought. [3] And if I departe alle my goodis in to the metis of pore men, and if I bitake my bodi, so that I brenne, and if I have not charite, it profitith to me no thing. [4] Charite is pacient, it is benygne; charite envyeth not, it doith not wickidli, it is not blowun, [5] it is not coveytouse, it sekith not tho thingis that ben hise owne, it is not stirid to wrathe, it thenkith not yvel, [6] it joyeth not on wickidnesse, but it joyeth togidere to treuthe; [7] it suffrith alle thingis, it bileveth alle thingis, it hopith alle thingis, it susteyneth alle thingis. Charite fallith nevere doun, [8] whether prophecies schulen be voided, ethir langagis schulen ceesse, ethir science schal be distried. [9] For a parti we knowun, and a parti we prophecien; [10] but whanne that schal come that is parfit, that thing that is of parti schal be avoidid. 'Whanne I was a litil child, I spak as a litil child, I undurstood as a litil child, I thoughte as a litil child; but whanne I was maad a man, I avoidide tho thingis that weren of a litil child. [12] And we seen now bi a myrour in derknesse, but thanne face to face; now I knowe of parti, but thanne I schal knowe, as I am knowun. [13] And now dwellen feith, hope, and charite, these thre; but the most of these is charite.'

c. 1395

From Tyndale's Translation

Though I spake with the tonges of men and angels, and yet had no love, I were even as soundynge brasse: or as a tynklynge cymball. [2] And though I coulde prophesy, and understode all secretes, and all knowledge: yee, yf I had all fayth, so that I coulde move mountayns oute of ther places, and yet had no love, I were nothinge. [3] And though I bestowed all my gooddes to fede the poore, and though I gave my body even that I burned, and yet had no love, it profeteth me nothinge.

[4] Love suffreth longe and is corteous. Love envieth not. Love doth not frowardly, swelleth not, [5] dealeth not dishonestly, seketh not her awne, is not provoked to anger, thinketh not evyll, [6] rejoyseth not in iniquite: but rejoyseth in the trueth, [7] suffreth all thinges, beleveth all thinges, hopeth all thinges, endureth in all thinges. [8] Though that prophesyinge fayle, other tonges shall cease, or knowledge vanysshe awaye, yet love falleth never awaye.

⁹ For oure knowledge is unparfect and oure prophesyinge is unperfect. ¹⁰ But when that which is parfect, is come, then that which is unparfect, shall be done awaye. ¹¹ When I was a chylde, I spake as a chylde, I understode as a chylde, I ymagened as a chylde. But assone as I was a man, I put away chyldeshnes. ¹² Now we se in a glasse, even in a darke speakynge: but then shall we se face to face. Now I knowe unparfectly: but then shall I knowe even as I am knowen. ¹³ Now abydeth fayth, hope, and love, even these thre: but the chefe of these is love.

1525; revised 1535

From The Great Bible

Though I spake with the tonges of men and of angels, and have no love, I am even as sounding brasse, or as a tynklinge cymball. ² And though I coulde prophesy, and understode all secretes, and all knowledge: yee yf I have all fayth, so that I can move mountayns oute of their places, and yet have no love, I am nothynge. ³ And though I bestowe all my goodes to fede the poore, and though I geve my body even that I burned, and yet have no love, it profyteth me nothynge.

⁴ Love suffreth longe, and is curteous. Love envyeth not. Love doth not frowardly, swelleth not, ⁵ dealeth not dishonestly, seketh not her awne, is not provoked to anger, thynketh no evyll, ⁶ rejoyseth not in iniquyte: but rejoyseth in the trueth, ⁷ suffreth all thynges, beleveth all thynges, hopeth all thynges, endureth all thynges. ⁸ Though that prophesyinges fayle, other tonges cease, or knowledge vanysshe awaye, yet love falleth never awaye.

⁹ For oure knowledge is unperfect, and oure prophesyinge is unperfect. ¹⁰ But when that whych is perfect, is come, then that whych is unperfect, shall be done awaye. ¹¹ When I was a chylde, I spake as a chylde, I understode as a chylde, I ymagined as a chylde. But assone as I was a man, I put awaye chyldeshnes. ¹² Nowe we se in a glasse, even in a darcke speakyng: but then shall we se face to face. Nowe I knowe unperfectly: but then shall I knowe even as I am knowen. ¹³ Nowe abydeth fayth, hope, and love, even these thre: but the chefe of these is love.

1539, revised 1540

From The Geneva Bible

Thogh I speake with the tongues of men and Angels, and have not love, I am as sounding brasse, or a tinkling cymbal. ² And thogh I had the gift of prophecie, and knewe all secretes and all knowledge, yea, if I had all faith, so that I colde remove mountaines and had not love, I were nothing. ³ And thogh I fede the poore with all my goods, and thogh I give my bodie, that I be burned, and have not love, it profiteth me nothing. ⁴ Love suffreth long: it is bountiful: love envieth not: love doeth not boast it self: it is not puffed up: ⁵ It disdaineth not: it seketh not her owne things: it is not provoked to anger: it thinketh not evil: ⁶ It rejoyceth not in iniquitie, but rejoyceth in the trueth. ⁷ It suffreth all things:

it beleveth all things: it hopeth all things: it endureth all things. [8] Love doeth never fall away, thogh that prophecyings be abolished, or the tongues cease or knowledge vanish away. [9] For we knowe in parte, and we prophecie in parte. [10] But when that which is perfite, is come, then that which is in parte, shalbe abolished. [11] When I was a childe, I spake as a childe, I understode as a childe, I thoght as a childe: but when I became a man, I put away childish things. [12] For now we se through a glasse darkely: but then shal we se face to face. Now I know in parte: but then shal I knowe even as I am knowen. [13] And now abideth faith, hope and love, even these thre: but the chiefest of these is love.

1560, revised 1602

From The Bishops' Bible

Though I speake with the tongues of men, and of Angels, and have not charitie, I am as sounding brasse, or as a tinckling cymbal. [2] And though I have prophecie, and understand all secrets, and all knowledge: yea, if I have all faith, so that I can remoove mountaines, and have not charitie, I am nothing. [3] And though I bestow all my goods to feed the poore, and though I give my body that I should be burned, and have not charitie, it profiteth me nothing. [4] Charitie suffereth long, and is courteous: Charitie envieth not, charity doth not frowardly, swelleth not, [5] Dealeth not dishonestly, seeketh not her owne, is not bitter, thinketh not evill, [6] Rejoyceth not in iniquitie, but rejoyceth in the trueth: [7] Suffreth all things, beleeveth all things, hopeth all things, endureth all things. [8] Though that prophecyings faile, either tongues cease, or knowledge vanish away, yet charitie falleth never away. [9] For our knowledge is unperfect, and our prophecying is unperfect: [10] But when that which is perfect is come, then that which is unperfect shalbe done away. [11] When I was a childe, I spake as a childe, I understood as a childe, I imagined as a childe: but assoone as I was a man, I put away childishnesse. [12] Now wee see in a glasse, even in a darke speaking: but then shall we see face to face. Now I know unperfectly: but then shall I know, even as I am knowen. [13] Now abideth faith, hope, and charitie, these three: but the chiefe of these is charitie.

1568, revised 1602

From The Douay-Rheims Version

If I speake with the tonges of men and of Angels, and have not charitie: I am become as sounding brasse, or a tinkling cymbal. [2] And if I should have prophecie, and knew al mysteries, and al knowledge, and if I should have al faith so that I could remove mountaines, and have not charitie, I am nothing. [3] And if I should distribute al my goods to be meate for the poore, and if I should deliver my body so that I burne, and have not charitie, it doth profit me nothing.

[4] Charitie is patient, is benigne: Charitie envieth not, dealeth not perversly: is not puffed up, [5] is not ambitious, seeketh not her owne, is not provoked to anger, thinketh not evil: [6] rejoyceth not upon iniquitie, but rejoyceth with the

truth: [7] suffereth al things, beleeveth al things, hopeth al things, beareth al things. [8] Charitie never falleth away: whether prophecies shal be made voide, or tonges shal cease, or knowledge shal be destroied. [9] For in part we know, and in part we prophecie. [10] But when that shal come that is perfect, that shal be made voide that is in part. [11] When I was a litle one, I spake as a litle one, I understood as a litle one, I thought as a litle one. But when I was made a man, I did away the things that belonged to a litle one. [12] We see now by a glasse in a darke sort: but then face to face. Now I know in part: but then I shal know as also I am knowen. [13] And now there remaine, faith, hope, charitie, these three, but the greater of these is charitie.

1582

From The King James Authorized Version

Though I speak with the tongues of men and of angels, and have not charity, I am become as sounding brass, or a tinkling cymbal. [2] And though I have the gift of prophecy, and understand all mysteries, and all knowledge; and though I have all faith, so that [7] could remove mountains, and have no charity, I am nothing. [3] And though I bestow all my goods to feed the poor, and though I give my body to be burned, and have not charity, it profiteth me nothing. [4] Charity suffereth long, and is kind; charity envieth not; charity vaunteth not itself, is not puffed up, [5] doth not behave itself unseemly, seeketh not her own, is not easily provoked, thinketh no evil; [6] rejoiceth not in iniquity, but rejoiceth in the truth; [7] beareth all things, believeth all things, hopeth all things, endureth all things. [8] Charity never faileth: but whether there be prophecies, they shall fail; whether there be tongues, they shall cease; whether there be knowledge, it shall vanish away. [9] For we know in part, and we prophesy in part. [10] But when that which is perfect is come, then that which is in part shall be done away. [11] When I was a child, I spake as a child, I understood as a child, I thought as a child: but when I became a man, I put away childish things. [12] For now we see through a glass, darkly; but then face to face: now I know in part; but then shall I know even as also I am known. [13] And now abideth faith, hope, charity, these three; but the greatest of these is charity.

1611, in edition of 1873

The Psalms in English Verse

Of central importance to the Reformation's concern both with liturgical reconstruction and the unmediated availability of vernacular Scripture were the metrical versions of the Psalter. Martin Luther had versified the Psalms, and paraphrased them in verse chorales, to which he had also written melodies, in order that the entire congregation in church might sing in their own language, rather than passively partaking in a dispensed Latin incantation. The French poet Clément Marot had versified the Psalms in the 1530's; in Geneva, the congregational singing of the Psalms in verse was established early (although in 1559, when introduced into an English church, the practice was still thought a novelty). Then, too, sophisticated biblical scholarship wanted to make clear that the Psalms in the original Hebrew were poetry, not prose; that David the musician-shepherd-king had composed sacred verse, and that this should be demonstrated in translation. In addition, the purely private practice among poets (Sir Thomas Wyatt and the Earl of Surrey are examples) of versifying the Psalms was a kind of penitential exercise.

In 1562 Thomas Sternhold, John Hopkins, and others completed a version of the Psalms in what is still called "common meter"—the familiar ballad stanza rhymed *abcd*, in four-beat lines alternating with three-beat ones (also used, in more learnedly literary poetry, as "fourteeners"). From their first publication until 1640, some 280 editions of the Sternhold-Hopkins renderings appeared. Rival translations were constantly being attempted, and the Scottish church had its own. A great tradition of psalm paraphrase grew up, in which a free adaptation of a psalm text became a literary form of its own, as well as a hymn for eventual musical setting and liturgical use. Often poets of the first rank attempted paraphrases, both in Latin and English verse, as exercises at once stylistic and spiritual, and it is interesting to observe the way in which changing poetic conventions affect the way in which the poetry of the Bible is rendered, often at three or four removes, linguistically.

The Psalm 137 (136 in the Vulgate) is a powerful and moving chant of protest, containing an extremely compelling and popular image. It is the refusal of a captive people to sing their native songs for the amusement or even the serious delectation of their conquerors; hanging the harp on the trees is a gesture of that refusal, standing for locking away all one's gifts and talents and skills, to live only the saddest and simplest of lives under one's captors. The versions presented below reflect changes in formal style and structure, and in the organization of imagery, over the course of more than a century. The King James Version of Psalm 137 is given complete; thereafter, the section comprising verses 1 through 6 will be given from various translations and paraphrases. In the case of Campion, Bacon, Crashaw, Carew, and Denham, the relevant Headnotes should be consulted. This text appealed to a great many poets who paraphrased it alone, not as part of a group of versions of the Psalms; the subject of song (poetry, creative power) refused, abandoned, or lost must have had great personal appeal.

From The King James Authorized Version

1 By the rivers of Babylon, there we sat down, yea, we wept, when we remembered Zion.

2 We hanged our harps upon the willows in the midst thereof.

3 For there they that carried us away captive required of us a song; and they that wasted us required of us mirth, saying, Sing us one of the songs of Zion.

4 How shall we sing the Lord's song in a strange land?

5 If I forget thee, O Jerusalem, let my right hand forget her cunning.

6 If I do not remember thee, let my tongue cleave to the roof of my mouth; if I prefer not Jerusalem above my chief joy.

7 Remember, O Lord, the children of Edom in the day of Jerusalem; who said Rase it, rase it, even to the foundation thereof.

8 O daughter of Babylon, who art to be destroyed; happy *shall he be,* that rewardeth thee as thou hast served us.

9 Happy *shall he be,* that taketh and dasheth thy little ones against the stones.

1611

From The Second Wycliffite Version

The Hundred and six and thirtieth Salm

On the floodis of Babiloyne there we saten,
and wepten; while we bithoughten on Syon.
In salwes° in the myddil thereof, we hangiden
up our orguns.° For thei that ledden us
prisoners, axiden us there the wordis of songis.
And their that ledden awei us seiden: Synge
ye to us an ympne° of the songis of Syon. Hou
schule we singe a songe of the Lord, in an
alien lond? If I forgete thee, Jerusalem,
my right hond be gouun to forgeting. Mi
tunge cleve to my chekis, if I bithenke not
on thee.

c. 1390

From The Geneva Bible

By the rivers of Babel we sate, and there we wept, when we remembered Zion.
We hanged our harps upon the willows in the middes thereof.
When they that led us captives required of us songs and mirth, when we had
hanged up our harps, saying Sing us one of the songs of Zion.
How shall we sing, said we, a song of the Lord in a strange land.
If I forget thee, O Jerusalem, may my right hand forget to play.

1560

From The Douay-Rheims Version

Upon the rivers of Babylon, there we sat and wept: when we remembered Sion.
On the willows in the midst thereof we hung up our instruments.
For there they that led us into captivity required of us the words of songs.
And they that carried us away, said: Sing ye to us a hymn of the songs of Sion.
How shall we sing the song of the Lord in a strange land?
If I forget thee, O Jerusalem, may my right hand be forgotten.

salwes sallows, willows   **ympne** hymn
orguns instruments

Let my tongue cleave to my jaws if I do not remember thee:
If I make not Jerusalem the beginning of my joy.

1582–1610

By Thomas Sternhold and John Hopkins

Whenas we sat in Babylon,
   the rivers round about,
And in remembrance of Ziòn
   the tears for grief burst out.
We hanged our harps and instruments°
   the willow trees upon,
For in that place men for their use
   had planted many one.

Then they to whom we prisoners were
   said to us tauntingly:
Now let us hear your Hebrew songs
   and pleasant melody.
Alas, said we, who can once frame
   his sorrowful heart to sing
The praises of our loving God,
   thus under the strange king.

But yet if I Jerusalem
   out of my heart let slide,
Then let my fingers quite forget
   the warbling harp to guide;
And let my tongue within my mouth
   be tied for ever fast,
If that I joy before I see
   thy full deliverance past.

1562

By The Countess of Pembroke°

Nigh seated where the river flows
   That watereth Babel's thankful plain,
Which then our tears in pearlèd rows
   Did help to water with their rain,
The thought of Zion bred such woes

---

harps and instruments this not for poetic elaboration, but out of uncertainty about how to translate the Vulgate *organum* (the Hebrew, *kinnor*, means "harp")
The Countess of Pembroke Sir Philip Sidney's sister wrote this paraphrase entitled *"Super Flumina"* (the opening words of the Latin translation: *Super flumina Babylonis*). It was part of a number she did to complete Sidney's own paraphrase of half the Psalter. Based on French paraphrases, their version embraces an amazing array of verse forms and brings to the rendering of the text all of those arts of language which Sidney so loved. This text is from a manuscript copied by Sir John Davies.

That, though our harps we did retain,
Yet useless and untouchèd there
On willows only hanged they were.

Now while our harps were hangèd so,
   The men whose captives there we lay
Did on our griefs insulting go,
   And more to grieve us thus did say:
You that of music make such show,
   Come sing us now a Zion lay.
——O no, we have nor voice nor hand
For such a song, in such a land.

Though far I lie, sweet Zion hill,
   In foreign soil exiled from thee,
Yet let my hand forget his skill
   If ever thou forgotten be;
Yea, let my tongue fast gluèd still
   Unto my roof lie mute in me,
If thy neglect within me spring,
Or ought I do but Salem sing.
c. 1590?

By Thomas Campion°

As by the streams of Babylon
Far from our native soil we sat,
Sweet Zion, thee we thought upon,
And every thought a tear begat.

Aloft the trees that spring up there
Our silent harps we pensive hung.°
Said they that captived us: 'Let's hear
Some song which you in Zion sung.'

Is then the song of our God fit
To be profaned in foreign land?
O Salem, thee when I forget,
Forget his skill may my right hand.

Fast to the roof may cleave my tongue
If mindless I of thee be found,
Or if, when all my joys are sung,
Jerusalem be not the ground.°
         c. 1614

Thomas Campion from his undated *Two Books of Airs*
pensive hung calling attention, delicately, to the etymological connection, in Latin, of these two words (*pendere*, to hang)

ground A personally meaningful musical pun: "ground" means the bass part, and the repeated melody or harmonic structure presented there, over which "divisions" or improvised melodic material will be composed or played.

By Francis Bacon°

When as we sat all sad and desolate,
  By Babylon upon the river's side,
Eased from the tasks which in our captive state
    We were enforcèd daily to abide,
        Our harps we had brought with us to the field,
        Some solace to our heavy souls to yield.

But soon we found we failed of our account,
  For when our minds some freedom did obtain,
Straightways the memory of Zion Mount
    Did cause afresh our wounds to bleed again;
        So that with present griefs, and future fears,
        Our eyes burst forth into a stream of tears.

As for our harps, since sorrow struck them dumb,
  We hanged them on the willow-trees were near;
Yet did our cruel masters to us come,
    Asking of us some Hebrew songs to hear:
        Taunting us rather in our misery,
        Than much delighting in our melody.

Alas (said we) who can once force or frame
  His grievèd and oppressèd heart to sing
The praises of Jehovah's glorious name,
    In banishment, under a foreign king?
        In Zion is his seat and dwelling place,
        Thence doth he shew the brightness of his face.

Hierusalem, where God his throne hath set,
  Shall any hour absent thee from my mind?
Then let my right hand quite her skill forget,
    Then let my voice and words no passage find;
        Nay, if I do not thee prefer in all,
        That in the compass of my thoughts can fall.
    1624   1624–25

By Richard Crashaw°

On the proud banks of great Euphrates' flood
  There we sat, and there we wept:
Our harps that now no music understood

Francis Bacon Bacon did a whole set of paraphrases while "in a fit of sickness" in 1624; it
was common for writers to translate the penitential Psalms, at least, under such circumstances. Bacon uses a variety of meters; these
particular stanzas must have had a plaintive
connotation for him.

Richard Crashaw from *Steps to the Temple*
(1646). The baroque poet's emblematic energy
animates the harps, dramatizes the rhetoric,
and concentrates with extreme detail on the
treatment of verse 6.

Nodding on the willows slept,
    While unhappy, captived we,
    Lovely Zion, thought on thee.

They, they that snatched us from our country's breast
    Would have a song carved to their ears
In Hebrew numbers then (O cruel jest!)
    When harps and hearts were drowned in tears:
        Come, they cried, come sing and play
        One of Zion's songs today.

Sing? Play? to whom (ah!) shall we sing or play,
    If not, Jerusalem, to thee?
Ah thee, Jerusalem! ah, sooner may
    This hand forget the mastery
        Of music's dainty touch, than I
        The music of thy memory.

Which when I lose, O may at once my tongue
    Lose this same busy, speaking art,
Unperched, her vocal arteries unstrung,
    No more acquainted with my heart,
        On my dry palate's roof to rest,
        A withered leaf, an idle guest.
                1646

By Thomas Carew°

Sitting by the streams that glide
    Down by Babel's towering wall,
With our tears we filled the tide
    Whilst our mindful thoughts recall
    Thee, O Zion, and thy fall.

Our neglected harps unstrung,
    Not acquainted with the hand
Of the skillful tuner, hung
    On the willow trees that stand
    Planted in the neighbour land.

Yet the spiteful foe commands
    Songs of mirth, and bids us lay
To dumb harps, our captive hands
    And (to scoff our sorrows) say:
    'Sing us some sweet Hebrew lay.'

But say we, our holy strain
    Is too pure for heathen land,

Thomas Carew first published from manuscript in 1655. The harps are here "neglected"—a far cry from the door-slamming gesture of the Hebrew text.

Nor may we God's Hymnés profane,
  Or move either voice or hand
  To delight a savage band.

Holy Salem, if thy love
  Fall from my forgetful heart,
May the skill by which I move
  Strings of music, tuned with art,
  From my withered hand depart!

May my speechless tongue give sound
  To no accents, but remain
To my prison roof fast bound,
  In my sad soul entertain
  Mirth, till thou rejoice again!
                1655

By Sir John Denham°

When on Euphrates' banks we sate,
Deploring Zion's dolefull state,
Our harps to which we lately sang,
Mute as ourselves, on willows hang.

Our sadness thus our spoiler jeers:
'Change into mirth your sighs and tears,
And give us with your hands and tongues
One of your pleasant Hebrew songs.'

Oh! how can we our airs compose
And sing of God amongst his foes!
When I forget his sacred hill,
May my right hand forget her skill!

When I shall thy remembrance leave,
My tongue to her dry roof shall cleave;
All other joys I shall contemn,
Calling to mind Jerusalem.
before 1668   1714

By Nahum Tate and Nicholas Brady°

When we, our weary limbs to rest,
Sat down by proud Euphrates' stream,
We wept, with doleful thoughts oppressed,

Sir John Denham Famous during the later 17th and the 18th century for his stylistic elegance and power, Denham here neatly but unsubtly blares out all the undertones which make the original so poignant ("Mute as ourselves").

Nahum Tate and Nicholas Brady The complete Tate-Brady version was designed to supplant Sternhold and Hopkins for liturgical use, and to appeal to Restoration taste.

And Zion was our mournful theme.
Our harps, that when with joy we sung
Were wont their tuneful parts to bear,
With silent strings, neglected, hung
On willow trees that withered° there.

Meanwhile our foes, who all conspired
To triumph in our slavish wrongs,
Music and mirth of us required:
'Come sing us one of Zion's songs.'
How shall we tune our voice to sing?
Or touch our harps with skillful hands?
Shall hymns of joy to God our King
Be sung by slaves in foreign lands?

O Salem, once our happy seat!
When I of thee forgetful prove,
Let then my trembling hand forget
The speaking strings with art to move!
If I to mention thee forbear,
Eternal silence seize my tongue,
Or if I sing one cheerful air
Till thy deliverance is my song.
                                    1696

THE NEW WORLD

For the Renaissance mind, the end of the fifteenth century witnessed the dawn of the New World as well as the intellectual reawakening of the Ancient one. The exploration and colonization of the Western hemisphere and of parts of the Orient (the two "Indies," East and West) were initiated by the Spanish and Portuguese voyagers, and the British were in fact rather slow to develop and dispatch expeditionary fleets. The Venetian John Cabot, sailing under the English flag, attained the Labrador coast on a voyage that started from Bristol years after Columbus set out from Lisbon, but it was not until the second half of the sixteenth century that such expeditions as those of Sir Francis Drake (1540?–96), Sir John Hawkins (1532–95), Sir Martin Frobisher (1532?–94), and Sir Humphrey Gilbert (1509–38), planner of a Northeast Passage to the Orient, would be launched. Circumnavigations and exploratory routes followed for their own sake gave way to naval expeditions and the near-piracy committed against Spanish shipping in the West Indies by Drake, and subsequently to early colonizations, such as Sir Richard Grenville's attempt in Virginia in 1585, and Sir Walter Ralegh's in Guiana ten years later.

Accounts of all these voyages were published and republished during the course of the century. The body of Renaissance travel writing reveals a domestication of fable into fact, an encompassing of the marvelous by the truthful that is far in advance of

---

withered This word has cropped up before in these versions; here, the willows may have withered partially in the sentimental rhetoric of the adaptation, partially because of an unstated half-pun on "withies" (= "willows").

contemporary scientific description in many other areas. An important prototype for English travel literature was the *De Orbe Novo* (Of the New World) of Peter Martyr of Anghiera (*fl.* 1510), of which the first part was published in 1511. In 1555 Richard Eden (1521–76) translated the whole work as *The Decades of the New World or West India,* making available in English a systematic account of the voyages of Columbus and his followers. Such records are of particular interest to literary history because of the mythological contexts in which the natural history of the New World was interpreted. The more speculative accounts considered the relation between the primitive and the civilized, and emerged with a complex set of attitudes conditioned by the romanticizing of rustic simplicity in pastoral literature, the myth of the Golden Age, and so forth. These accounts fed back into formal literature in a variety of ways, ranging from the elaborate meditations of Montaigne's essay "Of Cannibals" (see the Introduction to the Renaissance) to some of the backgrounds for Shakespeare's *The Tempest.*

A clergyman named Richard Hakluyt (1553–1616), made aware of the poor reputation of English maritime enterprise while attached to the embassy in Paris, attempted to improve that reputation by collecting and publishing reports of English voyages. In 1589 he brought out his *Principal Navigations, Voyages and Discoveries of the English Nation* (greatly augmented in three volumes in 1598–1600). Accounts of the expeditions of the Cabots, Hawkins, Frobisher, Drake, Gilbert, Ralegh, and others were systematically gathered together, and Hakluyt's work was continued by Samuel Purchas (1575–1626) in several books, including *Hakluytus Posthumus or Purchas His Pilgrims* (1625).

The excerpts given below commence with some passages from Eden's *Decades,* including as a postscript a remarkable disquisition on the varied skin colors of aboriginal races which interprets the diversification, without any racial or colonial condescension, as part of the providential decoration and beautification of created nature. Following these are two longer passages. The first is from Thomas Hariot's *Brief and True Report of the New-found Land of Virginia* (1588) from Hakluyt's 1600 edition; Hariot was a mathematician and astronomer of great gifts, a friend of Marlowe, Ralegh, and Drake among others, who accompanied Grenville on the 1585 Virginia adventure. The last selection is from Hakluyt's reprinting of Sir Francis Drake's account of his landing in what is today called Drake's Bay, just north of San Francisco, in the course of his 1577–80 circumnavigation of the globe. Sailing in his flagship *Pelican* (later renamed *The Golden Hind*), he passed through the Strait of Magellan, sailed up the coast of South America, attacking Spanish shipping all the way, and finally, in an attempt to discover a passage into the Atlantic, went as far north as latitude 48, almost as far as Vancouver. Stopping on the way back at Drake's Bay, he named the whole California coast New Albion and claimed it in the Queen's name. His discussion of the Indians' responses to the landing is quite different from Hariot's, being both colder and less discerning.

From The Decades of the New World
or West India

[The Golden World] [1]

The inhabitants of these Islands have been ever so used to live at liberty, in play and pastime, that they can hardly away with the yoke of servitude, which they attempt to shake off by all means they may. And surely if they had received our religion, I would think their life most happy of all men, if they might therewith enjoy their ancient liberty. . . . Among these simple souls, a few clothes serve the naked; weights and measures are not needful to such as can [2] not skill of craft and deceit, and have not the use of pestiferous money . . . they seem to live in that golden world of which the old writers speak so much, wherein men lived simply and innocently without enforcement of laws, without quarrelling, judges and libels, content only to satisfy nature, without further vexation for knowledge of things to come.

[During his exploration of Cuba, Columbus is at one point [3] extremely moved by the directness and simplicity of the aborigines and wonders "if that land were not heaven, which brought forth such a kind of man?" The argument continues:]

For it is certain that among them the land is as common as the sun and water, and that Mine and Thine (the seeds of all mischief) have no place with them. They are content with so little, that in so large a country they have rather superfluity than scarceness, so that (as we have said before) they seem to live in the golden world without toil, living in open gardens, not entrenched with ditches, divided with hedges, or defended with walls. They deal truly with one another without laws, without books and without judges. They take him for an evil and mischievous man, which taketh pleasure in doing hurt to another. . . .

[Of the Color of the Indians]

One of the marvellous things that God useth in the composition of man is colour, which doubtless can not be considered without great admiration in beholding one to be white, and another black, being colours utterly contrary. Some likewise to be yellow, which is between black and white, and other of other colours, as it were of divers liveries.[4] And as these colours are to be marvelled at, even so is it to be considered how they differ from another as it were by degrees, forasmuch as some men are white after divers sorts of whiteness, yellow after divers manners of yellow, and black after divers sorts of blackness; and how from white they go to yellow by discolouring to brown and red, and to black by ash colour, and murrey [5] somewhat lighter than black; and tawny like unto the West Indians which are altogether in general either purple or tawny like unto sod quinces, or of the colour of chestnuts or olives— which colour is to them natural and not by their going naked, as many have thought, albeit their nakedness have somewhat helped them thereunto. There-

---

1. From the First Decade, Book II.
2. Know.
3. From the First Decade, Book III.
4. Official uniforms.
5. Mulberry-colored.

fore in like manner and with such diversity as men are commonly white in Europe and black in Africa, even with like variety are they tawny in these Indies, with divers degrees diversely inclining more or less to black or white. No less marvel is it to consider that men are white in Seville, and black at the cape of Buena Speranza, and of chestnut colour at the river of Plata, being all in equal degrees from the equinoctial line. Likewise that the men of Africa and Asia that live under the burnt line (called *Zona Torrida*) [6] are black, and not they that live beneath or on this side the same line as in Mexico, Yucatan, Quauhtema, Lian, Nicaragua, Panama, Santo Domingo, Paria, Cape, Saint Augustine, Lima, Quito and the other lands of Peru which touch in the same equinoctial. . . . It may seem that such variety of colours proceedeth of man, and not of the earth, which may well be although we be all born of Adam and Eve, and know not the cause why God hath ordained it, otherwise than to consider that his divine majesty hath done this as infinite other to declare his omnipotence and wisdom in such diversity of colours as appear not only in the nature of man, but the like also in beasts, birds and flowers, where diverse and contrary colours are seen in one little feather, or the leaves growing out of one little stalk. Another thing is also to be noted as touching these Indians, and this is that their hair is not curled as is the Moors' and Ethiopians' that inhabit the same clime; neither are they bald except very seldom, and that but little. All which things may give further occasion to philosophers to search the secrets of nature and complexions of men with the novelties of the new world. . . .

1555

From A Brief and True Report

[A Renaissance Traveler Describes the Religion of Indians in Virginia] In respect of us they are a people poor, and for want of skill and judgment in the knowledge and use of our things, do esteem our trifles before things of greater value. Notwithstanding, in their proper manner (considering the want of such means as we have), they seem very ingenious. For although they have no such tools, nor any such crafts, sciences, and arts as we, yet in those things they do, they show excellency of wit.[1] And by how much they upon due consideration shall find our manner of knowledges and crafts to exceed theirs in perfection, and speed for doing or execution, by so much the more is it probable that they should desire our friendship and love, and have the greater respect for pleasing and obeying us. Whereby may be hoped, if means of good government be used, that they may in short time be brought to civility and the embracing of true religion.

Some religion they have already, which although it be far from the truth, yet being as it is, there is hope it may be the easier and sooner reformed.

They believe that there are many gods, which they call *Mantoac*, but of

6. The torrid zone is the region of the earth's surface lying between the tropics of Capricorn and Cancer.

1. Intelligence.

different sorts and degrees, one only chief and great god, which hath been from all eternity. Who, as they affirm, when he purposed to make the world, made first other gods of a principal order to be as means and instruments to be used in the creation and government to follow, and after the sun, moon, and stars as petty gods, and the instruments of the other order more principal. First, they say, were made waters, out of which by the gods was made all diversity of creatures that are visible or invisible.

For mankind, they say a woman was made first which, by the working of one of the gods, conceived and brought forth children. And in such sort, they say, they had their beginning. But how many years or ages have passed since, they say they can make no relation, having no letters nor other such means as we to keep records of the particularities of times past, but only tradition from father to son.

They think that all the gods are of human shape, and therefore, they represent them by images in the forms of men, which they call *Kewasowok* (one alone is called *Kewas*). These they place in houses appropriate or temples, which they call *Machicomuck*, where they worship, pray, sing, and make many times offering unto them. In some *Machicomuck*, we have seen but one *Kewas*, in some two, and in other some three. The common sort think them to be also gods.

They believe also the immortality of the soul that, after this life as soon as the soul is departed from the body, according to the works it hath done, it is either carried to heaven, the habitat of gods, there to enjoy perpetual bliss and happiness, or else to a great pit or hole which they think to be in the furthest parts of their part of the world toward the sunset, there to burn continually. The place they call *Popogusso*.

For the confirmation of this opinion, they told me two stories of two men that had been lately dead and revived again. The one happened, but a few years before our coming into the country, of a wicked man, which having been dead and buried, the next day the earth of the grave being seen to move, was taken up again, who made declaration where his soul had been. That is to say, very near entering into *Popogusso*, had not one of the gods saved him, and gave him leave to return again and teach his friends what they should do to avoid that terrible place of torment. The other happened in the same year we were there, but in a town that was sixty miles from us, and it was told me for strange news, that one being dead, buried, and taken up again as the first, showed that although his body had lain dead in the grave, yet his soul was alive and had travelled far in a long broad way, on both sides whereof grew most delicate and pleasant trees, bearing more rare and excellent fruits, than ever he had seen before or was able to express, and at length came to most brave and fair houses, near which he met his father that had been dead before, who gave him great charge to go back again and show his friends what good they were to do to enjoy the pleasures of that place, which when he had done he should after come again.

What subtlety soever be in the *Wiroances* [2] and priests, this opinion worked so much in many of the common and simple sort of people, that it maketh them have great respect to their governors, and also great care what they do,

2. Wiroances, chieftains.

to avoid torment after death, and to enjoy bliss, although notwithstanding there is punishment ordained for malefactors, as stealers, whoremongers, and other sort of wicked-doers, some punished with death, some with forfeitures, some with beating, according to the greatness of the facts.

And this is the sum of their religion, which I learned by having special familiarity with some of their priests. Wherein they were not so sure grounded, nor gave such credit to their traditions and stories, but through conversing with us they were brought into great doubts of their own, and no small admiration of ours, with earnest desire in many, to learn more than we had means for want of perfect utterance in their language to express.

Most things they saw with us, as mathematical instruments, sea compasses, the virtue of the lodestone in drawing iron, a perspective glass [3] whereby was showed many strange sights, burning glasses, wild fireworks, guns, hooks, writing and reading, spring-clocks that seem to go of themselves, and many other things that we had were so strange unto them, and so far exceeded their capacities to comprehend the reason and means how they should be made and done, that they thought they were rather the works of gods than of men, or at the leastwise, they had been given and taught us by the gods. Which made many of them have such opinion of us, as that if they knew not the truth of God and religion already, it was rather to be had from us whom God so specially loved, than from a people that were so simple as they found themselves to be in comparison of us. Whereupon greater credit was given unto that we spoke of, concerning such matters.

Many times and in every town where I came, according as I was able, I made declaration of the contents of the Bible, that therein was set forth the true and only God, and his mighty works, that therein was contained the true doctrine of salvation through Christ, with many particulars of miracles and chief points of religion, as I was able then to utter, and thought fit for the time. And although I told them the book materially and of itself was not of any such virtue, as I thought they did conceive, but only the doctrine therein contained, yet would many be glad to touch it, to embrace it, to kiss it, to hold it to their breasts and heads, and stroke over all their body with it, to show their hungry desire of that knowledge which was spoken of.[4]

1600

From Drake's Account

[Sir Francis Drake Lands Near What Is Now San Francisco]
In this bay we anchored the seventeenth of June, and the people of the country, having their houses close by the water's side, showed themselves unto us, and sent a present to our general.

When they came unto us, they greatly wondered at the things which we

3. An early telescope Hariot had developed; the "strange sights" included magnification, image-inversion, etc. "Burning glasses," however, were concave mirrors used to concentrate solar heat.
4. This misinterpretation of the Indians' totemic attachment to the book itself is ironically generous; it represents what a Christian humanist who believed in natural reason would want to be true.

brought, but our general, according to his natural and accustomed humanity, courteously entreated them, and liberally bestowed on them necessary things to cover their nakedness, whereupon they supposed us to be gods, and would not be persuaded to the contrary. The presents which they sent unto our general were feathers and cawls of network.

Their houses are digged round about with earth, and have from the uttermost brims of the circle clifts [1] of wood set upon them, joining close together at the top like a spire steeple, which by reason of that closeness are very warm.

Their bed is the ground with rushes strawed on it, and, lying about the house, they have the fire in the middest.[2] The men go naked, the women take bulrushes and kemb [3] them after the manner of hemp, and thereof make their loose garments, which being knit about their middles hang down about their hips, having also about their shoulders a skin of deer, with the hair upon it. These women are very obedient and serviceable [4] to their husbands.

After they were departed from us, they came and visited us the second time, and brought with them feathers and bags of tobacco for presents. And when they came to the top of the hill, at the bottom whereof we had pitched our tents, they stayed themselves, where one appointed for speaker wearied himself with making a long oration, which done, they left their bows upon the hill and came down with their presents.

In the meantime the women remaining on the hill tormented themselves lamentably, tearing their flesh from their cheeks, whereby we perceived that they were about [5] a sacrifice. In the meantime our general, with his company, went to prayer and to reading of the Scriptures, at which exercise they were attentive and seemed greatly to be affected with it. But when they were come unto us they restored again unto us those things which before we had bestowed upon them.

The news of our being there being spread through the country, the people that inhabited round about came down, and amongst them the king himself, a man of a goodly stature and comely personage,[6] with many other tall and warlike men, before whose coming were sent two ambassadors to our general to signify that their king was coming, in doing of which message their speech was continued about half an hour. This ended, they by signs requested our general to send something by their hand to their king, as a token that his coming might be in peace. Wherein our general having satisfied them, they returned with glad tidings to their king, who marched to us with a princely majesty, the people crying continually after their manner, and, as they drew near unto us, so did they strive to behave themselves in their actions with comeliness.

In the forefront was a man of a goodly personage, who bare the sceptre or mace before the king, whereupon hanged two crowns, a less and a bigger, with three chains of a marvellous length. The crowns were made of knitwork wrought

1. Stakes (because cleft from branches): clearly, a tepee is being described.
2. Midst.
3. Comb.
4. Prepared to serve.
5. Engaged in.
6. Appearance.

artificially with feathers of divers colours. The chains were made of a bony substance, and few be the persons among them that are admitted to wear them, and of that number also the persons are stinted, as some ten, some twelve, etc. Next unto him which bare the sceptre was the king himself, with his guard about his person, clad with cony [7] skins and other skins. After them followed the naked common sort of people, every one having his face painted, some with white, some with black, and other colours, and having in their hands one thing or other for a present, not so much as their children but they also brought their presents.

In the meantime, our general gathered his men together, and marched within his fenced place, making against their approaching a very warlike show. They being trooped together in their order, and a general salutation being made, there was presently a general silence. Then he that bare the sceptre before the king, being informed by another whom they assigned to that office, with a manly and lofty voice proclaimed that which the other spake to him in secret, continuing half an hour, which ended and a general amen, as it were, given, the king, with the whole number of men and women (the children excepted), came down without any weapon, who descending to the foot of the hill set themselves in order.

In coming towards our bulwarks and tents, the sceptre-bearer began a song, observing his measures in a dance, and that with a stately countenance, whom the king with his guard, and every degree of persons following, did in like manner sing and dance, saving only the women, which danced and kept silence. The general permitted them to enter within our bulwark, where they continued their song and dance a reasonable time. When they had satisfied themselves, they made signs to our general to sit down, to whom the king and divers others made several orations, or rather supplication, that he would take their province and kingdom into his hand and become their king, making signs that they would resign unto him their right and title of the whole land and become his subjects. In which to persuade us the better, the king and the rest with one consent and with great reverence, joyfully singing a song, did set the crown upon his head, enriched his neck with all their chains, and offered unto him many other things, honouring him by the name of *Hioh*, adding thereunto, as it seemed, a sign of triumph, which thing our general thought not meet to reject, because he knew not what honour and profit it might be to our country. Wherefore in the name and to the use of her Majesty he took the sceptre, crown, and dignity of the said country in his hands, wishing that the riches and treasure thereof might so conveniently be transported to the enriching of her kingdom at home as it aboundeth in the same.

The common sort of the people, leaving the king and his guard with our general, scattered themselves together with their sacrifices among our people, taking a diligent view of every person; and such as pleased their fancy (which were the youngest) they, enclosing them about, offered their sacrifices unto them with lamentable weeping, scratching, and tearing the flesh from their faces with their nails, whereof issued abundance of blood. But we used signs to them of disliking this, and stayed their hands from force, and directed them

7. Rabbit.

upwards to the living God, whom only they ought to worship. They showed unto us their wounds, and craved help of them at our hands, whereupon we gave them lotions, plasters, and ointments agreeing to the state of their griefs, beseeching God to cure their diseases. Every third day they brought their sacrifices unto us, until they understood our meaning, that we had no pleasure in them. Yet they could not be long absent from us, but daily frequented our company to the hour of our departure, which departure seemed so grievous unto them that their joy was turned into sorrow. They entreated us that being absent we would remember them, and by stealth provided a sacrifice, which we misliked.[8]

Our necessary business being ended, our general with his company travelled up into the country to their villages, where we found herds of deer by a thousand in a company, being most large and fat of body.

1600

THE ENGLISH HUMANISTS

The authors in this brief selection would not have called themselves humanists or used the word humanism to describe their activities. The Italian scholars of a generation earlier, who coined the word humanist, meant by it a teacher of the *studia humanitatis*, that is to say, of the language, literature, and antiquities of ancient Rome and later of Greece. For them, though they despised "monkish" stupidity, narrow pedantry, and restricted, technical learning, the word had none of the secular connotations—implying an emphasis on profane, human values rather than on divine—which it began to acquire in the nineteenth century. Their chief concern was with sound and wholesome doctrine —religious, philosophical, and moral—so eloquently expressed that men would be persuaded to accept it and put its precepts into action. The sixteenth-century English-men who occupied themselves with the study of classical literature, science, and philosophy had all consciously set themselves to improve the quality of life in their country by this means.

When John Colet (1466?–1519), Dean of St. Paul's and son of a former Lord Mayor of London, decided in about 1508 to use his large private fortune for the foundation of a school in which 153 boys should receive a free education, he wrote into the statutes of the school a kind of manifesto of what an elementary education should consist of. His statutes were copied by other foundations in England during the century: they set the tone of learned piety (*pietas letterata*)—to use the Protestant term—which is characteristic of the country and the century. The boys are to be taught the Christian faith and "good literature." They are to read only "good authors, such as have the very [i.e. true] Roman eloquence, joined with wisdom," and their curriculum is to set aside the "barbarousness and corruption" of medieval authors ("ignorant, blind fools," Colet calls them), with their adulterated Latin, "which may rather be called blotterature than literature." The ultimate end of their schooling is to "increase . . . good Christian life and manners" in the children.

Colet's language reflects the strength and impatience of his temper: his statutes mirror his fervor for the morally good life and his zeal for the ancient tongues as they had been spoken and written in ancient Rome itself, before the ⌣ . Ages began with

8. Disliked.

its sack by the barbarians. The educational methods of his younger friend Thomas More were less formal, more private, and perhaps more subtle. More's "school" was his household, where every younger member, boy or girl, mastered Latin and Greek, so that Erasmus and others held it up as a model to the rest of Europe. Colet's aim, and his mode of putting it into operation, were more practical and more immediately productive: More's are at least as significant and, ultimately, effective. His unspoken intentions are in part embodied in his *Utopia*.

Both More and Colet lived through an age which seemed to be, as Erasmus put it, a golden one for the arts and letters—the early years of the young King Henry VIII's reign. Colet did not live to see what would have seemed to him, as it did to More, the disaster of England's severance, in religion, from the Church of Rome. Both had written the most significant part of their output in the international language of Latin; both were well known, Colet less than More, to learned circles in Europe. Both had been much influenced by European scholars and philosophers, Italian, French, and Netherlandish.

A consciousness of European contexts runs through the implicit and explicit patriotism which is a feature of the life and work of both Colet and More. They were, on the other hand, less concerned with the status of their own language. More, under the pressure of time and circumstance in later life, wrote his works of religious controversy, which had a specifically English reference, in English, but neither More nor Colet makes a deliberate, conscious effort to strengthen and improve the language part of their program.

The rise of English as a general, even as a learned, means of communication goes back to the fourteenth century, and the effort to strengthen and adorn it is constant among the poets and prose writers of the fifteenth. Translation had played a large part in this, as a practice by which one could expect to improve both the matter and the manner of vernacular writing. It continued to do so in the sixteenth century, growing more and more an accepted mode as the century went on.

Sir Thomas More's contemporary, Sir Thomas Elyot, is typical of the early phase of English "vernacular humanism." Like More, he was a lawyer—a member of the profession that the Italian professional humanist held in contempt for money-grubbing and bad Latin. He is the first of the English humanists to set down an extended program, in his case largely borrowed from Italian sources, for the training of English youth to serve the commonwealth. He also sets himself to enrich the English language by introducing Latin vocabulary and Greek syntax, seeking semantic wealth and pithy brevity to help him get his program across. Later in the century, the fondness for the learned word, to the exclusion rather than the augmentation of the English, was to result in the vogue for "inkhorn" terms, Latinized forms fetched out of the bottom of scholarly inkwells to increase the eloquence and expressiveness of the English language. It was this kind of thing that later provoked Sir John Cheke to the protest of his prefatory letter to Sir Thomas Hoby's translation of Castiglione's *Il Cortegiano*:

> I am of this opinion, that our own tongue should be written clean and pure, unmixed and unmangled with borrowing of other tongues, wherein if we take not heed betimes, ever borrowing and never repaying, she shall be fain to keep her house as bankrupt. . . .

Cheke had his own excesses in his search for a plain English for Englishmen to write. In his translation of the Gospel according to St. Matthew, he makes an attempt to produce a native English equivalent for the words he is translating, which will also cut away the Catholic associations of the usual words. So he replaces the Greek-derived "apostle" by its etymological equivalent, "frosent," i.e. from + sent; and "lunatic" by "mooned." The experiment is bizarre, but it reflects the concern that Cheke and his fellow scholars felt for their language and its role in the intellectual and religious life of the nation.

In other areas, too, English had been steadily gaining ground: by Cheke's day it was already the accepted language for professional writing, in legal and in scientific treatises for example. In 1582 Richard Mulcaster, speaking from the most conservative of professions, as headmaster of the same St. Paul's School that Colet had founded, can say: "I love Rome, but London better, I favour Italy, but England more, I honour the Latin, but I worship the English." Mulcaster was recognizing a *fait accompli* at the same time as he was framing a manifesto. By this time, the translators had done their work thoroughly and the patriots, like Roger Ascham, had also done their best to naturalize Latin rhetoric and make it speak with an English tongue.

In Ascham, concern for the language takes the form of a careful imitation of Ciceronian prose as the model for Latin composition—which was a Renaissance commonplace—and the attempt to apply the firm structural principles of Ciceronian rhetoric to the writing of English as well. Other experiments, such as the imitation of classical meters and the discarding of rhyme in English verse, did not meet with much success.

Ascham's enthusiasm for ancient Italy and Greece was not accompanied by a delight in modern Italy: in life and in doctrine she was an example to be avoided. For Ascham's friend Sir Thomas Hoby, Italian example, as represented in the finest of all the Renaissance "courtesy books," the works that set out the requirements of life in a truly civilized society, was above all an example to be followed. His translation of Castiglione's *Il Cortegiano* is a spirited achievement, far surpassing Elyot's earlier imitation of another Italian courtesy book in the sophistication of its doctrine and the elegance of its presentation.

The achievement of these men, their teachers and pupils, is to have brought English finally to the point where it could rival any of the languages of Europe as a literary medium. It was never the function of humanism to dwell in the past: the lessons which the humanists asked the classical past to give them in language and in wisdom were lessons which they hoped could be applied toward the perfection of the present. They sought to know Latin and Greek as the means both of bridging the gap between their own times and the glories of the past and of claiming kinship with it. The empire of England was rising to the point where it felt that it could challenge comparison with its ancestor, the Roman empire, in all the arts of peace and war.

The Headnote, text, and glosses for this section were prepared by J. B. Trapp.

SIR THOMAS MORE
1478?–1535

Thomas More, knighted by Henry VIII in 1521, was executed by Henry's order in 1535 and canonized four hundred years after his death. The son of a prominent lawyer who became a judge, he spent his early years in the household of Cardinal Morton, from whom he may have got some of his information about Richard III. After continuing his education at Oxford University he studied at the Inns of Court, where he completed his legal training, meanwhile living, without taking vows, among the Carthusian monks in London. His object was to test his religious vocation: and he characteristically chose the most austere of the orders with which to live. Finally opting for the law rather than the church, he rose rapidly in his profession, as a public man—Member of Parliament, an Under-Sheriff of the City of London (legal adviser to the Mayor and other officers)—and a favored counselor of Henry VIII. He went on several occasions as ambassador to Flanders and to France, became a member of the King's Council (1517), Under-Treasurer of England (1521), Speaker of the House of Commons (1523), and finally Lord Chancellor, the highest secular office in the kingdom, in 1529. In 1532 he resigned this office. More had always opposed the King's divorce from Catharine of Aragon, but his resignation was on the issue of Henry's claim, as a temporal ruler, to be Supreme Head of the Church. Two years of poverty and ill-health followed before More's arrest in 1534 and committal to the Tower. On July 1, 1535 he was tried and convicted of treason on perjured evidence; he was beheaded on July 6.

More was the friend and often the benefactor of most of the leading scholars in the England of his day, as well as being the most famous Englishman—the King and perhaps Cardinal Wolsey excepted—on the continent of Europe. His fame abroad he owed chiefly to his *Utopia,* written in Latin, partly during his embassy to Flanders in 1516 and partly on his return to London, and published at Louvain in 1516. Desiderius Erasmus, the great Dutch humanist scholar, with whom More had become friendly during his first visit to England in 1499, saw it through the press. Erasmus is partly responsible for More's European reputation, having attended to the publication of most of his Latin works—few of them published in More's native country in their author's lifetime—and made him known to correspondents. His pen-pictures of the man and the academy he had made of his home in London, where as much care was taken for the education of daughters as for that of his son and the other male members of the household, reflect the serenity and happiness, the rational, learned, but not solemn calm, that he and others found there, just as they found in the person of More himself a model and a stay.

Thomas More's first literary works were probably some English poems, followed by Latin epigrams, and, with Erasmus, translations of Lucian's Greek into Latin. His *Life of John Picus, Earl of Mirandula,* translated about 1505–10 for the instruction of a nun, tells us, by implication, much about the formation of More's character: his austerity, the evenness of his temper, his wit, his detachment, and his love of piety and learning.

For some years after this translation, More seems to have written little, presumably because of the demands of his career and of the four children born between about 1505 and 1509 to him and his first wife. (His second marriage, to a lady neither young nor beautiful, as he uncharitably put it, was contracted within a month of the early death of his first wife, probably about 1511. There were no more children.) But in 1515 More found himself on an embassy to Flanders with a little time on his hands. The result was *Utopia.* In its second book, written after his return to London, More debates the classic dilemma of the humanist scholar: whether, in occupying oneself in public affairs and the service of one's king, one is making better use of oneself and one's talents than in the pursuit of philosophic wisdom. It was the decision that More was himself faced with at just this time. Having married and acquired a family and having ruled out a monastic calling, he could not hope to lead the life of a detached scholar. But he could, as his experience so far had shown, make a lucrative career in the law. Like most of his fellow humanists, who both wrote and spoke the international language of Latin, he was in demand for embassies abroad as well as counsel at home. Should he serve his king or not? By 1517 he had decided and had entered Henry's service: twenty years later, on the point of execution, he was to protest that he had kept the oath he had taken to the King, dying "the King's good servant, but God's first."

The *Utopia* was followed by a historical masterpiece: the *History of Richard III*, which exists in two versions, Latin and English, and was probably written about 1517–18. There were also more Latin verses.

After 1520 More wrote little that was not official business or religious controversy, except for the devotional works, in English, that were probably produced almost entirely during the last year or two of his life. His career as a religious controversialist begins explicitly in the service of Henry VIII, whose reply to the tract by Martin Luther on the *Babylonian Captivity of the Church*—the reply that earned Henry the papal title of Defender of the Faith—was edited by More. Luther retorted and More replied, pseudonymously, in his Latin *Responsio ad Lutherum* (1523). Five years later, at the request of the Church in England, More again embarked on works of religious controversy, this time in English: he was licensed by the Bishop of London to read the Lutheran and other heretical books that were now being imported into England, and to refute their errors. The refutation runs to half a dozen books in six years, amounting to over three-quarters of a million words. Later still, in the little time that remained to him, he wrote his *Dialogue of Comfort in Tribulation*, in English, a debate between a pious old Hungarian nobleman and his nephew on how they are to behave in the face of the conquering and cruel Turk. The work clearly concerns More's own case, the theme being the proper conduct of a pious Catholic in the face of a tyrannical ruler. This book, and the *Treatise on the Passion*, a meditation begun in English and completed in Latin, are, with the exception of letters to his family and friends, the last works that More wrote.

Most of what More produced, in English or in Latin, was published in his lifetime, the most notable exceptions being the *Dialogue of Comfort* and the *Treatise on the Passion*, as well as the *History of Richard III*. All these were included in the edition of his collected English *Works*, brought out in London during the reign of Queen Mary, in 1557. Editions of his Latin works appeared in 1563, 1565 (the first complete edition, published at Louvain), 1566, and 1689, this last including the Latin biography by Thomas Stapleton, written in 1588.

We possess several sixteenth-century biographies of More in English, the shortest and in many ways the best being that of his son-in-law, William Roper, probably written in the 1550's, but not published until 1626. Roper's account of More's death is given below. The fullest is by Nicholas Harpsfield, written in 1558, first published in full in 1932.

Utopia

The book which made More famous immediately after it was published in 1516 came out in five more editions before 1520. It was translated into German in 1524, but did not appear in English until 1551, when Ralph Robinson made the version from which the following extracts are taken.

The first book of *Utopia* was written second, on More's return to England from his embassy, in the time he could snatch from the demands of a busy family and professional life. Its object is to point the contrast between a rationally ordered state, such as the far-off island commonwealth of the Utopians described in the second book, and the Europe of More's day, where all, from kings downward, are bent on self-aggrandizement and self-enrichment. Kings manipulate alliances, war with each other for territory, extort money from their subjects. Their subjects, in turn, oppress others of their subjects.

More's account of the exactions of the great landlords given in the *Utopia* takes us over some of the same grievances as the *Second Shepherds' Play* and *Piers Plowman*. Wealthy English landowners, dispossessing small farmers of their land so as to increase the pasture for sheep, create unemployment. The unemployed turn to beggary and theft as alternatives to starvation, and English justice, instead of using a system of forced labor as a means of punishment, adopts the foolish deterrent of hanging thieves, which does not, in fact, reduce their number. The sheep are the culprits: it is they that should be punished.

It is important to realize that in this account of the evils of his day as well as in the description of Utopia itself, More is no radical reformer, looking to see a system swept away and a bright new one put in its place. His view of society is of an ordered hierarchy and just keeping of degree, from the divinely invested, God-fearing king downward. It was to the keeping of that social order in its best and fairest form that More devoted himself both in theory and in practice and it is to full participation in that form that he invites the scholar and philosopher in the first book of his *Utopia*.

Like the first book, the second is put into the mouth of a chance-met traveler, Raphael Hythlodaeus, whose name is derived from Greek, like most of the names in the *Utopia*, and means "babbler." It describes the island state that this traveler found during the voyages that he made after he had parted company with his commander, Amerigo Vespucci, from whose accounts of Indian customs in his *New World* and *Four Voyages* some of the details of Utopian social organization and practices seem to have been taken. Hythlodaeus tells of a society where all is ordered according to the dictates of reason and of nature, where people do not say one thing and do another. It is therefore No-place (Greek *ou-*, not, *topos*, place) and the narrative throughout is conditioned by the favorite late medieval and Renaissance mode of defining by negatives in its exploration of the paradox of the irrational behavior of man, the rational, social animal. If the reasoned usages of *Utopia* sometimes strike us as too severe, we must remember that More is always saying "This happens nowhere."

This is the overriding condition of his "poetry," as his Protestant religious enemies were to call it. The *Utopia* is not, like Plato's *Republic* or *Laws*, to whose ideas and ultimately to whose literary form it owes so much, a serious account of an ideal or even a possible commonwealth. Its title, which may be the work of Erasmus rather than More, proclaims it *A little book, truly golden, not less useful than entertaining*, and it aims, in what was More's favorite mode, to use irony, wit, and satire as a means of making men see what is good and true. In form and in spirit it is much closer to Lucian of Samosata, the Greek satirist of the second century A.D., one of More's favorite authors, than it is to Plato. Lucian's dialogues aim to be entertaining as well as to explore a serious topic in an interesting way. More and Erasmus translated some of them together in 1505, and among those translated by More was the *Menippus*, which may well have given him the idea for *Utopia*. It opens with a serious discussion among friends and continues with a traveler's tale of a fabulous place (in this case Hell), the lessons of which are applied to the questions raised in the preliminary discussion.

More's serious wit never obscures the implied comparison between the virtuous pagans of Utopia with the professed Christians of Europe, who fall so short of standards of reasonable conduct, either pagan or Christian. Utopia demands that all its citizens participate for a set time in the agriculture which supplies the necessities of an unpretentious life from the labor of a six-hour day. Its social organization is patriarchal, in family units, with slaves for menial duties. All property is held in common and the Utopians are indifferent to money, gold, silver, and precious stones. All the activities of the citizens are carefully supervised, including travel, marriage, the care of the sick, the elimination of the old and infirm. The Utopians hate war, but if they cannot avoid it they try to minimize its harm to the state by shortening it by every means available, including treachery, and by hiring mercenaries to fight it for them. They are not afraid to do what is morally reprehensible in order to secure a greater good. In peace they keep faith, both public and private, and therefore have no need of laws and lawyers. They love knowledge and wisdom, they pursue happiness in "good and decent" pleasure, they worship a single god, and they believe in the immortality of the soul and the happiness of the life after death. They observe the greatest solemnity in the practice of their religion and are convinced of its truth, but they would abandon it for one that could be proved better.

In all this, More is saying, the Utopians are right and we in Christian Europe wrong. Utopia is nowhere: we can only wish that it were here, now, in our part of the world.

Utopia

From *Book I*

[Utopian Communism]

That is it which I meant (quoth he) when I said philosophy had no place among kings.

Indeed (quoth I) this school philosophy [1] hath not, which thinketh all things meet for every place. But there is another philosophy more civil,[2] which knoweth, as ye would say, her own stage, and thereafter ordering and behaving herself in the play that she hath in hand, playeth her part accordingly with comeliness, uttering nothing out of due order and fashion. And this is the philosophy that you must use. Or else whiles a comedy of Plautus [3] is playing, and the vile bondmen [4] scoffing and trifling among themselves, if you should suddenly come upon the stage in a philosopher's apparel, and rehearse out of Octavia [5] the place wherein Seneca disputeth with Nero: had it not been better

1. Academic. This is a reference to the medieval system of scholasticism, regarded as purely speculative and useless.
2. Relating to society; practical.
3. Roman writer of comedies, 254–184 B.C.
4. Slaves, who were characters in the play.
5. Lucius Annaeus Seneca, Roman Stoic philosopher and playwright, *c.* 5 B.C.–65 A.D., did not write the play *Octavia*, a historical drama. The dispute of Seneca and Nero in the second act concerns the royal and civic virtues that More deals with here. Seneca has been extolling retirement and withdrawal, but then turns to engagement as the better course.

for you to have played the dumb person,[6] than by rehearsing that, which served neither for the time nor place, to have made such a tragical comedy or gillimaufry?[7] For by bringing in other stuff that nothing apperttaineth to the present matter, you must needs mar and pervert the play that is in hand, though the stuff that you bring be much better. What part soever you have taken upon you, play that as well as you can and make the best of it: and do not therefore disturb and bring out of order the whole matter, because that another, which is merrier, and better, cometh to your remembrance. So the case standeth in a commonwealth, and so it is in the consultations of kings and princes. If evil opinions and naughty[8] persuasions cannot be utterly and quite plucked out of their hearts, if you cannot, even as you would, remedy vices, which use and custom hath confirmed: yet for this cause you must not leave and forsake the commonwealth: you must not forsake the ship[9] in a tempest, because you cannot rule and keep down the winds. No, nor you must not labour to drive into their heads new and strange informations, which you know well shall be nothing regarded with them that be of clean contrary minds. But you must with a crafty wile and a subtle train[10] study and endeavour yourself, as much as in you lieth, to handle the matter wittily[11] and handsomely[12] for the purpose, and that which you cannot turn to good, so to order it that it be not very bad. For it is not possible for all things to be well, unless all men were good. Which I think will not be yet this good many years.

By this means (quoth he) nothing else will be brought to pass, but whiles that I go about to remedy the madness of others, I should be even as mad as they. For if I would speak things that be true I must needs speak such things; but as for to speak[13] false things, whether that be a philosopher's part or no; I cannot tell, truly it is not my part. Howbeit this communication of mine, though peradventure it may seem unpleasant to them, yet can I not see why it should seem strange, or foolishly newfangled. If so be that I should speak those things that Plato feigneth in his weal public:[14] or that the Utopians do in theirs, these things though they were (as they be indeed) better, yet they might seem spoken out of place. Forasmuch as here amongst us, every man hath his possessions several[15] to himself, and there all things be common. But what was in my communication contained, that might not, and ought not in any place to be spoken? Saving that to them which have thoroughly decreed and determined with themselves to roam headlong the contrary way, it cannot be acceptable and pleasant, because it calleth them back, and showeth them the jeopardies. Verily if all things that evil and vicious manners have caused to

6. A regular role, the "thinking" part, in Greek and Roman drama.
7. Originally a dish made up of odds and ends of food, hodge-podge.
8. Wicked.
9. The ship of state is a regular metaphor, from Plato's *Republic* onward.
10. Device, strategy.
11. Wisely.
12. Suitably. This is the principle of "accommodation"—regular advice to civil philosophers not to insist on strict and pure virtue, but to bring princes to see what they must do by less direct means.
13. That is, as for speaking.
14. That is, commonwealth, i.e. Plato's *Republic,* the classic account of an ideal state.
15. Separate.

seem inconvenient and nought [16] should be refused, as things unmeet and re-proachful, then we must among Christian people wink at [17] the most part of all those things, which Christ taught us,[18] and so strictly forbade them to be winked at, that those things also which he whispered in the ears of his disciples, he commanded to be proclaimed in open houses.[19] And yet the most part of them is more dissident from the manners of the world nowadays, than my communication was. But preachers, sly and wily men, following your counsel (as I suppose) because they saw men evil willing [20] to frame their manners to Christ's rule, they have wrested [21] and perverted his doctrine, and like a rule of lead [22] have applied it to men's manners: that by some means at the least-ways, they might agree together. Whereby I cannot see what good they have done: but that men may more sickerly [23] be evil. And I truly should prevail even as much in king's councils. For either I must say otherways than they say, and then I were as good to say nothing, or else I must say the same that they say, and (as Mitio saith in Terence [24]) help to further their madness. For that crafty wile, and subtle train of yours, I cannot perceive to what purpose it serveth, wherewith you would have me to study and endeavour myself, if all things cannot be made good, yet to handle them wittily and handsomely for the purpose, that as far forth as is possible they may not be very evil. For there is no place to dissemble in, nor to wink in. Naughty counsels must be openly allowed and very pestilent decrees must be approved. He shall be counted worse than a spy, yea almost as evil as a traitor, that with a faint heart doth praise evil and noisome decrees. Moreover a man can have no occasion to do good, chancing into the company of them which will sooner make nought a good man, than be made good themselves: through whose evil company he shall be marred, or else if he remain good and innocent, yet the wickedness and foolishness of others shall be imputed to him, and laid in his neck.[25] So that it is impossible with that crafty wile and subtle train to turn anything to better. Wherefore Plato [26] by a goodly similitude [27] declareth, why wise men refrain to meddle in the commonwealth. For when they see the people swarm into the streets, and daily wet to the skin with rain, and yet cannot persuade them to go out of the rain and to take their houses, knowing well, that if they should

16. Worthless, wrong.
17. Close their eyes to.
18. Erasmus and others at this time were of the opinion that communism was according to Christ's intention: it was Aristotle who said that a commonwealth in which things are common cannot flourish.
19. Matthew 10:27: "What ye hear in the ear, that preach ye upon the housetops." Cf. Luke 12:3.
20. That is, of ill will.
21. Twisted.
22. The lead rule, or Lesbian rule, was a flexible measuring stick used by ancient Greek architects, so called because it could be bent to fit curved Lesbian mouldings. It was pro-verbial for the adaptation or accommodation of law to morals.
23. Surely, certainly.
24. Roman writer of comedies, d. 159 B.C. Mitio is a character in his play *Adelphi* (The Brothers).
25. That is, laid to his charge.
26. In the *Republic* 496.
27. That is, image.

go out to them, they should nothing prevail, nor win aught by it, but be wet also in the rain, they do keep themselves within their houses, being content that they be safe themselves, seeing they cannot remedy the folly of the people. Howbeit doubtless, Master More (to speak truly as my mind giveth me) [28] wheresoever possessions be private, where money beareth all the stroke,[29] it is hard and almost impossible that there the weal public may justly be governed, and prosperously flourish. Unless you think thus: that justice is there executed, where all things come into the hands of evil men; or that prosperity there flourisheth, where all is divided among a few; which few nevertheless do not lead their lives very wealthily, and the residue live miserably, wretchedly and beggarly.[30] Wherefore when I consider with myself and weigh in my mind the wise and godly ordinances of the Utopians, among whom with very few laws all things be so well and wealthily ordered, that virtue is had in price [31] and estimation, and yet, all things being there common, every man hath abundance of everything. Again on the other part,[32] when I compare with them so many nations ever making new laws, yet none of them all well and sufficiently furnished with laws; where every man calleth that he hath gotten, his own proper [33] and private goods; where so many new laws daily made be not sufficient for every man to enjoy, defend, and know from another man's that which he calleth his own; which thing the infinite controversies in the law, that daily rise never to be ended, plainly declare to be true. These things (I say) when I consider with myself, I hold well with Plato,[34] and do nothing marvel, that he would make no laws for them, that refused those laws, whereby all men should have and enjoy equal portions of wealths and commodities. For the wise man did easily foresee, that this is the one and only way to the wealth of a commonalty,[35] if equality of all things should be brought in and established. Which I think is not possible to be observed, where every man's goods be proper and peculiar [36] to himself. For where every man under certain titles and pretences draweth and plucketh to himself as much as he can, and so a few divide among themselves all the riches that there is, be there never so much abundance and store, there to the residue is left lack and poverty. And for the most part it chanceth, that this latter sort is more worthy to enjoy that state of wealth, than the other be: because the rich men be covetous, crafty and unprofitable.[37] On the other part the poor be lowly, simple, and by their daily labour more profitable to the commonwealth than to themselves. Thus I do fully persuade myself, that no equal and just distribution of things can be

28. As my feelings incline me.
29. That is, has the greatest influence.
30. Amerigo Vespucci had reported of the Indians that one of their happinesses was to have no private property, and no king or other ruler.
31. In high value.
32. That is, hand.
33. That is, individual.
34. The story is in Diogenes Laertius, *On the Lives of the Philosophers* (3rd century A.D.). Plato refused to go and govern the new city of the Arcadians and Thebans when he heard that property would not be held in common there.
35. Commonwealth.
36. Private.
37. Harmful.

made, nor that perfect wealth shall ever be among men, unless this propriety [38] be exiled and banished. But so long as it shall continue, so long shall remain among the most and best part of men the heavy and inevitable burden of poverty and wretchedness. Which, as I grant that it may be somewhat eased, so I utterly deny that it can wholly be taken away. For if there were a statute made, that no man should possess above a certain measure of ground,[39] and that no man should have in his stock above a prescript and appointed [40] sum of money: if it were by certain laws decreed, that neither the king should be of too great power, neither the people too proud and wealthy, and that offices should not be obtained by inordinate suit,[41] or by bribes and gifts: that they should neither be bought nor sold, nor that it should be needful for the officers, to be at any cost or charge in their offices: for so occasion is given to the officers by fraud and ravin [42] to gather up their money again,[43] and by reason of gifts and bribes the offices be given to rich men, which should rather have been executed of wise men: by such laws I say, like as sick bodies that be desperate and past cure, be wont with continual good cherishing to be kept and botched [44] up for a time: so these evils also might be lightened and mitigated. But that they may be perfectly cured, and brought to a good and upright state, it is not to be hoped for, whiles every man is master of his own to himself. Yea, and whiles you go about to do your cure of one part, you shall make bigger the sore of another part, so the help of one causeth another's harm: forasmuch as nothing can be given to any man unless that be taken from another.[45]

But I am of a contrary opinion (quoth I) for methinketh [46] that men shall never there live wealthily,[47] where all things be common. For how can there be abundance of goods, or of anything, where every man withdraweth his hand from labour? Whom the regard of his own gains driveth not to work, and the hope that he hath in other men's travails maketh him slothful. Then when they be pricked with poverty, and yet no man can by any law or right defend that for his own, which he hath gotten with the labour of his own hands, shall not there of necessity be continual sedition and bloodshed? Specially the authority and reverence of magistrates being taken away, which, what place it may have with such men among whom is no difference, I cannot devise. . . .

From *Book II*
[Utopian Contempt for Gold]

For it must needs be, that how far a thing is dissonant and disagreeing from the guise and trade [1] of the hearers, so far shall it be out of their belief. Howbeit, a wise and indifferent esteemer [2] of things will not greatly marvel per-

38. Private property, ownership.
39. Later legislation proposed just this in England (1548).
40. Prescribed and laid down.
41. Over-pressing solicitation.
42. Plunder, spoils.
43. Recoup themselves.
44. Patched.
45. Proverbial saying, from classical times onward.
46. It seems to me.
47. In plenty.

1. Manners and ways.
2. Impartial judge.

chance, seeing all their other laws and customs do so much differ from ours, if the use also of gold and silver among them be applied,[3] rather to their own fashions than to ours. I mean in that they occupy[4] not money themselves, but keep it for that chance, which as it may happen, so it may be that it shall never come to pass. In the meantime gold and silver, whereof money is made, they do so use,[5] as none of them doth more esteem it, than the very nature of the thing deserveth. And then who doth not plainly see how far it is under iron: as without the which men can no better live than without fire and water.[6] Whereas to gold and silver nature hath given no use, that we may not well lack:[7] if that the folly of men had not set it in higher estimation for the rareness sake. But of the contrary part, nature as a most tender and loving mother, hath placed the best and most necessary things open abroad: as the air, the water and the earth itself. And hath removed and hid farthest from us vain and unprofitable things. Therefore if these metals among them should be fast locked up in some tower, it might be suspected, that the prince and the council (as the people is ever foolishly imagining) intended by some subtlety[8] to deceive the commons, and to take same profit of it to themselves. Furthermore if they should make thereof plate and such other finely and cunningly[9] wrought stuff: if at any time they should have occasion to break it, and melt it again, and therewith to pay their soldiers' wages, they see and perceive very well, that men would be loath to part from those things, that they once began to have pleasure and delight in. To remedy all this they have found out a means, which, as it is agreeable to all their other laws and customs, so it is from ours, where gold is so much set by and so diligently kept, very far discrepant and repugnant: and therefore incredible, but only to them that be wise. For whereas they eat and drink in earthen and glass vessels, which indeed be curiously and properly[10] made, and yet be of very small value: of gold and silver they make commonly chamber pots, and other like vessels,[11] that serve for most vile uses, not only in their common halls, but in every man's private house. Furthermore of the same metals they make great chains, with fetters, and gyves[12] wherein they tie their bondmen.[13] Finally whosoever for any offence be infamed,[14] by their ears hang rings of gold, upon their fingers they wear rings of gold, and about their necks chains of gold, and in conclusion their heads be tied about with gold. Thus by all means that may be they procure to have gold and silver among them in reproach and infamy. And therefore these metals, which other nations do as grievously and sorrowfully forgo, as in a manner from their own lives: if they

3. Adapted.
4. Employ.
5. Vespucci reported that the Indians despised gold, silver, and gems.
6. See Ecclesiasticus 39:26: "The principal things for the whole use of life are water, fire, iron . . .". The argument is that the test of how natural a thing is, is how useful it is.
7. Endure the absence of.
8. Trick.
9. Cleverly.
10. Ingeniously and handsomely.
11. This is a regular praise of primitive peoples in the Renaissance: they are "natural" men and use only "natural," things, not what is more valuable than is necessary.
12. Shackles.
13. Slaves.
14. That is, disgraced.

should altogether at once be taken from the Utopians, no man there would think that he had lost the worth of one farthing. They gather also pearls by the seaside, and diamonds and carbuncles [15] upon certain rocks, and yet they seek not for them: but by chance finding them, they cut and polish them. And therewith they deck their young infants. Which like as in the first years of their childhood, they make much and be fond [16] and proud of such ornaments, so when they be a little more grown in years and discretion, perceiving that none but children do wear such toys and trifles: they lay them away even of their own shamefacedness, without any bidding of their parents: even as our children, when they wax [17] big, do cast away nuts, brooches, and puppets.[18] Therefore these laws and customs, which be so far different from all other nations, how divers fantasies also and minds [19] they do cause, did I never so plainly perceive, as in the ambassadors of the Anemolians.[20]

These ambassadors came to Amaurote [21] whiles I was there. And because they came to entreat [22] of great and weighty matters, those three citizens [23] apiece out of every city were come thither before them. But all the ambassadors of the next countries, which had been there before, and knew the fashions and manners of the Utopians, among whom they perceived no honour given to sumptuous and costly apparel, silks to be contemned, gold also to be infamed [24] and reproachful, were wont to come thither in very homely and simple apparel. But the Anemolians, because they dwell far thence and had very little acquaintance with them, hearing that they were all apparelled alike, and that very rudely and homely: thinking them not to have the things which they did not wear: being therefore more proud, than wise: determined in the gorgeousness of their apparel to represent very [25] gods, and with the bright shining and glistering of their gay clothing to dazzle the eyes of the silly poor Utopians. So there came in three ambassadors with one hundred servants all apparelled in changeable [26] colours: the most of them in silks: the ambassadors themselves (for at home in their own country they were noblemen) in cloth of gold, with great chains of gold, with gold hanging at their ears, with gold rings upon their fingers, with brooches and aglets [27] of gold upon their caps, which glistered full of pearls and precious stones: to be short, trimmed and adorned with all those things, which among the Utopians were either the punishment of bondmen, or the reproach of infamed persons, or else trifles for young children to play withal. Therefore it would have done a man good at his heart to have seen how proudly they displayed their peacock's feathers, how much they made

15. Rubies.
16. Foolish about.
17. Grow.
18. Dolls.
19. Intentions.
20. The name is derived from *anemos*, the Greek word for wind; thus, Windbags.
21. From Greek, "dark, dim": i.e. Shadow City, Ghost City, the capital of Utopia.
22. Negotiate.
23. The three wise men sent annually from every city to a parliament in the capital.
24. Despised.
25. True.
26. Either particolored or "shot-silk."
27. Small pendants.

of their painted[28] sheaths, and how loftily they set forth and advanced themselves, when they compared their gallant[29] apparel with the poor raiment of the Utopians. For all the people were swarmed forth into the streets. And on the other side it was no less pleasure to consider how much they were deceived, and how far they missed of their purpose, being contrariwise taken than they thought they should have been. For to the eyes of all the Utopians, except very few, which had been in other countries for some reasonable cause, all that gorgeousness of apparel seemed shameful and reproachful. Insomuch that they most reverently saluted the vilest and most abject of them for lords: passing over the ambassadors themselves without any honour: judging them by their wearing of golden chains to be bondmen. Yea you should have seen children also, that had cast away their pearls and precious stones, when they saw the like sticking upon the ambassadors' caps, dig and push their mothers under the sides, saying thus to them: 'Look, mother, how great a lubber[30] doth yet wear pearls and precious stones, as though he were a little child still.' But the mother, yea, and that also in good earnest: 'Peace, son,' saith she: 'I think he be some of the ambassadors' fools.' Some found fault at their golden chains, as to no use nor purpose, being so small and weak, that a bondman might easily break them, and again so wide and large, that when it pleased him, he might cast them off, and run away at liberty whither he would. But when the ambassadors had been there a day or two and saw so great abundance of gold so lightly esteemed, yea in no less reproach, than it was with them in honour: and besides that more gold in the chains and gyves of one fugitive bondman, than all the costly ornaments of them three was worth: they began to abate their courage, and for very shame laid away all that gorgeous array, whereof they were so proud. And specially when they had talked familiarly with the Utopians, and had learned all their fashions and opinions.

For they marvel that any men be so foolish, as to have delight and pleasure in the glistering of a little trifling stone, which may behold any of the stars, or else the sun itself. Or that any man is so mad, as to count himself the nobler for the smaller or finer thread of wool, which selfsame wool (be it now in never so fine a spun thread) did once a sheep wear: and yet was she all that time no other thing than a sheep. They marvel also that gold, which of the own nature is a thing so unprofitable, is now among all people in so high estimation, that man himself, by whom, yea and for the use of whom it is so much set by, is in much less estimation than the gold itself. . . .

[Utopian Marriage Customs]

. . . The woman is not married before she be eighteen[1] years old. The man is four years older before he marry.

If either the man or the woman be proved to have bodily offended before their marriage with another, he or she whether[2] it be is sharply punished.

28. Ornamented, embroidered.
29. Elegant.
30. Dolt.

1. This is rather old by the customs of More's day. Aristotle had set eighteen as the best age for a woman, but thirty-seven for a man.
2. Whichever.

And both the offenders be forbidden ever after in all their life to marry: unless the fault be forgiven by the prince's pardon. But both the goodman [3] and the goodwife of the house where that offence was done, as being slack and negligent in looking to their charge, be in danger of great reproach and infamy. That offence is so sharply punished, because they perceive, that unless they be diligently kept from the liberty of this vice, few will join together in the love of marriage, wherein all the life must be led with one, and also all the griefs and displeasures that come therewith must patiently be taken and borne. Furthermore in choosing wives and husbands they observe earnestly and straitly [4] a custom, which seemed to us very fond and foolish. For a sad [5] and an honest [6] matron showeth the woman, be she maid or widow, naked to the wooer.[7] And likewise a sage and discreet man exhibiteth the wooer naked to the woman. At this custom we laughed and disallowed [8] it as foolish. But they on the other part do greatly wonder at the folly of all other nations, which in buying a colt,[9] whereas a little money is in hazard,[10] be so chary and circumspect, that though he be almost all bare, yet they will not buy him, unless the saddle and all the harness be taken off, lest under those coverings be hid some gall or sore. And yet in choosing a wife, which shall be either pleasure, or displeasure to them all their life after, they be so reckless, that all the residue of the woman's body being covered with clothes, they esteem [11] her scarcely by one hand-breadth (for they can see no more but her face), and so do join her to them not without great jeopardy of evil agreeing together, if anything in her body afterward do offend and mislike [12] them.

For all men be not so wise, as to have respect to the virtuous conditions of the party.[13] And the endowments of the body cause the virtues of the mind more to be esteemed and regarded: yea even in the marriages of wise men. Verily so foul deformity may be hid under those coverings, that it may quite alienate and take away the man's mind from his wife, when it shall not be lawful for their bodies to be separate again. If such deformity happen by any chance after the marriage is consummate and finished, well, there is no remedy but patience. Every man must take his fortune, well-a-worth.[14] But it were well done that a law were made whereby all such deceits might be eschewed and avoided beforehand.

And this were they constrained more earnestly to look upon, because they

3. Head of the house.
4. Strictly.
5. Sober, respectable.
6. Good.
7. Plutarch reports that the Spartan lawgiver Lycurgus sanctioned this custom.
8. Disapproved of.
9. More took this comparison from Horace, who uses the horse-dealing image (*Satires* I.ii.83–105) in his argument that fornication is preferable to adultery. Married women are always over-dressed and you cannot see what is underneath. Prostitutes, on the other hand, show you enough to give you a good idea.
10. At stake.
11. Value.
12. Displease.
13. Person.
14. Alas.

only of the nations in that part of the world be content every man with one wife apiece.

And matrimony is there never broken, but by death; except adultery break the bond, or else the intolerable wayward manners of either party. For if either of them find themselves for any such cause grieved, they may by the licence of the council change and take another. But the other party liveth ever after in infamy and out of wedlock. But for the husband to put way his wife for no fault, but for that some mishap is fallen to her body, this by no means they will suffer. For they judge it a great point of cruelty, that anybody in their most need of help and comfort should be cast off and forsaken, and that old age, which both bringeth sickness with it, and is a sickness itself, should unkindly and unfaithfully be dealt withal.[15] But now and then it chanceth, whereas the man and the woman cannot well agree between themselves, both of them finding other, with whom they hope to live more quietly and merrily, that they by the full consent of them both be divorced asunder and new married to other. . . . For in all offences they count the intent and pretensed [16] purpose as evil as the act or deed itself, for they think that no let [17] ought to excuse him that did his best to have no let. They set great store by fools.[18] And as it is great reproach to do to any of them hurt or injury, so they prohibit not to take pleasure of foolishness. For that, they think, doth much good to the fools. And if any man be so sad [19] and stern, that he cannot laugh neither at their words, nor at their deeds, none of them be committed to his tuition; [20] for fear lest he would not order them gently and favourably enough, to whom they should bring no delectation (for other goodness in them is none) much less any profit should they yield him. To mock a man for his deformity, or for that he lacketh any part or limb of his body, is counted great dishonesty [21] and reproach, not to him that is mocked, but to him that mocketh, which [22] unwisely doth upbraid any man of that as a vice which was not in his power to eschew. Also as they count and reckon very little wit to be in him, that regardeth not natural beauty and comeliness, so to help the same with paintings,[23] is taken for a vain and a wanton pride, not without great infamy. For they know, even by very experience, that no comeliness of beauty doth so highly commend and advance the

15. With.
16. That is, designed. Cf. Matthew 5:28: "whosoever looketh on a woman to lust after her hath committed adultery already with her in his heart."
17. Hindrance.
18. That is, they take good care of their mental defectives and do not laugh at them for their deficiencies, but because they can sometimes do or say things that are funny, wise, or witty on account of their simplicity. The fool in a well-to-do English household of the time, such as More's, need not have been such a defective, but if he was, he would have been taken into that household as a protection against less merciful members of society as well as for his talents as simpleton-philosopher. More's own fool, Henry Patenson, appears in the family-group portrait by Holbein (Fig. 2), which indicates the value set by More on simplicity and jesting as sources of wisdom.
19. Sober.
20. Guardianship.
21. Wrong.
22. Who.
23. Cosmetics.

wives in the conceit of their husbands, as honest conditions [24] and lowliness. For as love is oftentimes won with beauty, so it is not kept, preserved and continued, but by virtue and obedience.[25] They do not only fear [26] their people from doing evil by punishments, but also allure them to virtue with rewards of honour. Therefore they set up in the market-place the images of notable men, and of such as have been great and bountiful benefactors to the commonwealth, for the perpetual memory of their good acts, and also that the glory and renown of the ancestors may stir and provoke their posterity to virtue. He that inordinately and ambitiously desireth promotions is left all hopeless for ever attaining any promotion as long as he liveth. They live together lovingly. For no magistrate [27] is either haughty or fearful.[28] Fathers they be called, and like fathers they use themselves. The citizens (as it is their duty) do willingly exhibit unto them due honour without any compulsion. Nor the prince himself is not known from the other by his apparel, nor by a crown or diadem, or cap of maintenance,[29] but by a little sheaf of corn [30] carried before him. And so a taper of wax is borne before the bishop, whereby only he is known. They have but few laws.[31] For to people so instruct and institute [32] very few do suffice. Yea this thing they chiefly reprove among other nations, that innumerable books of laws and expositions upon the same be not sufficient. But they think it against all right and justice that men should be bound to those laws, which either be in number more than be able to be read, or else blinder and darker, than that any man can well understand them. Furthermore they utterly exclude and banish all proctors,[33] and sergeants at the law; [34] which craftily handle matters, and subtly dispute of the laws. For they think it most meet,[35] that every man should plead his own matter, and tell the same tale before the judge that he would tell to his man of law. So shall there be less circumstance of words, and the truth shall sooner come to light; whiles [36] the judge with a discreet judgment doth weigh the words of him whom no lawyer hath instruct with deceit, and while he helpeth and beareth out simple wits against the false and malicious circumversions [37] of crafty children.[38] This is hard to be ob-

24. Good morals.
25. English civil law allowed a husband to beat his wife with whips and sticks.
26. Frighten.
27. High public official.
28. Terrifying.
29. A crimson velvet hat, lined with ermine, originally worn by dukes only, as a symbol of dignity.
30. Representing the abundance that the well-governed land ought to produce, as it did when the goddess Astraea was on earth in the Golden Age and there was no need of any law or constraint.
31. The number of laws was regarded as an index of corruption: the more corrupt the society, the greater the number of laws required.
32. Instructed and trained.
33. That is, an attorney in the ecclesiastical and admiralty courts. More was himself a lawyer, with a contempt for those who used the law for self-advancement and self-importance.
34. Highest degree of barrister (pleader in court).
35. Fitting.
36. Sometimes.
37. Twistings.
38. People, as in "children of Israel."

served in other countries, in so infinite a number of blind and intricate laws. But in Utopia every man is a cunning [39] lawyer. For (as I said) they have very few laws; and the plainer and grosser [40] that any interpretation is, that they allow as most just. For all laws (say they) be made and published only to the intent that by them every man should be put in remembrance of his duty. But the crafty and subtle interpretation of them can put very few in that remembrance (for they be but few that do perceive them), whereas the simple, the plain and gross meaning of the laws is open to every man.

Else as touching the vulgar [41] sort of the people, which be both most in number, and have most need to know their duties, were it not as good for them, that no law were made at all, as when it is made, to bring so blind [42] an interpretation upon it, that without great wit [43] and long arguing no man can discuss it? To the finding out whereof neither the gross judgment of the people can attain, neither the whole life of them that be occupied in working for their livings can suffice thereto. These virtues of the Utopians have caused their next neighbours and borderers, which live free and under no subjection (for the Utopians long ago, have delivered many of them from tyranny) to take magistrates of them, some for a year, and some for five years' space. Which when the time of their office is expired, they bring home again with honour and praise, and take new ones again with them into their country. These nations have undoubtedly very well and wholesomely [44] provided for their commonwealths. For seeing that both the making and the marring of the weal public doth depend and hang upon the manners of the rulers and magistrates, what officers could they more wisely have chosen, than those which cannot be led from honesty by bribes (for to them that shortly after shall depart thence into their own country money should be unprofitable) nor yet be moved either with favour, or malice towards any man, as being strangers, and unacquainted with the people? The which two vices of affection and avarice, where they take place in judgments, incontinent [45] they break justice,[46] the strongest and surest bond of a commonwealth. These peoples which fetch their officers and rulers from them, the Utopians call their fellows. And other to whom they have been beneficial, they call their friends. As touching leagues,[47] which in other places between country and country be so oft concluded, broken and made again, they never make none with any nation. For to what purpose serve leagues? say they. As though nature had not set sufficient love between man and man. And who so regardeth not nature, think you that he will pass for words? They be brought into this opinion chiefly, because that in those parts of the world, leagues between princes be wont to be kept and observed very slenderly. For

39. Knowledgeable.
40. Simpler, more obvious.
41. Ordinary.
42. Obscure.
43. Intellect.
44. Soundly.
45. Immediately.
46. The contrast between justice (the natural) and law (the actual) is emphasized throughout.
47. Alliances.

here in Europe,[48] and especially in these parts where the faith and religion of Christ reigneth, the majesty of leagues is everywhere esteemed holy and inviolable, partly through the justice and goodness of princes, and partly through the reverence of great bishops. Which like as they make no promise themselves but they do very religiously perform the same, so they exhort all princes in any wise to abide by their promises, and them that refuse or deny so to do, by their pontifical power and authority they compel thereto. And surely they think well [49] that it might seem a very reproachful thing, if in the leagues of them which by a peculiar [50] name be called faithful,[51] faith should have no place. But in that new found part of the world, which is scarcely so far from us beyond the line equinoctial [52] as our life and manners be dissident from theirs, no trust nor confidence is in leagues. But the more and holier ceremonies the league is knit up with, the sooner it is broken by some cavillation [53] found in the words, which many times of purpose be so craftily put in and placed, that the bands can never be so sure nor so strong, but they will find some hole open to creep out at, and to break both league and truth. The which crafty dealing, yea the which fraud and deceit, if they should know it to be practised among private men in their bargains and contracts, they would incontinent cry out at it with a sour countenance, as an offence most detestable, and worthy to be punished with a shameful death: yea even very they that advance themselves authors of like counsel given to princes. Wherefore it may well be thought, either that all justice is but a base and a low virtue, and which abaseth itself far under the high dignity of kings; or at the leastwise, that there be two justices, the one meet [54] for the inferior sort of the people, going afoot and creeping below on the ground, and bound down on every side with many bands because it shall not run at rovers; [55] the other a princely virtue, which like as it is of much higher majesty than the other poor justice, so also it is of much more liberty, as to the which nothing is unlawful that it lusteth after. These manners of princes (as I said) which be there so evil keepers of leagues, cause the Utopians, as I suppose, to make no leagues at all, which perchance would change their mind if they lived here. Howbeit they think that though leagues be never so faithfully observed and kept, yet the custom of making leagues was very evil begun.[56] For this causeth men (as though nations which be separate asunder, by the space of a little hill or a river, were coupled together by no society or bond of nature) to think themselves born adversaries and enemies one to another, and that it is lawful for the one to seek the death and destruction of the

48. More is referring ironically to such incidents as the treachery of the French king Louis XII and of Ferdinand V of Castile against Frederick of Naples, of Pope Julius II and his attempt to expel the French, his former allies, from Italy, and to the break-up of the Holy League which Julius had formed for this purpose.
49. Rightly.
50. Special.
51. That is, holy, Christian.
52. That is, the equator. There is no need of leagues and covenants among "natural" men like the Indians.
53. Legal quibble.
54. Fit.
55. That is, run wild. "To shoot at rovers" was an archery term meaning to shoot an arrow at random and not at any target.
56. That is, that it was bad to have begun the custom of making alliances.

other, if leagues were not: yea, and that after the leagues be accorded, friendship doth not grow and increase; but the licence of robbing and stealing doth still remain, as farforth as for lack of foresight and advisement[57] in writing the words of the league, any sentence or clause to the contrary is not therein sufficiently comprehended.[58] But they be of a contrary opinion. That is, that no man ought to be counted an enemy, which hath done no injury. And that the fellowship of nature is a strong league; and that men be better and more surely knit together by love and benevolence, than by covenants of leagues; by hearty affection of mind, than by words.

1515   1516–51

Life of Pico

The example of Giovanni Pico della Mirandola, 1463–94, the Italian nobleman, scholar, and philosopher, was of the greatest importance for Thomas More. He was the epitome of the handsome nobleman who was not haughty and proud but delighted in works of self-abasement and charity, who was learned but not puffed up and impious. He applied his knowledge of the classical and Eastern languages, and the knowledge he gained from Jewish scholars and from the Cabbala (Jewish esoteric interpretation of the Old Testament), to investigating the mysteries of the Christian faith. He died in the habit of a Dominican friar. His neoplatonic and Cabbalistic philosophy was of little interest to More, who saw him especially as a man who had achieved the correct detachment from the things of this world, because of his fervent love of Christ. At the time when he translated the life of Pico, by Giovanni Francesco Pico della Mirandola, nephew of the philosopher (written in 1495), More was perhaps still undecided whether to enter religious life himself. The translation dates from between 1505 and 1510 and was made for Joyce Leigh, a nun. This text is modernized from More's English *Works*, 1557.

From The Life of John Picus, Earl of Mirandula

Of the Voluntary Affliction and Paining[1] of his Own Body.

Over all this, many times (which is not to be kept secret) he gave alms[2] of his own body. We know many men which, as Saint Hierom[3] saith, put forth their hand to poor folk; but with the pleasure of the flesh they be overcomen. But he many days (and namely those days which represent unto us the passion and death that Christ suffered for our sake) beat and scourged his own flesh in the remembrance of that great benefit, and for cleansing of his old offences.

---

57. Consideration.
58. Contained.

1. That is, beating.
2. That is, expressions of pity for Christ and so for all that are afflicted.
3. St. Jerome (*c.* 342–420), Letter 54: i.e. men will give money and help to poor people, but will not deny themselves food, drink, and other pleasures, still less afflict themselves and mortify the flesh in atonement for sin.

Of his Placability or Benign Nature.

He was of cheer [4] alway merry, and of so benign nature that he was never troubled with anger. And he said once to his nephew, that whatsoever should happen (fell there never so great misadventure) he could never, as him thought,[5] be moved to wrath, but if [6] his chests perished, in which his books lay, that he had with great travail and watch [7] compiled. But forasmuch as he considered that he laboured only for the love of God and profit of his church, and that he had dedicate unto him all his works, his studies and his doings; and sith [8] he saw that, sith God is almighty, they could not miscarry but if it were either by his commandment or by his sufferance, he verily trusted, sith God is all good, that he would not suffer him to have that occasion of heaviness. O very happy mind, which none adversity might oppress, which no prosperity might enhance! Not the conning [9] of all philosophy was able to make him proud: not the knowledge of the Hebrew, Chaldee [10] and Arabie [11] language, beside Greek and Latin, could make him vainglorious: not his great substance,[12] not his noble blood, could blow up [13] his heart; not the beauty of his body, not the great occasion of sin, were able to pull him back into the voluptuous broad way that leadeth to hell. What thing was there of so marvellous strength, that might overturn the mind of him which now, as Seneca saith,[14] was gotten above fortune? as he which as well her favour as her malice hath set at nought, that he might be coupled with a spiritual knot unto Christ and his heavenly citizens.

How he eschewed Dignities.

When he saw many men with great labour and money desire and busily purchase the offices and dignities of the church (which are nowadays, alas the while, commonly bought and sold), himself refused to receive them, when two kings offered them. When another man offered him great worldly promotion, if he would go to the king's court, he gave him such an answer, 'that he should well know that he neither desired worship nor worldly riches, but rather set them at nought, that he might the more quietly give himself to study and the service of God.' This wise he persuaded that to a philosopher and him that seeketh for wisdom, it was no praise to gather riches, but to refuse them. . . .

c. 1505–10   1557

4. Behavior.
5. It seemed to him.
6. Unless.
7. Labor and care.
8. Since.
9. Knowledge.
10. Aramaic.
11. Arabic.
12. Wealth.
13. Make proud.
14. Lucius Annaeus Seneca, *c.* 5 B.C.–65 A.D., Roman Stoic philosopher and playwright, tutor to the Emperor Nero. The passage is the last sentence of his dialogue *On the Constancy of a Wise Man,* a favorite Renaissance text.

The History of King Richard III

More's *History of King Richard III* exists in both Latin and English, and was probably written between 1514 and 1518, when the author was much occupied with royal affairs and had just entered the service of Henry VIII, the second monarch of the new Tudor dynasty, established in 1485 by the defeat and death of Richard III, the usurper.

It is Thomas More who is chiefly responsible for the picture of Richard passed on by the propagandists for the Tudor monarchy and picked up by Shakespeare in his *Richard III*—and it may well be that the picture is a true one, though much controversy has ensued about Richard's character. More's detail is often scrupulously correct and he appears to make few mistakes, though he must have been working from hearsay. He used other contemporary historians, but his history is more of a work of art than theirs, with the central character of Richard closely modeled on the portrait of the Emperor Tiberius by the Roman historian Tacitus (b. about 55 A.D.). More takes every opportunity to present Richard as a tyrant and villain.

This text is modernized from More's English *Works*, 1557.

From The History of King Richard III

The Young King and His Brother Murdered

Now fell there mischiefs thick. And as the thing evil gotten is never well kept, through all the time of his reign never ceased there cruel death and slaughter, till his own destruction ended it. But as he finished his time with the best death and the most righteous, that is to wit his own, so began he with the most piteous and wicked, I mean the lamentable murder of his innocent nephews, the young King and his tender brother.[1] Whose death and final infortune hath natheless[2] so far come in question, that some remain yet in doubt whether they were in his days destroyed or no. Not for that only, that Perkin Warbeck[3] (by many folks' malice and more folks' folly, so long space abusing[4] the world) was as well with princes as the poorer people reputed and taken for the younger of those two; but for that also, that all things were in late days so covertly demeaned,[5] one thing pretended and another meant, that there was nothing so plain and openly proved, but that yet for the common custom of close and covert dealing, men had it ever inwardly suspect, as many well-counterfeited jewels make the true mistrusted. Howbeit concerning that opinion,[6] with the occasions moving either party, we shall have place more at large

1. There is still much controversy over whether Richard III was responsible for the murder of his nephews, the young King Edward V and his brother the Duke of York. More's is the fullest account, but it must be hearsay, for he was only five years old in August 1483, when the princes were murdered.
2. Nevertheless.
3. Perkin Warbeck (1474–99), an impostor, who first appeared, claiming the throne as the Duke of York, in 1491. He was aided by the enemies of the new king, Henry VII, who had defeated the usurper Richard III in 1485; but was finally hanged.
4. Deceiving.
5. Secretly carried on.
6. That is, that the Duke of York was still alive.

to entreat, if we hereafter happen to write the time of the late noble prince of famous memory King Henry the Seventh, or percase [7] that history of Perkin in any compendious process [8] by itself. But in the mean time for this present matter, I shall rehearse you the dolorous end of those babes, not after every way that I have heard, but after that way that I have so heard by such men, and by such means, as methinketh it were hard but it should be true.

King Richard after his coronation taking his way to Gloucester, to visit in his new honour the town of which he bare the name of his old,[9] devised, as he rode, to fulfil the thing which he before had intended. And forasmuch as his mind gave him, that his nephews living, men would not reckon that he could have right to the realm, he thought therefore without delay to rid them, as though the killing of his kinsmen could amend his cause and make him a kindly [10] king. Whereupon he sent one John Grene,[11] whom he specially trusted, unto Sir Robert Brakenbery,[12] constable of the Tower, with a letter and credence [13] also, that the same Sir Robert should in any wise put the two children to death. This John Grene did his errand unto Brakenbery kneeling before our Lady [14] in the Tower; who plainly answered that he would never put them to death, to die therefore: [15] with which answer John Grene returning, recounted the same to King Richard at Warwick yet in his way.[16] Wherewith he took such displeasure and thought, that the same night he said unto a secret [17] page of his: 'Ah, whom shall a man trust? Those that I have brought up myself, those that I had went [18] would most surely serve me, even those fail me, and at my commandment will do nothing for me.' 'Sir,' quoth his page, 'there lieth one of your pallet without, that I dare well say, to do your Grace pleasure, the thing were right hard that he would refuse'; meaning this by [19] Sir James Tyrell,[20] which was a man of right goodly personage, and for nature's gifts, worthy to have served a much better prince, if he had well served God, and by grace obtained as much truth and good will as he had strength and wit. The man had an high heart, and sore longed upward, not rising yet so fast as he had hoped, being hindered and kept under by the means of Sir Richard

7. Perhaps.
8. Short narrative.
9. That is, he was visiting in his new capacity as King Richard III the town his title had been taken from when he was Duke of Gloucester, Protector of England, during the reign of the child-king Edward V.
10. That is, a king by natural right.
11. Various candidates have been proposed for the owner of this common name.
12. That is, the governor of the Tower, who usually deputed his duties to the lieutenant. He was a creature of Richard's and had just been appointed to the post. He was killed with Richard at the Battle of Bosworth Field (1485).
13. Credentials.
14. That is, Brakenbery was at his devotions.
15. That is, even if he should be put to death for it.
16. That is, still going westward to Gloucester.
17. Intimate.
18. Believed.
19. Referring to.
20. 1445–1502, a strong Yorkist, taken into favor by Henry VII after Richard's death. He had been knighted in 1471, after the Battle of Tewkesbury, not, as More says below, by Richard for the murder of the princes. He was beheaded for treason in 1502.

Ratclife and Sir William Catesby; [21] which longing for no more partners of the Prince's favour, and namely [22] not for him, whose pride they wist would bear no peer,[23] kept him by secret drifts [24] out of all secret trust. Which thing this page well had marked and known. Wherefore this occasion offered of very special friendship, he took his time [25] to put him forward, and by such wise do him good, that all the enemies he had except the devil, could never have done him so much hurt. For upon this page's words King Richard arose . . . and came out into the pallet chamber; on which he found in bed Sir James and Sir Thomas Tyrell,[26] of person like and brethren of blood, but nothing of kin in conditions.[27] Then said the king merrily to them, 'What, sirs, be ye in bed so soon?' and calling up Sir James, brake [28] to him secretly his mind in this mischievous matter. In which he found him nothing strange.[29] Wherefore on the morrow he sent him to Brakenbery with a letter, by which he was commanded to deliver Sir James all the keys of the Tower for one night; to the end he might there accomplish the King's pleasure, in such thing as he had given him commandment. After which letter delivered and the keys received, Sir James appointed the night next ensuing [30] to destroy them, devising before and preparing the means.

The Prince, as soon as the Protector [31] left that name and took himself as King, had it showed unto him that he should not reign, but his uncle should have the crown. At which word the Prince sore abashed began to sigh and said: 'Alas, I would my uncle would let me have my life yet, though I lose my kingdom.' Then he that told him the tale, used him with good words and put him in the best comfort he could. But forthwith was the Prince and his brother both shut up, and all other removed from them, only one called Black Will or William Slaughter [32] except, set to serve them and to see them sure. After which time the Prince never tied his points,[33] nor ought rought [34] of himself, but with that young babe his brother, lingered in thought and heaviness [35] till this traitorous death delivered them of that wretchedness.

For Sir James Tyrell devised that they should be murdered in their beds. To the execution whereof he appointed Miles Forest,[36] one of the four that kept them, a fellow fleshed [37] in murder beforetime. To him he joined one

21. Richard's powerful supporters and most influential counselors, the "Cat" and the "Rat." Ratcliffe was killed at Bosworth, Catesby was executed by Henry VII three days afterward.
22. Especially.
23. They knew would brook no equal.
24. Schemes.
25. That is, when this occasion for getting into truly high favor presented itself, he took his opportunity.
26. Younger brother of Sir James, supporter of Henry VII.
27. Morals, personal qualities.
28. Disclosed to him privately.
29. Unwilling, standoffish.
30. Following.
31. That is, Richard.
32. The name exists in contemporary records.
33. Laces for holding doublet to hose.
34. Took care.
35. Sadness.
36. Also known from the records, like Dighton.
37. Initiated into, inured to.

John Dighton, his own horsekeeper, a big, broad, square, strong knave. Then all the other being removed from them, this Miles Forest and John Dighton about midnight (the sely [38] children lying in their beds) came into the chamber, and suddenly lapped [39] them up among the clothes, so bewrapped them and entangled them, keeping down by force the featherbed and pillows hard unto their mouths, that within a while smored [40] and stifled, their breath failing, they gave up to God their innocent souls into the joys of heaven, leaving to the tormentors their bodies dead in the bed. Which after that the wretches perceived, first by the struggling with the pains of death, and after long lying still to be thoroughly dead, they laid their bodies naked out upon the bed, and fetched Sir James to see them. Which,[41] upon the sight of them, caused those murderers to bury them at the stair foot, meetly [42] deep in the ground under a great heap of stones. Then rode Sir James in great haste to King Richard, and showed him all the manner of the murder; who gave him great thanks and, as some say, there made him knight. But he allowed not, as I have heard, the burying in so vile a corner, saying that he would have them buried in a better place, because they were a King's sons. Lo, the honourable courage [43] of a King! Whereupon, they say that a priest of Sir Robert Brakenbery took up the bodies again, and secretly interred them in such place as, by the occasion of his death which only knew it, could never since come to light.[44] Very truth is it and well known, that at such time as Sir James Tyrell was in the Tower for treason committed against the most famous prince King Henry the seventh, both Dighton and he were examined, and confessed the murder in the manner above written; but whither the bodies were removed they could nothing tell.

And thus as I have learned of them that much knew and little cause had to lie, were these two noble princes, these innocent tender children, born of most royal blood, brought up in great wealth, likely long to live to reign and rule in the realm, by traitorous tyranny taken, deprived of their estate, shortly shut up in prison, and privily slain and murdered, their bodies cast God wot [45] where, by the cruel ambition of their unnatural uncle and his dispiteous [46] tormentors. Which things on every part well pondered, God never gave this world a more notable example, neither in what unsurety standeth this worldly weal,[47] or what mischief worketh the proud enterprise [48] of an high heart, or finally what wretched end ensueth such dispiteous cruelty. For first, to begin with the ministers,[49] Miles Forest at Saint Martin's [50] piecemeal rotted away. Dighton indeed yet walketh on alive, in good possibility to be hanged ere he

38. Poor innocent.
39. Bundled.
40. Smothered.
41. Who.
42. Moderately.
43. Heart.
44. Skeletons came to light in 1674 which were identified as the princes'.
45. Knows.
46. Cruel.
47. Prosperity.
48. Undertaking.
49. That is, murderers.
50. St. Martin le Grand, in the City of London, a place of sanctuary—i.e. holy ground, where fugitives from justice, by medieval law, could be safe.

die. But Sir James Tyrell died at Tower Hill,[51] beheaded for treason. King Richard himself, as ye shall hereafter hear, slain in the field,[52] hacked and hewed of his enemies' hands, harried on horseback dead, his hair in despite [53] torn and tugged like a cur dog: and the mischief that he took, within less than three years of the mischief that he did. And yet all the mean time spent in much pain and trouble outward, much fear, anguish, and sorrow within. For I have heard by credible report of such as were secret with his chamberers,[54] that after this abominable deed done, he never had quiet in his mind, he never thought himself sure. Where he went abroad, his eyes whirled about, his body privily fenced,[55] his hand ever on his dagger, his countenance and manner like one alway ready to strike again; he took ill rest a-nights, lay long waking and musing, sore wearied with care and watch, rather slumbered [56] than slept, troubled with fearful dreams, suddenly sometimes started up, leaped out of his bed and ran about the chamber, so was his restless heart continually tossed and tumbled with the tedious [57] impression and stormy remembrance of his abominable deed.

c. 1514–18   1557

The Life of Sir Thomas More

William Roper was probably born in 1496, and married More's favorite daughter Margaret in 1521. He was rescued from the Lutheran heresy by More, became an eminent lawyer and Member of Parliament, and died in 1577. His *Life* of More was probably written about 1555 but not printed until 1626, and is the shortest and best early biography, its spare narrative bringing home the superb and studied dignity of More's trial and death. Roper also took a hand in the preparation of the collected edition of More's English *Works,* 1557. This text is based on that of S. W. Singer (1822), with corrections and interpolations from the edition of E. V. Hitchcock (1935).

51. The hill by the Tower of London, scene of public executions. Tyrell, as a knight, would be beheaded, not hanged.
52. In battle at Bosworth (1485).
53. Contempt.
54. Chamberlains, valets.
55. Secretly protected.
56. Dozed.
57. Painful.

From William Roper's The Life of Sir Thomas More

[The Death of More]

. . . So remained Sir Thomas More [1] in the Tower [2] more than a sevennight [3] after his judgment. From whence, the day before he suffered,[4] he sent his shirt of hair,[5] not willing to have it seen, to my wife, his dearly beloved daughter, and a letter, written with a coal,[6] contained in the foresaid book of his works,[7] plainly expressing the fervent desire he had to suffer on the morrow in these words following: 'I cumber you, good Margaret, much, but I would be sorry if it should be any longer than tomorrow. For tomorrow is St. Thomas' even,[8] and the Octave of St. Peter,[9] and therefore tomorrow long I to go to God; it were a day very meet and convenient for me. I never liked your manner towards me better, than when you kissed me last. For I like when daughterly love, and dear charity hath no leisure to look to worldly courtesy.'

And so upon the next morrow, being Tuesday, St. Thomas' even, and the Octave of St. Peter in the year of our Lord God 1535, according as he in his letter the day before had wished, early in the morning came to him Sir Thomas Pope,[10] his singular [11] friend, on message from the King [12] and his Council, that he should before nine of the clock the same morning suffer death, and that therefore forthwith he should prepare himself thereunto. 'Master Pope,' saith he, 'for your good tidings I most heartily thank you. I have been always much bounden to the King's Highness for the benefits and honours that he hath

---

1. On false evidence More had been tried and judged guilty of high treason in that he had refused to acknowledge the right of Henry VIII, a temporal king, to govern the church in England.

2. The Tower of London, where offenders against the king who were of the clergy, gentry, or nobility, were imprisoned.

3. More was actually executed not a week, but on the fifth day (July 6, 1535), after his trial.

4. That is, was executed. There is already an element here of seeing More as the saint that the Church made him four hundred years after his death, in 1935. Roper's use of "suffered" may be intended to recall the "passion," i.e. suffering and execution of others—like St. Cyprian below—who had died martyrs for the faith.

5. A shirt woven of hair cloth was worn next to the skin by penitents and religious persons to mortify the flesh, in remembrance of Christ's sufferings. More had attempted to conceal his wearing of such a thing—it was part of his lifelong preparation for death—even from his daughter Margaret, his favorite child.

6. A piece of either charcoal or mineral coal. More had previously been allowed the use of pen and paper and had written a great deal of devotional prose in the Tower.

7. The collected volume of his English writings, published in 1557.

8. The eve of the feast day commemorating removal of St. Thomas Becket's body to its shrine in Canterbury Cathedral in 1220. The martyrdom of St. Thomas (More's patron saint) occurred on December 29, 1170, and is commemorated on that day in the Church's calendar.

9. The eighth day, counting inclusively, after the feast day of St. Peter, the first Bishop of Rome and the first head of the Catholic Church (June 29). To More, St. Peter is a symbol of the unity and inviolability of the church for which he was prepared to die.

10. (1507?–59), a wealthy lawyer, founder of Trinity College, Oxford, and guardian of the young Princess Elizabeth.

11. Special.

12. Henry VIII.

still from time to time most bountifully heaped upon me, and yet more bound [13] I am to his Grace for putting me into this place, where I have had convenient time and space to have remembrance of my end, and so help me God most of all, Master Pope, am I bound to his Highness, that it pleaseth him so shortly to rid me out of the miseries of this wretched world. And therefore will I not fail earnestly to pray for his Grace both here, and also in another world.' 'The King's pleasure is further,' quoth Master Pope, 'that at your execution you shall not use many words'. 'Master Pope' (quoth he), 'you do well to give me warning of his Grace's pleasure. For otherwise I had purposed [14] at that time somewhat to have spoken, but of no matter wherewith his Grace, or any other, should have had cause to be offended. Nevertheless, whatsoever I intended, I am ready obediently to conform myself to his Grace's commandment. And I beseech you, good Master Pope, to be a mean [15] unto his Highness, that my daughter Margaret may be at my burial.' 'The King is content already' (quoth Master Pope) 'that your wife, children, and other your friends shall have liberty to be present thereat.' 'O how much beholden,' then said Sir Thomas More, 'am I to his Grace, that unto my poor burial vouchsafeth to have so gracious consideration.' Wherewithal Master Pope taking his leave of him, could not refrain from weeping, which Sir Thomas More perceiving, comforted him in this wise, 'Quiet yourself, good Master Pope, and be not discomforted. For I trust that we shall, once in heaven, see each other full merrily, where we shall be sure to live and love together in joyful bliss eternally.' Upon whose departure Sir Thomas More, as one that had been invited to some solemn feast, changed himself into his best apparel; which Master Lieutenant [16] espying, advised him to put it off, saying, that he that should have it was but a javel.[17] 'What Master Lieutenant' (quoth he), 'shall I account him a javel, that will do me this day so singular a benefit? [18] Nay, I assure you, were it cloth of gold, I would account it well bestowed on him, as St. Cyprian [19] did, who gave his executioner thirty pieces of gold.' And albeit at length, through Master Lieutenant's importunate persuasion, he altered his apparel, yet, after the example of that holy martyr St. Cyprian, did he of that little money that was left him, send one angel of gold to his executioner. And so was he by Master Lieutenant brought out of the Tower, and from thence led towards the place of execution, where, going up the scaffold, which was so weak that it was ready to fall, he said merrily to Master Lieutenant, 'I pray you, Master Lieutenant, see me safe up, and for my coming down let me shift for myself.' [20] Then desired he all

13. More is making a special point: he was the King's servant as well as his subject and always emphasized that he was so: he depends for all his benefits on the King. He is also emphasizing that he is keeping true order and degree in church and state: Henry is overturning it.

14. Intended.

15. Intermediary.

16. The effective governor of the Tower was so titled.

17. Worthless rogue.

18. That is, by helping him exchange his earthly life for eternal life.

19. Bishop of Carthage, executed 258 A.D., whose writings and views on the unity and powers of the church influenced More.

20. More was famous for his "merry tales" and jokes.

the people thereabout to pray for him, and to bear witness with him, that he should now there suffer death in and for the faith of the holy Catholic Church,[21] which done he kneeled down, and after his prayers said, turned to the executioner, and with a cheerful countenance spake thus to him. 'Pluck up thy spirits, man, and be not afraid to do thine office, my neck is very short. Take heed therefore thou strike not awry for saving of thine honesty.'

So passed Sir Thomas More out of his world to God upon the very same day in which himself had most desired. Soon after whose death came intelligence [22] thereof to the Emperor Charles,[23] whereupon he sent for Sir Thomas Elyot,[24] our English Ambassador, and said unto him, 'My Lord Ambassador, we understand that the King your master hath put his faithful servant and grave wise councillor Sir Thomas More to death.' Whereunto Sir Thomas Elyot answered, that he understood nothing thereof. 'Well,' said the Emperor, 'it is too true, and this will we say, that if we had been master of such a servant, of whose doings ourselves have had these many years no small experience, we would rather have lost the best city of our dominions, than have lost such a worthy councillor.' . . .

c. 1555   1626

SIR THOMAS ELYOT
c. 1490–1546

Born about 1490, probably in Wiltshire, of West Country gentlefolk, Elyot received an informal legal training as Clerk to the Justices of Assize on the Western Circuit (from 1511), and a formal legal education at the Middle Temple in London and at Oxford University. As a young man he came under the influence of Sir Thomas More, and frequented his house in Chelsea, where he met Thomas Linacre, who taught him Greek and medicine, and made the acquaintance of other scholars. Elyot held an important administrative post under Cardinal Wolsey—which he lost at Wolsey's fall in 1530. Retiring to his country estate, he wrote The Book Named the Governor, first published in 1531. This, probably together with his friendship with Thomas Cromwell, Henry's adviser, got him the appointment of ambassador to Emperor Charles V in 1531. In 1532 he was recalled from his mission, to pass the rest of his life in semi-retirement.

Elyot made translations from several Greek authors (he held views on the structural relations between the two languages), such as Plutarch, Isocrates, and St. Cyprian, as well as from the Latin of Giovanni Pico della Mirandola. He also compiled, among other works, a Latin-English dictionary (1538) and a medical treatise The Castle of Health (1534?). In these, as in The Governor, he has constantly before his eyes the responsibility to "divulgate or set forth" the sound and beneficial learning of ancient and modern authors in an English which should be equal in strength and efficacy to its content. One of his methods of achieving the required linguistic solidity was the

21. He was always clear that this was what he was dying for.
22. News.
23. Charles V, Holy Roman Emperor.
24. 1490?–1546. He was not ambassador at Charles's court in 1535, but had been in 1531–32.

imitation of Latin and Greek syntax; another, especially in *The Governor*, was to strengthen the expressive possibilities of English by deliberate borrowing from other languages, carefully signaled either by defining the word in question or by using the new word along with an English word of the same or similar meaning—as in "divulgate or set forth" above.

The Governor begins by defining a public weal—a commonwealth—as "a body living, compact or made of sundry estates and degrees of men, which is disposed by the order of equity and governed by the rule and moderation of reason," in which nobles, commons, and clergy are under the rule of a king, all ranged in and observing the harmony of order and degree which God has ordained. The "inferior governors" to the king are those whose training requires special attention: it is to their education proper from early childhood that Elyot's book, like Plato's before him, is devoted. They begin Latin and Greek at the age of seven and, by allurements rather than by threats and punishments, are taken through Homer, Virgil, Lucian, Aristophanes, Ovid, Cicero, Quintilian, Livy, Xenophon, Caesar, Aristotle, and Plato, so that they will be fully equipped to manage civil and military matters as well as to follow virtue and eschew vice. As a relaxation from serious matters such as these, the aspiring "governor" is to practice music, painting, and sculpture; and to take exercise at hunting, archery, and dancing. But even when taking his exercise, the student must be alive to the moral lessons available. Borrowing the ideas of Lucian of Samosata, Elyot maintains that the base dance (*basse danse*), for example, is no mere frivolous pleasure. Its patterns of movement are intimations of that true and permanent pattern, or Platonic idea, laid up in heaven, of perfect proportion and congruity. It can, besides, teach one lessons about the nature of virtue and its residence in the Aristotelian mean. The final two-thirds of Elyot's book are taken up with a consideration of the virtues necessary to a "governor" and with *exempla* of their exercise—majesty, affability, placability, humanity, benevolence, liberality, amity, justice, faith, fortitude, patience, magnanimity, constancy, temperance, and the rest.

Elyot's aim, as it was later to be Ascham's—and, with differences, Sir Thomas Hoby's —was to provide England with properly and liberally educated servants of the state, to counteract the effects of an aristocracy that despised learning and of a legal-administrative social unit whose training was too narrowly confined to the financially profitable technicalities of the law.

Like Hoby and Ascham, Elyot chose to write in English, for his countrymen, not in Latin for the educated world of Europe: he was less concerned to make England-as-she-was known to the larger learned community. His self-appointed task was to apply the civilizing influence of humanism to English life, so that England would be worthy to take her place at the head of nations.

The text of *The Governor* is based on that of the first edition of 1531. Spelling and punctuation have been modernized.

The Book Named the Governor

From *Book I*

XXI. Wherefore in the good order of dancing a man and a woman danceth together

It is diligently to be noted that the associating of man and woman in dancing, they both observing one number and time in their movings, was not begun without a special consideration, as well for the necessary conjunction of those two persons, as for the intimation of sundry virtues which be by them represented. And forasmuch as by the association of a man and a woman in dancing may be signified matrimony, I could in declaring the dignity and commodity [1] of that sacrament make entire volumes, if it were not so commonly known to all men, that almost every friar limiter [2] carrieth it written in his bosom. Wherefore, lest in repeating a thing so frequent and common my book should be as fastidious [3] or fulsome [4] to the readers as such merchant [5] preachers be now to their customers, I will reverently take my leave of divines. And for my part I will endeavour myself to assemble, out of the books of ancient poets and philosophers, matter as well apt [6] to my purpose as also new or at the least ways infrequent, or seldom heard of them that have not read very many authors in Greek and Latin.

But now to my purpose. In every dance, of a most ancient custom, there danceth together a man and a woman, holding each other by the hand or the arm, which betokeneth concord. Now it behoveth the dancers and also the beholders of them to know all qualities incident to a man, and also all qualities to a woman likewise appertaining.

A man in his natural perfection is fierce, hardy, strong in opinion, covetous of glory, desirous of knowledge, appetiting [7] by generation to bring forth his semblable. [8] The good nature of a woman is to be mild, timorous, tractable, benign, of sure remembrance, and shamefast. Divers other qualities of each of them might be found out, but these be most apparent, and for this time sufficient.

Wherefore, when we behold a man and a woman dancing together, let us suppose there to be a concord of all the said qualities, being joined together, as I have set them in order. And the moving of the man would be more vehement, of the woman more delicate, and with less advancing of the body, signifying the courage and strength that ought to be in a man, and the pleasant soberness that should be in a woman. And in this wise fierceness joined with mildness maketh severity; audacity with timorosity maketh magnanimity; wilful opinion and tractability (which is to be shortly persuaded and moved) maketh

---

1. Advantage, profit. Compare T. S. Eliot, *East Coker*—though the dance Elyot describes is not a vigorous country-dance.
2. A friar licensed to beg, hear confessions, and preach within a certain district. Such a person would deal only in the most commonplace and best-known doctrines.
3. Boring.
4. Superfluous.
5. That is, mendicant.
6. Relating.
7. Instinctively desiring, as a natural necessity.
8. That is, a child like him.

constancy a virtue; covetousness of glory adorned with benignity causeth honour; desire of knowledge with sure remembrance procureth sapience;[9] shamefastness joined to appetite of generation maketh continence, which is a mean[10] between chastity and inordinate lust. These qualities, in this wise being knit together and signified in the personages of man and woman dancing, do express or set out the figure of very[11] nobility; which in the higher estate it is contained, the more excellent is the virtue in estimation.

XXII. How dancing may be an introduction unto the first moral virtue, called prudence[12]

As I have already affirmed, the principal cause of this my little enterprise is to declare an induction[13] or mean,[14] how children of gentle nature or disposition may be trained into the way of virtue with a pleasant facility. And for as much as it is very expedient that there be mixed with study some honest[15] and moderate disport,[16] or at the least way recreation, to recomfort and quicken[17] the vital spirits,[18] lest they long travailing,[19] or being much occupied in contemplation or remembrance of things grave and serious, might happen to be fatigued, or perchance oppressed. And therefore Tully,[20] who unneth[21] found ever any time vacant from study, permitteth in his first book of *Offices*[22] that men may use play and disport, yet notwithstanding in such wise as they do use sleep and other manner of quiet, when they have sufficiently disposed earnest matters and of weighty importance.

Now because there is no pastime to be compared to that wherein may be found both recreation and meditation of virtue, I have among all honest pastimes, wherein is exercise of the body, noted dancing to be of an excellent utility, comprehending in it wonderful figures, or, as the Greeks do call them, *ideae*,[23] of virtues and noble qualities, and specially of the commodious[24] virtue called prudence, whom Tully defineth to be the knowledge of things which ought to be desired and followed,[25] and also of them which ought to be fled

9. Wisdom.

10. According to Aristotle, *Nicomachean Ethics* II.6 ff., virtue has a disposition to choose the middle between extremes, and finds its true nature in the mean.

11. True.

12. Prudence, wisdom, the first of the cardinal virtues, the others being justice, temperance, and fortitude. According to Aristotle, prudence was the virtue best adapted to the mean.

13. Inducement.

14. Means.

15. Good.

16. Pastime.

17. Enliven.

18. The rarefied substances which, according to medieval and Renaissance medicine, were sent from the heart by the arteries and pulses, so that they permeated the body and kept it vigorous. Overmuch study was held to be one of the greatest and most deadening dangers to the vital spirits.

19. Working, laboring.

20. Marcus Tullius Cicero.

21. Scarcely.

22. *De Officiis* (Of Moral Duties) I.29.

23. Ideal patterns.

24. Advantageous, beneficial.

25. *De Officiis* I.43.

from or eschewed. And it is named of Aristotle the mother of virtues; [26] of other philosophers it is called the captain or mistress of virtues; of some the housewife, for as much as by her diligence she doth investigate and prepare places apt and convenient, where other virtues shall execute their powers or offices. Wherefore, as Solomon saith,[27] like as in water be shown the visages of them that behold it, so unto men that be prudent the secrets of men's hearts be openly discovered. This virtue being so commodious to man, and, as it were, the porch of the noble palace of man's reason, whereby all other virtues shall enter, it seemeth to me right expedient, that as soon as opportunity may be found, a child or young man be thereto induced. And because that the study of virtue is tedious for the more part to them that do flourish in young years, I have devised how in the form of dancing, now late used in this realm among gentlemen, the whole description of this virtue prudence may be found out and well perceived, as well by the dancers as by them which standing by will be diligent beholders and markers, having first mine instruction surely graven in the table of their remembrance. Wherefore all they that have their courage stirred toward very honour or perfect nobility, let them approach to this pastime, and either themselves prepare them to dance, or else at the least way behold with watching eyes other that can dance truly, keeping just measure and time. But to the understanding of this instruction, they must mark well the sundry motions and measures, which in true form of dancing is to be specially observed.

The first moving in every dance is called honour,[28] which is a reverent inclination or curtsey, with a long deliberation or pause, and is but one motion, comprehending the time of three other motions, or setting forth of the foot. By that may be signified that at the beginning of all our acts, we should do due honour to God, which is the root of prudence; which honour is compact of these three things, fear, love, and reverence. And that in the beginning of all things we should advisedly, with some tract [29] of time, behold and foresee the success of our enterprise.

By the second motion,[30] which is two in number, may be signified celerity and slowness: which two, albeit they seem to discord in their effects and natural properties, and therefore they may be well resembled to the brawl [31] in dancing (for in our English tongue we say men do brawl, when between them is altercation in words), yet of them two springeth an excellent virtue whereunto we lack a name in English.

26. *Magna Moralia,* I.35.
27. Proverbs 27:19: "As in the water face answereth to face, so the heart of man to man."
28. "Honour" was the first movement of the base dance, a "grave and slow" dance in which the feet did not leave the ground. The man made his reverence by keeping the left foot firm on the floor, bending the right knee and placing the right foot behind the left leg, meanwhile saluting the company and his partner by taking off his hat. According to Elyot, the reverence occupies the time taken by three steps of the dance itself.
29. Delay.
30. The step known as "braule," one of the four basic steps in the base dance (Elyot makes them eight), which normally came either immediately after the reverence, or at the end of the dance, or both.
31. Elyot seems to be saying that the brawl is second in order, that movement is either fast or slow, that these are two opposites, and that they are therefore susceptible to mediation by the mean.

Wherefore I am constrained to usurp a Latin word,[32] calling it maturity: which word, though it be strange and dark, yet by declaring the virtue in a few more words, the name once brought in custom, shall be facile to understand as other words late coming out of Italy and France, and made denizens [33] among us.

Maturity [34] is a mean between two extremities, wherein nothing lacketh or exceedeth, and is in such estate that it may neither increase nor minish [35] without losing the denomination of maturity. The Greeks in a proverb do express it properly in two words, which I can none otherwise interpret in English, but 'Speed thee slowly.' [36]

Also of this word maturity sprang a noble and precious sentence,[37] recited by Sallust in the *Battle against Catiline*,[38] which is in this manner or like, 'Consult before thou enterprise anything, and after thou hast taken counsel, it is expedient to do it maturely.'

Maturum in Latin may be interpreted ripe or ready, as fruit when it is ripe, it is at the very point to be gathered and eaten. And every other thing, when it is ready, it is at the instant after to be occupied. Therefore that word maturity is translated to the acts of man, that when they be done with such moderation that nothing in the doing may be seen superfluous or indigent,[39] we may say that they be maturely done: reserving the words ripe and ready to fruit and other things separate from affairs, as we have now in usage. And this do I now remember for the necessary augmentation of our language.

In the most excellent and most noble emperor Octavius Augustus, in whom reigned all nobility, nothing is more commended than that he had frequently in his mouth this word *Matura*, 'Do maturely.' [40] As he should have said, 'Do neither too much nor too little, too soon nor too late, too swiftly nor slowly, but in due time and measure.'

Now I trust I have sufficiently expounded the virtue called maturity, which is the mean or mediocrity between sloth and celerity, commonly called speediness; and so have I declared what utility may be taken of a brawl in dancing.

1531

32. Elyot's method for augmentation and enrichment of the English language was to introduce a Latin word along with an English equivalent or explanation, so as to ease the process of assimilation.

33. Naturalized aliens.

34. Elyot probably took the word from the Roman encyclopedist Aulus Gellius' (c. 123–165 A.D.) *Attic Nights* X.11.

35. Diminish.

36. Speude bradeōs, as "Festina lente," a favorite saying of the Emperor Augustus.

37. Wise saying.

38. The *Bellum Catilinae* I.1, by the Roman historian Gaius Sallustius Crispus (86–34 B.C.).

39. Lacking.

40. Also from Aulus Gellius; cf. Suetonius (c. 69–c. 140 A.D.), *Life of Octavius Augustus* XXV.

BALDASSARE CASTIGLIONE
1478–1529

SIR THOMAS HOBY
1530–1566

Castiglione was born in Mantuan territory in 1478, his mother being a member of the Gonzaga family, lords of Mantua. He was educated in Milan under celebrated humanist teachers and later established himself at the court of Urbino, which Duke Federigo da Montefeltro, the great *condottiere* and patron of learning (1422–82: Fig. 4) himself the pupil of the greatest educators of his day, had made one of the most famous in Italy for all the peaceful and military arts. During the years he spent there, from 1504 until 1513, Castiglione served the reigning duke, Guidobaldo, as ambassador in France and England and wrote *Il Cortegiano*. In 1513, he was sent as ambassador from Urbino to the court of Pope Leo X, brother of Giuliano de' Medici, the Lord Julian of *The Courtier*. Here he became a friend of the painter Raphael (Fig. 5). Castiglione had married in 1516, and on the death of his wife after only four years of marriage he entered the priesthood and was sent as Papal Nuncio to Spain, where he won the friendship of Emperor Charles V. The sack of Rome by the Emperor's troops in 1527 affected Castiglione deeply: it signified—as it did for Sir Thomas More—the death of what he had lived and worked for, a truly Christian Europe, united and at peace with itself spiritually and materially. He retired from the imperial court and died at Toledo early in 1529.

Il Cortegiano was one of the most influential and most famous products of the Italian Renaissance: its examination of the make-up of the perfect courtier provided a much more exalted and sophisticated model for imitation than had hitherto been available—or indeed than was set out in its successors, such as Giovanni della Casa's *Galateo* or Stefano Guazzo's *Civile Converzatione*. It is, in form, a record of the discussions of four successive evenings by one of those assemblies of learned and cultured men for which the Duchess of Urbino, with the aid of the Lady Emilia de' Pii, had made Urbino famous. Castiglione himself modestly pretends to have been absent from among his friends on the occasion. They discussed, on the first evening, the birth and education of the perfect courtier; on the second, his social experience and behavior in the daily circumstances of life, and the accomplishments that he ought to cultivate; on the third, the perfection of the noblewoman. On the fourth evening— from whose record our extract is taken—the Platonist Pietro Bembo defined the nature of love and its power to ennoble, a favorite topic of philosophic discourse in the Renaissance.

Castiglione's views on *cortegiania*—"the form of courtiership most befitting a gentleman who lives in the courts of princes, through which he may know how to serve them perfectly in everything which is according to reason, so as to win favour from them and praise from others"—became those of Europe. Ophelia's praise of Hamlet is a kind of paraphrase of them:

> The courtier's, soldier's, scholar's, eye, tongue, sword:
> The expectancy and rose of the fair state,
> The glass of fashion and the mould of form.

Gabriel Harvey's note in his copy of Sir Thomas Hoby's translation, too, sums up the book and its ethos well, and we can be sure that it found its echo in the mind of

Harvey's friend Edmund Spenser: "Above all things it importeth a courtier to be graceful and lovely in countenance and behaviour; fine and discreet in discourse and entertainment; skilful and expert in letters and arms; active and gallant in every courtly exercise; nimble and speedy of body and mind; resolute, industrious and valorous in action; as profound and invincible in action as is possible; and withal ever generously bold, wittily pleasant, and full of life in his sayings and doings." It is to men such as this, who by elaborating and transforming the mediaeval chivalric ideal to realize their full potential for virtuous action in arts and arms, that others looked for the improvement of the quality of English life.

This was what Sir Thomas Hoby hoped his translation might effect. He may have come across the original before he began the travels in Germany, France, and Italy by which he completed the education begun at St. John's College, Cambridge, the Renaissance stronghold of Protestant scholarship, in 1545. But it is more likely that he did not make its acquaintance until he had reached Italy, by which time the book itself was some forty years old. Castiglione had written it between 1508 and 1516, though it had not been published until 1528, after long revision and circulation, in the Renaissance fashion, among his friends. Hoby's is a young man's work: his spirited translation reflects his enthusiasm for Italy and the impact made on him by the nobility of the original as well as the fact that he was, as his friend Roger Ascham put it, "well furnished with learning and very expert in knowledge of divers tongues." This knowledge was to serve him well later, when, after Elizabeth's succession and the re-establishment of Protestantism, he became a public servant. Hoby was English ambassador when he died at Paris in 1566. His translation, complete by 1554, when he was twenty-four, was not published until 1561.

The Book of the Courtier

Hoby's book is the first translation of a secular work which can be called a masterpiece of English prose, but important and influential as it is in this respect, it owed its popularity—and the four editions of 1561, 1577, 1588, and 1603 which it went through during Elizabeth's reign—chiefly to its doctrine. It would be, he felt, useful to all men. It would tell princes truths that their advisers dared not utter; it would be the cause of useful reflection in older men and, most important of all, it would be for young gentlemen "an encouraging to garnish their minds with moral virtues, and their bodies with comely exercises, and . . . both . . . with honest qualities." To ladies and gentlemen it would be "a mirror to deck and tire themselves with virtuous conditions, comely behaviour and honest entertainment toward all men." To every reader it would be "a storehouse of most necessary implements for the conversation, use and training up of man's life with courtly demeanours."

Hoby's purpose is patriotic, as his use of English itself would show. But language was the means to an end. He wants Englishmen to have the best of it, to have this valuable doctrine in their own tongue. Translation, according to others, he says, injures memory and hinders learning; for his part, he sees it as performing the exact opposite. The more members of the nobility and gentry to whom such excellent reading is available, the better. Like Sir Thomas Elyot, he believed that if only each of our learned men would "store the tongue according to his knowledge and delight above other men" with good content and good language, England would soon become the equal of the ancient commonwealths of Greece and Rome for wisdom and power, and English the equal of the ancient languages for eloquence. Hoby was less concerned than Elyot to naturalize words from other languages, and had some sympathy with the purist principles of Sir John Cheke (his Cambridge mentor and later his friend) as they are expressed in Cheke's prefatory letter to *The Courtier*. He did not, however, go all the way with Cheke in wishing English written pure, "unmixed and unmangled with borrowing of other tongues."

This linguistic patriotism, a marked feature of sixteenth-century humanism in Italy, Spain, France, and Germany, as well as England, is more explicit in Hoby than in Castiglione. On the other hand, the element of philosophic discussion, of embodiment of the ideal, though inevitably present, is subtly altered by the translation. *The Courtier* is more sophisticated, less earnest, than Elyot's *Governor* in its purpose, but Hoby has broadened, almost moralized, his original: his book was for the many, not the few. It was intended to help in the fashioning of a class of living men who would be fit, by the refinement of their natures brought about by their practice of virtue and the completeness of their education, to be the guides of the life of a country which had now entered into her full share of greatness. It was intended for the social unit of hereditary nobility and gentry combined, who were the rulers, under the monarch, of Tudor England.

Other translators followed Hoby's lead: Robert Peterson in 1576 with a version of Della Casa's *Galateo*, and George Pettie and Bartholomew Young with their rendering of Guazzo's *Civile Conversatione* in 1581–86. Both texts are more restricted in their scope and neither had the impact of Hoby's *Courtier*.

The most famous passage in *The Courtier* is Cardinal Bembo's superbly eloquent exposition of the nature of love according to the philosophy of neoplatonism, which concludes the fourth and final book just as the new day is beginning to show itself. True love, he tells the company, is born of the intellectual perception of the beautiful, which is also the good. It is this which can make a man more like an angel than the beast he resembles if he stops short in mere earthly love and the gratification of the senses. In true love, he is united with the divine. His soul desires the immortal, unchanging, ideal beauty that it knew before its descent into the gross material of the body.

The extract from Bembo's speech here given begins with a difficulty, raised by one of the speakers in the dialogue. It looks as if, he is made to say, the ideal courtier will have to be an older man, since the knowledge and counsel which are the essential part of his make-up are the virtues of maturity: they take time to acquire. Will this, the question is, make him unapt for love and to that extent a less than perfect courtier?

The text is that of the first edition as reprinted in the series *Tudor Translations*, 1900. Spelling and punctuation have been modernized.

The Book of the Courtier

From *Book IV*

Then M. Peter [1] after a while's silence, somewhat settling himself as though he should entreat upon [2] a weighty matter, said thus: 'My lords, to show that old men may love not only without slander, but otherwhile [3] more happily than young men, I must be enforced to make a little discourse to declare what love is, and wherein consisteth the happiness that lovers may have. Therefore I beseech you give the hearing with heedfulness, for I hope to make you understand that it were not unfitting for any man here to be a lover, in case he were fifteen or twenty years elder than M. Morello.' [4]

And here, after they had laughed awhile, M. Peter proceeded: 'I say, therefore, that according as it is defined of the wise men of old time,[5] love is nothing else but a certain coveting to enjoy beauty; and forsomuch as coveting longeth for nothing but for things known,[6] it is requisite that knowledge go evermore before coveting,[7] which of his own nature willeth the good,[8] but of himself is blind and knoweth it not. Therefore hath nature so ordained that to every virtue of knowledge [9] there is annexed a virtue of longing. And because in our soul there be three manner [10] ways to know, namely, by sense, reason, and understanding: [11] of sense there ariseth appetite or longing, which is common to us with brute beasts; of reason ariseth election or choice, which is proper to man; of understanding, by the which man may be partner with angels, ariseth

1. Master Peter is Pietro Bembo (1470–1547), the Venetian humanist scholar, poet, prose writer, historian, later a cardinal, whose most famous work, *Gli Asolani,* is a series of dialogues on the nature of love. Bembo, a Platonist in philosophy, is here expounding a doctrine of love which is based ultimately on Plato, especially on his *Symposium* and *Phaedrus,* but owes much to Renaissance commentators on them, especially to Marsilio Ficino (1433–99), the Florentine neoplatonist philosopher. There are also similarities with other Renaissance neoplatonist works, such as the *De Amore* (On Love) of Francesco Cattani da Diacceto.
2. Handle, deal with.
3. Sometimes.
4. Morello de' Riccardi da Ortona, elderly soldier of fortune and courtier, a skilled musical performer, later intervenes in the discussion. His contention is that old men can love as hotly and sensuously as young.
5. That is, especially Plato.
6. That is, perceived by the senses.
7. That is, we must perceive before we can desire.
8. Wishes for the good.
9. Power, faculty of perception.
10. Kinds of.
11. If we perceive only through the senses, so that our passions or appetites are roused, we are no better than the beasts, in whom the same process can take place. If, by the exercise of our reason, which is what distinguishes man from the beasts, we perceive that we have an alternative and exercise our power of choice, we have moved away from bestiality to human, rational behavior. If our perceptions are intellectual, via the understanding, we can grasp the true nature of things, and our will must necessarily become set on such things, i.e. on the divine ideas. In desiring these, we become like the angels. See Pico della Mirandola in *On the Dignity of Man,* where God tells man: "You shall have the power to degenerate to the lower brutish forms of life; and you shall also have the power to be reborn to the higher, or divine, according to the judgment [i.e. choice] of your soul."

will.[12] Even as therefore the sense knoweth not but sensible matters and that which may be felt, so the appetite or coveting only desireth the same; and even as the understanding is bent but to behold things that may be understood, so is that will only fed with spiritual goods. Man of nature endowed with reason, placed, as it were, in the middle between these two extremities, may, through his choice inclining to sense or reaching to understanding, come nigh to the coveting, sometime of the one, sometime of the other part. In these sorts therefore may beauty be coveted, the general name whereof may be applied to all things, either natural or artificial, that are framed in good proportion and due temper,[13] as their nature beareth.

'But speaking of the beauty that we mean, which is only it that appeareth in bodies, and especially in the face of man, and moveth this fervent coveting which we call love, we will term it an influence of the heavenly bountifulness, the which for all it stretcheth over all things that be created (like the light of the sun), yet when it findeth out a face well proportioned, and framed with a certain lively agreement of several colours, and set forth with lights and shadows, and with an orderly distance and limits of lines,[14] thereinto it distilleth itself and appeareth most well favoured, and decketh out and lighteneth the subject where it shineth with a marvellous grace and glistering, like the sunbeams that strike against beautiful plate of fine gold wrought and set with precious jewels, so that it draweth unto it men's eyes with pleasure, and piercing through them, imprinteth himself in the soul, and with an unwonted sweetness all to-stirreth [15] her and delighteth, and setting her on fire maketh her to covet him. When the soul then is taken with coveting to enjoy this beauty as a good thing, in case she suffer herself to be guided with the judgment of sense, she falleth into most deep errors, and judgeth the body in which beauty is discerned to be the principal cause thereof; whereupon to enjoy it she reckoneth it necessary to join as inwardly as she can with that body, which is false; and therefore whoso thinketh in possessing the body to enjoy beauty, he is far deceived, and is moved to it, not with true knowledge by the choice of reason, but with false opinion by the longing of sense. Whereupon the pleasure that followeth it is also false and of necessity full of errors. And therefore into one of the two vices run all those lovers that satisfy their unhonest [16] lusts with the women whom they love; for either as soon as they come to the coveted end, they not only feel a fullness and loathsomeness, but also conceive a hatred against the wight [17] beloved, as though longing repented him of his offence and acknowledged the deceit wrought him by the false judgment of sense, that made him believe the ill to be good, or else they continue in the very same coveting and greediness, as though they were not indeed come to the end which they sought for. And albeit through the blind opinion that hath made them drunken

12. According to Ficino, intellect (understanding) is pure and refined will.
13. That is, the best balance of elements, the constituents of all matter (earth, water, fire, and air), and of qualities (hot, cold, moist, dry), which determine the nature of all created things.
14. Outlines.
15. Moves strongly.
16. Morally wrong.
17. Person.

(to their seeming) [18] in that instant they feel a contentation,[19] as the diseased otherwhile, that dream they drink of some clear spring, yet be they not satisfied, nor leave off so. And because of possessing coveted goodness there arises always quietness and satisfaction in the possessor's mind, in case this were the true and right end of their coveting, when they possess it they would be at quietness and thoroughly satisfied, which they be not: but rather deceived through that likeness, they forthwith return again to unbridled coveting, and with the very same trouble which they felt at the first, they fall again into the raging and most burning thirst of the thing, that they hope in vain to possess perfectly.

'These kinds of lovers therefore love most unluckily,[20] for either they never come by their covetings, which is a great unluckiness, or else if they do come by them, they find they come by their hurt and end their miseries with other greater miseries, for both in the beginning and middle of this love, there is never other thing felt but afflictions, torments, griefs, pining, travail, so that to be wan, vexed with continual tears and sighs, to live with a discontented mind, to be always dumb, or to lament, to covet death, in conclusion to be most unlucky, are the properties which, they say, belong to lovers.

'The cause therefore of this wretchedness in men's minds is principally sense, which in youthful age beareth most sway, because the lustiness of the flesh and of the blood in that season addeth unto him even so much force as it withdraweth from reason. Therefore doth it easily train the soul to follow appetite or longing, for when she seeth herself drowned in the earthly prison, because she is set in the office to govern the body, she cannot of herself understand plainly at the first the truth of spiritual beholding. Wherefore to compass the understanding of things, she must go beg the beginning at the senses, and therefore she believeth them and giveth ear to them, and is contented to be led by them, especially when they have so much courage, that (in a manner) they enforce [21] her, and because they be deceitful they fill her with errors and false opinions. Whereupon most commonly it happeneth that young men be wrapped in this sensual love, which is a very rebel against reason, and therefore they make themselves unworthy to enjoy the favours and benefits which love bestoweth upon his true subjects. Neither in love feel they any other pleasures than what beasts without reason do, but much more grievous afflictions.

'Setting case therefore this to be so, which is most true, I say that the contrary chanceth to them of a more ripe age. For in case they, when the soul is not now so much weighed down with the bodily burden, and when the natural burning assuageth and draweth to [22] a warmth, if they be inflamed with beauty, and to it bend their coveting guided by reasonable choice, they be not deceived, and possess beauty perfectly, and therefore through the possessing of it, always goodness ensueth to them. Because beauty is good [23] and

18. Appearance.
19. Satisfaction.
20. Unhappily.
21. Take by violence, rape.
22. Approaches, becomes.
23. The identity of beauty and goodness is fundamental to Platonism: the beauty of earthly things should recall to the soul its memory of true, heavenly beauty.

consequently the true love of it is most good and holy, and evermore bringeth forth good fruits in the souls of them that with the bridle of reason [24] restrain the ill disposition of sense, the which old men can much sooner do than young.

'It is not therefore out of reason to say that old men may also love without slander and more happily than young men, taking notwithstanding this name old, not for the age at the pit's brink, nor when the canals [25] of the body be so feeble, that the soul cannot through them work her feats,[26] but when knowledge in us is in his right strength. And I will not also hide this from you: namely, that I suppose where sensual love in every age is naught,[27] yet in young men it deserveth excuse, and perhaps in some cases lawful; [28] for although it putteth them in afflictions, dangers, travails, and the unfortunateness that is said, yet are there many that to win them the goodwill of their ladies practise virtuous things, which for all they be not bent to a good end, yet are they good of themselves; and so of that much bitterness they pick out a little sweetness, and through the adversities which they sustain, in the end they acknowledge their error. As I judge therefore those young men that bridle their appetites, and love with reason, to be godly; so do I hold excused such as yield to sensual love, whereunto they be so inclined through the weakness and frailty of man—so [29] they show therein meekness, courtesy, and prowess, and the other worthy conditions that these lords have spoken of; and when those youthful years be gone and past, leave it off clean, keeping aloof from this sensual coveting as from the lowermost step of the stairs, by the which a man may ascend to true love. But in case after they draw in [30] years, once they reserve [31] in their cold heart the fire of appetites, and bring stout reason in subjection to feeble sense, it cannot be said how much they are to be blamed: for like men without sense they deserve with an everlasting shame to be put in the number of unreasonable living creatures, because the thoughts and ways of sensual love be far unsitting for ripe age.'

Here Bembo paused awhile, as though he would breathe him, and when all things were whist [32] M. Morello of Ortona said: 'And in case there were some old man more fresh and lusty and of a better complexion [33] than many young men, why would you not have it lawful for him to love with the love that young men love?'

The Duchess [34] laughed, and said: 'If the love of young men be so unlucky,

24. The metaphor comes ultimately from Plato's *Phaedrus*, but the actual expression "bridle of reason" is in Seneca, *Dialogues* III.iii.7 ("On Anger" I.7).
25. Passages along which the "spirits," the refined substances which permeate the body and make it live and act, can travel.
26. Perform its operations.
27. Wrong, worthless.
28. That is, rightly.
29. As long as.
30. Advance in.
31. Retain.
32. Quiet.
33. Bodily make-up.
34. Elisabetta Gonzaga (1471–1526), the beautiful and gifted wife of Guidobaldo da Montefeltro, Duke of Urbino, whose court, like that of his father Federigo, was famous for its splendor and love of learning. It was the custom of the guests there to meet in the evening after supper for music, dancing, and discussion, presided over by the Duchess, of subjects proposed by her.

why would you, M. Morello, that old men should also love with this unluckiness? But in case you were old, as these men say you be, you would not thus procure the hurt of old men.'

M. Morello answered: 'The hurt of old men, meseemeth, M. Peter Bembo procureth, who will have them to love after a sort that I for my part understand not; and, methink,[35] the possessing of this beauty which he praiseth so much, without the body, is a dream.'

'Do you believe, M. Morello,' quoth then Count Lewis,[36] 'that beauty is always so good a thing as M. Peter Bembo speaketh of?'

'Not I, in good sooth,' answered M. Morello. 'But I remember rather that I have seen many beautiful women of a most ill inclination, cruel and spiteful, and it seemeth that, in a manner, it happeneth always so, for beauty maketh them proud, and pride, cruel.'

Count Lewis said, smiling: 'To you perhaps they seem cruel, because they content you not with it that you would have. But cause M. Peter Bembo to teach you in what sort old men ought to covet beauty, and what to seek at their ladies' hands, and what to content themselves withal; and in not passing out of these bounds you shall see that they shall be neither proud nor cruel, and will satisfy you with what you shall require.'

M. Morello seemed then somewhat out of patience, and said: 'I will not know the thing that toucheth [37] me not. But cause you to be taught how the young men ought to covet this beauty that are not so fresh and lusty as old men be.'

Here Sir Frederick,[38] to pacify M. Morello and to break their talk, would not suffer Count Lewis to make answer, but interrupting him said: 'Perhaps M. Morello is not altogether out of the way in saying that beauty is not always good, for the beauty of women is many times cause of infinite evils in the world—hatred, war, mortality, and destruction, whereof the razing of Troy [39] can be a good witness; and beautiful women for the most part be either proud and cruel, as is said, or unchaste; but M. Morello would find no fault with that. There be also many wicked men that have the comeliness of a beautiful countenance, and it seemeth that nature hath so shaped them because they may be the readier to deceive, and that this amiable look were like a bait that covereth the hook.'

Then M. Peter Bembo: 'Believe not,' quoth he, 'but beauty is always good.'

Here Count Lewis, because he would return again to his former purpose, interrupted him and said: 'Since M. Morello passeth [40] not to understand that which is so necessary for him, teach it me, and show me how old men may

---

35. It seems to me.
36. Count Lodovico of Canossa (1476–1532), another of those attracted to the court of Urbino by its reputation for learning and refinement, came of a Veronese family. He was a relation and a close friend of Castiglione's, and became bishop of Tricarico and papal emissary to France. In France he became bishop of Bayeux and acted as ambassador for the French king to the pope.
37. Concerns.
38. Federigo Fregoso (b. 1480), soldier and poet, a relative of the Duke's, in exile from Genoa; later nominated archbishop of Salerno and became bishop of Gubbio.
39. On account of Helen.
40. That is, cares.

come by this happiness of love, for I will not care to be counted old, so it may profit me.' [41]

M. Peter Bembo laughed, and said: 'First will I take the error out of these gentlemen's mind, and afterward will I satisfy you also.' So beginning afresh: 'My Lords,' quoth he, 'I would not that with speaking all of beauty, which is a holy thing, any of us, as profane and wicked, should purchase him the wrath of God. Therefore, to give M. Morello and Sir Frederick warning, that they lose not their sight, as Stesichorus [42] did—a pain most meet for whoso dispraiseth beauty—I say that beauty cometh of God and is like a circle, the goodness whereof is the centre. And therefore, as there can be no circle without a centre, no more can beauty be without goodness. Whereupon doth very seldom an ill soul dwell in a beautiful body. And therefore is the outward beauty a true sign of the inward goodness, and in bodies this comeliness is imprinted, more and less, as it were, for a mark of the soul, whereby she is outwardly known; as in trees, in which the beauty of the buds giveth a testimony of the goodness of the fruit. And the very same happeneth in bodies, as it is seen that palmisters [43] by the visage know many times the conditions and otherwhile the thoughts of men. And, which is more, in beasts also a man may discern by the face the quality of the courage, which in the body declareth itself as much as it can. Judge you how plainly in the face of a lion, a horse, and an eagle, a man shall discern anger, fierceness, and stoutness; [44] in lambs and doves, simpleness and very [45] innocency; the crafty subtlety in foxes and wolves; and the like, in a manner, in all other living creatures.

'The foul,[46] therefore, for the most part be also evil, and the beautiful good. Therefore it may be said that beauty is a face pleasant, merry, comely, and to be desired for goodness; and foulness a face dark, uglesome, unpleasant, and to be shunned for ill. And in case you will consider all things, you shall find that whatsoever is good and profitable hath also evermore the comeliness of beauty. Behold the state of this great engine [47] of the world, which God created for the health and preservation of everything that was made: the

41. That is, as long as good may come of it for me, I shall not care if I am thought old.
42. Hoby's note: "a notable poet which lost his sight for writing against Helena and recanting had his sight restored him again." He lived probably during the 6th century B.C. Plato tells the story in his *Phaedrus* 243a.
43. That is, physiognomists, who professed to read the outward characteristics of the body as indications of the soul and interior constitution.
44. Courage.
45. Real, true.
46. Ugly.
47. "Universal frame"; cf. Lucretius' *machina mundi*. This part of Bembo's speech, on fitness, harmony, and proportion in all things, is imitated from Cicero's *De Oratore*, III.45, where Cicero is arguing that nature has contrived that what is useful is also dignified and beautiful. The map of the universe that is described is the pre-Copernican, "Ptolemaic," so called after the Greek astronomer and mathematician Claudius Ptolemaeus (2nd century A.D.). See Fig. 1. The cosmos has earth at its center, surrounded by the spheres of the other elements—water, air, and fire—in concentric circles. These are in turn surrounded, in this simplified diagram, by the spheres of the planets, seven in all, beginning with the moon. After these comes the firmament, with the signs of the zodiac; then the crystalline sphere and the sphere of the *primum mobile* (first moving), which governs the orbits of all the others. They are presided over by God, the unmoved, Prime Mover.

heaven round beset with so many heavenly lights; and in the middle the earth environed with the elements and upheld with the very weight of itself; the sun, that compassing about giveth light to the whole, and in winter season draweth to the lowermost sign, afterward by little and little climbeth again to the other part; the moon, that of him taketh her light, according as she draweth nigh or goeth farther from him; and the other five stars that diversely keep the very same course. These things among themselves have such force by the knitting together of an order so necessarily framed that, with altering them any one jot, they should all be loosed and the world would decay. They have also such beauty and comeliness that all the wits men have cannot imagine a more beautiful matter.

'Think now of the shape of man, which may be called a little world,[48] in whom every parcel [49] of his body is seen to be necessarily framed by art and not by hap,[50] and then the form altogether most beautiful, so that it were a hard matter to judge whether the members (as the eyes, the nose, the mouth, the ears, the arms, the breast, and in like manner the other parts) give either more profit [51] to the countenance and the rest of the body, or comeliness. The like may be said of all other living creatures. Behold the feathers of fowls, the leaves and boughs of trees, which be given them of nature to keep them in their being, and yet have they withal [52] a very great sightliness.

'Leave nature, and come to art. What thing is so necessary in sailing vessels as the forepart, the sides, the main yards, the mast, the sails, the stern, oars, anchors, and tacklings? All these things notwithstanding are so well-favoured in the eye that unto whoso beholdeth them they seem to have been found out as well for pleasure as for profit. Pillars and great beams uphold high buildings and palaces, and yet are they no less pleasureful unto the eyes of the beholders than profitable to the buildings. When men began to build, in the middle of temples and houses they reared the ridge of the roof, not to make the works to have a better show, but because the water might the more commodiously avoid [53] on both sides; yet unto profit there was forthwith adjoined a fair sightliness, so that if, under the sky where there falleth neither hail nor rain, a man should build a temple without a reared ridge, it is to be thought that it could have neither a sightly show nor any beauty.

'Beside other things, therefore, it giveth a great praise to the world in saying that it is beautful. It is praised in saying the beautiful heaven, beautiful earth, beautiful sea, beautiful rivers, beautiful woods, trees, gardens, beautiful cities, beautiful churches, houses, armies. In conclusion, this comely and holy beauty is a wondrous setting out of everything. And it may be said that good and beautiful be after a sort one self thing, especially in the bodies of men; of

48. The microcosm, man, framed by God with the same exactness and proportion as the universe, the macrocosm, all the parts and motions of one corresponding to those of the other, the body corresponding to the sensible, the soul to the intelligible world. Democritus, the pre-Socratic philosopher, is said to have originated the term microcosm; its first actual appearance is in Aristotle, *Physics* VIII.8. (See also Glossary.)
49. Part.
50. Chance.
51. Use.
52. Moreover.
53. Escape. Bembo is still quoting Cicero, *De Oratore* III.45.

the beauty whereof the nighest cause, I suppose, is the beauty of the soul; [54] the which, as a partner of the right and heavenly beauty, maketh sightly and beautiful whatever she toucheth, and most of all, if the body, where she dwelleth, be not of so vile a matter that she cannot imprint in it her property. Therefore beauty is the true monument and spoil of the victory of the soul, when she with heavenly influence beareth rule over material and gross nature, and with her light overcometh the darkness of the body.

'It is not, then, to be spoken that beauty maketh women proud or cruel, although it seem so to M. Morello. Neither yet ought beautiful women to bear the blame of that hatred, mortality,[55] and destruction which the unbridled appetites of men are the cause of. I will not now deny but it is possible also to find in the world beautiful women unchaste; yet not because beauty inclineth them to unchaste living, for it rather plucketh them from it, and leadeth them into the way of virtuous conditions, through the affinity that beauty hath with goodness; but otherwhile ill bringing up, the continual provocations of lovers' tokens, poverty, hope, deceits, fear, and a thousand other matters, overcome the steadfastness, yea, of beautiful and good women; and for these and like causes may also beautiful men become wicked.'

Then said the Lord Cesar: [56] 'In case the Lord Gaspar's [57] saying be true of yesternight, there is no doubt but the fair women be more chaste than the foul.'

'And what was my saying?' quoth the Lord Gaspar.

The Lord Cesar answered: 'If I do well bear in mind, your saying was that the women that are sued [58] to always refuse to satisfy him that sueth to them, but those that are not sued to, sue to others. There is no doubt but the beautiful women have always more suitors, and be more instantly laid at [59] in love, than the foul. Therefore the beautiful always deny, and consequently be more chaste than the foul, which, not being sued to, sue unto others.'

M. Peter Bembo laughed, and said: 'This argument cannot be answered to.'

Afterward he proceeded: 'It chanceth also, oftentimes, that as the other senses, so the sight is deceived and judgeth a face beautiful which indeed is not beautiful. And because in the eyes and in the whole countenance of some woman a man beholdeth otherwhile a certain lavish wantonness, painted with dishonest flickerings, many, whom that manner delighteth because it promiseth them an easiness to come by the thing that they covet, call it beauty; but indeed it is a cloaked unshamefastness,[60] unworthy of so honourable and holy a name.'

M. Peter Bembo held his peace, but those lords still were earnest upon him [61]

---

54. That internal beauty, beauty of the soul, was essential to external beauty, was fundamental Platonic doctrine.

55. Deadliness.

56. Cesare Gonzaga (c. 1475–1512), Castiglione's cousin and paragon of the noble virtues and practices of chivalry.

57. Gaspare Pallavicino (1486–1511), whose short life was marred by ill-health, is presented throughout the book as a misogynist and contender with Emilia de' Pii: their sparring may have been one of Shakespeare's sources for the contests of Beatrice and Benedick in *Much Ado About Nothing*.

58. Pressed, solicited.

59. Besieged.

60. Immodesty.

61. Begged him earnestly.

to speak somewhat more of this love and of the way to enjoy beauty aright, and at the last: 'Methink,' quoth he, 'I have showed plainly enough that old men may love more happily than young, which was my drift; therefore it belongeth not to me to enter any farther.'

Count Lewis answered: 'You have better declared the unluckiness of young men than the happiness of old men, whom you have not as yet taught what way they must follow in this love of theirs; only you have said that they must suffer themselves to be guided by reason, and the opinion of many is that it is unpossible for love to stand with reason.'

Bembo notwithstanding sought to make an end of reasoning,[62] but the Duchess desired him to say on, and he began thus afresh: 'Too unlucky were the nature of man, if our soul, in which this so fervent coveting may lightly [63] arise, should be driven to nourish it with that only which is common to her with beasts, and could not turn it to the other noble part, which is proper to her. Therefore, since it is so your pleasure, I will not refuse to reason upon this noble matter. And because I know myself unworthy to talk of the most holy mysteries of love, I beseech him to lead my thought and my tongue so that I may show this excellent Courtier how to love contrary to the wonted manner of the common ignorant sort. And even as from my childhood I have dedicated all my whole life unto him, so also now that my words may be answerable to the same intent, and to the praise of him: I say, therefore, that since the nature of man in youthful age is so much inclined to sense, it may be granted the Courtier, while he is young, to love sensually; but in case afterward also, in his riper years, he chance to be set on fire with this coveting of love, he ought to be good and circumspect, and heedful that he beguile not himself to be led willfully into the wretchedness that in young men deserveth more to be pitied than blamed; and contrariwise in old men, more to be blamed than pitied.

Therefore when an amiable countenance of a beautiful woman cometh in his sight, that is accompanied with noble conditions [64] and honest [65] behaviours, so that, as one practised in love, he wotteth [66] well that his hue [67] hath an agreement with hers, as soon as he is aware that his eyes snatch that image and carry it to the heart, and that the soul beginneth to behold it with pleasure, and feeleth within herself the influence that stirreth her and by little and little setteth her in heat, and that those lively [68] spirits that twinkle out through the eyes put continually fresh nourishment to the fire, he ought in this beginning to seek a speedy remedy and to raise up reason, and with her to fence the fortress of his heart, and to shut in such wise the passages against sense and appetites that they may enter neither with force nor subtle practice.

'Thus, if the flame be quenched, the jeopardy is also quenched. But in

62. Talk.
63. Quickly.
64. Moral qualities.
65. Good. The Italian is *gentile*.
66. Knows.
67. The Italian reads "blood." The sense is more than "coloring" and nearer the modern "character" or "temperament."
68. Vital spirits, the rarefied substance that sustains life.

case it continue or increase, then must the Courtier determine, when he per-
ceiveth he is taken, to shun thoroughly all filthiness of common love, and so
enter into the holy way of love with the guide of reason, and first consider
that the body where that beauty shineth is not the fountain from whence beauty
springeth, but rather because beauty is bodiless and, as we have said, an
heavenly shining beam, she loseth much of her honour when she is coupled with
that vile subject and full of corruption, because the less she is partner thereof,
the more perfect she is, and, clean sundered from it, is most perfect. And as
a man heareth not with his mouth, nor smelleth with his ears, no more can he
also in any manner wise enjoy beauty, nor satisfy the desire that she stirreth
up in our minds, with feeling, but with the sense unto whom beauty is the very
butt to level at, namely, the virtue of seeing. Let him lay aside, therefore, the
blind judgment of the sense, and enjoy with his eyes the brightness, the
comeliness, the loving sparkles, laughters, gestures, and all the other pleasant
furnitures of beauty, especially with hearing the sweetness of her voice, the
tunableness of her words, the melody of her singing and playing on instruments (in case the woman beloved be a musician), and so shall he with most
dainty food feed the soul through the means of these two senses which have
little bodily substance in them and be the ministers of reason,[69] without
entering farther toward the body with coveting unto any longing otherwise
than honest. Afterward let him obey, please, and honour with all reverence
his woman, and reckon her more dear to him than his own life, and prefer all
her commodities [70] and pleasures before his own, and love no less in her the
beauty of the mind than of the body. Therefore let him have a care not to
suffer her to run into any error, but with lessons and good exhortations seek
always to frame [71] her to modesty, to temperance, to true honesty, and so to
work that there may never take place in her other than pure thoughts and far
wide from all filthiness of vices. And thus in sowing of virtue in the garden of
that mind, he shall also gather the fruits of most beautiful conditions, and savour
them with a marvellous good relish. And this shall be the right engendering
and imprinting of beauty in beauty, the which some hold opinion to be the end
of love. In this manner shall our Courtier be most acceptable to his lady, and
she will always show herself toward him tractable, lowly,[72] and sweet in language, and as willing to please him as to be beloved of him; and the wills of
them both shall be most honest and agreeable, and they consequently shall
be most happy.'

Here M. Morello: 'The engendering,' quoth he, 'of beauty in beauty aright
were the engendering of a beautiful child in a beautiful woman; and I would
think it a more manifest token a great deal that she loved her lover, if she
pleased him with this than with the sweetness of language that you speak of.'

M. Peter Bembo laughed, and said: 'You must not, M. Morello, pass your
bounds. I may tell you it is not a small token that a woman loveth when she
giveth unto her lover her beauty, which is so precious a matter; and by the

69. Hearing and sight, in Ficino's system, are the least material of the senses and therefore
the nearest to divine perfection.
70. Advantage, interests.
71. Shape, direct.
72. Humble, modest.

ways that be a passage to the soul (that is to say, the sight and the hearing) sendeth the looks of her eyes, the image of her countenance, and the voice of her words, that pierce into the lover's heart and give a witness of her love.'

M. Morello said: 'Looks and words may be, and oftentimes are, false witnesses. Therefore whoso hath not a better pledge of love, in my judgment he is in an ill assurance. And surely I looked still that you would have made this woman of yours somewhat more courteous and free toward the Courtier than my Lord Julian [73] hath made his; but meseemeth ye be both of the property [74] of those judges that, to appear wise, give sentence against their own.'

Bembo said: 'I am well pleased to have this woman much more courteous toward my Courtier not young than the Lord Julian's is to the young; and that with good reason, because mine coveteth but honest matters, and therefore may the woman grant him them all without blame. But my Lord Julian's woman, that is not so assured of the modesty of the young man, ought to grant him the honest matters only, and deny him the dishonest. Therefore more happy is mine, that hath granted him whatsoever he requireth, than the other, that hath part granted and part denied. And because you may moreover the better understand that reasonable [75] love is more happy than sensual, I say unto you that selfsame things in sensual ought to be denied otherwhile, and in reasonable granted; because in the one they be honest, and in the other dishonest. Therefore the woman, to please her good lover, besides the granting him merry countenances, familiar and secret talk, jesting, dallying, hand-in-hand, may also lawfully and without blame come to kissing, which in sensual love, according to the Lord Julian's rules, is not lawful. For since a kiss is a knitting together both of body and soul,[76] it is to be feared lest the sensual lover will be more inclined to the part of the body than of the soul; but the reasonable lover wotteth well that although the mouth be a parcel of the body, yet is it an issue for the words that be the interpreters of the soul, and for the inward breath, which is also called the soul; and therefore hath a delight to join his mouth with the woman's beloved with a kiss—not to stir him to any unhonest desire, but because he feeleth that that bond is the opening of an entry to the souls, which, drawn with a coveting the one of the other, pour themselves by turn the one into the other's body, and be so mingled together that each of them hath two souls, and one alone so framed of them both ruleth, in a manner, two bodies. Whereupon a kiss may be said to be rather a coupling together of the soul than of the body, because it hath such force in her that it draweth her unto it, and, as it were, separateth her from the body. For this do all chaste lovers covet a kiss as a coupling of souls together. And therefore Plato, the divine lover, saith that in kissing his soul came as far as his lips to depart out of the body.[77] And because the separating of the soul from the

73. Giuliano de' Medici (1479–1516), youngest son of Lorenzo il Magnifico, Duke of Nemours, poet and close friend of Castiglione, in exile from Florence, like the rest of his family at the time. His funerary effigy by Michelangelo is in the New Sacristy of San Lorenzo in Florence.

74. Kind, nature.

75. Rational.

76. Because of the mingling of the breath in the touch of the lips.

77. This is an allusion to a poem in the *Greek Anthology* by one Plato, who is perhaps the same as Plato the philosopher.

matters of the sense, and the thorough coupling of her with matters of understanding, may be betokened by a kiss, Solomon saith [78] in his heavenly book
of ballads, "Oh that he would kiss me with a kiss of his mouth," to express
the desire he had that his soul might be ravished through heavenly love to
the beholding of heavenly beauty in such manner that, coupling herself inwardly with it, she might forsake the body.' . . .

1508–16 / 1554   1528–61

ROGER ASCHAM
1515–1568

Ascham was born in Yorkshire and entered St. John's College, Cambridge, in 1530.
He became friends with Sir John Cheke (1514–57), his tutor, and was made Fellow of
his College in 1534 and Reader in Greek in 1538, siding with Cheke on the "reforming"
side in the controversy about the pronunciation of Greek. He received a pension from
Henry VIII in 1545 on the publication of his *Toxophilus* and became Public Orator of
the University, charged with the duty of making Latin orations on great occasions,
in 1546. A staunch Protestant, he was tutor to Princess Elizabeth (later Queen) in
1548–49; secretary to Sir Richard Morison, ambassador of Edward VI to the Emperor,
in 1550–53, and Latin Secretary, managing diplomatic correspondence, to the Catholic
Queen Mary in 1553. He retained the post under Elizabeth, with whom he continued
daily reading of Latin and Greek authors. Ascham married in 1554 and died in 1568.
His two chief works are *Toxophilus*, a dialogue on archery (1545), and *The Schoolmaster* (posthumously published in 1570).

Ascham's overriding concern was that of his fellow humanists: to strengthen his native
country in all the arts of peace and of defense, providing men properly educated to
serve and govern her so as to keep her at the head of European nations. His reverence
for Cicero and for Renaissance Ciceronianism does not make him write his treatises in
Latin, though he tries to strengthen his language and enrich it by using classical models.
The gentlest and most enlightened of teachers, the first to speak openly against beating
as an incentive to learning, he lays his stress on the possible, on what can be done by
encouragement, even with apparently unpromising material. Ascham has no grand
schemes: what he asks is that "goodness of nature be joined to the wisdom of the
teacher, in leading young wits into a right and plain way of learning" so that "children,
kept up in God's fear and governed by his grace, may most easily be brought well to
serve God and their country, both by virtue and wisdom." The way to this virtue and
wisdom was through the study of Latin and Greek, both as models of the eloquence
without which a man can never persuade another to virtue, and as the storehouse of
practical and theoretical wisdom (see the application of Homer's story of Ulysses in
The Schoolmaster). Along with the enchantments of Italy, "Gothic," immoral literature
—such as medieval romances—must be disregarded. Ascham endorses Cheke's judgment that "God's holy Bible," Cicero, Plato, Aristotle, with the Greek orators Isocrates
and Demosthenes, are enough to make an excellent man.

Ascham's contemporaries speak of him as an engaging, agreeable man, apt to make
and keep friends. His prose, carefully framed and neat, reflects the man. Its syntax is

78. Song of Songs, 1:2. The Song had the philosophic status of divine wisdom on the
nature of love.

based on Ciceronian models, but its character is strongly English, its vocabulary free of the patriotic purism of Cheke, or the affected learning of "inkhorn" terms—learned borrowings—of other contemporaries. It is wholly at ease with itself.

The Schoolmaster

The first book of The Schoolmaster, from which these passages are taken, is an account of the principles on which boys should be taught, along with some examples of their successful application. The most effective way to writing good Latin is via the method of double translation. After this recommendation comes a description of the qualities to be sought in a pupil and of the means of enticing, rather than compelling, him to study. The whole curriculum is directed toward making the young fit for "virtuous action": the aim of the English humanist educator. To keep them on the right path, in literature as in life, they must be kept from both the sight and the practice of all that is vicious (e.g. the reading of Arthurian romances and the experience of Italy).

The second book of The Schoolmaster is chiefly concerned with the doctrine of imitation in particular stylistic terms, rather than the general and ethical modes of Book I. To learn languages and improve eloquence, Ascham prescribes translation and imitation of the best (i.e. Ciceronian) models, along with paraphrase and metaphrase (turning prose into verse, verse into prose), and summary.

Ascham names his own masters as Plato, Aristotle, and Cicero among the ancients; and Sir John Cheke and Johann Sturm, his friend the preceptor of Strasbourg, among the moderns. There is an unacknowledged pervasive tinge from Quintilian's (c. 35–c. 100 A.D.) De Institutione Oratoria—as in all Renaissance educators—with its insistence that the ideal orator must be "a good man, skilled in speaking." Plato's influence is strongest in the first book, where it is made clear that the proper bringing-up of children, from birth onward, not merely in schools, is the most important of social responsibilities, involving a just estimate of the nature of pleasure and of freedom and their place in education. In the second book, the presence of the Ciceronian Sturm and of Cicero himself are most strongly felt.

The text of the selections from Ascham is taken from The Whole Works, ed. J. A. Giles, 1864–65. Spelling and punctuation have been modernized.

The Schoolmaster

From Book I

. . . First, let him teach the child cheerfully and plainly the cause [1] and matter [2] of the letter; [3] then, let him construe [4] it into English so oft, as the child may easily carry away the understanding of it; lastly, parse [5] it over

1. The reason for and circumstances of its writing.
2. Content.
3. That is, of Cicero's, which is his assigned reading.
4. Translate.
5. Describe each word in it grammatically, stating its part of speech, its case, and its relation to the others.

perfitly.[6] This done thus, let the child, by and by, both construe and parse it over again; so that it may appear, that the child doubteth in nothing that his master taught him before. After this, the child must take a paper book, and sitting in some place, where no man shall prompt him, by himself, let him translate into English his former lesson. Then showing it to his master, let the master take from him his Latin book, and pausing an hour at the least, then let the child translate his own English into Latin again in another paper book. When the child bringeth it turned into Latin, the master must compare it with Tully's [7] book, and lay them both together; and where the child doth well, either in choosing or true placing of Tully's words, let the master praise him, and say, 'Here ye do well.' For I assure you, there is no such whetstone to sharpen a good wit, and encourage a will to learning, as is praise.

But if the child miss, either in forgetting a word, or in changing a good with a worse, or misordering the sentence, I would not have the master either frown or chide with him, if the child have done his diligence, and used no truantship therein. For I know by good experience, that a child shall take more profit of two faults gently warned of, than of four things rightly hit: for then the master shall have good occasion to say unto him; 'N.,[8] Tully would have used such a word, not this: Tully would have placed this word here, not there; would have used this case, this number, this person, this degree, this gender: he would have used this mood, this tense, this simple, rather than this compound; this adverb here, not there: he would have ended the sentence with this verb, not with that noun or participle,' &c.

In these few lines I have wrapped up the most tedious part of grammar; and also the ground of almost all the rules that are so busily taught by the master, and so hardly learned by the scholar, in all common schools; which, after this sort, the master shall teach without all error, and the scholar shall learn without great pain; the master being led by so sure a guide, and the scholar being brought into so plain and easy a way. And therefore we do not contemn rules, but we gladly teach rules; and teach them more plainly, sensibly, and orderly, than they be commonly taught in common schools. For when the master shall compare Tully's book with the scholar's translation, let the master, at the first, lead and teach his scholar to join the rules of his grammar book with the examples of his present lesson, until the scholar by himself be able to fetch out of his grammar every rule for every example; so as the grammar book be ever in the scholar's hand, and also used of him as a dictionary for every present use. This is a lively and perfit way of teaching of rules; where the common way used in common schools, to read the grammar alone by itself, is tedious for the master, hard for the scholar, cold and uncomfortable for them both.

Let your scholar be never afraid to ask you any doubt, but use discreetly the best allurements ye can to encourage him to the same; lest his overmuch fearing of you drive him to seek some misorderly shift; [9] as to seek to be helped by some other book, or to be prompted by some other scholar; and so go about to beguile you much and himself more.

6. Perfectly.
7. Marcus Tullius Cicero's.
8. *Nomen*, i.e. the child's name.
9. Wrong expedient.

[Ascham goes on to give Socrates' points for distinguishing good students. The first comes from Plato's *Republic* 455b; the next five from 535b ff. The final point seems to be Ascham's: it is not in Plato.]

And because I write English, and to Englishmen, I will plainly declare in English both what these words of Plato mean, and how aptly they be linked, and how orderly they follow one another.

1. Euphuēs

Is he, that is apt by goodness of wit, and appliable by readiness of will, to learning, having all other qualities of the mind and parts of the body, that must another day serve learning; not troubled, mangled, and halved, but sound, whole, full, and able to do their office; as, a tongue not stammering, or over-hardly drawing forth words, but plain and ready to deliver the meaning of the mind; a voice not soft, weak, piping, womanish, but audible, strong, and man-like; a countenance not wearish [10] and crabbed, but fair and comely; a per-sonage not wretched and deformed, but tall and goodly; for surely, a comely countenance with a goodly stature giveth credit to learning, and authority to the person; otherwise, commonly, either open contempt or private [11] disfavour doth hurt or hinder both person and learning; and even as a fair stone requireth to be set in the finest gold, with the best workmanship, or else it loseth much of the grace and price; even so excellence in learning, and namely divinity, joined with a comely personage, is a marvellous jewel in the world. And how can a comely body be better employed than to serve the fairest exercise of God's greatest gift? and that is learning. But commonly the fairest bodies are bestowed on the foulest purposes. . . .

2. Mnēmōn

Good of memory: a special part of the first note [12] *euphuēs*, and a mere benefit of nature; yet it is so necessary for learning, as Plato maketh it a separate and perfect note of itself, and that so principal a note, as without it all other gifts of nature do small service to learning. . . .

3. Philomathēs

Given to love learning: for though a child have all the gifts of nature at wish, and perfection of memory at will, yet if he have not a special love to learning, he shall never attain to much learning. . . .

4. Philoponos

Is he that hath a lust [13] to labour and a will to take pains: for if a child have all the benefits of nature, with perfection of memory, love, like, and praise learning never so much, yet if he be not of himself painful, he shall never attain unto it. And yet where love is present, labour is seldom absent, and namely in study of learning, and matters of the mind. . . .

5. Philēkoos

He that is glad to hear and learn of another: for otherwise he shall stick with great trouble, where he might go easily forward; and also catch hardly a very

10. Sickly, delicate.
11. Concealed
12. Sign.
13. Desire, pleasure.

little by his own toil, when he might gather quickly a good deal by another man's teaching. . . .

6. Zētētikos

He that is naturally bold to ask any question, desirous to search out any doubt; not ashamed to learn of the meanest, nor afraid to go to the greatest, until he be perfectly taught and fully satisfied. The seventh and last point is,

7. Philepainos

He that loveth to be praised for well doing, at his father or master's hand. A child of this nature will earnestly love learning, gladly labour for learning, willingly learn of other, boldly ask any doubt.

. . . Hear what Socrates in the same place doth more plainly say: [14] 'And therefore, my dear friend, bring not up your children in learning by compulsion and fear, but by playing and pleasure.' [15] And you that do read Plato as you should, do well perceive, that these be no questions asked by Socrates as doubts, but they be sentences,[16] first affirmed by Socrates as mere [17] truths, and after given forth by Socrates as right rules, most necessary to be marked, and fit to be followed of all them that would have children taught as they should. And in this counsel, judgment, and authority of Socrates I will repose myself, until I meet with a man of the contrary mind, whom I may justly take to be wiser than I think Socrates was.

Fond [18] schoolmasters neither can understand, nor will follow this good counsel of Socrates; but wise riders in their office can and will do both; which is the only cause that commonly the young gentlemen of England go so unwillingly to school, and run so fast to the stable. For in very deed, fond schoolmasters, by fear, do beat into them the hatred of learning; and wise riders, by gentle allurements, do breed up in them the love of riding. They find fear and bondage in schools, they feel liberty and freedom in stables; which causeth them utterly to abhor the one, and most gladly to haunt [19] the other. And I do not write this, that, in exhorting to the one, I would dissuade young gentlemen from the other; yea, I am sorry with all my heart that they be given no more to riding than they be. For of all outward qualities, to ride fair is most comely for himself, most necessary for his country; and the greater [20] he is in blood, the greater is his praise, the more he doth exceed all other therein. It was one of the three excellent praises amongst the noble gentlemen of the old Persians; 'Always to say truth, to ride fair, and shoot well': and so it was engraven upon Darius's tomb, as Strabo beareth witness:

> Darius the king lieth buried here,
> Who in riding and shooting had never peer.[21]

14. The Greek is omitted.
15. Plato, *Republic* 536e.
16. Wise sayings.
17. Simple.
18. Foolish.
19. Frequent.
20. More noble. Cf. Spenser, *The Faerie Queene* II.iv.1: "But chiefly skill to ride seemes a science / Proper to gentle blood. . . ."
21. Strabo, Greek historian and geographer (64 B.C.–c. 21 A.D.), in his *Geography* XV.iii.8.

But to our purpose: Young men, by any means losing the love of learning, when by time [22] they come to their own rule,[23] they carry commonly from the school with them a perfect hatred of their master, and a continual contempt of learning. If ten gentlemen be asked, why they forgot so soon in court, that which they were learning so long in school, eight of them, or let me be blamed, will lay the fault on their ill-handling by their schoolmasters.

. . .

And thus will in children, wisely wrought [24] withal, may easily be won to be very well willing to learn. And wit in children, by nature, namely memory, the only key and keeper of all learning, is readiest to receive, and surest to keep any manner of thing that is learned in youth. This, lewd [25] and learned, by common experience, know to be most true. For we remember nothing so well when we be old, as those things which we learned when we were young. And this is not strange, but common in all nature's works. . . .

Therefore, if to the goodness of nature be joined the wisdom of the teacher, in leading young wits into a right and plain way of learning; surely children, kept up in God's fear, and governed by his grace, may most easily be brought well to serve God and their country, both by virtue and wisdom.

. . .

Therefore, to love or to hate, to like or contemn, to ply [26] this way or that way to good or to bad, ye shall have as ye use a child in his youth.

And one example, whether love or fear doth work more in a child for virtue and learning, I will gladly report; which may be heard with some pleasure, and followed with more profit.

Before I went into Germany,[27] I came to Broadgate in Leicestershire, to take my leave of that noble lady Jane Grey,[28] to whom I was exceeding much beholding.[29] Her parents, the Duke [30] and Duchess, with all the household, gentlemen and gentlewomen, were hunting in the park. I found her in her chamber, reading *Phædo Platonis* [31] in Greek, and that with as much delight as some gentlemen would read a merry tale in Boccace.[32] After salutation, and duty done,[33] with some other talk, I asked her, why she would lose such pastime

22. In due time.
23. Reach their majority and independence.
24. Wisely worked on.
25. Ignorant.
26. Bend, mold.
27. Ascham went to Germany, as secretary to Sir Richard Morison, the English ambassador to the Emperor Charles V, in 1550. Ascham and Morison read Greek together. Ascham learned Italian and briefly visited Italy. He returned to England in September 1553, but his *Report on the State of Germany* was not published until after his death.
28. 1537–54, later married to Lord Guildford Dudley as part of a plot to supplant the Tudor dynasty upon the death of Edward VI. She was proclaimed queen in 1553, arrested for treason in the same year, and executed at Queen Mary's order in 1554. The pupil of Bishop John Aylmer, she could at 15 write Latin, Greek, French, and German, and she had begun to study Hebrew.
29. Obligated.
30. Of Suffolk.
31. Plato's dialogue *Phaedo*, concerned with the nature of the soul.
32. Giovanni Boccaccio (1313?–75), author of the *Decameron* and other works of amusement and of piety.
33. That is, proper exchange of courtesies.

in the park? Smiling, she answered me; 'I wiss,[34] all their sport in the park is but a shadow [35] to that pleasure that I find in Plato. Alas! good folk, they never felt what true pleasure meant.' 'And how came you, madam,' quoth I, 'to this deep knowledge of pleasure? and what did chiefly allure you unto it, seeing not many women, but very few men, have attained thereunto?' 'I will tell you,' quoth she, 'and tell you a truth, which perchance ye will marvel at. One of the greatest benefits that ever God gave me, is, that he sent me so sharp and severe parents, and so gentle a schoolmaster. For when I am in presence either of father or mother; whether I speak, keep silence, sit, stand, or go, eat, drink, be merry, or sad, be sewing, playing, dancing, or doing any thing else; I must do it, as it were, in such weight, measure, and number, even so perfectly, as God made the world; [36] or else I am so sharply taunted, so cruelly threatened, yea presently [37] sometimes with pinches, nips, and bobs,[38] and other ways (which I will not name for the honour I bear them) so without measure misordered,[39] that I think myself in hell, till time come that I must go to Mr. Elmer; [40] who teacheth me so gently, so pleasantly, with such fair allurements to learning, that I think all the time nothing whiles I am with him. And when I am called from him, I fall on weeping, because whatsoever I do else but learning, is full of grief, trouble, fear, and whole misliking unto me. And thus my book hath been so much my pleasure, and bringeth daily to me more pleasure and more, that in respect of it, all other pleasures, in very deed, be but trifles and troubles unto me.'

I remember this talk gladly, both because it is so worthy of memory, and because also it was the last talk that ever I had, and the last time that ever I saw that noble and worthy lady.

.   .   .

To join learning with comely exercises, Conte Baldesar Castiglione, in his book *Cortegiane*,[41] doth trimly [42] teach; which book advisedly [43] read and diligently followed but one year at home in England, would do a young gentleman more good, I wiss, than three years' travel abroad spent in Italy. And I marvel this book is no more read in the court than it is, seeing it is so well translated into English by a worthy gentleman, Sir Thomas Hobby,[44] who was many ways well furnished with learning, and very expert in knowledge of divers tongues.

34. Certainly; a corrupt form of Middle English *ywis*.
35. Lady Jane is playing with the platonic notion of worldly things being only shadowy replicas of divine and eternal ideas: physical pleasures are nothing compared with intellectual pleasures.
36. The perfect proportion of God's creation is expressed in the Wisdom of Solomon 11:20, an apocryphal book of the Old Testament: "Thou hast ordered all things in measure, number and weight."
37. On the spot.
38. Raps, blows.
39. Ill-treated.
40. John Aylmer (1521–94), later Bishop of London, a good Latin and Greek scholar and an exile during Mary's reign.
41. See above.
42. Finely, effectively.
43. With care and consideration.
44. See above.

[They forget, Ascham goes on, all the good they have learned, they become dulled to virtuous learning ever after, they lose the ability to tell good from evil, and they come to despise good men. The only preservative against this corruption is the study of virtue, which is so far neglected that young men go abroad to study vice.]

Sir Richard Sackville,[45] that worthy gentleman of worthy memory, as I said in the beginning, in the queen's privy chamber [46] at Windsor, after he had talked with me for the right choice of a good wit in a child for learning, and of the true difference betwixt quick and hard wits, of alluring young children by gentleness to love learning, and of the special care that was to be had to keep young men from licentious living; he was most earnest with me, to have me say my mind also, what I thought concerning the fancy that many young gentlemen of England have to travel abroad, and namely to lead a long life in Italy. His request, both for his authority and good will toward me, was a sufficient commandment unto me, to satisfy his pleasure with uttering plainly my opinion in that matter. 'Sir,' quoth I, 'I take going thither, and living there, for a young gentleman that doth not go under the keep [47] and guard of such a man, as both by wisdom can, and authority dare rule him, to be marvellous dangerous.'

And why I said so then, I will declare at large now, which I said then privately, and write now openly; not because I do contemn either the knowledge of strange and divers tongues, and namely [48] the Italian tongue (which, next the Greek and Latin tongue, I like and love above all other), or else because I do despise the learning that is gotten, or the experience that is gathered in strange countries; or for any private malice that I bear to Italy; which country, and in it namely Rome, I have always specially honoured; because time was, when Italy and Rome have been to the great good of us that now live, the best breeders and bringers up of the worthiest men, not only for wise speaking, but also for well doing, in all civil affairs, that ever was in the world. But now that time is gone; and though the place remain, yet the old and present manners do differ as far as black and white, as virtue and vice. Virtue once made that country mistress over all the world; vice now maketh that country slave to them that before were glad to serve it. All men seeth it; they themselves confess it, namely such as be best and wisest amongst them. For sin, by lust and vanity, hath and doth breed up everywhere, common contempt of God's word, private contention in many families, open factions in every city; and so making themselves bond to vanity and vice at home, they are content to bear the yoke of serving strangers abroad. Italy now, is not that Italy that it was wont to be; and therefore now not so fit a place as some do count it, for young men to fetch either wisdom or honesty from thence. For surely they will make others but bad scholars, that be so ill masters to themselves. Yet, if a gentleman will needs travel into Italy, he shall do well to look

---

45. Ascham's Preface contains an account of the conversation in the Queen's private apartment at Windsor Castle, and Sackville's urging, which prompted him to write his book. Sir Richard Sackville (d. 1566), cousin of Anne Boleyn, was Treasurer of the Exchequer.
46. Private apartment.
47. Guardianship, care.
48. Especially.

on the life of the wisest traveller that ever travelled thither, set out by the wisest writer [49] that ever spake with tongue, God's doctrine only excepted; and that is Ulysses [50] in Homer.

. . .

Therefore, if wise men will needs send their sons into Italy, let them do it wisely, under the keep and guard of him who, by his wisdom and honesty, by his example and authority, may be able to keep them safe and sound in the fear of God, in Christ's true religion, in good order, and honesty [51] of living; except they will have them run headlong into over-many jeopardies, as Ulysses had done many times, if Pallas [52] had not always governed him; if he had not used to stop his ears with wax, to bind himself to the mast of his ship,[53] to feed daily upon that sweet herb Moly,[54] with the black root and white flower, given unto him by Mercury to avoid all the enchantments of Circe. Whereby the divine poet Homer meant covertly (as wise and godly men do judge) that love of honesty and hatred of ill, which David more plainly doth call the fear of God, the only remedy against all enchantments of sin.[55]

I know divers noble personages, and many worthy gentlemen of England, whom all the Siren songs of Italy could never untwine from the mast of God's Word, nor no enchantment of vanity overturn them from the fear of God and love of honesty.

But I know as many, or more, and some sometime my dear friends (for whose sake I hate going into that country the more), who parting out of England fervent in the love of Christ's doctrine, and well furnished with the fear of God, returned out of Italy worse transformed than ever was any in Circe's court. I know divers, that went out of England, men of innocent life, men of excellent learning, who returned out of Italy, not only with worse manners, but also with less learning; neither so willing to live orderly, nor yet so able to speak learnedly, as they were at home, before they went abroad. . . .

ELIZABETHAN SONG AND LYRIC

Actual songs, and lyric poems which might or might not be intended for setting, come down to us in several ways. There are, first, the miscellanies, or anthologies of verse, starting with Richard Tottel's *Songs and Sonnets* (1557), although an earlier one called *The Court of Venus,* of which we have only fragments, was printed in the late 1530's.

49. Homer was thought of as a sort of encyclopedia of wise counsel.
50. Ulysses reached Sicily and Italy in the wanderings described by Homer in his *Odyssey.*
51. Goodness.
52. Athena was the protector of Ulysses.
53. *Odyssey* XII.153 ff. On Circe's advice, to avoid being seduced by the sirens' song and destroyed by them, Ulysses had his crew stop their ears with wax and bind him to the mast.
54. *Odyssey* X.302–6. Ulysses had set out to bring back his comrades, turned into swine by the wicked enchantress Circe, when Mercury warned him that he would suffer the same fate without the help of the herb moly. Later commentators on Homer saw the incident as an allegory of education, the purpose of which was to teach a man to act virtuously, and steer clear of evil.
55. Psalms 34:9 ff. (Vulgate 33:9 ff.).

The editing of Tottel's Miscellany, and the explanatory titles attached to the poems, indicate a sense of a style, and of norms of metrical smoothness, quite well established. A successor, *The Paradise of Dainty Devices,* went through ten editions between its first appearance, in 1576, and 1606; *A Gorgeous Gallery of Gallant Inventions* (1578); *A Handful of Pleasant Delights* (1584, but based on a much earlier collection); *The Phoenix Nest* (1592), which contains elegies on Sir Philip Sidney—the phoenix of the title, out of whose ashes arise the new English poems of the 1590's—and a variety of modish and more old-fashioned poems both; *England's Helicon* (1600), limited to pastoral poetry of all sorts; and Davison's *A Poetical Rhapsody* of 1602, containing "Pastorals and Eglogues, Odes and Madrigals," including a good many translations from classical poets—in all these anthologies we find poems duplicated elsewhere in collections of work by the individual poets represented in them, and many that are not.

Then, too, there are the songbooks, the poems with their printed music—either for voices or for instruments in polyphonic settings, or, later on (the first such collection is William Barley's *A New Book of Tablature* of 1596), for lute and voice and known as "airs." The poems appearing with their musical settings were usually anonymous, or at least unidentified, and scholars have been gradually attempting to identify the authorship of many remarkable poems. Perhaps at this point something should be said about what "song" as a literary term implies. The concept "lyric poetry" originally comes from a classical Greek distinction between solo songs, sung to the lyre, composed in short stanzas and usually erotic in character, and choral ode, composed in triads of long strophes and of a public, celebratory character when not occurring as part of tragedy or comedy. There were many other classical poetic styles: elegiac verse was composed in couplets (always unrhymed as in all classical verse) and was used for satire and epigram, inscriptions and witty or pointed observation. Iambic verse had other ranges of use, from speeches in plays to drinking songs and love lyrics. Then there was, of course, the continuous hexameter line of epic poetry, and the originally almost startling adaptation of it by Theocritus for his pastoral eclogues.

Latin poets followed and adapted these Greek models, but the actual association of meters with musical forms and styles began to disappear. The Renaissance, extremely self-conscious as it came to be about classical antiquity, sought to emulate it with a deliberate re-unification of music and poetry. England lagged behind the Continent in the development of its music after the death of John Dunstable (1390–1453), one of the most renowned musicians of his day. By the 1580's, however, Italian influences and the invigoration of a native tradition led to a remarkable burst of secular musical activity, and the emergence of a group of composers of the first rank, among them William Byrd, Orlando Gibbons, John Dowland, Thomas Weelkes, Thomas Morley, and others. Aside from solo keyboard and lute composition, their main activities were in the field of song. Madrigals were polyphonic settings of poetic texts for several singers, either unaccompanied or, more often, with instruments either doubling the voices or taking their parts. They were often florid, chromatic, and complex, and went to such lengths to avoid stanzaic repetition of different words to the same tune that they confined themselves to monostrophic poems, like sonnets, or else frequently set two stanzas of the same poem as two different madrigals. Airs, or solo songs, were written for voice and lute (although usually printed with four-part settings included). They were oriented more toward a performer-audience situation than the madrigals, whose musico-poetic delights would appeal primarily to the individual singer, hearing the complexities of the setting of the often-repeated words weaving around him. Airs, in addition, were primarily stanzaic: thus the composer found a text and set the first stanza, allowing the subsequent ones to be "sung to the same tune," as it were. In the case of frequently banal, metrically smooth poems this "fit" worked very well. In the case of Donne's *Songs and Sonnets*, the tense, wrenched, individualized rhythmic patternings of almost every line made stanzaic settings almost impossible, though there were several attempts; and with Donne's poems we begin to see texts whose musical settings can best be thought of as the verbal "music" of their own intense speech cadences.

By the 1580's, a variety of poetic conventions had become assimilated to the notion of "lyric poem," including "sonnets" in both the strict and loose senses (that is, the familiar fourteen-line iambic pentameter poems as well as any short, Petrarchan love poem), epigrams, pastoral lyrics, and so forth. A musician (as Donne puts it in "The Triple Fool"), "his art and voice to show, / Doth set and sing my pain"—and composers frequently raided miscellanies and anthologies as well as published books and poems in manuscript. Almost any poem might, after publication, show up in a musical setting, sometimes altered for the convenience of the composer.

THOMAS, LORD VAUX
1510–1556

The Agèd Lover Renounceth Love°

I loathe that° I did love,
    In youth that I thought sweet,
As time requires for my behove:°
    Methinks they are not meet.

My lusts they do me leave,
    My fancies all be fled,
And tract of time begins to weave
    Grey hairs upon my head.

For age with stealing steps
10   Hath clawed me with his crutch,
And lusty life away she leaps
    As there had been none such.

My Muse doth not delight
    Me as she did before,
My hand and pen are not in plight,
    As they have been of yore.

The Agèd Lover Renounceth Love The title is from Richard Tottel's Miscellany (1557), where the poem first appeared; it was an important anthology which first printed the poems of Wyatt and Surrey. In Tottel, this poem was printed in "poulter's measure," the quatrains arranged into alternating 12- and 14-syllable rhyming lines in couplets; the gravedigger in *Hamlet* V.i hums parts of it, half-misremembering.
that what
behove benefit

For reason me denies
   This youthly idle rhyme;
And day by day to me she cries:
20   'Leave off these toys in time.'

The wrinkles in my brow,
   The furrows in my face,
Say limping age will lodge him now
   Where youth must give him place.

The harbinger of death,
   To me I see him ride,
The cough, the cold, the gasping breath
   Doth bid me to provide

A pickaxe and a spade,
30   And eke° a shrouding sheet,
A house of clay for to be made
   For such a guest most meet.

Methinks I hear the clerk
   That knolls the carefull knell,
And bids me leave my woeful wark,
   Ere nature me compel.

My keepers knit the knot
   That youth did laugh to scorn,
Of me that clean shall be forgot
40   As I had not been born.

Thus must I youth give up,
   Whose badge I long did wear;
To them I yield the wanton cup
   That better may it bear.°

Lo, here the barèd skull,
   By whose bald sign I know
That stooping age away shall pull
   Which youthful years did sow.

For beauty with her band
   These crooked cares hath
50   wrought,
And shippèd me into the land
   From whence I first was brought.

And ye that bide behind,
   Have ye none other trust:
As ye of clay were cast by kind,°
   So shall ye waste to dust.
1557

eke also
by kind by nature

To them . . . bear I give up joy to those
who can manage it

NICHOLAS GRIMALD°

1519–1562

The Garden°

The issue of great Jove, draw near you Muses nine:°
Help us to praise the blissful plot of garden ground so fine.
The garden gives good food, and aid for leeches'° cure:
The garden, full of great delight, his master doth allure.
Sweet salad herbs be here, and herbs of every kind:
The ruddy grapes, the seemly fruits, be here at hand to find.
Here pleasance wanteth not, to make a man full fain:
Here marvellous the mixture is of solace and of gain.
To water sundry seeds, the furrow by the way
10 A running river, trilling down with liquor, can convey.
Behold, with lively hue fair flowers that shine so bright:
With riches, like the orient° gems, they paint the mould° in sight.
Bees, humming with soft sound (their murmur is so small),
Of blooms and blossoms suck the tops, on dewèd leaves they fall.
The creeping vine holds down her own bewedded elms,
And, wandering out with branches thick, reeds folded overwhelms.
Trees spread their coverts wide with shadows fresh and gay:
Full well their branchèd boughs defend° the fervent sun away.
Birds chatter, and some chirp, and some sweet tunes do yield:
20 All mirthful, with their songs so blithe, they make both air and field.
The garden, it allures; it feeds, it glads the sprite:
From heavy hearts all doleful dumps° the garden chaseth quite.
Strength it restores to limbs, draws and fulfills the sight,
With cheer revives the senses all, and maketh labour light.
O, what delights to us the garden ground doth bring?
Seed, leaf, flower, fruit, herb, bee, and tree, and more, then I may sing.

¹557

Nicholas Grimald Playwright as well as poet, Grimald was a heavy contributor to Tottel's *Miscellany*.
The Garden Probably a paraphrase of a Latin poem in praise of gardens, this poem in poulter's measure demonstrates the poetic plain style of the mid-century; it is at its best when listing or cataloguing.
Muses nine An invocation to the Muses in so trivial a piece is little more than throat-clearing, a kind of literary "ahem!"
leeches' physicians'
orient shining
mould earth
defend ward off
doleful dumps common phrase for clouds of spiritual depression (cf. modern "down in the dumps"), but coming to mean a kind of musical piece

CHIDIOCK TICHBORNE

1558?–1586

Tichborne's Elegy°

My prime of youth is but a frost of cares,
My feast of joy is but a dish of pain,
My crop of corn is but a field of tares,
And all my good is but vain hope of gain;
The day is past, and yet I saw no sun,
And now I live, and now my life is done.

My tale was heard and yet it was not told,
My fruit is fallen and yet my leaves are green,
My youth is spent and yet I am not old,
10   I saw the world and yet I was not seen;
My thread is cut and yet it is not spun,
And now I live, and now my life is done.

I sought my death and found it in my womb,
I looked for life and saw it was a shade,
I trod the earth and knew it was my tomb,
And now I die, and now I was but made;
My glass is full, and now my glass is run,
And now I live, and now my life is done.

                                                    1586

ANONYMOUS

[A Song from Ovid]°

Constant Penelope sends to thee, careless Ulysses.
Write not again, but come, sweet mate, thyself to revive me.
Troy we do much envy, we desolate lost ladies of Greece,
Not Priamus, nor yet all Troy can us recompense make.
Oh, that he had, when he first took shipping to Lacedaemon,
That adulter I mean, had been o'erwhelmed with waters.
Then had I not lain now all alone, thus quivering for cold,
Nor used this complaint, nor have thought the day to be so long.

                                                    1588

Tichborne's Elegy Usually subtitled "Written
with his own hand in the Tower before his
execution"; whether or not actually so written
by this conspirator in a plot against the Queen,
it was an extremely popular poem of the period,
being set to music many times. Its easy use of
oxymoron, alliterating pairs, and clichés like
the "womb-tomb" rhyme, undoubtedly helped
the supposed circumstances of its composition
to make it a favorite.

A Song from Ovid a translation from the first
book of Ovid's *Heroides* (*Hanc tua Penelope
lento mittit, Ulixe*) into purely quantitative
English verse, perhaps by Thomas Watson, and
set to music, with the unrhymed hexameters
used in the rhythm of the setting, by William
Byrd in his *Psalms, Sonnets and Songs of Sadness and Piety* (1588). To the modern ear, it
sounds like beautifully cadenced free verse.

ANONYMOUS

[Shadow and Substance]°

I heard a noise and wishèd for a sight,
I looked for life and did a shadow see
Whose substance was the sum of my delight,
Which came unseen, and so did go from me.
    Yet hath conceit persuaded my content
    There was a substance where the shadow went.

I did not play Narcissus in conceit,°
I did not see my shadow in a spring;
I know mine eyes were dimmed with no deceit,
10 I saw the shadow of some worthy thing:
    For, as I saw the shadow glancing by,
    I had a glimpse of something in mine eye.

But what it was, alas, I cannot tell,
Because of it I had no perfect view;
But as it was, by guess, I wish it well
And will until I see the same anew.
    Shadow, or she, or both, or choose you whither:
    Blest be the thing that brought the shadow hither!

                  c. 1597

ROBERT SOUTHWELL
1561–1595

The Burning Babe°

As I in hoary winter's night stood shivering in the snow,
Surprised I was with sudden heat which made my heart to glow;
And lifting up a fearful eye to view what fire was near,
A pretty babe all burning bright did in the air appear;
Who, scorchèd with excessive heat, such floods of tears did shed
As though his floods should quench his flames which with his tears
    were fed.°
'Alas,' quoth he, 'but newly born in fiery heats I fry,
Yet none approach to warm their hearts or feel my fire but I!
My faultless breast the furnace is, the fuel wounding thorns,
10 Love is the fire, and sighs the smoke, the ashes shame and scorns;

Shadow and Substance the present editors' title for an anonymous poem from a manuscript probably written in the late 1590's; "shadow" means, as it does throughout this period, an image or vision, rather than only a cast shade **in conceit** "in concept," imaginedly
The Burning Babe Southwell, a Jesuit martyr hanged for his activities in England (where he had returned from Douay in 1586), wrote religious verse in a rather archaic manner; this poem, printed variously in the rhymed "fourteeners" of mid-century verse as well as in ballad form, is perhaps the most famous piece of recusant verse, admired by Ben Jonson and Dylan Thomas alike.
Who . . . fed Notice the parody, in these lines, of Petrarchan language about love.

The fuel justice layeth on, and mercy blows the coals,
The metal in this furnace wrought are men's defiled souls,
For which, as now on fire I am to work them to their good,
So will I melt into a bath to wash them in my blood.'
With this he vanished out of sight and swiftly shrunk away,
And straight I callèd unto mind that it was Christmas day.

1602

ANONYMOUS

'Hark, All Ye Lovely Saints'°

Hark, all ye lovely saints above:
Diana hath agreed with Love
His fiery weapon to remove.
    Do you not see
    How they agree?
Then cease, fair ladies, why weep ye?

See, see your mistress bids you cease,
And welcome Love with love's increase:
Diana hath procured your peace.
10   Cupid hath sworn
    His bow forlorn
To break and bend, ere ladies mourn.

The First Stanza as set to Music:

Hark, all ye lovely saints above:
Diana hath agreed with Love, hath agreed with Love
His fiery weapon to remove. *Fa la la la la la,*
La, la, la——fa la la la la la, la, la,
La la la la la——la.
    Do you not see
    How they agree?
20 *Then cease, fair ladies, why weèp ye? why weep yè?*

1598

'Hark, All Ye Lovely Saints' This little song, from Thomas Weelkes's *Ballets and Madrigals to Five Voices* (1598), is like an epigram or motto for an emblematic picture of sexuality abandoned for chastity; it is set in a ballet or "fa-la," as they were called, a mixture of homophonic setting, with every voice singing chordally, the same words at the same time (like a hymn tune), and true fugal polyphony on the "fa-la-la's." We also give the text as set, with polyphonic parts in italic: notice how Weelkes has chosen to set the words "why weep ye?" polyphonically, perhaps to bring out the different contrastive stress accent which gives the phrase slightly different meanings.

THOMAS NASHE°

Litany in Time of Plague

Adieu, farewell earth's bliss,
This world uncertain is:
Fond are life's lustful joys,
Death proves them all but toys,
None from his darts can fly.
I am sick, I must die.
      Lord, have mercy on us!

Rich men, trust not in wealth,
Gold cannot buy you health;
Physic° himself must fade,
All things to end are made.
The plague full swift goes by.
I am sick, I must die.
      Lord, have mercy on us!

Beauty is but a flower
Which wrinkles will devour;
Brightness falls from the air,°
Queens have died young and fair,
Dust° hath closed Helen's eye.
I am sick, I must die.
      Lord, have mercy on us!

Strength stoops unto the grave,
Worms feed on Hector brave,
Swords may not fight with fate,
Earth still holds ope her gate.
Come! come! the bells do cry.°
I am sick, I must die.
      Lord, have mercy on us!

Wit with his wantonness
Tasteth death's bitterness;
Hell's executioner
Hath no ears for to hear
What vain art can reply.
I am sick, I must die.
      Lord, have mercy on us!

Thomas Nashe Novelist (*The Unfortunate Traveller, or Jack of Wilton,* published in 1594, a brilliant picaresque adventure), pamphleteer, and master of splendid prose invective, Nashe was one of the bright young "University wits" —including Robert Greene, George Peele, Marlowe, and his stolid polemical enemy, Gabriel Harvey—who flourished in the 1590's and many of whom died young.

Physic medical skill
Brightness falls from the air an image of darkening, although its place in the catalogue of decaying beauties has made for a suggested emendation to "hair"
Dust The Biblical "dust to dust" means, of course, mud, clay, not dry precipitate.
bells do cry parish bell ringing out a death (see Donne, "Meditation XVII")

Haste, therefore, each degree,°
To welcome destiny.
Heaven is our heritage,
Earth but a player's stage;°
Mount we unto the sky.
I am sick, I must die.
         Lord, have mercy on us!
                 1600

Autumn

Autumn hath all the summer's fruitful treasure;
Gone is our sport, fled is poor Croydon's° pleasure.
Short days, sharp days, long nights come on apace,
Ah! who shall hide us from the winter's face?
Cold doth increase, the sickness will not cease,
And here we lie, God knows, with little ease.
   From winter, plague, and pestilence, good Lord, deliver us!

London doth mourn, Lambeth° is quite forlorn;
Trades cry, woe worth that ever they were born.
The want of term° is town and city's harm;
Close chambers we do want, to keep us warm.
Long banishèd must we live from our friends;
This low-built house° will bring us to our ends.
   From winter, plague, and pestilence, good Lord, deliver us!
                 1600

ANONYMOUS

A Peddler's Song°

Fine knacks for ladies, cheap, choice, brave and new!
   Good pennyworths! but money cannot move.
I keep a fair but for the fair° to view;
   A beggar may be liberal of love.

degree social class
stage the old commonplace (see Spenser, *Amoretti* LIV)
Croydon's This and the following poem are both songs from Nashe's rather masque-like play, *Summer's Last Will and Testament*, performed in 1592 for the Archbishop of Canterbury at his palace in Croydon, south of London; the play represented the death of summer as occurring in Croydon, and it was performed while the plague raged in London.
Lambeth south of the Thames, seat of the archbishop's palace
want of term lack of an ending to the plague;

also, perhaps, suggesting that it is vacation, after Michaelmas term in the autumn
low built house the palace at Croydon; perhaps also, in a more medieval way, the human body
A Peddler's Song a magnificent poem, exemplifying a common genre (see Autolycus's songs from *A Winter's Tale*), which appeared, set for lute and voice by John Dowland, in 1600. The usual catalogue of the peddler's wares has erotic connotations, but here an uncharacteristic elevation of the plain over the fancy arises.
fair but for the fair the first "fair" meaning an open sale, a one-man fair; the second, of course, the girls who would be his customers

Though all my wares be trash, the heart is true,
   The heart is true,
   The heart is true.

Great gifts are guiles and look for gifts again;
   My trifles comes as treasures from my mind.
10 It is a precious jewel to be plain;
   Sometimes in shell the orient pearls we find.
Of others take a sheaf, of me a grain,
    Of me a grain,
    Of me a grain.

Within this pack pins, points, laces, and gloves,
   And divers toys° fitting a country fair.
But in my heart, where duty serves and loves,
   Turtles and twins, court's brood,° a heavenly pair.
Happy the heart that thinks of no removes,
20   Of no removes,
    Of no removes.
            1600

SIR THOMAS WYATT
1503–1542

"A hand that taught what might be said in rhyme," his follower, Surrey, said of him. Wyatt's inaugurating role in the establishment of Elizabethan poetic conventions is a strange one. Like many originators who forge the stylistic models from which others will work, there is a kind of awkwardness and tentativeness about even his best work. Wyatt, born in Kent and educated at St. John's College, Cambridge, was a courtier and diplomat whose travels to Italy and France in 1526 and 1527 acquainted him with the High Renaissance abroad. He served Henry VIII in various capacities, and was charged with treason, and acquitted, a year before his death. Wyatt's poems are of two sorts. The first—lyrics in short, tight stanzas of eight-syllable lines or less, written in an earlier tradition of song continued from the later fifteenth century—represents what the Elizabethan critic Puttenham called the poetry of the "courtly makers." These poems are metrically regular in the accentual-syllabic tradition which, after Chaucer, was lost (save by the Scottish poets) in all but the short lines of song meters. (We must remember that iambic pentameter had virtually to be rediscovered in the Tudor period. Chaucer was known and admired devoutly, but his iambic pentameter line was misread, even as late as Spenser's time, as a rough, accentual, four-beat "riding rhyme.") The second sort, Wyatt's translations and adaptations of Petrarch, not only brought the sonnet form to English but also sought to work out, from the Italian eleven-syllable line, a viable English equivalent. Wyatt's sonnets are written in a peculiar mixture of syllabic and accentual lines, but the majority of those lines move toward the normative verse pattern which he was able to bequeath to his follower, the Earl of Surrey.

----

toys both small objects and "fancies": compare our contemporary notions counter at a store **Turtles and twins . . . brood** turtle-doves and the "heavenly pair" of twins, Castor and Pollux of the constellation Gemini, were emblems of true love and constancy; the latter were the "brood" of Jove as the swan, and Leda

I Find No Peace°

I find no peace and all my war is done;
   I fear and hope, I burn and freeze like ice;
   I fly above the wind, yet can I not arise,
   And naught I have and all the world I seize on;
That° looseth nor locketh holdeth me in prison,
   And holdeth me not yet can I scape nowise;
   Nor letteth me live nor die at my devise,°
   And yet of death it giveth none occasion.
Without eyen° I see, and without tongue I plain;
10   I desire to perish, and yet I ask health;
   I love another, and thus I hate myself;
I feed me in sorrow, and laugh in all my pain.
   Likewise displeaseth me both death and life,
   And my delight is causer of this strife.

from ms. 1913

My Galley Chargèd with Forgetfulness°

My galley chargèd with forgetfulness
   Through sharp seas, in winter night doth pass
   Tween rock and rock;° and eke° mine enemy, alas,
   That is my lord steereth with cruelness.
And every oar a thought in readiness,
   As though that death were light in such a case.
   An endless wind doth tear the sail apace
   Of forcèd sighs and trusty fearfulness.
A rain of tears, a cloud of dark disdain,
10   Hath done the wearied cords° great hinderance,
   Wreathed with error and eke with ignorance.
The stars be hid that led me to this pain
   Drownèd is reason that should me consort,
   And I remain despairing of the port.

from ms. 1913

Farewell, Love

Farewell, Love, and all thy laws forever,—
   Thy baited hooks shall tangle me no more;
   Senec° and Plato call me from thy lore,

I Find No Peace from Petrarch (*In Vita*, Sonnet XC), helping to establish the subsequently popular vogue for talking in paradoxes, particularly about love—in a tradition going back before Petrarch to Sappho and Catullus—and represented in its clichéd form by poems like "Tichborne's Elegy" (see above)
that that which (love)
devise plan
eyen eyes

My Galley . . . Forgetfulness from Petrarch (*In Vita*, Sonnet CXXXVII)
tween rock and rock a reminiscence of Homeric navigational dangers; the whole poem transforms Horace's "Ship of the state" (*Odes* I.14) into a ship of self
eke also
cords rigging
Senec Seneca, the Roman Stoic philosopher and tragedian

To perfect wealth my wit for to endeavour.
In blind error when I did persever,
    Thy sharp repulse, that pricketh aye so sore,
    Hath taught me to set in trifles no store
    And scape forth since liberty is lever.°
Therefore farewell—go trouble younger hearts,
10   And in me claim no more authority;
    With idle youth go use thy property,
And thereon spend thy many brittle darts.
    For hitherto though I have lost all my time,
    Me lusteth° no longer rotten boughs to climb.

                              from ms. 1913

The Long Love That in My Thought Doth Harbour°

The long love that in my thought doth harbour,
And in my heart doth keep his residence,
Into my face presseth with bold pretence
And there encampeth spreading his banner.
She that me learns° to love and suffer
And wills that my trust and lust's negligence
Be reined° by reason, shame° and reverence
With his hardiness takes displeasure.
Wherewithal unto the heart's forest he flieth,
10 Leaving his enterprise with pain and cry,
And there him hideth, and not appeareth.
What may I do, when my master feareth,
But in the field with him to live and die?
For good is the life ending faithfully.

                              from ms. 1913

Blame Not My Lute°

Blame not my lute, for he must sound
Of this or that as liketh me,
For lack of wit the lute is bound
To give such tunes as pleaseth me.
Though my songs be somewhat strange
And speaks such words as touch thy change,
Blame not my lute.

---

lever preferable
Me lusteth I desire
The Long Love . . . Harbour an adaptation of
Petrarch (*In Vita*, Sonnet xci also translated
by Surrey; see below). The conceit of conqueror
Love occupying the poet's inner state, showing
his colors in self-revealing blushes, is typical
of the mythological psychologizing of Petrarchan
poetry.
learns teaches
reined restrained
shame proper modesty
Blame Not My Lute As in the following poem,
the lute, like the classical poet's lyre, stands
for poetic eloquence.

My lute, alas, doth not offend,
Though that perforce he must agree
¹⁰ To sound such tunes as I intend,
To sing to them that heareth me.
Then, though my songs be somewhat plain,
And toucheth some that use to feign,°
Blame not my lute.

My lute and strings may not deny
But as I strike they must obey:
Break not them then so wrongfully,
But wreak thyself some wiser way.
And though the songs which I indite°
²⁰ Do quit thy change with rightful spite,
Blame not my lute.

Spite asketh spite and changing change,
And falsèd faith must needs be known.
The fault so great, the case so strange,
Of right it must abroad be blown.°
Then since that by thine own desért°
My songs do tell how true thou art,
Blame not my lute.

Blame but thyself that hast misdone
³⁰ And well deservèd to have blame.
Change thou thy way so evil begun
And then my lute shall sound that same.
But if till then my fingers play,
By thy desért, their wonted way,
Blame not my lute.

Farewell, unknown, for though thou brake
My strings in spite, with great disdain,
Yet have I found out for thy sake
Strings for to string my lute again.
⁴⁰ And if perchance this foolish rhyme
Do make thee blush at any time,
Blame not my lute.
                from ms. 1913

My Lute, Awake!

My lute, awake! Perform the last
Labour that thou and I shall waste,
And end that I have now begun:

---

use to feign have elaborate and fancy manners   blown broadcast
indite compose   desert deserving

For when this song is sung and past,
My lute, be still, for I have done.

As to be heard where ear is none,
As lead to grave in marble stone,
My song may pierce her heart as soon.°
Should we then sigh or sing or moan?
10 No, no, my lute, for I have done.

The rocks do not so cruelly
Repulse the waves continually
As she my suit and affectiòn,
So that I am past remedy,
Whereby my lute and I have done.

Proud of the spoil that thou hast got
Of simple hearts, thorough° love's shot,
By whom, unkind,° thou hast them won—
Think not he hath his bow forgot,
20 Although my lute and I have done.

Vengeance shall fall on thy disdain
That makest but game on earnest pain.
Think not alone under the sun,
Unquit,° to cause thy lovers plain,°
Although my lute and I have done.

Perchance thee lie withered and old
The winter nights that are so cold,
Plaining in vain unto the moon.
Thy wishes then dare not be told.
30 Care then who list,° for I have done.

And then may chance thee to repent
The time that thou hast lost and spent
To cause thy lovers sigh and swoon.
Then shalt thou know beauty but lent,
And wish and want as I have done.

Now cease, my lute. This is the last
Labour that thou and I shall waste,
And ended is that we begun.
Now is this song both sung and past;
40 My lute, be still, for I have done.

from ms. 1913

As to . . . soon not until sounds are audible
without ears, or lead can carve marble, will my
eloquence touch her heart
thorough through

unkind unnatural
Unquit unrevenged
plain to lament
list wishes

Whoso List To Hunt°

Whoso list° to hunt, I know where is an hind,
  But as for me alas, I may no more—
  The vain travail hath wearied me so sore,
  I am of them that farthest cometh behind.
Yet may I, by no means, my wearied mind
  Draw from the deer, but as she fleeth afore,
  Fainting I follow. I leave off therefore,
  Since in a net I seek to hold the wind.
Who list her hunt, I put him out of doubt,
10 As well as I, may spend his time in vain.
  And graven with diamonds in letters plain
There is written her fair neck round about:
  '*Noli me tangere*,° for Caesar's I am,
  And wild for to hold, though I seem tame.'

                from ms. 1913

They Flee from Me°

They flee from me, that sometime did me seek,
With naked foot stalking in my chamber.
I have seen them, gentle, tame, and meek,
That now are wild, and do not remember
That sometime they put themselves in danger
To take bread at my hand, and now they range,
Busily seeking with a continual change.

Thanked be Fortune it hath been otherwise,
Twenty times better; but once in special,
10 In thin array, after a pleasant guise,
When her loose gown from her shoulders did fall,
And she me caught in her arms long and small,°
And therewith all sweetly did me kiss
And softly said, 'Dear heart, how like you this?'

It was no dream, I lay broad waking.
But all is turned, thorough my gentleness,
Into a strange fashion of forsaking;
And I have leave to go, of her goodness,
And she also to use newfangleness.°

Whoso List To Hunt from Petrarch (*Rime,* Sonnet cxc)
list wishes
'Noli me tangere "Don't touch me"; appropriating Latin of John 20:17 out of context—presumably the situation of Anne Boleyn, admired by Wyatt but already marked for Henry VIII's interest, is reflected here: Petrarch's conceit and what was thought to be an actual court intrigue blend in prototypical English Petrarchan fashion.

They Flee from Me This remarkable poem exists both in manuscript, as here given, and in a form slightly rewritten by Richard Tottel, in his *Miscellany* (1557), with the rough, experimental meter normalized into regular iambic pentameter, and a more rhetorically pointed ending.
long and small long and slender
newfangleness fashionable fickleness

20   But since that I so kindely° am served,
     I fain would know what she hath deserved.

                              from ms. 1913

HENRY HOWARD, EARL OF SURREY
1517–1547

Soldier, courtier from the time of his youth, in and out of favor with King Henry VIII who married, then beheaded, Surrey's cousin Catherine, the poet was finally executed himself, for treason, in 1547. He appears to have done translations into English verse when young, and was an admirer and younger friend of Wyatt. His own poems left a more palpable legacy than Wyatt's. The sonnets in Tottel's Miscellany (1557) are of the quatrain and couplet sort which became the standard English model. His is the first English blank verse, perhaps derived from an acquaintance with Italian poetry in this meter, and used with neoclassical appropriateness for a translation of two books of Virgil's *Aeneid*, published after his death, in 1557. Surrey's sonnets lack the experimental vigor of Wyatt's which appealed so much to the tastes of poetic modernism in the 1930's and '40's; they are marked instead by the smoothness and sophistication in handling the form used later by Shakespeare, the balance and measure of syntax and verse unit, and the absorption of classical styles and their lessons for English, which make him such a direct precursor of Sir Philip Sidney.

Alas, So All Things Now Do Hold Their Peace°

Alas, so all things now do hold their peace,
Heaven and earth disturbed in no-thing;
The beasts, the air, the birds their song do cease,
The nightès chair° the stars about do bring.
Calm is the sea: the waves work less and less;
So am not I, whom love, alas, doth wring,
Bringing before my face the great increase
Of my desires, whereat I weep and sing
In joy and woe as in a doubtful ease;
10 For my sweet thoughts sometime do pleasure bring,
But by and by the cause of my disease°
Gives me a pang that inwardly doth sting,
    When that I think what grief it is again
    To live and lack the thing should rid my pain.

                              1557

---

kindely appropriately. Rather sarcastic, of course, and Tottel's version of the last two lines uses the word in its modern sense, making it negative, and coarsening the tone: "But since that I unkindly so am served, How like you this? What hath she now deserved?"
Alas . . . peace a version of Petrarch's sonnet (*In Vita*, Sonnet CLXIV) which is, itself, worked up from the well-known set piece by Virgil translated below
nightès chair car, or chariot, of the night, i.e. the Great Bear; "nightès" is disyllabic
disease uneasiness

From Virgil's Aeneid

[The Night-Piece°]

It was then night: the sound and quiet sleep
Had through the earth the wearied bodies caught;
The woods, the raging seas were fallen to rest;
When that the stars had half their course declined
The fields whist;° beasts and fowls of divers hue,
And what so that in the broad lakes remained,
Or yet among the bushy thicks° of briar
Laid down to sleep by silence of the night,
710 Gan 'suage their cares, mindless of travels past.
Not so the sprite of this Phoenician:°
Unhappy she, that on no sleep could chance,
Nor yet night's rest enter in eye or breast.
Her cares redouble; love doth rise and rage again,°
And overflows with swelling storms of wrath.

                                    1557

[The Trojan Horse°]

'The Greeks' chieftains, all irkèd with the war
Wherein they wasted had so many years
20 And oft repulsed by fatal destiny,
By the divine science of Minerva
A huge horse made, high raisèd like a hill,
For their return a feignèd sacrifice:
The fame whereof so wandered it at point.°
Of cloven fir compacted were his ribs;
In the dark bulk they closed bodies of men
Chosen by lot, and did enstuff° by stealth
The hollow womb with armèd soldiers.

There stands in sight an isle, hight° Tenedon,
30 Rich, and of fame, while Priam's kingdom stood;
Now but a bay, and road unsure for ship.
Hither them secretly the Greeks withdrew,
Shrouding themselves under the desert shore.
And, weening° we they had been fled and gone
And with that wind had fet the land of Greece,
Troyè discharged her long continued dole.
The gates cast up, we issued out to play,
The Greekish camp desirous to behold,
The places void, and the forsaken coasts.

The Night-Piece a famous passage in Virgil, *Aeneid* IV.522–28 contrasting the quiet of night with Dido's anxiety when she knows Aeneas will desert her. It was imitated by Petrarch in the sonnet adapted by Surrey given above.
whist were silent
thicks thickets
this Phoenician Dido, queen of Carthage

Her cares . . . again This is a deliberate alexandrine, or twelve-syllable line.
The Trojan Horse This section is narrated by Aeneas at Dido's court.
at point aptly
enstuff to garrison with soldiers
hight named
weening knowing

40   Here Pyrrhus' band; there fierce Achilles pight;°
　　Here rode their ships; there did their battles join.
　　Astonied, some the scatheful gift beheld,
　　Behight° by vow unto the chaste Minerve,
　　All wondering at the hugeness of the horse.
　　The first of all Timoetes gan advise
　　Within the walls to lead and draw the same,
　　And place it eke amid the palace court:
　　Whether of guile, or Troyès fate it would.
　　Capys, with some of judgment more discreet,
50   Willed it to drown, or underset with flame
　　The suspect present of the Greeks' deceit,　,
　　Or bore and gauge the hollow caves uncouth:
　　So diverse ran the giddy people's mind.
　　Lo, foremost of a rout that followed him,
　　Kindled Laocoön° hasted from the tower,
　　Crying far off: "O wretched citizens!
　　What so great kind of frenzy fretteth you?
　　Deem ye the Greeks our enemies to be gone?
　　Or any Greekish gifts can you suppose
60   Devoid of guile? Is so Ulysses known?
　　Either the Greeks are in this timber hid,
　　Or this an engine is to annoy our walls,
　　To view our towers, and overwhelm our town.
　　Here lurks some craft. Good Troyans, give no trust
　　Unto this horse, for whatsoever it be,
　　I dread the Greeks—yea, when they offer gifts!"
　　And with that word, with all his force a dart
　　He lancèd then into that crooked womb
　　Which trembling stuck, and shook within the side:
70   Wherewith the caves gan hollowly resound.
　　And, but for Fates, and for our blind forecast,
　　The Greeks' device and guile had he descried:
　　Troy yet had stood, and Priam's towers so high.'

· · ·

1557

Love That Doth Reign and Live Within My Thought

Love, that doth reign and live within my thought,°
And built his seat within my captive breast,
Clad in the arms wherein with me he fought,

---

pight pitched (of tents)
Behight consecrated
Laocoön Son of Priam (king of Troy) and a priest of Apollo, he was punished by Athena for his attempts to warn the Trojans about the Wooden Horse, and died, with his sons, in the coils of two great serpents.
Love . . . thought adapted from the same Petrarchan sonnet (*In Vita,* Sonnet xci) as Wyatt's "The Long Love That in My Thought Doth Harbour"

Oft in my face he doth his banner rest.
But she that taught me love and suffer pain,
My doubtful hope and eke my hot desire
With shamefast° look to shadow and refrain,
Her smiling grace converteth straight to ire.
And coward Love, then, to the heart apace
10   Taketh his flight, where he doth lurk and plain,°
His purpose lost, and dare not show his face.
For my lord's guilt thus faultless bide I pain,
   Yet from my lord shall not my foot remove:
   Sweet is the death that taketh end by love.

1557

SIR PHILIP SIDNEY
1554–1586

If the humanist ideal of the fulfilled human being was a wisely and gracefully educated aristocrat, Sir Philip Sidney was almost the perfect courtier. A man who could stand for the condition of humanity, not by exemplifying a random sample but as a mirror and a mold of all the virtues, should possess many cultivated skills (as Castiglione argued in *Il Cortegiano*) tempered with that *sprezzatura,* or aristocratic carelessness, which would distinguish him from a professional, a mere hired hand. English humanist educators had prescribed formal intellectual training as being necessary to the art of government; and the arts of literature as they might be practiced in courtly poetry, certainly, were free of the taint of base handicrafts and household help that painting, architecture, and professional music-making still kept. Sidney was able in his short life to unite some of the separate concerns of court and university by informing his originally recreational writing with a range of purposes and concerns shared by his teachers and his friends like Spenser and Fulke Greville; and indeed, under the pressure of these concerns, moral and aesthetic, two of these projects actually got, in a sense, out of hand. His prose romance (now called *The Old Arcadia*) gave way, in his later rewriting of it, to something so much more complex that he could not complete it. His sonnet sequence, *Astrophel and Stella,* created a model not only for what would become a national literary fashion in the last decade of the century but also for an association of form, mythological and narrative elements, and tone of personal voice which would continue to influence English lyric poetry in the century after his death.

Sidney was born to an important family; his uncles were the Earls of Leicester and Warwick, his mother, an unusually well educated lady for her day, who was able to assist with the basic education of her son and his sister (later the Countess of Pembroke) at Penshurst, the family castle in Kent (see Ben Jonson's "To Penshurst"). Sidney later went to Shrewsbury School and to Oxford, but left his college, Christ Church, without taking a degree, in 1571. Thereafter he traveled extensively abroad assisting on diplomatic missions, fought in Ireland, and met many learned and influential men who would reinforce his commitments to the skills of knowledge, and to Protestantism. It was in that cause, as much as in the nationalist one, that he would die in Holland,

---

shamefast modest   **plain** lament

after being wounded at the Battle of Zutphen fighting the Spanish forces of his god-father, King Philip of Spain.

Sidney's friendships in England and abroad were literary as well as courtly and diplomatic, and the concern for the establishment of an English national literature which is apparent in his *Defence of Poesie* was deeply rooted in more than merely the contemporary arguments about style and form (poetic meter, in particular, was an important issue) that dominated critical writing about literature in his day. In 1578 he wrote an entertainment (somewhere between a masque and a pageant) for Queen Elizabeth's visit to the Earl of Leicester; in that year, too, he began work on the *Arcadia*, "This idle work of mine," as he referred to it, "this child which I am loth to father," his *sprezzatura* minimizing what must have been, even in a work probably designed at first to amuse his sister, a very deep commitment to a literary program. Based on an Italian prototype, the *Arcadia* of Sannazaro (1501), in alternating passages of prose and verse as well as on the five-act structure of classical comedy, Sidney's work uses the idyllic setting of pastoral tradition, the shipwrecks, abductions by pirates, usurpations, and mistaken identities of the Alexandrian romances like Heliodorus' *Aethiopian Romance*, for its plot. But its literary center is in the dialogues and debates, in the most rhetorical of prose styles, on such subjects as reason and passion, the active as opposed to the contemplative life, the duties of kingship, and other academic set pieces. Fully as important were the interspersed poems, on a variety of subjects and in a variety of forms and meters, including adaptations of Greek and Latin quantitative meter in the fashionably experimental way. Sidney finished *The Old Arcadia* in 1580; two years later, he began work on its never-to-be-finished revision to be called (from the title of its first posthumously published version) *The Countess of Pembroke's Arcadia* (1590), or *The New Arcadia*. It represented a new mode of seriousness, introducing just the confusion of genres which the *Defence* so deplored (it is, perhaps, a good candidate for Polonius's "tragical-comical-historical-pastoral" in *Hamlet*). After finishing two books and part of a very long third one, Sidney abandoned the project; it was reissued with some slight changes and the added last three books of *The Old Arcadia*. There was perhaps no way in which Sidney could handle the transformation of the brilliant but limited genre of the first book without the kind of fundamental re-thinking of the nature of a literary form which resulted in many of Shakespeare's plays, and *The Faerie Queene*.

The sonnets of *Astrophel and Stella*, started in 1581, probably finished the following year, circulated widely, like many poems of their age, in manuscript, and finally appeared in three unauthorized but influential editions in 1591. The first full Petrarchan sequence in English, it adopts both the Petrarchan fiction (Astrophil or -phel means "star-lover" in Greek; Stella is Latin for "star") and the meta-fiction, namely that the fiction exists merely to veil a literal autobiographical situation. In fact, the Petrarchan mythology exists to provide a muse, a psychology, and a set of relations and images; the use of biography is to support that myth. Penelope Devereux, to whom Sidney was briefly engaged when she was quite young, was the daughter of the Earl of Essex; she eventually married Lord Rich, rather unhappily. The identification of Stella with her is unquestioned, and if threads of "story" are carefully analyzed, some relation between them and possible meetings, confrontations, and partings in the lives of Sidney and Penelope during 1581–82 may be discerned. In several sonnets there are puns on her name (she "Hath no misfortune but that Rich she is," etc.) that would become almost mandatory in subsequent sonnet collections. Still, the Stella of the sequence is a mythical muse of lyric poetry, and of English lyric poetry struggling to justify itself in the light of antiquity and of Continental mastery of the classical tradition. Sidney's use not only of Petrarchan imagery but also of patternings of linguistic surface and depth which he had learned from the Renaissance study of rhetoric, is reinforced in these poems by a constant sense of personal presence, of a tone of voice of a speaker in a situation, which will lay the groundwork for the new kind of lyric of speech that first appears so dramatically in the poetry of John Donne.

Ye Goatherd Gods°

STREPHON   Ye goatherd gods, that love the grassy mountains,
Ye nymphs that haunt the springs in pleasant valleys,
Ye satyrs joyed with free and quiet forests,
Vouchsafe your silent ears to plaining music,
Which to my woes gives still an early morning,
And draws the dolour on till weary evening.

KLAIUS   O Mercury, foregoer to the evening,
O heavenly huntress° of the savage mountains,
O lovely star, entitled of the morning,°
While that my voice doth fill these woeful valleys,
Vouchsafe your silent ears to plaining music,
Which oft hath Echo tired in secret forests.

STREPHON   I, that was once free burgess° of the forests,
Where shade from sun, and sport I sought at evening,
I, that was once esteemed for pleasant music,
Am banished now among the monstrous mountains
Of huge despair, and foul affliction's valleys,
Am grown a screech owl to myself each morning.

KLAIUS   I, that was once delighted every morning,
Hunting the wild inhabiters of forests,
I, that was once the music of these valleys,
So darkened am that all my day is evening,
Heartbroken so that molehills seem high mountains
And fill the vales with cries instead of music.

STREPHON   Long since, alas, my deadly swannish music°
Hath made itself a crier of the morning,

Ye Goatherd Gods One of the songs (No. 71) from the *Old Arcadia*, sung by Strephon and Klaius, two foreign swains united by their love for Urania, who has left Arcadia, commanding them to remain there. A double sestina, it expands the original 39-line form that traditionally uses only the six terminal words of its first stanza as terminals throughout (permutations of their order generate the subsequent stanzas). The brilliance and fame of this poem depend upon the resonant evocations of overtones of meaning in the repetitions of *mountains—valleys—forests—music—morning—evening*.
huntress Diana (Artemis), virgin moon goddess
O lovely . . . morning Lucifer, the Morning Star
burgess free citizen
deadly swannish music The swan was supposed to sing only at its death.

And hath with wailing strength climbed highest mountains;
Long since my thoughts more desert be than forests,
Long since I see my joys come to their evening,
And state thrown down to overtrodden valleys.

KLAIUS   Long since the happy dwellers of these valleys
Have prayed me leave my strange exclaiming music
Which troubles their day's work and joys of evening;
Long since I hate the night, more hate the morning,
Long since my thoughts chase me like beasts in forests
And make me wish myself laid under mountains.

STREPHON   Meseems I see the high and stately mountains
Transform themselves to low dejected° valleys;
Meseems I hear in these ill-changèd forests
The nightingales do learn of owls their music;
Meseems I feel the comfort of the morning
Turned to the mortal serene° of an evening.

KLAIUS   Meseems I see a filthy cloudy evening
As soon as sun begins to climb the mountains;
Meseems I feel a noisome scent, the morning
When I do smell the flowers of these valleys;
Meseems I hear, when I do hear sweet music,
The dreadful cries of murdered men in forests.

STREPHON   I wish to fire the trees of all these forests;
I give the sun a last farewell each evening;
I curse the fiddling finders-out of music;
With envy I do hate the lofty mountains.
And with despite despise the humble valleys;
I do detest night, evening, day, and morning.

KLAIUS   Curse to myself my prayer is, the morning;
My fire is more than can be made with forests,
My state more base than are the basest valleys.
I wish no evenings more to see, each evening;
Shamèd, I hate myself in sight of mountains
And stop mine ears, lest I grow mad with music.

STREPHON   For she whose parts° maintained a perfect music,
Whose beauty shined more than the blushing morning,
Who much did pass in state the stately mountains,
In straightness passed the cedars of the forests,
Hath cast me, wretched, into eternal evening
By taking her two suns° from these dark valleys.

---

dejected humble, with the Latin sense also of
"cast down"
mortal serene deadly (perhaps, also, transient)
mist

parts with a pun on musical polyphonic parts,
or voices
suns her eyes

70 KLAIUS   For she, to whom compared, the Alps are valleys,
            She, whose least word brings from the spheres their music,
            At whose approach the sun rose in the evening,
            Who where she went bare in her forehead morning,
            Is gone, is gone, from these our spoiled forests,
            Turning to deserts our best pastured mountains.

STREPHON   These mountains witness shall, so shall these valleys,

KLAIUS   These forests eke,° made wretched by our music,
            Our morning hymn this is, and song at evening.

                                                    1580

THE OLD ARCADIA

At the beginning of *The Old Arcadia*, two princes from Thrace have wandered into
Arcadia on a long journey home. The cousins are named Pyrocles ("fire and glory")
and Musidorus ("the Muses' gift"), and the former falls in love with a picture of the
daughter of the Duke of Arcadia. Musidorus rebukes him for his distractedness and
"solitariness"; his answer follows. It culminates in a description of Arcadia as the
locus amoenus, the "lovely place," that concept which connects Renaissance pastoral
settings with such classical paradises as those of the Golden Age and the Hesperidean
garden.

From The Old Arcadia

These words spoken vehemently and proceeding from so dearly an esteemed
friend as Musidorus did so pierce poor Pyrocles, that his blushing cheeks did
witness with him, he rather could not help, than did not know his fault. Yet,
desirous by degrees to bring his friend to a gentler consideration of him, and
beginning with two or three broken sighs, answered him to this purpose: 'Excellent Musidorus, in the praises you gave me in the beginning of your speech I
easily acknowledge the force of your good will unto me. For, neither could you
have thought so well of me if extremity of love had not something dazzled your
eyes, nor you could have loved me so entirely, if you had not been apt to make
so great (though undeserved) judgement of me. And even so must I say of
those imperfections, to which though I have ever through weakness been subject, yet which you by the daily mending of your mind have of late been able
to look into, which before you could not discern, so that the change you spake
of falls not out by my impairing, but by your bettering. And yet under the leave
of your better judgment I must needs say thus much, my dear cousin, that I
find not myself wholly to be condemned, because I do not with a continual
vehemency follow those knowledges which you call the betterings of my mind.
For, both the mind itself must (like other things) sometimes be unbent, or else
it will be either weakened or broken, and these knowledges, as they are of good

eke also

use, so are they not all the mind may stretch itself unto. Who knows whether I feed not my mind with higher thoughts? Truly, as I know not all the particularities, so yet see I the bounds of all those knowledges; but the workings of the mind I find much more infinite than can be led unto by the eye, or imagined by any that distract their thoughts without themselves; and in such contemplations, or as I think more excellent, I enjoy my solitariness, and my solitariness perchance is the nurse of these contemplations. Eagles we see fly alone, and they are but sheep which always herd together. Condemn not therefore my mind sometime to enjoy itself, nor blame not the taking of such times as serve most fit for it.'

And here Pyrocles suddenly stopped, like a man unsatisfied in himself, though his wit might well have served to have satisfied another. And so looking with a countenance as though he desired he should know his mind without hearing him speak, and yet desirous to speak, to breathe out some part of his inward evil, sending again new blood to his face, he continued his speech in this manner.

'And lord, dear cousin,' said he, 'doth not the pleasantness of this place carry in itself sufficient reward for any time lost in it, or for any such danger that might ensue? Do you not see how everything conspires together to make this place a heavenly dwelling? Do you not see the grass, how in color they excell the emeralds, every one striving to pass his fellow, and yet they are all kept in an equal height? And see you not the rest of all these beautiful flowers, each of which would require a man's wit to know, and his life to express? Do not these stately trees seem to maintain their flourishing old age, with the only happiness of their seat being clothed with a continual spring, because no beauty here should ever fade? Doth not the air breathe health which the birds (both delightful both to the ear and eye) do daily solemnize with the sweet consent of their voices? Is not every echo here a perfect music? And these fresh and delightful brooks, how slowly they slide away, as, loath to leave the company of so many things united in perfection, and with how sweet a murmur they lament their forced departure. Certainly, certainly, cousin, it must needs be, that some goddess this desert belongs unto, who is the soul of this soil, for neither is any less than a goddess worthy to be shrined in such a heap of pleasures, nor any less than a goddess could have made it so perfect a model of the heavenly dwellings.'

And so he ended with a deep sigh, ruefully casting his eye upon Musidorus, as more desirous of pity than pleading.

1580

From Astrophel and Stella

I

Loving in truth, and fain in verse my love to show,°
That she, dear she, might take some pleasure of my pain,
Pleasure might cause her read, reading might make her know,

Loving . . . show This opening sonnet of the sequence is an original text about the notion of originality in English poetry (see Herbert's "Jordan II" for an elaboration on it); it is one of six sonnets in alexandrines, twelve-syllabled lines adapted from the standard French meter, in the collection.

Knowledge might pity win, and pity grace obtain,
I sought fit words to paint the blackest face of woe:
Studying inventions fine,° her wits to entertain,
Oft turning others' leaves, to see if thence would flow
Some fresh and fruitful showers upon my sunburned brain.°
But words came halting forth, wanting Invention's stay;
10 Invention, Nature's child, fled stepdame Study's blows;
And others' feet° still seemed but strangers in my way.
Thus, great with child to speak, and helpless in my throes,
    Biting my truant pen, beating myself for spite:
      'Fool,' said my Muse to me, 'look in thy heart, and write!'°

II

Not at the first sight, nor with a dribbed° shot,
Love gave the wound which, while I breathe, will bleed;
But known worth did in mine° of time proceed,
Till, by degrees, it had full conquest got.
I saw, and liked; I liked, but lovèd not;
I loved, but straight did not what Love decreed:
At length to Love's decrees I, forced, agreed,
Yet with repining at so partial lot.°
Now even that footstep° of lost liberty
10 Is gone, and now, like slave-born Muscovite,
I call it praise to suffer tyranny;
And now employ the remnant of my wit
    To make myself believe that all is well,
      While, with a feeling skill,° I paint my hell.

III

Let dainty wits cry on the Sisters nine,°
That bravely masked, their fancies may be told;
Or, Pindar's apes,° flaunt they in phrases fine,
Enamelling with pied flowers their thoughts of gold;
Or else let them in statelier glory shine,
Ennobling new-found tropes° with problems old;

inventions fine *Inventio* (here not the personified process, as in l. 8, but its results) is the first of the three phases of composition—with *dispositio,* or structure, and *elocutio,* or style—recognized in the Renaissance; these "fine" inventions, obviously, will not do for Stella's poet.
sunburned brain Astrophel's study of courtly verse ("Oft turning others' leaves") accounts for his "sunburned brain," for this striking phrase refers to an accepted Elizabethan figure for poetic imitation. Sidney draws out what is implied in the metaphor from Thomas Wilson's *Art of Rhetoric,* the parched sense of the man who has walked too long in the sun of the ancients.
feet metrical feet as well
'Fool . . . write' that is, look in your heart and find Stella's image there and write from that image, that source and origin of true poetry (that poetry, in fact, will be Petrarchan)

dribbed dribbled, random
mine tunnel dug to undermine fortified walls: just so time undermines emotional resistance
repining . . . lot complaining of a judgment so unfair to my side of the case
footstep footprint
feeling skill the skill bred of feeling; a skill that is itself sensible of the emotions it depicts
Let . . . nine "Let weaker, foppish minds appeal to the Muses." The strategy in this sonnet will be to authenticate Stella as the true Muse by rejecting the artifices of literature, particularly of all the fashionable theories of poetry of Sidney's day.
Pindar's apes French lyric poets like Ronsard, claiming to ape Pindar, the Greek master of choral lyric, by their use of the term "ode" and the "flowers" of rhetorical art.
tropes figures of thought (see Rhetoric in the Glossary)

Or with strange similes° enrich each line,
Of herbs or beasts which Ind or Afric hold.
For me, in sooth, no Muse but one I know;
10   Phrases and problems from my reach do grow,
And strange things cost too dear for my poor sprites.°
How then? Even thus: in Stella's face I read
What love and beauty be; then all my deed
But copying is, what, in her, Nature writes.

        V

It is most true that eyes are formed to serve
The inward light,° and that the heavenly part
Ought to be king, from whose rules who do swerve,
Rebels to nature, strive for their own smart.
It is most true, what we call Cupid's dart
An image is, which for ourselves we carve
And, fools, adore in temple of our heart,
Till that good god make church and churchmen starve.
True, that true beauty virtue is indeed,
10   Whereof this beauty can be but a shade,°
Which elements with mortal mixture breed.
True, that on earth we are but pilgrims made,°
    And should in soul up to our country move.
    True, and yet true that I must Stella love.

        XIV

Alas, have I not pain enough, my friend,
Upon whose breast a fiercer gripe doth tire°
Than did on him who first stole down the fire,°
While Love on me doth all his quiver spend—
But with your rhubarb° words ye must contend,
To grieve me worse, in saying that Desire
Doth plunge my well-formed soul even in the mire
Of sinful thoughts, which do in ruin end?
If that be sin which doth the manners° frame,
10   Well stayed with truth in word and faith of deed,
Ready of wit, and fearing naught but shame;
If that be sin, which in fixed hearts doth breed
    A loathing of all loose unchastity,
    Then love is sin, and let me sinful be.

strange similes the over-elaborate prose style
and exotic comparisons of the so-called Euphuistic style (see the selection from John Lyly)
sprites spirits
inward light reason, which ought to rule over
the whole person; yet love, by another convention, enters at the eye and imprints the
beloved's image on the heart
shade image or picture; a standard Platonic
theme

pilgrims made the medieval notion of life as
a mere pilgrimage to the eternal life beyond
death
gripe doth tire grip does rip
him who . . . fire Prometheus, punished by
being chained to a rock with a vulture to lunch
on his liver
rhubarb used as a bitter laxative
manners moral style

XV

You that do search for every purling spring
Which from the ribs of old Parnassus° flows,
And every flower, not sweet perhaps, which grows
Near thereabouts, into your poesy wring;°
You that do dictionary's method° bring
Into your rhymes, running in rattling rows;
You that poor Petrarch's long deceasèd woes
With newborn sighs and denizened° wit do sing:
You take wrong ways; those far-fet° helps be such
10 As do bewray° a want of inward touch,°
And sure at length stolen goods do come to light;
But if, both for your love and skill, your name
You seek to nurse at fullest breasts of Fame,
Stella behold, and then begin to indite.

XX

Fly, fly, my friends—I have my death wound—fly!
See there that boy, that murdering boy, I say,
Who, like a thief, hid in dark bush doth lie
Till bloody bullet get him wrongful prey.°
So tyrant he no fitter place could spy,
Nor so fair level in so secret stay,°
As that sweet black which veils the heavenly eye;
There himself with his shot he close° doth lay.
Poor passenger,° pass now thereby I did,
10 And stayed, pleased with the prospect of the place,
While that black hue from me the bad guest hid;
But straight I saw motions of lightning grace,
    And then descried the glistering of his dart;
    But ere I could fly thence, it pierced my heart.

XXV

The wisest scholar of the wight most wise°
By Phoebus' doom, with sugared sentence says
That Virtue, if it once met with our eyes,
Strange flames of love it in our souls would raise;
But, for that° man with pain this truth descries,

Parnassus the other Greek mountain of inspiration, on which were Delphi (Apollo's oracle) and the Castalian spring, like the Hippocrene spring on Mt. Helicon sacred to the Muses
poesy wring twist into your wreath, work into your poem
dictionary's method alliterative, lame lines, as below
denizened naturalized into English. Sidney, as a devout Petrarchan, is prophetically attacking his own weaker imitators-to-be, and doing so as part of a Petrarchan strategy—only a vision of the Lady is sufficiently heavenly inspiration,

and all literary methods are to be shunned.
far-fet farfetched
bewray betray
inward touch true imagination
Till . . . prey For the image of the "hunter hunted" see "Ye Goatherd Gods."
so fair . . . stay get such a good aim in so secret a place
close secretly
passenger passer-by
wight most wise wisest man: Socrates (declared so by Apollo, see next line); his wisest scholar, Plato
for that because

While he each thing in sense's balance weighs,
And so nor will nor can behold those skies
Which inward sun° to heroic mind displays,
Virtue of late, with virtuous care to stir
10 Love of herself, takes Stella's shape, that she
To mortal eyes might sweetly shine in her.
It is most true; for since I her did see,
    Virtue's great beauty in that face I prove,°
    And find the effect, for I do burn in love.

      XXVI
Though dusty wits dare scorn astrology,
And fools can think those lamps of purest light°
—Whose numbers, ways, greatness, eternity,
Promising wonders, wonder do invite—
To have for no cause birthright in the sky
But for to spangle the black weeds° of night;
Or for some brawl° which in that chamber high
They should still dance to please a gazer's sight.
For me, I do Nature unidle° know,
10 And know great causes great effects procure;
And know those bodies high reign on° the low.
And if these rules did fail, proof makes me sure,
    Who oft forejudge my after-following race°
    By only those two stars in Stella's face.

      XXVIII
You that with allegory's curious frame
Of others' children changelings use to make,°
With me those pains, for God's sake, do not take;
I list° not dig so deep for brazen fame.
When I say Stella, I do mean the same
Princess of beauty, for whose only sake
The reins of Love I love, though never slack,
And joy therein, though nations count it shame.
I beg no subject to use eloquence,°
10 Nor in hid ways do guide philosophy;
Look at my hands for no such quintessence;°
But know that I in pure simplicity
    Breathe out the flames which burn within my heart,
    Love only reading unto me this art.

inward sun See Sonnet V, l. 2n.
prove try out
lamps . . . light the stars
weeds garments
brawl branle, a ring-dance, hence appropriate
to the spheres' rotation
Nature unidle Nature to be active
reign on rule over, with a pun on "rain (influence—see Astrology in the Glossary) down
on"

race life, seen as a pursuit of a goal
You that . . . make you who misread poems
by taking them allegorically
list wish
I beg . . . eloquence I'm not out of ideas to
use my style for
quintessence Aside from the four earthly elements, there was ether, a non-material essence
which pervaded all matter, and which the
alchemists labored unsuccessfully to extract.

XXXIII

I might—unhappy word—oh me, I might,
And then would not, or could not, see my bliss;
Till now wrapped in a most infernal night,
I find how heavenly day (wretch) I did miss.
Heart, rent° thyself, thou dost thyself but right;
No lovely Paris made thy Helen his;
No force, no fraud robbed thee of thy delight,
Nor Fortune of thy fortune author is;
But to myself myself did give the blow,
10 While too much wit, forsooth, so troubled me
That I respects° for both our sakes must show;
And yet could not, by rising morn, foresee
    How fair a day was near—oh punished eyes,
    That I had been more foolish, or more wise!

XLIX

I on my horse, and Love on me, doth try
Our horsemanships, while by strange work I prove
A horseman to my horse, a horse to Love,
And now man's wrongs in me, poor beast, descry.°
The reins wherewith my rider doth me tie
Are humbled thoughts, which bit of reverence move,
Curbed in with fear, but with gilt boss° above
Of hope, which makes it seem fair to the eye.
The wand° is will; thou, fancy, saddle art,
10 Girt fast by memory; and while I spur
My horse, he spurs with sharp desire my heart;
He sits me fast, however I do stir;
    And now hath made me to his hand so right
    That in the manege° myself takes delight.

LXXI

Who will in fairest book of Nature know
How virtue may best lodged in beauty be,
Let him but learn of love to read in thee,
Stella, those fair lines which true goodness show.
There shall he find all vices' overthrow,
Not by rude force, but sweetest sovereignty
Of reason, from whose light those night-birds° fly,
That inward sun° in thine eyes shineth so.
And, not content to be perfection's heir
10 Thyself, dost strive all minds that way to move,
Who mark in thee what is in thee most fair.

rent tear
respects due regard
man's wrongs . . . descry I perceive marks of
a rider's cruelty on me
boss ornamental gold stud on the bit

wand whip
manege art of horsemanship
night-birds the vices
inward sun here, as throughout these sonnets,
reason; cf. Sonnets V and XXV

So while thy beauty draws the heart to love,
  As fast thy virtue bends that love to good.
  But, ah, Desire still cries, 'Give me some food.'
                                         1591

DEFENCE OF POESIE

In 1579 Stephen Gosson (1554–1624), having been converted to the prevailing Puritan view that all the arts were pernicious, published "a pleasant invective" against them entitled *The School of Abuse;* and, presuming on Sidney's more cultivated Puritan sympathies, dedicated it to him. Sidney, says Gabriel Harvey, scorned him for his labor, "if at least it be in the goodness of that nature to scorn." Thomas Lodge published a *Defence* (1579), and Sidney reacted in the present work, first published after his death in 1595, but probably written about 1582. Sidney had better things to do than to reply in detail to Gosson, who merely provided the occasion for what is recognized as the most distinguished work of Elizabethan criticism and literary theory, its only rival, Puttenham's *Art of English Poesie* (1589), being less brilliant and speculative, though very useful.

Sidney planned the work carefully on the lines of a classical forensic defense, but concealed the rigidity of its organization under a flow of easy civilized prose. He also, in gentlemanly manner, refrained from a parade of learning, though he evidently knew the leading Continental critics J. C. Scaliger and A. S. Minturno and was at home with the classics. His argument is notable for its emphasis not only on the superior power of poetry to instruct, but on its inspiration, a doctrine he has to deal with at its source in Plato. It is this power which enables the poet to surpass philosophers and historians in his service to society and to morality. And it is this power which surpasses even the one which Sidney sees in the poet, who, "lifted up with the vigour of his own invention, doth grow in effect another nature, in making things either better than nature bringeth forth, or, quite anew, forms such as never were in nature, as the Heroes, Demigods, Cyclops, Chimeras, Furies, and such like: so as he goeth hand in hand with nature, and enclosed within the narrow warrant of her gifts, but freely ranging only within the zodiac of his own wit." Sidney combines with his views on inspiration a notable defense of the utility of fiction, not only because it avoids the generalities of the philosopher and the insignificant particularities of the historian but also because it can speak without necessarily making assertions: *now, for the poet, he nothing affirms, and therefore never lieth.* Apart from this subtle defense of fiction, Sidney's most penetrating idea may be that the poet (though, following Aristotle, he calls him an imitator of nature) is in fact a creator, a second nature, dealing with essential ideas and not their copies. Here, as elsewhere, he manipulates the conflicting texts of Plato in favor of poetry. For the rest, his lively and good-humored attack on the poet-haters, and his survey, cool but not bitter, of the contemporary English literary scene, are conducted with an easy and unaffected elegance rather rare in the English prose of the period.

From Defence of Poesie

[The opening is light and anecdotal in manner, establishing the easy tone of a lively gentleman's conversation. Sidney then continues the work by speaking of the antiquity of poetry, and its dignity as the source of other forms of knowledge.]

First, truly, to all them that professing learning inveigh against poetry may justly be objected that they go very near to ungratefulness, to seek to deface that which, in the noblest nations and languages that are known, hath been the first light-giver to ignorance, and first nurse, whose milk by little and little enabled them to feed afterwards of tougher knowledges. And will they now play the hedgehog that, being received into the den, drove out his host, or rather the vipers, that with their birth kill their parents? Let learned Greece in any of her manifold sciences be able to show me one book before Musaeus, Homer, and Hesiod,[1] all three nothing else but poets. Nay, let any history be brought that can say any writers were there before them, if they were not men of the same skill, as Orpheus, Linus,[2] and some other are named, who, having been the first of that country that made pens deliverers of their knowledge to their posterity, may justly challenge to be called their fathers in learning, for not only in time they had this priority (although in itself antiquity be venerable) but went before them, as causes to draw with their charming sweetness the wild untamed wits to an admiration of knowledge, so as Amphion was said to move stones with his poetry to build Thebes, and Orpheus[3] to be listened to by beasts—indeed stony and beastly people.[4] So among the Romans were Livius Andronicus and Ennius.[5] So in the Italian language the first that made it aspire to be a treasure-house of science were the poets Dante, Boccaccio and Petrarch.[6] So in our English were Gower and Chaucer, after whom, encouraged and delighted with their excellent foregoing, others have followed, to beautify our mother tongue, as well in the same kind as in other arts.

This did so notably show itself, that the philosophers of Greece durst not a long time appear to the world but under the masks of poets. . . . And truly, even Plato,[7] whosoever well considereth shall find that in the body of his work, though the inside and strength were philosophy, the skin as it were and beauty depended most of poetry: for all standeth upon dialogues, wherein he feigneth many honest burgesses of Athens to speak of such matters, that if they had been set on the rack they would never have confessed them, besides his poetical

---

1. Musaeus (non-historical), supposed to have been a pupil of Orpheus (see Marlowe, *Hero and Leander*); Hesiod, 7th-century B.C., author of the didactic *Works and Days*.
2. Non-historical poet.
3. Amphion made the rocks, and Orpheus the trees, follow his harp and do his bidding.
4. An allegorical interpretation of the story; see the section The Renaissance Ovid.
5. L. Andronicus, Latin poet and playwright of 3rd century B.C.; Ennius, Latin epic poet, 239–169 B.C.
6. Dante Alighieri (1265–1321) used the vernacular for his *Commedia,* which included much contemporary learning; Giovanni Boccaccio (1313–75), humanist scholar and writer of tales; Francesco Petrarca (1304–74), learned poet and humanist.
7. Plato was cited by the opponents of poetry because he excluded poets from his *Republic* as liars; but he himself used fictive dialogues and myths in his philosophy. Medieval and Renaissance theories of allegory and of biblical interpretation frequently used the image of shell and kernel to stand for literal ("outer") meaning and inner, or figurative, truth.

describing the circumstances of their meetings, as the well ordering of a banquet, the delicacy of a walk, with interlacing mere tales, as Gyges' Ring [8] and others, which who knoweth not to be flowers of poetry did never walk into Apollo's garden.

And even historiographers [9] (although their lips sound of things done, and verity be written in their foreheads) have been glad to borrow both fashion and perchance weight of poets. So Herodotus entitled his history by the name of the nine Muses; [10] and both he and all the rest that followed him either stole or usurped of poetry their passionate describing of passions, the many particularities of battles, which no man could affirm, or, if that be denied me, long orations put in the mouths of great kings and captains, which it is certain they never pronounced. So that, truly, neither philosopher nor historiographer could at the first have entered into the gates of popular judgments, if they had not taken a great passport of poetry, which in all nations at this day, where learning flourisheth not, is plain to be seen, in all which they have some feeling of poetry.

.   .   .

Nature never set forth the earth in so rich tapestry as divers poets have done—neither with pleasant rivers, fruitful trees, sweet-smelling flowers, nor whatsoever else may make the too much loved earth more lovely. Her world is brazen, the poets only deliver a golden. But let those things alone, and go to man—for whom as the other things are, so it seemeth in him her uttermost cunning is employed—and know whether she have brought forth so true a lover as Theagenes,[11] so constant a friend as Pylades,[12] so valiant a man as Orlando,[13] so right a prince as Xenophon's Cyrus,[14] so excellent a man every way as Virgil's Aeneas. Neither let this be jestingly conceived because the works of the one be essential, the other in imitation or fiction; for any understanding knoweth the skill of the artificer standeth in that idea or foreconceit of the work and not in the work itself.[15] And that the poet hath that idea is mainifest, by delivering them forth in such excellency as he hath imagined them. Which delivering forth also is not wholly imaginative, as we are wont to say by them that build castles in the air: but so far substantially it worketh, not only to make a Cyrus, which had been but a particular excellency, as nature might have done, but to bestow a Cyrus upon the world, to make many Cyruses, if they will learn aright why and how that maker [16] made him.

Neither let it be deemed too saucy a comparison to balance the highest point of man's wit with the efficacy of nature; but rather give right honour to the heavenly maker of that maker, who, having made man to his own likeness, set

8. Gyges, a Lydian shepherd, gained possession of a ring that could make him invisible; he used it to seduce the queen and kill the king (Plato, Republic 359–60).
9. Historians.
10. The nine books of his history are named for the Muses.
11. Hero of the Greek romance Aethiopica by Heliodorus (3rd century A.D.)
12. Friend of Orestes; their fidelity was proverbial.
13. Hero of Ariosto's Orlando Furioso (1515).
14. Subject of Xenophon's Cyropaedia, The Education of Cyrus (early 4th century B.C.).
15. It does not follow that because the work is fictive the idea of it is not valid; it pre-exists the work and has substance, more even than a natural creation.
16. Sidney has previously explained that the Greeks called the poet the "maker."

him beyond and over all the works of that second nature: which in nothing he showeth so much as in poetry, when with the force of a divine breath he bringeth things forth far surpassing her doings, with no small argument to the incredulous of that first accursed fall of Adam, since our erected wit maketh us know what perfection is, and yet our infected will keepeth us from reaching unto it. . . . [Sidney proceeds to "a more ordinary opening" of the subject.]

Poesy therefore is an art of imitation, for so Aristotle termeth it [17] in his word *Mimesis*, that is to say, a representing, counterfeiting, or figuring forth—to speak metaphorically, a speaking picture; [18] with this end, to teach and delight. Of this have been three several kinds.

The chief, both in antiquity and excellency, were they that did imitate the inconceivable excellencies of God. Such were David in his Psalms; Solomon in his Song of Songs, in his Ecclesiastes, and Proverbs; Moses and Deborah in their Hymns,[19] and the writer of Job, which, beside other, the learned Emanuel Tremellius [20] and Franciscus Junius [21] do entitle the poetical part of the Scripture. Against these none will speak that hath the Holy Ghost in due holy reverence. In this kind, though in a full wrong divinity, were Orpheus, Amphion, Homer in his Hymns . . . [Sidney's second kind of poet is philosophical.]

. . . [The] third be they which most properly do imitate to teach and delight,[22] and to imitate borrow nothing of what is, hath been, or shall be; but range, only reined with learned discretion, into the divine consideration of what may be, and should be.[23] These be they that, as the first and most noble sort may justly be termed *Vates*,[24] so these are waited on in the excellentest languages and best understandings, with the foredescribed name of poets; for these indeed do merely make to imitate, and imitate both to delight and teach, and delight to move men to take that goodness in hand, which without delight they would fly as from a stranger, and teach, to make them know that goodness whereunto they are moved: which being the noblest scope to which ever any learning was directed, yet want there not idle tongues to bark at them.

These be subdivided into sundry more special denominations. The most notable be the heroic, lyric, tragic, comic, satiric, iambic, elegiac, pastoral, and certain others, some of these being termed according to the matter they deal with, some by the sorts of verses they liked best to write in; for indeed the greatest part of poets have apparelled their poetical inventions in that numbrous [25] kind of writing which is called verse—indeed but apparelled, verse being but an ornament and no cause to poetry, since there have been many most excellent poets that never versified, and now swarm many versifiers that need never answer to the name of poets. For Xenophon, who did imitate so excellently as to give us *effigiem justi imperii*, 'the portraiture of a just Empire,'

---

17. *Poetics* I.2, which Sidney probably got from Scaliger's *Poetices Libri Septem*.
18. The phrase has a long history, going back to Plutarch and beyond.
19. Exodus 15:1–19, Judges 5.
20. Jewish Bible scholar converted to Protestantism (1510–80).
21. Edited a Latin Bible with Tremellius (1545–1602).
22. The requirement of Horace, always endorsed.
23. Aristotle, *Poetics* IX.1–3; see note 29 below.
24. Latin; Sidney earlier translates "diviner, foreseer, or prophet."
25. Metrical.

under name of Cyrus (as Cicero saith of him), made therein an absolute heroical poem. So did Heliodorus in his sugared invention of that picture of love in Theagenes and Chariclea;[26] and yet both these writ in prose: which I speak to show that it is not rhyming and versing that maketh a poet, no more than a long gown maketh an advocate, who though he pleaded in armour should be an advocate and no soldier. But it is that feigning notable images of virtues, vices, or what else, with that delightful teaching, which must be the right describing note to know a poet by, although indeed the senate of poets hath chosen verse as their fittest raiment, meaning, as in matter they passed all in all, so in manner to go beyond them—not speaking, table-talk fashion or like men in a dream, words as they chanceably fall from the mouth, but peiz-ing [27] each syllable of each word by just proportion according to the dignity of the subject.

[Sidney now proceeds to the next task, the examination of poetry with respect to its rivals for the title of *Architectonikè*, the "mistress-knowledge." He finds that philosophy is too general, history too tied to particulars.]

The philosopher therefore and the historian are they which would win the goal, the one by precept, the other by example. But both, not having both, do both halt.[28] For the philosopher, setting down with thorny argument the bare rule, is so hard of utterance and so misty to be conceived, that one that hath no other guide but him shall wade in him till he be old before he shall find suffi-cient cause to be honest. For his knowledge standeth so upon the abstract and general, that happy is that man who may understand him, and more happy that can apply what he doth understand. On the other side the historian, want-ing the precept, is so tied, not to what should be but to what is, to the particular truth of things and not to the general reason of things, that his example draweth no necessary consequence, and therefore a less fruitful doctrine.

Now doth the peerless poet perform both: for whatsoever the philosopher saith should be done, he giveth a perfect picture of it in someone by whom he presupposeth it was done; so as he coupleth the general notion with the par-ticular example. A perfect picture I say, for he yieldeth to the powers of the mind an image of that whereof the philosopher bestoweth but a wordish de-scription: which doth neither strike, pierce, nor possess the sight of the soul so much as that other doth.

For as in outward things, to a man that had never seen an elephant or a rhinoceros, who should tell him most exquisitely all their shapes, colour, bigness, and particular marks, or of a gorgeous palace the architecture, with declaring the full beauties might well make the hearer able to repeat, as it were by rote, all he had heard, yet should never satisfy his inward conceits with being witness to itself of a true lively knowledge: but the same man, as soon as he might see those beasts well painted, or the house well in model, should straightways grow, without need of any description, to a judicial comprehending of them: so no doubt the philosopher with his learned definition—be it of virtue, vices, matters of public policy or private government—replenisheth the memory with many infallible grounds of wisdom, which, notwithstanding, lie dark before the imag-

26. See note 11.
27. Weighing.
28. Limp.

inative and judging power, if they be not illuminated or figured forth by the speaking picture of poesy.

[After explaining that even primitive cultures had poets, Sidney goes on to speak of the honorable names given to poets by the Greeks and Romans; he calls the Psalms a "divine poem." He thinks this right because, unlike other learned activities, poetry does not depend on nature but creates a second nature of its own.]

But now may it be alleged that, if this imagining of matters be so fit for the imagination, then must the historian needs surpass, who bringeth you images of true matters, such as indeed were done, and not such as fantastically or falsely may be suggested to have been done. Truly, Aristotle [29] himself, in his discourse of poesy, plainly determineth this question, saying that poetry is *Philosophoteron* and *Spoudaioteron*, that is to say, it is more philosophical and more studiously serious than history. His reason is, because poesy dealeth with *Katholou*, that is to say, with the universal consideration, and the history with *Kathekaston*, the particular: 'now,' saith he, 'the universal weighs what is fit to be said or done, either in likelihood or necessity (which the poesy considereth in his imposed names), and the particular only marks whether Alcibiades did, or suffered, this or that.' Thus far Aristotle: which reason of his, as all his, is most full of reason. For indeed, if the question were whether it were better to have a particular act truly or falsely set down, there is no doubt which is to be chosen, no more than whether you had rather have Vespasian's [30] picture right as he was, or at the painter's pleasure nothing resembling. But if the question be for your own use and learning, whether it be better to have it set down as it should be, or as it was, then certainly is more doctrinable the feigned Cyrus in Xenophon than the true Cyrus in Justin,[31] and the feigned Aeneas in Virgil than the right Aeneas in Dares Phrygius: [32] as to a lady that desired to fashion her countenance to the best grace, a painter should more benefit her to portrait a most sweet face, writing Canidia upon it, than to paint Canidia as she was, who, Horace sweareth, was foul and ill favoured.[33]

If the poet do his part aright, he will show you in Tantalus, Atreus,[34] and such like, nothing that is not to be shunned; in Cyrus, Aeneas, Ulysses, each thing to be followed; where the historian, bound to tell things as things were, cannot be liberal (without he will be poetical) of a perfect pattern, but, as in Alexander or Scipio himself, show doings, some to be liked, some to be misliked. And then how will you discern what to follow but by your own discretion, which you had without reading Quintus Curtius? [35]. . .

---

29. Aristotle (*Poetics* IX) says that poetry (by which he means "fiction" more generally) is *philosophoteron kai spoudaioteron* ("more philosophical and more serious") than history because it deals with the general, while history deals with the particular.

30. Roman emperor, 70–79 A.D.

31. Marcus Junianus Justinus, Roman historian of the 2nd century A.D.

32. A medieval account of the Trojan war, attributed to the non-existent eyewitness Dares Phrygius, was long thought to be older than Homer.

33. Canidia is a witch-like figure in Horace, *Epode* V and *Satires* I.8.

34. Tantalus was punished in hell by perpetual hunger and thirst though almost within reach of water and food, for his blasphemous ambition. He served his son Pelops as a dish to the gods. Atreus served his brother Thyestes a meal consisting of Thyestes' sons.

35. Author of a history of Alexander the Great in the 1st century A.D.

[Sidney develops the point that poetry uses the material of history, but more usefully, and argues that its supremacy lies in the fact that it not only instructs but moves its listeners to act on the instruction.]

Now therein of all sciences (I speak still of human, and according to the humane conceits) is our poet the monarch. For he doth not only show the way, but giveth so sweet a prospect into the way, as will entice any man to enter into it. Nay, he doth, as if your journey should lie through a fair vineyard, at the first give you a cluster of grapes, that, full of that taste, you may long to pass further. He beginneth not with obscure definitions, which must blur the margent [36] with interpretations, and load the memory with doubtfulness; [37] but he cometh to you with words set in delightful proportion, either accompanied with or prepared for, the well-enchanting skill of music; and with a tale forsooth he cometh unto you, with a tale which holdeth children from play, and old men from the chimney corner. And, pretending no more, doth intend the winning of the mind from wickedness to virtue: even as the child is often brought to take most wholesome things by hiding them in such other as have a pleasant taste: which, if one should begin to tell them the nature of aloes [38] or rhubarb they should receive, would sooner take their physic at their ears than at their mouth. So is it in men (most of which are childish in the best things, till they be cradled in their graves): glad they will be to hear the tales of Hercules, Achilles, Cyrus, and Aeneas; and, hearing them, must needs hear the right description of wisdom, valour, and justice; which, if they had been barely, that is to say philosophically, set out, they would swear they be brought to school again.

[Sidney now gives further examples of poetry's power to move.]

By these, therefore, examples and reasons, I think it may be manifest that the poet, with that same hand of delight, doth draw the mind more effectually than any other art doth: and so a conclusion not unfitly ensueth, that, as virtue is the most excellent resting place for all worldly learning to make his end of, so poetry, being the most familiar to teach it, and most princely to move towards it, in the most excellent work is the most excellent workman. . . .

[Sidney now considers objections to the different kinds of poetry: pastoral, elegiac, comic, tragic, lyric, epic; all of which he finds of social value, as well as productive of pleasure. He sums up:]

Since then poetry is of all human learning the most ancient and of most fatherly antiquity, as from whence other learnings have taken their beginnings; since it is so universal that no learned nation doth despise it, nor no barbarous nation is without it; since both Roman and Greek gave divine names unto it, the one of 'prophesying,' the other of 'making,' and that indeed that name of 'making' is fit for him, considering that whereas other arts retain themselves within their subject, and receive, as it were, their being from it, the poet only bringeth his own stuff, and doth not learn a conceit [39] out of a matter, but maketh matter for a conceit; since neither his description nor his end containeth any evil, the thing described cannot be evil; since his effects be so good as to

36. Margin.
37. Disputed points.
38. Bitter purgative; for "rhubarb" see *Astrophel and Stella*, Sonnet XIV, l. 5n.
39. Concept, idea; see Glossary.

teach goodness and to delight the learners; since therein (namely in moral doctrine, the chief of all knowledges) he doth not only far pass the historian, but, for instructing, is well-nigh comparable to the philosopher, and, for moving, leaves him behind him; since the Holy Scripture (wherein there is no uncleanness) hath whole parts in it poetical, and that even our Saviour Christ vouchsafed to use the flowers of it; since all his kinds are not only in their united forms but in their severed dissections fully commendable; I think (and think I think rightly) the laurel crown appointed for triumphing captains doth worthily (of all other learnings) honour the poet's triumph.[40] But because we have ears as well as tongues, and that the lightest reasons that may be will seem to weigh greatly, if nothing be put in the counterbalance, let us hear, and, as well as we can, ponder, what objections may be made against this art, which may be worthy either of yielding or answering.

[Sidney now turns on the *Mysomousoi*, poet-haters, first dealing with their more trivial objections and rhetorical point-scoring. Speech, next to reason, is our greatest gift, and verse is the highest form of speech. Then he begins the defense against more serious and specific charges.]

Now then go we to the most important imputations laid to the poor poets. For aught I can yet learn, they are these. First, that there being many other more fruitful knowledges, a man might better spend his time in them than in this. Secondly, that it is the mother of lies. Thirdly, that it is the nurse of abuse, infecting us with many pestilent desires, with a siren's sweetness drawing the mind to the serpent's tale of sinful fancy—and herein, especially, comedies give the largest field to ear (as Chaucer saith)[41]—how both in other nations and in ours, before poets did soften us, we were full of courage, given to martial exercises, the pillars of manlike liberty, and not lulled asleep in shady idleness with poets' pastimes. And lastly, and chiefly, they cry out with an open mouth, as if they outshot Robin Hood, that Plato banished them out of his Commonwealth.[42] Truly, this is much, if there be much truth in it. First, to the first, that a man might better spend his time is a reason indeed: but it doth (as they say) but *petere principium*: [43] for if it be, as I affirm, that no learning is so good as that which teacheth and moveth to virtue, and that none can both teach and move thereto so much as poetry, then is the conclusion manifest that ink and paper cannot be to a more profitable purpose employed. And certainly, though a man should grant their first assumption, it should follow (methinks) very unwillingly, that good is not good because better is better. But I still and utterly deny that there is sprung out of earth a more fruitful knowledge. To the second therefore, that they should be the principal liars, I answer paradoxically, but truly, I think truly, that of all writers under the sun the poet is the least liar, and, though he would, as a poet can scarcely be a liar. The astronomer, with his cousin the geometrician, can hardly escape, when they take upon them to

---

40. The laurel crown, worn by the central figure in a Roman triumph, was also claimed by poets.

41. Knight's Tale, l. 28: "I have, God wot, a large field to ere" (plow).

42. Gosson had stressed this point, which depends principally on *Republic* 607a, where Plato says that except for hymns there should be no poetry allowed in the republic, not even Homer.

43. "Beg the question."

measure the height of the stars. How often, think you, do the physicians lie, when they aver things good for sicknesses, which afterwards send Charon [44] a great number of souls drowned in a potion before they come to his ferry? And no less of the rest, which take upon them to affirm. Now, for the poet, he nothing affirms, and therefore never lieth. For, as I take it, to lie is to affirm that to be true which is false; so as the other artists, and especially the historian, affirming many things, can, in the cloudy knowledge of mankind, hardly escape from many lies. But the poet (as I said before) never affirmeth. The poet never maketh any circles about your imagination, to conjure you to believe for true what he writes. He citeth not authorities of other histories, but even for his entry calleth the sweet Muses to inspire into him a good invention; in truth, not laboring to tell you what is, or is not, but what should or should not be. And therefore, though he recount things not true, yet because he telleth them not for true, he lieth not . . . What child is there that, coming to a play, and seeing *Thebes* written in great letters upon an old door,[45] doth believe that it is Thebes? If then a man can arrive, at that child's age, to know that the poets' persons and doings are but pictures what should be, and not stories what have been, they will never give the lie to things not affirmatively but allegorically and figuratively written. And therefore, as in history, looking for truth, they go away full fraught with falsehood, so in poesy, looking for fiction, they shall use the narration but as an imaginative ground-plot of a profitable invention.

But hereto is replied, that the poets give names to men they write of, which argueth a conceit of an actual truth, and so, not being true, proves a falsehood. And doth the lawyer lie then, when under the names of 'John a Stile' and 'John a Noakes' [46] he puts his case? But that is easily answered. Their naming of men is but to make their picture the more lively, and not to build any history; painting men, they cannot leave men nameless. We see we cannot play at chess but that we must give names to our chessmen; and yet, methinks, he were a very partial champion of truth that would say we lied for giving a piece of wood the reverend title of a bishop. The poet nameth Cyrus or Aeneas no other way than to show what men of their fames, fortunes, and estates should do.

[Having dealt with the first two objections, that other kinds of knowledge are more profitable and that poets tell lies, Sidney turns to the charge that poetry can corrupt; he admits this, but treats it as a confirmation of the fact that it can also edify and improve. "But what, shall the abuse of a thing make the right use odious? Nay truly, though I yield that poetry may not only be abused, but that being abused, by the reason of his sweet charming force, it can do more hurt than any other army of words, yet shall it be so far from concluding that the abuse should give reproach to the abused, that contrariwise it is a good reason, that whatsoever, being abused, doth most harm, being rightly used (and upon the right use each thing conceiveth his title) doth most good."

He denies that poetry corrupts military virtue, arguing the contrary. And then he answers the fourth objection, which is made with the authority of Plato.]

But now indeed my burden is great; now Plato's name is laid upon me, whom, I must confess, of all philosophers I have ever esteemed most worthy of rev-

44. Ferryman of Hades who bore the newly arrived dead across the Styx.
45. It was a custom in the Elizabethan playhouse to indicate the place of the action thus.
46. Fictitious names used in certain kinds of suit in the English courts.

erence, and with great reason, since of all philosophers he is the most poetical. Yet if he will defile the fountain out of which his flowing streams have proceeded, let us boldly examine with what reasons he did it. First truly, a man might maliciously object that Plato, being a philosopher, was a natural enemy of poets.[47] For indeed, after the philosophers had picked out of the sweet mysteries of poetry the right discerning true points of knowledge, they forthwith, putting it in method, and making a school art of that which the poets did only teach by a divine delightfulness, beginning to spurn at their guides, like ungrateful prentices, were not content to set up shops for ' themselves, but sought by all means to discredit their masters; which by the force of delight being barred them, the less they could overthrow them the more they hated them. For indeed, they found for Homer seven cities strove who should have him for their citizen; where many cities banished philosophers as not fit members to live among them. For only repeating certain of Euripides' verses, many Athenians had their lives saved of the Syracusians,[48] when the Athenians themselves thought many philosophers unworthy to live. Certain poets, as Simonides and Pindarus, had so prevailed with Hiero the First, that of a tyrant they made him a just king,[49] where Plato could do so little with Dionysius, that he himself of a philosopher was made a slave.[50] But who should do thus, I confess, should requite the objections made against poets with like cavilation [51] against philosophers; as likewise one should do that should bid one read *Phaedrus* or *Symposium* in Plato, or the discourse of love in Plutarch, and see whether any poet do authorize abominable filthiness,[52] as they do. Again, a man might ask out of what commonwealth Plato did banish them. In sooth, thence where he himself alloweth community of women.[53] So as belike this banishment grew not for effeminate wantonness, since little should poetical sonnets be hurtful when a man might have what woman he listed. But I honour philosophical instructions, and bless the wits which bred them: so as they be not abused, which is likewise stretched to poetry.

St. Paul himself, who yet, for the credit of poets, allegeth [54] twice two poets, and one of them by the name of a prophet, setteth a watchword [55] upon philosophy—indeed upon the abuse. So doth Plato upon the abuse, not upon poetry. Plato found fault that the poets of his time filled the world with wrong opinions of the gods, making light tales of that unspotted essence, and therefore would not have the youth depraved with such opinions. Herein may much be said;

47. "There is an ancient quarrel between philosophy and poetry," *Republic* 607.
48. Plutarch (*Nicias* 29) says that the inhabitants of Syracuse in Sicily spared some of the survivors of the unsuccessful Athenian expedition against them (415 B.C.) because they were able to teach them some verses of Euripides, their favorite poet.
49. Hiero I, tyrant of Syracuse, 478–467 B.C., patronized these and other poets and accepted their counsel.
50. Plato went to Sicily in 390 B.C., but the monarch Dionysius disliked his views and is said to have caused him to be sold into slavery.
51. Caviling, quibbling.
52. Homosexual love.
53. Plato admired the physique of the Spartans, who held their women in common, *Republic* 449 ff.
54. St. Paul alludes to the Greek poets Aratus, Cleanthes, Epimenides, and Menander in Acts 17:28, Titus 1:12, and I Corinthians 15:22. Epimenides is called a prophet in Titus.
55. Advises caution.

let this suffice: the poets did not induce such opinions, but did imitate those opinions already induced. For all the Greek stories can well testify that the very religion of that time stood upon many and many-fashioned gods, not taught so by the poets, but followed according to their nature of imitation. Who list may read in Plutarch the discourses of Isis and Osiris, of the cause why oracles ceased, of the divine providence,[56] and see whether the theology of that nation stood not upon such dreams which the poets indeed superstitiously observed, and truly (since they had not the light of Christ) did much better in it than the philosophers, who, shaking off superstition, brought in atheism. Plato therefore (whose authority I had much rather justly construe than unjustly resist) meant not in general of poets, in those words of which Julius Scaliger saith, *Qua authoritate barbari quidam atque hispidi abuti velint ad poetas e republica exigendos;*[57] but only meant to drive out those wrong opinions of the Deity (whereof now, without further law, Christianity hath taken away all the hurtful belief), perchance (as he thought) nourished by the then esteemed poets. And a man need go no further than to Plato himself to know his meaning: who, in his dialogue called *Ion*,[58] giveth high and rightly divine commendation to poetry. So as Plato, banishing the abuse, not the thing, not banishing it, but giving due honour unto it, shall be our patron and not our adversary. For indeed I had much rather (since truly I may do it) show their mistaking of Plato (under whose lion's skin they would make an ass-like braying against poesy) than go about to overthrow his authority; whom, the wiser a man is, the more just cause he shall find to have in admiration; especially since he attributeth unto poesy more than myself do, namely, to be a very inspiring of a divine force, far above man's wit, as in the afore-named dialogue is apparent.

. . . even the Greek Socrates, whom Apollo confirmed to be the only wise man,[59] is said to have spent part of his old time in putting Aesop's fables into verses.[60] And therefore, full evil should it become his scholar Plato to put such words in his master's mouth against poets. But what need more? Aristotle writes the Art of Poesy: and why, if it should not be written? Plutarch teacheth the use to be gathered of them,[61] and how, if they should not be read? And who reads Plutarch's either history or philosophy, shall find he trimmeth both their garments with guards [62] of poesy. But I list not to defend poesy with the help of her underling historiography. Let it suffice that it is a fit soil for praise to dwell upon; and what dispraise may set upon it, is either easily overcome, or transformed into just commendation. So that, since the excellencies of it may be so easily and so justly confirmed, and the low-creeping objections so soon trodden down; it not being an art of lies, but of true doctrine; not of effeminateness, but of notable stirring of courage; not of abusing man's wit, but of strengthening man's wit; not banished, but honoured by Plato; let us rather

56. Titles of essays by Plutarch included in his *Moralia*.
57. "Which authority some rude and barbarous people would like to abuse in order to expel poets from the state."
58. The *Ion*, a somewhat ironical account of the inspiration of poet and reciter, was an important source of doctrine on poetic inspiration.
59. Through the Delphic oracle as reported in Plato's *Apology* 21.
60. Socrates is made to say so in Plato's *Phaedo* 61.
61. In "On Listening to Poetry" in *Moralia*.
62. Ornaments.

plant more laurels for to engarland our poets' heads (which honour of being laureate, as besides them only triumphant captains wear, is a sufficient authority to show the price they ought to be had in) than suffer the ill-favouring breath of such wrong-speakers once to blow upon the clear springs of poesy.

[Sidney now turns his attention to the contemporary state of English poetry, lamenting its decline, but praising some poets old and new.]

Chaucer, undoubtedly, did excellently in his *Troilus and Cressida;* of whom, truly, I know not whether to marvel more, either that he in that misty time could see so clearly, or that we in this clear age walk so stumblingly after him. Yet had he great wants, fit to be forgiven in so reverent antiquity. I account the *Mirror of Magistrates* [63] meetly furnished of beautiful parts, and in the Earl of Surrey's *Lyrics* many things tasting of a noble birth, and worthy of a noble mind. The *Shepherd's Calendar* [64] hath much poetry in his Eclogues, indeed worthy the reading, if I be not deceived. That same framing of his style to an old rustic language I dare not allow, since neither Theocritus in Greek, Virgil in Latin, nor Sannazaro in Italian did affect it. Besides these, do I not remember to have seen but few (to speak boldly) printed, that have poetical sinews in them: for proof whereof, let but most of the verses be put in prose, and then ask the meaning; and it will be found that one verse did but beget another, without ordering at the first what should be at the last; which becomes a confused mass of words, with a tingling sound of rhyme, barely accompanied with reason.

Our tragedies and comedies (not without cause cried out against), observing rules neither of honest civility nor of skillful poetry, excepting *Gorboduc* [65] (again, I say, of those that I have seen), which notwithstanding as [66] it is full of stately speeches and well-sounding phrases, climbing to the height of Seneca's style, and as full of notable morality, which it doth most delightfully teach, and so obtain the very end of poesy, yet in truth it is very defectious in the circumstances,[67] which grieveth me, because it might not remain as an exact model of all tragedies. For it is faulty both in place and time, the two necessary companions of

---

63. *The Mirror for Magistrates* was first published in 1559, then in 1563 with the famous Induction of Thomas Sackville, Earl of Dorset (1536–1608), and in many later editions. It contains metrical tragedies on the falls of great men, known generally, from the first example of the kind in Boccaccio's *De Casibus Virorum Illustrium,* as the *de casibus* theme. The collection had wide circulation in the period.

64. Spenser's book was dedicated to Sidney; see Headnote to *The Shepheardes Calender.*

65. *Gorboduc,* by Sackville and Thomas Norton, was first acted at the Inner Temple in 1561, and was the first regular English dramatic tragedy. It uses blank verse and has a political-historical theme, the horror of civil war, a topic much in Elizabethan minds. The bloody story, the division into five acts, the use of "sentences" or moral pronouncements, and the absence of violence on the stage, suggest the comparison with Seneca, but other elements such as the dumbshows and the English patriotic fervor are nothing like him. The influence of Seneca, whose Latin plays of the 1st century were more for recitation than action, was great in the Renaissance drama of Europe, but there was and is a tendency to overstate its effect on the development of English drama. It should be recalled that *Gorboduc* was written for amateur performers, the law students of the Middle Temple; that it has little influence on later popular drama; and that the themes of man's fall from good fortune and the need for patience (Seneca was a Stoic) have medieval counterparts not always easy to distinguish from it.

66. That.

67. Defective in the arrangement of the narrative.

all corporal actions. For where the stage should always represent but one place, and the uttermost time presupposed in it should be, both by Aristotle's precept and common reason,[68] but one day, there is both many days, and many places, inartificially imagined. But if it be so in *Gorboduc*, how much more in all the rest, where you shall have Asia of the one side, and Afric of the other, and so many other under-kingdoms, that the player, when he cometh in, must ever begin with telling where he is, or else the tale will not be conceived? Now ye shall have three ladies walk to gather flowers, and then we must believe the stage to be a garden. By and by we hear news of shipwreck in the same place, and then we are to blame if we accept it not for a rock. Upon the back of that comes out a hideous monster, with fire and smoke, and then the miserable beholders are bound to take it for a cave. While in the meantime two armies fly in, represented with four swords and bucklers, and then what hard heart will not receive it for a pitched field? Now, of time they are much more liberal, for ordinary it is that two young princes fall in love. After many traverses,[69] she is got with child, delivered of a fair boy; he is lost, groweth a man, falls in love, and is ready to get another child; and all this in two hours' space: which, how absurd it is in sense, even sense may imagine, and art hath taught, and all ancient examples justified, and, at this day, the ordinary players in Italy will not err in. . . .

But besides these gross absurdities, how all their plays be neither right trage-dies, nor right comedies, mingling kings and clowns, not because the matter so carrieth it, but thrust in clowns by head and shoulders, to play a part in majes-tical matters, with neither decency nor discretion, so as neither the admiration and commiseration, nor the right sportfulness, is by their mongrel tragicomedy obtained.[70] . . . So falleth it out that, having indeed no right comedy, in that comical part of our tragedy we have nothing but scurrility, unworthy of any chaste ears, or some extreme show of doltishness, indeed fit to lift up a loud laughter, and nothing else; where the whole tract of a comedy should be full of delight, as the tragedy should be still maintained in a well-raised admiration. But our comedians think there is no delight without laughter; which is very wrong, for though laughter may come with delight, yet cometh it not of delight, as though delight should be the cause of laughter; but well may one thing breed both together. Nay, rather in themselves they have, as it were, a kind of con-trariety: for delight we scarcely do but in things that have a conveniency to ourselves or to the general nature: laughter almost ever cometh of things most

68. Aristotle recommended (*Poetics* V) that the action should take place within the com-pass of twenty-four hours or little more. The other two "unities," of place and action, were inferred from Aristotle by 16th-century commentators after the rediscovery of the *Poetics* at the beginning of the 16th century.
69. Difficulties, setbacks.
70. Sidney's objection to the mixing of the genres would rule out most of Elizabethan drama, including Shakespeare. He thinks the effect of "admiration and commiseration" proper to tragedy (and going back to Aristotle's "pity and terror") cannot be mixed with low comedy, and that the result is neither one thing nor the other, since comedy has no business with clowning either. Tragicomedy as a mean between tragedy and comedy may have been discussed by Aristotle in a lost part of the *Poetics*, but he cannot have had in mind the mixture common in Elizabethan theater.

disproportioned to ourselves and nature. Delight hath a joy in it, either permanent or present. Laughter hath only a scornful tickling.

[Sidney next condemns the English lyric for its frigidity and general lack of
"forcibleness, or *Energia.*" He attacks excessive "euphuism" (see Headnote on
Lyly) in prose—the use of rigid rhetorical schemes and similes drawn from
bestiary and herbal lore. The English language lends itself so well to a flexible
and easy discourse ("being so easy of itself, and so void of those cumbersome
differences of cases, genders, moods and tenses which I think was a piece of
the Tower of Babylon's curse") that it should not be restricted artificially. Such
a language should meet every need, and English poetry in particular should be
elevated to its proper position.]

So that since the ever-praiseworthy poesy is full of virtue-breeding delightfulness, and void of no gift that ought to be in the noble name of learning; since
the blames laid against it are either false or feeble; since the cause why it is
not esteemed in England is the fault of poet-apes, not poets; since, lastly, our
tongue is most fit to honour poesy, and to be honoured by poesy; I conjure you
all that have had the evil luck to read this ink-wasting toy of mine, even in the
name of the Nine Muses, no more to scorn the sacred mysteries of poesy, no
more to laugh at the name of 'poets,' as though they were next inheritors to
fools, no more to jest at the reverent title of a 'rhymer'; but to believe, with
Aristotle,[71] that they were the ancient treasures of the Grecians' divinity; to
believe, with Bembus,[72] that they were first bringers-in of all civility; to believe,
with Scaliger, that no philosopher's precepts can sooner make you an honest
man than the reading of Virgil; [73] to believe, with Clauserus,[74] the translator
of Cornutus, that it pleased the heavenly Deity, by Hesiod and Homer, under
the veil of fables, to give us all knowledge, logic, rhetoric, philosophy, natural
and moral, and *Quid non?*,[75] to believe, with me, that there are many mysteries
contained in poetry, which of purpose were written darkly, lest by profane wits
it should be abused; [76] to believe, with Landin,[77] that they are so beloved of
the gods that whatsoever they write proceeds of a divine fury; lastly, to believe
themselves, when they tell you they will make you immortal by their verses.

[The work ends on a tone of light banter matching that of its opening.]

71. Aristotle doesn't exactly say this, only that the poets first gave an account of the gods
(*Metaphysics* 983 b); but the opinion was attributed to him by Renaissance authorities.
72. Pietro Bembo (1470–1547), humanist and defender of the vernacular, and prominent
character in Castiglione's *Il Cortegiano.*
73. Julius Caesar Scaliger (1484–1558), a great Renaissance polymath whose *Poetices
Libri Septem* (1561) Sidney knew well, argued for the supremacy of the epic and Virgil,
as well as for the unities in drama.
74. Conrad Clauser was the 16th-century translator of Lucius Annaeus Cornutus, a Roman
grammarian of the 1st century A.D., and made this quite ordinary claim in the Preface to
the translation.
75. "What not?"
76. Another common defense of obscurity in poetry, used, for example, of difficult allegory
and emblems.
77. Cristoforo Landino (1424–1504), Florentine humanist and author of a famous commentary on the *Aeneid* (in *Disputationes Camaldulenses,* 1475) from which the period
took much of its allegorization of Virgil, and Sidney this quotation.

FULKE GREVILLE, LORD BROOKE
1554–1628

"Servant to Queen Elizabeth, Councillor to King James, Friend to Sir Philip Sidney"—
the epitaph Greville wrote for himself points up the centers of importance for his
career. Born to a Warwickshire landowning family, he became Sidney's close friend
at school and shared his literary and political interests. He was profoundly shaken by
Sidney's death (he wrote a *Life of Sidney* not published until 1652). Working at court
as Treasurer of the Navy, then Chancellor of the Exchequer under James, he grew very
rich and was made a peer in 1621. Except for the unauthorized printing of a tragedy, his
works were all published posthumously in 1633. They include the remarkable collection of poems called *Caelica* ("heavenly one") written perhaps over a period of
twenty years ending, according to Geoffrey Bullough, Greville's modern editor, in
1600. Some of the poems are sonnets, some meditations and expositions in a strong
"plain style," but there is nothing of the Petrarchan sequence about them.

From Caelica

XLIV

The Golden Age was when the world was young,
Nature so rich, as earth did need no sowing,
Malice not known, the serpents had not stung,
Wit was but sweet affection's overflowing;

Desire was free, and beauty's first-begotten;
Beauty then neither net,° nor made by art,
Words out of thoughts brought forth, and not forgotten;
The laws were inward that did rule the heart.

The Brazen Age is now when earth is worn,
10   Beauty grown sick, Nature corrupt and nought,
Pleasure untimely dead as soon as born,
Both words and kindness° strangers to our thought:

If now this changing world do change her head,
Caelica, what have her new lords for to boast?
The old lord knows desire is poorly fed,
And sorrows not a wavering province lost,
    Since in the gilt age Saturn ruled alone,
    And in this painted, planets every one.°

                1633

C

In night when colours all to black are cast,
Distinction lost, or gone down with the light;

net caught in a net
kindness naturalness
Saturn . . . planets every one the Golden Age
was ruled by Saturn (see Golding's translation

of the passage from Ovid); now fate and
arbitrariness (symbolized by all the planets'
rule, or astrology) hold sway

The eye—a watch to inward senses placed,
Not seeing, yet still having power of sight—
Gives vain alarums° to the inward sense
Where fear, stirred up with witty tyranny,°
Confounds all powers, and through self-offence,
Doth forge and raise impossibility,
Such as in thick, depriving darknesses
10 Proper reflections of the error be,
And images of self-confusednesses
Which hurt imaginations only° see—
    And from this nothing seen, tells news of devils,
    Which but expressions be of inward evils.
                                    1633

Chorus Sacerdotum°

O wearisome condition of humanity!
Born under one law, to another bound:°
Vainly begot, and yet forbidden vanity,
Created sick, commanded to be sound:
What meaneth Nature by these diverse laws?
Passion and reason, self-division cause.
Is it the mark, or majesty of power
To make offences that it may forgive?
Nature herself doth her own self deflower,
10 To hate those errors she herself doth give;
For how should man think that, he may not do
If Nature did not fail, and punish too?
Tyrant to others, to herself unjust,
Only commands things difficult and hard,
Forbids us all things, which it knows is lust,
Makes easy pains, unpossible reward.
If Nature did not take delight in blood,
She would have made more easy ways to good.
We that are bound by vows, and by promotion,°
20 With pomp of holy sacrifice and rites,
To teach belief in good and still devotion,
To preach of Heaven's wonders, and delights:
Yet when each of us, in his own heart looks,
He finds the God there, far unlike his books.
1609   1633

alarums alarms
witty tyranny power of imagining
hurt imaginations only only hurt imaginations
Chorus Sacerdotum "chorus of priests," from
The Tragedy of Mustapha (1609). This famous
text was moved to the end of the play in
Greville's 1633 Works, following a previous
chorus attacking superstition, praising reason,
and affirming natural law.

Born under . . . bound natural law and God's
word
promotion ecclesiastical and political advancement, connected with "vows" or declarations
of faith. This attack on ritual and forms of
order, very Calvinist in tone, should be contrasted with the passage from Hooker on
Ceremony in Of the Laws of Ecclesiastical
Polity.

EDMUND SPENSER

1552–1599

Spenser was born in London in 1552, or soon after that date. Though connected with a noble family of Spencers, he was not himself richly born, and went to school as a "poore scholler." His school was the Merchant Taylors', then a new humanist foundation, and his headmaster was Richard Mulcaster, famous for his learning and his insistence that the boys study not only Latin, Greek, and Hebrew, but also English.

In 1569, assisted by a charitable grant, Spenser went to Pembroke Hall, Cambridge, a strongly Puritan college. He was a sizar, which meant that he had free meals in return for doing jobs about the college. His studies were in rhetoric, logic, and philosophy, and he would have had to take part in formal disputations. In the usual way he was graduated B.A. after four years and took the three-year M.A. course, including philosophy, astronomy, Greek, and mathematics. These studies were based on ancient authors—there was no formal study of modern languages.

Spenser had published poetry even before going to university—his translations of Petrarch and Du Bellay appeared in John Vandernoodt's *Theatre of Voluptuous Worldlings* in 1569. But the learning that was considered essential to poetry—Harvey was to insist that the heroic poet needed to be "a curious and universal scholar"— Cambridge provided, together with the warm ecclesiastical controversy that left its mark on his poetry, especially *The Shepheardes Calender*. His poetic interests were also developed by his friendship with Gabriel Harvey, a Fellow of the College. Harvey was a farmer's son, and at once learned and likable, pedantic and amusing. Later he became famous for his acrimonious pamphleteering exchanges with Thomas Nashe. At this time he shared with Spenser an interest in English versification, and wanted to introduce into English the quantitative prosody of Latin. His exchange of letters with Spenser on this point was published in 1580. Spenser experimented with quantitative meters, and sent them to Harvey with a request for fuller instruction, adding that Sidney and others were also trying them out. Little came of this, but Harvey happened in replying to mention some works by Spenser, whether complete, in progress, or projected; there seems to have been a large body of work, virtually all of which has perished. Harvey remarked that he preferred Spenser's Nine Comedies to a part of *The Faerie Queene* then in existence. He hoped Spenser would give up the attempt to write like Ariosto, regretting that he would not write prophetic and visionary poetry on the lines of St. John's Revelation. This indicates that what Harvey saw was not a part of Book I, which is largely based on Revelation, but something now embedded in Books III or IV. Replying, Spenser speaks of the "Areopagus." This group consisted of himself, Sidney, and Dyer, and was dedicated to the reform of English poetry; but he soon abandoned the attempt to introduce classical meter. Indeed he had already written the *Calender*, which, however experimental in language and techniques, is in the native tradition.

After being graduated M.A. in 1576, Spenser visited his noble kinsmen in Lancashire, and seems to have met Rosalind, a girl whom Harvey teases him about, and who figures in the *Calender* and even, many years later, in *Colin Clouts Come Home Againe*. In 1577 he probably made his first trip to Ireland, and returned to enter the service of the powerful Earl of Leicester—hence his acquaintance with Leicester's nephew Philip Sidney. He married Machabyas Childe in 1579, the year of the *Calender*, which he dedicated to Sidney. Sidney admired it, with reservations concerning the "old rustic language," which he expressed in his *Defence of Poesie*.

Now familiar with the court, Spenser began a bold satire, *Mother Hubberds Tale*, a beast fable with strong political implications—he was of the party which disliked Lord Burleigh and opposed the projected marriage of the Queen to the Duc d'Alençon. In 1580 he became secretary to Lord Grey de Wilton, the new Lord Deputy of Ireland; and apart from visits to London he spent the rest of his life in that country. Elizabeth's handling of the Irish problem is one of the least glorious aspects of her reign. Ireland was virtually a colony, harshly exploited by the English; and Spenser was as colonialist as the rest of them. The new men, coming in to serve their own interests, got on neither with the Catholic poor nor the old Anglo-Irish ruling class; they tried to impose Protestantism, English justice, and the kind of agriculture profitable to themselves on a nation that wanted none of them. The ensuing uprisings Lord Grey suppressed with great severity, and Spenser approved of this, as Book V of *The Fairie Queene* and, more explicitly, his prose work, *A Vewe of the Present State of Ireland*, written in 1596, show. He accompanied Grey on military expeditions intended to pacify the Irish, and may well have seen him in action as Justice, with his troops in the role of Talus (the impersonal agent of Justice in Book V). But Grey felt he had inadequate support in London, and resigned, amid much ill-feeling and backbiting, in 1582. Spenser stayed on, at first in Dublin, then, from 1588, on the 3000-acre estate he had acquired at Kilcolman, adjacent to the larger estate of Ralegh.

Spenser, though much involved with his job, made a literary friend in Lodowick Bryskett, another civil servant, and in Bryskett's book, *A Discourse of Civil Life*, published in 1606, we hear of a conversation between Spenser, Bryskett, and others, in which Spenser declines to discourse on moral philosophy because he has in hand a poem on that very subject, "in *heroical verse* under the title of a *Faerie Queene* . . . assigning to every vertue a Knight to be the patron and defender of the same." Even if Bryskett is using hindsight here, it would seem that Spenser in Dublin had decided on the general scheme and was writing the poem.

In 1589 his neighbor Ralegh induced Spenser to visit London with him, and to bring along the first three books of the big poem. The Queen liked them, and awarded him a pension of £50, quite a good sum at the time, though he was disappointed, as we see from *Colin Clout* and from the Proem to Book IV. They were published in 1590, and Spenser followed up their success by publishing several poems in the following year, among them the mythological fable *Muiopotmos*, the satire *Mother Hubberds Tale*, and *Daphnaida*, an elegy.

Back in Ireland, he was involved in difficult law-suits, but remained very productive. If the attribution is correct, he translated the pseudo-Platonic dialogue *Axiochus*, published in 1592. He courted and in 1594 married Elizabeth Boyle, and the publication of *Amoretti* (the sonnet sequence of about 1591–94) and the marriage poem *Epithalamion* followed in 1595. That year also saw the publication of *Colin Clout* and *Astrophell*, his elegy for Sidney. Meanwhile he was finishing Books IV, V, and VI of *The Faerie Queene*, which were published, together with the earlier books, in 1596. His interest in contemporary affairs was never greater than in these later Irish years, when he inserted very late into *The Faerie Queene* (V.xi) a piece of political allegory involving the Earl of Essex and Henry IV of France, and wrote the *Vewe*. In 1596 James VI of Scotland, who was to succeed Elizabeth in 1603, demanded Spenser's punishment for libeling his mother, Mary Queen of Scots, in the portrait of Duessa before

Mercilla (V.ix). No action was taken. Other works of this period were the *Fowre Hymnes* and *Prothalamion,* written for the double marriage of the daughters of the Earl of Worcester, a friend of Essex.

The continuation of *The Faerie Queen* brought Spenser no reward from the Queen, and after a spell in London he went back to Ireland, becoming Sheriff of Cork in 1598. The much-feared rebellion of Tyrone, who was later to help discredit Essex himself, broke out in 1598; Kilcolman was sacked, and Spenser fled to Cork and then to London. There, on January 6, 1599, he died, probably not, as Jonson said, "for lack of bread," but certainly much reduced. Essex paid for his funeral in Westminister Abbey, and poets threw elegies into his grave, near Chaucer's. The Queen ordered him a monument, but it was not erected; the Countess of Dorset provided one in 1620. It got Spenser's dates wrong, but contained the famous eulogy, "The Prince of Poets in His Tyme." It was restored in marble in 1778, with the dates corrected, and is still in the Abbey.

It is not easy to form a definite view of the personality of Spenser. He was scholarly in a poet's way; he was ambitious, and had, till the final debacle, a pretty successful worldly career. He must have been exceptionally industrious, combining diligence in his job with diligence in poetry, from which he sought material reward as well as glory. He was a literary adventurer, seeking in the past models for entirely original modern achievements, much as the voyagers did. He, like some of his poetry, constituted a reconciliation of opposites. His views on Ireland seem cruel, yet he was gentle. He had strong opinions on the subjection of women, as Book V shows, yet he broke off the composition of his major work to write *Epithalamion,* and most of his lifework is an act of worship offered to a woman. He was oppressed by signs of returning chaos in the world, but celebrated love as an inexhaustible source of beauty and order. He valued peace and courtesy, yet supported the war party. These real and apparent oppositions are characteristic of his great poem, and perhaps also of his personality.

The text of Spenser used here is that of J. C. Smith and E. de Selincourt in the Oxford Standard Authors. Punctuation, capitalization, and use of italic are unchanged, but *u* and *v* have been changed to conform to modern usage, and *j* replaces *i* in such words as *joy.*

The Shepheardes Calender

This work was at once recognized as a great landmark in the development of a national poetry, and it retains its historical importance in times when it is no longer especially to our taste. Spenser designed it on the grand scale. There is an eclogue for each month, starting (unusually, since the year was normally taken to begin in March) with January. E.K., the unidentified commentator (perhaps Gabriel Harvey) who provides miscellaneous humanist glosses to the work, divides the Eclogues into three groups, Plaintive, Recreative, Moral. The classification is occasionally hard to follow, but we can agree that the second, fifth, seventh, ninth, and tenth are Moral (and "mixed with some satirical bitterness"). There is some hint of a narrative. Colin Clout is Spenser, Hobbinol is Harvey, and Rosalind seems to have been a real person.

Traditionally the pastoral eclogue was allegorical, aiming, as Puttenham says in his *Art of English Poesy* (1589), "under the veil of homely persons, and in rude speeches, to insinuate and glance at greater matters." So that whether or no in Rosalind and Dido Spenser "shadows" Elizabeth, the Lobbin of the November Eclogue, certainly seems to be the Earl of Leicester; and in the ecclesiastical allegory, a special attribute of the Renaissance pastoral tradition, contemporary bishops are more or less transparently displayed. (Priests being pastors, poems about shepherds were a convenient way of complaining about their corruption, as Milton did in *Lycidas*.) So Spenser has a lot to say about the religious issues of the time, generally from the viewpoint of a moderate Anglicanism.

The true importance of the work was, however, poetic. The *Calender* was as original in its day as *The Waste Land* (a poem it also resembles in having a not altogether helpful commentary). Its language is strange, using many archaic words (some of which have subsequently returned to use); and this not only because of the custom that pastoral uses a rustic or "Doric" dialect, but also in an attempt to revive Chaucerian English, as, in France, the group of poets called the Pléiade had revived obsolete French words. Moreover, Spenser, like Sidney in the *Arcadia,* used a great variety of meters and stanzas; he did not carry on with those classical quantitative meters he had tried out earlier with Harvey, but instead developed the possibilities of the native manner, in homage to the dedicatee, Sidney (who liked the work but not the archaic diction).

For all its novelty, the *Calender* claims its inheritance from a long tradition, going back to the Alexandria of Theocritus, the Rome of Virgil, the Italy of Mantuan (1448–1516), and the France of Marot (1497–1544). The Tenth (October) Eclogue looks back to Virgil, who established a model for other poets by writing eclogues before rising to epic; it laments the condition of English poetry, praises its ideal dignity, and ends once again in pastoral retirement.

From The Shepheardes Calender

October°
Ægloga decima°

Argument

In Cuddie° is set out the perfecte paterne of a Poete, whiche finding no main-tenaunce of his state and studies, complayneth of the contempte of Poetrie, and the causes thereof: Specially having bene in all ages, and even amongst the most barbarous alwayes of singular accounpt and honor, and being indede so worthy and commendable an arte: or rather no arte, but a divine gift and heavenly

October The *Calender* is augmented by lengthy notes, attributed to E.K.—perhaps Gabriel Harvey, perhaps Edmund Kirke, perhaps Spenser himself, though he occasionally takes issue with the poem. This humanistic commentary, rhetorical, linguistic, mythological, suited the Renaissance pastoral, a learned kind; but there seems no need to reprint it in full here. Some of E.K.'s glosses are therefore incorporated in the notes of the present edition, and marked E.K. Others are omitted.
Ægloga decima Tenth Eclogue. E.K. says it

is an imitation of the sixteenth idyll of Theocritus, "wherein he reproved the Tyranne Hiero of Syracuse for his nigardise towarde Poetes . . . The style hereof as also that in Theocritus, is more loftye then the rest, and applyed to the heighte of Poeticall witte."
Cuddie E.K. doubts "whether by Cuddie be specified the authour selfe, or some other." **One** suggestion is the court poet Dyer, friend of Sidney. Cuddie can hardly be Spenser, to whom (as Colin) he defers in l. 88.

instinct not to bee gotten by laboure and learning, but adorned with both: and poured into the witte by a certaine ἐνθουσιασμός.° and celestiall inspiration, as the Author hereof els where at large discourseth, in his booke called the English Poete,° which booke being lately come to my hands, I mynde also by Gods grace upon further advisement to publish.

PIERCE

Cuddie, for shame hold up thy heavye head,
And let us cast with what delight to chace,
And weary thys long lingring *Phœbus* race.°
Whilome‸ thou wont the shepheards laddes to leade,   *formerly*
In rymes, in riddles, and in bydding base:°
Now they in thee, and thou in sleepe art dead.

CUDDIE

Piers, I have pypèd erst‸ so long with payne,   *lately*
That all mine Oten reedes° bene rent and wore:
And my poore Muse hath spent her sparèd‸ store,   *small*
10   Yet little good hath got, and much lesse gayne.
Such pleasaunce makes the Grashopper so poore,
And ligge so layd,° when Winter doth her straine.

The dapper° ditties, that I wont devise,
To feede youthes fancie, and the flocking fry,°
Delighten much: what I the bett for thy‸?   *as a result*
They han the pleasure, I a sclender prise.
I beate the bush, the byrds to them doe flye.
What good thereof to Cuddie can arise?

PIRES°

Cuddie, the prayse is better, then‸ the price,   *than*
20   The glory eke‸ much greater then the gayne: *also*
O what an honor is it, to restraine
The lust of lawlesse youth with good advice:°
Or pricke‸ them forth with pleasaunce of thy vaine,   *urge*
Whereto thou list their traynèd willes entice.   *snared*

Soone as thou gynst to sette thy notes in frame,
O how the rurall routes‸ to thee doe cleave: *crowds*
Seemeth thou dost their soule of sence bereave,°

ενθουσιασμος. *enthousiasmos,* the divine fury that transports the poet beyond himself
the English Poete lost treatise by Spenser
weary . . . race pass the time
bydding base country game
Oten reedes "Avena" (E.K.), the Latin for stalks, used by Virgil to mean the shepherd's pipe
ligge so layd "lye so faynt and unlustye" (E.K.), referring to the fable of the ant and the grasshopper
dapper "pretye" (E.K.)
fry "is a bold Metaphore, forced from the spawning fishes. For the multitude of young fish be called the frye" (E.K.).
Pires "Piers" is the normal form, used hereafter.
restraine . . . advice E.K. relates this to Plato, *Laws* 1, which speaks of poets inspiring young people—ravishing them with delight—and also, in a less heroic vein, amusing them with love poems and satires.
soule . . . bereave E.K. illustrates this with the story of how the musician Timotheus worked on the passions of Alexander, and by recalling that Plato advised against a certain musical mode as likely to enervate children. Cf. Dryden, *Alexander's Feast.*

All° as the shepheard,° that did fetch his dame   *just*
From *Plutoes* balefull bowre withouten leave:
His musicks might the hellish hound° did tame.

> **CUDDIE**
>
> So praysen babes the Peacoks spotted traine,
> And wondren at bright *Argus*° blazing eye:
> But who rewards him ere the more for thy?
> Or feedes him once the fuller by a graine?
> Sike° prayse is smoke, that sheddeth in the skye,   *such*
> Sike words bene wynd, and wasten soone in vayne.

> **PIERS**
>
> Abandon then the base and viler clowne,°   *rustic*
> Lyft up thy selfe out of the lowly dust:
> And sing of bloody Mars, of wars, of giusts,°   *jousts*
> Turne thee to those, that weld° the awful crowne.   *wield*
> To doubted Knights, whose woundlesse armour° rusts,
> And helmes unbruzèd wexen dayly browne.

> There may thy Muse display° her fluttryng wing,
> And stretch her selfe at large from East to West:
> Whither thou list in fayre *Elisa* rest,
> Or if thee please in bigger notes to sing,
> Advaunce the worthy° whome shee loveth best,
> That first the white beare to the stake did bring.

> And when the stubborne stroke of stronger stounds,°   *blows*
> Has somewhat slackt the tenor of thy string:
> Of love and lustihead tho° mayst thou sing,   *then*
> And carrol lowde, and leade the Myllers rownde,°
> All° were *Elisa* one of thilke same ring.   *Although*
> So mought our *Cuddies* name to Heaven sownde.

> **CUDDIE**
>
> Indeede the Romish *Tityrus,*° I heare,
> Through his *Mecænas* left his Oaten reede,
> Whereon° he earst° had taught his flocks to feede,   *formerly*
> And laboured lands to yield the timely eare,°

---

shepheard "Orpheus: of whom it is sayd, that by his excellent skil in Musick and Poetry, he recovered his wife Eurydice from hell" (E.K.).
hound Cerberus, three-headed watchdog of hell
Argus Juno set Argus, who had a hundred eyes, to watch over Jupiter's girl Io, but Mercury played him asleep with music, and killed him. Juno transferred his eyes to the tail of her bird, the peacock. "For those coloured spots indeede resemble eyes" (E.K.).
woundlesse armour "unwounded in warre, do rust through long peace" (E.K.).
display E.K. calls this "a poeticall metaphor," meaning that Queen Elizabeth affords him opportunity for "more Heroicall argument" either in herself or in her nobles.

the worthy "he meaneth . . . the Erle of Leycester" (E.K.); Leicester's arms bore a bear and a ragged (knotty) staff
Myllers rownde "a kind of daunce" (E.K.)
Tityrus "wel knowen to be Virgile, who by Maecenas means was brought into the favour of the Emperor Augustus, and by him moved to write in loftier kinde, then he had erst doen" (E.K.).
Whereon " . . . the three severall workes of Virgile [are] intended. For in teaching his flocks to feede, is meant his Aeglogues. In labouring of lands, is hys Bucoliques. In singing of wars and deadly dreade, is his divine Aeneis figured" (E.K.).
laboured . . . eare farmed

And eft⟩ did sing of warres and deadly drede,   *afterwards*
60   So as⟩ the Heavens did quake his verse to here.   *so well that*

But ah *Mecænas* is yclad in claye,
And great *Augustus* long ygoe is dead:
And all the worthies liggen⟩ wrapt in leade,   *lie*
That matter made for Poets on to play:
For ever, who in derring doe° were dreade,
The loftie verse of hem⟩ was loved aye.°   *about them*

But after° vertue gan for age to stoupe,
And mighty manhode brought a bedde of ease.
The vaunting Poets found nought worth a pease,⟩   *pea*
70   To put in preace⟩ among the learnèd troupe.   *crowd in*
Tho gan the streames of flowing wittes to cease,
And sonnebright honour pend in shamefull coupe.°

And if that any buddes of Poesie,
Yet of the old stocke gan to shoote agayne:
Or it mens follies mote be forst to fayne,°
And rolle with rest in rymes of rybaudrye:
Or as it sprong, it wither must agayne:
Tom Piper makes us better melodie.°

PIERS

O pierlesse Poesye, where is then thy place?
80   If nor in Princes pallace thou doe sitt:
(And yet is Princes pallace the most fitt)
Ne brest of baser birth doth thee embrace.
Then make thee winges of thine aspyring wit,
And, whence thou camst, flye backe to heaven apace.

CUDDIE

Ah *Percy* it is all to weake and wanne,
So high to sore, and make so large a flight:
Her peecèd pyneons° bene not so in plight,
For *Colin* fittes° such famous flight to scanne:
He, were he not with love so ill bedight,
90   Would mount as high, and sing as soote⟩ as Swanne.°   *sweetly*

PIERS

Ah fon,⟩ for love does teach him climbe so hie,   *fool*
And lyftes him up out of the loathsome myre:
Such immortall mirrhor,° as he doth admire,

in derring doe "in manhoode and chevalrie"
(E.K.)
For ever . . . aye E.K. repeats the Renaissance
commonplace that poets immortalize great men.
But after "he sheweth the cause of contempt of
poetry to be idlenesse and basenesse of mynd"
(E.K.)
pend . . . coupe "shut up in slouth, as in a
coope or cage" (E.K.)
follies . . . fayne go in for satire or comedy
Tom . . . melodie "An ironicall Sarcasmus,
spoken in derision of these rude wits, whych
make more account of a ryming rybaud, then

of skill grounded upon learning and judgment"
(E.K.); Tom Piper is the name for the rustic
musician who plays for morris dancing.
peecèd pyneons "unperfect skil" (E.K.); repaired wings (the wings having been impaired,
the hawk cannot fly well)
For . . . fittes it is more suitable for Colin
(Spenser)
soote . . . Swanne E.K. explains that the swan
sings only at death, but then "most pleasantly."
mirrhor "Beauty, which is an excellent object
of politicall spirites" (E.K.)

Would rayse ones mynd above the starry skie.
And cause a caytive corage° to aspire,
For lofty love doth loath a lowly eye.°

      CUDDIE

All otherwise the state of Poet stands,
For lordly love is such a Tyranne fell:
That where he rules, all power he doth expell.
100 The vaunted verse a vacant head demaundes,
Ne wont with crabbèd care the Muses dwell.
Unwisely weaves, that takes two webbes in hand.

Who ever casts to compasse weightye prise,
And thinks to throwe out thondring words of threate:
Let powre in lavish cups and thriftie bitts of meate,°
For *Bacchus* fruite is frend to *Phœbus* wise.
And when with Wine the braine begins to sweate,
The nombers flowe as fast as spring doth ryse.

Thou kenst not *Percie* howe the ryme should rage.
110 O if my temples were distaind⟩ with wine,°   *stained*
And girt in girlonds of wild Yvie twine,°
How I could reare the Muse on stately stage,
And teache her tread aloft in bus-kin° fine,
With queint *Bellona*° in her equipage.

But ah my corage cooles ere it be warme,
For thy,⟩ content us in thys humble shade: *wherefore*
Where no such troublous tydes⟩ han us assayde,   *opportunities*
Here we our slender pipes may safely charme.°

      PIERS

And when my Gates shall han their bellies layd:°
120 *Cuddie* shall have a Kidde to store his farme.

      Cuddies Embleme.°
      Agitante calescimus illo, &c.°
          1579

a . . . corage "a base and abject minde" (E.K.)
lofty . . . eye E.K. complains of the alliterative l's, saying that "this playing with the letter" is a fault in English as well as Latin, and labeling it *cacozelon.*
lavish . . . meate lots of wine and not much food
O if . . . wine "He seemeth here to be ravished with a poetical furie. For . . . the numbers rise so ful, and the verse groweth so big, that it seemeth he hath forgot the meanenesse of shepheards state and stile" (E.K., remembering that decorum required pastoral to keep to the low style, though allowing for exceptions)
wild . . . twine "for it is dedicated to Bacchus and therefore it is sayd that the Maenades (that is Bacchus franticke priestes) used in their sacrifice to carry Thyrsos, which were pointed staves or Javelins, wrapped about with ivie" (E.K.)

bus-kin the high boot worn in tragedy (E.K. explains at length)
queint Bellona "strange Bellona; the goddess of battaile" (E.K., who explains that she is Pallas, born fully armed from the head of Jupiter and strange for that and other reasons)
charme "temper and order" (E.K.), but also a word used of birdsong as late as Milton (see *Paradise Lost* IV.642)
their . . . layd dropped their young
Embleme motto
Agitante . . . &c. "Hereby is meant, as also in the whole course of this Aeglogue, that Poetry is a divine instinct and unnatural rage passing the reach of comen reason . . ." (E.K.). The quotation from Ovid, *Fasti* VI.5, *est deus in nobis, agitante calescimus illo*— "there is a god in us, his stirring warms us"— crops up repeatedly in Renaissance discussion of poetic inspiration.

Colin Clouts Come Home Againe

This pastoral has an autobiographical content. Published in 1595, it was written four years earlier, when Spenser returned to Ireland after the visit to London which resulted in the publication of the first three books of *The Faerie Queene*. Spenser (Colin) tells his shepherd friends, including Hobbinol, about the journey and his visit to Cynthia's court. He and The Shepherd of the Ocean (Ralegh) read their poems to each other, and Colin waited on the Queen. He describes the voyage, and the strange and beautiful country beyond the sea, where the arts are honored. Cynthia, who approved of Colin's "piping" (she gave Spenser £50), has a number of poets attending her, and is bountiful. But he leaves the court because, despite the presence of good men (such as Lobbin-Leicester), it is a place of wicked ambition. In reply to a question as to whether love exists at court as well as in the country, Colin says that at court it is blasphemed; commended for his insight into its true nature, he speaks the lines that follow. He remembers his love for Rosalind; then they fold their sheep and rest.

Colin Clout abandons the experimental diction of the *Calender*, being, as pastoral ought to be, in the "low" style (see *Decorum* in the Glossary) yet capable of eloquence. The lines here given provide a valuable account (in less space than the *Fowre Hymnes*) of Platonic love doctrine. Love is the power that binds and moves the whole world. These doctrines are ancient, but had been refurbished and sophisticated in the Renaissance. Here love is the heavenly power that made the world, resolved the contraries of chaos (hot and cold, moist and dry, etc.), ordered the elements, and arranged a creative coincidence of opposites, of which generative love is an example. Thus the earth was filled with animal life. But men, having reason, are guided not merely by animal passion but by a desire for beauty; and those who dishonor this ennobling love are condemned and outlawed by the god.

From Colin Clouts Come Home Againe

Of loves perfection perfectly to speake,
Or of his nature rightly to define,
Indeed (said *Colin*) passeth reasons reach,
And needs his priest t'expresse his powre divine.
For long before the world he was y'bore⸴   *born*
840 And bred above in *Venus* bosome deare:
For by his powre the world was made of yore,
And all that therein wondrous doth appeare.
For how should else things so far from attone⸴   *agreement*
And so great enemies as of⸴ them bee,   *among*
Be ever drawne together into one,
And taught in such accordance⸴ to agree?   *harmony*
Through him the cold began to covet heat,
And water fire; the light to mount on hie,
And th'heavie downe to peize;⸴ the hungry t'eat   *press down*
850 And voydnesse to seeke full satietie.
So being former foes, they wexèd⸴ friends,   *grow to be*

And gan by litle learne to love each other:
So being knit, they brought forth other kynds
Out of the fruitfull wombe of their great mother.
Then first gan heaven out of darknesse dread
For to appeare, and brought forth chearfull day:
Next gan the earth to shew her naked head,
Out of deep waters which her drownd alway.
And shortly after, everie living wight⸥   *creature*
860   Crept forth like wormes out of her slimie nature,
Soone as on them the Suns life giving light,
Had powred kindly⸥ heat and formall feature,⸥   *natural / regular shape*
Thenceforth they gan each one his like to love,
And like himselfe desire for to beget,
The Lyon chose his mate, the Turtle Dove
Her deare, the Dolphine his owne Dolphinet:
But man that had the sparke of reasons might,
More then the rest to rule his passiòn,
Chose for his love the fairest in his sight.
870   Like as himselfe was fairest by creatiòn.
For beautie is the bayt which with delight
Doth man allure, for to enlarge his kynd,
Beautie the burning lamp of heavens light,
Darting her beames into each feeble mynd:
Against whose powre, nor God nor man can fynd,
Defence, ne⸥ ward⸥ the daunger of the wound,   *nor / protect himself against*
But being hurt, seeke to be medicynd
Of her that first did stir that mortall stownd.⸥   *stroke*
Then do they cry and call to love apace,
880   With praiers lowd importuning the skie,
Whence he them heares, and when he list⸥ shew grace,   *wishes to*
Does graunt them grace that otherwise would die.
So love is Lord of all the world by right,
And rules the creatures by his powrfull saw:⸥   *command*
All being made the vassalls of his might,
Through secret sence which therto doth them draw.
Thus ought all lovers of their lord to deeme:
And with chaste heart to honor him alway:
But who so else doth otherwise esteeme,
890   Are outlawes, and his lore do disobay.
For their desire is base, and doth not merit,
The name of love, but of disloyall lust:
Ne amongst true lovers they shall place inherit,
But as Exuls⸥ out of his court be thrust.   *exiles*

.   .   .

1595

The Faerie Queene

Heroic poetry, which in the Renaissance was taken by most commentators to be the highest kind, was necessarily associated with the growth of nationalist feelings, since it attempted to achieve in the vernacular what Virgil had done for the Roman empire in Latin. This explains Spenser's interest not only in the ancient models but also in modern Italian and French poetry—he would learn what he could from renaissances that flowered earlier than the English. But it also explains why *The Faerie Queene*, for all its dreamy Romance landscape and narrative, is very much a poem of its moment. He was celebrating national or imperial power, and did so not only by placing its origins in a fictive British past but by justifying modern policies, ecclesiastical, political, and military. He had to make his poem relevant to the glories, real and imaginary, of the reign he chose to represent as climactic in history; but he could not ignore the dark side of the picture.

The Acts of Supremacy and Uniformity of 1559 gave the country a foundation of peace and order but alienated recusants. The loss of Calais in 1558 marked the end of English power in France; henceforth England would be more narrowly nationalistic, and its church, with the Queen at its head, reflected this development. It became the chief Protestant power and engaged in a long and mostly cold war with Spain, the chief Catholic power. Meanwhile the cities grew larger and the great men grew greater, but the reign of Elizabeth ended with years that were glorious only in some ways; they were also melancholy, anxious, and beset by social and economic problems.

Elizabeth was a great but difficult woman. Her failure to marry and produce an heir meant that over the long period when this was no longer even a possibility her reign was under threat of the Catholic Stuart claims, represented in life by Mary Queen of Scots, and in Spenser's poem by Duessa. Mary was beheaded in 1587, the Armada defeated in 1588; but the succeeding thirteen years continued to be anxious, and the last of the favorites, Essex, was executed in 1601 for rebelliously declaring his interest in the succession of Mary's son, James VI of Scotland.

The celebration of the Virgin Queen, which Spenser and others carried to such heights, was in origin a way of making the best of a bad situation, and was intimately, though not obviously, related to foreign and ecclesiastical policy, which would arguably have been much easier if the Queen had lost her virginity, since the disputed succession made all the problems more acute. The religious situation was political, and vice versa. When Elizabeth succeeded to the throne in 1558, the country had just lived through her father's dispute with Rome, the brief period of triumphant Protestantism under Edward VI, and the Catholic reaction under Mary. Elizabeth was by no means an extreme Protestant, and the settlement of 1559 was a compromise, which for years pleased neither Protestant nor Catholic. The church now claimed, in fact, to be both—a Catholic church purged by Protestant action, with the Queen as its governor. Conformity was required by law. The clergy had mostly changed doctrines with each new reign; they were undistinguished, often venal, and easily exploited by the great laymen who had made fortunes out of the dissolution of the monasteries. The new (or, as propaganda said, very old) church was in poor condition. It was rescued by a brilliant intellectual enterprise: Archbishop Jewel's apology for the church, Archbishop Parker's history of it, and Hooker's justification of its middle way in broad historical and theological terms (see *Of the Laws of Ecclesiastical Polity* below) created a myth which Spenser and others accepted. The English church was older than Rome, having been founded soon after the Crucifixion by Joseph of Arimathaea, and it was ruled by an empress who inherited the powers of Constantine, the emperor who Christianized the Roman empire. So, from the doctrinal confusion and worldly corruption he commented on in the *Calender*, Spenser moved on to the heroic situation of a nation in all respects the heir of Rome, a church which had restored primitive purity in an apocalyptic manner, and an empress who concentrated the universal empire in her reign over one people. Rejecting both the extremes, the Catholic enemy who threatened both inside and outside England, and the Puritanism he had known at Cambridge, with its mistrust of bishops and the Prayer Book, Spenser found himself in a position to write an Anglican epic. The enemy therein is, primarily, Catholicism, the usurping papacy (antichrist); in his myth they are destroyers of paradise, types of the perfidy and duplicity which beset fallen humanity. Truth is England, Falsehood Rome.

This is stated most clearly in Book I. But Spenser never calls the British restoration of Truth perfect. And the strength of the whole poem arises in part from his reconciling incompatible feelings and attitudes to his subject. The court is the fount of courtesy, but also corrupt. The world which has seen the restoration of the true church is also evil and decaying. A polarity of light and dark is essential to his mind. He delights in the changing forms and colors of life, while allowing that movement belongs to time, not eternity, and color to earth, not heaven. He celebrates fertility and generation, but allows that it is inseparable from "fleshly slime" (III.vi.3). Life is not only delightful, it is also a trial or initiation, a total temptation. Time, which makes the world changeable and delightful to the senses, is the drudge of eternity, and our main business is with that.

Whatever his stated subject, Spenser confronts a virtue with its opposites, dark with light; he invents myth after myth to celebrate opposites, and develops his great technical variety in order to accommodate them. The very length of the poem, its diffuseness, are functions of his need to make contraries meet in one: past and present, concord and discord, good and evil, time and eternity, light and dark. The inclusiveness of the poem is its most remarkable virtue. It lacks the gravity of Virgil, the speed and power of Ariosto, but as a "continued allegory" it has no rival. Spenser aims, as heroic poets were supposed to, at educating a gentleman in the virtues. But in doing so he used his allegorical powers to much greater effect than Ariosto and Tasso, even with all the help they got from their commentators, had wanted or been able to do. Sometimes he is simple, as in the House of Alma or the House of Holiness. Sometimes the allegory is thin, sometimes frankly popular, as in parts of the First Book, which are little different in design from the popular allegories of Lord Mayors' shows or celebrations of the Queen's birthday, or her reception at some country house. The symbolism of the First Book is especially popular; but Spenser is capable of deepening it until it remembles the learned allegory of Ben Jonson in his masques, so that Spenser is both "homely, churchwardenly," as C. S. Lewis calls him, and a profound philosophical allegorist, with elaborate allegorical programs that have still not been worked out.

The allegory, then, is multiform, sometimes thin, sometimes thick, always an aspect of a syncretic myth-making operation which for Spenser was the poet's way to tell the truth about everything—and that means about the state of affairs in the England of the 1580's and 1590's as well as in the whole frame of the world. Hence the blend, strange to us, of topicality and ethical generality; hence the sudden moves from shallow to very deep water. In a sense it could be said that this habitual allegorizing at one level or another makes Spenser more "medieval" than, say, Tasso; if so, the issue is not very important. The England of the Renaissance did retain, in spite of its efforts to be modern and humanist, much of the medieval spirit, and Chaucer was as important to Spenser as any other poet. But there was nevertheless a true modernism in Spenser's experimental, past-rifling methods. An employment of every resource—Ovidian my-thologizing, heroic convention, symbolism and allegory of whatever kind—to speak about the world as it is, about deep problems which, rightly expressed, are reflected in the movements from day to day of politicians and religious leaders, is in that sense modern.

A poem, to do all that, must have readers who understand its peculiar languages and its ways of achieving flexibility. Spenser's language is not modern; it corresponds to his device of thrusting all the action back into a remote past, where connections are easier to make, life being simpler. Thus did the Elizabethans restore in show and tournament the old language and symbolism of chivalry. The archaism of *The Faerie Queene* increases its range of meaning; the vagueness of its fairyland allows Spenser to fluctuate, as in a myth or a dream, between vagueness and sharp definition at will. The reader must collaborate: *The Faerie Queene* is a world and a great one to all who learn to move in it.

A Letter of the Authors

Spenser returned to London with Ralegh in 1589–90, and presumably wrote this Letter specially for the publication of Books I through III in 1590. Perhaps he did so in haste, for, valuable as it is, it contains some puzzles and inaccuracies. The account of Book II seems to conflict with the facts of the poem. The reference to "the twelve private morall vertues, as Aristotle hath devised" and again to Magnificence and "the xii other vertues" has long been debated. Is it twelve or thirteen? In any case Aristotle's *Nicomachean Ethics* has no such list of virtues; and furthermore the six Spenser actually treated—seven if one counts Constancy—do not match Aristotle; for example, Temperance is an Aristotelian virtue but Holiness is not. Perhaps the mistake about Book II arose from haste—in setting down the part of Guyon's story which precedes the narrative as we have it, he neglected to make the two exactly consistent. As to the virtues, he may have been thinking more loosely than at first appears when he spoke of using Aristotle's *Ethics*—or some of the many Christianizing commentaries on the book—as a scheme from which he could vary.

These difficulties do not cancel the great value of the Letter. Here is a summary of its argument: 1. mode of the work: allegory; 2. moral intention; justification of subject and method; 3. defense of allegorical poetry as morally beneficial ("ensample" better than "rule"); 4. "general intention" of portrait of Arthur and of the Faerie Queene and other "shadowings" of Elizabeth; 5. the other knights of the first three books; 6. difference between poetry and historiography—stories of Books I through III as they would be in a chronicle rather than a poem; 7. "other adventures inter-medled"; 8. conclusion: the Letter tries to establish the general design of a poem that might without this explanation seem "tedious and confused."

The Letter, in its general claims, is in the tradition of Renaissance apologias for epic poetry; see Sidney's remarks in the *Defence*. The object is to fashion gentlemen; moral precepts are easier to swallow if the pill is coated. The choice of Arthur fits the rule that the hero should be both great and of a remote time (more, he was an official ancestor of the Tudors and the last emperor of Britain before them; thus he was a hero of the type used by Virgil and the Italian heroic poets of the sixteenth century). Homer and, more importantly, Virgil provide models; Ariosto and Tasso maintained and modified their tradition in modern times; to cover all the ground he would need twenty-four books.

Teaching "by ensample," Spenser needs an exemplary hero. His Arthur, however, cannot be to Elizabeth what Aeneas was to Augustus, and the sex of his monarch led him into various "dark conceits." Arthur is Magnificence, which includes all the other virtues. Elizabeth is first the Faerie Queene, Glory, for which gentlemen should strive; secondly, "a most vertuous and beautifull Lady." The division reflects her two "persons," political and natural (Gloriana and Belphoebe), a division that goes deep in English constitutional theory. She is also present in other female characters. As for the knights, they have a virtue apiece; Spenser found some difficulty in working Arthur into a scheme already so elaborate.

In the "historiographical" rendering, Spenser allows only an occasional hint of allegorical intention—as when he speaks of Red Cross's armour as that of the soldier of Christ (*miles Christi,* Ephesians 6). He also states that some episodes are "accidents" rather than "intendments"—scenes and narratives that developed along the way without belonging to the master plan; but this does not mean that they have no allegorical meanings; Britomart, Marinell and Florimell, and Belphoebe certainly have, and so do "many the like."

Everybody wishes Spenser had said a bit more, and said it more clearly, in this Letter; but it is the first commentary ever written on the poem, and comes from the best-informed commentator; so it is certainly worth study.

A Letter of the Authors

expounding his *whole intention in the course of this worke: which* for that it giveth great light to the Reader, for the better understanding is hereunto annexed.

To the Right noble, and Valorous, Sir Walter Ralegh knight, Lo. Wardein of the Stanneryes, and her Majesties liefetenaunt of the County of Cornewayll.

Sir knowing how doubtfully[1] all Allegories may be construed, and this booke of mine, which I have entituled the Faery Queene, being a continued Allegory, or darke conceit,[2] I have thought good as well for avoyding of gealous[3] opinions

---

1. Ambiguously.
2. Homer and Virgil were interpreted as continuously allegorical; allegorical readings were attached to Ariosto by the poet himself and his commentators; Tasso insisted on his moral allegory. So it was right for heroic poetry to be allegorical, to have a meaning or meanings below the surface and therefore "dark." These meanings Spenser calls "conceits," meaning something between the modern "concepts" and the now obsolete "acute metaphorical discoveries." In a poem so long and loosely structured as *The Faerie Queene* the conceits cannot be uniformly dark—the allegorical significances vary from the transparent to the unfathomable.
3. Hostile, envious.

and misconstructions, as also for your better light in reading therof, (being so by you commanded,) to discover unto you the general intention and meaning, which in the whole course thereof I have fashioned, without expressing of any particular [4] purposes or by-accidents therein occasioned. The generall end therefore of all the booke is to fashion a gentleman or noble person in vertuous and gentle discipline: Which for that I conceived shoulde be most plausible and pleasing, being coloured with an historicall fiction, the which the most part of men delight to read, rather for variety of matter, then for profite of the ensample: I chose the historye of king Arthure, as most fitte for the excellency of his person, being made famous by many mens former workes, and also furthest from the daunger of envy, and suspition of present time. In which I have followed all the antique Poets historicall, first Homere, who in the Persons of Agamemnon and Ulysses hath ensampled a good governour and a vertuous man, the one in his Ilias, the other in his Odysseis:[5] then Virgil, whose like intention was to doe in the person of Aeneas: after him Ariosto[6] comprised them both in his Orlando: and lately Tasso[7] dissevered them againe, and formed both parts in two persons, namely that part which they in Philosophy call Ethice, or vertues of a private man, coloured in his Rinaldo.[8] The other named Politice in his Godfredo.[9] By ensample of which excellente Poets, I labour to pourtraict in Arthure, before he was king, the image of a brave knight, perfected in the twelve private morall vertues, as Aristotle hath devised, the which is the purpose of these first twelve bookes: which if I finde to be well accepted, I may be perhaps encoraged, to frame the other part of polliticke vertues in his person, after that hee came to be king. To some I know this Methode will seeme displeasaunt, which had rather have good discipline delivered plainly in way of precepts, or sermoned at large, as they use, then thus clowdily enwrapped in Allegoricall devises. But such, me seeme, should be satisfide with the use of these dayes, seeing all things accounted by their showes, and nothing esteemed of, that is not delightfull and pleasing to commune sence. For this cause is Xenophon[10] preferred before Plato, for that the one in the exquisite depth of his judgement, formed a Commune welth such as it should be, but the other in the person of Cyrus and the Persians fashioned a government such as might best be: So much more profitable and gratious is doctrine by ensample, then by rule. So have I laboured to doe in the person of Arthure: whome I conceive after his long education by Timon, to whom he was by Merlin delivered to be brought up, so soone as he was borne of the Lady Igrayne, to have seene in a dream or vision the Faery Queene, with

4. As opposed to general, meaning the "accidents" mentioned near the end of the letter.
5. *Iliad, Odyssey.*
6. Lodovico Ariosto (1474–1533), author of *Orlando Furioso* (1532), the formative heroic poem of the Renaissance; Spenser is closest to it in the many interlinked stories of Bks. III and IV.
7. Torquato Tasso (1544–95), author of *Gerusalemme Liberata* (1581), owing much to Ariosto but made graver and more explicitly Christian by the influence of the Counter-Reformation.
8. Hero of Tasso's poem in its dealings with personal morality.
9. Godfrey of Boulogne, hero of Tasso's poem in its dealings with political morality.
10. Xenophon's *Cyropaedia, The Education of Cyrus,* and Plato's *Republic;* see Sidney's *Defence of Poesie.*

whose excellent beauty ravished, he awaking resolved to seeke her out, and so being by Merlin armed, and by Timon throughly instructed, he went to seeke her forth in Faerye land.[11] In that Faery Queene I meane glory in my generall intention, but in my particular I conceive the most excellent and glorious person of our soveraine the Queene, and her kingdome in Faery land. And yet in some places els, I doe otherwise shadow [12] her. For considering she beareth two persons,[13] the one of a most royall Queene or Empresse, the other of a most vertuous and beautifull Lady, this latter part in some places I doe expresse in Belphœbe, fashioning her name according to your owne excellent conceipt of Cynthia,[14] (Phœbe and Cynthia being both names of Diana.) So in the person of Prince Arthure I sette forth magnificence in particular, which vertue for that (according to Aristotle and the rest) it is the perfection of all the rest, and conteineth in it them all, therefore in the whole course I mention the deedes of Arthure applyable to that vertue, which I write of in that booke. But of the xii. other vertues, I make xii. other knights the patrones, for the more variety of the history: Of which these three bookes contayn three, The first of the knight of the Redcrosse, in whome I expresse Holynes: The seconde of Sir Guyon, in whom I sette forth Temperaunce: The third of Britomartis a Lady knight, in whome I picture Chastity. But because the beginning of the whole worke seemeth abrupte and as depending upon other antecedents, it needs that ye know the occasion of these three knights severall adventures. For the Methode of a Poet historical is not such, as of an Historiographer. For an Historiographer discourseth of affayres orderly as they were donne, accounting as well the times as the actions, but a Poet thrusteth into the middest,[15] even where it most concerneth him, and there recoursing to the thinges forepaste, and divining of thinges to come, maketh a pleasing Analysis of all. The beginning therefore of my history, if it were to be told by an Historiographer, should be the twelfth booke, which is the last, where I devise that the Faery Queene kept her Annuall feaste xii. dayes, uppon which xii. severall dayes, the occasions of the xii. severall adventures hapned, which being undertaken by xii. severall knights, are in these xii books severally handled and discoursed. The first was this. In the beginning of the feast, there presented him selfe a tall clownishe [16] younge man, who falling before the Queen of Faries desired a boone (as the manner then was) which during that feast she might not refuse: which was that hee might have the atchievement of any adventure, which during that feaste should happen, that being graunted, he rested him on the floore, unfitte through his rusticity for a better place. Soone after entred a faire Ladye in mourning weedes, riding on a white Asse, with a dwarfe behind her leading a warlike steed, that bore the Armes of a knight, and his speare in the dwarfes hand. Shee falling before the Queene of Faeries, com-

---

11. "By the Faery land of the poem I mean England."

12. Portray.

13. Referring to the doctrine that the monarch had two persons, one private and mortal, one political and immortal ("the king is dead, long live the king"). Elizabeth is therefore represented as both Queen and Empress, and most virtuous and beautiful lady.

14. Ralegh's poem to the Queen, *Cynthia;* like Phoebe and Diana, a name of the goddess of the moon and of chastity.

15. *In medias res,* as Horace (*Ars Poetica,* 148) advises.

16. Rustic, unpolished.

playned that her father and mother an ancient King and Queene, had bene by an huge dragon many years shut up in a brasen Castle, who thence suffred them not to yssew: and therefore besought the Faery Queene to assygne her some one of her knights to take on him that exployt. Presently [17] that clownish person upstarting, desired that adventure: whereat the Queene much wondering, and the Lady much gainesaying,[18] yet he earnestly importuned his desire. In the end the Lady told him that unlesse that armour which she brought, would serve him (that is the armour of a Christian man specified by Saint Paul v. Ephes.) that he could not succeed in that enterprise, which being forthwith put upon him with dewe furnitures [19] thereunto, he seemed the goodliest man in al that company, and was well liked of the Lady. And eftesoones taking on him knighthood, and mounting on that straunge Courser, he went forth with her on that adventure: where beginneth the first booke, vz.

A gentle knight was pricking on the playne, &c.

The second day ther came in a Palmer bearing an Infant with bloody hands, whose Parents he complained to have bene slayn by an Enchaunteresse called Acrasia: and therfore craved of the Faery Queene, to appoint him some knight, to performe that adventure, which being assigned to Sir Guyon, he presently went forth with that same Palmer: which is the beginning of the second booke and the whole subject thereof. The third day there came in, a Groome who complained before the Faery Queene, that a vile Enchaunter called Busirane had in hand a most faire Lady called Amoretta, whom he kept in most grievous torment, because she would not yield him the pleasure of her body. Whereupon Sir Scudamour the lover of that Lady presently tooke on him that adventure. But being unable to performe it by reason of the hard Enchauntments, after long sorrow, in the end met with Britomartis, who succoured him, and reskewed his love.

But by occasion hereof, many other adventures are intermedled,[20] but rather as Accidents, then intendments. As the love of Britomart, the overthrow of Marinell, the misery of Florimell, the vertuousnes of Belphœbe, the lasciviousnes of Hellenora, and many the like.

Thus much Sir, I have briefly overronne [21] to direct your understanding to the wel-head of the History, that from thence gathering the whole intention of the conceit, ye may as in a handfull gripe al the discourse, which otherwise may happily [22] seeme tedious and confused. So humbly craving the continuaunce of your honorable favour towards me, and th'eternall establishment of your happines, I humbly take leave.

23. January. 1589.
Yours most humbly affectionate.
Ed. Spenser.

17. At once.
18. Protesting.
19. Equipment.
20. Mixed in.
21. Run through.
22. Perchance.

Book I

Spenser probably did not begin here; the parts of the work that Harvey saw in 1580 must, if they survive at all, be in the middle books, for the work in which Spenser was then attempting to "overgo" Ariosto can have had nothing to do with the Revelation of St. John, a topic which Harvey recommends, and which is central to Book I as we now have it. When he did settle to Book I he made it very different in tone, and also made it much more self-contained than the more Ariostan books; in fact, I is even more so than II, which is to a great degree modeled on it, and V, the other Book that comes closest.

Red Cross is the greatest of the knights, a saint rather than a mere hero, and occasionally the image of Christ. The historical scope of the Book (extended by more or less "dark conceits") is the whole history of the world from the Fall to the final overthrow of Satan. Its theology and religion are more directly expressed than in the other Books, and it speaks with far more urgency to the great themes of history, and notably the vicissitudes of the church on earth, than they.

Red Cross is St. George, slayer of the dragon; a figure who is both a type of Christ and a droll figure in folkplay and popular pageant, hero of great works of art and of the antique Mummers Play; patron saint of England. He rides into Spenser's poem, in medias res, with his usual pageant companions, the lady on the ass and the lamb. The scene is vague and dreamlike, and we can already see what Coleridge meant when he spoke of "the marvellous independence and true imaginative absence of all particular space and time" in The Faerie Queene. But that is only a half-truth. These characters from the village play and the Lord Mayor's Show, in their narrative of nightmare apparitions, dreamlike transfigurations, apparently fitful meanings, are going to serve a story which deals with the history of the human condition as it appeared in an age of apocalyptic climax, the late 1580's. We have the same fancy in our day, but do not express it, as Spenser did and Virgil had done, in a heroic poem about human destiny in the context of earthly power and heavenly providence; nor would we give the story a milieu of Arthurian romance, though we might envy the way in which it enables the poet to achieve those strange transitions and condensations which so remind us of the Freudian dreamwork.

Red Cross, though of the elect, is a sinner, everyman. Spenser emphasizes his fall into sin and despair by echoing the anti-Romanist article of his church: "that we are justified by faith alone is a most wholesome doctrine." Given grace to repent, Red Cross undertakes the imitation of Christ, redeems the parents of Una (Adam and Eve), slays the old Dragon, and harrows hell—becomes, in short, Christ, the object of his imitation, and marries his Bride, Una, the True Church (i.e. the Church of England). Such are the transformations of Spenser's world, and they are prepared for in the opening lines. Red Cross, who wears the apocalyptic "bloudie Cross" (Christ wore it in the battle in heaven, as shown in illuminated manuscripts of Revelation), is also called "Right faithful true," which, fidelis et verax, is the title of Christ in Revelation (19:11). And Red Cross, St. George, is also England, defender of the true faith.

Revelation is the ultimate source. Una is "the woman clothed with the sun" (Revelation 12:1), traditionally identified with the true church; Spenser speaks of her "sunshyny face" (I.xii.23) as the medieval illuminators showed her in a glory of light. She, like her prototype, flees into the wilderness (Revelation 12:6). Duessa plays multiplicity to Una's integrity, but is also the Whore of Babylon, the Scarlet Woman

(Revelation 17); the best possible illustrations of Spenser's eighth canto, where she rides the Beast, are in the medieval apocalypses. She is also the Church of Rome in the allegories of Reformation propaganda. Archimago is antichrist, the Beast from the Land of Revelation, the papacy. The tree and the water, representing the two out of the Catholic seven sacraments retained by the reformed church (communion and baptism) refresh Red Cross in his three-day battle with the Dragon; they come from Revelation 22. And these are only samples of Spenser's allusions to Revelation.

If one thinks of the number of times it has happened both before and after Spenser, it will seem less strange that reference should be made to Revelation—a vision of the end of the world—for historical and political purposes. The last book of the Bible was thought to contain in prophetic form the whole history of the church, and Spenser followed an English tradition when he favored a Protestant interpretation and one which made the true Catholic church the Church of England, the primitive church now restored after centuries of Romanist disfigurement. Una is that church, and also its head, Elizabeth I, who replaced the papacy which had usurped the royal chief priests, her ancestors, for so long. The overthrow of the antichrist Archimago and the false fallen church, Duessa, amounts to a restoration of Eden.

Thus Spenser embodies in his dreamlike romance story the imperial and ecclesiastical pretensions of the last of the Tudors. He associates his empress with a triumphant restoration of the true church on earth, and with the reuniting of church and state by a queen who liked to be thought of as a second Constantine, the emperor who 1200 years earlier had Christianized the Roman empire. The presumptuous bishops of Rome had set apart the secular and religious powers, but they had been ousted from England and a new emperor, a new Constantine, ruled all.

As Virgil had celebrated the culmination of empire in the *Aeneid,* so would Spenser in *The Faerie Queene,* and especially in Book I. But to do so he chooses not courtly or difficult materials; rather he builds into his heroic pattern the familiar figures and almost equally familiar interpretations of Revelation, and explains how universal history justifies the worship of imperial Elizabeth.* It is not surprising that when Colin Clout read the poem to her she "gan to take delight . . . and it desired at timely hours to hear."

* The dedication ran as follows: "To the most high, mightie and magnificent empresse renowmed for pietie, vertue, and all gratious government Elizabeth by the grace of God Queene of England Fraunce and Ireland and of Virginia, defendour of the faith, &c. Her Most humble servaunt Edmund Spenser doth in all Humilitie Dedicate, Present and Consecrate these his labours to live with the eternitie of her fame."

The First Booke of The Faerie Queene

Contayning, the Legende of the Knight of the Red Crosse, or *Of Holinesse*

1   Lo I the man, whose Muse whilome˃ did maske,   *formerly*
      As time her taught, in lowly Shepheards weeds,˃   *clothes*
      Am now enforst a far unfitter taske,

For trumpets sterne to chaunge mine Oaten reeds,°
And sing of Knights and Ladies gentle⟩ deeds;   *noble*
Whose prayses having slept in silence long,°
Me, all too meane, the sacred Muse areeds⟩   *counsels*
To blazon broad emongst her learned throng:
Fierce warres and faithfull loves shall moralize my song.

2   Helpe then, O holy Virgin chiefe of nine,°
     Thy weaker⟩ Novice to performe thy will,   *too weak*
     Lay forth out of thine everlasting scryne⟩   *record chest*
     The antique rolles, which there lye hidden still,
     Of Faerie knights and fairest *Tanaquill,*⟩   *Gloriana*
     Whom that most noble Briton Prince° so long
     Sought through the world, and suffered so much ill,
     That I must rue his undeserved wrong:
O helpe thou my weake wit, and sharpen my dull tong.

3   And thou most dreaded impe⟩ of highest *Jove,*   *child*
     Faire *Venus* sonne,° that with thy cruell dart
     At that good knight so cunningly didst rove,⟩   *shoot*
     That glorious fire it kindled in his hart,
     Lay now thy deadly Heben⟩ bow apart,   *ebony*
     And with thy mother milde, come to mine ayde:
     Come both, and with you bring triumphant *Mart,*°
     In loves and gentle jollities arrayd,
After his murdrous spoiles and bloudy rage allayd.⟩   *calmed*

4   And with them eke,⟩ O Goddesse heavenly bright,°   *also*
     Mirrour of grace and Majestie divine,
     Great Lady of the greatest Isle, whose light
     Like *Phœbus* lampe° throughout the world doth shine,
     Shed thy faire beames into my feeble eyne⟩,   *eyes*
     And raise my thoughts too humble and too vile,
     To thinke of that true glorious type° of thine,
     The argument of mine afflicted stile:
The which to heare, vouchsafe, O dearest dred° a-while.

For trumpets . . . reeds He changes from the
shepherd's pipe of pastoral to the trumpets of
heroic poetry. This first stanza imitates the
proem to Virgil's *Aeneid.* On Virgil's model it
became prescriptive for an epic poet to prepare
himself with pastoral.
And sing . . . long imitating the opening of
Ariosto's *Orlando Furioso*
O holy . . . nine Calliope, chief of the Muses,
presided over eloquence and heroic poetry;
represented in art with a trumpet in the right
hand, a book in the left.
most . . . Prince Arthur
sonne Cupid
Mart Mars, god of war and lover of Venus
Goddesse . . . bright Queen Elizabeth
Phœbus lamps the sun
true . . . type Gloriana, symbol of Queen Elizabeth
dearest dred object of greatest awe

Canto i°

The Patron of true Holinesse,
   Foule Errour doth defeate:
Hypocrisie him to entrappe,
   Doth to his home entreate.

1   A Gentle Knight was pricking⟩ on the plaine,   *spurring*
   Y cladd in mightie armes and silver shielde,
   Wherein old dints of deepe wounds did remaine,
   The cruell markes of many' a bloudy fielde;
   Yet armes till that time did he never wield:°
   His angry steede did chide his foming bitt,
   As much disdayning to the curbe to yield:
   Full jolly⟩ knight he seemd, and faire did sitt,   *brave*
As one for knightly giusts⟩ and fierce encounters fitt.   *jousts*

2   But on his brest a bloudie Crosse he bore,
   The deare remembrance of his dying Lord,
   For whose sweete sake that glorious badge he wore,
   And dead as living ever him ador'd:
   Upon his shield the like was also scor'd,
   For soveraine hope, which in his helpe he had:
   Right faithfull true° he was in deede and word,
   But of his cheere⟩ did seeme too solemne sad;   *expression*
Yet nothing did he dread, but ever was ydrad.⟩   *dreaded*

3   Upon a great adventure he was bond,⟩   *bound*
   That greatest *Gloriana* to him gave,
   That greatest Glorious Queene of *Faerie* lond,
   To winne him worship, and her grace to have,
   Which of all earthly things he most did crave;
   And ever as he rode, his hart did earne⟩   *yearn*
   To prove his puissance⟩ in battell brave   *strength*
   Upon his foe, and his new force to learne;
Upon his foe, a Dragon horrible and stearne.

4   A lovely Ladie° rode him faire beside,
   Upon a lowly Asse more white then snow,
   Yet she much whiter, but the same did hide
   Under a vele, that wimpled⟩ was full low,   *folded*
   And over all a blacke stole she did throw,
   As one that inly mournd: so was she sad,

Canto i When Red Cross and his companions seek shelter they enter a wood, symbol of the errors of human existence. Despite the lady's warning that he places too much confidence in unaided human strength, the knight provokes and fights with Error (heresy, corrupter of pure doctrine). In his difficulty he is advised "Add faith unto your force"—a tenet of the true religion which allowed no justification by works alone—and he forces Error to spew forth its heretical brood. His victory at the outset foreshadows the victory over the dragon at the end, as Christ's victory over Satan in the wilderness foreshadowed the final overthrow of the old dragon; but his lapse foretells the sins that lie ahead also. His first encounter with religious deceit and hypocrisy of the papal kind that plagued England till the Reformation follows immediately.

armes . . . wield He is wearing the old arms of the Christian soldier (see Headnote to Bk. I)

Right . . . true See Headnote.

Ladie Una, her radiance concealed by a veil

And heavie sat upon her palfrey slow:
Seemed in heart some hidden care she had,
And by her in a line˃ a milke white lambe she lad.   *leash*

5   So pure an innocent, as that same lambe,
    She was in life and every vertuous lore,
    And by descent from Royall lynage came
    Of ancient Kings and Queenes, that had of yore
    Their scepters stretcht from East to Westerne shore,
    And all the world in their subjection held;°
    Till that infernal feend with foule uprore
    Forwasted˃ all their land, and them expeld: *destroyed*
    Whom to avenge, she had this Knight from far compeld.˃ *summoned*

6   Behind her farre away a Dwarfe° did lag,
    That lasie seemd in being ever last,
    Or wearièd with bearing of her bag
    Of needments at his backe. Thus as they past,
    The day with cloudes was suddeine overcast,
    And angry *Jove* an hideous storme of raine
    Did poure into his Lemans lap° so fast,
    That every wight˃ to shrowd˃ it did constrain,   *creature / shelter*
    And this faire couple eke to shroud themselves were fain.

7   Enforst to seeke some covert nigh at hand,
    A shadie grove not far away they spide,
    That promist ayde the tempest to withstand:
    Whose loftie trees yclad with sommers pride,
    Did spred so broad, that heavens light did hide,
    Not perceable with power of any starre:
    And all within were pathes and alleies wide,
    With footing worne, and leading inward farre:
    Faire harbour that them seems; so in they entred arre.

8   And foorth they passe, with pleasure forward led,
    Joying to heare the birdes sweete harmony,
    Which therein shrouded from the tempest dred,
    Seemd in their song to scorne the cruell sky.
    Much can˃ they prayse the trees so straight and hy,   *did*
    The sayling Pine,° the Cedar proud and tall,
    The vine-prop Elme, the Poplar never dry,
    The builder Oake, sole king of forrests all,
    The Aspine good for staves, the Cypresse funerall.

---

by descent . . . held Una is both the true and primitive church and the daughter of Eden. She is the unfallen world (her name means One, the primal unity before numbers) and the church while still universal; Duessa is multiplicity and even on her own claim her father rules only the west (I.ii.22). The point is, politically, to establish, as Elizabethan churchmen always did, the truth of the position that the English church was older and purer than the Roman, which had usurped it.
Dwarfe perhaps signifies her human needs, as the lamb signifies her purity
Lemans lap mistress's lap; the earth
sayling Pine used by shipbuilders. This epic catalogue of trees is probably developed here from Chaucer's *Parlement of Foules*.

9   The Laurell, meed⌐ of mightie Conquerors   *prize*
    And Poets sage, the Firre that weepeth still,⌐   *always*
    The Willow worne of forlorne Paramours,
    The Eugh⌐ obedient to the benders will,   *yew*
    The Birch for shaftes, the Sallow⌐ for the mill,   *willow*
    The Mirrhe sweete bleeding in the bitter wound,°
    The warlike Beech, the Ash for nothing ill,
    The fruitfull Olive, and the Platane⌐ round,   *plane-tree*
  The carver Holme,° the Maple seeldom inward sound.

10 Led with delight, they thus beguile the way,
    Untill the blustring storme is overblowne;
    When weening⌐ to returne, whence they did stray,   *thinking*
    They cannot finde that path, which first was showne,
    But wander too and fro in wayes unknowne,
    Furthest from end then, when they neerest weene,
    That makes them doubt, their wits be not their owne:
    So many pathes, so many turnings seene,
  That which of them to take, in diverse doubt they been.

11 At last resolving forward still to fare,
    Till that some end they finde or⌐ in or out,   *either*
    That path they take, that beaten seemd most bare,
    And like to lead the labyrinth about;⌐   *out of*
    Which when by tract they hunted had throughout,
    At length it brought them to a hollow cave,
    Amid the thickest woods. The Champion stout⌐   *brave*
    Eftsoones⌐ dismounted from his courser brave,⌐   *at once / splendid*
  And to the Dwarfe a while his needlesse spere he gave.

12 Be well aware, quoth then that Ladie milde,
    Least suddaine mischiefe ye too rash provoke:
    The danger hid, the place unknowne and wilde,
    Breedes dreadfull doubts: Oft fire is without smoke,
    And perill without show: therefore your stroke
    Sir knight with-hold, till further triall made.
    Ah Ladie (said he) shame were to revoke
    The forward footing for⌐ an hidden shade: *because of*
  Vertue gives her selfe light, through darkenesse for to wade.°

13 Yea but (quoth she) the perill of this place
    I better wot⌐ then you, though now too late   *know*
    To wish you backe returne with foule disgrace,
    Yet wisedome warnes, whilest foot is in the gate,
    To stay the steppe, ere forcèd to retrate.
    This is the wandring wood, this *Errours den,*°

Mirrhe . . . wound Its resins were extracted for
perfume from cuts in the bark.
carver Holme holm-oak used for carving
Vertue . . . wade Compare the misplaced confidence of the Elder Brother in Milton's *Comus,*

ll. 372–73: "Virtue could see to do what Virtue
would / By her own radiant light . . ."
Errours den Error stands for heresy; old
heresies breed new ones which feed on them;
Spenser remembers Revelation 9:7–10.

A monster vile, whom God and man does hate:
Therefore I read⟩ beware. Fly fly (quoth then   *counsel*
The fearefull Dwarfe:) this is no place for living men.

14   But full of fire and greedy hardiment,⟩   *courage*
    The youthfull knight could not for ought be staide,
    But forth unto the darksome hole he went,
    And lookèd in: his glistring armor made
    A litle glooming light, much like a shade,
    By which he saw the ugly monster plaine,
    Halfe like a serpent horribly displaide,
But th'other halfe did womans shape retaine,
Most lothsom, filthie, foule, and full of vile disdaine.

15   And as she lay upon the durtie ground,
    Her huge long taile her den all overspred,
    Yet was in knots and many boughtes⟩ upwound,   *bends*
    Pointed with mortall sting. Of her there bred
    A thousand yong ones, which she dayly fed,
    Sucking upon her poisonous dugs, eachone
    Of sundry shapes, yet all ill favorèd:
    Soone as that uncouth⟩ light upon them shone,   *unfamiliar*
Into her mouth they crept, and suddain all were gone.

16   Their dam upstart, out of her den effraide,⟩   *scared*
    And rushed forth, hurling her hideous taile
    About her cursèd head, whose folds displaid
    Were stretcht now forth at length without entraile.⟩   *coils*
    She lookt about, and seeing one in mayle
    Armèd to point,⟩ sought back to turne againe;   *fully*
    For light she hated as the deadly bale,⟩   *harm*
    Ay wont in desert darknesse to remaine,
Where plaine none might her see, nor she see any plaine.

17   Which when the valiant Elfe° perceiv'd, he lept
    As Lyon fierce upon the flying pray,
    And with his trenchand⟩ blade her boldly kept   *sharp*
    From turning backe, and forcèd her to stay:
    Therewith enrag'd she loudly gan to bray,
    And turning fierce,⟩ her speckled taile advaunst,   *fiercely*
    Threatning her angry sting, him to dismay:
    Who nought aghast, his mightie hand enhaunst⟩:   *raised*
The stroke down from her head unto her shoulder glaunst.

18   Much daunted with that dint, her sence was dazd,
    Yet kindling rage, her selfe she gathered round,
    And all attonce her beastly body raizd
    With doubled forces high above the ground:

Elfe fairy (Harvey's early reference is to the
Elvish Queen)

Tho˃ wrapping up her wrethèd sterne arownd,   *then*
Lept fierce upon his shield, and her huge traine˃   *tail*
All suddenly about his body wound,
That hand or foot to stirre he strove in vaine:
God helpe the man so wrapt in *Errours* endlesse traine.˃ *deceit*

19 His Lady sad to see his sore constraint,
  Cride out, Now now Sir knight, shew what ye bee,
  Add faith unto your force, and be not faint:
  Strangle her, else she sure will strangle thee.
  That when he heard, in great perplexitie,
  His gall did grate for griefe˃ and high disdaine, *anger*
  And knitting all his force got one hand free,
  Wherewith he grypt her gorge with so great paine,
  That soone to loose her wicked bands did her constraine.

20 Therewith she spewd out of her filthy maw˃   *stomach*
  A floud of poyson horrible and blacke,
  Full of great lumpes of flesh and gobbets raw,
  Which stunck so vildly,˃ that it forst him slacke *vilely*
  His grasping hold, and from her turne him backe:
  Her vomit full of bookes and papers was,°
  With loathly frogs and toades, which eyes did lacke,°
  And creeping sought way in the weedy gras:
  Her filthy parbreake˃ all the place defilèd has. *vomit*

21 As when old father *Nilus* gins to swell
  With timely pride above the *Aegyptian* vale,
  His fattie˃ waves do fertile slime outwell,   *greasy*
  And overflow each plaine and lowly dale:
  But when his later spring˃ gins to avale,˃ *flood / subside*
  Huge heapes of mudd he leaves, wherein there breed
  Ten thousand kindes of creatures, partly male
  And partly female of his fruitfull seed;
  Such ugly monstrous shapes elsewhere may no man reed.˃° *see*

22 The same so sore annoyèd has the knight,
  That welnigh chokèd with the deadly stinke,
  His forces faile, ne˃ can no longer fight.   *nor*
  Whose corage when the feend perceiv'd to shrinke,
  She pourèd forth out of her hellish sinke
  Her fruitfull cursèd spawne of serpents small,
  Deformèd monsters, fowle, and blacke as inke,
  Which swarming all about his legs did crall,
  And him encombred sore, but could not hurt at all.

vomit . . . was referring to the voluminousness of religious controversy, especially in the 16th century
loathly . . . lacke Revelation 16:13: "And I saw three unclean spirits like frogs come out of the mouth of the dragon, and out of the mouth of the beast, and out of the mouth of the false prophet."
As when . . . reed (stanza 21) The Nile floods which ensure the fertility of the valley, were supposed on subsiding to leave behind such creatures as crocodiles, bred from the mud.

23 As gentle Shepheard in sweete even-tide,
        When ruddy *Phœbus* gins to welke> in west,   *fade*
        High on an hill, his flocke to vewen wide,
        Markes which do byte their hasty supper best;
        A cloud of combrous gnattes do him molest,
        All striving to infixe their feeble stings,
        That from their noyance> he no where can rest,   *irritation*
        But with his clownish hands their tender wings
    He brusheth oft, and oft doth mar their murmurings.

24 Thus ill bestedd,> and fearefull more of shame,   *situated*
        Then> of the certaine perill he stood in,   *than*
        Halfe furious> unto his foe he came,   *mad*
        Resolv'd in minde all suddenly to win,
        Or soone to lose, before he once would lin;>   *stop*
        And strooke at her with more than manly force,
        That from her body full of filthie sin
        He raft> her hatefull head without remorse;   *cut*
    A streame of cole black bloud forth gushèd from her corse.

25 Her scattred brood, soone as their Parent deare
        They saw so rudely falling to the ground,
        Groning full deadly, all with troublous feare,
        Gathred themselves about her body round,
        Weening their wonted entrance to have found
        At her wide mouth: but being there withstood
        They flockèd all about her bleeding wound,
        And suckèd up their dying mothers blood,
    Making her death their life, and eke her hurt their good.°

26 That detestáble sight him much amazde,
        To see th'unkindly Impes> of heaven accurst,   *young, brood*
        Devoure their dam; on whom while so he gazd,
        Having all satisfide their bloudy thurst,
        Their bellies swolne he saw with fulnesse burst,
        And bowels gushing forth: well worthy end
        Of such as drunke her life, the which them nurst;
        Now needeth him no lenger labour spend,
    His foes have slaine themselves, with whom he should contend.

27 His Ladie seeing all, that chaunst, from farre
        Approcht in hast to greet his victorie,
        And said, Faire knight, borne under happy starre,
        Who see your vanquisht foes before you lye;
        Well worthy be you of that Armorie,°
        Wherein ye have great glory wonne this day,
        And proov'd your strength on a strong enimie,

Making . . . good heresy as finally self-de-   **Armorie** the armor of the *miles Christi*
structive

Your first adventure: many such I pray,
And henceforth ever wish, that like succeed it may.

28 Then mounted he upon his Steede againe,
   And with the Lady backward⟩ sought to wend;⟩   *back / go*
   That path he kept, which beaten was most plaine,
   Ne ever would to any by-way bend,
   But still⟩ did follow one unto the end,   *always*
   The which at last out of the wood them brought.
   So forward on his way (with God to frend)
   He passèd forth, and new adventure sought;
   Long way he travellèd, before he heard of ought.

29 At length they chaunst to meet upon the way
   An agèd Sire,° in long blacke weedes⟩ yclad,   *garments*
   His feete all bare, his beard all hoarie gray,
   And by his belt his booke he hanging had;
   Sober he seemde, and very sagely sad,⟩   *grave*
   And to the ground his eyes were lowly bent,
   Simple in shew, and voyde of malice bad,
   And all the way he prayèd, as he went,
   And often knockt his brest, as one that did repent.

30 He faire the knight saluted, louting⟩ low,   *bowing*
   Who faire him quited,⟩ as that courteous was: *responded*
   And after asked him, if he did know
   Of straunge adventures, which abroad did pas.
   Ah my deare Sonne (quoth he) how should, alas,
   Silly⟩ old man, that lives in hidden cell,   *simple*
   Bidding his beades all day for his trespas,
   Tydings of warre and worldly trouble tell?
   With holy father sits not with such things to mell.⟩ *meddle*

31 But if of daunger which hereby doth dwell,
   And homebred evill ye desire to heare,
   Of a straunge man I can you tidings tell,
   That wasteth all this countrey farre and neare.
   Of such (said he) I chiefly do inquere,
   And shall you well reward to shew the place,
   In which that wicked wight⟩ his dayes doth weare:⟩   *creature / pass*
   For to all knighthood it is foule disgrace,
   That such a cursèd creature lives so long a space.

32 Far hence (quoth he) in wastfull wildernesse
   His dwelling is, by which no living wight
   May ever passe, but thorough⟩ great distresse.   *through*
   Now (sayd the Lady) draweth toward night,
   And well I wote,⟩ that your later⟩ fight   *know / recent*

---

agèd Sire The black-magician hermit occurs in   allegorical of the papacy; various popes were
other romances, but Spenser makes Archimago   accused by Protestant historians of black magic.

Ye all forwearied be: for what so strong,
But wanting⸗ rest will also want of might?   *lacking*
The Sunne that measures heaven all day long,
At night doth baite⸗ his steedes the *Ocean* waves emong.   *refresh*

33   Then with the Sunne take Sir, your timely rest,
And with new day new worke at once begin:
Untroubled night they say gives counsell best.
Right well Sir knight ye have advisèd bin,
(Quoth then that agèd man;) the way to win
Is wisely to advise:⸗ now day is spent;   *consider*
Therefore with me ye may take up your In⸗   *lodging*
For this same night. The knight was well content:
So with that godly father to his home they went.

34   A little lowly Hermitage it was,
Downe in a dale, hard by a forests side,
Far from resort of people, that did pas
In travell to and froe: a little wyde⸗   *away*
There was an holy Chappell edifyde,
Wherein the Hermite dewly wont to say
His holy things each morne and eventyde:
Thereby a Christall streame did gently play,
Which from a sacred fountaine wellèd forth alway.

35   Arrivèd there, the little house they fill,
Ne looke for entertainement,⸗ where none was: *food*
Rest is their feast, and all things at their will;⸗   *as they wish*
The noblest mind the best contentment has.
With faire discourse the evening so they pas:
For that old man of pleasing wordes had store,
And well could file his tongue as smooth as glas;
He told of Saintes and Popes, and evermore
He strowd an *Ave-Mary* after and before.

36   The drouping Night thus creepeth on them fast,
And the sad humour⸗ loading their eye liddes,   *heavy moisture*
As messenger of *Morpheus*° on them cast
Sweet slombring deaw, the which to sleepe them biddes.
Unto their lodgings then his guestes he riddes:⸗   *leads*
Where when all drownd in deadly⸗ sleepe he findes,   *death-like*
He to his study goes, and there amiddes
His Magick bookes and artes of sundry kindes,
He seekes out mighty charmes, to trouble sleepy mindes.

37   Then choosing out few wordes most horrible,
(Let none them read) thereof did verses frame,
With which and other spelles like terrible,
He bad awake blacke *Plutoes* griesly Dame,°

Morpheus god of dreams   **Plutoes . . . Dame** Hecate, goddess of witch-
                                              craft, wife of Pluto, god of the underworld

And cursed heaven, and spake reprochfull shame
Of highest God, the Lord of life and light;
A bold bad man, that dar'd to call by name
Great *Gorgon*,° Prince of darknesse and dead night,
At which *Cocytus* quakes, and *Styx*° is put to flight.

38   And forth he cald out of deepe darknesse dred
Legions of Sprights, the which like little flyes
Fluttring about his ever damnèd hed,
A-waite whereto their service he applyes,°
To aide his friends, or fray⟩ his enimies: *frighten*
Of those he chose out two, the falsest twoo,
And fittest for to forge true-seeming lyes;
The one of them he gave a message too,
The other by him selfe staide other worke to doo.

39   He making speedy way through spersèd⟩ ayre,   *dispersed*
And through the world of waters wide and deepe,
To *Morpheus* house doth hastily repaire.
Amid the bowels of the earth full steepe,
And low, where dawning day doth never peepe,
His dwelling is; there *Tethys*° his wet bed
Doth ever wash, and *Cynthia*° still⟩ doth steepe   *forever*
In silver deaw his ever-drouping hed,
Whiles sad Night over him her mantle black doth spred.

40   Whose double gates° he findeth lockèd fast,
The one faire fram'd of burnisht Yvory,
The other all with silver overcast;
And wakefull dogges before them farre do lye,
Watching to banish Care their enimy,
Who oft is wont to trouble gentle Sleepe.
By them the Sprite doth passe in quietly,
And unto *Morpheus* comes, whom drownèd deepe
In drowsie fit he findes: of nothing he takes keepe.⟩   *heed*

41   And more, to lulle him in his slumber soft,
A trickling streame from high rocke tumbling downe
And ever-drizling raine upon the loft,
Mixt with a murmuring winde, much like the sowne⟩   *sound*
Of swarming Bees, did cast him in a swowne:⟩   *faint*
No other noyse, nor peoples troublous cryes,
As still are wont t'annoy the wallèd towne,
Might there be heard: but carelesse Quiet lyes,
Wrapt in eternall silence farre from enemyes.

Gorgon Demogorgon, the original god, who
dwelt in darkness
Cocytus . . . Styx two of the five rivers of hell
A-waite . . . applyes wait to find out what job
he wants them to do
Tethys wife of Ocean

Cynthia moon goddess
double gates In *Odyssey* XIX the two gates
of sleep were of ivory and horn (here silver);
false dreams issued from the ivory gate, true
ones from the gate of horn.

42 The messenger approching to him spake,
     But his wast wordes returnd to him in vaine:
     So sound he slept, that nought mought⟩ him awake.   *might*
     Then rudely he him thrust, and pusht with paine,
     Whereat he gan to stretch: but he againe
     Shooke him so hard, that forcèd him to speake.
     As one then in a dreame, whose dryer⟩ braine   *too dry*
     Is tost with troubled sights and fancies weake,
  He mumbled soft, but would not all his silence breake.

43 The Sprite then gan more boldly him to wake,
     And threatned unto him the dreaded name
     Of *Hecate:* whereat he gan to quake,
     And lifting up his lumpish head, with blame⟩   *pain*
     Halfe angry askèd him, for what he came.
     Hither (quoth he) me *Archimago* sent,
     He that the stubborne Sprites can wisely tame,
     He bids thee to him send for his intent
  A fit⟩ false dreame, that can delude the sleepers sent.⟩   *suitable / senses*

44 The God obayde, and calling forth straight way
     A diverse⟩ dreame out of his prison darke,   *deceptive*
     Delivered it to him, and down did lay
     His heavie head, devoide of carefull carke,⟩   *worry*
     Whose sences all were straight benumbd and starke.⟩   *paralyzed*
     He backe returning by the Yvorie dore,
     Remounted up as light as chearefull Larke,
     And on his litle winges the dreame he bore
  In hast unto his Lord, where he him left afore.

45 Who all this while with charmes and hidden artes,
     Had made a Lady of that other Spright,
     And fram'd of liquid ayre her tender partes
     So lively, and so like⟩ in all mens sight,   *lifelike*
     That weaker⟩ sence it could have ravisht quight: *too weak*
     The maker selfe for all his wondrous witt,
     Was nigh beguilèd with so goodly sight:
     Her all in white he clad, and over it
  Cast a blacke stole, most like to seeme for *Una* fit.

46 Now when that ydle⟩ dreame was to him brought,   *mischievous*
     Unto that Elfin knight he bad him fly,
     Where he slept soundly void of evill thought,
     And with false shewes abuse his fantasy,°
     In sort as he him schoolèd privily:°
     And that new creature borne without her dew,⟩   *unnaturally*
     Full of the makers guile, with usage sly

---

fantasy imagination (in sleep the reason no longer controls it)   **In sort . . . privily** in the manner in which he had secretly taught him

He taught to imitate that Lady trew,˃   *honest*
Whose semblance she did carrie under feignèd hew.˃   *form*

47   Thus well instructed, to their worke they hast,
And comming where the knight in slomber lay,
The one upon his hardy head him plast,
And made him dreame of loves and lustfull play,
That nigh his manly hart did melt away,
Bathèd in wanton blis and wicked joy:
Then seemèd him his Lady by him lay,
And to him playnd,˃ how that false wingèd boy°   *complained*
Her chast hart had subdewd, to learne Dame pleasures toy.˃   *love play*

48   And she her selfe of beautie soveraigne Queene,
Faire *Venus* seemde unto his bed to bring
Her, whom he waking˃ evermore did weene˃   *when awake / believe*
To be the chastest flowre, that ay˃ did spring   *ever*
On earthly braunch, the daughter of a king,
Now a loose Leman˃ to vile service bound: *mistress*
And eke the *Graces*° seemed all to sing,
Hymen iô Hymen,° dauncing all around,
Whilst freshest *Flora*° her with Yvie girlond crownd.

49   In this great passion of unwonted lust,
Or wonted feare of doing ought amis,
He started up, as seeming to mistrust
Some secret ill, or hidden foe of his:
Loe there before his face his Lady is,
Under blake stole hyding her bayted hooke,
And as halfe blushing offred him to kis,
With gentle blandishment and lovely looke,
Most like that virgin true, which for her knight him took.

50   All cleane dismayd to see so uncouth˃ sight,   *unfamiliar*
And halfe enragèd at her shamelesse guise,
He thought have˃ slaine her in his fierce despight:˃   *to have / contempt*
But hasty heat tempring with sufferance˃ wise,   *patience*
He stayde his hand, and gan himselfe advise˃   *consider*
To prove his sense, and tempt her faignèd truth.
Wringing her hands in wemens pitteous wise,
Tho˃ can˃ she weepe, to stirre up gentle ruth,˃   *then / did / pity*
Both for her noble bloud, and for her tender youth.

51   And said, Ah Sir, my liege Lord and my love,
Shall I accuse the hidden cruell fate,

false . . . boy Cupid
Graces Aglaia, Thalia, Euphrosyne (see VI.x.
22): daughters of Venus by Bacchus; here
expressing in the false vision amity and joy
as at marriage. Renaissance mythography held
that "the unity of Venus is unfolded in the
trinity of the Graces."
Hymen iô Hymen ritual shout at Roman wedding, invoking the god of marriage
Flora goddess of flowers; present with the Graces
and Venus in Botticelli's Primavera

And mightie causes wrought in heaven above,
Or the blind God, that doth me thus amate,> *cast down*
For> hopèd love to winne me certaine hate? *instead of*
Yet thus perforce he bids me do, or die.
Die is my dew: yet rew> my wretched state *pity*
You, whom my hard avenging destinie
Hath made judge of my life or death indifferently.

52 Your owne deare sake forst me at first to leave
My Fathers kingdome, There she stopt with teares;
Her swollen hart her speach seemd to bereave,
And then againe begun, My weaker years> *extreme youth*
Captiv'd to fortune and frayle worldly feares,
Fly to your faith for succour and sure ayde:
Let me not dye in languor and long teares.
Why Dame (quoth he) what hath ye thus dismayd?
What frayes ye, that were wont to comfort me affrayd?

53 Love of your selfe, she said, and deare constraint> *strong compulsion*
Lets me not sleepe, but wast the wearie night
In secret anguish and unpittied plaint,
Whiles you in carelesse sleepe are drownèd quight.
Her doubtfull> words made that redoubted knight *questionable*
Suspect her truth: yet since no' untruth he knew,
Her fawning love with foule disdainefull spight
He would not shend,> but said, Deare dame I rew, *reprove*
That for my sake unknowne such griefe unto you grew.

54 Assure your selfe, it fell not all to ground;
For all so deare as life is to my hart,
I deeme your love, and hold me to you bound;
Ne let vaine feares procure your needlesse smart,
Where cause is none, but to your rest depart.
Not all content, yet seemd she to appease
Her mournefull plaintes, beguilèd of her art,
And fed with words, that could not chuse but please,
So slyding softly forth, she turnd as to her ease.

55 Long after lay he musing at her mood,
Much griev'd to thinke that gentle Dame so light,
For whose defence he was to shed his blood.
At last dull wearinesse of former fight
Having yrockt a sleepe his irkesome spright,> *spirit*
That troublous dreame gan freshly tosse his braine,
With bowres, and beds, and Ladies deare delight:
But when he saw his labour all was vaine,
With that misformèd> spright he backe returnd againe. *illicitly created*

[Deceived by the demonic imitator of Una, Red Cross in canto ii is parted from the Truth; when he sees the spirit Una again, this time in bed with a "young Squire" (another demon), he abandons her and leaves with the Dwarf. Una goes in pursuit, and is met by Archimago disguised as Red Cross—a false St. George, a false Holiness. Meanwhile Red Cross meets a scarlet lady, Duessa, who is in the company of Sans Foy (Faithless). The Saracen Sans Foy attacks Red Cross, who kills him. He consoles the lady, who tells him that she was

> Borne the sole daughter of an Emperour,
> He that the wide West under his rule has,
> And high hath set his throne where *Tiberis* doth pas.

That is, as we gathered from her scarlet dress and miter, she is the Roman church. (Una, the true and single church, is the daughter of one who ruled East and West; she is universal and single, Duessa partial, false, and divided.) She complains further that her betrothal to a great prince (Christ) was thwarted because he died and she could not find his body. She fell in with Sans Foy and his brothers, Sans Joy and Sans Loy (a trinity opposite to the Christian Faith, Hope, and Charity—faithless, loveless, lawless). This suggests, as Protestant propaganda often did, a league between Rome and the Moslems, who threatened Europe from the East. As a further lie she names herself Fidessa. Later Sans Loy is killed in Book II (the book of Temperance) and Sans Joy in Book III (the book of Chastity). Red Cross believes Duessa's story despite the warning of Fradubio (False Doubt), who has now been turned into a tree (captive to sin) because he fell in just this way to the wiles of Duessa. Canto ii deals with Red Cross's human lapse into sin and error, but also with the desertion of the original true faith by England.

Canto iii describes Una, now protected by a lion, sheltering in the House of Blind Devotion (the Roman faith, attended by superstition and clerical greed). Archimago, dressed as Red Cross, joins her, but is defeated in combat by Sans Loy, who also kills the lion and takes Una captive.

In canto iv Duessa leads Red Cross into the House of Pride, ruled over by Lucifera (Pride, for Lucifer fell because of that sin) and her six counselors, representing the other deadly sins. The formal pageant of the Seven Deadly Sins which follows is often conventional in detail, but Spenser handles it with vigor.]

From Canto iv

17   So forth she° comes, and to her coche does clyme,
    Adornèd all with gold, and girlonds gay,
    That seemd as fresh as *Flora* in her prime,
    And strove to match, in royall rich array,
    Great *Junoes* golden chaire, the which they say
    The Gods stand gazing on, when she does ride
    To *Joves* high house through heavens braspavèd way
    Drawne of faire Pecocks,° that excell in pride,
    And full of *Argus* eyes° their tailes dispredden wide.

she Lucifera
Pecocks Juno's chariot was represented as drawn by peacocks.
Argus eyes Argus had 100 eyes, and so Juno put him to watch over Io, a paramour of Jupiter's; Jupiter had Mercury lull all the eyes to sleep and kill Argus; Juno put his eyes on the peacock's tail.

18 But this was drawne of six unequall² beasts,   *dissimilar*
  On which her six sage Counsellours did ryde,
  Taught to obay their bestiall beheasts,°
  With like conditions to their kinds² applyde: *natures*
  Of which the first, that all the rest did guyde,
  Was sluggish *Idlenesse* the nourse of sin;
  Upon a slouthfull Asse he chose to ryde,
  Arayd in habit blacke, and amis² thin,   *hood*
Like to an holy Monck, the service to begin.

19 And in his hand his Portesse² still he bare,   *breviary*
  That much was worne, but therein little red,
  For of devotion he had little care,
  Still drownd in sleepe, and most of his dayes ded;
  Scarse could he once uphold his heavie hed,
  To looken, whether it were night or day:
  May seeme the wayne² was very evill led,   *coach, car*
  When such an one had guiding of the way,
That knew not, whether right he went, or else astray.

20 From wordly cares himselfe he did esloyne,²   *withdraw*
  And greatly shunnèd manly exercise,
  From every worke he chalengèd essoyne²,   *excuse*
  For contemplation sake: yet otherwise,
  His life he led in lawlesse riotise;
  By which he grew to grievous malady;
  For in his lustlesse² limbs through evill guise²   *feeble / way of life*
  A shaking fever raignd continually:
Such one was *Idlenesse*, first of this company.

21 And by his side rode loathsome *Gluttony*,
  Deformèd creature, on a filthie swyne,
  His belly was up-blowne with luxury,
  And eke with fatnesse swollen were his eyne,
  And like a Crane° his necke was long and fyne,²   *thin*
  With which he swallowed up excessive feast,
  For want whereof poore people oft did pyne;²   *starve*
  And al the way, most like a brutish beast,
He spuèd up his gorge, that all did him deteast.

22 In greene vine leaves he was right fitly clad;
  For other clothes he could not weare for heat,
  And on his head an yvie girland had,
  From under which fast trickled downe the sweat:
  Still as he rode, he somewhat² still did eat,   *something*
  And in his hand did beare a bouzing can,
  Of which he supt so oft, that on his seat

Taught . . . beheasts i.e. they were instructed to obey the animals, not control them
Crane Like most of the other detail, this is traditional; Gluttony was represented as having a long thin crane's neck, for the better enjoyment of food.

His dronken corse he scarse upholden can,
In shape and life more like a monster, then a man.°

23 Unfit he was for any worldly thing,
    And eke unhable once⸢ to stirre or go,⸢   *at all / walk*
    Not meet to be of counsell to a king,
    Whose mind in meat and drinke was drownèd so,
    That from his friend he seldome knew his fo:
    Full of diseases was his carcas blew,⸢   *livid*
    And a dry⸢ dropsie through his flesh did flow: *thirst-producing*
    Which by misdiet daily greater grew:
  Such one was *Gluttony,* the second of that crew.

24 And next to him rode lustfull *Lechery,*
    Upon a bearded Goat, whose rugged haire,
    And whally⸢ eyes (the signe of gelosy,)   *green-tinged*
    Was like the person selfe, whom he did beare:
    Who rough, and blacke, and filthy did appeare,
    Unseemely man to please faire Ladies eye;
    Yet he of Ladies oft was lovèd deare,
    When fairer faces were bid standen by:⸢   *aside*
  O who does know the bent of womens fantasy?

25 In a greene gowne he clothèd was full faire,
    Which underneath did hide his filthinesse,
    And in his hand a burning hart he bare,
    Full of vaine follies, and new fanglenesse⸢:   *vain novelty*
    For he was false, and fraught with ficklenesse,
    And learnèd had to love with secret lookes,
    And well could⸢ daunce, and sing with ruefulnesse,   *knew how to*
    And fortunes tell, and read in loving bookes,
  And thousand other wayes, to bait his fleshly hookes.

26 Inconstant man, that lovèd all he saw,
    And lusted after all, that he did love,
    Ne would his looser⸢ life be tide to law,   *too loose*
    But joyd weake wemens hearts to tempt and prove⸢   *try*
    If from their loyall loves he might them move;
    Which lewdnesse fild him with reprochfull paine
    Of that fowle evill,⸢ which all men reprove,   *syphilis*
    That rots the marrow, and consumes the braine:
  Such one was *Lecherie,* the third of all this traine.

27 And greedy *Avarice* by him did ride,
    Upon a Camell loaden all with gold;
    Two iron coffers hong on either side,
    With precious mettall full, as they might hold,

In greene . . . man (stanza 22) modeled on
Silenus, gluttonous and drunken attendant of
Bacchus

And in his lap an heape of coine he told;⌐   *counted*
For of his wicked pelfe his God he made,
And unto hell him selfe for money sold;
Accursed usurie was all his trade,
And right and wrong ylike in equall ballaunce waide.

28 His life was nigh unto deaths doore yplast,
And thred-bare cote, and cobled shoes he ware,
Ne scarse good morsell all his life did tast,
But both from backe and belly still did spare,
To fill his bags, and richesse to compare;⌐   *acquire*
Yet chylde ne kinsman living had he none
To leave them to; but thorough⌐ daily care   *through*
To get, and nightly feare to lose his owne,
He led a wretched life unto him selfe unknowne.

29 Most wretched wight, whom nothing might suffise,
Whose greedy lust did lacke in greatest store,⌐   *plenty*
Whose need had end, but no end covetise,
Whose wealth was want, whose plenty made him pore,
Who had enough, yet wishèd ever more;
A vile disease, and eke in foote and hand
A grievous gout tormented him full sore,
That well he could not touch, nor go, nor stand:
Such one was *Avarice*, the fourth of this faire band.

30 And next to him malicious *Envie* rode,
Upon a ravenous wolfe, and still did chaw
Betweene his cankred teeth a venemous tode,
That all the poison ran about his chaw;⌐   *jaw*
But inwardly he chawèd his owne maw⌐   *guts*
At neighbours wealth, that made him ever sad;
For death it was, when any good he saw,
And wept, that cause of weeping none he had,
But when he heard of harme, he wexèd wondrous glad.   *grew*

31 All in a kirtle of discolourd say⌐   *serge*
He clothèd was, ypainted full of eyes;
And in his bosome secretly there lay
An hatefull Snake, the which his taile uptyes
In many folds, and mortall sting implyes.⌐   *enfolds*
Still as he rode, he gnasht his teeth, to see
Those heapes of gold with griple⌐ Covetyse,   *grasping*
And grudgèd at the great felicitie
Of proud *Lucifera*, and his owne companie.

32 He hated all good workes and vertuous deeds,
And him no lesse, that any like did use,°
And who with gracious bread the hungry feeds,

that . . . use that did such good deeds

His almes for want of faith he doth accuse;
So every good to bad he doth abuse:
And eke the verse of famous Poets witt
He does backebite, and spightfull poison spues
From leprous mouth on all, that ever writt:
Such one vile *Envie* was, that fifte in row did sitt.

33   And him beside rides fierce revenging *Wrath*,
Upon a Lion, loth for to be led;
And in his hand a burning brond⟩ he hath,   *sword*
The which he brandisheth about his hed;
His eyes did hurle forth sparkles fiery red,
And starèd sterne on all, that him beheld,
As ashes pale of hew and seeming ded;
And on his dagger still his hand he held,
Trembling through hasty rage, when choler⟩ in him sweld.   *anger*

34   His ruffin⟩ raiment all was staind with blood,   *disorderly*
Which he had spilt, and all to rags yrent,⟩   *torn*
Through unadvizèd⟩ rashnesse woxen wood;⟩   *unreflecting / mad*
For of his hands he had no government,
Ne car'd for⟩ bloud in his avengement: *cared about*
But when the furious fit was overpast,
His cruell facts⟩ he often would repent;   *deeds*
Yet wilfull man he never would forecast,⟩   *foretell*
How many mischieves should ensue his heedlesse hast.

35   Full many mischiefes follow cruell *Wrath;*
Abhorrèd bloudshed, and tumultuous strife,
Unmanly murder, and unthrifty scath,⟩   *damage*
Bitter despight, with rancours rusty knife,
And fretting griefe the enemy of life;
All these, and many evils moe⟩ haunt ire,   *more*
The swelling Splene, and Frenzy raging rife,
The shaking Palsey, and Saint *Fraunces* fire:⟩   *erysipelas*
Such one was *Wrath*, the last of this ungodly tire.

36   And after all, upon the wagon beame⟩   *shaft*
Rode *Sathan*, with a smarting whip in hand,
With which he forward lasht the laesie teme,
So oft as *Slowth* still in the mire did stand.
Huge routs of people did about them band,
Showting for joy, and still before their way
A foggy mist had covered all the land;
And underneath their feet, all scattered lay
Dead sculs and bones of men, whose life had gone astray.

37   So forth they marchen in this goodly sort,
To take the solace⟩ of the open aire,   *recreation*
And in fresh flowring fields themselves to sport;

Emongst the rest rode that false Lady faire,
The fowle *Duessa*, next unto the chaire
Of proud *Lucifera*, as one of the traine:
But that good knight would not so nigh repaire,
Him selfe estraunging from their joyaunce vaine,
Whose fellowship seemd far unfit for warlike swaine.

.   .   .

[Immediately after the pageant, Red Cross encounters Sans Joy, representative of Despair, the deadliest of sins. Lucifera stops the fight and orders them to meet next day in the lists; Duessa attaches herself, lying as ever about Red Cross, to his enemy.

In canto v Red Cross defeats Sans Joy, but Duessa saves his life and takes him for treatment to Aesculapius in hell. Red Cross, seeing the dangers of the House of Pride, leaves.

Canto vi tells how Una is rescued from Sans Loy by a band of satyrs who, in "bootlesse zeale" worship her ass when she forbids them to worship her. Sir Satyrane, son of a lady and a savage man, arrives, admires Una's wisdom, and enables her to flee. Archimago announces that Sans Joy has killed Red Cross, and Sans Loy appears to fight with Satyrane. Una escapes. (Here is one of Spenser's loose ends, for Satyrane's fight is never finished, and when he turns up again in III.vii.28 it has been forgotten.) Perhaps the satyrs stand for natural religion, a good instinct misdirected; Satyrane for a good mixture of nature and instruction, which is capable, like the Reformed Church of England, of receiving the truth.

The seventh canto shows Red Cross tricked by Duessa into drinking of an enervating fountain—corrupt Gospel—after he has removed his Christian armor. While powerless, he is captured by Orgoglio, the Pride of Life, great enemy of Holiness. Orgoglio's mistress is Duessa, in her role as the Whore of Babylon, wearing the triple crown of the papacy. The Dwarf finds Una and tells her what is happening; as she laments, Prince Arthur arrives, and this super-hero is described for the first time. Spenser planned, roughly, to have Arthur intervene in about the seventh or eighth canto of each book; so it is in I, II, and V. Una tells him of her plight; her parents have been the captives of the dragon for four years (i.e. the 4000 years between the fall of Adam and the birth of Christ). Arthur goes to the rescue.]

Canto viii
Faire virgin to redeeme her deare
    brings Arthur to the fight:
Who slayes the Gyant, wounds the beast,
    and strips Duessa quight.

1   Ay me, how many perils doe enfold
        The righteous man, to make him daily fall?
        Were not, that heavenly grace doth him uphold,
        And stedfast truth acquite° him out of all.   *deliver*
        Her love is firme, her care continuall,
        So oft as he through his owne foolish pride,
        Or weakenesse is to sinfull bands° made thrall: *bonds*

Else should this *Redcrosse* knight in bands have dyde,
For whose deliverance she this Prince doth thither guide.

2   They sadly traveild thus, untill they came
    Nigh to a castle builded strong and hie:
    Then cryde the Dwarfe, lo yonder is the same,
    In which my Lord my liege doth lucklesse lie,
    Thrall' to that Gyants hatefull tyrannie: *slave*
    Therefore, deare Sir, your mightie powres assay.'   *try*
    The noble knight alighted by and by
    From loftie steede, and bad the Ladie stay,
To see what end of fight should him befall that day.

3   So with the Squire, th'admirer of his might,
    He marchèd forth towards that castle wall;
    Whose gates he found fast shut, ne' living wight   *nor*
    To ward' the same, nor answere commers call.   *guard*
    Then tooke that Squire an horne of bugle small,°
    Which hong adowne his side in twisted gold,
    And tassels gay. Wyde wonders° over all
    Of that same hornes great vertues weren told,
Which had approvèd' bene in uses manifold.   *proved*

4   Was never wight, that heard that shrilling sound,
    But trembling feare did feele in every vaine;
    Three miles it might be easie heard around,
    And Ecchoes three answerd it selfe againe:
    No false enchauntment, nor deceiptfull traine'   *trickery*
    Might once abide the terror of that blast,
    But presently was voide and wholly vaine:
    No gate so strong, no locke so firme and fast,
But with that percing noise flew open quite, or brast.'   *burst*

5   The same before the Geants gate he blew,
    That all the castle quakèd from the ground,
    And every dore of freewill open flew.
    The Gyant selfe dismaièd with that sownd,
    Where he with his *Duessa* dalliance' fownd,   *love making*
    In hast came rushing forth from inner bowre,
    With staring countenance sterne, as one astownd,
    And staggering steps, to weet, what suddein stowre'   *tumult*
Had wrought that horror strange, and dar'd his dreaded powre.

6   And after him the proud *Duessa* came,
    High mounted on her manyheaded beast,°
    And every head with fyrie tongue did flame,
    And every head was crownèd on his creast,
    And bloudie mouthèd with late cruell feast.

---

horne . . . small small wild ox's horn   such horns had been featured in Romance
Wyde wonders from the *Chanson de Roland;*   **High . . . beast** See Headnote to Bk. I.

That when the knight beheld, his mightie shild
Upon his manly arme he soone addrest,⌐   *adjusted*
And at him fiercely flew, with courage fild,
And eger greedinesse through every member thrild.

7   Therewith the Gyant buckled him to fight,
Inflam'd with scornefull wrath and high disdaine,
And lifting up his dreadfull club on hight,
Allarm'd with ragged snubbes⌐ and knottie graine,   *snags*
Him thought at first encounter to have slaine.
But wise and warie was that noble Pere⌐,   *peer*
And lightly leaping from so monstrous maine,⌐   *force*
Did faire avoide the violence him nere;
It booted nought, to thinke, such thunderbolts to beare.

8   Ne shame he thought to shunne so hideous might:
The idle stroke, enforcing furious way,
Missing the marke of his misaymèd sight
Did fall to ground, and with his⌐ heavie sway   *its*
So deepely dinted in the driven clay,
That three yardes deepe a furrow up did throw:
The sad earth wounded with so sore assay,⌐   *onslaught*
Did grone full grievous underneath the blow,
And trembling with strange feare, did like an earthquake show.

9   As when almightie *Jove* in wrathfull mood,
To wreake⌐ the guilt of mortall sins is bent,   *punish*
Hurles forth his thundring dart with deadly food,⌐   *hatred (feud)*
Enrold in flames, and smouldring dreriment,
Through riven cloudes and molten firmament;
The fierce threeforkèd engin⌐ making way,   *weapon*
Both loftie towres and highest trees hath rent,
And all that might his⌐ angrie passage stay,   *its*
And shooting in the earth, casts up a mount of clay.

10 His boystrous⌐ club, so buried in the ground,   *vast*
He could not rearen up again so light,
But that the knight him at avantage found,
And whiles he strove his combred clubbe to quight⌐   *free*
Out of the earth, with blade all burning bright
He smote off his left arme, which like a blocke
Did fall to ground, depriv'd of native might;
Large streames of bloud out of the trunckèd stocke
Forth gushed, like fresh water streame from riven rocke.

11 Dismaièd with so desperate deadly wound,
And eke impatient of unwonted paine,
He loudly brayd with beastly yelling sound,
That all the fields rebellowèd againe;
As great a noyse, as when in Cymbrian⌐ plaine   *Danish*

An heard of Bulles, whom kindly˃ rage doth sting,   *natural*
Do for the milkie mothers want complaine,°
And fill the fields with troublous bellowing,
The neighbour woods around with hollow murmur ring.

12   That when his deare *Duessa* heard, and saw
      The evill stownd,˃ that daungerd her estate,   *blow*
      Unto his aid she hastily did draw
      Her dreadfull beast, who swolne with bloud of late
      Came ramping forth with proud presumpteous gate,
      And threatned all his heads like flaming brands.˃   *torches*
      But him the Squire made quickly to retrate,
      Encountring fierce with single˃ sword in hand,   *only*
And twixt him and his Lord did like a bulwarke stand.

13   The proud *Duessa* full of wrathfull spight,
      And fierce disdaine, to be affronted so,
      Enforst her purple beast with all her might
      That stop˃ out of the way to overthroe,   *hindrance*
      Scorning the let˃ of so unequall foe: *obstruction*
      But nathemore˃ would that courageous swayne   *nevertheless . . . not*
      To her yeeld passage, gainst his Lord to goe,
      But with outrageous strokes did him restraine,
And with his bodie bard the way atwixt them twaine.

14   Then tooke the angrie witch her golden cup,°
      Which still she bore, replete with magick artes;
      Death and despeyre did many thereof sup,
      And secret poyson through their inner parts,
      Th'eternall bale˃ of heavie wounded harts;   *grief*
      Which after charmes and some enchauntments said,
      She lightly sprinkled on his weaker˃ parts;   *too weak*
      Therewith his sturdie courage soone was quayd,˃   *subdued*
And all his senses were with suddeine dread dismayd.

15   So downe he fell before the cruell beast,
      Who on his necke his bloudie clawes did seize,
      That life nigh crusht out of his panting brest:
      No powre he had to stirre, nor will to rize.
      That when the carefull˃ knight gan well avise,˃   *watchful / notice*
      He lightly left the foe, with whom he fought,
      And to the beast gan turne his enterprise;
      For wondrous anguish in his hart it wrought,
To see his lovèd Squire into such thraldome brought.

16   And high advauncing his bloud-thirstie blade,
      Stroke one of those deformèd heads so sore,°

Do . . . complaine lament the absence of cows
golden cup Revelation 17:4; the Whore carries
"a golden cup in her hand full of abominations
and filthiness of her fornication"
Stroke . . . sore Revelation 13:3: "And I saw

one of his heads as it were wounded to death";
the passage is related to the prophecy of the
bruising of the serpent's head (fulfilled at the
Crucifixion) in Genesis 3:15.

That of his puissance proud ensample made;
His monstrous scalpe downe to his teeth it tore,
And that misformèd shape mis-shapèd more:
A sea of bloud gusht from the gaping wound,
That⸃ her gay garments staynd with filthy gore,   *which*
And overflowèd all the field around;
That over shoes in bloud he waded on the ground.

17 Thereat he roarèd for exceeding paine,
    That to have heard, great horror would have bred,
    And scourging th'emptie ayre with his long traine,⸃   *tail*
    Through great impatience⸃ of his grievèd hed   *pain*
    His gorgeous ryder from her loftie sted⸃   *place*
    Would have cast downe, and trod in durtie myre,
    Had not the Gyant soone her succourèd;
    Who all enrag'd with smart and franticke yre,
    Came hurtling in full fierce, and forst the knight retyre.

18 The force, which wont in two to be disperst,
    In one alone left⸃ hand he now unites,   *remaining*
    Which is through rage more strong then both were erst;⸃   *formerly*
    With which his hideous club aloft he dites,⸃   *raises*
    And at his foe with furious rigour smites,
    That strongest Oake might seeme to overthrow:
    The stroke upon his shield so heavie lites,
    That to the ground it doubleth him full low:
    What mortall wight could ever beare so monstrous blow?

19 And in his fall his shield, that covered was,
    Did loose his vele by chaunce, and open flew:
    The light whereof, that heavens light did pas,⸃   *surpass*
    Such blazing brightnesse through the aier threw,
    That eye mote⸃ not the same endure to vew.   *might*
    Which when the Gyaunt spyde with staring eye,
    He downe let fall his arme, and soft withdrew
    His weapon huge, that heavèd was on hye
    For to have slaine the man, that on the ground did lye.

20 And eke the fruitfull-headed⸃ beast, amaz'd   *many-headed*
    At flashing beames of that sunshiny shield,
    Became starke blind, and all his senses daz'd,
    That downe he tumbled on the durtie field,
    And seem'd himselfe as conquerèd to yield.
    Whom when his maistresse proud perceiv'd to fall,
    Whiles yet his feeble feet for faintnesse reeld,
    Unto the Gyant loudly she gan call,
    O helpe *Orgoglio,* helpe, or else we perish all.

21 At her so pitteous cry was much amoov'd
    Her champion stout, and for to ayde his frend,

Againe his wonted angry weapon proov'd:ͽ   *tried*
But all in vaine: for he has read his end
In that bright shield, and all their forces spend
Themselves in vaine: for since that glauncing sight,
He hath no powre to hurt, nor to defend;
As where th'Almighties lightning brond does light,
It dimmes the dazèd eyen, and daunts the senses quight.

22   Whom when the Prince, to battell new addrest,
And threatning high his dreadfull stroke did see,
His sparkling blade about his head he blest,ͽ   *waved*
And smote off quite his right leg by the knee,
That downe he tombled; as an agèd tree,
High growing on the top of rocky clift,
Whose hartstrings with keene steele nigh hewen be,
The mightie trunck halfe rent, with ragged rift
Doth roll adowne the rocks, and fall with fearefull drift.ͽ   *impact*

23   Or as a Castle rearèd high and round,
By subtile engins and malitious slightͽ   *artifice*
Is underminèd from the lowest ground,
And her foundation forst, and feebled quight,
At last downe falles, and with her heapèd hight
Her hastie ruine does more heavie make,
And yields it selfe unto the victours might;
Sich was this Gyaunts fall, that seemd to shake
The stedfast globe of earth, as it for feare did quake.

24   The knight then lightly leaping to the pray,
With mortall steele him smot againe so sore,
That headlesse his unweldy bodie lay,
All wallowd in his owne fowle bloudy gore,
Which flowèd from his wounds in wondrous store.
But soone as breath out of his breast did pas,
That huge great body, which the Gyaunt bore,
Was vanisht quite, and of that monstrous mas
Was nothing left, but like an emptie bladder was.

25   Whose grievous fall, when false *Duessa* spide,
Her golden cup she cast unto the ground,
And crownèd mitre rudely threw aside;
Such piercing griefe her stubborne hart did wound,
That she could not endure that dolefull stound,ͽ   *affliction*
But leaving all behind her, fled away:
The light-foot Squire her quickly turnd around,
And by hard meanes enforcing her to stay,
So brought unto his Lord, as his deservèd pray.

26   The royall Virgin, which beheld from farre,
In pensive plight, and sad perplexitie,

The whole atchievement° of this doubtfull warre,   *course*
Came running fast to greet his victorie,
With sober gladnesse, and myld modestie,
And with sweet joyous cheare him thus bespake;
Faire braunch of noblesse, flowre of chevalrie,
That with your worth the world amazèd make,
How shall I quite° the paines, ye suffer for my sake?   *repay*

27   And you fresh bud of vertue springing fast,°
     Whom these sad eyes saw nigh unto deaths dore,
     What hath poore Virgin for such perill past,
     Wherewith you to reward? Accept therefore
     My simple selfe, and service evermore;
     And he that high does sit, and all things see
     With equall° eyes, their merites to restore,°   *just / reward*
     Behold what ye this day have done for mee,
     And what I cannot quite, requite with usuree.°   *interest*

28   But sith° the heavens, and your faire handeling°   *since /conduct*
     Have made you maister of the field this day,
     Your fortune maister eke with governing,°
     And well begun end all so well, I pray,
     Ne let that wicked woman scape away;
     For she it is, that did my Lord bethrall,
     My dearest Lord, and deepe in dongeon lay,
     Where he his better dayes hath wasted all.
     O heare, how piteous he to you for ayd does call.

29   Forthwith he gave in charge unto his Squire,
     That scarlot whore to keepen carefully;
     Whiles he himselfe with greedie° great desire   *eager*
     Into the Castle entred forcibly,
     Where living creature none he did espye;
     Then gan he lowdly through the house to call:
     But no man car'd to answere to his crye.
     There raignd a solemne silence over all,
     Nor voice was heard, nor wight was seene in bowre or hall.

30   At last with creeping crooked pace forth came
     An old old man, with beard as white as snow,
     That on a staffe his feeble steps did frame,
     And guide his wearie gate both too and fro:
     For his eye sight him failed long ygo,
     And on his arme a bounch of keyes he bore,
     The which unusèd rust did overgrow:
     Those were the keyes of every inner dore,
     But he could not them use, but kept them still in store.

And . . . fast addressed to the squire, Timias   **Your . . . governing** now take advantage of
                                                        your fortune, too, by exercising foresight

31   But very uncouth sight was to behold,
        How he did fashion his untoward pace,
        For as he forward moov'd his footing old,
        So backward still was turnd his wrincled face,
        Unlike to men, who ever as they trace,
        Both feet and face one way are wont to lead.
        This was the auncient keeper of that place,
        And foster father of the Gyant dead;
     His name *Ignaro*° did his nature right aread.˃   *reveal*

32   His reverend haires and holy gravitie
        The knight much honord, as beseemèd well,
        And gently askt, where all the people bee,
        Which in that stately building wont to dwell.
        Who answerd him full soft, he could not tell.
        Againe he askt, where that same knight was layd,
        Whom great *Orgoglio* with his puissaunce fell
        Had made his caytive thrall;˃ againe he sayde,   *slave*
     He could not tell: ne ever other answere made.

33   Then askèd he, which way he in might pas:
        He could not tell, againe he answerèd.
        Thereat the curteous knight displeasèd was,
        And said, Old sire, it seemes thou hast not red˃   *understood*
        How ill it sits with˃ that same silver hed   *becomes*
        In vaine to mocke, or mockt in vaine to bee:
        But if thou be, as thou art pourtrahèd
        With natures pen, in ages grave degree,˃   *solemn status*
     Aread˃ in graver wise, what I demaund of thee.   *answer*

34   His answere likewise was, he could not tell.
        Whose sencelesse speach, and doted ignorance
        When as the noble Prince had markèd well,
        He ghest his nature by his countenance,
        And calmd his wrath with goodly temperance.
        Then to him stepping, from his arme did reach
        Those keyes, and made himselfe free enterance.
        Each dore he openèd without any breach;
     There was no barre to stop, nor foe him to empeach.˃   *hinder*

35   There all within full rich arayd he found,
        With royall arras and resplendent gold.
        And did with store of every thing abound,
        That greatest Princes presence might behold.
        But all the floore (too filthy to be told)
        With bloud of guiltlesse babes, and innocents trew,
        Which there were slaine, as sheepe out of the fold,

Ignaro This Ignorance reflects Spenser's contempt for blind devotion—he showed it in
canto iv; Ignaro is silent and pious but lives
with and fosters Worldly Pride.

Defilèd was, that dreadfull was to vew,
And sacred ashes over it was strowèd new.

36 And there beside of marble stone was built
An Altare, carv'd with cunning imagery,
On which true Christians bloud was often spilt,
And holy Martyrs often doen to dye,⟩   *put to death*
With cruell malice and strong tyranny.
Whose blessèd sprites from underneath the stone
To God for vengeance cryde continually,°
And with great griefe were often heard to grone,
That hardest heart would bleede, to heare their piteous mone.

37 Through every rowme he sought, and every bowr,
But no where could he find that wofull thrall:
At last he came unto an yron doore,
That fast was lockt, but key found not at all
Emongst that bounch, to open it withall;
But in the same a little grate was pight,⟩   *placed*
Through which he sent his voyce, and lowd did call
With all his powre, to weet, if living wight
Were housèd therewithin, whom he enlargen⟩ might.   *set free*

38 Therewith an hollow, dreary, murmuring voyce
These piteous plaints and dolours did resound;
O who is that, which brings me happy choyce
Of death, that here lye dying every stound,⟩   *moment*
Yet live perforce in balefull darkenesse bound?
For now three Moones have changèd thrice° their hew,⟩   *shape*
And have beene thrice hid underneath the ground,
Since I the heavens chearefull face did vew,
O welcome thou, that doest of death bring tydings trew.

39 Which when that Champion heard, with percing point
Of pitty deare⟩ his hart was thrillèd⟩ sore,   *great / pierced*
And trembling horrour ran through every joynt,
For ruth of gentle knight so fowle forlore:⟩   *lost*
Which shaking off, he rent that yron dore,
With furious force, and indignation fell;
Where entred in, his foot could find no flore,
But all a deepe descent, as darke as hell,
That breathèd ever forth a filthie banefull smell.

40 But neither darkenesse fowle, nor filthy bands,⟩   *bonds*
Nor noyous⟩ smell his purpose could withhold,   *noxious*

Whose . . . continually At the opening of the
Fifth Seal St. John "saw under the altar the
souls of them that were slain for the word of
God . . . And they cried with a loud voice,
saying, How long, O Lord, holy and true, dost
thou not judge and avenge our blood . . . ?"
(Revelation 6:9–10); in this canto the apocalyptic theme is unusually evident.
three Moones . . . thrice three months, representing the three centuries between Pope Gregory
VII and Wyclif during which England was
supposed to have been under the domination of
the papacy

(Entire affection hateth nicer> hands)   *too fastidious*
But that with constant zeale, and courage bold,
After long paines and labours manifold,
He found the meanes that Prisoner up to reare;
Whose feeble thighes, unhable to uphold
His pinèd corse,> him scarse to light could beare,   *wasted corpse*
A ruefull spectacle of death and ghastly drere.>   *wretchedness*

41 His sad dull eyes deepe sunck in hollow pits,
Could not endure th'unwonted sunne to view;
His bare thin cheekes for want of better bits,>   *food*
And empty sides deceivèd of their dew,
Could make a stony hart his hap> to rew;   *luck*
His rawbone armes, whose mighty brawnèd bowrs>   *muscles*
Were wont to rive steele plates, and helmets hew,
Were cleane consum'd, and all his vitall powres
Decayd, and all his flesh shronk up like withered flowres.

42 Whom when his Lady saw, to him she ran
With hasty joy: to see him made her glad,
And sad to view his visage pale and wan,
Who earst> in flowres of freshest youth was clad.   *formerly*
Tho when her well of teares she wasted had,
She said, Ah dearest Lord, what evill starre
On you hath frownd, and pourd his influence bad,
That of your selfe ye thus berobbèd arre,
And this misseeming hew> your manly looks doth marre? *appearance*

43 But welcome now my Lord, in wele or woe,
Whose̎ presence I have lackt too long a day;
And fie on Fortune mine avowèd foe,
Whose wrathfull wreakes> them selves do now alay.>   *injuries / diminish*
And for these wrongs shall treble penaunce pay
Of treble good: good growes of evils priefe.>   *test, experience*
The chearelesse man, whom sorrow did dismay,
Had no delight to treaten> of his griefe;   *talk*
His long endurèd famine needed more reliefe.

44 Faire Lady, then said that victorious knight,
The things, that grievous were to do, or beare,
Them to renew, I wote, breeds no delight;°
Best musicke breeds delight in loathing eare:°
But th'onely good, that growes of passèd feare,
Is to be wise, and ware> of like agein.   *wary*
This dayes ensample hath this lesson deare

Them . . . delight remembering the famous
line (*Aeneid* II.3), in which Aeneas answers
Dido's request that he should tell the story of
his adventures: *Infandum, regina, jubes renovare*

dolorem ("Queen, you are commanding me to
renew unspeakable grief")
Best . . . eare although fine music can produce
pleasure even in the ear that resists it (this is
not true of the knight's story)

Deepe written in my heart with yron pen,
That blisse may not abide in state of mortall men.

45 Henceforth sir knight, take to you wonted strength,
    And maister these mishaps with patient might;
    Loe where your foe lyes stretcht in monstrous length,
    And loe that wicked woman in your sight,
    The roote of all your care, and wretched plight,
    Now in your powre, to let her live, or dye.
    To do her dye (quoth *Una*) were despight,
    And shame t'avenge so weake an enimy;
    But spoile her of her scarlot robe, and let her fly.

46 So as she bad, that witch they disaraid,
    And robd of royall robes, and purple pall,
    And ornaments that richly were displaid;
    Ne sparèd they to strip her naked all.
    Then when they had despoild her tire> and call,>   *dress / headdress*
    Such as she was, their eyes might her behold,
    That her misshapèd parts did them appall,
    A loathly, wrinckled hag, ill favoured, old,
    Whose secret filth good manners biddeth not be told.

47 Her craftie head was altogether bald,
    And as in hate of honorable eld,>   *old age*
    Was overgrowne with scurfe and filthy scald;>   *scabs*
    Her teeth out of her rotten gummes were feld,>   *fallen*
    And her sowre breath abhominably smeld;
    Her drièd dugs, like bladders lacking wind,
    Hong downe, and filthy matter from them weld;
    Her wrizled> skin as rough, as maple rind,   *wrinkled*
    So scabby was, that would have loathd all womankind.

48 Her neather parts, the shame of all her kind,>   *womenkind*
    My chaster Muse for shame doth blush to write;
    But at her rompe she growing had behind
    A foxes taile,° with dong all fowly dight;>   *covered*
    And eke her feete most monstrous were in sight;
    For one of them was like an Eagles claw,
    With griping talaunts armd to greedy fight,
    The other like a Beares uneven> paw: *rough*
    More ugly shape yet never living creature saw.

49 Which when the knights beheld, amazd they were,
    And wondred at so fowle deformèd wight.
    Such then (said *Una*) as she seemeth here,
    Such is the face of falshood, such the sight
    Of fowle *Duessa*, when her borrowed light

Foxes taile The fox was associated in contemporary polemic with the Catholic clergy; the
text was Song of Songs 2:15, supported by
Luke 13:32, where Jesus calls Herod a fox.

Is laid away, and counterfesaunce° knowne.   *deception*
Thus when they had the witch disrobèd quight,°
And all her filthy feature open showne,
They let her goe at will, and wander wayes unknowne.

50   She flying fast from heavens hated face,
      And from the world that her discovered wide,
      Fled to the wastfull wildernesse apace,
      From living eyes her open shame to hide,
      And lurkt in rocks and caves long unespide.
      But that faire crew of knights, and *Una* faire
      Did in that castle afterwards abide,
      To rest them selves, and weary powres repaire,
    Where store they found of all, that dainty was and rare.°

[In canto ix we hear Arthur's story of his love for Gloriana. He exchanges
gifts, Arthur's symbolizing the Eucharist, and Red Cross's the New Testament,
and Arthur leaves. Red Cross then meets Sir Trevisan, fleeing from the Cave of
Despair; he goes to the Cave and meets Despair, to whom he almost succumbs.
In terms of the spiritual allegory this passage describes a great crisis in the
career of what Milton calls the "wayfaring" Christian soul; despair is the greatest single threat to it. In terms of the historical allegory, following the exposure
of Duessa, it means the relapse into Romanism under Queen Mary, before the
Elizabethan Settlement established the true church for ever.]

From Canto ix

33   Ere long they come, where that same wicked wight°
      His dwelling has, low in an hollow cave,
      Farre underneath a craggie clift ypight,°   *placed*
      Darke, dolefull, drearie, like a greedie grave,
      That still for carrion carcases doth crave:
      On top whereof aye dwelt the ghastly Owle,
      Shrieking his balefull note, which ever drave
      Farre from that haunt all other chearefull fowle;
    And all about it wandring ghostes did waile and howle.

34   And all about old stockes and stubs of trees,
      Whereon nor fruit, nor leafe was ever seene,
      Did hang upon the ragged rocky knees°;   *crags*
      On which had many wretches hangèd beene,
      Whose carcases were scattered on the greene,
      And throwne about the cliffs. Arrivèd there,
      That bare-head knight for dread and dolefull teene,°   *grief*
      Would faine have fled, ne durst approchen neare,
    But th'other forst him stay, and comforted in feare.

disrobèd quight Revelation 17:16: "these shall
hate the whore, and shall make her desolate and
naked . . . ".
store . . . rare They confiscate the viciously

acquired wealth of Orgoglio and Duessa, which
figures the confiscation of monastic wealth in
the reign of Henry VIII.
wight Despair

35 That darkesome cave they enter, where they find
    That cursèd man, low sitting on the ground,
    Musing full sadly in his sullein mind;
    His griesie⁾ lockes, long growen, and unbound,   *gray*
    Disordred hong about his shoulders round,
    And hid his face; through which his hollow eyne
    Lookt deadly dull, and starèd as astound;
    His raw-bone cheekes through penurie and pine,⁾   *hunger*
Were shronke into his jawes, as⁾ he did never dine.   *as though*

36 His garments nought but many ragged clouts,⁾   *cloths*
    With thornes together pind and patchèd was,
    The which his naked sides he wrapt abouts;
    And him beside there lay upon the gras
    A drearie corse, whose life away did pas,
    All wallowd in his owne yet⁾ luke-warme blood,   *still*
    That from his wound yet wellèd fresh alas;
    In which a rustie knife fast fixèd stood,
And made an open passage for the gushing flood.

37 Which piteous spectacle, approving⁾ trew   *proving*
    The wofull tale that *Trevisan* had told,
    When as the gentle *Redcrosse* knight did vew,
    With firie zeale he burnt in courage bold,
    Him to avenge, before his bloud were cold,
    And to the villein said, Thou damnèd wight,
    The author of this fact,⁾ we here behold,   *deed*
    What justice can but judge against thee right,
With thine owne bloud to price⁾ his bloud, here shed in sight? *pay for*

38 What franticke fit (quoth he) hath thus distraught
    Thee, foolish man, so rash a doome⁾ to give?   *judgment*
    What justice ever other judgement taught,
    But he should die, who merites not to live?
    None else to death this man despayring drive,⁾   *drove*
    But his owne guiltie mind deserving death.
    Is then unjust to each his due to give?
    Or let him die, that loatheth living breath?
Or let him die at ease, that liveth here uneath?⁾   *uneasy*

39 Who travels by the wearie wandring way,
    To come unto his wishèd home in haste,
    And meetes a flood, that doth his passage stay,
    Is not great grace to helpe him over past,⁾   *to pass over*
    Or free his feet, that in the myre sticke fast?
    Most envious man, that grieves at neighbours good,
    And fond,⁾ that joyest in the woe thou hast,   *foolish*
    Why wilt not let him passe, that long hath stood
Upon the banke, yet wilt thy selfe not passe the flood?

40   He there does now enjoy eternall rest
          And happie ease, which thou doest want and crave,
          And further from it daily wanderest:
          What if some litle paine the passage have,
          That makes fraile flesh to feare the bitter wave?
          Is not short paine well borne, that brings long ease,
          And layes the soule to sleepe in quiet grave?
          Sleepe after toyle, port after stormie seas,
      Ease after warre, death after life° does greatly please.

41   The knight much wondred at his suddeine° wit,   *quick*
          And said, The terme of life is limited,
          Ne may a man prolong, nor shorten it;
          The souldier may not move from watchfull sted,°   *post*
          Nor leave his stand, untill his Captaine bed.°   *orders*
          Who life did limit by almightie doome,°   *judgment*
          (Quoth he) knowes best the terms establishèd;
          And he, that points° the Centonell his roome,°   *appoints / post*
      Doth license him depart at sound of morning droome.

42   Is not his deed, what ever thing is donne,
          In heaven and earth? did not he all create
          To die againe? all ends that was begonne.
          Their times in his eternall booke of fate
          Are written sure, and have their certaine date.°   *termination*
          Who then can strive with strong necessitie,
          That holds the world in his° still chaunging state,   *its*
          Or shunne the death ordaynd by destinie?
      When houre of death is come, let none aske whence, nor why.

43   The lenger life, I wote° the greater sin,   *think*
          The greater sin, the greater punishment:
          All those great battels, which thou boasts to win,
          Through strife, and bloud-shed, and avengèment,
          Now praysd, hereafter deare thou shalt repent:
          For life must life, and bloud must bloud repay.
          Is not enough thy evill life forespent?
          For he, that once hath missèd the right way,
      The further he doth goe, the further he doth stray.

44   Then do no further goe, no further stray,
          But here lie downe, and to thy rest betake,
          Th'ill to prevent, that life ensewen may.°
          For what hath life, that may it lovèd make,
          And gives not rather cause it to forsake?
          Feare, sicknesse, age, losse, labour, sorrow, strife,
          Paine, hunger, cold, that makes the hart to quake;

death . . . life This is Despair's "suddeine wit"—he smuggles this item, which is not parallel to the others, into his list; all his subsequent arguments have the same kind of rhetorical plausibility.
that . . . may that may follow life

And ever fickle fortune rageth rife,
All which, and thousands mo⁾ do make a loathsome life.   *more*

45 Thou wretched man, of death hast greatest need,
  If in true ballance thou wilt weigh thy state:
  For never knight, that darèd warlike deede,
  More lucklesse disaventures did amate:⁾   *overthrow*
  Witnesse the dongeon deepe, wherein of late
  Thy life shut up, for death so oft did call;
  And though good lucke prolongèd hath thy date,
  Yet death then, would the like mishaps forestall,
Into the which hereafter thou maiest happen fall.

46 Why then doest thou, O man of sin, desire
  To draw thy dayes forth to their last degree?
  Is not the measure of thy sinfull hire⁾   *service to sin*
  High heapèd up with huge iniquitie,
  Against the day of wrath, to burden thee?
  Is not enough, that to this Ladie milde
  Thou falsèd hast thy faith with perjurie,
  And sold thy selfe to serve *Duessa* vilde,⁾   *vile*
With whom in all abuse thou hast thy selfe defilde?

47 Is not he just, that all this doth behold
  From highest heaven, and beares an equall⁾ eye?   *impartial*
  Shall he thy sins up in his knowledge fold,
  And guiltie be of thine impietie?
  Is not his law, Let every sinner die:
  Die shall all flesh?° what then must needs be donne,
  Is it not better to doe willinglie,
  Then linger, till the glasse be all out ronne?
Death is the end of woes: die soone, O faeries sonne.

48 The knight was much enmovèd with his speach,
  That as a swords point through his hart did perse,
  And in his conscience made a secret breach,
  Well knowing true all, that he did reherse⁾   *recount*
  And to his fresh remembrance did reverse⁾   *bring back*
  The ugly vew of his deformèd crimes,
  That all his manly powres it did disperse,
  As he were charmèd with inchaunted rimes,
That oftentimes he quakt, and fainted oftentimes.

49 In which amazement, when the Miscreant
  Perceivèd him to waver weake and fraile,
  Whiles trembling horror did his conscience dant,⁾   *daunt*
  And hellish anguish did his soule assaile,

Is . . . flesh Despair naturally omits to mention
that God modified this sentence, or that He
forbade suicide.

To drive him to despaire, and quite to quaile,°   *be dismayed*
He shew'd him painted in a table° plaine,   *picture*
The damnèd ghosts, that doe in torments waile,
And thousand feends that doe them endlesse paine
With fire and brimstone, which for ever shall remaine.

50   The sight whereof so throughly him dismaid,
That nought but death before his eyes he saw,
And ever burning wrath before him laid,
By righteous sentence of th'Almighties law:
Then gan the villein him to overcraw,°   *exult over*
And brought unto him swords, ropes, poison, fire,
And all that might him to perdition draw;
And bad him choose, what death he would desire:
For death was due to him, that had provokt Gods ire.°

51   But when as none of them he saw him take,
He to him raught° a dagger sharpe and keene,   *handed*
And gave it him in hand: his hand did quake,
And tremble like a leafe of Aspin° greene,   *poplar*
And troubled bloud through his pale face was seene
To come, and goe with tydings from the hart,
As it a running messenger had beene.
At last resolv'd to worke his finall smart,
He lifted up his hand, that backe again did start.

52   Which when as *Una* saw, through every vaine
The crudled° cold ran to her well of life,   *congealed*
As in a swowne:° but soone reliv'd° againe,   *faint / revived*
Out of his hand she snatcht the cursèd knife,
And threw it to the ground, enragèd rife,°   *deeply*
And to him said, Fie, fie, faint harted knight,
What meanest thou by this reprochfull strife?
Is this the battell, which thou vauntst to fight
With that fire-mouthèd Dragon, horrible and bright?

53   Come, come away, fraile, feeble, fleshly wight,
Ne let vaine words bewitch thy manly hart,
Ne divelish thoughts dismay thy constant spright.
In heavenly mercies hast thou not a part?
Why shouldst thou then despeire, that chosen art?°
Where justice growes, there grows eke greater grace,°
The which doth quench the brond of hellish smart,°   *pain*

---

death . . . ire Red Cross has been deceived into the desperate belief that his sins are unforgivable and that he should therefore anticipate the judgment of God.
chosen art theological: he is one of God's Elect, chosen before the creation for heaven. This "single" predestinarianism—there is election to salvation but not to damnation—is the less rigid form of the Calvinist doctrine: see

Paradise Lost III.183 ff.: "Some I have chosen of peculiar grace / Elect above the rest; so is my will; / The rest shall hear me call, and oft be warned / Their sinful state, and to appease betimes / The incensed deity, while offered grace / Invites. . . ."
where . . . grace Una reminds him of the fact Despair wanted him to forget: God's justice is followed by even greater grace.

And that accurst hand-writing doth deface.
Arise, Sir knight arise, and leave this cursèd place.

54 So up he rose, and thence amounted⁾ streight.   *mounted*
    Which when the carle⁾ beheld, and saw his gust   *churl*
    Would safe depart, for all his subtill sleight,
    He chose an halter from among the rest,
    And with it hung himselfe, unbid⁾ unblest.   *unprayed for*
    But death he could not worke himselfe thereby;
    For thousand times he so himselfe had drest,⁾   *prepared*
    Yet nathelesse it could not doe him die,⁾   *kill him*
    Till he should die his last, that is eternally.

[In canto x Una brings Red Cross to the House of Holiness, an elaborate
allegorical set-piece. He meets the three theological virtues, Fidelia, Speranza,
and Charissa (Faith, Hope, and Charity), sketched with their emblematic
attributes and called the daughters of Cælia (Heaven). Then the "soule-diseasèd
knight" undergoes severe penance and performs, in an allegory of seven beads-
men in a hospital, the seven corporal works of mercy. This prepares him for
Contemplation. In the following passage Contemplation leads him to the top
of a holy mountain, compared to Sinai and the Mount of Olives, and also to
Parnassus, haunt of the Muses. He can see the Heavenly Jerusalem and compare it with its earthly counterpart, Cleopolis (London). Now he acquires his
saint's name and reluctantly leaves to finish his quest.]

    From Canto x
46 Thence forward by that painfull way they pas,
    Forth to an hill, that was both steepe and hy;
    On top whereof a sacred chappell was,
    And eke a litle Hermitage thereby,
    Wherein an agèd holy man did lye,
    That day and night said his devotión,
    Ne⁾ other worldly busines did apply;   *nor*
    His name was heavenly *Contemplatión*;
    Of God and godnesse was his meditatión.

47 Great grace that old man to him given had;
    For God he often saw from heavens hight,
    All⁾ were his earthly eyen both blunt and bad,   *although*
    And through great age had lost their kindly⁾ sight,   *natural*
    Yet wondrous quick and persant⁾ was his spright,   *penetrating*
    As Eagles eye, that can behold the Sunne:
    That hill they scale with all their powre and might,
    That his frayle thighes nigh wearie and fordonne⁾   *tired out*
    Gan faile, but by her helpe the top at last he wonne.

48 There they do finde that godly aged Sire,
    With snowy lockes adowne his shoulders shed,
    As hoarie frost with spangles doth attire
    The mossy braunches of an Oke halfe ded.

Each bone might through his body well be red,⸱   *seen*
And every sinew seene through his long fast:
For nought he car'd his carcas long unfed;
His mind was full of spirituall repast,
And pyn'd⸱ his flesh, to keepe his body low and chast.   *starved*

49   Who when these two approaching he aspide,
        At their first presence grew agrievèd sore,
        That forst him lay his heavenly thoughts aside;
        And had he not that Dame° respected more,⸱   *greatly*
        Whom highly he did reverence and adore,
        He would not once have movèd for the knight.
        They him saluted standing far afore;⸱   *far off*
    Who well them greeting, humbly did requight,
And askèd, to what end they clomb that tedious height.

50   What end (quoth she) should cause us take such paine,
        But that same end, which every living wight
        Should make his marke, high heaven to attaine?
        Is not from hence the way, that leadeth right
        To that most glorious house, that glistreth bright
        With burning starres, and everliving fire,
        Whereof the keyes are to thy hand behight⸱   *entrusted*
    By wise *Fidelia*? she doth thee require,
To shew it to this knight, according⸱ his desire.   *granting*

51   Thrise happy man, said then the father grave,
        Whose staggering steps thy steady hand doth lead,
        And shewes the way, his sinfull soule to save.
        Who better can the way to heaven aread,⸱   *show*
        Then thou thy selfe, that was both borne and bred
        In heavenly throne, where thousand Angels shine?
        Thou doest the prayers of the righteous sead⸱   *offspring*
    Present before the majestie divine,
And his avenging wrath to clemencie incline.

52   Yet since thou bidst, thy pleasure shalbe donne.
        Then come thou man of earth, and see the way,
        That never yet was seene of Faeries sonne,
        That never leads the traveiler astray,
        But after labours long, and sad delay,
        Brings them to joyous rest and endlesse blis.
        But first thou must a season fast and pray,
        Till from her bands the spright assoilèd⸱ is,   *released*
    And have her strength recur'd⸱ from fraile infirmitis.   *recovered*

53   That done, he leads him to the highest Mount;
        Such one, as that same mighty man of God,°

Dame Mercy, who is leading Red Cross   the Israelites in flight from Egypt (Exodus
man of God Moses, who parted the Red Sea for   14:21 ff.)

That bloud-red billowes like a wallèd front
On either side disparted° with his rod,   *parted*
Till that his army dry-foot through them yod,°   *went*
Dwelt fortie dayes upon; where writ in stone
With bloudy letters by the hand of God,
The bitter doome of death and balefull mone
He did receive, whiles flashing fire about him shone.°

54   Or like that sacred hill, whose head full hie,
     Adornd with fruitfull Olives all arownd,
     Is, as it were for endlesse memory
     Of that deare Lord, who oft thereon was fownd,
     For ever with a flowring girlond crownd:
     Or like that pleasaunt Mount, that is for ay
     Through famous Poets verse each where° renownd,   *everywhere*
     On which the thrise three learnèd Ladies° play
     Their heavenly notes, and make full many a lovely lay.

55   From thence, far off he unto him did shew
     A litle path, that was both steepe and long,
     Which to a goodly Citie led his vew;
     Whose wals and towres were builded high and strong
     Of perle and precious stone, that earthly tong
     Cannot describe, nor wit of man can tell;
     Too high a ditty for my simple song;
     The Citie of the great king hight it° well,   *it is called*
     Wherein eternall peace and happinesse doth dwell.

56   As he thereon stood gazing, he might° see   *could*
     The blessed Angels to and fro descend
     From highest heaven,° in gladsome companee,
     And with great joy into that Citie wend,
     As commonly° as friend does with his frend.   *familiarly*
     Whereat he wondred much, and gan enquere,
     What stately building durst so high extend
     Her loftie towres unto the starry sphere,
     And what unknowen nation there empeoplèd° were.   *established*

57   Faire knight (quoth he) *Jerusalem* that is,
     The new *Jerusalem*,° that God has built
     For those to dwell in, that are chosen his,
     His chosen people purg'd from sinfull guilt,
     With pretious bloud, which cruelly was spilt
     On cursèd tree, of that unspotted lam,
     That for the sinnes of all the world was kilt:

---

where writ . . . shone Moses received the tab-
lets of the Law on Mount Sinai (Exodus 24:
12 ff.).
thrise . . . Ladies the nine Muses, who lived on
Parnassus
to and fro . . . heaven Jacob dreamed he saw

a ladder stretching from earth to heaven, with
"the angels of God ascending and descending
on it" (Genesis 28:12).
new Jerusalem Hebrews 12:22–23; the Heavenly
City, here compared not with Jerusalem but
Gloriana's capital, in effect London

Now are they Saints all in that Citie sam,⸖   *together*
More deare unto their God, then younglings to their dam.

58 Till now, said then the knight, I weenèd⸖ well,   *thought*
That great *Cleopolis*,° where I have beene,
In which that fairest *Faerie Queene* doth dwell,
The fairest Citie was, that might be seene;
And that bright towre all built of christall cleene,⸖   *clear*
Panthea,° seemd the brightest thing, that was:
But now by proofe⸖ all otherwise I weene;   *test*
For this great Citie that does far surpas,
And this bright Angels towre quite dims that towre of glas.

59 Most trew, then said the holy agèd man;
Yet is *Cleopolis* for earthly frame,⸖   *structure*
The fairest peece, that eye beholden can:
And well beseemes all knights of noble name,
That covett in th'immortall booke of fame,
To be eternizèd, that same to haunt.⸖   *frequent*
And doen their service to that soveraigne Dame,
That glorie does to them for guerdon graunt:
For she is heavenly borne, and heaven may justly vaunt.⸖   *claim*

60 And thou faire ymp, sprong out from English race,
How ever now accompted Elfins sonne,°
Well worthy doest thy service for her grace,
To aide a virgin desolate foredonne.⸖   *ruined*
But when thou famous victorie hast wonne,
And high emongst all knights hast hong thy shield,
Thenceforth the suit⸖ of earthly conquest shonne,⸖   *pursuit / avoid*
And wash thy hands from guilt of bloudy field:
For bloud can nought but sin, and wars but sorrowes yield.

61 Then seeke this path, that I to thee presage,⸖   *point out*
Which after all⸖ to heaven shall thee send;   *finally*
Then peaceably thy painefull pilgrimage
To yonder same *Jerusalem* do bend,
Where is for thee ordaind a blessèd end:
For thou emongst those Saints, whom thou doest see,
Shalt be a Saint, and thine owne nations frend
And Patrone: thou Saint *George* shalt called bee,
Saint *George* of mery England, the signe of victoree.

62 Unworthy wretch (quoth he) of so great grace,
How dare I thinke such glory to attaine?
These that have it attaind, were in like cace

Cleopolis London
Panthea feminine version of Pantheon; a royal
palace, perhaps Greenwich, may be in Spenser's
mind
How . . . sonne Spenser wants Red Cross now

to be known as English; in the next stanza he
becomes, explicitly, St. George, patron saint
of England, slayer of the dragon, knight faithful true, and type of Christ. For explanation
see stanzas 64–66.

(Quoth he) as wretched, and liv'd in like paine.
But deeds of armes must I at last be faine,>   *willing*
And Ladies love to leave so dearely bought?
What need of armes, where peace doth ay remaine,
(Said he) and battailes none are to be fought?
As for loose loves are vaine, and vanish into nought.

63   O let me not (quoth he) then turne againe
Backe to the world, whose joyes so fruitlesse are;
But let me here for aye in peace remaine,
Or streight way on that last long voyage fare,
That nothing may my present hope empare.>   *impair*
That may not be° (said he) ne maist thou yit>   *yet*
Forgo that royall maides bequeathèd care,°
Who did her cause into thy hand commit,
Till from her cursèd foe thou have her freely quit.

64   Then shall I soone, (quoth he) so God me grace,
Abet> that virgins cause disconsolate,   *uphold*
And shortly backe returne unto this place,
To walke this way in Pilgrims poore estate.
But now aread, old father, why of late
Didst thou behight> me borne of English blood,   *call*
Whom all a Faeries sonne doen nominate?
That word shall I (said he) avouchen> good,   *prove*
Sith to thee is unknowne the cradle of thy brood.

65   For well I wote, thou springst from ancient race
Of *Saxon* kings, that have with mightie hand
And many bloudie battailes fought in place>   *there*
High reard their royall throne in *Britane* land,
And vanquisht them, unable to withstand:
From thence a Faerie thee unweeting> reft,>   *unconscious / stole*
There as thou slepst in tender swadling band,
And her base Elfin brood there for thee left.
Such men do Chaungelings call, so chaungd by Faeries theft.

66   Thence she thee brought into this Faerie lond,
And in an heapèd furrow did thee hyde,
Where thee a Ploughman all unweeting> fond,   *unexpectedly*
As he his toylesome teme that way did guyde,
And brought thee up in ploughmans state to byde,
Whereof *Georgos*° he thee gave to name;
Till prickt with courage, and thy forces pryde,°
To Faery court thou cam'st to seeke for fame,
And prove thy puissaunt armes, as seemes thee best became.

That . . . be Spenser uses the familar idea
that in life there must be a balance of the
active and the contemplative.

royall . . . care charge of that royal maid,
which has been entrusted to you
Georgos Greek for "farmer"
forces pryde confidence of your own strength

67   O holy Sire (quoth he) how shall I quight
         The many favours I with thee have found,
         That hast my name and nation red aright,
         And taught the way that does to heaven bound?ʾ   *lead*
         This said, adowne he lookèd to the ground,
         To have returnd, but dazèd were his eyne,
         Through passingʾ brightnesse, which did quite confound   *surpassing*
         His feeble sence, and too exceeding shyne.
     So darke are earthly things compard to things divine.

68   At last whenas himselfe he gan to find,
         To *Una* back he cast him to retire;
         Who him awaited still with pensive mind.
         Great thankes and goodly meedʾ to that good syre,   *reward*
         He thence departing gave for his paines hyre.
         So came to *Una*, who him joyd to see,
         And after litle rest, gan him desire,
         Of her adventure mindfull for to bee.
     So leave they take of *Cælia*, and her daughters three.

[The eleventh canto describes the battle of Red Cross with the Dragon. On the first day things go badly for the knight; the heat of battle makes his Christian armor intolerable to him. He is revived by water from the Well of Life, type of the sacrament of Baptism, one of the two sacraments admitted, of the Roman seven, by the reformed church.]

From Canto xi

29   It fortunèd (as faire it then befell)
         Behind his backe unweeting,ʾ where he stood,   *not noticed*
         Of auncient time there was a springing well,
         From which fast trickled forth a silver flood,
         Full of great vertues, and for med'cine good.
         Whylome,ʾ before that cursèd Dragon got   *formerly*
         That happie land, and all with innocent blood
         Defyld those sacred waves, it rightly hotʾ   *was called*
     The well of life, ne yet hisʾ vertues had forgot.   *its*

30   For unto life the dead it could restore,
         And guilt of sinfull crimes cleane wash away,
         Those that with sicknesse were infected sore,
         It could recure,ʾ and agèd long decay   *cure*
         Renew, as one were borne that very day.
         Both *Silo* this, and *Jordan* did excell,
         And th'English *Bath*, and eke the german *Spau*,
         Ne can *Cephise*, nor *Hebrus*° match this well:
     Into the same the knight backe overthrowen, fell.

Silo . . . Hebrus Siloam, the stream by which Jesus cured a blind man (John 9:7); Jordan, the crossing of which saved the Jews; Bath in England and Spa in Germany have therapeutic waters; Cephisus and the Thracian Hebrus were renowned for the purity of their waters.

31 Now gan the golden *Phœbus* for to steepe
 His fierie face in billowes of the west,
 And his faint steedes watred in Ocean deepe,
 Whiles from their journall᾿ labours they did rest,   *daily*
 When that infernall Monster, having kest᾿   *cast*
 His wearie foe into that living well,
 Can᾿ high advance his broad discolourèd brest,   *did*
 Above his wonted pitch, with countenance fell,
And clapt his yron wings, as victor he did dwell.᾿   *remain*

32 Which when his pensive Ladie saw from farre,
 Great woe and sorrow did her soule assay,᾿   *assault*
 As weening that the sad end of the warre,
 And gan to highest God entirely᾿ pray,   *earnestly*
 That fearèd chance from her to turne away;
 With folded hands and knees full lowly bent
 All night she watcht, ne once adowne would lay
 Her daintie limbs in her sad dreriment,᾿   *sorrow*
But praying still᾿ did wake, and waking did lament.   *always*

33 The morrow next gan early to appeare,
 That᾿ *Titan*᾿ rose to runne his daily race;   *when / the sun*
 But early ere the morrow next gan reare
 Out of the sea faire *Titans* deawy face,
 Up rose the gentle virgin from her place,
 And lookèd all about, if she might spy
 Her lovèd knight to move his manly pace:
 For she had great doubt of his safèty,
Since late she saw him fall before his enemy.

34 At last she saw, where he upstarted brave
 Out of the well, wherein he drenchèd lay;
 As Eagle fresh out of the Ocean wave,°
 Where he hath left his plumes all hoary gray,
 And deckt himselfe with feathers youthly gay,
 Like Eyas᾿ hauke up mounts unto the skies,   *fledgling*
 His newly budded pineons to assay,
 And marveiles at himselfe, still as he flies:
So new this new-borne knight to battell new did rise.

.   .   .

[The second day's fighting goes better at first, but the knight is again driven
back, to be revived this time by the Tree of Life, representing the sacrament
of Communion. This extract describes its effects, and the knight's preparation
for the third and last day of the battle, in which the dragon is killed. The fight
is a type of the victory of Christ over Satan in the Last Days.]

Eagle . . . wave "thy youth is renewed like
the eagle's" (Psalms 103:5). The eagle, in
bestiary lore, was supposed when old to fly
toward the sun and burn off his old feathers
before plunging into water and renewing his
youth; cf. Milton, *Areopagitica*.

46   There grew a goodly tree him faire beside,
         Loaden with fruit and apples rosie red,
         As they in pure vermilion had beene dide,°   *dyed*
         Whereof great vertues over all° were red:°   *everywhere / told*
         For happie life to all, which thereon fed,
         And life eke everlasting did befall:
         Great God it planted in that blessèd sted°   *place*
         With his almightie hand, and did it call
  The tree of life, the crime of our first fathers fall.°

47   In all the world like was not to be found,
         Save in that soile, where all good things did grow,
         And freely sprong out of the fruitfull ground,
         As incorrupted Nature did them sow,
         Till that dread Dragon all did overthrow.°
         Another like faire tree eke grew thereby,
         Whereof who so did eat, eftsoones did know
         Both good and ill:° O mornefull memory:
  That tree through one mans fault hath doen us all to dy.

48   From that first tree forth flowd, as from a well,
         A trickling streame of Balme,° most soveraine°   *curative*
         And daintie deare,° which on the ground still fell,   *precious*
         And overflowèd all the fertill plaine,
         As it had deawèd bene with timely raine:
         Life and long health that gratious ointment gave,
         And deadly woundes could heale, and reare againe
         The senselesse corse appointed° for the grave.   *prepared*
  Into that same he fell: which did from death him save.

49   For nigh thereto the ever damnèd beast
         Durst not approch, for he was deadly made,°
         And all that life preservèd, did detest:
         Yet he it oft adventur'd to invade. . . .

[Red Cross, type of Christ, now, in the final canto, harrows hell, restores Eden, and takes Una (the true church) as his betrothed bride. Details of the marriage feast derive from Revelation. Una appears in her full glory—as the true ancient church appears in the Church of England. Archimago arrives with a lying letter from Duessa, but is exposed and cast into a dungeon, like his prototype in Revelation. Finally Red Cross resumes his knightly role and returns to the service of Gloriana for six more years.]

The tree . . . fall planted next to the Tree of the Knowledge of Good and Evil in Eden (Genesis 2:9). Its benefits were lost through Adam's fall; it grows in the New Jerusalem (Revelation 22:2).
Till . . . overthrow referring to Satan, who caused the Fall

Whereof . . . ill This is the Tree of Knowledge of Good and Evil, of which Eve and Adam ate the fruit (Genesis 3:1–6).
Balme This balm is related in typology to the healing blood of Christ.
deadly made His being had affinity with death, not life.

From Canto xii

17   Then said that royall Pere in sober wise;°
    Deare Sonne, great beene the evils, which ye bore
    From first to last in your late enterprise,
    That I note,° whether prayse, or pitty more:
    For never living man, I weene, so sore
    In sea of deadly daungers was distrest;
    But since now safe ye seisèdʾ have the shore,   *reached*
    And well arrivèd are, (high God be blest)
Let us devize of ease and everlasting rest.

18   Ah dearest Lord, said then that doughty knight,
    Of ease or rest I may not yet devize;
    For by the faith, which I to armes have plight,
    I bounden am streight after this emprize,ʾ   *enterprise*
    As that your daughter can ye well advize,
    Backe to returne to that great Faerie Queene,
    And her to serve six yeares in warlike wize,ʾ   *wise*
    Gainst that proud Paynim king,° that workes her teene:ʾ *woe*
Therefore I oughtʾ crave pardon, till I there have beene. *must*

19   Unhappie falles that hard necessitie,
    (Quoth he) the troubler of my happie peace,
    And vowèd foe of my felicitie;
    Ne I against the same can justly preace:ʾ   *press*
    But since that bandʾ ye cannot now release,   *bond*
    Nor doen undo; (for vowes may not be vaine)
    Soone as the terme of those six yeares shall cease,
    Ye then shall hither backe returne againe,
The marriage to accomplish vowd betwixt you twain.

20   Which for my part I covet to performe,
    In sort asʾ through the world I did proclame,   *just as*
    That who so kild that monster most deforme,
    And him in hardy battaile overcame,
    Should have mine onely daughter to his Dame,ʾ   *wife*
    And of my kingdome heire apparaunt bee:
    Therefore since now to thee perteines the same,
    By dew desert of noble chevalree,
Both daughter and eke kingdome, lo I yield to thee.

21   Then forth he called that his daughter faire,
    The fairest Un' his onely daughter deare,
    His onely daughter, and his onely heyre;
    Who forth proceeding with sadʾ sober cheare,ʾ *solemn / appearance*
    As bright as doth the morning starre appeare

Then . . . wise Una's father is commenting on
Red Cross's story of his adventures.
I note I don't know whether to

Paynim king the enemies of the true church,
both the Romans and the Turks

Out of the East, with flaming lockes bedight,
To tell that dawning day is drawing neare,
And to the world does bring long wishèd light;
So faire and fresh that Lady shewd her selfe in sight.

22   So faire and fresh, as freshest flowre in May;
For she had layd her mournefull stole aside,
And widow-like sad wimple⸖ throwne away,   *veil*
Wherewith her heavenly beautie she did hide,
Whiles on her wearie journey she did ride;
And on her now a garment she did weare,
All lilly white, withoutten spot, or pride,⸖   *ornament*
That seemd like silke and silver woven neare,
But neither silke nor silver therein did appeare.°

23   The blazing brightnesse of her beauties beame,
And glorious light of her sunshyny face°
To tell, were as to strive against the streame.
My ragged rimes are all too rude and bace,
Her heavenly lineaments for to enchace.⸖   *adorn*
Ne wonder; for her owne deare lovèd knight,
All⸖ were she dayly with himselfe in place,⸖   *although / in the same place*
Did wonder much at her celestiall sight:
Oft had he seene her faire, but never so faire dight.

24   So fairely dight, when she in presence came,
She to her Sire made humble reverence,
And bowèd low, that⸖ her right well became,   *so that it*
And added grace unto her excellence:
Who with great wisedome, and grave eloquence
Thus gan to say. But eare⸖ he thus had said,   *before*
With flying speede, and seeming great pretence,⸖   *importance*
Came running in, much like a man dismaid,
A Messenger with letters, which his message said.

25   All in the open hall amazèd stood,
At suddeinnesse of that unwarie⸖ sight,   *unexpected*
And wondred at his breathlesse hastie mood.
But he for nought would stay his passage right⸖   *direct*
Till fast⸖ before the king he did alight;   *close*
Where falling flat, great humblesse he did make,
And kist the ground, whereon his foot was pight;⸖   *placed*
Then to his hands that writ he did betake,
Which he disclosing, red thus, as the paper spake.

26   To thee, most mighty king of *Eden* faire,
Her greeting sends in these sad lines addrest,

But . . . appeare The bride of the Lamb was arrayed in fine linen (Revelation 19:7–8). **glorious . . . face** Una, the woman clothed with the sun (Revelation 12:1), has now ended her time in the wilderness (12:6) and survived the persecution of the dragon (12:4); she emerges reclothed with the sun, the Bride of Christ, who, as the New Jerusalem, has a "light . . . like unto a stone most precious" (Revelation 21:11).

The wofull daughter, and forsaken heire
Of that great Emperour of all the West;
And bids thee be advizèd for the best,
Ere thou thy daughter linck in holy band
Of wedlocke to that new unknowen guest:
For he already plighted his right hand
Unto another love, and to another land.

27　To me sad mayd, or rather widow sad,
　　　He was affiauncèd long time before,
　　　And sacred pledges he both gave, and had,
　　　False erraunt knight, infámous, and forswore:
　　　Witnesse the burning Altars, which⸍ he swore,　　　　*by which*
　　　And guiltie heavens of his bold perjury,°
　　　Which though he hath polluted oft of yore,
　　　Yet I to them for judgement just do fly,
　　And them conjure⸍ t'avenge this shamefull injury.　　　　*beseech*

28　Therefore since mine he is, or free or bond,
　　　Or false or trew, or living or else dead,
　　　Withhold, O soveraine Prince, your hasty hond
　　　From knitting league with him, I you aread;⸍　　　　　*advise*
　　　Ne weene⸍ my right with strength adowne to tread,　　*don't think*
　　　Through weakenesse of my widowhed, or woe:
　　　For truth is strong, her rightfull cause to plead,
　　　And shall find friends, if need requireth soe,
　　So bids thee well to fare, Thy neither friend, nor foe, *Fidessa*.

29　When he these bitter byting words had red,
　　　The tydings straunge did him abashèd make,
　　　That still he sate long time astonishèd
　　　As in great muse, ne word to creature spake.
　　　At last his solemne silence thus he brake,
　　　With doubtfull eyes fast fixèd on his guest;
　　　Redoubted knight, that for mine onely sake
　　　Thy life and honour late adventurest,
　　Let nought be hid from me, that ought to be exprest.

30　What meane these bloudy vowes, and idle threats,
　　　Throwne out from womanish impatient mind?
　　　What heavens? what altars? what enragèd heates⸍　　　*passions*
　　　Here heapèd up with termes of love unkind,
　　　My conscience cleare with guilty bands° would bind?
　　　High God be witnesse, that I guiltlesse ame.
　　　But if your selfe, Sir knight, ye faultie find,
　　　Or wrappèd be in loves of former Dame,
　　With crime do not it cover, but disclose the same.

guiltie . . . perjury heavens tainted by the guilt　　**guilty bands** illicit bonds
of his perjury

31 To whom the *Redcrosse* knight this answere sent,
      My Lord, my King, be nought hereat dismayd,
      Till well ye wote by grave intendiment,˃   *consideration*
      What woman, and wherefore doth me upbrayd
      With breach of love, and loyalty betrayd.
      It was in my mishaps, as hitherward
      I lately traveild, that unwares I strayd
      Out of my way, through perils straunge and hard;
    That day should faile me, ere I had them all declard.

32 There did I find, or rather I was found
      Of this false woman, that *Fidessa* hight,
      Fidessa hight the falsest Dame on ground,˃   *anywhere*
      Most false *Duessa*, royall richly dight,
      That easie was t'invegle˃ weaker˃ sight: *deceive / too weak*
      Who by her wicked arts, and wylie skill,
      Too false and strong for earthly skill or might,
      Unwares me wrought unto her wicked will,
    And to my foe betrayd, when least I fearèd ill.

33 Then steppèd forth the goodly royall Mayd,
      And on the ground her selfe prostrating low,
      With sober countenaunce thus to him sayd;
      O pardon me, my soveraigne Lord, to show
      The secret treasons, which of late I know
      To have bene wroght by that false sorceresse.
      She onely she it is, that earst˃ did throw   *previously*
      This gentle knight into so great distresse,
    That death him did awaite in dayly wretchednesse.

34 And now it seemes, that she subornèd hath
      This craftie messenger with letters vaine,
      To worke new woe and improvided˃ scath,˃   *unlooked-for / harm*
      By breaking of the band betwixt us twaine;
      Wherein she usèd hath the practicke paine˃   *artful skill*
      Of this false footman, clokt with simplenesse,
      Whom if ye please for to discover plaine,
      Ye shall him *Archimago* find, I ghesse,
    The falsest man alive; who tries shall find no lesse.

35 The king was greatly movèd at her speach,
      And all with suddein indignation fraight,˃   *burdened*
      Bad on that Messenger rude hands to reach.
      Eftsoones the Gard, which on his state did wait,
      Attacht˃ that faitor˃ false, and bound him strait: *seized / impostor*
      Who seeming sorely chauffèd˃ at his band,   *chafed*
      As chained Beare, whom cruell dogs do bait,
      With idle˃ force did faine˃ them to withstand,   *futile / wish*
    And often semblaunce made to scape out of their hand.

36   But they him layd full low in dungeon deepe,°
      And bound him hand and foote with yron chains.
      And with continuall watch did warely keepe;
      Who then would thinke, that by his subtile trains
      He could escape fowle death or deadly paines?
      Thus when that Princes wrath was pacifide,
      He gan renew the late forbidden banes,⸽   *banns*
      And to the knight his daughter deare he tyde,
      With sacred rites and vowes for ever to abyde.

37   His owne two hands the holy knots did knit,
      That none but death for ever can devide;
      His owne two hands, for such a turne most fit,
      The housling⸽ fire did kindle and provide,   *sacramental*
      And holy water° thereon sprinckled wide;
      At which the bushy Teade⸽ a groome did light,   *torch*
      And sacred lampe in secret chamber hide,
      Where it should not be quenchèd day nor night,
      For feare of evill fates, but burnen ever bright.

38   Then gan they sprinckle all the posts with wine,
      And made great feast to solemnize that day;
      They all perfumde with frankencense divine,
      And precious odours fetcht from far away,
      That all the house did sweat with great aray:⸽   *adornment*
      And all the while sweete Musicke did apply
      Her curious⸽ skill, the warbling notes to play,   *intricate*
      To drive away the dull Meláncholy;
      The whiles one sung a song of love and jollity.

39   During the which there was an heavenly noise
      Heard sound through all the Pallace pleasantly,
      Like as it had bene many an Angels voice,
      Singing before th'eternall majesty,
      In their trináll triplicities° on hye;
      Yet wist no creature, whence that heavenly sweet⸽   *delight*
      Proceeded, yet each one felt secretly⸽   *inwardly*
      Himselfe thereby reft of his sences meet,⸽   *proper*
      And ravishèd with rare impression⸽ in his sprite.   *sensation*

40   Great joy was made that day of young and old,
      And solemne feast proclaimd throughout the land,
      That their exceeding merth may not be told:
      Suffice it heare by signes to understand

---

they . . . deepe "And he laid hold on the dragon, that old serpent, which is the devil, and Satan, and bound him a thousand years, and cast him into the bottomless pit, and shut him up, and set a seal upon him, that he should deceive the nations no more, till the thousand years should be fulfilled: and after that he must be loosed a little season" (Revelation 20:1–3). Hence Archimago's escape, and the fact that history does not end at this point. fire . . . water These rituals are borrowed from the ancient Roman marriage ceremony. trináll triplicities The angels were ranked in three groups of three orders.

The usuall joyes at knitting of loves band.
Thrise happy man the knight himselfe did hold,
Possessèd of his Ladies hart and hand,
And ever, when his eye did her behold,
His heart did seeme to melt in pleasures manifold.

41   Her joyous presence and sweet company
In full content he there did long enjoy,
Ne wicked envie, ne vile gealosy
His deare delights were able to annoy:
Yet swimming in that sea of blisfull joy,
He nought forgot, how he whilome⟩ had sworne,   *formerly*
In case he could⟩ that monstrous beast destroy,   *did*
Unto his Farie Queene backe to returne:
The which he shortly did, and *Una* left to mourne.

42   Now strike your sailes ye jolly Mariners,
For we be come unto a quiet rode,⟩   *harbor*
Where we must land some of our passengers,
And light this wearie vessell of her lode.
Here she a while may make her safe abode,
Till she repairèd have her tackles spent,⟩   *worn out*
And wants supplide. And then againe abroad
On the long voyage whereto she is bent:
Well may she speede and fairely finish her intent.

1590

Book II

The main theme of the Legend of Temperance is the control of the passions by the higher powers of the mind. In the *Nicomachean Ethics* Aristotle had distinguished between temperance and continence; the latter presupposes, as the former does not, the existence of strong desires that have to be overcome. Guyon seems to represent a mixture of these two virtues, and Spenser, who probably derived his knowledge of the *Ethics* from editions with Christian commentaries, does not keep rigidly to Aristotle's scheme. Temperance, in Christian thought, was one of the four cardinal virtues, the others being Prudence, Fortitude, and Justice; these, added to the theological virtues (Faith, Hope, and Charity), made up the seven which were set against the Seven Deadly Sins. Christian Temperance, like the other virtues, had its own emblems —the set square, the bridle, the wine mixed with water, or the mixing bowl itself— and Spenser uses them all. The very name of Guyon derives from that one of the four rivers of Eden—Gehon—which was allegorically associated with Temperance.

However, there are Aristotelian elements in the syncretic mix. Aristotle, as usual, defines the virtue as a mean between its excess and its deficiency, and Spenser uses this, together with the doctrine that the passions, which temperance and continence oppose, are divided into the angry and the desirous, the irascible and the concupiscible. Spenser illustrates this by concentrating on the irascible in the first six cantos and on the concupiscible in the second six. Even the condition Guyon finally attains to—

Heroic Virtue—is mentioned by Aristotle as the opposite—there is, exceptionally, no mean between them—of bestiality.

The conflicts involving Guyon take place in the human being; so there is much less supernatural activity in this than in the First Book, which it otherwise so closely parallels in design. Primarily Book II has to do with the moral activity of men in the natural world. (Temperance was a pagan virtue; holiness was known only to Christians, by revelation.) Guyon must keep to the golden mean, and has the Palmer, representing Right Reason, to aid him most of the time. Thus he is lower than Red Cross, a saint, and more like a pagan hero, such as Aeneas, whom he resembles also in his visit to the underworld. But it would be wrong to suggest that Spenser excludes Christianity. As we shall see, the quest of Guyon has strong Christian implications. The Second Book is an interesting example of a Renaissance phenomenon, the syncretic blend of pagan and Christian, set in a medieval (romance) form.

The Second Booke of The Faerie Queene

Contayning,
The Legend of Sir Guyon,
or
Of Temperaunce

1   Right well I wote° most mighty Soveraine,   *know*
         That all this famous antique history,
         Of some th'aboundance of an idle braine
         Will judgèd be, and painted forgery,
         Rather then matter of just° memory,   *true*
         Sith° none, that breatheth living aire, does know,   *since*
         Where is that happy land of Faery,
             Which I so much do vaunt,° yet no where show,   *publicize*
         But vouch° antiquities, which no body can know.   *assert*

2   But let that man with better sence advize,°   *consider*
         That of the world least part to us is red:°   *made known*
         And dayly how through hardy enterprize,
         Many great Regions are discoverèd,
         Which to late age were never mentionèd.
         Who ever heard of th'Indian *Peru*?
         Or who in venturous vessell measurèd
             The *Amazons* huge river now found trew?°
         Or fruitfullest *Virginia*° who did ever vew?

3   Yet all these were, when no man did them know;
         Yet have from wisest ages hidden beene:
         And later times things more unknowne shall show.

The Amazons . . . trew It was first navigated (in part) in 1540.   **Virginia** named for Elizabeth, the Virgin Queen, on Ralegh's return in 1584.

Why then should witlesse man so much misweene˃   *wrongly suppose*
That nothing is, but that which he hath seene?
What if within the Moones faire shining spheare?
What if in every other starre unseene
    Of other worldes he happily˃ should heare?   *by chance*
He wonder would much more: yet such to some appeare.

4. Of Faerie lond yet if he more inquire,
    By certaine signes here set in sundry place
    He may it find; ne let him then admire,˃   *be surprised*
    But yield˃ his sence to be too blunt and bace,   *confess*
    That no'te without an hound fine footing trace.°
    And thou, O fairest Princesse under sky,
    In this faire mirrhour maist behold thy face,
    And thine owne realmes in lond of Faery,
And in this antique Image thy great auncestry.

5   The which O pardon me thus to enfold
    In covert vele, and wrap in shadowes light,
    That feeble eyes your glory may behold,
    Which else could not endure those beames bright,
    But would be dazled with exceeding light.
    O pardon, and vouchsafe with patient eare
    The brave adventures of this Faery knight
    The good Sir *Guyon* gratiously to heare,
In whom great rule of Temp'raunce goodly doth appeare.

[The first canto of Book II, like that of I, establishes the nature of the quest assigned to the knight of the Book, Guyon, whose "Legend" is Temperance. The escaped Archimago directs Guyon and the Palmer to Duessa, posing as a girl raped by Red Cross; but the knights˃ recognize each other before Guyon prosecutes her revenge. They converse and part, Red Cross wishing Guyon luck as he sets out "like race to run." Beside a fountain they find Amavia with her baby Ruddymane, so called because his hands are stained with her blood. Amavia dies beside the body of her husband Mordant, victim of the enchantress Acrasia (Incontinence). Mordant (Mortdant: deathgiver) was like Adam infected by concupiscence with original sin. The fountain stands for divine law, which provides sin with its occasion to produce concupiscence in men (Romans 7:7). The burial of Amavia and Mordant represents the death of the Old Man. Ruddymane is baptized, but carries the stain contracted by his father. Guyon at first thinks it is a simple case of intemperance; the deeper Christian meaning is revealed to him by the Palmer in canto xi. The destruction of the Bower of Bliss in xii is not just the overthrow of incontinence, but of sin in the human heart. Spenser is building Temperance into a Christian rather than a pagan (Aristotelian) scheme.

The second canto offers a schematic allegory of the doctrine of the mean, in the House of Medina. Medina is the mean, her sisters Elissa ("deficient") and Perissa

no'te . . . trace can't follow the tracks without a hunting dog

("excessive") are the extremes. They have lovers who share their qualities; Perissa's is San Loy. Canto iii introduces Braggadocchio, who steals Guyon's horse, and Belphoebe—it is a sort of first installment of Book III. In the fourth canto Spenser deals with irascibility as the enemy of temperance; Furor (Anger) is bound, and Occasio (occasion, opportunity) has her tongue locked up. Other characters are Atin (Strife), Pyrochles ("fire disturbed" = incontinent anger), and Cymochles, his brother ("wave disturbed" = incontinent sex); these last two return later.

In canto v, amid more instances of anger and its occasions, Guyon over-throws Pyrochles. In vi there is a transition from irascibility to concupiscence, and Spenser starts it with the moralization: "A Harder lesson, to learne Continence / In joyous pleasure, then in grievous paine." Guyon, now without his Palmer, falls in with Phaedria (Greek, "glittering," but Spenser himself calls her "immodest Merth".) She sails about on the Idle Lake—loose mirth floating on idleness leads, says Spenser to "loose desire." She sings to her victim Cymochles of the beauty and plenty of the paradise she inhabits on a floating island (a forecast of the Bower of Bliss). Guyon, though courteous, has no difficulty in rejecting her charms. There is an inconclusive bout between Guyon and Cymochles; and we see Pyrochles, trying to drown himself to extinguish his anger, saved by Archimago. The rejection of sensual pleasure by Guyon, though easy, is part of the pattern of rejections that is completed in the seventh canto; note that he undergoes these temptations without the aid of the Palmer.]

Book II, Canto vii

This is the crucial canto of Book II. Mammon is the god of money, but of more than money: "God of the world and worldlings" he says; of all, in fact, that the virtuous soul must resist, including fame, power, and improper knowledge. The scheme of the canto has much in common with that of *Paradise Regained*, and of Marvell's "Dialogue Between the Resolved Soul and Created Pleasure." During his three-day tour of Mammon's underground realm, Guyon is followed by a terrible fiend who will tear him to pieces if he once weakens. He has no difficulty in rejecting riches, having chosen "another bliss . . . another end." Nor does he have much of a struggle at the Temple of Philotime ("love of earthly honor"), because he has plighted his troth to another lady ("heavenly honor"). The final temptation is that of the Garden of Proserpina: this is the temptation of forbidden knowledge—here, as in Milton and Marvell, the climactic temptation. Unmoved, he has undergone, like Christ in the wilderness, the *total* temptation (the temptation of sex came with Phaedria), and Mammon, his time expired, has to take him back to the light. Only then does he require succor, as Christ received it after his trial.

This is one of the great cantos; Lamb said that "the transitions in this episode are every whit as violent as in the most extravagant dream, and yet the waking judgment ratifies them." Its interpretation is, however, disputed. Some believe Guyon should not have accompanied Mammon, and that his doing so illustrates his inability to avoid the occasion of temptation. His error would be comparable to that of Red Cross in the Cave of Despair. But Milton, despite his error in thinking that the Palmer was with

Guyon, is likely to be right in his reading, when he says, in *Areopagitica*, that "our sage and serious poet Spenser . . . describing true temperance under the person of Guyon, brings him in with his palmer through the cave of Mammon, and the bower of earthly bliss, that he might see and know, and yet abstain."

In this episode Guyon is not being tempted by his own desires but by an external enemy; he is no more seeking the occasion of sin than Christ in the wilderness. His reward for withstanding the total temptation is Heroic Virtue, in the sense given to this term by the church when adapting it from Aristotle's *Ethics*; he now has a habit of good conduct that is second nature, and it fits him for deeds beyond the scope of the ordinarily virtuous man; he occupies a middle ground between such a man and a saint. As the victory over sin in the wilderness prepared Christ for the victory over death on the Cross, so Guyon's victory over Mammon makes possible the destruction of the Bower of Bliss. His faint, requiring angelic succor, is therefore not a sign of moral weakness, but of exhaustion at the end of this ordeal of initiation.

Canto vii

Guyon findes Mammon in a delve,
  Sunning his threasure hore:
Is by him tempted, and led downe,
  To see his secret store.

1   As Pilot well expert in perilous wave,
    That to a stedfast starre his course hath bent,
    When foggy mistes, or cloudy tempests have
    The faithfull light of that faire lampe yblent,˃   *blinded*
    And cover'd heaven with hideous dreriment,
    Upon his card˃ and compas firmes his eye,   *chart*
    The maisters˃ of his long experiment,˃   *agents / experience*
    And to them does the steddy helme apply,
  Bidding his wingèd vessell fairely forward fly:

2   So *Guyon* having lost his trusty guide,°
    Late left beyond that *Ydle lake*, proceedes
    Yet on his way, of none accompanide;
    And evermore himselfe with comfort feedes,
    Of his owne vertues, and prayse-worthy deedes.°
    So long he yode,˃ yet no adventure found,   *went*
    Which fame of her shrill trompet worthy reedes:˃   *considers*
    For still he traveild through wide wastfull ground,
  That nought but desert wildernesse shew'd all around.

3   At last he came unto a gloomy glade,
    Cover'd with boughes and shrubs from heavens light,
    Whereas he sitting found in secret shade
    An uncouth,˃ salvage, and uncivile wight,   *strange*
    Of griesly hew,˃ and fowle ill favour'd sight;˃   *shape / appearance*

lost . . . guide The absence of the Palmer is presumably to allow Guyon to undergo these tests without the help of a guide external to himself who would always represent the reasonable attitude, and so shield Guyon from the spiritual pressures besetting him; Jesus in the wilderness had no supernatural aid, was as if only a man.

And evermore . . . deedes sometimes thought very smug, but he is cheering himself up by counting all the support he has

His face with smoke was tand, and eyes were bleard,
His head and beard with sout were ill bedight,
His cole-blacke hands did seeme to have beene seard
In smithes fire-spitting forge, and nayles like clawes appeard.

4   His yron coate all overgrowne with rust,
    Whose underneath envelopèd with gold,
    Whose glistring glosse darkned with filthy dust,
    Well yet appearèd, to have beene of old
    A worke of rich entayle,⸖ and curious mould,   *carving*
    Woven with antickes⸖ and wild Imagery: *strange figures*
    And in his lap a masse of coyne he told,⸖   *counted*
    And turnèd upsidowne, to feede his eye
  And covetous desire with his huge threasury.

5   And round about him lay on every side
    Great heapes of gold, that never could be spent:
    Of which some were rude owre,⸖ not purifide   *ore*
    Of *Mulcibers*° devouring element;
    Some others were new driven,⸖ and distent⸖   *smelted / beaten*
    Into great Ingoes,⸖ and to wedges square;   *ingots*
    Some in round plates withouten moniment;⸖   *engraving*
    But most were stampt, and in their metall bare
  The antique shapes of kings and kesars⸖ straunge and rare.   *emperors*

6   Soone as he *Guyon* saw, in great affright
    And hast he rose, for to remove aside
    Those pretious hils from straungers envious sight,
    And downe them pourèd through an hole full wide,
    Into the hollow earth, them there to hide.
    But *Guyon* lightly to him leaping, stayd
    His hand, that trembled, as one terrifyde;
    And though him selfe were at the sight dismayd,
  Yet him perforce restraynd, and to him doubtfull sayd.

7   What art thou man, (if man at all thou art)
    That here in desert hast thine habitaunce,
    And these rich heapes of wealth doest hide apart
    From the worldes eye, and from her right usaunce?
    Thereat with staring eyes fixèd askaunce,
    In great disdaine, he answerd; Hardy Elfe,
    The darest vew my direfull countenaunce,
    I read⸖ thee rash, and heedlesse of thy selfe,   *perceive*
  To trouble my still⸖ seate,⸖ and heapes of pretious pelfe.   *quiet / place*

8   God of the world and worldlings I me call,
    Great *Mammon*,° greatest god below the skye,

Mulcibers Mulciber was Vulcan, the smith god; his element was fire.
Mammon "No man can serve two masters . . . Ye cannot serve God and mammon" (Matthew 6:24); his name means "wealth"; one has to choose between the world and heaven.

That of my plenty poure out unto all,
And unto none my graces do enuye:
Riches, renowme, and principality,
Honour, estate, and all this worldes good,
For which men swinck⟩ and sweat incessantly,   *labor*
Fro me do flow into an ample flood,
And in the hollow earth have their eternall brood.

9   Wherefore if me thou deigne to serve and sew,⟩   *follow*
At thy command lo all these mountains bee;
Or if to thy great⟩ mind, or greedy vew   *ambitious*
All these may not suffise, there shall to thee
Ten times so much be numbred francke and free.
  Mammon (said he) thy godheades vaunt° is vaine,
  And idle offers of thy golden fee;
  To them, that covet such eye-glutting gaine,
Proffer thy giftes, and fitter servaunts entertaine.

10 Me ill besits,⟩ that in der-doing armes,°   *besets*
And honours suit⟩ my vowèd dayes do spend,   *pursuit*
Unto thy bounteous baytes, and pleasing charmes,
With which weake men thou witchest, to attend:
Regard of worldly mucke doth fowly blend,⟩   *defile*
  And low abase the high heroicke spright,
  That joyes for crownes and kingdomes to contend;
  Faire shields, gay steedes, bright armes be my delight.
Those be the riches fit for an advent'rous knight.

11 Vaine glorious Elfe (said he) doest not thou weet,
That money can thy wantes at will supply?
Shields, steeds, and armes, and all things for thee meet
It can purvay in twinckling of an eye;
And crownes and kingdomes to thee multiply.
  Do not I kings create, and throw the crowne
  Sometimes to him, that low in dust doth ly?
  And him that raignd, into his rowme thrust downe,
And whom I lust,⟩ do heape with glory and renowne?   *please*

12 All otherwise (said he) I riches read,⟩   *understand*
And deeme them roote of all disquietnesse;°
First got with guile, and then preserv'd with dread,
And after spent with pride and lavishnesse,
Leaving behind them griefe and heavinesse.
  Infinite mischiefes of them do arize,
  Strife, and debate, bloudshed, and bitternesse,
  Outrageous wrong, and hellish covetize,
That noble heart as great dishonour doth despize.

---

godheades vaunt boast of divinity   roote . . . disquietnesse "the love of money is
der-doing armes feats of high courage   the root of all evil" (I Timothy 6:10)

13   Ne thine be kingdomes, ne the scepters thine;
     But realmes and rulers thou doest both confound,
     And loyall truth to treason doest incline;
     Witnesse the guiltlesse bloud pourd oft on ground,
     The crownèd often slain, the slayer cround,
     The sacred Diademe in peeces rent
     And purple robe⃒ gorèd with many a wound;   *imperial cloak*
     Castles surprizd, great cities sackt and brent:
So mak'st thou kings, and gaynest wrongfull governement.

14   Long were to tell the troublous stormes, that tosse
     The private state,⃒ and make the life unsweet: *private life*
     Who swelling sayles in Caspian sea doth crosse,
     And in frayle wood on *Adrian*⃒ gulfe doth fleet,⃒   *Adriatic / float*
     Doth not, I weene, so many evils meet.
     Then *Mammon* wexing wroth, And why then, said,
     Are mortall men so fond and undiscreet,
     So evil thing to seeke unto their ayd,
And having not complaine, and having it upbraid?⃒   *reproach it*

15   Indeede (quoth he) through fowle intemperaunce,
     Frayle men are oft captiv'd to covetise:
     But would they thinke, with how small allowaunce
     Untroubled Nature doth her selfe suffise,°
     Such superfluities they would despise,
     Which with sad cares empeach⃒ our native joyes: *impair*
     At the well head the purest streames arise:
     But mucky filth his⃒ braunching armes annoyes,⃒   *its / fouls*
And with uncomely weedes the gentle wave accloyes.⃒   *clogs*

16   The antique⃒ world,° in his first flowring youth,   *ancient*
     Found no defect in his Creatours grace,
     But with glad thankes, and unreprovèd truth,
     The gifts of soveraigne bountie did embrace:
     Like Angels life was then mens happy cace;
     But later ages pride, like corn-fed steed,
     Abusd her plenty, and fat swolne encreace
     To all licentious lust, and gan exceed
The measure of her meane, and naturall first need.

17   Then gan a cursèd hand the quiet wombe
     Of his great Grandmother with steele to wound,
     And the hid treasures in her sacred tombe,
     With Sacriledge to dig. Therein he found
     Fountaines of gold and silver to abound,

Untroubled . . . suffice Boethius, *The Consolation of Philosophy* II.5, was the classical statement of this idea.
The antique world also based on the famous passage in Boethius, *The Consolation of Philosophy* II.5, *Felix nimium prior aetas* ("Too happy was that first age"); Boethius was translated into English by two sovereigns, Alfred and Elizabeth. Spenser also knew well the opening pages of Ovid's *Metamorphoses*, which describe the Golden Age and the subsequent decline.

Of which the matter of his huge desire
And pompous pride eftsoones> he did compound;   *forth with*
Then avarice gan through his veines inspire>   *breathe*
His greedy flames, and kindled life-devouring fire.

18 Sonne (said he then) let be thy bitter scorne,
    And leave the rudenesse of that antique age
    To them, that liv'd therein in state forlorne;
    Thou that doest live in later times, must wage
    Thy workes for wealth, and life for gold engage.
    If then thee list my offred grace to use,
    Take what thou please of all this surplusage;
    If thee list not, leave have thou to refuse:
    But thing refused, do not afterward accuse.

19 Me list not> (said the Elfin knight) receave   *I choose not*
    Thing offred, till I know it well be got,°
    Ne wote> I, but thou didst these goods bereave   *nor know*
    From rightfull owner by unrighteous lot,>   *division*
    Or that bloud guiltinesse or guile them blot.
    Perdy> (quoth he), yet never eye did vew,   *indeed*
    Ne toung did tell, ne hand these handled not,
    But safe I have them kept in secret mew,>   *den*
    From heavens sight, and powre of all which them pursew.

20 What secret place (quoth he) can safely hold
    So huge a masse, and hide from heavens eye?
    Or where hast thou thy wonne,> that so much gold   *dwelling*
    Thou canst preserve from wrong and robbery?
    Come thou (quoth he) and see. So by and by
    Through that thicke covert he him led, and found
    A darkesome way, which no man could descry
    That deepe descended through the hollow ground,
    And was with dread and horrour compassèd around.

21 At length they came into a larger space,
    That stretcht it selfe into an ample plaine,
    Through which a beaten broad high way did trace,
    That streight did lead to *Plutoes* griesly raine:> *hideous realm*
    By that wayes side, there sate infernall Payne,°
    And fast beside him sat tumultuous Strife:
    The one in hand an yron whip did straine,>   *grip*
    The other brandishèd a bloudy knife,
    And both did gnash their teeth, and both did threaten life.

22 On thother side in one consort there sate,
    Cruell Revenge, and rancorous despight,

Me list . . . well got Aristotle, *Nicomachean Ethics* IV, says a good man will not take money from a tainted source; the concept was Christianized (as we see from the reply of Jesus to Satan in *Paradise Regained*) on an offer of food—Satan asks "wouldst thou not eat?" and the reply is "Thereafter as I like the giver" (II.321).
Payne These simple allegories are based on the description of hell in Virgil, *Aeneid* VI.273 ff.

Disloyall Treason, and hart-burning Hate,
But gnawing Gealosie out of their sight
Sitting alone, his bitter lips did bight,
And trembling Feare still to and fro did fly,
And found no place, where safe he shroud° him might,   *shelter*
Lamenting Sorrow did in darknesse lye,
And Shame his ugly face did hide from living eye.

23   And over them sad Horrour with grim hew,°   *shape*
    Did alwayes sore, beating his yron wings;
    And after him Owles and Night-ravens flew,
    The hatefull messengers of heavy things,
    Of death and dolour telling sad tidings;
    Whiles sad *Celeno*,° sitting on a clift,°   *cliff*
    A song of bale and bitter sorrow sings,
    That hart of flint a sunder could have rift:°   *split*
Which having ended, after him she flyeth swift.

24   All these before the gates of *Pluto* lay,
    By whom they passing, spake unto them nought.
    But th'Elfin knight with wonder all the way
    Did feed his eyes, and fild his inner thought.
    At last him to a litle dore he brought,
    That to the gate of Hell, which gapèd wide,
    Was next adjoyning, ne them parted ought:°
    Betwixt them both was but a little stride,
That did the house of Richesse from hell-mouth divide.

25   Before the dore sat self-consuming Care,
    Day and night keeping wary watch and ward,
    For feare least Force or Fraud should unaware
    Breake in, and spoile the treasure there in gard:
    Ne would he suffer Sleepe once thither-ward
    Approch, albe his drowsie den were next;
    For next to death is Sleepe to be compard:
    Therefore his house is unto his annext;
Here Sleep, there Richesse, and Hel-gate them both betwext.°

26   So soone as *Mammon* there arriv'd, the dore
    To him did open, and affoorded way;
    Him followed eke Sir *Guyon* evermore,
    Ne darkensse him, ne daunger might dismay.
    Soone as he entred was, the dore streight way
    Did shut, and from behind it forth there lept

Celeno a Harpy; in Virgil, *Aeneid* III.219 ff., an image of rapacity; she speaks like a prophetess of doom (cf. *Tempest* III.iii, the apparition of Ariel as Harpy before the "three men of sin")
ne . . . ought i.e. there was nothing between them

Here . . . betwext Spenser arranges the "houses" and hell-mouth as if in a picture or in a pageant; the "hell-mouth" was familiar on the popular stage, a large-toothed aperture, partly a whale's, partly a devil's mouth.

An ugly feend,° more fowle then dismall day,
The which with monstrous stalke behind him stept,
And ever as he went, dew watch upon him kept.

27 Well hopèd he, ere long that hardy guest,
If ever covetous hand, or lustfull eye,
Or lips he layd on thing, that likt⸾ him best,   *pleased*
Or ever sleepe his eye-strings did untye,
Should be his pray. And therefore still⸾ on hye   *always*
He over him did hold his cruell clawes,
Threatning with greedy gripe to do him dye
And rend in peeces with his ravenous pawes,
If ever he transgrest the fatal *Stygian*° lawes.

28 That houses forme within was rude and strong,
Like an huge cave hewne out of rocky clift,
From whose rough vaut⸾ the ragged breaches⸾ hong,   *vault / fissures*
Embost with massy gold of glorious gift,⸾   *quality*
And with rich metall loaded every rift,
That heavy ruine⸾ they did seeme to threat;   *fall*
And over them *Arachne*° high did lift
Her cunning web, and spred her subtile net,
Enwrappèd in fowle smoke and clouds more blacke then Jet.

29 Both roofe, and floore, and wals were all of gold,
But overgrowne with dust and old decay,
And hid in darkenesse, that none could behold
The hew⸾ thereof: for vew of chearefull day   *appearance*
Did never in that house it selfe display,
But a faint shadow of uncertain light;
Such as a lamp, whose life does fade away:
Or as the Moone cloathèd with clowdy night,
Does shew to him, that walkes in feare and sad affright.

30 In all that rowme was nothing to be seene,
But huge great yron chests and coffers strong,
All bard with double bends, that none could weene⸾   *think*
Them to efforce⸾ by violence or wrong;   *break open*
On every side they placèd were along.
But all the ground with sculs was scatterèd,
And dead mens bones, which round about were flong,
Whose lives, it seemèd, whilome⸾ there were shed,   *formerly*
And their vile carcases now left unburièd.

---

feend Probably Eurynomos, described first by Pausanias (*Description of Greece* X.28) but accessible in the well-known manual of Cartari, *Imagini degli Dei* (many 16th-century editions). He tore his victims to pieces. In the Eleusinian mystery ritual the candidate was followed by a similar fury and forbidden to turn around; this stresses the initiatory element in Guyon's visit to the Cave of Mammon. The Eleusinian rite involved three days in "hell." Hercules, the type-hero for Guyon, was an initiate. Of course the ancient mystery rituals were given Christian significances.
Stygian referring to Styx, the infernal river, and thus to hell
Arachne the spider

31 They forward passe, ne *Guyon* yet spoke word,
    Till that they came unto an yron dore,
    Which to them openèd of his owne accord,
    And shewd of richesse such exceeding store,
    As eye of man did never see before;
    Ne ever could within one place be found,
    Through all the wealth, which is, or was of yore,
    Could gatherèd be through all the world around,
And that above were added to that under ground.

32 The charge thereof unto a covetous Spright
    Commaunded was, who thereby did attend,
    And warily awaited day and night,
    From other covetous feends it to defend,
    Who it to rob and ransacke did intend.°   *wish*
    Then *Mammon* turning to that warriour, said;
    Loe here the worldès blis, loe here the end,
    To which all men do ayme, rich to be made:
Such grace now to be happy, is before thee laid.

33 Certes (said he) I n'ill° thine offred grace,   *do not want*
    Ne to be made so happy do intend:
    Another blis before mine eyes I place,
    Another happinesse, another end.
    To them, that list, these base regardes I lend:°   *give*
    But I in armes, and in atchievements brave,
    Do rather choose my flitting houres to spend,
    And to be Lord of those, that riches have,
Then them to have my selfe, and be their servile sclave.

34 Thereat the feend his gnashing teeth did grate,
    And griev'd, so long to lacke his greedy° pray;   *eagerly desired*
    For well he weenèd, that so glorious bayte
    Would tempt his guest, to take thereof assay:°   *trial*
    Had he so doen, he had him snatcht away,
    More light then Culver° in the Faulcons fist.   *dove*
    Eternall God thee save from such decay.
    But whenas *Mammon* saw his purpose mist,
Him to entrap unwares another way he wist.

35 Thence forward he him led, and shortly brought
    Unto another rowme,° whose dore forthright,
    To him did open, as it had beene taught:
    Therein an hundred raunges weren pight,°   *placed*
    And hundred fornaces all burning bright;
    By every fornace many feends did bide,
    Deformèd creatures, horrible in sight,

rowme This is Mammon's forge, based on the
forges of the Cyclops in Virgil, *Aeneid* VIII.418.

> And every feend his busie paines applide,
> To melt the golden metall, ready to be tride.   *refined*

36   One with great bellowes gatherèd filling aire,
     And with forst wind the fewell did inflame;
     Another did the dying bronds repaire
     With yron toungs, and sprinckled oft the same
     With liquid waves, fiers *Vulcans* rage to tame,
     Who maistring them, renewd his former heat;
     Some scumd the drosse, that from the metall came;
     Some stird the molten owre with ladles great;
> And every one did swincke, and every one did sweat.   *labor*

37   But when as earthly wight they present saw,
     Glistring in armes and battailous aray,
     From their whot worke they did themselves withdraw   *hot*
     To wonder at the sight: for till that day,
     They never creature saw, that came that way.
     Their staring eyes sparckling with fervent fire,
     And ugly shapes did nigh the man dismay,
     That were it not for shame, he would retire,
> Till that him thus bespake their soveraigne Lord and sire.

38   Behold, thou Faeries sonne, with mortall eye,
     That living eye before did never see: *that which*
     The thing, that thou didst crave so earnestly,
     To weet, whence all the wealth late shewd by mee,
     Proceeded, lo now is reveald to thee.
     Here is the fountaine of the worldès good:
     Now therefore, if thou wilt enrichèd bee,
     Avise thee well, and chaunge thy wilfull mood,   *consider*
> Least thou perhaps hereafter wish, and be withstood.   *lest*

39   Suffise it then, thou Money God (quoth hee)
     That all thine idle offers I refuse.
     All that I need I have; what needeth mee
     To covet more, then I have cause to use?
     With such vaine shewes thy worldlings vile abuse:
     But give me leave to follow mine emprise.   *enterprise*
     Mammon was much displeased, yet no'te he chuse,   *he could not*
     And beare the rigour of his bold mesprise,   *scorn*
> And thence him forward led, him further to entise.

40   He brought him through a darksome narrow strait,
     To a broad gate, all built of beaten gold:
     The gate was open, but therein did wait
     A sturdy villein, striding stiffe and bold,
     As if that highest God defie he would;
     In his right hand an yron club he held,
     But he himselfe was all of golden mould,

Yet had both life and sence, and well could weldͯ   *wield*
That cursèd weapon, when his cruell foes he queld.

41   *Disdayne* he callèd was, and did disdaine
      To be so cald, and who so did him call:
      Sterne was his looke, and full of stomackeͯ vaine,   *pride*
      His portaunceͯ terrible, and stature tall,   *bearing*
      Far passing th'hight of men terrestriall;
      Like an huge Gyant of the *Titans* race,
      That made him scorne all creatures great and small,
      And with his pride all others powre defaceͯ:   *abash*
More fit amongst blacke fiendes, then men to have his place.

42   Soone as those glitterand armes he did espye,
      That with their brightnesse made that darknesse light,
      His harmefull club he gan to hurtleͯ hye,   *brandish*
      And threaten batteill to the Faery knight;
      Who likewise gan himselfe to batteill dight,ͯ   *prepare*
      Till *Mammon* did his hasty hand withhold,
      And counseld him abstaine from perilous fight:
      For nothing might abash the villein bold,
Ne mortall steele emperce his miscreated mould.

43   So having him with reason pacifide,
      And the fiers Carleͯ commaunding to forbeare,   *churl*
      He brought him in. The rowme° was large and wide,
      As it some Gyeldͯ or solemne Temple weare: *guildhall*
      Many great golden pillours did upbeare
      The massy roofe, and riches huge sustayne,
      And every pillour deckèd was full deareͯ   *richly*
      With crownes and Diademes, and titles vaine,
Which mortall Princess wore, whiles they on earth did rayne.

44   A route of people there assemblèd were,
      Of every sort and nation under skye,
      Which with great uprore preacèd to draw nere   *pressed*
      To th'upper part, where was advauncèd hye
      A stately siegeͯ of soveraigne majestye;   *throne*
      And thereon sat a woman° gorgeous gay,
      And richly clad in robes of royaltye,
      Thatͯ never earthly Prince in such aray   *such that*
His glory did enhaunce, and pompous pride display.

45   Her face right wondrous faire did seeme to bee,
      Thatͯ her broad beauties beam great brightnes threw   *so that*
      Through the dim shade, that all men might it see:
      Yet was not that same her owne native hew,ͯ   *form*

The rowme Passing by Disdain, protector of the privileged, Guyon now embarks on the temptation of false honor and wordly power in the temple of Philotime ("love of honor"); Spenser makes the temple rather like a great monarch's court.
woman Philotime, a corrupt earthly version of heavenly honor, to which Guyon is committed

But wrought by art and counterfetted shew,
Thereby more lovers unto her to call;
Nath'lesse° most heavenly faire in deed and vew   *nevertheless*
She by creation was, till she did fall;
Thenceforth she sought for helps, to cloke her crime withall.

46   There, as in glistring glory she did sit,
She held a great gold chaine° ylinckèd well,
Whose upper end to highest heaven was knit,
And lower part did reach to lowest Hell;
And all that preace° did round about her swell,   *crowd*
To catchen hold of that long chaine, thereby
To clime aloft, and others to excell:
That was *Ambition,* rash desire to sty.°   *ascend*
And every lincke thereof a step of dignity.

47   Some thought to raise themselves to high degree,
By riches and unrightèous reward,
Some by close shouldring,° some by flatteree;   *intriguing*
Others through friends, others for base regard;°   *bribery*
And all by wrong wayes for themselves prepard.
Those that were up themselves, kept others low,
Those that were low themselves, held others hard,
Ne suffered them to rise or greater grow,
But every one did strive his fellow downe to throw.

48   Which whenas *Guyon* saw, he gan inquire,
What meant that preace about that Ladies throne,
And what she was that did so high aspire.
Him *Mammon* answerèd; That goodly one,
Whom all that folke with such contention,
Do flocke about, my deare, my daughter is;
Honour and dignitie from her alone
Derivèd are, and all this worldès blis
For which ye men do strive: few get, but many mis.

49   And faire *Philotime* she rightly hight,°   *is called*
The fairest wight that wonneth° under skye,   *lives*
But that this darksome neather world her light
Doth dim with horrour and deformitie,
Worthy of heaven and hye felicitie,
From whence the gods have her for envy thrust:
But sith thou hast found favour in mine eye,
Thy spouse I will her make, if that thou lust,°   *wish*
That she may thee advance for workes and merites just.

gold chaine When attached to the throne of Zeus in Homer's *Iliad* (VIII.19 ff.) the golden chain became, for later allegorists, a symbol of the order of divine creation with its grades and hierarchies; Philotime's gold chain is a human and wicked parody, representing only the struggle for worldly power; every link is a "step of dignity," that is, a degree of social rank by which earthly ambition seeks to ascend.

50   Gramercy *Mammon* (said the gentle knight)
      For so great grace and offred high estate;
      But I, that am fraile flesh and earthly wight,
      Unworthy match for such immortall mate
      My self well wote,˒ and mine unequall fate;˒   *know / inferior destiny*
      And were I not, yet is my trouth yplight,
      And love avowd to other Lady° late,˒   *lately*
      That to remove the same I have no might:˒   *power*
      To chaunge love causelesse is reproch to warlike knight.

51   *Mammon* emmovèd was with inward wrath;
      Yet forcing it to faine,˒ him forth thence led   *to dissimulate it*
      Through griesly shadowes by a beaten path,
      Into a gardin° goodly garnishèd
      With hearbs and fruits, whose kinds mote˒ not be red:˒   *can / told*
      Not such, as earth out of her fruitfull woomb
      Throwes forth to men, sweet and well savourèd,
      But direfull deadly blacke both leafe and bloom,
      Fit to adorne the dead, and decke the drery toombe.

52   There mournfull *Cypresse* grew in greatest store,
      And trees of bitter *Gall,* and *Heben*˒ sad,   *ebony*
      Dead sleeping *Poppy,* and blacke *Hellebore,*
      Cold *Coloquintida,* and *Tetra* mad,
      Mortall *Samnitis,* and *Cicuta* bad,°
      With which th' unjust *Atheniens* made to dy
      Wise *Socrates,* who thereof quaffing glad
      Pourd out his life, and last Philosophy
      To the faire *Critias*° his dearest Belamy.˒   *friend*

53   The *Gardin* of *Proserpina* this hight;˒   *was named*
      And in the midst thereof a silver seat,°
      With a thicke Arber goodly over dight,˒   *placed overhead*

other **Lady** Guyon courteously rejects the offer on the ground that he is betrothed to another lady, meaning the true "love of honor" in the heaven from which Philotime has fallen (see stanza 45 and, for Mammon's version of her fall, stanza 49).

gardin The Garden of Proserpina is the setting for Guyon's last temptation, which completes the others, so that they add up to a total temptation like that of Jesus in the wilderness. This is the temptation of *curiosity* (forbidden knowledge). The garden is based on the Grove of Persephone in Homer, *Odyssey* X; Spenser fills it with deathly herbs, taking a hint from Pausanias, (*Description of Greece* X.30). The herbs are appropriate to Proserpina in her character as Hecate, patroness of poisons.

Dead sleeping . . . bad Poppy is the source of narcotics; hellebrore is a plant supposed to cure madness; coloquintida is bitter-apple; tetra is deadly nightshade; samnitis is the savine-tree used to procure abortions; cicuta is hemlock.

Critias Though once a disciple, Critias was an enemy of Socrates; Spenser seems confused about what happens in Plato's *Phaedo.* Many involved explanations of this have been offered, and some say Spenser evidently did not know his Plato. But there is a simple explanation: Socrates speaks his last words to Crito; Crito closes his eyes. The dialogue *Crito* also deals with the last days of Socrates. Crito was a very old friend of the philosopher.

silver seat Not a simple invitation to sloth but the forbidden seat of the Eleusinian mysteries—the *mystes* could not sit in it lest they should seem to be imitating the mourning Ceres as she rested on her search for her daughter Proserpina. For his attempt to rape Proserpina Theseus was punished (*Aeneid* VI. 617–18) by perpetual imprisonment in an underworld chair; Pausanias describes a painting (XXIX.9) which shows Theseus in the Chair of Forgetfulness, now a punishment for knowing too much of forbidden matters. Spenser somehow discovered this allegorical sense; it fits his theme of initiation into the mystery (of Heroic Virtue) and goes well, of course, in the Garden of Proserpina.

In which she often usd from open heat
Her selfe to shroud,° and pleasures to entreat,°   *shelter / occupy*
Next thereunto did grow a goodly tree,   *herself with*
With braunches broad dispred and body great,
Clothèd with leaves, that none the wood mote° see   *could*
And loaden all with fruit as thicke as it might bee.

54   Their fruit were golden apples° glistring bright,
That goodly was their glory to behold,
On earth like never grew, ne living wight
Like ever saw, but° they from hence were sold;°   *unless / brought*
For those, which *Hercules* with conquest bold
Got from great *Atlas* daughters,° hence began,
And planted there, did bring forth fruit of gold:
And those with which th'*Eubœan* young man wan°   *won*
Swift *Atalanta,*° when through craft he her out ran.

55   Here also sprong that goodly golden fruit,
With which *Acontius*° got his lover trew,
Whom he had long time sought with fruitlesse suit:
Here eke that famous golden Apple grew,
The which emongst the gods false *Ate*° threw;
For which th'*Idæan* Ladies disagreed,
Till partiall *Paris* dempt° it *Venus* dew,   *judged*
And had of her, faire *Helen* for his meed,
That many noble *Greekes* and *Trojans* made to bleed.

56   The warlike Elfe much wondred at this tree,
So faire and great, that shadowèd all the ground,
And his broad braunches, laden with rich fee,
Did stretch themselves without° the utmost bound   *beyond*
Of this great gardin, compast with a mound,
Which over-hanging, they themselves did steepe,
In a blacke flood which flow'd about it round;
That is the river of *Cocytus*° deepe,
In which full many soules do endlesse waile and weepe.

---

golden apples These are underworld fruit that must not be eaten (the *mala Punica,* Punic apples or pomegranates, were Proserpina's food of the dead), but Spenser adds that the famous apples of myth all descended from them. The forbidden fruit represents a temptation like that of Eve's apple, which was eaten out of appetite, vainglory, and curiosity. Spenser relates its mythological descendants to the temptation of forbidden knowledge.
Hercules . . . daughters The apples of the Hesperides; Hercules in his eleventh labor had to get them from the tree of the daughters of Atlas (Hesperides); they were protected by a dragon. They became emblems of astronomical knowledge.
th'Eubœan . . . Atalanta Hippomenes won his race with the swift Atalanta by throwing golden

apples in her way; she stopped to pick them up and was beaten. These apples were Hesperidean. Atalanta had desecrated the shrine of the Great Mother (an image of the blasphemy of forbidden knowledge).
Acontius He wrote on an apple "I swear by Artemis that I will marry Acontius"; Cydippe picked the apple up, read the message aloud, and was bound by the oath, though she tried blasphemously to get out of it.
Ate goddess of Discord. She produced the apple which was the prize to be awarded by Paris to the most beautiful of three goddesses; in return for Helen he gave it to Venus. His abduction of Helen caused the Trojan War. Allegorically this apple was a symbol of insane contempt for divine wisdom.
Cocytus river of hell

57   Which to behold, he clomb up to the banke,
      And looking downe, saw many damnèd wights,
      In those sad waves, which direfull deadly stanke,
      Plongèd continually of° cruell Sprights,   *by*
      That with their pitteous cryes, and yelling shrights,°   *shrieks*
      They made the further shore resounden° wide: *echo*
      Emongst the rest of those same ruefull sights,
      One cursèd creature he by chaunce espide,
  That drenchèd lay full deepe, under the Garden side.

58   Deepe was he drenchèd to the upmost chin,
      Yet gapèd still, as coveting to drinke
      Of the cold liquor, which he waded in,
      And stretching forth his hand, did often thinke
      To reach the fruit, which grew upon the brincke:
      But both the fruit from hand, and floud from mouth
      Did flie abacke, and made him vainely swinke:°   *labor*
      The whiles he sterv'd° with hunger and with drouth   *died*
  He daily dyde, yet never throughly° dyen couth.°   *completely / could*

59   The knight him seeing labour so in vaine,
      Askt who he was, and what he ment thereby:
      Who groning deepe, thus answerd him againe;
      Most cursèd of all creatures under skye,
      Lo *Tantalus,*° I here tormented lye:
      Of whom high *Jove* wont° whylome° feasted bee, *was accustomed / once*
      Lo here I now for want of food doe dye:
      But if that thou be such, as I thee see,
  Of grace I pray thee, give to eat and drinke to mee.

60   Nay, nay, thou greedie *Tantalus* (quoth he)
      Abide the fortune of thy present fate,
      And unto all that live in high degree,
      Ensample be of mind intemperate,
      To teach them how to use their present state.
      Then gan the cursèd wretch aloud to cry,
      Accusing highest *Jove* and gods ingrate,
      And eke blaspheming heaven bitterly,
  As authour of unjustice, there to let him dye.

61   He lookt a little further, and espyde
      Another wretch, whose carkasse deepe was drent°   *submerged*
      Within the river, which the same did hyde:
      But both his hands most filthy feculent,°   *foul*

Tantalus His punishment derives from *Odyssey* XI. A type of avarice, but also of intemperate and blasphemous knowledge, for he served the gods a dish made of the body of his son Pelops in order to test their immortality; also, as a guest of Jupiter, he heard secrets of divine knowledge and reported them to men. Ovid says he revealed the Eleusinian secrets, and Pausanias shows him suffering in hell with those who revealed or despised these mysteries. Guyon in stanza 60 says he is an example of "mind intemperate"; Spenser is not talking about greed or avarice.

Above the water were on high extent,°   *extended*
And faynd° to wash themselves incessantly: *pretended*
Yet nothing cleaner were for such intent,
But rather fowler seemèd to the eye;
So lost his labour vaine and idle industry.

62 The knight him calling, askèd who he was,
    Who lifting up his head, him answerd thus:
    I *Pilate*° am the falsest Judge, alas,
    And most unjust, that by unrighteous
    And wicked doome, to Jewes despiteous
    Delivered up the Lord of life to die,
    And did acquite a murdrer felonous;
    The whiles my hands I washt in puritie,
    The whiles my soule was soyld with foule iniquitie.

63 Infinite moe,° tormented in like paine   *more*
    He there beheld, too long here to be told:
    Ne *Mammon* would there let him long remaine,
    For terrour of the tortures manifold,
    In which the damnèd soules he did behold,
    But roughly him bespake. Thou fearefull foole,
    Why takest not of that same fruit of gold,
    Ne sittest downe on that same silver stoole,
    To rest thy wearie person, in the shadow coole.

64 All which he did, to doe him deadly fall
    In frayle intemperance through sinfull bayt;
    To which if he inclinèd had at all,
    That dreadfull feend, which did behind him wayt,
    Would him have rent in thousand peeces strayt:
    But he was warie wise in all his way,
    And well perceivèd his deceiptfull sleight,
    Ne suffred lust his safetie to betray:
    So goodly did beguile the Guyler° of the pray.   *deceiver*

65 And now he has so long remainèd there,
    That vitall powres gan wexe both weake and wan,
    For want of food, and sleepe, which two upbeare,
    Like mightie pillours, this fraile life of man,
    That none without the same enduren can.
    For now three dayes of men were full outwrought,°   *completed*
    Since he this hardie enterprize began:
    For thy° great *Mammon* fairely he besought,   *therefore*
    Into the world to guide him backe, as he him brought.

Pilate the type of judicial corruption. When Christ said "To this end was I born, and for this cause came I into the world, that I should bear witness unto the truth. Every one that is of the truth heareth my voice," Pilate replied "What is truth?" (John 18:37–38); by releasing Barabbas he denied divine truth.

66   The God, though loth, yet was constraind t'obay,
        For lenger time, then that, no living wight
        Below the earth, might suffred be to stay:
        So backe againe, him brought to living light.
        But all so soone as his enfeebled spright
        Gan sucke this vitall aire into his brest,
        As overcome with too exceeding might,
        The life did flit away out of her nest,
And all his senses were with deadly fit opprest.

        From Canto viii°
        Sir Guyon laid in swowne is by
            Acrates sonnes despoyld,
        Whom Arthur soone hath reskewed
            And Paynim brethren foyld.

1   And is there care in heaven? and is there love
        In heavenly spirits to these creatures bace,
        That may compassion of their evils move?
        There is: else much more wretched were the cace
        Of men, then beasts. But O th' exceeding grace
        Of highest God, that loves his creatures so,
        And all his workes with mercy doth embrace,
        That blessèd Angels, he sends to and fro,
To serve to wicked man, to serve his wicked foe.°

2   How oft do they, their silver bowers leave,
        To come to succour us, that succour want?˃   *lack*
        How oft do they with golden pineons,˃ cleave   *wings*
        The flitting˃ skyes, like flying Pursuivant,˃   *changing / messenger*
        Against foule feends to aide us millitant?
        They for us fight, they watch and dewly ward,
        And their bright Squadrons round about us plant,
        And all for love, and nothing for reward:
O why should heavenly God to men have such regard?°

[In canto viii the Palmer returns, but Arthur has to rescue Guyon from the
attack of Pyrochles and Cymochles, perhaps representing the threat of a temporary insurrection of irascibility and concupiscence in his weakened state. Canto
ix has a full-scale allegorical treatment of the House of Alma (the soul), also
called the House of Temperance. The well-regulated human body is here
described under the transparent allegory of a great house with its services, interconnections, sewers, etc. But it is besieged by enemies; and in xi (the interven-

Canto viii Spenser opens with a passage commenting on the fact that Guyon, in his faint, is
tended by an angel (stanzas 5–8). So was Christ
after his victory over sin in the wilderness; he
had overcome, says St. Augustine, temptation
by the lust of the flesh; by vainglory; and by
curiosity. These are all the temptations. (Augustine says this in a Homily on Psalm 8, which
Spenser quotes in these stanzas.) Guyon is now
confirmed in Heroic Virtue, having withstood
his initiatory trial; his virtues are now those of

the purged soul, a little lower than sanctity,
which Red Cross achieved, but higher than
ordinary virtues, and qualifying for the category
first invented by Aristotle, and later Christianized, namely, Heroic Virtue.
blessèd . . . foe "ministering spirits, sent forth
to minister for them who shall be heirs of salvation" (Hebrews 1:14)
O why . . . regard "What is man, that thou
art mindful of him? and the son of man, that
thou visitest him?" (Psalms 8:4)

ing canto is a long account of Elizabeth's legendary ancient British ancestors)
Spenser describes the siege, the assault on the human body of its enemies, led
by Maleger (Latin: *aeger*, sick). This is one of the great passages of *The
Faerie Queene*; Maleger is Spenser's most nightmarish figure—"like a ghost
he seemed, whose grave clothes were unbound"—and Arthur's combat with this
unkillable but apparently lifeless shadow has real horror. It represents the un-
stoppable onslaught of ills brought on by Adam's intemperance.

Canto xii brings Guyon to the climax of his quest, the Bower of Bliss, home
of Acrasia, Intemperance herself. But it takes a long voyage to get there, and
the account of it serves to recapitulate much of the Book. Guyon and the Palmer
sail past Phaedria, for example, and many other *exempla* of intemperance. At
the Bower they encounter many spurious beauties provided by art to conceal
the truth that it is an evil structure calling for merciless purgation. The Porter
is Genius, but not the benign Genius of "life and generation" we meet in
Epithalamion; in fact he is the exact opposite, "the foe of life," and Guyon
knocks over his winebowl and breaks his staff. Within, the Bower is a false version of the Earthly Paradise.]

From Canto xii

50 Thus being entred, they behold around
    A large and spacious plaine, on every side
    Strowèd with pleasauns,° whose faire grassy ground   *pleasances*
    Mantled with greene, and goodly beautifide
    With all the ornaments of *Floraes* pride,
    Wherewith her mother Art, as halfe in scorne
    Of niggard Nature, like a pompous bride
    Did decke her, and too lavishly adorne,
When forth from virgin bowre she comes in th' early morne.

51 Thereto the Heavens alwayes Joviall,°
    Lookt on them lovely, still in stedfast state,
    Ne suffred storme nor frost on them to fall,
    Their tender buds or leaves to violate,
    Nor scorching heat, nor cold intemperate°
    T'afflict the creatures, which therein did dwell,
    But the milde aire with season moderate
    Gently attempred, and disposd so well,
That still it breathèd forth sweet spirit and holesome smell.

52 More sweet and holesome, then the pleasaunt hill
    Of *Rhodope,*° on which the Nimphe, that bore
    A gyaunt babe, her selfe for griefe did kill;

Joviall under the influence of the planet Jupiter,
producing joy and happiness
Nor . . . intemperate Spenser represents the
place somewhat conventionally as an Earthly
Paradise and, like Milton in *Paradise Lost* IV,
enforces the idea by saying that this is better
than all the others; but he includes various
indications—not only Guyon's determination
to have nothing to do with the pleasures of
the place—to suggest that it is the scene of

abuses as well as of the natural plenty proper
to paradises. Hence the "wanton wreathings";
but especially he places Excess in the foreground,
for the lavish gifts of nature are being abused,
as later they are by Comus.
Rhodope mountain in Thrace into which Rhodope was turned for claiming to be more
beautiful than Juno; she bore Neptune a giant
son

Or the Thessalian *Tempe,*° where of yore
Faire *Daphne*° *Phœbus* hart with love did gore;
Or *Ida,*° where the Gods lov'd to repaire,
When ever they their heavenly bowres forlore;
Or sweet *Parnasse,* the haunt of Muses faire;
Or *Eden* selfe, if ought with *Eden* mote˘ compaire.   *can*

53   Much wondred *Guyon* at the faire aspect
        Of that sweet place, yet suffred no delight
        To sincke into his sence, nor mind affect,
        But passèd forth, and lookt still forward right,
        Bridling his will, and maistering his might:
        Till that he came unto another gate;
        No gate, but like one, being goodly dight
        With boughes and braunches, which did broad dilate
Their clasping armes, in wanton wreathings intricate.

54   So fashionèd a Porch with rare device,
        Archt over head with an embracing vine,
        Whose bounches hanging downe, seemed to entice
        All passers by, to tast their lushious wine,
        And did themselves into their hands incline,
        As freely offering to be gatherèd:
        Some deepe empurpled as the *Hyacint,*˘   *sapphire*
        Some as the *Rubine,*˘ laughing sweetly red,   *ruby*
Some like faire *Emeraudes,* not yet well ripenèd.

55   And them amongst, some were of burnisht gold,
        So made by art, to beautifie the rest,
        Which did themselves emongst the leaves enfold,
        As lurking from the vew of covetous guest,
        That the weake bowes, with so rich load opprest,
        Did bow adowne, as over-burdenèd.
        Under that Porch a comely dame did rest,
        Clad in faire weedes,˘ but fowle disorderèd,   *garments*
And garments loose, that seemd unmeet for womanhed.

56   In her left hand a Cup of gold she held,
        And with her right the riper fruit did reach,
        Whose sappy liquor, that with fulnesse sweld,
        Into her cup she scruzd,˘ with daintie breach   *squeezed*
        Of her fine fingers, without fowle empeach,˘   *detriment*
        That so faire wine-presse made the wine more sweet:
        Thereof she usd to give to drinke to each,
        Whom passing by she happenèd to meet:
It was her guise,˘ all Straungers goodly so to greet.   *manner*

Tempe Orpheus by his music led trees to the
mountain valley in Thessaly, famous for its
groves and walks.

Daphne She escaped Phoebus Apollo in Tempe
by being turned into a laurel.
Ida Cretan mountain, frequented by gods during
the Trojan war

57   So she to *Guyon* offred it to tast;
        Who taking it out of her tender hond,
        The cup to ground did violently cast,
        That all in peeces it was broken fond,
        And with the liquor stainèd all the lond:
        Whereat *Excesse* exceedingly was wroth,
        Yet no'teʾ the same amend, ne yet withstond,   *could not*
        But suffrèd him to passe, all were she loth;
     Who nought regarding her displeasure forward goth.

58   There the most daintie Paradise on ground,
        It selfe doth offer to his sober eye,
        In which all pleasures plenteously abound,
        And none does others happinesse envye:
        The painted flowres, the trees upshooting hye,
        The dales for shade, the hilles for breathing space,
        The trembling groves, the Christall running by;
        And that, which all faire workes doth most aggrace,
     The art, which all that wrought, appearèd in no place.°

59   One would have thought, (so cunningly, the rude,
        And scornèd parts were mingled with the fine,)
        That nature had for wantonesse ensudeʾ   *imitated*
        Art, and that Art at nature did repine;
        So striving each th' other to undermine,
        Each did the others worke more beautifie;
        So diff'ring both in willes, agreed in fine:ʾ   *in the end*
        So all agreed through sweete diversitie,
     This Gardin to adorne with all varietie.

60   And in the midst of all, a fountaine stood,
        Of richest substaunce, that on earth might bee,
        So pure and shiny, that the silver flood
        Through every channell running one might see;
        Most goodly it with curious imageree
        Was over-wrought, and shapes of naked boyes,
        Of which some seemd with lively jollitee,
        To fly about, playing their wanton toyes,ʾ   *games*
     Whilest others did them selves embayʾ in liquid joyes.   *bathe*

61   And over all, of purest gold was spred,
        A trayle of yvie in his native hew:ʾ   *appearance*
        For the rich mettall was so colourèd,
        That wight, who did not well avis'd it vew,
        Would surely deeme it to be yvie trew;
        Low his lascivious armes adown did creepe,
        That themselves dipping in the silver dew,

The art . . . place exactly translated from Tasso, *Gerusalemme Liberata* (the main inspiration of this canto). Spenser's meaning is not that art is lower than nature, as some critics say; the fault in the paradise lies in the human uses to which it is put, not in its design.

Their fleecy flowres they tenderly did steepe,
Which drops of Christall seemd for wantonès to weepe.

62 Infinit streames continually did well
    Out of this fountaine, sweet and faire to see,
    The which into an ample laver⸴ fell,   *basin*
    And shortly grew to so great quantitie,
    That like a little lake it seemd to bee;
    Whose depth exceeded not three cubits hight,
    That through the waves one might the bottom see,
  All pav'd beneath with Jaspar shining bright,
That seemd the fountaine in that sea did sayle upright.

63 And all the margent round about was set,
    With shady Laurell trees, thence to defend⸴   *fend off*
    The sunny beames, which on the billowes bet,⸴   *beat*
    And those which therein bathèd, mote offend.
    As *Guyon* hapned by the same to wend,
    Two naked Damzelles he therein espyde,
    Which therein bathing, seemèd to contend,
    And wrestle wantonly, ne car'd to hyde,
Their dainty parts from vew of any, which them eyde.

64 Sometimes the one would lift the other quight
    Above the waters, and then downe againe
    Her plong, as over maisterèd by might,
    Where both awhile would covered remaine,
    And each the other from to rise⸴ restraine;   *rising*
    The whiles their snowy limbes, as through a vele,
    So through the Christall waves appearèd plaine:
    Then suddeinly both would themselves unhele,⸴   *uncover*
And th'amorous sweet spoiles to greedy eyes revele.

65 As that faire Starre,° the messenger of morne,
    His deawy face out of the sea doth reare:
    Or as the *Cyprian* goddesse,° newly borne
    Of th'Oceans fruitfull froth, did first appeare:
    Such seemèd they, and so⸴ their yellow heare   *in the same way*
    Christalline humour⸴ dropped downe apace.   *water*
    Whom such when *Guyon* saw, he drew him neare,
    And somewhat gan relent his earnest pace,
His stubborne brest gan secret pleasaunce to embrace.°

66 The wanton Maidens him esyping, stood
    Gazing a while at his unwonted guise;⸴   *behavior*
    Then th'one her selfe low duckèd in the flood,

---

faire Starre the Morning Star (Venus)
Cyprian goddesse Venus, born of the union of Saturn's semen and the ocean
His stubborne . . . embrace Guyon's momentary lust for the girls in the fountain recalls the lapses of his pagan (but Christianized) prototype Hercules; but Right Reason (the Palmer) enables temperance to overcome concupiscence.

Abasht, that her a straunger did avise:˃   *look at*
But th'other rather higher did arise,
And her two lilly paps aloft displayd,
And all, that might his melting hart entise
To her delights, she unto him bewrayd:˃   *displayed*
The rest hid underneath, him more desirous made.

67   With that, the other likewise up arose,
And her faire lockes, which formerly were bownd
Up in one knot, she low adowne did lose:˃   *unloose*
Which flowing long and thick, her cloth'd arownd,
And th'yvorie in golden mantle gown:
So that faire spectacle from him was reft,
Yet that, which reft it, no lesse faire was fownd:
So hid in lockes and waves from lookers theft,
Nought but her lovely face she for his looking left.

68   Withall she laughèd, and she blusht withall,
That blushing to her laughter gave more grace,
And laughter to her blushing, as did fall:
Now when they spide the knight to slacke his pace,
Them to behold, and in his sparkling face
The secret signes of kindled lust appeare,
Their wanton meriments they did encreace,
And to him beckned, to approach more neare,
And shewd him many sights, that courage˃ cold could reare.   *desire*

69   On which when gazing him the Palmer saw,
He much rebukt those wandring eyes of his,
And counseld well, him forward thence did draw.
Now are they come nigh to the *Bowre of blis*
Of her fond favorites so nam'd amis:
When thus the Palmer; Now Sir, well avise;
For here the end of all our travell is:
Here wonnes˃ Acrasia, whom we must surprise,   *lives*
Else she will slip away, and all our drift˃ despise.   *plans*

70   Eftsoones they heard a most melodious sound,
Of all that mote delight a daintie eare,
Such as attonce might not on living ground,
Save in this Paradise, be heard elsewhere:
Right hard it was, for wight, which did it heare,
To read,˃ what manner musicke that mote bee: *tell*
For all that pleasing is to living eare,
Was there consorted in one harmonee,
Birdes, voyces, instruments, windes, waters, all agree.

71   The joyous birdes shrouded in chearefull shade,
Their notes unto the voyce attempred sweet;
Th'Angelicall soft trembling voyces made

To th'instruments divine respondence meet;
The silver sounding instruments did meet
With the base° murmure of the waters fall: *bass*
The waters fall with difference discreet,
Now soft, now loud, unto the wind did call:
The gentle warbling wind low answerèd to all.°

72 There, whence that Musick seemèd heard to bee,
     Was the faire Witch her selfe now solacing,
     With a new Lover, whom through sorceree
     And witchcraft, she from farre did thither bring:
     There she had him now layd a slombering,
     In secret shade, after long wanton joyes:
     Whilst round about them pleasauntly did sing
     Many faire Ladies, and lascivious boyes,
That ever mixt their song with light licentious toyes.

73 And all that while, right over him she hong,
     With her false eyes fast fixèd in his sight,
     As seeking medicine, whence she was stong,°
     Or greedily depasturing° delight: *consuming*
     And oft inclining downe with kisses light,
     For feare of waking him, his lips bedewed,
     And through his humid eyes did sucke his spright,
     Quite molten into lust and pleasure lewd;
Wherewith she sighèd soft, as if his case she rewd.

74 The whiles some one did chaunt this lovely lay;°
     Ah see, who so faire thing doest faine to see,
     In springing flowre the image of thy day;
     Ah see the Virgin Rose, how sweetly shee
     Doth first peepe forth with bashfull modestee,
     That fairer seemes, the lesse ye see her may;
     Lo see soone after, how more bold and free
     Her bared bosome she doth broad display;
Loe see soone after, how she fades, and falles away.

75 So passeth, in the passing of a day,
     Of mortall life the leafe, the bud, the flowre,
     Ne more doth flourish after first decay,
     That earst was sought to decke both bed and bowre,

The joyous . . . all This stanza of natural and artificial harmony Spenser developed from Tasso, *Gerusalemme Liberata* XVI.2, though that leaves out the instruments and voices; however, Tasso includes these when he writes a rather similar stanza (XVIII.8); hence if Spenser is really, as some critics say, making the combination of artificial and natural music seem sinister, Tasso, whose sinister intent is hard to see, preceded him.
seeking . . . stong seeking a cure from that which hurt her

lay Translated from Tasso (XVI.14–15), where it is sung by a bird. The theme—*carpe diem*, seize the day—is ancient, and so is the group of figures attached to the rose. The beauty of the "lovely lay" emphasizes, like the beauty of the approaches to the Bower, the powerful forces against which Temperance must fight. The theme occurs in many poems which have not the moralistic context of Spenser's, but Comus's use of the rose-figure in Milton's masque is very like this one (ll. 742–43).

Of many a Ladie, and many a Paramowre:
Gather therefore the Rose, whilest yet is prime,
For soone comes age, that will her pride deflowre:
Gather the Rose of love, whilest yet is time,
Whilest loving thou mayst lovèd be with equall crime.˃   *sin*

76   He ceast, and then gan all the quire of birdes
Their diverse notes t'attune unto his lay,
As in approvance of his pleasing words.
The constant paire heard all, that he did say,
Yet swarvèd˃ not, but kept their forward way,   *swerved*
Through many covert groves, and thickets close,
In which they creeping did at last display˃   *discover*
That wanton Ladie, with her lover lose,
Whose sleepie head she in her lap did soft dispose.

77   Upon a bed of Roses she was layd,
As faint through heat, or dight to pleasant sin,
And was arayd, or rather disarayd,
All in a vele of silke and silver thin,
That hid no whit her alablaster˃ skin,   *alabaster*
But rather shewd more white, if more might bee:
More subtile web *Arachne* cannot spin,
Nor the fine nets, which oft we woven see
Of scorchèd deaw, do not in th'aire more lightly flee.

78   Her snowy brest was bare to readie spoyle
Of hungry eies, which n'ote˃ therewith be fild,   *could not*
And yet through languor of her late sweet toyle,
Few drops, more cleare then Nectar, forth distild,
That like pure Orient perles adowne it trild,
And her faire eyes sweet smyling in delight,
Moystenèd their fierie beames, with which she thrild
Fraile harts, yet quenchèd not; like starry light
Which sparckling on the silent waves, does seeme more bright.

79   The young man sleeping by her, seemd to bee
Some goodly swayne of honorable place,
That certes it great pittie was to see
Him his nobilitie so foule deface;
A sweet regard, and amiable grace,
Mixèd with manly sternnesse did appeare
Yet sleeping, in his well proportiond face,
And on his tender lips the downy heare
Did now but freshly spring, and silken blosomes beare.

80   His warlike armes, the idle instruments
Of sleeping praise, were hong upon a tree,
And his brave shield, full of old moniments,˃   *figures*
Was fowly ra'st,˃ that none the signes might see;   *erased*

Ne for them, ne for honour carèd hee,
Ne ought, that did to his advancement tend,
But in lewd loves, and wastfull luxuree,
His dayes, his goods, his bodie he did spend:
O horrible enchantment, that him so did blend.°   *blind*

81   The noble Elfe, and carefull Palmer drew
So nigh them, minding nought, but lustfull game,
That suddein forth they on them rusht, and threw
A subtile° net,° which onely°for the same   *fine / specially*
The skilfull Palmer formally° did frame.°   *expressly / design*
So held them under fast, the whiles the rest
Fled all away for feare of fowler shame.
The faire Enchauntresse, so unwares opprest,
Tryde all her arts, and all her sleights, thence out to wrest.

82   And eke her lover strove: but all in vaine;
For that same net so cunningly was wound,
That neither guile, nor force might it distraine.°   *break*
They tooke them both, and both them strongly bound
In captive bandes, which there they readie found:
But her in chaines of adamant he tyde;
For nothing else might keepe her safe and sound;
But *Verdant*° (so he hight) he soone untyde,
And counsell sage in steed thereof° to him applyde.   *of constraint*

83   But all those pleasant bowres and Pallace brave,
Guyon broke downe, with rigour pittilesse;
Ne ought their goodly workmanship might save
Them from the tempest of his wrathfulnesse,
But that their blisse he turn'd to balefulnesse:
Their groves he feld, their gardins did deface,
Their arbers spoyle, their Cabinets° suppresse,   *bowers*
Their banket houses burne, their buildings race,°   *raze*
And of the fairest late, now made the fowlest place.

84   Then led they her away, and eke that knight
They with them led, both sorrowfull and sad:
The way they came, the same retourn'd they right,
Till they arrivèd, where they lately had
Charm'd those wild-beasts,° that rag'd with furie mad.
Which now awaking, fierce at them gan fly,
As in their mistresse reskew, whom they lad;
But them the Palmer soone did pacify.
Then *Guyon* askt, what meant those beastes, which there did ly.

net borrowed from *Odyssey* VIII. 276 ff., where Hephaestus (Vulcan) traps his wife Aphrodite (Venus) in bed with Ares (Mars) by a similar stratagem
Verdant perhaps because in the spring of his life; perhaps "spring (or life)-giving," as Mordant, Acrasia's earlier lover, was "death-giving"
wild-beasts They met these beasts on the way in stanza 39.

85 Said he, These seeming beasts are men indeed,
    Whom this Enchauntresse hath transformèd thus,
    Whylome⸾ her lovers, which her lusts did feed,   *formerly*
    Now turned into figures hideous,
    According to their mindes like monstruous.°
    Sad end (quoth he) of life intemperate,
    And mournefull meed of joyes delicious:
    But Palmer, if it mote thee so aggrate,⸾   *please*
    Let them returnèd be unto their former state.

86 Streight way he with his vertuous staffe them strooke,
    And streight of beasts they comely men became;
    Yet being men they did unmanly looke,
    And starèd ghastly, some for inward shame,
    And some for wrath, to see their captive Dame:
    But one above the rest in speciall,
    That had an hog beene late, hight *Grille*° by name,
    Repinèd greatly, and did him miscall,
    That had from hoggish forme him brought to naturall.

87 Said *Guyon*, See the mind of beastly man,
    That hath so soone forgot the excellence
    Of his creation, when he life began,
    That now he chooseth, with vile difference,
    To be a beast, and lacke intelligence.
    To whom the Palmer thus, The donghill kind
    Delights in filth and foule incontinence:
    Let *Grill* be *Grill*, and have his hoggish mind,
    But let us hence depart, whilest wether serves and wind.

                                                         1590

Book III

Book III is the Legend of Chastity, a Book of Love, and very different structurally from I and II, being in this regard closely linked to IV. It may be that parts of it are earlier than I and II, and belong to a time when Spenser was much more interested in writing a poem like Ariosto's *Orlando Furioso*, which has, though with greater pace and dash, a similar interweaving of many stories. Spenser here combines the tales of Britomart and Artegall, Marinell and Florimell, Belphoebe and Timias, with that of Scudamour and Amoret and many others. Amoret is chaste married love, and Scuda-

---

According . . . monstruous Acrasia is modeled on Homer's Circe, who turns men into beasts. Allegorically, the cup she offers gives a man his choice between two extremes between which, according to Aristotle, there is no mean: Bestiality and Heroic Virtue. Acrasia's victims chose Bestiality, and so are transformed into beasts.
Grille According to Plutarch, in his *Whether the Beasts Have Use of Reason*, one of Odys-

seus' comrades refused to be turned back into a man. This was Gryllus. The story was known in England from a book called *Circe*, translated from Italian and published in 1557. Guyon uses Grille as an occasion to reflect on the willingness of some men to forgo their rank above the beast and next to the angels; the Palmer abandons him, since some men do, through incontinence, lose even the desire to be restored to humanity.

mour finally achieves her at the end of the Book, but only in the 1590 edition of Books I to III; in 1596 Spenser canceled the last five stanzas and replaced them by three new ones postponing the union.

In Book III Elizabeth is celebrated in her second person, not as Queen but as "a most virtuous and beautifull Lady," namely Belphoebe. Spenser can include in a treatment of love philosophical considerations wider and higher than relations between men and women; he glories in love as the bringer of fertility and order in the whole world. Thus the Virgin Queen can be the patroness and exemplar of plenty, fertility, order, while remaining a devotee of virginity; her twin sister, Amoret, expresses the other kind of chastity, which is consistent with married love.

The cosmic and moral implications of love are present also in the parts of the Book Spenser calls, in the Letter to Ralegh, "Accidents"; one is "the over-throw of Marinell, the misery of Florimell," a story that runs on into Book V. Florimell is based on Ariosto's Angelica, who is always being chased and who has an evil double, as Florimell has a Snowy Florimell imitating her. Her allegorical significance is not clear, but she seems to be a type of the beauty of natural creation, the opposite but also the complement of the chaotic sea (Marinell) out of which Love was born.

[In the opening canto Spenser follows his now established procedure—the departing Guyon meets the knight of the new Book, the maiden warrior Britomart, and she beats him in fight because Chastity, her virtue, is higher than Temperance, Guyon's. But she presides over the Book much less firmly than Guyon over his, and comes into her own only at the end. The first canto also contains a key to the whole Book in the account of Castle Joyeous, the abode of Malecasta, which is full of emblems of unchastity. Britomart defeats Malecasta's champions. Cantos ii and iii establish the relation between Britomart and Artegall (knight of Justice in Book V) to Elizabeth, and iv is about Marinell and Florimell and ends with a beautiful apostrophe to Night. Canto v describes the healing of the squire Timias by Belphoebe (probably a reference to the quarrel between Ralegh and the Queen). Canto vi is the "core" canto, and one of the most important in the entire poem.]

Book III, Canto vi

This canto, which has strong associations with the Mutability Cantos, contains a charming, newly invented myth and a philosophical allegory which is not only hard to interpret but also, in some respects, central to the poem, and the source of much that we consider "Spenserian"; if The Faerie Queene in any sense adds up to a great poem much depends upon these stanzas; they tell us about the color of the poet's mind and the way he had learned to speak a philosophy of life through mythological fictions.

The Garden of Adonis is about the great opposites that everybody knows about in his own life; we experience continuity but also change; we know that humanity, like plant life, survives, but also that as individuals we die. In short, life is mutable but also constant. The Renaissance poet will express this felt knowledge by making a myth which brings the opposites into a unity. Spenser will explain that the forms are sempiternal, that is, perpetual though lacking the final immutable stillness of eternity.

They are deathless but do not possess being-for-ever. The matter which these forms assume is separated from them by death. He represents the forms as plants in a nursery garden, and the matter that clothes them comes from a chaos like that which God used as material for the creation. This matter is eternal; love produces its union with form, so that the world is stocked with generated beings; and Time produces their separation. The generative *cycle* is quasi-immortal; the individual elements of it are not.

Consequently the species, neither eternal nor of time, occupies a third realm in between them. It partakes both of mutability and the unchangingness of the eternal: "by succession made perpetuall, / Transformed oft and chaunged diverslie." The symbol of this realm is Adonis; he is the entire biological cycle, dying and living on, in time and out of it.

Like all myths, as Claude Lévi-Strauss sees them, Spenser's is not an answer to a problem, but a way of containing it, making it humanly acceptable. Through culture man is aware of and dreads death; here culture and nature confront each other, and the myth allows the mind to condone the confrontation: the problem is not solved but acceptably formulated. So essential is this problem to Spenser's whole view of the world that he restates it in an analogous myth in Book VII.

It is disastrous to try to give this canto exact philosophical meanings. It is a myth, and the use of philosophical concepts and language is incidental to that kind of explanation. But a few notes on the more abstract-sounding stanzas may be helpful. The seminary (as described in stanzas 33–38) is analogous to the Platonic *anima mundi* or world-soul, from which come the forms that give created things their characteristic shapes ("hews") when joined with matter from chaos. When Spenser says "the substance is eterne" he is not trying, as a philosopher using such language would, to distinguish between "matter" and "substance"; for him they mean much the same thing, substance being a little more specific, and meaning matter in so far as it has a relation to form.

When Spenser says that it is the forms which suffer under time, and that if it were otherwise the voluptuous delights of the garden would be immortal, we understand him well enough without troubling to ask why, since the wearing out of the forms takes place in "the state of life," there has to be an allegorical figure of Time inside the garden as well. The introduction of that figure into an Earthly Paradise is in itself a myth; it represents the confrontation of human knowledge of fact and human hope.

It is Adonis himself, in the famous stanza 47, who elicits from Spenser his most determined effort to spell out discursively the knowledge which is implicit in his myth. Adonis was killed by the boar, but lives. Instead of representing him in the traditional way as dying annually and annually reviving, like vegetation, Spenser crushes together his mortality and immortality; in explaining this he has to be aphoristic: "All be he subject to mortalitie, / Yet is eterne in mutabilitie, / And by succession made perpetuall." For this reason he is called "the Father of all formes"; he represents the condition under which, though the living die, they still have life. Meanwhile the additional myth of Cupid and Psyche relates the pleasure of generation to the most exalted idea of love, seen as following the mutable course of the passion in life and in time. In the Mutability Cantos the relation of eternity to time is more fully considered.

Canto vi°
The birth of faire Belphœbe and
Of Amoret is told.
The Gardins of Adonis° fraught
With pleasures manifold.

1   Well may I weene, faire Ladies, all this while
    Ye wonder, how this noble Damozell°
    So great perfections did in her compile,
    Sith that in salvage˃ forests she did dwell,   *wild*
    So farre from court and royall Citadell,
    The great schoolmistresse of all curtesy:
    Seemeth that such wild woods should far expell
    All civill usage and gentility,
And gentle sprite deforme with rude rusticity.

2   But to this faire *Belphœbe°* in her berth
    The heavens so favourable were and free,˃   *unencumbered*
    Looking with myld aspect° upon the earth,
    In th'*Horoscope* of her nativitee,
    That all the gifts of grace and chastitee
    On her they pourèd forth of plenteous horne;°
    Jove laught on *Venus* from his soveraigne see,˃   *throne*
    And *Phœbus* with faire beames did her adorne,
And all the *Graces°* rockt her cradle being borne.

3   Her berth was of the wombe of Morning dew,
    And her conception of the joyous Prime˃   *spring*
    And all her whole creation did her shew
    Pure and unspotted from all loathly crime,˃   *sin*
    That is ingenerate˃ in fleshly slime.   *inborn*
    So was this virgin borne, so was she bred,
    So was she trayned up from time to time,°
    In all chast vertue, and true bounti-hed
Till to her dew perfection she was ripenèd.

4   Her mother was the faire *Chrysogonee,°*
    The daughter of *Amphisa,°* who by race
    A Faerie was, yborne of high degree,
    She bore *Belphœbe,* she bore in like cace
    Faire *Amoretta* in the second place:
    These two were twinnes, and twixt them two did share
    The heritage of all celestiall grace.

Gardins of Adonis originally little pots of flowers which sprang up and in a few days withered, symbols of the death of Adonis used by women who mourned him, like Thammuz, as a god who died and was annually revived. Spenser hardly has them in mind when he constructs his big allegory of what is "eterne in mutabilitie."
Damozell Belphoebe
Belphœbe "handsome-radiant"

aspect This is the relative position of the planets as it determines their influence (see *Astrology* in the Glossary).
pourèd . . . horne as if from a cornucopia
Graces See I.i.48n.
from time to time through the stages of growth
Chrysogonee "golden-born"
Amphisa "of double nature" (natural and supernatural)

That all the rest it seem'd they robbèd bare
Of bountie, and of beautie, and all vertues rare.

5   It were a goodly storie,° to declare,
By what straunge accident faire *Chrysogone*
Conceiv'd these infants, and how them she bare,
In this wild forrest wandring all alone,
After she had nine moneths fulfild and gone:
For not as other wemens commune brood,
They were enwombèd in the sacred throne
Of her chaste bodie, nor with commune food,
As other wemens babes, they suckèd vitall blood.

6. But wondrously they were begot, and bred
Through influence of th'heavens fruitfull ray,
As it in antique bookes is mentionèd.
It was upon a Sommers shynie day,
When *Titan* faire his beamès did display,
In a fresh fountaine, farre from all mens vew,
She bath'd her brest, the boyling heat t' allay;
She bath'd with roses red, and violets blew,
And all the sweetest flowres, that in the forrest grew.

7   Till faint through irkesome wearinesse, adowne
Upon the grassie ground her selfe she layd
To sleepe, the whiles a gentle slombring swowne⟩   *faint*
Upon her fell all naked bare displayd;
The sunne-beames bright upon her body playd,
Being through former bathing mollifide,⟩   *softened*
And pierst into her wombe, where they embayd⟩   *pervaded*
With so sweet sence and secret power unspide,
That in her pregnant flesh they shortly fructifide.

8   Miraculous may seeme to him, that reades
So straunge ensample of conceptión;
But reason teacheth that the fruitfull seades
Of all things living, through impressión
Of the sunbeames in moyst complexión,
Doe life conceive and quickned are by⟩ kynd: *according to*
So after *Nilus* inundatión,°
Infinite shapes of creatures men do fynd,
Informèd in the mud, on which the Sunne hath shynd.

9   Great father he of generation
Is rightly cald, th'author of life and light;
And his faire sister for creation
Ministreth matter fit, which tempred right

---

storie This is a myth of Spenser's invention,
made to give a narrative explanation of the
sinless birth of Belphoebe and Amoret, and
their separate and different educations.
Nilus inundation See I.i.21n.

With heate and humour,ᐢ breedes the living wight. *moisture*
So sprong these twinnes in wombe of *Chrysogone*,
Yet wist she nought thereof, but sore affright,
Wondred to see her belly so upblone,
Which still increast, till she her terme had full outgone.

10   Whereof conceiving shame and foule disgrace,
    Albeᐢ her guiltlesse consciènce her cleard, *although*
    She fled into the wildernesse a space,
    Till that unweeldy burden she had reard,
    And shund dishonor, which as death she feard:
    Where wearie of long travell, downe to rest
    Her selfe she set, and comfortably cheard,ᐢ *encouraged*
    There a sad cloud of sleepe her overkest,ᐢ *overcast*
And seizèd every sense with sorrow sore opprest.

11   It fortunèd, faire *Venus* having lost
    Her little sonne, the wingèd god of love,
    Who for some light displeasure, which him crost,
    Was from her fled, as flitᐢ as ayerie Dove, *swift*
    And let her blisfull bowre of joy above,
    (So from her often he had fled away,°
    When she for ought him sharpely did reprove,
    And wandred in the world in strange aray,
Disguiz'd in thousand shapes, that none might him bewray.ᐢ) *reveal*

12   Him for to seeke, she left her heavenly hous,
    The house of goodly formes and faire aspects,
    Whence all the world derives the glorious
    Features of beautie, and all shapes select,
    With which high God his workmanship hath deckt;
    And searchèd every way, through which his wings
    Had borne him, or his tractᐢ she moteᐢ detect: *track / could*
    She promist kisses sweet, and sweeter things
Unto the man, that of him tydings to her brings.

13   First she him sought in Court, where most he used
    Whylomeᐢ to haunt, but there she found him not; *formerly*
    But many there she found, which sore accused
    His falsehood, and with foule infámous blot
    His cruell deedes and wicked wyles did spot:
    Ladies and Lords she every where mote heare
    Complayning, how with his empoysned shot
    Their wofull harts he wounded had whyleare,ᐢ *earlier*
And so had left them languishing twixt hope and feare.

14   She then the Citties sought from gate to gate,
    And every one did aske, did he him see;

So . . . away Spenser is imitating an idyll of the Alexandrian poet Moschus, called *Love the Runaway.* Venus seeks Cupid in court, city, and country, the three divisions of society, and must now try the wilds.

And every one her answerd, that too late
He had him seene, and felt the crueltie
Of his sharpe darts and whot artillerie;
And every one threw forth reproches rife
Of his mischíevous deedes, and said, That hee
Was the disturber of all civill᾿ life,   *city*
The enimy of peace, and author of all strife.

15   Then in the countrey she abroad him sought,
And in the rurall cottages inquirèd,
Where also many plaints to her were brought,
How he their heedlesse harts with love had fyrèd,
And his false venim through their veines inspyrèd;
And eke the gentle shepheard swaynes, which sat
Keeping their fleecie flockes, as they were hyrèd,
She sweetly heard complaine, both how and what
Her sonne had to them doen; yet she did smile thereat.

16   But when in none of all these she him got,
She gan avize,᾿ where else he mote᾿ him hyde: *consider / might*
At last she her bethought, that she had not
Yet sought the salvage woods and forrests wyde,
In which full many lovely Nymphes abyde,
Mongst whom might be, that he did closely lye,
Or that the love of some of them him tyde:
For thy,᾿ she thither cast her course t'apply,   *wherefore*
To search the secret haunts of *Dianes* company.

17   Shortly unto the wasteful woods she came,
Whereas she found the Goddesse with her crew,
After late chace of their embrewèd᾿ game,   *blood-stained*
Sitting beside a fountaine in a rew,᾿   *row*
Some of them washing with the liquid dew
From off their dainty limbes the dustie sweat,
And soyle which did deforme their lively hew;᾿   *form*
Others lay shaded from the scorching heat;
The rest upon her person gave attendance great.

18   She having hong upon a bough on high
Her bow and painted quiver, had unlaste
Her silver buskins from her nimble thigh,
And her lancke loynes ungirt, and brests unbraste,
After her heat the breathing cold to taste;
Her golden lockes, that late in tresses bright
Embreaded were for hindring of her haste,
Now loose about her shoulders hong undight,᾿   *loose*
And were with sweet *Ambrosia* all besprinckled light.

19   Soone as she *Venus* saw behind her backe,
She was asham'd to be so loose surprized,

And woxe halfe wroth against her damzels slacke,
That had not her thereof before avized,°   *warned*
But suffred her so carelesly disguized°   *adorned*
Be overtaken. Soone her garments loose
Upgath'ring, in her bosome she comprized,°   *drew together*
Well as she might, and to the Goddesse rose,
Whiles all her Nymphes did like a girlond her enclose.°

20 Goodly she gan faire *Cytherea* greet,   *Venus*
    And shortly askèd her, what cause her brought
    Into that wildernesse for her unmeet,°   *unsuitable*
    From her sweete bowres, and beds with pleasures fraught:
    That suddein change she strange adventure thought.
    To whom halfe weeping, she thus answerèd,
    That she her dearest sonne *Cupído* sought,
    Who in his frowardnesse° from her was fled;   *peevishness*
    That she repented sore, to have him angerèd.

21 Thereat *Diana* gan to smile, in scorne
    Of her vaine plaint, and to her scoffing sayd;
    Great pittie sure, that ye be so forlorne
    Of your gay sonne, that gives ye so good ayd
    To your disports:° ill mote ye bene apayd°   *sports / requited*
    But she was more engrievèd, and replide;
    Faire sister, ill beseemes it to upbrayd
    A dolefull heart with so disdainfull pride;
    The like that mine, may be your paine another tide.°   *time*

22 As you in woods and wanton wildernesse
    Your glory set, to chace the salvage beasts,
    So my delight is all in joyfulnesse,
    In beds, in bowres, in banckets, and in feasts:
    And ill becomes you with your loftie creasts,°   *helmets*
    To scorne the joy, that *Jove* is glad to seeke;
    We both are bound to follow heavens beheasts,
    And tend our charges with obeisance meeke:
    Spare, gentle sister, with reproch my paine to eeke.°   *augment*

23 And tell me, if that ye my sonne have heard,
    To lurke emongst your Nymphes in secret wize;
    Or keepe° their cabins: much I am affeard,   *watch*
    Least he like one of them him selfe disguize,
    And turne his arrowes to their exercize:
    So may he long himself full easie hide:
    For he is faire and fresh in face and guize,°   *appearance*
    As any Nymph (let not it be envyde.)°   *grudged*
    So saying every Nymph full narrowly she eyde.

Whiles . . . enclose The story of Venus sur-   who did so in Ovid, *Metamorphoses* III; and
prising Diana is adapted from that of Actaeon,   this line is almost a translation of III.180.

24   But *Phœbe* therewith sore was angerèd,
   And sharply said; Goe Dame, goe seeke your boy,
   Where you him lately left, in *Mars* his bed;
   He comes not here, we scorne his foolish joy,
   Ne lend we leisure to his idle toy:°   *game*
   But if I catch him in this company,
   By *Stygian* lake I vow, whose sad annoy°   *injuriouness*
   The Gods doe dread, he dearely shall abye.° *pay for it*
Ile clip his wanton wings, that he no more shall fly.

25   Whom when as *Venus* saw so sore displeased,
   She inly sory was, and gan relent,
   What she had said: so her she soone appeased,
   With sugred words and gentle blandishment,
   Which as a fountaine from her sweet lips went,
   And wellèd goodly forth, that in short space
   She was well pleasd, and forth her damzels sent,
   Through all the woods, to search from place to place,
If any tract of him or tydings they mote trace.

26   To search the God of love, her Nymphes she sent
   Throughout the wandring forrest every where:
   And after them her selfe eke with her went
   To seeke the fugitive, both farre and nere,
   So long they sought, till they arrivèd were
   In that same shadie covert, whereas lay
   Faire *Crysogone* in slombry traunce whilere:
   Who in her sleepe (a wondrous thing to say)
Unwares had borne two babes, as faire as springing day.

27   Unwares she them conceiv'd, unwares she bore:
   She bore withouten paine, that she conceived
   Withouten pleasure: ne her need implore
   Lucinaes aide:° which when they both perceived,
   They were through wonder nigh of sense bereaved,
   And gazing each on other, nought bespake:
   At last they both agreed, her seeming grieved° *unwell*
   Out of her heavy swowne not to awake,
But from her loving side the tender babes to take.

28   Up they them tooke, each one a babe uptooke,
   And with them carried, to be fosterèd;
   Dame *Phœbe* to a Nymph her babe betooke,
   To be upbrought in perfect Maydenhed,
   And of her selfe her name *Belphœbe* red:° *gave*
   But *Venus* hers thence farre away convayd,
   To be upbrought in goodly womanhed,

Lucinaes aide Juno, in the capacity of patron
of women in labor, was called Lucina.

And in her litle loves stead,⟩ which was strayd,   *place*
Her *Amoretta* cald,° to comfort her dismayd.

29   She brought her to her joyous Paradize,
        Where most she wonnes,⟩ when she on earth does dwel.   *lives*
        So faire a place, as Nature can devize:
        Whether in *Paphos*,° or *Cytheron*° hill,
        Or it in *Gnidus*° be, I wote not well; ˙
        But well I wote by tryall,⟩ that this same   *experience*
        All other pleasant places doth excell,
        And callèd is by her lost lovers name
    The *Gardin* of *Adonis*, farre renowmd by fame.

30   In that same Gardin all the goodly flowres,
        Wherewith dame Nature doth her beautifie,
        And decks the girlonds of her paramoures,
        Are fetcht: there is the first seminarie⟩   *seed nursery*
        Of all things, that are borne to live and die,
        According to their kindes. Long worke it were,
        Here to account the endlesse progenie
        Of all the weedes,⟩ that bud and blossome there;   *plants*
    But so much as doth need, must needs be counted here.

31   It sited was in fruitfull soyle of old,
        And girt in with two walles on either side;
        The one of yron, the other of bright gold,
        That none might thorough⟩ breake, nor overstride: *through*
        And double gates it had, which opened wide,
        By which both in and out men moten⟩ pas;   *could*
        Th'one faire and fresh, the other old and dride:
        Old *Genius* the porter of them was,
    Old *Genius*, the which a double nature has.

32   He letteth in, he letteth out to wend,⟩   *go*
        All that to come into the world desire;
        A thousand thousand naked babes attend
        About him day and night, which do require,
        That he with fleshly weedes would them attire:
        Such as him list, such as eternall fate
        Ordainèd hath, he clothes with sinfull mire,°
        And sendeth forth to live in mortall state,
    Till they againe returne backe by the hinder gate.

33   After that they againe returnèd beene,
        They in that Gardin planted be againe;

And in . . . cald Lacking Cupid (Amor), she called the baby Amoretta.
Paphos town in Cyprus, sacred to Venus
Cytheron mountain where Venus was worshiped
Gnidus Cnidus in Doria, where stood the statue of Venus by Praxiteles

sinful mire flesh; matter; so called because the world is fallen, but also because, in neoplatonism, matter is evil in so far as it is remote from spirit

And grow afresh, as they had never seene
Fleshly corruption, nor mortall paine.
Some thousand yeares so doen they there remaine;
And then of him are clad with other hew,⸼   *forms*
Or sent into the chaungefull world againe,
Till thither they returne, where first they grew:
So like a wheele around they runne from old to new.

34   Ne needs there Gardiner to set, or sow,
        To plant or prune: for of their owne accord
        All things, as they created were, doe grow,
        And yet remember well the mightie word,
        Which first was spoken by th'Almightie lord,
        That bad them to increase and multiply:°
        Ne doe they need with water of the ford,
        Or of the clouds to moysten their roots dry;
For in themselves eternall moisture they imply.⸼   *contain*

35   Infinite shapes of creatures there are bred,
        And uncouth⸼ formes, which none yet ever knew,   *unknown, strange*
        And every sort is in a sundry⸼ bed   *separate*
        Set by it selfe, and ranckt in comely rew:⸼   *row*
        Some fit for reasonable soules° t'indew,⸼   *put on*
        Some made for beasts, some made for birds to weare,
        And all the fruitfull spawne of fishes hew
        In endlesse rancks along enraungèd were,
That seem'd the *Oceán* could not containe them there.

36   Daily they grow, and daily forth are sent
        Into the world, it to replenish more;
        Yet is the stocke not lessenèd, nor spent,
        But still remaines in everlasting store,
        As it at first created was of yore,
        For in the wide wombe of the world there lyes,
        In hatefull darkenesse and in deepe horrore,
        An huge eternal *Chaos,* which supplyes
The substances of natures fruitfull progenyes.

37   All things from thence doe their first being fetch,
        And borrow matter, whereof they are made,
        Which when as forme and feature it does ketch,⸼   *take*
        Becomes a bodie, and doth then invade⸼   *enter*
        The state of life, out of the griesly⸼ shade.   *ghastly*
        That substance is eterne, and bideth so,
        Ne when the life decayes, and forme does fade,
        Doth it consume, and into nothing go,
But chaungèd is, and often altred to and fro.

increase and multiply Genesis 1:22   **reasonable soules** human souls; below them
                                                    there is no reason

38   The substance is not chaunged, nor alterèd,
          But th'only> forme and outward fashión;>   *only the / appearance*
      For every substance is conditioned
          To change her hew, and sundry formes to don,
      Meet for her temper and complexión:
      For formes are variable and decay,
          By course of kind,> and by occasión;>   *nature / accident*
      And that faire flowre of beautie fades away,
      As doth the lilly fresh before the sunny ray.

39   Great enimy to it, and to all the rest,
          That in the *Gardin* of *Adonis* springs,
      Is wicked *Time*, who with his scyth addrest,>   *equipped*
          Does mow the flowring herbes and goodly things,
      And all their glory to the ground downe flings,
          Where they doe wither, and are fowly mard:
      He flyes about, and with his flaggy> wings   *drooping*
          Beates downe both leaves and buds without regard,
      Ne ever pittie may relent his malice hard.

40   Yet pittie often did the gods relent,
          To see so faire things mard, and spoylèd quight:
      And their great mother *Venus* did lament
          The losse of her deare brood, her deare delight:
      Her hart was pierst with pittie at the sight,
          When walking through the Gardin, them she spyde,
      Yet no'te> she find redresse for such despight.   *knew not how to*
          For all that lives, is subject to that law:
      All things decay in time, and to their end do draw.

41   But were it not, that *Time* their troubler is,
          All that in this delightfull Gardin growes,
      Should happie be, and have immortall bliss.
          For here all plentie, and all pleasure flowes,
      And sweet love gentle fits emongst them throwes,
          Without fell rancor, or fond gealosie;
      Franckly each paramour> his leman> knowes.   *lover / mistress*
          Each bird his mate, ne any does envie>   *resent*
      Their goodly meriment, and gay felicitie.

42   There is continuall spring, and harvest there
          Continuall, both meeting at one time:°
      For both the boughes doe laughing blossomes beare,
          And with fresh colours decke the wanton Prime,>   *spring*
      And eke attonce the heavy trees they clime,
          Which seeme to labour under their fruits lode:
      The whiles the joyous birdes make their pastime

Continuall . . . time another feature of the Earthly Paradise. To contrast this with the Bower of Bliss in II.xii is a favorite topic: here is good generative sexuality, where God's commandment to increase and multiply is obeyed with joy and not corrupted by sinister luxury.

Emongst the shadie leaves, their sweet abode,
And their true loves without suspition⸍ tell abrode.   *fear*

43   Right in the middest of that Paradise,
        There stood a stately Mount, on whose round top
        A gloomy grove of mirtle trees did rise,
        Whose shadie boughes sharpe steele did never lop,
        Nor wicked beasts their tender buds did crop,
        But like a girlond compassèd the hight,
        And from their fruitfull sides sweet gum did drop,
        That all the ground with precious deaw bedight,
    Threw forth most dainty odours, and most sweet delight.

44   And in the thickest covert of that shade,
        There was a pleasant arbour, not by art.
        But of the trees owne inclination⸍ made,   *bending*
        Which knitting their rancke⸍ braunches part to part,   *luxuriant*
        With wanton yvie twyne entrayld athwart,
        And Eglantine, and Caprifole⸍ emong,   *honeysuckle*
        Fashiond above within their inmost part,
        That nether⸍ *Phœbus* beams could through them throng,   *neither*
    Nor *Aeolus* sharp blast could worke them any wrong.

45   And all about grew every sort of flowre,
        To which sad lovers were transformed of yore;
        Fresh *Hyacinthus,*° *Phœbus* paramoure,
        And dearest love,
        Foolish *Narcisse,*° that likes the watry shore,
        Sad *Amaranthus,*° made a flowre but late,
        Sad *Amaranthus,* in whose purple gore
        Me seemes I see *Amintas*° wretched fate,
    To whom sweet Poets verse hath given endlesse date.

46   There wont faire *Venus* often to enjoy
        Her deare *Adonis* joyous company,
        And reape sweet pleasure of the wanton boy;
        There yet, some say, in secret he does ly,
        Lappèd in flowres and pretious spycery,
        By her hid from the world, and from the skill⸍   *knowledge*
        Of *Stygian* Gods,⸍ which doe her love envy;   *gods of hell*
        But she her selfe, when ever that she will,
    Possesseth him, and of his sweetnesse takes her fill.

47   And sooth it seemes they say: for he may not
        For ever die, and ever burièd bee
        In balefull night, where all things are forgot;

Hyacinthus killed while playing quoits with Apollo, who made the flower that sprang from his blood an emblem of his mourning
Narcisse Narcissus, who died of self-love and was transformed into a flower

Amaranthus from the flower so called because it does not fade; there is no myth of Amaranthus
Amintas a pastoral name for Sir Philip Sidney, whose death was celebrated by many elegies

All be⸱ he subject to mortalitie,   *even though*
Yet is eterne in mutabilitie,
And by succession made perpetuall,
Transformèd oft, and chaungèd diverslie:
For him the Father of all formes, they call;
Therefore needs mote he live, that living gives to all.

48 There now he liveth in eternall blis,
      Joying his goddesse, and of her enjoyd:
      Ne feareth he henceforth that foe of his,
      Which with his cruell tuske him deadly cloyd:⸱   *pierced*
      For that wilde Bore, the which him once annoyd,⸱   *injured*
      She firmely hath emprisonèd for ay,
      That her sweet love his malice mote avoyd,
      In a strong rocky Cave, which is they say,
    Hewen underneath that Mount, that none him losen⸱ may.   *loose*

49 There now he lives in everlasting joy,
      With many of the Gods in company,
      Which thither haunt,⸱ and with the wingèd boy   *visit*
      Sporting himselfe in safe felicity:
      Who when he hoth with spoiles and cruelty
      Ransackt the world, and in the wofull harts
      Of many wretches set his triumphes hye,
      Thither resorts, and laying his sad darts
    Aside, with faire *Adonis* playes his wanton parts.

50 And his true love faire *Psyche*° with him playes,
      Faire *Psyche* to him lately reconcyld,
      After long troubles and unmeet upbrayes,⸱   *unsuitable reproaches*
      With which his mother *Venus* her revyld,
      And eke himselfe her cruelly exyld:
      But now in stedfast love and happy state
      She with him lives, and hath him borne a chyld,
      Pleasure,° that doth both gods and men aggrate,
    Pleasure, the daughter of *Cupid* and *Psyche* late.

51 Hither great *Venus* brought this infant faire,
      The younger daughter of *Chrysogonee,*
      And unto *Psyche* with great trust and care
      Committed her, yfosterèd to bee,
      And trainèd up in true feminitee:
      Who no lesse carefully her tenderèd,
      Then her owne daughter *Pleasure,* to whom shee

Psyche (Greek, "breath" and "soul") The myth of Cupid and Psyche originates in *The Golden Ass* of Apuleius, and from the outset had allegorical significance; Psyche is the Soul, joined, after many trials, with the love of God. **Pleasure** Apuleius called the daughter of Cupid and Psyche Voluptas (Pleasure). See Milton's adaptation, in which he had Spenser much in mind, in the Epilogue to *Comus.* Cupid visits Psyche only at night and she never sees him; trying to do so, she spills hot oil from a lamp on the sleeping god, and he leaves her. In her search for him she has to perform almost impossible tasks set by Venus, but finally succeeds.

Made her companion, and her lessonèd
In all the lore of love, and goodly womanhead.

52 In which when she to perfect ripenesse grew,
    Of grace and beautie noble Paragone,°   *model*
    She brought her forth into the worldes vew,
    To be th'ensample of true love alone,
    And Lodestarre of all chaste affectióne,
    To all faire Ladies, that doe live on ground.
    To Faery court she came, where many one
    Admyred her goodly haveour,° and found   *behavior*
His feeble hart wide launchèd° with loves cruell wound.   *pierced*

53 But she to none of them her love did cast,
    Save to the noble knight Sir *Scudamore,*
    To whom her loving hart she linkèd fast
    In faithfull love, t'abide for evermore,
    And for his dearest sake endurèd sore,
    Sore trouble of an hainous enimy;
    Who her would forcèd have to have forlore°   *abandoned*
    Her former love, and stedfast loialty,
As ye may elsewhere read that ruefull history.

. . .

[The remainder of Book III continues Florimell's story, and introduces other *exempla* of love. So, in canto vii, Satyrane rescues the Squire of Dames, who has been set the impossible task of finding many chaste women (this has humor, somewhat rare in Spenser). The ninth canto contains the story of Malbecco, an impotent miser who keeps a jealous eye on his pretty young wife Hellenore. Satyrane says knowingly: "Extremely mad the man I surely deeme, / That weenes with watch and hard restraint to stay / A womans will, which is disposed to go astray" (stanza 6). And go astray she does, with Paridell, Satyrane's traveling companion. (The girl's name derives from that of Helen, Paridell's from Paris.) At first Malbecco will not let them into his house, though the weather is very bad. Britomart shows up, fights with Paridell, forms an allegiance with him, and finally succeeds with him in making Malbecco let them in. They sit at the table. The dinner is the occasion for an intense flirtation between Hellenore and Paridell, and a discourse on the history of the Trojans after the fall of their city; they founded first Rome and then London.]

From Canto ix

27 They sate to meat, and *Satyrane* his chaunce
    Was her before,° and *Paridell* besyde;
    But he him selfe° sate looking still askaunce,
    Gains *Britomart,* and ever closely eyde
    Sir *Satyrane,* that glaunces might not glyde:

his chaunce . . . before it happened that he   **he him selfe** Malbecco
sat opposite her

But his blind eye, that syded *Paridell*,
All his demeasnure,° from his sight did hyde: *behavior*
On her faire face so did he feede his fill,
And sent close messages of love to her at will.

28 And ever and anone, when none was ware,
With speaking lookes, that close embassage° bore,   *message*
He rov'd° at her, and told his secret care: *shot*
For all that art he learnèd had of yore.
Ne was she ignoraunt of that lewd lore,
But in his eye his meaning wisely red,
And with the like him answerd evermore:
She sent at him one firie dart, whose hed
Empoisned was with privy lust, and gealous dred.

29 He from that deadly throw made no defence,
But to the wound his weake hart opened wyde;
The wicked engine° through false influence,   *weapon*
Past through his eyes, and secretly did glyde
Into his hart, which it did sorely gryde.°   *pierce*
But nothing new to him was that same paine,
Ne paine at all; for he so oft had tryde
The powre thereof, and lov'd so oft in vaine,
That thing of course he counted,° love to entertaine.

30 Thenceforth to her he sought to intimate
His inward griefe, by meanes to him well knowne,
Now *Bacchus* fruit out of the silver plate
He on the table dasht, as overthrowne,
Or of the fruitfull liquor overflowne,
And by the dauncing bubbles did divine,
Or therein write to let his love be showne;
Which well she red out of the learnèd line,
A sacrament prophane in mistery of wine.°

31 And when so of his hand the pledge she raught,°
The guilty cup she fainèd to mistake,°
And in her lap did shed her idle draught,
Shewing desire her inward flame to slake:
By such close signes they secret way did make
Unto their wils, and one eyes watch escape;
Two eyes him needeth, for to watch and wake,
Who lovers will deceive. Thus was the ape,
By their faire handling, put into *Malbeccoes* cape.°

That . . . counted he regarded such suffering
as a necessary part of
A sacrament . . . wine based on Ovid's account
of Paris and Helen in a similar situation, *Heroides* XVII.75 ff., where the word *Amo* ("I love
you") is traced in wine. The sacrament is
"profane" because of the use of wine in the
communion service, where it relates to divine
love and the blood of Christ.
of . . . raught took the winecup from his hand
mistake not get good hold of
ape . . . cape Malbecco was made a fool of

32 Now when of meats and drinks they had their fill,
    Purpose was movèd by that gentle Dame,
    Unto those knights adventurous, to tell
    Of deeds of armes, which unto them became,
    And every one his kindred, and his name.
    Then *Paridell,* in whom a kindly⟩ pryde   *natural*
    Of gracious speach, and skill his words to frame
    Abounded, being glad of so fit tyde⟩   *occasion*
Him to commend to her, thus spake, of all well eyde.

33 *Troy,* that art now nought, but an idle name,
    And in thine ashes buried low dost lie,
    Though whilome⟩ far much greater then thy fame,   *formerly*
    Before that angry Gods, and cruell skye
    Upon thee heapt a direfull destinie,
    What boots it boast thy glorious descent,
    And fetch from heaven thy great Genealogie,
    Sith all thy worthy prayses being blent,⟩   *defiled*
Their of-spring hath embaste,⟩ and later glory shent.⟩ *debased / disgraced*

34 Most famous Worthy of the world, by whome
    That warre was kindled, which did *Troy* inflame,
    And stately towres of *Ilion* whilome
    Brought unto balefull ruine, was by name
    Sir *Paris* far renowmd through noble fame,
    Who through great prowesse and bold hardinesse,
    From *Lacedæmon*° fetcht the fairest Dame,⟩   *Helen*
    That ever *Greece* did boast, or knight possesse,
Whom *Venus* to him gave for meed⟩ of worthinesse.   *reward*

35 Faire *Helene,* flowre of beautie excellent,
    And girlond of the mighty Conquerours,
    That madest many Ladies deare lament
    The heavie losse of their brave Paramours,
    Which they far off beheld from *Trojan* toures,°
    And saw the fieldes of faire *Scamander*° strowne
    With carcases of noble warrioures,
    Whose fruitlesse lives were under furrow sowne,
And *Xanthus*° sandy bankes with bloud all overflowne.

36 From him my linage I derive aright,
    Who long before the ten yeares siege of *Troy,*
    Whiles yet on *Ida* he a shepheard hight,⟩   *was called*
    On faire *Oenone*° got a lovely boy,
    Whom for remembraunce of her passèd joy,

Lacedæmon Sparta, where Helen was the wife of the king, Menelaus
toures Helen and the other ladies watched the fighting from the towers of Troy
Scamander river flowing through the plain before Troy

Xanthus another name for Scamander
Oenone nymph of Ida, and first love of Paris before he was awarded Helen (see Tennyson, *Oenone*)

She of his Father *Parius* did name;
Who, after *Greekes* did *Priams* realme° destroy,
Gathred the *Trojan* reliques° sav'd from flame,
And with them sayling thence, to th'Isle of *Paros* came.

37   That was by him cald *Paros,* which before
     Hight *Nausa,* there he many yeares did raine,
     And built *Nausicle°* by the *Pontick°* shore,
     The which he dying left next in remaine
     To *Paridas* his sonne.
     From whom I *Paridell* by kin descend;
     But for faire Ladies love, and glories gaine,
     My native soile have left, my dayes to spend
In sewing˃ deeds of armes, my lives and labours end.   *pursuing*

38   Whenas the noble *Britomart* heard tell
     Of *Trojan* warres, and *Priams* Citie sackt,°
     The ruefull story of Sir *Paridell,*
     She was empassiond at that piteous act,
     With zelous envy of Greekes cruell fact,˃   *deed*
     Against that nation, from whose race of old
     She heard, that she was lineally extract:
     For noble *Britons* sprong from *Trojans* bold,
And *Troynovant°* was built of old *Troyes* ashes cold.

39   Then sighing soft awhile, at last she thus:
     O lamentable fall of famous towne,
     Which raignd so many yeares victorious,
     And of all *Asie* bore the soveraigne crowne,
     In one sad night consumd, and throwen downe:
     What stony hart, that heares thy haplesse fate,
     Is not empierst with deepe compassiowne,
     And makes ensample of mans wretched state,
That floures so fresh at morne, and fades at evening late?

40   Behold, Sir, how your pitifull complaint
     Hath found another partner of your payne:
     For nothing may impresse so deare constraint,˃   *distress*
     As countries cause, and commune foes disdayne
     But if it should not grieve you, backe agayne
     To turne your course, I would to heare desyre,
     What to *Aeneas* fell; sith that men sayne
     He was not in the Cities wofull fyre
Consum'd, but did him selfe to safètie retyre.

Priams realme Troy
Trojan reliques the palladium, on which the
safety of Troy depended, and which Aeneas
(not Paris) saved and took to Rome
Nausicle the city of Nausa
Pontick Black Sea
Priams . . . sackt Spenser is varying the story

as he knew it from Virgil's *Aeneid* and other
sources.
Troynovant New Troy = London. It was a
commonplace in popular history and also in
propaganda that the British were descended
from the Trojans, just as the Romans were—
a myth shared by many other countries.

41 *Anchyses* sonne begot of *Venus* faire,°
    (Said he,) out of the flames for safegard fled,
    And with a remnant did to sea repaire,
    Where he through fatall errour° long was led
    Full many yeares, and weetlesse wanderèd
    From shore to shore, emongst the Lybicke⁒ sands,   *Libyan*
    Ere rest he found. Much there he sufferèd,
    And many perils past in forreine lands,
To save his people sad from victours vengefull hands.

42 At last in *Latium*° he did arrive,
    Where he with cruell warre was entertaind
    Of th'inland folke, which sought him backe to drive,
    Till he with old *Latinus* was constraind,
    To contract wedlock: (so the fates ordaind.)
    Wedlock contract in bloud, and eke in blood
    Accomplishèd, that many deare⁒ complained:°   *sadly*
    The rivall slaine, the victour through the flood
Escapèd hardly, hardly praisd his wedlock good.

43 Yet after all, he victour did survive,
    And with *Latinus* did the kingdome part.
    But after, when both nations gan to strive,
    Into their names the title to convart,
    His sonne *Iülus* did from thence depart,
    With all the warlike youth of *Trojans* bloud,
    And in long *Alba*° plast his throne apart,
    Where faire it florishèd, and long time stoud,
Till *Romulus* renewing it,° to *Rome* remoud.

44 There there (said *Britomart*) a fresh appeard
    The glory of the later world to spring,
    And *Troy* againe out of her dust was reard,
    To sit in second seat of soveraigne king,
    Of all the world under her governing.
    But a third kingdome yet is to arise,
    Out of the *Trojans* scatterèd of-spring,
    That in all glory and great enterprise,
Both first and second *Troy* shall dare to equalise.

45 It *Troynovant* is hight, that with the waves
    Of wealthy *Thamis*⁒ washèd is along,   *Thames*
    Upon whose stubborne neck, whereat he raves
    With roring rage, and sore him selfe does throng,⁒   *crush*

Anchyses . . . faire Aeneas
fatall errour wanderings decreed by fate
Latium part of Italy near the Tiber
Wedlock . . . complaind refers to the wars
between Aeneas and Latinus, king of Latium,
and their settlement by Aeneas' marriage with
Lavinia, daughter of Latinus; Juno said this

would result in bloodshed, because Turnus of
the Rutilians wanted Lavinia. Turnus tried to
expel Aeneas, but was killed by him.
long Alba city built in Latium by Aeneas'
son Ascanius, extending along the hill Albinus
it the Trojan dynasty, which now moved to
Rome

That all men feare to tempt his billowes strong,
She fastned hath her foot, which standes so hy,
That it a wonder of the world is song
In forreine landes, and all which passen by,
Beholding it from far, do thinke it threates the skye.

46 The *Trojan Brute*° did first that Citie found,
    And Hygate made the meare˃ thereof by West,   *boundary*
    And *Overt*˃ gate by North: that is the bound   *open*
    Toward the land; two rivers bound the rest.
    So huge a scope at first him seemèd best,
    To be the compasse of his kingdomes seat:
    So huge a mind could not in lesser rest,
    Ne in small meares containe his glory great,
    That *Albion*° had conquerèd first by warlike feat.

47 Ah fairest Lady knight, (said *Paridell*)
    Pardon I pray my heedlesse oversight,
    Who had forgot, that whilome˃ I heard tell   *once*
    From agèd *Mnemon;*° for my wits bene light.
    Indeed he said (if I remember right,)
    That of the antique *Trojan* stocke, there grew
    Another plant, that raught˃ to wondrous hight,   *reached*
    And far abroad his mighty branches threw,
    Into the utmost Angle of the world he knew.

48 For that same *Brute,* whom much he did advaunce˃   *praise*
    In all his speach, was *Sylvius* his sonne,
    Whom having slaine, through luckles arrowes glaunce
    He fled for feare of that he had misdonne,
    Or else for shame, so fowle reproch to shonne,
    And with him led to sea an youthly trayne,
    Where wearie wandring they long time did wonne,˃   *dwell*
    And many fortunes prov'd in th'*Ocean* mayne,
    And great adventures found, that now were long to sayne.˃   *say*

49 At last by fatall course they driven were
    Into an Island spatious and brode,
    The furthest North, that did to them appeare:
    Which after rest they seeking far abrode,
    Found it the fittest soyle for their abode,
    Fruitfull of all things fit for living foode,
    But wholy wast, and void of peoples trode,
    Save an huge nation of the Geaunts broode,°
    That fed on living flesh, and druncke mens vitall blood.

50 Whom he through wearie wars and labours long,
    Subdewd with losse of many *Britons* bold:

Brute Brutus, in legendary history the first   Mnemon Memory personified
king of Britain, and great-grandson of Aeneas   Geaunts broode Brutus, arriving in Britain
Albion Britain   found it populated only by giants.

In which the great *Goemagot*° of strong
Corineus,° and *Coulin*° of *Debon*° old
Were overthrowne, and layd on th'earth full cold,
Which quakèd under their so hideous masse,
A famous history to be enrold
In everlasting moniments° of brasse,   *records*
That all the antique Worthies merits far did passe.

51 His worke great *Troynovant,* his worke is eke
Faire *Lincolne,* both renowmèd far away,
That who from East to West will endlong seeke,
Cannot two fairer Cities find this day,
Except *Cleopolis:*° so heard I say
Old *Mnemon.* Therefore Sir, I greet you well
Your countrey kin, and you entirely pray
Of pardon for the strife, which late befell
Betwixt us both unknowne. So ended *Paridell.*

52 But all the while, that he these speaches spent,
Upon his lips hong faire Dame *Hellenore,*
With vigilant regard, and dew attent,°   *attention*
Fashioning worlds of fancies evermore
In her fraile wit, that now her quite forlore:°   *deserted*
The whiles unwares away her wondring eye,
And greedy eares her weake hart from her bore:
Which he perceiving, ever privily
In speaking, many false belgardes° at her let fly.   *loving looks*

53 So long these knights discoursed diversly,
Of straunge affaires, and noble hardiment,
Which they had past with mickle jeopardy,
That now the humid night was farforth spent,
And heavenly lampes were halfendeale° ybrent: *half*
Which th'old man seeing well, who too long thought
Every discourse and every argument,
Which by the houres he measurèd, besought
Them go to rest. So all unto their bowres were brought.

[In canto x Paridell outwits Malbecco, and elopes with "this second Hellene,"
having stolen his wealth and set fire to his house. Malbecco, fruitlessly pursuing
them, falls in with the sham knight Braggadocchio and his servant Trompart,
who take up his cause. Paridell abandons Hellenore, who is discovered by
Malbecco in a new role, as the queen of a group of satyrs, greatly enjoying
their sexual performances; she turns Malbecco down, and he goes off, finding

Goemagot Gogmagog: giant, later split into
Gog and Magog, whose effigies stand outside
the Guildhall in the City of London
Corineus Trojan who conquered Gogmagog and
was awarded Cornwall for his pains
Coulin a giant

Debon the hero who overcame Coulin, and was
awarded Devonshire (Spenser had already
made these points about Corineus and Debon in
II.xii.12)
Cleopolis here the city of Gloriana, temporarily
distinct from London (Troynovant)

himself a cave, where he lives miserably and for ever; for "he has quight / Forgot he was a man, and *Gealosie* is hight." So ends one of the oddest and most lascivious of Spenser's "accidents."

Canto xi brings Britomart to the aid of Scudamour, lamenting the imprisonment of Amoret in the house of Busirane, an enchanter named for Busiris, a cruel pharaoh who slew all strangers. To enter one must pass through a flame; Britomart does so, but Scudamour cannot, his desires not being sufficiently pure. Britomart, inside, inspects Busirane's tapestries, dealing with Jupiter's love affairs, and those of the other gods. There is also an altar dedicated to Cupid, "Victor of the Gods," at which the inhabitants of the house blasphemously worship. The motto *Be bold* is emblazoned everywhere, except in one place, where it reads *Be not too bold*, which seems to refer to an English nursery rhyme—behind *that* door are skeletons and tubs of blood. Britomart prepares her weapons. She is about to perform for Unchastity what Guyon did for Intemperance.]

Book III, Canto xii

Allegorically the Mask of Cupid represents the disordered passions which intervene in love relationships, as between Amoret and Scudamour—she, though the perfect bride, tormented by the charms of Busirane, he out of control and unable to act for her preservation. Spenser emphasizes that the procession of Cupid's attendants is a masque, that is, a show of allegorical figures with allegorical intent, presented as a dance which displays their attributes. Masques were courtly entertainments, and involved dancing in which the characters of the masque joined with the audience; but here he is content with that part of the presentation which exhibited, in the known language of symbols, some complex moral proposition. In this respect it could be called a pageant with equal correctness. In fact some of Spenser's allegorical detail is borrowed from Petrarch's pageant *The Triumph of Love*. The "triumph" was a Renaissance courtly form related to the masque.

Although there is a real debt to courtly entertainments of a kind he must often have seen, Spenser is here, no more than anywhere else, willing to tie himself strictly to what could be presented in such a show, as the plight of Amoret sufficiently proves. With the masque itself Spenser combines the story of Britomart's intrusion, which is the stuff of romantic narrative: the storm, the fire, the arras depicting Cupid's triumphs, the baffling of the hero by a closed door, the reversal of the enchanter's charms, and the extinguishing of the fire are all romance themes.

Cupid here has a different aspect from that displayed in the allegory of Cupid and Psyche in III.vi. Spenser uses Venus in similarly contradictory (or complementary) ways. The cruelty of the wrong kind of love, in which passion predominates, is his theme. He wanted, as in the last cantos of Books I and II, a great set piece, this time an image of the love in which chastity has no part, but which succumbs to passion and madness; and he has his knight come in and abolish this image, and take prisoner the enchanter who forged it.

From Canto xii
The maske of Cupid, and th'enchaunted
   Chamber are displayd.
Whence Britomart redeemes faire
   Amoret, through charmes decayd.

1   Tho when as chearelesse Night ycovered had
      Faire heaven with an universall cloud,
      That every wight dismayd with darknesse sad,
      In silence and in sleepe themselves did shroud,
      She heard a shrilling Trompet sound aloud,
      Signe of nigh battell, or got victory;
      Nought therewith daunted was her courage proud,
      But rather stird to cruell enmity,
   Expecting ever, when some foe she might descry.

2   With that, an hideous storme of winde arose,
      With dreadfull thunder and lightning atwixt,
      And an earth-quake, as if it streight would lose
      The worlds foundations from his centre fixt;
      A direfull stench of smoke and sulphure mixt
      Ensewd, whose noyance fild the fearefull sted,⌐   *place*
      From the fourth houre of night untill the sixt;
      Yet the bold *Britonesse* was nought ydred,
   Though much emmov'd, but stedfast still perseverèd.

3   All suddenly a stormy whirlwind blew
      Throughout the house, that clappèd every dore,
      With which that yron wicket open flew,
      As it with mightie levers had bene tore:
      And forth issewd, as on the ready flore
      Of some Theàtre, a grave personage,
      That in his hand a branch of laurell bore,
      With comely haveour and count'nance sage,
   Yclad in costly garments, fit for tragicke Stage.

4   Proceeding to the midst, he still did stand,
      As if in mind he somewhat had to say,
      And to the vulgar beckning with his hand,
      In signe of silence, as to heare a play,
      By lively actions he gan bewray⌐   *expound*
      Some argument of matter passionèd;
      Which doen, he backe retyrèd soft away,
      And passing by, his name discoverèd,
   Ease,° on his robe in golden letters cypherèd.

5   The noble Mayd, still standing all this vewd,
      And merveild at his strange intendiment,⌐   *design*

Ease is the "presenter" of the masque, as the
Attendant Spirit is of Milton's *Comus;* he makes
the preliminary announcement stating the theme.

With that a joyous fellowship issewd
Of Minstrals, making goodly meriment,
With wanton Bardes, and Rymers impudent,
All which together sung full chearefully
A lay of loves delight, with sweet concent.˃   *harmony*
After whom marcht a jolly company,
In manner of a maske, enragèd orderly.

6   The whiles a most delitious harmony,
        In full straunge notes was sweetly heard to sound,
        That the rare sweetnesse of the melody
        The feeble senses wholly did confound,
        And the fraile soule in deepe delight nigh dround:
        And when it ceast, shrill trompets loud did bray,
        That their report did farre away rebound,˃   *echo*
        And when they ceast, it gan againe to play,
    The whiles the maskers marchèd forth in trim aray.

7   The first was *Fancy*,° like a lovely boy,
        Of rare aspect, and beautie without peare;
        Matchable either to that ympe˃ of *Troy*,   *child*
        Whom Jove did love, and chose his cup to beare,°
        Or that same daintie lad, which was so deare
        To great *Alcides*,° that when as he dyde,
        He wailèd womanlike with many a teare,
        And every wood, and every valley wyde
    He fild with *Hylas*° name; the Nymphes eke *Hylas* cryde.

8   His garment neither was of silke nor say,˃   *fine wool*
        But painted plumes, in goodly order dight,
        Like as the sunburnt *Indians* do aray
        Their tawney bodies, in their proudest plight.˃   *attire*
        As those same plumes, so seemd he vaine and light,
        That by his gate˃ might easily appeare;   *gait*
        For still he far'd as dauncing in delight,
        And in his hand a windy fan did beare,
    That in the idle aire he mov'd still here and there.

9   And him beside marcht amorous *Desyre*,
        Who seemd of riper yeares, then th'other Swaine,
        Yet was that other swayne this elders syre,
        And gave him being, commune to them twaine:
        His garment was disguisèd˃ very vaine,˃   *worn / foolishly*
        And his embrodered Bonet sat awry;
        Twixt both his hands few sparkes he close did straine,

---

Fancy, fantasy, imagination, especially strong in lovers; he wears feathers, symbols of lightness and uncertainty
ympe . . . beare Ganymede, cupbearer of Jupiter, very beautiful

Alcides Hercules
Hylas Hercules' page, abducted by nymphs; for this Hercules mourned

Which still he blew, and kindled busily,
That soone they life conceiv'd, and forth in flames did fly.

10   Next after him went *Doubt*, who was yclad
     In a discolour'd cote, of straunge disguyse,˃   *fashion*
     That at his backe a brode Capuccio˃ had,   *hood*
     And sleeves dependant *Albanese*-wyse:°
     He lookt askew with his mistrustfull eyes,
     And nicely˃ trode, as thornes lay in his way,   *delicately*
     Or that the flore to shrinke he did avyse,˃   *consider*
     And on a broken reed he still˃ did stay   *ever*
     His feeble steps, which shrunke, when hard theron he lay.˃   *trod*

11   With him went *Daunger*,° cloth'd in raggèd weed,
     Made of Beares skin, that him more dreadfull made,
     Yet his owne face was dreadfull, ne did need
     Straunge˃ horrour, to deforme his griesly shade;   *external*
     A net in th'one hand, and a rustie blade
     In th'other was, this Mischiefe, that Mishap;
     With th'one his foes he threatned to invade,˃   *stab*
     With th'other he his friends ment to enwrap:
     For whom he could not kill, he practizd to entrap.

12   Next him was *Feare*, all arm'd from top to toe,
     Yet thought himselfe not safe enough thereby,
     But feard each shadow moving to and fro,
     And his owne armes when glittering he did spy,
     Or clashing heard, he fast away did fly,
     As ashes pale of hew, and wingyheeld;
     And evermore on daunger fixt his eye,
     Gainst whom he alwaies bent a brasen shield,
     Which his right hand unarmèd fearefully did wield.

13   With him went *Hope* in rancke, a handsome Mayd,
     Of chearefull looke and lovely to behold;
     In silken samite˃ she was light arayd,   *rich silk*
     And her faire lockes were woven up in gold;
     She alway smyld, and in her hand did hold
     An holy water Sprinckle, dipt in deowe,
     With which she sprinckled favours manifold,
     On whom she list, and did great liking sheowe,
     Great liking unto many, but true love to feowe.˃   *few*

14   And after them *Dissemblance*˃ and *Suspect*˃   *dissimulation / suspicion*
     Marcht in one rancke, yet an unequall paire:
     For she was gentle, and of milde aspect,
     Courteous to all, and seeming debonaire,

Albanese-wyse in the Albanian fashion (?)
Daunger a regular attendant on Love. It means, in this context, the unapproachability of a lady, her creation around herself of hostility toward a lover; in IV.x.17 and also here it has to do with the withholding of love from a suitor.

Goodly adornèd, and exceeding faire:
Yet was that all but paintèd, and purloynd,
And her bright browes were deckt with borrowed haire:
Her deedes were forgèd, and her words false coynd,
And alwaies in her hand two clewes of silke she twynd.

15　But he was foule, ill favourèd, and grim,
　　　Under his eyebrowes looking still askaunce;
　　　And ever as *Dissemblance* laught on him,
　　　He lowrd on her with daungerous eyeglaunce;
　　　Shewing his nature in his countenance;
　　　His rolling eyes did never rest in place,
　　　But walkt each where, for feare of hid mischaunce,
　　　Holding a lattice° still⸀ before his face,　　　　　　　*always*
　　Through which he still did peepe, as forward he did pace.

16　Next him went *Griefe*, and *Fury* matcht yfere,⸀　　　*together*
　　　Griefe all in sable sorrowfully clad,
　　　Downe hanging his dull head, with heavy chere,
　　　Yet inly being more, then⸀ seeming sad:　　　　　　　*than*
　　　A paire of Pincers in his hand he had,
　　　With which he pinchèd people to the hart,
　　　That from thenceforth a wretched life they lad,
　　　In wilfull languor and consuming smart,
　　Dying each day with inward wounds of dolours dart.

17　But *Fury* was full ill apparelèd
　　　In rags, that naked nigh she did appeare,
　　　With ghastly lookes and dreadfull drerihed,⸀　　　　*gloom*
　　　For from her backe her garments she did teare,
　　　And from her head oft rent her snarlèd heare:
　　　In her right hand a firebrand she did tosse
　　　About her head, still roming here and there;
　　　As a dismayèd Deare in chace embost,⸀　　　　　*hard pressed*
　　Forgetfull of his safety, hath his right way lost.

18　After them went *Displeasure* and *Pleasance*,
　　　He looking lompish and full sullein sad,
　　　And hanging downe his heavy countenance;
　　　She chearefull fresh and full of joyance glad,
　　　As if no sorrow she ne felt ne drad;
　　　That evill matchèd paire they seemd to bee:
　　　An angry Waspe th'one in a viall had
　　　Th'other in hers an hony-lady Bee;
　　Thus marchèd these six couples forth in faire degree.

19　After all these there marcht a most faire Dame,°
　　　Led of two grysie⸀ villeins, th'one *Despight*,⸀　　　*grim / spite*

---

lattice Suspect carries it because of a pun on the Italian *gelosia* or French *jalousie*, meaning both "jealousy" and "Venetian blind." **Dame** Amoret; the picture of her is reminiscent of some in the emblem books (see Glossary).

The other clepèd *Cruelty* by name:
She dolefull Lady, like a dreary Spright,
Cald by strong charmes out of eternall night,
Had deathes owne image figurd in her face,
Full of sad signes, fearefull to living sight;
Yet in that horror shewd a seemely grace,
And with her feeble feet did move a comely pace.

20   Her brest all naked, as net⌐ ivory,   *pure*
Without adorne of gold or silver bright,
Wherewith the Craftesman wonts it beautify,
Of her dew honour was despoylèd quight,
And a wide wound therein (O ruefull sight)
Entrenchèd deepe with knife accursèd keene,
Yet⌐ freshly bleeding forth her fainting spright,   *still*
(The worke of cruell hand) was to be seene,
That dyde in sanguine red her skin all snowy cleene.

21   At that wide orifice her trembling hart
Was drawne forth, and in silver basin layd,
Quite through transfixèd with a deadly dart,
And in her bloud yet steeming fresh embayd.⌐   *bathed*
And those two villeins, which her steps upstayd,
When her weake feete could scarcely her sustaine,
And fading vitall powers gan to fade,
Her forward still with torture did constraine,
And evermore encreasèd her consuming paine.

22   Next after her the wingèd God himselfe
Came riding on a Lion ravenous,
Taught to obay the menage⌐ of that Elfe,   *handling*
That man and beast with powre imperious
Subdeweth to his kingdome tyrannous:
His blindfold eyes° he bad a while unbind,
That his proud spoyle of that same dolorous
Faire Dame he might behold in perfect kind;
Which seene, he much rejoyced in his cruell mind.

23   Of which full proud, himselfe up rearing hye,
He lookèd round about with sterne disdaine;
And did survay his goodly company:
And marshalling the evill ordered traine,
With that the darts which his right hand did straine,
Full dreadfully he shooke that all did quake,
And clapt on hie his coulourd wingès twaine,
That all his many⌐ it affraide did make: *company*
Tho⌐ blinding him⌐ againe, his way he forth did take.   *then / himself*

---

blindfold eyes Cupid was never blindfolded in antiquity; later he was so represented to imply the blindness of erotic choice, though in more mystical writings his blindness was said to show that love is above the intellect.

24 Behinde him was *Reproch, Repentance, Shame;*
    Reproch the first, *Shame* next, *Repent* behind:
    Repentance feeble, sorrowfull, and lame:
    Reproch despightfull, carelesse, and unkind;
    Shame most ill favour, bestiall, and blind:
    Shame lowrd, *Repentance* sigh'd, *Reproch* did scould;
    Reproch sharpe stings, *Repentance* whips entwind,
    Shame burning brond-yrons in her hand did hold:
All three to each unlike, yet all made in one mould.

25 And after them a rude confusèd rout
    Of persons flockt, whose names is⟩ hard to read: *it is*
    Emongst them was sterne *Strife*, and *Anger* stout,
    Unquiet *Care*, and fond *Unthriftihead*,
    Lewd *Losse of Time*, and *Sorrow* seeming dead,
    Inconstant *Chaunge*, and false *Disloyaltie*,
    Consuming *Riotise*, and guilty *Dread*
    Of heavenly vengeance, faint *Infirmitie*,
Vile *Povertie*, and lastly *Death* with infamie.

26 There were full many moe like maladies,
    Whose names and natures I note readen well,⟩   *cannot well say*
    So many moe, as there be phantasies
    In wavering wemens wit, that none can tell,
    Or paines in love, or punishments in hell;
    All which disguizèd marcht in masking wise,
    About the chamber with that Damozell,
    And then returnèd, having marchèd thrise,
Into the inner roome, from whence they first did rise.

27 So soone as they were in, the dore streight way
    Fast lockèd, driven with that stormy blast,
    Which first it opened; and bore all away.
    Then the brave Maid, which all this while was plast
    In secret shade, and saw both first and last,
    Issewèd forth, and went unto the dore,
    To enter in, but found it lockèd fast:
    It vaine she thought with rigorous uprore
For to efforce, when charmes had closèd it afore.

28 Where force might not availe, there sleights and art
    She cast to use, both fit for hard emprize;
    For thy⟩ from that same roome not to depart   *because*
    Till morrow next, she did her selfe avize,⟩   *counsel*
    When that same Maske againe should forth arize.
    The morrow next appeard with joyous cheare,
    Calling men to their daily exercize,
    Then she, as morrow fresh, her selfe did reare
Out of her secret stand, that day for to out weare.

29 All that day she outwore in wandering,
        And gazing on that Chambers ornament,
        Till that againe the second evening
        Her covered with her sable vestiment,
        Wherewith the worlds faire beautie she hath blent:˒   *extinguished*
        Then when the second watch was almost past,
        That brasen dore flew open, and in went
        Bold *Britomart*, as she had late forecast,˒   *planned*
    Neither of idle shewes, nor of false charmes aghast.

30 So soone as she was entred, round about
        She cast her eies, to see what was become
        Of all those persons, which she saw without:
        But lo, they streight were vanisht all and some,˒   *entirely*
        Ne living wight she saw in all that roome,
        Save that same woefull Ladie, both whose hands
        Were bounden fast, that did her ill become,
        And her small wast girt round with yron bands,
    Unto a brasen pillour, by the which she stands.

31 And her before the vile Enchaunter sate,
        Figuring straunge charácters of his art,
        With living bloud he those charácters wrate,
        Dreadfully dropping from her dying hart,
        Seeming transfixèd with a cruell dart,
        And all perforce to make her him to love.
        Ah who can love the worker of her smart?˒   *pain*
        A thousand charmes he formerly did prove;˒   *try*
    Yet thousand charmes could not her stedfast heart remove.

32 Soone as that virgin knight he saw in place,
        His wicked bookes in hast he overthrew,
        Not caring his long labours to deface,˒   *spoil*
        And fiercely ronning to that Lady trew,
        A murdrous knife out of his pocket drew,
        The which he thought, for villeinous despight,
        In her tormented bodie to embrew:˒   *plunge*
        But the stout Damzell to him leaping light,
    His cursèd hand withheld, and maisterèd his might.

33 From her, to whom his fury first he ment,˒   *intended*
        The wicked weapon rashly he did wrest,
        And turning to her selfe his fell intent,
        Unwares it strooke into her snowie chest,
        That little drops empurpled her faire brest.
        Exceeding wroth therewith the virgin grew,
        Albe˒ the wound were nothing deepe imprest,   *although*
        And fiercely forth her mortall blade she drew,
    To give him the reward for such vile outrage dew.

34 So mightily she smote him, that to ground
      He fell halfe dead; next stroke him should have slaine,
      Had not the Lady, which by him stood bound,
      Dernely⸀ unto her callèd to abstaine,   *dismally*
      From doing him to dy. For else her paine
      Should be remedilesse, sith⸀ none but hee,   *since*
      Which wrought it, could the same recure⸀ againe.   *cure*
      Therewith she stayd her hand, loth stayd to bee;
For life she him envyde,⸀ and long'd revenge to see.   *begrudged*

35 And to him said, Thou wicked man, whose meed
      For so huge mischiefe, and vile villany
      Is death, or if that ought do death exceed,
      Be sure, that nought may save thee from to dy,
      But if that thou this Dame doe presently
      Restore unto her health, and former state;
      This doe and live, else die undoubtedly.
      He glad of life, that lookt for death but late,
Did yield himselfe right willing to prolong his date.

36 And rising up, gan streight to overlooke
      Those cursèd leaves, his charmes backe to reverse;
      Full dreadfull things out of that balefull booke
      He red, and measur'd many a sad verse,
      That horror gan the virgins hart to perse,
      And her faire locks up starèd stiffe on end,
      Hearing him those same bloudy lines reherse;
      And all the while he red, she did extend
Her sword high over him, if ought⸀ he did offend.   *lest in anyway*

37 Anon she gan perceive the house to quake,
      And all the dores to rattle round about;
      Yet all that did not her dismaièd make,
      Nor slacke her threatfull hand for daungers dout,⸀   *fear*
      But still with stedfast eye and courage stout
      Abode, to weet what end would come of all.
      At last that mightie chaine, which round about
      Her tender waste was wound, adowne gan fall,
And that great brasen pillour broke in peeces small.

38 The cruell steele, which thrild⸀ her dying hart,   *pierced*
      Fell softly forth, as of his owne accord,
      And the wyde wound, which lately did dispart⸀   *divide*
      Her bleeding brest, and riven bowels gor'd,
      Was closèd up, as it had not bene bor'd,
      And every part to safèty full sound,
      As she were never hurt, was soone restor'd:
      Tho⸀ when she felt her selfe to be unbound,   *then*
And perfect hole,⸀ prostrate she fell unto the ground.   *whole*

39   Before faire *Britomart,* she fell prostrate,
      Saying, Ah noble knight, what worthy meed
      Can wretched Lady, quit⸢ from wofull state,   *redeemed*
      Yield you in liew of this your gratious deed?
      Your vertue selfe her owne reward shall breed,
      Even immortall praise, and glory wyde,
      Which I your vassall, by your prowesse freed,
      Shall through the world make to be notifyde,
And goodly well advance,⸢ that goodly well was tryde.⸢   *make known /*
                                                            proved

40   But *Britomart* uprearing her from ground,
      Said, Gentle Dame, reward enough I weene
      For many labours more, then I have found,
      This, that in safety now I have you seene,
      And meane of your deliverance have beene:
      Henceforth faire Lady comfort to you take,
      And put away remembrance of late teene;
      In stead thereof know, that your loving Make,⸢   *mate*
Hath no lesse griefe endurèd for your gentle sake.

41   She much was cheard to heare him mentiònd,
      Whom of all living wights she lovèd best.
      Then laid the noble Championesse strong hond
      Upon th'enchaunter, which had her distrest
      So sore, and with foule outrages opprest:
      With that great chaine, wherewith not long ygo
      He bound that pitteous Lady prisoner, now relest,
      Himselfe she bound, more worthy to be so,
And captive with her led to wretchednesse and wo.

42   Returning backe, those goodly roomes, which erst⸢   *recently*
      She saw so rich and royally arayd,
      Now vanisht utterly, and cleane subverst⸢   *overthrown*
      She found, and all their glory quite decayd,
      That sight of such a chaunge her much dismayd.
      Thence forth descending to that perlous Porch,
      Those dreadfull flames she also found delayd,⸢   *quenched*
      And quenchèd quite, like a consumèd torch,
That erst all entrers won⸢ so cruelly to scorch.   *used*

43   More° easie issew⸢ now, then entrance late   *exit*
      She found: for now that fainèd dreadfull flame,

More The following three stanzas were inserted in the edition of 1596 to replace the five with which Spenser had originally ended the Book. In the first version Britomart finds Scudamour, as usual, in distress, but when he sees Amoret in good health he runs to her and embraces her. They seemed grown together like a hermaphrodite, and Britomart half envies them, knowing that she is to be denied such happiness. Spenser makes no use of these stanzas when Scudamour and Amoret finally do meet again in IV.ix. It has been suggested (see Proem to IV) that he changed them because he was afraid of offending Burleigh any further; but more probably he had further use, in the interlocking stories that also make up Book IV, for Scudamour and Amoret.

Which chokt the porch of that enchaunted gate,
And passage bard to all, that thither came,
Was vanisht quite, as it were not the same,
And gave her leave at pleasure forth to passe.
Th'Enchaunter selfe, which all that fraud did frame,
To have efforst the love of that faire lasse,
Seeing his worke now wasted deepe engrievèd was.

44   But when the victoresse arrivèd there,
Where late she left the pensife *Scudamore,*
With her owne trusty Squire, both full of feare,
Neither of them she found where she them lore:⁊   *left*
Thereat her noble hart was stonisht sore;
But most faire *Amoret,* whose gentle spright
Now gan to feede on hope, which she before
Conceivèd had, to see her owne deare knight,
Being thereof beguyld was fild with new affright.

45   But he sad man, when he had long in drede
Awayted there for *Britomarts* returne,
Yet saw her not nor signe of her good speed,
His expectation to despaire did turne,
Misdeeming sure that her those flames did burne;
And therefore gan advize⁊ with her old Squire,   *decide*
Who her deare nourslings losse no lesse did mourne,
Thence to depart for further aide t'enquire:
Where let them wend at will, whilest here I doe respire.⁊   *take a breather*

                  1590

Book IV

It may be that in the course of writing Book IV Spenser found that the Ariostan scheme of interlocked stories was less suitable to his purposes than the more monolithic organization of I and II. Book IV is the least compelling part of the poem, despite its connections with the brilliant Book III. It is the Legend of Friendship, and attempts to express the Renaissance mystique of friendship; the simplest expression Spenser gives it occurs in the opening stanza of canto ix:

Hard is the doubt, and difficult to deeme,
When all three kinds of love together meet,
And do dispart⁊ the heart with powre extreme,   *divide*
Whether⁊ shall weigh the balance down; to weet   *which*
The deare affection unto kindred sweet,
Or raging fire of love to woman kind,
Or zeale of friends combynd with vertues meet.
But of them all the band⁊ of vertuous mind   *bond*
Me seemes the gentle hart should most assurèd bind.

> For naturall affection soone doth cesse,
>   And quenchèd is with *Cupids* greater flame:
>   But faithfull friendship doth them both suppresse,
>   And them with maystring discipline doth tame,
>   Through thoughts aspyring to eternall fame.
>   For as the soule doth rule the earthly masse,
>   And all the service of the bodie frame,
>   So love of soule doth love of bodie passe,
> No lesse than perfect gold surmounts the meanest brasse.

This is the kind of friendship that makes Shakespeare's Valentine, in *Two Gentlemen of Verona*, offer to give up his girl Silvia to his friend Proteus, who has just tried to rape her; except that Spenser always insists that true friendship is between virtuous equals.

The nominal heroes of this book are Cambel and Triamond, borrowed from Chaucer's unfinished Squire's Tale; but Spenser diversifies that story in order to provide many different examples of love and friendship. Many of these are carried over from III: the False Florimell, Florimell and Marinell, Britomart and Artegall, Timias and Belphoebe, Scudamour and Amoret. Guyon and Braggadocchio, Satyrane and Archimago also return. The cancellation of the original conclusion made it possible to continue Scudamour's adventures, and to show him in the House of Care, a famous passage which is given below.

In the Proem to IV, which serves as an introduction to the second installment of the whole poem, Books IV through VI, Spenser refers to the censure of Lord Burleigh, Elizabeth's Lord Chancellor and the most powerful man in England, and offers a spirited defense, saying that his work is not for such readers but for those who, like the Queen, understand love, and the utility of examples which show what is right by exposing what is wrong.

The Fourth Booke of The Faerie Queene

Contayning, The Legend of Cambel and Triamond, or Of Friendship

1   The rugged forhead that with grave foresight
      Welds⟩ kingdomes causes, and affaires of state,°   *wields*
      My looser rimes (I wote) doth sharply wite,⟩   *blame*
      For praising love, as I have done of late,
      And magnifying⟩ lovers deare debate;   *glorifying*
      By which fraile youth is oft to follie led,
      Through false allurement of that pleasing baite,
      That better were in vertues disciplèd,
      Then with vaine poemes weeds⟩ to have their fancies fed.   *blooms*

The rugged . . . state William Cecil, Lord
Burleigh

2   Such ones ill judge of love, that cannot love,
    Ne in their frosen hearts feele kindly° flame: *natural*
    For thy° they ought not thing unkowne reprove,   *therefore*
    Ne naturall affection faultlesse blame,
    For fault of few that have abusd the same.
    For it of honor and all vertue is
    The roote, and brings forth glorious flowres of fame,
    That crowne true lovers with immortall blis,
The meed of them that love, and do not live amisse.

3   Which who so list looke backe to former ages,
    And call to count the things that then were donne,
    Shall find, that all the workes of those wise sages,
    And brave exploits which great Heroès wonne,
    In love were either ended or begunne:
    Witnesse the father of Philosophie,
    Which to his *Critias,*° shaded oft from sunne,
    Of love full manie lessons did apply,
The which these Stoicke censours cannot well deny.

4   To such therefore I do not sing at all,
    But to that sacred Saint my soveraigne Queene,
    In whose chast breast all bountie naturall,
    And treasures of true love enlockèd beene,
    Bove all her sexe that ever yet was seene;
    To her I sing of love, that loveth best,
    And best is lov'd of all alive I weene:
    To her this song most fitly is addrest,
The Queene of love, and Prince of peace from heaven blest.

5   Which that she may the better deigne to heare,
    Do thou dred infant, *Venus* dearling dove,°
    From her high spirit chase imperious feare,
    And use of awfull Majestie remove:
    In sted thereof with drops of melting love,
    Deawd with ambrosiall kisses, by thee gotten
    From thy sweete smyling mother from above,
    Sprinckle her heart, and haughtie courage° soften,   *spirit*
That she may hearke to love, and reade this lesson often.

[In this Book Atè (Strife) and Concord contend for mastery. Atè fills Scudamour with rage and misery by persuading him that Britomart has stolen the
affections of Amoret. It is in this frame of mind that Scudamour enters the
House of Care. Care is a blacksmith who makes instruments to torment the
unquiet soul.]

Critias meaning Crito; see II.vii.52n   **dove** Cupid

From Canto v

32   So as they travellèd, the drouping night
         Covered with cloudie storme and bitter showre,
         That dreadfull seem'd to every living wight,
         Upon them fell, before her timely howre;
         That forcèd them to seeke some covert bowre,
         Where they might hide their heads in quiet rest,
         And shrowd their persons from that stormie stowre.
         Not farre away, not meete for any guest
     They spide a little cottage, like some poore mans nest.

33   Under a steepe hilles side it placèd was,
         There where the mouldred earth had cav'd the banke;
         And fast beside a little brooke did pas
         Of muddie water, that like puddle stanke,
         By which few crookèd sallowes⁷ grew in ranke: *willows*
         Whereto approaching nigh, they heard the sound
         Of many yron hammers beating ranke,⁷   *violently*
         And answering their wearie turnes around,
     That seemèd some blacksmith dwelt in that desert ground.

34   There entring in, they found the goodman selfe,
         Full busily unto his worke ybent;
         Who was to weet a wretched wearish⁷ elfe,   *wizened*
         With hollow eyes and rawbone cheekes forspent,
         As if he had in prison long bene pent:
         Full blacke and griesly did his face appeare,
         Besmeard with smoke that nigh his eye-sight blent;⁷   *blinded*
         With rugged beard, and hoarie shaggèd heare,
     The which he never wont to combe, or comely sheare.

35   Rude was his garment, and to rags all rent,
         Ne better had he, ne for better cared:
         With blistred hands emongst the cinders brent,
         And fingers filthie, with long nayles unpared,
         Right fit to rend the food, on which he fared.
         His name was *Care;* a blacksmith by his trade,
         That neither day nor night from working spared,
         But to small purpose yron wedges made;
     Those be unquiet thoughts, that carefull minds invade.

36   In which his worke he had six servants prest,
         About the Andvile standing evermore,
         With huge great hammers, that did never rest
         From heaping stroakes, which thereon sousèd⁷ sore: *struck*
         All sixe strong groomes, but one then other more;
         For by degrees they all were disagreed;
         So likewise did the hammers which they bore,
         Like belles in greatnesse orderly succeed,
     That he which was the last, the first did farre exceede.

37   He like a monstrous Gyant seem'd in sight,
         Farre passing *Bronteus*, or *Pyracmon*° great,
         The which in *Lipari*° doe day and night
         Frame thunderbolts for *Joves* avengefull threate.
         So dreadfully he did the andvile beat,
         That seem'd to dust he shortly would it drive:
         So huge his hammer and so fierce his heat,
         That seem'd a rocke of Diamond it could rive,
    And rend a sunder quite, if he thereto list strive.

38   Sir *Scudamour* there entring, much admired
         The manner of their worke and wearie paine;
         And having long beheld, at last enquired
         The cause and end thereof: but all in vaine;
         For they for nought would from their worke refraine,
         Ne let his speeches come unto their eare.
         And eke the breathfull bellowes blew amaine,⸢   *powerfully*
         Like to the Northren winde, that⸢ none could heare: *so that*
    Those *Pensifenesse* did move; and *Sighes* the bellows weare.

39   Which when that warriour saw, he said no more,
         But in his armour layd him downe to rest:
         To rest he layd him downe upon the flore,
         (Whylome⸢ for ventrous Knights the bedding best)   *formerly*
         And thought his wearie limbs to have redrest.
         And that old agèd Dame,° his faithfull Squire,
         Her feeble joynts layd eke a downe to rest;
         That needed much her weake age to desire,
    After so long a travell, which them both did tire.

40   There lay Sir *Scudamour* long while expecting,
         When gentle sleepe his heavie eyes would close;
         Oft chaunging sides, and oft new place electing,
         Where better seem'd he mote himselfe repose;
         And oft in wrath he thence againe uprose;
         And oft in wrath he layd him downe againe.
         But wheresoever he did himselfe dispose,
         He by no meanes could wishèd ease obtaine:
    So every place seem'd painefull, and ech changing vaine.

41   And evermore, when he to sleepe did thinke,
         The hammers sound his senses did molest;
         And evermore, when he began to winke,
         The bellowes noyse disturb'd his quiet rest,
         Ne suffred sleepe to settle in his brest.
         And all the night the dogs did barke and howle
         About the house, at sent⸢ of stranger guest: *scent*

Bronteus . . . Pyracmon two of the Cyclops   **agèd Dame** Glaucè, serving as squire to Scuda-
who forged the thunderbolts of Zeus   mour
Lipari Lipara, one of the Lipari islands off
Sicily

And now the crowing Cocke, and now the Owle
Lowde shriking him afflicted to the very sowle.

42   And if by fortune any litle nap
    Upon his heavie eye-lids chaunst to fall,
    Eftsoones one of those villeins him did rap
    Upon his headpeece with his yron mall;˃   *mallet*
    That he was soone awakèd therewithall,
    And lightly started up as one affrayd;
    Or as if one him suddenly did call.
    So oftentimes he out of sleepe abrayd,˃   *awoke*
And then lay musing long, on that him ill apayd.˃   *pleased*

43   So long he muzèd, and so long he lay,
    That at the last his wearie sprite opprest
    With fleshly weaknesse, which no creature may
    Long time resist, gave place to kindly rest,
    That all his senses did full soone arrest:
    Yet in his soundest sleepe, his dayly feare
    His ydle braine gan busily molest,
    And made him dreame those two° disloyall were:
The things that day most minds, at night doe most appeare.

44   With that, the wicked carle the maister Smith
    A paire of redwhot yron tongs did take
    Out of the burning cinders, and therewith
    Under his side him nipt, that forst to wake,
    He felt his hart for very paine to quake,
    And started up avengèd for to be
    On him, the which his quiet slomber brake:
    Yet looking round about him none could see;
Yet did the smart remaine, though he himselfe did flee.

45   In such disquiet and hartfretting payne,
    He all that night, that too long night did passe.
    And now the day out of the Ocean mayne
    Began to peepe above this earthly masse,
    With pearly dew sprinkling the morning grasse:
    Then up he rose like heavie lumpe of lead,
    That in his face, as in a looking glasse,
    The signes of anguish one mote plainely read,
And ghesse the man to be dismayd with gealous dread.

46   Unto his lofty steede he clombe anone,
    And forth upon his former voiage fared,
    And with him eke that agèd Squire attone;˃   *together*
    Who whatsoever perill was prepared,
    Both equall paines and equall perill shared:
    The end whereof and daungerous event

those two Britomart and Amoret

Shall for another canticle be spared.
But here my wearie teeme nigh over spent
Shall breath it selfe awhile, after so long a went.ʾ   *journey*

[In the sixth canto Britomart and Artegall fall in love; upon their union depend
not only the future happiness of Britain but much of Spenser's Fifth Book. In vii
Belphoebe saves Amoret from the attentions of a wicked "salvage" man (some
are good, some bad as Caliban). He represents the intrusion of bestial lust into
the world of love, a fallen world in which virtuous friendship is nobler than the
love of women. Yet the core of the Book is really not any example of male friendship but Scudamour's account, in canto x, of his first wooing and winning of
Amoret. He forces access into the Temple of Venus, past Doubt, Delay, and
Danger, who make for the unapproachability of virtuous women, and comes
upon a paradise of pleasure and innocent friendship. In the Temple itself,
Concord reconciles the passions of love and hate, as she holds together the
conflicting elements in the frame of the world. The goddess now appears as
Hermaphrodite, symbolizing the union of opposites in the love of man and
woman (Spenser had used the idea figuratively in the original conclusion to
Book III). The prayer of the lover to Venus is based on the great invocation
to Venus of Lucretius in his *De Rerum Natura*: "alma Venus, Venus genetrix,"
giver of pleasure and fertility throughout the creation. Scudamour echoes him.
In the lap of Womanhood, flanked by appropriate female qualities, he sees
Amoret; the goddess smiles on him and he leads his woman away. This is an
allegory of proper courtship; a little forcefulness is required to break down
the good customary prohibitions. It is also an allegory of love as Spenser understands it, for instance in *Epithalamion* and Book III of *The Faerie Queene*. It
is a power transcending physical relations, being the source of order and fertility in all things. As it affects men and women it is a source of delight, but
needs checks, and is subject to being overbalanced by sexual passion; this
episode is a flashback, and precedes the disasters of Book III, in which Scudamour is parted from Amoret by Busirane, who stands for the unregulated
desire that came between them on their wedding night. At the end of Book
IV he still hasn't got her back.]

From Canto x

23   In such luxurious plentie of all pleasure,
      It seem'd a second paradise° to ghesse,
      So lavishly enricht with natures threasure,
      That if the happie soules, which doe possesse
      Th'Elysian fields, and live in lasting blesse,
      Should happen this with living eye to see,
      They soone would loath their lesser happinesse,
      And wish to life return'd againe to bee,
      That in this joyous place they mote have joyance free.

24   Fresh shadowes, fit to shroud from sunny ray;
      Faire lawnds, to take the sunne in season dew;

second paradise We have now seen several such
paradises; note how their purport changes with
the context, just as does the significance of Cupid
and Venus.

Sweet springs, in which a thousand Nymphs did play;
Soft rombling brookes, that gentle slomber drew;
High reared mounts, the lands about to vew;
Low looking dales, disloignd° from common gaze;   *distant*
Delightfull bowres, to solace lovers trew;
False Labyrinthes, fond runners eyes to daze;
All which by nature made did nature selfe amaze.

25   And all without were walkes and alleyes dight°   *adorned*
With divers trees, enrang'd in even rankes;
And here and there were pleasant arbors pight.°   *placed*
And shadie seates, and sundry flowring bankes,
To sit and rest the walkers wearie shankes,
And therein thousand payres of lovers walkt,
Praysing their god, and yeelding him great thankes,
Ne ever ought but of their true loves talkt,
Ne ever for rebuke or blame of any balkt.°   *stopped*

26   All these together by themselves did sport
Their spotlesse pleasures, and sweet loves content.
But farre away from these, another sort
Of lovers lincked in true harts consent;
Which lovèd not as these, for like intent,
But on chast vertue grounded their desire,
Farre from all fraud, or faynèd blandishment;
Which in their spirits kindling zealous fire,
Brave thoughts and noble deeds did evermore aspire.

27   Such were great *Hercules,* and *Hylas*° deare;
Trew *Jonathan,* and *David*° trustie tryde;
Stout *Theseus,* and *Pirithous*° his feare;°   *companion*
Pylades and *Orestes*° by his syde;
Myld *Titus* and *Gesippus*° without pryde;
Damon and *Pythias* whom death could not sever:°
All these and all that ever had bene tyde
In bands of friendship, there did live for ever,
Whose lives although decay'd, yet loves decayèd never.

28   Which when as I, that never tasted blis,
Nor happie howre, beheld with gazefull eye,
I thought there was none other heaven then this;
And gan their endlesse happinesse envye,
That being free from feare and gealosye,

Hylas boy lover of Hercules; he was either
drowned or carried away by nymphs
Jonathan, and David I Samuel 18
Theseus, and Pirithous a friendship cemented
by war against the Centaurs and by the attempted
rape of Proserpina from the underworld
Pylades and Orestes the classical type of friendship; Pylades helped Orestes revenge his father

Agamemnon by killing his mother Clytemnestra
and her lover Aegisthus
Titus and Gesippus The story of Titus and
Giseppus is in the Tenth Day of Boccaccio's
Decameron; Titus accused himself of a murder
for which Giseppus had accepted responsibility.
Damon . . . sever Damon stood as hostage for
his friend Pythias when the latter was under
sentence of death.

Might frankely there their loves desire possesse;
Whilest I through paines and perlous jeopardie,
Was forst to seeke my lifes deare patronesse:
Much dearer be the things, which come through hard distresse.

29   Yet all those sights, and all that else I saw,
    Might not my steps withhold, but that forthright
    Unto that purposd place I did me draw,
    Where as my love was lodgèd day and night:
    The temple of great *Venus*, that is hight
    The Queene of beautie, and of love the mother,
    There worshippèd of every living wight;
    Whose goodly workmanship farre past all other
That ever were on earth, all were they˘ set together.   *as if they were*

30   Not that same famous Temple of *Diane*,°
    Whose hight all *Ephesus* did oversee,
    And which all *Asia* sought with vowes prophane,
    One of the worlds seven wonders sayd to bee,
    Might match with this by many a degree:
    Nor that, which that wise King of *Jurie* framed,
    With endlesse cost, to be th'Almighties see;˘   *abode*
    Nor all that else through all the world is named
To all the heathen Gods, might like to this be clamed.

31   I much admyring that so goodly frame,
    Unto the porch approcht, which open stood;
    But therein sate an amiable Dame,
    That seem'd to be of very sober mood,
    And in her semblant˘ shewed great womanhood: *appearance*
    Strange was her tyre;˘ for on her head a crowne   *headdress*
    She wore much like unto a Danisk hood,°
    Poudred with pearle and stone, and all her gowne
Enwoven was with gold, that raught˘ full low a downe.   *reached*

32   On either side of her, two young men stood,
    Both strongly arm'd, as fearing one another;
    Yet were they brethren both of halfe the blood,
    Begotten by two fathers of one mother,
    Though of contrarie natures each to other:
    The one of them hight *Love*, the other *Hate*,
    Hate was the elder, *Love* the younger brother;
    Yet was the younger stronger in his state
Then th'elder, and him maystred still in all debate.

33   Nathlesse that Dame so well them tempred both,
    That she them forcèd hand to joyne in hand,
    Albe that *Hatred* was thereto full loth,

Temple of Diane Acts 19   **Danisk hood** Danish headdress, perhaps distinctive in shape

And turn'd his face away, as he did stand,
Unwilling to behold that lovely band.°   *bond*
Yet she was of such grace and vertuous might,
That her commaundment he could not withstand,
But bit his lip for felonous despight,
And gnasht his yron tuskes at that displeasing sight.

34 Concord° she cleepèd° was in common reed,°   *called / speech*
Mother of blessèd *Peace,* and *Friendship* trew;
They both her twins, both borne of heavenly seed,
And she her selfe likewise divinely grew;
The which right well her workes divine did shew:
For strength, and wealth, and happinesse she lends,
And strife, and warre, and anger does subdew:
Of litle much, of foes she maketh frends,
And to afflicted minds sweet rest and quiet sends.

35 By her the heaven is in his course contained,
And all the world in state unmovèd stands,
As their Almightie maker first ordained.
And bound them with inviolable bands;
Else would the waters overflow the lands,
And fire devoure the ayre, and hell them quight,°   *revenge, pay back*
But that she holds them with her blessèd hands.
She is the nourse of pleasure and delight,
And unto *Venus* grace the gate doth open right.°

36 By her I entring halfe dismayèd was,
But she in gentle wise me entertayned,
And twixt her selfe and *Love* did let me pas;
But *Hatred* would my entrance have restrayned,
And with his club me threatned to have brayned,
Had not the Ladie with her powrefull speach
Him from his wicked will uneath° refrayned;   *with difficulty*
And th'other eke his malice did empeach,°   *hinder*
Till I was throughly past the perill of his reach.

37 Into the inmost Temple thus I came,
Which fuming all with frankensence I found,
And odours rising from the altars flame,
Upon an hundred marble pillors round
The roofe up high was rearèd from the ground,
All deckt with crownes, and chaynes, and girlands gay,
And thousand pretious gifts worth many a pound,
The which sad lovers for their vowes did pay;
And all the ground was strow'd with flowres, as fresh as May.

Concord Placing her between love and hate as mediator, Spenser is remembering the ancient principle that concord issues from the resolution of discords; it is stated in Boethius, *The Consolation of Philosophy* II.8, which he knew, and also by Chaucer in *Troilus and Criseyde* III.1751 ff., and The Knight's Tale, ll. 2990 ff. Spenser puts it into the *Hymne of Heavenly Love,* ll. 76 ff.

unto . . . right without the resolution of the discord of opposites there can be no love between men and women

38   An hundred Altars round about were set,
         All flaming with their sacrifices fire,
         That with the steme thereof the Temple swet,˃   *sweated*
         Which rould in clouds to heaven did aspire,
         And in them bore true lovers vowes entire:
         And eke an hundred brasen caudrons bright,
         To bath in joy and amorous desire,
         Every of which was to a damzell hight;˃   *assigned*
For all the Priests were damzels, in soft linnen dight.

39   Right in the midst the Goddesse selfe did stand
         Upon an altar of some costly masse,
         Whose substance was uneath˃ to understand: *difficult*
         For neither pretious stone, nor durefull brasse,
         Nor shining gold, nor mouldring clay it was;
         But much more rare and pretious to esteem,
         Pure in aspect, and like to christall glasse,
         Yet glasse was not, if one did rightly deeme,
But being faire and brickle,˃ likest glasse did seeme.   *brittle*

40   But it in shape and beautie did excell
         All other Idoles, which the heathen adore,
         Farre passing that, which by surpassing skill
         Phidias did make in *Paphos* Isle° of yore,
         With which that wretched Greeke, that life forlore,˃   *abandoned*
         Did fall in love: yet this much fairer shined,
         But covered with a slender veile afore;
         And both her feete and legs together twyned
Were with a snake, whose head and tail were fast combyned.

41   The cause why she was covered with a vele,
         Was hard to know, for that her Priests the same
         From peoples knowledge labour'd to concele.
         But sooth it was not sure for womanish shame,
         Nor any blemish, which the worke mote blame;˃   *disfigure*
         But for, they say, she hath both kinds in one,
         Both male and female, both under one name:°
         She syre and mother is her selfe alone,
Begets and eke conceives, ne needeth other none.

42   And all about her necke and shoulders flew
         A flocke of litle loves, and sports, and joyes,
         With nimble wings of gold and purple hew;
         Whose shapes seem'd not like to terrestriall boyes,
         But like to Angels playing heavenly toyes;˃   *games*

that . . . Isle the statue made by Praxiteles at Cnidos, which first showed Venus naked; a youth fell in love with it
Both . . . name The name is Hermaphroditus, son of Hermes and Aphrodite, who was made one body with the nymph Salmacis in love. The Venus of this name sums up the male-female generative process over which the goddess traditionally presides; as Spenser puts it in *Colin Clout*, ll. 801-2: "For Venus selfe doth solely couples seem, / Both male and female through commixture join'd." Hairy Venuses in women's dress are recorded in antiquity.

The whilest their eldest brother was away,
Cupid their eldest brother; he enjoyes
The wide kingdome of love with Lordly sway,
And to his law compels all creatures to obay.

43   And all about her altar scattered lay
Great sorts° of lovers piteously complayning,   *groups*
Some of their losse, some of their loves delay,
Some of their pride, some paragons disdayning,
Some fearing fraud, some fraudulently fayning,
As every one had cause of good or ill.
Amongst the rest some one through loves constrayning,
Tormented sore, could not containe it still,
But thus brake forth, that all the temple it did fill.

44   Great *Venus,* Queene of beautie and of grace,
The joy of Gods and men, that under skie
Doest fayrest shine, and most adorne thy place,
That with thy smyling looke doest pacifie
The raging seas, and makst the stormes to flie;
Thee goddesse, thee the winds, the clouds doe feare,
And when thou spredst thy mantle forth on hie,
The waters play and pleasant lands appeare,
And heavens laugh, and al the world shews joyous cheare.

45   Then doth the dædale° earth throw forth to thee
Out of her fruitfull lap aboundant flowres,
And then all living wights, soone as they see
The spring breake forth out of his lusty bowres,
They all doe learne to play the Paramours;
First doe the merry birds, thy prety pages
Privily prickèd with thy lustfull powres,
Chirpe loud to thee out of their leavy cages,
And thee their mother call to coole their kindly rages.

46   Then doe the salvage beasts begin to play
Their pleasant friskes, and loath their wonted food;
The Lyons rore, the Tygres loudly bray,
The raging Buls rebellow through the wood,
And breaking forth, dare tempt the deepest flood,
To come where thou doest draw them with desire:
So all things else, that nourish vitall blood,
Soone as with fury thou doest them inspire,
In generation seeke to quench their inward fire.

47   So all the world by thee at first was made,
And dayly yet thou doest the same repayre:

dædale intricately constructed, as if by Daedalus,
the great artificer who built the labyrinth at
Cnossos

Ne ought on earth that merry is and glad,
Ne ought on earth that lovely is and fayre,
But thou the same for pleasure didst prepayre.
Thou art the root of all that joyous is,
Great God of men and women, queene of th'ayre,
Mother of laughter, and welspring of blisse,
O graunt that of my love at last I may not misse.

48 So did he say: but I with murmure soft,
That none might heare the sorrow of my hart,
Yet inly groning deepe and sighing oft,
Besought her to graunt ease unto my smart,
And to my wound her gratious help impart.
Whilest thus I spake, behold with happy eye
I spyde, where at the Idoles feet apart
A bevie of fayre damzels close did lye,
Wayting when as the Antheme should° be sung on hye.

49 The first of them did seeme of ryper yeares,
And graver countenance then all the rest;
Yet all the rest were eke her equall peares,
Yet unto her obayèd all the best.
Her name was *Womanhood,* that she exprest
By her sad⸂ semblant⸂ and demeanure wyse: *serious / appearance*
For stedfast still her eyes did fixèd rest,
Ne rov'd at randon after gazers guyse,⸂   *fashion*
Whose luring baytes oftimes doe heedlesse harts entyse.

50 And next to her sate goodly *Shamefastnesse,*
Ne ever durst her eyes from ground upreare,
Ne never once did looke up from her desse,⸂   *dais*
As if some blame of evill she did feare,
That in her cheekes made roses oft appeare.
And her against sweet *Cherefulnesse* was placed,
Whose eyes like twinkling stars in evening cleare,
Were deckt with smyles, that all sad humors chaced,
And darted forth delights, the which her goodly graced.

51 And next to her sate sober *Modestie,*
Holding her hand upon her gentle hart;
And her against sate comely *Curtesie,*
That unto every person knew her part;
And her before was seated overthwart⸂   *opposite*
Soft *Silence,* and submisse⸂ *Obedience,*   *submissive*
Both linckt together never to dispart,⸂   *part*
Both gifts of God not gotten but from thence,
Both girlonds° of his Saints against their foes offence.

Wayting . . . should waiting for the anthem to be   **girlonds** adornments (which protect them from foes)

52   Thus sate they all a round in seemely rate:>   *manner*
      And in the midst of them a goodly mayd,
      Even in the lap of *Womanhood* there sate,
      The which was all in lilly white arayd,
      With silver streames amongst the linnen stray'd;
      Like to the Morne, when first her shyning face
      Hath to the gloomy world it selfe bewray'd,
      That same was fayrest *Amoret* in place,
    Shyning with beauties light, and heavenly vertues grace.

53   Whom soone as I beheld, my hart gan throb,
      And wade in doubt, what best were to be donne:
      For sacrilege me seem'd the Church to rob,
      And folly seem'd to leave the thing undonne,
      Which with so strong attempt I had begonne.
      Tho> shaking off all doubt and shamefast feare,   *then*
      Which Ladies love I heard had never wonne
      Mongst men of worth, I to her steppèd neare,
    And by the lilly hand her labour'd up to reare.

54   Thereat that formost matrone me did blame,
      And sharpe rebuke, for being over bold;
      Saying it was to Knight unseemely shame,
      Upon a recluse> Virgin to lay hold,   *in seclusion*
      That unto *Venus* services were sold.>   *given*
      To whom I thus, Nay but it fitteth best,
      For *Cupids* man with *Venus* mayd to hold,
      For ill your goddesse services are drest
    By virgins, and her sacrifices let to rest.

55   With that my shield I forth to her did show,
      Which all that while I closely had conceld;
      On which when *Cupid* with his killing bow
      And cruell shafts emblazond she beheld,
      At sight thereof she was with terror queld,
      And said no more: but I which all that while
      The pledge of faith, her hand engagèd held,
      Like warie Hynd> within the weedie soyle,   *laborer*
    For no intreatie would forgoe so glorious spoyle.

56   And evermore upon the Goddesse face
      Mine eye was fixt, for feare of her offence,
      Whom when I saw with amiable grace
      To laugh at me, and favour my pretence,>   *claim*
      I was emboldned with more confidence,
      And nought for nicenesse> nor for envy sparing,   *scrupulousness*
      In presence of them all forth led her thence,
      All looking on, and like astonisht staring,
    Yet to lay hand on her, not one of all them daring.

57 She often prayd, and often me besought,
        Sometime with tender teares to let her goe,
        Sometime with witching smyles: but yet for nought,
        That ever she to me could say or doe,
        Could she her wishèd freedome fro me wooe;
        But forth I led her through the Temple gate,
        By which I hardly past with much adoe:
        But that same Ladie which me friended late
    In entrance, did me also friend in my retrate.

58 No lesse did *Daunger* threaten me with dread,
        When as he saw me, maugre° all his powre,   *despite*
        That glorious spoyle of beautie with me lead,
        Then *Cerberus,* when *Orpheus* did recoure°   *recover*
        His Leman° from the Stygian Princes boure.
        But evermore my shield did me defend,
        Against the storme of every dreadfull stoure°:   *conflict*
        Thus safely with my love I thence did wend.
    So ended he his tale, where I this Canto end.

                            1596

[The main business of the concluding cantos is to bring together Florimell
and Marinell. Canto xi is a big set-piece, which Spenser had possibly had for
some years in a drawer, describing the marriage of the rivers Thames and
Medway. It fits, in general, the theme of concord resolving discord, but emphasizes the loose-knit quality of IV; the union of Florimell and Marinell (of
sea and land) also fits the theme, but neither the characters nor the theme
have the centrality and the climactic quality one finds at the conclusion of
the earlier books. However, Alastair Fowler, in his study of the numerological
patterns of *The Faerie Queene* (*Spenser and the Numbers of Time,* 1964),
claims that on the basis of such patterns he sees the fourth "as in many ways
the most unified of all the books of *The Faerie Queene.*"]

Book V

In this Book Spenser reverts to a scheme more like that of I and II: in fact his
examination of the nature of Justice may be his most schematic. He also crowds in
allusions to contemporary affairs. He opens with a proem lamenting the changes that
have come over the world since the departure of Astraea, goddess of Justice, at the
end of the Golden Age. The present age is of stone. Not only human affairs, but even
the movements of the planets, have grown very irregular. Justice now comes from
princes, for example from Elizabeth, the returned Astraea (Virgil, in his most famous
prophetic eclogue, the fourth, had predicted this: "iam redit et Virgo"—and now
Astraea returns; and a mystique of Astraeanism grew up around the Queen).

Leman Eurydice, temporarily brought back from
the underworld by the music of her husband
Orpheus

The Fifth Booke of The
Faerie Queene

Contayning, The Legend of Artegall, *or Of Justice*

1 So oft as I with state of present time,
  The image of the antique world compare,
  When as mans age was in his freshest prime,
  And the first blossome of faire vertue bare,
  Such oddes I finde twixt those, and these which are,
  As that, through long continuance of his course,
  Me seemes the world is runne quite out of square,
  From the first point of his appointed sourse,
And being once amisse growes daily wourse and wourse.

2 For from the golden age, that first was named,
  It's now at earst˄ become a stonie one;   *lately*
  And men themselves, the which at first were framed
  Of earthly mould, and form'd of flesh and bone,
  Are now transformèd into hardest stone:
  Such as behind their backs (so backward bred)
  Were throwne by *Pyrrha* and *Deucalione*:°
  And if then those may any worse be red,˄   *called*
They into that ere long will be degenderèd.

3 Let none then blame me, if in discipline
  Of vertue and of civill uses lore,
  I doe not forme them to the common line
  Of present dayes, which are corrupted sore,
  But to the antique use, which was of yore,
  When good was onely for it selfe desyrèd,
  And all men sought their owne, and none did more;
  When Justice was not for most meed outhyrèd,
But simple Truth did rayne, and was of all admyrèd.

4 For that which all men then did vertue call,
  Is now cald vice; and that which vice was hight,
  Is now hight vertue, and so us'd of all:
  Right now is wrong, and wrong that was is right,
  As all things else in time are chaungèd quight.
  Ne wonder; for the heavens revolution
  Is wandred farre from where it first was pight,˄   *placed*
  And so doe make contrarie constitution
Of all this lower world, toward his dissolution.

5 For who so list into the heavens looke,
  And search the courses of the rowling spheares,
  Shall find that from the point, where they first tooke

Pyrrha . . . Deucalione They escaped like Noah
and his family from a general deluge; later an
oracle told them to throw stones over their
shoulders, from which grew men and woman to
restock the world.

Their setting forth, in these few thousand yeares
They all are wandred much;° that plaine appeares.
For that same golden fleecy Ram, which bore
Phrixus and *Helle*° from their stepdames feares,
Hath now forgot, where he was plast of yore,
And shouldred hath the Bull, which fayre *Europa*° bore.

6   And eke the Bull hath with his bow-bent horne
    So hardly butted those two twinnes of *Jove*,°
    That they have crusht the Crab,° and quite him borne
    Into the great *Nemæan* lions grove.°
    So now all range, and doe at randon rove
    Out of their proper places farre away,
    And all this world with them amisse doe move,
    And all his creatures from their course astray,
Till they arrive at their last ruinous decay.

7   Ne is that same great glorious lampe of light,
    That doth enlumine all these lesser fyres,°
    In better case, ne keepes his course more right,
    But is miscaried with the other Spheres.
    For since the term of fourteene hundred yeres,
    That learnèd *Ptolomæe* his hight did take,°
    He is declynèd from that marke of theirs,
    Nigh thirtie minutes to the Southerne lake;
That makes me feare in time he will us quite forsake.

8   And if to those Ægyptian wisards old,
    Which in Star-read° were wont have best insight,   *star-lore*
    Faith may be given, it is by them told,
    That since the time they first tooke the Sunnes hight,
    Foure times his place he shifted hath in sight,
    And twice hath risen, where he now doth West,
    And wested twice, where he ought rise aright.°
    But most is *Mars* amisse of all the rest,
And next to him old *Saturne*,° that was wont be best.

---

wandred much Spenser bases his lament for the decay of the world on the apparent disorder of the heavens. Ptolemy of Alexandria, whose astronomy with modifications survived until Copernicus, recorded the obliquity of the ecliptic (the apparent course of the sun through the sky relative to the equator) and between 130 A.D. and Spenser's time it had decreased somewhat. Consequently it was possible to say that the sun, Mars, and Saturn got progressively out of line as time went by, and that the signs of the zodiac, through which sun and planets pass, were jostling one another, so that the heavens as well as the earth were in decay. Further speculation of the kind occurs in VII.vi.50 ff., on which see note.
Phrixus and Helle Brother and sister who, fleeing the cruelty of Ino their stepmother, escaped on a golden-fleeced flying ram—Aries, of the zodiac; all the zodiacal signs were attached to myths.

Europa carried off by Jupiter in the form of a bull—the sign of Taurus
twinnes of Jove Castor and Pollux, sons of Jove by Leda—the sign of Gemini
Crab sign of Cancer
Nemæan lions grove sign of Leo; killing the Nemaean lion was one of the labors of Hercules
enlumine . . . fyres the stars were thought to store light from the sun
his . . . take determined the obliquity of the sun's ecliptic
And . . . aright These impossible phenomena were alleged by Herodotus (b. 404 B.C.) in his *History* II.142.
Mars . . . Saturne They have the most eccentric planetary orbits except for Mercury: see VII. vii.51n; and in Spenser's time it was assumed these orbits must normally be circular (elliptical orbits were proved by Kepler in 1609).

9   For during *Saturnes* ancient raigne° it's sayd,
      That all the world with goodnesse did abound:
      All lovèd vertue, no man was affrayd
      Of force, ne fraud in wight was to be found:
      No warre was knowne, no dreadfull trompets sound,
      Peace universall rayn'd mongst men and beasts,
      And all things freely grew out of the ground:
      Justice sate high ador'd with solemne feasts,
    And to all people did divide her dred beheasts.

10   Most sacred vertue she of all the rest,
      Resembling God in his imperiall might;
      Whose soveraine powre is herein most exprest,
      That both to good and bad he dealeth right,
      And all his workes with Justice hath bedight.
      That powre he also doth to Princes lend,
      And makes them like himselfe in glorious sight,
      To sit in his owne seate, his cause to end,
    And rule his people right, as he doth recommend.

11   Dread Soverayne Goddesse, that doest highest sit
      In seate of judgement, in th'Almighties stead,
      And with magnificke might and wondrous wit
      Doest to thy people righteous doome° aread,°   *judgment / deliver*
      That furthest Nations filles with awfull dread,
      Pardon the boldnesse of thy basest thrall,
      That dare discourse of so divine a read,
      As thy great justice praysèd over all:
    The instrument whereof loe here thy *Artegall.*°

[The action of V is supposed to occur after the departure of Astraea; the administration of justice has fallen to such as Bacchus and Hercules and Artegall (Artegalle was a mythical British king, and the name could mean "equal to Arthur"). By his union with Britomart, Artegall would establish (as Arthur did, according to Tudor historians) a line of British kings stretching to the Tudors. He represents pure justice, enforcing the law with the aid of Talus, an iron man with a flail, a sort of one-giant police force who executes the decisions of the law. Artegall's quest is to destroy Grantorto (Great Wrong) and release Irena (meaning both "peace" and "Ireland"). On the pattern of I, the first canto contains a miniature of the quest; Sangliere is forced by justice to carry around the head of the lady he has killed. Then Artegall and Talus suppress men who buy and sell justice, and go on to deal with a mad revolutionary giant who proposes a communism of the sort then proposed by extreme Protestant sects. Artegall explains that the elimination of inequality among men would destroy order and harmony. The people are mutinous at this, but Talus

---

Saturnes . . . raigne The *Saturnia regna* of Virgil's fourth Eclogue constituted the Age of Gold, the first age, as described earlier by Hesiod *(Works and Days)*, and by Ovid at the outset of the *Metamorphoses;* Astraea then lived on earth.
Artegall Knight of Justice and hero of Bk. V

subdues them. Here Spenser is expressing a commonplace of the age: justice depends on a recognition of the divinely ordered inequality of all creation.

The third canto interpolates the marriage, finally, of Florimell, and the exposure of Braggadocchio; Guyon at last retrieves his horse. In the fourth there are *exempla* of distributive justice (there were two branches, distributive and corrective) and in the fifth, Artegall, lapsing like Red Cross, imitates Hercules (with whom all Renaissance heroes have something in common) by falling under the spell of a woman, Radigund. The unnatural situation—for women are naturally the inferiors of men—is underlined by his effeminate dress and his woman's occupation, spinning. The only exception to the rule, that women must not be masters, is when Heaven lifts a woman "to lawfull soveraintie" (v.25)—a necessary and prudent, but also, in England, a common view. Britomart hears from Talus about Artegall's plight, and sets out to rescue him, stopping at Isis' church for spiritual support.

As in earlier books, the seventh is the core canto. The Isis allegory is brief and mysterious. Probably it deals with equity—"that part of Justice, which is Equity." In Elizabethan England the Courts of Chancery and Star Chamber were courts of equity. Chancery was "the conscience of the Queen" as represented by her Lord Chancellor; unlike the courts of justice it was not bound by precedent, and it accumulated great power. Star Chamber dealt with criminal causes such as sedition touching the monarch's security, and was also powerful. Chancery could remedy injustices that found no remedy in common law, for example, when a poor man was wronged by a nobleman who could pack the jury. Common lawyers resented the growth of the power of Chancery and associated it with growing absolutism. Star Chamber was the more hated, and Parliament abolished it in 1641.

In Spenser's myth, his Temple of Justice, he borrows from Plutarch's allegory of Isis and Osiris. Isis was identified with justice, with Astraea, and with matter (see III.vi). Osiris is justice without benefit of equity, as in the common law courts. Equity is like matter, and justice gives it mutable forms. The priests of Isis are jurists. Their abstinence from wine, described earlier as the blood of the rebel Titans, stands for their opposition to riot and recusancy. The foot on the crocodile and the wand signify the control of justice by equity, in both civil and criminal causes (Chancery and Star Chamber). The crocodile is law-without-equity, such as Artegall, incapable on his own of imperial equity, has thus far practiced.

The dream of Britomart changes her from priest to empress, robed in imperial purple, crowned with the sun, fount (if you saw it her way) of equity and ancestress of Elizabeth. The tempest and fire are rebellions against her, suppressed by the crocodile, the law of England. Perhaps the crocodile's impatience suggests the discontent of common lawyers with the prerogative or equity courts. The union of Britomart and the crocodile is that of justice and equity in the imperial person of the Queen. The priestly interpreter explains that the crocodile is Artegall, justice-without-equity; his union with equity completes the imperial justice of the Queen, and the Isis allegory allies this to the function of love in ordering and maintaining the frame of the whole world. So, at any rate, one might venture to read this passage, which is perhaps at this date the "darkest" in the whole poem, and the one about which least is certainly known.]

From Canto vii

1   Nought is on earth more sacred or divine,
      That Gods and men doe equally adore,
      Then this same vertue, that doth right define:
      For th'hevens themselves, whence mortal men implore
      Right in their wrongs, are rul'd by righteous lore
      Of highest Jove, who doth true justice deale
      To his inferiour Gods, and evermore
      Therewith containes his heavenly Commonweale:
   The skill whereof to Princes hearts he doth reveale.

2   Well therefore did the antique world invent,
      That Justice was a God of soveraine grace,
      And altars unto him, and temples lent,
      And heavenly honours in the highest place;
      Calling him great *Osyris*, of the race
      Of th'old Ægyptian Kings, that whylome° were;   *once*
      With faynèd colours shading° a true case: *painting*
      For that *Osyris*, whilest he livèd here,
   The justest man alive, and truest did appeare.°

3   His wife was *Isis*, whom they likewise made
      A Goddesse of great powre and soverainty,
      And in her person cunningly did shade
      That part of Justice, which is Equity,°
      Whereof I have to treat here presently.
      Unto whose temple when as *Britomart*
      Arrivèd, shee with great humility
      Did enter in, ne could that night depart;
   But *Talus* mote not be admitted to her part.°

4   There she receivèd was in goodly wize
      Of many Priests, which duely did attend
      Uppon the rites and daily sacrifize,
      All clad in linnen robes with silver hemd;
      And on their heads with long locks comely kemd,°
      They wore rich Mitres shapèd like the Moone,
      To shew that *Isis* doth the Moone portend;
      Like as *Osyris* signifies the Sunne.
   For that they both like race in equall justice runne.

5   The Championesse them greeting, as she could,°   *knew how*
      Was thence by them into the Temple led;
      Whose goodly building when she did behould,

The justest . . . appeare This is the "euhemer-
ist" explanation of Osiris: that is, it treats his
myth as a version of the life of a hero.
That . . . Equity Spenser is adapting Plutarch's
myth, in his usual freely creative way, to allow
of this justice-equity interpretation.
But Talus . . . part Talus is excluded because

equity thinks it "better to reforme then to cut
off the ill."
And . . . kemd Plutarch's priests are shaven;
Spenser is borrowing from an account of the
priesthood of Rhea (vowed to chastity and
dressed as women) or some other priesthood—
why he does so is a matter for guessing.

Borne uppon stately pillours, all dispred
With shining gold, and archèd over hed,
She wondred at the workemans passing skill,
Whose like before she never saw nor red;
And thereuppon long while stood gazing still,
But thought, that she thereon could never gaze her fill.

6   Thence forth unto the Idoll they her brought,
     The which was framèd all of silver fine,
     So well as could with cunning hand be wrought,
     And clothèd all in garments made of line,°   *linen*
     Hemd all about with fringe of silver twine.
     Uppon her head she wore a Crowne of gold,
     To shew that she had powre in things divine;
     And at her feete a Crocodile° was rold,
     That with his wreathèd taile her middle did enfold.

7   One foote was set uppon the Crocodile,
     And on the ground the other fast did stand,
     So meaning to suppresse both forgèd guile,
     And open force: and in her other hand
     She stretchèd forth a long white sclender wand.
     Such was the Goddesse; whom when *Britomart*
     Had long beheld, her selfe uppon the land
     She did prostrate, and with right humble hart,
     Unto her selfe her silent prayers did impart.

8   To which the Idoll as it were inclining,
     Her wand did move with amiable looke,
     By outward shew her inward sence desining.°   *indicating*
     Who well perceiving, how her wand she shooke,
     It as a token of good fortune tooke.
     By this the day with dampe was overcast,
     And joyous light the house of *Jove*° forsooke: *sky*
     Which when she saw, her helmet she unlaste,
     And by the altars side her selfe to slumber plaste.

9   For other beds the Priests there usèd none,
     But on their mother Earths deare lap did lie,
     And bake° their sides uppon the cold hard stone,   *harden*
     T'enure them selves to sufferaunce thereby
     And proud rebellious flesh to mortify.
     For by the vow of their religión
     They tied were to stedfast chastity,
     And continence of life, that all forgon,°   *given up*
     They mote the better tend to their devotion.

10   Therefore they mote not taste of fleshly food,
     Ne feed on ought, the which doth bloud containe,

Crocodile In Plutarch the crocodile stands not for Osiris but for Typhon, the irrational part of the soul; again Spenser is transforming an existing myth for his own purposes.

Ne drinke of wine, for wine they say is blood,
Even the bloud of Gyants, which were slaine,
By thundring Jove in the Phlegrean plaine:°
For which the earth° (as they the story tell)
Wroth with the Gods, which to perpetuall paine
Had damn'd her sonnes, which gainst them did rebell,
With inward grief and malice did against them swell.

11 And of their vitall bloud, the which was shed
Into her pregnant bosome, forth she brought
The fruitfull vine, whose liquor blouddy red
Having the mindes of men with fury fraught,
Mote in them stirre up old rebellious thought,
To make new warre against the Gods againe:
Such is the powre of that same fruit, that nought
The fell contagion may thereof restraine,
Ne within reasons rule, her madding mood containe.

12 There did the warlike Maide her selfe repose,
Under the wings of *Isis* all that night,
And with sweete rest her heavy eyes did close,
After that long daies toile and weary plight.
Where whilest her earthly parts with soft delight
Of sencelesse sleepe did deeply drownèd lie,
There did appeare unto her heavenly spright
A wondrous vision, which did close implie⟩   *secretly sum up*
The course of all her fortune and posteritie.

13 Her seem'd, as she was doing sacrifize
To *Isis,* deckt with Mitre on her hed,
And linnen stole after those Priestès guize,⟩   *fashion*
All sodainely she saw transfigurèd
Her linnen stole to robe of scarlet red,
And Moone-like Mitre to a Crowne of gold,
That even she her selfe much wonderèd
At such a chaunge, and joyed to behold
Her selfe, adorn'd with gems and jewels manifold.

14 And in the midst of her felicity,
An hideous tempest seemèd from below,
To rise through all the Temple sodainely,
That from the Altar all about did blow
The holy fire, and all the embers strow
Uppon the ground, which kindled privily,
Into outragious flames unwares did grow,

the bloud . . . plaine Throughout the Book the giants or Titans are symbols of lawlessness and rebellion. Jupiter overthrew their rebellion at Phlegra, near Naples—the many volcanic cones of the area are supposed to be the places where the Titans were thrown to earth. Plutarch says that vines sprang from their blood, so that wine is their rebellious blood.
The earth Gaea, Earth, mother of the Titans

That all the Temple put in jeopardy
Of flaming, and her selfe in great perplexity.

15   With that the Crocodile, which sleeping lay
     Under the Idols feete in fearelesse bowre,
     Seem'd to awake in horrible dismay,
     As being troubled with that stormy stowre;'   *disturbance*
     And gaping greedy wide, did streight devoure
     Both flames and tempest: with which growen great,
     And swolne with pride of his owne peerelesse powre,
     He gan to threaten her likewise to eat;
     But that the Goddesse with her rod him backe did beat.

16   Tho turning all his pride to humblesse meeke,
     Him selfe before her feete he lowly threw,
     And gan for grace and love of her to seeke:
     Which she accepting, he so neare her drew,
     That of his game she soone enwombèd grew,
     And forth did bring a Lion of great might;
     That shortly did all other beasts subdew.
     With that she wakèd, full of fearefull fright,
     And doubtfully dismayd through that so uncouth' sight.   *strange*

17   So thereuppon long while she musing lay,
     With thousand thoughts feeding her fantasie,
     Untill she spide the lampe of lightsome day,
     Up-lifted in the porch of heaven hie.
     Then up she rose fraught with melancholy,
     And forth into the lower parts did pas;
     Whereas the Priestes she found full busily
     About their holy things for morrow Mas:
     Whom she saluting faire, faire resaluted was.

18   But by the change of her unchearefull looke,
     They might perceive, she was not well in plight;
     Or that some pensivenesse to heart she tooke.
     Therefore thus one of them, who seem'd in sight
     To be the greatest, and the gravest wight,
     To her bespake; Sir Knight it seemes to me,
     That thorough evill rest of this last night,
     Or ill apayd;' or much dismayd ye be,   *satisfied*
     That by your change of cheare is easie for to see.

19   Certes (sayd she) sith ye so well have spide
     The troublous passion of my pensive mind,
     I will not seeke the same from you to hide,
     But will my cares unfolde, in hope to find
     Your aide, to guide me out of errour blind.
     Say on (quoth he) the secret of your hart:
     For by the holy vow, which me doth bind,

      I am adjur'd, best counsell to impart
      To all, that shall require my comfort in their smart.⟩   *pain*

20   Then gan she to declare the whole discourse
      Of all that vision, which to her appeard,
      As well as to her minde it had recourse.⟩   *came back*
      All which when he unto the end had heard,
      Like to a weake faint-hearted man he fared,
      Through great astonishment of that strange sight;
      And with long locks up-standing, stifly stared
      Like one adawèd⟩ with some dreadfull spright.   *terrified*
   So fild with heavenly fury, thus he her behight.⟩   *named*

21   Magnificke Virgin, that in queint disguise
      Of British armes doest maske thy royall blood,
      So to pursue a perillous emprize,⟩   *adventure*
      How couldst thou weene, through that disguizèd hood,
      To hide thy state from being understood?
      Can from th'immortall Gods ought hidden bee?
      They doe thy linage, and thy Lordly brood;
      They doe thy sire, lamenting sore for thee;
      They doe thy love, forlorne in womens thraldome see.

22   The end whereof, and all the long event,
      They doe to thee in this same dreame discover.
      For that same Crocodile doth represent
      The righteous Knight, that is thy faithfull lover,
      Like to *Osyris* in all just endever.
      For that same Crocodile *Osyris* is,
      That under *Isis* feete doth sleepe for ever:
      To shew that clemence oft in things amis,
   Restraines those sterne behests, and cruell doomes of his.

23   That Knight shall all the troublous stormes asswage,
      And raging flames, that many foes shall reare,
      To hinder thee from the just heritage
      Of thy sires Crowne, and from thy countrey deare.
      Then shalt thou take him to thy lovèd fere,⟩   *mate*
      And joyne in equall portion of thy realme.
      And afterwards a sonne to him shalt beare,
      That Lion-like shall shew his powre extreame.
   So blesse thee God, and give thee joyance of thy dreame.

24   All which when she unto the end had heard,
      She much was easèd in her troublous thought,
      And on those Priests bestowèd rich reward:
      And royall gifts of gold and silver wrought,
      She for a present to their Goddesse brought.
      Then taking leave of them, she forward went,
      To seeke her love, where he was to be sought;

Ne rested till she came without relent
Unto the land of Amazons, as she was bent.

. . .

1596

[Fortified by the divine prediction of her powers, Britomart defeats Radigund, overthrows the unnatural "liberty of women," and frees Artegall. They go on to perform various tasks, in which the allegorical content grows more and more political; canto viii treats of the war with Spain, the Soudan being the king of Spain and his wife Adicia (Greek, injustice). There is a transparent allusion to the defeat of the Armada (1588), and other matters of contemporary history. The ninth canto concerns Lord Grey's campaign against the Irish, and, in the trial of Duessa at the court of Mercilla, an allegory of Elizabeth's condemnation of Mary Queen of Scots. Equity does not mean indiscriminate forgiveness; Mercilla, with the lion from Britomart's dream at her feet and in all the trappings of majesty, stands for equity, with the lion as her servant the common law. Arthur leaves her court to do her business in the Netherlands, against the Spanish forces of the papal antichrist, and the eleventh canto describes greater successes against them than were ever achieved in history. Arthur visits the Temple of Geryon, or injustice, which balances that of Isis, and slays the beast under its altar. Finally Artegall fulfills his quest in a welter of topical allegory, killing the tyrant Grantorto and restoring Irena to her throne—an outcome sought for but not achieved by Grey and later Essex, who went to Ireland in 1599 to implement Grey's hard-line policies (here supported) but failed. On his way home Artegall is assailed by Envy, Detraction, and the Blatant Beast— the object of the quest in Book VI—by way of allusion to the ill repute of Grey on his return from Ireland.

The intrusion of so much topical material does the Book no good in the eyes of a modern reader, and in general it is a poor relation of Book I. But the triple portraits of Isis, Mercilla, and Grantorto are finely done and related, as the best of Spenser's set pieces are, like sections of some great fresco, such as that in the Palazzo Púbblico at Urbino.]

Book VI

Book VI is the legend of Courtesy; the knight Calidore must quest after the Blatant Beast. As in I, II, and V, the knight meets his predecessor in canto i, and in this opening there is a seed of all the rest. After encountering many *exempla* of courtesy and discourtesy Calidore drops out, rather as Red Cross did, in mid-course, going into a "pastoral truancy" and neglecting his quest. But the tone of the Book is new; it lacks deep allegories like those in the "core" cantos of earlier Books. Instead Spenser includes something quite different, the scene in which the Graces appear to Colin Clout, as given below.

Spenser means more by "courtesy" than agreeableness of manner. In his Proem he distinguishes between that, and something more noble and inclusive. Courtesy is a gentleman's or nobleman's standard of conduct, the virtue which poems of this kind were meant to develop, when they undertook, as Spenser did in the Letter to Ralegh, "to fashion a gentleman or noble person in vertuous and gentle discipline." Gentle birth was a prerequisite for its possession; even courteous savages will turn out to have been well born. Of course, the gentle can fall into discourtesy.

Courtesy, in the full sense of "civility" or "gentleness" given it by the Elizabethans, is *noblesse oblige*—what makes for decency, honor, and harmony in civil and military life. It was a fashionable subject, and courtesy books abounded, Castiglione's *The Courtier*, which Hoby translated into English, being only the most famous. Their precepts—aimed at fashioning gentlemen by example and ethical instruction—Spenser takes over in this Book, translating them into a romance narrative which, more than his others, approximates to the mood and style of Greek romance, and especially to the novella *Daphnis and Chloe* of Longus (probably 3rd century B.C.). He was also remembering the courtesy of Sidney, and the example of his prose-epic *Arcadia*. There is every reason to think that Shakespeare in turn was affected by Book VI when he wrote his final plays.

Calidore is bound to put down slander and evil speaking at its source, but also to demonstrate the gentleness of the gentleman: to be mild when that is appropriate, to champion women, show politeness to inferiors, and oppose all manifestations of discourtesy. In the course of some strange stories we see him doing this, chastising a churl for cutting off people's hair, righting the wrongs of ladies. He meets Childe Tristram, a wild young man of the forest, and at once detects his royal birth. He tends a wounded knight, and, by a knightly equivocation, saves a lady, caught in a compromising position with her lover, from her father's anger. Stumbling on a secluded pair of lovers, he manages to convince them that his intentions are innocent, and when the lady, Serena, is carried off by the Blatant Beast, he rescues her. The lover, Calepine, then takes Serena to the castle of Sir Turpine, a discourteous knight who refuses them admittance. Turpine and Calepine fight, and Calepine is saved by a courteous "salvage man," who also turns out to have been nobly born. The savage cures Calepine's wounds, but the knight gets lost, and Serena, traveling now with the savage, meets Arthur with Timias (Ralegh), who is being slandered (an allusion to Ralegh's fall into royal disfavor when he secretly married the lady-in-waiting Elizabeth Throckmorton). Timias and Serena are cured of the wound of slander by a hermit's psychological counseling; Arthur and the savage defeat Turpine and courteously allow him and his wife Blandina to live; but on a recurrence of treachery Arthur hangs Turpine by his heels from a tree. Meanwhile Timias and Serena meet Mirabella, who is undergoing a grotesque punishment for treating her lovers discourteously. Timias is captured by Disdain, and Arthur frees him. Calepine turns up just in time to save Serena from a band of cannibals who are admiring her naked body as a prelude to consuming it—this is one of the most sensual passages in the poem; the prurience of these savages represents a great enemy of courtesy.

Having neglected Calidore for a long time, Spenser now returns to him, describing his "truancy," his sojourn in the idyllic pastoral retreat of Pastorella and her (supposed) father Meliboee. The knight lives the life of pastoral content, described by Meliboee in lines (ix.20–21) that may have been in Shakespeare's mind when he conducted his lighthearted but searching examination of the pastoral conventions in *As You Like It*. Meliboee attacks gardens, emblems of the interference of art with nature, rather as Marvell's Mower does (see below). Calidore accepts the pastoral life, and when a rustic swain of Pastorella's grows jealous, he treats him with courtesy. The girl begins to love Calidore, but Spenser reminds us that his time is not his own, and that he should not be "Unmyndful of his vow and high beheast." Yet it is in the midst of this premature retirement from the life of action that he is blessed with the vision of the maidens dancing around the three Graces to the music of Colin Clout, representing Spenser himself.

The Graces usually appear in a group, usually with one facing the spectator. Here (in vi. x. 1–28) they represent the civil delight which good love spreads through human society—they are often associated with Venus—and are the opposites of the vices associated with discourtesy. The presence of Colin makes this a rare autobiographical interlude, strangely occurring at a crucial point in the Book; Spenser places his own love at the center, and shows himself singing her praises. He seems to be saying that his labors on the huge poem were interrupted by the personal matters described in the *Amoretti* and *Epithalamion,* poems which must have caused him to break off the epic in Book VI. He himself has been guilty of a "pastoral truancy," and in stanza 27 he asks pardon of the Queen for introducing this passage in praise of her "poore handmayd," for, after all, he had spent his life celebrating her greater glory. The girl is almost certainly Elizabeth Boyle, though some say she is the Rosalind of *The Shepheardes Calender* and *Colin Clout;* the tone of the poet's praise of her, mediator of delight and virtue through love, is close to that of *Epithalamion.*

     From Canto x
     Calidore sees the Graces daunce,
       To Colins melody:
     The whiles his Pastorell is led,
       Into captivity.

1   Who now does follow the foule *Blatant Beast,*
     Whilest *Calidore* does follow that faire Mayd,
     Unmyndfull of his vow and high beheast,
     Which by the Faery Queene was on him layd,
     That he should never leave, nor be delayd
     From chacing him, till he had it attchieved?
     But now entrapt of love, which him betrayd,
     He mindeth more, how he may be relieved
With grace from her, whose love his heart hath sore engrieved.

2   That from henceforth he meanes no more to sew°   *follow*
     His former quest, so full of toile and paine;
     Another quest, another game in vew
     He hath, the guerdon° of his love to gaine: *reward*
     With whom he myndes for ever to remaine,
     And set his rest amongst the rusticke sort,
     Rather then hunt still after shadowes vaine
     Of courtly favour, fed with light report
Of every blaste, and sayling alwaies in the port.°

3   Ne certes mote he greatly blamèd be,
     From so high step to stoupe unto so low.

sayling . . . port prevented by headwinds from
getting anywhere

For who had tasted once (as oft did he)
The happy peace, which there doth overflow,
And prov'd the perfect pleasures, which doe grow
Amongst poore hyndes,⁊ in hils, in woods, in dales,   *country folk*
Would never more delight in painted show
Of such false blisse, as there is set for stales,⁊   *baits*
T'entrap unwary fooles in their eternall bales.⁊   *evils*

4   For what hath all that goodly glorious gaze
  Like to one sight, which *Calidore* did vew?
  The glaunce whereof their dimmèd eies would daze,
  That never more they should endure the shew
  Of that sunne-shine, that makes them looke askew.
  Ne ought in all that world of beauties rare,
  (Save onely *Glorianaes* heavenly hew⁊   *form*
  To which what can compare?) can it compare;°
The which as commeth now, by course I will declare.

5   One day as he did raunge the fields abroad,
  Whilest his faire *Pastorella* was elsewhere,
  He chaunst to come, far from all peoples troad,⁊   *tread*
  Unto a place, whose pleasaunce did appere
  To passe all others, on the earth which were:
  For all that ever was by natures skill
  Devized to worke delight, was gathered there,
  And there by her were pourèd forth at fill,
As if this to adorne, she all the rest did pill.⁊   *plunder*

6   It was an hill plaste in an open plaine,
  That round about was bordered with a wood
  Of matchlesse hight, that seem'd th'earth to disdaine,
  In which all trees of honour stately stood,
  And did all winter as in sommer bud,°
  Spredding pavilions for the birds to bowre,
  Which in their lower braunches sung aloud;
  And in their tops the soring hauke did towre,⁊   *perch high*
Sitting like King of fowles in majesty and powre.

7   And at the foote thereof, a gentle flud
  His silver waves did softly tumble downe,
  Unmard with ragged mosse or filthy mud,
  Ne mote wylde beastes, ne mote the ruder clowne
  Thereto approach, ne filth mote therein drowne:
  But Nymphes and Faeries by the bancks did sit,
  In the woods shade, which did the waters crowne,
  Keeping all noysome things away from it,
And to the waters fall tuning their accents fit.

---

can . . . compare can rival it   **all winter . . . bud** yet another view of the
Earthly Paradise

8   And on the top thereof a spacious plaine
      Did spred it selfe, to serve to all delight,
      Either to daunce, when they to daunce would faine,
      Or else to course about their bases light;°
      Ne ought there wanted, which for pleasure might
      Desirèd be, or thence to banish bale:
      So pleasauntly the hill with equall hight,
      Did seeme to overlooke the lowly vale;
   Therefore it rightly cleepèd was mount *Acidale*.°

9   They say that *Venus*, when she did dispose
      Her selfe to pleasaunce, usèd to resort
      Unto this place, and therein to repose
      And rest her selfe, as in a gladsome port,
      Or with the Graces there to play and sport;
      That even her owne Cytheron,° though in it
      She usèd most to keepe her royall court,
      And in her soveraine Majesty to sit,
   She in regard hereof° refusde and thought unfit.

10 Unto this place when as the Elfin Knight
      Approcht, him seemèd that the merry sound
      Of a shrill pipe he playing heard on hight,
      And many feete fast thumping th'hollow ground,
      That through the woods their Eccho did rebound.
      He nigher drew, to weete what mote it be;
      There he a troupe of Ladies dauncing found
      Full merrily, and making gladfull glee,
   And in the midst of Shepheard piping he did see.

11 He durst not enter into th'open greene,
      For dread of them unwares to be descryde,
      For breaking of their daunce, if he were seene;
      But in the covert of the wood did byde,
      Beholding all, yet of them unespyde.
      There he did see, that pleasèd much his sight,
      That even he himselfe his eyes envyde,
      An hundred naked maidens lilly white,
   All raungèd in a ring, and dauncing in delight.

12 All they without were raungèd in a ring,
      And dauncèd round; but in the midst of them
      Three other Ladies did both daunce and sing,
      The whilest the rest them round about did hemme,
      And like a girlond did in compasse stemme

---

to course . . . light to play the game of prisoner's base
Acidale the name of the Muses' fountain (see *Epithalamion*, l. 310) but here transferred to the hill because of its association with Greek

akades, "carefree," or because of Latin *acies*, sight, view, here combined with *dale*
Cytheron Cythera, Venus' island, was sometimes confused with the mountain Citheron in Greece.
in regard hereof compared with this

And in the middest of those same three, was placed
Another Damzell, as a precious gemme,
Amidst a ring most richly well enchaced,
That with her goodly presence all the rest much graced.

13   Looke how the Crowne, which *Ariadne* wore
Upon her yvory forehead that same day,
That *Theseus* her unto his bridale bore,
When the bold *Centaures* made that bloudy fray,
With the fierce *Lapithes,* which did them dismay;
Being now placèd in the firmament,
Through the bright heaven doth her beams display,
And is unto the starres an ornament,
Which round about her move in order excellent.°

14   Such was the beauty of this goodly band,
Whose sundry parts were here too long to tell:
But she that in the midst of them did stand,
Seem'd all the rest in beauty to excell,
Crownd with a rosie girlond, that right well
Did her beseeme. And ever, as the crew
About her daunst, sweet flowres, that far did smell,
And fragrant odours they uppon her threw;
But most of all, those three did her with gifts endew.

15   Those were the Graces, daughters of delight,
Handmaides of *Venus,* which are wont to haunt⟩   *sojourn*
Uppon this hill, and daunce there day and night:
Those three to men all gifts of grace do graunt,
And all, that *Venus* in her selfe doth vaunt,
Is borrowèd of them. But that faire one,
That in the midst was placed paravaunt,⟩   *in foremost place*
Was she to whom that shepheard pypt alone,
That made him pipe so merrily, as never none.

16   She was to weete⟩ that jolly Shepheards lasse,   *to wit*
Which pipèd there unto that merry rout,
That jolly shepheard, which there pipèd, was
Poore *Colin Clout* (who knowes not *Colin Clout*?)
He pypt apace, whilest they him daunst about.
Pype jolly shepheard, pype thou now apace
Unto thy love, that made thee low to lout:⟩   *bow*
Thy love is present there with thee in place,
Thy love is there advaunst to be another Grace.

17   Much wondred *Calidore* at this straunge sight,
Whose like before his eye had never seene,
And standing long astonishèd in spright,

Looke how . . . excellent (stanza 13) refers
to the constellation, but the fight Spenser
mentions occurred at the wedding of Pirithous
and Hippodamia

And rapt with pleasaunce, wist not what to weene;
Whether it were the traine of beauties Queene,
Or Nymphes, or Faeries, or enchaunted show,
With which his eyes mote have deluded beene.
Therefore resolving, what it was, to know,
Out of the wood he rose, and toward them did go.

18 But soone as he appearèd to their vew,
They vanisht all away out of his sight,
And cleane were gone, which way he never knew;
All save the shepheard, who for fell despight
Of that displeasure, broke his bag-pipe quight,
And made great mone for that unhappy turne.
But *Calidore*, though no lesse sory wight,
For that mishap, yet seeing him to mourne,
Drew neare, that he the truth of all by him mote learne.

19 And first him greeting, thus unto him spake,
Haile jolly shepheard, which thy joyous dayes
Here leadest in this goodly merry make,›   *merrymaking*
Frequented of these gentle Nymphes alwayes,
Which to thee flocke, to heare thy lovely layes;
Tell me, what mote these dainty Damzels be,
Which here with thee doe make their pleasant playes?
Right happy thou, that mayst them freely see:
But why when I them saw, fled they away from me?

20 Not I so happy, answerd then that swaine,
As thou unhappy, which them thence didst chace,
Whome by no meanes thou canst recall againe,
For being gone, none can them bring in place,
But whom they of themselves list so to grace.
Right sory I, (saide then Sir *Calidore*,)
That my ill fortune did them hence displace.
But since things passèd none may now restore,
Tell me, what were they all, whose lacke thee grieves so sore.

21 Tho› gan that shepheard thus for to dilate;   *then*
Then wote thou shepheard, whatsoever thou bee,
That all those Ladies, which thou sawest late,
Are *Venus* Damzels, all within her fee,›   *service*
But differing in honour and degree:
They all are Graces, which on her depend,
Besides a thousand more, which ready bee
Her to adorne, when so she forth doth wend:
But those three in the midst, doe chiefe on her attend.

22 They are the daughters of sky-ruling Jove,
By him begot of faire *Eurynome*,°

Eurynome daughter of Ocean and mother of
the Graces

The Oceans daughter, in this pleasant grove,
As he this way comming from feastfull glee,
Of *Thetis* wedding with *Æacidee,*°
In sommers shade him selfe here rested weary.
The first of them hight mylde *Euphrosyne,*
Next faire *Aglaia,* last *Thalia* merry:
Sweete Goddesses all three which me in mirth do cherry.˃   *cheer*

23   These three on men all gracious gifts bestow,
    Which decke the body or adorne the mynde,
    To make them lovely or well favoured show,
    As comely carriage, entertainement˃ kynde,   *behavior to others*
    Sweete semblaunt,˃ friendly offices that bynde,   *demand*
    And all the complements of curtesie:
    They teach us, how to each degree and kynde
    We should our selves demeane,˃ to low, to hie;   *conduct*
To friends, to foes, which skill men call Civility.

24   Therefore they alwaies smoothly seeme to smile,
    That we likewise should mylde and gentle be,
    And also naked are, that without guile
    Or false dissemblaunce all them plaine may see,
    Simple and true from covert malice free:
    And eeke them selves so in their daunce they bore,
    That two of them still froward˃ seem'd to bee,   *turned away*
    But one still tòwards shew'd her selfe afore;
That good should from us goe, then come in greater store.

25   Such were those Goddesses, which ye did see;
    But that fourth Mayd, which there amidst them traced,
    Who can aread,˃ what creature mote she bee,   *tell*
    Whether a creature, or a goddesse graced
    With heavenly gifts from heven first enraced?˃   *implanted*
    But what so sure she was, she worthy was,
    To be the fourth with those three other placed:
    Yet was she certes but a countrey lasse,
Yet she all other countrey lasses farre did passe.

26   So farre as doth the daughter of the day,°
    All other lesser lights in light excell,
    So farre doth she in beautyfull array,
    Above all other lasses beare the bell,˃   *gains victory*
    Ne lesse in vertue that beseemes her well,
    Doth she exceede the rest of all her race,
    For which the Graces that here wont to dwell,
    Have for more honor brought her to this place,
And gracèd her so much to be another Grace.

Æacidee Peleus, son of Aeacus, whose wedding
(he married Thetis) was attended by the gods

daughter of the day the evening (and morning)
star, Venus

27   Another Grace she well deserves to be,
         In whom so many Graces gathered are,
         Excelling much the meane of her degree;
         Divine resemblaunce, beauty soveraine rare,
         Firme Chastity, that spight ne blemish dare;
         All which she with such courtesie doth grace,
         That all her peres cannot with her compare,
         But quite are dimmèd when she is in place.
       She made me often pipe and now to pipe apace.ˀ   *copiously*

28   Sunne of the world, great glory of the sky,
         That all the earth doest lighten with thy rayes,
         Great *Gloriana*, greatest Majesty,
         Pardon thy shepheard, mongst so many layes,
         As he hath sung of thee in all his dayes,
         To make one minimeˀ of thy poore handmayd,   *musical note*
         And underneath thy feete to place her prayse,
         That when thy glory shall be farre displayd
       To future age of her this mention may be made.

                              · · ·

                            1596

[The pastoral calm is abruptly broken when brigands attack the settlement and
carry off Pastorella, Meliboee, and others. Then the brigands fight with slavers,
and all their prisoners are killed except Pastorella, whom Calidore rescues from
under a heap of bodies. The courtesy of innocence, he has discovered, is too
vulnerable; in the wicked world we have there must be men of chivalry perpetually ready for the defense of innocence and courtesy. Pastorella, identified
by a birthmark, is restored to her noble parents; Calidore captures the Blatant
Beast, but it escapes, and, says Spenser, waxes even more mischievous and
outrageous, not even sparing poets.

   On this inconclusive note, introduced as a sad afterthought in the last four
stanzas, the unfinished poem comes to a stop, except for the fragment of another Book which was published in 1609. This is made up of the Two Cantos
of Mutability, and the publisher guesses that they are part of a legend of
Constancy, labeling them cantos vi, vii, and viii 1–2 of that Book.]

Two Cantos of Mutability

It appears most likely that Spenser wrote these as the "core" cantos, leaving the rest
of the work, which would have to be devoted more to narrative, for later completion;
for example, there is no reason why the Garden of Adonis canto in Book III should not
have been written separately and in advance. The view that these are early and rejected
drafts seems incomprehensible, considering that they contain Spenser's finest philosophical poetry.

   Canto vi proposes the topic of Change or Mutability, opposite of Constancy, and calls Mutability a daughter of the Titans (charged in Book V with the guilt of having brought rebellion and intemperance into the world). She has altered the original order of creation, defaced Nature and Justice, and brought death into life; she is, in fact under one aspect, the image of the disaster of the Fall. Having ruined earth, she aspires to the heavens which are beyond the moon, below which her power is admitted by all. First she claims the moon, whose sphere is the border between the two worlds; an eclipse strikes terror and creates the fear that Chaos is coming again. Mercury investigates for Jupiter, who explains to the heavenly powers that a Titan's daughter is again challenging them. Mutability arrives to state her claim. Jupiter admires her beauty, but chides her, asserting his obvious preeminence. She claims a hearing in a higher court, that of Nature, and a hearing is appointed, to be held on Arlo Hill in Spenser's Ireland.

Spenser now makes a myth, based on Ovid, to explain why this beautiful place (used in the previous Book as the dancing place of the Graces) should have lost some of its original loveliness and innocence. Then, in canto vii, the hearing is described.

The success of these cantos depends on Spenser's ability to convert philosophical explanations into myths of his own devising, and therefore fitting the basic patterns of his imagination. Scholarship has said much about the sources—in Ovid, Lucretius, the neo-platonists, in Boethius, the mainstay of medieval philosophy, and even in the thought of Spenser's contemporary, Giordano Bruno, who spent some time in London and Oxford before being condemned as a heretic by the Inquisition. Probably he depended on no particular source—philosophically, what he says on this subject both here and in III.vi is not very different from the speech of Theseus at the end of Chaucer's Knight's Tale: God is stable and eternal, but has decreed that "speces of thinges and progressiouns / Shullen enduren by successiouns, / And nat eterne be, withoute lye." But the whole joint development of thought and myth—or thought-in-myth—is Spenserian.

Ovid, the classic poet of mutability (his greatest work is the *Metamorphoses*), was in Spenser's mind; he borrowed from Ovid not only Nature (again see the opening lines of the *Metamorphoses*), trimming it with other material from the long tradition, but also three strands of narrative: the challenge of Mutability, the story of Faunus in vi, and the pageant of times and seasons in vii. From Ovid he also borrowed a speech attributed to Pythagoras on the subject of change. But he is not a "classical" poet; he admits medieval elements, and also understands things in a Christian sense. The relation of Time and Eternity—the root problem, since time is the agent of change—he sees in a Christian light, remembering the great medieval commonplaces. Here the answer is quite like that of III.vi. Adonis, though "subject to mortalitee / Yet is eterne in mutabilitie, / And by succession made perpetuall." Boethius said that "all things rejoice to return again to their own nature," and that in the long run they do not change except insofar as change may bring them to the perfection potential in their natures. This also implies change and decay; but the two things are complementary, and mutability is the servant of the eternality of things.

Mutability may reflect, as Spenser often does, contemporary convictions of the rapid decay of the world, but she also represents something that delighted him, which is why he makes her beautiful, and why this myth goes very deep with him. "All change is sweet," he says in *Muiopotmos,* and, at the very end of the poem, "for all that moveth, doth in *Change* delight." The beauty and variety of the physical world are a consequence of mutability. Thus Mutability has the better arguments, and Jupiter merely storms; Nature ends the dispute only by means of a mysterious answer, but one in which gnomic language underlines what mythological invention has already achieved, the reconciliation of opposites.

From Canto vii

3   Now, at the time that was before agreed,
    The Gods assembled all on *Arlo*° hill;
    As well those that are sprung of heavenly seed,
    As those that all the other world doe fill,
    And rule both sea and land unto their will:
    Onely th'infernall Powers might not appeare;
    As well for horror of their count'naunce ill,
    As for th'unruly fiends which they did feare;
    Yet *Pluto* and *Proserpina*° were present there.

4   And thither also came all other creatures,
    What-ever life or motion doe retaine,
    According to their sundry kinds of features;
    That *Arlo* scarsly could them all containe;
    So full they fillèd every hill and Plaine:
    And had not *Natures* Sergeant (that is *Order*)
    Them well disposèd by his busie paine,
    And raungèd farre abroad in every border,
    They would have causèd much confusion and disorder.

5   Then forth issewed (great goddesse) great dame *Nature*°
    With goodly port and gracious Majesty;
    Being far greater and more tall of stature
    Then any of the gods or Powers on hie:
    Yet certès by her face and physnomy,
    Whether she man or woman inly were,
    That could not any creature well descry:
    For, with a veile that wimpled᾿ every where   *covered*
    Her head and face was hid, that mote to none appeare.

6   That some doe say was so by skill devizèd,
    To hide the terror of her uncouth᾿ hew,   *unknown*
    From mortall eyes that should be sore agrizèd;᾿   *horrified*
    For that her face did like a Lion shew,
    That eye of wight could not indure to view:
    But others tell that it so beautious was,
    And round about such beames of splendor threw,
    That it the Sunne a thousand times did pass,
    Ne could be seene, but like an image in a glass.

Arlo hill near Spenser's estate at Kilcolman
Pluto and Proserpina king and queen of hell
dame Nature As he suggests, Spenser owes something to Alanus, *De Planctu Naturae*, and more directly to Chaucer's *Parlement of Foules* for this figure. The veil and the hermaphroditism probably come from Plutarch's Isis and Osiris, on which he also drew for III.vi and V.x vii; and just as the philosophical argument partly parallels that of III.vi, so the presentation of the figure of Nature is reminiscent of the hermaphrodite Venus of IV.x. Here he succeeds marvelously in attributing to Nature beauty and terror, mystery and authority, fertility and order.

7   That well may seemen true: for, well I weene
      That this same day, when she on *Arlo* sat,
      Her garment was so bright and wondrous sheene,˃   *fair*
      That my fraile wit cannot devize to what
      It to compare, nor finde like stuffe to that,
      As those three sacred *Saints*, though else most wise,
      Yet on mount *Thabor* quite their wits forgat,
      When they their glorious Lord in strange disguise
   Transfigur'd sawe;° his garments so did daze their eyes.

8   In a fayre Plaine upon an equall˃ Hill,   *symmetrical*
      She placèd was in a paviliόn;
      Not such as Craftes-men by their idle˃ skill   *vain*
      Are wont for Princes states to fashiόn:
      But th'earth her self of her owne motiόn,
      Out of her fruitfull bosome made to growe
      Most dainty trees; that, shooting up anon,
      Did seeme to bow their bloosming heads full lowe,
   For homage unto her, and like a throne did shew.

9   So hard it is for any living wight,
      All her array and vestiments to tell,
      That old *Dan Geffrey*° (in whose gentle spright
      The pure well head of Poesie did dwell)
      In his *Foules parley*° durst not with it mel,
      But it transferd to *Alane,*° who he thought
      Had in his *Plaint of kindes*° describ'd it well:
      Which who will read set forth so as it ought,
   Go seek he out that *Alane* where he may be sought.

10   And all the earth far underneath her feete
      Was dight with flowres, that voluntary grew
      Out of the ground, and sent forth odours sweet;
      Tenne thousand mores˃ of sundry sent and hew,   *roots, plants*
      That might delight the smell, or please the view;
      The which, the Nymphes, from all the brooks thereby
      Had gathered, which° they at her foot-stoole threw;
      That richer seem'd then any tapestry,
   That Princes bowres adorne with painted imagery.

11   And *Mole*° himself, to honour her the more,
      Did deck himself in freshest faire attire,

---

those three . . . sawe Matthew 17:1–2, Mark 9:6: "And after six days Jesus taketh Peter, James and John his brother, and bringeth them up into a high mountain apart, and was transfigured before them: and his face did shine with the sun, and his raiment was white as the light . . . they were sore afraid"
Dan Geffrey Chaucer
Foules parley The Parlement of Foules
Alane Alanus de (ab) Insulis, Alain de l'Isle (c.1128–1203), French Cistercian theologian, author of satirical poem cited in the following line.
Plaint of kinds De Planctu Naturae; Chaucer says: "And right as Aleyn, in the Pleynt of Kinde, / Devyseth Nature of aray and face, / In swich aray men mighten hir ther finde" (The Parlement of Foules, ll. 316–18)
which redundant syntactically, and also metrically if one says gatherèd
Mole forest near Kilcolman

And his high head, that seemeth alwaies hore
With hardned frosts of former winters ire,
He with an Oaken girlond now did tire,°   *dress*
As if the love of some new Nymph late seene,
Had in him kindled youthfull fresh desire,
And made him change his gray attire to greene;
Ah gentle *Mole!* such joyance hath thee well beseene.°   *become*

12 Was never so great joyance since the day,
    That all the gods whylome° assembled were,   *once*
    On *Hæmus hill*° in their divine array,
    To celebrate the solemne bridall cheare,
    Twixt *Peleus,* and dame *Thetis*° pointed° there;   *appointed*
    Where *Phœbus* self, that god of Poets hight,
    They say did sing the spousall hymne full cleere,
    That all the gods were ravisht with delight
Of his celestiall song, and Musicks wondrous might.

13 This great Grandmother of all creatures bred
    Great *Nature,* ever young yet full of eld,
    Still mooving, yet unmovèd from her sted;°   *position*
    Unseene of any, yet of all beheld;°
    Thus sitting in her throne as I have teld,
    Before her came dame *Mutabilitie;*
    And being lowe before her presence feld,°   *fallen*
    With meek obaysance and humilitie,
Thus gan her plaintif Plea, with words to amplifie;

14 To thee O greatest goddesse, onely° great,   *alone*
    An humble suppliant loe, I lowely fly
    Seeking for Right, which I of thee entreat;
    Who Right to all dost deale indifferently,
    Damning all Wrong and tortious° Injurie,   *wrongful*
    Which any of thy creatures doe to other
    (Oppressing them with power, unequally)
    Sith of them all thou art the equall° mother,   *impartial*
And knittest each to each, as brother unto brother.

15 To thee therefore of this same *Jove* I plaine,°   *complain*
    And of his fellow gods that faine to be,
    That challenge° to themselves the whole worlds raign; *claim*
    Of which, the greatest part is due to me,
    And heaven it selfe by heritage in Fee:°   *right of inheritance*
    For, heaven and earth I both alike do deeme,
    Sith heaven and earth are both alike to thee;

Hæmus hill hill in Thessaly
Peleus . . . Thetis See XI.x.22n.
ever young . . . beheld This reconciliation of
opposites in Nature states the main theme of
the Mutability Cantos, and one of Spenser's
most radically important poetic preoccupations.

Furthermore, in her ability to be "Still mooving,
yet unmovèd from her sted," Nature contains
the secret answer to Mutability, who cannot
understand the possibility of reconciling stillness
and movement, or time and eternity.

And, gods no more then men thou doest esteeme:
For, even the gods to thee, as men to gods do seeme.

16   Then weigh, O soveraigne goddesse, by what right
         These gods do claime the worlds whole soveraity;
         And that˃ is onely˃ dew unto thy might   *that which / solely*
         Arrogate to themselves ambitiously:
         As for the gods owne principality,
         Which *Jove* usurpes unjustly; that to be
         My heritage, *Jove's* self cannot deny,
         From my great Grandsire *Titan*, unto mee,
       Deriv'd by dew descent; as is well knowen to thee.

17   Yet mauger˃ *Jove,* and all his gods beside,   *in spite of*
         I doe possesse the worlds most regiment;˃   *rule*
         As, if ye please it into parts divide,
         And every parts inholders˃ to convent,˃   *tenants / summon*
         Shall to your eyes appeare incontinent.˃   *immediately*
         And first, the Earth (great mother of us all)
         That only˃ seems unmov'd and permanent,   *alone*
         And unto *Mutability* not thrall;
       Yet is she chang'd in part, and eeke in generall.°

18   For, all that from her springs, and is ybredde,
         How-ever fayre it flourish for a time,
         Yet see we soone decay; and, being dead,
         To turne again unto their earthly slime:
         Yet, out of their decay and mortall crime,°
         We daily see new creatures to arize;
         And of their Winter spring another Prime,˃   *spring*
         Unlike in forme, and chang'd by strange disguise:
       So turne they still about, and change in restlesse wise.

19   As for her tenants; that is, man and beasts,
         The beasts we daily see massácred dy,
         As thralls and vassalls unto mens beheasts:˃   *commands*
         And men themselves doe change continually,
         From youth to eld, from wealth to poverty,
         From good to bad, from bad to worst of all.
         Ne doe their bodies only flit and fly:
         But eeke their minds (which they immortall call)
       Still change and vary thoughts, as new occasions fall.

20   Ne is the water in more constant case;
         Whether those same on high, or these belowe.°
         For, th'Ocean moveth stil,˃ from place to place;   *always*

Yet . . . generall The arguments of Mutability
derive partly from the teaching of Pythagoras
in Ovid, *Metamorphoses* XV, on the theme
omnia mutantur, all things are changed.

mortall crime This is the association, inevitable
in the period, between mutability and the consequences of the Fall.
on high . . . belowe Genesis 1:7

And every River still doth ebbe and flowe:
Ne any Lake, that seems most still and slowe;
Ne Poole so small, that can his smoothnesse holde,>   *maintain*
When any winde doth under heaven blowe;
With which, the clouds are also tost and roll'd;
Now like great Hills; and, streight, like sluces, them unfold.

21 So likewise are all watry living wights
Still tost, and turnèd, with continuall change.
Never abyding in their stedfast plights.>   *fixed conditions*
The fish, still floting, doe at randon range,
And never rest; but evermore exchange
Their dwelling places, as the streames them carrie:
Ne have the watry foules a certaine grange,>   *dwelling*
Wherein to rest, ne in one stead> do tarry;   *place*
But flitting still doe flie, and still their places vary.

22 Next is the Ayre: which who feeles not by sense
(For, of all sense it is the middle meane)°
To flit still? and, with subtill influence
Of this thin spirit,° all creatures to maintaine,
In state of life? O weake life! that does leane
On thing so tickle> as th'unsteady ayre;   *unstable*
Which every howre is chang'd, and altred cleane>   *completely*
With every blast that bloweth fowle or faire:
The faire doth it prolong; the fowle doth it impaire.

23 Therein the changes infinite beholde,
Which to her creatures every minute chaunce;
Now, boyling hot: streight, friezing deadly cold:
Now, faire sun-shine, that makes all skip and daunce:
Streight, bitter storms and balefull countenance,
That makes them all to shiver and to shake:
Rayne, hayle, and snowe do pay> them sad penance,   *inflict on*
And dreadfull thunder-claps (that makes them quake)
With flames and flashing lights that thousand changes make.

24 Last is the fire: which, though it live for ever,
Ne can be quenchèd quite; yet, every day,
Wee see his parts, so soone as they do sever,
To lose their heat, and shortly to decay;
So, makes himself his owne consuming pray.
Ne any living creatures doth he breed:°
But all, that are of others bredd,° doth slay;
And, with their death, his cruell life dooth feed;
Nought leaving but their barren ashes, without seede.

---

middle meane medium, e.g. for scent and hearing
spirit monosyllabic

Ne . . . breed The salamander was sometimes excepted.
of others bredd bred of the other elements

25   Thus, all these fower° (the which the ground-work bee
     Of all the world, and of all living wights)
     To thousand sorts of *Change* we subject see.
     Yet are they chang'd (by other wondrous slights⌐)   *tricks*
     Into themselves,⌐ and lose their native mights;   *each other*
     The Fire to Aire, and th'Ayre to Water sheere,⌐   *bright*
     And Water into Earth: yet Water fights
     With Fire, and Aire with Earth approaching neere:
   Yet all are in one body, and as one appeare.

26   So, in them all raignes *Mutabilitie*;
     How-ever these, that Gods themselves do call,
     Of them doe claime the rule and soveranty:
     As, *Vesta,* of the fire æthereall;°
     Vulcan, of this, with us so usuall;°
     Ops,° of the earth; and *Juno* of the Ayre;
     Neptune, of Seas; and Nymphes, of Rivers all.
     For, all those Rivers to me subject are:
   And all the rest, which they usurp, be all my share.

27   Which to approven true, as I have told,
     Vouchsafe, O goddesse, to thy presence call
     The rest which doe the world in being hold:
     As, times and seasons of the yeare that fall:
     Of all the which, demand in generall,
     Or judge thy selfe, by verdit⌐ of thine eye,   *verdict*
     Whether to me they are not subject all.
     Nature did yeeld thereto; and by-and-by,
   Bade *Order* call them all, before her Maiesty.

            .   .   .

[There follows a lavish pageant of the Seasons, the Months, Day and Night, the Hours, and Life and Death. Mutability resumes her plea.]

47   When these were past, thus gan the *Titanesse*;
     Lo, mighty mother, now be judge and say,
     Whether in all thy creatures more or lesse⌐   *greater or smaller*
     CHANGE doth not raign and beare the greatest sway:
     For, who sees not, that *Time* on all doth pray?
     But *Times* do change and move continually.
     So nothing here long standeth in one stay:
     Wherefore, this lower world who can deny
   But to be subject still to *Mutabilitie?*

48   Then thus gan *Jove*; Right true it is, that these
     And all things else that under heaven dwell
     Are chaung'd of *Time*, who doth them all disseise⌐   *deprive*

---

fower the four elements, earth, water, air, fire, of which everything is constituted
Vesta . . . æthereall Vesta, goddess of holy fire, and so of the celestial fires of the heavens

Vulcan . . . usual Vulcan the smith, so god of the fire on earth, which is used for manufacture
Ops identified with Rhea and Gaea, names of the earth goddess

Of being: But, who is it (to me tell)
That *Time* himselfe doth move and still compell
To keepe his course? Is not that namely wee
Which poure that vertue˃ from our heavenly cell,   *influence*
That moves them all, and makes them changèd be?
So them we gods doe rule, and in them also thee.

49   To whom, thus *Mutability:* The things
Which we see not how they are mov'd and swayd,
Ye may attribute to your selves as Kings,
And say they by your secret powre are made:
But what we see not, who shall us perswade?
But were they so, as ye them faine to be,
Mov'd by your might, and ordred by your ayde;
Yet what if I can prove, that even yee.
Your selves are likewise chang'd, and subject unto mee?

50   And first, concerning her that is the first,
Even you faire *Cynthia,*° whom so much ye make
Joves dearest darling, she was bread and nurst
On *Cynthus* hill, whence she her name did take:
Then is she mortall borne, how-so ye crake;˃   *boast*
Besides, her face and countenance every day
We changèd see, and sundry forms partake,
Now hornd, now round, now bright, now brown and gray:
So that *as changefull as the Moone* men use to say.

51   Next, *Mercury,* who though he lesse appeare
To change his hew,˃ and alwayes seeme as one;   *form*
Yet, he his course doth altar˃ every yeare,   *alter*
And is of late far out of order gone:°
So *Venus* eeke, that goodly Paragone,
Though faire all night, yet is she darke all day;
And *Phœbus* self, who lightsome is alone,˃   *alone is*
Yet is he oft eclipsèd by the way,
And fills the darkned world with terror and dismay.

52   Now *Mars* that valiant man is changèd most:
For, he some times so far runs out of square,
That he his way doth seem quite to have lost,
And cleane without his usuall sphere to fare;
That even these Star-gazers stonisht are
At sight thereof, and damne their lying bookes:
So likewise, grim Sir *Saturne* oft doth spare

Cynthia moon goddess, so called from Cynthus, a mountain in Delos. Spenser treats the moon as a planet, and goes on to deal with the other six of the old system: Mercury, Venus, the sun, Mars, Saturn, and Jupiter.
out of order gone See notes on V, Proem, where Spenser confines his remarks on eccentric orbits to the sun, Mars, and Saturn. That Mercury, much harder to observe, was also eccentric, was a fairly recent discovery, and perhaps Spenser caught up with it between the writing of V and of these cantos. Of course all such eccentricities were consequent upon the mistaken view that planetary orbits were circular (see also the opening lines of Donne's "Good Friday, 1613. Riding Westward").

His sterne aspect, and calme his crabbèd lookes:
So many turning cranks these have, so many crookes.°

53 But you *Dan Jove*, that only constant are,
    And King of all the rest, as ye do clame,
    Are you not subject eek to this misfare?'   *misfortune*
    Then let me aske you this withouten blame,'   *offense*
    Where were ye borne? some say in *Crete* by name,
    Others in *Thebes*, and others other-where;°
    But wheresoever they comment' the same,   *lyingly invent*
    They all consent that ye begotten were,
And borne here in this world, ne other can appeare.

54 Then are ye mortall borne, and thrall to me,
    Unlesse the kingdome of the sky yee make'   *argue*
    Immortall, and unchangeable to bee;
    Besides, that power and vertue which ye spake,
    That ye here worke, doth many changes take,
    And your owne natures change: for, each of you.
    That vertue have, or this, or that to make,
    Is checkt and changèd from his nature trew,
By others opposition or obliquid view.°

55 Besides, the sundry motions of your Spheares,
    So sundry waies and fashions as clerkes faine,
    Some in short space, and some in longer yeares;
    What is the same but alteration plaine?
    Onely the starrie skie° doth still remaine:
    Yet do the Starres and Signes therein still move,°
    And even it self is mov'd, as wizards saine.°
    But all that moveth, doth mutation love:
Therefore both you and them to me I subject prove.

56 Then since within this wide great *Universe*
    Nothing doth firme and permanent appeare,
    But all things tost and turnèd by transverse:'   *haphazardly*
    What then should let,' but I aloft should reare   *hinder*
    My Trophee, and from all, the triumph beare?
    Now judge then (O thou greatest goddesse trew!)

---

cranks . . . crooks turnings and windings (alluding to the progressively more complex hypotheses of epicycles introduced to justify the Ptolemaic system in the light of observed eccentricities)

some . . . other-where There were conflicting traditions about Jupiter's birthplace, Crete, Thebes, and Arcadia being claimants: Natalis Comes, the Renaissance mythographer known to Spenser, sums up the matter as "very contentious."

each of you . . . view The influences of which the planets are capable are qualified and changed by their action on one another; *opposition* is the relation between two planets when their longitude differs by 180 degrees; an *obliquid* relation is more obliquely directed.

the starry skie the "crystalline" sphere of the fixed stars, held to be immutable and pure

Starres . . . move The movement referred to resulted from the effect on terrestrial observation of the precession of the equinoxes (cf. V, Proem).

it self . . . saine the crystalline sphere itself moves, according to astronomers. Ptolemy said that "inasmuch as the stars maintain their relative distances we may justly call them fixed, yet inasmuch as the whole sphere to which they are attached is in motion, the word 'fixed' is but little appropriate."

According as thy selfe doest see and heare,
And unto me addoom⁀ that is my dew;   *adjudicate*
That is the rule of all, all being rul'd by you.

57   So having ended, silence long ensewed,
        Ne *Nature* to or fro spake for a space,
        But with firme eyes affixt, the ground still viewed.
        Meane while, all creatures, looking in her face,
        Expecting th'end of this so doubtfull case,
        Did hang in long suspence what would ensew,
        To whether⁀ side should fall the soveraigne place: *which*
        At length, she looking up with chearefull view,
    The silence brake, and gave her doome in speeches few.

58   I well consider all that ye have sayd,
        And find that all things stedfastnes doe hate
        And changèd be: yet being rightly wayd⁀   *considered*
        They are not changèd from their first estate;
        But by their change their being doe dilate:
        And turning to themselves at length againe,
        Doe worke their owne perfection so by fate:
        Then over them Change doth not rule and raigne;
    But they raigne over change, and doe their states maintaine.

59   Cease therefore daughter further to aspire,
        And thee content thus to be rul'd by me:
        For thy decay thou seekst by thy desire;°
        But time shall come that all shall changèd bee,
        And from thenceforth, none no more change shall see.
        So was the *Titaness* put downe and whist,⁀   *silenced*
        And *Jove* confirm'd in his imperiall see.⁀   *throne*
        Then was that whole assembly quite dismist,
    And *Natur's* selfe did vanish, whither no man wist.⁀   *knew*

   The viii. Canto, unperfite⁀   *unfinished*

1   When I bethinke me on that speech whyleare,⁀   *recent*
        Of *Mutability,* and well it way:
        Me seemes, that though she all unworthy were
        Of the Heav'ns Rule; yet very sooth to say,
        In all things else she beares the greatest sway.
        Which makes me loath this state of life so tickle,⁀   *unstable*
        And love of things so vaine to cast away;
        Whose flowring pride, so fading and so fickle,
    Short⁀ *Time* shall soon cut down with his consuming sickle.   *who shortens*

2   Then gin I thinke on that which Nature sayd,
        Of that same time when no more *Change* shall be,

For . . . desire by your own wish to subject   your own decay, since you will have to be
everything to mutability you unwittingly seek   mutable too

> But stedfast rest of all things firmely stayd
> Upon the pillours of Eternity,
> That is contrayr to *Mutabilitie*:
> For, all that moveth, doth in *Change* delight:
> But thence-forth all shall rest eternally
> With Him that is the God of Sabbaoth° hight:°   *called*
> O that great Sabbaoth God, graunt me that Sabaoths sight.°

1609

Amoretti

Amoretti means "little cupids"; Spenser's sonnet sequence, published in 1595 with the *Epithalamion*, is not only a collection of "little loves" (or expressions thereof), but a carefully constructed series of glimpses into the quasi-fictional sonnet world, part private and autobiographical, part mythological and shared with Sidney, Daniel, Drayton, and Shakespeare. Spenser married Elizabeth Boyle before the publication of the collection, and the poems seem to comprehend this cycle of courtship and marriage, interlaced with the cycle of the secular and liturgical year and even of phases of poetic work (numbers 33 and 80 refer to the unfinished *Faerie Queene*). Spenser's form combines French and English verse traditions in linking the sonnet quatrains with common rhymes (the interlocking of *The Faerie Queene* stanza) and maintaining or breaking the octave-sestet division at will (abab bcbc cdcd ee). Rhetorically less dynamic than the sonnets of Sidney or Shakespeare, they nevertheless present in a subtle way a variety of tones and stances.

From Amoretti

I

> Happy ye leaves° when as those lilly hands,
>   which hold my life in their dead doing° might,   *killing*
>   shall handle you and hold in loves soft bands,
>   lyke captives trembling at the victors sight.
> And happy lines, on which with starry light,
>   those lamping° eyes will deigne sometimes to look   *flashing*
>   and reade the sorrowes of my dying spright,°   *spirit*
>   written with teares in harts close° bleeding book.   *secret*
> And happy rymes bath'd in the sacred brooke,
>   of *Helicon*° whence she derivèd is,
>   when ye behold that Angels blessèd looke,
>   my soules long lackèd foode, my heavens blis.

10

God of Sabbath God of Hosts
Sabaoths sight Spenser may mean "grant me sight of the Lord on the last day," but more probably he means *Sabbath* in the sense of eternity—the stillness that will follow the tumult of the six days of the world's history.
leaves pages of the book of the *Amoretti*; similarly the "lines" and "rymes"

the sacred . . . Helicon the fountain of Hippocrene on Mt. Helicon, sacred to the Muses, the mythical "source" (which word itself originally means "spring") of poetry, here "sacred" because of the Petrarchan heavenly associations with the sonneteer's muse

Leaves, lines, and rymes, seeke her to please alone,
  whom if ye please, I care for other none.
          1595

xv

Ye tradefull Merchants, that with weary toyle,
  do seeke most pretious things to make your gain;
  and both the Indias° of their treasures spoile,
  what needeth you to seeke so farre in vaine?
For loe my love doth in her selfe containe
  all this worlds riches that may farre be found,
  if Saphyres,° loe her eies be Saphyres° plaine,   *clear*
  if Rubies, loe hir lips be Rubies sound:
If Pearles, hir teeth be pearles both pure and round;
10 if Yvorie, her forhead yvory weene;   *beautiful*
  if Gold, her locks are finest gold on ground;
  if silver, her faire hands are silver sheene.
But that which fairest is, but few behold,
  her mind adornd with vertues manifold.
          1595

xvi

One day as I unwarily did gaze
  on those fayre eyes my loves immortall light:
  the whiles my stonisht hart stood in amaze,
  through sweet illusion of her lookes delight.
I mote° perceive how in her glauncing sight,   *could*
  legions of loves° with little wings did fly:
  darting their deadly arrowes fyry bright,
  at every rash beholder passing by.
One of those archers closely° I did spy,   *secretly*
10 ayming his arrow at my very hart:
  when suddenly with twincle° of her eye,   *blink*
  the Damzell broke his misintended dart.
Had she not so doon, sure I had bene slayne,
  yet as it was, I hardly° scap't with paine.   *scarcely*
          1595

LIV

Of this worlds Theatre° in which we stay,
  My love lyke the Spectator ydly sits

Indias both East and West Indies
Saphyres This blazon of the Lady's beauties may stem from the comparisons of those of the beloved to rare artifacts in the Song of Songs 5:10–16, but it also reflects a contemporary convention: it is hard to believe that Shakespeare's Sonnet CXXX is not, particularly in ll. 3–4, parodying this poem.
loves The "amoretti," little cupids, fly along the "eyebeams" which interlock two lovers' gazes (see Donne, "The Ecstasy," for a complex use of this lore; behind Spenser's use of it lies the serious doctrine in his own *Hymne in Honour of Beautie,* ll. 231–45).
worlds Theatre The *theatrum mundi* commonplace, likening reality to a play, God to the author and director, the world to a set, and people to actors (the final curtain is, inevitably, Apocalypse), goes back originally to Plato; it is most familiar through Jaques's "All the world's a stage" speech in *As You Like It,* although it is uncommon in Petrarchan sonnets.

beholding me that all the pageants° play,
    disguysing diversly my troubled wits.
Sometimes I joy when glad occasion fits,
    and mask in myrth lyke to a Comedy:
soone after when my joy to sorrow flits,
    I waile and make my woes a Tragedy.
Yet she beholding me with constant eye,
10   delights not in my merth° nor rues my smart:°   *mirth*
but when I laugh she mocks, and when I cry
    she laughs, and hardens evermore her hart.
What then can move her? if nor merth nor mone,°   *moan*
    she is no woman, but a sencelesse stone.

                    1595

LXIII

After long stormes and tempests sad assay,°
    Which hardly I endurèd heretofore:
in dread of death and daungerous dismay,
    with which my silly barke° was tossèd sore:
I doe at length descry the happy shore,
    in which I hope ere long for to arryve;
fayre soyle it seemes from far and fraught with store°
    of all that deare and daynty is alyve.
Most happy he that can at last atchyve
10   the joyous safety of so sweet a rest:
whose least delight sufficeth to deprive
    remembrance of all paines which him opprest.
All paines are nothing in respect of this,
    all sorrowes short that gaine eternall blisse.

                    1595

LXIV

Comming to kisse her lyps, (such grace I found)
    me seemd I smelt a gardin of sweet flowres:°
that dainty odours from them threw around
    for damzels fit to decke their lovers bowres.
Her lips did smell lyke unto Gillyflowers,
    her ruddy cheekes lyke unto Roses red:
her snowy browes lyke budded Bellamoures,
    her lovely eyes lyke Pincks° but newly spred.   *carnations*
Her goodly bosome lyke a Strawberry bed,
10   her neck lyke to a bounch of Cullambynes:°   *columbine*
her brest lyke lillyes, ere theyr leaves be shed,
    her nipples lyke yong blossomd Jessemynes.°   *jasmines*

---

pageants parts in the productions
rues my smart pities my sorrow
sad assay painful encounter (with storms)
silly barke innocent or simple ship: this is a
commonplace (see Wyatt's "My Galley Chargèd
with Forgetfullness")

fraught with store bounteously supplied
gardin of sweet flowres another sort of blazon
or catalogue, going back to another source in
Song of Songs (4:12–15), describing the lover
as an enclosed garden

Such fragrant flowres doe give most odorous smell,
  but her sweet odour did them all excell.

1595

LXXV

One day I wrote her name upon the strand,   *beach*
  but came the waves and washèd it away:
  agayne I wrote it with a second hand,
  but came the tyde, and made my paynes his pray.   *prey*
Vayne man, sayd she, that doest in vaine assay,
  a mortall thing so to immortalize,
  for I my selve shall lyke to this decay,
  and eek my name bee wypèd out lykewize.   *also*
Not so, (quod I) let baser things devize   *contrive*
10 to dy in dust, but you shall live by fame:
  my verse your vertues rare shall eternize,°
  and in the hevens wryte your glorious name.
Where whenas death shall all the world subdew,
  our love shall live, and later life renew.

1595

Epithalamion

Epithalamion was published with the *Amoretti* in 1595. An epithalamion is a marriage song, and Spenser combines conventional features of the genre with strong personal applications, for he wrote the poem about his own wedding, to his second wife, Elizabeth Boyle. The wedding songs of Catullus are the type, and, as in Jonson in the masque *Hymenaei* and Herrick later, there are ceremonies and figures belonging more to a Roman than an English wedding; but Spenser, in the Renaissance manner, blends with these purely Christian figures, and also breaks with tradition in making the bridegroom the singer of the song.

In apparently freely flowing stanzas, Spenser invokes the Muses and follows the events of the wedding day, much in the Latin manner; the effect is of controlled abundance, an ordered joy appropriate to marriage and that desire of generation which is the honorable gift of the earthly Venus. And this effect is not impaired by the knowledge, recently achieved, that the poem has an elaborate hidden numerological structure. A. Kent Hieatt has demonstrated that the twenty-three stanzas and the envoy stand for the hours of the day, the last eight being the night hours, for the day of the wedding is the summer solstice. The day hours have the refrain, "The woods shall to me answer"; the night hours, "The woods no more shall answer." There are 365 long lines, one for each day of the year. There are other evidences of strict design, but the demands it made on Spenser did not prevent his achieving what C. S. Lewis calls "festal sublimity," any more than similar patterns, even more recently discovered in *The Faerie Queene,* cramp or diminish it.

---

eternize Poetry's ability to perpetuate beautiful lives in myth even longer than can statues or inscriptions in stone is an old theme (cf. Shakespeare's Sonnet LV: "Not marble, nor the gilded monuments"), and especially suited to the delight sonnet sequences took in referring to themselves.

Epithalamion

Ye learnèd sisters° which have oftentimes
Beene to me ayding, others° to adorne:
Whom ye thought worthy of your gracefull° rymes,
That even the greatest did not greatly scorne
To heare theyr names sung in your simple layes,
But joyèd in theyr prayse.
And when ye listˀ your owne mishaps to mourne,   *choose*
Which death, or love, or fortunes wreck did rayse,
Your string could soone to sadder tenor° turne,
10 And teach the woods and waters to lament
Your dolefull dreriment.ˀ   *grief*

Now lay those sorrowfull complaints aside,
And having all your heads with girland crownd,
Helpe me mine owne loves prayses to resound,
Ne let the same of any be envideˀ   *grudged*
So Orpheus did for his owne bride,°
So I unto my selfe alone will sing,
The woods shall to me answer and my Eccho ring.

Early before the worlds light giving lampe,
20 His golden beame upon the hils doth spred,
Having disperst the nights unchearefull dampe,
Doe ye awake, and with fresh lusty hed,ˀ   *vigor*
Go to the bowre of my belovèd love,
My truest turtle dove,
Bid her awake; for Hymen° is awake,
And long since ready forth his maske to move,°
With his bright Teadˀ that flames with many a flake,ˀ   *torch / spark*
And many a bachelor to waite on him,
In theyr fresh garments trim.
30 Bid her awake therefore and soone her dight,ˀ   *dress*
For lo the wishèd day is come at last,
That shall for al the paynes and sorrowes past,
Pay to her usuryˀ of long delight: *interest*
And whylest she doth her dight,
Doe ye to her of joy and solace sing,
That all the woods may answer and your eccho ring.

Bring with you all the Nymphes that you can heare°
Both of the rivers and the forrests greene:
And of the sea that neighbours to her neare,°
40 Al with gay girlands goodly wel beseene.ˀ   *provided*

learnèd sisters the Muses
others e.g. Queen Elizabeth
gracefull conferring grace
sadder tenor graver mood, deeper note
So . . . bride Orpheus can plausibly be supposed to have provided an epithalamion for Eurydice.

Hymen god of marriage
his maske to move to lead the procession of revelers
that . . . heare that can hear you
sea . . . neare Elizabeth Boyle had been staying at Youghal near the sea.

And let them also with them bring in hand,
Another gay girland
For my fayre love of lillyes and of roses,
Bound truelove wize° with a blew silke riband.   *where*
And let them make great store of bridale poses,
And let them eeke bring store of other flowers
To deck the bridale bowers.
And let the ground whereas˃ her foot shall tread,   *where*
For feare the stones her tender foot should wrong
50 Be strewed with fragrant flowers all along,
And diapred˃ lyke the discolorèd˃ mead.   *strewn with flowers / multicolored*
Which done, doe at her chambre dore awayt,
For she will waken strayt,
The whiles doe ye this song unto her sing,
The woods shall to you answer and your Eccho ring.

Ye Nymphes of Mulla° which with carefull heed,
The silver scaly trouts doe tend full well;
And greedy pikes which use therein to feed,
(Those trouts and pikes all others doo excell)
60 And ye likewise which keepe the rushy lake,
Where none doo fishes take,
Bynd up the locks the which hang scatterd light,
And in his waters which your mirror make,
Byhold your faces as the christall bright,
That when you come whereas my love doth lie,
No blemish she may spie.
And eke ye lightfoot mayds which keepe the deere,
That on the hoary mountayne use to towre,°
And the wylde wolves which seeke them to devoure,
70 With your steele darts doo chace from comming neer
Be also present heere,
To helpe to decke her and to help to sing,
That all the woods may answer and your eccho ring.

Wake, now my love, awake; for it is time,
The Rosy Morne long since left Tithones bed,°
All ready to her silver coche to clyme,
And Phœbus gins to shew his glorious hed.
Hark how the cheerefull birds do chaunt theyr laies
And carroll of loves praise.
80 The merry Larke hir mattins sings aloft,
The thrush replyes, the Mavis˃ descant° playes.   *thrush*
The Ouzell˃ shrills, the Ruddock˃ warbles soft,   *blackbird / robin*
So goodly all agree with sweet consent,

---

truelove wize in a love knot
Mulla now the river Awbeg, which flows near
Kilcolman
towre live high up
Tithones bed Tithonus is the husband of the

Dawn; this is a stock expression, going back
to Homer.
descant melody or counterpoint written above
a simple musical theme. The concept of birds
is a medieval convention.

To this dayes merriment.
Ah my deere love why doe ye sleepe thus long,
When meeter were that ye should now awake,
T'awayt the comming of your joyous make,°   *mate*
And hearken to the birds lovelearnèd song,
The deawy leaves among.
90   For they of joy and pleasance to you sing,
That all the woods them answer and theyr eccho ring.

My love is now awake out of her dreame,
And her fayre eyes like stars that dimmèd were
With darksome cloud, now shew theyr goodly beames
More bright then Hesperus his head doth rere.
Come now ye damzels, daughters of delight,
Helpe quickly her to dight.
But first come ye fayre houres which were begot
In Joves sweet paradice, of Day and Night,°
100   Which doe the seasons of the yeare allot,
And al that ever in this world is fayre
Doe make and still° repayre.   *ever*
And ye three handmayds of the Cyprian Queene,°
The which doe still adorne her beauties pride,
Helpe to addorne my beautifullest bride:
And as ye her array, still throw betweene
Some graces to be seene,
And as ye use° to Venus, to her sing,   *do as a rule*
The whiles the woods shal answer and your eccho ring.

110   Now is my love all ready forth to come,
Let all the virgins therefore well awayt,
And ye fresh boyes that tend upon her groome
Prepare your selves; for he is comming strayt.
Set all your things in seemely good aray
Fit for so joyfull day,
The joyfulst day that ever sunne did see.
Faire Sun, shew forth thy favourable ray,
And let thy lifull° heat not fervent be   *life-bestowing*
For feare of burning her sunshyny face,
120   Her beauty to disgrace.
O fayrest Phœbus, father of the Muse,
If ever I did honour thee aright,
Or sing the thing, that mote thy mind delight,
Doe not thy servants simple boone refuse,
But let this day let this one day be myne,
Let all the rest be thine.
Then I thy soverayne prayses loud wil sing,
That all the woods shal answer and theyr eccho ring.

of **Day and Night** more usually of Zeus and   **three . . . Queene** the Graces, attendant on
Themis—a little invention of Spenser's   Venus, as in *The Faerie Queene* VI.x

Harke how the Minstrels gin to shrill aloud
130   Their merry Musick that resounds from far,
The pipe, the tabor, and the trembling Croud,°   *fiddle*
That well agree withouten breach or jar.°   *discord*
But most of all the Damzels doe delite,
When they their tymbrels smyte,
And thereunto doe daunce and carrol sweet,
That all the sences they doe ravish quite,
The whyles the boyes run up and downe the street,
Crying aloud with strong confusèd noyce,°   *noise*
As if it were one voyce.
140   Hymen io Hymen,° Hymen they do shout,
That even to the heavens theyr shouting shrill
Doth reach, and all the firmament doth fill,
To which the people standing all about,
As in approvance doe thereto applaud
And loud advaunce her laud,°   *praise*
And evermore they Hymen Hymen sing,
That al the woods them answer and theyr eccho ring.

Loe where she comes along with portly° pace   *stately*
Lyke Phœbe° from her chamber of the East,
150   Arysing forth to run her mighty race,
Clad all in white, that seemes a virgin best.   *becomes*
So well it her beseemes° that ye would weene
Some angell she had beene.
Her long loose yellow locks lyke golden wyre,
Sprinckled with perle, and perling flowres a tweene,
Doe lyke a golden mantle her attyre,
And being crownèd with a girland greene,
Seeme lyke some mayden Queene.
Her modest eyes abashèd to behold
160   So many gazers, as on her do stare,
Upon the lowly ground affixèd are.
Ne dare lift up her countenance too bold,
But blush to heare her prayses sung so loud,
So farre from being proud.
Nathlesse doe ye still loud her prayses sing.
That all the woods may answer and your eccho ring.

Tell me ye merchants daughters did ye see
So fayre a creature in your towne before,
So sweet, so lovely, and so mild as she,
170   Adornd with beautyes grace and vertues store,
Her goodly eyes° lyke Saphyres shining bright,

Hymen io Hymen traditional wedding cry (see
The Faerie Queen I.i.48)
Phoebe moon goddess, who borrows from her
brother Phoebus the sun, "which is as a bridegroom coming out of his chamber, and rejoiceth
as a strong man to run a race" (Psalms 15:5):
Spenser transfers all this to the virgin bride
goodly eyes This begins a conventional catalogue
of beauties known as the blazon; cf. Sonnet XV.

recalls song of Soloman

Her forehead yvory white,
Her cheekes lyke apples which the sun hath rudded,°   *reddened*
Her lips lyke cherryes charming men to byte,
Her brest like to a bowle of creame uncrudded,°   *uncurdled*
Her paps lyke lyllies budded,
Her snowie necke lyke to a marble towre,
And all her body like a pallace fayre,
Ascending uppe with many a stately stayre,
180   To honors seat and chastities sweet bowre.°
Why stand ye still ye virgins in amaze,
Upon her so to gaze,
Whiles ye forget your former lay to sing,
To which the woods did answer and your eccho ring.

But if ye saw that which no eyes can see,
The inward beauty of her lively spright,°   *spirit*
Garnisht with heavenly guifts of high degree,
Much more then would ye wonder at that sight,
And stand astonisht lyke to those which red°   *saw*
190   Medusaes mazeful hed.°
There dwels sweet love and constant chastity,
Unspotted fayth and comely womanhood,
Regard of honour and mild modesty,
There vertue raynes as Queen in royal throne,
And giveth lawes alone.°
The which the base affections° doe obay,   *passions*
And yeeld theyr services unto her will,
Ne thought of thing uncomely ever may
Thereto approach to tempt her mind to ill.
200   Had ye once seene these her celestial threasures,
And unrevealèd pleasures,
Then would ye wonder and her prayses sing,
That al the woods should answer and your echo ring.

Open the temple gates unto my love,
Open them wide that she may enter in,
And all the postes adorne° as doth behove,°   *as is fitting*
And all the pillours deck with girlands trim,
For to recyve this Saynt with honour dew,
That commeth in to you.
210   With trembling steps and humble reverence,
She commeth in, before th'almighties vew,
Of her ye virgins learne obedience,
When so ye come into those holy places,
To humble your proud faces:

honors . . . bowre the head, which controls the rest
Medusaes . . . hed Medusa was a Gorgon, whose terrible head turned the beholder to stone;
the bride's spirit would be awe-inspiring.
giveth . . . alone alone commands
postes adorne Roman wedding custom, surviving in poetry

Bring her up to th'high altar, that she may
The sacred ceremonies there partake,
The which do endlesse matrimony make,
And let the roring Organs loudly play
The praises of the Lord in lively notes,
220 The whiles with hollow throates
The Choristers the joyous Antheme sing,
That al the woods may answere and their eccho ring.

Behold whiles she before the altar stands
Hearing the holy priest that to her speakes
And blesseth her with his two happy hands,
How the red roses flush up in her cheekes,
And the pure snow with goodly vermill stayne,
Like crimsin dyde in grayne,   *thoroughly*
That even th'Angels which continually,
230 About the sacred Altare doe remaine,°
Forget their service and about her fly;
Ofte peeping in her face that seemes more fayre,
The more they on it stare.
But her sad eyes still fastened on the ground,   *grave*
Are governèd with goodly modesty,
That suffers not one looke to glaunce awry,
Which may let in a little thought unsownd.
Why blush ye love to give to me your hand,
The pledge of all our band?   *bond*
240 Sing ye sweet Angels, Alleluya sing,°
That all the woods may answere and your eccho ring.

Now al is done; bring home the bride againe,
Bring home the triumph of our victory,
Bring home with you the glory of her gaine,   *of gaining her*
With joyance bring her and with jollity.
Never had man more joyfull day then this,
Whom heaven would heape with blis.
Make feast therefore now all this live long day,
This day for ever to me holy is,
250 Poure out the wine without restraint or stay,
Poure not by cups, but by the belly full,
Poure out to all that wull,   *want*
And sprinkle all the postes and wals with wine,°
That they may sweat, and drunken be withall.
Crowne ye God Bacchus with a coronall,   *garland*
And Hymen also crowne with wreathes of vine,
And let the Graces daunce unto the rest;
For they can doo it best:

remaine Revelation 7:11
Sing . . . sing Revelation 19:1. Spenser remembers the marriage in Revelation, which was
so important in the conclusion of *The Faerie Queene* I.
sprinkle . . . wine another Roman custom

The whiles the maydens doe theyr carroll sing,
260   To which the woods shal answer and theyr eccho ring.

Ring ye the bels, ye yong men of the towne,
And leave your wonted᠈ labors for this day: *usual*
This day is holy; doe ye write it downe,
That ye for ever it remember may.
This day the sunne is in his chiefest hight,
With Barnaby the bright,°
From whence declining daily by degrees,
He somewhat loseth of his heat and light,
When once the Crab behind his back he sees.°
270   But for this time it ill ordainèd was,
To chose the longest day in all the yeare,
And shortest night, when longest fitter weare:
Yet never day so long, but late᠈ would passe.   *at last*
Ring ye the bels, to make it weare away,
And bonefiers° make all day,
And daunce about them, and about them sing
That all the woods may answer, and your eccho ring.

Ah when will this long weary day have end,
And lende me leave to come unto my love?
280   How slowly do the houres theyr numbers spend?
How slowly does sad Time his feathers move?
Hast thee O fayrest Planet° to thy home
Within the Westerne fome:
Thy tyrèd steedes long since have need of rest.
Long though it be, at last I see it gloome,᠈   *darken*
And the bright evening star with golden creast
Appeare out of the East.
Fayre childe of beauty, glorious lampe of love
That all the host of heaven in rankes doost lead,
290   And guydest lovers through the nightes dread,
How chearefully thou lookest from above,
And seemst to laugh atweene thy twinkling light
As joying in the sight
Of these glad many which for joy doe sing,
That all the woods them answer and their eccho ring.

Now ceasse ye damsels your delights forepast;᠈   *over*
Enough is it, that all the day was youres:
Now day is doen, and night is nighing fast:
Now bring the Bryde into the brydall boures.
300   Now night is come, now soone her disaray,

---

the sunne . . . bright St. Barnabas day, June
11, was till the revision of the calendar the
summer solstice.
the Crab . . . sees The sun moved out of Cancer into Leo in mid-June.

bonefiers midsummer bonfires, a surviving pagan
custom
Planet The sun was regarded as a planet in
Ptolemaic astronomy.

And in her bed her lay;
Lay her in lillies and in violets,
And silken courteins over her display,>   *spread*
And odourd sheetes, and Arras> coverlets.   *tapestry*
Behold how goodly my faire love does ly
In proud humility;
Like unto Maia,° when as Jove her tooke,
In Tempe,° lying on the flowry gras,
Twixt sleepe and wake, after she weary was,
310 With bathing in the Acidalian° brooke.
Now it is night, ye damsels may be gon,
And leave my love alone,
And leave likewise your former lay to sing:
The woods no more shal answere, nor your eccho ring.

Now welcome night, thou night so long expected,
That long daies labour doest at last defray,>   *pay for*
And all my cares, which cruell love collected,
Hast sumd in one, and cancellèd for aye:
Spread thy broad wing over my love and me,
320 That no man may us see,
And in thy sable mantle us enwrap,
From feare of perrill and foule horror free.
Let no false treason seeke us to entrap,
Nor any dread disquiet once annoy
The safety of our joy:
But let the night be calme and quietsome,
Without tempestuous storms or sad afray:
Lyke as when Jove with fayre Alcmena lay,
When he begot the great Tirynthian groome:°
330 Or lyke as when he with thy selfe° did lie,
And begot Majesty.°
And let the mayds and yongmen cease to sing:
Ne let the woods them answer, nor theyr eccho ring.

Let no lamenting cryes, nor dolefull teares,
Be heard all night within nor yet without:
Ne let false whispers, breeding hidden feares,
Breake gentle sleepe with misconceivèd dout.
Let no deluding dreames, nor dreadful sights
Make sudden sad affrights;
340 Ne let housefyres, nor lightnings helpelesse> harmes,   *incurable*

Maia one of the seven Pleiades; she gave birth
to Hermes (Mercury) after the encounter described
Tempe beautiful vale in Thessaly
Acidalian Acidalia was a fountain sacred to
Venus.
Lyke . . . groome Alcmena, wife of Amphit-
ryon, spent a night of love, magically prolonged to the length of three nights, with
Jupiter, and conceived Hercules, who was born
at Tiryns and served as a super-groom in the
cleaning of the Augean stables.
thy selfe Night
begot Majesty Spenser made up this little
myth himself.

Ne let the Pouke,° nor other evill sprights,
Ne let mischívous witches with theyr charmes,
Ne let hob Goblins, names whose sence we see not,
Fray us with things that be not,
Let not the shriech Oule, nor the Storke be heard:
Nor the night Raven° that still° deadly yels,   *ever*
Nor damnèd ghosts cald up with mighty spels,
Nor griesly vultures make us once affeard:
Ne let th'unpleasant Quyre of Frogs still° croking   *always*
350   Make us to wish theyr choking.
Let none of these theyr drery accents sing;
Ne let the woods them answer, nor theyr eccho ring.

But let stil Silence trew night watches keepe,
That sacred peace may in assurance rayne,
And tymely sleep, when it is tyme to sleepe,
May poure his limbs forth on your° pleasant playne,
The whiles an hundred little wingèd loves,°
Like divers fethered doves,
Shall fly and flutter round about your bed,
360   And in the secret darke, that° none reproves,   *when*
Their prety stealthes shal worke, and snares shal spread
To filch away sweet snatches of delight,
Conceald through covert night.
Ye sonnes of Venus, play your sports at will,
For greedy pleasure, carelesse of your toyes,°   *tricks*
Thinks more upon her paradise of joyes,
Then what ye do, albe it good or ill.
All night therefore attend your merry play,
For it will soone be day:
370   Now none doth hinder you, that say or sing,
Ne will the woods now answer, nor your Eccho ring.

Who is the same, which at my window peepes?
Or whose is that faire face, that shines so bright,
Is it not Cinthia,° she that never sleepes,
But walkes about high heaven al the night?
O fayrest goddesse, do thou not envy
My love with me to spy:
For thou likewise didst love, though now unthought,°   *unremembered*
And for a fleece of woll, which privily,
380   The Latmian shephard° once unto thee brought,
His pleasures with thee wrought.
Therefore to us be favorable now;

Pouke puck, Robin Goodfellow, mischievous
and malevolent fairy
Oule . . . Storke . . . night Raven birds of
ill-omen, all foretelling death except the stork,
believed to avenge adultery
your Night's

loves cupids, "amoretti"
Cinthia the moon; there was a new moon on
June 9, two days before the wedding
Latmian shephard Endymion lay with Diana
on Mount Latmos; in most versions it was Pan
who won her with a fleece of wool.

And sith of wemens labours thou hast charge,
And generation goodly dost enlarge,
Encline thy will t'effect our wishfull vow,
And the chast wombe informe with timely seed,
That may our comfort breed:
Till which we cease our hopefull hap⸃ to sing,   *luck*
Ne let the woods us answere, nor our Eccho ring.

390   And thou great Juno, which with awful might
The lawes of wedlock still dost patronize,°
And the religion⸃ of the faith first plight⸃   *bond / pledged*
With sacred rites hast taught to solemnize:
And eeke for comfort often callèd art
Of women in their smart,⸃   *labor pains*
Eternally bind thou this lovely band,
And all thy blessings unto us impart.
And thou glad Genius,° in whose gentle hand,
The bridale bowre and geniall° bed remaine,
400   Without blemish or staine,
And the sweet pleasures of theyr loves delight
With secret ayde doest succour and supply,
Till they bring forth the fruitfull progeny,
Send us the timely fruit of this same night.
And thou fayre Hebe,° and thou Hymen free,
Grant that it may so be.
Til which we cease your further prayse to sing,
Ne any woods shal answer, nor your Eccho ring.

And ye high heavens, the temple of the gods,
410   In which a thousand torches flaming bright
Doe burne, that to us wretched earthly clods,
In dreadful darknesse lend desirèd light;
And all ye powers which in the same remayne,
More then we men can fayne,
Poure out your blessing on us plentiously,
And happy influence upon us raine,
That we may raise a large posterity,
Which from the earth, which they may long possesse,
With lasting happinesse,
420   Up to your haughty pallaces may mount,
And for the guerdon of theyr glorious merit
May heavenly tabernacles there inherit,
Of blessèd Saints for to increase the count.
So let us rest, sweet love, in hope of this,

Juno . . . patronize *Juno pronuba,* goddess of marriage. Lucina, on whom women called in childbirth, was a name applied to both Diana and Juno.
Genius the patron of generation, as in *The Faerie Queene* III.vi 31–33

geniall Latin expression for marriage bed, place of generation
Hebe goddess of youth, not traditionally associated with weddings

And cease till then our tymely joyes to sing,
The woods no more us answer, nor our eccho ring.

Song made in lieu of many ornaments,°
With which my love should duly have bene dect,⟩   *decked*
Which cutting off through hasty accidents,°
430   Ye would not stay your dew time to expect,
But promist both to recompens,
Be unto her a goodly ornament,
And for short time an endlesse moniment.°

1595

SIR WALTER RALEGH
1552–1618

Born to a Devon family, he attended Oriel College, Oxford, for a while, served as a soldier in France and Ireland, returned to London, and lived in the Middle Temple. He became a favorite of the Queen, who elevated him and made him rich. His careers were many: as a courtier, he was a precursor of the later "dandy"; as a sailor and entrepreneur, he explored Guiana, founded the first Virginia colony, and attacked the Spanish fleet at Cadiz in 1596. As an intellectual, his association with Chapman, Marlowe, and Hariot in a group referred to as the "School of Night" earned him a reputation for atheism (for a suggestion of the precise flavor of his fame, see the sketch of him by John Aubrey, below). After being the Queen's protégé for a decade, he was dropped (so the story went) because of his seduction of one of the Queen's attendants, Elizabeth Throckmorton. James I, who eventually had him beheaded for treason, imprisoned him in the Tower for thirteen years, during which time he worked on scientific and historical projects. The poems published in his lifetime appeared in anthologies (his long poem, *Cynthia*, in praise of Queen Elizabeth, is lost, except for a fragment); his comprehensive historical work is *The History of the World*.

From The History of the World
Book I, Chapter II, Section V

That man is, as it were, a little world: [1] with a digression touching our mortality.

Man, thus compounded and formed by God, was an abstract or model, or brief story of the universal, in whom God concluded the creation and work of the world, and whom he made the last and most excellent of his creatures, being

---

ornaments wedding presents; the envoy makes apologetic reference to the occasion of the poem
hasty accidents accidents of haste (perhaps the date had to be brought forward)

short . . . **moniment** immortal record of the one day it records and schematically represents

1. This section forms part of the theoretical opening of Ralegh's huge, meditative *History of the World*, unfinished (like its subject), and published first in 1614. The part reproduced here is as elaborate a statement as one could want of the received idea of man as microcosm, or little world (see Fig. 22).

internally endued with a divine understanding, by which he might contemplate and serve his Creator, after whose image he was formed, and endued with the powers and faculties of reason and other abilities, that thereby also he might govern and rule the world, and all other God's creatures therein. And whereas God created three sorts of living natures, to wit, angelical, rational, and brutal; giving to angels an intellectual, and to beasts a sensual nature, he vouchsafed unto man both the intellectual of angels, the sensitive of beasts, and the proper rational belonging unto man,[2] and therefore, saith Gregory Nazianzen,[3] *Homo est utriusque naturæ vinculum:* 'Man is the bond and chain which tieth together both natures.' And because in the little frame of man's body there is a representation of the universal, and (by allusion) a kind of participation of all the parts thereof, therefore was man called *microcosmos,* or the little world. *Deus igitur hominem factum, velut alterum quendam mundum, in brevi magnum, atque exiguo totum, in terris statuit:* 'God therefore placed in the earth the man whom he had made, as it were another world, the great and large world in the small and little world.'[4] For out of earth and dust was formed the flesh of man, and therefore heavy and lumpish; the bones of his body we may compare to the hard rocks and stones, and therefore strong and durable, of which Ovid:[5]

> Inde genus durum sumus, experiensque laborum,
> Et documenta damus qua simus origine nati.

> From thence our kind hard-hearted is,
>   Enduring pain and care,
> Approving, that our bodies of
>   A stony nature are.

His blood, which disperseth itself by the branches of veins through all the body, may be resembled to those waters which are carried by brooks and rivers over all the earth; his breath to the air; his natural heat to the enclosed warmth which the earth hath in itself—which, stirred up by the heat of the sun, assisteth nature in the speedier procreation of those varieties which the earth bringeth forth; our radical moisture, oil, or balsamum (whereon the natural heat feedeth and is maintained) is resembled to the fat and fertility of the earth; the hairs of man's body, which adorns, or overshadows it, to the grass, which covereth the upper face and skin of the earth; our generative power, to nature, which produceth all things; our determinations,[6] to the light, wandering, and unstable clouds, carried every where with uncertain winds; our eyes, to the light of the sun and moon; and the beauty of our youth, to the flowers of the spring, which, either in a very short time, or with the sun's heat, dry up and wither away, or the fierce puffs of wind blow them from the stalks; the thoughts of our mind, to the motion of angels; and our pure understanding (formerly called *mens,* and that which always looketh upwards) to those intellectual natures which are always present with God; and, lastly, our immortal souls (while they are

---

2. Another received notion of Renaissance psychology, derived from Aristotle's statement of it in his *Physics.*
3. St. Gregory of Nazianzus (*c.* 328–390), bishop and theologian.
4. Ralegh is quoting from St. Augustine, *The City of God.*
5. *Metamorphoses* I.414–15.
6. Resolutions.

righteous) are by God himself beautified with the title of his own image and similitude. And although, in respect of God, there is no man just, or good, or righteous (for, *in angelis deprehensa est stultitia,* 'Behold, he found folly in his angels,' saith Job [7]) yet, with such a kind of difference as there is between the substance and the shadow,[8] there may be found a goodness in man: which God being pleased to accept, hath therefore called man the image and similitude of his own righteousness. In this also is the little world of man compared, and made more like the universal (man being the measure of all things—*Homo est mensura omnium rerum,* saith Aristotle [9] and Pythagoras) that the four complexions resemble the four elements,[10] and the seven ages of man the seven planets; whereof our infancy is compared to the moon, in which we seem only to live and grow, as plants; the second age to Mercury, wherein we are taught and instructed; our third age to Venus, the days of love, desire, and vanity; the fourth to the sun, the strong, flourishing, and beautiful age of man's life; the fifth to Mars, in which we seek honour and victory, and in which our thoughts travel to ambitious ends; the sixth age is ascribed to Jupiter, in which we begin to take account of our times, judge of ourselves, and grow to the perfection of our understanding; the last and seventh to Saturn, wherein our days are sad, and overcast, and in which we find by dear and lamentable experience, and by the loss which can never be repaired, that of all our vain passions and affections past, the sorrow only abideth: our attendants are sicknesses, and variable infirmities; and by how much the more we are accompanied with plenty, by so much the more greedily is our end desired, whom when time hath made unsociable to others, we become a burden to ourselves: being of no other use, than to hold the riches we have from our successors. In this time it is, when (as aforesaid) we, for the most part, and never before, prepare for our eternal habitation, which we pass on unto with many sighs, groans, and sad thoughts, and in the end, by the workmanship of death, finish the sorrowful business of a wretched life; towards which we always travel both sleeping and waking; neither have those beloved companions of honour and riches any power at all to hold us any one day by the glorious promise of entertainments; but by what crooked path soever we walk, the same leadeth on directly to the house of death, whose doors lie open at all hours, and to all persons. For this tide of man's life, after it once turneth and declineth, ever runneth with a perpetual ebb and falling stream, but never floweth again: our leaf once fallen, springeth no more; neither doth the sun or the summer adorn us again, with the garments of new leaves and flowers.

> Redditur arboribus florens revirentibus ætas;
> Ergo non homini, quod fuit ante, redit.[11]

---

7. Job 4:18.
8. A traditional way of phrasing a contrast between matter and the mere image of matter.
9. In the *Metaphysics* I.1053b which mentions Protagoras, not "Pythagoras"; this idea was also treated by Plato in the *Theaetetus.*
10. The four "complexions" or temperaments (sanguine, choleric, phlegmatic, and melancholy) are actually generated by combinations of the elements (see *Renaissance Psychology* in the Glossary).
11. From an elegy on the death of Maecenas by Albinovanus, a minor poet of the Augustan age.

To which I give this sense.

> The plants and trees made poor and old
> By winter envious,
> The spring-time bounteous
> Covers again from shame and cold:
> But never man repaired again
> His youth and beauty lost,
> Though art, and care, and cost,
> Do promise nature's help in vain.

And of which Catullus, Epigram 53.[12]

> Soles occidere et redire possunt:
> Nobis cum semel occidit brevis lux,
> Nox est perpetua una dormienda.

> The sun may set and rise:
> But we contrarywise
> Sleep after our short light
> One everlasting night.

For if there were any baiting place, or rest, in the course or race of man's life, then, according to the doctrine of the Academics,[13] the same might also perpetually be maintained. But as there is a continuance of motion in natural living things, and as the sap and juice, wherein the life of plants is preserved, doth evermore ascend or descend; so is it with the life of man, which is always either increasing towards ripeness and perfection, or declining and decreasing towards rottenness and dissolution.

1614

A Description of Love

Now what is love? I pray, tell.
It is that fountain and that well,
Where pleasure and repentance dwell.
It is perhaps that sauncing° bell,
That tolls all in to heaven or hell:
And this is love, as I hear tell.

Yet what is love? I pray thee say.
It is a work on holy-day;
It is December matched with May;
10   When lusty bloods, in fresh array
Hear ten months after of the play:
And this is love, as I hear say.

12. A famous passage from the "Vivamus mea Lesbia, atque amemus," adapted by Ben Jonson and Thomas Campion (see "Come, My Celia" and "My Sweetest Lesbia").
13. The philosophic descendants of Plato, down to the Roman Cicero.

sauncing the Sanctus bell, rung during that portion of the Mass

Yet what is love? I pray thee sayn.
It is a sunshine mixed with rain;
It is a tooth-ache, or like pain;
It is a game where none doth gain;
The lass saith no, and would full fain:°
And this is love, as I hear sayn.

20 Yet what is love? I pray thee say.
It is a yea, it is a nay,
A pretty kind of sporting fray;
It is a thing will soon away;
Then take the vantage while you may:
And this is love, as I hear say.

Yet what is love? I pray thee show.
A thing that creeps, it cannot go;
A prize that passeth to and fro;
A thing for one, a thing for mo;
And he that proves° must find it so:
30 And this is love, sweet friend, I trow.

                            1593

Answer to Marlowe°

If all the world and love were young,
And truth in every shepherd's tongue,
These pretty pleasures might me move
To live with thee and be thy love.

Time drives the flocks from field to fold,
When rivers rage and rocks grow cold,
And Philomel° becometh dumb;
The rest complain of cares to come.

The flowers do fade, and wanton fields
10 To wayward winter reckoning yields;
A honey tongue, a heart of gall,
Is fancy's spring, but sorrow's fall.

Thy gowns, thy shoes, thy beds of roses,
Thy cap, thy kirtle,° and thy posies
Soon break, soon wither, soon forgotten,
In folly ripe, in reason rotten.

Thy belt of straw and ivy buds,
Thy coral clasps and amber studs,

---

fain be glad to, with a pun on "feign" (pretend)
proves tries it out
Answer to Marlowe See "The Passionate

Shepherd to His Love," and Donne, "The Bait."
Philomel the nightingale
kirtle dress

All these in me no means can move
20 To come to thee and be thy love.

But could youth last and love still breed,
Had joys no date nor age no need,
Then these delights my mind might move
To live with thee and be thy love.

1600

On the Life of Man

What is our life? a play° of passion,
Our mirth the music of division;°
Our mothers' wombs the tiring-houses° be
Where we are dressed for this short comedy;
Heaven the judicious, sharp spectator is
That sits and marks still who doth act amiss;
Our graves that hide us from the searching sun
Are like drawn curtains when the play is done:
Thus march we, playing, to our latest° rest,
10 Only we die in earnest, that's no jest.

1612

GEORGE CHAPMAN
1559–1634

Born in 1559 of Hertfordshire yeomanry, Chapman may have attended Oxford, but if so, left without taking a degree. After some time abroad, probably fighting in the Low Countries, he returned to England, and his circle there included Marlowe, Sir Walter Ralegh, and the mathematicians Roydon and Hariot, a group of advanced thinkers, religiously and intellectually, who may have constituted what is called "The School of Night," after the title of Chapman's first published work, *The Shadow of Night* (1594). An obscure and difficult poem, it presents an antithetical reading of the mythological significance and moral import of chaos, night, and darkness. *Ovid's Banquet of Sense*, a mythological narrative with neoplatonic philosophical interpolations, appeared the following year. By 1598, when his completion of Marlowe's unfinished *Hero and Leander* appeared, he was an established dramatist. But he is best known for his magnificent translation of Homer (the *Iliad* appearing in 1611, the *Odyssey* in 1614–15), the first done in the rhymed fourteeners of earlier sixteenth-century tradition, the second in the heroic couplets that replaced them as the equivalent of heroic Greek and Latin verse. His concern in all his poetry was for the philosophical interpretation of received ancient mythology; in his conclusion to *Hero and Leander*, we see him turning erotic narrative into moral speculation.

---

play This is a version of the *theatrum mundi* theme (see Spenser's *Amoretti*, Sonnet LIV) but a grim, half-mocking one; the first line puns on "passion plays", as religious drama.

division in the musical sense, free counterpoint based on a theme
tiring-houses dressing rooms
latest last

From Hero and Leander°

The Third Sestiad

THE ARGUMENT OF THE THIRD SESTIAD

Leander to the envious light
Resigns his night-sports with the night,
And swims the Hellespont again.
Thesme,° the deity sovereign
Of customs and religious rites,
Appears, improving° his delights,
Since nuptial honours he neglected;
Which straight he vows shall be effected.
Fair Hero, left devirginate,
Weighs, and with fury wails her state:
But with her love and woman's wit
She argues and approveth it.

New light gives new directions,° fortunes new
To fashion our endeavours that ensue—
More harsh, at least more hard, more grave and high
Our subject runs, and our stern Muse must fly.
Love's edge is taken off, and that light flame,
Those thoughts, joys, longings, that before became
High unexperienced blood, and maids' sharp plights,
Must now grow staid, and censure the delights,
That, being enjoyed, ask judgment; now we praise,
As having parted: evenings crown the days.
    And now, ye wanton Loves, and young Desires,
Pied Vanity, the mint of strange attires,
Ye lisping Flatteries, and obsequious Glances,
Relentful° Musics, and attractive Dances,
And you detested Charms constraining love!
Shun love's stoln° sports by that these lovers prove.
    By this, the sovereign of heaven's golden fires,
And young Leander, lord of his desires,
Together from their lover's arms arose:
Leander into Hellespontus throws
His Hero-handled body, whose delight
Made him disdain each other epithite.
And so amidst the enamoured waves he swims,
The god of gold° of purpose gilt his limbs,

10

20

Hero and Leander See Marlowe's two Sestiads, below.
Thesme from the Greek *thesmos*, meaning "law": we shall see her named Ceremony below
improving reproving, condemning
New light . . . directions Chapman, starting out on the morning after Hero and Leander's first night of making love, connects his changing

subject—the legitimization of human passion in moral order—with a narrative new day's dawning.
Relentful relaxing, calming
stoln stolen
god of gold Apollo, because, here, the power of sunlight is imagined as creating it

That, this word *gilt* including double sense,
The double guilt of his incontinence
Might be expressed, that had no stay to employ
The treasure which the love-god let him joy
In his dear Hero, with such sacred thrift
30 As had beseemed so sanctified a gift;
But, like a greedy vulgar prodigal,
Would on the stock dispend,° and rudely fall,
Before his time, to that unblessèd blessing
Which, for lust's plague, doth perish with possessing:
Joy graven in sense,° like snow in water, wastes;
Without preserve of virtue, nothing lasts.
What man is he, that with a wealthy eye
Enjoys a beauty richer than the sky,
Through whose white skin, softer than soundest sleep,
40 With damask eyes the ruby blood doth peep,
And runs in branches through her azure veins,
Whose mixture and first fire his love attains;
Whose both hands limit both love's deities,°
And sweeten human thoughts like paradise;
Whose disposition silken is and kind.
Directed with an earth-exempted mind—
Who thinks not heaven with such a love is given?
And who, like earth, would spend that dower of heaven,
With rank desire to joy it all at first?
50 What simply kills our hunger, quencheth thirst,
Clothes but our nakedness and makes us live,
Praise doth not any of her favours give
But what doth plentifully minister
Beauteous apparel and delicious cheer,
So ordered that it still excites desire,
And still gives pleasures freeness to aspire,
The palm of Bounty ever moist preserving—
To Love's sweet life this is the courtly carving.°
Thus Time and all-states-ordering Ceremony°
60 Had banished all offence: Time's golden thigh°
Upholds the flowery body of the earth
In sacred harmony, and every birth
Of men and actions makes legitimate;
Being used aright, the use of time is fate.
    Yet did the gentle flood transfer once more
This prize of love home to his father's shore,
Where he unlades himself of that false wealth

---

dispend spend wastefully
graven in sense at a purely sensual level
deities Venus and Cupid
courtly carving showing the proper courtesy
all-states-ordering Ceremony the goddess will
appear shortly

Time's golden thigh the golden thigh, traditional
attribute of Pythagoras; here given to Time
because Pythagoras discovered numerical proportion, the "sacred harmony" on which the
order of creation depends

That makes few rich—treasures composed by stealth;
And to his sister, kind Hermione
70 (Who on the shore kneeled, praying to the sea
For his return), he all love's goods did show,
In Hero seized° for him, in him for Hero.
    His most kind sister all his secrets knew,
And to her, singing, like a shower, he flew,
Sprinkling the earth, that to their tombs took in
Streams dead for love, to leave his ivory skin,
Which yet a snowy foam did leave above,
As soul to the dead water that did love;
And from thence did the first white roses spring
80 (For love is sweet and fair in every thing),
And all the sweetened shore, as he did go,
Was crowned with odorous roses, white as snow.
Love-blest Leander was with love so filled,
That love to all that touched him he instilled;
And as the colours of all things we see,
To our sight's powers communicated be,
So to all objects that in compass came
Of any sense he had, his senses' flame
Flowed from his parts with force so virtual,
90 It fired with sense things mere° insensual.
    Now, with warm baths and odours comforted,
When he lay down, he kindly kissed his bed,
As consecrating it to Hero's right,
And vowed thereafter, that whatever sight
Put him in mind of Hero or her bliss,
Should be her altar to prefer° a kiss.
    Then laid he forth his late-enrichèd arms,
In whose white circle Love writ all his charms,
And made his characters° sweet Hero's limbs,
100 When on his breast's warm sea she sideling° swims;
And at those arms, held up in circle, met,
He said, 'See, sister, Hero's carquenet!'°
Which she had rather wear about her neck
Than all the jewels that do Juno deck.
    But, as he shook with passionate desire
To put in flame his other secret fire,
A music so divine did pierce his ear,
As never yet his ravished sense did hear;
When suddenly a light of twenty hues
110 Brake through the roof, and, like the rainbow, views
Amazed Leander: in whose beams came down

seized settled, established
mere totally
to prefer on which to proffer

characters the letters in which magician love
writes his charms
sideling sideways
carquenet jeweled collar or necklace

The goddess Ceremony,° with a crown
Of all the stars; and Heaven with her descended:
Her flaming hair to her bright feet extended,
By which hung all the bench of deities;
And in a chain,° compact° of ears and eyes,
She led Religion: all her body was
Clear and transparent as the purest glass,
For she was all presented to the sense:
120 Devotion, Order, State, and Reverence,
Here shadows were; Society, Memory;
All which her sight made live, her absence die.
A rich disparent pentacle° she wears,
Drawn full of circles and strange characters.
Her face was changeable to every eye;
One way looked ill, another graciously;
Which while men viewed they cheerful were and holy,
But looking off, vicious and melancholy.
The snaky paths to each observed law
130 Did Policy° in her broad bosom draw.
One hand a mathematic crystal° sways,
Which, gathering in one line a thousand rays
From her bright eyes, Confusion burns to death,
And all estates of men distinguisheth:
By it Morality and Comeliness
Themselves in all their sightly figures dress.
Her other hand a laurel rod applies,
To beat back Barbarism and Avarice,
That followed eating earth and excrement
140 And human limbs; and would make proud ascent
To seats of gods, were Ceremony slain.
The Hours and Graces bore her glorious train;
And all the sweets of our society
Were sphered and treasured in her bounteous eye.
Thus she appeared, and sharply did reprove
Leander's bluntness in his violent love:
Told him how poor was substance without rites,
Like bills unsigned; desires without delights;
Like meats unseasoned; like rank corn that grows
150 On cottages, that none or reaps or sows;
Not being with civil forms confirmed and bounded,

---

goddess Ceremony This allegorical figure is
Chapman's own, but she represents powerful
forces in the Renaissance world view; see the
relevant passage from Hooker's *Of the Laws of
Ecclesiastical Polity*, below; also, Prospero's
insistence on ceremonious marriage, *The Tempest* IV.
chain a version of the famous concept of the
Great Chain of Being, derived from Homer's
vision of Zeus' golden chain by which all the
other gods, earth, and sea were connected in
order and by which he could draw them all up
to Olympus. Spenser refers to it in *The Faerie
Queene* II.vii.46 as the "faire cheyne of love"
and Milton in the Second Prolusion as the
"universal concord and sweet union of all things
which Pythagoras poetically figures as harmony."
compact compounded
disparent pentacle multicolored five-pointed
star, emblematic of magical power
Policy governmental and legal manipulations
mathematic crystal probably a convex lens

For human dignities and comforts founded;
But loose and secret all their glories hide;
Fear fills the chamber. Darkness decks the bride.

.   .   .

1598

From Homer's Odyssey

[The Gardens of Alcinoüs°]
Without the hall, and close upon the gate,
A goodly orchard-ground was situate,
Of near ten acres; about which was led
A lofty quickset.᾽ In it flourishèd   *hedge*
High and broad fruit trees, that pomegranates bore,
Sweet figs, pears, olives; and a number more
Most useful plants did there produce their store;
Whose fruits the hardest winter could not kill,
160 Nor hottest summer wither. There was still
Fruit in his proper season all the year.
Sweet Zephyr breathed upon them blasts that were
Of varied tempers. These he made to bear
Ripe fruits, these blossoms. Pear grew after pear,
Apple succeeded apple, grape the grape,
Fig after fig came; time made never rape
Of any dainty there. A sprightly vine
Spread here his root, whose fruit a hot sunshine
Made ripe betimes; here grew another green.
170 Here some were gathering, here some pressing, seen.
A large-allotted several° each fruit had;
And all the adorned grounds their appearance made
In flower and fruit, at which the king did aim
To the precisest order he could claim.
    Two fountains graced the garden; of which one
Poured out a winding stream that over-run

The Gardens of Alcinoüs In the *Odyssey* VII.
85–135 the hero, after being washed up on the
shores of Phaeacia, proceeds to the palace of its
ruler, where he is beautifully entertained, and
where he narrates all of the adventures befall-
ing him from the time of leaving Troy to his stay
on Calypso's island. Phaeacia is a version of the
Great Good Place, and Odysseus is tempted
by its bounties (and by the innocent loveliness
of Nausicaa, Alcinous' daughter) to remain.
For the Renaissance, the Phaeacian gardens
were a classical parallel to the biblical Eden,
along with the Elysian Fields,
        Where Rhadamanthus rules, and where
        men live
    A never-troubled life, where snow, nor
    showers,

Nor irksome Winter spends his
    fruitless powers,
But from the ocean Zephyr still resumes
A constant breath, that all the fields
    perfumes.
                            (*Odyssey* IV. 762–66)
Visions of the pastoral realm involved this
garden world (see the passage from Sidney's
Old Arcadia, above), and English gardening
traditions were acutely aware of the literary
and pictorial background of their art. What
became the Continental formal garden in the
17th and 18th centuries, laid out geo-
metrically and schematically, corresponds to the
Phaeacian gardens; the English tradition, the
carefully arranged appearance of haphazard-
ness, can be thought of as mimetic of Eden.
several perhaps "a place allocated to it"

The grounds for their use chiefly; the other went
Close by the lofty palace gate, and lent
The city his sweet benefit. And thus
180   The Gods the court deckt of Alcinoüs.

1614

CHRISTOPHER MARLOWE
1564–1593

Marlowe was the son of a Canterbury shoemaker. Scholarships took him to the King's School, Canterbury, and then to Corpus Christi College, Cambridge, in 1580. He graduated B.A. in 1584, and satisfied requirements for the M.A. by March 1587; but the authorities withheld the degree. At this point there was an extraordinary intervention by the Queen's Privy Council, which explained that Marlowe did not, as the University apparently supposed, intend to go to Rheims, considered the center of Catholic conspiracy against Elizabeth, and that "he had done her Majestie good service," adding that the Queen thought it wrong for Marlowe to suffer because of this. He took the degree.

The University had probably expected him to take holy orders, and suspected that he was about to leave, a convert to Catholicism, for the English seminary at Rheims. In fact he had already been employed by the Government on some secret political mission. Thus, Marlowe's career as a playwright, which also began at Cambridge, was from the start superimposed on a more underground existence.

Tamburlaine (1587), with its superman hero and its "mighty line," practically invented English tragedy and its blank-verse medium. But its author apparently continued to lead a double life; two years later he was involved in a fatal sword fight, in London. Not surprisingly he acquired a reputation for violent manners, and also for "atheism." His friend Thomas Kyd, trying to explain some compromising papers found in the room they had shared, said after Marlowe's death that the poet would "jest at the divine scriptures, gibe at prayers," and the informer Richard Baines accused him of many "atheistical" remarks, such as "Christ was a bastard and his mother dishonest" or "the first beginning of religion was only to keep men in awe." (In Elizabethan English the term atheism applied to any extreme manifestation of impiety.) Baines also reported a remark suggestive of homosexuality, and *Edward II* (c. 1591), Marlowe's history play, shows discreet interest in the theme.

Marlowe's death in a way fitted this kind of life. In his last year, probably, he wrote *Doctor Faustus* and was perhaps working on *Hero and Leander* when, in May 1593, the Privy Council ordered his arrest. He was awaiting examination by them and reporting daily when, on May 30, he went to a Deptford tavern with Ingram Frizer, Nicholas Skeres, and Robert Poley. Frizer and Skeres were agents and swindlers, Poley a double-agent. After supper there was a quarrel about the check, and Marlowe, seizing Frizer's dagger, wounded him; whereupon Frizer stabbed him to death, later successfully pleading self-defense. Marlowe was twenty-nine years old.

As a poet Marlowe achieved both celebrity and infamy; he was "the Muses' darling" but also creator of "that atheist Tamburlaine"; he was "by profession a scholar . . . but by practice a playmaker, and a Poet of scurrility." His "high astounding terms"— as he calls them in the Prologue to *Tamburlaine*—and his admiration for the ambitious "overreacher" hero and the "Machiavel" introduced the great period of English drama and gave expression to that hubris attendant on the revaluation of human power we associate with the Renaissance. In the highly original *Jew of Malta*—"tragic farce" as T. S. Eliot called it—the aim of ambition is money; in *Doctor Faustus* it is knowledge. Thus Marlowe displays his heroes reacting to most of the temptations that Satan can contrive; and the culminating temptation, as in Andrew Marvell's "Dialogue Between Resolved Soul and Created Pleasure," in Spenser's Cave of Mammon, and in *Paradise Regained*, is the scholar's temptation, forbidden knowledge. The difference between Marlowe and the others is that his heroes do not resist the temptations, and he provides us, not with a negative proof of virtue and obedience to divine law, but with positive examples of what happens in their absence. Thus, whatever his intentions may have been, and however much he flouted convention, Marlowe's themes are finally reducible to the powerful formulae of contemporary religion and morality. The interest of the plays, except perhaps Part I of *Tamburlaine*, derives largely from an exhibition of heroic and unavailing resistance, which releases great moral and dramatic energy. In the poems, based on an Ovid liberated from the old moralizing, we can see that energy operating without such severe resistance, in verse that is self-delighting, strong and easy.

Doctor Faustus

By common consent Marlowe's greatest play, *Doctor Faustus*, can nevertheless try the reader's patience. One difficulty is that we are often uncertain about the authenticity of what we are reading. Marlowe collaborated with at least one other writer, and there are, broadly, two distinct versions of the play. The first, published in 1604, is probably based on the players' memories of a touring version, shorter than the original but including extra clowning scenes. The other, of 1616, was probably based on the original manuscripts but including theatrical revisions; unfortunately the editors also used the text of 1604 and made cuts and changes. Only since W. W. Greg published his edition in 1950 has it been possible to feel any assurance that one has something fairly close to what Marlowe and his collaborator wrote. The whole basis of Greg's "conjectural reconstruction" has recently been called into question by Fredson T. Bowers in an important article, but for the time being Greg's is the text on which secondary editions must depend.

We cannot now blame later interfering hands for the mixing of very bad with very fine material. From the beginning the play must have had scenes of second-rate farce, and there can never have been a version in which Faustus did not use his powers to absurdly trivial ends. For one thing, it was part of the conception that such a bargain could not be of high human use. Furthermore, the foolery that intervenes between the strong opening and the wonderful closing scene paid off in the popular theater, if not in terms of dramatic art. Marlowe left these scenes to the collaborator, perhaps Samuel Rowley, who knew how to write for the clowns and devils, and how to use the properties—the dragon, for example—of the Admiral's Men. He himself handled most, but not all, of the serious material; F. P. Wilson calculates that he was responsible for not more than 825 lines.

The comic material is developed from *The Damnable Life and Deserved Death of*

Doctor John Faustus, published in 1592—a free translation of a Lutheran German original of 1587. The *Damnable Life* was thus an anti-Catholic work, and the authors eked it out by referring also to that great English work of anti-papal propaganda, Foxe's *Acts and Monuments* (1563).

If the theme of the play can be reduced to a simple proposition, some words from *The Damnable Life* might serve: "Give none blame but thine own self-will, thy proud and aspiring mind, which both brought thee into the wrath of God and utter damnation." This is the moral, but it is of course complicated by Marlowe's ability to give powerfully attractive accounts of "proud and aspiring minds." The Faust story acquired a quasi-mythical status as an *exemplum* of the soul that yields to the last temptation of Satan, the temptation of knowledge.

This was a theme of high interest in Marlowe's time. The ecclesiastical ban on *curiositas*—the desire for forbidden knowledge—was constant, but the line between the licit and the wicked was differently drawn at different times and by different sects. In general the principle was that all knowledge which did not contribute to the salvation of the soul was wrong, whether sought out of pride or ambition. Yet knowledge of the creation—God's second book—could be good; where "curiosity" began and pious inquiry into the creatures left off was a question. In Marvell's "Dialogue Between the Resolved Soul and Created Pleasure" the tempter says

> Thou shalt know each hidden cause
>   And see the future time;
> Try what depth the center draws,
>   And then to heaven climb.

but the Resolved Soul rejects this; it would not help him to heaven, except in the sense that Faustus takes a trip to its frontiers with Mephostophilis. Faustus, on the other hand, accepts, for purely worldly reasons. He wants everything the good soul rejects: money, women, power. "The god thou serv'st is thine own appetite," he confesses. None of the questions to which, as a scholar, he values the answers are properly dealt with by Mephostophilis, and the devil, in Marlowe's parts of the play, does not conceal the pains of hell—the price of this essentially trivial and imperfect learning. So Faustus damns himself; his curiosity, like Eve's in *Paradise Lost* a tributary of pride, is proof against his occasional motions of repentance.

The greatness of the play lies not in its compliance with religious wisdom but in the resistance, not only of Faustus but of the very verse he speaks, to the law which must subdue him. There is, for example, a crisis when the demonic Helen appears; the Old Man has moved him, but the second apparition of Helen results from his deliberate choice; and by carnally embracing a demon he excludes "the grace of heaven," as the Old Man observes. Thus Faustus sins only by his own choice, here as elsewhere. But the address to Helen: "Was this the face that launched a thousand ships?" illustrates the resistance of the senses and poetry to the law. So in the opening, when Faustus, proud and inconsiderate in his scholarly ambition, rejects all human learning, and all the warnings of divinity, and wantonly sets out on his self-destructive course—"A sound magician is a demi-god"—his folly has a kind of poetic splendor; so has his blasphemy, when he uses the last words of Christ on the cross in sealing his bargain with Lucifer. Nearly all the rest till Helen comes—even the fine talk about astrology—is dross. Then, in Faustus's last speech, the first great tragic monologue of the English stage, we find a verse of Ovid, transplanted from its amorous context into this scholar's agony—a last poignant testimony of the struggle of the intellect and senses against the law.

It is as scholar and poet that the closing Chorus laments Faustus. The description, and the lament, fit Marlowe as well; learning, virtuosity in erotic and tragic verse, violence in action, a humane magniloquence not yet free of the religious bonds that restricted it: these are characteristic not only of the play and its author, but also of what we understand when we speak of "Renaissance Man."

Doctor Faustus

DRAMATIS PERSONAE

CHORUS

DR. JOHN FAUSTUS
WAGNER, *his servant, a student*
CORNELIUS ⎫
VALDES   ⎬ *his friends, magicians*
THREE SCHOLARS, *students under Faustus*
OLD MAN
POPE ADRIAN
RAYMOND, *King of Hungary*
BRUNO, *the rival Pope*
CARDINALS OF FRANCE AND PADUA
ARCHBISHOP OF RHEIMS
CHARLES V, *Emperor of Germany*
MARTINO   ⎫
FREDERICK ⎬ *knights at the Emperor's court*
BENVOLIO   ⎭
DUKE OF SAXONY
DUKE OF VANHOLT
DUCHESS OF VANHOLT

ROBIN
DICK
VINTNER
HORSE-COURSER
CARTER
HOSTESS
GOOD ANGEL
BAD ANGEL (*Spirit*)
MEPHOSTOPHILIS
LUCIFER
BELZEBUB
SPIRITS PRESENTING THE SEVEN DEADLY SINS
    ALEXANDER THE GREAT
    ALEXANDER'S PARAMOUR
    DARIUS, *King of Persia*
    HELEN OF TROY

DEVILS, CUPIDS, BISHOPS, MONKS, FRIARS, LORDS, SOLDIERS, ATTENDANTS

[PROLOGUE]

CHORUS

> Not marching in the fields of Thrasimene,°
> Where Mars did mate° the warlike Carthagens,
> Nor sporting in the dalliance of love
> In courts of kings where state° is overturned,
> Nor in the pomp of proud audacious deeds,
> Intends our muse° to vaunt his heavenly verse.

Thrasimene Lake Trasimene, scene of Hannibal's victory over Rome (217 B.C.), presumably treated in some lost play

mate ally with
state government
muse poet

Only this, Gentles: we must now perform
The form of Faustus' fortunes, good or bad.
And now to patient judgements we appeal,
And speak for Faustus in his infancy.
Now is he born, of parents base of stock,
In Germany, within a town called Rhode.°
At riper years to Wittenberg° he went,
Whereas° his kinsmen chiefly brought him up.
So much he profits in divinity,
The fruitful plot of scholarism° graced,
That shortly he was graced with doctor's name,
Excelling all whose sweet delight disputes
In heavenly matters of theology.
Till swol'n with cunning of a self-conceit,°
His waxen wings did mount above his reach,
And melting,° heavens conspired his overthrow.
For falling to a devilish exercise,
And glutted now with learning's golden gifts,
He surfeits upon cursèd necromancy;
Nothing so sweet as magic is to him,
Which he prefers before his chiefest bliss:°
And this the man that in his study sits.   *Exit.*

[SCENE I]

FAUSTUS *in his study.*°

FAUSTUS   Settle thy studies, Faustus, and begin
To sound the depth of that thou wilt profess.
Having commenced,° be a divine in show,°
Yet level° at the end of every art
And live and die in Aristotle's works.°
Sweet Analytics,° 'tis thou hast ravished me.
Bene disserere est finis logices.°
Is to dispute well logic's chiefest end?
Affords this art no greater miracle?
Then read no more, thou hast attained that end.
A greater subject fitteth Faustus' wit:

Rhode Roda (now Stadtroda) in central Germany
Wittenberg German university (Luther was an alumnus)
Whereas where
plot of scholarism garden of scholarship
cunning . . . self-conceit intellectual pride arising from arrogance
melting when they melted; Marlowe is thinking of Icarus
chiefest bliss heaven
in his study The curtain has been drawn, revealing Faustus in the alcove at the back of the stage.
commenced taken a degree
in show ostensibly
level aim
Aristotle's works These still dominated the university curriculum, though they were increasingly challenged.
Analytics Aristotle's work on the nature of proof
Bene . . . logices "To argue well is the end of logic"; not from Aristotle but his 16th-century opponent Ramus

Bid *on kai me on*° farewell; Galen,° come.
Seeing, *ubi desinit philosophus, ibi incipit medicus.*°
Be a physician, Faustus, heap up gold
And be eternized° for some wondrous cure.
Summum bonum medicinae sanitas:°
The end of physic is our body's health.
Why Faustus, hast thou not attained that end?
Is not thy common talk sound aphorisms?°
20   Are not thy bills° hung up as monuments,
Whereby whole cities have escaped the plague,
And thousand desperate maladies been cured?
Yet art thou still but Faustus, and a man.
Couldst thou make men to live eternally,
Or being dead, raise them to life again,
Then this profession were to be esteemed.
Physic, farewell. Where is Justinian?°
Si una eademque res legatur duobus,
Alter rem, alter valorem rei°—*etc.,*
30   A petty case of paltry legacies!
Exhaereditare filium non potest pater, nisi°—
Such is the subject of the Institute°
And universal body of the law.
This study fits a mercenary drudge,
Who aims at nothing but external trash,°
Too servile and illiberal for me.
When all is done divinity is best.
Jerome's Bible,° Faustus, view it well.
Stipendium peccati mors est.° Ha! *Stipendium, etc.,*
40   The reward of sin is death. That's hard.
Si pecasse negamus, fallimur, et nulla est in nobis veritas.°
If we say that we have no sin we deceive ourselves, and there is no truth
    in us. Why then, belike we must sin, and so consequently die.°
Ay, we must die an everlasting death.
What doctrine call you this? *Che sera, sera.*
What will be, shall be. Divinity, adieu!
These metaphysics of magicians
And necromantic books are heavenly;
Lines, circles, signs, letters and characters:
50   Ay, these are those that Faustus most desires.

---

on kai me on being and not being (Greek)
Galen Greek writer on medicine (*c.* 129–199 A.D.)
ubi desinit . . . medicus "where the philosopher leaves off, the doctor begins" (Aristotle, *De Sensu*)
eternized made immortal
Summum . . . sanitas translated in next line
aphorisms medical precepts
bills prescriptions
Justinian 6th-century Roman emperor who codified the law
Si una . . . rei "if one and the same thing is bequeathed to two persons, one shall have

the thing itself, the other the value of the thing"
Exhaereditare . . . nisi "a father cannot disinherit his son unless"
Institute Justinian's collection is called the *Institutes;* these Latin quotations derive from it.
trash money
Jerome's Bible the Vulgate, Latin Bible formerly used by Catholics, based on the translation of St. Jerome completed in 405 A.D.
Stipendium . . . est Romans 6:23
Si . . . veritas 1 John 1:8
Why then . . . die Faustus omits considering the Christian doctrine of redemption.

O what a world of profit and delight,
Of power, of honour, of omnipotence,
Is promised to the studious artisan!°
All things that move between the quiet° poles
Shall be at my command. Emperors and kings
Are but obeyed in their several° provinces.
Nor can they raise the wind or rend the clouds.
But this dominion that exceeds in this
Stretcheth as far as doth the mind of man:
60   A sound magician is a demi-god.
Here tire,° my brains to get° a deity.

Enter WAGNER.

Wagner, commend me to my dearest friends,
The German Valdes and Cornelius.
Request them earnestly to visit me.

WAGNER   I will sir.   *Exit*

FAUSTUS   Their conference° will be a greater help to me
Than all my labours, plod I ne'er so fast.

Enter the ANGEL *and* SPIRIT.°

GOOD ANGEL   O Faustus, lay that damnèd book aside,
And gaze not on it lest it tempt thy soul,
70   And heap God's heavy wrath upon thy head.
Read, read the scriptures: that is blasphemy.

BAD ANGEL   Go forward, Faustus, in that famous art
Wherein all nature's treasury is contained.
Be thou on earth as Jove° is in the sky,
Lord and commander of these elements.   *Exeunt* ANGELS.

FAUSTUS   How am I glutted with conceit° of this!
Shall I make spirits fetch me what I please,
Resolve me of all ambiguities,
Perform what desperate enterprise I will?
80   I'll have them fly to India for gold,
Ransack the ocean for orient pearl,
And search all corners of the new-found world
For pleasant fruits and princely delicates;°
I'll have them read me strange philosophy,
And tell the secrets of all foreign kings;
I'll have them wall all Germany with brass,°
And make swift Rhine circle fair Wittenberg;
I'll have them fill the public schools with silk,
Wherewith the students shall be bravely clad;

---

artisan artist; here, practitioner of magic
quiet motionless
several respective
tire tire yourselves
get beget
conference conversation
Spirit Bad Angel (devil)

Jove God
conceit the idea
delicates delicacies
wall . . . brass The 13th-century English scholar-alchemist Roger Bacon, in Robert Greene's play *Friar Bacon and Friar Bungay* (1594), planned to wall England thus.

90   I'll levy soldiers with the coin they bring,
And chase the Prince of Parma° from our land,
And reign sole king of all the provinces.
Yea, stranger engines for the brunt of war
Than was the fiery keel at Antwerp's bridge°
I'll make my servile spirits to invent.
Come, German Valdes and Cornelius,
And make me blest with your sage conference.

Enter VALDES *and* CORNELIUS.

Valdes, sweet Valdes and Cornelius!
Know that your words have won me at the last
100   To practise magic and concealèd arts.
Yet not your words only but mine own fantasy°
That will receive no object for my head,
But ruminates on necromantic skill.
Philosophy is odious and obscure,
Both law and physic are for petty wits;
Divinity is basest of the three,
Unpleasant, harsh, contemptible and vile.
'Tis magic, magic that hath ravished me.
Then, gentle friends, aid me in this attempt,
110   And I, that have with concise syllogisms
Gravelled° the pastors of the German church
And made the flowering pride of Wittenberg
Swarm to my problems as the infernal spirits
On sweet Musaeus° when he came to hell,
Will be as cunning as Agrippa° was,
Whose shadows made all Europe honour him.
VALDES   Faustus, these books, thy wit and our experience
Shall make all nations to canónize us.
As Indian Moors obey their Spanish lords,
120   So shall the spirits of every element
Be always serviceable to us three.
Like lions shall they guard us when we please,
Like Almain rutters° with their horsemen's staves,
Or Lapland giants trotting by our sides;
Sometimes like women or unwedded maids,
Shadowing more beauty in their airy brows
Than has the white breasts of the Queen of Love.
From Venice shall they drag huge argosies,
And from America the golden fleece°

Prince of Parma Spanish governor of the Netherlands provinces 1579–92, and enemy of the
English
fiery keel . . . bridge a fireship that destroyed
the bridge Parma had built over the Scheldt
fantasy imagination
Gravelled brought down

Musaeus legendary Greek poet, perhaps here
confused with Orpheus
Agrippa Cornelius Agrippa (1485–1535), humanist and mage
Almain rutters German cavalry
the golden fleece object of Jason's voyage in
the *Argo*, but Marlowe is thinking of the
treasure fleets of Philip II of Spain

130   That yearly stuffs old Philip's treasury,
            If learned Faustus will be resolute.
    FAUSTUS   Valdes, as resolute am I in this
            As thou to live, therefore object it not.°
    CORNELIUS   The miracles that magic will perform
            Will make thee vow to study nothing else.
            He that is grounded in astrology,
            Enriched with tongues, well seen° in minerals,
            Hath all the principles magic doth require.
            Then doubt not, Faustus, but to be renowned,
140   And more frequented for this mystery
            Than heretofore the Delphian oracle.
            The spirits tell me they can dry the sea,
            And fetch the treasure of all foreign wrecks—
            Ay, all the wealth that our forefathers hid
            Within the massy entrails of the earth
            Then tell me, Faustus, what shall we three want?
    FAUSTUS   Nothing, Cornelius! O, this cheers my soul.
            Come, show me some demonstrations magical,
            That I may conjure in some lusty° grove,
150   And have these joys in full possession.
    VALDES   Then haste thee to some solitary grove,
            And bear wise Bacon's and Abanus' works,°
            The Hebrew Psalter and New Testament;°
            And whatsoever else is requisite
            We will inform thee ere our conference cease.
    CORNELIUS   Valdes, first let him know the words of art,
            And then, all other ceremonies learned,
            Faustus may try his cunning° by himself.
    VALDES   First I'll instruct thee in the rudiments,
160   And then wilt thou be perfecter than I.
    FAUSTUS   Then come and dine with me, and after meat
            We'll canvass every quiddity° thereof,
            For ere I sleep, I'll try what I can do.
            This night I'll conjure, though I die therefore.   *Exeunt omnes.*

        [SCENE II]

        Enter two SCHOLARS.

    1 SCHOLAR   I wonder what's become of Faustus, that was wont to make our
        schools ring with *sic probo.*°

object it not do not object to it
well seen well versed
lusty pleasant
Bacon's and Abanus' works Roger Bacon (see
l. 86n) and Pietro d'Abano (1250?–1316?),
Italian philospher and magician
Hebrew . . . Testament Psalms 22 and 51, and

the opening words of St. John's gospel, were
used in conjuring spirits.
cunning skill
quiddity fine point
sic probo "thus I prove it" (used in scholastic
disputation)

Enter WAGNER.

2 SCHOLAR That shall we presently° know. Here comes his boy.

1 SCHOLAR How now, sirrah, where's thy master?

WAGNER God in heaven knows.

2 SCHOLAR Why, dost not thou know then?

WAGNER Yes, I know, but that follows not.

1 SCHOLAR Go to, sirrah, leave your jesting and tell us where he is.

WAGNER That follows not by force of argument, which you, being licentiates,°
10 should stand° upon; therefore acknowledge your error and be attentive.

2 SCHOLAR Then you will not tell us?

WAGNER You are deceived, for I will tell you. Yet if you were not dunces, you
would never ask me such a question. For is he not *corpus naturale?* And is
not that *mobile?*° Then wherefore should you ask me such a question? But
that I am by nature phlegmatic, slow to wrath and prone to lechery (to love,
I would say), it were not for you to come within forty foot of the place of
execution,° although I do not doubt but to see you both hanged the next
sessions. Thus, having triumphed over you, I will set my countenance like a
precisian,° and begin to speak thus: Truly, my dear brethren, my master is
20 within at dinner with Valdes and Cornelius, as this wine, if it could speak,
would inform your worships. And so the Lord bless you, preserve you and
keep you, my dear brethren.   *Exit.*

1 SCHOLAR O Faustus, then I fear that which I have long suspected
That thou art fallen into that damnèd art
For which they two are infamous through the world.

2 SCHOLAR Were he a stranger, not allied to me,
The danger of his soul would make me mourn.
But come, let us go and inform the Rector;°
It may be his grave counsel may reclaim him.

1 SCHOLAR I fear me nothing will reclaim him now.

2 SCHOLAR Yet let us see what we can do.   *Exeunt.*

[SCENE III]

Thunder. Enter LUCIFER *and four* DEVILS *[above].* FAUSTUS *to them with
this speech.*

FAUSTUS Now that the gloomy shadow of the night,
Longing to view Orion's drizzling looks,°
Leaps from the antarctic° world unto the sky,
And dims the welkin° with her pitchy breath,

---

presently immediately
licentiates qualified to go on to the master's or
doctor's degree
stand rely
corpus naturale . . . mobile *corpus naturale
seu mobile* ("a natural body and as such
capable of movement") was the Aristotelian
definition of the subject matter of physics;
Wagner had picked it up from his betters.

place of execution dining room, but he carries
on the criminal sense
precisian puritan
Rector head of the University
Orion's . . . looks Orion was traditionally a
rainy constellation
Now that . . . antarctic a strange supposition,
that night comes on from the south
welkin sky

Faustus, begin thine incantations
And try if devils will obey thy hest,°
Seeing thou hast prayed and sacrificed to them.
Within this circle is Jehovah's name
Forward and backward anagrammatized:
10 The abbreviated names of holy saints,
Figures of every adjunct° to the heavens,
And characters° of signs and erring stars°
By which the spirits are enforced to rise.
Then fear not, Faustus, to be resolute
And try the utmost magic can perform.   *Thunder.*

Sint mihi dei Acherontis propitii; valeat numen triplex Jehovae; ignei, aerii,
aquatici, terreni spiritus salvete! Orientis princeps, Belzebub inferni ardentis
monarcha, et Demogorgon, propitiamus vos, ut appareat, et surgat, Me-
phostophilis.   *Dragon [appears above.]*

20 *Quid tu moraris? Per Jehovam, Gehannam, et consecratam aquam quam nunc*
spargo; signumque crucis quod nunc facio; et per vota nostra, ipse nunc surgat
nobis dicatus Mephostophilis.°

Enter a DEVIL.°

I charge thee to return and change thy shape,
Thou art too ugly to attend on me.
Go, and return an old Franciscan friar,
That holy shape becomes a devil best.   *Exit* DEVIL.
I see there's virtue in my heavenly words!
Who would not be proficient in this art?
How pliant is this Mephostophilis,
30 Full of obedience and humility,
Such is the force of magic and my spells.
Now, Faustus, thou art conjurer laureate,°
That canst command great Mephostophilis.
Quin redis, Mephostophilis, fratris imagine!°

Enter MEPHOSTOPHILIS.

MEPHOSTOPHILIS   Now Faustus, what wouldst thou have me do?
FAUSTUS   I charge thee wait upon me whilst I live,
To do whatever Faustus shall command,
Be it to make the moon drop from her sphere,
Or the ocean to overwhelm the world.

hest command
adjunct heavenly body
characters Rays from the stars were thought to
mark certain earthly objects, giving them magical power in the hands of the adept.
signs and erring stars signs of the Zodiac and
planets
Sint . . . Mephostophilis "May the gods of
hell be favorable to me; farewell to the threefold spirit of God; hail, spirits of fire, air,
water and earth! O prince of the East [Lucifer],
Beelzebub monarch of burning hell, and De-

mogorgon, we beseech you that Mephostophilis
should appear and rise. Why do you delay?
By Jehovah, hell, and the holy water that I
now sprinkle; by the sign of the cross that I
now make; and by our prayers, may Mephostophilis himself now rise, compelled to obey
us."
Devil Mephostophilis in devilish form
laureate singled out for honors
Quin . . . imagine "Why do you not return,
Mephostophilis, in the likeness of a friar?"

40

MEPHOSTOPHILIS   I am a servant to great Lucifer,
And may not follow thee without his leave;
No more than he commands must we perform.
FAUSTUS   Did not he charge thee to appear to me?
MEPHOSTOPHILIS   No, I came now hither of mine own accord.
FAUSTUS   Did not my conjuring speeches raise thee? Speak.
MEPHOSTOPHILIS   That was the cause, but yet *per accidens;*°
For when we hear one rack° the name of God,
Abjure the scriptures and his saviour Christ,
We fly in hope to get his glorious soul;
Nor will we come unless he use such means
Whereby he is in danger to be damned.
Therefore the shortest cut for conjuring
Is stoutly to abjure the Trinity
And pray devoutly to the prince of hell.°
FAUSTUS   So Faustus hath already done, and holds this principle:
There is no chief but only Belzebub,
To whom Faustus doth dedicate himself.
This word 'damnation' terrifies not him,
For he confounds hell in Elysium.°
His ghost be with the old philosophers.°
But leaving these vain trifles of men's souls,
Tell me, what is that Lucifer, thy lord?
MEPHOSTOPHILIS   Arch-regent and commander of all spirits.
FAUSTUS   Was not that Lucifer an angel once?
MEPHOSTOPHILIS   Yes Faustus, and most dearly loved of God.
FAUSTUS   How come it then that he is prince of devils?
MEPHOSTOPHILIS   O, by aspiring pride and insolence,
For which God threw him from the face of heaven.
FAUSTUS   And what are you that live with Lucifer?
MEPHOSTOPHILIS   Unhappy spirits that fell with Lucifer,
Conspired against our God with Lucifer,
And are for ever damned with Lucifer.
FAUSTUS   Where are you damned?
MEPHOSTOPHILIS   In hell.
FAUSTUS   How comes it then that thou art out of hell?
MEPHOSTOPHILIS   Why, this is hell, nor am I out of it.°
Think'st thou that I who saw the face of God
And tasted the eternal joys of heaven,
Am not tormented with ten thousand hells

---

per accidens i.e. not the essential cause but an incidental contribution; a scholastic expression
rack torment
For when . . . hell (ll. 47–54) In this speech Mephostophilis clarifies an important point; it is not conjuring itself that damns a man, but the evidence it provides that he is a likely subject for diabolic treatment; consequently the bond Faustus signs is not in itself irrevocable; he must damn himself otherwise.

confounds . . . Elysium does not distinguish between hell and Elysium (the pagan afterworld)
old philosophers who lived before the Redemption and neither knew of nor could go to Heaven
this is hell . . . it Cf. Milton's Satan, "Which way I fly is Hell; my self am Hell" (*Paradise Lost* IV.75); other Miltonic resemblances will be noticed.

80   In being deprived of everlasting bliss?°
           O Faustus, leave these frivolous demands,
           Which strikes a terror to my fainting soul.
FAUSTUS   What, is great Mephostophilis so passionate°
           For being deprivèd of the joys of heaven?
           Learn thou of Faustus manly fortitude,
           And scorn those joys thou never shalt possess.
           Go, bear these tidings to great Lucifer,
           Seeing Faustus hath incurred eternal death
           By desperate thoughts against Jove's deity.
90   Say he surrenders up to him his soul,
           So° he will spare him four and twenty years,
           Letting him live in all voluptuousness,
           Having thee ever to attend on me,
           To give me whatsoever I shall ask,
           To tell me whatsoever I demand,
           To slay mine enemies and aid my friends
           And always be obedient to my will.
           Go, and return to mighty Lucifer,
           And meet me in my study at midnight,
100   And then resolve me of thy master's mind.
MEPHOSTOPHILIS   I will, Faustus.   *Exit.*
FAUSTUS   Had I as many souls as there be stars,
           I'd give them all for Mephostophilis.
           By him I'll be great emperor of the world,
           And make a bridge through the moving air
           To pass the ocean with a band of men;
           I'll join the hills that bind the Afric shore,
           And make that country continent to° Spain,
           And both contributory° to my crown.
110   The Emperor shall not live but by my leave,
           Nor any potentate of Germany.
           Now that I have obtained what I desire
           I'll live in speculation° of this art
           Till Mephostophilis return again.   *Exit.*
           [*Exeunt* LUCIFER *and* DEVILS.]

[SCENE IV]

Enter WAGNER *and the* CLOWN [ROBIN].

WAGNER   Come hither, sirrah boy.
ROBIN   Boy? O disgrace to my person! Zounds, boy in your face! You have seen
many boys with such pickadevants,° I am sure.

---

deprived . . . bliss traditionally the most painful punishment of the damned
passionate sorrowful
So on condition that

continent to continuous with
contributory i.e. paying tribute
speculation contemplation
pickadevants pointed beards

WAGNER   Sirrah, hast thou no comings in?°

ROBIN   Yes, and goings out° too, you may see, sir.

WAGNER   Alas, poor slave, see how poverty jests in his nakedness. I know the
villain's out of service and so hungry that I know he would give his soul to
the devil for a shoulder of mutton, though it were blood-raw.

ROBIN   Not so neither. I had need to have it well roasted, and good sauce to it,
10   if I pay so dear, I can tell you.

WAGNER   Sirrah, wilt thou be my man and wait on me? And I will make thee
go like *Qui mihi discipulus*.°

ROBIN   What, in verse?

WAGNER   No, slave, in beaten silk° and stavesacre.°

ROBIN   Stavesacre? That's good to kill vermin; then belike if I serve you I shall
be lousy.

WAGNER   Why, so thou shalt be whether thou dost it or no; for, sirrah, if thou
dost not presently bind thyself to me for seven years, I'll turn all the lice
about thee into familiars° and make them tear thee in pieces.

20   ROBIN   Nay sir, you may save yourself a labour, for they are as familiar with me
as if they paid for their meat and drink, I can tell you.

WAGNER   Well sirrah, leave your jesting and take these guilders.°

ROBIN   Yes, marry sir, and I thank you too.

WAGNER   So, now thou art to be at an hour's warning, whensoever and wheresoever the devil shall fetch thee.

ROBIN   Here, take your guilders, I'll none of 'em.

WAGNER   Not I, thou art pressed;° prepare thyself, for I will presently raise up
two devils to carry thee away. Banio! Belcher!

ROBIN   Belcher? And° Belcher come here, I'll belch him! I am not afraid of a
30   devil.

Enter two DEVILS, *and the* CLOWN *runs up and down crying.*

WAGNER   How now, sir, will you serve me now?

ROBIN   Ay, good Wagner; take away the devil then.

WAGNER   Spirits, away!   *Exeunt* [DEVILS].
              Now, sirrah, follow me.

ROBIN   I will sir. But hark you master, will you teach me this conjuring occupation?

WAGNER   Ay sirrah, I'll teach thee to turn thyself to a dog, or a cat, or a mouse,
or a rat, or anything.

ROBIN   A dog, or a cat, or a mouse, or a rat! O brave, Wagner.

WAGNER   Villain, call me Master Wagner, and see that you walk attentively,
40   and let your right eye be always diametrally° fixed upon my left heel, that
thou mayst *quasi vestigiis nostris insistere*.°

ROBIN   Well sir, I warrant you.   *Exeunt.*

comings in earnings, income
goings out expenses
Qui . . . discipulus "You who are my pupil"
(opening words of a didactic poem for school-
boys, used in Elizabethan schools)
beaten silk embroidered silk; Wagner means
he will beat him
stavesacre flea powder

familiars attendant devils
guilders Dutch money
pressed hired, drafted
And if
diametrally directly
quasi . . . insistere "follow as it were in our
footsteps"

[SCENE V]

Enter FAUSTUS *in his study.*

FAUSTUS   Now, Faustus, must thou needs be damned?
And canst thou not be saved.
What boots it then to think on God or heaven?
Away with such vain fancies, and despair;
Despair in God, and trust in Belzebub.
Now go not backward; no, Faustus, be resolute.
Why waver'st thou? O something soundeth in mine ears,
'Abjure this magic, turn to God again.'
Ay, and Faustus will turn to God again.
10   To God? He loves thee not.
The God thou serv'st is thine own appetite,
Wherein is fixed the love of Belzebub.
To him, I'll build an altar and a church,
And offer lukewarm blood of new-born babes.

Enter the two ANGELS.

GOOD ANGEL   Sweet Faustus, leave that execrable art.
FAUSTUS   Contrition, prayer, repentance, what of these?
GOOD ANGEL   O they are means to bring thee unto heaven.
BAD ANGEL   Rather illusions, fruits of lunacy,
That make men foolish that do trust them most.
20   GOOD ANGEL   Sweet Faustus, think of heaven and heavenly things.
BAD ANGEL   No, Faustus, think of honour and of wealth.   *Exeunt* ANGELS.
FAUSTUS   Of wealth!
Why, the signory° of Emden° shall be mine!
When Mephostophilis shall stand by me,
What God can hurt me? Faustus, thou art safe;
Cast no more doubts. Mephostophilis, come,
And bring glad tidings from great Lucifer.
Is it not midnight? Come Mephostophilis!
Veni,° veni, Mephostophile!

Enter MEPHOSTOPHILIS.

30   Now tell me, what saith Lucifer, thy lord?
MEPHOSTOPHILIS   That I shall wait on Faustus whilst he lives,
So he will buy my service with his soul.
FAUSTUS   Already Faustus hath hazarded that for thee.
MEPHOSTOPHILIS   But now thou must bequeath it solemnly,
And write a deed of gift with thine own blood,
For that security craves Lucifer.
If thou deny it, I must back to hell.
FAUSTUS   Stay, Mephostophilis, and tell me

signory lordship   **Veni** come
Emden large northwest German port, trading
with England

FAUSTUS   What good will my soul do thy lord?

40   MEPHOSTOPHILIS   Enlarge his kingdom.

FAUSTUS   Is that the reason why he tempts us thus?

MEPHOSTOPHILIS   *Solamen miseris, socios habuisse doloris.*°

FAUSTUS   Why, have you any pain, that torture other?°

MEPHOSTOPHILIS   As great as have the human souls of men.
But tell me, Faustus, shall I have thy soul?
And I will be thy slave and wait on thee,
And give thee more than thou hast wit to ask.

FAUSTUS   Ay, Mephostophilis, I'll give it him.

MEPHOSTOPHILIS   Then, Faustus, stab thy arm courageously,

50   And bind thy soul, that at some certain day
Great Lucifer may claim it as his own,
And then be thou as great as Lucifer.

FAUSTUS   Lo, Mephostophilis, for love of thee
Faustus hath cut his arm, and with his proper° blood
Assures his soul to be great Lucifer's,
Chief lord and regent of perpetual night.
View here this blood that trickles from mine arm,
And let it be propitious for my wish.

MEPHOSTOPHILIS   But, Faustus,

60   Write it in manner of a deed of gift.

FAUSTUS   Ay, so I will. But, Mephostophilis,
My blood congeals and I can write no more!

MEPHOSTOPHILIS   I'll fetch thee fire to dissolve it straight.   *Exit.*

FAUSTUS   What might the staying of my blood portend?
Is it unwilling I should write this bill?
Why streams° it not that I may write afresh?
'Faustus gives to thee his soul': ah, there it stayed!
Why shouldst thou not? Is not thy soul thine own?
Then write again: 'Faustus gives to thee his soul.'

Enter MEPHOSTOPHILIS *with the chafer*° *of fire.*

70   MEPHOSTOPHILIS   See Faustus, here is fire; set it on.

FAUSTUS   So, now the blood begins to clear again;
Now will I make an end immediately.

MEPHOSTOPHILIS   What will not I do to obtain his soul!

FAUSTUS   *Consummatum est:*° this bill is ended,
And Faustus hath bequeathed his soul to Lucifer.
But what is this inscription on mine arm?
Homo fuge!° Whither should I flie?
If unto God, he'll throw me down to hell.
My senses are deceived: here's nothing writ!

Solamen . . . doloris "it is a comfort to the wretched to have companions in distress"
that torture other you that torture others
proper own
streams The word is used of Christ's blood in the closing scene.

chafer portable grate
Consummatum est "it is finished"; last words of Christ on the Cross, John 20:30
Homo fuge fly, O man

80 O yes, I see it plain. Even here is writ
      Homo fuge! Yet shall not Faustus fly.
MEPHOSTOPHILIS   I'll fetch him somewhat to delight his mind.   *Exit.*

      Enter DEVILS, *giving crowns and rich apparel to* FAUSTUS; *they dance
      and then depart. Enter* MEPHOSTOPHILIS.

FAUSTUS   What means this show? Speak, Mephostophilis.
MEPHOSTOPHILIS   Nothing, Faustus, but to delight thy mind,
      And let thee see what magic can perform.
FAUSTUS   But may I raise such spirits when I please?
MEPHOSTOPHILIS   Ay, Faustus, and do greater things than these.
FAUSTUS   Then Mephostophilis, receive this scroll,
      A deed of gift, of body and of soul:
90   But yet conditionally, that thou perform
      All covenants and articles between us both.
MEPHOSTOPHILIS   Faustus, I swear by hell and Lucifer
      To effect all promises between us made.
FAUSTUS   Then hear me read it, Mephostophilis.
      On these conditions following:
      'First, that Faustus may be a spirit in form and substance.
      'Secondly, that Mephostophilis shall be his servant, and at his command.
100   'Thirdly, that Mephostophilis shall do for him, and bring him whatsoever.
      'Fourthly, that he shall be in his chamber or house invisible.
      'Lastly, that he shall appear to the said John Faustus at all times in
      what form or shape soever he please.
      'I John Faustus of Wittenberg, doctor, by these presents, do give both
      body and soul to Lucifer, Prince of the East, and his minister Mephostophilis,
      and furthermore grant unto them that, four-and-twenty years being expired,
      the articles above written inviolate,° full power to fetch or carry the said
      John Faustus, body and soul, flesh, blood or goods, into their habitation
      wheresoever.
110   'By me John Faustus.'
MEPHOSTOPHILIS   Speak, Faustus, do you deliver this as your deed?
FAUSTUS   Ay, take it, and the devil give thee good on it.
MEPHOSTOPHILIS   Now, Faustus, ask what thou wilt.
FAUSTUS   First will I question with thee about hell.
      Tell me, where is the place that men call hell?
MEPHOSTOPHILIS   Under the heavens.
FAUSTUS   Ay, so are all things else; but whereabouts?
MEPHOSTOPHILIS   Within the bowels of these elements,
      Where we are tortured and remain for ever.
120   Hell hath no limits, nor is circumscribed
      In one self place,° but where we are is hell,
      And where hell is, there must we ever be.
      And to be short, when all the world dissolves
      And every creature shall be purified,

inviolate, not having been violated   one self place one and the same place

All places shall be hell that is not heaven.

FAUSTUS   I think hell's a fable.

MEPHOSTOPHILIS   Ay, think so still, till experience change thy mind.

FAUSTUS   Why, does thou think that Faustus shall be damned?

MEPHOSTOPHILIS   Ay, of necessity, for here's the scroll
130   In which thou hast given thy soul to Lucifer.

FAUSTUS   Ay, and body too, but what of that?
          Think'st thou that Faustus is so fond° to imagine
          That after this life there is any pain?
          Tush, these are trifles and mere old wives' tales.

MEPHOSTOPHILIS   But I am an instance to prove the contrary,
          For I tell thee I am damned, and now in hell.

FAUSTUS   Nay, and this be hell, I'll willingly be damned.
          What, sleeping, eating, walking and disputing?
          But leaving this, let me have a wife, the fairest maid in Germany, for
140   I am wanton and lascivious, and cannot live without a wife.

MEPHOSTOPHILIS   How, a wife? I prithee, Faustus, talk not of a wife.

FAUSTUS   Nay, sweet Mephostophilis, fetch me one, for I will have one.

MEPHOSTOPHILIS   Well, thou wilt have one. Sit there till I come: I'll fetch thee
          a wife in the devil's name.   [*Exit.*]

          Enter with a DEVIL *dressed like a woman, with fireworks.*

          Tell me, Faustus, how dost thou like thy wife?

FAUSTUS   A plague on her for a hot whore.

MEPHOSTOPHILIS   Marriage is but a ceremonial toy,
          And if thou lovest me, think no more of it.
          I'll cull thee out the fairest courtesans
150   And bring them every morning to thy bed:
          She whom thine eye shall like, thy heart shall have,
          Were she as chaste as was Penelope,°
          As wise as Saba,° or as beautiful
          As was bright Lucifer before his fall.
          Hold, take this book, peruse it thoroughly:
          The iterating° of these lines brings gold,
          The framing of this circle on the ground
          Brings thunder, whirlwinds, storm and lightning.°
          Pronounce this thrice devoutly to thyself
160   And men in harness° shall appear to thee,
          Ready to execute what thou command'st.

FAUSTUS   Thanks, Mephostophilis. Yet fain would I have a book wherein I
          might behold all spells and incantations, that I might raise up spirits when
          I please.

MEPHOSTOPHILIS   Here they are in this book.   *There turn to them.*

FAUSTUS   Now would I have a book where I might see all characters and

---

fond foolish
Penelope the faithful wife of Ulysses
Saba Queen of Sheba

iterating repetition
lightning trisyllabic; pronounced **light-en-ing**
harness armor

planets of the heavens, that I might know their motions and dispositions.°
MEPHOSTOPHILIS   Here they are too.   *Turn to them.*
FAUSTUS   Nay, let me have one book more, and then I have done, wherein I
170   might see all plants, herbs and trees that grow upon the the earth.
MEPHOSTOPHILIS   Here they be.
FAUSTUS   Oh thou art deceived.
MEPHOSTOPHILIS   Tut, I warrant° thee.   *Turn to them.*
                                                                Exeunt.

[SCENE VI°]

Enter FAUSTUS *in his study, and* MEPHOSTOPHILIS.

FAUSTUS   When I behold the heavens then I repent,
          And curse thee, wicked Mephostophilis,
          Because thou hast deprived me of those joys.
MEPHOSTOPHILIS   'Twas thine own seeking, Faustus, thank thyself.
          But think'st thou heaven is such a glorious thing?
          I tell thee, Faustus, it is not half so fair
          As thou or any man that breathes on earth.
FAUSTUS   How prov'st thou that?
MEPHOSTOPHILIS   'Twas made for man; then he's more excellent.
10   FAUSTUS   If heaven was made for man, 'twas made for me.
          I will renounce this magic and repent.

Enter the two ANGELS.

GOOD ANGEL   Faustus, repent; yet God will pity thee.
BAD ANGEL   Thou art a spirit;° God cannot pity thee.
FAUSTUS   Who buzzeth° in mine ears I am a spirit?
          Be I a devil, yet God may pity me;
          Yea, God will pity me if I repent.
BAD ANGEL   Ay, but Faustus never shall repent.   *Exeunt* ANGELS.
FAUSTUS   My heart's so hardened I cannot repent.
          Scarce can I name salvation, faith or heaven,
20   But fearful echoes thunders in mine ears
          'Faustus, thou art damned'; then swords and knives,
          Poison, guns, halters and envenomed steel
          Are laid before me to dispatch myself.
          And long ere this I should have done the deed,
          Had not sweet pleasure conquered deep despair.
          Have not I made blind Homer sing to me
          Of Alexander's love and Oenon's death?°
          And hath not he, that built the walls of Thebes

---

dispositions situations
warrant assure
Scene VI A scene, presumably comic, has apparently been lost from the position between V and VI.

spirit demon, devil
buzzeth muttereth
Alexander's . . . death Alexander (Paris) loved Oenone but deserted her when offered Helen.

> With ravishing sound of his melodious harp,°
> 30   Made music with my Mephostophilis?
> Why should I die then, or basely despair?
> I am resolved, Faustus shall not repent.
> Come, Mephostophilis, let us dispute again,
> And reason of divine astrology.
> Speak, are there many spheres above the moon?
> Are all celestial bodies but one globe,
> As is the substance of this centric earth?

MEPHOSTOPHILIS   As are the elements, such are the heavens,
> Even from the moon unto the empyreal orb,°
> 40   Mutually folded in each other's spheres,
> And jointly move upon one axle-tree,
> Whose terminé° is termed the world's wide pole.
> Nor are the names of Saturn, Mars or Jupiter
> Feigned, but are erring stars.

FAUSTUS   But have they all one motion, both *situ et tempore*?°

MEPHOSTOPHILIS   All move from east to west in four and twenty hours upon the poles of the world, but differ in their motions upon the poles of the zodiac.°

FAUSTUS   These slender questions Wagner can decide!
> 50   Hath Mephostophilis no greater skill?
> Who knows not the double motion of the planets,
> That the first is finished in a natural day,
> The second thus: Saturn in thirty years, Jupiter in twelve, Mars in four, the Sun, Venus and Mercury in a year, the Moon in twenty-eight days. These are freshmen's suppositions.° But tell me, hath every sphere a dominion or *intelligentia*?°

MEPHOSTOPHILIS   Ay.

FAUSTUS   How many heavens or spheres are there?

MEPHOSTOPHILIS   Nine, the seven planets, the firmament, and the empyreal
> 60   heaven.

FAUSTUS   But is there not *coelum igneum*?° *et cristallinum*?°

MEPHOSTOPHILIS   No, Faustus, they be but fables.

FAUSTUS   Resolve me then in this one question. Why are not conjunctions,° oppositions,° aspects,° eclipses, all at one time, but in some years we have more, in some less?

MEPHOSTOPHILIS   *Per inaequalem motum, respectu totius.*°

---

he . . . harp Amphion's harp made the stones move together to form the wall of Thebes.
Even . . . orb from the sphere of the moon, closest of the "planets," to the empyrean, beyond their spheres and that of the fixed stars, where God is
terminé extremity
situ et tempore as to both position and time
poles of the zodiac common axle on which all spheres revolve
freshmen's suppositions elementary assumptions as taught to first-year students
dominion or intelligentia angel that controls the motion of a planet within its sphere
coelum igneum sphere of fire, a cosmological

hypothesis often regarded skeptically at this time
et cristallinum crystalline sphere, an extra sphere, brought in to explain astronomical observations in conflict with Ptolemaic principles
conjunctions apparent proximity of heavenly bodies
oppositions extreme apparent divergence
aspects Such relative positions were called *aspects.*
Per inaequalem . . . totius "on account of their unequal movement with respect to the whole"

FAUSTUS   Well, I am answered. Now tell me, who made the world?

MEPHOSTOPHILIS   I will not.

FAUSTUS   Sweet Mephostophilis, tell me.

70   MEPHOSTOPHILIS   Move° me not, Faustus.

FAUSTUS   Villain, have not I bound thee to tell me anything?

MEPHOSTOPHILIS   Ay, that is not against our kingdom:
This is. Thou art damned, think thou of hell.

FAUSTUS   Think, Faustus, upon God, that made the world.

MEPHOSTOPHILIS   Remember this—   *Exit.*

FAUSTUS   Ay, go, accursèd spirit to ugly hell.
'Tis thou hast damned distressèd Faustus' soul.
Is't not too late?

Enter the two ANGELS.

BAD ANGEL   Too late.

80   GOOD ANGEL   Never too late, if Faustus will repent.

BAD ANGEL   If thou repent, devils will tear thee in pieces.

GOOD ANGEL   Repent, and they shall never raze° thy skin.   *Exeunt* ANGELS.

FAUSTUS   Ah, Christ my saviour, my saviour,
Help to save distressèd Faustus' soul.

Enter LUCIFER, BELZEBUB, *and* MEPHOSTOPHILIS.

LUCIFER   Christ cannot save thy soul, for he is just;
There's none but I have interest in° the same.

FAUSTUS   O what art thou that look'st so terribly?

LUCIFER   I am Lucifer, and this is my companion prince in hell.

FAUSTUS   O Faustus, they are come to fetch thy soul.

90   BELZEBUB   We are come to tell thee thou dost injure us.

LUCIFER   Thou call'st on Christ contrary to thy promise.

BELZEBUB   Thou shouldst not think on God.

LUCIFER   Think on the devil.

BELZEBUB   And his dam too.

FAUSTUS   Nor will I henceforth. Pardon me in this,
And Faustus vows never to look to heaven,
Never to name God or to pray to him,
To burn his scriptures, slay his ministers,
And make my spirits pull his churches down.

100   LUCIFER   So shalt thou show thyself an obedient servant,
And we will highly gratify thee for it.

BELZEBUB   Faustus, we are come from hell in person to show thee some pastime. Sit down and thou shalt behold the Seven Deadly Sins appear to thee in their own proper shapes and likeness.

FAUSTUS   That sight will be as pleasant to me as Paradise was to Adam the first day of his creation.

LUCIFER   Talk not of Paradise or Creation, but mark the show. Go, Mephostophilis, fetch them in.

Move anger   **interest in** claim upon
raze graze

Enter the SEVEN DEADLY SINS [*led by a Piper*].

BELZEBUB   Now, Faustus, question them of their names and dispositions.

110   FAUSTUS   That shall I soon. What are thou, the first?

PRIDE   I am Pride. I disdain to have any parents. I am like to Ovid's flea,° I can creep into every corner of a wench; sometimes like a periwig I sit upon her brow; next, like a necklace I hang about her neck; then, like a fan of feathers, I kiss her; and then, turning myself to a wrought° smock, do what I list. But fie, what a smell is here! I'll not speak another word, unless the ground be perfumed and covered with cloth of arras.°

FAUSTUS   Thou art a proud knave indeed. What art thou, the second?

COVETOUSNESS   I am Covetousness, begotten of an old churl in a leather bag; and might I now obtain my wish, this house, you and all, should turn to gold,

120   that I might lock you safe into my chest. O my sweet gold!

FAUSTUS   And what are thou, the third?

ENVY   I am Envy, begotten of a chimney-sweeper and an oyster-wife.° I cannot read and therefore wish all books burned. I am lean with seeing others eat: O that there would come a famine over all the world, that all might die, and I live alone; then thou shouldst see how fat I'd be. But must thou sit and I stand? Come down, with a vengeance!

FAUSTUS   Out, envious wretch. But what art thou, the fourth?

WRATH   I am Wrath. I had neither father nor mother. I leapt out of a lion's mouth when I was scarce an hour old, and ever since have run up and down

130   the world with these case° of rapiers, wounding myself when I could get none to fight withal. I was born in hell, and look to it, for some of you shall be° my father.

FAUSTUS   And what art thou, the fifth?

GLUTTONY   I am Gluttony. My parents are all dead, and the devil a penny they have left me, but a small pension, and that buys me thirty meals a day and ten bevers:° a small trifle to suffice nature. I come of a royal pedigree: my father was a gammon of bacon and my mother was a hogshead of claret wine. My godfathers were these: Peter Pickle-herring and Martin Martlemas-beef.° But my godmother, O, she was an ancient gentle-woman, and well-beloved

140   in every good town and city; her name was Mistress Margery March-beer.° Now, Faustus, thou hast heard all my progeny,° wilt thou bid me to supper?

FAUSTUS   No, I'll see thee hanged; thou wilt eat up all my victuals.

GLUTTONY   Then the devil choke thee.

FAUSTUS   Choke thyself, Glutton. What art thou, the sixth?

SLOTH   Hey ho, I am Sloth. I was begotten on a sunny bank, where I have lain ever since, and you have done me great injury to bring me from thence. Let me be carried thither again by Gluttony and Lechery. Hey ho! I'll not speak a word more for a king's ransom.

Ovid's flea an elegy on a flea, erroneously attributed to Ovid; the lover envies the flea who has the freedom of his mistress's body; cf. John Donne's "The Flea"
wrought embroidered
cloth of arras rich tapestry (too fine for floor-covering)
chimney-sweeper and an oyster-wife consequently black and smelly

case pair
shall be is sure to prove
bevers snacks
Martlemas-beef On November 11, Martlemas or Martinmas, the feast of St. Martin of Tours, cattle were slaughtered for salting.
March-beer strong beer brewed in March
progeny line

150 FAUSTUS   And what are you, Mistress Minx, the seventh and last?

LECHERY   Who, I sir? I am one that loves an inch of raw mutton° better than an ell of fried stockfish, and the first letter of my name begins with Lechery.°

LUCIFER   Away to hell! Away, on, piper! *Exeunt the* SEVEN SINS [*and the Piper*]

FAUSTUS   O how this sight doth delight my soul.

LUCIFER   But Faustus, in hell is all manner of delight.

FAUSTUS   O might I see hell and return again safe, how happy were I then!

LUCIFER   Faustus, thou shalt; at midnight I will send for thee. Meanwhile, peruse this book and view it thoroughly, and thou shalt turn thyself into what
160   shape thou wilt.

FAUSTUS   Thanks, mighty Lucifer; this will I keep as chary° as my life.

LUCIFER   Now, Faustus, farewell.

FAUSTUS   Farewell, great Lucifer. Come, Mephostophilis.

Exeunt omnes, several° ways.

[SCENE VII]

Enter the CLOWN [ROBIN].

ROBIN   What, Dick, look to the horses there till I come again. I have gotten one of Doctor Faustus' conjuring books, and now we'll have such knavery as passes.°

Enter DICK.

DICK   What, Robin, you must come away and walk the horses.

ROBIN   I walk the horses? I scorn it, 'faith. I have other matters in hand. Let the horses walk themselves and they will. *A per se a, t.h.e. the: o per se o, deny orgon, gorgon.*° Keep further from me, O thou illiterate and unlearned hostler.

DICK   'Snails,° what hast thou got there? A book? Why, thou canst not tell
10   ne'er a word on it.

ROBIN   That thou shalt see presently. Keep out of the circle, I say, lest I send you into the hostry° with a vengeance.

DICK   That's like, 'faith. You had best leave your foolery, for an° my master come, he'll conjure you, 'faith!

ROBIN   My master conjure me? I'll tell thee what, an my master come here, I'll clap as fair a pair of horns° on his head as e'er thou sawest in thy life.

DICK   Thou need'st not do that, for my mistress hath done it.

ROBIN   Ay, there be of us here, that have waded as deep into matters as other men, if they were disposed to talk.

20 DICK   A plague take you! I thought you did not sneak up and down after her for nothing. But I prithee tell me, in good sadness,° Robin, is that a conjuring book?

inch . . . mutton penis
first letter . . . Lechery a common facetious expression
chary carefully
several different
as passes as beats everything
A per se . . . gorgon having difficulty in read-

ing, he spells out: *a* by itself spells *a*; *t,h,e* spells *the*; *o* by itself spells *o*; *Demogorgon*
'Snails God's nails
hostry hostelry, inn
an if
pair of horns the sign of a cuckold
in good sadness to be serious

ROBIN   Do but speak what thou'lt have me to do, and I'll do it. If thou'lt dance
naked, put off thy clothes and I'll conjure thee about presently. Or if thou'lt
go but to the tavern with me, I'll give thee white wine, red wine, claret wine,
sack, muscadine,° malmesey° and whippincrust,° hold—belly—hold,° and
we'll not pay one penny for it.

DICK   O brave! Prithee, let's to it presently, for I am as dry as a dog.

ROBIN   Come, then, let's away.   *Exeunt.*

[CHORUS I]

CHORUS

> Learnèd Faustus,
> To find the secrets of astronomy
> Graven in the book of Jove's high firmament,
> Did mount him up to scale Olympus top,
> Where sitting in a chariot burning bright,
> Drawn by the strength of yokèd dragons' necks,
> He views the clouds, the planets, and the stars,
> The tropics, zones, and quarters of the sky,
> From the bright circle of the hornèd moon,
10 > Even to the height of *Primum Mobile.*°
> And whirling round with this circumference,
> Within the concave compass of the pole,
> From east to west his dragons swiftly glide,
> And in eight days did bring him home again.
> Not long he stayed within his quiet house,
> To rest his bones after his weary toil,
> But new exploits do hale him out again,
> And mounted then upon a dragon's back,
> That with his wings did part the subtle air,
20 > He now is gone to prove° cosmography,
> That measures coasts and kingdoms of the earth;
> And as I guess will first arrive at Rome,
> To see the Pope and manner of his court,
> And take some part of holy Peter's feast,
> The which this day° is highly solemnized.   *Exit*

[SCENE VIII]

Enter FAUSTUS *and* MEPHOSTOPHILIS.

FAUSTUS   Having now, my good Mephostophilis,
> Passed with delight the stately town of Trier,
> Environed round with airy mountain tops,
> With walls of flint, and deep-entrenchèd lakes,°

muscadine muscatel
malmesey a strong sweet wine
whippincrust hippocras, a special wine
hold—belly—hold a bellyful
From . . . Mobile i.e. from the lowest to the
highest of the spheres, *Primum Mobile* being

the First Mover which imparted motion to all
the rest
prove put to the test
this day June 29th, the feast of St. Peter
lakes moats

Not to be won by any conquering prince;
From Paris next, coasting the realm of France,
We saw the river Main fall into Rhine,
Whose banks are set with groves of fruitful vines;
Then up to Naples, rich Campania,°
With buildings fair and gorgeous to the eye,
Whose streets straight forth° and paved with finest brick,
Quarters the town in four equivalents.
There saw we learned Maro's golden tomb,°
The way he cut,° an English mile in length,
Thorough a rock of stone in one night's space.
From thence to Venice, Padua and the rest,
In the midst of which a sumptuous temple° stands,
That threats the stars with her aspiring top,
Whose frame is paved with sundry coloured stones,
And roofed aloft with curious work in gold.
Thus hitherto hath Faustus spent his time.
But tell me now, what resting place is this?
Hast thou, as erst I did command,
Conducted me within the walls of Rome?

MEPHOSTOPHILIS   I have, my Faustus, and for proof thereof,
This is the goodly palace of the Pope;
And 'cause we are no common guests,
I choose his privy chamber for our use.

FAUSTUS   I hope his Holiness will bid us welcome.

MEPHOSTOPHILIS   All's one, for we'll be bold with his venison.
But now, my Faustus, that thou mayest perceive
What Rome contains for to delight thine eyes,
Know that this city stands upon seven hills,
That underprop the groundwork of the same;
Just through the midst runs flowing Tiber's stream,
With winding banks that cut it in two parts,
Over the which four stately bridges lean,
That make safe passage to each part of Rome.
Upon the bridge° called Ponte Angelo
Erected in a castle passing strong,
Where thou shalt see such store of ordinance
As that the double cannons forged of brass
Do match the number of the days contained
Within the compass of one complete year;
Beside the gates and high pyrámidès,°
That Julius Caesar brought from Africa.

FAUSTUS   Now by the kingdoms of infernal rule,

Naples . . . Campania an erroneous identification
straight forth in straight lines
Maro's . . . tomb Virgil (Maro) was buried near Naples.
The way he cut Virgil had a great reputation during the Middle Ages, as a necromancer, and was supposed to have cut the tunnel running through the promontory where he was buried.
sumptuous temple St. Mark's at Venice
Upon the bridge This is inaccurate; the Castel Sant' Angelo is not on the bridge.
pyramides actually an obelisk brought from Egypt by Caligula

Of Styx, of Acheron, and the fiery lake
Of ever-burning Phlegethon,° I swear
50   That I do long to see the monuments
And situation of bright-splendent Rome.
Come, therefore, let's away.
MEPHOSTOPHILIS Nay stay, my Faustus. I know you'd see the Pope,
And take some part of holy Peter's feast,
The which in state and high solemnity
This day is held through Rome and Italy
In honour of the Pope's triumphant victory.
FAUSTUS Sweet Mephostophilis, thou pleasest me.
Whilst I am here on earth let me be cloyed
60   With all things that delight the heart of man.
My four-and-twenty years of liberty
I'll spend in pleasure and in dalliance,
That Faustus' name, whilst this bright frame doth stand,
May be admirèd through the furthest land.
MEPHOSTOPHILIS 'Tis well said, Faustus. Come then, stand by me,
And thou shalt see them come immediately.
FAUSTUS Nay stay, my gentle Mephostophils,
And grant me my request, and then I go.
Thou knowest within the compass of eight days
70   We viewed the face of heaven, of earth and hell;
So high our dragons soared into the air,
That looking down, the earth appeared to me
No bigger than my hand in quantity.
There did we view the kingdoms of the world,
And what might please mine eye, I there beheld.
Then in this show let me an actor be,
That this proud Pope may Faustus' cunning see.
MEPHOSTOPHILIS Let it be so, my Faustus, but first stay
And view their triumphs° as they pass this way.
80   And then devise what best contents thy mind
By cunning in thine art to cross the Pope,
Or dash the pride of this solemnity,
To make his monks and abbots stand like apes,
And point like antics° at his triple crown,
To beat the beads about the friars' pates,
Or clap huge horns upon the cardinals' heads,
Or any villainy thou canst devise,
And I'll perform it, Faustus. Hark, they come!
This day shall make thee be admired in Rome.

Enter the CARDINALS *and* BISHOPS, *some bearing crosiers,*° *some the
pillars;*° MONKS *and* FRIARS *singing their procession. Then the* POPE *and*
RAYMOND° *King of Hungary with Bruno*° *led in chains.*

Styx . . . Phlegethon the three rivers of Hades
triumphs ceremonial parades
antics grotesques
crosiers crosses carried by bishops

pillars symbols of the cardinal's dignity
Raymond not historical
Bruno fictitious antipope; probably based on
Victor IV in Foxe's *Acts and Monuments*

POPE   Cast down our footstool.

90 RAYMOND   Saxon Bruno, stoop,
         Whilst on thy back his Holiness ascends
         Saint Peter's chair and state° pontifical.

BRUNO   Proud Lucifer, that state belongs to me:
         But thus I fall to Peter, not to thee.

POPE   To me and Peter shalt thou grovelling lie,
         And crouch before the papal dignity.
         Sound trumpets then, for thus Saint Peter's heir
         From Bruno's back ascends Saint Peter's chair.

                            A flourish° while he ascends.

         Thus, as the gods creep on with feet of wool
100   Long ere with iron hands° they punish men,
         So shall our sleeping vengeance now arise,
         And smite with death thy hated enterprise.
         Lord cardinals of France and Padua,
         Go forthwith to our holy consistory,°
         And read amongst the statutes décretál,°
         What by the holy council held at Trent°
         The sacred synod° hath decreed for him
         That doth assume the papal government,
         Without election and a true consent.
110   Away, and bring us word with speed!

1 CARDINAL   We go, my lord.

                                   Exeunt CARDINALS.

POPE   Lord Raymond.   [*The* POPE *and* RAYMOND *converse.*]

FAUSTUS Go, haste thee, gentle Mephostophilis,
         Follow the cardinals to the consistory,
         And as they turn their superstitious books,
         Strike them with sloth and drowsy idleness,
         And make them sleep so sound that in their shapes
         Thyself and I may parley with this Pope,
         This proud confronter of the Emperor,°
120   And in despite of all his holiness
         Restore this Bruno to his liberty
         And bear him to the states of Germany.

MEPHOSTOPHILIS   Faustus, I go.

FAUSTUS   Dispatch it soon,
         The Pope shall curse that Faustus came to Rome.

                            Exeunt FAUSTUS *and* MEPHOSTOPHILIS.

BRUNO   Pope Adrian, let me have some right of law:
         I was elected by the Emperor.

POPE   We will depose the Emperor for that deed,

---

state throne
flourish fanfare of trumpets
feet . . . hands proverb: "God comes with
woollen feet but strikes with iron hands"
consistory meeting place of the papal consistory
or senate
statutes décretál papal decrees

council . . . Trent council held in 1543–63
and launching the Counter-Reformation
synod general council
confronter . . . Emperor The pope has captured the Holy Roman Emperor's nominee
for the papacy.

And curse the people that submit to him.
Both he and thou shalt stand excommunicate,
130   And interdict° from Church's privilege
And all society of holy men.
He grows too proud in his authority,
Lifting his lofty head above the clouds
And like a steeple overpeers the Church.
But we'll pull down his haughty insolence,
And as Pope Alexander, our progenitor,
Stood on the neck of German Frederick,°
Adding this golden sentence to our praise,
That Peter's heirs should tread on emperors
140   And walk upon the dreadful adder's back,
Treading the lion and the dragon down,
And fearless spurn the killing basilisk,
So will we quell that haughty schismatic,
And by authority apostolical
Depose him from his regal government.

BRUNO   Pope Julius swore to princely Sigismund,°
For him and the succeeding popes of Rome,
To hold the emperors their lawful lords.

POPE   Pope Julius did abuse the Church's rites,
150   And therefore none of his decrees can stand.
Is not all power on earth bestowed on us?
And therefore though we would we cannot err.
Behold this silver belt, whereto is fixed
Seven golden keys° fast sealed with seven seals,
In token of our seven-fold power from heaven,
To bind or loose, lock fast, condemn or judge,
Resign° or seal, or whatso pleaseth us.
Then he and thou, and all the world, shall stoop,
Or be assurèd of our dreadful curse,
160   To light as heavy as the pains of hell.

Enter FAUSTUS *and* MEPHOSTOPHILIS, *like the cardinals.*

MEPHOSTOPHILIS   Now tell me, Faustus, are we not fitted well?

FAUSTUS   Yes, Mephostophilis, and two such cardinals
Ne'er served a holy pope as we shall do.
But whilst they sleep within the consistory,
Let us salute his reverend Fatherhood.

RAYMOND   Behold, my lord, the cardinals are returned.

POPE   Welcome, grave fathers, answer presently:
What have our holy council there decreed
Concerning Bruno and the Emperor,

---

interdict forbidden
Pope Alexander . . . Frederick Pope Alexander
III (1159–81) compelled the Emperor Frederick Barbarossa to stoop to him; Foxe reports the pope as quoting Psalms 91:13: "Thou
shalt walk upon the adder and on the basilisk,
and shalt tread down the lion and the dragon."
Pope . . . Sigismund fictitious
keys of St. Peter
Resign unseal

170   In quittance° of their late conspiracy
    Against our state and papal dignity?
FAUSTUS Most sacred patron of the Church of Rome,
    By full consent of all the synod
    Of priests and prelates, it is thus decreed:
    That Bruno and the German Emperor
    Be held as lollards° and bold schismatics
    And proud disturbers of the Church's peace.
    And if that Bruno by his own assent,
    Without enforcement of the German peers,
180   Did seek to wear the triple diadem
    And by your death to climb Saint Peter's chair,
    The statutes décretal have thus decreed:
    He shall be straight condemned of heresy
    And on a pile of faggots burnt to death.
POPE It is enough. Here, take him to your charge,
    And bear him straight to Ponte Angelo,
    And in the strongest tower enclose him fast.
    Tomorrow, sitting in our consistory
    With all our college of grave cardinals,
190   We will determine of his life or death.
    Here, take his triple crown° along with you,
    And leave it in the Church's treasury.
    Make haste again,° my good lord cardinals,
    And take our blessing apostolical.
MEPHOSTOPHILIS So, so, was never devil thus blessed before.
FAUSTUS Away, sweet Mephostophilis, be gone:
    The cardinals will be plagued for this anon.

       Exeunt FAUSTUS *and* MEPHOSTOPHILIS [*with* BRUNO].

POPE Go presently and bring a banquet forth
    That we may solemnize Saint Peter's feast,
200   And with Lord Raymond, King of Hungary,
    Drink to our late and happy victory.   *Exeunt.*

[SCENE IX]

A sennet° while the banquet is brought in; and then enter FAUSTUS *and*

MEPHOSTOPHILIS *in their own shapes.*

MEPHOSTOPHILIS Now, Faustus, come prepare thyself for mirth;
    The sleepy cardinals are hard at hand
    To censure° Bruno, that is posted hence,

quittance requital of
lollards heretics; originally the followers of Wyclif
triple crown Bruno had apparently acquired a papal tiara.

again back again
sennet trumpet flourish
censure judge

And on a proud-placed steed as swift as thought
Flies o'er the Alps to fruitful Germany,
There to salute the woeful Emperor.

FAUSTUS   The Pope will curse them for their sloth today,
That slept both Bruno and his crown away.
But now, that Faustus may delight his mind,
And by their folly make some merriment,
Sweet Mephostophilis, so charm me here,
That I may walk invisible to all,
And do what e'er I please unseen of any.

MEPHOSTOPHILIS   Faustus, thou shalt. Then kneel down presently:
Whilst on thy head I lay my hand,
And charm thee with this magic wand.
First wear this girdle, then appear
Invisible to all are here.
The planets seven, the gloomy air,
Hell, and the Furies' forkèd hair,°
Pluto's blue fire° and Hecat's tree,°
With magic spells so compass thee,
That no eye may thy body see.
So, Faustus, now for all their holiness,
Do what thou wilt, thou shalt not be discerned.

FAUSTUS   Thanks, Mephostophilis. Now, friars, take heed
Lest Faustus make your shaven crowns to bleed.

MEPHOSTOPHILIS   Faustus, no more; see where the cardinals come.

Enter POPE *and all the* LORDS [*and* ARCHBISHOP OF RHEIMS]. *Enter the*
CARDINALS *with a book.*

POPE   Welcome, lord cardinals. Come, sit down.
Lord Raymond, take your seat. Friars, attend,
And see that all things be in readiness
As best beseems this solemn festival.

1 CARDINAL   First, may it please your sacred holiness
To view the sentence of the reverend synod
Concerning Bruno and the Emperor?

POPE   What needs this question? Did I not tell you
Tomorrow we would sit i' the consistory
And there determine of his punishment?
You brought us word even now, it was decreed
That Bruno and the cursèd Emperor
Were by the holy Council both condemned
For loathèd lollards and base schísmatics.
Then wherefore would you have me view that book?

1 CARDINAL   Your grace mistakes. You gave us no such charge.

RAYMOND   Deny it not; we all are witnesses
That Bruno here was late delivered you,

---

forkèd hair the tongues of the snakes on the   **Pluto's blue fire** the sulphurous flames of hell
Furies' heads   **Hecat's tree** the gallows-tree

With his rich triple crown to be reserved°
And put into the Church's treasury.

BOTH CARDINALS   By holy Paul, we saw them not.

50   POPE   By Peter, you shall die
Unless you bring them forth immediately.
Hale them to prison, lade° their limbs with gyves!°
False prelates, for this hateful treachery,
Cursed be your souls to hellish misery.   [*Exit* CARDINALS, *guarded.*]

FAUSTUS   So, they are safe. Now Faustus, to the feast;
The Pope had never such a frolic guest.

POPE   Lord Archbishop of Rheims, sit down with us.

ARCHBISHOP   I thank your holiness.

FAUSTUS   Fall to;° the devil choke you an° your spare.

60   POPE   Who's that spoke? Friars, look about.

FRIARS   Here's nobody, if it like your holiness.

POPE   Lord Raymond, pray fall to. I am beholding
To the Bishop of Milan for this so rare a present.

FAUSTUS   I thank you, sir.   *Snatch it.*

POPE   How now? Who snatched the meat from me?
Villains, why speak you not?
My good Lord Archbishop, here's a most dainty dish
Was sent me from a cardinal in France.

FAUSTUS   I'll have that too.   [*Snatch it.*]

70   POPE   What lollards do attend our holiness
That we receive such great indignity? Fetch me some wine.

FAUSTUS   Ay, pray do, for Faustus is a-dry.

POPE   Lord Raymond, I drink unto your grace.

FAUSTUS   I pledge your grace.   [*Snatch the cup.*]

POPE   My wine gone too? Ye lubbers,° look about
And find the man that doth this villainy,
Or by our sanctitude you all shall die.
I pray, my lords, have patience at this
Troublesome banquet.

80   ARCHBISHOP   Please it your holiness, I think it be some ghost crept out of
purgatory, and now is come unto your holiness for his pardon.

POPE   It may be so.
Go, then, command our priests to sing a dirge
To lay the fury of this same troublesome ghost.

                                        The POPE *crosseth himself.*

FAUSTUS   How now? Must every bit be spiced with a cross?
Well, use that trick no more, I would advise you.   *Cross again.*
Well, there's the second time; aware° the third:
I give you fair warning.   *Cross again.*
                        Nay then take that!

reserved kept safe
lade load
gyves fetters; shackles
Fall to start eating

an if
lubbers clumsy fools
aware beware

FAUSTUS *hits him a box of the ear.*

POPE   Oh, I am slain! Help me, my lords.
Oh come, and help to bear my body hence.
Damned be this soul for ever for this deed!

Exeunt the POPE *and his train.*

90   MEPHOSTOPHILIS   Now, Faustus, what will you do now? For I can tell you,
you'll be cursed with bell, book and candle,°
FAUSTUS   Bell, book and candle, candle, book and bell,
Forward and backward, to curse Faustus to hell.

Enter the FRIARS *with bell, book and candle, for the dirge.*

FRIAR   Come, brethren, let's about our business with good devotion.   *Sing this.*
Cursed be he that stole his holiness' meat from the table.
Maledicat Dominus!°
Cursed be he that struck his holiness a blow on the face.
Maledicat Dominus!
Cursed be he that took Friar Sandelo a blow on the pate.
100   *Maledicat Dominus!*
Cursed be he that disturbeth our holy dirge.
Maledicat Dominus!
Cursed be he that took away his holiness' wine.
Maledicat Dominus!

[FAUSTUS *and* MEPHOSTOPHILIS] *beat the* FRIARS, *fling
fireworks among them, and exeunt* [omnes].

[SCENE X]

Enter CLOWN [ROBIN] *and* DICK, *with a cup.*

DICK   Sirrah, Robin we were best look that your devil can answer the stealing
of this same cup, for the vintner's boy follows us at the hard heels.°
ROBIN   'Tis no matter, let him come; an he follow us, I'll so conjure him, as he
was never conjured in his life, I warrant him. Let me see the cup.

Enter VINTNER.

DICK   Here 'tis. Yonder he comes! Now Robin, now or never show thy cunning.
VINTNER   O, are you here? I am glad I have found you. You are a couple of fine
companions! Pray where's the cup you stole from the tavern?
ROBIN   How, how? We steal a cup? Take heed of what you say; we look not
10   like cup-stealers, I can tell you.
VINTNER   Never deny, for I know you have it, and I'll search you.
ROBIN   Search me? Ay, and spare not. [*Aside*] Hold the cup, Dick. Come,
come, search me, search me.   [VINTNER *searches him.*]
VINTNER   Come on sirrah, let me search you now.

---

bell, book and candle an excommunication
ritual: the bell is tolled, the book closed, the
candle extinguished

Maledicat Dominus "May the Lord curse him"
at the hard heels right at our heels

DICK Ay, ay, do, do. [*Aside*] Hold the cup, Robin. I fear not your searching; we scorn to steal your cups, I can tell you.   [VINTNER *searches him.*]

VINTNER Never outface me for the matter,° for sure the cup is between you two.

ROBIN Nay, there you lie; 'tis beyond us both.

20 VINTNER A plague take you! I thought 'twas your knavery to take it away. Come, give it me again.

ROBIN Ay, much!° When, can you tell?° Dick, make me a circle, and stand close at my back, and stir not for thy life. Vintner, you shall have your cup back anon. Say nothing, Dick. *O per se, o; Demogorgon, Belcher and Mephostophilis!*

> *Enter* MEPHOSTOPHILIS.

MEPHOSTOPHILIS You princely legions of infernal rule,
    How am I vexèd by these villains' charms!
    From Constantinople have they brought me now,
    Only for pleasure of these damnèd slaves.   [*Exit* VINTNER.]

30 ROBIN By lady sir, you have had a shrewd journey of it. Will it please you to take a shoulder of mutton to supper, and a tester° in your purse, and go back again?

DICK Ay, I pray you heartily, sir, for we called you but in jest, I promise you.

MEPHOSTOPHILIS To purge the rashness of this cursèd deed
    First, be thou turnèd to this ugly shape,
    For apish° deeds transformèd to an ape.

ROBIN O brave, an ape! I pray sir, let me have the carrying of him about to show some tricks.

40 MEPHOSTOPHILIS And so thou shalt: be thou transformed to a dog, and carry him upon thy back. Away, be gone!

ROBIN A dog? That's excellent: let the maids look well to their porridge-pots, for I'll into the kitchen presently. Come, Dick, come.

> *Exeunt the two* CLOWNS.

MEPHOSTOPHILIS Now with the flames of ever-burning fire
    I'll wing myself and forthwith fly amain°
    Unto my Faustus to the great Turk's court.   *Exit.*

[CHORUS 2]

CHORUS

> When Faustus had with pleasure ta'en the view
> Of rarest things and royal courts of kings,
> He stayed his course° and so returnèd home,
> Where such as bare his absence but with grief—
> I mean his friends and nearest companions—
> Did gratulate° his safety with kind words;

Never . . . matter don't try to brazen the matter out with me
Ay, much derisive
When, can you tell derisive
tester sixpence

apish foolish, ridiculous
amain speedily
stayed his course interrupted his traveling
gratulate rejoice at

And in their conference of that befell,
Touching his journey through the world and air,
They put forth questions of astrology,
Which Faustus answered with such learnèd skill
As they admired and wondered at his wit.
Now is his fame spread forth in every land:
Amongst the rest, the Emperor is one,
Carolus the Fifth,° at whose palace now
Faustus is feasted 'mongst his noblemen.
What there he did in trial of his art,
I leave untold: your eyes shall see performed.   *Exit.*

[SCENE XI]

Enter MARTINO *and* FREDERICK *at several doors.*

MARTINO   What ho, officers, gentlemen!
Hie to the presence° to attend the Emperor.
Good Frederick, see the rooms be voided straight,°
His majesty is coming to the hall;
Go back, and see the state° in readiness.
FREDERICK   But where is Bruno, our elected Pope,
That on a fury's back came post from Rome?
Will not his grace consort° the Emperor?
MARTINO   Oh, and with him comes the German conjurer.
The learnèd Faustus, fame of Wittenberg,
The wonder of the world for magic art;
And he intends to show great Carolus
The race of all his stout progenitors,
And bring in presence of his majesty
The royal shapes and warlike semblances
Of Alexander and his beauteous paramour.
FREDERICK   Where is Benvolio?
MARTINO   Fast asleep, I warrant you.
He took his rouse° with stoups° of Rhenish wine
So kindly yesternight to Bruno's health,
That all this day the sluggard keeps his bed.
FREDERICK   See, see, his window's ope. We'll call to him.
MARTINO   What ho, Benvolio?

Enter BENVOLIO *above at a window in his nightcap, buttoning.*

BENVOLIO   What a devil ail you two?
MARTINO   Speak softly, sir, lest the devil hear you;
For Faustus at the court is late arrived,

Carolus the Fifth Charles V, Emperor from
1519–1556
presence audience chamber
voided straight cleared at once
state throne
consort accompany
took his rouse drank heavily
stoups measures

And at his heels a thousand furies wait
To accomplish whatsoever the doctor please.

BENVOLIO   What of this?

30   MARTINO   Come, leave thy chamber first, and thou shalt see
This conjurer perform such rare exploits
Before the Pope and royal Emperor
As never yet was seen in Germany.

BENVOLIO   Has not the Pope enough of conjuring yet?
He was upon the devil's back late enough,
And if he be so far in love with him,
I would he would post with him to Rome again.

FREDERICK   Speak, wilt thou come and see this sport?

BENVOLIO   Not I.

40   MARTINO   Wilt thou stand in thy window and see it, then?

BENVOLIO   Ay, and I fall not asleep i' the meantime.

MARTINO   The Emperor is at hand, who comes to see
What wonders by black spells may compassed be.

BENVOLIO   Well, go you attend the Emperor. I am content for this once to
thrust my head out at a window, for they say if a man be drunk overnight the
devil cannot hurt him in the morning. If that be true, I have a charm in my
head shall control° him as well as the conjurer, I warrant you.

A sennet. [*Enter*] *Charles the German* EMPEROR, BRUNO, [*Duke of*]
SAXONY, FAUSTUS, MEPHOSTOPHILIS, *and* ATTENDANTS.

EMPEROR   Wonder of men, renowned magician,
Thrice-learnèd Faustus, welcome to our court.

50   This deed of thine, in setting Bruno free
From his and our professèd enemy,
Shall add more excellence unto thine art,
Than if by powerful necromantic spells
Thou couldst command the world's obedience.
For ever be beloved of Carolus;
And if this Bruno thou hast late redeemed,
In peace possess the triple diadem
And sit in Peter's chair, despite of chance,°
Thou shalt be famous through all Italy,

60   And honoured of the German emperor.

FAUSTUS   These gracious words, most royal Carolus,
Shall make poor Faustus to his utmost power
Both love and serve the German Emperor,
And lay his life at Holy Bruno's feet.
For proof whereof, if so your grace be pleased,
The doctor stands prepared by power of art
To cast his magic charms that shall pierce through
The ebon gates of ever-burning hell,
And hale the stubborn furies from their caves,

control subdue   **chance** fortune

70   To compass whatsoe'er your grace commands.

BENVOLIO   Blood, he speaks terribly! But for all that, I do not greatly believe
    him; he looks as like a conjurer as the Pope to a costermonger.°

EMPEROR   Then, Faustus, as thou late didst promise us,
    We would behold that famous conqueror,
    Great Alexander, and his paramour,
    In their true shapes and state majestical,
    That we may wonder at their excellence.

FAUSTUS   Your majesty shall see them presently.
    Mephostophilis, away!

80   And with a solemn noise of trumpets' sound,
    Present before this royal Emperor
    Great Alexander and his beauteous paramour.

MEPHOSTOPHILIS   Faustus, I will.   *Exit* MEPHOSTOPHILIS.

BENVOLIO   Well, master doctor, an your devils come not away quickly, you
    shall have me asleep presently. Zounds, I could eat myself for anger, to
    think I have been such an ass all this while, to stand gaping after the devil's
    governor, and can see nothing.

FAUSTUS   I'll make you feel something anon, if my art fail me not.
    My lord, I must forewarn your majesty

90   That when my spirits present the royal shapes
    Of Alexander and his paramour,
    Your grace demand no questions of the king,
    But in dumb silence let them come and go.

EMPEROR   Be it as Faustus please, we are content.

BENVOLIO   Ay, ay, and I am content too. And thou bring Alexander and his
    paramour before the Emperor, I'll be Actaeon° and turn myself to a stag.

FAUSTUS   And I'll play Diana, and send you the horns presently.°

SENNET   *Enter at one door the Emperor* ALEXANDER, *at the other* DARIUS; *they
    meet;* DARIUS *is thrown down;* ALEXANDER *kills him, takes off his crown,
    and, offering to go out, his* PARAMOUR *meets him; he embraceth her and
    sets* DARIUS' *crown upon her head, and coming back, both salute the*
    EMPEROR, *who, leaving his state, offers to embrace them, which* FAUSTUS
    seeing, suddenly stays him. Then trumpets cease and music sounds.

    My gracious lord, you do forget yourself;
    These are but shadows, not substantial.

100   EMPEROR   O pardon me, my thoughts are ravished so
    With sight of this renownèd emperor,
    That in mine arms I would have compassed him.
    But, Faustus, since I may not speak to them,
    To satisfy my longing thoughts at full,
    Let me this tell thee: I have heard it said
    That this fair lady, whilst she lived on earth,
    Had on her neck a little wart or mole;

costermonger man who sells fruit, fish, etc. from
a barrow in the street
Actaeon saw Diana bathing and was turned into

a stag for punishment; his own hounds killed
him.
send . . . presently Cf. vii. 16n.

How may I prove that saying to be true?

FAUSTUS   Your majesty may boldly go and see.

110   EMPEROR   Faustus, I see it plain,
And in this sight thou better pleasest me
Than if I gained another monarchy.

FAUSTUS   Away, be gone.   *Exit Show.*
See, see, my gracious lord, what strange beast is yon, that thrusts this head out at window?

EMPEROR   O, wondrous sight! See, Duke of Saxony,
Two spreading horns most strangely fastenèd
Upon the head of young Benvolio!

SAXONY   What, is he asleep or dead?

120   FAUSTUS   He sleeps, my lord, but dreams not of his horns.

EMPEROR   This sport is excellent. We'll call and wake him.
What ho, Benvolio!

BENVOLIO   A plague upon you! Let me sleep awhile.

EMPEROR   I blame thee not to sleep much,° having such a head of thine own.

SAXONY   Look up, Benvolio, 'tis the Emperor calls.

BENVOLIO   The Emperor? Where? O, zounds, my head!

EMPEROR   Nay, and thy horns hold, 'tis no matter for thy head, for that's armed sufficiently.

FAUSTUS   Why, how now, sir knight? What, hanged by the horns? This is most
130   horrible! Fie, fie, pull in your head for shame, let not all the world wonder at you.

BENVOLIO   Zounds, doctor, is this your villainy?

FAUSTUS   O say not so, sir. The doctor has no skill,
No art, no cunning, to present these lords
Or bring before this royal Emperor
The mighty monarch, warlike Alexander.
If Faustus do it, you are straight resolved
In bold Actaeon's shape to turn a stag.
And therefore, my lord, so please your majesty,
140   I'll raise a kennel of hounds shall hunt him so
As all his footmanship° shall scarce prevail
To keep his carcass from their bloody fangs.
Ho, Belimote, Argiron, Asterote!

BENVOLIO   Hold, hold! Zounds, he'll raise up a kennel of devils, I think, anon. Good my lord, entreat for me. 'Sblood, I am never able to endure these torments.

EMPEROR   Then, good master doctor,
Let me entreat you to remove his horns:
He has done penance now sufficiently.

150   FAUSTUS   My gracious lord, not so much for injury done to me, as to delight your majesty with some mirth, hath Faustus justly requited this injurious° knight; which being all I desire, I am content to remove his horns. Mephostophilis, transform him. And hereafter, sir, look you speak well of scholars.

I blame . . . much I don't much blame you for   footmanship skill in the running
sleeping   injurious insulting

BENVOLIO   Speak well of ye? 'Sblood, and scholars be such cuckhold-makers
    to clap horns of honest men's head o' this order,° I'll ne'er trust smooth faces
    and small ruffs° more. But an° I be not revenged for this, would I might be
    turned to a gaping oyster and drink nothing but salt water.
EMPEROR   Come, Faustus, while the Emperor lives,
160   In recompense of this thy high desert,
        Thou shalt command the state of Germany,
        And live beloved of mighty Carolus.   *Exeunt omnes.*

    [SCENE XII]

    Enter BENVOLIO, MARTINO, FREDERICK, *and* SOLDIERS.

MARTINO   Nay, sweet Benvolio, let us sway thy thoughts
        From this attempt against the conjurer.
BENVOLIO   Away, you love me not, to urge me thus.
        Shall I let slip so great an injury,
        When every servile groom jests at my wrongs,
        And in their rustic gambols° proudly say
        'Benvolio's head was graced with horns today'?
        O may these eyelids never close again
        Till with my sword I have that conjurer slain.
10   If you will aid me in this enterprise,
        Then draw your weapons and be resolute;
        If not, depart: here will Benvolio die,
        But Faustus' death shall quit my infamy.
FREDERICK   Nay, we will stay with thee, betide° what may,
        And kill that doctor if he come this way.
BENVOLIO   Then, gentle Frederick, hie thee to the grove,
        And place our servants and our followers
        Close in an ambush there behind the trees.
        By this, I know, the conjurer is near:
20   I saw him kneel and kiss the Emperor's hand,
        And take his leave, laden with rich rewards.
        Then, soldiers, boldly fight; if Faustus die,
        Take you the wealth, leave us the victory.
FREDERICK   Come, soldiers, follow me unto the grove.
        Who kills him shall have gold and endless love.

                    Exit FREDERICK *with the* SOLDIERS.

BENEVOLIO   My head is lighter than it was by the horns,
        But yet my heart's more ponderous than my head,
        And pants until I see that conjurer dead.
MARTINO   Where shall we place ourselves, Benvolio?

---

o' this order in this manner
smooth faces and small ruffs Scholars often
avoided the beards and large ruffs of the
courtier.

But an unless if
gambols frolics
betide happen

30   BENVOLIO   Here will we stay to bide the first assault.
             O were that damnèd hell-hound but in place,
             Thou soon shouldst see me quit° my foul disgrace.

     Enter FREDERICK.

     FREDERICK   Close, close! The conjurer is at hand,
             And all alone comes walking in his gown.
             Be ready then, and strike the peasant down.
     BENVOLIO   Mine be that honour, then; now sword, strike home.
             For horns he gave, I'll have his head anon.

     Enter FAUSTUS *with the false head.*

     MARTINO   See, see, he comes.
     BENVOLIO   No words. This blow ends all.
             Hell take his soul; his body thus must fall.
                                              [*Strikes* FAUSTUS.]

     FAUSTUS   O!
40   FREDERICK   Groan you, master doctor?
     BENVOLIO   Break may his heart with groans! Dear Frederick, see,
             Thus will I end his griefs immediately.   [*Cuts off his head.*]
     MARTINO   Strike with a willing hand; his head is off.
     BENVOLIO   The devil's dead; the Furies now may laugh.
     FREDERICK   Was this that stern aspect, that awful frown,
             Made the grim monarch of infernal spirits
             Tremble and quake at his commanding charms?
     MARTINO   Was this that damnèd head, whose art° conspired
50   Benvolio's shame before the Emperor?
     BENVOLIO   Ay, that's the head, and here the body lies,
             Justly rewarded for his villainies.
     FREDERICK   Come, let's devise how we may add more shame
             To the black scandal of his hated name.
     BENVOLIO   First, on his head, in quittance of my wrongs,
             I'll nail huge forkèd horns, and let them hang
             Within the window where he yoked° me first,
             That all the world may see my just revenge.
     MARTINO   What use shall we put his beard to?
60   BENVOLIO   We'll sell it to a chimney-sweeper; it will wear out ten birchen
             brooms, I warrant you.
     FREDERICK   What shall his eyes do?
     BENVOLIO   We'll put out his eyes, and they shall serve for buttons to his lips,
             to keep his tongue from catching cold.
     MARTINO   An excellent policy!° And now, sirs, having divided him, what shall
             the body do?   [FAUSTUS *stands up*]
     BENVOLIO   Zounds, the devil's alive again!
     FREDERICK   Give him his head, for God's sake!

---

quit repay   **yoked** the horns held his head fast, like the
art wit   yoke of oxen
                                  policy trick

FAUSTUS   Nay, keep it. Faustus will have heads and hands,
70   Ay, all your hearts to recompense this deed.
            Knew you not, traitors, I was limited°
            For four-and-twenty years to breathe on earth?
            And had you cut my body with your swords,
            Or hewed this flesh and bones as small as sand,
            Yet in a minute had my spirit returned,
            And I had breathed a man made free from harm.
            But wherefore do I dally° my revenge?
            Asteroth, Belimoth, Mephostophilis!

Enter MEPHOSTOPHILIS *and other* DEVILS.

            Go, horse these traitors on your fiery backs,
80   And mount aloft with them as high as heaven;
            Thence pitch them headlong to the lowest hell.
            Yet stay, the world shall see their misery,
            And hell shall after plague their treachery.
            Go, Belimoth, and take this caitiff° hence,
            And hurl him in some lake of mud and dirt.
            Take thou this other, drag him through the woods
            Amongst the pricking thorns and sharpest briars,
            Whilst with my gentle Mephostophilis,
            This traitor flies unto some steepy rock,
90   That rolling down may break the villain's bones
            As he intended to dismember me.
            Fly hence, dispatch my charge immediately.
FREDERICK   Pity us, gentle Faustus! Save our lives!
FAUSTUS   Away!
FREDERICK   He must needs go that the devil drives.°

                                Exeunt SPIRITS *with the* KNIGHTS.

Enter the ambushed SOLDIERS.

1 SOLDIER   Come, sirs, prepare yourselves in readiness.
            Make haste to help these noble gentlemen.
            I heard them parley with the conjurer.
2 SOLDIER   See where he comes; dispatch and kill the slave.
FAUSTUS   What's here? An ambush to betray my life!
100   Then Faustus, try thy skill. Base peasants, stand!
            For lo, these trees remove at my command,
            And stand as bulwarks twixt yourselves and me,
            To shield me from your hated treachery.
            Yet, to encounter this your weak attempt,
            Behold an army comes incontinent.°

            FAUSTUS *strikes the door,*° *and enter a* DEVIL *playing on a drum; after
            him another bearing an ensign; and divers with weapons;* MEPHO-

---

limited allowed the extent of   **He . . . drives** proverbial
dally trifle with, delay over   **incontinent** immediately
caitiff wretch   **the door** at the back of the stage

STOPHILIS *with fireworks. They set upon the* SOLDIERS *and drive them out.*   [*Exit* FAUSTUS.]

[SCENE XIII]

Enter at several doors BENVOLIO, FREDERICK, *and* MARTINO, *their heads and faces bloody and besmeared with mud and dirt, all having horns on their heads.*

MARTINO   What ho, Benvolio!

BENVOLIO   Here, what, Frederick, ho!

FREDERICK   O help me, gentle friend; where is Martino?

MARTINO   Dear Frederick, here,
Half smothered in a lake of mud and dirt,
Through which the furies dragged me by the heels.

FREDERICK   Martino, see, Benvolio's horns again!

MARTINO   O misery! How now, Benvolio?

BENVOLIO   Defend me, heaven! Shall I be haunted still?

10   MARTINO   Nay, fear not, man; we have no power to kill.

BENVOLIO   My friends transformèd thus! O hellish spite!
Your heads are all set with horns!

FREDERICK   You hit it right:
It is your own you mean; feel on your head.

BENVOLIO   Zounds, horns again!

MARTINO   Nay, chafe not, man, we all are sped.°

BENVOLIO   What devil attends this damned magician,
That, spite of spite,° our wrongs are doubled?°

FREDERICK   What may we do, that we may hide our shames?

BENVOLIO   If we should follow him to work revenge,
He'd join long asses' ears to these huge horns,

20   And make us laughing stocks to all the world.

MARTINO   What shall we then do, dear Benvolio?

BENVOLIO   I have a castle joining near these woods,
And thither we'll repair and live obscure,
Till time shall alter these our brutish shapes.
Sith° black disgrace hath thus eclipsed our fame,
We'll rather die with grief, than live with shame.   *Exeunt omnes.*

[SCENE XIV]

Enter FAUSTUS *and the* HORSE-COURSER° *and* MEPHOSTOPHILIS.

HORSE-COURSER   I beseech your worship accept of these forty dollars.

FAUSTUS   Friend, thou canst not buy so good a horse for so small a price; I have no great need to sell him, but if thou likest him for ten dollars more, take him, because I see thou hast a good mind to him.

sped done for
spite of spite in spite of everything
doubled trisyllabic; pronounced dou-ble-ed
Sith since

Horse-courser horse-dealer (with traditional reputation like a used-car salesman's)

HORSE-COURSER   I beseech you sir, accept of this. I am a very poor man, and
have lost very much of late by horse-flesh, and this bargain will set me up
again.

FAUSTUS   Well, I will not stand° with thee, give me the money. Now sirrah,
I must tell you, that you may ride him o'er hedge and ditch, and spare him
10   him not; but, do you hear, in any case, ride him not into the water.°

HORSE-COURSER   How sir, not into the water? Why, will he not drink of all
waters?°

FAUSTUS   Yes, he will drink of all waters, but ride him not into the water; o'er
hedge and ditch or where thou wilt, but not into the water. Go bid the ostler
deliver him unto you—and remember what I say.

HORSE-COURSER   I warrant you, sir. O joyful day! Now am I a made man for
ever.   *Exit.*

FAUSTUS   What art thou, Faustus, but a man condemned to die?
Thy fatal time° draws to a final end.
20   Despair doth drive distrust into my thoughts;
Confound° these passions with a quiet sleep.
Tush, Christ did call the thief upon the cross,°
Then rest thee, Faustus, quiet in conceit.°   *He sits to sleep.*

Enter the HORSE-COURSER, *wet.*

HORSE-COURSER   O what a cozening° doctor was this! I, riding my horse into
the water, thinking some hidden mystery had been in the horse, I had nothing
under me but a little straw, and had much ado to escape drowning. Well,
I'll go rouse him, and make him give me my forty dollars again. Ho, sirrah
doctor, you cozening scab!° Master doctor, awake, and rise, and give me my
money again, for your horse is turned to a bottle° of hay. Master doctor!
30   *He pulls off his leg.*
Alas, I am undone; what shall I do? I have pulled off his leg.

FAUSTUS   O help, help! The villain hath murdered me.

HORSE-COURSER   Murder or not murder, now he has but one leg I'll outrun him,
and cast this leg into some ditch or other.   [*Exit.*]

FAUSTUS   Stop him, stop him, stop him—ha, ha, ha! Faustus hath his leg again,
and the horse-courser a bundle of hay for his forty dollars.

Enter WAGNER.

How now Wagner, what news with thee?

WAGNER   If it pleases you, the Duke of Vanholt doth earnestly entreat your
company, and hath sent some of his men to attend you with provision fit for
40   your journey.

FAUSTUS   The Duke of Vanholt's an honourable gentleman, and one to whom
I must be no niggard of my cunning. Come away.   *Exeunt.*

---

stand haggle
ride . . . water Running water breaks witches'
spells.
drink . . . waters go anywhere
fatal time time allotted by fate
Confound disperse

Christ . . . cross Luke 23:39–43
conceit mind
cozening cheating
scab villain
bottle bundle

[SCENE XV]

Enter Clown [ROBIN], DICK, HORSE-COURSER, *and a* CARTER.

CARTER   Come, my masters, I'll bring you to the best beer in Europe. What ho, hostess. Where be these whores?°

Enter HOSTESS.

HOSTESS   How now, what lack you? What, my old guests, welcome!

ROBIN   Sirrah Dick, dost thou know why I stand so mute?

DICK   No, Robin, why is it?

ROBIN   I am eighteen pence on the score;° but say nothing, see if she have forgotten me.

HOSTESS   Who's this, that stands so solemnly by himself? What, my old guest!

10 ROBIN   Oh, hostess, how do you? I hope my score stands still.

HOSTESS   Ay, there's no doubt of that, for methinks you make no haste to wipe it out.

DICK   Why, hostess, I say, fetch us some beer.

HOSTESS   You shall presently. Look up into the hall there, ho!°   *Exit.*

DICK   Come, sirs, what shall we do now till mine hostess comes?

CARTER   Marry, sir, I'll tell you the bravest tale how a conjurer served me. You know Doctor Fauster?

HORSE-COURSER   Ay, a plague take him. Here's some on's have cause to know him. Did he conjure thee too?

20 CARTER   I'll tell you how he served me. As I was going to Wittenberg t'other day, with a load of hay, he met me and asked me what he should give me for as much hay as he could eat. Now, sir, I, thinking that a little would serve his turn, bade him take as much as he would for three-farthings. So he presently gave me my money and fell to eating; and, as I am a cursen° man, he never left eating till he had eat up all my load of hay.

ALL   O monstrous, eat a whole load of hay!

ROBIN   Yes, yes, that may be, for I have heard of one that h'as eat a load of logs.°

HORSE-COURSER   Now, sirs, you shall hear how villainously he served me. I

30 went to him yesterday to buy a horse of him, and he would by no means sell him under forty dollars. So, sir, because I knew him to be such a horse as would run over hedge and ditch and never tire, I gave him his money. So when I had my horse, Doctor Fauster bade me ride him night and day and spare him no time. 'But,' quoth he, 'in any case ride him not into the water.' Now, sir, I thinking the horse had some quality that he would not have me know of, what did I but rid him into a great river, and when I came just in the midst, my horse vanished away, and I sat straddling upon a bottle of hay.

ALL   O brave° doctor!

40 HORSE-COURSER   But you shall hear how bravely° I served him for it: I went me home to his house, and there I found him asleep. I kept-a-hallowing and

---

whores servants
on the score an old debt still charged against him
Look . . . ho She instructs the maids to attend to the customers.

cursen Christian
eat . . . logs been drunk
brave excellent
bravely well

whooping in his ears, but all could not wake him. I, seeing that, took him by the leg and never rested pulling, till I had pulled me his leg quite off, and now 'tis at home in mine hostry.

ROBIN   And has the doctor but one leg, then? That's excellent, for one of his devils turned me into the likeness of an ape's face.

CARTER   Some more drink, hostess.

ROBIN   Hark you, we'll into another room and drink a while, and then we'll go seek out the doctor.   *Exeunt omnes.*

[SCENE XVI]

Enter the DUKE OF VANHOLT, *his* DUCHESS, [SERVANTS,] FAUSTUS *and* MEPHOSTOPHILIS.

DUKE   Thanks, master doctor, for these pleasant sights. Nor know I how sufficiently to recompense your great deserts in erecting that enchanted castle in the air, the sight whereof so delighted me, as nothing in the world could please me more.

FAUSTUS   I do think myself, my good lord, highly recompensed in that it pleaseth your grace to think but well of that which Faustus hath performed. But, gracious lady, it may be that you have taken no pleasure in those sights; therefore, I pray you tell me, what is the thing you most desire to have: be it in the world, it shall be yours. I have heard that great-bellied women do
10   long for things are° rare and dainty.

DUCHESS   True, master doctor, and since I find you so kind, I will make known unto you what my heart desires to have; and were it now summer, as it is January, a dead time of the winter, I would request no better meat° than a dish of ripe grapes.

FAUSTUS   This is but a small matter; go, Mephostophilis, away.

                                                                    Exit MEPHOSTOPHILIS.

Madame, I will do more than this for your content.

Enter MEPHOSTOPHILIS *again with the grapes.*

Here, now taste ye these; they should be good, for they come from a far country, I can tell you.

DUKE   This makes me wonder more than all the rest, that at this time of the
20   year, when every tree is barren of his fruit, from whence you had these ripe grapes.

FAUSTUS   Please it your grace, the year is divided into two circles over the whole world, so that when it is winter with us, in the contrary circle it is likewise summer with them, as in India, Saba° and such countries that lie far east, where they have fruit twice a year. From whence, by means of a swift spirit that I have, I had these grapes brought as you see.

DUCHESS   And trust me, they are the sweetest grapes that e'er I tasted.

                                                    The CLOWNS *bounce*° *at the gate within.*

are that are
meat food

Saba Sheba
bounce knock loudly

DUKE   What rude disturbers have we at the gate?
30   Go, pacify their fury. Set it ope,
         And then demand of them what they would have.

                    They knock again and call out to talk with FAUSTUS.

SERVANT   Why, how now, masters? What a coil° is there? What is the reason°
    you disturb the Duke?

DICK   We have no reason for it, therefore a fig for him.°

SERVANT   Why, saucy varlets, dare you be so bold?

HORSE-COURSER   I hope, sir, we have wit enough to be more bold than welcome.

SERVANT   It appears so. Pray be bold elsewhere, and trouble not the Duke.

DUKE   What would they have?

SERVANT   They all cry out to speak with Doctor Faustus.

40 CARTER   Ay, and we will speak with him.

DUKE   Will you sir? Commit° the rascals.

DICK   Commit with° us! He were as good commit with his father as commit
    with us.

FAUSTUS   I do beseech your grace let them come in.
         They are good subject for a merriment.

DUKE   Do as thou wilt, Faustus; I give thee leave.

FAUSTUS   I thank your grace.

         Enter the CLOWN [ROBIN], DICK, CARTER, *and* HORSE-COURSER.

         Why, how now, my good friends?
         Faith, you are too outrageous,° but come near;
         I have procured your pardons. Welcome all.

50 ROBIN   Nay, sir, we will be welcome for our money, and we will pay for what
    we take. What ho! Give's half-a-dozen of beer here, and be hanged.

FAUSTUS   Nay, hark you, can you tell me where you are?

CARTER   Ay, marry can I; we are under heaven.

SERVANT   Ay, but, sir sauce-box, know you in what place?

HORSE-COURSER   Ay, ay, the house is good enough to drink in. Zounds, fill us
    some beer or we'll break all the barrels in the house and dash out all your
    brains with your bottles.

FAUSTUS   Be not so furious; come, you shall have beer.
         My lord, beseech you give me leave awhile.
60   I'll gage° my credit, 'twill content your grace.

DUKE   With all my heart, kind doctor, please thyself;
         Our servants and our court's at thy command.

FAUSTUS   I humbly thank your grace. Then fetch some beer.

HORSE-COURSER   Ay, marry, there spake a doctor indeed, and, 'faith, I'll drink
    a health to thy wooden leg for that word.

FAUSTUS   My wooden leg? What dost thou mean by that?

CARTER   Ha, ha, ha! Dost thou hear him, Dick? He has forgot his leg.

---

coil disturbance
reason with a pun on the homophone *raisin*—
which leads to the fig
a fig for him expression of contempt. They don't
realize that the room they have got into is the
Court.

Commit take to prison
Commit with have sexual intercourse
outrageous violent
gage wager

HORSE-COURSER   Ay, ay, he does not stand much upon° that.

FAUSTUS   No, 'faith, not much upon a wooden leg.

70   CARTER   Good Lord, that flesh and blood should be so frail with your worship! Do not you remember a horse-courser you sold a horse to?

FAUSTUS   Yes, I remember I sold one a horse.

CARTER   And do you remember you bid he should not ride into the water?

FAUSTUS   Yes, I do very well remember that.

CARTER   And do you remember nothing of your leg?

FAUSTUS   No, in good sooth.

CARTER   Then I pray remember your curtsy.°

FAUSTUS   I thank you, sir.   [He bows.]

CARTER   'Tis not so much worth; I pray you, tell me one thing.

80   FAUSTUS   What's that?

CARTER   Be both your legs bedfellows every night together?

FAUSTUS   Wouldst thou make a colossus° of me, that thou askest me such questions?

CARTER   No, truly, sir; I would make nothing of you, but I would fain know that.

    Enter HOSTESS *with drink.*

FAUSTUS   Then I assure thee certainly they are.

CARTER   I thank you, I am fully satisfied.

FAUSTUS   But wherefore dost thou ask?

CARTER   For nothing, sir—but methinks you should have a wooden bedfellow
90   of one of 'em.

HORSE-COURSER   Why, do you hear, sir, did not I pull off one of your legs when you were asleep?

FAUSTUS   But I have it again now I am awake. Look you here, sir.

ALL   O horrible! Had the doctor three legs?

CARTER   Do you remember, sir, how you cozened me and eat up my load of—
                                            FAUSTUS *charms him dumb.*

DICK   Do you remember how you made me wear an ape's—

HORSE-COURSER   You whoreson conjuring scab, do you remember how you
99   cozened me with a ho—

ROBIN   Ha' you forgotten me? You think to carry it away° with your hey-pass and re-pass.° Do you remember the dog's fa—   *Exeunt* CLOWNS.

HOSTESS   Who pays for the ale? Hear you, master doctor, now you have sent away my guests, I pray who shall pay me for my a—   *Exit* HOSTESS.

DUCHESS   My lord,
    We are much beholding to this learnèd man.

DUKE   So are we, madam, which we will recompense
    With all the love and kindness that we may.
    His artful sport drives all sad thoughts away.   *Exeunt.*

---

stand much upon set great store by
curtsy to curtsy was "to make a leg"
colossus The Colossus of Rhodes was an enormous statue bestriding the harbor.

carry it away carry it off
hey-pass and re-pass juggler's exclamations

[SCENE XVII]

Thunder and lightning. Enter DEVILS *with covered dishes.*
MEPHOSTOPHILIS *leads them into* FAUSTUS' *study. Then enter* WAGNER.

WAGNER   I think my master means to die shortly.
He hath made his will, and given me his wealth,
His house, his goods, and store of golden plate,
Besides two thousand ducats ready coined.
And yet methinks, if that death were near,
He would not banquet and carouse and swill
Amongst the students, as even now he doth,
Who are at supper with such belly-cheer
As Wagner ne'er beheld in all his life.
10   See where they come; belike the feast is ended.   *Exit.*

Enter FAUSTUS, MEPHOSTOPHILIS, *and two or three* SCHOLARS.

1 SCHOLAR   Master Doctor Faustus, since our conference about fair ladies,
which was the beautifullest in all the world, we have determined with ourselves that Helen of Greece was the admirablest lady that ever lived. Therefore master doctor, if you will do us so much favour, as to let us see that peerless dame of Greece, whom all the world admires for majesty, we should
think ourselves much beholding unto you.

FAUSTUS   Gentlemen,
For that I know your friendship is unfeigned,
And Faustus' custom is not to deny
20   The just requests of those that wish him well,
You shall behold that peerless dame of Greece,
No otherways for pomp and majesty,
Than when Sir Paris crossed the seas with her,
And brought the spoils to rich Dardania.°
Be silent then, for danger is in words.

Music sounds. MEPHOSTOPHILIS *brings in* HELEN; *she passeth over the
stage.*

2 SCHOLAR   Too simple is my wit to tell her praise,
Whom all the world admires for majesty.
3 SCHOLAR   No marvel though the angry Greeks pursued
With ten years war the rape of such a queen,
30   Whose heavenly beauty passeth all compare.
1 SCHOLAR   Since we have seen the pride of nature's works,
And only° paragon of excellence,
Let us depart; and for this glorious deed
Happy and blest be Faustus evermore.

Enter an OLD MAN.

FAUSTUS   Gentlemen, farewell: the same wish I to you.   *Exeunt* SCHOLARS.
OLD MAN   O gentle Faustus, leave this damnèd art,

Dardania Troy   **only** sole

This magic, that will charm thy soul to hell,
And quite bereave thee of salvation.
Though thou hast now offended like a man,
40   Do not perséver in it like a devil.
Yet, yet, thou hast an amiable soul,
If sin by custom grow not into nature.°
Then, Faustus, will repentance come too late,
Then thou art banished from the sight of heaven;
No mortal can express the pains of hell.
It may be this my exhortation
Seems harsh and all unpleasant; let it not,
For, gentle son, I speak it not in wrath,
Or envy of thee, but in tender love,
50   And pity of thy future misery;
And so have hope, that this my kind rebuke,
Checking° thy body, may amend thy soul.

FAUSTUS   Where art thou, Faustus? Wretch, what hast thou done?
Damned art thou, Faustus, damned: despair and die.
Hell claims his right, and with a roaring voice
Says 'Faustus, come, thine hour is almost come'

                    MEPHOSTOPHILIS *gives him a dagger.*°
And Faustus now will come to do thee right.°

OLD MAN   O stay, good Faustus, stay thy desperate stops!
I see an angel hovers o'er thy head,
60   And with a vial full of precious grace,
Offers to pour the same into thy soul.
Then call for mercy and avoid despair.

FAUSTUS   O friend, I feel thy words
To comfort my distressèd soul.
Leave me awhile to ponder on my sins.

OLD MAN   Faustus, I leave thee, but with grief of heart,
Fearing the ruin of thy hapless soul.   *Exit.*

FAUSTUS   Accursed Faustus, where is mercy now?
I do repent, and yet I do despair.
70   Hell strives with grace for conquest in my breast;
What shall I do to shun the snares of death?

MEPHOSTOPHILIS   Thou traitor, Faustus, I arrest thy soul
For disobedience to my sovereign lord.
Revolt,° or I'll in piecemeal tear thy flesh.

FAUSTUS   I do repent I e'er offended him.
Sweet Mephostophilis, entreat thy lord
To pardon my unjust presumption,
And with my blood again I will confirm
The former vow I made to Lucifer.

---

custom . . . nature often opposed in Renaissance thought. Here "custom" means "habit," and the warning is against sin's becoming "second nature."
Checking reproving

dagger Suicide would suit the devil's purposes well.
do thee right pay you your due
Revolt turn back (to the devil)

80 MEPHOSTOPHILIS   Do it then, Faustus, with unfeignèd heart,
    Lest greater dangers do attend thy drift.°
 FAUSTUS   Torment, sweet friend, that base and agèd man
    That durst dissuade me from thy Lucifer,
    With greatest torment that our hell affords.
 MEPHOSTOPHILIS   His faith is great: I cannot touch his soul,
    But what I may afflict his body with
    I will attempt, which is but little worth.
 FAUSTUS   One thing, good servant, let me crave of thee,
    To glut the longing of my heart's desire,
90   That I may have unto my paramour
    That heavenly Helen which I saw of late,
    Whose sweet embracings may extinguish clear°
    Those thoughts that do dissuade me from my vow,
    And keep mine oath I made to Lucifer.
 MEPHOSTOPHILIS   This, or what else my Faustus shall desire,
    Shall be performed in twinkling of an eye.

   Enter HELEN *again, passing over between two* CUPIDS.

 FAUSTUS   Was this the face that launched a thousand ships,
    And burnt the topless° towers of Ilium?
    Sweet Helen, make me immortal with a kiss:
100   Her lips suck forth my soul, see where it flies.
    Come, Helen, come, give me my soul again.
    Here will I dwell, for heaven is in these lips,
    And all is dross that is not Helena.

   Enter OLD MAN.

    I will be Paris, and for love of thee
    Instead of Troy shall Wittenberg be sacked,
    And I will combat with weak Menelaus,°
    And wear thy colours on my plumèd crest.
    Yea, I will wound Achilles in the heel,°
    And then return to Helen for a kiss.
110   O, thou art fairer than the evening's air,
    Clad in the beauty of a thousand stars.
    Brighter art thou than flaming Jupiter,
    When he appeared to hapless Semele:°
    More lovely than the monarch of the sky,
    In wanton Arethusa's azured arms,°
    And none but thou shalt be my paramour.

        Exeunt [FAUSTUS *and* HELEN].

 OLD MAN   Accursèd Faustus, miserable man,

---

drift away from his allegiance
clear entirely
topless so high as to seem to have no tops
Menelaus Helen's Greek husband
in the heel where alone he was vulnerable
Semele She asked Jupiter to appear to her in

his full glory as a god; when he did, she was consumed by the lightning and thunderbolts that attended him.
More lovely . . . arms Arethusa, a nymph, was changed into a fountain; thus, the sun reflected in the water.

That from thy soul exclud'st the grace of heaven,
And fliest the throne of his tribunal seat.

Enter the DEVILS.

120 Satan begins to sift° me with his pride,
As in this furnace God shall try my faith.
My faith, vile hell, shall triumph over thee!
Ambitious fiends, see how the heavens smiles
At your repulse, and laughs your state to scorn.
Hence, hell, for hence I fly unto my God. *Exeunt.*

[SCENE XVIII]

Thunder. Enter LUCIFER, BELZEBUB, *and* MEPHOSTOPHILIS [*above.*]

LUCIFER   Thus from infernal Dis° do we ascend
To view the subjects of our monarchy,
Those souls which sin seals the black sons of hell,
'Mong which as chief, Faustus, we come to thee,
Bringing with us lasting damnation
To wait upon thy soul; the time is come
Which makes it forfeit.
MEPHOSTOPHILIS   And this gloomy night,
Here in this room will wretched Faustus be.
BELZEBUB   And here we'll stay,
10 To mark him how he doth demean° himself.
MEPHOSTOPHILIS   How should he, but in desperate lunacy?
Fond worldling, now his heart-blood dries with grief,
His conscience kills it, and his labouring brain
Begets a world of idle fantasies
To overreach the devil. But all in vain:
His store of pleasures must be sauced with pain.
He and his servant Wagner are at hand.
Both come from drawing Faustus' latest will.
See where they come.

Enter FAUSTUS *and* WAGNER.

20 FAUSTUS   Say, Wagner, thou hast perused my will:
How dost thou like it?
WAGNER   Sir, so wondrous well,
As in all humble duty I do yield
My life and lasting service for your love.

Enter the SCHOLARS.

FAUSTUS   Gramercies,° Wagner. Welcome, gentlemen.   [*Exit* WAGNER.]
1 SCHOLAR   Now, worthy Faustus, methinks your looks are changed.

sift test   **demean** conduct
Dis the underworld   **Gramercies** thanks

FAUSTUS Ah gentlemen!

2 SCHOLAR What ails Faustus?

FAUSTUS Ah, my sweet chamber-fellow, had I lived with thee, then had I lived
30   still, but now must die eternally. Look, sirs, comes he not, comes he not?

1 SCHOLAR O my dear Faustus, what imports this fear?

2 SCHOLAR Is all our pleasure turned to melancholy?

3 SCHOLAR He is not well with being over-solitary.

2 SCHOLAR If it be so, we'll have physicians, and Faustus shall be cured.

3 SCHOLAR 'Tis but a surfeit,° sir, fear nothing.

FAUSTUS A surfeit of deadly sin, that hath damned both body and soul.

2 SCHOLAR Yet Faustus, look up to heaven, and remember God's mercy is infinite.

FAUSTUS But Faustus' offence can ne'er be pardoned; the serpent that tempted
40   Eve may be saved, but not Faustus. O gentlemen, hear with patience and
tremble not at my speeches. Though my heart pants and quivers to remember
that I have been a student here these thirty years—O would I had never seen
Wittenberg, never read book! And what wonders I have done all Germany
can witness, yea all the world—for which Faustus hath lost both Germany
and the world, yea heaven itself, heaven, the seat of God, the throne of the
blessed, the kingdom of joy; and must remain in hell for ever. Hell, ah hell
for ever! Sweet friends, what shall become of Faustus, being in hell for ever?

2 SCHOLAR Yet Faustus, call on God.

50 FAUSTUS On God, whom Faustus hath abjured? On God, whom Faustus hath
blasphemed? Ah my God—I would weep, but the devil draws in my tears.
Gush forth blood instead of tears, yea, life and soul! O, he stays my tongue.
I would lift up my hands, but see, they hold them, they hold them.

ALL Who, Faustus?

FAUSTUS Why, Lucifer and Mephostophilis: Ah gentlemen, I gave them my
soul for my cunning.

ALL God forbid.

FAUSTUS God forbade it indeed, but Faustus hath done it. For the vain pleasure
60   of four-and-twenty years hath Faustus lost eternal joy and felicity. I writ
them a bill° with mine own blood; the date is expired; this is the time, and
he will fetch me.

1 SCHOLAR Why did not Faustus tell us of this before, that divines might have
prayed for thee?

FAUSTUS Oft have I thought to have done so, but the devil threatened to tear
me in pieces if I named God, to fetch me body and soul if I once gave ear to
divinity; and now 'tis too late. Gentlemen, away, lest you perish with me.

2 SCHOLAR Oh what may we do to save Faustus?

70 FAUSTUS Talk not of me, but save yourselves and depart.

3 SCHOLAR God will strengthen me. I will stay with Faustus.

1 SCHOLAR Tempt not God, sweet friend, but let us into the next room and pray
for him.

FAUSTUS Ay, pray for me, pray for me. And what noise soever you hear, come
not unto me, for nothing can rescue me.

---

surfeit overindulgence in food or drink   **bill** deed

2 SCHOLAR   Pray thou, and we will pray, that God may have mercy upon thee.
FAUSTUS   Gentlemen, farewell. If I live till morning, I'll visit you. If not,
   Faustus is gone to hell.
ALL   Faustus, farewell.   *Exeunt* SCHOLARS.
80   MEPHOSTOPHILIS   Ay, Faustus, now thou hast no hope of heaven,
         Therefore despair, think only upon hell,
         For that must be thy mansion, there to dwell.
FAUSTUS   Oh, thou bewitching fiend, 'twas thy temptation
         Hath robbed me of eternal happiness.
MEPHOSTOPHILIS   I do confess it, Faustus, and rejoice.
         'Twas I that, when thou were it i' the way to heaven,
         Damned up thy passage; when thou took'st the book
         To view the scriptures, then I turned the leaves
         And led thine eye.
90   What, weep'st thou? 'Tis too late, despair. Farewell.
         Fools that will laugh on earth, must weep in hell.   *Exit.*

   Enter the GOOD *and the* BAD ANGEL *at several doors.*

GOOD ANGEL   O Faustus, if thou hadst given ear to me
         Innumerable joys had followed thee.
         But thou didst love the world.
BAD ANGEL   Gave ear to me,
         And now must taste hell's pains perpetually.
GOOD ANGEL   O, what will all thy riches, pleasures, pomps,
         Avail thee now?
BAD ANGEL   Nothing but vex thee more,
         To want in hell, that had on earth such store.
                              Music while the throne° descends.
GOOD ANGEL   O, thou hast lost celestial happiness,
100   Pleasures unspeakable, bliss without end.
         Hadst thou affected sweet divinity,
         Hell, or the devil, had had no power on thee.
         Hadst thou kept on that way, Faustus, behold
         In what resplendent glory thou hadst sat
         In yonder throne, like those bright shining saints,
         And triumphed over hell. That hast thou lost,
         And now, poor soul, must thy good angel leave thee:
         The jaws of hell are open to receive thee.   *Exit [the throne ascends].*
                                                 Hell is discovered.°
BAD ANGEL   Now, Faustus, let thine eyes with horror stare
110   Into that vast perpetual torture-house.
         There are the furies tossing damnèd souls
         On burning forks; there bodies boil in lead;
         There are live quarters° broiling on the coals
         That ne'er can die; this ever-burning chair

throne chair let down from roof of stage on
ropes and representing the throne Faustus might
have had in heaven
Hell is discovered Curtain is drawn to reveal

perhaps a painted backcloth, perhaps some other
image of hell.
quarters quartered bodies

Is for o'er-tortured souls to rest them in;
These, that are fed with sops of flaming fire,
Were gluttons, and loved only delicates,
And laughed to see the poor starve at their gates.
But yet all these are nothing: thou shalt see
120   Then thousand tortures that more horrid be.
FAUSTUS   O, I have seen enough to torture me.
BAD ANGEL   Nay, thou must feel them, taste the smart of all:
He that loves pleasure must for pleasure fall.
And so I leave thee, Faustus, till anon:
Then wilt thou tumble in confusión.   *Exit [Hell is concealed].*
                                                       The clock strikes eleven.

FAUSTUS   Ah Faustus,
Now hast thou but one bare hour to live,
And then thou must be damned perpetually.
Stand still, you ever-moving spheres of heaven,
130   That time may cease and midnight never come.
Fair nature's eye, rise again, and make
Perpetual day; or let this hour be but
A year, a month, a week, a natural day,
That Faustus may repent and save his soul.
O lente, lente, currite noctis equi!°
The stars move still, time runs, the clock will strike.
The devil will come, and Faustus must be damned.
O I'll leap up to my God! Who pulls me down?
See, see, where Christ's blood streams in the firmament!°
140   One drop would save my soul, half a drop. Ah, my Christ!
Rend not my heart for naming of my Christ!
Yet will I call on him. O spare me, Lucifer!
Where is it now? 'Tis gone:
And see where God stretcheth out his arm,
And bends his ireful brows.
Mountains and hills, come, come, and fall on me,
And hide me from the heavy wrath of God.
No, no!
Then will I headlong run into the earth.
Earth gape! O no, it will not harbour me.
You stars that reigned at my nativity,
Whose influence hath allotted death and hell,
Now draw up Faustus like a foggy mist
Into the entrails of yon labouring clouds,
That when they vomit forth into the air,
160   My limbs may issue from their smoky mouths,
So that° my soul may but ascend to heaven.

                                                       The watch strikes.

O lente . . . equi "O run slowly, slowly, horses
of the night"; the lover who says this in Ovid,
Amores I.xiii.40, wants to prolong the night in
his mistress's arms.

Christ's blood . . . firmament See above, Scene
V, l. 66n.
So that if only

Ah, half the hour is passed: 'twill all be passed anon.
O God,
If thou wilt not have mercy on my soul,
Yet for Christ's sake, whose blood hath ransomed me,
Impose some end to my incessant pain;
Let Faustus live in hell a thousand years,
A hundred thousand, and at last be saved!
Oh, no end is limited° to damnèd souls.
170   Why wert thou not a creature wanting soul?
Or why is this immortal that thou hast?
Ah, Pythagoras' metempsychosis,° were that true
This soul should fly from me and I be changed
Unto some brutish beast: all beasts are happy,
For when they die
Their souls are soon dissolved in elements;
But mine must live still° to be plagued in hell.
Cursed be the parents that engendered me!
No, Faustus, curse thyself, curse Lucifer
180   That hath deprived thee of the joys of heaven.

The clock striketh twelve.

It strikes, it strikes! Now body, turn to air,
Or Lucifer will bear thee quick° to hell!

Thunder and lightning.

O soul, be changed to little water-drops
And fall into the ocean, ne'er be found.

Enter DEVILS.

My God, my God! Look not so fierce on me!
Adders and serpents, let me breathe awhile!
Ugly hell, gape not! Come not, Lucifer;
I'll burn my books!°—Ah, Mephostophilis!

Exeunt with him.

[SCENE XIX]

Enter the SCHOLARS.

1 SCHOLAR   Come gentlemen, let us go visit Faustus,
For such a dreadful night was never seen
Since first the world's creation did begin.
Such fearful shrieks and cries were never heard;
Pray heaven the doctor have escaped the danger.
2 SCHOLAR   Oh help us, heaven! See, here are Faustus' limbs,
All torn asunder by the hand of death.
3 SCHOLAR   The devils whom Faustus served have torn him thus:

---

limited appointed
metempsychosis Pythagoras' theory that at death
the soul passed into some other creature

still forever
quick alive
books (of magic)

10 For 'twixt the hours of twelve and one, methought
I heard him shriek and call aloud for help,
At which self time the house seemed all on fire
With dreadful horror of these damnèd fiends.

2 SCHOLAR   Well, Gentlemen, though Faustus' end be such
As every Christian heart laments to think on,
Yet, for he was a scholar once admired
For wondrous knowledge in our German schools,
We'll give his mangled limbs due burial,
And all the students clothed in mourning black
Shall wait upon his heavy° funeral.   *Exeunt.*

[EPILOGUE]

CHORUS

Cut is the branch that might have grown full straight,
And burnèd is Apollo's laurel bough,°
That sometime° grew within this learnèd man.
Faustus is gone: regard his hellish fall,
Whose fiendful fortune may exhort the wise
Only to wonder° at unlawful things,
Whose deepness doth entice such forward wits,
To practise more than heavenly power permits.   [*Exit.*]

Terminat hora diem, terminat Author opus.°

FINIS.

1604, 1616

Hero and Leander

The brief epic, or epyllion as it is sometimes called, is a genre with its roots in classical antiquity—such works as Catullus' poem on the lock of Berenice, and more particularly the individual narratives of Ovid's *Heroides*—and, in particular, in an Alexandrian tradition, opposed to the "epic" proportions of Homeric narrative, favoring the verse tale of one episode. The Elizabethan literary type of Ovidian mythological verse narrative inaugurated by Marlowe's *Hero and Leander* and Shakespeare's *Venus and Adonis* is a typically Renaissance invention. Alternately pictorial, sententious, delightedly lascivious, didactically moralizing, and interpretively mythographic, the erotic epyllia of the late sixteenth and early seventeenth century discharged those twinned Renaissance obligations to instruct and delight. They followed not only classical models, but contemporary interpretive and emblematic traditions as well. A passage from Marston's *The Metamorphosis of Pygmalion's Image* (given in The Renaissance Ovid) illustrates

heavy sorrowful
Apollo's laurel bough Apollo is the god of learning; his tree is the laurel or bay, thus associated with learning and poetry.
sometime once

Only to wonder be content with merely wondering
Terminat . . . opus "The hour ends the day, the author ends his work."

the kind of pointing-up of an Ovidian story which even the poorer sort of imagination could effect.

Marlowe's unfinished poem, only two cantos of which survive, is based upon a fifth-century (A.D.) version of the story by Musaeus, as well as on Ovid's *Heroides*. It is both witty and lush, picturesque and ironic; its moralization is all in the realm of erotic psychology and no censorious notes intrude. Marlowe's two "Sestiads" were first published five years after his death, in 1598; the same year, they were brought out again with George Chapman's vastly different completion, in which a whole exterior moral realm is introduced with more philosophic and mythographic intensity than narrative sophistication.

Hero and Leander

From *First Sestiad*°

On Hellespont, guilty of true love's blood,°
In view and opposite, two cities stood,
Sea-borderers, disjoined by Neptune's might;
The one Abydos, the other Sestos hight.°
At Sestos Hero dwelt; Hero the fair,
Whom young Apollo courted for her hair,°
And offered as a dower his burning throne,
Where she should sit for men to gaze upon.
The outside of her garments were of lawn,°
10   The lining purple silk, with gilt stars drawn;
Her wide sleeves green, and bordered with a grove
Where Venus in her naked glory strove
To please the careless and disdainful eyes
Of proud Adonis, that before her lies.
Her kirtle blue, whereon was many a stain,
Made with the blood of wretched lovers slain.
Upon her head she ware° a myrtle° wreath,
From whence her veil reached to the ground beneath.
Her veil was artificial flowers and leaves,
20   Whose workmanship both man and beast deceives.
Many would praise the sweet smell as she passed,
When 'twas the odour which her breath forth cast;
And there for honey, bees have sought in vain,
And, beat from thence, have lighted there again.
About her neck hung chains of pebble-stone,
Which, lightened by her neck, like diamonds shone.

Sestiad Marlowe's own term for the books of this poem, from "Sestos"
Hellespont . . . blood Helle drowned in the Dardanelles while riding on a golden ram.
hight named
Whom . . . hair Marlowe's invented anecdote
lawn a fine linen. Marlowe is describing an allegorical costume like that in a court masque or emblematic picture assembled from various

symbolic modes: thus green sleeves are conventionally erotic, but blend into a picture of Venus' grove; Hero is Venus' votary; she also wears buskins, boots worn by the classically derived personages of masques, pageants, and pictures.
ware wore
myrtle signifying sexual love

She ware no gloves, for neither sun nor wind
Would burn or parch her hands, but to her mind°
Or warm or cool them, for they took delight
30 To play upon those hands, they were so white.
Buskins° of shells all silverèd, used she,
And branched with blushing coral to the knee,
Where sparrows perched, of hollow pearl and gold,
Such as the world would wonder to behold—
Those with sweet water oft her handmaid fills,
Which, as she went, would chirrup through the bills.
Some say, for her the fairest Cupid pined,
And looking in her face, was strooken blind.°
But this is true: so like was one the other,
40 As he imagined Hero was his mother;
And oftentimes into her bosom flew,
About her naked neck his bare arms threw,
And laid his childish head upon her breast,
And with still° panting rocked, there took his rest.
So lovely fair was Hero, Venus' nun,°
As Nature wept, thinking she was undone,
Because she took more from her than she left
And of such wondrous beauty her bereft:
Therefore, in sign her treasure suffered wrack,
50 Since Hero's time hath half the world been black.
Amorous Leander, beautiful and young,
(Whose tragedy divine Musaeus° sung)
Dwelt at Abydos; since him dwelt there none
For whom succeeding times make greater moan.
His dangling tresses that were never shorn,
Had they been cut and unto Colchos° borne,
Would have allured the venturous youth of Greece
To hazard more than for the Golden Fleece.
Fair Cynthia° wished his arms might be her sphere;°
60 Grief makes her pale, because she moves not there.
His body was as straight as Circe's wand;
Jove might have sipped out nectar from his hand.°

to her mind as she was minded to
Buskins See l. 9n.
strooken blind In Renaissance images, Eros or
Cupid is shown blindfolded because "Love is
blind," passion clouds understanding, etc.,
although a commentator like Pico della Mirandola (1463–94), the Florentine humanist,
would point to Love's blindness as a tran-
scendence of the senses (like the blindfold on
Justice, allowing her to ignore interest). A
great painting by Titan (1477?–1576) shows
Venus blindfolding her son Cupid, while another
unblinded Cupid looks on—perhaps a picture
of a "blind" sensuous love and a "seeing,"
higher one. In the light of all this background,
Marlowe's anti-mythological joke becomes more

pointed. See Francis Bacon's "Cupid, or the
Atom."
still constant
nun votary
Musaeus 5th-century (A.D.) author of Marlowe's
original, confused with a mythical, earlier,
Homeric sort of bard
Colchos Colchis, home of the Golden Fleece,
sought by the Argonauts on one of the great
quests of myth
Cynthia the moon
sphere orbit
Jove . . . hand like Ganymede, Jupiter's cup-
bearer. There is intense sexual interest both in
this description of Leander, and in the homosexual episode with Neptune in the Second
Sestiad (see below).

Even as delicious meat is to the taste,
So was his neck in touching, and surpassed
The white of Pelops' shoulder.° I could tell ye
How smooth his breast was, and how white his belly,
And whose immortal fingers did imprint
That heavenly path, with many a curious° dint,
That runs along his back; but my rude pen
70 Can hardly blazon° forth the loves of men,
Much less of powerful gods—let it suffice
That my slack muse sings of Leander's eyes,
Those orient° cheeks and lips, exceeding his
That leapt into the water for a kiss
Of his own shadow,° and despising many,
Died ere he could enjoy the love of any.
Had wild Hippolytus° Leander seen,
Enamoured of his beauty had he been;
His presence made the rudest peasant melt,
80 That in the vast uplandish country dwelt.
The barbarous Thracian soldier, moved with naught,
Was moved with him, and for his favour sought.
Some swore he was a maid in man's attire,
For in his looks were all that men desire:
A pleasant smiling cheek, a speaking eye,
A brow for love to banquet royally;
And such as knew he was a man, would say,
'Leander, thou art made for amorous play:
Why art thou not in love, and loved of all?
90 Though thou be fair, yet be not thine own thrall.'

[In the remainder of the First Sestiad, Leander has fallen in love with Hero at
the temple of Venus. In II, they meet and embrace, but she will allow him
nothing more than passionate kissing. He leaves, and returns home, still longing
for Hero, who is "As loath to see Leander going out."]

From *Second Sestiad*

And now the sun that through the horizon peeps,
100 As pitying these lovers, downward creeps,
So that in silence of the cloudy night,
Though it was morning, did he take his flight.
But what the secret trusty night concealed,
Leander's amorous habit soon revealed;
With Cupid's myrtle was his bonnet crowned,
About his arms the purple riband wound
Wherewith she wreathed her largely spreading hair;

Pelops' shoulder It was of ivory.
curious exquisite
blazon to catalogue admiringly
orient shining

shadow image; this is about Narcissus
Hippolytus He preferred the hunt to the bed
of Phaedra.

Nor could the youth abstain, but he must wear
The sacred ring wherewith she was endowed,
110   When first religious chastity she vowed;
Which made his love through Sestos to be known,
And thence unto Abydos sooner blown
Than he could sail; for incorporeal Fame,
Whose weight consists in nothing but her name,
Is swifter than the wind, whose tardy plumes
Are reeking water and dull earthly fumes.
Home, when he came, he seemed not to be there,
But like exiled heir thrust from his sphere,
Set in a foreign place; and straight from thence,
120   Alcides° like, by mighty violence
He would have chased away the swelling main
That him from her unjustly did detain.
Like as the sun in a diameter
Fires and inflames objects removed far,
And heateth kindly, shining laterally,
So beauty sweetly quickens when 'tis nigh,
But being separated and removed,
Burns where it cherished, murders where it loved.
Therefore even as an index to a book,
130   So to his mind was young Leander's look.
Oh, none but gods have power their love to hide;
Affection by the countenance is descried.
The light of hidden fire itself discovers,
And love that is concealed betrays poor lovers.
His secret flame apparently was seen;
Leander's father knew where he had been,
And for the same mildly rebuked his son,
Thinking to quench the sparkles new begun.
But love, resisted once, grows passionate,
140   And nothing more than counsel lovers hate:
For as a hot proud horse° highly disdains
To have his head controlled, but breaks the reins,
Spits forth the ringled° bit, and with his hooves
Checks° the submissive ground, so he that loves,
The more he is restrained, the worse he fares.
What is it now but mad Leander dares?
'Oh Hero, Hero!' thus he cried full oft,
And then he got him to a rock aloft,
Where having spied her tower, long stared he on't
150   And prayed the narrow toiling Hellespont
To part in twain, that he might come and go,
But still the rising billows answered 'No.'

Alcides Hercules   ringled ringed
horse Cf. the analogous section from Shake-   Checks stamps
speare's *Venus and Adonis*.

With that he stripped him to the ivory skin,
And crying, 'Love, I come!' leaped lively° in.
Whereat the sapphire-visaged god° grew proud,
And made his capering Triton sound aloud,
Imagining that Ganymede,° displeased,
Had left the heavens; therefore on him he seized.
Leander strived; the waves about him wound,
160   And pulled him to the bottom, where the ground
Was strewed with pearl, and in low coral groves
Sweet singing mermaids sported with their loves
On heaps of heavy gold, and took great pleasure
To spurn in careless sort° the shipwreck treasure.
For here the stately azure palace stood
Where kingly Neptune and his train abode.
The lusty god embraced him, called him love,
And swore he never should return to Jove.
But when he knew it was not Ganymede,
170   (For under water he was almost dead)
He heaved him up, and looking on his face,
Beat down the bold waves with his triple mace,
Which mounted up, intending to have kissed him,
And fell in drops like tears, because they missed him.
Leander, being up, began to swim,
And looking back, saw Neptune follow him;
Whereat aghast, the poor soul gan to cry,
'Oh, let me visit Hero ere I die!'
The god put Helle's bracelet on his arm,
180   And swore the sea should never do him harm.
He clapped his plump cheeks, with his tresses played,
And smiling wantonly, his love bewrayed.°
He watched his arms, and as they opened wide
At every stroke, betwixt them would he slide
And steal a kiss, and then run out and dance,
And as he turned, cast many a lustful glance,
And threw him gaudy toys to please his eye,
And dive into the water, and there pry
Upon his breast, his thighs, and every limb,
190   And up again, and close beside him swim,
And talk of love. Leander made reply,
'You are deceived, I am no woman, I.'
Thereat smiled Neptune, and then told a tale
How that a shepherd, sitting in a vale,
Played with a boy so lovely, fair, and kind,
As for his love both earth and heaven pined;
That of the cooling river durst not drink

---

lively smartly   **sort** fashion
god Neptune   **bewrayed** revealed
Ganymede Jupiter's cup-bearer

Lest water nymphs should pull him from the brink;
And when he sported in the fragrant lawns,
200   Goat-footed satyrs and up-staring fauns
Would steal him thence. Ere half this tale was done,
'Ay me,' Leander cried, 'the enamoured sun,
That now should shine on Thetis'° glassy bower,
Descends upon my radiant Hero's tower.
O, that these tardy arms of mine were wings!'
And as he spake, upon the waves he springs.
Neptune was angry that he gave no ear,
And in his heart revenging malice bare:
He flung at him his mace, but as it went
210   He called it in, for love made him repent.
The mace returning back, his own hand hit,
As meaning to be venged for darting it.
When this fresh bleeding wound Leander viewed,
His colour went and came, as if he rued
The grief which Neptune felt. In gentle breasts
Relenting thoughts, remorse, and pity rests;
And who have hard hearts and obdurate minds
But vicious, harebrained, and illiterate hinds?
The god, seeing him with pity to be moved,
220   Thereon concluded that he was beloved.
(Love is too full of faith, too credulous,
With folly and false hope deluding us.)
Wherefore, Leander's fancy to surprise,
To the rich ocean for gifts he flies.
'Tis wisdom to give much; a gift prevails
When deep persuading oratory fails.
   By this, Leander, being near the land,
Cast down his weary feet and felt the sand.
Breathless albeit he were, he rested not
230   Till to the solitary tower he got,
And knocked and called, at which celestial noise
The longing heart of Hero much more joys
Than nymphs or shepherds when the timbrel rings,
Or crooked dolphin when the sailor sings°
She stayed not for her robes, but straight arose,
And drunk with gladness, to the door she goes,
Where seeing a naked man, she screeched for fear,
—Such sights as this to tender maids are rare—
And ran into the dark herself to hide.
240   Rich jewels in the dark are soonest spied;
Unto her was he led, or rather drawn,
By those white limbs which sparkled through the lawn.°

Thetis' Neptune's daughter, a sea nymph   Arion, shipwrecked, charmed a dolphin with his
Or crooked . . . sings The mythical lyre-player   music; it bore him to shore.
                                                lawn her sheer dress

The nearer that he came, the more she fled,
And seeking refuge, slipped into her bed.
Whereon Leander sitting, thus began,
Through numbing cold all feeble, faint and wan:
   'If not for love, yet, love, for pity sake,
Me in thy bed and maiden bosom take;
At least vouchsafe these arms some little room,
250 Who, hoping to embrace thee, cheerly° swum;
This head was beat with many a churlish billow,
And therefore let it rest upon thy pillow.'
Herewith affrighted Hero shrunk away,
And in her lukewarm place Leander lay,
Whose lively heat like fire from heaven fet,°
Would animate gross clay, and higher set
The drooping thoughts of base declining souls,
Than dreary° Mars carousing nectar bowls.
His hands he cast upon her like a snare;
260 She, overcome with shame and sallow fear,
Like chaste Diana, when Actaeon spied her,
Being suddenly betrayed, dived down to hide her.
And as her silver body downward went,
With both her hands she made the bed a tent,
And in her own mind thought herself secure,
O'ercast with dim and darksome coverture.
And now she lets him whisper in her ear,
Flatter, entreat, promise, protest, and swear;
Yet ever as he greedily assayed
270 To touch those dainties, she the harpy played,
And every limb did as a soldier stout
Defend the fort and keep the foeman out;
For though the rising ivory mount he scaled,
Which is with azure circling lines empaled,
Much like a globe (a globe may I term this,
By which love sails to regions full of bliss)
Yet there with Sisyphus° he toiled in vain,
Till gentle parley did the truce obtain.
Wherein Leander on her quivering breast,
280 Breathless spoke something, and sighed out the rest;
Which so prevailed, as he with small ado
Enclosed her in his arms and kissed her too.
And every kiss to her was as a charm,
And to Leander as a fresh alarm,°
So that the truce was broke, and she, alas,
(Poor silly maiden) at his mercy was.
Love is not full of pity (as men say)

cheerly happily
fet fetched
dreary gory

Sisyphus punished in Hades by having to roll
a stone uphill continuously
alarm battle cry

But deaf and cruel where he means to prey.
Even as a bird, which in our hands we wring,
290 Forth plungeth and oft flutters with her wing,
She trembling strove; this strife of hers (like that
Which made the world)° another world begat
Of unknown joy. Treason was in her thought,
And cunningly to yield herself she sought.
Seeming not won, yet won she was at length—
In such wars women use but half their strength.
Leander now, like Theban Hercules,
Entered the orchard of the Hesperides,
Whose fruit none rightly can describe but he
300 That pulls or shakes it from the golden tree.°
And now she wished this night were never done,
And sighed to think upon the approaching sun,
For much it grieved her that the bright daylight
Should know the pleasure of this blessed night,
And them like Mars and Erycine° displayed
Both in each other's arms chained as they laid,°
Again she knew not how to frame her look,
Or speak to him who in a moment took
That which so long, so charily she kept,
310 And fain by stealth away she would have crept,
And to some corner secretly have gone,
Leaving Leander in the bed alone.
But as her naked feet were whipping out,
He on the sudden clinged her so about,
That mermaid-like unto the floor she slid:
One half appeared, the other half was hid.
Thus near the bed she blushing stood upright.
And from her countenance behold ye might
A kind of twilight break, which through the hair,
320 As from an orient cloud, glimpse here and there;
And round about the chamber this false morn
Brought forth the day before the day was born.
So Hero's ruddy cheek Hero betrayed,
And her all naked to his sight displayed,
Whence his admiring eyes more pleasure took
Than Dis° on heaps of gold fixing his look.
By this, Apollo's° golden harp began
To sound forth music to the ocean,

---

made the world Love and Strife, according to a Greek philosophical tradition, governed the patterning of the four elements in the organization of the world from chaos.
Leander . . . tree Gathering the golden apples guarded by Atlas' daughters was the last of the Labors of Hercules; the golden fruit was associated in the Renaissance with the Earthly Paradise, and Marlowe cleverly uses the allusion here to tell of Leander's final sexual possession of Hero without actual pornographic description.
Erycine a name for Venus
laid lay
Dis Pluto, god of the underworld, and hence of minerals
Apollo's as song god and lord of the stringed instruments

Which watchful Hesperus no sooner heard,
330 But he the day-bright-bearing car° prepared,
And ran before, as harbinger of light,
And with his flaring beams mocked ugly Night
Till she, o'ercome with anguish, shame, and rage,
Danged° down to hell her loathsome carriage.

      Desunt nonnulla.°
        1598

The Passionate Shepherd to His Love°

Come live with me and be my love,
And we will all the pleasures prove°
That valleys, groves, hills, and fields,
Woods, or steepy mountain yields.

And we will sit upon the rocks,
Seeing the shepherds feed their flocks,
By shallow rivers to whose falls
Melodious birds sings madrigals.°

And I will make thee beds of roses
10 And a thousand fragrant posies,
A cap of flowers, and a kirtle °
Embroidered all with leaves of myrtle.

A gown made of the finest wool
Which from our pretty lambs we pull;
Fair lined slippers for the cold,
With buckles of the purest gold

A belt of straw and ivy buds,
With coral clasps and amber studs;
And if these pleasures may thee move,
20 Come live with me, and be my love.

The shepherd° swains shall dance and sing
For thy delight each May morning
If these delights thy mind may move,
Then live with me and be my love.
        1599–1600

---

car chariot
Danged hurled
Desunt nonnulla "some are missing" (the other Sestiads); see George Chapman's continuation, above
The Passionate Shepherd to His Love an invitation to the pastoral realm where nature outdoes art; see Ralegh's answer to it, above, and Donne's "The Bait"

prove test by experiencing
madrigals the natural harmony of the pastoral world; notice the complex and perverted use of it in the Bower of Bliss in Spenser's *Faerie Queene* II.xii
kirtle dress
shepherd The 1600 text gives "shepherds'."

SAMUEL DANIEL

1562–1619

An enterprising and remarkably productive Elizabethan man of letters, Daniel came from a musical Somerset family, studied at Oxford, traveled abroad, and became a member of the literary circle of the Countess of Pembroke, Sir Philip Sidney's sister. He was involved in the establishment of the sonneteering tradition of the last decade of the century, publishing in 1591—along with the first appearance of Sidney's *Astrophel and Stella* sonnets—a group of twenty-eight of his own. In 1592 a full collection entitled *Delia* appeared. Their form is usually said to have influenced Shakespeare's choice of the three-quatrain-and-couplet model set up by Surrey, but there seem to be occasional similarities in a shared condensed syntax and rhythmic structures as well. Daniel wrote narrative, history, lofty disquisition, tragedy, and pastoral drama, all in assured and competent verse, as well as a famous prose essay, *A Defence of Rhyme,* in answer to Thomas Campion's attack on vernacular traditions of versifying. He wrote masques for the Jacobean court, and like his contemporary, Drayton, kept revising his sonnets and other poems, hardening and purifying the diction.

Care-charmer Sleep

Care-charmer Sleep, son of the sable Night,
Brother to Death, in silent darkness born,
Relieve my languish° and restore the light,
With dark forgetting of my cares, return.
And let the day be time enough to mourn
The shipwreck of my ill-adventured youth;
Let waking eyes suffice to wail their scorn
Without the torment of the night's untruth.
Cease, dreams, the images of day-desires,
To model forth the passions of the morrow;
Never let rising sun approve you liars,
To add more grief to aggravate° my sorrow.
    Still let me sleep, embracing clouds in vain,
    And never wake to feel the day's disdain.

1592–94

A Pastoral°

Oh happy golden age
Not for° that rivers ran
With streams of milk, and honey dropped from trees;

---

languish drooping enfeeblement
aggravate make heavier
A Pastoral translated from a chorus in Torquato Tasso's pastoral drama, *Aminta* (1573); see "The Golden Age" in The Renaissance Ovid, above, and the chorus from Guarini's *Il Pastor*

Fido (1590) translated by Sir Richard Fanshawe. Daniel here adapts the Italian 7- and 11-syllable lines to English, keeping the rhyme scheme.
Not for not (golden or happy) because . . .

Not that the earth did gauge°
Unto the husbandman
Her voluntary fruits,° free without fees;
Not for no cold did freeze,
Nor any cloud beguile
The eternal flowering spring
10   Wherein lived everything
And whereon the heavens perpetually did smile;
Not for no ship had brought
From foreign shores or wars or wares° ill sought—

But only for that name,
That idle name of wind,
That idol of deceit, that empty sound
Called Honour,° which became
The tyrant of the mind
And so torments our nature without ground,
20   Was not yet vainly found;
Nor yet sad griefs imparts
Amidst the sweet delights
Of joyful amorous wights,°
Nor were his hard laws known to free-born hearts;
But golden laws like these
Which Nature wrote: 'That's lawful which doth please.'

Then amongst flowers and springs
Making delightful sport,
Sat lovers without conflict, without flame;
30   And nymphs and shepherds sings,
Mixing in wanton sort
Whisperings with songs, then kisses with the same
Which from affection came;
The naked virgin then
Her roses fresh reveals
Which now her veil conceals,
The tender apples in her bosom seen;
And oft in rivers clear
The lovers with their loves consorting were.

40   Honour, thou first didst close
The spring of all delight,
Denying water to the amorous thirst;
Thou taught'st fair eyes to lose
The glory of their light,
Restrained from men, and on themselves reversed.

gauge pledge
voluntary fruits no work was needed for human
sustenance
or . . . or either . . . or
Honour in the sense of sexual chasity, here
viewed in its negative aspect of coyness, reticence, and prudery—all bred by the knowledge
that sexual enjoyment is forbidden. Tasso's
point is that the most important thing about
the Golden Age is that everything was permitted,
and thus lovely; see *Paradise Lost* IV.312–18.
wights people

Thou in a lawn° didst first
Those golden hairs encase
Late° spread unto the wind;
Thou mad'st loose grace unkind,
50 Gav'st bridle to their words, art to their pace.°
Oh Honour, is it thou
That mak'st that stealth which love doth free allow?

It is thy work that brings
Our griefs and torments thus,
But thou, fierce lord of nature and of love,
The qualifier of kings,
What dost thou here with us
That are below thy power, shut from above?
Go, and from us remove:
60 Trouble the mighty's sleep!
Let us, neglected, base,
Live still without thy grace,
And the use of the ancient happy ages keep.
Let's love—this life of ours
Can make no truce with time, that all devours.
Let's love! The sun doth set and rise again,
But whenas our short light
Comes once to set, it makes eternal night.°

1592, 1601

MICHAEL DRAYTON
1563–1631

Drayton is essentially an Elizabethan in the line of Spenser. Born in Warwickshire, brought up as a page in a noble house, he composed fashionable sonnets (*Idea's Mirror*, 1594), pastorals, and historical narrative in the 1590's. Never achieving favor or influence at the Jacobean court, he depended upon patronage (such as that of the Countess of Bedford, Donne's admirer) for support of his growingly ambitious projects. Notable among these was the massive topographical, historical poem *Poly-Olbion* (1612–13) covering England, county by county, and his post-Spenserian pastoral narrative *Nymphidia* (1627). *The Muses' Elizium* (1630) represents a last flowering of mythopoetic tradition at the edge of a narrower, wittier period of mythological poetry. The sonnets printed below are from the revised *Idea* of 1619.

From The Muses' Elizium

The Description of Elizium°

A Paradise on earth is found,
Though far from vulgar sight,
Which with those pleasures doth abound
That it *Elizium*° hight.

Where, in delights that never fade,
The Muses lullèd be,
And sit at pleasure in the shade
Of many a stately tree,

Which no rough tempest makes to reel
10 Nor their straight bodies bows,
Their lofty tops do never feel
The weight of winter's snows.

In groves that evermore are green
No falling leaf is there,
But Philomel° (of birds the queen)
In music spends the year.

The merle upon her myrtle perch
There to the mavis sings,
Who from the top of some curled birch
20 Those notes redoubled rings.

There daisies damask° every place
Nor once their beauties lose,
That when proud Phoebus hides his face
Themselves they scorn to close.

The pansy and the violet here,
As seeming to descend
Both from one root, a very pair,
For sweetness yet contend

And, pointing to a pink to tell
30 Which bears it, it is loath
To judge it; but replies, for smell
That it exceeds them both;

Wherewith displeased they hang their heads
So angry soon they grow,

The Description of Elizium This is the introductory poem to *The Muses' Elizium*, blending Renaissance themes of the earthly paradise with such classical motifs as the Elysian Fields and the Gardens of Alcinous from Bk. 7 of the *Odyssey*, into a vision of the paradise of poetry. **Elizium** Its name mixes that of the classical Elysian Fields with the late Queen Elizabeth's, the implication being that the Elizabethan period was a poetical Golden Age.
Philomel Philomela, who was changed into a nightingale
damask ornament

And from their odoriferous beds
Their sweets at it they throw.

The winter here a summer is,
No waste is made by time,
Nor doth the autumn ever miss
40   The blossoms of the prime.°

The flower that Júly forth doth bring
In April here is seen,
The primrose that puts on the spring
In Júly decks each green.

The sweets for sovereignty contend
And so abundant be,
That to the very earth they lend
And bark of every tree.

Rills rising out of every bank
50   In wild meanders strain,
And playing many a wanton prank
Upon the speckled plain,

In gambols and lascivious gyres°
Their time they still bestow,
Nor to the fountaines none retires;
Nor on their course will go

Those brooks with lilies bravely decked,
So proud and wanton made
That they their courses quite neglect,
60   And seem as though they stayed

Fair Flora in her state to view
Which through these lilies looks,
Or as those lilies leaned to show
Their beauties to the brooks.

That Phoebus in his lofty race
Oft lays aside his beams
And comes to cool his glowing face
In these delicious streams.

Oft spreading vines climb up the cleeves°
70   Whose ripened clusters there
Their purple liquid drop, which drives
A vintage through the year.

Those cleeves whose craggy sides are clad
With trees of sundry suits,

prime spring. Compare this with the Garden of
Adonis in Spenser's *Faerie Queene* III.vi.

lascivious gyres erotic twistings
cleeves cliffs

Which make continual summer glad,
Even bending with the fruits,

Some ripening, ready some to fall,
Some blossomed, some to bloom,
Like gorgeous hangings on the wall
80   Of some rich, princely room:

Pomegranates, lemons, citrons, so
Their laded branches bow,
Their leaves in number that outgo
Nor roomth° will them allow.

There in perpetual summer's shade,
Apollo's prophets sit,
Among the flowers that never fade,
But flourish like their wit;

To whom the nymphs upon their lyres,
90   Tune many a curious lay,
And with their most melodious choirs
Make short the longest day.

The thrice three virgins heavenly clear,
Their trembling timbrels sound,
Whilst the three comely Graces there
Dance many a dainty round,°

Decay nor age there nothing knows;
There is continual youth,
As time on plant or creatures grows
100   So still their strength reneweth.

The poets' paradise this is,
To which but few can come;
The Muses' only bower of bliss°
Their dear *Elizium.*

Here happy souls (their blessed bowers,
Free from the rude resort
Of beastly people) spend the hours,
In harmless mirth and sport.

Then on to the Elizian plains
110   Apollo doth invite you
Where he provides with pastoral strains,
In Nymphals° to delight you.

1630

roomth room
Whilst . . . round Cf. Calidore's vision of the maidens dancing around the three graces to the music of Colin Clout in *The Faerie Queene* VI.x.
bower of bliss alludes to Spenser's in *The*

Faerie Queene II.xii, but with no negative overtones
Nymphals The pastoral narratives which follow Drayton calls "Nymphals" rather than "songs," as elsewhere.

From Idea

VII

How many paltry, foolish, painted things,
That now in coaches trouble every street,
Shall be forgotten, whom no poet sings,
Ere they be well wrapped in their winding sheet!
Where I to thee eternity shall give,
When nothing else remaineth of these days,
And queens hereafter shall be glad to live
Upon the alms of thy superfluous praise.
Virgins and matrons reading these my rhymes
10   Shall be so much delighted with thy story
That they shall grieve they lived not in these times,
To have seen thee, their sex's only glory.
    So shalt thou fly above the vulgar throng,
    Still to survive in my immortal song.
                1619

VIII

There's nothing grieves me but that age should haste
That in my days I may not see thee old:
That where those two clear, sparkling eyes are placed
Only two loopholes then I might behold;
That lovely archèd, ivory, polished brow
Deface with wrinkles that I might but see;
Thy dainty hair, so curled and crispèd now
Like grizzled moss upon some agèd tree;
Thy cheek, now flush with roses, sunk and lean;
10   Thy lips, with age as any wafer thin;
Thy pearly teeth out of thy head so clean,
That when thou feed'st thy nose shall touch thy chin.
    These lines that now thou scorn'st, which should delight thee,
    Then would I make thee read, but to despite thee.
                1619

LVI

Since there's no help, come let us kiss and part;
Nay, I have done, you get no more of me,
And I am glad, yea glad with all my heart
That thus so cleanly I myself can free;
Shake hands forever, cancel all our vows,
And when we meet at any time again,
Be it not seen in either of our brows
That we one jot of former love retain.
Now at the last gasp of love's latest breath,
10   When, his pulse failing, Passion° speechless lies,

Passion These personifications make up a kind
of allegorical picture or sculptured group, almost
the parody of a Pietà.

When Faith is kneeling by his bed of death,
And Innocence is closing up his eyes,
  Now if thou wouldst, when all have given him over,
  From death to life thou mightst him yet recover.

1619

WILLIAM SHAKESPEARE
1564–1616

Shakespeare was baptized on April 26, 1564, at Stratford-on-Avon, Warwickshire. His father John was a Stratford tradesman, called in legal documents a "glover," but also a dealer in timber and wool, the main commodity of the nearby Cotswold area. A man of substance and father of eight children, John owned property in Stratford, and was an official of the town, but he suffered a period of reverses, some possibly caused by his recusancy—he remained Catholic when it was dangerous and costly to do so. He got over this, and in 1596 he was granted the arms of a gentleman, probably at William Shakespeare's request. He died in 1601.

Shakespeare almost certainly attended Stratford Grammar School, where the teaching was mostly of Latin grammar and rhetoric, and where he would have read Terence, the Latin dramatist from whom the rules of dramatic structure—which he knew but did not slavishly obey—ultimately derived. He went to neither university, but married the pregnant Anne Hathaway, eight years his senior, in November 1582; their daughter Susanna was christened in May 1583, and their twins, Judith and Hamnet, in February 1585.

Nothing is known about his going to London, but he almost certainly was there by 1589; by 1592 he had written Henry VI and was well enough known to be attacked as an upstart actor by the pamphleteer Greene in his Groatsworth of Wit.

The London theaters closed when deaths from plague reached a certain figure each week, and there was an especially bad epidemic in the years 1592–94. During this time the existing companies went on tour, collapsed, and lost their principal writers. Shakespeare wrote his narrative poems, Venus and Adonis and The Rape of Lucrece, during this time. Both poems were dedicated to the Earl of Southampton (1573–1624), a patron of literature and the friend of the Queen's favorite, the Earl of Essex, in whose rebellion (1601) Southampton was to take part. Although he is a favored candidate for the role of dedicatee and friend in Shakespeare's Sonnets, no positive connection between them other than the dedications of Venus and Adonis and The Rape of Lucrece has ever been proved. Evidently, however, during the plague years Shakespeare was seeking or enjoying the protection of this powerful nobleman.

When the plague abated, the companies sorted themselves out into two—the Admiral's Men and the Lord Chamberlain's Men (named for their official sponsors at court—they were in fact liveried servants of these aristocrats). The great actor Alleyn went to the Admiral's Men; Burbage, his rival, to the Lord Chamberlain's. Shakespeare joined Burbage, and remained with the company for the rest of his working life. When King James I took it over (1603) as the King's Men he became, technically, a servant of the king. The grant of arms to his father in 1596 made Shakespeare himself a gentleman, and in the following year he was rich enough to buy a large house in Stratford.

Before the formation of the Lord Chamberlain's Men Shakespeare had probably written *Henry VI, Richard II,* and *Titus Andronicus.* His early plays for the new company were *The Comedy of Errors, The Taming of the Shrew, The Two Gentlemen of Verona,* and *Love's Labour's Lost.* He must have been extremely busy in this period, as "sharer" (shareholder) in the company, actor, and principal playwright. By 1599 he had also written *Romeo and Juliet, Richard II, King John, The Merchant of Venice,* the two parts of *Henry IV, Henry V, Much Ado About Nothing,* and *The Merry Wives of Windsor.*

In 1599 the lease of their house, The Theatre, expired, and in an operation of considerable ingenuity and enterprise Shakespeare's company forestalled the demolition men sent in by the landlord, rapidly dismantled the building, and shipped it across the Thames to Bankside, where they built a new playhouse with the old timbers and called it The Globe. Shakespeare was registered as owner of one-tenth share. In this theater were played most of his masterpieces, including all the main tragedies: *Julius Caesar, Hamlet, Othello, King Lear, Macbeth, Antony and Cleopatra, Coriolanus,* and *Timon of Athens* (if it was performed at all). The Globe also saw the première of *As You Like It* and *Twelfth Night,* of the "problem" plays, *Troilus and Cressida, All's Well That Ends Well,* and *Measure for Measure,* and Shakespeare's final plays, *Pericles, Cymbeline, The Winter's Tale,* and *The Tempest.* There were two more works, in which Shakespeare was a collaborator, *Two Noble Kinsmen* and *Henry VIII,* during a performance of which the theater burnt down when a blank cannon shot set fire to the thatch, on June 29, 1613.

In the preceding few years, from about 1609, the King's Men had also performed indoors in the more sophisticated Blackfriars Theatre; this certainly affected the kind of play they wanted and got from Shakespeare and the younger playwrights Beaumont and Fletcher. But The Globe was his true arena, the "wooden O" which contained and fed his imagination.

Shakespeare retired to Stratford around 1610; *The Winter's Tale* and *The Tempest* were probably written there. He continued his business life, and records of lawsuits— Shakespeare appears always to have enjoyed litigation—survive from the period between his retirement and his death, at the age of fifty-two, on April 23, 1616.

Shakespeare apparently took little care to be published, except with *Venus and Adonis* and *The Rape of Lucrece;* even the authorized quartos of the plays published during his life time are badly and carelessly printed. The *Sonnets* were published without his consent or care, and his mysterious poem "The Phoenix and Turtle," which appeared in an anthology in 1601, is almost the only work he willingly published after 1593. A great part of his work remained in manuscript until his colleagues John Heminges and Henry Condell brought out in 1623 the collection we now call the First Folio. This large book contains, in texts of varying authority, all the plays we now attribute to Shakespeare except *Pericles,* which was added in the third edition (Third Folio) of 1664.

Venus and Adonis

This was Shakespeare's first published work (he calls it "the first heir of my invention" in the dedication). The first edition of 1593 is one of the few things he is likely to have seen carefully through the press, for it was dedicated to a noble patron—the young Earl of Southampton—and needed to be presented in a form that would please him. Ten more editions appeared in the next twenty-four years; the poem presumably achieved this degree of success because of its fashionable eroticism.

Venus and Adonis belongs to the genre of erotic epyllion, of which other examples are Marlowe's *Hero and Leander* (see the Headnote to that poem) and Marston's *Pygmalion's Image*. The immediate appeal lies, broadly speaking, in the wittily erotic handling of the theme; yet these poems were capable of bearing some allegorical freight, and Shakespeare's does so. Such poetry is Ovidian (see The Renaissance Ovid) and "etiological," that is, providing mythical explanations for, say, the existence of a particular flower. The ostensible "cause" of Shakespeare's poem is thus to account for the anemone, said to have grown out of Adonis' blood after the boar has killed him. But this is merely the occasion for a display of rhetorical, decorative, and serio-comic poetry.

Shakespeare uses a variant of the Venus-Adonis myth which (as in Titian's painting) makes Adonis reluctant, and Venus the outrageous wooer (see also *Hero and Leander* I.12–14). This adds to the piquancy of the narrative, and also enables the author to make observations, at once eloquent and singularly moral, about love and lust. So the poem is not without seriousness, but there is little of the high seriousness which colors Spenser's treatment of the theme in *The Faerie Queene* III.vi, or Milton's in the Epilogue to *Comus*.

Venus and Adonis has two notable digressions, one on the hunting of the hare, and one on the stallion of Adonis (part of the latter is given below). Venus has already wooed Adonis, the "flint-hearted boy," by praising his beauty and by using arguments employed by Shakespeare in the early sonnets ("Thou wast begot, to get it is thy duty"). He resists, showing both sexual coldness and some effeminacy ("The sun doth burn my face, I must remove"); then, rejecting Venus' suggestions of sexual pleasure, he tries but fails to recover his horse, whose amorous attitude to the stray mare makes an interesting contrast with Adonis' attitude to Venus. This use of a contrasting example to add, without explicit comment, a dimension to the theme, is a sophistication similar in some ways to the author's use of dramatic subplots, in others to techniques later identified as "baroque"—though the *ecphrasis*, as it is called, is an ancient device. In this case, as with the hare, Shakespeare mingles Italianate refinement with down-to-earth detail and observation.

After this digression the poem continues for nearly nine hundred lines more; Adonis expatiates on his unripeness, on the crime of lust, on his desire to hunt the boar; Venus argues back unavailingly. He leaves her ("Look how a bright star shooteth from the sky, / So glides he in the night from Venus' eye" are lines made famous by Coleridge as an example of the operation of imagination, as opposed to fancy) and is killed. Venus lengthily laments his death, decrees that "Sorrow on love hereafter shall attend," and clutches his flower to her bosom.

From Venus and Adonis°

'Fondling,'° she saith, 'since I have hemmed thee here
230 Within the circuit of this ivory pale,°
I'll be a park, and thou shalt be my deer:°
Feed where thou wilt, on mountain or in dale;
    Graze on my lips, and if those hills be dry,
    Stray lower, where the pleasant fountains° lie.

'Within this limit° is relief° enough,
Sweet bottom grass° and high delightful plain,
Round rising hillocks, brakes obscure and rough,°
To shelter thee from tempest and from rain:
    Then be my deer, since I am such a park,
240   No dog shall rouse° thee, though a thousand bark.'

At this Adonis smiles as in disdain,
That° in each cheek appears a pretty dimple;
Love made those hollows, if himself were slain,°
He might be buried in a tomb so simple,
    Foreknowing well, if there he came to lie,
    Why there love lived, and there he could not die.

These lovely caves, these round enchanting pits,
Opened their mouths to swallow Venus' liking:°
Being mad before, how doth she now for wits?
250 Struck dead before, what needs a second striking?
    Poor queen of love, in thine own law forlorn,°
    To love a cheek that smiles at thee in scorn!

Now which way shall she turn? what shall she say?
Her words are done, her woes the more increasing;
The time is spent, her object° will away,
And from her twining arms doth urge releasing.
    'Pity,' she cries, 'some favour, some remorse!'°
    Away he springs, and hasteth to his horse.

But lo from forth a copse that neighbours by,°
260 A breeding jennet,° lusty, young and proud,
Adonis' trampling courser doth espy,
And forth she rushes, snorts and neighs aloud:
    The strong-necked steed being tied unto a tree,
    Breaketh his rein, and to her straight goes he.

Venus and Adonis Venus forces Adonis to dismount, and woos him ardently without success; now she embraces him and links her fingers behind him.
Fondling foolish one
hemmed enclosed
pale fence
deer pun on "dear"
limit precinct
relief pasture
fountains . . . bottom grass . . . brakes obscure and rough This kind of punning gave the poem its reputation for naughtiness; *bottom:* meadow, *brakes:* thickets.
rouse drive from cover
That so that
if . . . slain so that if he himself were killed
liking desire
in thine . . . forlorn deprived in a matter which you're supposed to control
object Adonis
remorse mercy
neighbours by lies near by
breeding jennet small Spanish mare

419

Imperiously he leaps, he neighs, he bounds,
And now his woven girths he breaks asunder;
The bearing° earth with his hard hoof he wounds,
Whose hollow womb resounds like heaven's thunder;
    The iron bit he crusheth 'tween his teeth,
270   Controlling what he was controllèd with.°

His ears up-pricked, his braided hanging mane
Upon his compassed° crest now stand on end;
His nostrils drink the air, and forth again
As from a furnace, vapours doth he send;
    His eye which scornfully glisters like fire,
    Shows his hot courage° and his high desire.

Sometimes he trots, as if he told° the steps,
With gentle majesty and modest pride;
Anon he rears upright, curvets° and leaps,
280   As who should say 'Lo thus my strength is tried:
    And this I do to captivate the eye
    Of the fair breeder that is standing by.'

What recketh° he his rider's angry stir,°
His flattering 'holla' or his 'Stand, I say'?
What cares he now for curb or pricking spur,
For rich caparisons° or trappings gay?
    He sees his love, and nothing else he sees,
    For nothing else with his proud sight agrees.

Look when a painter would surpass the life
290   In limning out° a well-proportioned steed,
His art with nature's workmanship at strife,
As if the dead the living should exceed:
    So did this horse excel a common one,
    In shape, in courage, colour, pace and bone.°

Round-hoofed, short-jointed, fetlocks shag° and long,
Broad breast, full eye, small head, and nostril wide,
High crest, short ears, straight legs and passing strong,
Thin mane, thick tail, broad buttock, tender hide:
    Look what a horse should have he did not lack,
300   Save a proud rider on so proud a back.

Sometimes he scuds far off, and there he stares;
Anon he starts at stirring of a feather.
To bid the wind a base° he now prepares,

---

bearing that bears his weight
Imperiously . . . with Cf. the use of a horse as
emblem of sexual desire in Marlowe, *Hero and
Leander* II.141–45.
compassed arched
courage lust
told counted
curvets prances

recketh cares
stir agitation
caparisons ornamental harness
limning out drawing, painting
bone frame
shag rough, untrimmed
bid . . . base challenge the wind to a chase

And where° he run or fly, they know not whether,°
   For through his mane and tail the high wind sings,
   Fanning the hairs, who wave like feathered wings.

He looks upon his love, and neighs unto her:
   She answers him, as if she knew his mind.
   Being proud, as females are, to see him woo her,
310 She puts on outward strangeness,° seems unkind,
   Spurns at his love, and scorns the heat he feels,
   Beating his kind° embracements with her heels.

Then like a melancholy malcontent,°
   He vails° his tail that like a falling plume
   Cool shadow to his melting buttock lent;
   He stamps, and bites the poor flies in his fume.°
   His love perceiving how he was enraged,
   Grew kinder, and his fury was assuaged.

His testy° master goeth about° to take him,
320 When lo the unbacked° breeder, full of fear,
   Jealous of catching,° swiftly doth forsake him;
   With her the horse, and left Adonis there:
   As they were mad unto the wood they hie them,
   Outstripping crows that strive to overfly them.

. . .

1593?   1593

The Rape of Lucrece

This poem, like *Venus and Adonis,* was dedicated to the Earl of Southampton, in terms which may suggest that Shakespeare had improved his acquaintance with the nobleman in the intervening year. Published in a careful text in 1594, it had five more editions in the next twelve years.

   Lucrece is longer and more weighty than *Venus,* being the "graver labour" he had promised Southampton in the dedication to the earlier poem. It is a narrative tragedy of extreme schematic and rhetorical elaboration. The theme is roughly that of Sonnet CXXIX, "The expense of spirit in a waste of shame / Is lust in action." The action is simple: Tarquin, inflamed by the virtuous Lucrece, accepts her hospitality and then rapes her; she requires of her husband an oath of revenge, and then commits suicide. The expulsion of the Tarquins and the end of the Roman monarchy follow.

   Shakespeare extends this material to 1855 lines by dwelling on the struggle in Tarquin's mind between desire and dishonor ("Thus graceless holds he disputation / 'Tween frozen conscience and hot burning will"), his guilt, Lucrece's sense of disgrace, and her invocations to Night, Opportunity, and Time, of which the last is given

---

where whether
whether which
outward strangeness show of indifference
kind both loving and according to nature
melancholy malcontent The melancholy man
and the malcontent were fashionable social types.

vails droops
fume irritation
testy angry
goeth about tries
unbacked unbroken
Jealous of catching anxious not to be caught

here. (With characteristic virtuosity it touches on most of the commonplaces associated with the subject.) The work is further extended by a long and significant digression in which she describes a wall-hanging depicting the fall of Troy.

No other work of Shakespeare resembles this early ambitious and learned poem. Its extensive working out of schemes and topics is matched by nothing in the plays (*Titus Andronicus,* the closest of the tragedies in time and theme, is also closest in treatment). It contains much, in the description of both action and passion, in the seizing of narrative and moral opportunities, that is remarkably fine; it touches on matters which were many times to preoccupy the later dramatist; but it represents with *Venus and Adonis* the starting point of a career Shakespeare never followed, for he gave it up as soon as the theaters reopened and enabled him to resume his dramatic work.

From The Rape of Lucrece

'Mis-shapen Time,° copesmate° of ugly Night,
Swift subtle post,° carrier of grisly Care,
Eater of youth, false slave to false delight,
Base watch° of woes, sin's pack-horse, virtue's snare!
Thou nursest all, and murderest all that are:
930 O hear me then, injurious shifting° Time!
  Be guilty of my death, since of° my crime.

'Why hath thy servant Opportunity°
Betrayed the hours thou gavest me to repose,
Cancelled my fortunes and enchainèd me
To endless date° of never-ending woes?
Time's office is to fine° the hate of foes,
  To eat up errors by Opinion° bred,
  Not spend the dowry of a lawful bed.°

'Time's glory is to calm contending kings,
940 To unmask falsehood and bring truth° to light,
To stamp the seal of time in agèd things,
To wake the morn and sentinel° the night,
To wrong the wronger till he render right,°
  To ruinate° proud buildings with thy hours,
  And smear with dust their glittering golden towers;

Time Lucrece, having inveighed against Night and Opportunity, now formally accuses Time, which is almost a favorite topic of Shakespeare's; see especially Sonnets XII, XIX, LXIV.
copesmate companion
post messenger
watch watchman (who counts woes like hours)
shifting moving; cheating
since of since you were guilty of
Opportunity occasion (closely related to time: "Whoever plots the sin, thou pointst the season," l. 879).
Cancelled . . . date cancelled an existing contract with fortune and substituted another, with

no expiry date, to sorrow
fine bring to an end
Opinion belief unsupported by real knowledge (the word usually had a disparaging sense at this time)
spend . . . bed squander the future of a virtuous marriage
truth often called "the daughter of time"
sentinel stand watch over
To wrong . . . right to afflict the guilty with later misfortunes so as to produce a change of conscience
ruinate reduce to ruins

'To fill with worm-holes stately monuments,
To feed Oblivion° with decay of things,
To blot old books and alter their contents,
To pluck the quills from ancient ravens'° wings,
950   To dry the old oak's sap and cherish springs,
　　　To spoil antiquities of hammered steel,
　　　And turn the giddy round of fortune's wheel;°

'To show the beldam° daughters of her daughter,
To make the child a man, the man a child,
To slay the tiger that doth live by slaughter,
To tame the unicorn and lion wild,
To mock the subtle in themselves beguiled,°
　　　To cheer the ploughman with increaseful crops,
　　　And waste huge stones with little water-drops.

960   'Why workest thou mischief in thy pilgrimage,
Unless thou couldst return to make amends?
One poor retiring minute° in an age
Would purchase thee a thousand thousand friends,
Lending him wit that to bad debtors lends:°
　　　O this dread night, wouldst thou one hour come back,
　　　I could prevent this storm and shun thy wrack!

'Thou ceaseless lackey to eternity,°
With some mischance cross° Tarquin in his flight;
Devise extremes beyond extremity,°
970   To make him curse this cursèd crimeful night.
Let ghastly shadows his lewd eyes affright,
　　　And the dire thought of his committed evil
　　　Shape every bush a hideous shapeless devil.

'Disturb his hours of rest with restless trances,
Afflict him in his bed with bedrid° groans;
Let there bechance him pitiful mischances,
To make him moan, but pity not his moans,
Stone him with hardened hearts harder than stones,
　　　And let mild women to him lose their mildness,
980   　　Wilder to him than tigers in their wildness.

'Let him have time to tear his curlèd hair,
Let him have time against himself to rave,
Let him have time of time's help to despair,

Oblivion later, in *Troilus and Cressida* III.
iii.144–45: "Time hath, my lord, a wallet at his
back, / Wherein he puts alms for oblivion"
ravens' Ravens were supposed to live three times
as long as humans.
fortune's wheel Fortune is usually represented
with a wheel, on which some mount and some
fall.
beldam old woman
To mock . . . beguiled by providing a simpler
outcome than they expected

retiring minute a minute in which time goes
backward
Lending . . . lends giving him a glimpse of
the future which would prevent his making that
mistake
ceaseless . . . eternity Eternity is the "standing
now"; time does the moving, and is its agent.
cross interfere with
extremes . . . extremity the wildest contin-
gencies
bedrid bedridden

Let him have time to live a loathèd slave,
Let him have time a beggar's orts° to crave,
   And time to see one that by alms doth live
   Disdain to him disdainèd scraps to give.

'Let him have time to see his friends his foes,
And merry fools to mock at him resort;
990 Let him have time to mark how slow time goes
In time of sorrow, and how swift and short
His time of folly and his time of sport:
   And ever let his unrecalling° crime
   Have time to wail the abusing of his time.

1594   1594

The Phoenix and Turtle

In 1601 appeared a quarto called *Love's Martyr: Or, Rosalin's Complaint. Allegorically shadowing the truth of Love, in the constant Fate of the Phoenix and Turtle, etc.* After describing the main part of the work, the title goes on to say that it also includes *some new compositions, of severall moderne Writers . . . upon the first Subject: viz. The Phoenix and Turtle.*

Among much else, *Love's Martyr* contains a story of how a Turtledove, sorrowing for his dead mate, meets the Phoenix; and how they decide to die together in a fire of sweet wood. The Turtle goes first, then the Phoenix; and the event is reported by a nearby pelican. To this muddled poem of Robert Chester's, Ben Jonson, Shakespeare, and others, for unknown reasons, consented to add their shorter pieces.

Chester was celebrating his patron Sir John Salisbury as the Turtledove (Constancy) and his wife as the Phoenix (Love), and the daughter of that union. The other contributors, including Shakespeare, treat his new-made myth with great freedom. Shakespeare appears to have found in it an occasion to combine the image of the phoenix with a bird-funeral of the kind known in folklore; one analogue to his poem is "Cock Robin." But in doing so he also wrote his most obscure and metaphysical poem.

Shakespeare's birds have "no posterity"—even the phoenix this time does not arise from its ashes. There may be a topical issue to explain this—the execution of Essex (the approach of the Phoenix Elizabeth to death)—but it has not been satisfactorily adduced. The best course is to read the poem for its own sake—in rhythm, movement of thought, and lexical inventiveness a great work and itself a phoenix.

The birds assemble (ll. 1–20), appropriately if conceitedly characterized; then follows the anthem, which gives way to a simpler funeral song, into the tercets of which it modulates with unprecedented musical effect. Most of the obscurities of language and idea occur in the anthem, which F. T. Prince has in mind when he calls the work "a marriage between intense emotion and almost unintelligible fantasy." It is a meditation on the question, which so often arises in a quite different way in Donne, of the identity of separate persons in love. Shakespeare adapts scholastic terms used in the discussion of the persons of the Trinity, which, though distinct, are not divided; but in the

orts **scraps of food**   unrecalling **irrevocable**

course of the adaptation he stretches many English words—*property, selfsame, mine, either, neither*—to fit contexts of exalted argument remote from their daily uses. This practice and the unclued context of the whole make of *The Phoenix and Turtle* one of the least explicable and most beautiful poems in the language.

The Phoenix and Turtle

Let the bird of loudest lay,°
On the sole Arabian tree,°
Herald sad and trumpet° be,
To whose sound chaste wings obey.°

But thou shrieking harbinger,°
Foul precurrer° of the fiend,
Augur° of the fever's end,
To this troop come thou not near.

From this session interdict°
10   Every fowl of tyrant wing,°
Save the eagle, feathered king;
Keep the obsequy° so strict.°

Let the priest in surplice white,
That defunctive music can,°
Be the death-divining swan,
Lest the requiem lack his right.°

And thou treble-dated° crow,
That thy sable gender mak'st,
With the breath thou giv'st and tak'st,°
20   'Mongst our mourners shalt thou go.

Here the anthem doth commence:
Love and Constancy is dead;
Phoenix and the turtle fled
In a mutual flame from hence.

So they loved as° love in twain
Had the essence but in one;

---

of loudest lay that can sing loudest
sole Arabian tree As there was but one phoenix, so he had a unique tree, probably a palm; in Greek *phoinix* means both "phoenix" and "palm."
trumpet trumpeter
To . . . obey to whose sound the wings of virtuous birds are obedient
shrieking harbinger screech-owl
precurrer precursor
Augur prophet, soothsayer; the screech-owl foreboded death
interdict forbid

tyrant wing prey
obsequy funeral
strict restricted
the priest . . . can The swan sang only before its own death: it "knows how to sing funeral music."
right either the "rite" provided by the swan or "what is due to the requiem"
treble-dated long-lived
thy sable . . . tak'st Crows were thought to mate at the mouth and lay their eggs there.
as so that

Two distincts, division none:°
Number there in love was slain.°

30 Hearts remote, yet not asunder;
Distance, and no space was seen
Twixt this turtle and his queen:
But in them it were a wonder.°

So between them love did shine
That the turtle saw his right°
Flaming in the phoenix' sight;
Either was the other's mine.°

Property° was thus appalled,
That the self was not the same;°
Single nature's double name
40 Neither two nor one was called.°

Reason, in itself confounded,°
Saw division grow together,°
To themselves, yet either neither,°
Simple were so well compounded:°

That it cried, 'How true a twain
Seemeth this concordant one!°
Love hath reason, Reason none,
If what parts can so remain.'°

Whereupon it made this threne°
50 To the phoenix and the dove,
Co-supremes° and stars of love,
As chorus to their tragic scene:

Beauty, Truth, and Rarity,
Grace in all simplicity,
Here enclosed in cinders lie.

Death is now the phoenix nest,
And the turtle's loyal breast
To eternity doth rest,

Two . . . none two distinct, but not divided,
persons. Scholastically the terms are used of
the relations between the three persons of the
Trinity.
Number . . . slain Mathematically it is said
that "one is no number," so when two become
one, number is slain.
But . . . wonder in any other case but theirs
it would have been a marvel
right love returned, as was due to him
mine selfhood (not "source of wealth")
Property the natural order in which each thing
is itself
self . . . same splits up "selfsame" in order to
emphasize the uniqueness of this situation.
Single . . . called not one, because their persons remain distinct; not two, because they are
not divided

confounded because these matters defy normal
logic
grow together resolve into unity
yet either neither expresses, unparaphraseably,
the positive and negative of each selfhood in this
relation.
Simple . . . compounded The substance of the
soul is simple, but here a compound retains the
qualities of the simple.
How true . . . one This harmonious "one" is
really a new kind of two, with the integrity of
unity.
Love . . . remain Love is more reasonable than
reason if it can give to the compound and divide
the virtues of the simple unity.
threne funeral song; from the Greek, *threnos*
Co-supremes joint rulers

Leaving no posterity:
60 'Twas not their infirmity,
It was married chastity.

Truth may seem, but cannot be;°
Beauty brag, but 'tis not she;
Truth and Beauty buried be.

To this urn let those repair
That are either true or fair;
For these dead birds sigh a prayer.

1601   1601

The Sonnets

Shakespeare's sonnets were written over an indeterminate period and published together in 1609, after the vogue of sonneteering was over. Unlike Spenser's *Amoretti* or
Sidney's *Astrophel and Stella* they revolve about no central mythical lady, named and
constantly invoked; instead, we have a constellation of three figures providing a far
greater ironic and dramatic range than the traditional relation of lover-poet to lady-
muse. A blond young aristocrat, a dark lady, and a rival poet, none totally trustworthy,
all ambiguously admirable, inhabit these sonnets, which, throughout, are haunted by
the theme of time and its effects on people, things and buildings, human relationships.
They attracted much misguided critical attention because of the belief that they were
autobiographical and because of the mystery (but probably trivial import) of the dedication to an unknown "Mr. W. H." Their compact language, range of tone, profound
word-play, and intense moral vision are unsurpassed by any of the regular sonnet
sequences of Sidney, Spenser, or Drayton. The early poems of the cycle urge the
young man to marry and have children; later on, there is a group addressed to the
lady; toward the end, obvious complications occur.

XII

When I do count the clock that tells the time,°
And see the brave° day sunk in hideous night;
When I behold the violet past prime,°
And sable curls o'er-silvered all with white;
When lofty trees I see barren of leaves,
Which erst from heat did canopy the herd,
And summer's green all girded up° in sheaves
Borne on the bier with white and bristly beard;°
Then of thy beauty do I question make

Truth . . . be henceforth there can be only the
appearance, not the reality, of truth
count . . . time mark the passage of the hours
brave resplendent, finely attired
past prime faded
girded up with a girdle about his waist, the
image being that of an old man being carried to
his grave
And summer's . . . beard the green corn, now
ripe, harvested, the imagery making the sheaves
a conceited image of death

10 That thou among the wastes of time° must go,
    Since sweets° and beauties do themselves forsake°
    And die as fast as they see others grow;
        And nothing 'gainst Time's scythe can make defence
        Save breed° to brave° him when he takes thee hence.

XVIII

Shall I compare thee to a summer's day?°
Thou art more lovely and more temperate:
Rough winds do shake the darling buds of May,
And summer's lease hath all too short a date:°
Sometime too hot the eye of heaven shines,
And often is his gold complexion dimmed,
And every fair from fair sometime declines,
By chance or nature's changing course untrimmed;°
But thy eternal summer shall not fade
10 Nor lose possession of that fair thou owest,°
Nor shall Death brag thou wander'st in his shade,
When in eternal lines° to time thou growest:°
    So long as men can breathe or eyes can see,
    So long lives this, and this gives life to thee.

XIX

Devouring Time, blunt thou the lion's paws,
And make the earth devour her own sweet brood;
Pluck the keen teeth from the fierce tiger's jaws,
And burn the long-lived phoenix in her blood;°
Make glad and sorry seasons as thou fleet'st,
And do whate'er thou wilt, swift-footed Time,
To the wide world and all her fading sweets:°
But I forbid thee one most heinous crime—
Oh carve not with thy hours my love's fair brow
10 Nor draw no lines there with thine ántique° pen;
Him in thy course untainted do allow
For beauty's pattern to succeeding men.
        Yet do thy worst, old Time: despite thy wrong
        My love shall in my verse ever live young.

wastes of time the things time has destroyed	**lines** such as the lines of this poem and the other sonnets
sweets blossoms	**growest** becomes a part of
forsake undo	**phoenix . . . blood** The first three lines describe Time's action on living things that change and die; the phoenix also comes to the end of its years, although it is instantly reborn from its own funeral pyre.
breed offspring	
brave defy	
day may mean the period (or season) of a summer, as in the expression "in my day"	
date the period of a lease	
untrimmed stripped of beauty	**sweets** flowers
that . . . owest that beauty thou possessest (ownest)	**ántique** ancient, with a play on "antic" or "fantastic"

XX

A woman's face with nature's own hand painted
Hast thou, the master-mistress° of my passion;
A woman's gentle heart, but not acquainted
With shifting change as is false women's fashion;
An eye more bright than theirs, less false in rolling,°
Gilding the object whereupon it gazeth;
A man in hue° all hues in his controlling,
Which steals men's eyes and women's souls amazeth:
And for a woman wert thou first created,—
10   Till nature as she wrought thee fell a-doting,
And by addition me of thee defeated,°
By adding one thing° to my purpose nothing.
     But since she pricked° thee out for women's pleasure,
     Mine be thy love and thy love's use° their treasure.

XXIX

When, in disgrace with Fortune and men's eyes,
I all alone beweep my outcast state,°
And trouble deaf heaven with my bootless° cries,
And look upon myself and curse my fate,
Wishing me like to one more rich in hope,
Featured like him,° like him with friends possessed,
Desiring this man's art and that man's scope,
With what I most enjoy contented least;
Yet in these thoughts myself almost despising
10   Haply I think on thee, and then my state,
Like to the lark at break of day arising
From sullen° earth, sings hymns at heaven's gate:
     For thy sweet love remembered such wealth brings
     That then I scorn to change my state with kings.

XXX

When to the sessions° of sweet silent thought
I summon up remembrance of things past,
I sigh the lack of many a thing I sought,
And with old woes new wail my dear time's waste:
Then can I drown an eye, unused to flow,
For precious friends hid in death's dateless° night,

master-mistress both the oxymoron "boy-girl"
and, as if unhyphenated, "sovereign mistress"
rolling roving
hue form
defeated defrauded
one thing male sex
pricked selected; also "prick" as in modern
slang for penis
use sexual practice
state Here, as in all the sonnets, the meaning

shifts from "condition in life" through "state
of being" (l. 10) to "stately."
bootless unavailing
like him like yet another person
sullen dull, heavy
sessions of a law court. The legal conceit turns
on words like "dateless," "cancelled," "expense," "account," etc., and suggests the poet
being called to account, as steward, for the
estate of his life.
dateless endless

And weep afresh love's long since cancelled woe,
And moan the expense° of many a vanished sight:
Then can I grieve at grievances foregone,°
10   And heavily° from woe to woe tell° o'er
The sad account of fore-bemoanèd moan,
Which I new pay as if not paid before.
　　But if the while I think on thee, dear friend,°
　　All losses are restored and sorrows end.

XXXIII

Full many a glorious morning have I seen
Flatter° the mountain tops with sovereign eye,
Kissing with golden face the meadows green,
Gilding pale streams with heavenly alchemy,
Anon permit the basest clouds to ride
With ugly rack° on his celestial face,
And from the fórlorn world his visage hide,
Stealing unseen to west with this disgrace:°
Even so my sun one early morn did shine
10   With all triumphant° splendour on my brow;
But out alack, he was but one hour mine:
The region° cloud hath masked him from me now.
　　Yet him for this my love no whit disdaineth:
　　Suns of the world may stain,° when heaven's sun staineth.

LIII

What is your substance, whereof are you made,
That millions of strange shadows° on you tend?
Since every one hath, every one, one shade,
And you, but one, can every shadow lend.
Describe Adonis,° and the counterfeit
Is poorly imitated after you;
On Helen's cheek all art of beauty set,°
And you in Grecian tires° are painted new.
Speak of the spring and foison° of the year:
10   The one doth shadow of your beauty show,
The other as your bounty doth appear,
And you in every blessèd shape we know.

expense loss
foregone gone by
heavily sadly
tell reckon
dear friend the first use of this term in the *Sonnets*
Flatter brighten, cheer up (as the sovereign's smile would a courtier)
rack drifting; a mass of clouds driven before the wind; cf. *The Tempest* IV.i.156
this disgrace i.e. the concealing clouds
triumphant glorious

region region of the air
stain grow dim
strange shadows external, foreign images. The word-play is on "shadow and substance" meaning "appearance vs. reality"; in l. 10, the word takes on its modern sense of "cast shade."
Adonis See notes to *Venus and Adonis*, above.
On Helen's . . . set put the best makeup on the face of the most beautiful woman ever
tires attire, costume, dress
foison autumnal harvest

In all external grace you have some part,
But you like none, none you for constant heart.

LV

Not marble, nor the gilded monuments
Of princes shall outlive this powerful rhyme;
But you shall shine more bright in these contents
Than unswept stone besmeared with sluttish time.°
When wasteful° war shall statues overturn,
And broils° root out the work of masonry,
Nor Mars his sword° nor war's quick° fire shall burn
The living record of your memory.
'Gainst death and all oblivious° enmity
10 Shall you pace forth: your praise° shall still find room
Even in the eyes of all posterity
That wear this world out° to the ending doom.
    So, till the judgment that yourself arise,
    You live in this,° and dwell in lovers' eyes.

LXIV

When I have seen by Time's fell hand defaced
The rich proud cost of outworn buried age;
When sometime lofty towers I see down razed,
And brass eternal° slave to mortal° rage;
When I have seen the hungry ocean gain
Advantage on the kingdom of the shore,
And the firm soil win of the watery main,
Increasing store° with loss and loss with store;
When I have seen such interchange of state,°
10 Or state itself confounded to decay,
Ruin hath taught me thus to ruminate
That Time will come and take my love away.
    This thought is as a death, which cannot choose
    But weep to have that which it fears to lose.

LXVI

Tired with all these for restful death I cry
As to behold Desert° a beggar born,
And needy Nothing trimmed in jollity,°

---

unswept . . . time The stone bore an inscription to the dead man, the letters of which had become obscured ("sluttish" = dirty) in the course of time.
wasteful destructive
broils battles
Nor . . . sword "Destroy" is understood.
quick lively
oblivious bringing to oblivion
praise glory
wear . . . out outlast

this these lines of poetry
brass eternal Eternal brass as opposed, syntactically, to "mortal rage"—this patterning of noun-adjective:adjective-noun, called chiasmus, is typically Elizabethan.
mortal both "deadly" and "subject to death"
store abundance
state condition; also "estate"; also "grandeur" (as in the next line)
Desert a personification of one who is deserving
jollity fine costume

And purest Faith° unhappily forsworn,
And gilded Honour shamefully misplaced,
And maiden Virtue rudely strumpeted,°
And right Perfection wrongfully disgraced,
And Strength by limping Sway disablèd,
And Art made tongue-tied by Authority,
10   And Folly, Doctor-like,° controlling° Skill,
And simple Truth miscalled Simplicity,°
And captive Good attending captain Ill:
    Tired with all these, from these would I be gone
    Save that, to die, I leave my love alone.

LXXIII

That time of year thou mayst in me behold
When yellow leaves, or none, or few, do hang
Upon those boughs which shake against the cold,
Bare ruined choirs where late the sweet birds sang:°
In me thou see'st the twilight of such day
As after sunset fadeth in the west,
Which by and by black night doth take away,
Death's second self that seals up all in rest:
In me thou see'st the glowing of such fire
10   That on the ashes of his youth doth lie
As the death-bed whereon it must expire,
Consumed with that which it was nourished by:°
    This thou perceivest, which makes thy love more strong
    To love that well which thou must leave ere long.

LXXXVI

Was it the proud full sail of his° great verse,
Bound for the prize of all-too-precious you,
That did my ripe thoughts in my brain inhearse,°
Making their tomb the womb wherein they grew?
Was it his spirit, by spirits taught to write
Above a mortal pitch, that struck me dead?
No, neither he, nor his compeers by night
Giving him aid, my verse astonishèd:
He, nor that affable familiar ghost°
10   Which nightly gulls° him with intelligence,°

Faith fidelity; also True Religion
strumpeted called a whore
Doctor-like pedant-like
controlling also with a sense of rebuking, censuring
Simplicity stillness
Bare . . . sang The trees are likened to arching ruins, half-opened to the sky, of the choirs of gothic monastery churches; the sweet birds literally sang in the summer trees, and, figuratively, sang as choir boys, perhaps, in the choir stalls of the church in the image; notice the sequence in the quatrains of autumn—sundown —dying fire.
Consumed . . . by "consumed with life," as with passion; also perhaps consumed by the nourishing fire; the image is one of embers hotter than they look
his some rival poet: George Chapman has been suggested
inhearse entomb
familiar ghost some spirit attending the rival; perhaps a poetic predecessor
gulls deceives
intelligence secret information

As victors of my silence cannot boast,
I was not sick of any fear from thence:
But when your countenance filled up his line,
Then lacked I matter; that° enfeebled mine.

LXXXVII

Farewell—thou art too dear° for my possessing,
And like enough thou knowest thy estimate:°
The charter° of thy worth gives thee releasing;
My bonds in thee are all determinate.°
For how do I hold thee but by thy granting?
And for that riches where is my deserving?
The cause of this fair gift in me is wanting,
And so my patent° back again is swerving.°
Thy self thou gavest, thy own worth then not knowing;
10 Or me, to whom thou gavest it, else mistaking:°
So thy great gift, upon misprision° growing,
Comes home again on better judgment making.°
  Thus have I had thee as a dream doth flatter:
  In sleep a king, but waking no such matter.

XCIV

They that have power to hurt and will do none,
That do not do the thing they most do show,°
Who moving others are themselves as stone,
Unmovèd, cold, and to temptation slow;
They rightly do inherit heaven's graces,°
And husband nature's riches from expense;°
They are the lords and owners of their faces,
Others but stewards° of their excellence.
The summer's flower is to the summer sweet,
10 Though to itself it only live and die;
But if that flower with base infection meet,
The basest weed outbraves° his dignity:
  For sweetest things turn sourest by their deeds.
  Lilies that fester smell far worse than weeds.°

XCVII

How like a winter hath my absence been
From thee, the pleasure of the fleeting year!
What freezings have I felt, what dark days seen!—

---

that "that this was true"
dear expensive; also, "aristocratic"
estimate worth
charter privilege
determinate ended
patent grant of a monopoly
is swerving returns to you
mistaking overestimating
misprision misjudgment

on better judgment making on your judging
better
show look as if they could do
heaven's graces the favors of heaven
husband . . . expense protect from wastefulness
stewards officials who manage estates for the
owners; "their" refers to "they" in l. 1
outbraves makes a finer show than
Lilies . . . weeds a line from an old play

What old December's bareness everywhere!
And yet this time removed° was summer's time:
The teeming autumn big with rich increase°
Bearing the wanton° burthen of the prime,°
Like widowed wombs after their lords' decease.
Yet this abundant issue seemed to me
But hope of orphans, and unfathered fruit;
For summer and his pleasures wait on° thee,
And thou away the very birds are mute;
    Or if they sing, 'tis with so dull a cheer
    That leaves look pale, dreading the winter's near.

10

CVI

When in the chronicle of wasted time
I see descriptions of the fairest wights,°
And beauty making beautiful old rhyme
In praise of ladies dead and lovely knights,
Then in the blazon° of sweet beauty's best—
Of hand, of foot, of lip, of eye, of brow—
I see their antique pen would have expressed
Even such a beauty as you master now.
So all their praises are but prophecies
Of this our time, all you prefiguring;
And for they looked but with divining eyes
They had not skill enough your worth to sing:
    For we which now behold these present days
    Have eyes to wonder, but lack tongues to praise.

10

CVII

Not mine own fears, nor the prophetic soul
Of the wide world dreaming on things to come
Can yet the lease° of my true love control,
Supposed as forfeit to a cónfined doom.
The mortal moon hath her eclipse endured,°
And the sad augurs mock their own presage;
Incertainties now crown themselves assured,
And peace proclaims olives° of endless age.
Now with the drops of this most balmy time
My love looks fresh; and Death to me subscribes,
Since spite of him I'll live in this poor rhyme
While he insults o'er° dull and speechless tribes:

10

time removed time of separation
increase offspring, crops
wanton playful; luxuriant
prime spring
wait on attend, as at court
wights people
blazon poetic cataloguing of a person's beauties and virtues, publicly displayed
lease period or term of lease

The mortal moon . . . endured Some historical crisis has passed—whether the Spanish Armada, sailing in a crescent (defeated in 1588), a lunar eclipse, or some crisis of the Queen—making "mortal" mean "deadly" or "able to die."
olives olive branch of peace (ever since the dove flew back to Noah's ark with one when the flood had abated)
insults o'er triumphs over

And thou in this shalt find thy monument
When tyrants' crests and tombs of brass are spent.

CXVI

Let me not to the marriage of true minds
Admit impediments:° love is not love
Which alters when it alteration finds,
Or bends with the remover to remove.°
Oh no! it is an ever-fixèd mark°
That looks on tempests and is never shaken;
It is the star to every wandering bark,
Whose worth's unknown although his height be taken.°
Love's not Time's fool, though rosy lips and cheeks
10 Within his bending° sickle's compass come;
Love alters not with his brief hours and weeks,
But bears it out° even to the edge of doom.
    If this be error and upon me proved,
    I never writ, nor no man ever loved.

CXXI

'Tis better to be vile than vile esteemed,
When not to be receives reproach of being,
And the just pleasure lost which is so deemed°
Not by our feeling but by others' seeing.
For why should others' false adulterate eyes
Give salutation to my sportive blood?°
Or on my frailties why are frailer spies,
Which in their wills count bad what I think good?
No: I am that I am,° and they that level°
10 At my abuses reckon up their own;
I may be straight though they themselves be bevel;°
By their rank° thoughts my deeds must not be shown,—
    Unless this general evil° they maintain:
    All men are bad and in their badness reign.

CXXIX

The expense of spirit in a waste of shame°
Is lust° in action; and till action, lust°

Let . . . impediments an echo of the marriage service. The "impediments" are change of circumstance (l. 3) and inconstancy (l. 4).
bends . . . remove withdraws when its object does
an . . . mark a beacon
height be taken altitude be known
bending bent; also "causing the grass of youthful beauty to bend"
bears it out endures
so deemed either "vile," in which case the unjust condemnation of the love by outsiders wrecks its pleasure; or "just pleasure," in which case the outsiders ("others") approve of the love although the sonneteer doesn't

Give salutation . . . blood mockingly hail my sexual activity
I am that I am I am what I am (apparently echoing the words of God from the burning bush to Moses, Exodus 3:14)
level aim a weapon
bevel crooked
rank lewd
general evil i.e. the following moral formula: "All men are bad . . ." etc.
The expense . . . shame abstractly, characterizing lust; concretely, sexual "spending" (orgasm) to no purpose in a shameful waste (the theme of *post coitum triste*—"sorrow after sex")
lust grammatical subject of the first sentence

Is perjured, murderous, bloody, full of blame,
Savage, extreme, rude,° cruel, not to trust;
Enjoyed no sooner but despisèd straight;
Past reason hunted; and no sooner had,
Past reason hated, as a swallowed bait
On purpose laid to make the taker mad;
Mad in pursuit, and in possession so;
10   Had, having, and in quest to have, extreme;
A bliss in proof;° and proved, a very woe;
Before, a joy proposed; behind, a dream.
      All this the world well knows, yet none knows well
      To shun the heaven that leads men to this hell.

CXXX

My mistress' eyes are nothing like the sun;
Coral is far more red than her lips' red;
If snow be white, why then her breasts are dun;°
If hairs be wires, black wires grow on her head;
I have seen roses damasked,° red and white,
But no such roses see I in her cheeks;
And in some perfumes is there more delight
Than in the breath that from my mistress reeks;°
I love to hear her speak, yet well I know
10   That music hath a far more pleasing sound;
I grant I never saw a goddess go
(My mistress when she walks treads on the ground).
      And yet by heaven I think my love as rare
      As any she belied with false compare.

CXXXV

Whoever hath her wish, thou hast thy *Will*,°
And *Will* to boot, and *Will* in overplus:
More than enough am I that vex thee still,
To thy sweet *Will* making addition thus.
Wilt thou whose *Will* is large and spacious
Not once vouchsafe to hide my *Will* in thine?
Shall *Will* in others seem right gracious,
And in my *Will* no fair acceptance shine?
The sea, all water, yet receives rain still,
10   And in abundance addeth to his store:
So thou being rich in *Will* add to thy *Will*
One *Will* of mine to make thy large *Will* more.

---

rude brutal
in proof experienced
dun tan. The whole poem is an anti-blazon, actually a Petrarchan "anti-Petrarchan" device.
roses damasked pink roses, but also perhaps patterned in the symbolic colors of passion and purity

reeks emanates (with no sense of "stinks")
Will volition; desire; passionate feeling ("wit and will" meant something like "thought and feeling"); the auxiliary verb; and, in this sonnet, both the poet's own name, and sexual member (but of both sexes—as if modern slang "dick" meant both penis and vagina)

Let no unkind no fair° beseechers kill;
Think all but one, and me in that one *Will.*

CXXXVIII

When my love swears that she is made of truth°
I do believe her, though I know she lies,°
That she might think me some untutored youth
Unlearnèd in the world's false subtleties.
Thus vainly thinking that she thinks me young,
Although she knows my days are past the best,
Simply° I credit her false-speaking tongue:
On both sides thus is simple truth suppressed.
But wherefore says she not she is unjust?°
10 And wherefore say not I that I am old?
Oh, love's best habit° is in seeming trust,
And age, in love,° loves not to have years told.
    Therefore I lie with her,° and she with me,
    And in our faults by lies we flattered be.

CXLIV

Two loves I have, of comfort and despair,
Which like two spirits do suggest me still:°
The better angel is a man right fair,°
The worser spirit a woman coloured ill.°
To win me soon to hell, my female evil
Tempteth my better angel from my side,
And would corrupt my saint to be a devil,
Wooing his purity with her foul pride.
And whether that my angel be turned fiend
10 Suspect I may, yet not directly tell;
But being both from me, both to each friend,
I guess one angel in another's hell:°
    Yet this shall I ne'er know, but live in doubt
    Till my bad angel fire my good one out.°

CXLVI

Poor soul, the centre of my sinful earth,°
(Foiled by)° these rebel powers that thee array,°
Why dost thou pine within and suffer dearth,

---

fair legitimate
made of truth "faithful to me," as well as "truth-telling"
she lies "sleeps around," as well as "tells lies"
Simply like a simpleton, unconditionally, absolutely
unjust unfaithful
habit costume
in love also, "in re love"
lie with her "lie to her"; also, "sleep with her"
suggest me still tempt me ever
fair light-haired and -complexioned; beautiful; honest (modern "fair" as "just")

coloured ill a brunette
hell the prison zone in barley-break, a game like prisoner's base; also, as in a story in the *Decameron* of Giovanni Boccaccio (1313–75), "the devil in hell" as his sexual member in hers
fire . . . out reject him; also, to give him venereal disease (only when the friend shows signs of this will it be clear that he slept with her)
earth flesh, body
(Foiled by) an emendation; the original phrase is a misprint
array both "deck out" and "afflict"

Painting thy outward walls so costly gay?
Why so large cost, having so short a lease,
Dost thou upon thy fading mansion spend?
Shall worms, inheritors of this excess,
Eat up thy charge? Is this thy body's end?
Then, soul, live thou upon thy servant's loss,
10   And let that° pine to aggravate° thy store;
Buy terms° divine in selling hours of dross;
Within be fed, without be rich no more:
    So shalt thou feed on Death, that feeds on men,
    And Death once dead there's no more dying then.°

Songs from the Plays

The songs in Shakespeare's plays represent almost every sixteenth-century lyrical mode.
They follow, adapt, parody, and transform conventions of courtly lyric, ballad, pastoral
song, air, masque lyric, and others, sometimes quoting or reworking familiar words
or following familiar tunes. In plays, the role of song varies: does a character ask for
music, in the course of the action, from musicians? does he sing himself? to another
person? is the singing an aside or soliloquy? Shakespeare often condensed central
themes of plays in phrases in the songs (consider "benefits forgot" and its meaning
in As You Like it).

Tell Me Where Is Fancy Bred?°

Tell me where is fancy bred,
Or in the heart or in the head?
How begot, how nourishèd?
        Reply, reply!
It is engendered in the eyes,
With gazing fed; and fancy dies
In the cradle where it lies.
        Let us all ring fancy's knell:
        I'll begin it—Ding, dong, bell.
10   Ding, dong, bell.

that "that one," the servant body
aggravate increase
terms years or decades of a lease
And Death . . . then Cf. I Corinthians 15:54–
55.
Tell Me Where Is Fancy Bred? from The Mer-

chant of Venice (1596–97), III.ii; sung by
Portia's musicians as Bassanio makes his choice
of a lead casket over a silver or gold one, thus
winning her. The opening rhymes are all on
"lead."

Dirge°

Fear no more the heat o' the sun
    Nor the furious winter's rages;
Thou thy worldly task hast done,
    Home art gone, and ta'en thy wages;
Golden lads and girls all must,
As chimney-sweepers,° come to dust.°

Fear no more the frown o' the great,
    Thou art past the tyrant's stroke;
Care no more to clothe and eat,
10   To thee the reed is as the oak:
The sceptre, learning, physic,° must
All follow this and come to dust.

Fear no more the lightning flash,
    Nor the all-dreaded thunder-stone;°
Fear not slander, censure rash;
    Thou hast finished joy and moan:
All lovers young, all lovers must
Consign to thee and come to dust.

No exorciser harm thee!
20   Nor no witchcraft charm thee!
Ghost unlaid forbear thee!
    Nothing ill come near thee!
Quiet consummation have,
And renownèd be thy grave.

Dialogue in Praise of the Owl and Cuckoo°

Spring

When daisies pied° and violets blue
    And lady-smocks all silver-white
And cuckoo-buds of yellow hue
    Do paint the meadows with delight,
The cuckoo then, on every tree,
Mocks married men; for thus sings he,
    Cuckoo,°

Dirge from *Cymbeline* (1610–11), IV.ii; ceremonially chanted by Guiderius and Arviragus over Imogen, believed dead
chimney-sweepers a secondary meaning: slang in Warwickshire for "dandelions"
come to dust both literal and figurative ashes: "Man, thou art dust, and into dust thou shalt return"
physic medical learning
thunder-stone believed to cause its sound

Dialogue in Praise of the Owl and Cuckoo from the ironically tinged happy ending of *Love's Labours Lost* (1594–95), which defers the concluding marriages for a year. The spring song sounds a "word of fear," the night and winter one, "a merry note."
pied varicolored
Cuckoo The cuckoo's cry sounds like the "cuckold" he thereby rebukes.

439

Cuckoo, cuckoo! O word of fear
Unpleasing to a married ear!

10 When shepherds pipe on oaten straws,
        And merry larks are ploughmen's clocks,
When turtles tread, and rooks, and daws,
        And maidens bleach their summer smocks,
The cuckoo then, on every tree,
Mocks married men; for thus sings he,
            Cuckoo,
Cuckoo, cuckoo! O word of fear,
Unpleasing to a married ear!

Winter

When icicles hang by the wall,
        And Dick the shepherd blows his nail,°
And Tom bears logs into the hall,
        And milk comes frozen home in pail,
When blood is nipped, and ways be foul,°
Then nightly sings the staring owl,
            Tu-whit, to-who,
            A merry note,
While greasy Joan doth keel° the pot.

10 When all aloud the wind doth blow,
        And coughing drowns the parson's saw,°
And birds sit brooding in the snow,
        And Marian's nose looks red and raw,
When roasted crabs° hiss in the bowl,
Then nightly sings the staring owl,
            Tu-whit, to-who,
            A merry note,
While greasy Joan doth keel the pot.

Who Is Silvia?°

Who is Silvia? what is she,
    That all our swains commend her?
Holy, fair, and wise is she;
    The heaven such grace did lend her,
That she might admirèd be.

Is she kind as she is fair?
    For beauty lives with kindness:
Love doth to her eyes repair

---

blows his nail to warm his fingers
ways . . . foul roads be impassable
keel scrape out
saw proverb
crabs crabapples

Who Is Silvia? from *Two Gentlemen of Verona*
(1594–95), IV.ii; a formal serenade sung in the
play by hired musicians (for Thurio, who will
not get Silvia anyway)

10　To help him of his blindness,°
　　And being helped, inhabits there.

　　Then to Silvia let us sing
　　　　That Silvia is excelling;
　　She excels each mortal thing
　　　　Upon the dull earth dwelling.
　　To her let us garlands bring.

Take, O Take Those Lips Away°

Take, O take those lips away,
　　That so sweetly were forsworn;
And those eyes, the break of day,
　　Lights that do mislead the morn:
But my kisses bring again,
　　　　Bring again,
Seals of love, but sealed in vain,
　　　　Sealed in vain.

O Mistress Mine°

O mistress mine, where are you roaming?
O, stay and hear; your true-love's coming,
　　That can sing both high and low.
Trip no further, pretty sweeting;
Journeys end in lovers meeting,
　　Every wise man's son doth know.

What is love? 'tis not hereafter;
Present mirth hath present laughter;
　　What's to come is still unsure:
In delay there lies no plenty;
Then come kiss me, sweet and twenty!
　　Youth's a stuff will not endure.

When That I Was and a Little Tiny Boy°

When that I was and a little tiny boy,
　　With hey, ho, the wind and the rain,

blindness See note to Marlowe's *Hero and Leander* I.38n.
Take, O Take Those Lips Away from *Measure for Measure* (1604), IV.i; sung at the jilted Mariana's first entrance, by a boy, indicating her pitiable state

O Mistress Mine from *Twelfth Night* (1601), II.iii; sung by Feste, the clown
When That I Was and a Little Tiny Boy an epilogue to *Twelfth Night*, again sung by Feste

A foolish thing was but a toy,°
 For the rain it raineth every day.

But when I came to man's estate,
 With hey, ho, the wind and the rain,
'Gainst knaves and thieves men shut their gate,
 For the rain it raineth every day.

But when I came, alas! to wive,
 With hey, ho, the wind and the rain,
By swaggering could I never thrive,
 For the rain it raineth every day.

But when I came unto my beds,
 With hey, ho, the wind and the rain,
With tosspots still had drunken heads,
 For the rain it raineth every day.

A great while ago the world begun,
 With hey, ho, the wind and the rain;
But that's all one, our play is done,
 And we'll strive to please you every day.

Under the Greenwood Tree°

 Under the greenwood tree
 Who loves to lie with me,
 And turn his merry note
 Unto the sweet bird's throat,
Come hither, come hither, come hither:
  Here shall he see
  No enemy
But winter and rough weather.°

 Who doth amibition shun
 And loves to live in the sun,
 Seeking the food he eats,
 And pleased with what he gets,
Come hither, come hither, come hither:
  Here shall he see
  No enemy
But winter and rough weather.

A foolish . . . toy a fool's bauble was nothing
serious
Under the Greenwood Tree from *As You Like It*

(1599), II.v; sung by Touchstone, the clown, to
celebrate the forest of Arden
No enemy . . . weather even his realistic, anti-
pastoral country is better than court life

Blow, Blow, Thou Winter Wind°

Blow, blow, thou winter wind,
Thou are not so unkind
   As man's ingratitude;
Thy tooth is not so keen
Because thou art not seen,
   Although thy breath be rude.
Heigh-ho! sing heigh-ho, unto the green holly:
Most friendship is feigning, most loving mere folly:
   Then heigh-ho! the holly!
10   *This life is most jolly.*

Freeze, freeze, thou bitter sky
That dost not bite so nigh
   As benefits forgot:
Though thou the waters warp,°
Thy sting is not so sharp
   As friend remembered not.
Heigh-ho! etc.

Autolycus' Song°

When daffodils begin to peer,°
   With heigh, the doxy° over the dale!
Why, then comes in the sweet of the year
   For the red blood reigns in the winter's pale.

The white sheet bleaching on the hedge,°
   With heigh, the sweet birds, O how they sing!
Doth set my pugging° tooth on edge,
   For a quart of ale is a dish for a king.

The lark that tirra lirra chants,
10   With heigh, with heigh, the thrush and the jay!
Are summer songs for me and my aunts°
   While we lie tumbling in the hay.

Blow, Blow, Thou Winter Wind from *As You Like It* II.vii
warp by freezing
Autolycus' Song from *The Winter's Tale* (1609–10), IV.ii; Autolycus, a thief (his name that of Mercury's son), sings this to himself
peer appear
doxy girl

The white . . . hedge Laundry left out to dry and whiten in the sun was often snatched by wandering peddlers like Autolycus, cloth of any kind being most valuable. For the thief, such sheets would indeed be blossoms to be plucked.
pugging stealing
aunts girls

Autolycus as Peddler°

Lawn° as white as driven snow,
Cyprus° black as e'er was crow,
Gloves as sweet as damask roses,
Masks for faces and for noses,
Bugle-bracelet, necklace amber,
Perfume for a lady's chamber,
Golden quoifs and stomachers°
For my lads to give their dears,
Pins and poking sticks° of steel
—What maids lack from head to heel.
Come buy of me, come; come buy, come buy,
Buy lads, or else your lasses cry.

The Tempest

The first play in the First Folio is *The Tempest,* although it was the last Shakespeare wrote unaided. The publishers took exceptional care with its preparation, as if, in putting it at the head of the section of comedies, and so first in the book, they were treating it as a showpiece.

Ever since it was discovered to be the last of Shakespeare's plays, *The Tempest* has attracted special attention as a kind of culmination of his work, the final statement of the greatest of dramatists. The attempts of nineteenth- and twentieth-century critics to find in it an allegory of Shakespeare's life or thoughts vary in subtlety and constitute an enormous range of interpretations. Perhaps we should react to these not by choosing one against the others but by arguing that the very fact of its lending itself, however partially, to such allegories, proves the play to have the rare quality of *suggesting* to the spectator or reader that he must make his own contribution, must complete the work in his own imagination. The play is perhaps the most remarkable example of qualities all good Shakespeareans learn to attribute to his finest work: patience and reticence. Patience is that ability to suffer and survive interpretation without which no work of art can achieve classic status and have direct relevance to the lives of successive generations. Reticence is the quality of not speaking out, not simplifying the text to the point where its meanings become more or less explicit, but leaving unsettled potential conflicts and complexities of meaning. Anyone who studies Verdi's *Otello,* great masterpiece though it is, will see that in comparison Shakespeare's *Othello* is reticent. Anyone who knows the history of *King Lear* criticism will understand the sense in which *King Lear* is patient. *The Tempest,* so resistant to interpretation, so full of possible but never fully spoken meanings, exemplifies both characteristics; which is why it preserves its unique status in the canon of Shakespeare's work.

Autolycus as Peddler *The Winter's Tale* IV.iii; disguised as a thief, he sings a conventional peddler's song (see "Fine Knacks for Ladies," above)
Lawn fine linen
Cyprus a thin crape

quoifs and stomachers close-fitting caps, and parts of bodices
poking sticks metal rods used to iron ruffs; given the next line, perhaps with a bawdy overtone

It is, of course, possible to relate it to other plays of Shakespeare, and especially to the romances—*Pericles*, *Cymbeline*, and *The Winter's Tale*, with which it is usually classified. These works all came into being because of the revival of an old form of dramatic romance. The element of masque, the dominant form of courtly entertainment in King James's reign, which is particularly strong in *The Tempest*, suggests not only that the King's Men were often engaged for masques at court but also that the play may have been written with the Blackfriars Theatre in mind; for these things, with their scenes and machines, their dancing and music, could be done better in the smaller, artificially-lighted indoor theater with its courtly audiences than in the big open-air house. If we speak of *The Tempest* as a romance, we need to bear all this in mind: the dramatic romance was not a subtle or courtly form, but it rapidly became so in the years leading up to *The Tempest*.

The history of the changes whereby simple romance could be made adequate to the purposes of Shakespeare In *The Tempest* may be seen from his own work. *Pericles* is formally an adaptation of a simpler romance narrative enormously sophisticated by Shakespeare in the interests of the beautiful scene of recognition between Marina and Pericles which is its climax. *Cymbeline* displays examples of Shakespeare's most mature and difficult blank verse, but also exploits with a deliberate false naïveté the Romance themes of lost sons and miraculous multiple recognitions. *The Winter's Tale* dramatizes a romantic novella, changing out of recognition its naïve philosophy but preserving its extensive Romance chronology and also developing its "pastoral" possibilities; again the climax is a miraculous recognition scene, more improbable than anything in the novella.

The Tempest is the story of a magician prince and his daughter put to sea in a leaky boat and taking possession of an island where, twelve years later, amid fantastic displays of the prince's supernatural powers, the wrongs of the past are righted at the final recognition. But this time Shakespeare has taken up the themes of royal children, of marvelous rescue from death, of reconciliation a generation later between enemies —in a different way. He has made the form *intensive;* this play alone of Shakespeare's is played in something like the same time as that taken by the events it enacts, and the text draws our attention to this. Such tautness of dramatic form—which nevertheless allows multiple plotting, a masque, and spectacular and climactic *coups de théâtre* like the apparition of Ariel as a Harpy—makes this play, for all its thematic resemblances to the other romances, uniquely surprising in design and suggestive in meaning. Nowhere else does Shakespeare use so much music, so many pantomimic devices, yet there is always a sense of the imminence of the catastrophe. Nowhere else does he juxtapose so abruptly verses which enact the turbulent human passions of anger, remorse, and fear—the verse, one might say, of *Coriolanus* and parts of *Cymbeline*—with the limpid, stylized grief of Ferdinand ("This music crept by me upon the waters") and the unearthly songs of Ariel. *The Tempest* is, finally, *sui generis*, the only play of its kind, and nothing we can learn about it will alter that.

At the level of fact, as of reasonable conjecture, we can, however, offer some relevant information. Shakespeare in 1610 evidently saw certain accounts, both published and unpublished, of a wreck in the Bermudas a year earlier. He had read a lot about voyages to the New World, but this occurrence was especially interesting because he knew people connected with the Virginia Company; the *Sea-Adventure* was bound for Virginia when she ran ashore in a gale and was lodged between two rocks; the colonists escaped with their lives and much of the ship's stores. William Strachey's

True Reportory of the Wrack, written in 1610 but not published till 1625, gives the most important account of the wreck and subsequent adventures. Shakespeare uses Strachey's description of St. Elmo's fire in Ariel's account of the storm, as well as other borrowings.

The importance of these allusions is not that Shakespeare was being very topical, but that the New World colonies deeply stirred his imagination. The Virginia Company had, of course, an economic interest which was served best by regarding the colonies as the natural domain of the European Christian. One of the books Shakespeare read calls the natives "human beasts." When Prospero says he was set upon his island "to be the lord on it" (V.i.162), he is talking like a colonist; when he discovers that on Caliban's "nature / Nurture will never stick," he is repeating what many colonial adventurers had reported; and when Caliban complains that he had been helpful with fresh water and fish-dams we recall that this was also admitted by the colonists, who added that the natives soon turned treacherous.

In this way *The Tempest* alludes to the new colonial problem; it also repeats some of the moralizations of the adventurers, who called the wreck a "tragicall comaedie," and rejoiced that what had seemed "a punishment against evil" was "but a medicine." Discussing the quarrels and mutinies in Virginia, they showed they had learned the lesson that "every inordinate soul soon becomes his own punishment." (Compare Gonzalo's "their great guilt . . . now 'gins to bite the spirits," III.iii.104–6.) Strachey calls the Bermudas "these unfortunate (yet fortunate) Ilands"—for all their terrors they proved a place of deliverance. (Compare Gonzalo's expressions in V.i.206 ff.)

But *The Tempest* does not take place in the New World—the island is somewhere between Tunis and Naples in the Mediterranean—and like everybody else Shakespeare interpreted the astonishing news from America in accordance with already existing Old World ideas. For example, Caliban, though his name is probably an anagram of "cannibal," is based on the wild man or *Wodewose* of European tradition—treacherous, lecherous, without language. It was easy to relate the savages to this type, which was traditionally held to be in an intermediate position between man and beast, natural in a bad sense. However, there are, for example in Spenser, good and bad wild men; and the travelers and others who speculated on the matter were divided into those who believed that "natural" men—without Christianity or civility—would be better and more beautiful, or wickeder and more ugly, than Europeans. Montaigne, whose essay "Of Cannibals" is paraphrased by Gonzalo in II.i.143 ff., was of the first party. Shakespeare is more ambiguous. Prospero's "Art," represented by his magical powers, is incapable of civilizing Caliban ("You taught me language; and my profit on't / Is, I know how to curse," I.ii.365–66), and Caliban is the dupe of Stephano and a traitor to his lord. He was given the same education as Miranda, but tried to rape her and was unrepentant. Yet he is not as base as the wicked Italians, who illustrate the saying *corruptio optimi pessima*, the corruption of the best is the worst corruption. Miranda's "brave new world" is the old one, in which man, though redeemed and beautiful in comparison with the world of mere nature, can be corrupt. Although art as well as grace can be added to nature, as by grafting finer fruit is made to grow on natural stocks, there is a corruption worse than the natural; and this the art of Prospero must try to purge. The purity possible to those who live above nature is Miranda's; her assurance that beautiful souls inhabit beautiful bodies ('There's nothing ill can dwell in such a temple," I.ii.460, and "How beauteous mankind is!," V.i.183) is not in accord with the facts, any more than the notion of the noble savage. And

Prospero, having failed with Caliban, must try with the Italian noblemen. He does not, it appears, wholly succeed.

Prospero has a "project," like an alchemist; the action of the play represents the climactic stage of the experiment. He saves his enemies, unharmed, from a tempest of his own causing; and will, if he can, regenerate them and by a marriage union prevent further strife. He is technically in charge of the whole experiment, stage-managing, or "presenting" the wanderings of the various parties, the great apparition of Ariel, the masques, the punishment of the vulgar rebels, and the final confrontation with Alonso and Sebastian. But Shakespeare will not allow the play to become too inertly schematic. Prospero is passionate, even bad-tempered. His excitement in the long expository scene (I.ii) is reflected in the disturbed verses which recount the past, his severe admonitions to Miranda, his nervous rage with Caliban and harshness to Ariel. So, later, his mind is "troubled" (IV.i.160); he rejoices in having his enemies at his mercy (IV.i.263), but also speaks the great lines from Ovid which are his farewell to magic arts, and the famous elegiac set piece after the masque. He is naggingly insistent about the need for Miranda and Ferdinand not to anticipate marriage; and his forgiveness of his brother Antonio is hardly in the mood of gentle reconciliation occasionally called characteristic in these romances—"most wicked sir, whom to call brother / Would even infect my mouth" (V.i.130–31). Miranda's more innocent re-actions he learns to treat pityingly.

Such are the cross-currents of meaning and tone that make it impossible for any-body to announce boldly what The Tempest is about. Like all the best plays of Shake-speare, it is reticent on that point. When you think it may declare itself as having a particular theme, it frustrates the expectation by suddenly modulating into a different narrative manner, a different verse style. Thus the stage realism of the opening scene is followed by the scene of Prospero's agitated reminiscence, and when that threatens to become a forceful account of some political usurpation, the verse shifts it into a new mode of fairy tale at I.ii.44. Soon we meet Ariel and Caliban, for each of whom Shakespeare invented an idiomatic poetry; and then Ferdinand (I.ii.390), his strange water-music deriving from Ariel's uncanny song, "Full fadom five." This is a slight indication of the range of the play's voices; one needs to add the cheerful solemnity of Gonzalo's, the guilty sorrow of Alonso's, the Macbeth-like whispers of Antonio's and Sebastian. Ariel speaks as scourge and minister as well as fretful sprite, Caliban as a native of a good place and not only as a savage, Prospero as artist but also as fallible, vindictive, regretful man. Miranda's are the expressions of a perfectly innocent high-born wonder no less true for its brokenness; Ferdinand greets her as a goddess, she him as a god, and it is Prospero who suggests that there is ignorance in this innocence. The play does not imply that he must be right, and it does not call him wrong; it leaves us to follow, and choose between, the swirling changes of tone and emphasis, the clues that cross each other and prevent any from becoming dominant, ideological. This is the reticence that accompanies the classic's patience, and this marvelous play, so well endowed with both, may stand here as representative of Shakespeare's highest achievements.

The Tempest

The Scene, an uninhabited Island

Names of the Actors

ALONSO, *King of Naples*
SEBASTIAN, *his brother*
PROSPERO, *the right Duke of Milan*
ANTONIO *his brother, the usurping*
    Duke of Milan
FERDINAND, son to the King of Naples
GONZALO, *an honest old Counsellor*
ADRIAN *and* FRANCISCO, *Lords*
CALIBAN, *a savage and deformed slave*
TRINCULO, *a jester*
STEPHANO, *a drunken butler*

MASTER OF A SHIP
BOATSWAIN
MARINERS
MIRANDA, *daughter to Prospero*
ARIEL, *an airy spirit*
IRIS
CERES
JUNO   ⎱SPIRITS
NYMPHS
REAPERS ⎰

ACT I

SCENE I   [*On a ship at sea*]:° *a tempestuous noise of thunder and lightning heard.*

Enter a SHIP-MASTER *and a* BOATSWAIN.

SHIP-MASTER Boatswain!
BOATSWAIN Here, master: what cheer?
SHIP-MASTER Good: speak to the mariners: fall to it, yarely,° or we run ourselves aground: bestir, bestir.   *Exit.*

Enter MARINERS.

BOATSWAIN Heigh, my hearts! cheerly, cheerly, my hearts! yare, yare! Take in the topsail. Tend to the master's whistle.° Blow till thou burst thy wind, if room° enough!

Enter ALONSO, SEBASTIAN, ANTONIO, FERDINAND, GONZALO, *and others.*

10 ALONSO Good boatswain, have care. Where's the master? Play the men.°
BOATSWAIN I pray now, keep below.
ANTONIO Where is the master, boatswain?
BOATSWAIN Do you not hear him? You mar our labour: keep your cabins: you do assist the storm.
GONZALO Nay, good, be patient.
BOATSWAIN When the sea is. Hence! What cares these roarers° for the name of King? To cabin: silence! trouble us not.

[**On a ship at sea**] Square brackets in stage directions mean that the words enclosed are editorial additions to the copy-text, which is that of the First Folio of 1623, here called F.
yarely briskly

whistle used for giving orders by the Master
room sea-room
Play the men be courageous; or, make the men work (*ply* the men)
cares care
roarers toughs, hooligans (meaning the waves)

GONZALO Good, yet remember whom thou hast aboard.

20 BOATSWAIN None that I more love than myself. You are a counsellor; if you can command these elements to silence, and work the peace of the presence,° we will not hand a rope more; use your authority: if you cannot, give thanks you have lived so long, and make yourself ready in your cabin for the mischance of the hour, if it so hap. Cheerly, good hearts! Out of our way, I say.   *Exit.*

GONZALO I have great comfort from this fellow: methinks he hath no drowning mark° upon him; his complexion is perfect gallows.° Stand fast,
30 good Fate, to his hanging: make the rope of his destiny our cable, for our own doth little advantage.° If he be not born to be hanged, our case is miserable.   *Exeunt.*

Re-enter BOATSWAIN.

BOATSWAIN Down with the topmast! yare! lower, lower! Bring her to try with main-course° [*A cry within*]. A plague upon his howling! they are louder than the weather or our office.

Re-enter SEBASTIAN, ANTONIO, *and* GONZALO.

Yet again! what do you here? Shall we give o'er, and drown? Have you a mind to sink?

40 SEBASTIAN A pox o' your throat, you bawling, blasphemous, incharitable dog!

BOATSWAIN Work you, then.

ANTONIO Hang, cur! hang, you whoreson, insolent noise-maker. We are less afraid to be drowned than thou art.

GONZALO I'll warrant him for° drowning, though the ship were no stronger than a nutshell, and as leaky as an unstanched wench.°

BOATSWAIN Lay her a-hold,° a-hold! set her two courses;° off to sea again; lay
50 her off.

Enter MARINERS *wet.*

MARINERS All lost, to prayers, to prayers! all lost!

BOATSWAIN What, must our mouths be cold?

GONZALO The King and Prince at prayers, let's assist them,
For our case is as theirs.

SEBASTIAN   I'm out of patience.

ANTONIO We are merely° cheated of our lives by drunkards:
This wide-chapped rascal,—would thou mightst lie drowning
The washing of ten tides!

GONZALO   He'll be hanged yet,
Though every drop of water swear against it,

presence F has *present*, but *presence* (meaning the immediate vicinity of the king and court) is probable; his counselors would be responsible for keeping order in this area.
drowning mark mole or other blemish thought to indicate by its position the person's likeliest mode of death, here drowning
perfect gallows he will hang rather than drown
little advantage helps us little

Bring . . . main-course make her heave to
for i.e. against
unstanched wench loose (literally "leaky") woman
a-hold hove-to
courses sails; lacking sea-room to heave to, he tries to take the ship to sea
merely absolutely

And gape at wid'st to glut him.
[*A confused noise within:* 'Mercy on us!'—
'We split, we split!'—'Farewell, my wife and children!'—
'Farewell, brother!'—'We split, we split, we split!']

ANTONIO   Let's all sink wi' the King.

SEBASTIAN   Let's take leave of him.   *Exeunt* ANTONIO *and* SEBASTIAN

GONZALO   Now would I give a thousand furlongs of sea for an acre of barren
ground, long heath, broom, furze,° anything. The wills above be done!
but I would fain die a dry death.   *Exeunt.*

SCENE II [*The Island. Before* PROSPERO's *Cell.*]

Enter PROSPERO *and* MIRANDA.

MIRANDA   If by your Art, my dearest father, you° have
Put the wild waters in this roar, allay them.
The sky, it seems, would pour down stinking pitch,
But that the sea, mounting to the welkin's° cheek,
Dashes the fire out. O, I have suffered
With those that I saw suffer! a brave vessel,
(Who had, no doubt, some noble creature in her,)
Dashed all to pieces. O, the cry did knock
Against my very heart! Poor souls, they perished!
Had I been any god of power, I would
Have sunk the sea within the earth, or ere
It should the good ship so have swallowed, and
The fraughting° souls within her.

PROSPERO   Be collected:
No more amazement:° tell your piteous° heart
There's no harm done.

MIRANDA   O, woe the day!

PROSPERO   No harm.
I have done nothing but in care of thee,
Of thee, my dear one; thee, my daughter, who
Art ignorant of what thou art; nought knowing
Of whence I am, nor that I am more better°
Than Prospero, master of a full poor cell,
And thy no greater father.

MIRANDA   More to know
Did never meddle° with my thoughts.

PROSPERO   'Tis time
I should inform thee farther. Lend thy hand,
And pluck my magic garment from me.—So:

                                          Lays down his mantle.

Lie there, my Art.° Wipe thou thine eyes; have comfort.

---

broom, furze F has *browne firrs.*
you deferential, used by Miranda to her father,
who usually addresses her as "thou"
welkin's firmament's
fraughting forming the cargo

amazement terror
piteous full of pity
more better of higher rank
meddle mingle
my Art i.e. the robe, symbol of his art

The direful spectacle of the wrack,° which touched
The very virtue° of compassion in thee,
I have with such provision in mine Art
So safely ordered, that there is no soul°—
No, not so much perdition° as an hair
Betid° to any creature in the vessel
Which thou heard'st cry, which thou saw'st sink. Sit down;
For thou must now know farther.

MIRANDA   You have often
Begun to tell me what I am, but stopped,
And left me to bootless inquisition,°
Concluding 'Stay: not yet.'

PROSPERO   The hour's now come;
The very minute bids thee ope thine ear;
Obey, and be attentive. Canst thou remember
A time before we came unto this cell?
40   I do not think thou canst, for then thou wast not
Out° three years old.

MIRANDA   Certainly, sir, I can.

PROSPERO   By what? by any other house or person?
Of any thing the image tell me, that
Hath kept with thy remembrance.

MIRANDA   'Tis far off,
And rather like a dream than an assurance
That my remembrance warrants.° Had I not
Four or five women once that tended me?

PROSPERO   Thou hadst, and more, Miranda. But how is it
That this lives in thy mind? What seest thou else
50   In the dark backward and abysm of time?°
If thou rememberest aught ere thou camest here,
How thou camest here thou mayst.

MIRANDA   But that I do not.

PROSPERO   Twelve year since, Miranda, twelve year since,
Thy father was the Duke of Milan, and
A prince of power.

MIRANDA   Sir, are not you my father?

PROSPERO   Thy mother was a piece° of virtue, and
She said thou wast my daughter; and thy father
Was Duke of Milan; and his only heir
And princess, no worse issued.

MIRANDA   O the heavens!
60   What foul play had we, that we came from thence?
Or blessed was't we did?

---

wrack wreck
virtue essence
soul Prospero is about to say something like "lost," but changes the direction of his sentence.
perdition loss
Betid happened

bootless inquisition fruitless inquiry
Out fully
an assurance . . . warrants a certainty my memory guarantees
backward . . . time dark abyss of time past
piece perfect specimen

PROSPERO   Both, both, my girl:
By foul play, as thou say'st, were we heaved thence,
But blessedly holp° hither.
MIRANDA   O, my heart bleeds
To think o' the teen° that I have turned you to,
Which is from° my remembrance! Please you, farther.
PROSPERO   My brother, and thy uncle, called Antonio,—
I pray thee, mark me, that a brother should
Be so perfidious!—he whom next thyself
Of all the world I loved, and to him put
70   The manage of my state; as at that time
Through all the signories it was the first,
And Prospero the prime duke, being so reputed
In dignity, and for the liberal Arts
Without a parallel; those being all my study,
The government I cast upon my brother,
And to my state grew stranger, being transported
And rapt in secret studies° thy false uncle—
Dost thou attend me?
MIRANDA   Sir, most heedfully.
PROSPERO   Being once perfected how to grant suits,
80   How to deny them, who to advance, and who
To trash for over-topping,° new created
The creatures that were mine, I say, or changed 'em,
Or else new formed 'em; having both the key
Of officer and office, set all hearts i' the state
To what tune pleased his ear;° that now he was
The ivy which had hid my princely trunk,
And sucked my verdure out on it.° Thou attend'st not?
MIRANDA   O, good sir, I do.
PROSPERO   I pray thee, mark me.
I, thus neglecting worldly ends, all dedicated
90   To closeness and the bettering of my mind
With that which, but by being so retired,
O'er-prized all popular rate, in my false brother
Awaked an evil nature; and my trust,
Like a good parent, did beget of him
A falsehood in its contrary, as great

---

holp helped
teen trouble
from absent from
My brother . . . studies (ll. 66–77) Prospero
loses the thread of this speech, which may be
summarized: My brother Antonio—note his
amazing treachery—the person I loved best in
the world except for you, so that I entrusted
him with the management of my estate, which
was the chief one in North Italy and I the
senior duke by virtue of my position and my
learning . . . to this brother I delegated the
government, caring not for my dukedom but
for my studies.

trash for over-topping keep in check for being
over-bold; "trash" means a cord used in training hounds
set . . . ear The musical image grows out of
the word *key*.
Being . . . on it (ll. 79–87) having mastered
the art of dealing with suitors, advancing some,
disappointing others, so arranging things that
those already in office by my favor became
his dependents—having got the measure of all
the jobs and the men who did them, he ran
the state exactly as he pleased; he was to me
as ivy to the noble oak, concealing and enfeebling it

As my trust was; which had indeed no limit,
A confidence sans bound.° He being thus lorded,°
Not only with what my revénue yielded,
But what my power might else exact,° like one
100   Who having into° truth, by telling of it,°
Made such a sinner of his memory,
To credit his own lie, he did believe
He was indeed the duke; out o' the substitution,
And executing the outward face of royalty,
With all prerogative;°—hence his ambition growing,—
Dost thou hear?

MIRANDA   Your tale, sir, would cure deafness.

PROSPERO   To have no screen between this part he played
And him he played it for,° he needs will be
Absolute Milan.° Me, poor man, my library
110   Was dukedom large enough: of temporal° royalties
He thinks me now incapable; confederates,
So dry° he was for sway, wi' the King of Naples
To give him annual tribute, do him homage,
Subject his coronet to his crown, and bend
The dukedom, yet unbowed,—alas, poor Milan!—
To most ignoble stooping.

MIRANDA   O the heavens!

PROSPERO   Mark his condition,° and the event;° then tell me
If this might be a brother.

MIRANDA   I should sin
To think but nobly of my grandmother:
Good wombs have borne bad sons.

120 PROSPERO   Now the condition.
This King of Naples, being an enemy
To me inveterate, hearkens my brother's suit;
Which was, that he, in lieu o' the premises°
Of homage and I know not how much tribute,
Should presently° extirpate me and mine
Out of the dukedom, and confer fair Milan,
With all the honours, on my brother: whereon,
A treacherous army levied, one midnight
Fated to the purpose, did Antonio open

I . . . sans bound (ll. 89–97) the fact of my retirement, in which I neglected wordly affairs and gave myself to secret studies of a kind beyond the understanding and esteem of the people, brought out a bad side in my brother's nature; consequently the great, indeed boundless, trust I placed in him gave rise on his part to a disloyalty equally great, just as it can happen that a virtuous father may have a vicious son
lorded made a lord of
else exact otherwise extort
into unto
it i.e. his own lie

executing . . . prerogative carrying out the public duties of royalty with full power
him . . . for i.e. himself
Absolute Milan Duke, not merely Duke's substitute
temporal worldly, as opposed to spiritual
dry thirsty
condition terms on which the deal with Naples was concluded
event outcome
in lieu o' the premises in return for the undertaking
presently immediately

130   The gates of Milan; and, i' the dead of darkness,
      The ministers° for the purpose hurried thence
      Me and thy crying self.

MIRANDA   Alack, for pity!
      I, not remembering how I cried out then,
      Will cry it o'er again: it is a hint°
      That wrings mine eyes to it.

PROSPERO   Hear a little further,
      And then I'll bring thee to the present business
      Which now's upon us; without the which, this story
      Were most impertinent.°

MIRANDA   Wherefore did they not
      That hour destroy us?

PROSPERO   Well demanded, wench:
140   My tale provokes that question. Dear, they durst not,
      So dear the love my people bore me; nor set
      A mark so bloody on the business; but
      With colours fairer painted their foul ends.
      In few,° they hurried us aboard a bark,
      Bore us some leagues to sea; where they prepared
      A rotten carcass of a butt,° not rigged,
      Nor tackle, sail, nor mast; the very rats
      Instinctively have quit it: there they hoist us,
      To cry to the sea that roared to us; to sigh
150   To the winds, whose pity, sighing back again,
      Did us but loving wrong.

MIRANDA   Alack, what trouble
      Was I then to you!

PROSPERO   O, a cherubin
      Thou wast that did preserve me. Thou didst smile,
      Infusèd with a fortitude from heaven,
      When I have decked° the sea with drops full salt,
      Under my burthen groaned; which raised in me
      An undergoing stomach,° to bear up
      Against what should ensue.

MIRANDA   How came we ashore?

PROSPERO   By Providence divine.
160   Some food we had, and some fresh water, that
      A noble Neapolitan, Gonzalo,
      Out of his charity,° who being then appointed
      Master of this design, did give us, with
      Rich garments, linens, stuffs and necessaries,
      Which since have steaded much;° so, of his gentleness,

---

ministers those employed
hint occasion
impertinent not to the purpose
In few to be brief
butt tub (contemptuous); a clumsy boat
decked adorned; note the intrusion here of an

artificial, conceited manner
undergoing stomach spirit of endurance
charity love, but in a wider sense than the
modern; see The English Bible section
steaded much stood us in good stead

Knowing I loved my books, he furnished me
From mine own library with volumes that
I prize above my dukedom.

MIRANDA   Would I might
But ever° see that man!

PROSPERO   Now I arise:

170   Sit still, and hear the last of our sea-sorrow.
Here in this island we arrived; and here
Have I, thy schoolmaster, made thee more profit
Than other princess'° can, that have more time
For vainer hours, and tutors not so careful.

MIRANDA   Heavens thank you for it! And now, I pray you, sir,
For still 'tis beating in my mind, your reason
For raising this sea-storm?

PROSPERO   Know thus far forth.
By accident most strange, bountiful Fortune
(Now my dear lady) hath mine enemies

180   Brought to this shore; and by my prescience°
I find my zenith doth depend upon
A most auspicious star,° whose influence
If now I court not, but omit, my fortunes
Will ever after droop. Here cease more questions:
Thou art inclined to sleep; 'tis a good dulness,
And give it way: I know thou canst not choose.

                                        MIRANDA *sleeps.*

Come away, servant, come. I am ready now.
Approach, my Ariel, come.

Enter ARIEL.

ARIEL   All hail, great master! grave sir, hail! I come

190   To answer thy best pleasure; be it to fly,
To swim, to dive into the fire, to ride
On the curled clouds, to thy strong bidding task
Ariel and all his quality.°

PROSPERO   Hast thou, spirit,
Performed to point° the tempest that I bade thee?

ARIEL   To every article.
I boarded the king's ship; now on the beak,°
Now in the waist,° the deck,° in every cabin,
I flamed amazement:° sometime I'd divide,
And burn in many places; on the topmast,

200   The yards and boresprit,° would I flame distinctly,

But ever only someday
princess' princesses
prescience foreknowledge
my zenith . . . star I am reaching the highest
point in my fortunes—my star is in its most
favorable aspect
quality attendant spirits

to point exactly
beak prow
waist amidships
deck poop
flamed amazement struck terror by appearing as
flames (as lightning and St. Elmo's fire)
boresprit bowsprit

Then meet and join. Jove's lightnings, the precursors
O' the dreadful thunder-claps, more momentary
And sight-outrunning were not: the fire and cracks
Of sulphurous roaring the most mighty Neptune
Seem to besiege, and make his bold waves tremble,
Yea, his dread trident shake.

PROSPERO   My brave spirit!
Who was so firm, so constant, that this coil°
Would not infect his reason?

ARIEL   Not a soul
But felt a fever of the mad, and played
210   Some tricks of desperation. All but mariners
Plunged in the foaming brine, and quit the vessel,
Then all afire with me: the King's son, Ferdinand,
With hair up-staring,°—then like reeds, not hair,—
Was the first man that leaped; cried, 'Hell is empty,
And all the devils are here.'

PROSPERO   Why, that's my spirit!
But was not this nigh shore?

ARIEL   Close by, my master.

PROSPERO   But are they, Ariel, safe?

ARIEL   Not a hair perished;
On their sustaining° garments not a blemish,
But fresher than before: and, as thou bad'st me,
220   In troops I have dispersed them 'bout the isle.
The King's son have I landed by himself;
Whom I left cooling of the air with sighs
In an odd angle° of the isle, and sitting,
His arms in this sad knot.°

PROSPERO   Of the King's ship,
The mariners, say how thou hast disposed,
And all the rest o' the fleet.

ARIEL   Safely in harbour
Is the King's ship; in the deep nook, where once
Thou call'dst me up at midnight to fetch dew
From the still-vexed Bermoothes,° there she's hid:
230   The mariners all under hatches stowed;
Who, with a charm joined to their suffered labour,°
I have left asleep: and for the rest o' the fleet,
Which I dispersed, they all have met again,
And are upon the Mediterranean flote,°
Bound sadly home for Naples;
Supposing that they saw the King's ship wracked,
And his great person perish.

---

coil turmoil
up-staring standing on end
sustaining upholding
angle corner

in . . . knot folded
still-vexed Bermoothes always stormy Bermudas
suffered labour the labor they have undergone
flote sea

PROSPERO   Ariel, thy charge
 Exactly is performed: but there's more work.
 What is the time o' the day?
ARIEL   Past the mid season.
240 PROSPERO   At least two glasses.° The time 'twixt six and now
 Must by us both be spent most preciously.
ARIEL   Is there more toil? Since thou dost give me pains,
 Let me remember thee what thou hast promised,
 Which is not yet performed me.
PROSPERO   How now? moody?
 What is it thou canst demand?
ARIEL   My liberty.
PROSPERO   Before the time be out? no more!
ARIEL   I prithee,
 Remember I have done thee worthy service;
 Told thee no lies, made no mistakings,° served
 Without or° grudge or grumblings: thou didst promise
 To bate° me a full year.
250 PROSPERO   Dost thou forget
 From what a torment I did free thee?
ARIEL   No.
PROSPERO   Thou dost, and think'st it much to tread the ooze°
 Of the salt deep,
 To run upon the sharp wind of the north,
 To do me business in the veins o' the earth°
 When it is baked° with frost.
ARIEL   I do not, sir.
PROSPERO   Thou liest, malignant thing! Hast thou forgot
 The foul witch Sycorax, who with age and envy°
 Was grown into a hoop?° hast thou forgot her?
ARIEL   No, sir.
260 PROSPERO   Thou hast. Where was she born? speak; tell me.
ARIEL   Sir, in Argier.°
PROSPERO   O, was she so? I must
 Once in a month recount what thou hast been,
 Which thou forget'st. This damned witch Sycorax,
 For mischiefs manifold, and sorceries terrible
 To enter human hearing, from Argier,
 Thou knowest, was banished: for one thing she did°
 They would not take her life. Is not this true?
ARIEL   Ay, sir.
PROSPERO   This blue-eyed° hag was hither brought with child,

---

glasses hours; turns of the hourglass
made no mistakings F has *made thee no mistakings.*
or either
bate let me off
ooze slimy bottom
veins o' the earth Contemporary cosmology held that there were subterranean waters in the earth like veins and arteries in the body.
baked hardened
envy malignity
grown into a hoop bent double
Argier Algiers
one thing she did some good service; or, being with child
blue-eyed sign of exhaustion or pregnancy

270 And here was left by the sailors. Thou, my slave,
As thou report'st thyself, wast then her servant;
And, for° thou wast a spirit too delicate
To act her earthy° and abhorred commands,
Refusing her grand hests,° she did confine thee,
By help of her more potent ministers,°
And in her most unmitigable rage,
Into a cloven pine; within which rift
Imprisoned thou didst painfully remain
A dozen years; within which space she died,
280 And left thee there; where thou didst vent° thy groans
As fast as mill-wheels strike. Then was this island—
Save for the son that she did litter here,
A freckled whelp hag-born—not honoured with
A human shape.

ARIEL   Yes, Caliban her son.

PROSPERO   Dull thing, I say so; he, that Caliban,
Whom now I keep in service. Thou best knowest
What torment I did find thee in; thy groans
Did make wolves howl, and penetrate the breasts
Of ever-angry bears: it was a torment
290 To lay upon the damned, which Sycorax
Could not again undo: it was mine Art,
When I arrived and heard thee, that made gape
The pine, and let thee out.

ARIEL   I thank thee, master.

PROSPERO   If thou more murmur'st, I will rend an oak,
And peg thee in his knotty entrails, till
Thou hast howled away twelve winters.

ARIEL   Pardon, master:
I will be correspondent° to command,
And do my spriting gently.°

PROSPERO   Do so; and after two days
I will discharge thee.

ARIEL   That's my noble master!
300 What shall I do? say what; what shall I do?

PROSPERO   Go make thyself like a nymph o' the sea:
Be subject to
No sight but thine and mine; invisible
To every eyeball else. Go take this shape,
And hither come in it: go: hence
With diligence.   *Exit* ARIEL.
Awake, dear heart, awake! thou hast slept well;
Awake!

---

for because
earthy Sycorax and Caliban are associated with
earth, Ariel with air and fire.
hests commands

ministers demonic agents
vent utter
correspondent compliant
gently without complaint

MIRANDA   The strangeness of your story put
                 Heaviness° in me.

PROSPERO   Shake it off. Come on;
310   We'll visit Caliban my slave, who never
                 Yields us kind answer.

MIRANDA   'Tis a villain, sir,
                 I do not love to look on.

PROSPERO   But, as 'tis,
                 We cannot miss° him: he does make our fire,
                 Fetch in our wood, and serves in offices°
                 That profit us. What, ho! slave! Caliban!
                 Thou earth, thou! speak.

CALIBAN   [*Within*] There's wood enough within.

PROSPERO   Come forth, I say! there's other business for thee;
                 Come, thou tortoise! when?

                 Re-enter ARIEL *like a water-nymph.*

                 Fine apparition! My quaint° Ariel,
                 Hark in thine ear.

320   ARIEL   My lord, it shall be done.   *Exit.*

PROSPERO   Thou poisonous slave, got by the devil himself°
                 Upon thy wicked dam, come forth!

                 Enter CALIBAN.

CALIBAN   As wicked° dew as e'er my mother brushed
                 With raven's feather° from unwholesome fen
                 Drop on you both! a south-west° blow on ye
                 And blister you all o'er!

PROSPERO   For this, be sure, tonight thou shalt have cramps,
                 Side-stitches that shall pen thy breath up; urchins°
                 Shall for that vast of night that they may work,
330   All exercise on thee;° thou shalt be pinched
                 As thick as honeycomb, each pinch more stinging
                 Than bees that made 'em.°

CALIBAN   I must eat my dinner.
                 This island's mine, by Sycorax my mother,
                 Which thou tak'st from me. When thou camest first,
                 Thou strok'st me, and made much of me; wouldst
                     give me
                 Water with berries° in it; and teach me how

Heaviness drowsiness
miss do without
offices services
quaint elegant, ingenious
got . . . himself Caliban was the result of a
union between witch and devil.
wicked baneful
raven's feather The raven (*corax*) was a bird of
ill-omen.

south-west the pestilence-bearing wind
urchins hedgehogs, goblins in the shape of
hedgehogs
Shall for . . . thee shall, during the dead of
night which is the period during which they
are allowed to operate, all torment you
'em the cells of the honeycomb
berries The Bermudan castaways used berries
to make drinks.

To name the bigger light, and how the less,°
That burn by day and night: and then I loved thee,
And showed thee all the qualities o' the isle,
340   The fresh springs, brine-pits, barren place and fertile:
Cursed be I that did so! All the charms
Of Sycorax, toads, beetles, bats,° light on you!
For I am all the subjects that you have,
Which first was mine own King: and here you sty me°
In this hard rock, whiles you do keep from me
The rest o' the island.

PROSPERO   Thou most lying slave,
Whom stripes° may move, not kindness! I have used thee,
Filth as thou art, with human care; and lodged thee
In mine own cell, till thou didst seek to violate
350   The honour of my child.

CALIBAN   O ho, O ho! would it had been done!
Thou didst prevent me; I had peopled else
This isle with Calibans.

MIRANDA   Abhorrèd slave,
Which any print° of goodness wilt not take,
Being capable of° all ill! I pitied thee,
Took pains to make thee speak, taught thee each hour
One thing or other: when thou didst not, savage,
Know thine own meaning, but wouldst gabble like
A thing most brutish, I endowed thy purposes
360   With words that made them known. But thy vile race,°
Though thou didst learn, had that in it which good natures
Could not abide to be with; therefore wast thou
Deservedly confined into this rock,
Who hadst deservèd more than a prison.

CALIBAN   You taught me language; and my profit on it
Is, I know how to curse. The red plague° rid° you
For learning me your language!

PROSPERO   Hag-seed, hence!
Fetch us in fuel; and be quick, thou 'rt best,
To answer other business.° Shrug'st thou, malice?°
370   If thou neglect'st, or dost unwillingly
What I command, I'll rack thee with old° cramps,
Fill all thy bones with achès, make thee roar,
That beasts shall tremble at thy din.

CALIBAN   No, 'pray thee.
[Aside] I must obey: his Art is of such power,

---

bigger light . . . less sun and moon; see
Genesis 1:16
toads, beetles, bats all associated with witches
sty me keep me pent up
stripes lashes
print impression
capable of apt to receive the impression of
race hereditary nature; contrasted with the
"good natures" of the next line

red plague bubonic plague; called after the
color of the sores
rid destroy
thou'rt . . . business it will be best for you
to do the jobs assigned you
malice malicious thing
old severe

It would control° my dam's god, Setebos,°
And make a vassal of him.

PROSPERO   So, slave; hence!   *Exit* CALIBAN.

Re-enter ARIEL, *invisible, playing and singing;* FERDINAND *following.*

ARIEL'S SONG

> *Come unto these yellow sands,*
>   *And then take hands:*
> *Courtsied when you have and kissed*
380   *The wild waves whist:°*
> *Foot it featly° here and there,*
>   *And sweet sprites bear*
> *The burthen. Hark, hark.*

Burthen° dispersedly.° *Bow-wow.*
ARIEL   *The watch dogs bark:*

Burthen dispersedly. *Bow-wow.*

ARIEL   *Hark, hark! I hear*
The strain of strutting chanticleer

Cry—Burthen dispersedly. *Cock a diddle dow.*

390 FERDINAND   Where should this music be? i' the air or the earth?
It sounds no more: and, sure, it waits upon°
Some god o' the island. Sitting on a bank,
Weeping again° the King my father's wrack,
This music crept by me upon the waters,
Allaying both their fury and my passion
With its sweet air: thence° I have followed it,
Or it hath drawn me rather. But 'tis gone.
No, it begins again.

ARIEL *sings.*

> *Full fadom° five thy father lies;*
400   *Of his bones are coral made;*
> *Those are pearls that were his eyes:*
>   *Nothing of him that doth fade,*
> *But doth suffer a sea-change*
>   *Into something rich and strange.°*
> *Sea-nymphs hourly ring his knell:*

Burthen: *Ding-dong.*

ARIEL   *Hark! now I hear them,—Ding-dong, bell.*

---

control overcome
Setebos Patagonian god mentioned by a travel writer
Courtsied . . . whist either "when you have curtsied to and kissed your partner, the sea remaining quiet," or, "when you have curtsied and kissed the sea into silence"
featly gracefully
Burthen refrain

dispersedly not in unison
waits upon attends
again indicates intensity as well as repetition
thence from the water's edge
fadom fathom
Nothing . . . strange Every part of his body that is otherwise doomed to decay is transformed into some rich or rare sea-substance.

Full fad-om five thy fa - ther lies; of his bones are cor - al__ made; those are pearls that were his eyes noth - ing of him that doth fade, but doth suf - fer a sea - change In - to some-thing rich and strange. Sea nymphs hour-ly ring his knell; Hark, now I hear them, Hark__ now I hear them, Ding, Dong Bell Ding Dong Ding Dong Bell

Ding Dong Ding Dong   Bell   Ding Dong Ding Dong   Bell.

This setting of "Full Fadom Five", like that of "Where the Bee Sucks" in Act V
(for voice and unfigured bass line), is by Robert Johnson (1583?–1633), a composer
known for his music for plays and masques. These settings may well have been written
for the first production, although they were first published in an arrangement for three
voices in John Wilson's *Cheerful Airs* (1659). The unfigured bass simply gave the lowest
musical line; the songs could be sung as given, with a bass viol accompaniment, or
with a lute (filling in other lines and chords), or by a group of instruments (this is a
little like the modern practice of printing a popular song with guitar chords). In "Full
Fadom Five" there is a fugue-like imitation in the voice and bass parts, and we can be
certain that other instruments took up the melody as well. The effect of the whole
would be that of chiming bells.

FERDINAND   The ditty° does remember° my drowned father.
            This is no mortal business, nor no sound
410   That the earth owes:°—I hear it now above me.
PROSPERO   The fringèd curtains of thine eye advance,°
            And say what thou seest yond.
MIRANDA   What is it? a spirit?
            Lord, how it looks about! Believe me, sir,
            It carries a brave° form. But 'tis a spirit.
PROSPERO   No, wench; it eats and sleeps and hath such senses
            As we have, such. This gallant which thou seest
            Was in the wrack; and, but° he's something stained
            With grief (that's beauty's canker°) thou mightst call him
            A goodly person: he hath lost his fellows,
            And strays about to find 'em.
420 MIRANDA   I might call him
            A thing divine; for nothing natural°
            I ever saw so noble.
PROSPERO   [*Aside*] It goes on,° I see,
            As my soul prompts it. Spirit, fine spirit! I'll free thee
            Within two days for this.
FERDINAND   Most sure the goddess°
            On whom these airs attend! Vouchsafe my prayer

ditty words of the song
remember commemorate
owes owns
fringèd curtains . . . advance eyelids . . . lift
up
brave splendid
but except that
canker disease of roses

natural in the realm of nature as opposed to
spirit
It goes on my plan (that Miranda should love
Ferdinand) is working out
Most sure the goddess virtually a translation
of Virgil's *O dea certe*, *Aeneid* I.328, often used
in romance; Miranda's response (ll. 430–31)
is also modeled on the passage

May know if you remain upon this island;
And that you will some good instruction give
How I may bear me° here: my prime° request,
Which I do last pronounce, is, O you wonder!°
If you be maid or no?

430   MIRANDA   No wonder, sir;
But certainly a maid.

FERDINAND   My language! heavens!
I am the best of them that speak this speech,
Were I but where 'tis spoken.

PROSPERO   How? the best?
What wert thou, if the King of Naples heard thee?

FERDINAND   A single° thing, as I am now, that wonders
To hear thee speak of Naples. He does hear me;
And that he does I weep: myself am Naples,°
Who with mine eyes, never since at ebb, beheld
The King my father wracked.

MIRANDA   Alack, for mercy!

440   FERDINAND   Yes, faith, and all his lords; the Duke of Milan
And his brave° son being twain.

PROSPERO   [*Aside*] The Duke of Milan
And his more braver daughter could control° thee,
If now 'twere fit to do it. At the first sight
They have changed eyes.° Delicate Ariel,
I'll set thee free for this. [*To* FERDINAND] A word, good sir;
I fear you have done yourself some wrong:° a word.

MIRANDA   Why speaks my father so ungently? This
Is the third man° that e'er I saw; the first
That e'er I sighed for: pity move my father
To be inclined my way!°

450   FERDINAND   O, if a virgin,
And your affection not gone forth, I'll make you
The Queen of Naples.

PROSPERO   Soft, sir! one word more.
[*Aside*] They are both in either's powers: but this swift business
I must uneasy make, lest too light winning°
Make the prize light.° [*To* FERDINAND] One word more; I charge thee
That thou attend me: thou dost here usurp
The name thou ow'st° not; and hast put thyself
Upon this island as a spy, to win it
From me, the lord on it.

---

bear me conduct myself
prime most important
wonder a play on Miranda's name, which Ferdinand doesn't yet know
single solitary
myself am Naples Ferdinand thinks his father is dead and that he himself is King of Naples.
brave gallant. There is no further mention of Antonio's son in the play and this may be a slip.

control confute
changed eyes fallen in love
you have done yourself some wrong ironically polite way of saying "You're mistaken"
third man the others are Prospero and Caliban
inclined my way persuaded to my wishes
light winning easy success
light undervalued
ow'st ownest

FERDINAND   No, as I am a man.

460 MIRANDA   There's nothing ill can dwell in such a temple:°
    If the ill spirit have so fair a house,
    Good things will strive to dwell with it.°

PROSPERO   Follow me.
    Speak not you for him: he's a traitor. Come;
    I'll manacle thy neck and feet together:
    Sea-water shalt thou drink; thy food shall be
    The fresh-brook mussels, withered roots, and husks
    Wherein the acorn cradled. Follow.

FERDINAND   No;
    I will resist such entertainment° till
    Mine enemy has more power.

                  He draws, and is charmed from moving.

MIRANDA   O dear father,
470 Make not too rash a trial of him, for
    He's gentle, and not fearful.°

PROSPERO   What! I say,
    My foot my tutor?° Put thy sword up, traitor;
    Who mak'st a show, but dar'st not strike, thy conscience
    Is so possessed with guilt: come from thy ward;°
    For I can here disarm thee with this stick°
    And make thy weapon drop.

MIRANDA   Beseech you, father.

PROSPERO   Hence! hang not on my garments.

MIRANDA   Sir, have pity;
    I'll be his surety.

PROSPERO   Silence! one word more
    Shall make me chide thee, if not hate thee. What!
480 An advocate for an impostor! hush!
    Thou think'st there is° no more such shapes as he,
    Having seen but him and Caliban: foolish wench!
    To° the most of men this is a Caliban,
    And they to him are angels.

MIRANDA   My affections°
    Are then most humble; I have no ambition
    To see a goodlier° man.

PROSPERO   Come on; obey:
    Thy nerves° are in their infancy again,
    And have no vigour in them.

There's nothing . . . temple Conventional neo-platonic doctrine—that the beautiful body houses a beautiful soul—is expressed by Miranda though qualified by Prospero later; but for the same reason Caliban and Sycorax are ugly.
Good things . . . with it suggesting that this is absurd
entertainment hospitality (ironical)
gentle . . . fearful high-born and not cowardly
My foot my tutor? shall you, so much my inferior, presume to instruct me? (Prospero thinks of himself as the head)
come from thy ward abandon your posture of defense
stick magic staff
is are
To in comparison with
affections feelings
goodlier more handsome
nerves sinews

FERDINAND   So they are:
My spirits,° as in a dream, are all bound up.
490   My father's loss, the weakness which I feel,
The wrack of all my friends, nor° this man's threats,
To whom I am subdued, are° but light to me,
Might I but through my prison once a day
Behold this maid: all corners else o' the earth
Let liberty make use of;° space enough
Have I in such a prison.
PROSPERO   [Aside] It works. [To FERDINAND] Come on.
[To ARIEL] Thou hast done well, fine Ariel! Follow me;
Hark what thou else shalt do me.
MIRANDA   Be of comfort;
My father's of a better nature, sir,
500   Than he appears by speech: this is unwonted°
Which now came from him.
PROSPERO   Thou shalt be as free
As mountain winds: but then exactly do
All points of my command.
ARIEL   To the syllable.
PROSPERO   Come, follow. Speak not for him.   Exeunt.

ACT II

SCENE I [Another part of the Island.]

Enter ALONSO, SEBASTIAN, ANTONIO, GONZALO, ADRIAN, FRANCISCO, and
others.

GONZALO   Beseech you, sir, be merry; you have cause,
So have we all, of joy; for our escape
Is much beyond our loss. Our hint of° woe
Is common; every day, some sailor's wife,
The masters of some merchant,° and the merchant,°
Have just our theme of woe; but for the miracle,
I mean our preservation, few in millions
Can speak like us: then wisely, good sir, weigh
Our sorrow with our comfort.
ALONZO   Prithee, peace.
10   SEBASTIAN [Aside to ANTONIO]   He receives comfort like cold porridge.°
ANTONIO [Aside to SEBASTIAN]   The visitor° will not give him o'er° so.

---

spirits energies; animal spirits, which convey
nourishment and so strength to the body
nor Grammar confused; it would be clear if
this were and.
are Read would be.
all corners . . . use of those who are free may
have all the rest of the world; my prison, if I
could see Miranda, would be all the space I
needed

unwonted unaccustomed
hint of occasion for
some merchant some merchant vessel
merchant owner of the vessel
porridge made of pease; so there is a pun on
Alonso's word, "peace"
visitor one who comforts the infirm
give him o'er cease to administer his advice

SEBASTIAN [*Aside to* ANTONIO]   Look, he's winding up the watch of his wit; by
and by it will strike.°

GONZALO   Sir,—

SEBASTIAN [*Aside to* ANTONIO]   One: tell.°

GONZALO   When every grief is entertained that's offered,
Comes to the entertainer°—

SEBASTIAN   A dollar.°

GONZALO   Dolour comes to him, indeed: you have spoken truer than you pur-
20   posed.

SEBASTIAN   You have taken it wiselier° than I meant you should.

GONZALO   Therefore, my lord,—

ANTONIO   Fie, what a spendthrift is he of his tongue!

ALONZO   I prithee, spare.°

GONZALO   Well, I have done: but yet,—

SEBASTIAN   He will be talking.

ANTONIO   Which, of he or Adrian, for a good wager, first begins to crow?

SEBASTIAN   The old cock.

30   ANTONIO   The cockerel.°

SEBASTIAN   Done. The wager?

ANTONIO   A laughter.°

SEBASTIAN   A match!

ADRIAN   Though this island seem to be desert,—

ANTONIO   Ha, ha, ha!

SEBASTIAN   So: you're paid.°

ADRIAN   Uninhabitable, and almost inaccessible,—

SEBASTIAN   Yet,—

40   ANTONIO   He could not miss it.

ADRIAN   It must needs be of subtle, tender and delicate temperance.°

ANTONIO   Temperance° was a delicate wench.

SEBASTIAN   Ay, and a subtle; as he most learnedly delivered.

ADRIAN   The air breathes upon us here most sweetly.

SEBASTIAN   As if it had lungs, and rotten ones.

ANTONIO   Or as 'twere perfumed by a fen.

GONZALO   Here is everything advantageous to life.

ANTONIO   True; save means to live.

50   SEBASTIAN   Of that there's none, or little.

GONZALO   How lush and lusty° the grass looks! how green!

ANTONIO   The ground, indeed, is tawny.°

SEBASTIAN   With an eye of green° in it.

ANTONIO   He misses not much.

---

strike Striking or "repeating" watches were invented about 1510.
tell count
When . . . entertainer he who makes a point of accepting every occasion for grief that presents itself gets—
dollar sum of money (punning on the word Gonzalo speaks next)
wiselier more cleverly, more sagely
spare your words

cockerel i.e. Adrian
A laughter The winner is to have the right to laugh at the loser.
paid Antonio has had his laugh; in F Sebastian is given l. 35, Antonio l. 36.
temperance climate
Temperance a (Puritan) woman's name
lush and lusty fresh and luxuriant
tawny parched brown
eye of green having green patches

SEBASTIAN   No; he doth but mistake° the truth totally.

GONZALO   But the rarity of it is,—which is indeed almost beyond credit,°—

SEBASTIAN   As many vouched rarities° are.

GONZALO   That our garments, being, as they were, drenched in the sea, hold,
notwithstanding, their freshness and glosses, being rather new-dyed than
stained with salt water.

ANTONIO   If but one of his pockets could speak, would it not say he lies?

SEBASTIAN   Ay, or very falsely pocket up° his report.

GONZALO   Methinks our garments are now as fresh as when we put them on
first in Afric, at the marriage of the King's fair daughter Claribel to the
King of Tunis.

SEBASTIAN   'Twas a sweet marriage, and we prosper well° in our return.

ADRIAN   Tunis was never graced before with such a paragon to their Queen.

GONZALO   Not since widow Dido's° time.

ANTONIO   Widow! a pox o' that! How came that widow in? widow Dido!

SEBASTIAN   What if he had said 'widower Æneas'° too? Good Lord, how you
take it!

ADRIAN   'Widow Dido' said you? you make me study of that:° she was of
Carthage, not of Tunis.°

GONZALO   This Tunis, sir, was Carthage.

ADRIAN   Carthage?

GONZALO   I assure you, Carthage.

ANTONIO   His word is more than the miraculous harp.°

SEBASTIAN   He hath raised the wall, and houses too.

ANTONIO   What impossible matter will he make easy next?

SEBASTIAN   I think he will carry this island home in his pocket, and give it his
son for an apple.

ANTONIO   And, sowing the kernels of it in the sea, bring forth more islands.

GONZALO   Ay.°

ANTONIO   Why, in good time.

GONZALO   Sir,° we were talking that our garments seem now as fresh as when
we were at Tunis at the marriage of your daughter, who is now Queen.

ANTONIO   And the rarest that e'er came there.

SEBASTIAN   Bate,° I beseech you, widow Dido.

ANTONIO   O, widow Dido! ay, widow Dido.

GONZALO   Is not, sir, my doublet as fresh as the first day I wore it? I mean, in
a sort.°

---

mistake punning on *miss* in previous line
credit belief
vouched rarities strange travelers' tales, vouched
for by the teller
pocket up conceal (referring to the remark
about Gonzalo's pocket, which could act as
mouthpiece for the suit and tell a different
story)
we prosper well ironical, of course
widow Dido's She was the widow of Sychaeus
when she met Aeneas, but the expression is
found ridiculous.
widower Æneas Aeneas was a widower just as
Dido was a widow—why not mention that,
too?

study of that give some thought to that
Tunis The site of the ancient Carthage was
near to, but not identical with, that of modern
Tunis; so Gonzalo is wrong.
more . . . harp Only the *walls* of Thebes rose
to the music of Amphion's harp, whereas Gonzalo, by identifying Carthage and Tunis, fabri-
cates a whole city.
Ay Gonzalo reaffirms his position on Tunis and
Carthage (F has *I*).
Sir he addresses the King
Bate make an exception of
sort up to a point

100 ANTONIO That sort was well fished for.°

GONZALO When I wore it at your daughter's marriage?

ALONSO You cram these words into mine ears against
    The stomach of my sense.° Would I had never
    Married my daughter there! for, coming thence,
    My son is lost, and, in my rate,° she too,
    Who is so far from Italy removed
    I ne'er again shall see her. O thou mine heir
    Of Naples and of Milan, what strange fish
    Hath made his meal on thee?

FRANCISCO   Sir, he may live:
110   I saw him beat the surges° under him,
    And ride upon their backs; he trod the water,
    Whose enmity he flung aside, and breasted
    The surge most swoln that met him; his bold head
    'Bove the contentious waves he kept, and oared
    Himself with his good arms in lusty stroke
    To the shore, that o'er his wave-worn basis° bowed,
    As stooping to relieve him: I not doubt
    He came alive to land.

ALONSO   No, no, he's gone.

SEBASTIAN Sir, you may thank yourself for this great loss,
120   That would not bless our Europe with your daughter,
    But rather loose° her to an African;
    Where she, at least, is banished from your eye,
    Who hath cause to wet the grief on it.°

ALONSO   Prithee, peace.

SEBASTIAN You were kneeled to, and importuned otherwise,
    By all of us; and the fair soul herself
    Weighed° between loathness° and obedience, at
    Which end o' the beam should bow. We have lost your son,
    I fear, for ever: Milan and Naples have
    Mo° widows in them of this business' making
130   Than we bring men to comfort them:
    The fault's your own.

ALONSO   So is the dearest° o' the loss.

GONZALO My lord Sebastian,
    The truth you speak doth lack some gentleness,
    And time° to speak it in: you rub the sore,
    When you should bring the plaster.°

SEBASTIAN   Very well.

That . . . for the word "sort" was a lucky catch, and saved Gonzalo from an outright lie **stomach of my sense** The King compares Gonzalo's persistence in plying him with consolations to that of a man who forces food on a reluctant recipient.
rate estimation
surges waves
basis base

loose mate (contemptuous)
Who . . . on it obscure: probably "weep for the grief her loss has caused you"
Weighed balanced
loathness reluctance
Mo more
dearest bitterest
time appropriate time
plaster dressing

ANTONIO And most chirurgeonly.°

GONZALO It is foul weather in us all, good sir,
When you are cloudy.

SEBASTIAN   Foul° weather?

ANTONIO   Very foul.

GONZALO Had I plantation° of this isle, my lord,—

ANTONIO He'd sow it with nettle-seed.

140 SEBASTIAN   Or docks, or mallows.°

GONZALO And were the King on it, what would I do?

SEBASTIAN 'Scape being drunk for want of wine.

GONZALO I' the commonwealth° I would by contraries°
Execute all things; for no kind of traffic°
Would I admit; no name of magistrate;
Letters° should not be known; riches, poverty,
And use of service,° none; contract, succession,°
Bourn,° bound of land, tilth,° vineyard, none;
No use of metal, corn, or wine, or oil;

150 No occupation;° all men idle, all;
And women too, but innocent and pure:
No sovereignty;—

SEBASTIAN   Yet he would be King on it.

ANTONIO The latter end of his commonwealth forgets the beginning.

GONZALO All things in common° Nature should produce
Without sweat or endeavour: treason, felony,
Sword, pike, knife, gun, or need of any engine,°
Would I not have; but Nature should bring forth,
Of its own kind, all foison,° all abundance,

160 To feed my innocent people.

SEBASTIAN No marrying 'mong his subjects?

ANTONIO None, man; all idle; whores and knaves.

GONZALO I would with such perfection govern, sir,
To excel the Golden Age.

SEBASTIAN   'Save his Majesty!

ANTONIO Long live Gonzalo!

GONZALO   And,—do you mark me, sir?

ALONSO Prithee, no more: thou dost talk nothing° to me.

GONZALO I do well believe your highness; and did it to minister occasion° to
these gentlemen, who are of such sensible° and nimble lungs that they

170 always use to laugh at nothing.

---

chirurgeonly surgeon-like
Foul The point of this exchange is lost—perhaps
Sebastian looks mockingly at the fineness of
the weather.
plantation colonization; Antonio takes it in the
other sense of "planting"
nettle-seed . . . docks . . . mallows common
English weeds
commonwealth The passage that follows is based
on Montaigne's essay "Of Cannibals" as translated by John Florio.
by contraries doing the opposite of what is
usually done

traffic trade
Letters literacy
use of service the employment of servants
succession inheritance of property
Bourn boundry
tilth tillage
occupation working at a trade
in common for ownership
engine military weapon
foison abundance
nothing empty nonsense
minister occasion afford opportunity
sensible sensitive

ANTONIO   'Twas you we laughed at.

GONZALO   Who in this kind of merry fooling am nothing to you: so you may continue, and laugh at nothing still.

ANTONIO   What a blow was there given!

SEBASTIAN   An it had not fallen flat-long.°

GONZALO   You are gentlemen of brave mettle;° you would lift the moon out of her sphere, if she would continue in it five weeks without changing.°

Enter ARIEL *(invisible) playing solemn music.*

180   SEBASTIAN   We would so, and then go a-batfowling.°

ANTONIO   Nay, good my lord, be not angry.

GONZALO   No, I warrant you; I will not adventure° my discretion so weakly. Will you laugh me asleep, for I am very heavy?°

ANTONIO   Go sleep, and hear us.°

All sleep except ALONSO, SEBASTIAN, *and* ANTONIO

ALONSO   What, all so soon asleep! I wish mine eyes
　　　　Would, with themselves, shut up my thoughts: I find
　　　　They are inclined to do so.

SEBASTIAN   　　　　　　　Please you, sir,
　　　　Do not omit° the heavy offer of it:
190   　　　　It seldom visits sorrow; when it doth,
　　　　It is a comforter.

ANTONIO   　　　　　　　We two, my lord,
　　　　Will guard your person while you take your rest,
　　　　And watch your safety.

ALONSO   　　　　　　　Thank you.—Wondrous heavy.

ALONSO *sleeps. Exit* ARIEL.

SEBASTIAN   What a strange drowsiness possesses them!

ANTONIO   It is the quality° o' the climate.

SEBASTIAN   　　　　　　　Why
　　　　Doth it not then our eyelids sink? I find not
　　　　Myself disposed to sleep.

ANTONIO   　　　　　　　Nor I; my spirits are nimble.
　　　　They fell together all, as by consent;
　　　　They dropped, as by a thunder-stroke. What might,
200   　　　　Worthy Sebastian?—O, what might?—No more:—
　　　　And yet methinks I see it in thy face,
　　　　What thou shouldst be: the occasion speaks° thee; and
　　　　My strong imagination sees a crown
　　　　Dropping upon thy head.

SEBASTIAN   　　　　　　　What, art thou waking?°

ANTONIO   Do you not hear me speak?

---

flat-long with the flat of the sword
brave mettle fine spirit
you would lift . . . changing you'd have the moon out of the heavens if she'd stay still a little longer
a-batfowling hunting birds with a light (in this case, the moon), toward which they fly and are beaten down with clubs

adventure risk
heavy drowsy
hear us hear us laughing
omit neglect
quality characteristic
occasion speaks opportunity invites
waking awake

SEBASTIAN   I do; and surely
It is a sleepy language, and thou speak'st
Out of thy sleep. What is it thou didst say?
This is a strange repose, to be asleep
With eyes wide open; standing, speaking, moving,
And yet so fast asleep.
ANTONIO   Noble Sebastian,
Thou let'st thy fortune sleep—die, rather; wink'st°
Whiles thou art waking.
SEBASTIAN   Thou dost snore distinctly;
There's meaning in thy snores.
ANTONIO   I am more serious than my custom: you
Must be so too, if heed me; which to do
Trebles thee o'er.°
SEBASTIAN   Well, I am standing water.°
ANTONIO   I'll teach you how to flow.°
SEBASTIAN   Do so: to ebb
Hereditary sloth instructs me.
ANTONIO   O,
If you but knew how you the purpose cherish°
Whiles thus you mock it! how, in stripping it,
You more invest it!° Ebbing men, indeed,
Most often do so near the bottom run
By their own fear of sloth.
SEBASTIAN   Prithee, say on:
The setting of thine eye and cheek° proclaim
A matter° from thee; and a birth, indeed,
Which throes° thee much to yield.
ANTONIO   Thus, sir:
Although this lord of weak remembrance,° this,
Who shall be of as little memory
When he is earthed,° hath here almost persuaded,—
For he's a spirit of persuasion, only
Professes to persuade,°—the King his son's alive,
'Tis is as impossible that he's undrowned
As he that sleeps here swims.
SEBASTIAN   I have no hope°
That he's undrowned.
ANTONIO   O, out of that 'no hope'
What great hope have you! no hope that way is
Another way so high a hope, that even

210
220
230

wink'st closest thine eyes
Trebles thee o'er triples thy greatness
standing water slack water between tides
flow continuing the tide figure—flow rather than ebb
cherish value, enhance
invest it clothe it (while you think that by playing it cool you're stripping or minimizing it)
setting . . . cheek serious look on your face

A matter something of weight
throes gives pain
weak remembrance poor memory
Who shall . . . earthed who will himself be unremembered when he is buried
Professes to persuade makes a profession of persuasion
hope expectation. Antonio takes it in a more modern sense.

Ambition cannot pierce a wink beyond,
But doubt discovery there.° Will you grant with me
That Ferdinand is drowned?

SEBASTIAN   He's gone.

ANTONIO   Then tell me,
Who's the next heir of Naples?

240 SEBASTIAN   Claribel.

ANTONIO   She that is Queen of Tunis; she that dwells
Ten leagues beyond man's life;° she that from Naples
Can have no note,° unless the sun were post,°—
The man i' the moon's too slow,—till new-born chins
Be rough and razorable; she that from whom°
We all were sea-swallowed, though some cast° again,
And by that destiny to perform an act
Whereof what's past is prologue; what to come,
In yours and my discharge.°

SEBASTIAN   What stuff is this! how say you?

250 'Tis true, my brother's daughter's Queen of Tunis;
So is she heir of Naples; 'twixt which regions
There is some space.

ANTONIO   A space whose every cubit°
Seems to cry out, 'How shall that Claribel
Measure us° back to Naples? Keep in Tunis,
And let Sebastian wake.' Say this were death
That now hath seized them;° why, they were no worse
Than now they are. There be that can rule Naples
As well as he that sleeps; lords that can prate
As amply and unnecessarily

260 As this Gonzalo; I myself could make
A chough of as deep chat.° O, that you bore°
The mind that I do! what a sleep were this
For your advancement! Do you understand me?

SEBASTIAN   Methinks I do.

ANTONIO   And how does your content
Tender° your own good fortune?

SEBASTIAN   I remember
You did supplant your brother Prospero.

ANTONIO   True:
And look how well my garments sit upon me;
Much feater° than before: my brother's servants

Ambition . . . there Ambition cannot set its
eye on higher object (than the crown) and even
there must have difficulty in discerning the goal
Ten leagues . . . life ten leagues farther than
one might journey in a lifetime
note communication
post messenger
from whom in coming from whom
cast vomited forth
perform . . . act . . . prologue . . . dis-

charge theatrical expressions; "to discharge a
part" was the common phrase
cubit ancient measure; 18 to 22 inches
us i.e. the cubits
Keep stay (the cubits address Claribel)
them the sleepers
I myself . . . chat I could teach a jackdaw to
talk as profoundly as he does
bore had
Tender regard
feater more gracefully

Were then my fellows; now they are my men.
270   SEBASTIAN   But for your conscience.
ANTONIO   Ay, sir; where lies that? if 'twere a kibe,°
'Twould put me to my slipper:° but I feel not
This deity in my bosom: twenty consciences,
That stand 'twixt me and Milan, candied° be they,
And melt, ere they molest! Here lies your brother,
No better than the earth he lies upon,
If he were that which now he's like, that's dead;
Whom I, with this obedient steel, three inches of it,
Can lay to bed for ever; whiles you, doing thus,
280   To the perpetual wink° for aye might put
This ancient morsel,° this Sir Prudence, who
Should not upbraid our course. For all the rest,
They'll take suggestion° as a cat laps milk;
They'll tell the clock to any business that
We say befits the hour.°
SEBASTIAN   Thy, case, dear friend,
Shall be my precedent; as thou got'st Milan,
I'll come by Naples. Draw thy sword: one stroke
Shall free thee from the tribute which thou payest;
And I the King shall love thee.
ANTONIO   Draw together;
290   And when I rear my hand, do you the like,
To fall it° on Gonzalo.
SEBASTIAN   O, but one word.   *They talk apart.*

Re-enter ARIEL *invisible, with music and song.*

ARIEL   My master through his Art foresees the danger
That you, his friend,° are in; and sends me forth,—
For else his project dies,—to keep them living.
                                        Sings in GONZALO's *ear.*

        While you here do snoring lie,
        Open-eyed conspiracy
            His time doth take.
        If of life you keep a care,
        Shake off slumber, and beware:
            Awake, Awake!
300

ANTONIO   Then let us both be sudden.°
GONZALO [*Waking*]   Now, good angels
        Preserve the King!   *The others wake.*
ALONSO   Why, how now? ho; awake?—Why are you drawn?

kibe sore, usually on the heel
put in slipper force me to wear a slipper
candied frozen solid
perpetual wink everlasting sleep
ancient morsel Gonzalo
suggestion prompting

tell . . . hour pretend that whatever we propose is opportune
fall it let it fall
friend Gonzalo
sudden prompt in action

Wherefore this ghastly looking?

GONZALO   What's the matter?

SEBASTIAN   Whiles we stood here securing your repose,
 Even now, we heard a hollow burst of bellowing
 Like bulls, or rather lions: did it not wake you?
 It struck mine ear most terribly.

ALONSO   I heard nothing.

ANTONIO   O, 'twas a din to fright a monster's ear,
310 To make an earthquake! sure, it was the roar
 Of a whole herd of lions.

ALONSO   Heard you this, Gonzalo?

GONZALO   Upon mine honour, sir, I heard a humming,°
 And that a strange one too, which did awake me:
 I shaked you, sir, and cried: as mine eyes opened,
 I saw their weapons drawn:—there was a noise,
 That's verily.° 'Tis best we stand upon our guard,
 Or that we quit this place: let's draw our weapons.

ALONSO   Lead off this ground; and let's make further search
 For my poor son.

GONZALO   Heavens keep him from these beasts!
 For he is, sure, i' the island.

320 ALONSO   Lead away.

ARIEL   Prospero my lord shall know what I have done:
 So, King, go safely on to seek thy son.   *Exeunt.*

SCENE II [*Another part of the Island.*]

Enter CALIBAN *with a burthen of wood. A noise of thunder heard.*

CALIBAN   All the infections that the sun sucks up°
 From bogs, fens, flats, on Prosper fall, and make him
 By inch-meal° a disease! his spirits hear me,
 And yet I needs must curse. But they'll nor pinch,
 Fright me with urchin-shows,° pitch me i' the mire,
 Nor lead me, like a firebrand,° in the dark
 Out of my way, unless he bid 'em: but
 For every trifle are they set upon me;
 Sometime like apes, that mow° and chatter at me,
10 And after bite me; then like hedgehogs, which
 Lie tumbling in my barefoot way, and mount
 Their pricks° at my footfall; sometime am I
 All wound° with adders, who with cloven tongues
 Do hiss me into madness.

humming he heard Ariel's song
verily (to speak) truly
sucks up Disease-bearing mists were thought
to be sucked from bogs and fens by the sun.
inch-meal inch by inch

urchin-shows apparitions of goblins
firebrand will-o'-the-wisp, *ignis fatuus*
mow make faces
pricks quills
wound twined about with

Enter TRINCULO.

> Lo, now, lo!
> Here comes a spirit of his, and to torment me
> For bringing wood in slowly. I'll fall flat;
> Perchance he will not mind me.

TRINCULO   Here's neither bush nor shrub, to bear off° any weather at all, and
20   another storm brewing; I hear it sing i' the wind: yond same black cloud,
yond huge one, looks like a foul bombard° that would shed his liquor.
If it should thunder as it did before, I know not where to hide my head:
yond same cloud cannot choose but fall by pailfuls. What have we here?
a man or a fish? dead or alive? A fish: he smells like a fish; a very ancient
and fish-like smell; a kind of, not of the newest Poor-John.° A strange
fish! Were I in England° now, as once I was, and had but this fish
painted,° not a holiday fool there but would give a piece of silver: there
would this monster make a man;° any strange beast there makes a man:
when they will not give a doit° to relieve a lame beggar, they will lay
30   out ten to see a dead Indian.° Legged like a man! and his fins like arms!
Warm o' my troth! I do now let loose my opinion, hold it no longer:
this is no fish, but an islander, that hath lately suffered° by a thunder-
bolt. [*Thunder*] Alas, the storm is come again! my best way is to creep
under his gaberdine;° there is no other shelter hereabout: misery
acquaints a man with strange bed-fellows. I will here shroud till the
dregs of the storm be past.

Enter STEPHANO, *singing: a bottle in his hand.*

> *I shall no more to sea, to sea,*
> *Here shall I die ashore,—*

This is a very scurvy tune to sing at a man's funeral; well, here's my
40   comfort.   *Drinks. Sings.*

> *The master, the swabber, the boatswain, and I,*
> *The gunner, and his mate,*
> *Loved Mall,° Meg, and Marian, and Margery,*
> *But none of us cared for Kate:*
> *For she had a tongue with a tang,*
> *Would cry to a sailor, Go hang!*
> *She loved not the savour of tar nor of pitch;*
> *Yet a tailor might scratch her where'er she did itch.*
> *Then to sea, boys, and let her go hang!*

50   This is a scurvy tune too: but here's my comfort.   *Drinks.*
CALIBAN   Do not torment me:—O!

---

bear off ward off
bombard large leather bottle
Poor-John dried hake, a fish similar to cod
England where exhibitions of monsters were popular
painted on a board and hung outside a fair-booth
make a man make a man's fortune (with pun

on the other sense)
doit small coin
Indian Indians were often so exhibited, and usually died early.
suffered been killed
gaberdine cloak
Mall diminutive form of Mary

STEPHANO   What's the matter? Have we devils here? Do you put tricks upon us with salvages° and men of Ind,° ha? I have not scaped drowning, to be affeard now of your four legs; for it hath been said, As proper a man° as ever went on four legs cannot make him give ground; and it shall be said so again, while Stephano breathes at' nostrils.

CALIBAN   The spirit torments me:—O!

STEPHANO   This is some monster of the isle with four legs, who hath got, as I take it, an ague.° Where the devil should he learn° our language? I
60   will give him some relief, if it be but for that. If I can recover° him, and keep him tame, and get to Naples with him, he's a present° for any emperor that ever trod on neat's leather.°

CALIBAN   Do not torment me, prithee; I'll bring my wood home faster.

STEPHANO   He's in his fit now, and does not talk after the wisest. He shall taste of my bottle: if he have never drink wine afore, it will go near to remove his fit. If I can recover him, and keep him tame, I will not take too much for him;° he shall pay for him that hath him and that soundly.

CALIBAN   Thou dost me yet but little hurt; thou wilt anon, I know it by thy trembling:° now Prosper works upon thee.
70   STEPHANO   Come on your ways; open your mouth; here is that which will give language to you, cat:° open your mouth; this will shake your shaking, I can tell you, and that soundly: you cannot tell who's your friend: open your chaps° again.

TRINCULO   I should know that voice: it should be—but he is drowned; and these are devils:—O defend me!

STEPHANO   Four legs and two voices,—a most delicate monster! His forward voice, now, is to speak well of his friend; his backward voice is to utter foul speeches and to detract.° If all the wine in my bottle will recover him, I will help° his ague. Come:—Amen!° I will pour some in thy
80   other mouth.

TRINCULO   Stephano!

STEPHANO   Doth thy other mouth call me? Mercy, mercy! This is a devil, and no monster: I will leave him; I have no long spoon.°

TRINCULO   Stephano! If thou beest Stephano, touch me, and speak to me; for I am Trinculo,—be not afeard,—thy good friend Trinculo.

STEPHANO   If thou beest Trinculo, come forth: I'll pull thee by the lesser legs: If any be Trinculo's legs, these are they. Thou art very Trinculo indeed! How camest thou to be the siege° of this moon-calf?° can he vent° Trinculos?

salvages savages
men of Ind Indians
As proper a man as fine a fellow
ague fever
should he learn can he have learned
recover restore
present Great men of the period liked to collect dwarfs and other unusual species.
neat's-leather cowhide (the expression was proverbial)
I will . . . for him no price I get for him will be too much
trembling Caliban takes this as a sign that the

tormentor is in process of being possessed prior to starting work on him.
cat alluding to the proverb "Ale (liquor) will make a cat speak"
chaps jaws
detract slander
help cure
Amen that's enough for one mouth
long spoon proverb: "He that would eat with the devil must have a long spoon"
siege excrement
moon-calf monstrosity, deformed by the influence of the moon
vent excrete

90   TRINCULO   I took him to be killed with a thunder-stroke. But art thou not
     drowned, Stephano? I hope, now, thou art not drowned. Is the storm
     over-blown? I hid me under the dead moon-calf's gaberdine for fear of
     the storm. And art thou living, Stephano? O Stephano, two Neapolitans
     scaped!

STEPHANO   Prithee, do not turn me about; my stomach is not constant.°

CALIBAN [*Aside*]   These be fine things,° an if° they be not sprites.
     That's a brave° god, and bears celestial liquor:
     I will kneel to him.

STEPHANO   How didst thou scape? How camest thou hither? swear, by this
100 bottle, how thou camest hither. I escaped upon a butt of sack,° which
     the sailors heaved o'erboard, by this bottle! which I made of the bark
     of a tree with mine own hands, since I was cast ashore.

CALIBAN   I'll swear, upon that bottle, to be thy true subject; for the liquor
     is not earthly.

STEPHANO   Here; swear, then, how thou escapedst.

TRINCULO   Swum ashore, man, like a duck: I can swim like a duck, I'll be
     sworn.

STEPHANO   Here, kiss the book.° Though thou canst swim like a duck, thou
     art made like a goose.

110 TRINCULO   O Stephano, hast any more of this?

STEPHANO   The whole butt, man: my cellar is in a rock by the seaside, where
     my wine is hid. How now, moon-calf! how does thine ague?

CALIBAN   Hast thou not dropped from heaven?

STEPHANO   Out o' the moon,° I do assure thee: I was the man i' the moon
     when time was.°

CALIBAN   I have seen thee in her, and I do adore thee:
     My mistress showed me thee, and thy dog, and thy bush.

STEPHANO   Come, swear to that; kiss the book: I will furnish it anon with new
     contents: swear.

120 TRINCULO   By this good light, this is a very shallow monster; I afeard of him?
     A very weak monster! The man i' the moon! A most poor credulous
     monster! Well drawn,° monster, in good sooth!°

CALIBAN   I'll show thee every fertile inch° o' the island; and I will kiss thy
     foot: I prithee, be my god.

TRINCULO   By this light, a most perfidious and drunken monster! when his
     god's asleep, he'll rob his bottle.

CALIBAN   I'll kiss thy foot; I'll swear myself thy subject.

STEPHANO   Come on, then; down, and swear.

TRINCULO   I shall laugh myself to death at this puppy-headed monster. A
130 most scurvy monster! I could find in my heart to beat him,—

---

constant steady
fine things Note the similarity of Caliban's
reaction to the sight of Trinculo and Stephano,
and Miranda's to the noblemen, especially
Ferdinand.
an if if
brave fine
sack sherry-like wine; such a butt is mentioned
in one of the narratives of the Bermuda wreck

kiss the book Trinculo raises the bottle to his
lips.
Out o' the moon Stephano was not the first
voyager to tell this to the natives.
when time was once upon a time
Well drawn a good pull at the wine
in good sooth truly
every fertile inch Twelve years earlier he had
done this for Prospero.

STEPHANO   Come, kiss.

TRINCULO   But that the poor monster's in drink. An abominable monster!

CALIBAN   I'll show thee the best springs; I'll pluck thee berries;
I'll fish for thee, and get thee wood enough.
A plague upon the tyrant° that I serve!
I'll bear him no more sticks, but follow thee,
Thou wondrous man.

TRINCULO   A most ridiculous monster, to make a wonder of a poor drunkard!

CALIBAN   I prithee, let me bring thee where crabs° grow;
And I with my long nails will dig thee pig-nuts;°
Show thee a jay's nest, and instruct thee how
To snare the nimble marmoset;° I'll bring thee
To clustering filberts,° and sometimes I'll get thee
Young scamels° from the rock. Wilt thou go with me?

STEPHANO   I prithee now, lead the way, without any more talking. Trinculo,
the King and all our company else being drowned, we will inherit° here:
here; bear my bottle: fellow Trinculo, we'll fill him by and by again.

CALIBAN   *Sings drunkenly.*

   Farewell, master; farewell, farewell!

TRINCULO   A howling monster; a drunken monster!

CALIBAN   *No more dams I'll make for fish;*
   Nor fetch in firing
      At requiring;
   Nor scrape trenchering,° nor wash dish:
      'Ban, 'Ban, Cacaliban
   Has a new master:—get a new man.

Freedom, high-day!° high-day, freedom! freedom, high-day, freedom!

STEPHANO   O brave monster! lead the way.   *Exeunt.*

ACT III

SCENE I [*Before* PROSPERO'S *Cell.*]

Enter FERDINAND, *bearing a log.*

FERDINAND   There be some sports are painful, and their labour
Delight in them sets off:° some kinds of baseness
Are nobly undergone; and most poor° matters
Point to rich ends. This my mean task
Would be as heavy to me as odious, but
The mistress which I serve quickens° what's dead,

---

tyrant usurper
crabs crab-apples
pig-nuts earthnuts
marmoset small monkey (called "good meat" by colonists)
filberts trees bearing hazel nuts
scamels The word is not recorded elsewhere: either a bird or a shellfish.

inherit take possession
trenchering "trenchers" (dishes) collectively; cf. housing, clothing
high-day meaningless cry of joy and pleasure
There . . . off in some arduous sports the pleasure they give cancels our pains
most poor the poorest
quickens gives life to

And makes my labour pleasures: O, she is
Ten times more gentle than her father's crabbed,°
And he's composed of harshness. I must remove
Some thousands of these logs, and pile them up,
Upon a sore injunction:° my sweet mistress
Weeps when she sees me work, and says, such baseness
Had never like executor.° I forget:
But these sweet thoughts do even refresh my labours,
Most busy least when I do it.°

Enter MIRANDA; *and* PROSPERO [*at a distance, unseen*].

MIRANDA   Alas, now, pray you,
Work not so hard: I would the lightning had
Burnt up those logs that you are enjoined° to pile!
Pray, set it down, and rest you: when this burns,
'Twill weep° for having wearied you. My father
Is hard at study; pray, now, rest yourself:
He's safe for these three hours.
FERDINAND   O most dear mistress,
The sun will set before I shall discharge°
What I must strive to do.
MIRANDA   If you'll sit down,
I'll bear your logs the while: pray give me that;
I'll carry it to the pile.
FERDINAND   No, precious creature;
I had rather crack my sinews, break my back,
Than you should such dishonour undergo,
While I sit lazy by.
MIRANDA   It would become me
As well as it does you: and I should do it
With much more ease; for my good will is to it,
And yours it is against.
PROSPERO   Poor worm, thou art infected!°
This visitation° shows it.
MIRANDA   You look wearily.
FERDINAND   No, noble mistress: 'tis fresh morning with me
When you are by at night. I do beseech you,—
Chiefly that I might set it in my prayers,—
What is your name?
MIRANDA   Miranda.—O my father,
I have broke your hest° to say so!
FERDINAND   Admired° Miranda!

10

20

30

---

crabbed bad-tempered
Upon . . . injunction under a severe penalty
Had . . . executor was never carried out by so
noble a person
Most busy . . . it F: *Most busie lest, when I
do it;* unsolved crux, perhaps corrupt, perhaps
meaning "My work is hardest when I think of
her least"

enjoined commanded
weep by exuding sap
discharge fulfill
infected by love, as by the plague
visitation visit; also used of a plague epidemic
hest order
admired playing on the meaning of her name:
"worthy of admiration"

Indeed the top of admiration! worth
What's dearest to the world! Full many a lady
40   I have eyed with best regard,° and many a time
The harmony of their tongues hath into bondage
Brought my too diligent ear: for several° virtues°
Have I liked several women; never any
With so full soul, but some defect in her
Did quarrel with the noblest grace° she owed,°
And put it to the foil:° but you, O you,
So perfect and so peerless, are created
Of every creature's best!°

MIRANDA   I do not know
One of my sex: no woman's face remember,
50   Save, from my glass, mine own; nor have I seen
More that I may call men than you, good friend,
And my dear father: how features are abroad,°
I am skilless of;° but, by my modesty,
The jewel in my dower, I would not wish
Any companion in the world but you;
Nor can imagination form a shape,
Besides yourself, to like of.° But I prattle
Something too wildly, and my father's precepts
I therein do forget.

FERDINAND   I am, in my condition,°
60   A prince, Miranda; I do think, a King;
I would not so!—and would no more endure
This wooden slavery° than to suffer
The flesh-fly blow° my mouth. Hear my soul speak:
The very instant that I saw you, did
My heart fly to your service; there resides,
To make me slave to it; and for your sake
Am I this patient log-man.

MIRANDA   Do you love me?

FERDINAND   O heaven, O earth, bear witness to this sound,
And crown what I profess with kind event,°
70   If I speak true! if hollowly,° invert
What best is boded me° to mischief! I,
Beyond all limit of what else i' the world,
Do love, prize, honour you.

MIRANDA   I am a fool
To weep at what I am glad of.

---

best regard attentive gaze
several different
virtues qualities
noblest grace finest attribute
owed owned
put . . . foil spoiled, overthrew it
every creature's best a common Elizabethan
love-compliment
abroad out in the world

skilless of ignorant of
like of be pleased with
condition rank
wooden slavery menial task of wood-carrying
blow foul, sully
kind event favorable outcome
hollowly insincerely
What . . . me the best fortune has in store for
me

PROSPERO   Fair encounter
        Of two most rare affections!° Heavens rain grace
        On that which breeds between 'em!°
FERDINAND   Wherefore weep you?
MIRANDA   At mine unworthiness, that dare not offer
        What I desire to give; and much less take
        What I shall die to want.° But this is trifling;°
80   And all the more it° seeks to hide itself,
        The bigger bulk it shows. Hence, bashful cunning!
        And prompt me, plain and holy innocence!
        I am your wife, if you will marry me;
        If not, I'll die your maid:° to be your fellow
        You may deny me; but I'll be your servant,
        Whether you will or no.
FERDINAND   My mistress, dearest;
        And I thus humble ever.
MIRANDA   My husband, then?
FERDINAND   Ay, with a heart as willing
        As bondage e'er of freedom:° here's my hand.
90 MIRANDA   And mine, with my heart in it: and now farewell
        Till half an hour hence.
FERDINAND   A thousand thousand!°
                    Exeunt. FERDINAND _and_ MIRANDA _severally._
PROSPERO   So glad of this as they I cannot be,
        Who are surprised with all;° but my rejoicing
        At nothing can be more. I'll to my book;
        For yet, ere supper-time, must I perform
        Much business appertaining.°   _Exit._

        SCENE II [_Another part of the Island._]

        Enter CALIBAN, STEPHANO, _and_ TRINCULO.

STEPHANO   Tell not me;°—when the butt is out, we will drink water; not a
        drop before: therefore bear up, and board 'em.° Servant-monster, drink
        to me.
TRINCULO   Servant-monster! the folly° of this island! They say there's but five
        upon this isle: we are three of them; if the other two be brained° like
        us, the state totters.
STEPHANO   Drink, servant-monster, when I bid thee: thy eyes are almost set°
        in thy head.

affections dispositions
that which . . . 'em i.e. love and/or children
want be without
trifling using words unequal to her true feelings
it her love
maid with two senses, "virgin" and "servant"
with . . . freedom as eagerly as the captive
longs for freedom
thousand "farewells"
surprised with all taken unawares by all these
developments (or _withal,_ by this)

appertaining relating (to the marriage and what
must lead up to it)
Tell not me don't talk to me (about saving
liquor)
bear up and board 'em naval order, here
meaning "drink up"
folly freak
brained equipped with brains
set disappearing, like the setting sun. Trinculo
takes it in a different sense.

TRINCULO Where should they be set else? he were a brave monster indeed, if
10   they were set in his tail.
STEPHANO My man-monster hath drowned his tongue in sack: for my part, the
          sea cannot drown me; I swam, ere I could recover° the shore, five-and-
          thirty leagues off and on. By this light, thou shalt be my lieutenant,
          monster, or my standard.°
TRINCULO Your lieutenant, if you list; he's no standard.
STEPHANO We'll not run,° Monsieur Monster.
TRINCULO Nor go° neither; but you'll lie,° like dogs, and yet say nothing
          neither.
20 STEPHANO Moon-calf, speak once in thy life, if thou beest a good moon-calf.
CALIBAN   How does thy honour? Let me lick thy shoe: I'll not serve him, he is
          not valiant.
TRINCULO Thou liest, most ignorant monster: I am in case° to justle a con-
          stable.° Why, thou deboshed° fish, thou, was there ever man a coward
          that hath drunk so much sack as I to-day? Wilt thou tell a monstrous lie,
          being but half a fish and half a monster?
CALIBAN   Lo, how he mocks me! wilt thou let him, my lord?
30 TRINCULO 'Lord,' quoth he? That a monster should be such a natural!°
CALIBAN   Lo, lo, again! bite him to death, I prithee.
STEPHANO Trinculo, keep a good tongue in your head: if you prove a mutineer,
          —the next tree! The poor monster's my subject, and he shall not suffer
          indignity.
CALIBAN   I thank my noble lord. Wilt thou be pleased to hearken once again
          to the suit I made to thee?
STEPHANO Marry, will I: kneel and repeat it; I will stand, and so shall Trinculo.

          Enter ARIEL, *invisible.*

40 CALIBAN   As I told thee before, I am subject to a tyrant,° a sorcerer, that by
          his cunning hath cheated me of the island.
ARIEL   Thou liest.
CALIBAN   Thou liest, thou jesting monkey,° thou:
          I would my valiant master would destroy thee!
          I do not lie.
STEPHANO Trinculo, if you trouble him any more in 's tale, by this hand, I will
          supplant° some of your teeth.
TRINCULO Why, I said nothing.
50 STEPHANO Mum, then, and no more. Proceed.
CALIBAN   I say, by sorcery he got this isle;
          From me he got it. If thy greatness will
          Revenge it on him,—for I know thou dar'st,
          But this thing° dare not,—

recover reach
standard standard-bearer, but as Caliban can
hardly stand, Trinculo puns on the word
run from the enemy; but also because they are
staggering
go walk
lie lie down; tell lies
in case in a condition

justle a constable Trinculo is drunk enough
to rough up a law officer
deboshed debauched
natural idiot
tyrant usurper
Thou liest . . . monkey Caliban thinks the previous remark came from Trinculo.
supplant uproot
this thing Trinculo

STEPHANO   That's most certain.

CALIBAN   Thou shalt be lord of it, and I'll serve thee.

STEPHANO   How now shall this be compassed?° Canst thou bring me to the
party?°

CALIBAN   Yea, yea, my lord: I'll yield him thee asleep,
60   Where thou mayst knock a nail into his head.

ARIEL   Thou liest; thou canst not.

CALIBAN   What a pied° ninny's this! Thou scurvy patch!°
I do beseech thy greatness, give him blows,
And take his bottle from him: when that's gone,
He shall drink nought but brine; for I'll not show him
Where the quick freshes° are.

STEPHANO   Trinculo, run into no further danger: interrupt the monster one
word further, and, by this hand, I'll turn my mercy out o' doors, and
70   make a stock-fish° of thee.

TRINCULO   Why, what did I? I did nothing. I'll go farther off.

STEPHANO   Didst thou not say he lied?

ARIEL   Thou liest.

STEPHANO   Do I so? take thou that. [*Beats him.*] As you like this, give me the
lie° another time.

TRINCULO   I did not give the lie. Out o' your wits, and hearing too? A pox o'
your bottle! this can sack and drinking do. A murrain° on your monster,
and the devil take your fingers!

80   CALIBAN   Ha, ha, ha!

STEPHANO   Now, forward with your tale.—Prithee, stand further off.°

CALIBAN   Beat him enough: after a little time,
I'll beat him too.

STEPHANO   Stand farther.—Come, proceed.

CALIBAN   Why, as I told thee, 'tis a custom with him
I' the afternoon to sleep: there° thou mayst brain him,
Having first seized his books; or with a log
Batter his skull, or paunch° him with a stake,
Or cut his wezand° with thy knife. Remember
90   First to possess° his books; for without them
He's but a sot,° as I am, nor hath not
One spirit to command: they all do hate him
As rootedly as I. Burn but° his books.
He has brave útensils,°—for so he calls them,—
Which, when he has a house, he'll deck withal.°
And that° most deeply to consider is

---

compassed brought about
party person concerned
pied particolored (referring to jester's motley)
patch fool, jester
freshes springs of fresh water
stock-fish salted cod, beaten with a club before
cooking
give me the lie call me a liar
murrain disease of cattle
stand further off to Trinculo, to prevent him

from interrupting; or to Caliban because he
smells
there at that time
paunch disembowel
wezand windpipe
possess seize
sot ignoramus
Burn but only be sure to burn; burn only
utensils household goods
deck withal furnish it with
that that which is

The beauty of his daughter; he himself
Calls her a nonpareil:° I never saw a woman,
But only Sycorax my dam and she;
100   But she as far surpasseth Sycorax
As greatest does least.

STEPHANO   Is it so brave a lass?

CALIBAN   Ay, lord; she will become thy bed, I warrant,
And bring thee forth brave brood.

STEPHANO   Monster, I will kill this man: his daughter and I will be king and
queen,—save our graces!—and Trinculo and thyself shall be viceroys.
Dost thou like the plot,° Trinculo?

TRINCULO   Excellent.

STEPHANO   Give me thy hand: I am sorry I beat thee; but, while thou livest,
110   keep a good tongue in thy head.

CALIBAN   Within this half hour will he be asleep:
Wilt thou destroy him then?

STEPHANO   Ay, on mine honour.

ARIEL   This will I tell my master.

CALIBAN   Thou mak'st me merry; I am full of pleasure:
Let us be jocund: will you troll the catch°
You taught me but whi! -ere?°

STEPHANO   At thy request, monster, I will do reason, any reason.°—Come on,
Trinculo, let us sing.   *Sings.*

            Flout 'em and scout° 'em,
120   *And scout 'em and flout 'em;*
                Thought is free.°

CALIBAN   That's not the tune.

                    ARIEL *plays the tune on a tabor° and pipe.*

STEPHANO   What is this same?

TRINCULO   This is the tune of our catch, played by the picture of Nobody.°

STEPHANO   If thou beest a man, show thyself in this likeness: if thou beest a
devil, take it as thou list.°

TRINCULO   O, forgive me my sins!

STEPHANO   He that dies pays all debts: I defy thee. Mercy upon us!

130   CALIBAN   Art thou afeard?

STEPHANO   No, monster, not I.

CALIBAN   Be not afeard; the isle is full of noises,°
Sounds and sweet airs, that give delight, and hurt not.
Sometimes a thousand twangling instruments
Will° hum about mine ears; and sometime voices,
That, if I then had waked° after long sleep,

---

nonpareil without an equal
plot in the modern sense; but *plot* was also the
summary of a play's action
troll the catch sing the round
while-ere a short time ago
any reason anything within reason
scout on first occurrence F reads *cout* (jeer at),
which is possible
Thought is free thought can't be censored
(proverbial)

tabor little drum
picture of Nobody Personifying Nobody was a
very old joke, and pictures of Nobody usually
consist of empty suits of clothes.
take it as thou list take it anyway you like (old
saying: "the devil take it")
noises music
Will . . . had waked . . . Will . . . methought
. . . waked . . . cried Note illogical sequence
of tenses for special effect.

Will° make me sleep again: and then, in dreaming,
The clouds methought° would open; and show riches
Ready to drop upon me; that, when I waked,°
I cried° to dream again.

STEPHANO   This will prove a brave kingdom to me, where I shall have my music for nothing.

CALIBAN   When Prospero is destroyed.

STEPHANO   That shall be by and by: I remember the story.

TRINCULO   The sound is going away; let's follow it, and after do our work.

STEPHANO   Lead, monster; we'll follow. I would I could see this taborer; he lays it on.

TRINCULO   Wilt come?° I'll follow, Stephano.   *Exeunt.*

SCENE III [*Another part of the Island.*]

Enter ALONSO, SEBASTIAN, ANTONIO, GONZALO, ADRIAN, FRANCISCO, etc.

GONZALO   By 'r lakin,° I can go no further, sir;
My old bones ache: here's a maze trod, indeed,
Through forth-rights° and meanders!° By your patience,
I needs must rest me.

ALONSO   Old lord, I cannot blame thee,
Who am myself attached° with weariness,
To the dulling of my spirits:° sit down, and rest.
Even here I will put off° my hope, and keep it
No longer for my flatterer: he is drowned
Whom thus we stray to find; and the sea mocks
Our frustrate° search on land. Well, let him go.

ANTONIO [*Aside to* SEBASTIAN]   I am right glad that he's so out of hope.
Do not, for one repulse, forego the purpose
That you resolved to effect.

SEBASTIAN [*Aside to* ANTONIO]   The next advantage
Will we take throughly.°

ANTONIO [*Aside to* SEBASTIAN]   Let it be tonight;
For, now they are oppressed with travel, they
Will not, nor cannot, use such vigilance
As when they are fresh.

SEBASTIAN [*Aside to* ANTONIO]   I say, tonight: no more.

Solemn and strange music; and PROSPER *on the top° (invisible).° Enter several strange Shapes, bringing in a banquet;° and dance about it with gentle actions of salutations; and inviting the King, etc., to eat,° they depart.*

Wilt come? addressed to Caliban
lakin "Ladykin," i.e. the Virgin Mary
forth-rights straight paths
meanders winding paths
attached seized
spirits vital powers
put off divest myself of
frustrate vain
throughly thoroughly

on the top on the upper stage, or possibly in a higher place
(invisible) not, of course, to the audience
banquet a light meal; stage magicians often conjured up banquets
to eat Banquets could stand allegorically for all voluptuous temptation and for that which the virtuous man would refuse to partake of.

ALONSO   What harmony is this? My good friends, hark!

GONZALO   Marvellous sweet music!

20 ALONSO   Give us kind keepers,° heavens!—What were these?

SEBASTIAN   A living drollery.° Now I will believe
        That there are unicorns; that in Arabia
        There is one tree, the phoenix' throne; one phoenix°
        at this hour reigning there.

ANTONIO   I'll believe both;
        And what does else want credit,° come to me,
        And I'll be sworn 'tis true: travellers ne'er did lie,°
        Though fools at home condemn 'em.

GONZALO   If in Naples
        I should report this now, would they believe me?
        If I should say, I saw such islanders,—

30   For, certes,° these are people of the island,—
        Who, though they are of monstrous° shape, yet, note,
        Their manners° are more gentle, kind, than of
        Our human generation you shall find
        Many, nay, almost any.

PROSPERO   [*Aside*] Honest° lord,
        Thou hast said well; for some of you there present
        Are worse than devils.

ALONSO   I cannot too much muse°
        Such shapes, such gesture, and such sound, expressing—
        Although they want the use of tongue—a kind
        Of excellent dumb discourse.

PROSPERO   [*Aside*] Praise in departing.°

FRANCISCO   They vanished strangely.

40 SEBASTIAN   No matter, since
        They have left their viands° behind; for we have stomachs.°—
        Will it please you taste of what is here?

ALONSO   Not I.

GONZALO   Faith, sir, you need not fear. When we were boys,
        Who would believe that there were mountaineers
        Dew-lapped like bulls, whose throats had hanging at 'em
        Wallets of flesh?° or that there were such men
        Whose heads stood in their breasts?° which now we find

---

keepers guardian angels
living drollery puppet show in which the figures are alive
unicorns . . . phoenix frequent wonders in travelers' tales, myth, and folklore. There was only one Phoenix, in the "sole Arabian tree"; it renewed itself from the ashes of its funeral pyre; see above, "The Phoenix and Turtle."
want credit is difficult to believe
travellers . . . lie The lies of travelers were famous.
certes certainly
monstrous unnatural
manners in a wider sense than ours

Honest honorable
muse wonder at
Praise in departing "don't praise your host till the entertainment's over" (proverbial)
viands food
stomachs appetites
Wallets of flesh exaggerated account of goiter found in some mountain areas; "wallet" is cognate with "wattle"
heads . . . breasts These monsters go back beyond Mandeville to Pliny; and Othello on his travels met "men whose heads / Do grow beneath their shoulders."

Each putter-out of five for one° will bring us
Good warrant of.

ALONSO   I will stand to, and feed,
50   Although my last: no matter, since I feel
The best° is past. Brother, my lord the duke,
Stand to, and do as we.

Thunder and lightning. Enter ARIEL *like a Harpy;*° *claps his wings upon the table; and, with a quaint device,*° *the banquet vanishes.*

ARIEL   You are three men of sin, whom Destiny,—
That hath to instrument° this lower world
And what is in it,—the never-surfeited° sea
Hath caused to belch up you; and on this island,
Where man doth not inhabit,—you 'mongst men
Being most unfit to live. I have made you mad;
And even with such-like valour° men hang and drown
Their proper° selves.

ALONSO, SEBASTIAN, *etc., draw their swords.*
60   You fools! I and my fellows
Are ministers° of Fate: the elements,
Of whom your swords are tempered, may as well
Wound the loud winds, or with bemocked-at-stabs
Kill the still-closing° waters, as diminish
One dowle° that's in my plume: my fellow-ministers
Are like° invulnerable.° If° you could hurt,
Your swords are now too massy° for your strengths,
And will not be uplifted. But remember—
For that's my business to you—that you three
70   From Milan did supplant good Prospero:
Exposed unto the sea, which hath requit° it,
Him and his innocent child: for which foul deed
The powers, delaying, not forgetting, have
Incensed the seas and shores, yea, all the creatures,°
Against your peace. Thee of thy son, Alonso,
They have bereft; and do pronounce by me

putter-out . . . one Travelers could take out a form of insurance, leaving a premium which would be forfeited if they failed to return, but which would be repaid fivefold if they came back with proof that they had reached the stated destination.
best best part of my life
Harpy In Virgil's *Aeneid* III.255 ff. harpies devour and befoul the food of Aeneas and his friends, and the harpy Celaeno speaks a prophecy on which Ariel's is ultimately based; allegorically the harpy confronted a man with his guilty past.
quaint device ingenious contrivance. Perhaps Ariel, descending in a "machine," covered the table with his wings, and a stagehand, concealed under the table, removed a panel and whisked the banquet out of sight below.
to instrument as its instrument

never-surfeited A surfeit—eating too much—would be a normal cause of belching up, but the sea is always hungry, and a special intervention of Destiny was necessary to cause it to vomit forth the "men of sin" on this occasion.
such-like valour a false courage, of the kind that leads people to suicide
proper own
ministers agents
still-closing that always close up again
dowle small feather
like likewise
invulnerable as were Virgil's harpies
If even if
massy heavy
requit paid back
Incensed roused
creatures created things

Ling'ring perdition°—worse than any death
Can be at once—shall step by step attend
You and your ways; whose wraths to guard you from—
80   Which here, in this most desolate isle, else° falls°
Upon your heads,—is nothing but heart-sorrow
And a clear° life ensuing.

*He vanishes in thunder; then, to soft music, enter the Shapes again, and
dance, with mocks and mows,° and carrying out the table.*

PROSPERO   Bravely° the figure of this Harpy hast thou
Performed, my Ariel; a grace it had devouring:°
Of my instruction hast thou nothing bated°
In what thou hadst to say: so, with good life°
And observation strange,° my meaner ministers°
Their several kinds have done.° My high charms work,
And these mine enemies are all knit up
90   In their distractions:° they now are in my power;
And in these fits I leave them, while I visit
Young Ferdinand,—whom they suppose is drowned,—
And his and mine loved darling.   *Exit.*
GONZALO   I' the name of something holy, sir, why stand you
In this strange stare?
ALONSO   O, it is monstrous, monstrous!
Methought the billows spoke, and told me of it;
The winds did sing it to me; and the thunder,
That deep and dreadful organ-pipe, pronounced
The name of Prosper: it did bass my trespass.°
100   Therefor my son i' the ooze° is bedded; and
I'll seek him deeper than e'er plummet sounded,
And with him there lie mudded.   *Exit.*
SEBASTIAN   But one fiend at a time,
I'll fight their legions o'er.°
ANTONIO   I'll be thy second.
                                        Exeunt SEBASTIAN *and* ANTONIO.
GONZALO   All three of them are desperate: their great guilt,
Like poison given to work a great time after,°
Now 'gins to bite the spirit. I do beseech you,

Ling'ring perdition slow wasting away
else otherwise
falls fall
clear blameless
mocks and mows mocking gestures and grimaces
Bravely finely
a grace . . . devouring either: it was graceful
in the act of devouring the banquet (Virgil's
harpies do so, but Ariel presumably merely
caused it to disappear); or: it had a devouring
(ravishing) grace
bated left out
good life a comment on Ariel's powers as an
actor
observation strange unusual attentiveness

meaner ministers the spirits, subservient to
Ariel, who played in the banquet scene
Their . . . done have performed the tasks their
natures suited them for
knit up . . . distractions entangled in their
madness
bass my trespass provide the bass part in the
chorus in which nature described my sin
ooze sea mud
o'er to the last
Like poison . . . after The Elizabethan was
credulous about poisons, especially in the hands
of Italians, and it was thought possible that
there were some that acted after a long interval.

That are of suppler joints, follow them swiftly,
And hinder them from what this ecstasy°
May now provoke them to.

ADRIAN   Follow, I pray you.   *Exeunt omnes.*

ACT IV

SCENE I [*Before* PROSPERO'*s Cell.*]

Enter PROSPERO, FERDINAND, *and* MIRANDA.

PROSPERO   If I have too austerely punished you,
Your compensation makes amends; for I
Have given you here a third of mine own life,°
Or that for which I live; who once again
I tender° to thy hand: all thy vexations
Were but my trials of thy love, and thou
Hast strangely° stood the test: here, afore Heaven,
I ratify this my rich gift. O Ferdinand,
Do not smile at me that I boast her off,°
10   For thou shalt find she will outstrip all praise,
And make it halt° behind her.

FERDINAND   I do believe it
Against an oracle.°

PROSPERO   Then, as my gift,° and thine own acquisition
Worthily purchased,° take my daughter: but
If thou dost break her virgin-knot° before
All sanctimonious° ceremonies may
With full and holy rite be ministered,
No sweet aspersion° shall the heavens let fall
To make this contract grow;° but barren hate,
20   Sour-eyed disdain and discord shall bestrew°
The union of your bed with weeds so loathly
That you shall hate it both: therefore take heed,
As Hymen's lamp shall light you.°

FERDINAND   As I hope
For quiet days, fair issue° and long life,

---

ecstasy madness
a third . . . life Either he thinks of Miranda, his dead wife, and himself as the whole; or Miranda, Milan, and himself; or that he has spent a third of his life bringing up Miranda; or that he has a third of his life to come, and that Miranda alone gives it value.
tender hand over
strangely wonderfully well
boast her off cry up her praises
halt limp
Against an oracle even if an oracle should declare otherwise
gift F: *guest*

purchased earned, won
break her virgin-knot take her maidenhead; from the symbolic loosening of the girdle in Roman custom, *virgineam dissoluit zonam,* "he untied her virgin belt or girdle"
sanctimonious holy
aspersion sprinkling (ritual sense)
grow into a happy and fruitful marriage
bestrew flowers—not weeds—were customarily scattered on the bridal bed
As . . . light you as you hope that the torch of the marriage god will burn clear as a good omen at your marriage; F has *lamps*
issue children

With such love as 'tis now, the murkiest den,
The most opportune place, the strong'st suggestion°
Our worser genius° can,° shall never melt
Mine honour into lust, to° take away
The edge of that day's celebration
30   When I shall think, or° Phoebus' steeds are foundered,°
Or Night kept chained below.°

PROSPERO   Fairly spoke.
Sit, then, and talk with her; she is thine own.
What, Ariel! my industrious servant, Ariel!

Enter ARIEL.

ARIEL   What would my potent master? here I am.
PROSPERO   Thou and thy meaner fellows your last service
Did worthily perform; and I must use you
In such another trick.° Go bring the rabble,°
O'er whom I give thee power, here to this place:
Incite them to quick motion; for I must
40   Bestow upon the eyes of this young couple
Some vanity° of mine Art: it is my promise,
And they expect it from me.

ARIEL   Presently?°
PROSPERO   Ay, with a twink.°
ARIEL   Before you can say, 'come,' and 'go,'
And breathe twice, and cry, 'so, so,'
Each one, tripping on his toe,
Will be here with mop and mow.°
Do you love me, master? no?
PROSPERO   Dearly, my delicate Ariel. Do not approach
Till thou dost hear me call.
50   ARIEL   Well, I conceive.°   *Exit.*
PROSPERO   Look thou be true;° do not give dalliance°
Too much the rein: the strongest oaths are straw
To the fire in' the blood: be more abstemious,
Or else, good night your vow!

FERDINAND   I warrant you, sir;
The white cold virgin snow upon my heart
Abates the ardour of my liver.°

PROSPERO   Well.
Now come, my Ariel! bring a corollary,°

suggestion temptation
worser genius bad angel; everybody had a
good one and a bad one
can is capable of
to so as to
or either
foundered gone lame
below below the horizon, from which it ascends
at sunset
trick magic device
rabble the inferior spirits

vanity trifle
Presently at once
with a twink in the twinkling of an eye
mop and mow grin and grimace
conceive understand
true faithful to your promise
dalliance lovemaking
liver thought to be the seat of the passion of
love
corollary extra man, supernumerary

Rather than want° a spirit: appear, and pertly!°
No tongue! all eyes! be silent.   *Soft music.*

Enter IRIS.°

60   IRIS   *Ceres, most bounteous lady, thy rich leas*°
Of wheat, rye, barley, vetches, oats, and pease;
Thy turfy mountains, where live nibbling sheep,
And flat meads thatched with stover,° them to keep;
Thy banks with pionèd and twillèd° brims,
Which spongy April° at thy hest betrims,°
To make cold° nymphs chaste crowns; and thy broom-groves,°
Whose shadow the dismissèd bachelor° loves,
Being lass-lorn;° thy pole-clipt° vinëyard;
And thy sea-marge,° sterile and rocky-hard,
70   *Where thou thyself dost air;—the queen o' th' sky,*
Whose wat'ry arch° and messenger° am I,
Bids thee leave these;° and with her sovereign grace,

JUNO *descends.*°

Here, on this grass-plot, in this very place,
To come and sport:—her peacocks° fly amain:°
Approach, rich Ceres, her to entertain.

Enter CERES.

CERES   *Hail, many-coloured messenger, that ne'er*
Dost disobey the wife of Jupiter;
Who, with thy saffron° wings, upon my flowers
Diffusest honey-drops, refreshing showers;
80   *And with each end of thy blue bow dost crown*
My bosky° acres and my unshrubbed down,°
Rich scarf to my proud earth; why hath thy queen
Summoned me hither, to this short-grassed green?
IRIS   *A contract of true love to celebrate;*
And some donation° freely to estate°
On the blest lovers.

---

want lack
pertly smartly
Enter Iris What follows is a reduced form of
court masque (See Headnote to *Pleasure Rec-*
onciled to Virtue, below) appropriate to a
betrothal; it cannot end, as masques should,
with a dance involving the spectators; however,
it is what was called a "show," as was the
spectacular episode in III.iii.
Ceres goddess of grain and harvest
leas meadows
thatched . . . stover covered with a growth of
grass used as winter fodder
pionèd and twillèd Meaning is uncertain but
most likely man-made embankments with
branches laid criss-cross on the top.
spongy April April is traditionally a showery
month.
betrims adorns

cold sexually pure
broom-groves gorse-clumps (perhaps)
dismissèd bachelor rejected lover
lass-lorn deprived of his girl
pole-clipt pruned
sea-marge seashore
wat'ry arch rainbow
messenger Iris traditionally had this role.
these the places mentioned
Juno descends presumably begins her descent
from the roof
peacocks sacred to Juno, whose chariot they
drew
amain swiftly
saffron yellow
bosky wooded
unshrubbed down hilly country without trees
donation gift
estate bestow

CERES   *Tell me, heavenly bow,*
If Venus or her son, as thou dost know,
Do now attend the queen?° Since they did plot
The means that dusky Dis° my daughter got,
90   *Her and her blind boy's° scandalled° company*
I have forsworn.
IRIS   *Of her society*
Be not afraid: I met her deity
Cutting the clouds towards Paphos,° and her son
Dove-drawn° with her. Here thought they to have done
Some wanton charm upon this man and maid,
Whose vows are, that no bed-right shall be paid°
Till Hymen's torch be lighted: but in vain;
Mars's hot minion° is returned again;
Her waspish-headed° son has broke his arrows,
100   *Swears he will shoot no more, but play with sparrows,°*
And be a boy right out.°
CERES   *Highest queen of state,*
Great Juno comes; I know her by her gait.
JUNO   *How does my bounteous sister? Go with me*
To bless this twain, that they may prosperous be,
And honoured in their issue.

They sing:

JUNO   *Honour, riches, marriage-blessing,*
Long continuance, and increasing,
Hourly joys be still° upon you!
Juno sings her blessings on you.
110 CERES   *Earth's increase, foison° plenty,*
Barns and garners never empty;
Vines with clust'ring bunches growing;
Plants with goodly burthen bowing;
Spring come to you at the farthest
In the very end of harvest!°
Scarcity and want shall shun you;
Ceres' blessing so is on you.

FERDINAND   This is a most majestic vision, and
Harmonious charmingly. May I be bold
To think these spirits?

---

dusky Dis Pluto; dusky because king of the underworld; he abducted Persephone (Proserpina in Latin) to be his queen for half the year
blind boy's Cupid's
scandalled tainted with scandal, disgraceful
Paphos center of the cult of Venus, in Cyprus
Dove-drawn doves were sacred to Venus and drew her chariot
bed-right . . . paid marital intercourse take place

hot minion lustful mistress
waspish-headed peevish
sparrows also associated with Venus, and thought to be lustful
right out outright, altogether
still always
foison harvest
Spring . . . harvest i.e. may you have no winter

120   PROSPERO   Spirits, which by mine Art
          I have from their confines° called to enact
          My present fancies.°
      FERDINAND   Let me live here ever;
          So rare a wondered father and a wise°
          Makes this place Paradise.

                      JUNO *and* CERES *whisper, and send* IRIS *on employment.*
                      Sweet, now, silence!
          Juno and Ceres whisper seriously;
          There's something else to do: hush, and be mute,
          Or else our spell is marred.
      IRIS   *You nymphs, called Naiads, of the windring° brooks,*
          With your sedged crowns° and ever-harmless looks,
130   *Leave your crisp° channels, and on this green land*
          Answer your summons; Juno does command:
          Come, temperate° nymphs, and help to celebrate
          A contract of true love; be not too late.

              Enter certain NYMPHS.

          You sunburned sicklemen,° of August weary,
          Come hither from the furrow, and be merry:
          Make holiday; your rye-straw hats put on,
          And these fresh° nymphs encounter every one
          In country footing.°

              Enter certain Reapers, properly habited: they join with the Nymphs in
              a graceful dance; towards the end whereof PROSPERO *starts suddenly,*
              and speaks; after which, to a strange, hollow, and confused noise, they
              heavily° vanish.

      PROSPERO [*Aside*] I had forgot that foul conspiracy
140   Of the beast Caliban and his confederates
          Against my life: the minute of their plot
          Is almost come. [*To the* SPIRITS] Well done! avoid;° no more!
      FERDINAND   This is strange: your father's in some passion
          That works° him strongly.
      MIRANDA   Never till this day
          Saw I him touched with anger, so distempered.
      PROSPERO   You do look, my son, in a moved sort,°
          As if you were dismayed: be cheerful, sir.
          Our revels° now are ended. These our actors,

---

confines natural limits
fancies imaginative entertainments
wondered . . . wise father so to be wondered
at (or so capable of producing wonders) and
also wise (some copies of F have *wife*, which
creates an analogy between the island and the
Garden of Eden, with Prospero as God the
Father and Miranda as Eve)
windring portmanteau of "wandering" and
"winding"
sedged crowns garlands of sedge
crisp covered with little waves

temperate chaste (which is why Naiads, nymphs
of the cool water, are summoned)
sicklemen reapers
fresh young
encounter . . . footing partner in a country
dance
heavily dejectedly
avoid begone
works agitates
moved sort troubled state
revels common name for such entertainments

As I foretold you, were all spirits, and
150 Are melted into air, into thin air:
And, like the baseless fabric° of this vision,
The cloud-capped towers, the gorgeous palaces,
The solemn temples, the great globe itself,
Yea, all which it inherit,° shall dissolve,
And, like this insubstantial pageant° faded,
Leave not a rack° behind. We are such stuff
As dreams are made on;° and our little life
Is rounded with° a sleep. Sir, I am vexed;°
Bear with my weakness; my old brain is troubled:
160 Be not disturbed with my infirmity:
If you be pleased, retire into my cell,
And there repose: a turn or two I'll walk,
To still my beating° mind.
FERDINAND, MIRANDA   We wish your peace.   *Exeunt.*
PROSPERO   Come with a thought.° I thank thee. Ariel: come.

Enter ARIEL.

ARIEL   Thy thoughts I cleave to.° What's thy pleasure?
PROSPERO   Spirit,
We must prepare to meet with Caliban.
ARIEL   Ay, my commander: when I presented° Ceres,
I thought to have told thee of it; but I feared
Lest I might anger thee.
170 PROSPERO   Say again, where didst thou leave these varlets?°
ARIEL   I told you, sir, they were red-hot with drinking;
So full of valour that they smote the air
For breathing in their faces; beat the ground
For kissing of their feet; yet always bending°
Towards their project. Then I beat my tabor;
At which, like unbacked° colts, they pricked their ears,
Advanced° their eyelids, lifted up their noses
As° they smelt music: so I charmed their ears,
That, calf-like, they my lowing followed, through
180 Toothed briers, sharp furzes, pricking goss,° and thorns,
Which entered their frail shins: at last I left them
I' the filthy-mantled° pool beyond your cell,
There dancing up to the chins, that the foul lake

---

baseless fabric structure without foundation. The comparison that follows between "revels" and the whole world was an old commonplace, here given powerful elegiac expression; cf. Spenser, *Amoretti*, Sonnet 54.
inherit possess, occupy
pageant term applied to elaborate and temporary allegorical show
rack cloud
on of
rounded with rounded off by; or, crowned with
vexed emotionally troubled
beating agitated

Come with a thought Prospero has only to think his wish that Ariel should come.
Thy thoughts . . . cleave to Ariel confirms this.
presented acted the part of Ceres; or, as Iris, the "presenter" of the masque, introduced Ceres
varlets rascals
bending directly their way
unbacked unbroken
Advanced opened
As As if
goss gorse
filthy-mantled covered with filthy scum

O'erstunk their feet.°
PROSPERO   This was well done, my bird.
Thy shape invisible retain thou still:
The trumpery° in my house, go bring it hither,
For stale° to catch these thieves.
ARIEL   I go, I go.   *Exit.*
PROSPERO   A devil, a born devil, on whose nature
Nurture° can never stick; on whom my pains,
190   Humanely taken, all, all lost, quite lost;
And as with age his body uglier grows,
So his mind cankers.° I will plague them all,
Even to roaring.

Re-enter ARIEL, *loaden with glistering apparel, etc.*

Come, hang them on this line.°
PROSPERO *and* ARIEL *remain, invisible.*

Enter CALIBAN, STEPHANO, *and* TRINCULO, *all wet.*

CALIBAN   Pray you, tread softly, that the blind mole may not
Hear a foot fall: we now are near his cell.
STEPHANO   Monster, your fairy, which you say is a harmless fairy, has done
little better than played the Jack° with us.
with us.
TRINCULO   Monster, I do smell all horse-piss; at which my nose is in great
200   indignation.
STEPHANO   So is mine. Do you hear, monster? If I should take displeasure
against you, look you,—
TRINCULO   Thou wert but a lost monster.
CALIBAN   Good my lord, give me thy favour still.
Be patient, for the prize I'll bring thee to
Shall hoodwink this mischance:° therefore speak softly.
All's hushed as midnight yet.
TRINCULO   Ay, but to lose our bottles in the pool,—
STEPHANO   There is not only disgrace and dishonour in that, monster, but an
210   infinite loss.
TRINCULO   That's more to me than my wetting: yet this is your harmless fairy,
monster.
STEPHAN   I will fetch off my bottle, though I be o'er ears for my labour.
CALIBAN   Prithee, my King, be quiet. Seest thou here,
This is the mouth o' the cell: no noise, and enter.
Do that good mischief which may make this island
Thine own for ever, and I, thy Caliban,
For aye thy foot-licker.

O'erstunk their feet smelled worse than their
feet
trumpery rubbishy clothes
stale bait, decoy
Nurture education, civility
cankers grows diseased

line lime-tree
played the Jack played the knave; played the
jack o' lantern (will-o'-the-wisp)
hoodwink this mischance put this mischance
out of sight

STEPHANO   Gives me thy hand. I do begin to have bloody thoughts.

220 TRINCULO   O King Stephano! O peer! O worthy Stephano!° look what a wardrobe here is for thee!

CALIBAN   Let it alone, thou fool; it is but trash.

TRINCULO   O, ho, monster! we know what belongs to a frippery.° O King
Stephano!

STEPHANO   Put off that gown, Trinculo; by this hand, I'll have that gown.

TRINCULO   Thy grace shall have it.

CALIBAN   The dropsy drown this fool!° what do you mean
To dote thus on such luggage?° Let 't° alone,
And do the murther first: if he awake,
230   From toe to crown he'll fill our skins with pinches,
Make us strange stuff.°

STEPHANO   Be you quiet, monster. Mistress line, is not this my jerkin? Now is
the jerkin under the line: now, jerkin, you are like to lose your hair, and
prove a bald jerkin.°

TRINCULO   Do, do;° we steal by line and level,° an't like your grace.

STEPHANO   I thank thee for that jest; here's a garment for it: wit shall not go
unrewarded while I am King of this country. 'Steal by line and level' is
an excellent pass of pate;° there's another garment for it.

TRINCULO   Monster, come, put some lime° upon your fingers, and away with
240   the rest.

CALIBAN   I will have none on it: we shall lose our time,
And all be turned to barnacles,° or to apes
With foreheads villainous° low.

STEPHANO   Monster, lay-to your fingers: help to bear this away where my hogshead of wine is, or I'll turn you out of my kingdom: go to, carry this.

TRINCULO   And this.

STEPHANO   Ay, and this.

*A noise of hunters heard. Enter divers Spirits, in shape of dogs and
hound, hunting them about;* PROSPERO *and* ARIEL *setting them on.*

PROSPERO   Hey, Mountain, hey!

ARIEL   Silver! there it goes, Silver!

250 PROSPERO   Fury, Fury! there, Tyrant,° there! hark, hark!

CALIBAN, STEPHANO, *and* TRINCULO *are driven out.*

Go charge my goblins that they grind their joints

O King . . . Stephano refers to old ballad
"King Stephen was a worthy peer," which Iago
sings in *Othello*.
frippery old-clothes shop. Trinculo is saying he
knows the contents of such shops, and denies
that these clothes are of that kind.
The dropsy . . . fool Dropsy is an excessive
accumulation of fluid in the body. Caliban
wants him to drown internally since he escaped
drowning in the sea.
luggage encumbrance
Let't F has "let's"
strange stuff when he's done with us we'll look
even stranger than the clothes
Now is . . . bald jerkin The jerkin is under the

tree (line=equator) and diseases contracted in
the tropics caused loss of hair.
Do, do expressing some kind of amusement at
the joke?
steal . . . level according to the rule, systematically (carrying on the punning on *line*)
an't like if it please
pass of pate thrust of wit
lime birdline
barnacles a kind of geese, supposed to hatch
from barnacles on ships' timbers
villainous wretchedly
Mountain . . . Silver . . . Fury . . . Tyrant
names of hounds

With dry convulsions;° shorten up their sinews
With aged cramps;° and more pinch-spotted° make them
Than pard° or cat o' mountain.°
ARIEL   Hark, they roar!
PROSPERO   Let them be hunted soundly. At this hour
Lies° at my mercy all mine enemies:
Shortly shall all my labours end, and thou
Shalt have the air at freedom: for a little
260   Follow, and do me service.   *Exeunt.*

ACT V

SCENE I [*Before the Cell of* PROSPERO.]

Enter PROSPERO *in his magic robes, and* ARIEL.

PROSPERO   Now does my project gather to a head:°
My charms crack not;° my spirits obey; and time
Goes upright with his carriage.° How's the day?
ARIEL   On the sixth hour; at which time, my lord,
You said our work should cease.
PROSPERO   I did say so,
When first I raised the tempest. Say, my spirit,
How fares the King and his followers?
ARIEL   Confined together
In the same fashion as you gave in charge,
Just as you left them; all prisoners, sir,
10   In the line-grove which weather-fends° your cell;
They cannot budge till your release.° The King,
His brother, and yours, abide all three distracted.
And the remainder mourning over them,
Brimful of sorrow and dismay; but chiefly
Him that you termed, sir, 'The good old lord, Gonzalo';
His tears runs° down his beard, like winter's drops
From eaves of reeds.° Your charm so strongly works° 'em,
That if you now beheld them, your affections
Would become tender.
PROSPERO   Dost thou think so, spirit?
ARIEL   Mine would, sir, were I human.°
20   PROSPERO   And mine shall.
Hast thou, which art but air, a touch, a feeling
Of their afflictions, and shall not myself,

dry convulsions convulsions in which bone grinds on bone
aged cramps cramps such as the aged suffer
pinch-spotted bruised all over with pinches from the goblins
pard leopard
cat' o' mountain catamount, lynx
Lies lie
project . . . head experiment reach its final phase (alchemical)

crack not don't go wrong (the alchemist's retort might "crack" at this point)
time . . . carriage time's burden is light; we are near the end
weather-fends protects from the weather
your release you release them
runs run
reeds a thatched roof
works moves, agitates
were I human Ariel, a spirit of air, can only imagine human feelings.

One of their kind, that relish all as sharply
Passion as they,° be kindlier° moved than thou art?
Though with their high wrongs° I am struck to the quick,
Yet with my nobler° reason 'gainst my fury
Do I take part: the rarer° action is
In virtue° than in vengeance: they being penitent,
The sole drift of my purpose doth extend
30   Not a frown further.° Go release them, Ariel:
My charms I'll break, their senses I'll restore,
And they shall be themselves.

ARIEL   I'll fetch them, sir.   *Exit.*

PROSPERO   Ye elves° of hills, brooks, standing lakes, and groves;
And ye that on the sands with printless foot°
Do chase the ebbing Neptune,° and do fly him
When he comes back; you demi-puppets° that
By moonshine do the green sour ringlets° make,
Whereof the ewe not bites; and you whose pastime
Is to make midnight mushrooms,° that rejoice
40   To hear the solemn curfew;° by whose aid—
Weak masters° though ye be—I have bedimmed
The noontide sun, called forth the mutinous winds,
And 'twixt the green sea and the azured vault°
Set roaring war: to the dread rattling thunder
Have I given fire, and rifted Jove's stout oak
With his own bolt; the strong-based promontory
Have I made shake, and by the spurs° plucked up
The pine and cedar: graves at my command
Have waked their sleepers, oped, and let 'em forth
50   By my so potent Art. But this rough magic
I here abjure; and, when I have required
Some heavenly music,—which even now I do,—
To work mine end upon their senses, that
This airy charm is for, I'll brake my staff,
Bury it certain fadoms in the earth,
And deeper than did ever plummet sound
I'll drown my book.°   *Solemn music.*

Re-enter ARIEL *before: then* ALONSO, *with a frantic gesture,*° *attended
by* GONZALO; SEBASTIAN *and* ANTONIO *in like manner, attended by* ADRIAN

---

relish . . . they am wholly as sensitive as they
to suffering
kindlier more suitably to human nature
high wrongs great injuries inflicted on me
nobler i.e. nobler than passion
rarer finer
virtue as contrasted with *vengeance*, the Christian virtue of forgiveness
Not a frown further no further than I have gone, not by so much as a look of displeasure
Ye elves . . . ll. 33–58. In this farewell to magic Shakespeare paraphrases very closely Ovid, *Metamorphoses* VII.197–209, using the original as well as Golding's translation.
printless foot foot that leaves no print

Neptune ocean
demi-puppets quasi-puppets; elves the size of puppets
green sour ringlets "fairy rings," caused by mycelium under the surface. Apparently sheep do not avoid them.
mushrooms grow overnight, so their nurture is attributed to elves
curfew After curfew tolls, spirits and elves can walk abroad.
masters the magician's demonic agents
azured vault blue sky
spurs roots
book which is necessary to his magic
gesture demeanor

and FRANCISCO: *they all enter the circle which* PROSPERO *had made, and
there stand charmed; which* PROSPERO *observing, speaks:*

A solemn air, and the best comforter
To an unsettled fancy, cure thy brains,
Now useless, boiled° within thy skull! There stand,
For you are spell-stopped.
Holy Gonzalo, honourable man,
Mine eyes, even sociable to the show of thine,
Fall fellowly drops.° The charm dissolves apace;
And as the morning steals upon the night,
Melting the darkness, so their rising senses
Begin to chase the ignorant fumes that mantle°
Their clearer reason. O good Gonzalo,
My true preserver, and a loyal sir
To him thou follow'st! I will pay° thy graces
Home° both in word and deed. Most cruelly
Didst thou, Alonso, use me and my daughter:
Thy brother was a furtherer in the act.
Thou art pinched for it now, Sebastian. Flesh and blood,
You, brother mine, that entertained° ambition,
Expelled remorse and nature; whom,° with Sebastian—
Whose inward pinches therefore are most strong—
Would here have killed your King; I do forgive thee,
Unnatural though thou art. Their understanding
Begins to swell;° and the approaching tide
Will shortly fill the reasonable shore,°
That now lie° foul and muddy. Not one of them
That yet looks on me, or would know me: Ariel,
Fetch me the hat and rapier in my cell:
I will discase me,° and myself present
As I was sometime° Milan:° quickly, spirit;

ARIEL *sings and helps to attire him.*

Thou shalt ere long be free.

*Where the bee sucks, there suck I:
In a cowslip's bell lie;
There I couch° when owls do cry.
On the bat's back I do fly
After summer° merrily.
Merrily, merrily shall I live now
Under the blossom that hangs on the bough.*

boiled seething; F: *boile*
Mine eyes . . . drops my eyes, in sympathy
with the tears visible in yours, let fall sympa-
thetic drops
mantle shroud, obscure
pay repay
Home thoroughly
entertained welcomed
whom who

swell rise like the tide
reasonable shore shore of reason, now empty
and dry
lie lies
discase me take off my cloak
sometime formerly
Milan Duke of Milan
couch lie
After summer in pursuit of summer

un - der   the   blos - som   that   hangs   on   the   bough.

This setting of "Where the Bee Sucks" is by Robert Johnson. (See Note on "Full Fadom Five," Act I, Scene II.)

PROSPERO   Why, that's my dainty Ariel! I shall miss thee;
But yet thou shalt have freedom: so, so, so.
To the King's ship, invisible as thou art:
There shalt thou find the mariners asleep
Under the hatches; the master and the boatswain
100   Being awake,° enforce them to this place,
And presently, I prithee.
ARIEL   I drink the air° before me, and return
Or ere your pulse twice beat.   *Exit.*
GONZALO   All torment, trouble, wonder and amazement
Inhabits here: some heavenly power guide us
Out of this fearful country!
PROSPERO   Behold, sir King,
The wrongèd Duke of Milan, Prospero:
For more assurance° that a living Prince
Does now speak to thee, I embrace thy body;
110   And to thee and thy company I bid
A hearty welcome.
ALONSO   Whether° thou be'st he or no,
Or some enchanted trifle° to abuse° me,
As late I have been, I not know: thy pulse
Beats, as of flesh and blood; and, since I saw thee,
The affliction of my mind amends, with which,
I fear, a madness held me: this must crave—
An if this be at all—a most strange story.
Thy dukedom I resign, and do entreat
Thou pardon me my wrongs.—But how should Prospero
Be living and be here?
120   PROSPERO   First, noble friend,
Let me embrace thine age, whose honour cannot
Be measured or confined.
GONZALO   Whether this be
Or be not, I'll not swear.
PROSPERO   You do yet taste

Being awake having awakened them   enchanted trifle apparition raised by an en-
drink the air devour the way   chanter
For more assurance to make thee more sure   abuse delude, deceive
Whether F: *Where*

Some subtleties° o' the isle, that will not let you
Believe things certain.° Welcome, my friends all!
[*Aside to* SEBASTIAN *and* ANTONIO] But you, my brace of lords,
   were I so minded,
I here could pluck° his highness' frown upon you,
And justify° you traitors: at this time
I will tell no tales.

SEBASTIAN [*Aside*]   The devil speaks in him.

PROSPERO   No.

130   For you, most wicked sir, whom to call brother
Would even infect my mouth, I do forgive
Thy rankest fault,—all of them; and require
My dukedom of thee, which perforce, I know,
Thou must restore.

ALONSO   If thou be'st Prospero,
Give us particulars of thy preservation;
How thou hast met us here, whom three hours since°
Were wracked upon this shore; where I have lost—
How sharp the point of this remembrance is!—
My dear son Ferdinand.

PROSPERO   I am woe° for it, sir.

140 ALONSO   Irreparable is the loss; and patience
Says it is past her cure.

PROSPERO   I rather think
You have not sought her help, of whose soft grace
For the like loss I have her sovereign° aid,
And rest myself content.

ALONSO   You the like loss!

PROSPERO   As great to me as late;° and, súpportable
To make the dear° loss, have I means much weaker°
Than you may call to comfort you, for I
Have lost my daughter.

ALONSO   A daughter?
O heavens, that they were living both in Naples,
150   The King and Queen there! that° they were, I wish
Myself were mudded in that oozy bed
Where my son lies. When did you lose your daughter?

PROSPERO   In this last tempest. I perceive, these lords
At this encounter do so much admire,°
That they devour their reason,° and scarce think

---

taste . . . subtleties The normal meaning of
subtleties is qualified by a secondary sense,
"elaborate confections of sugar," hence the
word *taste*.
things certain real, non-magical things
pluck bring down
justify prove
three hours since calling attention to the short
time taken by the events of the play
woe sorry

sovereign all-healing
As great to me as late as great to me and as
recent (as yours to you)
dear heavy
much weaker Alonso has a child left; or,
Miranda will live at Naples
that provided that
admire wonder
devour their reason are open-mouthed with
wonder

Their eyes do offices of truth,° their words
Are natural breath:° but, howsoe'er you have
Been justled from your senses, know for certain
That I am Prospero, and that very duke
160   Which was thrust forth of° Milan; who most strangely
Upon this shore, where you were wracked, was landed,
To be the lord on it. No more yet of this;
For 'tis a chronicle of day by day,
Not a relation for a breakfast, nor
Befitting this first meeting. Welcome, sir;
This cell's my court: here have I few attendants,
And subjects none abroad:° pray you, look in.
My dukedom since you have given me again,
I will requite you with as good a thing;
170   At least bring forth a wonder,° to content ye
As much as me my dukedom.

Here PROSPERO *discovers*° FERDINAND *and* MIRANDA *playing at chess.*

MIRANDA   Sweet lord, you play me false.°
FERDINAND   No, my dearest love,
I would not for the world.
MIRANDA   Yes, for a score of kingdoms you should wrangle,
And I would call it fair play.°
ALONSO   If this prove
A vision° of the island, one dear son
Shall I twice lose.
SEBASTIAN   A most high miracle!°
FERDINAND   Though the seas threaten, they are merciful;
I have cursed them without cause.
ALONSO   Now all the blessings
180   Of a glad father compass thee about!
Arise,° and say how thou cam'st here.
MIRANDA   O, wonder!
How many goodly creatures are there here!
How beauteous mankind is! O brave new world,
That has such people in it!
PROSPERO   'Tis new to thee.
ALONSO   What is this maid with whom thou wast at play?
Your eld'st° acquaintance cannot be three hours:°
Is she the goddess that hath severed us,
And brought us thus together?
FERDINAND   Sir, she is mortal;

do offices of truth report the world truly
natural breath the ordinary speech of human beings
of from
abroad outside this cell, about the island
wonder apparently announcing another "trick," really about to display Miranda (the wonder) and Ferdinand
discovers draws back a curtain to display
play me false cheat me

fair . . . play i.e. if we were playing for a stake of twenty kingdoms you'd cheat and I'd call it fair play
vision illusion
miracle Sebastian has the right reaction.
Arise Ferdinand has knelt for a paternal blessing.
eld'st longest
three hours another reminder

But by immortal Providence she's mine:
190   I chose her when I could not ask my father
For his advice, nor thought I had one. She
Is daughter to this famous Duke of Milan,
Of whom so often I have heard renown,
But never saw before; of whom I have
Received a second life; and second father
This lady makes him to me.

ALONSO   I am hers:°
But, O, how oddly will it sound that I
Must ask my child forgiveness!

PROSPERO   There, sir, stop:
Let us not burthen our remembrance'° with
A heaviness° that's gone.

200   GONZALO   I have inly wept,
Or should have spoke ere this. Look down, you gods,
And on this couple drop a blessed crown!
For it is you that have chalked forth° the way
Which brought us hither.

ALONSO   I say, Amen, Gonzalo!

GONZALO   Was Milan° thrust from Milan, that his issue
Should become Kings of Naples! O, rejoice
Beyond a common joy, and set it down
With gold on lasting pillars: in one voyage
Did Claribel her husband find at Tunis,
210   And Ferdinand, her brother, found a wife
Where he himself was lost, Prospero his dukedom
In a poor isle, and all of us ourselves
When no man was his own.°

ALONSO [*To* FERDINAND *and* MIRANDA]   Give me your hands:
Let grief and sorrow still° embrace° his heart
That doth not wish you joy!

GONZALO   Be it so! Amen!

Re-enter ARIEL, *with the Master and Boatswain amazedly following.*

O, look, sir, look, sir! here is more of us:
I prophesied, if a gallows were on land,
This fellow could not drown. Now, blasphemy,°
That swear'st grace o'erboard,° not an oath on shore?
220   Hast thou no mouth by land? What is the news?

BOATSWAIN   The best news is, that we have safely° found
Our King, and company; the next, our ship—

hers her father
remembrance' F: *remembrances*
heaviness sadness
chalked forth marked out
Was . . . (ll. 205–12) Gonzalo, rejoicing that
all the ills resulting from the crime against
Prospero should be canceled, and good come
of them, has a sort of exaltation, and this
speech greatly affects the overall tone of the
play.

no man was his own nobody was in command
of himself; now they have found themselves
again
still always
embrace cling to
blasphemy blasphemous fellow
swear'st grace o'erboard by thy profanity drivest
grace out of the ship
safely in a state of safety

Which, but three glasses° since, we gave out split—
Is tight and yare° and bravely rigged, as when
We first put out to sea.

ARIEL [*Aside to* PROSPERO]   Sir, all this service
Have I done since I went.

PROSPERO [*Aside to* ARIEL]   My tricksy° spirit!

ALONSO   These are not natural events; they strengthen
From strange to stranger.° Say, how came you hither?

BOATSWAIN   If I did think, sir, I were well awake,
230   I'd strive to tell you. We were dead of sleep,°
And—how we know not—all clapped under hatches;
Where, but even now, with strange and several° noises
Of roaring, shrieking, howling, jingling chains,
And mo° diversity of sounds, all horrible,
We were awaked; straightway, at liberty;°
Where we, in all our trim,° freshly beheld
Our royal, good, and gallant ship; our master
Cap'ring° to eye her:—on a trice,° so please you,
Even in a dream, were we divided from them,
And were brought moping° hither.

240 ARIEL [*Aside to* PROSPERO]   Was it well done?

PROSPERO [*Aside to* ARIEL] Bravely,° my diligence.° Thou shalt be free.

ALONSO   This is as strange a maze as e'er men trod;
And there is in this business more than nature
Was ever conduct of:° some oracle°
Must rectify our knowledge.

PROSPERO   Sir, my liege,
Do not infest° your mind with beating° on
The strangeness of this business; at picked° leisure
Which shall be shortly single,° I'll resolve you,°
Which to you shall seem probable,° of every
250   These happened accidents;° till when, be cheerful,
And think of each thing well.° [*Aside to* ARIEL] Come hither, spirit:
Set Caliban and his companions free;
Untie the spell. [*Exit* ARIEL] How fares my gracious sir?
There are yet missing of your company
Some few odd lads that you remember not.

---

three glasses three hours (another reminder)
yare shipshape, ready for sea
tricksy nimble, clever
strengthen . . . stranger increase in strangeness
of sleep asleep
several separate, different
mo more
at liberty no longer confined under hatches
in all our trim our clothes in good shape; some read *her trim* and refer the phrase to the ship
Cap'ring dancing for joy
on a trice in an instant
moping dazed
Bravely splendidly

diligence diligent one
more . . . of more than unaided nature could arrange
oracle source of more than natural information
infest torment, annoy
beating dwelling agitatedly
picked leisure a free time we shall choose
single continuous
resolve you explain to you
Which . . . probable in a manner you'll accept as plausible
every . . . accidents each one of these occurrences
think . . . well give a favorable interpretation to everything

Re-enter ARIEL, *driving in* CALIBAN, STEPHANO, *and* TRINCULO, *in their stolen apparel.*

STEPHANO   Every man shift for all the rest,° and let no man take care for himself; for all is but fortune.—Coragio,° bully-monster, coragio!

TRINCULO   If these be true spies° which I wear in my head, here's a goodly
260   sight.

CALIBAN   O Setebos, these be brave spirits indeed!
How fine° my master is! I am afraid
He will chastise me.

SEBASTIAN   Ha, ha!
What things are these, my lord Antonio?
Will money buy 'em?

ANTONIO   Very like; one of them
Is a plain fish, and, no doubt, marketable.

PROSPERO   Mark but the badges° of these men, my lords,
Then say if they be true.° This mis-shapen knave,
His mother was a witch; and one so strong
270   That could control the moon, make flows and ebbs,
And deal in her command, without her power.°
These three have robbed me; and this demi-devil—
For he's a bastard one°—had plotted with them
To take my life. Two of these fellows you
Must know and own;° this thing of darkness I
Acknowledge mine.

CALIBAN   I shall be pinched to death.

ALONSO   Is not this Stephano, my drunken butler?

SEBASTIAN   He is drunk now: where had he wine?

ALONSO   And Trinculo is reeling ripe:° where should they
280   Find this grand liquor that hath gilded 'em?°—
How comest thou in this pickle?°

TRINCULO   I have been in such pickle,° since I saw you last, that, I fear me, will never out of my bones: I shall not fear fly-blowing.°

SEBASTIAN   Why, how now, Stephano!

STEPHANO   O, touch me not;—I am not Stephano, but a cramp.

PROSPERO   You'ld be King o' the isle, sirrah?

STEPHANO   I should have been a sore° one, then.

ALONSO   This is as strange a° thing as e'er I looked on.

Every man . . . rest inversion of the saying, "Every man for himself"
Coragio courage
true spies trustworthy eyes
fine Prospero is magnificently dressed in ducal robes.
badges device indicating to which lord a servant belonged (the stolen clothes are thus a proof of the conspirators' dishonesty)
true honest
deal . . . power act in the moon's sphere of authority with a power beyond that of the moon herself (the witch Medea in Ovid's *Metamorphoses* VII.207 had this power)

demi-devil . . . one Caliban was begotten by the devil on a witch; he is a half-devil and a bastard.
own acknowledge
reeling ripe so drunk he reeled as he walked
grand liquor . . . 'em The "grand liquor" is sack, but here Alonso alludes to the elixir the alchemists make gold; "gilded" refers to this metaphor but also means "flushed."
pickle mess
pickle preservative
fly-blowing being pickled, he is safe from the flies that corrupt fresh meat
sore severe; also aching
as strange a F: *a stranger*

Pointing to CALIBAN.

290 PROSPERO   He is disproportioned in his manners°
As in his shape. Go, sirrah, to my cell;
Take with you your companions; as you look
To have my pardon, trim it handsomely.
CALIBAN   Ay, that I will; and I'll be wise hereafter,
And seek for grace.° What a thrice-double ass
Was I, to take this drunkard for a god,
And worship this dull fool!
PROSPERO   Go to; away!
ALONSO   Hence, and bestow your luggage° where you found it.
SEBASTIAN   Or stole it, rather.
300 PROSPERO   Sir, I invite your Highness and your train
To my poor cell, where you shall take your rest
For this one night; which, part of it, I'll waste°
With such discourse as, I not doubt, shall make it
Go quick away: the story of my life,
And the particular accidents° gone by
Since I came to this isle: and in the morn
I'll bring you to your ship, and so to Naples,
Where I have hope to see the nuptial°
Of these our dear-beloved solemnized;
310 And thence retire me to my Milan, where
Every third thought shall be my grave.
ALONSO   I long
To hear the story of your life, which must
Take° the ear strangely.
PROSPERO   I'll deliver° all;
And promise you calm seas, auspicious gales,
And sail° so expeditious, that shall catch
Your royal fleet far off.° [*Aside to* ARIEL] My Ariel, chick,°
That is thy charge: then to the elements°
Be free, and fare thou well! Please you, draw near.   *Exeunt omnes.*

EPILOGUE°

Spoken by PROSPERO.

Now my charms are all o'erthrown,
And what strength I have's mine own,

manners conduct, morality
grace pardon, favor
luggage rubbish, encumbrance
waste spend
accidents incidents
nuptial nuptials, wedding ceremony
Take captivate
deliver tell
sail voyage
far off far off though it already is
chick term of endearment
elements Ariel's natural habitat
Epilogue Although this is valuable material for those who would read the play as an allegory, it is basically the traditional appeal for applause, expressed in figures derived from the action of the play that has just ended. The actor who played Prospero has now, he says, no power to release himself from a spell which can only be broken when the audience applauds; and he prays for this as a grace that will help him avoid the sin of despair and set him free of his faults (as an actor). This he asks in the language of the Lord's Prayer; as the audience hopes for pardon itself, so it should award it to him.

Which is most faint: now, 'tis true,
I must be here confined° by you,
Or sent to Naples. Let me not,
Since I have my dukedom got,
And pardoned the deceiver, dwell
In this bare island by your spell;
But release me from my bands°
10 *With the help of your good hands:°*
Gentle breath° of yours my sails
Must fill, or else my project° fails,
Which was to please. Now I want
Spirits to enforce, Art to enchant;
And my ending is despair,
Unless I be relieved by prayer,°
Which pierces° so, that it assaults
Mercy itself,° and frees° all faults.
*   As you from crimes° would pardoned be,*
20 *   Let your indulgence° set me free.*   *Exit.*
      1611   1623

THOMAS CAMPION
1567–1620

One of the greatest writers of song in English, Campion, a student of law and medicine, was also a composer and poet. He published the bulk of his work in several books of airs between 1601 and 1617. He also wrote court masques and a good deal of Latin verse. Campion used the form of the stanzaic song to embody a variety of Renaissance poetic genres, including Petrarchan poems, epigrams, hymns, pastoral lyrics. His musical settings for solo voice and lute are graceful and typical of their style. While as a composer he is far less remarkable, particularly in his lute accompaniments, than the great lutenist John Dowland, his poems are unsurpassed for their smoothness and freshness, which still provide great rhetorical power. In an effort to augment such power John Donne was concurrently eschewing the rhythmic evenness of song texts, with their adaptability for musical setting, for the "strong lines" of his *Songs and Sonnets*.

Campion remained more or less in a Sidneyan tradition. He wrote a treatise on quantitative verse, suggesting a way of counting long and short syllables in English different from the usual Elizabethan methods but, like them, opting for unrhymed verse. His splendid collections of songs ignore these prescriptions.

confined as Ariel was
bands bonds
hands their clapping would break the spell
Gentle breath kindly comment on the performance
project his, parallel to but distinct from, Prospero's
prayer the petition he is now making
pierces is so penetrating
assaults Mercy itself "Prayers . . . break open heaven's gate" was a proverb.
frees wins pardon for
crimes sins
indulgence kindness; also remission for sins

My Sweetest Lesbia°

My sweetest Lesbia, let us live and love.
And, though the sager sort our deeds reprove,
Let us not weigh them. Heaven's great lamps do dive
Into their west, and straight again revive.
But soon as once set is our little light,
Then must we sleep one ever-during night.

If all would lead their lives in love like me,
Then bloody swords and armour should not be.
No drum nor trumpet peaceful sleeps should move,
Unless alarm came from the camp of Love.
But fools do live and waste their little light,
And seek with pain their ever-during night.

When timely death my life and fortune ends,
Let not my hearse be vexed with mourning friends.
But let all lovers, rich in triumph, come
And with sweet pastimes grace my happy tomb.
And, Lesbia, close up thou my little light,
And crown with love my ever-during night.

                                    1601

Follow Your Saint

Follow your saint, follow with accents sweet;
Haste you, sad notes, fall at her flying feet.
There, wrapped in cloud of sorrow, pity move,
And tell the ravisher of my soul I perish for her love.
But if she scorns my never-ceasing pain,
Then burst with sighing in her sight and ne'er return again.

All that I sung still to her praise did tend,
Still she was first, still she my songs did end.
Yet she my love and music both doth fly,
The music that her echo is and beauty's sympathy.
Then let my notes pursue her scornful flight:
It shall suffice that they were breathed and died for her delight.

                                    1601

My Sweetest Lesbia An adaptation of Catullus'
famous *Vivamus mea Lesbia, atque amemus;*
compare it with Ben Jonson's version in "Come,
My Celia" to see how Campion's use of the
varied refrain helps him build a stanzaic song.

Rose-cheeked Laura°

Rose-cheeked Laura, come
Sing thou smoothly with thy beauty's
Silent music, either other°
    Sweetly gracing.

Lovely forms do flow
From concent° divinely framed;
Heaven is music, and thy beauty's
    Birth is heavenly.

These dull notes we sing
10 Discords need for helps to grace them;
Only beauty purely loving
    Knows no discord,

But still moves delight,
Like clear springs renewed by flowing,
Ever perfect, ever in them-°
    selves eternal.
        1602

Mistress, Since You So Much Desire

Mistress, since you so much desire
To know the place of Cupid's fire,
In your fair shrine that flame doth rest,
Yet never harboured in your breast.
It bides not in your lips so sweet,
Nor where the rose and lilies meet,
    But a little higher,
There, there, O there, lies Cupid's fire.

E'en in those starry piercing eyes,
10 There Cupid's sacred fire lies.
Those eyes I strive not to enjoy,
For they have power to destroy.
Nor woo I for a smile or kiss,
So meanly triumphs not my bliss.
    But a little higher
I climb to crown my chaste desire.
        1601

Rose-cheeked Laura an example of the "lyrical" metrical forms from Campion's *Observations in the Art of English Poesy* (1602), in which he tried to reconstitute English meter on a kind of quantitative basis, although the modern reader can hear it is unrhymed, stressed trochaic **either other** each one the other
concent harmony
them- This kind of hyphenation across the last two lines of a stanza occurs in Greek Sapphic verse, from which this form is derived.

Beauty, Since You So Much Desire°

Beauty, since you so much desire
To know the place of Cupid's fire,
About you somewhere doth it rest,
Yet never harboured in your breast,
Nor gout-like in your heel or toe.
What fool would seek Love's flame so low?
    But a little higher,
There, there, O there lies Cupid's fire.

10 Think not, when Cupid most you scorn,
Men judge that you of ice were born.
For though you cast Love at your heel,
His fury yet sometime you feel.
And whereabout, if you would know,
I tell you still, not in your toe,
    But a little higher,
There, there, O there lies Cupid's fire.

               c. 1618

There Is a Garden in Her Face

There is a garden in her face
    Where roses and white lilies grow;
A heavenly paradise° is that place,
    Wherein these pleasant fruits do flow.°
There cherries grow which none may buy,
Till 'Cherry-ripe'° themselves do cry.

These cherries fairly do enclose
    Of orient pearl° a double row,
Which when her lovely laughter shows,
10   They look like rose-buds filled with snow;
Yet them no peer nor prince can buy,
Till 'Cherry-ripe' themselves do cry.

Her eyes like angels watch them still;
    Her brows like bended bows° do stand,
Threatening with piercing shafts to kill

Beauty, Since You So Much Desire This poem is an erotic parody of the idealized, Petrarchan "Mistress, Since You So Much Desire" which precedes it in this text; here, the lady's eyes as the place of love give way to her genital region, much as in Donne's "Love's Progress." **There is . . . paradise** no mere hyperbole, for the garden and its treasures, the fruit and jewels of Eden and the Hesperides garden with its golden apples, are guarded by angels against re-entry
flo'w abound, echoing the biblical "flowing with milk and honey"

'**Cherry-ripe**' This was the conventional advertising street cry of cherry-peddlers in London. Campion not only quotes the phrase but, in his musical setting of this poem, quotes the b-natural—c—d—d—d melody of the street cry on the words "cherry ripe, ripe, ripe" in the completed song; the point is only that one mayn't kiss the lady until those same lips invite the kiss.
orient pearl shining pearls; her teeth
bended bows a traditional conceit

512

All that presume with eye or hand
Those sacred cherries to come nigh,
Till 'Cherry-ripe' themselves do cry.
1617

This is Campion's own setting, for lute and voice, of the preceding poem. The little melodic fragment to "cherry ripe ripe ripe" was the street-cry actually sung to these words by London cherry vendors, and Campion works it into the vocal part just as he works the words into the conceit of his text.

Thrice Toss These Oaken Ashes in the Air°

Thrice toss these oaken ashes in the air.
Thrice sit thou mute in this enchanted chair.
Then thrice three times tie up this true love's knot,
And murmur soft: She will, or she will not.

Go burn these poisonous weeds in yon blue fire,
These screech-owl's feathers and this prickling briar,
This cypress gathered at a dead man's grave,
That all thy fears and cares and end may have.

Then come, you fairies, dance with me a round;
10   Melt her hard heart with your melodious sound.
In vain are all the charms I can devise;
She hath an art to break them with her eyes.

                              c. 1618

Thrice Toss These Oaken Ashes This song is an
incantation or spell, invoking traditional fairy
magic (like pulling petals from a daisy and saying "He loves me, he loves me not"); the

world of magic, it will be observed, defers to
the conventional Petrarchan power of the lady's
eyes.

When to Her Lute Corinna Sings

When to her lute Corinna° sings,
Her voice revives the leaden strings,
And doth in highest notes appear
As any challenged echo clear.
But when she doth of mourning speak,
Even with her sighs the strings do break.

And as her lute doth live or die,
Led by her passion, so must I.
For when of pleasure she doth sing,
10   My thoughts enjoy a sudden spring;
But if she doth of sorrow speak,
Even from my heart the strings° do break.

                   1601

Never Weather-beaten Sail

Never weather-beaten sail more willing bent to shore,
Never tired pilgrim's limbs affected slumber more,
Than my weary sprite° now longs to fly out of my troubled breast.
O come quickly, sweetest Lord, and take my soul to rest.

Ever blooming are the joys of Heaven's high Paradise.
Cold age deafs not there our ears, nor vapour dims our eyes;
Glory there the sun outshines, whose beams the blessed only see.
O come quickly, glorious Lord, and raise my sprite° to thee.

                   c. 1613

JOHN DONNE
1572–1631

Donne was born early in 1572, son of a prosperous London merchant and a mother not only Catholic but connected by marriage to Sir Thomas More; her brother, Jasper Heywood, translator of Seneca, was imprisoned for his part in a Jesuit mission to England, and Donne's own brother Henry died in prison in 1593 after being arrested for concealing a priest. The poet was justified in claiming that his family had suffered heavily "for obeying the teachers of the Roman Doctrine" (*Pseudo-Martyr,* an anti-Jesuit polemic of 1610). His early education was Catholic, and although he came to reject it (especially in its Jesuit form) his thinking and his temperament were affected by his Catholic training throughout his life.

    As a Catholic, Donne could not take a degree, though he spent three years at Oxford, and three at Cambridge; in the early 1590's he was a student at the Inns of Court, in

---

Corinna an ancient Greek lyric poetess. Her name is used for the Petrarchan lady in the guise of musician who plays on her lover like an instrument.

the strings Because of a pun on the Latin words for "heart" and "string," the concept of "heart-strings" was a Renaissance cliché.
sprite spirit

London, then more a university than a law school; he studied law, languages, and theology from four in the morning till ten, and in his spare time was, we are told, a great visitor of ladies and a theatergoer. In these years he wrote the Elegies and Satires, and some of the *Juvenilia* and of the *Songs and Sonnets*. He traveled in Europe and took part in two naval expeditions before becoming, in 1598, secretary to the powerful Sir Thomas Egerton; but his good prospects of worldly success were ended by his secret marriage with Ann More, Egerton's niece, in 1601. For years he lived miserably and sought patronage—Lucy, Countess of Bedford and Sir Robert Drury were among his most important benefactors—and worked at anti-Romanist polemic as assistant to Morton, a clergyman who was to become the bishop of Durham. In 1610 his financial difficulties were eased; he published *Pseudo-Martyr* and the satire *Ignatius His Conclave,* also directed against the Jesuits. To this period belong also the two *Anniversaries* commemorating Elizabeth Drury (1611, 1612) and *Biathanatos,* a casuistic work on suicide which he did not publish. His chief theological work, *Essays in Divinity,* was written in 1614 but remained unpublished till after his death.

Although he had probably declared for the Anglican religion by 1602, Donne resisted royal pressure to take orders until 1615, after which his ecclesiastical advancement was rapid. Henceforth he wrote few poems—even the *Holy Sonnets* are, for the most part, earlier than the date of his ordination. His wife died in 1617, at a time when he was achieving fame as a preacher. He became Dean of St. Paul's in 1621, and so completed the rejection of "the mistress of my youth, Poetry" for "the wife of mine age, Divinity." In 1623 he had a serious illness, during which he wrote his *Devotions upon Emergent Occasions* and two famous hymns. But the great sermons— ten volumes of them in the standard edition—were his chief work in these years. They often allude to his own life—the deaths of his wife and daughter, his own departure abroad, his remorse at past sins, even, in the famous *Death's Duel,* preached to King Charles I in Lent 1631, his own death. His friend Walton made much of his histrionic composure on his deathbed, and did much to confirm the traditional view of Donne as a sort of St. Augustine, who, after a wild youth, settled for preaching, piety, and remorse. This is too simple, for Donne was an ambitious man, a man with many friends in the world; there must have been a certain piquancy in the thought that the libertine poems still circulating around London had come from the pen of the somber and powerful preacher in St. Paul's; yet the same intellectual ambitions and interests, the same wit, animate both. "Wit / He did not banish, but transplanted it," says one of his elegists; for wit was certainly a quality as highly valued in sermons as in love poems.

The best way to understand what is meant by Donne's "wit" is to work at the poems. For they require work; they depend upon one's understanding how the fantastic argument is advanced by the pseudo-logic of analogy and far-fetched allusion. After that one can begin to admire the complexity of tone, the countercurrents of secondary meaning, the ingenuity of the prodigally invented stanza forms, and the "masculine persuasive force," as Donne himself called it, of the language. To be thus "harsh"— Donne's own word again—was a duty imposed on satirists; to be conceited and harsh was a requirement of the funeral elegy, of which Donne wrote many. What is more unusual is the employment of "strong lines" and scholastic argument in love poetry, especially in a poet whose voice is capable of combining a masculine tenderness with colloquial power and both with obscure argument. Such combination—of apparent spontaneity and fine-drawn ratiocination, of amorous élan with verse forms of wantonly ingenious difficulty—characterize the finest of the poems to a degree that sets them apart from all predecessors and imitators, no matter how cogently resemblances are argued.

This does not mean, of course, that Donne was an absolute innovator. Many of his poems are on topics which occur in other sixteenth- and early seventeenth-century verse—"The Flea" and "The Dream," for example—and the conceits of Petrarchanism, like some standard emblems, recur, though in modified forms. Donne was harsher than the others—Jonson scolded him for it—and also wittier and more skeptical.

It might also be said that he was more "modern"; but this is a difficult concept. Wit, the *discordia concors*, was not modern. Nor was obscurity—Jonson said Donne would perish for not being understood, but he is much less obscure than his contemporary Chapman, and even the mellifluous Spenser is on occasion virtually impenetrable. Furthermore, the modernity of Donne's references to "new philosophy"—specifically Copernicanism—has been much exaggerated; his chief sources of learned imagery are the doctrines of the Schoolmen, law, and alchemy. For all his learning he was traditionally skeptical about the power of the human mind to know truth.

Where, then, does this modernity, so much admired by the nineteenth and twentieth centuries, lie? Partly in the new cult of an old wit, which affected poetry and preaching throughout Europe in these years; partly in a new kind of obscurity, deriving not from a manipulation of secret mythic meanings but from the representation of passionate thinking; partly from a skepticism which, despite its deep religious roots, took a modern form in Montaigne and Donne. Donne's rejection of the learning that depends on unaided human sense is essential to his religion; we see it expressed with extravagance in the lines here extracted from the *Second Anniversary*, and with more gravity in the Easter-Day Sermon. In the same way he distinguished between human "custom," which has no divine support, and the law; and his ultimate rejection of the church of Rome depended on this distinction. But when erotic poetry is subjected to the same skepticism the effect is very different; for "custom" is what controls normal "bourgeois" sexual relations, and "law" is natural inclination. In short, the skeptic can, in these matters, reject convention and the vast superstructure of human sanctions as matters of opinion, not of true knowledge of the natural law. The consequence of this rejection is libertine poetry.

Yet even libertine poetry is ancient; and in the Elegies, the warmest of his poems, Donne is imitating Ovid. Nor is his amorous verse all concerned with the paradoxes and problems that arise from the conflict of desire with authority; he often has a recognizably more serious tone, and draws on the lore of Renaissance Platonism to illustrate the union of lovers' souls and the relationship between soul and body.

All we can say, then, is that Donne's modern contained much of the past, as modernity always does. What, in the end, preserves him is that his poetry is full of his powerful mind; and that the projection of his mind into poetry is immediate and, whatever the subject, witty or passionate or both.

It would not do to end this brief general introduction without a word more about Donne's religion, which preoccupied him through most of his life and long survived his active career as a poet. The third Satire is an urgent statement of the importance, there and then, of discovering a true religion. His choice of the English church as nearest to the true primitive and catholic was no doubt made possible by the labors of Hooker and other apologists. Donne held to the English middle course, the *via media*, supporting all attempts to persuade others to join it, for the rest of his life.

His chosen church avoided the errors of Rome, but maintained its contact with the ancient learning and forms; it cherished tradition without accumulated error, the Fathers but not their follies. He rejected the extreme Calvinists with detestation, but, like them, knew his Augustine. He saw the dangers of learned controversy: "It is the text that saves us; the interlineary glosses, and the marginal notes, and the *variae lectiones*, controversies and perplexities, undo us." Although his sermons seem very learned, it is worth noticing that he patiently explains his meanings, and repeats the explanations; he was an enormously popular preacher, and his distinction as a church-man lies in that and in his piety, for he was not a distinguished theologian. The wit—fineness of mind—and passion of the erotic poetry lived on, not only into the religious poetry but, suitably adapted to a larger audience, into the great sermons also. "His fancy," said his biographer Izaak Walton, "was unimitably high, equalled only by his great wit . . . He was by nature highly passionate." The words will serve to explain why, as beneficiaries of the twentieth-century revival of Donne and the scholarship which has cleared his text and illustrated his meanings, we continue to value him so highly, and perhaps occasionally to marvel that the smallish city of London, in one lifetime, contained such different poets as Marlowe, Spenser, Shake-speare, Jonson, and Donne.

We sometimes hear of a School of Donne, and there were certainly admirers and imitators, of whom the best was also the last of any merit, Abraham Cowley (1618–67). What will not do is to include the other so-called Metaphysical poets—men of the stature and idiosyncrasy of Herbert, Vaughan, Crashaw, Marvell—under such a head-ing. The conceit of Donne degenerated into a joke; the ultimate ancestor of such a work as the young Dryden's *Elegy on Lord Hastings* may be the conceit-powered funeral elegies of Donne, or even the *Anniversaries*, but a remarkable decline has occurred.

At the same time the concept of wit underwent important changes. As an admired quality it was no longer primarily a matter of acuteness, the power to make unforeseen metaphors and arguments; the concept grew more general, closer to Pope's "What oft was thought. . . ." So conceited, "strong-lined" poetry went out of fashion, as did "Senecan" prose and the witty sermon. Dr. Johnson's study of Donne's wit in his *Life of Cowley*, hostile, penetrating, even in its way just, shows him conversant with the Donnean idea of wit, but also disapproving; the best he can say is that to write as these men did it "was at least necessary to think." Pope knew the Satires, but smoothed them out, and Donne's poetry came to be thought of as at best interesting primitive work. The revival, depending on atrocious texts, was an achievement of the nineteenth century; Coleridge read deeply in the verse and prose, saying some harsh things about the verse but soliciting admiration also, especially for "The Ecstasy" and *Satire 3*. Later Browning, and George Eliot, and then many poets of the later years of the century, helped to build up a cult. Grierson's edition of 1912 made good texts and informed commentary available, and by the time T. S. Eliot wrote his famous essay "The Metaphysical Poets" in 1923, there were easily available ways of speaking and writing about this exciting poet. These we tend, wrongly, to attribute to Eliot himself. For a while modern criticism treated the disappearance of Donne's colloquial intensity from English poetry as a symptom of a general cultural disaster, called by Eliot a "dissociation of sensibility"; later he revised his views on Donne, and some-what changed that concept, in itself neither original nor historically valid; but the association of Donne with it, and with critical campaigns against Milton, still persists in some quarters. It is not harmless, for it imposes false ways of reading both Donne and Milton, which is why these notes say so little, and that skeptically, about the cultural and scientific crisis identified with Donne's verse, and so much, relatively, about Donne's own skepticism.

From Juvenilia: Or Paradoxes and Problems°

Problem: Why Does the Pox So Much Affect to Undermine the Nose?°

Paracelsus° perchance saith true, that every disease hath his exaltation° in some part certain. But why this in the nose? Is there so much mercy in this disease that it provides that one should not smell his own stink? Or hath it but the common fortune that, being begot and bred in obscurest and secretest places (because therefore his serpentine crawling and insinuation should not be suspected nor seen), he comes soonest into great place, and is more able to destroy the worthiest member than a disease better born? Perchance as mice defeat elephants° by gnawing their *proboscis* (which is their nose), this wretched Indian vermin practiceth to do the same upon us. Or as the ancient furious custom and connivancy° of some laws that° one might cut off their nose whom he deprehended in adultery, was but a type of this; and that now, more charitable laws having taken away all revenge from particular hands, this common magistrate and executioner is come to do the same office invisibly? Or by withdrawing this conspicuous part, the nose, it warns us from all adventuring upon that coast—for it is as good a mark to take in a flag, as to hang one out. Possibly Heat, which is more potent and active than Cold, thought herself injured, and the Harmony of the World out of tune, when Cold was able to show the high-way to noses in Muscovia, except she found the means to do the same in other countries. Or because by the consent of all, there is an analogy, proportion and affection between the nose and that part where this disease is first contracted, and therefore Heliogabalus° chose not his minions° in the bath but by the nose. And Albertus° had a knavish meaning when he preferred great noses. And the licentious poet° was *Naso Poeta.* I think this reason is nearest truth:° that the nose is most compassionate with this part

Paradoxes and Problems The paradox was a fashionable exercise throughout Europe, and Donne's early interest in it is reflected in some of the *Songs and Sonnets.*
Why Does . . . Nose While the point of the "paradox" as a literary exercise was to argue contrary to the received view, the problem of these "problems" was to produce as many ingenious and funny "explanations" as possible for a phenomenon that, presumably, could not be explained. The pox, syphilis, frequently resulted in facial disfigurement; as the erotic and mercantile disease (it was believed to have been brought to Europe from the Caribbean by explorers) it led to much grim humor.
Paracelsus (Theophrastus Bombastus von Hohenheim, 1493–1541), Swiss alchemist and physician

exaltation most powerful manifestation
mice . . . elephants or so the belief was
connivancy literally, "winking at," overlooking, and pretending not to
that so that
deprehended apprehended
Heliogabalus (204–222 A.D.), wildly depraved Roman emperor
minions literally, "cuties," male sexual partners
Albertus St. Albertus Magnus (Albert von Böllstadt, 1193?–1280), scholastic philosopher and St. Thomas Aquinas's teacher
licentious poet Ovid, whose full name was Publius Ovidus Naso
nearest truth He certainly does not; this is like the "But seriously, now," of the stand-up comic.

—except this be nearer: that it is reasonable that this disease in particular should affect the most eminent and perspicuous part, which in general doth affect to take hold of the most eminent and conspicuous men.

1633

Elegies

The chief model of the Elizabethan love elegy was the *Amores* of Ovid; Marlowe had made these fashionable, and the tradition was crossed with that of the witty, paradoxical, Italian love poetry of the period. Donne's Elegies, of which two are given here, belong to his early twenties, being attributable to the early 1590's, when he was a student at Lincoln's Inn. He outdoes Ovid in his witty dedication to physical pleasure; and the Elegies differ from the *Songs and Sonnets* not only in their adherence to the iambic pentameter couplet but in the unspiritual ruthlessness that for the most part characterizes their attitude to love. Not all the Elegies have the sexual directness and plain-spokenness of these two, but they will serve to demonstrate one extreme of his love poetry.

Elegy XVIII: Love's Progress°

Whoever loves, if he do not propose
The right true end of love, he's one that goes
To sea for nothing but to make him sick.
And love's a bear-whelp° born, if we o'er-lick
Our love, and force it new strange shapes to take,
We err, and of a lump a monster make.
Were not a calf a monster that were grown
Faced like a man, though better than his own?°
Perfection is in unity: prefer°
One woman first, and then one thing in her.
I, when I value gold, may think upon
The ductileness, the application,°
The wholesomeness, the ingenuity,°
From rust, from soil, from fire ever free,
But if I love it, 'tis because 'tis made
By our new nature,° use, the soul of trade.
    All these in women we might think upon
(If women had them) and yet love but one.
Can men more injure women than to say
They love them for that, by which they are not they?

₁₀

₂₀

Love's Progress refused a license in 1633; first printed in 1661 and with Donne's other poems in 1669
bear-whelp supposed to be born a shapeless lump which the mother licked into shape
though . . . own even though a man's face is in itself better than a calf's
application uses it is put to
ingenuity noble quality
new nature human custom (or, as he calls it, *use*)

Makes virtue woman? must I cool my blood
Till I both be, and find one, wise and good?
May barren angels love so. But if we
Make love to woman, virtue is not she,
As beauty's not, nor wealth. He that strays thus
From her to hers,° is more adulterous
Than if he took her maid. Search every sphere
And firmament, our Cupid is not there.°
He's an infernal god and underground
30   With Pluto dwells, where gold and fire° abound.
Men to such gods, their sacrificing coals
Did not in altars lay, but pits and holes.
Although we see celestial bodies move
Above the earth, the earth we till and love:
So we her airs contemplate, words and heart,
And virtues; but we love the centric part.°
        Nor is the soul more worthy, or more fit
For love than this,° as infinite as it.
But in attaining this desirèd place
40   How much they stray, that set out at the face!
The hair a forest is of ambushes,
Of springes, snares, fetters and manacles;
The brow becalms us when 'tis smooth and plain,
And when 'tis wrinkled, shipwrecks us again;
Smooth, 'tis a paradise, where we would have
Immortal stay, and wrinkled 'tis our grave.
The nose like to the first meridian° runs
Not 'twixt an east and west, but 'twixt two suns;
It leaves a cheek, a rosy hemisphere
50   On either side, and then directs us where
Upon the Islands Fortunate° we fall,
(Not faint Canary,° but ambrosial°)
Her swelling lips; to which when we are come,
We anchor there, and think ourselves at home,
For they seem all: there sirens' songs, and there
Wise Delphic oracles do fill the ear;
There in a creek where chosen pearls do swell,
The remora,° her cleaving tongue doth dwell.
These, and the glorious promontory, her chin
60   O'erpast; and the strait Hellespont between

from her to hers from her essential self to her
mere attributes
Search . . . there no heavenly body is called
after Cupid
gold with fire Deep in the earth, in the realm
of the god of hell, are gold and heat, both
necessary to love.
pits and holes . . . centric part *doubles en-
tendres*
this the vagina
springes small traps for game

first meridian first circle of longitude, which
(at the Canary Islands) divided the eastern and
western hemispheres
Islands Fortunate mythical happy islands west
of Gibraltar; usually identified with the Canaries
faint Canary the light sweet wine of the
Canaries
ambrosial Ambrosia was the food of the gods.
remora sucking-fish, supposed to be able to
stop ships

The Sestos and Abydos° of her breasts,
(Not of two lovers,° but two loves the nests)
Succeeds a boundless sea, but yet thine eye
Some island moles may scattered there descry;
And sailing towards her India,° in that way
Shall at her fair Atlantic navel stay;
Though thence the current be thy pilot made,
Yet ere thou be where thou wouldst be embayed,°
Thou shalt upon another forest set,
70 Where many shipwreck, and no further get.
When thou art there, consider what this chase
Misspent by thy beginning at the face.
　　Rather set out below, practise my art,
Some symmetry° the foot hath with that part
Which thou dost seek, and is thy map for that
Lovely enough to stop, but not stay at:
Least subject to disguise and change it is;
Men say the Devil never can change his.°
It is the emblem that hath figurèd
80 Firmness;° 'tis the first part that comes to bed.
Civility, we see, refined the kiss
Which at the face begun, transplanted is
Since to the hand, since to the imperial knee,
Now at the papal foot delights to be.°
If kings think that the nearer way,° and do
Rise from the foot, lovers may do so too;
For as free spheres° move faster far than can
Birds, whom the air resists, so may that man
Which goes this empty and ethereal way,
90 Than if at beauty's elements he stay.
Rich Nature hath in women wisely made
Two purses,° and their mouths aversely° laid;
They then, which to the lower tribute owe,
That way which that exchequer looks, must go.
He which doth not, his error is as great,
As who by clyster° gave the stomach meat.

1669

Sestos and Abydos towns on the opposite shores of the Hellespont; cf. Marlowe's *Hero and Leander* above
two lovers Hero and Leander
India the orient, source of riches
embayed See Carew, "A Rapture," ll. 85–90, below.
symmetry likeness of shape
his his cloven foot
emblem . . . firmness The foot was used as an emblem of *firmitas*.

Civility . . . to be polite manners have made our kissing more subservient; kissing on the face descends to hand-kissing, then to kissing the emperor's knee and the pope's foot
the nearer way the shortest way to what they want
free spheres the heavenly bodies, which encounter no resistance from the air
Two purses the mouth and the vagina
aversely at different angles
clyster enema

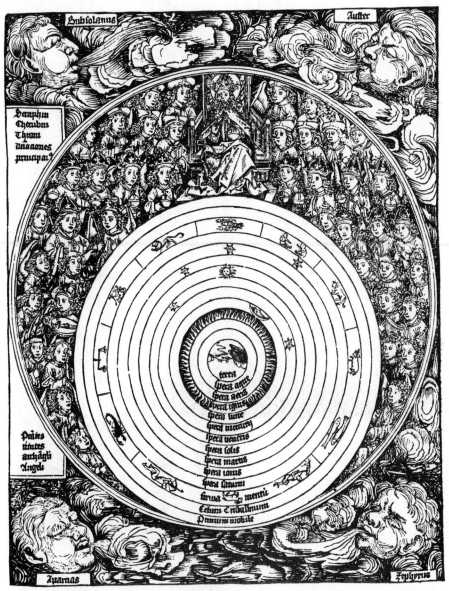

1. The "Ptolemaic" Universe: the spheres from earth to Prime Mover, with God at the top, surrounded by choiring angels, and with the four winds in their corners. From Hartmann Schedel, *Liber Chronicarum* ("Nuremberg Chronicle"), 1493.

2. *Sir Thomas More and His Household* (c. 1527), by Hans Holbein the Younger (1497/8–1543), the German artist who served as court painter to Henry VIII. *Oeffentliche Kunstsammlung*, Basel.

3. *Sir Thomas Elyot* (c. 1527–28),
also drawn by Holbein.
*By permission of Her Majesty the Queen,
Copyright reserved.*

4. Guidobaldo da Montefeltro as a boy, with his father Federigo, Duke of Urbino, painted about 1476 by the Flemish artist Joos van Wassenhove called Justus van Ghent (active c. 1460–80). *Anderson-Art Reference Bureau.*

THE WORLD OF *THE COURTIER*

5. Raphael's portrait of Baldassare Castiglione (c. 1514–15). *Photo Bulloz.*

6. Allegory in Portraiture: Sir John Luttrell (1550), after the painting by Hans Eworth (c. 1520–73). Here shown wading waist-high amid shipwreck, Luttrell, a naval adventurer, looks up at the allegorical figure of Peace surrounded by her attendants. On his wrist is a bracelet with a Latin motto, which would be translated "Money deterred him not, nor did danger wreck him." On the rock at the left are the English verses:

> More than the rock amid the raging seas
> The constant heart no danger dreads, nor fears.

It has recently been suggested that the allegory of Peace also refers specifically to a treaty made with France in 1550. *Luttrell Estates, Ltd.*

7. Queen Elizabeth I and the Three Goddesses (1569), by the monogrammist "HE." Like
so much mythological poetry and, in particular, like the masques and entertainments of
the Jacobean period, this emblematic painting portrays the Queen as Paris, in the famous
episode from Greek mythology in which he awards the apple to Aphrodite (Venus) and is
rewarded with Helen of Troy—and the Trojan War. Here the Queen awards the prize (the
apple "for the fairest" as her orb of power) to herself; the goddesses are, *left* to *right*,
Juno (crowned but with her scepter cast down and with her left shoe come off), Minerva
(armed), and Venus (nude, as always, and accompanied by Cupid). In the background is
Windsor Castle. *By permission of Her Majesty the Queen, Copyright reserved.*

8. Queen Elizabeth (c. 1592), by Marcus Gheeraerts the Younger (1561–1635). The so-called "Ditchley Portrait," probably commemorating an entertainment given the Queen at his house in Oxfordshire by Sir Henry Lee, her Master of the Armoury and probable author of the sonnet appearing in fragmentary form on the right. It hails her as "The prince of light," toward which the figure of the Queen faces, away from stormy clouds ("Thunder, the image of that power divine," says the inscription). She stands on a map of England, with her feet near Ditchley, in fact. *National Portrait Gallery*, London.

9. Sir Walter Ralegh (1588); to the right of his head, a crescent moon facing downward, perhaps in allusion to Queen Elizabeth as Cynthia, the moon goddess and muse of Ralegh's unfinished cycle of poems. The painter has not been definitely identified. *National Portrait Gallery.*

10. A Burning Lover. A miniature by Nicholas Hilliard (c. 1547–1619) depicting a man in his shirt, conventionally ear-ringed, holding a locket probably containing his mistress's picture, and surrounded by the metaphorical fires of his passion. *Victoria and Albert Museum, ·London.*

11. A Courtly Sonneteer. This Hilliard miniature, c. 1588, shows an unidentified young man leaning against a tree among roses. The Latin motto, *Dat poenas laudata fides,* proclaims that the lover's vaunted faith in love has given him suffering, a typical formula. *Victoria and Albert Museum.*

12. An Elizabethan Musing, c. 1590. This later miniature by Isaac Oliver (1568?–1617) shows a young man beneath a tree in solitude away from the social life in the house and garden behind him. It has been suggested that the melancholy with which the figure is tinged has some relation to that of the figure of Democritus (also seated beneath a tree) on the title page of Burton's *Anatomy of Melancholy* (see Fig. 17). *By permission of Her Majesty the Queen, Copyright reserved.*

13. Shakespeare, engraving by Martin Droeshout (b. 1601) on a title page of the First Folio. *The Granger Collection.*

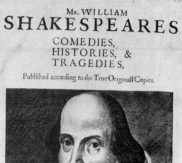

14. Ben Jonson, by an anonymous seventeenth-century painter. *The Granger Collection.*

15. John Donne (c. 1595), as a melancholic lover—"that picture of mine" he said in disposing of it in his will, "which was taken in the shadows." The large, floppy hat and the undone collar were both marks of the distracted lover in a usually tightly laced age. The inscription, to an unidentified lady, implores her to light up his shadow: *Illumina tenebras nostras domina* (Enlighten our darkness, lady)—a parody, in fact, of the Latin text translated in the (Anglican) Book of Common Prayer as "Lighten our darkness, we beseech thee, Lord." *National Portrait Gallery.*

16. *Melancholy.* The celebrated engraving by Albrecht Dürer (1471–1528), with its emblematic bat, dog, abandoned scientific and speculative instruments, makes of this brooding, dark angel as personal a myth of the internalized imagination as Milton's in "Il Penseroso" or Burton's in the *Anatomy. The Metropolitan Museum of Art, Harris Brisbane Dick Fund, 1943,* New York.

17. *The Anatomy of Melancholy*, title page of the 1628 edition. Surrounding the text are images of melancholic types: on the *left*, the Lover; on the *right*, the Hypochondriac; *above*, *center*, the Scholar. The Lover may be compared, for his hat and crossed arms, with the portrait of Donne in Figure 15. "Democritus Jr.," the pseudonymous Burton, appears at lower center. *New York Public Library, Arents Collection.*

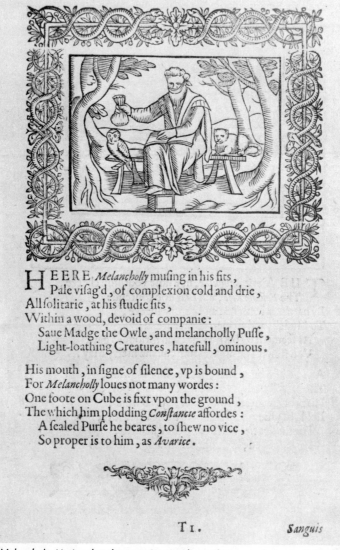

HEERE *Melancholly* mufing in his fits,
    Pale vifag'd, of complexion cold and drie,
Allfolitarie, at his ftudie fits,
Within a wood, devoid of companie:
    Saue Madge the Owle, and melancholly Puffe,
    Light-loathing Creatures, hatefull, ominous.

His mouth, in figne of filence, vp is bound,
For *Melancholly* loues not many wordes:
One foote on Cube is fixt vpon the ground,
The which him plodding *Conftancie* affordes:
    A fealed Purfe he beares, to fhew no vice,
    So proper is to him, as *Auarice.*

T I.   *Sanguis*

18. *Melancholy.* Notice that the text gives readings of various elements of the picture.

Emblems of the Four Temperaments from Henry Peacham's emblem book *Minerva Brittana*, 1610. *Yale University Library*, New Haven, Conn.

T HE Aierie *Sanguine*, in whose youthfull cheeke,
   The *Peſtane Roſe*, and *Lilly* doe contend :
By nature is benigne , and gentlie meeke ,
To Muſick , and all merriment a frend ;
   As ſeemeth by his flowers , and girlondes gay ,
   Wherewith he dightes him , all the merry May .

And by him browzing , of the climbing vine ,
The luſtfull *Goate* is ſeene , which may import ,
His pronenes both to women , and to wine ,
Bold , bounteous , frend vnto the learned ſort ;
   For ſtudies fit , beſt louing , and belou'd ,
   Faire-ſpoken , baſhfull , ſeld in anger moou'd .

                                        Cholera

19. *The Sanguine Temperament.*

NEXT *Choller* ſtandes, reſembling moſt the fire,
   Of ſwarthie yeallow, and a meager face;
With Sword a late, vnſheathed in his Ire:
Neere whome, there lies, within a little ſpace,
   A ſterne ei'de Lion, and by him a ſheild,
   Charg'd with a flame, vpon a crimſon feild.

We paint him young, to ſhew that paſſions raigne,
The moſt in heedles, and vnſtaied youth:
That Lion ſhowes, he ſeldome can refraine,
From crueli deede, devoide of gentle ruth:
   Or hath perhaps, this beaſt to him aſſign'd,
   As bearing moſt, the braue and bounteous mind.

T 2.   *Phlegma*

20. The Choleric.

HEERE *Phlegme* sits coughing on a Marble seate,
    As Citie-vsurers before their dore :
Of Bodie grosse , not through excesse of meate,
But of a Dropsie, he had got of yore :
    His slothfull hand , in's bosome still he keepes ,
    Drinkes , spits , or nodding , in the Chimney sleepes .

Beneath his feete , there doth a *Tortoise* crall ,
For slowest pace , Sloth's Hieroglyphick here ,
For Phlegmatique , hates Labour most of all ,
As by his course araiment , may appeare :
    Nor is he better furnished I find ,
    With Science , or the virtues of the mind .

21. *The Phlegmatic.*

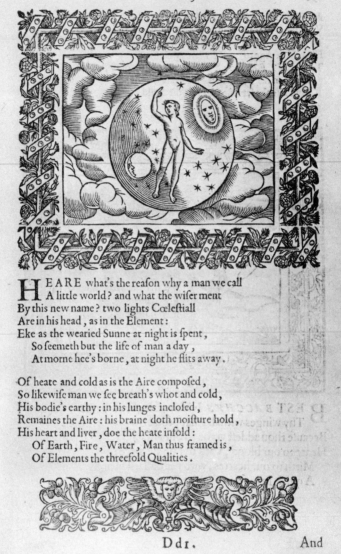

HEARE what's the reafon why a man we call
A little world? and what the wifer ment
By this new name? two lights Cœleftiall
Are in his head, as in the Element:
Eke as the wearied Sunne at night is fpent,
   So feemeth but the life of man a day,
   At morne hee's borne, at night he flits away.

Of heate and cold as is the Aire compofed,
So likewife man we fee breath's whot and cold,
His bodie's earthy: in his lunges inclofed,
Remaines the Aire: his braine doth moifture hold,
His heart and liver, doe the heate infold:
   Of Earth, Fire, Water, Man thus framed is,
   Of Elements the threefold Qualities.

22. Man the Microcosm, another emblem from *Minerva Brittana*. Compare with the treatment of the human microcosm in Donne's "I am a little world made cunningly," and in Browne and Ralegh. *Yale University Library.*

Virgil. in Fragm.
de littera y.
*Quisquis enim duros
casus virtutis amore
Vicerit, ille sibi lau-
démque decusque pa-
rabit.
At qui desidiä luxúm-
que sequetur inertem,
Dum fugit oppositos in-
cauta mente labores,
Turpis, inopsque simul,
miserabile transiget
aeuum.*

W̲H̲E̲N̲ H̲E̲R̲C̲V̲L̲E̲S̲, was dowtfull of his waie,
     Inclosed rounde, with vertue, and with vice:
With reasons firste, did vertue him assaie,
The other, did with pleasures him entice:
     They longe did striue, before he coulde be wonne,
     Till at the lengthe, A̲L̲C̲I̲D̲E̲S̲ thus begonne.

Oh pleasure, thoughe thie waie bee smoothe, and faire,
And sweete delightes in all thy courtes abounde:
Yet can I heare, of none that haue bene there,
That after life, with fame haue bene renoum'de:
     For honor hates, with pleasure to remaine,
     Then houlde thy peace, thow wastes thie winde in vaine.

But heare, I yeelde oh vertue to thie will,
And vowe my selfe, all labour to indure,
For to ascende the steepe, and craggie hill,
The toppe whereof, whoe so attaines, is sure
     For his rewarde, to haue a crowne of fame:
     Thus H̲E̲R̲C̲V̲L̲E̲S̲, obey'd this sacred dame.

                                Pana

23. The Choice of Hercules, a mythological emblem expounded in an almost homiletic way, from Geoffrey Whitney's *Choice of Emblems*, 1586. See also Ben Jonson's *Pleasure Reconciled to Virtue. Yale University Library.*

By Studiousnesse, *in* Vertue's *waies*
Men gaine an universall-praise.

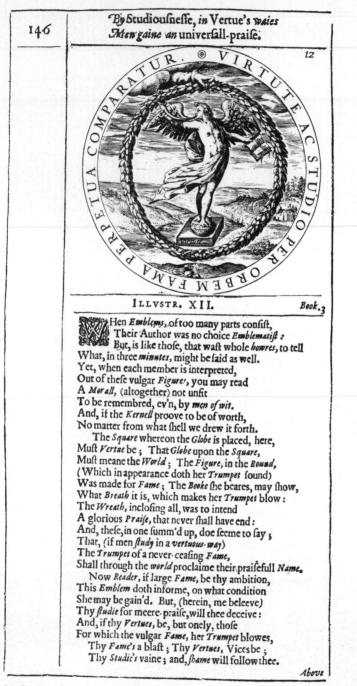

12

VIRTUTE AC STUDIO PER ORBEM FAMA PERPETUA COMPARATUR.

ILLVSTR. XII.   Book. 3

Hen *Emblems,* of too many parts confift,
    Their Author was no choice *Emblematift :*
    But, is like thofe, that waft whole *howres,* to tell
What, in three *minutes,* might be faid as well.
Yet, when each member is interpreted,
Out of thefe vulgar *Figures,* you may read
A *Morall,* (altogether) not unfit
To be remembred, ev'n, by *men of wit.*
And, if the *Kernell* proove to be of worth,
No matter from what fhell we drew it forth.

    The *Square* whereon the *Globe* is placed, here,
Muft *Vertue* be ; That *Globe* upon the *Square,*
Muft meane the *World* ; The *Figure,* in the *Round,*
(Which in appearance doth her *Trumpet* found)
Was made for *Fame* ; The *Booke* fhe beares, may fhow,
What *Breath* it is, which makes her *Trumpet* blow :
The *Wreath,* inclofing all, was to intend
A glorious *Praife,* that never fhall have end :
And, thefe, in one fumm'd up, doe feeme to fay ;
That, (if men *ftudy* in a *vertuous-way*)
The *Trumpet* of a never-ceafing *Fame,*
Shall through the *world* proclaime their praifefull *Name.*

    Now *Reader,* if large *Fame,* be thy ambition,
This *Emblem* doth informe, on what condition
She may be gain'd. But, (herein, me beleeve)
Thy *ftudie* for meere-praife, will thee deceive :
And, if thy *Vertues,* be, but onely, thofe
For which the vulgar *Fame,* her *Trumpet* blowes,
    Thy *Fame's* a blaft ; Thy *Vertues,* Vicesbe ;
    Thy *Studie's* vaine ; and, *fhame* will follow thee.

Above

24. Study and Fame. George Wither's *A Collection of Emblems,* 1635, contains this rather plodding reading of a complex symbol. It may amuse the modern reader to follow it step by step.

If Safely, *thou desire to goe,*
Bee nor too swift, *nor* overslow.

60

ILLVSTR. X.   Book. 2

Vr *Elders*, when their meaning was to shew
A *native-speedinesse* (in Emblem wise)
The picture of a *Dolphin-Fish* they drew;
Which, through the waters, with great swiftnesse, flies.
An *Anchor*, they did figure, to declare
Hope, stayednesse, or a *grave-deliberation:*
And therefore when those two, united are,
It giveth us a two-fold Intimation.
For, as the *Dolphin* putteth us in minde,
That in the Courses, which we have to make,
Wee should not be, to *slothfulnesse* enclin'd;
But, swift to follow what we undertake:
So, by an *Anchor* added thereunto,
Inform'd wee are, that, to maintaine our *speed*,
Hope, must bee joyn'd therewith (in all we doe)
If wee will undiscouraged proceed.
It sheweth (also) that, our *speedinesse*,
Must have some *staydnesse*; lest, when wee suppose
To prosecute our aymes with good successe,
Wee may, by *Rashnesse*, good endeavors lose.
    They worke, with most securitie, that know
The *Times*, and best *Occasions* of *delay*;
When, likewise, to be neither *swift*, nor *slow*;
And, when to practise all the *speed*, they may.
For, whether calme, or stormie-passages,
(Through this life's *Ocean*) shall their *Bark* attend;
This *double Vertue*, will procure their ease:
And, them, in all necessities, befriend.
    By *Speedinesse*, our works are timely wrought;
    By *Staydnesse*, they, to passe are, safely, brought.

They,

25. *Festina Lente* (Make haste slowly). The device of a dolphin curled about an anchor
first in classical times and as ascribed to the Emperor Augustus. In the Renaissance it becomes a dialectical resolution of the opposites of anchored steadfastness and
joyful, bounding motion. The great Venetian printer Aldus Manutius used it as his device.
This version, from Wither's book of emblems, uses the conventional symbolism of the
anchor as Hope and, later, as Faith.

26. Emblem and Poem

The engraved title page of Ralegh's *History of the World,* 1614, shows an allegorical figure of History, labeled in Latin "mistress of life" and bearing aloft the globe, which remains beneath the Eye of Providence; History tramples Death and Oblivion, and is attended by Experience and Truth (naked as always). Ben Jonson wrote the poem "The Mind of the Frontispiece to a Book" to accompany, and gloss, the picture:

> From Death and dark Oblivion, ne'er the same
> > The Mistress of Man's life, grave History
> Raising the World to Good or Evil Fame
> > Doth vindicate it to eternity.
> Wise Providence would so: that nor the good
> > Might be defrauded, nor the great secured,
> But both might know their ways were understood
> > When Vice alike in time with Virtue dured.
> Which makes that (lighted by the beamy hand
> > Of Truth that searcheth the most hidden springs
> And guided by Experience, whose straight wand
> > Doth mete, whose line doth sound, the depth of things),
> She cheerfully supporteth what she rears
> > Assisted by no strengths but are her own,
> Some note of which each varied pillar bears,
> > By which, as proper titles, she is known:
> Time's witness, Herald of Antiquity,
> > The Light of Truth, and Life of Memory.

New York Public Library, Rare Book Division.

27. The Entry of Comus, from Jonson's *Pleasure Reconciled to Virtue*, one of the designs by Inigo Jones (1573–1652) for the masque. *Courtauld Institute*, London.

28. *Queen Henrietta Maria as Chloris* in Ben Jonson's *Chlorida*, 1631, another Inigo Jones drawing of a costume design to illustrate the stage direction: "In the most eminent place of the Bower sat the goddess Chloris, accompanied with fourteen Nymphs, their apparell white, embroidered with silver, trimmed at the shoulders with great leaves of green, embroidered with gold, falling one under the other. . . . their headties of flowers mixed with silver and gold, with sprigs of egrets among, and from the top of their dressing a thin veil hanging down." *Courtauld Institute of Art*, London.

29. The young Milton, at age twenty or twenty-one, in 1629. *National Portrait Gallery.*

30. Milton at thirty-six or thirty-seven, the frontispiece to the *Poems*, 1645, as engraved by William Marshall. In reaction Milton wrote the Greek inscription at the bottom: "This picture was drawn by an unskillfull hand (you'd say,) looking at its original and not recognizing the true copy [pun on *engraving*]. Friends, laugh at the bad picture by a worthless engraver." *New York Public Library, Rare Book Division.*

31. *King Charles I on Horseback*. Sir Anthony Van Dyck (1599–1641), who lived in England from 1632 until his death, served as painter to Charles I, a great collector and connoisseur. Van Dyck's various portraits of him capture a range of the King's qualities, such as hauteur and refinement; in this equestrian portrait (163?) he is depicted in a manner derived from Titian's Emperor Charles V, but not literally denoting the head of a conquering army so much as suggesting, with almost Platonist imagery, a higher soul controlling powerful passions. *National Gallery*, London.

32. *Charles I and James, Duke of York, 1647.* Portrait by Sir Peter Lely (1618–80) of the doomed King and his heir suggested an almost emblematic reading to the Cavalier poet Richard Lovelace, who wrote of it:

> See what a clouded Majesty! and eyes
> Whose glory through their mist doth brighter rise!
> See what an humble bravery doth shine,
> And grief triumphant breaking through each line; . . .
> That mightiest Monarchs by this shaded book
> May copy out their proudest, richest look.

From "To My Worthy Friend Mr. Peter Lilly"

Country Life, London.

33. The Cavalier Temper. Though most often thought of as a court painter to Charles II, the Dutch artist Sir Peter Lely, who came to London in 1643, was active during the Commonwealth as well. This exotic vision of nymphs at a fountain seems an apt counterpart to the poetic world of Thomas Carew's "A Rapture." *Dulwich College Picture Gallery*, London.

34. St. Teresa in Ecstasy

> His is the dart must make the death
> Whose stroke shall taste thy hallowed breath;
> A dart thrice dipped in that rich flame
> Which writes thy spouse's radiant name
> Upon the roof of heaven. . . .

From Richard Crashaw's "A Hymn to the Name
and Honour of the Admirable Saint Teresa, . . ."

The great baroque vision of *The Ecstasy of St. Teresa* by Gianlorenzo Bernini (1598–1680) (in the Cornaro Chapel of Santa Maria della Vittoria, in Rome) took form in 1645–52, and its amazing theatrical use of natural lighting from above to play about flesh, drapery, and gilded, carved rays of celestial light parallels Crashaw's imagery in representing the rapid transience of the ecstatic moment. Compare with Crashaw's "The Flaming Heart." *Alinari-Scala.*

35. Oliver Cromwell, painted by Robert Walker (c. 1605–60) in a format derived, like Lely's of Charles I and his son, from Van Dyck's division of the scene into two areas, one backed by hanging drapery, the other by outdoor sky. It is ironic that Walker should **have** used the courtly pictorial conventions to depict the Court's destroyer. *National Portrait Gallery.*

36. Andrew Marvell (1658), by Adriaen Hanneman. (c. 1601–71). *The Granger Collection*.

37. Rubens's Ceiling, detail of the center end panel representing *The Benefits of the Government of James I.* James crowned and wreathed by angelic figures; *below*, Minerva (as Wisdom) defends the throne against Mars (as War) who crushes the King's enemies. Mercury, *left*, points toward their Hell, and above him Peace embraces Plenty. *Department of the Environment, Crown Copyright reserved.*

38. Interior view of the Banqueting House, Whitehall, designed by Inigo Jones (1573–1652) and completed in 1622 for James I. It was the scene of court masques by Ben Jonson and others until 1635, at which time the ceiling by Peter Paul Rubens (1577–1640), commissioned by Charles I, was installed. *A. F. Kersting.*

Elegy XIX: To His Mistress Going to Bed°

Come, Madam, come, all rest my powers defy,
Until I labour, I in labour lie.
The foe oft-times having the foe in sight,
Is tired with standing° though they never fight.
Off with that girdle, like heaven's zone° glistering,
But a far fairer world encompassing.
Unpin that spangled breastplate° which you wear,
That the eyes of busy fools may be stopped there.
Unlace yourself, for that harmonious chime°
10 Tells me from you, that now 'tis your bed time.
Off with that happy busk,° which I envy,
That still can be, and still can stand so nigh.
Your gown going off, such beauteous state reveals,
As when from flowery meads the hill's shadow steals.
Off with that wiry coronet° and show
The hairy diadem which on you doth grow;
Now off with those shoes, and then safely tread
In this love's hallowed temple, this soft bed.
In such white robes heaven's angels used to be
20 Received by men; thou angel bring'st with thee
A heaven like Mahomet's paradise;° and though°
Ill spirits walk in white, we easily know
By this these angels from an evil sprite:
Those set our hairs, but these our flesh upright.
   Licence my roving hands, and let them go
Before, behind, between, above, below.
O my America, my new found land,
My kingdom, safeliest when with one man manned,°
My mine of precious stones, my empery,°
30 How blessed am I in this discovering thee!
To enter in these bonds,° is to be free;
Then where my hand is set, my seal shall be.°
   Full nakedness, all joys are due to thee.
As souls unbodied, bodies unclothed must be,
To taste whole joys.° Gems which you women use
Are like Atalanta's balls,° cast in men's views,

To His Mistress Going to Bed refused license in 1633; published 1669
standing waiting to fight; here: having an erection
heaven's zone Orion's belt (*zona* = girdle)
spangled breastplate stomacher, which covered the breast and was, often jeweled
chime she had a chiming watch
busk corset
wiry coronet band of metal worn round the brow
Mahomet's paradise a place of sensual bliss (for men)
though even though

manned inhabited, served
empery empire
these bonds her arms
where . . . shall be having signed the contract he will seal it; having put his hand on her sex he will complete that transaction also
As souls . . . whole joys as souls must be divested of bodies to taste heavenly joy, so bodies must be divested of clothes
Atalanta's balls Hippomenes defeated the unbeatable Atalanta in a race by throwing three golden apples in her path; she stopped to pick them up.

That when a fool's eyes lighteth on a gem,
His earthly soul may covet theirs, not them.
Like pictures, or like books' gay coverings made
40   For laymen,° are all women thus arrayed;
Themselves are mystic books, which only we
Whom their imputed grace will dignify°
Must see revealed. Then since I may know,
As liberally, as to a midwife, show
Thyself: cast all, yea, this white linen hence,
There is no penance due to innocence.°
   To teach thee, I am naked first, why then
What need'st thou have more covering than a man.

                                        1669

Songs and Sonnets

First published in 1633, two years after Donne's death, these poems circulated in
manuscript during the poet's lifetime. Their first audience was a small, sophisticated,
no doubt rather "fast" group of like-minded young men, willing to be tested by
fantastic argument, admiring what Donne himself called, in a squib called *The
Courtier's Library*, "itchy outbreaks of far-fetched wit." This much may be said without
prejudice to the great variety of tone in the poems: they all ask one to admire their
ingenuity, their skill in overcoming the difficulties placed in the way of complicated
argument by the arbitrarily difficult stanza forms. Yet some really are "songs," and
were sung; others fail, as so many of the poems of later poets who imitated them fail,
by being nothing but ingenious. The selection of poems that follows excludes several
such relative failures.

   Nevertheless, it would be dangerous to argue that only the more "serious" poems
are good; just as it is dangerous to divide the poems, as some do, into two groups,
rakish poems written before 1600, more subtle and serious poems written after 1602.
Occasionally dates can be conjectured; some of these dates are after 1600, and the
tone of the poems is different from that of the more libertine Elegies, which belong to
the 1590's. But there is no certainty, and for that reason no dates of composition are
appended to the poems in this selection.

The Good Morrow

   I wonder by my troth, what thou and I
      Did, till we loved? were we not weaned till then,
   But sucked on country° pleasures, childishly?

laymen who cannot understand the contents
imputed grace . . . dignify to the elect women
will impute the grace necessary to this revelation, as Christ, in Calvinist doctrine, imputes
to his elect the grace necessary to salvation
There . . . innocence the white linen of penitence is inappropriate, since you are doing no
sin. Another much-favored reading is: "Here is
no penance, much less innocence"—you are
neither a penitent nor an innocent, and so have
no occasion to wear white.
country rustic

Or snorted° we in the seven sleepers' den?°
'Twas so; but this,° all pleasures fancies be.
If ever any beauty I did see,
Which I desired, and got, 'twas but a dream of thee.

And now good morrow to our waking souls,
Which watch not one another out of fear;
10   For love, all love of other sights controls,°
And makes one little room, an every where.
Let sea-discoverers to new worlds have gone,
Let maps° to others, worlds on worlds have shown,
Let us possess one world, each hath one, and is one.

My face in thine eye, thine in mine appears,
And true plain hearts do in the faces rest;
Where can we find two better hemispheres°
Without sharp north, without declining west?
Whatever dies, was not mixed equally;°
20   If our two loves be one, or, thou and I
Love so alike that none do slacken, none can die.°

1633

The Sun Rising°

Busy old fool, unruly sun,
Why dost thou thus,
Through windows, and through curtains call on us?
Must to thy motions lovers' seasons run?
Saucy pedantic wretch, go chide
Late school-boys, and sour prentices,
Go tell court-huntsmen,° that the King will ride,
Call country ants° to harvest offices;°
Love, all alike, no season knows, nor clime,
10   Nor hours, days, months, which are the rags° of time.

Thy beams, so reverend, and strong
Why shouldst thou think?
I could eclipse and cloud them with a wink,
But that I would not lose her sight so long:
If her eyes have not blinded thine,

snorted snored
seven sleepers' den Seven young Christians
were walled up in a cave during the persecution of Decius (249) and did not die but
slept for 187 years.
but this except for this
controls inhibits
maps charts of the heavens
two better hemispheres together they make
the whole world, and as hemispheres they lack
the disadvantages of the geographical ones,
which have to include the cold north and the
west where the sun sets
Whatever . . . equally Death, in Galen's teach-

ing, results from imbalance of elements within
the body.
Love . . . die each matches the perfection of
the other's love to a degree that prevents either
from waning; neither can die
The Sun Rising follows the tradition, beginning
with Ovid, of the lover's address to the sun,
but differs in its irreverence.
court-huntsmen who hunt with King James, and
also hunt office
country ants rural drudges
offices tasks
rags fragments, divisions

Look, and tomorrow late, tell me,
Whether both the Indias° of spice and mine
Be where thou left'st them, or lie here with me.
Ask for those kings whom thou saw'st yesterday,
20   And thou shalt hear, All here in one bed lay.

She is all states, and all princes, I,
Nothing else is.
Princes do but play us; compared to this,
All honour's mimic; all wealth alchemy.°
Thou sun art half as happy as we,
In that the world's contracted thus;
Thine age asks ease, and since thy duties be
To warm the world, that's done in warming us.
Shine here to us, and thou art everywhere;
30   This bed thy centre° is, these walls, thy sphere.

1633

The Canonization°

For God's sake hold your tongue, and let me love,
Or chide my palsy, or my gout,
My five grey hairs, or ruined fortune flout,
With wealth your state, your mind with arts improve,
Take you a course,° get you a place,°
Observe his Honour,° or his Grace,°
Or the King's real, or his stamped face°
Contemplate; what you will, approve,°
So you will let me love.

10   Alas, alas, who's injured by my love?
What merchant's ships have my sighs° drowned?
Who says my tears° have overflowed his ground?
When did my colds° a forward spring remove?
When did the heats° which my veins fill
Add one more to the plaguy bill?°
Soldiers find wars, and lawyers find out still
Litigious men, which quarrels move,
Though she and I do love.

---

both the Indias the East and West Indies, the
first for perfumes and spices, the second for
gold
alchemy fake gold
centre of his universe; that around which he
revolves
The Canonization The martyrs of love become
saints.
Take . . . course get yourself a career
place appointment at court
his Honor some lord

his Grace some bishop
King's . . . face the King in person (as to a
sycophant) or as he appears on money (as to
a businessman)
approve try, experience
sighs . . . tears . . . colds . . . heats the conventional Petrarchan hyperboles for lovesick-
ness used as an argument that their love affects
nobody else's business
plaguy bill lists of plague victims posted weekly

Call us what you will, we are made such by love;
20   Call her one, me another fly,
We are tapers too,° and at our own cost die,°
    And we in us find the Eagle and the Dove.
        The Phoenix riddle° hath more wit
        By us; we two being one, are it.
So to one neutral thing both sexes fit,°
    We die and rise the same, and prove
    Mysterious by this love.

We can die by it, if not live by love,
    And if unfit for tombs and hearse
30   Our legend be, it will be fit for verse;
    And if no piece of chronicle° we prove,
        We'll build in sonnets° pretty rooms;
        As well a well-wrought urn° becomes
The greatest ashes, as half-acre tombs,°
    And by these hymns, all shall approve°
    Us canonized for love:

And thus invoke us;° 'You whom reverend love
    Made one another's hermitage;
You, to whom love was peace, that now° is rage;
40   Who did the whole world's soul contract, and drove
        Into the glasses of your eyes
        (So made such mirrors, and such spies,
That they did all to you epitomize),
    Countries, towns, courts:° beg from above°
    A pattern° of your love!'
                1633

Lovers' Infiniteness°

If yet I have not all thy love,
Dear, I shall never have it all,
I cannot breathe one other sigh, to move,
Nor can entreat one other tear to fall.
All my treasure, which should purchase thee,

fly . . . tapers too not only moths but flames
die with the common double meaning: have orgasm
Eagle . . . Dove the predatory and the meek
Phoenix riddle The Phoenix was reborn out of its own ashes, not by sex, and so contained in one individual the male and female principles; cf. Shakespeare, *The Phoenix and Turtle*, above.
So . . . fit in such measure do both sexes meet in one neutral thing (that)
die and rise with secondary sexual sense
Mysterious worthy of reverence, like religious mysteries
chronicle history
sonnets love poems

urn . . . tombs taking the urn as the love lyric, the tomb as the chronicle of worldly achievement
approve allow
invoke us pray to them as saints
now in the world you have left
Who did . . . courts who reduced the entire animating principle of the world to yourselves, concentrated all society into your own eyes, which accordingly mirrored and epitomized it
beg from above pray on behalf (for)
pattern model
Lovers' Infiniteness the three-stage argument often found in Donne

Sighs, tears, and oaths, and letters I have spent,
Yet no more can be due to me,
Than at the bargain made was meant.
If then thy gift of love were partiàl,
10   That some to me, some should to others fall,
Dear, I shall never have thee all.

Or if then thou gavest me all,
All was but all, which thou hadst then;
But if in thy heart, since, there be or shall
New love created be, by other men,
Which have their stocks entire, and can in tears,
In sighs, in oaths, and letters outbid me,
This new love may beget new fears,
For, this love was not vowed by thee.
20   And yet it was, thy gift being general,
The ground, thy heart is mine; whatever shall
Grow there, dear, I should have it all.

Yet I would not have all yet,
He that hath all can have no more,
And since my love doth every day admit
New growth, thou shouldst have new rewards in store;
Thou canst not every day give me thy heart,
If thou canst give it, then thou never gav'st it:
Love's riddles° are, that though thy heart depart,
30   It stays at home, and thou with losing sav'st it:°
But we will have a way more liberal,
Than changing hearts, to join them, so we shall
Be one, and one another's all.

1633

Song°

Sweetest love, I do not go,
For weariness of thee,
Nor in hope the world can show
A fitter love for me;
But since that I
Must die at last, 'tis best,
To use my self in jest
Thus by feigned deaths to die.

Yesternight the sun went hence,
10   And yet is here today,
He hath no desire nor sense,

riddles paradoxes. They are adapted from Matthew 16:25: ". . . whosoever will save his life
shall lose it."

Song Like several other Donne poems, this one
exists in a contemporary musical setting.

Nor half so short a way:
　　Then fear not me,
But believe that I shall make
Speedier journeys, since I take
　　More wings and spurs than he.

O how feeble is man's power,
　　That if good fortune fall,
Cannot add another hour,
20　　Nor a lost hour recall!
　　　But come bad chance,
And we join to it our strength,
And we teach it art and length,
　　Itself o'er us to advance.°

When thou sigh'st, thou sigh'st not wind,
　　But sigh'st my soul away,
When thou weep'st, unkindly kind,
　　My life's blood doth decay.
　　　It cannot be
30 That thou lov'st me, as thou say'st,
If in thine my life thou waste,
　　Thou art the best of me.°

Let not thy divining° heart
　　Forethink me any ill,
Destiny may take thy part,
　　And may thy fears fulfil;
　　　But think that we
Are but turned aside to sleep;
They who one another keep
40　　Alive, ne'er parted be.
　　　　　1633

A Fever°

Oh do not die, for I shall hate
　　All women so when thou art gone,
That thee I shall not celebrate
　　When I remember, thou wast one.

But yet thou canst not die, I know,
　　To leave this world behind, is death;
But when thou from this world wilt go,
　　The whole world vapours with thy breath.

But come . . . advance but if bad luck comes we lend it our strength, and teach it how to torment us protractedly, so that it triumphs over us
the best of me in expending her soul in sighs and tears she is wasting him, since she is his life
divining prophetic, foreseeing
A Fever The basic conceit—that the death of a mistress destroys the world—is Petrarchan.

Or if, when thou, the world's soul,° go'st,
10   It stay, 'tis but thy carcase then,
The fairest woman, but thy ghost,
But corrupt worms, the worthiest men.

Oh wrangling schools, that search what fire
Shall burn this world,° had none the wit
Unto this knowledge to aspire,
That this her fever might be it?

And yet she cannot waste by this,
Nor long bear this torturing wrong,
For much corruption needful is
20   To fuel such a fever long.°

These burning fits but meteors be,
Whose matter in thee is soon spent.
Thy beauty, and all parts, which are thee,
Are unchangeable firmament.°

Yet 'twas of my mind, seizing thee,
Though it in thee cannot perséver.°
For I had rather owner be
Of thee one hour, than all else ever.

1633

Air and Angels°

Twice or thrice had I loved thee,
Before I knew thy face or name;
So in a voice, so in a shapeless flame,
Angels affect us oft, and worshipped be;
    Still° when, to where thou wert, I came,
Some lovely glorious nothing° I did see,
    But since my soul, whose child love is,
Takes limbs of flesh, and else could nothing do,°
    More subtle° than the parent is
10   Love must not be, but take a body too,
    And therefore what thou wert, and who

---

world's soul ani̇ma mundi, a Platonic concept
what fire . . . world The Stoics, and later the
Schoolmen, disputed the nature of the final conflagration.
much . . . long The heat of fevers was thought
to proceed from corruption caused by conflict
between elements in the body.
These burning . . . firmament Meteors were
thought to be exhaled from the earth and
consumed in the sphere of fire (cf. *Dr. Faustus*
vi.61n.); their corruptibility is contrasted with
the incorruptibility of the heavens.
seizing taking possession of (legal)
perséver persist
Air and Angels The argument of the poem de-

pends on the difference of purity between air
and angels: air, the purest form of matter, cannot be quite as pure as angels, which are spirit.
One of Donne's most difficult poems.
Still always
some . . . nothing He saw her as he might an
angel, without the specific form angels take on
when, to be visible to those they visit, they
wear a "body of air"; the point is that his
first love for her lacked this physical or material
element.
could nothing do Cf. end of "The Ecstasy"; the
soul acts through the senses.
subtle ethereal

I bid love ask, and now
That it assume thy body, I allow,
And fix itself in thy lip, eye, and brow.

Whilst thus to ballast love I thought,
And so more steadily to have gone,
With wares which would sink admiration,
I saw, I had love's pinnace° overfraught,
Every thy hair for love to work upon
20 Is much too much, some fitter must be sought;
For, nor° in nothing, nor in things
Extreme, and scatt'ring bright, can love inhere;
Then as an angel, face and wings
Of air, not pure as it, yet pure doth wear,
So thy love may be my love's sphere;°
Just such disparity
As is 'twixt air and angels' purity,
'Twixt women's love and men's will ever be.°
1633

The Anniversary

All kings, and all their favourites,
All glory of honours, beauties, wits
The sun itself, which makes times as they pass,
Is elder by a year now than it was
When thou and I first one another saw:
All other things to their destruction draw,
Only our love hath no decay;
This, no tomorrow hath, nor yesterday,
Running it never runs from us away,
10 But truly keeps his first, last, everlasting day.

Two graves must hide thine and my corse,
If one might, death were no divorce,
Alas, as well as other princes, we
(Who prince enough in one another be),
Must leave at last in death, these eyes, and ears,
Oft fed with true oaths, and with sweet salt tears;
But souls where nothing dwells but love
(All other thoughts being inmates°) then shall prove°
This, or a love increasèd there above,°
20 When bodies to their graves, souls from their graves remove.

pinnace small ship; now he has gone too far
in associating love with specific physical detail
nor neither
sphere in the relation of the planet (material)
to the angel-intelligence (spiritual) which informs and guides it
Just . . . ever be The compromise, whereby

love is not reduced to materiality—the woman's
way—nor left in an angelic shapelessness and
spirituality—men's way—is represented by the
angel wearing his body of air.
inmates lodgers
prove experience
above in heaven

And then we shall be throughly blessed,
   But we no more, than all the rest.°
Here upon earth, we are kings, and none but we
Can be such kings, nor of such subjects° be;
Who is so safe as we? where none can do
Treason to us, except one of us two.
   True and false fears let us refrain,
Let us love nobly, and live, and add again
Years and years unto years, till we attain
30 To write threescore; this is the second of our reign.

                                        1633

The Dream°

Dear love, for nothing less than thee
Would I have broke this happy dream,
      It was a theme
For reason, much too strong for phantasy,°
Therefore thou waked'st me wisely; yet
My dream thou brokest not, but continued'st it;
Thou art so truth,° that thoughts of thee suffice,
To make dreams truths, and fables histories;
Enter these arms, for since thou thought'st it best,
10 Not to dream all my dream, let's act the rest.

As lightning, or a taper's light,
Thine eyes, and not thy noise waked me;
      Yet I thought thee
(For thou lov'st truth) an angel, at first sight,
But when I saw thou saw'st my heart,
And knew'st my thoughts, beyond an angel's art,°
When thou knew'st what I dreamed, when thou knew'st when
Excess of joy would wake me, and cam'st then,
I must confess, it could not choose but be
20 Profane,° to think thee anything but thee.

Coming and staying showed thee, thee,
But rising makes me doubt, that now,
      Thou art not thou.
That love is weak, where fear's as strong as he;
'Tis not all spirit, pure, and brave,

---

no more . . . rest the doctrine that in heaven each is blessed with contentment according to his capacity
of such subjects subjects of such kings
The Dream based on the topic of the waking to find at one's bedside a mistress of whom one has been dreaming; as old as Ovid, but here newly handled
too strong . . . phantasy The fantasy or im-agination continues to produce images in sleep, when the reason cannot process them.
truth so absolutely the truth itself (many editions read *true*)
knew'st . . . art not even angels, but only God himself, can read one's inmost thoughts
Profane with a hint that she is more God than angel

If mixture it of fear, shame, honour,° have.
Perchance as torches which must ready be,
Men light and put out,° so thou deal'st with me,
Thou cam'st to kindle, goest to come;° then I
30 Will dream that hope again, but else would die.

                                        1633

A Valediction: Of Weeping

          Let me pour forth
My tears before thy face, whilst I stay here,°
For thy face coins them,° and thy stamp they bear,
And by this mintage they are something worth,
          For thus they be
          Pregnant of thee;
Fruits of much grief they are, emblems° of more,
When a tear falls, that thou° falls which it bore,
So thou and I are nothing then, when on a divers shore.°

10   On a round ball
A workman that hath copies by, can lay
An Europe, Afric, and an Asia,
And quickly make that, which was nothing, all,°
          So doth each tear,
          Which thee doth wear,
A globe, yea world by that impression grow,
Till thy tears mixed with mine do overflow
This world, by waters sent from thee, my heaven dissolvèd so.°

          O more than moon,°
20 Draw not up seas to drown me in thy sphere,
Weep me not dead, in thine arms, but forbear
To teach the sea, what it may do too soon;
          Let not the wind
          Example find,
To do me more harm, than it purposeth;
Since thou and I sigh one another's breath,
Whoe'er sighs most, is cruellest, and hastes the other's death.

                                        1633

honour as usual in Donne, the enemy of love
torches . . . put out A torch that has been
burning ignites more easily.
come come back
whilst I stay here while I'm still with you
coins them Each tear, bearing her reflected
image, is like a coin.
emblems prophetic images (the next lines explain why)
that thou that image of you
on a divers shore in different countries
nothing, all By pasting maps of the countries of

the world on a blank globe he is converting
nothing (the zero of the globe) into everything
(the world).
Till . . . dissolved so Their tears combine to
form a flood and inundate the world of the
tear—it is a world because it bears her image.
She is his heaven, which dissolves as the sky did
for the Flood.
more than moon She is more powerful than the
moon and should not raise a tide that would
drown him.

Love's Alchemy°

Some that have deeper digged love's mine than I,
Say, where his centric happiness doth lie:
    I have loved, and got,° and told,°
But should I love, get, tell, till I were old,
I should not find that hidden mystery;
    Oh, 'tis imposture all:
And as no chemic yet the elixir got,
    But glorifies his pregnant pot,
    If by the way to him befall
10 Some odoriferous thing, or medicinal,°
    So, lovers dream a rich and long delight,
    But get a winter-seeming summer's night.

Our ease, our thrift, our honour, and our day,°
Shall we, for this vain bubble's shadow pay?
    Ends love in this, that my man,°
Can be as happy as I can; if he can
Endure the short scorn of a bridegroom's play?
    That loving wretch that swears,
'Tis not the bodies marry, but the minds,
20   Which he in her angelic finds,
    Would swear as justly, that he hears,
In that day's° rude hoarse minstrelsy, the spheres.°
Hope not for mind in women; at their best
    Sweetness and wit, they are but mummy, possessed.°

                   1633

The Flea°

Mark but this flea, and mark in this,
How little that which thou deny'st me is;
Me it sucked first, and now sucks thee,
And in this flea, our two bloods mingled be;
Confess it, this cannot be said°

Love's Alchemy entitled *Mummy* in many MSS
got acquired
told counted
no chemic . . . medicinal No alchemist ever
achieved the quintessence, but all the same
praises his fertile retort if, along the way, he
makes a chance discovery, of a perfume or a
medicine (a common remark about alchemists).
winter-seeming . . . night at once short and
cold
our day our life wasted day by day in sexual
acts
man servant
short scorn brief indignity
that day's the wedding day's
the spheres music of the spheres (see Glossary)

mummy, possessed like a dead body (from
which the soul has departed) occupied by a
demon; i.e. even when they seem to have wit,
they are only well-preserved flesh with substitute (and devilish) minds
The Flea an ancient theme for ribald love-
poems, dating back to Ovid (cf. *Dr. Faustus*
vi.111n.); but Donne's treatment, making the
flea a symbol of the desired union of his and his
mistress's blood, is original. The action of the
poem is in three stages: first, the poet draws a
moral from the flea; second, the woman proposes to kill it; third, she has done so. He makes
the maximum capital out of each stage by
fertility of argument.
said called

A sin, or shame, or loss of maidenhead,
   Yet this enjoys before it woo,
   And pampered swells with one blood made of two,
   And this, alas, is more than we would do.°

10   Oh stay, three lives in one flea spare,
Where we almost, nay more than married are.
This flea is you and I, and this
Our marriage bed, and marriage temple is;
Though parents grudge, and you, we are met,
And cloistered in these living walls of jet.
   Though use° make you apt to kill me,
   Let not to this, self murder added be,
   And sacrilege, three sins° in killing three.

Cruel and sudden, hast thou since
20   Purpled thy nail, in blood of innocence?
In what could this flea guilty be,
Except in that drop which it sucked from thee?
Yet thou triumph'st, and say'st that thou
Find'st not thyself, nor me the weaker now;
   'Tis true, then learn how false, fears be;
   Just so much honour, when thou yield'st to me,
   Will waste, as this flea's death took life from thee.

                         1633

A Nocturnal upon S. Lucy's Day,
Being the Shortest Day°

'Tis the year's midnight, and it is the day's,
Lucy's, who scarce seven hours herself unmasks,
   The sun is spent, and now his flasks°
   Send forth light squibs,° no constant rays;
     The world's whole sap is sunk:
The general balm° the hydroptic° earth hath drunk,
Whither, as to the bed's-feet,° life is shrunk,
Dead and interred; yet all these seem to laugh,
Compared with me, who am their epitaph.

10   Study me then, you who shall lovers be
At the next world, that is, at the next spring:°

more . . . do They don't want an ensuing pregnancy.
use habit
three sins murder, suicide, sacrilege
A Nocturnal upon S. Lucy's Day . . . December 13, then the shortest day of the year, the winter solstice, when the sun entered the sign of the Goat (Capricorn). The Gregorian calendar was not adopted in England till 1752, by which eleven days were added to the date. St. Lucy's festival is celebrated with lights, and candles.

flasks The stars were thought to store up the sun's light as flasks store gunpowder.
light squibs weak flashes
sap . . . balm preservative essences of living things
hydroptic pathologically thirsty
bed's-feet A patient huddling at the foot of the bed was thought to be near death.
world . . . spring spring as *renovatio mundi*, rebirth of the world

For I am every dead thing,
In whom love wrought new alchemy.°
    For his art did express°
A quintessence° even from nothingness,°
From dull privations, and lean emptiness;
He ruined me,° and I am re-begot
Of absence, darkness, death;° things which are not.

All° others, from all° things, draw all° that's good,
20 Life, soul, form, spirit, whence they being have;
    I, by love's limbeck,° am the grave
    Of all,° that's nothing.° Oft a flood
        Have we two wept, and so
Drowned the whole world, us two;° oft did we grow
To be two chaoses, when we did show
Care to aught else;° and often absences
Withdrew our souls; and made us carcases.

But I am by her death (which word wrongs her)
Of the first nothing, the elixir grown;°
30   Were I a man, that I were one,
    I needs must know; I should prefer,
        If I were any beast,
Some ends, some means; yea plants, yea stones detest,
And love,° all, all some properties invest;°
If I an ordinary nothing were,
As° shadow, a light, and body must be here.

But I am none;° nor will my sun° renew.
You lovers, for whose sake, the lesser sun°
    At this time to the Goat is run
40   To fetch new lust,° and give it you,
        Enjoy your summer all;
Since she enjoys her long night's festival,°

new alchemy which, unlike the old, is concerned with the principle of deadness rather than the principle of life
express distill, extract (alchemical)
quintessence elixir, principle
from nothingness unlike "old" alchemy, which dealt with allness
He ruined me he broke down my substance (alchemical)
I am . . . death I am reconstituted by the forms of nothingness ("re-begot" is alchemical)
limbeck alembic, the distilling flask used by alchemists
All . . . nothing the basic conceit of the poem
Oft a flood . . . us two By weeping they have drowned the images of each other in their eyes (see "Valediction: Of Weeping" above); "flood" is another alchemical term.
show . . . else concerned ourselves about matters external to us, so causing our souls which having given form to our material bodies, to vacate them, leaving them chaoses
Of the first . . . grown become the quintessence not of chaos but of the primal nothing which preceded the institution of chaos (matter without form) by God
Were I . . . love If I were a man I should know it, because men have a rational soul; if a beast, I should have a sensitive soul, and make certain choices; if a plant, with only a vegetative soul, I could choose nutriment. Even (magnetic) stones, with no souls at all, attract and repel.
all . . . invest everything else is endowed with *some* properties
As such as
none nonce usage to suggest absolute nothingness
my sun his lady
lesser sun the sun
to the Goat . . . lust to the sign of Capricorn to bring back lust, always associated with the goat
long night's festival dark sleep of death, which this, the longest night of the year, fittingly commemorates

Let me prepare towards her,° and let me call
This hour her vigil, and her eve, since this
Both the year's, and the day's deep midnight is.

1633

The Bait

Come live with me, and be my love,
And we will some new pleasures prove
Of golden sands, and crystal brooks,
With silken lines, and silver hooks.

There will the river whispering run
Warmed by thy eyes, more than the sun.
And there th'enamoured fish will stay,
Begging themselves they may betray.

When thou wilt swim in that live bath,
10   Each fish, which every channel hath,
Will amorously to thee swim,
Gladder to catch thee, than thou him.

If thou, to be so seen, be'st loth,
By sun, or moon, thou darkenest both,
And if myself have leave to see,
I need not their light, having thee.

Let others freeze with angling reeds,
And cut their legs, with shells and weeds,
Or treacherously poor fish beset,
20   With strangling snare, or windowy net:

Let coarse bold hands, from slimy nest
The bedded fish in banks out-wrest,
Or curious traitors, sleavesilk flies°
Bewitch poor fishes' wandering eyes.

For thee, thou need'st no such deceit,
For thou thyself art thine own bait,
That fish, that is not catched thereby,
Alas, is wiser far than I.

1633

prepare towards her fit myself by meditation
for her feast
vigil service the night before a festival
The Bait A reply—by no means the first—to
Marlowe's *The Passionate Shepherd to His Love*
(cf. Ralegh's *Reply*). Walton quotes all three
in *The Compleat Angler,* Donne's being of
course especially appropriate; Walton thought
it showed Donne "could make soft and smooth
verses when he thought fit." It is also a
piscatory pastoral, substituting the world of
the fisherman for that of the shepherd.
sleavesilk flies artificial flies made of silk thread
separable into finer filaments

The Apparition

When by thy scorn,° O murderess, I am dead,
And that thou think'st thee free
From all solicitation from me,
Then shall my ghost come to thy bed,
And thee, feigned vestal,° in worse arms shall see;
Then thy sick taper will begin to wink,
And he whose thou art then, being tired before,
Will, if thou stir, or pinch to wake him, think
     Thou call'st for more,
10 And in false sleep will from thee shrink,
And then poor aspen° wretch, neglected thou
Bathed in a cold quicksilver sweat wilt lie
     A verier ghost than I;
What I will say, I will not tell thee now,
Lest that preserve thee; and since my love is spent,
I had rather thou shouldst painfully repent,
Than by my threatenings rest still innocent.

                       1633

A Valediction: Forbidding Mourning

As virtuous men pass mildly away,
   And whisper to their souls, to go,
Whilst some of their sad friends do say,
   The breath goes now, and some say, no:

So let us melt, and make no noise,
   No tear-floods, nor sigh-tempests move,
'Twere profanation of our joys
   To tell the laity our love.

Moving of th' earth° brings harms and fears,
10   Men reckon what it did and meant,
But trepidation of the spheres,°
   Though greater far, is innocent.°

Dull súblunary° lovers' love
   (Whose soul is sense°) cannot admit
Absence, because it doth remove
   Those things which elemented° it.

---

by thy scorn Donne takes up the Petrarchan theme of the lover dying of his mistress's scorn but gives it new dramatic force.
vesta holy virgin
aspen trembling (like a poplar leaf in the wind)
Moving of th'earth earthquakes
trepidation of the spheres libration of the ninth or crystalline sphere, which accounted for the precession of the equinoxes
innocent does no harm
sublunary below the moon, therefore more corrupt than the heavens
Whose soul is sense not mind; it therefore requires contact
elemented composed

But we by a love, so much refined,
   That our selves know not what it is,
Inter-assurèd of the mind,
20   Care less, eyes, lips, and hands to miss.

Our two souls therefore, which are one,
   Though I must go, endure not yet
A breach, but an expansion,
   Like gold to aery thinness beat.

If they be two, they are two so
   As stiff twin compasses° are two,
Thy soul the fixed foot, makes no show
   To move, but doth, if th'other do.

And though it in the centre sit,
30   Yet when the other far doth roam,
It leans, and hearkens after it,
   And grows erect, as that comes home.

Such wilt thou be to me, who must
   Like the other foot, obliquely run;
Thy firmness makes my circle just,
   And makes me end, where I begun.°
           1633

The Ecstasy°

Where, like a pillow on a bed,
   A pregnant bank swelled up, to rest
The violet's reclining head,°
   Sat we two, one another's best;

Our hands were firmly cemented
   With a fast balm, which thence did spring,°
Our eye-beams twisted, and did thread
   Our eyes, upon one double string;°

compasses a familiar emblem, denoting constancy in change
end . . . begun complete circle
The Ecstasy The title means "standing outside," as the souls here are represented as doing; long periods of this were thought inadvisable, though the experience offered unmediated knowledge of divine truth. The argument concerns the power of the ecstatic joint soul of the lovers to know the truth about love when outside their bodies, but the man urges a return to the physical. Opinion is divided about the full tone and sense of the poem: to some it is a central statement of the poet's love-metaphysic, and deeply serious; to others it is an example of what Dryden called his power to "perplex the minds of the fair sex with the nice speculations of philosophy." At one extreme is the reading which takes the last line as referring merely to the return of the souls to the inanimate bodies; at the other, the view that the whole poem is a fantastic seduction. In fact the opinion that the last line connotes sexual activity does not imply cynicism, and there is no good reason not to treat the poem as both serious *and* persuasive to love. See also William Cartwright's "No Platonic Love."
Where . . . head a traditional, though quickly sketched, *locus amoenus:* setting for pastoral or garden love-making or love-talk
Our . . . spring sweat; a moist palm was an index of sexual desire
Our . . . string The light-rays, thought of as emerging from the eyes, twist together so that the eyes are like beads on a string.

So to intergraft° our hands, as yet
10   Was all our means to make us one,
And pictures in our eyes to get°
    Was all our propagatiòn.°

As 'twixt two equal armies, Fate
    Suspends uncertain victory,°
Our souls, (which to advance their state,°
    Were gone out), hung 'twixt her, and me.

And whilst our souls negotiate° there,
    We like sepulchral statues lay;
All day, the same our postures were,
20   And we said nothing, all the day.

If any, so by love refined,
    That he soul's language understood,
And by good love were grown all mind,
    Within convenient distance stood,

He (though he knew not which soul spake
    Because both meant, both spake the same)
Might thence a new concoction° take,
    And part far purer than he came.

This ecstasy doth unperplex
30   (We said) and tell us what we love,°
We see by this, it was not sex,
    We see we saw not what did move:°

But as all several° souls contain
    Mixture of things, they know not what,°
Love, these mixed souls doth mix again,
    And makes both one, each this and that.°

A single violet transplant,
    The strength, the colour, and the size,
(All which before was poor, and scant,)
40   Redoubles still, and multiplies.°

When love, with one another so
    Interinanimates two souls,

intergraft graft one on the other; grafting—cf. Marvell, "Mower against Gardens"—was a sexual figure
pictures . . . get The reflection of one's face in an eye into which one is gazing was sometimes called a baby—hence get = beget.
propagatiòn five syllables
'twixt . . . victory The uncertainty of the outcome of a battle is represented by an image of Victory hanging between them.
state dignity
negotiate as in a parley before battle
concoction purification of metals by heat, of the physique by refinement of the animal spirits; see below

what we love the true object of their love
what did move what the true motive was
several distinct
Mixture . . . what the functions of the soul being both physical and spiritual, it must be of compounded nature which we cannot know exactly
Love . . . that The new single soul, made up of two, is also mixed, but has advantages explained later: that the two souls of lovers become one is a Platonic commonplace.
A single . . . multiplies either the violet propagates itself on transplantation, or grows richer double flowers

That abler soul, which thence doth flow,
    Defects of loneliness controls.°

We then, who are this new soul, know,
    Of what we are composed, and made,
For, th'atomies° of which we grow,
    Are souls, whom no change can invade.°

But O alas, so long, so far
50   Our bodies why do we forbear?
They are ours, though they are not we, we are
    The intelligences, they the sphere.°

We owe them thanks, because they thus,
    Did us, to us, at first convey,
Yielded their forces, sense,° to us,
    Nor are dross to us, but allay.°

On man heaven's influence works not so,
    But that it first imprints the air,°
So soul into the soul may flow,
60   Though it to body first repair.

As our blood labours to beget
    Spirits, as like souls as it can,°
Because such fingers need° to knit
    That subtle° knot, which makes us man:

So must pure lovers' souls descend
    T'affections,° and to faculties,°
Which sense may reach and apprehend,°
    Else a great prince in prison lies.°

To our bodies turn we then, that so
70   Weak men on love revealed may look;°
Love's mysteries in souls do grow,
    But yet the body is his book.°

And if some lover, such as we,
    Have heard this dialogue of one,

Defects . . . controls overcomes the imperfections of separateness
atomies components
Are . . . invade Unlike the body, the soul is not subject to change; this completes the argument for the advantages of pure soul-union, and there is now a sharp turn in the poem.
we are . . . sphere Souls are to bodies as the angel-intelligence-spirit is to the planet—matter—it controls; cf. "Air and Angels" above.
forces, sense They have given up their power of movement to enable the souls to experience non-physical union.
dross . . . allay not the waste left over after metallurgical refinement but that which, in an alloy, makes the gold serviceable
heaven's . . . air The influence of the stars on men was held to occur through the medium of air; and angels (cf. "Air and Angels") took a

body of air, "not pure as it," when appearing to men.
Spirits . . . can The animal spirits, "concocted" or refined from the blood, serve as a medium between matter and spirit, body and soul.
need are needed
subtle fine, impalpable
affections feelings, passions
faculties power of the body
Which . . . apprehend with which sense has contact and relation
Else . . . lies otherwise the new soul is impotent, has no agents
weak . . . look As the truths of religions accommodate themselves to weak men through revelation, so physical activity will make evident a love which otherwise would not be so.
body is his book as the Bible makes evident the truths of religion

Let him still mark us, he shall see
    Small change, when we are to bodies gone.°

                                    1633

The Funeral

Whoever comes to shroud me, do not harm
        Nor question much
That subtle wreath of hair, which crowns my arm;
The mystery, the sign you must not touch,
        For 'tis my outward soul,
Viceroy to that, which then to heaven being gone,
        Will leave this to control,
And keep these limbs, her° provinces, from dissolution.

For if the sinewy thread° my brain lets fall
10   Through every part,
Can tie those parts, and make me one of all;°
These hairs which upward grew, and strength and art
        Have from a better brain,
Can better do it; except° she meant that I
        By this should know my pain,
As prisoners then are manacled, when they're condemned to die.

Whate'er she meant by it, bury it with me,
        For since I am
Love's martyr, it might breed idolatry,
20   If into others' hands these relics came;
        As 'twas humility
To afford to it all that a soul can do,°
        So, 'tis some bravery,°
That since you would save none of me, I bury some of you.

                                    1633

Farewell to Love°

        Whilst yet to prove,°
I thought there was some deity in love
    So did I reverence, and gave
Worship; as atheists at their dying hour
Call, what they cannot name, an unknown power,

some lover . . . gone The refined lover of line
21 will see that there is little difference between
our loving before and after we used our bodies.
her the soul's
sinewy thread the nerves by which the brain
transmits messages to the body
make . . . all unite my several parts into a
whole person
except unless

To afford . . . do to credit it with the powers
of a soul
bravery bravado
Farewell to Love Not positively ascribed to
Donne in the 1633 edition; it is probably by
him but may represent a draft rather than a
finished poem.
Whilst . . . prove while still inexperienced

As ignorantly did I crave:
    Thus when
Things not yet known are coveted by men,
  Our desires give them fashion,° and so
10 As they wax lesser, fall, as they size, grow.°

    But, from late° fair
His highness sitting in a golden chair,°
  Is not less cared for after three days
By children, than the thing° which lovers so
Blindly admire, and with such worship woo;
    Being had, enjoying it decays:°
      And thence,
What before pleased them all, takes but one sense,°
  And that so lamely, as it leaves behind
20 A kind of sorrowing dullness to the mind.°

    Ah cannot we,
As well as cocks and lions° jocund be,
  After such pleasures? Unless wise
Nature decreed (since each such act, they say,
Diminisheth the length of life a day)
    This; as she would man should despise
      The sport,
Because that other curse of being short,
  And only for a minute made to be
30 Eager, desires to raise posterity.°

    Since so,° my mind
Shall not desire what no man else can find,
  I'll no more dote and run
To pursue things which had endamaged me.
And when I come where moving beauties° be,
  As men do when the summer's sun
    Grows great,
Though I admire their greatness, shun their heat;
  Each place can afford shadows. If all fail,
40 'Tis but applying worm-seed° to the tail.°

            1633

Our . . . fashion we imagine them to accord with our wishes
As . . . grow they decline as our desire reduces, grow as our desire expands
late some recent
His highness . . . chair gingerbread effigy of a prince sold to children at a fair
the thing sex
Being . . . decays once had, the enjoyment of it wanes
What . . . sense what formerly pleased all the senses now captivates only one (touch)
A kind . . . mind referring to the saying "omne animal post coitum triste" (all animals are sad after sex)
cocks and lions The medical authority Galen

exempts these animals from the general rule.
Unless . . . posterity perhaps the most difficult passage in Donne, and possibly corrupt—"unless nature, because every act of sex is said to reduce one's life by a day, wisely arranged that men should feel contemptuous of sex when the act is over; since its other disadvantage (its brevity) would otherwise lead us to do it too often." Here "desires to raise posterity" is taken to mean "wants the act to beget other successive acts."
so it is so
moving beauties beauties who rouse my desire
worm-seed an anaphrodisiac
tail penis

The Relic°

When my grave is broke up again
Some second guest to entertain,
(For graves have learned that woman-head°
To be to more than one a bed)
        And he that digs it, spies
A bracelet of bright hair about the bone,
        Will he not let us alone,
And think that there a loving couple lies,
Who thought that this device might be some way
To make their souls, at the last busy day,°
Meet at this grave, and make a little stay?

If this fall° in a time, or land,
Where mis-devotion° doth command,
Then, he that digs us up, will bring
Us, to the Bishop, and the King,
        To make us relics; then
Thou shalt be a Mary Magdalen,° and I
        A something else° thereby;
All women shall adore us, and some men;
And since at such time, miracles are sought,
I would have that age by this paper° taught
What miracles we harmless lovers wrought.

First, we loved well and faithfully,
Yet knew not what we loved, nor why,
Difference of sex no more we knew,
Than our guardian angels° do;
        Coming and going,° we
Perchance might kiss, but not between those meals;
        Our hands ne'er touched the seals,
Which nature, injured by late law, sets free:°
These miracles we did; but now alas,
All measure, and all language, I should pass,
Should I tell what a miracle she was.

                1633

10   (line number)
20   (line number)
30   (line number)

The Relic Cf. "The Funeral"; the situation is the same, but at a somewhat later time.
woman-head woman-like behavior
last busy day the Resurrection
this fall the digging up of my body should happen
mis-devotion false religious practices, such as the use of relics
a Mary Magdalen in art represented as having golden hair, and in her youth could have given lovers such tokens

a something else contemptuous for Mary's lover; or, scandalously, "Jesus Christ," represented in that role
this paper this poem
guardian angels having no sexuality
Coming and going arriving and departing
seals . . . free prohibitions on sexual conduct which do not exist in nature, but which law and custom have, at a later time of the world, imposed

544

Satire III

Donne wrote five satires in the 1590's, a time when they were greatly in vogue (publication of satire was inhibited in 1598). Partly because of a mistaken etymology which related satire to *Satyr*, the Elizabethan practitioners affected a very rough style, harsh and "snarling," as appropriate to an uncouth natural speaker commenting on the evil sophistication of city life. Hence the violently misplaced accents, hypermetric syllables, and forced rhymes, not to speak of the farfetched images and emphasis on vice and ugliness, of Donne's satires. The ancient model was Horace, whose satires are colloquial in manner and have similar themes, but are not, in this sense, "harsh."

The third Satire is unlike the others, not in manner but in theme. It concerns the necessity for choosing a religion, a necessity nonetheless paramount because the decision is not one to be made hastily. This was Donne's own position as a young man; he said he "used no inordinate haste, nor precipitation, in binding my conscience to any local religion" (*Pseudo-Martyr*), but nevertheless regarded the choice as of great urgency. He seems to have regarded himself as Protestant from about the turn of the century; this poem probably belongs to 1595. It is unique in the impassioned immediacy of its religious argument; it is part satiric railing against men's unwillingness to give priority to their most urgent concerns, part sarcasm at the expense of contemporary religious follies, and partly virile exhortation. Above all it considers, in the very voice of urgent meditation, the harsh and solemn necessity of choice imposed upon the serious Christian in an age when doctrinal differences were reflected in political power-struggles. It reminds us that the poet of the Elegies was, at the same time, profoundly concerned to use his mind and poetic powers on what seemed to him the greatest single issue, that of the true religion.

Satire III

Kind pity chokes my spleen;° brave scorn° forbids
Those tears to issue which swell my eye-lids,
I must not laugh, nor weep sins, and be wise;°
Can railing° then cure these worn° maladies?
Is not our mistress fair religion,
As worthy of all our soul's devotion,
As virtue was to the first blinded age?°
Are not heaven's joys as valiant to assuage
Lusts, as earth's honour° was to them? Alas,
10 As we do them in means, shall they surpass
Us in the end, and shall thy father's spirit
Meet blind philosophers in heaven, whose merit

---

spleen the source of scornful laughter
brave scorn the flaunting scorn of the satirist
I must . . . wise If I'm to be wise I mustn't, it seems, either laugh about sins or weep over them
railing ranting, shouting down
worn hackneyed

first blinded age Before Christ the philosophers, denied the light of revelation, worshipped virtue; we should surely think as well of religion as they did of virtue.
earth's honour which was all they had, whereas we have the bliss of heaven

Of strict life may be imputed faith,° and hear
Thee, whom he taught so easy ways and near
To follow, damned? O if thou dar'st, fear this;
This fear great courage, and high valour is.
Dar'st thou aid mutinous Dutch,° and dar'st thou lay
Thee in ships' wooden sepulchres, a prey
To leaders' rage, to storms, to shot, to dearth?
20 Dar'st thou dive seas, and dungeons° of the earth?
Hast thou courageous fire to thaw the ice
Of frozen north discoveries?° and thrice
Colder than salamanders,° like divine
Children in th'oven,° fires of Spain, and the line,°
Whose countries limbecks° to our bodies be,
Canst thou for gain bear? and must every he
Which cries not, 'Goddess!' to thy mistress, draw,
Or eat thy poisonous words? courage of straw!
O desperate coward, wilt thou seem bold, and
30 To thy foes and his° (who made thee to stand
Sentinel in his world's garrison) thus yield,
And for forbidden wars, leave th'appointed field?
Know thy foes: the foul Devil, he, whom thou
Strivest to please, for hate, not love, would allow
Thee fain, his whole realm to be quit;° and as
The world's all parts wither away and pass,
So the world's self, thy other loved foe, is
In her decrepit wane,° and thou loving this,
Doest love a withered and worn strumpet; last,
40 Flesh (itself's death)° and joys which flesh can taste,
Thou lovest; and thy fair goodly soul, which doth
Give this flesh power to taste joy, thou dost loathe.
    Seek true religion. O where? Mirreus°
Thinking her unhoused here, and fled from us,
Seeks her at Rome, there, because he doth know
That she was there a thousand years ago,
He loves her rags° so, as we here obey
The statecloth where the Prince sate yesterday.°
Crants° to such brave° loves will not be enthralled,

blind . . . faith though not justified by faith,
since they lived before Christ, they may be in
heaven because their pagan virtues qualify
them—are imputed to them as faith
mutinous Dutch The Dutch resisted their Spanish overlords, and the English sometimes assisted
them.
dungeon mines, caves
frozen . . . discoveries attempts to find a northwest passage to the Pacific
salamanders lizards supposed to live in fire
divine . . . oven Shadrach, Meshach, and Abed-
nego, who survived the ordeal of the fiery
furnace into which Nebuchadnezzar cast them
fires . . . line the Inquisition and tropical heat
limbecks alchemical stills

his God's
the foul . . . quit Satan, whom you try to
please, would willingly grant you his whole
kingdom, but for hate, not love
decrepit wane Donne often recurs to the view
that the world is declining into its last age.
(itself's death) the sins of the flesh bring
about its destruction
Mirreus the Romanist; perhaps latinized from
"Mreo," anagram of "Rome"
rags ceremonial survivals
statecloth . . . yesterday the canopy over the
chair of state; the throne was reverenced even
in the monarch's absence
Crants Calvinist
brave showy

50   But loves her only, who at Geneva° is called
      Religìon, plain, simple, sullen, young,
      Contemptuous, yet unhandsome; as among
      Lecherous humours,° there is one that judges
      No wenches wholesome, but coarse country drudges.
      Graius° stays still at home here, and because
      Some preachers, vile ambitious bawds,° and laws
      Still new like fashions,° bid him think that she
      Which dwells with us, is only° perfect, he
      Embraceth her, whom his godfathers will
60   Tender to him, being tender,° as wards still
      Take such wives as their guardians offer, or
      Pay values.° Careless Phrygius° doth abhor
      All, because all cannot be good, as one
      Knowing some women whores, dares marry none.
      Gracchus° loves all as one, and thinks that so
      As women do in divers countries go
      In divers habits, yet are still one kind,
      So does, so is religion; and this blind-
      ness too much light breeds;° but unmovèd thou
70   Of force must one, and forced but one allow;
      And the right; ask thy father° which is she,
      Let him ask his; though truth and falsehood be
      Near twins, yet truth a little elder is;°
      Be busy to seek her, believe me this,
      He's not of none, nor worst, that seeks the best.°
      To adore, or scorn an image, or protest,°
      May all be bad; doubt wisely; in strange way°
      To stand inquiring right, is not to stray;
      To sleep, or run wrong is. On a huge hill,
80   Cragged, and steep, Truth stands, and he that will
      Reach her, about must, and about must go;
      And what the hill's suddenness resists, win so;°
      Yet strive so, that before age, death's twilight,
      Thy soul rest, for none can work in that night,°

Geneva center of Calvinism
lecherous humours men of lecherous tastes
Graius Greek; perhaps because the Greeks
worshipped "an unknown God"—Acts 17–23
—and sought novelty
ambitious bawds pimps seeking advancement
by selling their girl
Still . . . fashions always changing, like fashions (the variety of English laws aimed at
securing conformity)
only alone
Tender . . . tender offer to him in his infancy
Pay values Wards who refused the marriage
proposed for them by their guardians had to pay
a fine; so, under the Act of Uniformity of
1559, did people who refused to attend the
parish church.
Phrygius who turns against all religion

Gracchus named for the Roman Gracchi, who
were democrats; a liberal, unwisely tolerant
bindness . . . breeds too much light breeds this
blindness
ask thy father "Ask thy father and he will
show thee," Deuteronomy 32:7
a little elder is the need is to get back to the
facts of the true primitive church; heresy is
almost but not quite as old
He's . . . best he's not of no religion, nor of
the worst religion, who seeks the best religion
protest be Protestant
in strange way on an unfamilar road
And what . . . so thus achieve what the steep-
ness of the hill tries to prevent
that night "the night cometh, when no man can
work" (John 9:4)

To will implies delay, therefore now do.
Hard deeds, the body's pains; hard knowledge too
The mind's endeavours reach,° and mysteries
Are like the sun, dazzling, yet plain to all eyes.°
Keep the truth which thou hast found; men do not stand
90 In so ill case° here, that God hath with his hand
Signed king's blank-charters° to kill whom they hate,
Nor are they vicars,° but hangmen to Fate.
Fool and wretch, wilt thou let thy soul be tied
To man's laws, by which she shall not be tried
At the last day? Or will it then boot thee
To say a Philip,° or a Gregory,°
A Harry,° or a Martin° taught thee this?
Is not this excuse for mere° contraries,
Equally strong; cannot both sides say so?
100 That thou mayest rightly obey power, her bounds know;
Those past, her nature, and name is changed;° to be
Then humble to her is idolatry.
As streams are, power is; those blessed flowers that dwell
At the rough stream's calm head, thrive and prove well,
But having left their roots, and themselves given
To the stream's tyrannous rage, alas are driven
Through mills, and rocks, and woods, and at last, almost
Consumed in going, in the sea are lost:
So perish souls, which more choose men's unjust
Power from God claimed, than God himself to trust.

                                                    from MS. 1802

The Second Anniversary

Donne wrote two *Anniversaries* to commemorate the death at fourteen of Elizabeth
Drury in 1610. The girl's father, Sir Robert, was his benefactor, but he never met the
girl. These strange poems—Donne's longest, and interesting experiments in the prolongation during lengthy structured works of the fantastic conceited style of the
funeral elegy—were regarded at the time as excessive; Ben Jonson is reported as
saying that "Donne's Anniversary was profane and full of blasphemies; that he had
told Mr. Donne, if it had been written of the Virgin Mary it had been something; to
which he answered, that he described the Idea of a Woman, and not as she was."

    The poems, especially the second, use an elaborate system of linked formal medita-
tions. The first, *An Anatomy of the World,* treats the girl as the embodiment of all that

---

Hard deeds . . . reach as the labor of the
body achieves severe physical tasks, so that
of the mind achieves hard knowledge
mysteries . . . eyes the fact that we can never
comprehend them doesn't alter the fact that
they are visibly there
so ill case such an evil condition
blank-charters Richard II made wealthy men
sign promises to pay money to him, and to
leave the sum blank; here the idea is extended
to death warrants which could be filled in at
the whim of the ruler.

vicars deputies
Philip Philip II of Spain
Gregory Pope Gregory VII (who in the 11th
century established papal power over secular
rulers) or Gregory XIII or Gregory XIV (contemporary popes)
Harry Henry VIII
Martin Luther
mere absolute
nature . . . changed to tyranny

men forfeited at the Fall, and imagines the world as a corpse following the departure of its soul. The second, *The Progress of the Soul,* dwells on the advantages enjoyed by the soul after death by comparison with "the incommodities of the soul in this life." The extract is from a section dealing with a theme Donne often treated, the uselessness and partiality of earthly knowledge in comparison with the full knowledge of essentials that the soul will achieve in heaven.

From The Second Anniversary

Poor soul, in this thy flesh what dost thou know?
Thou know'st thyself so little, as thou know'st not,
How thou didst die, nor how thou wast begot.
Thou neither know'st, how thou at first cam'st in,
Nor how thou took'st the poison of man's sin.°
Nor dost thou, (though thou know'st, that thou art so)
260 By what way thou art made immortal, know.
Thou art too narrow, wretch, to comprehend
Even thyself; yea though thou wouldst but bend
To know thy body. Have not all souls thought
For many ages, that our body is wrought
Of air, and fire, and other elements?
And now they think of new ingredients,°
And one soul thinks one, and another way
Another thinks, and 'tis an even lay.
Know'st thou but how the stone doth enter in
270 The bladder's cave, and never break the skin?
Know'st thou how blood, which to the heart doth flow,
Doth from one ventricle to th'other go?°
And for the putrid stuff, which thou dost spit,
Know'st thou how thy lungs have attracted it?
There are no passages, so that there is
(For aught thou know'st) piercing of substances.°
And of those many opinions which men raise
Of nails and hairs,° dost thou know which to praise?
What hope have we to know our selves, when we
280 Know not the least things, which for our use be?
We see in authors, too stiff to recant,
A hundred controvèrsies of an ant;
And yet one watches, starves, freezes, and sweats,
To know but catechisms and alphabets
Of unconcerning° things, matters of fact;

how . . . sin whether from the parents or by direct infusion—an old controversy
new ingredients The old Galenist view was that earth, water, and fire were balanced in man; the Paracelsan novelty lay in making the constituents chemical, e.g. sulfur, mercury, etc.
blood . . . go Harvey's discoveries were published in 1628.

piercing of substances transmission of matter through solid resistances
opinions . . . hairs whether or no they were organic or waste matter
unconcerning trivial; a magnificent statement of the argument

How others on our stage their parts did act;
What Caesar did, yea, and what Cicero said.
Why grass is green, or why our blood is red,
Are mysteries which none have reached unto.
290   In this low form,° poor soul, what wilt thou do?
When wilt thou shake off this pedántery,
Of being taught by sense and fantasy?°
Thou look'st through spectacles; small things seem great
Below; but up unto the watch-tower get,
And see all things despoiled of fallacies:
Thou shalt not peep through lattices of eyes,
Nor hear through labyrinths of ears, nor learn
By circuit,° or collections° to discern.
In heaven thou straight know'st all, concerning it,°
And what concerns it not, shalt straight forget.

1612

The Holy Sonnets

It seems probable that all these sonnets, except for three in the Westmoreland manuscript, belong to about 1609–11, that is, before Donne's ordination. These other three are later: one on the death of his wife (1617), one on the defeat of the Protestants at the battle of the White Mountain in 1620, and one uncertain, but presumably late. Of the remaining sixteen, four are additional to the two sequences of six which appeared in the first edition of 1633. Their order in that edition is the correct one, as Dame Helen Gardner showed when she restored and justified it in her 1952 Oxford edition of Donne's *Divine Poems*.

The first six, here represented by II, IV, V, and VI, are meditations on the Last Judgment; the second six, of which only X is given here, meditate on the Atonement and on the love owed by man to God and to his neighbor, and plead the intervention of God in the subject's life. The Jesuit meditation, based on the prescriptions of St. Ignatius Loyola, was designed to involve all the powers of the soul, including the senses, in the contemplation of some religious object or moment—the subject's own deathbed, for example, or the Crucifixion or, as in IV, the Last Judgment. Donne adapts this form of meditation to an Italian sonnet form, usually with a clear break at the *volta*, after the eighth line, and a change of tone in the sestet, which is quieter and more reflective than the octave. It was admirably suited to his powers, providing for passionate and excited as well as for devotional language and rhythms.

II

Oh my black soul! now thou art summonèd
By sickness, death's herald, and champion;
Thou art like a pilgrim, which abroad hath done
Treason, and durst not turn° to whence he is fled,
Or like a thief, which till death's doom be read,

low form humble condition
sense and fantasy by the evidence of the senses as treated by the fancy or imagination, i.e. by fallible human instruments

circuit roundabout processes
collections inferences
it heaven
turn return

Wisheth himself deliverèd from prison;
But damned and haled to executiòn,
Wisheth that still he might be imprisonèd;
Yet grace, if thou repent, thou canst not lack;
10   But who shall give thee that grace to begin?°
Oh make thyself with holy mourning black,
And red with blushing, as thou art with sin;
Or wash thee in Christ's blood, which hath this might
That being red, it dyes red souls to white.

IV

At the round earth's imagined corners,° blow
Your trumpets, angels, and arise, arise
From death, you numberless infinities
Of souls, and to your scattered bodies go,
All whom the flood did, and fire shall o'erthrow,
All whom war, dearth, age, agues, tyrannies,
Despair, law, chance, hath slain, and you whose eyes
Shall behold God, and never taste death's woe.°
But° let them sleep, Lord, and me mourn a space,
10   For, if above all these, my sins abound,
'Tis late to ask abundance of thy grace,°
When we are there; here on this lowly ground,
Teach me how to repent; for that's as good
As if thou hadst sealed° my pardon, with thy blood.

V

If poisonous minerals, and if that tree,
Whose fruit threw death on else immortal us,
If lecherous goats, if serpents envious
Cannot be damned;° alas, why should I be?
Why should intent or reason, born in me,
Make sins, else equal, in me more heinous?
And mercy being easy, and glorious
To God, in his stern wrath, why threatens he?
But who am I,° that dare dispute with thee
10   O God? Oh! of thine only worthy blood,°
And my tears, make a heavenly lethean° flood,
And drown in it my sin's black memory;
That thou remember them, some claim as debt,°
I think it mercy, if thou wilt forget.

---

grace to begin prevenient grace, without which the repentance which gains further grace is impossible
imagined corners Revelation 7:1
never . . . woe I Corinthians 15:51–52
But the characteristic change of tone for the sestet
sins . . . grace Romans 6:1
sealed confirmed
If . . . be damned Only men, who have reason, can be damned; cf. *Dr. Faustus* XVIII. 171 ff.

But who am I Changing tone in sestet, he reproves himself for arguing with God's dispensations.
thine . . . blood thy blood which is alone worthy
lethean Lethe was the river of Hades out of which souls drank forgetfulness of their previous existence.
That . . . debt some ask for their sins to be remembered, and so included in the debt Christ discharged

VI

Death be not proud, though some have callèd thee
Mighty and dreadful, for, thou art not so,
For, those, whom thou think'st, thou dost overthrow,
Die not, poor death, nor yet canst thou kill me;
From rest and sleep, which but thy pictures be,
Much pleasure, then from thee, much more must flow,°
And soonest our best men with thee do go,°
Rest of their bones, and soul's delivery.
Thou art slave to fate, chance, kings, and desperate men,
10   And dost with poison, war, and sickness dwell,
And poppy,° or charms can make us sleep as well,
And better than thy stroke; why swell'st thou then?
One short sleep past, we wake eternally,
And death shall be no more, Death thou shalt die.

X

Batter my heart, three-personed° God; for, you
As yet but knock, breathe, shine, and seek to mend;
That I may rise, and stand, o'erthrow me, and bend
Your force, to break, blow, burn, and make me new.
I, like an usurped town, to another due,°
Labour to admit you, but oh, to no end,
Reason your viceroy in me, me should defend,
But is captivèd, and proves weak or untrue,
Yet dearly I love you,° and would be loved fain,
10   But am bethrothed unto your enemy,
Divorce me, untie, or break that knot again,
Take me to you, imprison me, for I
Except you enthral° me, never shall be free,
Nor ever chaste, except you ravish me.

XIX

Oh, to vex° me, contraries meet in one:
Inconstancy unnaturally hath begot
A constant habit; that when I would not
I change in vows, and in devotiòn.
As humorous° is my contritiòn
As my profane love,° and as soon forgot:
As riddlingly distempered,° cold and hot,

From rest . . . flow if we derive pleasure from
rest and sleep, which are only images of death,
how much more should we get from death itself
soonest . . . go the good die without fuss
poppy opiate
swell'st puff yourself up
three-personed the trinity
to another due owing allegiance to someone
other than the usurper, in this case the devil
Yet . . . you For the sestet the figure changes
to one of love, marriage and rape.
enthral take prisoner
vex trouble
humorous changeable, whimsical
As . . . love rare instance of Donne's relating
sacred and profane love
riddlingly distempered puzzlingly disproportioned

As praying, as mute; as infinite, as none.
I durst not view heaven yesterday; and today
10   In prayers, and flattering speeches I court God:
Tomorrow I quake with true fear of his rod.
So my devout fits come and go away
Like a fantastic ague:° save that here
Those are my best days, when I shake with fear.°

1633

Good Friday, 1613. Riding Westward°

Let man's soul be a sphere, and then, in this,
The intelligence that moves, devotion is,
And as the other spheres, by being grown
Subject to foreign motions, lose their own,
And being by others hurried every day,
Scarce in a year their natural form obey:
Pleasure or business, so, our souls admit
For their first mover, and are whirled by it.°
Hence is't, that I am carried towards the west
10   This day, when my soul's form° bends toward the east.
There I should see a sun, by rising set,°
And by that setting endless day beget;°
But that Christ on this Cross, did rise and fall,
Sin had eternally benighted all.
Yet dare I almost be glad, I do not see
That spectacle of too much weight for me.
Who sees God's face, that is self life,° must die;°
What a death were it then to see God die?°
It made his own lieutenant° Nature shrink,
20   It made his footstool crack,° and the sun wink.
Could I behold those hands which span the poles,
And turn° all spheres at once, pierced with those holes?
Could I behold that endless height which is
Zenith° to us, and to our antipodes,°

fantastic ague capricious fever; agues, caused by malaria, struck at intervals
best . . . fear the difference from an ague is that in that case one's worst days are the days on which one shakes
Good Friday, 1613. . . . a meditation actually composed on a journey taken that day from Warwickshire to Montgomery in Wales
Let . . . whirled by it as the angel-intelligence moves its heavenly body, so the devotion moves man's soul; and as the regular motion of heavenly bodies is affected by external forces, so that they are rarely in their proper orbits, so the forces of business or pleasure take over from devotion and move us in directions not proper to us

soul's form devotion
by rising set . . . beget Christ coming into the world and dying; by so doing he creates the possibility of eternal life
self life the essence of life
must die Exodus 33:20
die the *rime riche*, unusual in English verse
lieutenant deputy
footstool crack Isaiah 66:1 and, for the earthquake at the Crucifixion, Matthew 27:51
turn An alternative reading, "tune," would make this refer to the music of the spheres.
Zenith . . . antipodes the highest point to us and also to those who inhabit the other side of the world

Humbled below us? or that blood which is
The seat of all our souls, if not of his,°
Made dirt of dust,° or that flesh which was worn,
By God, for his apparel, ragged, and torn?
If on these things I durst not look, durst I
30   Upon his miserable mother cast mine eye,
Who was God's partner here, and furnished thus
Half of that sacrifice, which ransomed us?
Though these things, as I ride, be from mine eye,
They are present yet unto my memory,
For that looks towards them; and thou look'st towards me,
O Saviour, as thou hang'st upon the tree;
I turn my back to thee, but to receive
Corrections, till thy mercies bid thee leave.
O think me worth thine anger, punish me,
40   Burn off my rusts, and my deformity,
Restore thine image,° so much, by thy grace,
That thou mayst know me, and I'll turn my face.

                                        1633

Hymn to God My God, in My Sickness°

Since I am coming to that holy room,°
    Where, with thy choir of saints for evermore,
I shall be made thy music; as I come
    I tune the instrument here at the door,
    And what I must do then, think now before.

Whilst my physicians by their love° are grown
    Cosmographers, and I their map, who lie
Flat on this bed, that by them may be shown
    That this is my south-west discovery°
10   Per fretum febris,° by these strains to die,

I joy, that in these straits, I see my west;°
    For, though their currents yield return to none,
What shall my west hurt me? As west and east
    In all flat maps (and I am one) are one,
    So death doth touch the resurrection.

The seat . . . of his whether or no the blood is,
as some say, the seat of the soul, Christ's
blood is certainly the seat of ours
Made . . . dust turned into mud by mixing
with dust
Restore thine image (by punishment) make
anew your likeness in me
Hymn to God, in My Sickness According to
Walton this was written by Donne on his death-
bed, but more likely it dates, like "A Hymn
to God the Father," from his illness of 1623.

holy room heaven
love attentive care to his body
Cosmographers geographers
south-west discovery The south is hot, the west
"declining"—cf. "The Good Morrow"—and so
the discovery of a southwest passage to the East
is an emblem of death by fever.
Per fretum febris fretum is both "heat" and
"strait": through the hot strait of fever
my west my death (his east will be the resurrection)

Is the Pacific Sea° my home? Or are
   The eastern riches?° Is Jerusalem?°
Anyan,° and Magellan, and Gibraltàr,
   All straits, and none but straits, are ways to them,°
20   Whether where Japhet dwelt, or Cham, or Shem.°

We think that Paradise and Calvary,
   Christ's cross, and Adam's tree, stood in one place;°
Look Lord, and find both Adams met in me;
   As the first Adam's sweat surrounds my face,
   May the last Adam's blood my soul embrace.

So, in his purple wrapped receive me Lord,
   By these his thorns° give me his other crown;
And as to others' souls I preached thy word,
   Be this my text, my sermon to mine own,
30   Therefore that° he may raise the Lord throws down.

                     1635

A Hymn to God the Father°

I

Wilt thou forgive that sin where I begun,
   Which is my sin, though it were done before?°
Wilt thou forgive that sin, through which I run,°
   And do run still:° though still° I do deplore?
      When thou hast done, thou hast not done,°
         For I have more.

II

Wilt thou forgive that sin which I have won
   Others to sin? and, made my sin their door?
Wilt thou forgive that sin which I did shun
10   A year, or two, but wallowed in a score?
      When thou hast done, thou hast not done,
         For I have more.

Pacific Sea which could stand for heavenly
peace
eastern riches standing for heaven
Jerusalem standing, as always, for the Heavenly
City
Anyan Annam, then thought of as a strait
dividing Asia from America
All straits . . . to them all the ways to heaven
are "straits"
Japhet . . . Cham . . . Shem The world was
divided between the sons of Noah: Japhet got
Europe, Ham Africa, and Shem Asia.
Paradise . . . one place This myth is recorded
elsewhere, but seems not to have been wide-
spread, though Donne refers to it twice.

these his thorns the poet's sufferings which resemble Christ's
Therefore that in order that
A Hymn to God the Father according to Walton,
written during the serious illness of 1623 which
also produced the *Devotions.* A contemporary
musical setting by John Hilton survives.
my sin . . . before the sin of his parents, by
which original sin was transmitted to him
still always
When . . . done When you've done that you've
not finished / When you've done that you've
still not gained Donne

III

I have a sin of fear, that when I have spun
  My last thread, I shall perish on the shore;
But swear by thy self, that at my death thy son°
  Shall shine as he shines now, and heretofore;
    And, having done that, thou hast done,
      I fear no more.

1633

Devotions upon Emergent Occasions

From Meditation X

This is Nature's nest of Boxes: the Heavens contain the earth, the earth, cities, cities, men. And all these are concentric: the common center to them all is decay, ruin; only that is eccentric which was never made; only that place or garment rather, which we can imagine, but not demonstrate—that light which is the very emanation of the light of God, in which the saints shall dwell, with which the saints shall be apparelled—only that bends not to this center, this ruin; that which was not made of Nothing is not threatened with this annihilation. All other things are, even angels, even our souls: they move upon the same poles, they bend to the same center, and if they were not made immortal by preservation, their nature could not keep them from sinking to this center, annihilation.

Meditation XVII

Nunc lento sonitu dicunt, Morieris [1]
Now this bell, rolling softly for another, says to me, Thou must die

Perchance he for whom this bell [2] tolls may be so ill as that he knows not it tolls for him; and perchance I may think myself so much better than I am, as that they who are about me and see my state, may have caused it to toll for me, and I know not that. The church is catholic, universal; so are all her actions; all that she does belongs to all. When she baptizes a child, that action concerns me, for that child is thereby connected to that Head which is my Head too, and engraffed [3] into that body, whereof I am a member.[4] And when she buries a man, that action concerns me. All mankind is of one author, and is one volume; when one man dies, one chapter is not torn out of the book, but trans-

---

thy son a pun which makes Christ = the sun

1. Literally, "Now they say with their slow sounding, 'Thou shalt die.' "
2. Passing-bell.
3. Grafted.
4. The church.

lated [5] into a better language, and every chapter must be so translated; God employs several translators; some pieces are translated by age, some by sickness, some by war, some by justice; but God's hand is in every translation; and his hand shall bind up all our scattered leaves again for that library where every book shall lie open to one another. As therefore the bell that rings to a sermon calls not upon the preacher only, but upon the congregation to come, so this bell calls us all; but how much more me, who am brought so near the door by this sickness. There was a contention as far as a suit [6] (in which both piety and dignity, religion and estimation, [7] were mingled) which of the religious orders should ring to prayers first in the morning; and it was determined, that they should ring first that rose earliest. If we understand aright the dignity of this bell that tolls for our evening prayer, we would be glad to make it ours by rising early, in that application, that it might be ours as well as his whose indeed it is. The bell doth toll for him that thinks it doth; and though it intermit [8] again, yet from that minute that that occasion wrought upon him, he is united to God. Who casts not [9] up his eye to the sun when it rises? But who takes off his eye from a comet when that breaks out? Who bends not [9] his ear to any bell which upon any occasion rings? But who can remove it from that bell which is passing a piece of himself out of this world? No man is an island, entire of itself; every man is a piece of the continent, a part of the main; [10] if a clod be washed away by the sea, Europe is the less, as well as if a promontory were, as well as if a manor [11] of thy friend's or of thine own were. Any man's death diminishes me, because I am involved in mankind; and therefore never send to know for whom the bell tolls; it tolls for thee. Neither can we call this a begging of misery or a borrowing of misery, as though we were not miserable enough of ourselves, but must fetch in more from the next house, in taking upon us the misery of our neighbours. Truly it were an excusable covetousness if we did; for affliction is a treasure, and scarce any man hath enough of it. No man hath affliction enough that is not matured and ripened by it, and made fit for God by that affliction. If a man carry treasure in bullion, or in a wedge of gold, and have none coined into current monies, his treasure will not defray him as he travels. Tribulation is treasure in the nature of it, but it is not current money in the use of it, except we get nearer and nearer our home, heaven, by it. Another man may be sick too, and sick to death, and this affliction may lie in his bowels, as gold in a mine, and be of no use to him; but this bell, that tells me of his affliction, digs out and applies that gold to me, if by this consideration of another's danger, I take mine own into contemplation, and so secure myself by making my recourse to my God, who is our only security.

1624

5. Punning on the etymological sense, "carried over."
6. Which went as far as legal action.
7. Self-esteem.
8. Break off.
9. These words may be intrusive; the sense is stronger without them.
10. Mainland.
11. Estate.

Sermons

By the end of his life, when he was Dean of St. Paul's, Donne's chief fame was as a preacher. His sermons form a vast bulk, and nowadays they are mostly read by scholars seeking, and finding, enlightenment concerning what they value more highly, namely, the poems; but they are, in themselves, a great achievement. They are not all of equal importance or profundity; some were for learned audiences, some for large; some are relatively perfunctory, some terrifying. The liturgical season, the particular occasion, affect the tone. Like most preachers of his time, Donne was preoccupied by sin and death; he confesses his melancholy and his desire for extinction. "I preach the sense of God's indignation on mine own soul." But there is joy also, and humanity. Above all there is a learned wit, which relates the old to the young Donne, and both to the other great preachers of his day. He followed the general scheme employed in the very long sermons of the time, but expected his audience, in the midst of their instruction, to follow his puns and allusions, as well as to respond to the immense eloquence he could produce when he thought fit.

It is impossible to select one brief passage and expect it to give any notion of Donne the preacher; the famous final sermon *Death's Duel* is not really characteristic, and too many anthologists have, by choosing only purple passages, given a positively false impression. What follows here is from a fine but not spectacular sermon on a central text, which happens to be in the chapter chosen to illustrate the development of the English Bibles. There is just about enough of it to enable the reader to see how Donne handled a text, and how he defined and enriched his theme for an audience which, though made up of better listeners than any preacher could find today, nevertheless needed the preacher's summations, repetitions, and explanations, if they were to follow him.

From A Sermon Preached at St. Paul's for Easter-Day, 1628

> 'For now we see through a glass darkly, but then face to face; now I know in part, but then I shall know even as also I am known.'[1]

These two terms in our text, *nunc* and *tunc*, now and then, now in a glass, then face to face, now in part, then in perfection, these two secular[2] terms, of which one designs the whole age of this world from the creation to the dissolution thereof, for all that is comprehended in this word *now*, and the other designs the everlastingness of the next world, for that incomprehensibleness is comprehended in the other word *then*—these two words that design two such ages are now met in one day, in this day in which we celebrate all resurrections in the root in the resurrection of our Lord and Saviour Christ Jesus blest forever. For the first term, *now*, 'Now in a glass, now in part,' is intended most especially of that very act which we do now at this present, that is, of the ministry of the Gospel, of declaring God in his ordinance, of preaching his word, 'Now,' in

---

1. I Corinthians 13:12—"glass" = "mirror." See the section The English Bible.
2. Relating to ages.

this ministry of his Gospel, 'we see in a glass, we know in part'; and then the *then,* the time of seeing face to face and knowing as we are known is intended of that time which we celebrate this day, the day of resurrection, the day of judgement, the day of the actual possession of the next life. So that this day this whole Scripture is fulfilled in your ears; for now, now in this preaching, you have some sight, and then, then when that day comes which in the first root thereof we celebrate this day, you shall have a perfect sight of all; 'Now we see through a glass,' etc.

That therefore you may the better know him when you come to see him face to face than by having seen him in a glass now, and that your seeing him now in his ordinance [3] may prepare you to see him then in his essence, proceed we thus in the handling of these words. First, that there is nothing brought into comparison, into consideration, nothing put into the balance, but the sight of God, the knowledge of God; it is not called a better sight, nor a better knowledge, but there is no other sight, no other knowledge proposed or mentioned or intimated or imagined but this; all other sight is blindness, all other knowledge is ignorance; [4] and then we shall see how there is a twofold sight of God and a twofold knowledge of God proposed to us here; a sight and a knowledge here in this life, and another manner of sight and another manner of knowledge in the life to come; for here we see God *in speculo,* in a glass, that is, by reflection, and here we know God *in ænigmate,* says our text, darkly, so we translate it, that is, by obscure presentations, and therefore it is called a knowledge but in part; but in heaven our sight is face to face, and our knowledge is to know as we are known.

For our sight of God here, our theatre, the place where we sit and see him, is the whole world, the whole house and frame of nature, and our medium, our glass, is the book of creatures, and our light, by which we see him, is the light of natural reason. And then for our knowledge of God here, our place, our academy, our university is the church, our medium is the ordinance of God in his church, preaching and sacraments; and our light is the light of faith. Thus we shall find it to be for our sight and for our knowledge of God here. But for our sight of God in heaven, our place, our sphere is heaven itself, our medium is the patefaction,[5] the manifestation, the revelation of God himself, and our light is the light of glory. And then for our knowledge of God there, God himself is all; God himself is the place, we see him in him; God is our medium, we see him by him; God is our light; not a light which is his, but a light which is he; not a light which flows from him, no, nor a light which is in him, but that light which is he himself. Lighten our darkness, we beseech thee, O Lord, O Father of lights, that in thy light we may see light,[6] that now we see this through this thy glass, thy ordinance, and by the good of this hereafter face to face.

The sight is so much the noblest of all the senses as that it is all the senses.[7] As the reasonable soul of man, when it enters, becomes all the soul of man, and

---

3. Explained in next paragraph.
4. See *The Second Anniversary,* ll. 254 ff.
5. Making plain.
6. Psalms 36:9.
7. The usual view; the senses ran down from sight through hearing, smell, taste, and touch.

he hath no longer a vegetative and a sensitive soul but all is that one reasonable soul;[8] so, says St. Augustine, and he exemplifies it by several pregnant places of Scripture, *Visus per omnes sensus recurrit,* all the senses are called seeing; as there is *videre et audire,* 'St. John turned to see the sound';[9] and there is *gustate et videte,* 'Taste and see how sweet the Lord is';[10] and so of the rest of the senses, all is sight. Employ then this noblest sense upon the noblest object, see God; see God in everything, and then thou needst not take off thine eye from beauty, from riches, from honour, from anything. St. Paul speaks here of a diverse seeing of God. Of seeing God in a glass, and seeing God face to face; but of not seeing God at all, the apostle speaks not at all.

When Christ took the blind man by the hand,[11] though he had then begun his cure upon him, yet he asked him if he saw aught. Something he was sure he saw; but it was a question whether it were to be called a sight, for he saw men but as trees. The natural man[12] sees beauty and riches and honour, but yet it is a question whether he sees them or no, because he sees them but as a snare. But he that sees God in them sees them to be beams and evidences of that beauty, that wealth, that honour, that is in God, that is in God himself. The other blind man that importuned Christ, 'Jesus, thou son of David, have mercy upon me,' when Christ asked him, 'What wilt thou that I shall do unto thee?' had presently that answer, 'Lord, that I may receive my sight';[13] and we may easily think that if Christ had asked him a second question, 'What wouldst thou see when thou hast received thy sight?' he would have answered, 'Lord, I will see thee'; for when he had his sight and Christ said to him, 'Go thy way,' he had no way to go from Christ, but, as the text says there, 'He followed him.' All that he cared for was seeing, all that he cared to see was Christ. Whether he would see a peace or a war may be a statesman's problem; whether he would see plenty or scarcity of some commodity may be a merchant's problem; whether he would see Rome or Spain grow in greatness may be a Jesuit's problem; but whether I had not rather see God than anything is no problematical matter. All sight is blindness, that was our first; all knowledge is ignorance till we come to God, is our next consideration.

The first act of will is love, says the School;[14] for till the will love, till it would have something, it is not a will. But then, *amare nisi nota non possumus;* it is impossible to love anything till we know it. First our understanding must present it as *verum,* as a known truth, and then our will embraces it as *bonum,* as good, and worthy to be loved. Therefore the philosopher[15] concludes easily, as a thing that admits no contradiction, that naturally all men desire to know, that they may love. But then, as the addition[16] of an honest man varies the signification with the profession and calling of the man—for he is an honest man at court that oppresses no man with his power, and at the exchange he is

8. Man has the first, which comprehends the others; animals the second and third.
9. Revelation 1:12.
10. Psalms 34:8.
11. Mark 8:23.
12. Man without religion, seeing by the light of nature.
13. Mark 10:46–51.
14. The scholastic philosophy.
15. St. Augustine.
16. Description.

the honest man that keeps his word, and in an army the valiant man is the honest man—so the addition of learning and understanding varies with the man; the divine, the physician, the lawyer are not qualified, not denominated by the same kind of learning. But yet, as it is for honesty, there is no honest man at court or exchange or army if he believe not in God; so there is no knowledge in the physician nor lawyer if he know not God. Neither does any man know God except he know him so as God hath made himself known, that is, in Christ. Therefore, as St. Paul desires to know nothing else,[17] so let no man pretend to know anything but Christ crucified; that is, crucified for him, made his. In the eighth verse of this chapter he says, 'Prophecy shall fail, and tongues shall fail, and knowledge shall vanish'; but this knowledge of God in Christ made mine, by being crucified for me, shall dwell with me forever. And so from this general consideration all sight is blindness, all knowledge is ignorance, but of God, we pass to the particular consideration of that twofold sight and knowledge of God expressed in this text, 'Now we see through a glass,' etc.

First then we consider—before we come to our knowledge of God—our sight of God in this world, and that is, says our apostle, *in speculo*, 'We see as in a glass.' But how do we see in a glass? Truly, that is not easily determined. The old writers in the optics said that when we see a thing in a glass, we see not the thing itself but a representation only; all the later men say we do see the thing itself but not by direct but by reflected beams. It is a useless labour for the present to reconcile them. This may well consist with both, that as that which we see in a glass assures us that such a thing there is, for we cannot see a dream in a glass, nor a fancy, nor a chimera, so this sight of God, which our apostle says we have in a glass, is enough to assure us that a God there is.

This glass is better than the water; the water gives a crookedness and false dimensions to things that it shows;[18] as we see by an oar when we row a boat, and as the poet describes a wry and distorted face, *qui faciem sub aqua, Phœbe, natantis habes*, that he looked like a man that swam under water. But in the glass which the apostle intends we may see God directly, that is, see directly that there is a God. And therefore St. Cyril's addition in this text is a diminution; *videmus quasi in fumo*, says he, we see God as in a smoke; we see him better than so; for it is a true sight of God, though it be not a perfect sight, which we have this way. This way our theatre, where we sit to see God, is the whole frame of nature; our medium, our glass in which we see him is the creature; and our light by which we see him is natural reason.

Aquinas calls this theatre, where we sit and see God, the whole world; and David compasses the world and finds God everywhere and says at last, 'Whither shall I fly from thy presence? If I ascend up into heaven, thou art there';[19] at Babel they thought to build to heaven; but did any man ever pretend to get above heaven? Above the power of the winds, or the impression of other malignant meteors, some high hills are got. But can any man get above the power of God? 'If I take the wings of the morning, and dwell in the uttermost parts of the sea, there thy right hand shall hold me and lead me.' If we sail to the waters above the firmament, it is so too. Nay, take a place which

17. I Corinthians 2:2.
18. The phenomenon of refraction.
19. Psalms 139:8.

God never made, a place which grew out of our sins, that is, hell; yet, 'If we make our bed in hell, God is there too.' It is a woeful inn to make our bed in, hell; and so much the more woeful as it is more than an inn, an everlasting dwelling. But even there God is; and so much more strangely than in any other place because he is there without any emanation of any beam of comfort from him who is the God of all consolation or any beam of light from him who is the Father of all lights. In a word, whether we be in the eastern parts of the world, from whom the truth of religion is passed, or in the western, to which it is not yet come; whether we be in the darkness of ignorance, or darkness of the works of darkness, or darkness of oppression of spirit in sadness; the world is the theatre that represents God, and everywhere every man may, nay, must see him.

The whole frame of the world is the theatre, and every creature the stage, the medium, the glass in which we may see God. 'Moses made the laver in the tabernacle of the looking glasses of women.' [20] Scarce can you imagine a vainer thing—except you will except the vain lookers-on in the action—than the looking glasses of women; and yet Moses brought the looking glasses of women to a religious use, to show them that came in the spots of dirt which they had taken by the way, that they might wash themselves clean before they passed any farther.

There is not so poor a creature but may be the glass to see God in. The greatest flat glass that can be made cannot represent anything greater than it is. If every gnat that flies were an archangel, all that could but tell me that there is a God; and the poorest worm that creeps tells me that. If I should ask the basilisk,[21] how camest thou by those killing eyes? he would tell me, thy God made me so; and if I should ask the slow-worm, how camest thou to be without eyes? he would tell me, thy God made me so. The cedar is no better a glass to see God in than the hyssop [22] upon the wall; all things that are, are equally removed from being nothing; and whatsoever hath any being is by that very being a glass in which to see God, who is the root and the fountain of all being. The whole frame of nature is the theatre, the whole volume of creatures is the glass, and the light of nature, reason, is our light; which is another circumstance.

Of these words, John 1:9, 'That was the true light that lighteth every man that cometh into the world,' the slackest sense that they can admit gives light enough to see God by. If we spare St. Chrysostom's sense, that that light is the light of the Gospel and of grace, and that that light considered in itself and without opposition in us does enlighten, that is, would enlighten every man if that man did not wink [23] at that light; if we forbear St. Augustine's sense, that light enlightens every man, that is, every man that is enlightened is enlightened by that light; if we take but St. Cyril's sense, that this light is the light of natural reason, which, without all question, 'enlighteneth every man that comes into the world'; yet have we light enough to see God by that light in the theatre of nature and in the glass of creatures. God affords no man the comfort, the false comfort of atheism. He will not allow a pretending atheist the power to flatter

20. Exodus 38:8: "laver" = washbowl.
21. Fabulous dragon that killed by looking at its victim.
22. Aromatic herb.
23. Close his eyes.

himself so far as seriously to think there is no God. He must pull out his own eyes and see no creature before he can say, he sees no God; he must be no man and quench his reasonable soul before he can say to himself, there is no God. The difference between the reason of man and the instinct of the beast is this, that the beast does but know, but the man knows that he knows.[24] The bestial atheist will pretend that he knows there is no God; but he cannot say that he knows that he knows it; for his knowledge will not stand the battery[25] of an argument from another nor a ratiocination from himself. He dares not ask himself, who is it that I pray to in a sudden danger if there be no God? Nay, he dares not ask, who is it that I swear by in a sudden passion if there be no God? Whom do I tremble at and sweat under at midnight and whom do I curse by next morning if there be no God? It is safely said in the School, *media perfecta ad quæ ordinantur*, how weak soever those means which are ordained by God seem to be, and be indeed in themselves, yet they are strong enough to those ends and purposes for which God ordained them.

And so for such a sight of God as we take the apostle to intend here, which is to see that there is a God, the frame of nature, the whole world is our theatre, the book of creatures is our medium, our glass, and natural reason is light enough. But then for the other degree, the other notification of God, which is the knowing of God, though that also be first to be considered in this world, the means is of a higher nature than served for the sight of God; and yet whilst we are in this world it is but *in ænigmate*, in an obscure riddle, a representation, darkly, and in part, as we translate it.

As the glass which we spoke of before was proposed to the sense, and so we might see God, that is, see that there is a God, this *ænigma* that is spoken of now, this dark similitude and comparison, is proposed to our faith; and so far we know God, that is, believe in God in this life but by enigmas, by dark representations and allusions. Therefore says St. Augustine that Moses saw God, in that conversation which he had with him in the mount, *sevocatus ab omni corporis sensu*, removed from all benefit and assistance of bodily senses—he needed not that glass, the help of the creature; and more than so, *ab omni significativo æenigmate spiritus*, removed from all allusions or similitudes or representations of God which might bring God to the understanding and so to the belief; Moses knew God by a more immediate working than either sense or understanding or faith. Therefore says that father, *per speculum et ænigma*, by this which the apostle calls a glass and this which he calls *ænigma*, a dark representation, *intelliguntur omnia accommodata ad notificandum deum*, he understands all things by which God hath notified himself to man, by the glass to his reason, by the *ænigma* to his faith. And so for this knowing of God by way of believing in him—as for seeing him our theatre was the world, the creature was our glass, and reason was our light—our academy to learn this knowledge is the church, our medium is the ordinance and institution of Christ in his church, and our light is the light of faith in the application of those ordinances in that church.

This place then where we take our degrees in this knowledge of God, our

24. See "A Nocturnal upon S. Lucy's Day," ll. 30–31.
25. Assault.

academy, our university for that, is the church; for, though as there may be some few examples given of men that have grown learned who never studied at university; so there may be some examples of men enlightened by God and yet not within that covenant which constitutes the church; yet the ordinary place for degrees is the university, and the ordinary place for illumination in the knowledge of God is the church. Therefore did God, who ever intended to have his kingdom of heaven well peopled, so powerfully, so miraculously enlarge his way to it, the church, that it prospered as a wood which no feeling, no stubbing could destroy. We find in the acts of the church five thousand martyrs executed in a day; and we find in the Acts of the Apostles five thousand brought to the church by one sermon; still our christenings were equal to our burials at least. . . .

1628   1640

BEN JONSON
1572–1637

Born in the same year as Donne, Ben Jonson was to exert an equally strong shaping force on the poetry of his century. The son of a London bricklayer, he attended Westminster school under the scholar and antiquary William Camden, soldiered in Flanders, and returned to the London stage, first as an actor, then as the major playwright of *Sejanus* (1603), *Volpone* (1606), *Epicoene* (1609), *The Alchemist* (1610), *Bartholomew Fair* (1614), and other plays. As a poet he produced as well a major corpus of verse—lyric, satiric, epigrammatic, elegiac—informed by his vast and profound knowledge of the Latin and Greek classics, as well as by his own remarkable sense of language's control of thought and feeling in poetry. Appropriateness, order, structure, all brought his wit under the control of rhetorical and dialectical patterns based, but elaborated, on the classics. His influence reached through his immediate followers and friends—Herrick, the Cavalier poets, Waller—to Dryden at the other end of the century. Jonson's ambitiousness and self-regard enabled him to publish, in 1616, a folio edition of his *Works* (a word used hitherto only for the *Opera* or dead classical authors), containing epigrams, songs from plays, masques, and a selection of his favorite poems called *The Forest;* a posthumous edition of 1640–41 added more masques and a larger group of poems called *The Underwood.* After the accession of James I in 1603, Jonson became responsible for the writing of masques and entertainments at court, at annual revels and state occasions; and his twenty-eight masques form a major body of imaginative achievement, particularly in the mythopoetic directions which his plays and his other verse rarely sought to take. In the fables and animated moral emblems of his masques, Jonson links up Spenserian traditions with their eventual rebirth in the poetry of Milton.

But it is the public, instructive character both of his poetry and of his sense of the poet's role in society which distinguishes Jonson from Donne; the latter poet was our language's genius of the private, and his idiosyncratic revisions of the available Petrarchan phrases, attitudes, and expressive forms create what we think of as the personal voice. Jonson wrote personal poems, but always as the kind of public spokesman that his classical forebears, Horace and Pindar, led him to try to be. When he felt that, after the accession of Charles I, he could no longer speak to England by influencing its center, the crown, he betook himself more and more to his immediate circle, the so-called Tribe of Ben which included not only most of the best minor poets of the middle of the century, but scholars and statesmen as well. The wisdom and flexibility of his voice is continually evident in the wide range of his forms and lyric types as well as in the constancy of his instructive power, even in moments of self-mockery as poet and as man.

To the Memory of My Beloved, the Author Mr. William Shakespeare:°

and What He Hath Left Us

To draw no envy (Shakespeare) on thy name,
    Am I thus ample° to thy book, and fame,
While I confess thy writings to be such
    As neither Man nor Muse can praise too much.
'Tis true, and all men's suffrage.° But these ways
    Were not the paths I meant unto thy praise:
For seeliest° ignorance on these may light,
    Which, when it sounds at best, but echoes right;
Or blind affection, which doth ne'er advance
10   The truth, but gropes, and urgeth all by chance;
Or crafty malice might pretend this praise,
    And think to ruin, where it seemed to raise.
These are, as some infamous bawd or whore,
    Should praise a matron. What could hurt her more?
But thou art proof against them, and indeed
    Above the ill fortune of them, or the need,
I, therefore will begin. Soul of the age!
    The applause! delight! the wonder of our stage!
My Shakespeare, rise; I will not lodge thee by
20   Chaucer or Spenser, or bid Beaumont lie
A little further, to make thee a room:°
    Thou art a monument without a tomb,
And art alive still, while thy book doth live,
    And we have wits to read, and praise to give.
That I not mix thee so, my brain excuses,
    I mean with great, but disproportioned muses;
For, if I thought my judgment were of years,
    I should commit thee surely with thy peers,
And tell, how far thou didst our Lyly° outshine,
30   Or sporting Kyd,° or Marlowe's mighty line.

To the Memory . . . Shakespeare prefixed to the Shakespeare First Folio of 1623
ample liberal
suffrage consent (as by vote)
seeliest silliest
make thee a room in Westminster Abbey, where all these poets are ceremoniously entombed
Lyly See Headnote on John Lyly.
Kyd Thomas Kyd (1558–94), author of heavy melodrama; "sporting" is a sarcastic pun on "kidding"

And though thou hadst small Latin and less Greek,°
   From thence to honour thee, I would not seek
For names; but call forth thundering Aeschylus,
   Euripides and Sophocles° to us,
Paccuvius, Accius,° him° of Cordova dead,
   To life again, to hear thy buskin° tread,
And shake a stage: Or, when thy socks° were on,
   Leave thee alone, for the comparison
Of all that insolent Greece or haughty Rome
40   Sent forth, or since did from their ashes come.
Triumph, My Britain, thou hast one to show,
   To whom all scenes of Europe homage owe.
He was not of an age, but for all time!
   And all the muses still were in their prime,
When like Apollo he came forth to warm
   Our ears, or like a Mercury to charm!
Nature herself was proud of his designs,
   And joyed to wear the dressing of his lines!
Which were so richly spun and woven so fit,
50   As,° since, she will vouchsafe no other wit:
The merry Greek, tart Aristophanes,°
   Neat Terence,° witty Plautus, now not please,
But antiquated, and deserted lie
   As they were not of nature's family.
Yet must I not give nature all: thy art,
   My gentle Shakespeare, must enjoy a part,
For though the poet's matter nature be,
   His art doth give the fashion; and that he
Who casts° to write a living line, must sweat
60   (Such as thine are), and strike the second heat
Upon the muses' anvil, turn the same
   (And himself with it), that he thinks to frame,
Or for the laurel, he may gain a scorn;
   For a good poet's made, as well as born.
And such wert thou. Look how the father's face
   Lives in his issue; even so, the race
Of Shakespeare's mind, and manners brightly shines
   In his well turnèd, and true-filèd lines:
In each of which, he seems to shake a lance,°
70   As brandished at the eyes of ignorance.

---

small Latin and less Greek as compared with Jonson's own massive classical learning; as compared with our own, he had a good knowledge of Latin
Aeschylus, Euripides and Sophocles the three great Greek tragedians
Paccuvius, Accius Roman tragedians
him Seneca, Roman tragic poet and philosopher who strongly influenced Elizabethan dramatists; he was born, and died, at Corduba

buskin emblematic high boot of tragedy, worn by actors in the classical drama
socks the low shoes or slippers of comedy
As that
Aristophanes great Greek comic playwright
Terence with Plautus, greatest and most influential Roman comedians
casts sets out
shake a lance shake a spear (an old gag)

Sweet Swan of Avon!° what a sight it were
  To see thee in our waters yet appear,
And make those flights upon the banks of Thames,
  That so did take Eliza° and our James!
But stay, I see thee in the hemisphere
  Advanced and made a constellation there!
Shine forth, thou star of poets, and with rage°
  Or influence,° chide, or cheer the drooping stage;
Which, since thy flight from hence, hath mourned like night,
80   And déspairs day, but for thy volume's light.

1623

To the Immortal Memory and Friendship of That Noble Pair Sir Lucius Cary and Sir H. Morison°

THE TURN°

Brave infant of Saguntum,° clear°
Thy coming forth in that great year,
When the prodigious Hannibal did crown
His rage, with razing your immortal town.
Thou, looking then about,
Ere thou wert half got out,
Wise child, didst hastily return,
And madest thy mother's womb thine urn.°
How summed a circle didst thou leave mankind
10 Of deepest lore,° could we the center find!

THE COUNTERTURN

Did wiser nature draw thee back,
From out the horror of that sack,
Where shame, faith, honour, and regard of right
Lay trampled on; the deeds of death and night,
Urged, hurried forth, and hurled°

Swan of Avon He makes Shakespeare a swan because that most noble and serene of birds, "fair, upward and direct" as Jonson puts it elsewhere, in flight, was reputed to sing magnificently at its death; this poem celebrates a posthumous volume of Shakespeare's works, and its metamorphic image is that of the constellations Cygnus (as the lyre of Orpheus, in classical tradition, became Lyra).
Eliza Queen Elizabeth
rage rapture or enthusiasm
influence the way stars affected human lives; see *Astrology* in the Glossary
To . . . Sir Lucius Cary and Sir H. Morison Viscount Falkland, philosophically inclined, died fighting for the king in 1643; Morison was his brother-in-law who died prematurely in 1629.
The Turn Jonson is self-consciously writing the first Pindaric ode in English, and he labels the triads with literal translations of "strophe," "antistrophe," and "epode."
infant of Saguntum Pliny tells this anecdote of a newborn baby in a town besieged by Hannibal in 219 B.C., starting the second Punic War.
clear famous (was); perhaps with a sense of "pure"
urn funeral urn
How summed . . . lore how full of meaning would be your circle emblem, your "in my end is my beginning"
hurled hurled themselves

Upon the affrighted world:
Sword, fire, and famine, with fell fury met;
And all on utmost ruin set;
As, could they but life's miseries foresee,
20   No doubt all infants would return like thee?

THE STAND

For, what is life, if measured by the space,°
Not by the act?°
Or maskèd man, if valued by his face,
Above his fact?°
Here's one outlived his peers,
And told forth fourscore years;
He vexèd time, and busied the whole state,
Troubled both foes and friends,
But ever to no ends.
30   What did this stirrer, but die late?
How well at twenty had he fallen or stood!
For three of his fourscore, he did no good.

THE TURN

He entered well, by virtuous parts,°
Got up and thrived with honest arts;
He purchased friends, and fame, and honours then,
And had his noble name advanced with men,
But weary of that flight,
He stooped in all men's sight
To sordid flatteries, acts of strife,
40   And sunk in that dead sea of life
So deep, as he did then death's waters sup,
But that the cork of title buoyed him up.

THE COUNTERTURN

Alas, but Morison fell young:
He never fell; thou fallest, my tongue.
He stood, a soldier to the last right end,
A perfect patriot, and a noble friend,
But most a virtuous son.
All offices were done
By him, so ample, full, and round,
50   In weight, in measure, number, sound,
As though his age imperfect might appear,
His life was of humanity the sphere.°

space length
act action
fact deed
virtuous parts he was well-born

sphere Circles were symbols of perfection as
were spheres; in Ptolemaic astronomy, they were
planetary orbits.

THE STAND

Go now, and tell° out days summed up with fears,
And make them years;
Produce thy mass of miseries on the stage,
To swell thine age;
Repeat of things a throng,
To show thou hast been long,
Not lived; for life doth her great actions spell,
60   By what was done and wrought
In season, and so brought
To light: her measures° are how well
Each syllable answered, and was formed, how fair:
These make the lines of life, and that's her air.°

THE TURN

It is not growing like a tree
In bulk, doth make man better be,
Or standing long an oak, three hundred year,
To fall a log, at last, dry, bald, and sear;
A lily of a day
70   Is fairer far in May,
Although it fall and die that night:
It was the plant and flower of light.
In small proportions, we just beauties see,
And in short measures, life may perfect be.

THE COUNTERTURN

Call, noble Lucius, then for wine
And let thy looks with gladness shine;
Accept this garland, plant it on thy head,
And think, nay know, thy Morison's not dead.
He leaped the present age,
80   Possessed with holy rage,
To see that bright eternal day,
Of which we priests and poets say
Such truths, as we expect for happy men,
And there he lives with memory; and Ben°

THE STAND

Jonson, who sung this of him, ere he went
Himself to rest,

tell count
measures how we judge lives, punning on poetic
meter (thus "syllable" means each moment or
deed)
air fashion, manner; also, perhaps, "tune" (setting words in those "lines")

Ben a shocking enjambment, separating "Ben"
(as he would be known in his circle of friends)
from "Ben Jonson" (his public self) "who
wrote this" public, celebratory, instructive form
of poem, the ode

Or taste a part of that full joy he meant
To have expressed,
In this bright asterism,°
90 Where it were friendship's schism,
(Were not his Lucius long with us to tarry)
To separate these twi-
Lights, the Dioscuri,°
And keep the one half from his Harry.
But fate doth so altérnate the design,
Whilst that in heaven, this light on earth must shine.

THE TURN

And shine as you exalted are,
Two names of friendship, but one star,
Of hearts the union. And those not by chance
100 Made, or indentured,° or leased out to advance
The profits for a time.
No pleasures vain did chime,
Of rimes, or riots, at your feasts,
Orgies of drink, or feigned protests,
But simple love of greatness, and of good,
That knits brave minds, and manners, more than blood.

THE COUNTERTURN

This made you first to know the Why
You liked, then after, to apply
That liking; and approach so one the tother,°
110 Till either grew a portion of the other,
Each styled by his end,
The copy of his friend.
You lived to be the great surnames,
And titles, by which all made claims
Unto the virtue: Nothing perfect done,
But as a Cary or a Morison.

THE STAND

And such a force the fair example had,
As they that saw
The good, and durst not practise it, were glad
120 That such a law
Was left yet to mankind,
Where they might read, and find
Friendship, in deed, was written, not in words;
And with the heart, not pen,

---

asterism constellation
To separate . . . Dioscuri Again, the enjambment "separates," here the Dioscuri (Castor and
Pollux, the constellation Gemini), as death has
parted these twin lights, Cary and Morison.
indentured contracted out
tother other

Of two so early° men,
Whose lines her rolls° were, and recórds,
Who, ere the first down bloomèd on the chin,
Had sowed these fruits, and got the harvest in.
                                        1640

Ode to Himself°

    Come leave the loathèd stage,
    And the more loathsome age,
Where pride and impudence in faction knit
    Usurp the chair of wit:
Indicting and arraigning every day,
    Something they call a play.
  Let their fastidious, vain
  Commission of the brain,
Run on and rage, sweat, censure, and condemn:
10 They were not made for thee, less thou for them.

    Say that thou pourest 'em wheat,
    And they would acorns eat:
'Twere simple° fury, still thyself to waste
    On such as have no taste,
To offer them a surfeit of pure bread,
    Whose appetites are dead.
  No, give them grains° their fill,
  Husks, draff° to drink, and swill:
If they love lees,° and leave the lusty wine,
20 Envy them not, their palate's with the swine.°

    No doubt a mouldy tale,
    Like *Pericles*,° and stale
As the shrive's° crusts, and nasty as his fish,
    Scraps out of every dish.
Thrown forth and raked into the common tub,°
    May keep up the Play Club.
  Broome's° sweepings do as well
  There as his master's meal,
For who the relish of these guests will fit
30 Needs set them but the alms-basket of wit.

    And much good do't ye then,
    Brave plush and velvet men

---

early young
rolls archives
Ode to Himself written after the failure of his
play *The New Inn* in 1629
simple simpleminded
grains brewers' residue
draff refuse
lees dregs

the swine as in "neither cast ye your pearls before swine" (Matthew 7:6)
Pericles Shakespeare's play, first printed in 1609
shrive's sheriff's—this means jail food
common tub scraps for the poor
Broome's Richard Brome, Jonson's ex-servant,
now a playwright

Can feed on orts;° and safe in your scene clothes,
    Dare quit upon your oaths
The stagers, and the stage-wrights too; your peers,
    Of stuffing your large ears
    With rage of comic socks,°
    Wrought upon twenty blocks,°
Which, if they're torn, and foul, and patched enough,
40   The gamesters share your guilt,° and you their stuff.

    Leave things so prostitute,
    And take the Alcaic lute,°
Or thine own Horace, or Anacreon's lyre;°
    Warm thee by Pindar's fire,°
And though thy nerves° be shrunk and blood be cold,
    Ere years have made thee old,
    Strike that disdainful heat
    Throughout, to their defeat:
As curious fools, and envious of thy strain,
50   May blushing swear, no palsy's in thy brain.°

    But when they hear thee sing
    The glories of thy king;
His zeal to God, and his just awe of men,
    They may be bloodshaken, then
Feel such a flesh-quake to possess their powers,
    That no tuned harp like ours,
    In sound of peace or wars,
    Shall truly hit the stars
When they shall read the acts of Charles° his reign,
60   And see his chariot triumph 'bove his wain.°
                1631, 1640

A Fit of Rime Against Rime°

Rime, the rack° of finest wits,
That expresseth but by fits,°
    True conceit.°
Spoiling senses of their treasure,
Cozening judgment with a measure,
    But false weight.°

orts scraps
socks low shoes of classical comedy
blocks both shoe molds and blockheads
guilt punning on "gilt" (gilded, flashy fake)
Alcaic lute lyric poetry; Alcaeus (l. 600 B.C.)
invented a lyric meter, used frequently in Latin
by Horace
Anacreon's lyre lyric poetry again; for the
Anacreontic poems, see note on Lovelace's "The
Grasshopper"
Pindar's fire odes, like the one he is writing,
based on Pindar
nerves sinews, muscles

no palsy's . . . brain Jonson had been paralyzed by a stroke in 1628.
Charles Charles I assumed the throne in 1625.
wain wagon (the Big Dipper, called "Charles's
Wain"); also, his "wane," or decline
Rime Our modern "rhyme" preserves in its
spelling the etymology from the Greek "rhythm,"
but "rime" is older in English and French.
rack wreck; also, "torturing device"
fits cantos of a poem; also, "fitfully"
conceit thought
Cozening . . . weight cheating like a crooked
merchant, by being metrical but trivial

Wresting words from their true calling;
Propping verse for fear of falling
     To the ground.
10 Jointing syllables, drowning letters,
Fastening vowels, as with fetters
     They were bound!
Soon as lazy thou wert known,
All good poetry hence was flown,
     And art banished.
For a thousand years together
All Parnassus° green did wither,
     And wit vanished.
Pegasus° did fly away,
20 At the wells no muse did stay,
     But bewailed
So to see the fountain dry,
And Apollo's music die,
     All light failed!
Starveling° rimes did fill the stage,
Not a poet in an age
     Worth crowning.
Not a work deserving bays,°
Nor a line deserving praise,
30   Pallas° frowning;
Greek was free from rime's infection,
Happy Greek by this protection
     Was not spoiled.
Whilst the Latin, queen of tongues,
Is not yet free from rime's wrongs,
     But rests foiled.°
Scarce the hill again doth flourish,
Scarce the world a wit doth nourish
     To restore
40 Phoebus° to his crown again,
And the muses to their brain
     As before.
Vulgar° languages that want
Words, and sweetness, and be scant
     Of true measure,
Tyrant rime hath so abused
That they long since have refused
     Other ceasure;°
He that first invented thee

Parnassus the Muses' mountain
Pegasus winged horse of poetry, whose hoof struck open Hippocrene, a fountain on Helicon, the Muses' other hill
Starveling weak, shoddy
bays laurel crown for poetic glory
Pallas Athena

foiled stabbed, and so defeated. The point is that classical Greek never developed rhyme, while medieval Latin did.
Phoebus Apollo
Vulgar vernacular
other ceasure other ways of ending lines (than with rhyming words)

50   May his joints tormented be,
              Cramped forever;
        Still may syllables jar with time,
        Still may reason war with rime,
              Resting never.
        May his sense when it would meet
        The cold tumor in his feet°
              Grow unsounder.
        And his title be long fool,°
        That in rearing such a school
60   Was the founder.
                    1640

The Hourglass°

        Do but consider this small dust,
            Here running in the glass,
                By atoms moved;°
            Could you believe that this,
                The body was
                    Of one that loved?
        And in his mistress' flame, playing like a fly,
            Turned to cinders by her eye?
            Yes, and in death, as life unblessed,
10   To have't expressed,
            Even ashes of lovers find no rest.
                    1640

Epigram from Petronius

        Doing° a filthy pleasure is, and short,
            And done, we straight repent us of the sport.
        Let us not then rush blindly on unto it,
            Like lustful beasts, that only know to do it;
        For lust will languish, and that heat decay;
            But thus, thus keeping endless holiday
        Let us together closely lie, and kiss:
            There is no labour, nor no shame in this.
        This hath pleased, doth please and long will please; never
10   Can this decay, but is beginning ever.
                    1640

feet punning on "metrical feet"
fool a labored joke: "arse" (ass) means "fool";
"ars longa, vita brevis" ("art is long, life
short"), a famous tag
 The Hourglass a typical emblem poem: compare
it with Herbert's "Church Monuments" below

By atoms moved not atoms in the modern sense,
but those identical smallest units of matter
which the Renaissance learned of from Lucretius
Doing fucking

To Penshurst°

Thou art not, Penshurst, built to envious show
  Of touch° or marble, nor canst boast a row
Of polished pillars, or a roof of gold;
  Thou hast no lanthorn,° whereof tales are told,
Or stairs, or courts; but standest an ancient pile,
  And these grudged at,° art reverenced the while.
Thou joyest in better marks,° of soil, of air,
  Of wood, of water: therein thou art fair.
Thou hast thy walks for health, as well as sport;
10   Thy Mount,° to which the Dryads do resort,
Where Pan and Bacchus their high feasts have made
  Beneath the broad beech and the chestnut shade,
The taller tree, which of a nut was set,
  At his great birth,° where all the Muses met.
There, in the writhèd bark, are cut the names
  Of many a Sylvan, taken with his flames.°
And thence, the ruddy Satyrs oft provoke
  The lighter Fauns, to reach thy Lady's oak.°
Thy copse, too, named of Gamage,° thou hast there,
20   That never fails to serve thee seasoned deer
When thou wouldst feast, or exercise thy friends.
  The lower land that to the river bends,
Thy sheep, thy bullocks, kine, and calves do feed;
  The middle grounds thy mares and horses breed.
Each bank doth yield thee coneys,° and the tops
  Fertile of wood, Ashore and Sidney's copse,°
To crown thy open table doth provide
  The purpled pheasant with the speckled side.
The painted partridge lies in every field,
30   And, for thy mess, is willing to be killed;
And if the high swollen Medway° fail thy dish,
  Thou hast thy ponds that pay thee tribute fish,
Fat, agèd carps, that run into thy net.
  And pikes, now weary their own kind to eat,
As loath, the second draught° or cast to stay,°
  Officiously,° at first, themselves betray.
Bright eels that emulate them and leap on land,

Penshurst In Kent, the home of the Sidney family (although only from 1552); Sir Robert Sidney, Sir Philip's younger brother, was then head of the household. See Waller's poem praising the same great house, Denham's *Cooper's Hill*, Marvell's "Upon Appleton House," and Pope's "Windsor Forest" for the tradition of the topographical poem.
touch black marble
lanthorn lantern: small, glassed-in cupola atop a building
grudged at begrudged ("they are envied; you, lacking them, are not")
marks boundaries
Mount some hill on the grounds

his great birth Sir Philip Sidney's (November 30, 1554)
Sylvan . . . flames country people who fell in love (as if love "flamed" out of Sidney's sonnets)
Lady's oak under which Lady Leicester started into labor with her son, Sir Robert Sidney
Gamage after Barbara Gamage, the owner's wife, who fed deer there
coneys rabbits
Ashore . . . copse two wooded areas
Medway the river beside the estate
draught drawing-in of the fishing net
stay await
Officiously dutifully

Before the fisher or into his hand.°
Then hath thy orchard fruit, thy garden flowers,
40   Fresh as the air and new as are the hours.
The early cherry, with the later plum,
   Fig, grape, and quince, each in his time doth come;
The flushing apricot and woolly peach
   Hang on thy walls° that° every child may reach.
And though thy walls be of the country stone,
   They are reared with no man's ruin, no man's groan.
There's none that dwell about them wish them down;
   But all come in, the farmer, and the clown;°
And no one empty-handed to salute
50   Thy lord and lady, though they have no suit.°
Some bring a capon, some a rural cake,
   Some nuts, some apples; some that think they make
The better cheeses bring them; or else send
   By their ripe daughters whom they would commend
This way to husbands, and whose baskets bear
   An emblem of themselves,° in plum or pear.
But what can this (more than express their love)
   Add to thy free provisions, far above
The need of such? whose liberal board doth flow
60   With all that hospitality doth know!
Where comes no guest, but is allowed to eat
   Without his fear,° and of thy Lord's own meat,
Where the same beer and bread and self-same wine
   That is his Lordship's shall be also mine.
And I not fain to sit (as some, this day,
   At great men's tables) and yet dine away.°
Here no man tells° my cups; nor, standing by,
   A waiter doth my gluttony envý,
But gives me what I call and lets me eat,
70   He knows, below, he shall find plenty of meat.
Thy tables hoard not up for the next day,
   Nor when I take my lodging need I pray
For fire, or lights, or livery:° all is there;
   As if thou, then, wert mine, or I reigned here,
There's nothing I can wish, for which I stay.
   That found King James, when hunting late this way,
With his brave son, the Prince,° they saw thy fires
   Shine bright on every hearth as° the desires
Of thy Penates° had been set on flame

into his hand These extravagances and those that follow are all quasi-paradisiacal images of natural plenitude in a rural life more like Adam's than like a fallen human farmer's.
Hang on thy walls Trees were espaliered for decoration; this is Jonson's conceit.
that so that
clown peasant
suit petition
emblem of themselves picture of their ripeness and roundness
fear (of poisoning)
dine away still hungry, have to go out for a meal
tells counts
livery provision
Prince James I's son, Prince Henry, died in November of 1612.
as as if
Penates Roman household gods

80   To entertain them; or the country came,
      With all their zeal, to warm their welcome here.
          What (great, I will not say, but) sudden cheer
      Didst thou, then, make them! and what praise was heaped
          On thy good lady, then! who, therein, reaped
      The just reward of her high huswifery;
          To have her linen, plate, and all things nigh,
      When she was far: and not a room, but dressed,
          As if it had expected such a guest!
      These, Penshurst, are thy praise, and yet not all.
90   Thy lady's noble, fruitful, chaste withall.
      His children thy great lord may call his own:
          A fortune in this age but rarely known.
      They are and have been taught religion; thence
          Their gentler spirits have sucked innocence.
      Each morn and even they are taught to pray
          With the whole household, and may, every day,
      Read, in their virtuous parents noble parts,
          The mysteries of manners, arms, and arts.
      Now Penshurst, they that will proportion° thee
100   With other edifices, when they see
      Those proud, ambitious heaps, and nothing else,
          May say, their lords have built, but thy lord dwells.
                                              1616

Song: To Celia°

      Come, my Celia, let us prove,°
      While we may, the sports of love;
      Time will not be ours forever:
      He, at length, our good will sever.
      Spend not then his gifts in vain:
      Suns that set may rise again;
      But if once we lose this light,
      'Tis with us perpetual night.
      Why should we defer our joys?
10   Fame and rumour are but toys.
      Cannot we delude the eyes
      Of a few poor household spies?
      Or his easier ears beguile,°
      So removèd by our wile?
      'Tis no sin love's fruit to steal,
      But the sweet theft to reveal:
      To be taken, to be seen,
      These have crimes accounted been.
                                        1606

proportion compare
To Celia from *Volpone* (1606), III.vii, where
it is sung as a seduction song and reflects the
play's themes of acquisition and deceit. It is
based on Catullus' fifth ode (see Campion's

"My Sweetest Lesbia").
prove experience
his . . . beguile Volpone, the seducer, is aware
that the lady's husband is listening.

Rather quick.

Voice

Come my   Ce - li - a, let   us   prove,
Spend not   then   his_____ gifts   in   vain;

Piano

While   we   may,   the sweets   of   love.   Time__
Suns   that   set   may   rise   a - gain,   But__

__ will   not   be   ours   for   ev - er,   He   at   length__
__ if   we   once   lose   this   light   'Tis   with   us__

*

__ our   good_____ will   se - ver.
__ per - pe - - - - tual   night.

*2

* Small notes second time.

*2 No G second time.

Why should we de - fer our joys? Fame and
Ru - mour_ are but toys. Can - not we_ de - lude the
eyes Of a few poor house-hold spies? Or_ his eas - ier ears_
_ be - guile, Thus re - mov - ed by our wile?

This is the setting of the poem by Alfonso Ferrabosco (c. 1575–1628), for lute and solo voice, from his 1609 book of airs. Although a contemporary piece, this was probably not the sort of more simplified setting that might have been used for the song in *Volpone*.

To the Same°

Kiss me, sweet: the wary lover
Can your favours keep, and cover,
When the common courting jay
All your bounties will betray.
Kiss again: no creature comes.
Kiss, and score up wealthy sums
On my lips, thus hardly sundered
While you breathe. First give a hundred,
Then a thousand, then another
Hundred, then unto the tother
Add a thousand, and so more,
Till you equal with the store
All the grass that Rumney° yields,
Or the sand in Chelsea fields,
Or the drops in silver Thames,
Or the stars that gild his streams
In the silent summer-nights,
When youths ply their stolen delights,
That the curious may not know
How to tell° them, as thy flow,
And the envious, when they find
What their number is, be pined.°
                              1616

Song: To Celia

Drink to me only with thine eyes,
    And I will pledge° with mine;
Or leave a kiss but in the cup,
    And I'll not look for wine.
The thirst that from the soul doth rise
    Doth ask a drink divine:
But might I of Jove's nectar sup,
    I would not change for thine.°
I sent thee, late, a rosy wreath,
    Not so much honouring thee,
As giving it a hope that there
    It could not withered be.
But thou thereon didst only breathe
    And sent'st it back to me,
Since when it grows, and smells, I swear,
    Not of itself, but thee.
                              1616

To the Same from Catullus' seventh ode
Rumney famous pasture grounds in Kent
tell count
pined miserable

pledge drink a toast
But . . . thine except for the nectar of the
gods, I'd not swap my "drinks" of you for anything

On My First Son

Farewell, thou child of my right hand° and joy;
  My sin was too much hope of thee, loved boy.
Seven years thou wert lent to me, and I thee pay,
  Exacted by thy fate, on the just day.°
O, could I lose all father now! For why
  Will man lament the state he should envy?
To have so soon 'scaped world's and flesh's rage,
  And, if no other misery, yet age?
Rest in soft peace,° and asked, say here doth lie
10 Ben. Jonson, his best piece of poetry:°
For whose sake, henceforth, all his vows be such,
  As what he loves may never like too much.

                                        1616

Epitaph on S. P.° a Child of Queen Elizabeth's Chapel

Weep with me, all you that read
  This little story,
And know, for whom a tear you shed,
  Death's self is sorry.
'Twas a child, that so did thrive
  In grace and feature,
As Heaven and Nature seemed to strive
  Which owned the creature.
Years he numbered scarce thirteen
10 When Fates turned cruel,
Yet three filled zodiacs° had he been
  The stage's jewel,
And did act, what now we moan,
  Old men so duly,
As, sooth, the Parcae° thought him one,
  He played so truly.
So, by error, to his fate
  They all consented;
But viewing him since (alas, too late)
20 They have repented.
And have sought, to give new birth,
  In baths° to steep him;

---

right hand Jonson's boy, who died of the plague
in 1603 at the age of 7, was likewise Benjamin
(in Hebrew, "son of the right hand").
just day Day of Judgment
Rest . . . peace the "requiescat in pace"
poetry Jonson has in mind the Greek etymology
of *poesis*, "making" or "creation."

S. P. Salomon Pavy, a boy actor
zodiacs 1600–1602, his three brief years on the
stage
Parcae the Fates
baths Aeson, father of Jason (he of the Golden
Fleece) was restored from decrepitude by a
magical bath.

But, being so much too good for earth,
   Heaven vows to keep him.
        1616

To William Roe°

Roe (and my joy to name), thou art now to go,
   Countries and climes, manners and men to know,
To extract, and choose the best of all these known,
   And those to turn to blood and make thine own.
May winds as soft as breath of kissing friends
   Attend thee hence, and there may all thy ends,
As the beginning here, prove purely sweet
   And perfect in a circle always meet.°
So when we, blessed with thy return, shall see
10   Thyself, with thy first thoughts, brought home by thee,
We each to other may this voice inspire:
   This is that good Aeneas, passed through fire,
Through seas, storms, tempests; and embarked for hell,
   Came back untouched. This man hath travelled° well.
        1616

Inviting a Friend to Supper

Tonight, grave sir, both my poor house, and I
   Do equally desire your company;
Not that we think us worthy such a guest,
   But that your worth will dignify our feast
With those that come, whose grace may make that seem
   Something, which else could hope for no esteem.
It is the fair acceptance, sir, creates
   The entertainment perfect, not the cates.°
Yet shall you have, to rectify your palate,
10   An olive, capers, or some better salad
Ushering the mutton; with a short-legged hen,
   If we can get her, full of eggs, and then
Lemons, and wine for sauce; to these, a coney°
   Is not to be despaired of, for our money;
And, though fowl now be scarce, yet there are clerks,
   The sky not falling, think we may have larks.
I'll tell you of more, and lie, so you will come:
   Of partridge, pheasant, woodcock, of which some

To William Roe as he was setting out on a
journey
circle always meet Compare Donne's compass
image in "A Valediction: Forbidding Mourning."

travelled also "travailed," labored
cates delicacies (cf. "caterer")
coney rabbit

May yet be there, and godwit, if we can;
20   Knat, rail, and ruff° too. Howsoe'r, my man
Shall read a piece of Virgil, Tacitus,
      Livy, or of some better book to us,
Of which we'll speak our minds, amidst our meat;°
      And I'll profess no verses to repeat.
To this, if aught appear which I not know of,
      That will the pastry, not my paper, show of.
Digestive cheese and fruit there sure will be;
      But that which most doth take my Muse and me,
Is a pure cup of rich Canary wine,
30   Which is the Mermaid's° now, but shall be mine;
Of which had Horace, or Anacreon tasted,
      Their lives, as do their lines, till now had lasted.
Tobacco,° nectar, or the Thespian spring,°
      Are all but Luther's beer° to this I sing.
Of this we will sup free, but moderately,
      And we will have no Pooley, or Parrot° by,
Nor shall our cups make any guilty men;
      But, at our parting we will be as when
We innocently met. No simple word
40   That shall be uttered at our mirthful board,
Shall make us sad next morning or affright
      The liberty that we'll enjoy tonight.

                                    1616

Songs From Plays

Slow, Slow Fresh Fount°

Slow, slow, fresh fount, keep time with my salt tears;
Yet slower, yet, Oh faintly, gentle springs!
List to the heavy part the music bears,
Woe weeps out her division,° when she sings.
          Droop herbs and flowers;
          Fall grief in showers;
Our beauties are not ours. Oh, I could still
Like melting snow upon some craggy hill,
10   Drop, drop, drop, drop,
Since nature's pride is now a withered daffodil.

                                    1601

godwit . . . Knat . . . rail . . . ruff   game
birds
meat meal
Mermaid's the Mermaid Tavern, convivial home
of Jonson's circle
Tobacco "Drinking" meant smoking it.
Thespian spring another of the Muses' fountains
Luther's beer bad German beer (as opposed to
his wine)

Pooley, or Parrot famous government informers
(Pooley, or Poley, was present at Marlowe's
murder)
Slow, Slow Fresh Fount from *Cynthia's Revels*
(1601)
division musical improvisation or variation based
on a stated theme ("dividing" its long notes),
like a jazz soloist's "chorus"

Queen and Huntress°

Queen and huntress, chaste and fair,
Now the sun is laid to sleep,
Seated in thy silver chair,
State in wonted manner keep:
  Hesperus° entreats thy light,
  Goddess excellently bright.

Earth, let not thy envious shade
Dare itself to interpose;
Cynthia's shining orb was made
10 Heaven to clear° when day did close:
  Bless us then with wishèd sight,
  Goddess excellently bright.

Lay thy bow of pearl apart,
And thy crystal-shining quiver;
Give unto the flying hart°
Space to breathe, how short soever:
  Thou that mak'st a day of night,
  Goddess excellently bright.

Clerimont's Song°

Still to be neat, still to be dressed
As° you were going to a feast;
Still to be powdered, still perfumed—
Lady, it is to be presumed,
Though art's hid causes are not found,
All is not sweet, all is not sound.

Give me a look, give me a face,
That makes simplicity a grace;
Robes loosely flowing, hair as free:
10 Such sweet neglect more taketh me
Than all the adulteries° of art;
They strike mine eyes, but not my heart.

Queen and Huntress from the concluding masque in *Cynthia's Revels.* Cynthia (Diana), goddess of the moon and of hunting, symbolized Queen Elizabeth.
Hesperus the Evening Star
clear brighten
hart male deer, with the usual pun

Clerimont's Song from *Epicoene, or The Silent Woman* (1609), I.i. Compare Herrick's "Delight in Disorder" with this praise of "naturalness" based on a late Latin poem.
As as if
adulteries adulterations

Pleasure Reconciled to Virtue

The court masque was, for Jonson, a supreme form in which to exercise what he felt were the moral and political obligations of poetry. The Jacobean and Caroline masque had evolved from staged court dances and entertainments, and came to include dancing, singing, allegorical scenery and costume, and an elaborate mythology (put together, like pictures of the great Italian Renaissance painters, out of classical myths, Christian materials, and their combined interpretations and inter-associations). All this centered on the monarch or other presiding figure, and involved the audience in many ways: as spectators, students of the emblematic lesson being taught, hearers of music, and, finally, as participating dancers themselves. The "masquers" were members of the court or state family, elaborately dressed in symbolic costume; they joined the richly, but not allegorically, dressed spectators in the revels, the occurrence of which, for Jonson and other writers of masques, could figure forth the interaction of myth and reality, of poetry and actual moral order as centered on the monarch. The stage scenery and effects were most complex—transformation scenes, involving both illusionistic sets and complex machinery, were frequent—and Jonson worked with Inigo Jones, the great architect and stage designer, falling out with him when it became apparent that Charles I, unlike his intellectual father, preferred more spectacle and less poetic coherence in his masques.

Pleasure Reconciled to Virtue was Charles's first masque (as the young Prince, he led the masquers). Its mythology is based on the Choice of Hercules (himself a centrally important heroic figure for the English Renaissance): as a youth, he met two tall women at a crossroads; each offered him a different future. Pleasure promised him delight, Virtue, a life of toil crowned with glory (in some versions of the legend, Pleasure inevitably, trivially, is called Vice). Jonson gives his spectators a complex, animated emblem of moral fulfillment in "reconciling" the two personifications: when what is good and what is delightful, "pleasure and profit," are indistinguishable, life is being properly conducted (a lesson, we must remember, being taught a royal court on Twelfth Night, traditional time of revelry). In the action, we have first, an antimasque ("antic masque" or "anti-masque") of Comus, a big comic fatso, figure of overindulgence and the monstrosity of its moral shape; next, a second antimasque of pygmies; then Hercules appears and banishes the monsters, is crowded by Mercury, and gives way in the action to Daedalus (here standing for skill in design, music, and, of course, Jonson's own art), leading the masquers through the grand masquing dances. The symbolic action occurs not merely in the text, but in the audience's controlled reactions to it—watching the dance, joining it, and somehow, *thereby*, understanding it. Milton knew this masque, and transformed its low-comic figure into someone very different in *Comus*. Our text owes much to Stephen Orgel's splendid edition.

Pleasure Reconciled to Virtue

A Masque. As it was presented at court before King James, 1618

The scene was the mountain ATLAS,° *who had his top ending in the figure of an old man, his head and beard all hoary and frost as if his shoulders were*

Atlas mountain mythologically placed in Libya, the transformed state of the giant who was said to support the earth on his shoulders

covered with snow; the rest wood and rock. A grove of ivy at his feet, out of which, to a wild music of cymbals, flutes and tabers, is brought forth COMUS,°
the god of cheer, or the belly, riding in triumph, his head crowned with roses and other flowers, his hair curled; they that wait upon him crowned with ivy, their javelins done about with it; one of them going with HERCULES *his bowl bare before him, while the rest presented him with this*

HYMN

10   Room, room, make room for the bouncing belly,
    First father of sauce, and deviser of jelly,
    Prime master of arts, and the giver of wit,
    That found out the excellent engine, the spit,
    The plow, and the flail, the mill, and the hopper,°
    The hutch,° and the bolter,° the furnace, and copper,°
    The oven, the bavin,° the mawkin,° the peel,°
    The hearth, and the range, the dog and the wheel.°
    He, he first invented the hogshead and tun,°
    The gimlet and vise° too, and taught 'em to run.
20   And since, with the funnel, an Hippocras bag°
    He's made of himself, that now he cries swag.°
    Which shows, though the pleasure be but of four inches,
    Yet he is a weasel, the gullet that pinches,
    Of any delight, and not spares from this back
    Whatever to make of the belly a sack.°
    Hail, hail, plump paunch, O the founder of taste
    For fresh meats, or powdered, or pickle, or paste;
    Devourer of broiled, baked, roasted or sod,°
    And emptier of cups, be they even or odd;
30   All which have now made thee so wide i' the waist
    As scarce with no pudding thou art to be laced;°
    But eating and drinking until thou dost nod,
    Thou break'st all thy girdles, and break'st forth a god.

To this, the Bowl-bearer

Do you hear, my friends? to whom did you sing all this now? Pardon me only that I ask you, for I do not look for an answer; I'll answer myself: I know it is

---

Comus from the Greek "kōmos" ("carousal");
late mythic figure of a winged, rose-crowned
youth; Jonson adds attributes of a monster
turned all belly (by the Circe-like power of
satire)
hopper for receiving grain in a mill
hutch sifting bin. All these terms will follow a
process, from milling to cooking, paralleling
that of the alimentary tract.
bolter sifter
copper pot
bavin kindling brushwood for bakers' ovens
mawkin baker's mop
peel baker's shovel
dog . . . wheel treadmill to turn a roasting
spit

tun keg
vise for tapping kegs
Hippocras bag for straining spiced wine punch
cries swag shows his swag-belly, his pendulous
paunch
which shows . . . sack though the pleasure of
swilling only adds four inches to the waistline,
the gullet won't give up its delights, even to
make it easier for the back to bear the weight
of the huge tummy
sod boiled
As scarce . . . laced you're too fat (even stuff-
ing more pudding into you—which can't be
done) to be laced up

now such a time as the saturnals° for all the world, that every man stands under the eaves of his own hat and sings what please him; that's the right and the liberty of it. Now you sing of god Comus here, the Belly-god. I say it is well, and I say it is not well. It is well as it is a ballad, and the belly worthy of it,
40   I must needs say, an 'twere forty yards of ballad more—as much ballad as tripe.° But when the belly is not edified by it, it is not well; for where did you ever read or hear that the belly had any ears? Come, never pump for an answer, for you are defeated. Our fellow Hunger there, that was as ancient a retainer to the belly as any of us, was turned away from being unseasonable (not unreasonable, but unseasonable) and now is he (poor thin-gut) fain to get his living with teaching of starlings, magpies, parrots and jackdaws, those things he would have taught the belly. Beware of dealing with the belly; the belly will not be talked to, especially when he is full. Then there is no venturing upon Venter;° he will blow you all up; he will thunder indeed, la: some in
50   derision call him the father of farts. But I say he was the first inventor of great ordnance,° and taught us to discharge them on festival days. Would we had a fit feast for him, i' faith, to show his activity: I would have something now fetched in to please his five senses, the throat, or the two senses, the eyes. Pardon me for my two senses; for I that carry Hercules' bowl i' the service may see double by my place, for I have drunk like a frog today. I would have a tun now brought in to dance, and so many bottles about him. Ha! You look as if you would make a problem of this. Do you see? Do you see? a problem: why bottles? and why a tun? and why a tun? and why bottles to dance? I say that men that drink hard and serve the belly in any place of quality (as The Jovial Tinkers, or
60   The Lusty Kindred)° are living measures of drink, and can transform themselves, and do every day, to bottles or tuns when they please; and when they ha' done all they can, they are, as I say again (for I think I said somewhat like it afore) but moving measures of drink; and there is a piece° i' the cellar can hold more than all they. This will I make good if it please our new god but to give a nod; for the belly does all by signs, and I am all for the belly, the truest clock i' the world to go by.

> *Here the first antimasque° after which,*

HERCULES   What rites are these? Breeds earth more monsters yet?
        Antaeus° scarce is cold: what can beget
70   This store?° And stay! such contraries upon her?°
        Is earth so fruitful of her own dishonour?
        Or 'cause his vice was inhumanity,
        Hopes she by vicious hospitality
        To work an expiation first? and then
        (Help, Virtue!) these are sponges, and not men.

---

saturnals the Roman Saturnalia, a feast of licentious revelry, corresponding to Twelfth Night, which concluded the period of Christmas revels (this masque was written for Twelfth Night, 1618)
tripe guts
Venter Latin for tummy
ordnance artillery
The Jovial . . . Kindred perhaps taverns

piece barrel
antimasque It was danced by men costumed as bottles and a barrel.
Antaeus a giant whose power came from touching Earth, his mother; Hercules held him off the ground and crushed him to death
store abundance
her Earth. "Contraries" are monsters.

Bottles? Mere vessels? Half a tun of paunch?
How? and the other half thrust forth in haunch?
Whose feast? the belly's? Comus'? and my cup
Brought in to fill the drunken orgies up?

80 And here abused, that was the crowned reward
Of thirsty heroes after labour hard?
Burdens and shames of nature, perish, die!
—For yet you never lived, but in the sty
Of vice have wallowed, and in that swine's strife
Been buried under the offence of life.
Go, reel and fall under the load you make,
Till your swollen bowels burst with what you take.
Can this be pleasure, to extinguish man?
Or so quite change him in his figure? Can

90 The belly love his pain, and be content
With no delight but what's a punishment?
These monsters plague themselves, and fitly, too,
For they do suffer what and all they do.
But here must be no shelter, nor no shroud
For such: sink grove, or vanish into cloud!

*At this the whole grove vanished, and the whole music° was discovered,
sitting at the foot of the mountain, with* PLEASURE *and* VIRTUE *seated
above them. The choir invited* HERCULES *to rest with this*

SONG

100   Great friend and servant of the good,
                   Let cool awhile thy heated blood,
                      And from thy mighty labour cease.
                         Lie down, lie down,
                   And give thy troubled spirits peace,
                      Whilst Virtue, for whose sake
                Thou dost this godlike travail take,
                   May of the choicest herbage make,
                      Here on this mountain bred,
                         A crown, a crown
110   For thy immortal head.

Here HERCULES *being laid down at their feet, the second antimasque,
which was of* PIGMIES, *appeared.*

1ST PIGMY   Antaeus dead! and Hercules yet live!
Where is this Hercules? What would I give
To meet him now? Meet him? nay three such other,
If they had hand in murder of our brother?°
With three? with four? with ten? Nay, with as many

music *the orchestra and choir, whose members,
like the actors and singers, were professionals
(the masquers were not)*

brother *The fabled Pygmies of antiquity were
also distorted sons of Earth.*

As the name yields?° Pray anger there be any
Whereon to feed my just revenge, and soon
120   How shall I kill him? Hurl him 'gainst the moon,
And break him in small portions? Give to Greece
His brain, and every tract of earth a piece?

2ND PIGMY   He is yonder.

1ST PIGMY   Where?

3RD PIGMY   At the hill foot, asleep.

1ST PIGMY   Let one go steal his club.

2ND PIGMY   My charge, I'll creep.

4TH PIGMY   He's ours.

1ST PIGMY   Yes, peace.

3RD PIGMY   Triumph, we have him, boy.

4TH PIGMY   Sure, sure, he is sure.

1ST PIGMY   Come, let us dance for joy.

*At the end of their dance they thought to surprise him; when suddenly,
being awaked by the music, he roused himself, they all ran into holes.*

SONG°

130   Wake, Hercules, awake: but heave up thy black eye,
'Tis only asked from thee to look and these will die,
                    Or fly.
            Already they are fled,
            Whom scorn had else left dead.

At which MERCURY *descended from the hill with a garland of poplar°
to crown him.*

MERCURY   Rest still, thou active friend of Virtue: these
Should not disturb the peace of Hercules.
Earth's worms and honour's dwarfs, at too great odds,
140   Prove,° or provoke the issue of the gods.
See, here a crown the agèd hill hath sent thee,
My grandsire Atlas, he that did present thee
With the best sheep that in his fold were found,
Or golden fruit in the Hesperian ground,°
For rescuing his fair daughters, then the prey
Of a rude pirate, as thou cam'st this way;
And taught thee all the learning of the sphere,
And how, like him,° thou might'st the heavens up-bear,
As that thy labour's virtuous recompense.
150   He, though a mountain now, hath yet the sense

---

as many . . . yields Various ancient local
heroes were called "Hercules" and assimilated
to his cult.
Song sung by the choir
poplar In another story, Hercules crowned himself with poplar leaves from the Aventine Hill;
Jonson here associates it with Atlas (see below).
Prove test

Hesperian ground In a garden, Atlas' three
daughters, the Hesperides, guarded the golden
apples whose acquisition was the last of the
labors of Hercules.
like him Hercules had carried the world for
Atlas for a while, and duped him into taking on
the burden again.

Of thanking thee for more, thou being still
Constant to goodness, guardian of the hill;
Antaeus, by thee suffocated here,
And the voluptuous Comus, god of cheer,
Beat from his grove, and that defaced. But now
The time's arrived that Atlas told thee of—how,
By unaltered law, and working of the stars,
There should be a cessation of all jars°
'Twixt Virtue and her noted opposite,
160   Pleasure; that both should meet here in the sight
Of Hesperus,° the glory of the west,
The brightest star, that from his burning crest
Lights all on this side the Atlantic seas
As far as to thy pillars,° Hercules.
See where he shines: Justice and Wisdom placed
About his throne, and those with Honour graced,
Beauty and Love. It is not with his brother
Bearing the world, but ruling such another
Is his renown.° Pleasure, for his delight
170   Is reconciled to Virtue, and this night
Virtue brings forth twelve princes have° been bred
In this rough mountain and near Atlas' head,
The hill of knowledge; one and chief of whom°
Of the bright race of Hesperus is come,
Who shall in time the same that he is be,
And now is only a less light than he.
These now she° trusts with Pleasure, and to these
She gives an entrance to the Hesperides,
Fair Beauty's garden; neither can she fear
180   They should grow soft or wax effeminate here,
Since in her sight and by her charge all's done,
Pleasure the servant, Virtue looking on.

*Here the whole choir of music called the twelve masquers forth from
the lap of the mountain, which then opened with this*

SONG°

       Ope agèd Atlas, open then thy lap,
       And from thy beamy bosom strike a light,
       That men may read in thy mysterious map
            All lines
190   And signs
       Of royal education and the right.

---

jars discords
Hesperus the Evening Star, here symbolically associated with King James
pillars the Strait of Gibraltar
ruling . . . renown being king of "another world" (England), paralleling Atlas carrying his world

have who have
chief of whom Prince Charles, who was the chief masquer
she Virtue
Song sung and danced, Pleasure probably leading the way; this was the entrance of the masquers

> See how they come and show,
> That are but born to know.
> Descend,
> Descend,
> Though pleasure lead,
> Fear not to follow;
> They who are bred
> Within the hill
> Of skill
> May safely tread
> What path they will:
> No ground of good is hollow.

200

In their descent from the hill DAEDALUS° *came down before them, of whom* HERCULES *questioned* MERCURY.

HERCULES   But Hermes,° stay a little, let me pause.
Who's this that leads?
MERCURY   A guide that gives them laws
To all their motions: Daedalus the wise.
HERCULES   And doth in sacred harmony comprise
His precepts?
MERCURY   Yes.
HERCULES   They may securely prove°
Then any labyrinth, though it be of love.

210

Here, while they put themselves in form, DAEDALUS *had his first*

SONG

> Come on, come on; and where you go,
> So interweave the curious knot,°
> As even the observer scarce may know
> Which lines are Pleasure's and which not.
> First, figure out the doubtful way
> At which awhile all youth should stay,
> Where she and Virtue did contend
> Which should have Hercules to friend.°
> Then, as all actions of mankind
> Are but a labyrinth or maze,
> So let your dances be entwined,
> Yet not perplex men unto gaze;°

220

Daedalus great designer and artificer who built the labyrinth for Minos; here he descends from the "hill of skill' to preside over the remainder of the masque
Hermes "Mercury" in Greek
prove experience
curious knot complex choreographic interweaving of lines of dancers. The masquers are literally acting out Daedalus' metaphorical in-

structions in this part of the masque, and it will be hard to tell pleasures and virtues apart. See the emblem of Hercules (Fig. 23).
Hercules to friend referring to the Choice of Hercules (see Headnote). The episode of the Choice has happened in the past, and Hercules represents a moral being already tested.
unto gaze into bewilderment

But measured, and so numerous° too,
    As men may read each act you do,
    And when they see the graces meet,
        Admire the wisdom of your feet.
230   For dancing is an exercise
        Not only shows the mover's wit,
    But maketh the beholder wise,°
        As he hath power to rise to it.

The first dance.

After which DAEDALUS *again.*

SONG 2

O more, and more; this was so well
    As praise wants half his voice to tell;
        Again yourselves compose,°
240   And now put all the aptness on
        Of figure, that proportion
            Or colour can disclose—°
    That if those silent arts° were lost,
        Design and picture, they might boast
            From you a newer ground,°
        Instructed by the heightening sense
            Of dignity and reverence
                In your true motions found:
    Begin, begin; for look, the fair
250   Do longing listen to what air°
            You form your second touch,°
    That they may vent their murmuring hymns
    Just to the tune you move your limbs,
            And wish their own were such.
    Make haste, make haste, for this
        The labyrinth of beauty is.

The second dance.

That ended, DAEDALUS.

SONG 3

260   It follows now you are to prove°
        The subtlest maze of all, that's love,

numerous "numbered," like English verse (both
"measured" and stress-accented)
wise by understanding its symbolic significance
compose rearrange
And now . . . disclose arrange your postures
and expressions with the same skill that design
and painting use

silent arts architectural design and pictures are
silent poetry
ground basis (conceptually); base (architec-
turally); underlaid color (in painting); bass
(musically)
air melody
touch passage of music
prove try out

And if you stay too long,
The fair will think you do 'em wrong.
Go, choose among,° but with a mind
As gentle as the stroking wind
Runs o'er the gentler flowers.
And so let all your actions smile,
As if they meant not to beguile
The ladies, but the hours.

270

Grace, laughter and discóurse may meet,
And yet the beauty not go less:°
For what is noble should be sweet,
But not dissolved in wantonness.
Will you° that I give the law
To all your sport, and sum it?°
It should be such should° envy draw,
But ever overcome it.

Here they danced with the ladies, and the whole revels° followed; which
ended, MERCURY *called to him° in this following speech, which was after*

280

repeated in song by two trebles, two tenors, a bass and the whole chorus.

SONG 4

An eye of looking back were well,
Or any murmur that would tell
Your thoughts, how you were sent
And went,
To walk with Pleasure, not to dwell.
These, these are hours by Virtue spared
Herself, she being her own reward,
But she will have you know

290

That though
Her sports be soft, her life is hard.
You must return unto the hill,
And there advance
With labour, and inhabit still
That height and crown
From whence you ever may look down
Upon triumphèd° Chance.
She, she it is, in darkness shines.
'Tis she that still herself refines,

300

By her own light, to every eye
More seen, more known when Vice stands by.
And though a stranger here on earth,

---

among among them
go less be worth less
will you do you wish
sum it sum it up
should that should
revels the part of the masque in which the

"beholders" would, literally, "rise to it" (see
l. 233) and join with the masquers in the
dancing, which would go on a good while
him Daedalus
triumphèd triumphed-over

In heaven she hath her right of birth.
There, there is Virtue's seat,°
Strive to keep her your own;
'Tis only she can make you great,
Though place° here make you known.

*After which, they danced their last dance, and returned into the scene,
which closed and was a mountain again as before.*

The End.
1618   1640

WILLIAM DRUMMOND OF HAWTHORNDEN
1585–1649

He attended the University of Edinburgh, became laird of Hawthornden in 1610,
corresponded with Drayton and Ben Jonson (who visited him in 1618–19, and whose
remarks Drummond dutifully recorded in a set of *Conversations*), wrote epigrammatic
verse and religious meditation (the prose *Cypress Grove*, published in 1623), and,
towards the end of his life, political pamphlets for the Royalist cause. His 1616 *Poems*
contain sonnets, songs, and epigrams strangely called "madrigals," arranged in
Petrarchan sections following the life and then the death of the beloved lady. His
religious poems appeared in *Flowers of Sion,* in 1623.

Madrigal°

Like the Idalian Queen,°
Her hair about her eyne,°
With neck and breasts' ripe apples to be seen,
At first glance of the morn
In Cyprus' gardens gathering those fair flowers
Which of her blood were born,
I saw, but fainting saw, my paramours.
The Graces naked danced about the place,
The winds and trees amazed
10   With silence on her gazed,
The flowers did smile, like those upon her face,
And as their aspine° stalks those fingers band,
(That she might read my case)
A hyacinth I wished me in her hand.
                              1616

---

seat official place
place status, rank
Madrigal Drummond uses this term in a peculiar way, to mean short, epigrammatic poems,
more usually perhaps written in heroic couplets,
but here comprising one strophe or stanza with

varying line lengths, an Italian conception.
Idalian Queen Venus; Idalia, on Cyprus, was
the center of her cult
eyne eyes
aspine trembling

Madrigal

This life which seems so fair
Is like a bubble blown up in the air
By sporting children's breath,
Who chase it everywhere,
And strive who can most motion it bequeath;
And though it sometime seem of its own might,
Like to an eye of gold, to be fixed there,
And firm to hover in that empty height,
That only is because it is so light;
10 But in that pomp it doth not long appear,
    For even when most admired, it in a thought,
      As swelled from nothing, doth dissolve in nought.

                    1616

On Mary Magdalen°

Those eyes (dear Lord) once brandons° of desire,
Frail scouts betraying what they had to keep,
Which their own heart, then others, set on fire,
Their traitorous black before thee here outweep:
Those locks, of blushing deeds the fair attire,
Smooth-frizzled waves, sad shelves which shadow deep,
Soul-stinging serpents in gilt curls which creep,
To touch thy sacred feet do now aspire.
In seas of care behold a sinking bark,
10 By winds of sharp remorse unto thee driven:
O, let me not exposed by ruin's mark,
My faults confessed (Lord) say they are forgiven.
    —Thus sighed to Jesus the Bethanian° fair,
      His tear-wet feet still drying with her hair.

                    1623

WILLIAM BROWNE OF TAVISTOCK
1591?–1643?

Browne was born in Devon and educated at Exeter College, Oxford, and the Inner Temple. His sense of place, of the natural scene of the West Country, combined with his deep love of the Sidneyan and Spenserian poetic traditions to allow him, like Drayton and his friend George Wither, to continue that tradition well into the seventeenth century. He was in the service of the Pembroke family, and collaborated on a book of pastorals called *The Shepherd's Pipe* (1614); his major work, *Britannia's Pastorals*, appeared in 1613 (Pt. I) and 1616 (Pt. II). Part III was not printed until 1852.

On Mary Magdalen The weeping figure of the Magdalene, or her very tears, were a favorite subject for baroque poetry (see Crashaw's verse on this subject).

brandons torches
Bethanian Mary Magdalene (from the town of Bethany)

On the Death of Marie, Countess of Pembroke

Underneath this sable hearse
Lies the subject of all verse:
Sidney's sister, Pembroke's mother;
Death, ere thou has slain another,
Fair, and learned, and good as she,
Time shall throw a dart at thee.

Marble piles let no man raise
To her name for after days;
Some kind woman borne as she,
10   Reading this, like Niobe°
Shall turn marble, and become
Both her mourner and her tomb.

                                    1623

To Pyrrha°

Tell me, Pyrrha, what fine youth,
      All perfumed and crowned with roses,
To thy chamber thee pursueth,
      And thy wanton arm encloses?

What is he thou now hast got,
      Whose more long and golden tresses
Into many a curious knot
      Thy more curious finger dresses?

How much will he wail his trust,
10   And, forsook, begin to wonder,
When black winds shall billows thrust,
      And break all hopes in sunder!

Fickleness of winds he knows
      Very little that doth love thee;
Miserable are all those
      That affect thee ere they prove thee.

I, as one from shipwreck freed,
      To the ocean's mighty ranger
Consecrate my dropping weed,
20   And in freedom think of danger.

                              from MS. 1894

Niobe Mourning the death of her twelve children, she was transformed into a rocky mountain spring, forever weeping.

To Pyrrha imitated from Horace; compare Milton's version of the same Latin original

From Britannia's Pastorals

[Aletheia Arises from the Corpse of Fida's Hind°]

As that Arabian bird° (whom all admire)
Her exequies prepared and funeral fire,
Burnt in a flame conceivèd from the sun,
And nourishèd with slips of cinnamon,
Out of her ashes hath a second birth,
And flies abroad, a wonderment on earth:
So from the ruins of this mangled creature
Arose so fair and so divine a feature,
That Envy for her heart would dote upon her;
10 Heaven could not choose but be enamoured on her:
Were I a star, and she a second sphere,
I'd leave the other, and be fixèd there.
Had fair Arachne° wrought this maiden's hair,
When she with Pallas did for skill compare,
Minerva's work had never been esteemed,
But this had been more rare and highly deemed;
Yet gladly now she would reverse her doom,
Weaving this hair within a spider's loom.
Upon her forehead, as in glory, sat
20 Mercy and Majesty, for wondering at,
As pure and simple as Albania's snow,
Or milk-white swans which stem the streams of Po:
Like to some goodly foreland, bearing out
Her hair, the tufts which fringed the shore about.
And lest the man which sought those coasts might slip,
Her eyes like stars did serve to guide the ship.
Upon her front (heaven's fairest promontory)
Delineated was the authentic story
Of those elect, whose sheep at first began
To nibble by the springs of Canaan:
30 Out of whose sacred loins (brought by the stem
Of that sweet singer of Jerusalem)
Came the best Shepherd° ever flocks did keep,
Who yielded up his life to save his sheep.
   O thou Eterne! by whom all beings move,
Giving the springs beneath, and springs above;
Whose finger doth this universe sustain,
Bringing the former and the latter rain;

Aletheia Arises . . . Hind from the fourth song
of Book I of Browne's Spenserian poem (ll.
155–224), describing the birth of Aletheia
(Truth), daughter of Time, from the remains of
Fida's (Faith's) dead deer, killed by the monster Riot

bird the phoenix
Arachne challenged Athena (here called both
"Pallas" and "Minerva") to a weaving contest,
lost, and was turned into a spider.
Shepherd Christ, of the "stem" of David the
psalmist

Who dost with plenty meads and pastures fill,
40   By drops distilled like dew on Hermon° hill:
Pardon a silly swain, who (far unable
In that which is so rare, so admirable)
Dares on an oaten pipe thus meanly sing
Her praise immense, worthy a silver string.
And thou which through the desert and the deep,
Didst lead thy chosen like a flock of sheep:
As sometime by a star thou guided'st them,
Which fed upon the plains of Bethlehem;
So by thy sacred Spirit direct my quill,
50   When I shall sing ought of thy holy hill,
That times to come, when they my rhymes rehearse,
May wonder at me, and admire my verse:
For who but one rapt in celestial fire,
Can by his Muse to such a pitch aspire,
That from aloft he might behold and tell
Her worth, whereon an iron pen might dwell?
    When she was born, Nature in sport began
To learn the cunning of an artisan,
And did vermilion with a white compose,
60   To mock herself and paint a damask rose.
But scorning Nature unto Art should seek,
She spilt her colours on this maiden's cheek.
Her mouth the gate from whence all goodness came,
Of power to give the dead a living name.
Her words embalmèd in so sweet a breath,
That made them triumph both on Time and Death;
Whose fragrant sweets, since the chameleon knew,
And tasted of, he to this humour grew,
Left other elements, held this so rare,
70   That since he never feeds on ought but air.

1613

SEVENTEENTH-CENTURY LYRIC MODES

With Jacobean verse traditions, music and lyric verse begin to part company, although there are still interconnections. Certainly the court masque remains a unifying force in the Caroline period as well, and the many volumes of "Airs and Dialogues" by such composers as William and Henry Lawes continue to set witty courtly verse much as the madrigalists and lutenist composers had set Petrarchan poetry in the earlier period. But lyric verse forms came to be used for epigrammatic purposes, and the development of the ode from Jonson through Cowley was that of an expository

Hermon The reference here is to Psalms 133:3 "As the dew of Hermon and as the dew that descended upon the mountains of Zion: for there the Lord commanded the blessing, even life for evermore."

form. Below are a number of Jacobean and Caroline poems representing forms as diverse as song, inscription, and elegy, and exemplifying both the so-called strong lines of the school of Donne, and the gradually developing smoothness (as in Denham) of the later part of the century.

ANONYMOUS

Tom o' Bedlam °

From the hag and hungry goblin
That into rags would rend ye,
The spirit that stands by the naked man
In the Book of Moons° defend ye,
That of your five sound senses
You never be forsaken,
Nor wander from yourselves with Tom
Abroad to beg your bacon,
    While I do sing, Any food, any feeding,
10   Feeding, drink, or clothing;
    Come dame or maid, be not afraid,
    Poor Tom will injure nothing.

Of thirty bare years have I
Twice twenty been enragèd,
And of forty been three times fifteen
In durance soundly cagèd
On the lordly lofts of Bedlam
With stubble soft and dainty,
Brave bracelets° strong, sweet whips ding dong
20 With wholesome hunger plenty,
    And now I sing, etc.

With a thought I took for Maudlin°
And a cruse of cockle pottage,°
With a thing thus tall, sky bless you all,
I befell into this dotage.
I slept not since the Conquest,
Till then I never wakèd,
Till the roguish boy of love where I lay

Tom o' Bedlam This amazing poem from a manuscript commonplace—or literary scrap-book —of about 1620 is the greatest example of the mad song, or dramatic expression of a conventionalized view of insanity, before Blake. The protagonist is the stock figure of the out-patient from Bedlam (Bethlehem Hospital, the London madhouse), a wandering beggar, asking for alms and insisting he is harmless. Edgar in *King Lear* becomes this same "Poor Tom" in his manic guise. This song moves from the rhetoric of begging and confessional to a kind of triumphant expression of an autonomous visionary.
Book of Moons an astrological treatise for fortune-telling
bracelets handcuffs; like the "lordly lofts" and the dainty stubble, this is ironic
Maudlin British pronunciation of "Magdalene," hence, some whore, or sex personified
cockle pottage weed stew

Me found and strip't me nakèd.
30   And now I sing, etc.

When I short have shorn my sow's face
And swigged my horny barrel,°
In an oaken inn I pound° my skin
As a suit of gilt apparel;
The moon's my constant mistress
And the lovely owl my marrow;°
The flaming drake° and the night crow° make
Me music to my sorrow.
          While I do sing, etc.

40 The palsy plagues my pulses
When I prig° your pigs or pullen,°
Your culvers° take, or matchless° make
Your Chanticleer or Sullen.°
When I want provant° with Humphrey°
I sup, and when benighted,
I repose in Paul's° with waking souls
Yet never am affrighted.
          But I do sing, etc.

I know more than Apollo,°
50 For oft when he lies sleeping
I see the stars at bloody wars
In the wounded welkin weeping;
The moon embrace her shepherd,°
And the Queen of Love° her warrior,
While the first doth horn the star of morn,°
And the next the heavenly Farrier.°
          While I do sing, etc.

The gypsies, Snap and Pedro,
Are none of Tom's comradoes,
60 The punk° I scorn and the cutpurse° sworn,
And the roaring boy's° bravadoes.
The meek, the white, the gentle
Me handle, touch, and spare not;
But those that cross Tom Rynosseross

horny barrel leather flask
pound impound (as if it were a suit he could pawn for a night's lodging)
marrow mate
flaming drake flaming dragon: a meteor
night crow an owl, here a maddened alternative to the nightingale
prig steal. This and other words in the poem are from thieves' or gypsies' cant, or slang.
pullen chickens
culvers doves
matchless without their hens
Sullen Solon, like Chanticleer, a rooster
provant provender, food

Humphrey "dining with Duke Humphrey" meant "going hungry"
Paul's the haunted churchyard of St. Paul's
Apollo here, as the sun god
shepherd Endymion, lover of Cynthia or Diana
Queen of Love Venus; her "warrior" was Mars
horn . . . morn by enclosing the Morning Star in the horns of the crescent moon
Farrier Vulcan, Venus' husband, who is "horned," or cuckolded
punk whore
cutpurse pickpocket
roaring boy's juvenile gang member's

Do what the panther dare not.
  Although I sing, etc.

With an host of furious fancies
Whereof I am commander,
With a burning spear and a horse of air,
70 To the wilderness I wander.
By a knight of ghosts and shadows
I summoned am to a tourney
Ten leagues beyond the wide world's end:
Methinks it is no journey.
   Yet will I sing, etc.
     c. 1620

FRANCIS QUARLES°

Emblem IV°

 I am my beloved's, and his desire is towards me.°

Like to the arctic needle,° that doth guide
 The wandering shade by his magnetic power,
And leaves his silken gnomon° to decide
 The question of the controverted hour,
First frantics up and down from side to side,
  And restless beats his crystalled ivory case
  With vain impatience; jets° from place to place,
And seeks the bosom of his frozen bride;
  At length he slacks his motion, and doth rest
10 His trembling point at his bright pole's belovèd breast.

Even so my soul, being hurried here and there,
 By every object that presents delight,
Fain would be settled, but she knows not where;
 She likes at morning what she loathes at night:
She bows to honour, then she lends an ear
  To that sweet swan-like voice of dying pleasure,
  Then tumbles in the scattered heaps of treasure;
Now flattered with false hope, now foiled with fear:
  Thus finding all the world's delight to be
20 But empty toys, good God, she points alone to thee.

Francis Quarles [1592–1644] a civil servant and author of prose tracts defending church and king
Emblem IV from Quarles's *Emblems, Divine and Moral,* the Fifth Book (1635, and countless editions thereafter—it was one of the most popular books of verse in the century). The *imprese* or pictures in this part of Quarles's book were taken from the Jesuit Herman Hugo's *Pia Desideria* (1624); the poems are Quarles's (see *Emblem* in the Glossary).

I am . . . me Canticles 7:10
arctic needle compass needle. The conceit is extremely complex, comparing the wavering and vertical tilt of the needle to that of the soul.
gnomon the vertical finger of a sundial. Here, the vertical silk thread or thin metallic pin on which the transverse needle is hung becomes momentarily a sundial hand for the compass's clock-face.
jets throws itself about

But hath the virtued steel° a power to move?
  Or can the untouched needle point aright?
Or can my wandering thoughts forbear to rove,
  Unguided by the virtue of thy sprite?°
Oh hath my laden soul the art to improve
    Her wasted talent, and, unraised, aspire
    In this sad moulting time of her desire?
Not first beloved, have I the power to love?
    I cannot stir but as thou please to move me,
30 Nor can my heart return thee love until thou love me.

The still commandress° of the silent night
  Borrows her beams from her bright brother's eye;
His fair aspéct fills her sharp horns with light,
  If he withdraw, her flames are quenched and die:
Even so the beams of thy enlightening sprite,
    Infused and shot into my dark desire,
    Inflame my thoughts, and fill my soul with fire,
That I am ravished with a new delight;
    But if thou shroud thy face, my glory fades,
40 And I remain a nothing, all composed of shades.

Eternal God! O thou that only art,
  The sacred fountain of eternal light,
And blessed loadstone of my better part,
  O thou, my heart's desire, my soul's delight!
Reflect upon my soul, and touch my heart,
    And then my heart shall prize no good above thee;
    And then my soul shall know thee; knowing, love thee;
And then my trembling thoughts shall never start
    From thy commands, or swerve the least degree,
50 Or once presume to move, but as they move in thee.

EPIGRAM 4

My soul, thy love is dear; 'twas thought a good
And easy penn'worth° of thy Saviour's blood;
But be not proud; all matters rightly scanned,
'Twas over-bought: 'twas sold at second hand.
               1635

---

virtued steel magnetized (and thus, empowered)   **commandress** the moon
steel   **penn'worth** pennyworth
sprite spirit

THOMAS RANDOLPH°

Upon Love Fondly Refused for Conscience's Sake°

Nature, Creation's law, is judged by sense,
  Not by the tyrant conscience.
Then our commission gives us leave to do,
  What youth and pleasure prompts us to:
For we must question else heaven's great decree,
  And tax it with a treachery,
If things made sweet to tempt our appetite
  Should with a guilt stain the delight.
Higher powers rule us, ourselves can nothing do;
10 Who made us love, made it lawful too.
It was not love, but love transformed to vice,
  Ravished by envious avarice,
Made women first impropriate:° all were free:
  Enclosures men's inventions be.
In the golden age no action could be found
  For trespass on my neighbour's ground:
'Twas just with any fair to mix our blood;
  The best is most diffusive good.
She that confines her beams to one man's sight,
20 Is a dark lanthorn° to a glorious light.
Say, does the virgin-spring less chaste appear,
  'Cause many thirsts are quenchèd there?
Or have you not with the same odours met,
  When more have smelt your violet?
The Phœnix is not angry at her nest,
  'Cause her perfumes make others blest.
Though incense to the eternal gods be meant,
  Yet mortals rival in the scent.
Man is the lord of creatures, yet we see
30 That all his vassals' loves are free,
The severe wedlock's letters do not bind
  The pard's° inflamed and amorous mind;
But that he may be like a bridegroom led
  Even to the royal lion's bed.
The birds may for a year their loves confine,
  But make new choice each Valentine.°

Thomas Randolph [1603–1635] in his own day, almost the most famous poetical son of Ben Jonson's circle, Randolph was wildly praised, even after his death, as an *enfant terrible*. His posthumous collected *Poems* (1638) went through a great many editions.
Upon Love Fondly Refused for Conscience's Sake This poem takes up the garden theme in a typically lascivious Cavalier mode, its meter based on that of a Horatian epode which Randolph had translated. See Andrew Marvell's "The Mower Against Gardens" as an answer to, and revision of, Randolph's treatment of grafting in horticulture to produce new species and more plenteous growth; it is written in the same meter.
impropriate indecorous; unchaste
lanthorn lantern
pard's leopard's
Valentine Birds supposedly took new mates on St. Valentine's Day.

If our affections then more servile be
   Than are our slaves, where is man's sovereignty?
Why, then, by pleasing more, should you less please,
40   And spare the sweets, being more sweet than these?
If the fresh trunk have sap enough to give
   That each insertive° branch may live;
The gardener grafts not only apples there,
   But adds the warden° and the pear.
The peach and apricot together grow,
   The cherry and the damson too,
Till he hath made by skilful husbandry
   An entire orchard of one tree.°
So lest our paradise perfection want,
50   We may as well inoculate° as plant.
What's conscience but a beldame's midnight theme,
   Or nodding nurse's idle dream?
So feigned as are the goblins, elves, and fairies
   To watch their orchards and their dairies.
For who can tell, when first her reign begun?
   In the state of innocence was none:
And since large conscience (as the proverb shows)
   In the same sense with bad one goes,
The less the better then, whence this will fall,
60   'Tis to be perfect to have none at all.
Suppose it be a virtue rich and pure,
   'Tis not for spring or summer, sure.
Nor yet for autumn; love must have his prime,
   His warmer heats and harvest-time.
Till we have flourished, grown, and reaped our wishes;
   What conscience dares oppose our kisses?
But when time's colder hand leads us near home,
   Then let that winter-virtue come:
Frost is till then prodigious; we may do
70   What youth and pleasure prompts us to.

1638

insertive inserted in grafting. This whole passage plays on the sexual connotation of putting a twig into a slot cut in another branch.
warden a kind of pear
one tree the Roman writer Pliny mentions in a letter a remarkable tree in the gardens at Tivoli which, by tricks of grafting, was made to bear grapes, pomegranates, apples, pears, figs, nuts, and berries all at once.
inoculate to graft by budding

JOHN CLEVELAND°

On the Memory of Mr. Edward King, Drowned in the Irish Seas°

I like not tears in tune, nor do I prize
His artificial grief who scans his eyes.
Mine weep down pious beads, but why should I
Confine them to the Muse's rosary?
I am no poet here; my pen's the spout
Where the rain-water of mine eyes runs out
In pity of that name, whose fate we see
Thus copied out in grief's hydrography.°
The Muses are not mermaids, though upon
His death the ocean might turn Helicon.°   10
The sea's too rough for verse: who rhymes upon't
With Xerxes strives to fetter the Hellespont.°
My tears will keep no channel, know no laws
To guide their streams, but like the waves, their cause,
Run with disturbance till they swallow me
As a description of his misery.
But can his spacious virtue find a grave
Within the imposthumed° bubble of a wave?
Whose learning if we found, we must confess
The sea but shallow and him bottomless.   20
Could not the winds, to countermand thy death,
With their whole card of lungs° redeem thy breath?
Or some new island in thy rescue peep
To heave thy resurrection from the deep,
That so the world might see thy safety wrought
With no less wonder than thyself was thought?
The famous Stagirite,° who in his life
Had Nature as familiar as his wife,
Bequeathed his widow to survive with thee,
Queen Dowager of all philosophy—   30
An ominous legacy, that did portend
Thy fate and predecessor's second end.°
Some have affirmed that what on earth we find,
The sea can parallel in shape and kind.

John Cleveland [1613–1658] a late and extravagant Metaphysical poet, whose name became attached to empty and overworked conceits (called by Dryden "Clevelandisms")
On the Memory of Mr. Edward King . . . Seas from *Justa Edouardo King*, a set of elegies by various hands on the young Cambridge poet, drowned in the Irish Sea. Cleveland's elaborate, highly wrought, and rhetorical poem should be compared with "Lycidas," Milton's contribution to the same volume.
hydrography literally, "water-writing"
Helicon actually, the mountain sacred to poetry: the fountain on it was called Hippocrene (formed when Pegasus' hoof struck the hilltop)

Hellespont the strait joining the Propontis or Sea of Marmora with the Aegean (see Marlowe's *Hero and Leander*). Xerxes, the 5th-century Persian emperor, bridged it for his invading troops by putting causeways over ranks of ships.
imposthumed swollen, both as in a festering pustule and as with pride
card of lungs Cleveland is thinking of old maps which represented the four winds in puffing pictures at each corner.
Stagirite Aristotle
second end alluding to a mythical story that Aristotle drowned himself in a body of water whose complex tidal schedule he could not calculate

Books, arts, and tongues were wanting, but in thee
Neptune hath got an university.
We'll dive no more for pearls; the hope to see
Thy sacred reliques of mortality
Shall welcome storms, and make the seaman prize
40   His shipwreck now more than his merchandise.
He shall embrace the waves and to thy tomb
As to a royaler exchanges shall come.
What can we now expect? Water and fire,
Both elements our ruin do conspire,
And that dissolves us which doth us compound.
One Vatican was burnt,° another drowned.
We of the gown our libraries must toss°
To understand the greatness of our loss;
Be pupils to our grief, and so much grow
50   In learning as our sorrows overflow.
When we have filled the runlets° of our eyes,
We'll issue it forth and vent such elegies
As that our tears shall seem the Irish Seas,
We floating islands, living Hebrides.°

1638

Mark Antony

Whenas the nightingale chanted her vespers,
And the wild forester couched on the ground,
Venus invited me in the evening whispers
Unto a fragrant field with roses crowned,
    Where she before had sent
    My wishes' complement;
    Unto my heart's content
    Played with me on the green.
      Never Mark Antony
10   Dallied more wantonly
      With the fair Egyptian Queen.

First on her cherry cheeks I mine eyes feasted,
Thence fear of surfeiting made me retire;
Next on her warmer lips, which when I tasted,
My duller spirits made active as fire.
    Then we began to dart,
    Each at another's heart,
    Arrows that knew no smart,
    Sweet lips and smiles between.
20   Never Mark, &c.

burnt The Vatican Library was never burned;
Cleveland is referring (either erroneously or
wittily) to the great library at Alexandria,
burned by Caesar.
toss turn (as the pages of books)

runlets kegs
floating . . . Hebrides a linking of Delos, the
mythical birthplace of Apollo, with the Hebrides,
near which King drowned

Wanting a glass to plait her amber tresses,
Which like a bracelet rich deckèd mine arm,
Gaudier than Juno wears whenas she graces
Jove with embraces more stately than warm;
    Then did she peep in mine
    Eyes' humour° crystalline;
    I in her eyes was seen,
    As if we one had been.
      Never Mark, &c.

30 Mystical grammar of amorous glances;
Feeling of pulses, the physic of love;
Rhetorical courtings and musical dances;
Numbering of kisses arithmetic prove;°
    Eyes like astronomy;
    Straight-limbed geometry;
    In her art's ingeny°
    Our wits were sharp and keen.
      Never Mark Antony
      Dallied more wantonly
40   With the fair Egyptian Queen.

              1647

WILLIAM STRODE°
1602?–1645

On Chloris Walking in the Snow

I saw fair Chloris walk alone
Where feathered rain came softly down:
Then Jove descended from his tower
To court her in a silver shower;°
The wanton snow flew to her breast
Like little birds into their nest,
But overcome with whiteness there,
For grief it thawed into a tear;
Then, falling down her garment hem,
For grief it freezed into a gem.

              1632

humour bodily fluid
prove test
ingeny wit, in the 17th-century sense of creative
intelligence
William Strode author of a tragi-comedy, *The*

Floating Island, produced at Oxford in 1636.
This poem is from a songbook by Walter Porter.
a silver shower with a tactful nod to the myth
of Danaë, mother of Perseus, whom Jupiter
possessed in the form of a shower of gold

SIR RICHARD FANSHAWE°

1608–1666

The Golden Age°

Fair Golden Age! when milk was the only food,
And cradle of the infant world the wood
(Rocked by the winds); and the untouched flocks did bear
Their dear young for themselves! None yet did fear
The sword or poison; no black thoughts begun
T'eclipse the light of the eternal Sun:
Nor wandring pines unto a foreign shore
Or war, or riches (a worse mischief), bore.
That pompous sound, Idol of vanity,
10 Made up of Title, Pride, and Flattery,
Which they call Honour° whom Ambition blinds,
Was not as yet the tyrant of our minds.
But to buy real goods with honest toil
Amongst the woods and flocks, to use no guile,
Was honour to those sober souls that knew
No happiness but what from virtue grew.
Then sports and carols amongst brooks and plains
Kindled a lawful flame in nymphs and swains.
Their hearts and tongues concurred, the kiss and joy
20 Which were most sweet, and yet which least did cloy
Hymen bestowed on them. To one alone
The lively roses of delight were blown;
The thievish lover found them shut on trial,
And fenced with prickles of a sharp denial.
Were it in cave or wood, or purling Spring,
Husband and Lover signified one thing.
   Base present age, which dost with thy impure
Delights the beauty of the soul obscure:
Teaching to nurse a dropsy in the veins:
30 Bridling the look, but givest desire the reins.
Thus, like a net that spread and covered lies
With leaves and tempting flowers, thou dost disguise
With coy and holy arts a wanton heart;
Makest life a Stage-play, virtue but a part:
Nor thinkest it any fault love's sweets to steal,
So from the world thou canst the theft conceal.°
   But thou that art the King of Kings, create

Sir Richard Fanshawe translated the fourth book of the *Aeneid* in Spenserian stanzas, the Portuguese Camoëns's *Lusiads* (1665), and selections from Horace.

The Golden Age a translation of a famous chorus from Battista Guarini's *Il Pastor Fido* (The Faithful Shepherd), combining material from Ovid and Horace (see Golding's version, above)

Honour sexual honor, modesty; here seen as a product of guilt in a fallen world. Cf. Daniel, "A Proposal," Carew's "Rapture," and *Paradise Lost* IV. 314–18.

theft conceal probably a reminiscence of Ben Jonson's "To Celia"

In us true honour: Virtue's all the state
Great souls should keep. Unto these cells return
40 Which were thy court, but now thy absence mourn:
From their dead sleep with thy sharp goad awake
Them who, to follow their base wills, forsake
Thee, and the glory of the ancient world.
     Let's hope: our ills have truce till we are hurled
From that: Let's hope, the sun that's set may rise,
And with new light salute our longing eyes.

                                   1647

WILLIAM CARTWRIGHT°
1611–1643

No Platonic Love°

Tell me no more of minds embracing minds,
     And hearts exchanged for hearts;
That spirits spirits meet, as winds do winds,
     And mix their subtlest parts;
That two unbodied essences may kiss,
And then like angels, twist and feel one bliss.

I was that silly thing that once was wrought
     To practise this thin love;
I climbed from sex to soul, from soul to thought;
10   But thinking there to move,
Headling I rolled from thought to soul, and then
From soul I lighted at the sex again.

As some strict down-looked men pretend to fast
     Who yet in closets eat,
So lovers who profess they spirits taste,
     Feed yet on grosser meat;
I know they boast they souls to souls convey,
Howe'er they meet, the body is the way.

Come, I will undeceive thee: they that tread
20   Those vain aërial ways
Are like young heirs and alchemists, misled
     To waste their wealth and days;
For searching thus to be forever rich,
They only find a medicine for the itch.

                                   1651

William Cartwright one of the most popular
young poets and preachers in the Oxford of
his day, admired by the king and one of Ben
Jonson's favorite "sons"

No Platonic Love a parody of John Donne's
"The Ecstasy"

AURELIAN TOWNSHEND°
c. 1583–1651?

A Dialogue Betwixt Time and a Pilgrim°

PILGR. Aged man, that mows these fields.
TIME. Pilgrim speak, what is thy will?
PILGR. Whose soil is this that such sweet pasture yields?
      Or who art thou whose foot stand never still?
      Or where am I? TIME. In love.
PILGR. His lordship lies above.
TIME. Yes and below, and round about
      Where in all sorts of flowers are growing
    Which as the early spring puts out,
10   Time falls as fast a mowing.
PILGR. If thou art Time, these flowers have lives,
      And then I fear,
    Under some lilly she I love
      May now be growing there.
TIME. And in some thistle or some spire of grass,
    My scythe thy stalk before hers come may pass.
PILGR. Will thou provide it may? TIME. No.
PILGR. Allege the cause.
TIME. Because time cannot alter but obey fate's laws.
20 CHO. Then happy those whom fate, that is the stronger,
    Together twists their threads, and yet draws hers the longer.

                       1653

JAMES SHIRLEY°
1596–1666

Dirge°

The glories of our blood and state
    Are shadows, not substantial things,
There is no armour against fate,
    Death lays his icy hand on Kings;
        Scepter and crown,
        Must tumble down,
And in the dust be equal made,
With the poor crooked scythe and spade.

Aurelian Townshend An associate of Lord Herbert of Cherbury and Thomas Carew, he composed some lyrics and two masques (1632). A Dialogue . . . Pilgrim The form of this lyric is that of the 17th-century musical dialogue, for two voices and harpsichord or lute accompaniment, which explains why the final moralization is given to a "chorus"; the biblical text behind the figure of Time as a mower is Isaiah 40:6: "All flesh is grass."
James Shirley a copious dramatist, who also published a collected Poems in 1646
Dirge from The Contention of Ajax and Ulysses

611

Some men with swords may reap the field,
10   And plant fresh laurels where they kill,
But their strong nerves° at last must yield,
    They tame but one another still;
        Early or late,
        They stoop to fate,
And must give up the murmuring breath,
When they, pale captives, creep to death.

The garlands wither on your brow,
    Then boast no more your mighty deeds;
Upon death's purple° altar now,
20   See where the victor-victim bleeds,
        Your heads must come,
        To the cold tomb;
Only the actions of the just
Smell sweet, and blossom in their dust.

                1659

SIR JOHN DENHAM°
1615–1669

From Cooper's Hill

My eye, descending from the hill,° surveys
Where Thames amongst the wanton valleys strays.
Thames, the most loved of all the ocean's sons,
By his old sire, to his embraces runs,
Hasting to pay his tribute to the sea,
Like mortal life to meet eternity.
Though with those streams he no resemblance hold,
Whose foam is amber and their gravel gold;
His genuine, and less guilty° wealth to explore,
10 Search not his bottom, but survey his shore,
O'er which he kindly spreads his spacious wing,
And hatches plenty for the ensuing spring.

Not then destroys it with too fond a stay,
Like mothers which their infants overlay;
Nor with a sudden and impetuous wave,
Like prófuse kings, resumes° the wealth he gave.
No unexpected inundations spoil

nerves sinews; muscles
purple red
Sir John Denham royalist, playwright, friend
of Waller, and regarded in the Augustan age
as a major figure. *Cooper's Hill,* his topographical poem, was first published in a pirated
edition.

hill Cooper's Hill, in Surrey, overlooking the
Thames, about 7 miles from Windsor
less guilty because it is the wealth of agriculture and mercantile trade, with a pun on "gilt,"
for gilded
resumes repossesses

The mower's hopes, nor mock the plowman's toil;
But God-like his unwearied bounty flows:
20 First loves to do, then loves the good he does.°
Nor are his blessings to his banks confined,
But free and common as the sea or wind;
When he to boast, or to disperse his stores,
Full of the tributes of his grateful shores,
Visits the world, and in his flying towers°
Brings home to us, and makes the Indies ours;
Finds wealth where 'tis, bestows it where it wants,°
Cities in deserts, woods in cities plants,
So that to us no thing, no place is strange,
30 While his fair bosom is the world's exchange.
O could I flow like thee, and make thy stream
My great example, as it is my theme!
Though deep, yet clear, though gentle, yet not dull,
Strong without rage, without o'er-flowing, full.°

                    1642–1665

ROBERT HERRICK
1591–1674

Son of a London goldsmith, Herrick was apprenticed early to a rich uncle, also a goldsmith, but at the late age of twenty-two he went to Cambridge. He took B.A. and M.A. degrees, was ordained in 1623, and for the next six years led a life centering on London, where he was a devoted member of Ben Jonson's circle and the companion of literary courtiers. In 1629 he obtained the living of Dean Prior in Devonshire, and took up the life of a country clergyman, never feeling totally in tune with his surroundings. "More discontents I never had, / Since I was born, than here, / Where I have been and, still am, sad / In this dull Devonshire" he wrote, and yet it was perhaps just this sense of alienation from London, and from the cultural cosmopolis which the Tribe of Ben had meant for him, which led to the extensiveness of his output of verse. *Hesperides* (published with *Noble Numbers* in 1648), named for the golden apples whose gathering was Hercules' task, were the fruits of a poetic paradise located somewhere in his world of classical reading: his more than 1400 short poems (some, admittedly, consisting of a single couplet) sprang from an antique ground of Horace, Catullus, Martial, the Anacreontic poems, and the epigrams of the Greek Anthology, which provided form, tone of voice, allusions, images, and strategies of rhetoric. Subject and scene came often from the rural life around him, often from memories of a learned and convivial London life. It was as if, in a mild kind of exile,

---

First loves . . . does alluding to God in Genesis 1:4–31: "And God saw the light, that it was good," and so on.
flying towers of square-rigged merchant ships
wants is lacking
O could . . . o'erflowing, full These lines were to become extremely important and widely known in the later 17th and the early 18th

century; not only did their rhetoric, diction, and syntax seem to suggest the model of how heroic couplets should be written, but their tactful use of images about language ("clear," "deep," etc.) derived from aspects of moving (eloquence) or standing (thought) water were strikingly attractive, although Dr. Johnson later confessed himself to be unimpressed.

he could reconstruct an imaginative life from the convivial and amatory wit of writers whose world he seldom makes any attempt to accommodate to Christian thought. His religious poems parallel the *Hesperides* in their use of scriptural allusion as a taking-off point, but though their diction and style are quite similar, their modes never interpenetrate, as in the poetry of Donne or Crashaw. Herrick was ejected from his parish (he was a Royalist) in 1647, apparently lived in London, and returned to his "discontents in Devon" in 1660, where, by his own admission, "I ne'er invented such / Ennobled numbers for the press / Than where I loathed so much." Herrick never wrote much after the publication of *Hesperides* and *Noble Numbers*.

From Hesperides

The Argument° of His Book

I sing of brooks, of blossoms, birds and bowers;
Of April, May, of June and Júly flowers.
I sing of May-poles, hock-carts,° wassails, wakes,°
Of bridegrooms, brides and of their bridal cakes.
I write of youth, of love, and have access
By these, to sing of cleanly wantonness.
I sing of dews, of rains, and piece by piece,
Of balm, of oil, of spice, of ambergris.°
I sing of times trans-shifting; and I write
10   How roses first came red, and lilies white.
I write of groves, of twilights, and I sing
The court of Mab,° and of the Fairy King.°
I write of hell; I sing (and ever shall)
Of heaven, and hope to have it after all.
                    1648

To the Virgins, To Make Much of Time

Gather ye rosebuds while ye may,
    Old time is still a-flying;
And this same flower that smiles today,
    Tomorrow will be dying.

The glorious lamp of heaven, the sun,
    The higher he's a-getting,
The sooner will his race be run,
    And nearer he's to setting.

Argument summary of the contents of a piece of writing
hock-carts that brought in the last of the harvest
wakes parish festivals
ambergris perfume base from the spout of whales
Mab Queen of the Fairies
King Oberon

That age is best which is the first,
10   When youth and blood are warmer,
But being spent, the worse, and worst
     Times still succeed the former.

Then be not coy, but use your time,
     And while ye may, go marry:
For having lost but once your prime,
     You may forever tarry.
                    1648

Corinna's Going A-Maying°

Get up, get up for shame; the blooming morn
Upon her wings presents the god unshorn.°
          See how Aurora° throws her fair
          Fresh-quilted colours through the air!
          Get up, sweet slug-a-bed, and see
          The dew-bespangling herb and tree.
Each flower has wept, and bowèd toward the east,
Above an hour since; yet you not dressed,
          Nay! not so much as out of bed?
10   When all the birds have matins° said,
          And sung their thankful hymns: 'tis sin,
          Nay, profanation to keep in,
When as a thousand virgins on this day,
Spring, sooner than the lark, to fetch in may.°

Rise; and put on your foliage, and be seen
To come forth, like the springtime, fresh and green
          And sweet as Flora. Take no care
          For jewels for your gown or hair;
          Fear not: the leaves will strew
20   Gems in abundance upon you;
Besides, the childhood of the day has kept,
Against° you come, some orient° pearls unwept:
          Come, and receive them while the light
          Hangs on the dew-locks of the night:
          And Titan° on the eastern hill
          Retires himself, or else stands still
Till you come forth. Wash, dress, be brief in praying:
Few beads° are best when once we go a-maying.

Corinna's Going A-Maying like "To the Virgins
. . ." a treatment of the famous theme of
carpe diem ("seize the day"), but a much more
elaborate one, involving an injunction to rise
up early in the morning of one's youth to gather
these special symbolic blossoms on May-day
god unshorn the ever-young sun god, Apollo,
with his long hair streaming

Aurora goddess of the dawn
matins morning prayers
may the white hawthorn, emblematic of marriage
(white for purity, thorns for the danger of pain)
Against until
orient shining; orient pearls were the best
Titan the sun
beads of a rosary

Come, my Corinna, come; and coming, mark
30 How each field turns a street; each street a park
  Made green, and trimmed with trees; see how
  Devotion gives each house a bough,
  Or branch; each porch, each door, ere this,
   An ark, a tabernacle is,
Made up of white-thorn° neatly interwove;
As if here were those cooler shades of love.
  Can such delights be in the street,
  And open fields, and we not see't?
  Come, we'll abroad; and let's obey
40   The proclamation made for May:
And sin no more, as we have done, by staying;
But my Corinna, come, let's go a-maying.

There's not a budding boy or girl this day,
But is got up, and gone to bring in may.
  A deal of youth, ere this, is come
  Back, and with white-thorn laden home.
  Some have dispatched their cakes and cream,
  Before that we have left to dream;°
And some have wept, and wooed, and plighted troth,
50 And chose their priest, ere we can cast off sloth.
  Many a green-gown has been given;°
  Many a kiss, both odd and even:
  Many a glance too has been sent
  From out the eye, love's firmament;
Many a jest told of the keys betraying
This night, and locks picked,° yet we are not a-maying.

Come, let us go, while we are in our prime;
And take the harmless folly of the time.
  We shall grow old apace, and die
60   Before we know our liberty.
  Our life is short; and our days run
  As fast away as does the sun:
And as a vapour, or a drop of rain
Once lost, can ne'er be found again:
  So when or you or I are made
  A fable, song, or fleeting shade,
  All love, all liking, all delight
  Lies drowned with us in endless night.
Then while time serves, and we are but decaying,
70 Come, my Corinna, come, let's go a-maying.

     1648

white-thorn The may, the white hawthorn sanctifies houses into churches in the religion of nature worship—the "old religion" behind the "old religion" of Catholicism.
left to dream left off dreaming

green-gown . . . given gowns grass-stained from amorous rolling about
locks picked literally, and figuratively by phallic keys

Upon Julia's Clothes

Whenas in silks my Julia goes,
Then, then (methinks) how sweetly flows
That liquefaction of her clothes.

Next, when I cast mine eyes and see
That brave° vibration each way free,
O how that glittering taketh me!

                              1648

Delight in Disorder°

A sweet disorder in the dress
Kindles in clothes a wantonness:
A lawn° about the shoulders thrown
Into a fine distraction:
An erring lace, which here and there
Enthralls the crimson stomacher:°
A cuff neglectful, and thereby
Ribbands° to flow confusèdly:
A winning wave (deserving note)
In the tempestuous petticoat:
A careless shoestring, in whose tie
I see a wild civility:
Do more bewitch me than when art
Is too precise in every part.

                              1648

The Night-Piece, To Julia

Her eyes the glow-worm lend thee;
The shooting stars attend thee;
     And the elves also,
     Whose little eyes glow
Like the sparks of fire, befriend thee.

No will-o'-the-wisp mis-light thee;
Nor snake or slow-worm° bite thee;
     But on, on thy way,
     Not making a stay,
Since ghost there's none to affright thee.

brave bright
Delight in Disorder This poem reflects the changing aesthetic of dress in the Caroline period, as tight sleeves, corseting, and stiff, formal hair styles gave way to an equally carefully-arranged appearance of looseness.
lawn a scarf of fine linen

erring lace . . . stomacher The stomacher was a separate piece of cloth held in place across the front of the bodice by lacing; here, the lace must wander haphazardly across it.
ribbands ribbons
slow-worm a kind of lizard

Let not the dark thee cumber;°
What though the moon does slumber?
   The stars of the night
   Will lend thee their light,
Like tapers clear without number.

Then, Julia, let me woo thee,
Thus, thus to come unto me;
   And when I shall meet
   Thy silvery feet,
20 My soul I'll pour into thee.
           1648

The Mad Maid's Song°

Good morrow to the day so fair;
   Good morning sir to you;
Good morrow to mine own torn hair
   Bedabbled with the dew.

Good morning to this primrose too;
   Good morrow to each maid;
That will with flowers the tomb bestrew,
   Wherein my love is laid.

Ah woe is me, woe, woe is me,
10   Alack and welladay!
For pity, sir, find out that bee,
   Which bore my love away.

I'll seek him in your bonnet brave;°
   I'll seek him in your eyes;
Nay, now I think they've made his grave
   In the bed of strawberries.

I'll seek him there; I know, ere this,
   The cold, cold earth doth shake° him;
But I will go, or send a kiss
20   By you, sir, to awake him.

Pray hurt him not; though he be dead,
   He knows well who do love him,
And who with green turfs rear his head,
   And who do rudely move him.

He's soft and tender (pray take heed);
   With bands of cowslips bind him;
And bring him home, but 'tis decreed
   That I shall never find him.
           1648

cumber trouble
The Mad Maid's Song See also "Tom o' Bedlam," above.

brave splendid
shake chill

To Anthea, Who May Command Him Anything

Bid me to live, and I will live
    Thy protestant to be:
Or bid me love, and I will give
    A loving heart to thee.

A heart as soft, a heart as kind,
    A heart as sound and free
As in the whole world thou canst find,
    That heart I'll give to thee.

Bid that heart stay, and it will stay,
10   To honour thy decree;
Or bid it languish quite away,
    And't shall do so for thee.

Bid me to weep, and I will weep,
    While I have eyes to see;
And having none, yet I will keep
    A heart to weep for thee.

Bid me despair, and I'll despair,
    Under that cypress° tree;
Or bid me die, and I will dare
20   E'en death, to die for thee.

Thou art my life, my love, my heart,
    The very eyes of me;
And hast command of every part,
    To live and die for thee.
                    1648

From Noble Numbers

The White Island, or Place of the Blessed

In this world, the isle of dreams,
While we sit by sorrow's streams,
Tears and terrors are our themes,
        Reciting;

But when once from hence we fly,
More and more approaching nigh
Unto young eternity,
        Uniting

In that whiter island, where
10 Things are evermore sincere;
Candour° here and lustre there
        Delighting:

---

cypress emblematic of death

candour literally, a white glow; also in its verbal sense of frankness

There no monstrous fancies shall
Out of hell an horror call
To create, or cause at all,
　　Affrighting;

There, in calm and cooling sleep
We our eyes shall never steep,
But eternal watch shall keep,
20　　Attending

Pleasures such as shall pursue
Me immortalized, and you,
And fresh joys as never, too,
　　Have ending.
　　　　1648

THOMAS CAREW
1594?–1640

Carew, whose name is generally pronounced 'Cary' and who may have sounded it that way himself, was born to a well-connected and influential family, studied at Merton College, Oxford, and at the Middle Temple, and spent his life in various subsidiary diplomatic posts (such as secretary to Lord Herbert of Cherbury) and, finally, attached to Charles I's court, for which he wrote his celebrated masque *Coelum Britannicum* in 1633. An amorous courtier and a dedicated and skillful poet, he was devoted to both Ben Jonson and to John Donne, both of whom he knew and allowed to influence and shape his work. His elegy on the death of Donne is a major statement of the Caroline poetic temper, employing language and paradoxical concepts derived from Donne to praise him. His great "Rapture" poem is a masterpiece of erotic vision strengthened, rather than kept in check by, the action of wit. Its sexual topography heightens that of Renaissance epic with the intense precision of Donne and the Italian Giambattista Marino, who influenced both Carew and Crashaw; its language quotes, alludes to, and expands upon that of Donne as Jonsonian tradition was doing with Horace, Catullus, the Anacreontic poems, and Martial, and as the sonneteers of the 1590's did with Petrarch.

A Rapture

I will enjoy thee now, my Celia, come,
And fly with me to Love's Elysium.°
The giant, Honour, that keeps cowards out,
Is but a masquer,° and the servile rout

Elysium Compare this erotic paradise with Drayton's "The Muses' Elizium" above, and with the descriptions of the Golden Age by Daniel and Fanshawe.

masquer Honour is only an allegorical figure in a court masque.

Of baser subjects only bend in vain
To the vast idol; whilst the nobler train
Of valiant lovers daily sail between
The huge Colossus' legs,° and pass unseen
Unto the blissful shore. Be bold and wise,
10 And we shall enter: the grim Swiss° denies
Only to tame fools a passage, that not know
He is but form, and only frights in show
The duller eyes that look from far; draw near,
And thou shalt scorn what we were wont to fear.
We shall see how the stalking pageant° goes
With borrowed legs, a heavy load to those
That made and bear him: not, as we once thought,
The seed of gods, but a weak model wrought
By greedy men, that seek to enclose the common,°
20 And within private arms impale free woman.
    Come, then, and mounted on the wings of Love
We'll cut the flitting air, and soar above
The monster's° head, and in the noblest seats
Of those blest shades quench and renew our heats.
There shall the Queens of Love and Innocence,
Beauty and Nature, banish all offence
From our close ivy-twines; there I'll behold
Thy barèd snow and thy unbraided gold;
There my enfranchised hand° on every side
30 Shall o'er thy naked polished ivory slide.
No curtain there, though of transparent lawn,
Shall be before thy virgin-treasure drawn;
But the rich mine, to the inquiring eye
Exposed, shall ready still for mintage lie;
And we will coin young Cupids. There a bed
Of roses and fresh myrtles shall be spread
Under the cooler shade of cypress groves;
Our pillows of the down of Venus' doves,
Whereon our panting limbs we'll gently lay,
40 In the faint respites of our active play;
That so our slumbers may in dreams have leisure
To tell the nimble fancy our past pleasure,
And so our souls that cannot be embraced
Shall the embraces of our bodies taste.
Meanwhile the bubbling stream shall court the shore,
The enamoured chirping wood-choir shall adore

Colossus' legs the Colossus of Rhodes, one of the Wonders of the ancient world, popularly supposed to have straddled the entrance to the harbor
Swiss the Vatican's Swiss Guards, known for their height
pageant the show of Honour
common a town's or village's farm or grazing land. The conceit is of enclosure and continues to pun on "pale" (for "fence") in the next line; cf. *Venus and Adonis*, ll. 229–40.
monster's Honour's
enfranchised hand recalls Donne's "License my roving hands, and let them go / Before, behind, between, above, below" (see Elegy XIX: "To His Mistress going to Bed")

In varied tunes the Deity of Love;
The gentle blasts of western winds shall move
The trembling leaves, and through their close boughs breathe
50   Still music, whilst we rest ourselves beneath
Their dancing shade; till a soft murmur, sent
From souls entranced in amorous languishment,
Rouse us, and shoot into our veins fresh fire,
Till we in their sweet ecstasy expire.
     Then, as the empty bee, that lately bore
Into the common treasure all her store,
Flies 'bout the painted field with nimble wing,
Deflowering the fresh virgins of the spring,°
So will I rifle all the sweets that dwell
60   In my delicious paradise, and swell
My bag with honey, drawn forth by the power
Of fervent kisses from each spicy flower.
I'll seize the rose-buds in their perfumed bed,
The violet knots, like curious mazes spread
O'er all the garden, taste the ripened cherry,
The warm firm apple, tipped with coral berry;
Then will I visit with a wandering kiss
The vale of lilies and the bower of bliss:°
And where the beauteous region doth divide
70   Into two milky ways, my lips shall slide
Down those smooth alleys, wearing as I go
A tract° for lovers on the printed snow;
Thence climbing o'er the swelling Apennine,°
Retire into thy grove of eglantine,°
Where I will all those ravished sweets distill
Through Love's alembic,° and with chemic° skill
From the mixed mass one sovereign balm derive,
Then bring that great elixir to thy hive.
     Now in more subtle wreaths I will entwine
80   My sinewy thighs, my legs and arms with thine;
Thou like a sea of milk shalt lie displayed,
Whilst I the smooth, calm ocean invade
With such a tempest, as when Jove of old
Fell down on Danaë in a storm of gold;
Yet my tall pine shall in the Cyprian strait°
Ride safer at anchor, and unlade her freight:
My rudder with thy bold hand, like a tried
And skillful pilot, thou shalt steer, and guide
My bark into love's channel, where it shall

---

virgins of the spring untasted flowers; notice how the honey-making image then stands for physical sex in the next lines
bower of bliss Spenser's phrase, here used without a negative moral cast; see *The Faerie Queene* II.xii
tract both pathways and treatise
Apennine Italy's central mountain range; the lady's belly
eglantine sweetbriar; here, the pubic hair
Love's alembic alchemists' distilling flask; the image is Donne's
chemic alchemical
Cyprian straight the vagina; Cyprus was Venus' birthplace

90 Dance, as the bounding waves do rise or fall.
    Then shall thy circling arms embrace and clip
    My willing body, and thy balmy lip
    Bathe me in juice of kisses, whose perfume
    Like a religious incense shall consume,
    And send up holy vapours to those powers
    That bless our loves and crown our sportful hours,
    That with such halcyon° calmness fix our souls
    In steadfast peace, as no affright controls.
    There no rude sounds shake us with sudden starts;
100 No jealous ears, when we unrip our hearts,
    Suck our discourse in; no observing spies
    This blush, that glance traduce;° no envious eyes
    Watch our close meetings; nor are we betrayed
    To rivals by the bribèd chambermaid.
    No wedlock bonds unwreathe our twisted loves;
    We seek no midnight arbour, no dark groves
    To hide our kisses: there the hated name
    Of husband, wife, lust, modest, chaste or shame,
    Are vain and empty words, whose very sound
110 Was never heard in the Elysian ground.
    All things are lawful there that may delight
    Nature or unrestrainèd appetite;
    Like and enjoy, to will and act is one:
    We only sin when Love's rites are not done.
        The Roman Lucrece° there reads the divine
    Lectures of Love's great master, Aretine,°
    And knows as well as Lais° how to move
    Her pliant body in the act of love.
    To quench the burning ravisher, she hurls
120 Her limbs into a thousand winding curls,
    And studies artful postures, such as be
    Carved on the bark of every neighbouring tree
    By learnèd hands, that so adorned the rind
    Of those fair plants, which, as they lay entwined,
    Have fanned their glowing fires. The Grecian dame,°
    That in her endless web toiled for a name
    As fruitless as her work, doth there display
    Herself before the youth of Ithaca,
    And the amorous sport of gamesome nights prefer
130 Before dull dreams of the lost traveller.
    Daphne hath broke her bark, and that swift foot
    Which the angry gods had fastened with a root
    To the fixed earth doth now unfettered run

---

halcyon kingfisher, associated with calm waters
traduce slander
Lucrece Shakespeare's Roman heroine, an emblem of chastity; in Carew's bower she is reading pornography
Aretine Pietro Aretino (1492–1566) was famous for, among other things, his sonnets made to go

with Giulio Romano's paintings describing various positions of sexual intercourse.
Lais a courtesan of antiquity
Grecian dame Odysseus' Penelope who, to keep her suitors at bay, unravelled at night the weaving she had done in the day, upon whose completion she was to have chosen one of them

To meet the embraces of the youthful Sun.
She hangs upon him like his Delphic lyre;
Her kisses blow the old, and breathe new fire;
Full of her god, she sings inspired lays,
Sweet odes of love, such as deserve the bays,°
Which she herself was. Next her, Laura° lies
140   In Petrarch's learnèd arms, drying those eyes
That did in such sweet smooth-paced numbers° flow,
As made the world enamoured of his woe.
These, and ten thousand beauties more, that died
Slave to the tyrant, now enlargèd deride
His cancelled laws, and for their time misspent
Pay into Love's exchequer double rent.
 Come then, my Celia, we'll no more forbear
To taste our joys, struck with a panic fear,
But will depose from his imperious sway
150   This proud usurper, and walk free as they,
With necks unyoked; nor is it just that he
Should fetter your soft sex with chastity,
Which Nature made unapt for abstinence;
When yet this false impostor can dispense
With human justice and with sacred right,
And, maugre° both their laws, command me fight
With rivals or with emulous loves that dare
Equal with thine their mistress' eyes or hair.
If thou complain of wrong, and call my sword
160   To carve out thy revenge, upon that word
He bids me fight and kill, or else he brands
With marks of infamy my coward hands,
And yet religion bids from bloodshed fly,
And damns me for that act. Then tell me why
This goblin Honour, which the world adores,
Should make men atheists, and not women whores.

1640

An Elegy upon the Death of Doctor Donne, Dean of Paul's°

Can we not force from widowed poetry,
Now thou art dead (great Donne) one elegy
To crown thy hearse?° Why yet did we not trust,
Though with unkneaded dough-baked prose, thy dust,

---

bays laurel crowns for poetic achievement
Laura Petrarch's muse
numbers metrical verses
maugre despite
An Elegy . . . Paul's This poem was first
printed in the 1633 edition of Donne's poems.

crown thy hearse It was actually the practice
to attach poems praising the dead to the funeral
hearse, like wreaths, further enforcing the 17th-
century association of flowers and poetry, poesy
and posies.

Such as the unscissored° churchman from the flower
Of fading rhetoric, short-lived as his hour,
Dry as the sand that measures it, should lay
Upon the ashes, on the funeral day?
Have we no voice, nor tune? Didst thou dispense
10   Through all our language both the words and sense?
'Tis a sad truth. The pulpit may her plain
And sober Christian precepts still retain;
Doctrines it may, and wholesome uses, frame,
Grave homilies and lectures, but the flame
Of thy brave soul (that shot such heat and light
As burnt our earth, and made our darkness bright,
Committed holy rapes upon our will,
Did through the eye the melting heart distil,
And the deep knowledge of dark truths so teach
20   As sense might judge, what fancy could not reach)
Must be desired for ever. So the fire
That fills with spirit and heat the Delphic choir,°
Which, kindled first by thy Promethean° breath,
Glowed here a while, lies quenched now in thy death.
The Muses' garden with pedantic weeds
O'erspread, was purged by thee; the lazy seeds
Of servile imitation thrown away,
And fresh invention planted; thou didst pay
The debts of our penurious bankrupt age;
30   Licentious thefts, that make poetic rage
A mimic fury, when our souls must be
Possessed, or with Anacreon's° ecstasy
Or Pindar's,° not their own; the subtle cheat
Of sly exchanges,° and the juggling feat
Of two-edged words, or whatsoever wrong
By ours was done the Greek or Latin tongue,
Thou hast redeemed, and opened us a mine
Of rich and pregnant fancy; drawn a line
Of masculine° expression, which had good
40   Old Orpheus seen, or all the ancient brood
Our superstitious fools admire and hold
Their lead more precious than thy burnished gold,
Thou hadst been their exchequer, and no more
They each in other's dust had raked for ore.
Thou shalt yield no precedence, but of time

unscissored untonsured
Delphic choir the Muses, led by Apollo
Promethean Prometheus stole fire, symbolizing
all crafts and skills, from the gods to give to
men, and was punished for his pains with
greater pains.
Anacreon's the Greek poet to whom were
wrongly ascribed the poems that served as a
model for so much Cavalier verse

Pindar's the great Greek choral, public poet
sly exchanges Perhaps plays upon the Latin
sense of English words.
masculine referring not to sexuality, but to
stylistic power. In differing ages it could imply
anything from decorum to the "strong lines"
of Metaphysical verse which Carew is praising.

And the blind fate of language, whose tunèd chime
More charms the outward sense; yet thou mayst claim
From so great disadvantage greater fame,
Since to the awe of thy imperious wit
50   Our stubborn language bends, made only fit
With her tough thick-ribbed hoops to gird about
Thy giant fancy, which had proved too stout
For their soft melting phrases. As in time
They had the start, so did they cull the prime
Buds of invention many a hundred year,
And left the rifled fields, besides the fear
To touch their harvest; yet from those bare lands
Of what is purely thine, thy only hands,
(And that their smallest work) have gleanèd more
60   Than all those times and tongues could reap before.
    But thou art gone, and thy strict laws will be
Too hard for libertines in poetry;
They will recall the goodly exiled train
Of gods and goddesses, which in thy just reign
Were banished nobler poems; now with these,
The silenced tales i' the *Metamorphoses*,°
Shall stuff their lines, and swell the windy page,
Till verse, refined by thee in this last age,
Turn ballad-rhyme, or those old idols be
70   Adored again with new apostasy.°
    O, pardon me, that break with untuned verse
The reverend silence that attends thy hearse,
Whose awful solemn murmurs were to thee,
More than these faint lines, a loud elegy,
That did proclaim in a dumb eloquence
The death of all the arts; whose influence,
Grown feeble, in these panting numbers° lies
Gasping short-winded accents, and so dies.
So doth the swiftly turning wheel not stand
80   In the instant we withdraw the moving hand,
But some small time retain a faint weak course,
By virtue of the first impulsive force;
And so, whilst I cast on thy funeral pile
The crown of bays,° oh, let it crack awhile,
And spit disdain, till the devouring flashes
Suck all the moisture up, then turn to ashes.
    I will not draw the envy to engross°
All thy perfections, or weep all the loss;
Those are too numerous for an elegy,

Metamorphoses Ovid's epic, a repository of classical myth (see The Renaissance Ovid) **apostasy** All of these religious terms, applied to the holy company of good poetry, parallel Donne's use of them for images of love. **numbers** verses **bays** laurel (the poet's crown) **engross** copy out (a legal term)

90 And this too great to be expressed by me.
Though every pen should share a distinct part,
Yet art thou theme enough to tire all art;
Let others carve the rest, it shall suffice
I on thy tomb this epitaph incise:

> Here lies a king, that ruled as he thought fit
> The universal monarchy of wit;
> Here lie two flamens,° and both those, the best,
> Apollo's first, at last, the true God's priest.

1633

Upon a Ribband°

This silken wreath, which circles in mine arm,
Is but an emblem of that mystic charm
Wherewith the magic of your beauties binds
My captive soul, and round about it winds
Fetters of lasting love. This hath entwined
My flesh alone; that hath impaled my mind.
Time may wear out these soft weak bands, but those
Strong chains of brass Fate shall not discompose.
This holy relic may preserve my wrist,
10 But my whole frame doth by that power subsist:
To that my prayers and sacrifice, to this
I only pay a superstitious kiss.
This but the idol, that's the deity;
Religion there is due; here, ceremony.
That I receive by faith, this but in trust;
Here I may tender duty: there, I must.
This order as a layman I may bear,
But I become Love's priest when that I wear.
This moves like air; that as the centre stands;
20 That knot your virtue tied; this but your hands.
That, Nature framed; but this was made by Art;
This makes my arm your prisoner; that, my heart.

1640

RICHARD LOVELACE
1618–1657

Lovelace is perhaps the Cavalier poet *par excellence*. Born to a prominent Kentish family, a social and literary success at Oxford, personally gorgeous enough for the King and Queen to have caused him to be given an M.A. while on an Oxford visit, he lived a country life of learning and enjoyments. In 1642 he was imprisoned for petition-

---

flamens priests   **Ribband** ribbon

ing the Long Parliament in the King's cause, was released, fought in France against
the Spanish, returned, was imprisoned again by the Puritan government, was released
after ten months, and died in obscurity. The volume called *Lucasta* was published in
1649. Lovelace's poems celebrate Love as the child of Beauty and War (Cupid's father
was Mars in some versions of the myth) and are full of an awareness of the fragility
of the life they celebrate, and of the possibilities of erotic joy and delight in emblematic readings of animals and pictures.

The Grasshopper°

To my noble friend, Mr. Charles Cotton

ODE°

O thou that swing'st upon the waving hair
   Of some well-fillèd oaten beard,
Drunk every night with a delicious tear
   Dropped thee from heaven, where now th'art reared:

The joys of earth and air are thine entire,
   That with thy feet and wings dost hop and fly;
And, when thy poppy works, thou dost retire
   To thy carved acorn-bed to lie.

Up with the day, the sun thou welcomest then,
10   Sport'st in the gilt plats° of his beams,
And all these merry days makest merry: men,
   Thyself, and melancholy streams.

But ah, the sickle!° Golden ears are cropped;
   Ceres and Bacchus bid good night;°
Sharp frosty fingers all your flowers have topped,
   And what scythes spared, winds shave off quite.

Poor verdant fool! and now green ice! thy joys
   Large and as lasting as thy perch of grass,
Bid us lay in 'gainst winter, rain, and poise°
20   Their floods with an o'erflowing glass.

Thou best of men and friends! we will create
   A genuine summer in each other's breast,
And spite of this cold time and frozen fate,
   Thaw us a warm seat to our rest.

The Grasshopper In Aesop, the silly grasshopper fiddles and sings all summer long, while
the wise ant lays up stores for the winter which
will kill the careless singer. In the Greek poems
called Anacreontic, the grasshopper is praised
for his love of drinking—the wine of dew—and
his song.
Ode alluding to the Anacreontic poems, one of
which is translated by Lovelace's first three
stanzas (see Abraham Cowley's translation of
the Anacreontic poem in this volume)
plats braids
sickle of autumnal mowers, of Time, thus perhaps of the Puritan world cutting down the
Cavalier one
Ceres . . . night bid farewell to these gods of
food and drink, plenitude and joy
poise balance

Our sacred hearths shall burn eternally
    As vestal flames; the North Wind, he
Shall strike his frost-stretched wings, dissolve, and fly
    This Aetna° in epitome.

30 Dropping December shall come weeping in,
    Bewail the usurping° of his reign;
But when in showers of old Greek° we begin,
    Shall cry he hath his crown again.

Night as clear Hesper° shall our tapers whip
    From the light casements where we play,
And the dark hag from her black mantle strip,
    And stick there everlasting day.

Thus richer than untempted kings are we,
    That asking nothing, nothing need:
Though lord of all what seas embrace, yet he
40   That wants° himself is poor indeed.

                1649

La Bella Bona Roba°

I cannot tell who loves the skeleton
Of a poor marmoset,° naught but bone, bone.
Give me a nakedness with her clothes on.

Such whose white-satin upper coat of skin,
Cut upon velvet rich incarnadin,°
Has yet a body (and of flesh) within.

Sure it is meant good husbandry in men,
Who so incorporate with aery lean,°
To repair their sides, and get their rib again.

10 Hard hap unto that huntsman that decrees
Fat joys for all his sweat, whenas he sees,
After his 'say,° naught but his keeper's fees.

Then Love, I beg, when next thou takest thy bow,
Thy angry shafts, and dost heart-chasing° go,
Pass rascal deer,° strike me the largest doe.

                1649

Aetna the famous Sicilian volcano
usurping perhaps an allusion to the Long Parliament's ban in 1644 of Christmas celebrations as paganism
old Greek perhaps Hippocras, a spiced wine drink
Hesper the Evening Star. The syntax of this line is puzzling: "Our tapers shall, like Hesper, whip night away from our windows."
wants lacks

La Bella Bona Roba a common expression for a whore, but, literally, a pleasantly plump girl
marmoset slang for prostitute
incarnadin flesh-colored
lean leanness (in women)
'say "assay," taken of the deer's flesh to check its quality
heart-chasing punning on "hart"
rascal deer were thin and too poor to hunt

Song

To Lucasta, Going to the Wars

Tell me not, sweet, I am unkind,°
  That from the nunnery
Of thy chaste breast and quiet mind,
  To war and arms I fly.

True, a new mistress now I chase,
  The first foe in the field;
And with a stronger faith embrace
  A sword, a horse, a shield.

Yet this inconstancy is such
10   As you too shall adore;
I could not love thee, dear, so much,
  Loved I not honour more.

          1649

The Snail

Wise emblem of our politic world,
Sage snail, within thine own self curled,
Instruct me softly to make haste,°
Whilst these my feet go slowly fast.
  Compendious snail! thou seemst to me
Large Euclid's strict epitome;°
And in each diagram, dost fling
Thee from the point unto the ring.
A figure now triangular,
10 An oval now, and now a square;
And then a serpentine dost crawl,
Now a straight line, now crooked, now all.
  Preventing rival of the day,
Th'art up and openest thy ray,
And ere the morn cradles the moon,
Th'art broke into a beauteous noon.
Then, when the sun sups in the deep,
Thy silver horns ere Cynthia's peep,
And thou, from thine own liquid bed,
20 New Phoebus, heavest thy pleasant head.
  Who shall a name for thee create,

---

unkind unnatural, as well as in the modern sense
softly to make haste A famous tag, *festina lente* ("make haste slowly"), usually attributed to the Emperor Augustus, was frequently applied to the snail's slow pace; this whole poem is an expanded emblem verse.
Euclid's strict epitome because it embraces, in its slow motions, all the geometric figures, including the spiral of its shell

630

Deep riddle of mysterious state?
Bold nature, that gives common birth
To all products of sea and earth,
Of thee, as earthquakes, is afraid,
Nor will thy dire delivery aid.
   Thou thine own daughter, then, and sire,
That son and mother art entire,
That big still with thy self dost go,
30 And livest an aged embryo;
That like the cubs of India,
Thou from thy self a while dost play;
But frighted with a dog or gun,
In thine own belly thou dost run,
And as thy house was thine own womb,
So thine own womb concludes thy tomb.
   But now I must (analyzèd king)
Thy economic virtues sing;
Thou great staid husband still within,
40 Thou thee, that's thine, dost discipline;
And when thou art to progress bent,
Thou movest thy self and tenement,
As warlike Scythians travelled, you
Remove your men and city too;
Then, after a sad dearth and rain,
Thou scatterest thy silver train;
And when the trees grow naked and old,
Thou clothest them with cloth of gold,
Which from thy bowels thou dost spin,
50 And draw from the rich mines within.
   Now hast thou changed thee saint, and made
Thy self a fane° that's cupola'd
And in thy wreathèd cloister thou
Walkest thine own grey friar too;
Strict, and locked up, th'art hood all o'er,
And ne'er eliminatest thy door.
On salads thou dost feed severe,
And 'stead of beads thou droppest a tear,
And when to rest each calls the bell,
60 Thou sleepest within thy marble cell;
Where, in dark contemplation placed,
The sweets of nature thou dost taste;
Who now with time thy days resolve,
And in a jelly thee dissolve;
Like a shot star, which doth repair
Upward, and rarify the air.
          1659–60

fane temple

Love Made in the First Age: °
To Chloris

In the nativity of time,
Chloris, it was not thought a crime
   In direct Hebrew° for to woo.
Now we make love, as all on fire,
Ring retrograde our lewd desire,
   And court in English backward too.

Thrice happy was the golden age,
When compliment was construed rage,
   And fine words in the center hid;
10 When cursèd *No* stained no maid's bliss
And all discourse was summed in *Yes,*
   And nought forbade, but to forbid.

Love then unstinted love did sip,
And cherries plucked fresh from the lip,
   On cheeks and roses free he fed;
Lasses like autumn plums did drop,
And lads indifferently did crop
   A flower and a maidenhead.

Then unconfinèd each did tipple
20 Wine from the bunch, milk from the nipple,
   Paps tractable as udders were;
Then equally the wholesome jellies
Were squeezed from olive trees and bellies,
   Nor suits° of trespass did they fear.

A fragrant bank of strawberries,
Diapered with violet's eyes
   Was table, tablecloth, and fare;
No palace to the clouds did swell,
Each humble princess then did dwell
30   In the piazza of her hair.

Both broken faith and the cause of it,
All-damning gold, was damned to the pit;
   Their troth, sealed with a clasp and kiss,
Lasted until that éxtreme day
In which they smiled their souls away,
   And, in each other, breathed new bliss.

Love Made in the First Age This poem is a
libertine elaboration of the theme of unfallen
eros in the Golden Age: see the treatments of
it by Ovid, Daniel, and Fanshawe above.
direct Hebrew The Renaissance believed Hebrew
to have been the original language spoken in
Paradise; the fracturing of Speech into myriad
languages after the Tower of Babel is Lovelace's
image for how guilt ruined sex after an initial
age of perfection was over. Hebrew reads from
right to left: this forms the basis for the conceit
in the first stanza.
suits lawsuits

Because no fault, there was no tear;
No groan did grate the granting ear;
   No false foul breath their delicate smell:
40 No serpent kiss poisoned the taste,
Each touch was naturally chaste,
   And their mere sense a miracle.

Naked as their own innocence,
And unembroidered from offence
   They went, above poor riches, gay;
On softer than the cygnet's down,
In beds they tumbled of their own;
   For each within the other lay.

Thus did they live: thus did they love,
50 Repeating only joys above;
   And angels were, but with clothes on,
Which they would put off cheerfully,
To bathe them in the galaxy,
   Then gird them with the heavenly zone.

Now, Chloris, miserably crave
The offered bliss you would not have,
   Which evermore I must deny,
Whilst ravished with these noble dreams,
And crownèd with mine own soft beams,
60   Enjoying of myself I lie.
           1659–60

EDMUND WALLER
1606–1687

Waller's reputation, along with that of Sir John Denham, could not outlast the Augustan period which claimed them as true progenitors of proper verse—for just so long did "Denham's strength and Waller's sweetness," in Pope's phrase, remain celebrated models. Waller himself was born to a wealthy country family, attended Eton, Cambridge for a while, and Lincoln's Inn; then he was elected to Parliament, and made a wealthy marriage to a lady whose fortune he inherited upon her early death. Although a Parliamentarian at first, he veered to the Royalist cause. He became involved in a plot to seize London for the crown, was exposed, joined the English exiles in Paris in 1643, was pardoned in 1651, and after the Restoration again became involved in court life and government. His literary sphere was Jonsonian, he was a member of the circle of Lucius Cary, Viscount Falkland (celebrated in Jonson's great Pindaric ode). In our own day, Ezra Pound has praised and imitated Waller, perhaps in recognition of all sorts of affinities.

Song

Go, lovely Rose—
Tell her that wastes her time and me
    That now she knows,
When I resemble her to thee,
    How sweet and fair she seems to be.

    Tell her that's young
And shuns to have her graces spied
    That, hadst thou sprung
In deserts where no men abide,
10   Thou must have uncommended died.

    Small is the worth
Of beauty from the light retired:
    Bid her come forth,
Suffer herself to be desired,
    And not blush so to be admired.

    Then die that she
The common fate of all things rare
    May read in thee;
How small a part of time they share
20   That are so wondrous sweet and fair!

                                    1645

At Penshurst°

Had Sacharissa° lived when mortals made
Choice of their deities, this sacred shade
Had held an altar to her power, that gave
The peace and glory which these alleys have;
Embroidered so with flowers where she stood,
That it became a garden of a wood.
Her presence has such more than human grace,
That it can civilize the rudest place;
And beauty too, and order, can impart,
10 Where nature ne'er intended it, nor art.
The plants acknowledge this, and her admire,
No less than those of old did Orpheus' lyre;°
If she sit down, with tops all towards her bowed,
They round about her into arbours crowd;
Or if she walk, in even ranks they stand,
Like some well-marshalled and obsequious band.

At Penshurst See Ben Jonson's poem to the same house.
Sacharissa literally, "sweet one," Waller's name in his poems for Lady Dorothy Sidney, whom he courted unsuccessfully
Orpheus' lyre His fabulous music made the trees dance.

Amphion° so made stones and timber leap
Into fair figures from a cónfused heap,
And in the symmetry of her parts is found
20   A power like that of harmony in sound.
    Ye lofty beeches, tell this matchless dame
That if together ye fed all one flame,
It could not equalize the hundredth part
Of what her eyes have kindled in my heart!
Go, boy, and carve this passion on the bark
Of yonder tree,° which stands the sacred mark
Of noble Sidney's birth; when such benign,
Such more than mortal-making stars did shine,
That there they cannot but for ever prove
30   The monument and pledge of humble love;
His humble love whose hopes shall ne'er rise higher,
Than for a pardon that he dares admire.

1645

Of English Verse

Poets may boast, as safely vain,
Their works shall with the world remain;
Both, bound together, live or die,
The verses and the prophecy.

But who can hope his lines should long
Last in a daily changing tongue?
While they are new, envy prevails;
And as that dies, our language fails.

When architects have done their part,
10   The matter may betray their art;
Time, if we use ill-chosen stone,
Soon brings a well-built palace down.

Poets that lasting marble seek,
Must carve in Latin, or in Greek;
We write in sand, our language grows,
And, like the tide, our work o'erflows.

Chaucer his sense can only boast;
The glory of his numbers lost!°
Years have defaced his matchless strain;
20   And yet he did not sing in vain.

Amphion a parallel mythological figure: his music charmed the stones of the walls of Thebes into place
tree the one planted in honor of Sir Philip Sidney's birth

numbers lost Even in Waller's time, it was not understood that Chaucer's verse was iambic pentameter.

The beauties which adorned that age,
The shining subjects of his rage,°
Hoping they should immortal prove,
Rewarded with success his love.

This was the generous poet's scope;
And all an English pen can hope,
To make the fair approve his flame,
That can so far extend their fame.

Verse, thus designed, has no ill fate,
30   If it arrive but at the date°
Of fading beauty; if it prove
But as long-lived as present love.

1693

ABRAHAM COWLEY
1618–1667

Abraham Cowley is perhaps best remembered as Samuel Johnson's epitome of the Metaphysical school, for it is in his Life of Cowley that the famous remarks on Donne appear. As a writer of "strong lines," Cowley certainly sounds a dying fall, and it is in his more public and expository manner that he seems interesting now. Born to a London middle-class family, he attended Westminster School and Trinity College, Cambridge, became a close friend of Crashaw, traveled abroad for the Royalist cause and was imprisoned upon his return to England in 1655. Following his release, he studied medicine, and after 1660 experienced a private restoration in the return of his Cambridge fellowship and the gift of some land by the Queen, to which he retired to write essays and to concern himself with the Royal Society, in whose foundation he was interested. His "Pindaric" odes are, in fact, the first irregular odes in English, and it was this form which Dryden bequeathed to the differing uses of posterity.

Cowley's Metaphysical lyrics were published in The Mistress (1647), to considerable acclaim; in 1656 he published his attempt at a large-scale biblical epic in heroic couplets, Davideis, and his collected Poems. The posthumous Works appeared in 1668.

Ode° of Wit

Tell me, O tell, what kind of thing is wit,°
    Thou who master art of it.
For the first matter° loves variety less;

---

rage poetic ardor
date terminal date, or end. The whole phrase is strangely reminiscent of the language of Shakespeare's sonnets.
Ode This is not one of Cowley's "Pindaric" odes, but, like them, it flourishes its title to suggest a public poem, almost an essay.
wit Between the death of Queen Elizabeth and

about 1750, the word "wit" undergoes shifts of meaning; Cowley's opening question, conscious of this, is more than a mere rhetorical device.
first matter In classical creation theories, chaos contained matter, but without orderly differentiation even of qualities and attributes; thus it would love variety, but wit loves it even more.

Less women love't, either in love or dress.
   A thousand different shapes it bears,
   Comely in thousand shapes appears.
Yonder we saw it plain; and here 'tis now,
Like spirits in a place, we know not how.

London that vents of false ware so much store,°
10   In no more ware deceives us more.
For men led by the colour and the shape,
Like Zeuxis' birds, fly to the painted grape;°
   Some things do through our judgment pass
   As through a multiplying° glass.
And sometimes, if the object be too far,
We take a falling meteor for a star.

Hence 'tis a wit, that greatest word of fame,
   Grows such a common name,
And wits by our creation they become,
20 Just so, as titular bishops made at Rome.°
   'Tis not a tale, 'tis not a jest
   Admired with laughter at a feast,
Nor florid talk, which can that title gain:
The proofs of wit forever must remain.

'Tis not to force some lifeless verses meet
   With their five gouty feet.°
All everywhere, like man's, must be the soul,
And reason the inferior powers control.°
   Such were the numbers° which could call
30   The stones into the Theban wall.°
Such miracles are ceased, and now we see
No towns or houses raised by poetry.

Yet 'tis not to adorn and gild each part
   That shows more cost than art.
Jewels at nose and lips but ill appear;
Rather than all thing wit, let none be there.
   Several° lights will not be seen
   If there be nothing else between;
Men doubt, because they stand so thick i' the sky,
40 If those be stars which paint the galaxy.

---

vents . . . store abounds with fakes
Zeuxis' birds . . . grape the most famous anecdote about Greek painting: Zeuxis, a 5th-century B.C. painter, painted grapes so realistically that birds flew to them
multiplying magnifying
made at Rome bishops with titles but not present at their distant sees
feet of iambic pentameter verse
All . . . control Just as the human soul was thought to be diffused throughout the body (except by Descartes, who located it in the inaccessible pineal gland), so must poetic power be generally dispersed throughout, and in mastery of, the mere arts of language.
numbers meter and music
which could . . . wall Amphion, an Orpheus-like figure, charmed the stones of the walls of Thebes into place with his playing.
Several distinct, separate

'Tis not when two like words make up one noise,°
　Jests for Dutch men, and English boys.
In which who finds out wit, the same may see
In anagrams and acrostics° poetry.
　　Much less can that have any place
　　At which a virgin hides her face.
Such dross the fire must purge away: 'tis just
The author blush, there where the reader must.

'Tis not such lines as almost crack the stage,
50　　When Bajazet° begins to rage.
Nor a tall metaphor in the Oxford way,°
Nor the dry chips of short-lunged Seneca.°
　　Nor upon all things to obtrude,
　　And force some odd similitude.
What is it then, which like the Power Divine
We only can by negatives define?

In a true piece of wit all things must be,
　　Yet all things there agree,
As in the ark, joined without force or strife,
60　All creatures dwelt, all creatures that had life;
　　Or as the primitive forms of all
　　(If we compare great things with small)
Which without discord or confusion lie,
In that strange mirror of the Deity.°

But Love that moulds one man up out of two,
　　Makes me forget and injure you.
I took you for myself sure when I thought
That you in anything were to be taught.
　　Correct my error with thy pen,
70　　And if any ask me then,
What thing right wit and height of genius° is,
I'll only show your lines, and say, ' 'Tis this.'

　　　　　　　　　　　　　1656

The Grasshopper°

Happy insect, what can be
In happiness compared to thee?
Fed with nourishment divine,
The dewy morning's gentle wine!
Nature waits upon thee still,
And thy verdant cup does fill;

one noise and sound: he means puns
acrostics poems and initial letters of whose lines
spell out a message
Bajazet defeated potentate in Marlowe's *Tamburlaine the Great*
tall . . . way high-flown, bombastic rhetoric
Seneca The Roman tragedian's style was more
terse.

mirror of the Deity perhaps the hyaline stone
in Revelation 4:6
genius in the sense of "wit" (which, in Italian,
is "ingegno")
The Grasshopper a translation of the Anacreontic
poem from which Lovelace derives his remarkable "The Grasshopper." Cowley expands con-
siderably on the original.

'Tis filled wherever thou dost tread,
Nature's self's thy Ganymede.°
Thou dost drink and dance and sing,
10   Happier than the happiest king!°
All the fields which thou dost see,
All the plants, belong to thee;
All that summer hours produce,
Fertile made with early juice.
Man for thee does sow and plow,
Farmer he, and landlord thou!
Thou dost innocently joy,
Nor does thy luxury° destroy;
The shepherd gladly heareth thee,
20   More harmonious than he.
Thee country hinds with gladness hear,
Prophet of the ripened year!
Thee Phœbus° loves and does inspire;
Phœbus is himself thy sire.
To thee of all things upon earth
Life is no longer than thy mirth.
Happy insect, happy thou,
Dost neither age nor winter know.
But when thou'st drunk and danced and sung
30   Thy fill the flowery leaves among,
Voluptuous and wise withal,
Epicurean animal!°
Sated with thy summer feast,
Thou retirest to endless rest.
                1656

The Praise of Pindar° in Imitation of Horace His Second Ode, Book 4

Pindarum quisquis studet œmulari, &.

Pindar is imitable by none;
    The phoenix Pindar° is a vast species alone.
Whoe'er but Dædalus with waxen wings could fly
And neither sink too low nor soar too high?°
        What could he who followed claim
    But of vain boldness the unhappy fame,

Ganymede Zeus' cup-bearer
Happier . . . king Again, see what use Lovelace makes of this.
luxury lust ("luxuria" was one of the seven deadly sins)
Phœbus Apollo, as lord of stringed music; grasshoppers were always thought of as fiddling, never piping (perhaps because of biological fact).
Epicurean animal The Greek philosopher Epicurus was taken as the proverbial theoretican of enjoyment.

The Praise of Pindar one of Cowley's programmatic "Pindaric" or "irregular" odes
phoenix Pindar there is only one phoenix, it is individual and species in one; this is the first of the bird images in the poem
Daedalus . . . high the fabulous artificer of antiquity, who built the labyrinth for Minos in which to hide the Minotaur, and escaped out of it on wax wings; his son, Icarus, flew too high, his wings melted, and down he fell

And by his fall a sea to name?
Pindar's unnavigable song,
Like a swollen flood from some steep mountain, pours along;
10   The ocean meets with such a voice
From his enlargèd mouth as drowns the ocean's noise.

So Pindar does new words and figures roll
Down his impetuous dithyrambic° tide,
      Which in no channel deigns to abide,
      Which neither banks nor dikes control.
      Whether the immortal gods he sings
      In a no less immortal strain,
Or the great acts of god-descended kings,
Who in his numbers° still survive and reign,
20   Each rich embroidered line,
      Which their triumphant brows around
      By his sacred hand is bound,
Does all their starry diadems outshine.

Whether at Pisa's race° he please
To carve in polished verse the conquerors' images,
Whether the swift, the skillful, or the strong
Be crownèd in his nimble, artful, vigorous song,
Whether some brave young man's untimely fate
In words worth dying for he celebrate,
30   Such mournful and such pleasing words
As joy to his mother's and his mistress' grief affords,
      He bids him live and grow in fame;
      Among the stars he sticks his name;
The grave can but the dross of him devour,
So small is death's, so great the poet's power.

Lo, how the obsequious wind and swelling air
      The Theban swan° does upwards bear
Into the walks of clouds, where he does play,
And with extended wings opens his liquid way,
40   Whilst, alas, my timorous Muse
      Unambitious tracks pursues;
      Does, with weak, unballast° wings,
      About the mossy brooks and springs,
      About the trees' new-blossomed heads,
      About the gardens' painted beds,
      About the fields and flowery meads,
      And all inferior beauteous things,
         Like the laborious bee,
      For little drops of honey flee,
50   And there with humble sweets contents her industry.

1656

dithyrambic inspired, ecstatic
numbers verses
Pisa's race the Olympic games

Theban swan Pindar; see Ben Jonson's poem
to Shakespeare
unballast unsteady

ANDREW MARVELL

1621–1678

Marvell, the son of a Yorkshire Calvinist clergyman, was educated at Hull Grammar School and Trinity College, Cambridge. At eighteen he was temporarily converted to Roman Catholicism; at twenty he lost his Cambridge appointment. When the Civil War began in 1642 he was traveling in Europe. At the end of the war he found himself on the winning anti-Royalist side, and became tutor, at Nunappleton in Yorkshire, to Mary Fairfax, daughter of the victorious Commonwealth general. Later he was tutor to William Dutton, Cromwell's prospective son-in-law, and traveled with Dutton; in 1657 he became Latin Secretary as a colleague of Milton. In 1659, after the death of Cromwell, he became Member of Parliament for Hull, and held the seat till his death, serving also as secretary to English embassies in Russia, Denmark, and Sweden.

A bachelor, a man of violent temper, and in his later years a powerful controversialist, Marvell seems to have written his lyric poetry by the early 1650's; his satirical verse and prose belong to the Restoration period, and for a long time his reputation was primarily as a patriot, satirist, and prose-writer. The appearance in 1681 of his *Miscellaneous Poems* attracted little notice. His lyric poetry, then out of fashion, is highly individual yet related, in close and interesting ways, to that of Jonson, Carew, Lovelace, and Randolph. His range and virtuosity are greater than any of theirs, except Jonson's; and the central comment on his lyric verse is T. S. Eliot's: "Marvell's best verse is the product of European, that is to say Latin, culture," and from this he derives his *wit* and his *magniloquence*. His wit Eliot speaks of as "a tough reasonableness beneath the slight lyric grace," which, playing over "the great traditional commonplaces of European literature," renews them. Thus we have transferred from his political to his poetic reputation the words of his epitaph, which grant him "wit and learning, with a singular penetration and strength of judgment."

A Dialogue Between the Resolved Soul and Created Pleasure°

> Courage my soul, now learn to wield
> The weight of thine immortal shield.°
> Close on thy head thy helmet° bright.
> Balance thy sword° against the fight.
> See where an army, strong as fair,
> With silken banners° spreads the air.
> Now, if thou be'st that thing divine,
> In this day's combat let it shine:
> And show that nature wants an art
> To conquer one resolvèd heart.

10

A Dialogue . . . Pleasure The tempter, in this schematic poem, deploys against the Resolved Soul all the elements of the total temptation suffered by Christ in the wilderness. First the senses are the targets, and the Chorus intervenes at line 45 to comment on their successful resistance. Then follow the temptations of voluptuous sex, money, glory, and forbidden knowledge. Having overcome these, the Soul has

defeated all temptation, and the Chorus ends the work by proclaiming this fact.
shield . . . helmet . . . sword "the whole armour of God" (Ephesians 6:11, 13, 16, 17) worn by the *miles Christi*, soldier of Christ and his imitator
army . . . banners "terrible as an army with banners," Song of Songs 6:4

PLEASURE   Welcome the creation's guest,
            Lord of earth, and heaven's heir.
            Lay aside that warlike crest,
            And of nature's banquet share:
            Where the souls of fruits and flowers
            Stand prepared to heighten yours.°

SOUL   I sup above, and cannot stay
        To bait° so long upon the way.

PLEASURE   On these downy pillows lie,
20   Whose soft plumes will thither fly;
            On these roses strowed so plain°
            Lest one leaf° thy side should strain.

SOUL   My gentler rest is on a thought,
        Conscious of doing what I ought.

PLEASURE   If thou be'st with perfumes pleased,
            Such as oft the gods appeased,
            Thou in fragrant clouds shalt show
            Like another god below.

SOUL   A soul that knows not to presume
30   Is heaven's and its own perfume.

PLEASURE   Everything does seem to vie
            Which should first attract thine eye;
            But since none deserves that grace,
            In this crystal° view *thy* face.

SOUL   When the Creator's skill is prized,
        The rest is all but earth disguised.

PLEASURE   Hark how music then prepares
            For thy stay° these charming airs;
            When the posting winds recall,
40   And suspend the river's fall.

SOUL   Had I but any time to lose,
        On this I would it all dispose.
        Cease, Tempter. None can chain a mind
        Whom this sweet chordage° cannot bind.

CHORUS   *Earth cannot show so brave a sight*
          As when a single soul does fence
          The batteries of alluring sense,
          And Heaven views it with delight.
              Then persevere, for still new charges sound;
50   *And if thou overcom'st thou shalt be crowned.*

Where the souls . . . yours where the essences
of fruits and flowers will be ready to stimulate
your (lower or sensitive) soul
bait pause for refreshment
plain flat
one leaf remembering the Sybarite who was
made uncomfortable by a crumpled rose petal
(a tale told by Seneca)
crystal looking-glass
stay sustenance
chordage bonds, musical chords

PLEASURE   All this fair and soft and sweet,
            Which scatteringly doth shine,
            Shall within one beauty° meet,
            And she be only thine.

SOUL   If things of sight such heavens be,
        What heavens are those we cannot see?

PLEASURE   Wheresoe'er thy foot shall go
            The minted gold shall lie;
            Till thou purchase all below,
60   And want new worlds to buy.

SOUL   Were't not a price who'd value gold?
        And that's worth nought that can be sold.

PLEASURE   Wilt thou all the glory have
            That war or peace commend?
            Half the world shall be thy slave,
            The other half thy friend.

SOUL   What friends, if to my self untrue?
        What slaves, unless I captive you?

PLEASURE   Thou shalt know each hidden cause,°
70   And see the future time;
            Try what depth the centre° draws,
            And then to heaven climb.

SOUL   None thither mounts by the degree°
        Of knowledge, but humility.

CHORUS   *Triumph, triumph, victorious soul;*
          The world has not one pleasure more:°
          The rest does lie beyond the pole,
          And is thine everlasting store.
                    1681

A Dialogue Between the Soul and Body°

SOUL   Oh, who shall from this dungeon raise
        A soul enslaved so many ways?
        With bolts of bones; that fettered stands
        In feet, and manacled in hands;°
        Here blinded with an eye, and there

within one beauty remembering the painter
Zeuxis who brought together the beauties of
many models in his portrait of Helen
cause antecedent of natural phenomenon
centre of the earth
degree ladder (pun on academic sense)
not . . . more all temptations are exhausted,
as in Luke 4:13
A Dialogue . . . Body For the theme see

Galatians 5:17: "the flesh lusteth against the
spirit, and the spirit against the flesh: and these
are contrary the one to the other."
bolts . . . hands The soul sees the organs of
the body as having, for it, exactly the opposite
of their obvious functions; the feet *fetter*, the
hands *manacle* (Latin, *manus*, hand), the eye
blinds, and the ear deafens.

Deaf with the drumming of an ear;
A soul hung up, as 'twere, in chains
Of nerves and arteries and veins;
Tortured, besides each other part,
In a vain head and double heart.°

BODY   Oh, who shall me deliver whole
From bonds of this tyrannic soul?
Which stretched upright, impales° me so
That mine own precipice I go;
And warms and moves this needless° frame,
A fever could but do the same.
And, wanting where its spite to try,
Has made me live to let me die.
A body that could never rest,
Since this ill spirit it possessed.

SOUL   What magic° could me thus confine
Within another's grief to pine?
Where whatsoever it complain,
I feel, that cannot feel, the pain.°
And all my care itself employs,
That to preserve which me destroys.
Constrained not only to endure
Diseases, but, what's worse, the cure;
And ready oft the port° to gain,
Am shipwrecked into health again.

BODY   But physic yet could never reach
The maladies° thou me dost teach:
Whom first the cramp of hope does tear,
And then the palsy shakes of fear;
The pestilence of love does heat,
Or hatred's hidden ulcer eat.
Joy's cheerful madness does perplex,
Or sorrow's other madness vex;
Which knowledge forces me to know,
And memory will not forgo.
What but a soul could have the wit
To build me up for sin so fit?
So architects do square and hew
Green trees that in the forest grew.°

1681

head . . . heart these words used by the soul in their figurative instead of their organic senses, the head egotistic, the heart treacherous
impales The soul, responsible for the body's motion, holds it reluctantly upright, like a man impaled.
needless that doesn't need it
magic Magicians—like Prospero—could confine spirits within trees.

whatsoever . . . pain whatever ill the body complains of, I experience the pain, although (except for my connection with it) I am immaterial and so impervious to pain
port death
maladies spiritual ills
So . . . grew just as architects take naturally round trees and make square pillars of them

The Nymph Complaining for the Death of Her Fawn°

The wanton troopers° riding by
Have shot my fawn, and it will die.
Ungentle men! They cannot thrive
To kill thee. Thou ne'er didst alive
Them any harm, alas, nor could
Thy death yet do them any good.
I'm sure I never wished them ill,
Nor do I for all this, nor will;
But if my simple prayers may yet
10 Prevail with heaven to forget
The murder, I will join my tears
Rather than fail. But oh, my fears!
It cannot die so.° Heaven's King
Keeps register of everything,
And nothing may we use in vain.
Ev'n beasts must be with justice slain,
Else men are made their deodands;°
Though they should wash their guilty hands,
In this warm life-blood, which doth part
20 From thine, and wound me to the heart,
Yet could they not be clean, their stain
Is dyed in such a purple grain.
There is not such another in
The world to offer for their sin.

    Unconstant Sylvio, when yet
I had not found him counterfeit,
One morning (I remember well)
Tied in this silver chain and bell,
Gave it to me: nay, and I know
30 What he said then; I'm sure I do:
Said he, 'Look how your huntsman here
Hath taught a fawn to hunt his dear.'°
But Sylvio soon had me beguiled;

The Nymph . . . Fawn This is in a tradition
of poems lamenting the deaths of pets, but,
as the commentaries show, it lends itself to
partial allegorical readings. Given the naïve
narrator, and her occasionally portentous vocabulary, the meanings waver between simple
and apparently complex; and the references
to the Song of Songs, though simple, bring
into play the various, voluminous, and intermit-
tent allegories attached to that work. ("My
beloved is mine and I am his: he feedeth
among the lilies . . . turn, my beloved, and
be thou like a roe or a young hart . . . my
beloved is gone down into his garden, to the
bed of spices, to feed in the gardens, and to
gather lilies . . . I am the rose of Sharon, and
the lily of the valleys. . . ." Song of Songs,
2.1, etc.) In the same way it is we, not the
nymph, who feel the mixture of innocence and
presumption in her adopting the stance of
Niobe weeping for her children, and of the
Virgin at the foot of the Cross. Hence our
difficulty in assimilating the strangeness of
this poem. T. S. Eliot best expresses our sense
of it when he says that Marvell takes "a
slight affair, the feeling of a girl for her pet,
and gives it a connexion with that inexhaustible
and terrible nebula of emotion which surrounds
all our exact and practical passions and mingles
with them."
troopers soldiers on the Commonwealth side
so i.e., forgotten
deodands any chattel that caused the death
of a man was forfeit to the crown for charity;
the same should apply to men who kill beasts
unjustly
dear dear-deer

This waxèd tame, while he grew wild,
And quite regardless of my smart,
Left me his fawn, but took his heart.°
   Thenceforth I set myself to play
My solitary time away
With this, and very well content,
Could so mine idle life have spent;
For it was full of sport and light
Of foot and heart, and did invite
Me to its game: it seemed to bless
Itself in me; how could I less
Than love it? Oh, I cannot be
Unkind to a beast that loveth me.
   Had it lived long, I do not know
Whether it too might have done so
As Sylvio did; his gifts might be
Perhaps as false, or more, than he;
But I am sure, for aught that I
Could in so short a time espy,
Thy love was far more better than
The love of false and cruel men.
   With sweetest milk and sugar, first
I it at mine own fingers nursed;
And as it grew, so every day
It waxed more white and sweet than they.
It had so sweet a breath! And oft
I blushed to see its foot more soft
And white, shall I say than my hand?
Nay, any lady's of the land.
   It is a wondrous thing how fleet
'Twas on those little silver feet;
With what a pretty skipping grace
It oft would challenge me the race;
And when it had left me far away,
'Twould stay, and run again, and stay;
For it was nimbler much than hinds,
And trod as if on the four° winds.
   I have a garden of my own,
But so with roses overgrown,
And lilies, that you would it guess
To be a little wilderness;
And all the springtime of the year
It only lovèd to be there.
Among the beds of lilies I
Have sought it oft, where it should lie,
Yet could not, till itself would rise,

40

50

60

70

heart heart-hart   four disyllabic

80 Find it, although before mine eyes;
    For in the flaxen lilies' shade,
    It like a bank of lilies laid.
    Upon the roses it would feed,
    Until its lips e'en seemed to bleed;
    And then to me 'twould boldly trip,
    And print those roses on my lip.
    But all its chief delight was still
    On roses thus itself to fill,
    And its pure virgin limbs to fold
90 In whitest sheets of lilies cold:
    Had it lived long, it would have been
    Lilies without, roses within.
        O help! O help! I see it faint
    And die as calmly as a saint!
    See how it weeps! the tears do come
    Sad, slowly dropping like a gum.
    So weeps the wounded balsam;° so
    The holy frankincense doth flow;
    The brotherless Heliades°
100 Melt in such amber tears as these.
        I in a golden vial will
    Keep these two crystal tears, and fill
    It till it do o'erflow with mine;
    Then place it in Diana's shrine.
        Now my sweet fawn is vanished to
    Whither the swans and turtles go,
    In fair Elysium to endure,
    With milk-white lambs and ermines pure.
    O do not run too fast; for I
110 Will but bespeak thy grave, and die.
        First, my unhappy statue shall
    Be cut in marble, and withal
    Let it be weeping, too; but there
    Th' engraver sure his art may spare;
    For I so truly thee bemoan
    That I shall weep, though I be stone,°
    Until my tears, still dropping, wear
    My breast, themselves engraving there.
    There at my feet shalt thou be laid,
120 Of purest alabaster made;
    For I would have thine image be
    White as I can, though not as thee.
                    1681

balsam both the balsam-tree and its resin
Heliades the three daughters of the sun god
Helios who, after mourning the death of their

brother Phaeton, were changed into amber-
dropping trees
stone like the weeping Niobe, who was turned
to stone

To His Coy Mistress°

Had we but world enough, and time,
This coyness, Lady, were no crime.
We would sit down, and think which way
To walk, and pass our long love's day.
Thou by the Indian Ganges' side
Shouldst rubies find; I by the tide
Of Humber° would complain. I would
Love you ten years before the Flood,
And you should, if you please, refuse
10 Till the Conversion of the Jews.°
My vegetable° love should grow
Vaster than empires and more slow;
An hundred years should go to praise
Thine eyes, and on thy forehead gaze;
Two hundred to adore each breast,
But thirty thousand to the rest;
An age at least to every part,
And the last age should show your heart.
For, Lady, you deserve this state,°
20 Nor would I love at lower rate.

    But at my back I always hear
Time's wingèd chariot° hurrying near;
And yonder all before us lie
Deserts of vast eternity.
Thy beauty shall no more be found,
Nor, in thy marble vault, shall sound
My echoing song; then worms shall try
That long-preserved virginity,
And your quaint° honour turn to dust,
30 And into ashes all my lust:
The grave's a fine and private place,
But none, I think, do there embrace.

    Now therefore, while the youthful hue
Sits on thy skin like morning dew,
And while thy willing soul transpires

To His Coy Mistress The theme is ancient: seize the day, there is no love-making in hell. Even the catalogue of a girl's charms (*blazon*, see Glossary) is old, though here merely sketched in derisive rejection of her notion that she exists in a world where there is plenty of time. The ultimate source is a poem by Asclepiades in the Greek Anthology: "You spare your maidenhead, and to what profit? For when you come to Hades you will not find your lover, girl. Among the living are the delights of Venus; but, maiden, we shall lie in the underworld mere bones and dust." Marvell's lover is masculine and physical, at war with time and with metaphysical notions of love. The abstraction "virginity" is, for him, a hymen, a physical obstacle; so is "quaint honour"; even "quaint" puns on "cunt". The girl must see the terrifying Time of the conclusion as her enemy too.
Humber river on which stands Hull, Marvell's home town
Conversion of the Jews thought to be one of the concluding events of history
vegetable growing as slowly as vegetation
state ceremonial treatment
Time's . . . chariot Time is often winged, and often has a chariot; only Marvell, apparently, gives him both attributes at once.
quaint fastidious (for pun, see first note)

At every pore with instant fires,°
Now let us sport us while we may,
And now, like amorous birds of prey,
Rather at once our time devour
40 Than languish in his slow-chapt° power.
Let us roll all our strength and all
Our sweetness up into one ball,
And tear our pleasures with rough strife
Thorough° the iron gates of life;
Thus, though we cannot make our sun
Stand still, yet we will make him run.°

1681

The Definition of Love°

My love is of a birth as rare
As 'tis, for object, strange and high;
It was begotten by Despair
Upon Impossibility.

Magnanimous Despair alone
Could show me so divine a thing,
Where feeble Hope could ne'er have flown,
But vainly flapped its tinsel wing.

And yet I quickly might arrive
10 Where my extended soul° is fixed;
But Fate does iron wedges drive,
And always crowds itself betwixt.

For Fate with jealous eyes does see
Two perfect loves, nor lets them close;°
Their union would her ruin be,
And her tyrannic power depose.

And therefore her decrees of steel
Us as the distant poles have placed
(Though Love's whole world on us doth wheel),
20 Not by themselves to be embraced;

willing . . . fires her coyness cannot prevent her amorous spirit from showing in her flushed face
slow-chapt power power of his devouring jaws
Thorough through
Let us roll . . . run discontinuous and urgent. The first two lines suggest a pomander, the next couplet a forcing of pleasure out of the dull constriction of ordinary life; and the last says the lovers cannot treat the sun like Joshua, who made it stand still, but should treat it like David, who made it come forth like a bridegroom to run his race.

The Definition of Love Not very like other "Definitions of Love" in the period; rather a poem on the known topic, "in love despair is nobler than hope," developed by metaphysical conceits to the point where the structure of nature would have to be changed to bring the lovers together; a situation in which the lover takes despairing pride
extended soul It resides in his mistress, not in him.
close unite

Unless the giddy heaven fall,
And earth some new convulsion tear,
And, us to join, the world should all
Be cramped into a planisphere.°

As lines, so loves, oblique may well
Themselves in every angle greet;
But ours, so truly parallel,
Though infinite, can never meet.

Therefore the love which us doth bind,
30 But Fate so enviously debars,
Is the conjunction of the mind,
And opposition° of the stars.

                    1681

The Picture of Little T. C.°
In a Prospect of Flowers

See with what simplicity
This nymph begins her golden days!
In the green grass she loves to lie,
And there with her fair aspect tames
The wilder flowers, and gives them names;°
But only with the roses plays,
        And them does tell
What colour best becomes them, and what smell.

Who can foretell for what high cause
10 This darling of the gods° was born?
Yet this is she whose chaster laws
The wanton Love shall one day fear,
And under her command severe
See his bow broke and ensigns torn.
        Happy, who can
Appease this virtuous enemy of man!

Oh then let me in time compound,
And parley with those conquering eyes,
Ere they have tried their force to wound;
20 Ere with their glancing wheels they drive
In triumph over hearts that strive,
And them that yield but° more despise.
        Let me be laid
Where I may see thy glories from some shade.

---

planisphere map of the worlds or heavens projected on a plane surface
conjunction . . . opposition astrological terms—
the proximity and the maximum separation of
planets
T. C. perhaps Theophila Cornewall (b. 1644)

gives them names traditionally Adam's task in
Paradise (see Genesis 2:19)
darling of the gods Theophila means "dear to
the gods."
but only

Meantime, whilst every verdant thing
Itself does at thy beauty charm,
Reform the errors of the spring:
Make that the tulips may have share
Of sweetness, seeing they are fair;
30   And roses of their thorns disarm;
     But most procure
That violets may a longer age endure.

.   But, O young beauty of the woods,
Whom nature courts with fruits and flowers,
Gather the flowers, but spare the buds,
Lest Flora, angry at thy crime,
To kill her infants in their prime,
Do quickly make the example yours;
     And ere we see,
40   Nip in the blossom all our hopes and thee.

                 1681

The Mower Against Gardens°

Luxurious° man, to bring his vice in use,°
   Did after him the world seduce,
And from the fields the flowers and plants allure,
   Where Nature was most plain and pure.
He first enclosed within the gardens square
   A dead and standing pool of air,
And a more luscious earth for them did knead,
   Which stupefied them while it fed.
The pink grew then as double as his mind;
10   The nutriment did change the kind.
With strange perfumes he did the roses taint;
   And flowers themselves were taught to paint.°
The tulip white did for complexion seek,
   And learned to interline its cheek;
Its onion root they then so high did hold,°
   That one was for a meadow sold:°
Another world was searched through oceans new,
   To find the *Marvel of Peru;*°

The Mower Against Gardens Gardens could be good (the art that improves nature) or bad (the art that corrupts nature). Grafting can be good when it improves the natural stock; or bad, since the gardener is acting like a pander. Gardens can be the settings for debauchery or for meditation. These antitheses are frequent in the poetry of this period. Randolph's poem "Upon Love Fondly Refused for Conscience's Sake" is on the libertine side. Marvell, using the same Horatian epode measure, puts the other case, using many of the same instances but in the contrary sense. He makes his speaker a mower, who belongs to the fields outside the house and garden, and so not corrupt.
Luxurious lecherous, sinful
bring . . . use to make a profit on his sin
paint apply make-up
hold value
one . . . sold At the height of Dutch tulipomania in the 1630's bulbs were bought for huge prices; the Mower naturally chooses "a meadow" to represent something of high value.
Marvel of Peru *Mirabilis jalapa* or *peruviana,* then an exotic flower

And yet these rarities might be allowed
20   To man, that sovereign thing and proud,
Had he not dealt between° the bark and tree,
    Forbidden mixtures° there to see.
No plant now knew the stock from which it came;
    He grafts upon the wild the tame,
That the uncertain and adulterate fruit
    Might put the palate in dispute.
His green seraglio has its eunuchs too,
    Lest any tyrant him outdo;
And in the cherry he does Nature vex,
30   To procreate without a sex.°
'Tis all enforced, the fountain and the grot,
    While the sweet fields do lie forgot,
Where willing Nature does to all dispense
    A wild and fragrant innocence;
And fauns and fairies do the meadows till
    More by their presence than their skill.
Their statues polished by some ancient hand,
    May to adorn the gardens stand;
But, howsoe'er the figures do excel,
40   The Gods themselves with us do dwell.

                                        1681

Damon the Mower

Hark how the mower Damon sung,
With love of Juliana stung!
While everything did seem to paint
The scene more fit for his complaint:
Like her fair eyes the day was fair;
But scorching like his am'rous care:
Sharp like his scythe his sorrow was,
And withered like his hopes the grass.

'Oh what ususual heats are here,
10   Which thus our sunburned meadows sear!
The grasshopper its pipe gives o'er;
And hamstringed° frogs can dance no more:
But in the brook the green frog wades,
And grasshoppers seek out the shades.
Only the snake, that kept within,
Now glitters in its second skin.

dealt between acted as pander for   **To . . . sex** probably a reference to a stoneless
Forbidden mixtures Cf. Deuteronomy 22:9.   cherry
                                        hamstringed lamed (by the heat)

'This heat the sun could never raise,
Nor Dog Star so inflames the days.
It from an higher beauty grow'th,
20 Which burns the fields and mower both:
Which made the Dog,° and makes the sun
Hotter than his own Phaëton.°
Not July causeth these extremes,
But Juliana's scorching beams.

'Tell me where I may pass the fires
Of the hot day, or hot desires.
To what cool cave shall I descend,
Or to what gelid fountain bend?
Alas! I look for ease in vain,
30 When remedies themselves complain;
No moisture but my tears do rest,
Nor cold but in her icy breast.

'How long wilt thou, fair Shepherdess,
Esteem me, and my presents less?
To thee the harmless snake I bring,
Disarmèd of its teeth and sting;
To thee chameleons changing hue,
And oak leaves tipped with honey dew.
Yet thou, ungrateful, hast not sought
40 Nor what they are, nor who them brought.

'I am the mower Damon, known
Through all the meadows I have mown.
On me the morn her dew distills
Before her darling daffodils:
And, if at noon my toil me heat,
The sun himself licks off my sweat;
While, going home, the evening sweet
In cowslip-water° bathes my feet.

'What though the piping shepherd stock
50 The plains with an unnumbered flock,
This scythe of mine discovers wide
More ground than all his sheep do hide.
With this the golden fleece I shear
Of all these closes° every year.
And though in wool more poor than they,
Yet am I richer far in hay.

'Nor am I so deformed to sight,°
If in my scythe I lookèd right;

made the Dog perhaps "mads the Dog" (Sirius)
Phaëton who failed to control the horses of
the sun
cowslip-water used by ladies to cleanse the skin
closes enclosed fields

deformed to sight using his scythe as a mirror,
whereas Virgil's Corydon, in the phrase Marvell
translates, was using a calm sea

In which I see my picture done,
60   As in a crescent moon the sun.
The deathless fairies take me oft
To lead them in their dances soft;
And, when I tune myself to sing,
About me they contract their ring.°

'How happy might I still have mowed,
Had not Love here his thistles sowed!
But now I all the day complain,
Joining my labour to my pain;
And with my scythe cut down the grass,
70   Yet still my grief is where it was;
But, when the iron blunter grows,
Sighing I whet my scythe and woes.'

While thus he threw his elbow round,
Depopulating all the ground,
And, with his whistling scythe, does cut
Each stroke between the earth and root,
The edgèd steel by careless chance
Did into his own ankle glance;
And there among the grass fell down,
80   By his own scythe, the mower mown.

'Alas!' said he, 'these hurts are slight
To those that die by Love's dispite.
With shepherd's-purse,° and clown's-all-heal,°
The blood I stanch, and wound I seal.
Only for him no cure is found,
Whom Juliana's eyes do wound.
'Tis death alone that this must do:
For Death, thou art a mower too.'

                    1681

The Mower to the Glowworms

Ye living lamps, by whose dear light
The nightingale does sit so late,
And studying all the summer-night,
Her matchless songs does meditate;

Ye country comets, that portend
No war, nor prince's funeral,°
Shining unto no higher end
Than to presage the grass's fall;°

ring the "fairy-ring" caused by certain fungi
shepherd's-purse a weed supposed to check
bleeding
clown's-all-heal a nettle thought to heal wounds

funeral Comets were supposed to signify the
death of great men.
grass's fall Glowworms were thought to appear
only when the hay was ripe for cutting.

Ye glowworms, whose officious° flame
10   To wand'ring mowers shows the way,
That in the night have lost their aim,
And after foolish fires° do stray;

Your courteous lights in vain you waste,
Since Juliana here is come,
For she my mind hath so displaced
That I shall never find my home.

                                        1681

The Garden°

How vainly men themselves amaze
To win the palm, the oak, or bays;°
And their uncessant labours see
Crowned from some single herb or tree:
Whose short and narrow-vergèd shade
Does prudently their toils upbraid;
While all flowers and all° trees do close°
To weave the garlands of repose.

Fair Quiet, have I found thee here,
10   And Innocence, thy sister dear!
Mistaken long, I sought you then
In busy companies of men.
Your sacred plants, if here below,
Only among the plants will grow.
Society is all but rude,
To this delicious solitude.°

No white nor red° was ever seen
So amorous as this lovely green.°
Fond lovers, cruel as their flame,
20   Cut in these trees their mistress' name:
Little, alas, they know or heed
How far these beauties hers exceed!
Fair trees, wheresoe'er your barks I wound,
No name shall but your own° be found.

officious attentive
foolish fires the *ignis fatuus* or will-o'-the-wisp.
Marsh-gas spontaneously ignited, was thought
to "mislead night wanderers."
The Garden The garden, like the biblical
"paradise of pleasure," satisfies the senses but
also calls for contemplation of the source of
these delights. It is not a libertine garden; there
is no woman in it, and the poem echoes the
misogynist tradition that Adam was better off
without Eve. The garden's color, green, is
good; other colors are not. Eventually the mind
withdraws from all that pleases the senses and
contemplates the source of pure light, broken
on earth (as the Platonists declared), into
variety. There is a return to the green pleasures
of the garden.

palm . . . oak . . . bays honors awarded for
war, statesmanship, poetry
all . . . all . . . as opposed to the *single* of
l. 4
close unite
Society . . . solitude paradoxical, since society
is usually thought more "polished" than retirement
white . . . red emblematic of female beauty
green by association, emblematic of solitude
and the absence of women
No . . . own since the trees are lovelier than
the girls, we should cut *their* names, not the
girls', in the barks

When we have run our passion's heat,°
Love hither makes his best retreat.°
The gods, that mortal beauty chase,
Still° in a tree did end their race:
Apollo hunted Daphne so,
30   Only that she might laurel grow;
And Pan did after Syrinx speed,
Not as a nymph, but for a reed.°

What wondrous life in this I lead!
Ripe apples drop about my head;
The luscious clusters of the vine
Upon my mouth do crush their wine;
The nectarine and curious peach
Into my hands themselves do reach;
Stumbling on melons, as I pass,
40   Ensnared with flowers, I fall on grass.°

Meanwhile the mind from pleasure less°
Withdraws into its happiness;
The mind, that ocean° where each kind
Does straight its own resemblance find;
Yet it creates, transcending these,
Far other worlds and other seas,°
Annihilating all that's made
To a green thought in a green shade.°

Here at the fountain's sliding foot,
50   Or at some fruit-tree's mossy root,
Casting the body's vest aside,
My soul into the boughs does glide:
There, like a bird, it sits and sings,
Then whets° and combs its silver wings,
And, till prepared for longer flights,°
Waves in its plumes the various light.°

Such was that happy garden-state,
While man there walked without a mate:°
After a place so pure and sweet,

heat ardor; race
retreat both military and religious senses
Still always
Apollo . . . reed contrary to the myth, which
represents Apollo as frustrated when Daphne
turned into a laurel, so with the story of Pan
and Syrinx, who escaped him by turning into
a reed
fall on grass harmlessly, unlike Adam
from . . . less experiencing less pleasure in
nature than the senses (and so turning inward)
ocean It was supposed that the sea contained
creatures parallel to all found on land; the
implication is that the mind is equipped in

advance to recognize everything in the world.
Yet . . . seas beyond this, the imagination
creates forms with no equivalents in reality
Annihilating . . . shade making the visible
world seem as nothing compared with what can
be imagined by the contemplative
whets preens
Till . . . flight resting, in its ascent, between
the created and the intelligible worlds
various light neoplatonic image of the white
light of eternity broken into color in the
temporal world
Such . . . mate the Garden of Eden before the
creation of Eve

60   What other help could yet be meet!°
But 'twas beyond a mortal's share
To wander solitary there:
Two paradises 'twere in one
To live in paradise alone.

How well the skillful gardener drew,
Of flowers and herbs, this dial new;°
Where, from above, the milder sun
Does through a fragrant° zodiac run;
And, as it works, the industrious bee
70   Computes its time° as well as we!
How could such sweet and wholesome hours
Be reckoned but with herbs and flowers!

                  1681

From Upon Appleton House°

And now to the abyss I pass
370   Of that unfathomable grass,
Where men like grasshoppers appear,
But grasshoppers are giants° there:
They, in their squeaking laugh, contemn
Us as we walk more low than them;
And, from the precipices tall
Of the green spires, to us do call.

To see men through this meadow dive
We wonder how they rise alive;
As, under water, none does know
380   Whether he fall through it or go;
But as the mariners that sound
And show upon their lead the ground,°
They bring up flowers so to be seen,
And prove they've at the bottom been.

help . . . meet "And the LORD God said, It is
not good that the man should be alone; I will
make him an help meet for him" (Genesis
2:18).
dial new new style of sundial (the whole
garden)
milder . . . fragrant The sun is filtered through
trees and on to green plants.
time pun on "thyme"
Upon Appleton House Appleton House, the
home of Lord Fairfax, was once a priory but
at the time a brick mansion with a center block
and two wings. There was a large park, including watermeadows of the River Wharfe. The
poem is a somewhat unusual member of a
genre praising country houses and their lords.
Marvell uses a "conceited" manner, corresponding as nearly as anything in English to the
French *précieux* poetry. The house may represent its master, and Order, but Marvell
applies to his theme a fantastic wit and many
elaborate set pieces—on the house itself, its
Catholic history, the garden, the mowing of
the meadows (here extracted), the woods
meet for contemplation (given here in part),
the river, and Maria Fairfax, his pupil. The
whole is what the French called a *tableau
fantasque*, sustained with extraordinary wit and
learning; some 200 lines must serve to give
an impression of the whole, which has 776.
At the outset the poet moves into the deep
grass that is about to be mown.
grasshoppers . . . giants Cf. Numbers 13:33.
ground mud from seabed

No scene that turns with engines strange
Does oftener than these meadows change:
For when the sun the grass hath vexed,
The tawny mowers enter next;
Who seem like Israelites to be,
390   Walking on foot through a green sea.
To them the grassy deeps divide,
And crowd a lane to either side.°

With whistling scythe and elbow strong,
These massacre the grass along;
While one, unknowing, carves the rail,°
Whose yet unfeathered quills her fail.
The edge all bloody from its breast
He draws, and does his stroke detest;
Fearing the flesh untimely mowed°
400   To him a fate as black forebode.

But bloody Thestylis, that waits
To bring the mowing camp° their cates,°
Greedy as kites has trussed it up,
And forthwith means on it to sup;
When on another quick° she lights,
And cries, 'He° called us Israelites;
But now, to make his saying true,
Rails rain for quails, for manna dew.'°

Unhappy birds! what does it boot
410   To build below the grasses' root,
When lowness is unsafe as height,
And chance o'ertakes what scapeth spite?
And now your orphan parents' call
Sounds your untimely funeral.
Death-trumpets creak in such a note,
And 'tis the sourdine° in their throat.

Or sooner hatch or° higher build!
The mower now commands the field,
In whose new traverse° seemeth wrought
420   A camp of battle newly fought:
Where, as the meads with hay, the plain
Lies quilted o'er with bodies slain;
The women that with forks it fling,
Do represent the pillaging.

crowd . . . side crowd to either side to form
a lane, as the Red Sea did for the Israelites
rail corn crake, land bird
untimely mowed Cf. "Damon the Mower," l. 88.
mowing camp The mowers are thought of as
soldiers.
cates food
quick alive

He the poet, in l. 389, of whom she has somehow got knowledge
quails . . . dew Exodus 16:13–14
sourdine hoarse low trumpet, or mute producing
this effect
Or either
traverse passage cut through the field

And now the careless victors play,
Dancing the triumphs of the hay;°
Where every mower's wholesome heat
Smells like an Alexander's sweat,°
Their females fragrant as the mead
430 Which they in fairy circles° tread:
When at their dance's end they kiss,
Their new-made hay not sweeter is.

When after this 'tis piled in cocks,
Like a calm sea it shows the rocks;
We wondering in the river near
How boats among them safely steer.
Or, like the desert Memphis° sand,
Short pyramids of hay do stand.
And such° the Roman camps° do rise
440 In hills for soldiers' obsequies.

This scene again withdrawing° brings
A new and empty face of things;
A levelled space, as smooth and plain
As cloths° for Lely° stretched to stain.
The world when first created sure
Was such a table rase° and pure;
Or rather such is the *toril*°
Ere the bulls enter at Madril.°

For to this naked equal flat,
450 Which Levellers° take pattern at,°
The villagers in common° chase
Their cattle, which it closer rase;
And what below the scythe increased°
Is pinched yet nearer by the beast.
Such, in the painted world, appeared
Davenant with the universal Herd.°

They seem within the polished grass
A landskip drawn in looking-glass;°
And shrunk in the huge pasture show

hay country dance (with a pun)
Alexander's sweat According to Plutarch this had a "passing delightful savor."
fairy circles See "Damon the Mower," l. 64.
Memphis Egyptian city near Pyramids
such in the same manner
Roman camps tumuli now known to be of ancient British origin
scene . . . withdrawing continues theatrical figure of l. 385
cloths canvases
Lely Sir Peter Lely, Dutch portrait painter who went to England in 1641. See Fig. 33.
table rase *tabula rasa*
toril bullring
Madril Madrid

Levellers egalitarian political party, favoring the leveling out of rank, parliamentary representation, etc.
take pattern at use as a model
in common The meadow is for common grazing.
what . . . increased what grew lower than the scythe could cut
Davenant . . . Herd In Sir William Davenant's admired contemporary epic *Gondibert* there is a description of a painting of the Six Days of Creation; on the sixth day "an universal Herd appears."
landskip . . . glass landscape shown in a painting reflected in a mirror and thus reduced in size

460   As spots, so shaped, on faces do.
  Such fleas, ere they approach the eye,
  In multiplying glasses lie;°
  They feed so wide, so slowly move,
  As constellations do above.

  Then to conclude these pleasant acts,
  Denton° sets ope its cataracts;
  And makes the meadow truly be
  (What it but seemed before) a sea.
  For, jealous of its lord's long stay,
470   It tries t'invite him thus away.
  The river in itself is drowned
  And isles the astonished cattle round.

  Let others tell the paradox,
  How eels now bellow in the ox;
  How horses at their tails do kick,
  Turned as they hang to leeches° quick;
  How boats can over bridges sail,
  And fishes do the stables scale;
  How salmons trespassing are found,
480   And pikes are taken in the pound.

  But I, retiring from the flood,
  Take sanctuary in the wood;
  And, while it lasts, myself embark
  In this yet green, yet growing ark;
  Where the first carpenter° might best
  Fit timber for his keel have pressed;°
  And where all creatures might have shares,
  Although in armies, not in pairs.

  The double wood of ancient stocks
490   Linked in, so thick an union locks,
  It like two pedigrees appears,
  On one hand Fairfax, th' other Veres;
  Of whom though many fell in war,°
  Yet more to heaven shooting are:
  And, as they Nature's cradle decked,
  Will in green age her hearse expect.

  When first the eye this forest sees
  It seems indeed as wood not trees:
  As if their neighbourhood° so old
500   To one great trunk them all did mould.

Such . . . lie so do fleas appear on the glass
before one looks at them through a microscope
Denton river flowing through the meadow
leeches Horsehairs in water were supposed to
turn into eels or leeches.

first carpenter Noah
pressed commandeered
fell in war were cut down to satisfy the war-
time demand for timber
neighbourhood proximity

There the huge bulk takes place, as meant
To thrust up a fifth element;°
And stretches still so closely wedged
As if the night within were hedged.

Dark all without it knits; within
It opens passable and thin;
And in as loose an order grows
As the Corinthian° porticoes.
The arching boughs unite between
510   The columns of the temple green;
And underneath the wingèd choirs
Echo about their tunèd fires.

The nightingale does here make choice
To sing the trials of her voice.
Low shrubs she sits in, and adorns
With music high the squatted thorns.
But highest oaks stoop down to hear,
And listening elders prick the ear.
The thorn, lest it should hurt her, draws
520   Within the skin its shrunken claws.

But I have for my music found
A sadder, yet more pleasing sound:
The stock doves, whose fair necks are graced
With nuptial rings, their ensigns chaste;
Yet always, for some cause unknown,
Sad pair, unto the elms they moan.
O why should such a couple mourn,
That in so equal flames do burn!

Then as I careless on the bed
530   Of gelid strawberries do tread,
And through the hazels thick espy
The hatching throstle's shining eye,
The heron from the ash's top
The eldest of its young lets drop,
As if it, stork-like,° did pretend
That tribute to its Lord to send.

But most the hewel's° wonders are,
Who here has the holt-felster's° care.
He walks still upright from the root,
540   Measuring the timber with his foot;
And all the way, to keep it clean,

---

fifth element of different substance from the other four: earth, water, air, fire
Corinthian most ornate of the Greek architectural orders, also associated with moral laxity (hence "looseness")

stork-like The stork was supposed to leave one of its young behind as tribute to the owner.
hewel's green woodpecker's
holt-felster's woodcutter's

Doth from the bark the wood-moths glean.
He, with his beak, examines well
Which fit to stand and which to fell.

The good he numbers up, and hacks;
As if he marked them with the ax.
But where he, tinkling with his beak,
Does find the hollow oak to speak,
That for his building he designs,
550   And through the tainted side he mines.°
Who could have thought the tallest oak
Should fall by such a feeble stroke!

Nor would it, had the tree not fed
A traitor worm, within it bred.
(As first our flesh corrupt within
Tempts impotent and bashful sin.)
And yet that worm triumphs not long,
But serves to feed the hewel's young;
While the oak seems to fall content,
560   Viewing the treason's punishment.

Thus I, easy philosopher,
Among the birds and trees confer;
And little now to make me wants,
Or of the fowls or of the plants.
Give me but wings as they, and I
Straight floating on the air shall fly:
Or turn me but, and you shall see
I was but an inverted tree.°

. . .

1681

An Horatian Ode upon Cromwell's Return from Ireland°

The forward° youth that would appear
Must now° forsake his Muses dear,
    Nor in the shadows sing
    His numbers languishing:
'Tis time to leave the books in dust,

---

mines burrows
tree "Man is like an inverted tree" is an old
commonplace.
An Horatian Ode . . . Written between May
and July 1650, after Cromwell's return from
Ireland and before his Scottish campaign,
which began in July. Marvell had in mind
certain odes of Horace, and the *Pharsalia* of
Lucan, which is about Julius Caesar and
Pompey (Caesar also violated "ancient rights,"
as Charles I did). What makes this the greatest of political poems in English is its weight
and control. Whether, as seems most likely,

Marvell was at the time of writing committed
to Cromwell, or whether the lines on the King's
execution are not merely part of the rhetorical
strategy but express sympathy for his cause,
we feel principally a strong mind and a mature
wit at work in the representation of a great
historical crisis. The poem is soaked in history,
not only English but imperial; and the force of
its political realism is no greater than the gravity
with which it deploys its sense of history, and of
what has been lost.
forward ambitious
now in times like these

And oil th' unusèd armour's rust,
    Removing from the wall
        The corslet of the hall.
So restless Cromwell could not cease
10   In the inglorious arts of peace,
        But through adventurous war
            Urgèd his active star;
And like the three-forked lightning, first
Breaking the clouds where it was nursed,
        Did thorough° his own side°
            His fiery way divide.
For 'tis all one to courage high,
    The emulous or enemy;
        And with such to inclose
20   Is more than to oppose.°
Then burning through the air he went,
And palaces and temples rent;
        And Cæsar's° head at last
            Did through his laurels° blast.
'Tis madness to resist or blame
The force of angry heaven's flame;
        And, if we would speak true,
            Much to the man is due,
Who, from his private gardens, where
30   He lived reservèd and austere
        (As if his highest plot
            To plant the bergamot),°
Could by industrious valour climb
To ruin the great work of time,
        And cast the kingdoms old
            Into another mould;
Though Justice against Fate complain,
And plead the ancient rights in vain;
        But those do hold or break,
40   As men are strong or weak.
Nature, that hateth emptiness,
Allows of penetration° less,
        And therefore must make room
            Where greater spirits come.
What field of all the civil wars,
Where his were not the deepest scars?
        And Hampton shows what part
            He had of wiser art;

---

thorough through
side party. But the lightning tears through its
own body, namely, the cloud.
with . . . oppose to pen him in will produce
an even more violent reaction than to fight
against him

Cæsar's Charles I, beheaded in 1649
laurels supposed to be proof against lightning
bergamot kind of pear
penetration occupation of same space by two
bodies at the same time

Where, twining subtle° fears with hope,
50 He wove a net of such a scope
  That Charles himself might chase
  To Carisbrooke's° narrow case,°
That thence the Royal Actor° borne
The tragic scaffold might adorn;
  While round the armèd bands
  Did clap° their bloody hands.
He nothing common did, or mean,
Upon that memorable scene,
  But with his keener° eye
60   The axe's edge did try;°
Nor called the gods with vulgar spite
To vindicate his helpless right;
  But bowed his comely head
  Down, as upon a bed.°
This was that memorable hour
Which first assured the forcèd° power;
  So, when they did design
  The Capitol's first line,
A bleeding head, where they begun,
70 Did fright the architects to run;
  And yet in that the state
  Foresaw its happy fate.°
And now the Irish are ashamed
To see themselves in one year° tamed;
  So much one man can do
  That does both act and know.°
They° can affirm his praises best,
And have, though overcome, confessed
  How good he is, how just,
80   And fit for highest trust,
Nor yet grown stiffer with command,
But still in the republic's hand—
  How fit is he to sway
  That can so well obey!
He to the Commons' feet presents
A kingdom for his first year's rents;
  And, what he may,° forbears
  His fame, to make it theirs;

subtle finely woven
Carisbrooke's In 1648 Charles fled from Hampton Court to Carisbrooke in the Isle of Wight, but did not receive the welcome he expected, and was made prisoner; but it seems not to be true that Cromwell engineered this.
case cage
Actor This theatrical figure continues in *scaffold, clap, scene.*
clap Some said the soldiers were told to clap to render the King's last words inaudible.
keener than the ax's edge; *acies* is Latin for both "eyesight" and "blade." The King's eyes were said to be very bright on the scaffold, and he asked about the sharpness of the ax.
try test
bowed . . . bed Arrangements to drag his head down by force were unnecessary.
forcèd gained by force
So . . . fate This myth about the building of the Roman Capitol is in Pliny.
in one year Cromwell's Irish campaign lasted from August 1649 to May 1650.
act and know excel in action as in contemplation
They the Irish
what he may as far as he can

And has his sword and spoils ungirt,
90 To lay them at the public's skirt:
   So when the falcon high
   Falls heavy from the sky,
She, having killed, no more does search
But on the next green bough to perch;
   Where, when he first does lure,
   The falconer has her sure.
What may not, then, our isle presume,
While victory his crest does plume?
   What may not others fear,
100 If thus he crown each year?
A Cæsar he, ere long, to Gaul,
To Italy an Hannibal,
   And to all states not free
   Shall climactèric° be.
The Pict° no shelter now shall find
Within his party-coloured° mind,
   But from this valour sad°
   Shrink underneath the plaid;
Happy if in the tufted brake
110 The English hunter him mistake,°
   Nor lay his hounds in near
   The Caledonian° deer.
But thou, the war's and fortune's son,
March indefatigably on!
   And for the last effect,
   Still keep thy sword erect;
Besides the force it has to fright
The spirits of the shady night,°
   The same arts that did gain
120 A power must it maintain.
        1681

GEORGE HERBERT
1593–1633

George Herbert's greatness as a religious poet came in some measure from his struggle with the temptations of poetry itself. His carefully arranged collection of English poems called *The Temple* was published posthumously in 1633, and had gone through thirteen editions by 1709, influencing Crashaw, Vaughan, and Traherne—to mention only three of his followers—in a variety of ways. Herbert was born of a distinguished family, the younger brother of Lord Herbert of Cherbury; he was educated at Westminster School

---

climacteric critical; marking an epoch
Pict Scots tribe
party-coloured variously colored (suggested by "Pict" and its similarity to the Latin verb "to paint"), that is, changeable
sad severe

mistake because of his camouflaging colors
Caledonian Scottish
force . . . night not because of the uplifted cross-hilt, but because the sun glitters on the blade

and Trinity College, Cambridge, elected to a fellowship and a readership after that, and served as a member of Parliament for two years. In 1630 he became rector of Bemerton, near Salisbury, and it was apparently during the last years of his life that almost all of his English poems were composed.

The Temple is an astonishing work, reflecting at once a discontent with the fashions of complex, post-Petrarchan amatory verse which we loosely call the Metaphysical tradition, and a brilliant and subtle use of all those arts of image-making and rhetoric practiced by Donne and used by Herbert to cast doubt on the purity of any discourse which would employ them. *The Temple* is in one sense a constant attempt, in poem after poem, to make poetry do the work of prayer and devotion. They substitute for the Petrarchan poet's implicit pleading to his muse to grant authenticity to the poems he writes for her a prayer to God for their own moral genuineness. In another way, these poems go to make up a private liturgy of the vicarage, a day-to-day meditative regimen attuned not to canonical hours or days, but to a personal array of occasions. The poems present a spectrum of almost celestial variety: not only is the range of versification and stanza form amazing (every poem is in some formal way unique), but the centers of meditative attention in them vary widely as well.

Almost every aspect of clerical life becomes an emblem for Herbert: parts of the church building, on the one hand, sections of biblical text, on the other. Scriptural allusions and quotations abound, as do a host of formal figurative devices—ways of making the printed text of the poem itself the *impresa*, or picture, of the emblem they make up, as well as the *motto*, or caption. Herbert may have been influenced in his sense of formal variety by the songs from Sir Philip Sidney's *Arcadia*, and by the metrical psalm paraphrases of Sidney and his sister, the Countess of Pembroke (see The Psalms in English Verse, above). Herbert's poetic world is ever-conscious of music as well, and he employs the word "sing" in a way parallel to, but very different from, the Jonsonian, neoclassical poet's use to mean "write poetry."

From The Temple

Love-joy

As on a window late I cast mine eye,
I saw a vine drop grapes with *J* and *C*
Annealed° to every bunch. One standing by
Asked what it meant; I, who am never loth
To spend my judgment, said, It seemed to me
To be the body and the letters both
Of *Joy* and *Charity*. 'Sir, you have not missed,'
The man replied; 'It figures° JESUS CHRIST.'

1633

Annealed the grapes are in a stained-glass window   **figures** both in the sense of "pictures" and of "symbolizes"

The Altar°

A broken ALTAR, Lord, thy servant rears,
Made of a heart, and cémented with tears;
　　Whose parts are as thy hand did frame;
　　No workman's tool hath touched the same.°
　　　　　A　　HEART　　alone
　　　　　Is　　such　　a　　stone
　　　　　As　　　nothing　　but
　　　　　Thy　power　doth　cut.
　　　　　Wherefore　each　part
10　　　　Of　my　hard　heart
　　　　　Meets　in　this　frame,
　　　　　To　praise　thy　Name;
　　That, if I chance to hold my peace,
　　These stones to praise thee may not cease.
O let thy blessèd SACRIFICE be mine,
And　santify　this　ALTAR　to　be　thine.
　　　　　　　　　　　　　1633

Denial°

　　　When my devotions could not pierce
　　　　　　　　Thy silent ears;
　　Then was my heart broken, as was my verse:
　　　　　My breast was full of fears
　　　　　　　　And disorder:

　　　My bent thoughts, like a brittle bow,
　　　　　　　　Did fly asunder:
　　Each took his way; some would to pleasures go,
　　　　　Some to the wars and thunder
10　　　　　　　　　Of alarms.

　　　'As good go any where,' they say,
　　　　　　　　'As to benumb
　　Both knees and heart, in crying night and day,
　　　　　Come, come, my God, O come,
　　　　　　　　But no hearing.'

　　　O that thou shouldst give dust a tongue
　　　　　　　　To cry to thee,
　　And then not hear it crying! all day long
　　　　　My heart was in my knee,
20　　　　　　　　But no hearing.

Therefore my soul lay out of sight,
Untuned, unstrung;
My feeble spirit, unable to look right,
Like a nipped blossom, hung
Discontented.

O cheer and tune my heartless breast,
Defer no time;
That so thy favours granting my request,
They and my mind may chime,
30   And mend my rhyme.

1633

Easter-Wings°

Lord, who createdst man in wealth and store,°
Though foolishly he lost the same,
Decaying more and more,
Till he became
Most poor:
With thee
O let me rise
As larks, harmoniously,
And sing this day thy victories:
10   Then shall the fall further the flight in me.

My tender age in sorrow did begin:
And still with sicknesses and shame
Thou didst so punish sin,
That I became
Most thin.
With thee
Let me combine,
And feel this day thy victory:
For, if I imp° my wing on thine,
20   Affliction shall advance the flight in me.

1633

Easter-Wings based on a Greek poem shaped
like Cupid's wings. Notice how, when turned so
that the lines are vertical, the two stanzas
resemble a pair of angels rising upward, seen
from behind; as printed regularly, it is in a
lozenge shape whose "meaning" is "first narrow,
then widen" or a meaning of Easter: "descent
in order that there may be ascent."
store abundance
imp to graft feathers on a falcon's damaged
wing

Our Life Is Hid with Christ in God

COLOSS. 3. 3.°

My words and thoughts do both express this notion,
That *Life* hath with the sun a double motion.°
The first *Is* straight, and our diurnal friend,
The other *Hid*, and doth obliquely bend.
One life is wrapped *In* flesh, and tends to earth:
The other winds towards *Him*, whose happy birth
Taught me to live here so, *That* still one eye
Should aim and shoot at that which *Is* on high:
Quitting with daily labour all *My* pleasure,
To gain at harvest an eternal *Treasure.*

1633

The Pearl°

MATTH. 13. 45

I know the ways of Learning; both the head
And pipes that feed the press,° and make it run;
What reason hath from nature borrowèd,
Or of itself, like a good huswife, spun
In laws and policy; what the stars conspire;
What willing nature speaks, what forcéd by fire;
Both the old discoveries, and the new-found seas,
The stock and surplus, cause and history;
All these stand open, or I have the keys:
Yet I love thee.

I know the ways of Honour, what maintains
The quick returns of courtesy and wit:
In vies of favours whether° party gains,
When glory° swells the heart, and mouldeth it
To all expressions both of hand and eye,
Which on the world a true-love-knot° may tie,
And bear the bundle, wheresoe'er it goes;
How many drams of spirit there must be
To sell my life unto my friends or foes:
Yet I love thee.

Coloss. 3. 3. the text: "For ye are dead, and your life is hid with Christ in God"
double motion the sun's two apparent motions, revolution and rotation. The poem's "oblique" motion "is hid" in the italicized iambic pentameter line got by reading diagonally, as the spirit "is hid" in the flesh, the figurative in the literal. **The Pearl** The text behind this is Matthew 13: 45–46, likening the kingdom of heaven to "one pearl of great price," for which a wise merchant

"went out and sold all that he had and bought it."
press wine or olive press imagined as a printing press
whether which
glory ambition
true-love-knot a token of faithful love; the ambitious heart is pledged to the world—and stuck with it

I know the ways of Pleasure, the sweet strains,
The lullings and the relishes° of it;
The propositions of hot blood and brains;
What mirth and music mean; what love and wit
Have done these twenty hundred years, and more:
I know the projects of unbridled store:°
My stuff is flesh, not brass; my senses live,
And grumble oft, that they have more in me
Than he that curbs them, being but one to five:
30   Yet I love thee.

I know all these, and have them in my hand:
Therefore not sealèd,° but with open eyes
I fly to thee, and fully understand
Both the main sale, and the commodities;
And at what rate and price I have thy love;
With all the circumstances that may move
Yet through these labyrinths, not my groveling wit,
But thy silk twist° let down from heaven to me
Did both conduct and teach me, how by it
40   To climb to thee.
                    1633

The Church-Floor°

Mark you the floor? that square and speckled stone,
        Which looks so firm and strong,
            Is *Patience;*

And th'other black and grave, wherewith each one
        Is checkered all along,
            Humility;

The gentle rising, which on either hand
        Leads to the Choir above,
            Is *Confidence;*

10 But the sweet cément, which in one sure band
        Ties the whole frame, is *Love*
            And *Charity.*

Hither sometimes Sin steals, and stains
        The marble's neat and curious veins
But all is cleansèd when the marble weeps.

relishes musical ornamentation
store wealth
sealèd In falconry, birds' eyes were sewn closed
during training.
silk twist thread
The Church-Floor a meditative reading of the

checkerboard marble floor of the church. The
change of form in the last eight lines follows
a shift from the presentation of an emblem
to its interpretation; it is almost as if ll. 1–12
were picture, and 13–20, motto or text.

Sometimes Death, puffing at the door,
Blows all the dust about the floor,
But while he thinks to spoil the room, he sweeps.
Blest be the Architect, whose art
20   Could build so strong in a weak heart.

1633

Aaron°

Holiness on the head,
Light and perfections on the breast,
Harmonious bells below, raising the dead
To lead them unto life and rest:
Thus are true Aarons dressed.

Profaneness in my head,
Defects and darkness in my breast,
A noise of passions ringing me for dead
Unto a place where is no rest:
10   Poor priest thus am I dressed.

Only another head
I have, another heart and breast,
Another music, making live not dead,
Without whom I could have no rest:
In him I am well dressed.

Christ is my only head,
My alone only heart and breast,
My only music, striking me even dead;°
That to the old man I may rest,
20   And be in him new dressed.

So holy in my head,
Perfect and light in my dear breast,
My doctrine tuned by Christ (who is not dead,
But lives in me while I do rest):
Come people; Aaron's dressed.

1633

Aaron a meditation as though while putting on
vestments, remembering the garments of Aaron,
the first high priest (see Exodus 28)

dead As a clapper strikes a bell, Christ's music
strikes dead the sinner in man.

Sonnet°

My God, where is that ancient heat towards thee,
    Wherewith whole shoals of martyrs once did burn,
    Besides their other flames? Doth poetry
Wear Venus' livery? only serve her turn?
Why are not sonnets made of thee? and lays
    Upon thine altar burnt? Cannot thy love
    Heighten a spirit to sound out thy praise
As well as any she? Cannot thy Dove
Outstrip their Cupid easily in flight?
    Or, since thy ways are deep, and still the same,
    Will not a verse run smooth that bears thy name?
Why doth that fire, which by thy power and might
    Each breast does feel, no braver° fuel choose
    Than that, which one day worms may chance refuse?
    1610   1670

The Pulley°

    When God at first made man,
Having a glass of blessings standing by,
'Let us' (said he) 'pour on him all we can:
Let the world's riches, which dispersèd lie,
    Contract into a span.'°

    So strength first made a way;
Then beauty flowed, then wisdom, honour, pleasure:
When almost all was out, God made a stay,
Perceiving that alone of all his treasure
    Rest° in the bottom lay.

    'For if I should' (said he)
'Bestow this jewel also on my creature,
He would adore my gifts instead of me,
And rest in Nature, not the God of Nature:
    So both should losers be.

    'Yet let him keep the rest,
But keep them with repining° restlessness:
Let him be rich and weary, that at least,
If goodness lead him not, yet wariness
    May toss him to my breast.'
    1633

Sonnet from *The Life of Herbert* by Izaak
Walton, who says that Herbert sent it to his
mother as a New Year's gift when he was
seventeen, from Cambridge
braver handsomer
The Pulley which draws man up to God on
either side, as long as on the other there is a
compensating descent. This poem plays on the
myth of Pandora's box, in a later version of
which all the divine blessings escape from
it, leaving only hope; here, Herbert makes the
gift of restlessness (withholding of rest) a
kind of hope.
span the width of a man's hand
Rest repose, but punning on "what remains"
repining complaining

The Collar°

I struck the board,° and cried, 'No more,
    I will abroad!
What? shall I ever sigh and pine?
My lines and life are free, free as the road,
    Loose as the wind, as large as store.°
       Shall I be still in suit?°
Have I no harvest but a thorn
To let me blood, and not restore
What I have lost with cordial° fruit?
10   Sure there was wine
Before my sighs did dry it; there was corn
    Before my tears did drown it.
Is the year only lost to me?
    Have I no bays° to crown it?
No flowers, no garlands gay? all blasted?
    All wasted?
Not so, my heart: but there is fruit,
    And thou hast hands.
Recover all thy sigh-blown age
20 On double pleasures: leave thy cold dispute
Of what is fit, and not. Forsake thy cage,
    Thy rope of sands,°
Which petty thoughts have made, and made to thee
    Good cable, to enforce and draw,
       And be thy law,
While thou didst wink and wouldst not see.
       Away; take heed:
       I will abroad.
Call in thy death's head° there; tie up thy fears.
30   He that forbears
    To suit and serve his need,
       Deserves his load.'
But as I raved and grew more fierce and wild
    At every word,
Me thoughts I heard one calling, 'Child!'
    And I replied, 'My Lord.'

1633

The Collar an emblem of discipline and restraint, perhaps also punning on "choler" as "anger"
board dining table (where he is serving)
store abundance
in suit in attendance
cordial restorative

bays laurel crown for poetic excellence
rope of sands This startling image of a connection unable to withstand the slightest tug has an almost proverbial force.
death's head the *memento mori* skull as a meditational reminder of death

A Wreath°

A wreathèd garland of deservèd praise,
Of praise deservèd, unto thee I give,
I give to thee, who knowest all my ways,
My crooked winding ways, wherein I live,
Wherein I die, not live: for live is straight,
Straight as a line, and ever tends to thee,
To thee, who art more far above deceit,
Than deceit seems above simplicity.
Give me simplicity, that I may live,
10   So live and like, that I may know thy ways,
Know them and practise them: then shall I give
For this poor wreath, give thee a crown of praise.

                                        1633

Ana-⎰ Mary ⎱gram°
⎱ Army ⎰

How well her name an *Army* doth present,
In whom the *Lord of Hosts* did pitch his tent!

                                        1633

Jordan (I)°

Who says that fictions only and false hair
Become a verse? Is there in truth no beauty?
Is all good structure in a winding stair?
May no lines pass, except they do their duty
    Not to a true, but painted chair?°

Is it no verse, except 'enchanted groves'°
And 'sudden arbours' shadow° coarse-spun lines?
Must 'purling° streams' refresh a lover's loves?
Must all be veiled, while he that reads, divines,
10   Catching the sense at two removes?

A Wreath Not only are the lines "interwoven" by means of locking repeated words, but also the poem "curls around" the central quatrain about straightness and directness, ll. 9–12 matching in their rhyme-words ll. 4–1.
Ana-gram Herbert may be thinking of an image from Hebrews 8:1–2.
Jordan (I) This and the following poem, both praising the plain over the artful, refer in their titles to Jordan (the language of piety) as an alternative to Helicon's fountain (literary poetry), Jordan's rough waters being more healing than smooth classical streams (see the anecdote in II Kings 5:1–14).
May . . . chair must all poetry defer to pictures of the world?
'enchanted groves' The phrases in quotes are used in two ways: designating elements in an over-elaborate garden, and as their equivalents —fancy clichés in poems.
shadow both "shade" and "provide images for"
purling curling, swiftly-running (of streams); a stitching (in knitting or sewing)

674

Shepherds are honest people: let them sing.
Riddle who list,° for me, and pull for prime;°
I envy no man's nightingale or spring;
Nor let them punish me with loss of rhyme,
　　Who plainly say, 'My God, My King.'

1633

Jordan (II)°

When first my lines of heavenly joys made mention,
Such was their lustre, they did so excell,
That I sought out quaint words, and trim invention;°
My thoughts began to burnish,° sprout, and swell,
Curling with metaphors a plain intention,
Decking the sense, as if it were to sell.

Thousands of notions in my brain did run,
Offering their service, if I were not sped;°
I often blotted° what I had begun:
10　This was not quick° enough, and that was dead.
Nothing could seem too rich to clothe the sun,
Much less those joys which trample on his head.°

As flames do work and wind, when they ascend,
So did I weave my self into the sense.
But while I bustled, I might hear a friend
Whisper, 'How wide° is all this long pretense!°
There is in love a sweetness ready penned:
Copy out only that, and save expense.'

1633

Paradise°

I bless thee, Lord, because I GROW
Among thy trees, which in a ROW
To thee both fruit and order ow.

What open force, or hidden CHARM
Can blast° my fruit, or bring me HARM
While the enclosure is thine ARM?

list wish
pull for prime draw for a winning hand at
cards; "go for broke"
Jordan (II) transformation of the Petrarchan
theme of inspiration, following Sidney's opening
sonnet of *Astrophel and Stella*
quaint . . . invention Cf. Sidney's *Astrophel
and Stella*, Sonnets I, II, XV.
burnish spread
sped well-equipped with them
blotted blotted out, effaced

quick alive, lively
joys . . . head Christian alternatives to the
sun's—the world's—plenitude
wide wide of the mark
pretense striving
Paradise Adam and Eve in paradise needed
only to "prune and pare" the abundant growth;
work was gardening, not agriculture; each
tercet of this poem pares down its rhyme
word into the two others.
blast wither

Enclose me still for fear I START;
Be to me rather sharp and TART,
Than let me want° thy hand and ART.

10   When thou dost greater judgments SPARE,
And with thy knife but prune and PARE,
Even fruitful trees more fruitful ARE.

Such sharpness shows the sweetest FREND: °
Such cuttings rather heal than REND;
And such beginnings touch° their END.

1633

Church Monuments°

While that my soul repairs to her devotion,
Here I entomb my flesh, that it betimes
May take acquaintance of this heap of dust,
To which the blast of Death's incessant motion,
Fed with the exhalation° of our crimes,
Drives all at last. Therefore I gladly trust

My body to this school, that it may learn
To spell° his elements, and find his birth
Written in dusty heraldry and lines; °
10   Which dissolution sure doth best discern,
Comparing dust with dust, and earth with earth.
These laugh at jet and marble, put for signs,

To sever the good fellowship of dust,
And spoil the meeting—what shall point out them,
When they shall bow and kneel and fall down flat
To kiss those heaps which now they have in trust?
Dear flesh, while I do pray, learn here thy stem°
And true descent, that, when thou shalt grow fat,

And wanton in thy cravings, thou mayst know
20   That flesh is but the glass° which holds the dust
That measures all our time, which also shall
Be crumbled into dust. Mark here below
How tame these ashes are, how free from lust,
That thou mayst fit thyself against° thy fall.

1633

want lack
Frend friend (the old spelling preserved in this case)
touch with a sense of "color" or "tinge," and of "join"
Church Monuments a meditation on the carved tombs in churches, of "jet and marble" and sometimes ruined and crumbling, containing the "dust" to which the dust of human flesh returns
exhalation ironically paralleling the divine ex-

halation which animated the first Adamic dust
spell spell out half-obscured inscriptions
lines genealogical lines of descent, as well as the actual carved ones on the tomb
stem ancestry
glass hourglass of Time's emblem; made of marble, it too will crumble. There is a surprising echo of the biblical "All flesh is grass" (Isaiah 40:6), with the hardened, monumental "glass" substituted.
fit thyself against make ready for

Prayer (I)°

Prayer the Church's banquet,° Angels' age,°
  God's breath in man returning to his birth,
  The soul in paraphrase,° heart in pilgrimage,
The Christian plummet sounding heaven and earth;
Engine against the Almighty, sinners' tower,
  Reversèd thunder, Christ-side-piercing spear,
  The six-day's-world° transposing in an hour,
A kind of tune, which all things hear and fear;
Softness, and peace, and joy, and love, and bliss,
10   Exalted manna,° gladness of the best,
  Heaven in ordinary, man well dressed,°
The milky way, the bird of paradise,°
  Church-bells beyond the stars heard, the soul's blood,
  The land of spices; something understood.

1633

Virtue

Sweet day, so cool, so calm, so bright,
The bridal of the earth and sky:
The dew shall weep thy fall tonight;
       For thou must die.

Sweet rose, whose hue angry° and brave°
Bids the rash gazer wipe his eye:
Thy root is ever in its grave,
       And thou must die.

Sweet spring, full of sweet days and roses,
10 A box where sweets° compacted lie;
My music shows ye have your closes,°
       And all must die.

Only a sweet and virtuous soul,
Like seasoned timber, never gives;
But though the whole world turn to coal,°
       Then chiefly lives.

1633

Prayer (I) The whole poem (with no predicate verb) is itself a brilliant series of paraphrases.
banquet a light refreshment between meals (i.e. prayer is a snack between one Holy Communion and the next)
Angels' age an eternity
paraphrase with a sense of an expansion of an original (rather than, as in modern usage, a compression)
six-day's-world Creation took six days; also, the world occupies six days of the week, but not the Sabbath; "transposing" that world suggests making any of the six days into the seventh.

Exalted manna The biblical manna fell from heaven; this kind rises to it.
Heaven . . . dressed God at the table, and man prepared as a dish for Him
bird of paradise from the legend that this bird had no feet and so never touched the ground
angry red
brave splendid
sweets perfumes
closes musical cadences
turn to coal become cinders and ashes in the conflagration of the Day of Judgment

Love (III)

Love bade me welcome: yet my soul drew back,
    Guilty of dust and sin.
But quick-eyed Love,° observing me grow slack
    From my first entrance in,
Drew nearer to me, sweetly questioning,
    If I lacked any thing.

'A guest,' I answered, 'worthy to be here':
    Love said, 'You shall be he.'
'I the unkind, ungrateful? Ah my dear,
    I cannot look on thee.'
Love took my hand, and smiling did reply,
    'Who made the eyes but I?'

'Truth Lord, but I have marred them: let my shame
    Go where it doth deserve.'
'And know you not,' says Love, 'who bore the blame?'
    'My dear, then I will serve.'
'You must sit down,' says Love,' and taste my meat:°
    So I did sit and eat.

1633

RICHARD CRASHAW
1612/13–1649

If Crashaw is indeed, as Douglas Bush has remarked, the "one conspicuous English incarnation of the 'baroque sensibility,'" it is perhaps because of his association with just those aspects of European baroque which are easiest to identify across national and formal boundaries. An enthusiastic Roman Catholic convert at a historical moment when Anglicanism could suffice for many, his mature work was influenced by Jesuit Latin poetry and by the Italian of Giambattista Marino (1569–1625). His religious verse is far more excitedly sensual than a good deal of Caroline erotic poetry. His use of the paradox of self-contradiction and of excruciatingly insistent conceits was energized by a belief that only by the intensification of the concrete realms—of body, picture, or thing—could the abstract ones of soul and significance be released.

Crashaw was born in London, the son of a Yorkshire clergyman, and educated at the Charterhouse and at Pembroke College, Cambridge; he became a fellow of Peterhouse in 1635, is thought to have taken orders by 1639, was associated with High Church intellectuals like Nicholas Ferrar and with Abraham Cowley. In 1643, like Cowley, he abandoned his fellowship before being ejected from it. He went abroad,

---

quick-eyed Love As opposed to the blind or blindfolded Cupid of Renaissance erotic imagery, Caritas or Divine Love is characterized as "quick-" (or "living-") eyed; the whole poem plays on this contrast; for the blindness of Amor or Cupid, see Marlowe's *Hero and Leander* I.38n.

meat repast, as almost always in the 17th century; here, the love-feast, or *agapē*, of the early Christians, manifesting itself in Holy Communion, which the priest both serves and takes himself

became a Catholic in 1645, it is believed, lived among the royalist émigrés in Paris, and finally went to Rome, where he entered Cardinal Pallotta's service. Perhaps because of a lack of political sophistication, he was sent to a post at Loreto, where he died (as a result, it was almost inevitably rumored in England at the time, of poisoning). His earliest published poems were his Latin epigrams, including a now-famous line "explaining" Christ's transformation of water to wine at the marriage in Cana (John 2:1–10): the embarrassed nymph inhabiting the water caught sight of God, and blushed. In 1646 and 1648 appeared two versions of *Steps to the Temple* (the allusion being to the title of George Herbert's 1633 collection) and, in 1652, the posthumous *Carmen Deo Nostro*. Some of his more intense secular poetry, like the grand "Music's Duel," shares with his devotional verse a delight in expressive energy itself, banishing good taste and rhetorical control as a Cavalier love lyrist would banish prudence, a delight that found no strength save at the brink of rage, no fullness save in overflow.

Music's Duel°

Now Westward Sol had spent the richest beams
Of noon's high glory, when hard by the streams
Of Tiber, on the scene of a green plat,°
Under protection of an oak, there sat
A sweet lute's-master, in whose° gentle airs
He lost the day's heat and his own hot cares.
   Close in the covert of the leaves there stood
A nightingale, come from the neighbouring wood
(The sweet inhabitant of each glad tree,
10 Their muse, their siren, harmless siren she):
There stood she listening, and did entertain
The music's soft report, and mould the same
In her own murmurs, that whatever mood°
His curious° fingers lent, her voice made good.
The man perceived his rival and her art,
Disposed to give the light-foot lady sport
Awakes his lute, and 'gainst the fight to come
Informs it, in a sweet praeludium,°
Of closer strains, and ere the war begin,
20 He lightly skirmishes on every string
Charged with a flying touch,° and straightway she
Carves out her dainty voice as readily
Into a thousand sweet distinguished tones,
And reckons up in soft divisions,°

Music's Duel a wildly elaborate version of a Latin original by the Jesuit Famianus Strada, itself frequently translated as an epitome of the conflict between art and nature.
plat plot
whose the lute's. The pun on "airs" ("tunes," thus the lute's "breezes") inaugurates the continuous word-play on technical musical terms throughout the poem.
mood also means musical mode, or key
curious complicatedly artful
praeludium prelude, first movement in a suite of instrumental pieces
touch a passage of music
divisions improvised expansions of a theme

Quick volumes of wild notes, to let him know
By that shrill taste, she could do something too.
  His nimble hands instinct then taught each string
A capering cheerfulness, and made them sing
To their own dance; now negligently rash
30 He throws his arm, and with a long drawn dash°
Blends all together, then distinctly trips
From this to that, then quick returning skips
And snatches this again, and pauses there.
She° measures every measure, everywhere
Meets art with art; sometimes as if in doubt
Not perfect yet, and fearing to be out
Trails her plain ditty in one long-spun note
Through the sleek passage of her open throat:
A clear unwrinkled° song, then doth she point it
40 With tender accents, and severely joint it
By short diminutives, that being reared
In controverting warbles° evenly shared,
With her sweet self she wrangles; he amazed
That from so small a channel should be raised
The torrent of a voice, whose melody
Could melt into such sweet variety,
Strains higher yet; that tickled with rare art
The tattling strings (each breathing in his part)
Most kindly do fall out; the grumbling bass
50 In surly groans disdains the treble's grace.
The high-perched treble° chirps at this and chides,
Until his finger (moderator) hides
And closes the sweet quarrel rousing all
Hoarse, shrill, at once, as when the trumpets call
Hot Mars to the harvest of death's field, and woo
Men's hearts into their hands; this lesson too
She gives him back; her supple breast thrills out
Sharp airs, and staggers in a warbling doubt
Of dallying sweetness, hovers o'er her skill,
60 And folds in waved notes° with a trembling bill,
The pliant series of her slippery song.
Then starts she suddenly into a throng
Of short thick sobs, whose thundering volleys float
And roll themselves over her lubric° throat
In panting murmurs, stilled° out of her breast,
That ever-bubbling spring, the sugared nest
Of her delicious soul, that there does lie

---

dash in lute notation, the sign for a stroked chord
She the bird
unwrinkled In musical notation, all half and
quarter notes would look "unwrinkled" on the
page, not having the tails or ligatures of shorter-
valued notes.
diminutives . . . warbles ornamentation

treble The highest lute string was single, the
others, double (octaves or unisons).
waved notes with runs of sixteenth and thirty-
second notes, looking like waves on the page
lubric smooth, slippery
stilled distilled

Bathing in streams of liquid melody,
Music's best seed plot, when in ripened airs
70 A bold-headed harvest fairly rears
His honey-dropping tops, plowed by her breath
Which there reciprocally laboureth
In that sweet soil. It seems a holy choir
Founded to the name of great Apollo's lyre,
Whose silver roof rings with the sprightly notes
Of sweet-lipped angel imps, that swill their throats
In cream of morning Helicon,° and then
Prefer° soft anthems to the ears of men,
To woo them from their beds, still murmuring
80 That men can sleep while they their matins sing
(Most divine service! whose so early lay
Prevents° the eyelids of the blushing day).
There might you hear her kindle her soft voice
In the close murmur of a sparkling noise,
And lay the groundwork of her hopeful song,
Still keeping in the forward stream, so long,
Till a sweet whirlwind (striving to get out)
Heaves her soft bosom, wanders round about,
And makes a pretty earthquake in her breast,
90 Till the fledged notes° at length forsake their nest,
Fluttering in wanton shoals, and to the sky,
Winged with their own wild echoes, prattling fly.
She opes the floodgate and lets loose a tide
Of streaming sweetness, which in state doth ride
On the waved back of every swelling strain,
Rising and falling in a pompous train.
And while she thus discharges a shrill peal
Of flashing airs, she qualifies their zeal
With the cool epode of a graver note,°
100 Thus high, thus low, as if her silver throat
Would reach the brazen voice of war's hoarse bird;
Her little soul is ravished, and so poured
Into loose ecstasies that she is placed
Above herself,° music's enthusiast.

    Shame now and anger mixed a double stain
In the musician's face; 'Yet once again,
Mistress I come; now reach a strain, my lute,
Above her mock, or be forever mute.
Or tune a song of victory to me,
110 Or to thyself sing thine own obsequy.'°

Helicon the Muses' and Apollo's mountain
Prefer proffer, extend
Prevents precedes
fledged notes The notes are fledgling birds (1)
because they are daughters of (produced by)
the nightingale; (2) because in notation their
tails (they being eighth and sixteenth notes)
look wing-like (compare comic-book representations of singing).
graver note lower, as well as more weighty, tone
Above herself "Ecstasy" is literally, in Greek,
"standing outside" (oneself); here, the bird has
"overdone it," too.
obsequy funeral rite

So said, his hands sprightly as fire he flings,
And with a quavering coyness° tastes° the strings.
The sweet-lipped sisters° musically frighted,
Singing their fears are fearfully delighted.
Trembling as when Apollo's golden hairs°
Are fanned and frizzled, in the wanton airs
Of his own breath: which married to his lyre
Doth tune the spheres, and make heaven's self look higher.
From this to that, from that to this he flies,
120   Feels Music's pulse in all her arteries,
Caught in a net which there Apollo spreads,
His fingers struggle with the vocal threads,
Following those little rills, he sinks into
A sea of Helicon; his hand does go
Those parts of sweetness, which with nectar drop,
Softer than that which pants in Hebe's cup.°
The humorous° strings expound his learnèd touch
By various glosses;° now they seem to grutch°
And murmur in a buzzing din, then jingle
130   In shrill-tongued accents, striving to be single.°
Every smooth turn, every delicious stroke
Gives life to some new grace; thus doth h'invoke
Sweetness by all her names; thus, bravely thus
(Fraught with a fury so harmonious)
The lute's light genius° now does proudly rise,
Heaved on the surges of swollen rhapsodies.
Whose flourish (meteor-like) doth curl the air
With flash of high-borne fancies,° here and there
Dancing in lofty measures, and anon
140   Creeps on the soft touch of a tender tone,
Whose trembling murmurs melting in wild airs
Runs to and fro, complaining his sweet cares
Because those precious mysteries that dwell
In music's ravished soul he dare not tell,
But whisper to the world: thus do they vary
Each string his note, as if they meant to carry
Their master's blessed soul (snatched out at his ears
By a strong ecstasy)° through all the spheres
Of Music's heaven; and seat it there on high
150   In th' Empyraeum° of pure harmony.

quavering coyness "Quavers" is British usage
for eighth notes, and "coy" means quiet and
reserved here.
tastes "Tastar de corde" was a kind of lute prelude.
sweet-lipped sisters the strings ("sisters," being
parallel and like Graces or Muses)
hairs sunbeams
Hebe's cup held by the gods' cup-bearer
humorous lively and intelligent (as students)
glosses footnotes like this one

grutch grouch, complain
single The double lute strings jangle and buzz
together in loud passages.
genius spirit
fancies imaginative thoughts and, musically,
"fantasias," free compositions
ecstasy Music was thought to ravish men's souls
by drawing them out through the ears.
Empyraeum the outermost of the concentric
heavens in Greek astronomy, later thought of
also as the brightest region

At length (after so long, so loud a strife
Of all the strings, still breathing the best life
Of blessed variety attending on
His finger's fairest revolution
In many a sweet rise, many as sweet a fall)
A full-mouth diapason° swallows all.
   This done, he lists what she would say to this,
And she although her breath's late exercise
Had dealt too roughly with her tender throat,
Yet summons all her sweet powers for a note
Alas! in vain! for while (sweet soul) she tries
To measure all those wild diversities
Of chattering strings, by the small size of one
Poor simple voice, raised in a natural tone,
She fails, and failing grieves, and grieving lies.
She dies, and leaves her life the victor's prize,
Falling upon his lute—Oh fit to have
(That lived so sweetly) dead, so sweet a grave!

160

1646

From The Weeper°

    Hail, sister springs!
    Parents of silver-footed rills!
    Ever bubbling things!
    Thawing crystal! snowy hills,
Still spending, never spent! I mean
Thy fair eyes, sweet Magdalene!

    Heavens thy fair eyes be;
    Heavens of ever-falling stars.
    'Tis seed-time still with thee,
    And stars thou sowest, whose harvest dares
Promise the earth to countershine
Whatever makes heaven's forehead fine.

    But we're deceivèd all.
    Stars indeed they are too true,
    For they but seem to fall
    As Heaven's other spangles do.
It is not for our earth and us
To shine in things so precious.

10

---

diapason octave
The Weeper This string of glittering epigrams
was first published in 1646 and later revised,
but even in its later form lacks total coherence;
the editors have excerpted from it, omitting the
following stanzas of the 1652 text: 13–16, 20–
27. The poem was printed with an emblem of
the weeping Mary Magdalene above a winged,
bleeding heart, with this motto: "Lo, where a
wounded heart with bleeding eyes conspire: / Is
she a flaming fountain, or a weeping fire?" The
tears of the repentant Magdalene are a wide-
spread image especially identified with baroque;
for the story of her washing the feet of Jesus, her
presence at the Crucifixion, and her discovery of
his resurrection, see Matthew 27-28.

Upwards thou dost weep:
20   Heaven's bosom drinks the gentle stream.
Where the milky rivers creep,
Thine floats above and is the cream.°
Waters above the Heavens, what they be
We are taught best by thy tears and thee.

Every morn from hence
A brisk cherub something sips
Whose sacred influence°
Adds sweetness to his sweetest lips.
Then to his music. And his song
30   Tastes of this breakfast all day long.

Not in the evening's eyes
When they red with weeping are
For the sun that dies,
Sits sorrow with a face so fair;
Nowhere but here did ever meet
Sweetness so sad, sadness so sweet.

When sorrow would be seen
In her brightest majesty
(For she is a queen)
40   Then is she dressed by none but thee.
Then, and only then, she wears
Her proudest pearls; I mean, thy tears.

The dew no more will weep
The primrose's pale cheek to deck,
The dew no more will sleep
Nuzzled in the lily's neck;
Much rather would it be thy tear,
And leave them both to tremble here.

There's no need at all
50   That the balsam-sweating bough
So coyly should let fall
His médicinable° tears; for now
Nature hath learnt to extract a dew
More sovereign and sweet from you.

Yet let the poor drops weep,
(Weeping is the ease of woe)
Softly let them creep,
Sad that they are vanquished so.
They, though to others no relief,
60   Balsam may be for their own grief.

cream of the Milky Way
influence used in an astrological sense to mean
the emanations of the stars

medicinable Many aromatic gums or balms were
used in medicine.

Such the maiden gem
By the purpling vine put on,
Peeps from her parent stem
And blushes at the bridegroom sun.
This watery blossom of thy eyen,
Ripe, will make the richer wine.

When some new bright guest
Takes up among the stars a room,
And Heaven will make a feast,
70   Angels with crystal vials come
And draw from these full eyes of thine
Their master's water, their own wine.

   . . .

But can these fair floods be
Friends with the bosom fires that fill thee?
Can so great flames agree
100   Eternal tears should thus distill thee?
Oh floods, oh fires! oh suns, oh showers!
Mixed and made friends by Love's sweet powers.°

'Twas his well-pointed dart
That digged these wells and dressed this vine,
And taught the wounded heart
The way into these weeping eyen.°
Vain loves avaunt! bold hands forbear!
The lamb hath dipped his white foot here.

And now where'er he° strays
110   Among the Galilean mountains
Or more unwelcome ways,
He's followed by two faithful fountains,
Two walking baths, two weeping motions,
Portable and compendious oceans.

Oh thou, thy Lord's fair store!
In thy so rich and rare expenses,
Even when he showed most poor,
He might provoke the wealth of princes:
What prince's wantonest pride e'er could
120   Wash with silver, wipe with gold?°

   . . .

Love's sweet powers Notice the shift from Christian to adapted classical imagery here: the power of Love (with that of Strife) first arranged the elements out of chaos; in the next stanza, Love will be the traditional Eros with bow and arrow, but here made to stand for Christian *caritas,* divine love.
eyen eyes. In Petrarchan and neoplatonist traditions, Cupid's arrows hit one in the eye (love occurs proverbially "at first sight," not at first hearing, or touch).
he Jesus, who is now "love" incarnate. The image at the end of this stanza is a famous conceit, widely extravagant and perched on the edge of the ridiculous.
with gold her hair, with which Jesus' feet were dried

Say, ye bright brothers,
The fugitive sons of those fair eyes,
Your fruitful mother's!
What make you here? what hopes can 'tice°
You to be born? what cause can borrow
You from those nests of noble sorrow?

Whither away so fast?
170   For sure the sordid° earth
Your sweetness cannot taste
Nor does the dust deserve your birth.
Sweet, whither haste you then? oh say
Why you trip so fast away?

'We go not to seek
The darlings of Aurora's bed,
The rose's modest cheek,
Nor the violet's humble head,
Though the field's eyes too weepers be
180 Because they want° such tears as we.

Much less mean we to trace
The fortune of inferior gems,
Preferred to some proud face
Or perched upon feared diadems.
Crowned heads are toys. We go to meet
A worthy object, our Lord's feet.'
      1646, 1648, 1652

On Our Crucified Lord, Naked and Bloody

Th'have left thee naked, Lord, O that they had!
This garment, too, I would they had denied;
Thee with thyself they have too richly clad,
Opening the purple° wardrobe of thy side.
    O never could be found garments too good
    For thee to wear, but these, of thy own blood.
        1640

'tice entice
sordid dirty
want lack

purple This usually means "red" in 17th-century English, not "violet"; thus the "royal purple" was a powerful crimson.

Upon Our Saviour's Tomb Wherein Never Man Was Laid

How Life and Death in Thee
> Agree?
Thou had'st a virgin Womb
> And Tomb.
A Joseph° did betroth
> Them both.
> 1646

Upon the Infant Martyrs

To see both blended in one flood;
The mother's milk, the children's blood,
Makes me doubt if Heaven will gather
Roses hence, or lilies rather.
> 1646

The Flaming Heart

Along with the weeping Magdalene, a favorite figure for Crashaw's baroque meditation was Saint Teresa of Avila (1515–82), the Spanish Carmelite nun, whose mystical autobiography would have been known to him in an English translation published in 1642. Her ecstatic vision of angelic penetration is enshrined in Bernini's great sculpture in the church of Santa Maria della Vittoria in Rome; she wrote of an angel appearing to her "in a corporeal form" with "a long dart of gold in his hand; and at the end of the iron below, me thought, there was a little fire; and I conceived that he thrust it some several times through my very heart, after such a manner as that it passed the very inwards of my bowels. And when he drew it back, me thought, it carried away as much as it had touched within me, and left all that which remained wholly inflamed with a great love of almighty God." The figuring forth of divine possession in sexual terms appealed strongly to the concretely emblematic and the paradoxical elements of Crashaw's imagination, and in two poems about her he responded to ecstasy in a controlled linguistic frenzy of his own, a religious equivalent of the energies of "Music's Duel." (See Fig. 34.)

Joseph Joseph of Arimathea, who laid Jesus away in the tomb which he soon vacated, and Joseph, Mary's husband. William Butler Yeats's nasty little epigram, "A Stick of Incense," is based on this conceit.

From The Flaming Heart

Upon the book and picture of the seraphical Saint Teresa, as she is usually
expressed with a seraphim° beside her.

Well-meaning readers, you that come as friends
And catch the precious name this piece pretends;
Make not too much haste to admire
That fair-cheeked fallacy° of fire.
That is a seraphim, they say,
And this the great Teresia.
Readers, be ruled by me, and make
Here a well-placed and wise mistake:
You must transpose the picture quite,
10   And spell it wrong to read it right;
Read *him* for her and *her* for him;
And call the saint the seraphim.

     .   .   .

    Do then as equal right requires,
Since his the blushes be, and hers the fires,
Resume and rectify thy rude design;
40   Undress thy seraphim into mine.
Redeem this injury of thy art:
Give him the veil, give her the dart.
    Give him the veil, that he may cover
The red cheeks of a rivalled lover,
Ashamed that our world now can show
Nests of new seraphims here below.
    Give her the dart, for it is she
(Fair youth) shoots both thy shaft and thee.
Say, all ye wise and well-pierced hearts
50   That live and die amidst her darts,
What is it your tasteful spirits prove
In that rare life of her, and love?
Say and bear witness: sends she not
A seraphim at every shot?
What magazines of immortal arms there shine!
Heaven's great artillery in each love-spun line.
Give then the dart to her who gives the flame;
Give him the veil, who kindly takes the shame.
    But if it be the frequent fate
60   Of worse faults to be fortunate;
If all's prescription, and proud wrong
Harkens not to an humble song;
For all the gallantry of him,
Give me the suffering seraphim.

---

seraphim The form is a Hebrew plural ("seraph"
is the correct singular), but the mistake is
conventional in English.

fallacy The emblem is wrong; only the following
paradoxical twisting of things into their opposites will makes the true significance emerge.

His be the bravery of all those bright things,
The glowing cheeks, the glistering wings;
The rosy hand, the radiant dart;
Leave her alone the flaming heart.
    Leave her that; and thou shalt leave her
70 Not one loose shaft, but love's whole quiver.
For in love's field was never found
A nobler weapon than a wound.
Love's passives are his activest part,
The wounded is the wounding heart.
O heart! the equal poise° of love's both parts,
Big like° with wounds and darts,
Live in these conquering leaves; live all the same
And walk through all tongues one triumphant flame:
Live here, great heart, and love and die and kill,
80 And bleed and wound, and yield and conquer still.

. . .

1648

HENRY VAUGHAN
1621/22–1695

Henry Vaughan was the elder twin of Thomas Vaughan, the alchemist and hermetist, later satirized in Swift's *The Tale of a Tub*. They were born and bred in Breconshire, Wales, and Vaughan called himself "Silurist" after the ancient British tribe which had lived there. The twins went, as Welshmen did and still do, to Jesus College, Oxford. But Henry took no degree, and his subsequent study of the law was, according to his own testimony, ended by the Civil War, in which he saw military service on the Royalist side. He married, and published volumes of poetry: *Poems* in 1646, *Olor Iscanus* (Swan of Usk, the local river) in 1651; most of the poems to be found in this book were written at least four years earlier.

Partly through his brother's work, partly through his own study, Henry grew familiar with hermetic and alchemical lore. This fed into the entirely new kind of poetry he began to write—possibly after a serious illness—in the late 1640's, poetry which appeared in *Silex Scintillans* (*The Sparkling Flint;* 1650) and in the second part added to that work in 1655. For the second part he wrote a Preface condemning strongly the abuse of wit in the writing of irreligious poetry, and commended the work of Herbert, in whose steps he proposed to follow. He did so; it has been said that Vaughan's debt to Herbert is the greatest any English poet owes to another. After *Silex Scintillans* he produced some prose, devotional meditations, a medical treatise, and a last volume of verse, *Thalia Rediviva* (1678), which makes no difference to his reputation.

Vaughan's masterpieces are, then, in *Silex,* and belong to a few years of his life from about 1650 to 1655. His imperfections are often pointed out: he can begin a poem with Herbertian directness (sometimes on a Herbertian text) but not always quite control it as Herbert did; he is repetitive and sometimes too vague. But his

---

poise weight, value   **Big like** equally full of

merits are quite clear; he has a wholly distinctive resonance, and complex new meanings rise up and follow his peculiar voice. On the face of it there is a unique blend of Christian devotional and neoplatonic ideas and images; go deeper and there is more, a power—perhaps not wholly conscious—to form images, each carrying a strong charge of devotional meaning, into constellations which occur nowhere else, so that even the biblical allusions are strongly colored by the strange and strong imagination which brings them together. An example would be the unique transformation of an already ravishing passage from the Song of Songs in *Night,* or the ubiquitous associations of stars, clouds, veils, tombs, darkness, and plants, some of which are briefly indicated in the notes.

Vaughan's distinction is of a kind hardly to be found outside his lifetime. The new science, and the purgation from the humanist tradition of mysticism and pseudoscience, introduced a world in which poetry of his kind was all but impossible. With none of the Continental afflatus of Crashaw, he had much in common with Herbert, though he is less neat, less liturgical, less proverbial, and more strange than that spiritually more consistent and intellectually more powerful poet; nonetheless, his best works stand with theirs as among the greatest of seventeenth-century devotional poetry.

Religion°

My God, when I walk in those groves
　　And leaves thy spirit doth still fan,
I see in each shade that there grows
　　An angel talking with a man.

Under a juniper,° some house,
　　Or the cool myrtle's canopy;°
Others beneath an oak's green boughs,°
　　Or at some fountain's bubbling eye.°

Here Jacob dreams, and wrestles;° there
10　　Elias by a raven is fed;°
Another time by the angel, where
　　He brings him water with his bread.

In Abraham's tent° the wingèd guests
　　(Oh how familiar then was heaven!)
Eat, drink, discourse, sit down, and rest,
　　Until the cool and shady even.

Religion In groves which Vaughan can still think of as holy, he imagines free conversation between men and angels, and remembers that God also spoke directly to men. Why is this no longer so? Has the Incarnation, providing us with a Mediator, rendered such encounters unnecessary? He denies this. Religion has grown corrupt, but at its source still bears miraculous benefits; he prays that the spring be cleansed, or that we be led to its source.
juniper There an angel spoke to the sleeping Elijah (I Kings 19:5).

myrtle's canopy Zechariah 1:11
oak's . . . boughs There an angel spoke to Gideon (Judges 6:11).
fountain's . . . eye There an angel accosted Hagar, Sarah's maid (Genesis 16:7).
Here . . . wrestles with an angel, Genesis 32:24 ff.; his dream of the ladder, Genesis 28:12 ff.
Elias . . . fed I Kings 17; Elias = Elijah
In Abraham's tent Genesis 18:1 ff., where the angels bearing the promise that Sarah will be fruitful accept refreshments

Nay Thou Thyself, my God, in fire,
 Whirlwinds and clouds, and the soft voice,°
Speak'st there so much, that I admire°
20 We have no conference in these days.

Is the truce broke? or 'cause we have
 A Mediator now with Thee,
Dost Thou therefore old treaties waive,
 And by appeals from Him decree?°

Or is't so, as some green heads° say,
 That now all miracles must cease?
Though Thou has promised they should stay
 The tokens of the Church and peace.

No, no; Religion is a spring
30 That from some secret, golden mine
Derives her birth, and thence doth bring
 Cordials in every drop, and wine.

But in her long and hidden course,
 Passing through the Earth's dark veins,
Grows still from better unto worse,
 And both her taste and colour stains;

Then drilling on, learns to increase
 False echoes and confusèd sounds,
And unawares doth often seize
40 On veins of sulphur underground;

So poisoned, breaks forth in some clime,
 And at first sight doth many please;
But drunk,° is puddle or mere slime,
 And 'stead of physic, a disease.

Just such a tainted sink we have,
 Like that Samaritan's dead well;°
Nor must we for the kernel crave
 Because most voices like the shell.

Heal then these waters, Lord; or bring Thy flock,
50 Since these are troubled, to the springing rock;
Look down, Great Master of the feast; Oh shine,
And turn once more our water into wine!°

---

fire . . . voice fire: Exodus 3:2; whirlwind: Job 38:1; clouds: Exodus 24:16; soft voice: I Kings 19:12
admire wonder
Is . . . decree Does the existence of Jesus Christ as our Mediator imply that the old covenant between God and man (Genesis 9: 12–13, Exodus 31:13–17, Numbers 25:13) is invalid?
green heads immature thinkers

drunk when we drink it
Samaritan's . . . well Jesus said to the Samaritan woman at the well, "Whosoever drinketh of this water shall thirst again: But whosoever drinketh of the water that I shall give him shall never thirst" (John 4:13–14).
water into wine The idea of water (religion) miraculously purified leads Vaughan, in the concluding petition, to remember line 32, and also the miracle at Cana, John 2:1–11.

CANT. CAP. 4. VER. 12.

My sister, my spouse is as a garden enclosed, as a spring shut up, and a
    fountain sealed up.°

1650

The Retreat°

Happy those early days! when I
Shined in my angel-infancy,
Before I understood this place
Appointed for my second race,°
Or taught my soul to fancy ought
But a white, celestial thought;
When yet I had not walked above
A mile or two from my first love,
And looking back—at that short space—
Could see a glimpse° of His bright face;
When on some gilded cloud, or flower,
My gazing soul would dwell an hour,
And in those weaker glories spy
Some shadows° of eternity;
Before I taught my tongue to wound
My conscience with a sinful sound,
Or had the black art to dispense
A several° sin to every sense,
But felt through all this fleshly dress
Bright shoots of everlastingness.°
    Oh how I long to travel back,
And tread again that ancient track!
That I might once more reach that plain,
Where first I left my glorious train;°
From whence the enlightened spirit sees
That shady city of palm trees.°
But ah! my soul with too much stay°

10

20

My sister . . . sealed up Here as elsewhere Vaughan adds a verse of the Song of Songs (4:12), a work subjected to multiple allegorical interpretation. The sister-spouse is the Church, bride of Christ; here the verse is apposite because the spouse is compared to "a spring shut up."

The Retreat Vaughan seems to have believed in something like the Platonic notion of a prior existence which, in childhood and less often later, we can recall; in the innocence of childhood he is close to the divine source (represented, again in neoplatonic terms, as a white radiance), can see images of eternity in the world; and feels, in his mortal flesh, the truth of his immortality. This after-vision of the Heavenly City is lost as maturity brings on its sins. The similarity of the basic idea to that of

Wordsworth's *Ode on the Intimations of Immortality* is often noticed, and Wordsworth knew Vaughan's poem.

second race The first "race" (life, nation, contest) was in heaven.

glimpse a favorite word of Vaughan's referring to the human power of briefly intuiting divinity

shadows images, reflections

several separate

Bright . . . everlastingness Like other expressions that sound idiosyncratic to Vaughan, this is borrowed—from the essayist Owen Felltham.

train companions, or way of life

shady . . . trees Jericho, as Moses saw it from the top of Pisgah; here a type of the Heavenly City (Deuteronomy 34:1–4)

stay from having stayed too long

Is drunk, and staggers in the way.
    Some men a forward motion love,
30 But I by backward steps would move
    And when this dust falls to the urn,
    In that state I came, return.°

                    1650

Corruption°

Sure it was so. Man in those early days
    Was not all stone and earth;
He shined a little, and by those weak rays
    Had some glimpse of his birth.°
He saw Heaven o'er his head, and knew from whence
    He came, condemnèd hither;
And, as first love draws strongest, so from hence
    His mind sure progressed thither.
Things here were strange unto him: sweat and till,
10   All was a thorn or weed:
Nor did those last, but, like himself, died still°
    As soon as they did seed.
They seemed to quarrel with him, for that act
    That felled him foiled them all:°
He drew the curse upon the world, and cracked
    The whole frame with his fall.
This made him long for home, as loth to stay
    With murmurers and foes;
He sighed for Eden, and would often say,
20   'Ah! what bright days were those!'
Nor was Heaven cold unto him; for each day
    The valley or the mountain
Afforded visits, and still paradise lay
    In some green shade or fountain.
Angels lay lieger° here; each bush and cell,
    Each oak and highway knew them;
Walk but the fields, or sit down at some well,
    And he was sure to view them.°

return would return
Corruption Vaughan looks back, not to childhood as in "The Retreat," but to an earlier stage in history, when man had easier access to the divine, and remembered his heavenly origin. He then charts the decline of such powers, explaining that in falling, man also corrupted nature, which became mortal and also the cause of man's labor. Still man longed for his immortal home and still had encounters with angels, and paradisal intimations from nature (as in "Religion" and "The Retreat"), whereas now man is in despair, will not help himself, and demands that fate end his life. God does not communicate; man lives in sin and darkness; but the trumpet will sound for the last day and the restoration of heaven and light.
He shined . . . birth Vaughan thought of the soul as a divine spark; here its light affords a "glimpse" (see note on "The Retreat") of heaven. "Ray" was another favorite word.
still always
that act . . . all the Fall, as explained in succeeding lines
lieger a resident, not merely visiting, ambassador
view them exactly the same idea in "Religion"

Almighty Love! where art Thou now? Mad man
30   Sits down and freezeth on;
He raves, and swears to stir nor fire nor fan,
   But bids the thread be spun.°
I see thy curtains are close-drawn; thy bow
   Looks dim, too, in the cloud;
Sin triumphs still, and man is sunk below
   The centre,° and his shroud.
All's in deep sleep and night: thick darkness lies
   And hatcheth° o'er thy people—
But hark! what trumpet's that? what angel cries,
40   'Arise! thrust in Thy sickle'?°

              1650

The World°

I saw Eternity the other night
Like a great ring of pure and endless light,°
   All calm as it was bright;
And round beneath it, Time in hours, days, years,
   Driven by the spheres°
Like a vast shadow moved; in which the world
   And all her train° were hurled.
The doting lover in his quaintest° strain
   Did there complain;
10 Near him, his lute, his fancy, and his flights,°
   Wit's sour delights;
With gloves and knots, the silly snares of pleasure,
   Yet his dear treasure,
All scattered lay, while he his eyes did pour°
   Upon a flower.

The darksome statesman, hung with weights and woe
Like a thick midnight fog, moved there so slow,
   He did nor stay, nor go;
Condemning thoughts—like sad eclipses—scowl
20   Upon his soul,

thread be spun The Fates spun the thread of men's lives.
centre of the earth; the lowest place, where corruption gathers
hatcheth places a hatch
Arise . . . sickle Revelation 14:18. The angel that has power over fire cried to another, "Thrust in thy sharp sickle, and gather the clusters of the vine of the earth; for her grapes are fully ripe" (note the surprising assonance of people / sickle, expressively replacing a rhyme).
The World The basic contrast is between Eternity, symbolized by the circle, and Time, in which various types of folly, emblematically represented, are described; the question of access from Time to Eternity is handled in the enigmatic conclusion.
ring . . . light The circle was the usual emblem of eternity, having no begining or end; by calling it a *ring*, Vaughan prepares for the nuptial figure introduced later.
Driven . . . spheres According to Plato (*Timaeus*), time is identified with the movement of the heavenly bodies.
train followers, companions
quaintest most highly wrought
flights of rhetoric
pour he poured his eyes; pored over

And clouds of crying witnesses without
    Pursued him with one shout.
Yet digged the mole,° and lest his ways be found,
    Worked under ground,
Where he did clutch his prey; but one° did see
    That policy:
Churches and altars fed him, perjuries
    Were gnats and flies;
It rained about him blood and tears, but he
30   Drank them as free.°

The fearful miser on a heap of rust
Sat pining all his life there, did scarce trust
    His own hands with the dust,
Yet would not place one piece above, but lives
    In fear of thieves.
Thousands there were as frantic as himself,
    And hugged each one his pelf;°
The downright epicure° placed heaven in sense,
    And scorned pretence;
40 While others, slipped into a wide excess,
    Said little less;
The weaker sort slight, trivial wares enslave,
    Who think them brave;°
And poor, despisèd Truth sat counting° by
    Their victory.

Yet some,° who all this while did weep and sing,
And sing and weep, soared up into the ring;
    But most would use no wing.
Oh fools, said I, thus to prefer dark night
50   Before true light!
To live in grots and caves, and hate the day
    Because it shows the way;
The way, which from this dead and dark abode
    Leads up to God;
A way where you might tread the sun, and be
    More bright than he!
But as I did their madness so discuss,
    One whispered thus,
'This ring the Bridegroom did for none provide,
60   But for His bride.'°

mole the statesman, at his devious work
one God
as free as freely as they came
pelf lucre, wealth
epicure The word derives from the philosopher
Epicurus but came to mean simply one who
makes pleasure the highest good, that is, "places
heaven in sense." See Glossary.
brave fine, splendid
counting estimating

some Vaughan's adepts or mystics, who can
"walk to the sky" during their lives
His bride the Church: "I John saw the holy city,
new Jerusalem, coming down from God out of
heaven, prepared as a bride adorned for her
husband . . . And there came unto me one of
the seven angels . . . saying, Come hither, I
will show you the bride, the Lamb's wife"
(Revelation 21:2, 9)

JOHN, CAP. 2 VER. 16, 17

All that is in the world, the lust of the flesh, the lust of the eyes, and the pride
of life, is not of the Father, but is of the world.

And the world passeth away, and the lusts thereof; but he that doeth the will
of God abideth for ever.

1650

[They Are All Gone into the World of Light]°

They are all gone into the world of light!
    And I alone sit lingering here;
Their very memory is fair and bright
    And my sad thoughts doth clear.

It grows and glitters in my cloudy breast,
    Like stars° upon some gloomy grove,
Or those faint beams in which this hill is dressed
    After the sun's remove.

I see them walking in an air of glory,
10   Whose light doth trample on my days:
My days, which are at best but dull and hoary,
    Mere glimmering and decays.

Oh holy hope, and high humility,
    High as the heavens above!
These are your walks, and you have showed them me
    To kindle my cold love.

Dear, beauteous death! the jewel of the just,
    Shining nowhere but in the dark,
What mysteries do lie beyond thy dust,
20   Could man outlook that mark!

He that hath found some fledged bird's° nest, may know
    At first sight, if the bird be flown;
But what fair well or grove° he sings in now,
    That is to him unknown.

And yet, as angels in some brighter dreams
    Call to the soul when man doth sleep,
So some strange thoughts transcend our wonted themes,
    And into glory peep.°

They . . . Light The souls of the dead are in
the world of light, heaven; the poet is meditat-
ing on the place of the soul in the darkness
of the world, from which death will free it;
he petitions for light, as he does for the pure
water at the end of "Religion"—either here
or, by the intervention of death, in heaven.
stars Vaughan often compares the dead to
stars; here the memory of them is a faint
light to him.
fledged bird's image of the winged soul
well or grove as in "Religion" and "corruption" associated with holy places
peep another favorite word of Vaughan's used,
like *glimpse*, of the faint intimation of immortality available to the soul

If a star were confined into a tomb,°
30   Her captive flames must needs burn there;
But when the hand that locked her up gives room,
    She'll shine through all the sphere.

Oh father of eternal life, and all
   Created glories under thee!
Resume° thy spirit from this world of thrall
    Into true liberty.

Either disperse these mists, which blot and fill
   My pérspective° still as they pass:
Or else remove me hence unto that hill
40   Where I shall need no glass.

             1655

The Night°

JOHN 3:2°
Through that pure virgin shrine,
That sacred veil° drawn o'er thy glorious noon,
That men might look and live, as glow-worms shine
    And face the moon,°
  Wise Nicodemus saw such light
  As made him know his God by night.

  Most blest believer he!
Who in that land of darkness and blind eyes
Thy long-expected healing wings° could see,
10   When thou didst rise,
  And, what can never more be done,
  Did at midnight speak with the sun!

  Oh who will tell me where
He found thee at that dead and silent hour?
What hallowed solitary ground did bear
    So rare a flower,
  Within whose sacred leaves did lie
  The fullness of the deity?

star . . . tomb characteristic; cf. opening of "Cock-Crowing," below
Resume take back
perspective telescope, optic glass
The Night Nicodemus saw his God through the veil of the flesh of Jesus, saw, in the dark, the light. The poem praises night and secrecy, the meeting of Nicodemus with Jesus not in the Temple but in some dark grove. Night is the time of prayer; it is also, in a famous mystical text, an image of God considered as dazzlingly dark; and Vaughan finally petitions for death, the darkest of nights, in which he will be with God as Nicodemus was.

John 3:2 The gospel text tells how Nicodemus, a Pharisee, "came to Jesus by night, and said unto him, Rabbi, we know that thou art a teacher come from God," and was told that a man must be born again to enter into the kingdom of God.
veil See "Cock-crowing," below, l. 37n.
That men . . . moon That men might survive its brilliance ("there shall no man see me, and live," Exodus 33:20) and live with their own small light as glowworms can with the moon, though not the sun.
healing wings Malachi 4:2: "unto you that fear my name shall the Sun of righteousness arise with healing in his wings"

No mercy-seat of gold,
20 No dead and dusty cherub, nor carved stone,°
But His own living works did my Lord hold°
    And lodge alone;
  Where trees and herbs did watch and peep
  And wonder, while the Jews did sleep.°

    Dear night! this world's defeat;
The stop to busy fools; care's check and curb;
The day of spirits; my soul's calm retreat
    Which none disturb!
  Christ's progress, and his prayer time;°
30 The hours to which high heaven doth chime;

    God's silent, searching flight;
When my lord's head is filled with dew, and all
His locks are wet with the clear drops of night;°
    His still, soft call;°
  His knocking time;° the soul's dumb watch,
  When spirits their fair kindred catch.°

    Were all my loud, evil days
Calm and unhaunted as is thy dark tent,
Whose peace but by some angel's wing or voice
40   Is seldom rent,
  Then I in heaven all the long year
  Would keep, and never wander here.

    But living where the sun
Doth all things wake, and where all mix and tire
Themselves and others, I consent and run
    To every mire,
  And by this world's ill-guiding light,
  Err more than I can do by night.

    There is in God—some say—
50 A deep but dazzling darkness,° as men here
Say it is late and dusky, because they
    See not all clear.

No mercy-seat . . . stone not in the Temple
hold keep to
Where trees . . . sleep The notion is of vegetation being awake and growing in the night, here aware of Jesus as the Jews, who set much store by the Temple rejected in the preceding lines, were not.
his prayer time Jesus prayed at night in Gethsemane while the disciples slept.
my lord's head . . . night Song of Songs 5:2: "I sleep, but my heart waketh: it is the voice of my beloved that knocketh, saying, Open to me, my sister, my love, my dove, my undefiled: for my head is filled with dew, and my locks with the drops of night." This image of the Beloved is even more beautiful if one sees it as a figure for the star-filled night sky.
still . . . call I Kings 19:12.
knocking time Revelation 3:20: "Behold I stand at the door, and knock"
spirits . . . catch perhaps the contact between living and dead mentioned in "They Are All Gone . . ."
deep . . . darkness The mystical tradition venerated the works of Dionysius the Areopagite (Pseudo-Dionysius), who spoke of heavenly truths which lay "hidden in the dazzling obscurity of the secret Silence, outshining all brilliance with the intensity of their darkness"; and this was a common theme in Renaissance neoplatonic thought.

Oh for that night, where I in Him
Might live invisible and dim!
                    1655

Cock-Crowing°

Father of lights!° what sunny seed,°
What glance of day hast thou confined
Into this bird? To all the breed
This busy ray° thou hast assigned;
      Their magnetism works all night,°
      And dreams of Paradise and light.

Their eyes watch for the morning-hue,
Their little grain,° expelling night,
So shines and sings, as if it knew
10 The path unto the house of light.°
      It seems their candle, howe'er done,
      Was tinned° and lighted at the sun.

If such a tincture, such a touch,
So firm a longing can impour,°
Shall thy own image° think it much
To watch for thy appearing hour?
      If a mere blast so fill the sail,
      Shall not the breath of God prevail?

Oh thou immortal light and heat,
20 Whose hand so shines through all this frame,
That by the beauty of the seat,
We plainly see who made the same;

Cock-Crowing One of the most "hermetic" of Vaughan's poems, and directly indebted to his brother Thomas's treatise *Anima Magica Abscondita* (1650): "for she [the soul] is guided in her operations by a spiritual, metaphysical grain, a seed or glance of light . . . descending from the first Father of Lights" (see Elizabeth Holmes, *Henry Vaughan and the Hermetic Philosophy,* 1932). Hermetic and other occult doctrines combine in Vaughan with a traditional Christianity and a reflective use of Bible texts; he is in no way an adherent of some rival or heretical sect. The occasional strangeness of his idiom, like the range of inference he can suggest in what are otherwise plain scriptural allusions, is due to this commingling with Christianity of imagery from an independent tradition much cultivated in the mid-17th century, and regarded partly as a complement to the new science, and partly as a complement to traditional Christian devotion. Thus "Cock-Crowing," though one of his strangest poems, is not only similar in method to his others, but an orthodox act of Christian devotion.

Father of lights See the quotation from Thomas Vaughan, but also James 1:17, "Every good gift . . . cometh down from the Father of lights."
seed Vaughan's use of this word, like his brother's, is idiosyncratic but related to other mystical usages; it means, roughly, the same as *ray* (in l. 4) and "spark," an element of divinity within the soul, and here within the cock, which, responding to the first light, is an emblem of man's recognition of the heavenly light, and a symbol of the Resurrection (it has alchemical significance also).
ray See preceding note on *seed.*
magnetism . . . night Magnetism, important in the science and occult learning of the day, is a figure for the "sympathies" uniting distant objects; here the power of the "rays" to make the cocks dream of the origin of the rays.
grain seed
house of light Cf. Thomas Vaughan's treatise *Aula Lucis, or, The House of Light* (1652).
tinned kindled
impour pour in
thy own image man

Seeing thy seed abides in me,
Dwell thou in it, and I in thee!

To sleep without thee is to die;
Yea, 'tis a death partakes of hell;
For where thou dost not close the eye
It never opens, I can tell.
In such a dark, Egyptian border,°
30   The shades of death dwell, and disorder.

If joys and hopes and earnest throes,
And hearts whose pulse beats still° for light,
Are given to birds, who but thee knows
A love-sick soul's exalted flight?
Can souls be tracked by any eye
But his, who gave them wings to fly?

Only this veil° which thou hast broke,
And must be broken yet in me,
This veil, I say, is all the cloak,
40   And cloud which shadows thee from me.
This veil thy full-eyed love denies,
And only gleams and fractions spies.

Oh take it off! make no delay,
But brush me with thy light, that I
May shine unto a perfect day,
And warm me at thy glorious eye.
Oh take it off! or till it flee,
Though with no lily,° stay with me!
                    1655

THOMAS TRAHERNE
1637–1674

Traherne's poems and those of his prose works which we find of interest were unpublished during the seventeenth century; in 1896–97, manuscripts of his poetry and
of a remarkable group of prose meditations arranged in groups of a hundred were
discovered on a London bookstall. The poems were at first attributed to Henry
Vaughan (whose work they resemble rather more than Vaughan's does that of George
Herbert), but Bertram Dobell, who published them in 1903, ascribed them to Traherne.

dark . . . border Exodus 10:21–2
still always
veil Vaughan was fond of this word, and the
idea of light, for instance starlight, concealed
behind a veil; in II Corinthians 3:13 ff. the veil
is over the heart of the Jews in their reading
of the Old Testament, but will be taken away
when that heart "shall turn to the Lord."
Vaughan means that the Law has been superseded—the Old Testament revealed to be a
preparation for the New—and that a similar
process must happen in his own soul. Elsewhere

Vaughan quotes Hebrews 10:19–20: "Having
. . . boldness to enter into the holiest by the
blood of Jesus, By a new and living way,
which he hath consecrated for us, through the
veil, that is to say, his flesh." Perhaps Vaughan
means here: be rid of the flesh, as Jesus was.
Though . . . lily Song of Songs 2:16: "My
beloved . . . feedeth among the lilies." The
point is that he is no lily, but a weed, as in a
similar use of this text in his prose work
The Mount of Olives.

Seven years later, another manuscript turned up at the British Museum, containing some of these same poems somewhat reworked by Traherne's brother, Philip, who had prepared the work for the publication it was not, in its own time, to receive. We know little of Traherne's life: son of a Herefordshire shoemaker, he was sent to Oxford (Brasenose, B.A. 1656), took orders (the living of Credenhill in his native Herefordshire was his), then became chaplain, in London and in Hereford, to Sir Orlando Bridgeman, Lord Keeper of the Great Seal. He published some polemical and devotional works in 1673, and some were published posthumously, but his truly remarkable achievement comprises the "centuries" or hundreds of devotional meditations. For their time, they are direct and unadorned, proceeding by intuitive leaps more than through evolving conceits; at their best, they are amazingly powerful, particularly in the evocation of childhood, a world which, as Philippe Ariès has shown us in his *Centuries of Childhood*, would not conceptually evolve until the later eighteenth century. It is the privileged condition which Traherne ascribes to the incompleteness of childhood, and the imaginative possibilities he sees in contemplating the mistakes children make in reading the world about them, that have caused critics to liken him to Blake and Wordsworth, whom he in fact does not very much resemble. "When I was a child," says St. Paul, "I spake as a child, I understood as a child, I thought as a child: but when I became a man, I put away childish things" (I Corinthians 13:11); and the point of the passage is about completeness and maturation as types of fulfilled, redeemed knowledge. But Traherne would see a loss rather than a gain in the putting away; it is that loss which he reveals in some of the prose passages and in many of his somewhat prolix, structurally uncomfortable poems, which nevertheless represent in their own way a final stage of the Metaphysical devotional poetry springing from Donne and Herbert.

Shadows° in the Water

In unexperienced° infancy
Many a sweet mistake doth lie:
Mistake though false, intending° true;
A *seeming* somewhat more than *view;*
    That doth instruct the mind
    In things that lie behind,
And many secrets to us show
Which afterwards we come to know.

Thus did I by the water's brink
10 Another world beneath me think;
And while the lofty spacious skies
Reversèd there abused mine eyes,
    I fancied other feet
    Came mine to touch and meet;
As by some puddle I did play°
Another world within it lay.

Shadows images
unexperienced inexperienced
intending meaning

As by . . . play as if nearby some puddle I played in

Beneath the water people drowned,
Yet with another heaven° crowned,
In spacious regions seemed to go
20   Freely moving to and fro:
    In bright and open space
    I saw their very face;
Eyes, hands, and feet they had like mine;
Another sun did with them shine.

'Twas strange that people there should walk,
And yet I could not hear them talk:
That through a little watery chink,
Which one dry ox or horse might drink,
    We other worlds should see,
30   Yet not admitted be;
And other confines there behold
Of light and darkness, heat and cold.

I called them oft, but called in vain;
No speeches we could entertain:
Yet did I there expect to find
Some other world, to please my mind.
    I plainly saw by these
    A new Antipodes,°
Whom, though they were so plainly seen,
40   A film kept off that stood between.

By walking men's reversed feet
I chanced another world to meet;
Though it did not to view exceed
A phantasm, 'tis a world indeed,
    Where skies beneath us shine,
    And earth by art divine
Another face presents below,
Where people's feet against ours go.

Within the regions of the air,
50   Compassed about with heavens fair,
Great tracts of land there may be found
Enriched with fields and fertile ground;
    Where many numerous hosts,
    In those far distant coasts,
For other great and glorious ends,
Inhabit, my yet unknown friends.

Oh ye that stand upon the brink,
Whom I so near me, through the chink,
With wonder see: what faces there,
60   Whose feet, whose bodies, do ye wear?

---

another heaven Cf. Eve's vision of herself reflected in *Paradise Lost* IV.459.

Antipodes the reciprocal but antithetical world at the diametric opposite of the globe

I, my companions, see
  In you another me.
They seemed others, but are we;
Our second selves those shadows be.

Look how far off those lower skies
Extend themselves! scarce with mine eyes
I can them reach. Oh ye, my friends,
What secret borders on those ends?
    Are lofty heavens hurled
    'Bout your inferior° world?
Are ye the representatives
Of other peoples' distant lives?

Of all the playmates which I knew
That here I do the image view
In other selves, what can it mean?
But that below the purling stream
    Some unknown joys there be
    Laid up in store for me;
To which I shall, when that thin skin
Is broken, be admitted in.

            from MS., pub. 1903

From Centuries of Meditations

(*The First Century*)

3

I will open my mouth in parables: I will utter things that have been kept secret from the foundation of the world. Things strange, yet common; incredible, yet known; most high, yet plain; infinitely profitable, but not esteemed. Is it not a great thing that you should be heir of the world? Is it not a very enriching verity, in which the fellowship of the Mystery which from the beginning of the world hath been hid in God, lies concealed? The thing hath been from the creation of the world, but hath not been so explained, as that the interior beauty should be understood.[1] It is my design, therefore, in such a plain manner to unfold it, that my friendship may appear in making you possessor of the whole world.

(*The Third Century*)

1

Will you see the infancy of this sublime and celestial greatness? Those pure and virgin apprehensions I had from the womb, and that divine light wherewith I was born are the best unto this day, wherein I can see the universe. By the gift of God they attended me into the world, and by his special favour I remember them till now. Verily they seem the greatest gifts his wisdom could

___

inferior lower
1. Compare this with Sir Thomas Browne's "I love to lose myself in a mystery," from the *Religio Medici*.

bestow, for without them all other gifts had been dead and vain. They are unattainable by book, and therefore I will teach them by experience. Pray for them earnestly: for they will make you angelical and wholly celestial. Certainly Adam in Paradise had not more sweet and curious apprehensions of the world than I when I was a child.

2

All appeared new, and strange at the first, inexpressibly rare and delightful and beautiful. I was a little stranger, which at my entrance into the world was saluted and surrounded with innumerable joys. My knowledge was divine. I knew by intuition those things which since my apostasy I collected again by the highest reason. My very ignorance was advantageous. I seemed as one brought into the estate of innocence. All things were spotless and pure and glorious: yea, and infinitely mine, and joyful and precious. I knew not that there were any sins, or complaints, or laws. I dreamed not of poverties, contentions, or vices. All tears and quarrels were hidden from mine eyes. Everything was at rest, free and immortal. I knew nothing of sickness or death or rents or exaction, either for tribute or bread. In the absence of these I was entertained like an angel with the works of God in their splendour and glory, I saw all in the peace of Eden; heaven and earth did sing my Creator's praises, and could not make more melody to Adam than to me. All time was eternity, and a perpetual Sabbath. Is it not strange that an infant should be heir of the whole world, and see those mysteries which the books of the learned never unfold?

3

The corn was orient [2] and immortal wheat, which never should be reaped, nor was ever sown. I thought it had stood from everlasting to everlasting. The dust and stones of the street were as precious as gold: the gates were at first the end of the world. The green trees when I saw them first through one of the gates transported and ravished me, their sweetness and unusual beauty made my heart to leap, and almost mad with ecstasy, they were such strange and wonderful things. The men! Oh what venerable and reverend creatures did the aged seem! Immortal cherubims! [3] And young men glittering and sparkling angels, and maids strange seraphic pieces of life and beauty! Boys and girls tumbling in the street, and playing, were moving jewels. I knew not that they were born or should die; but all things abided eternally as they were in their proper places. Eternity was manifest in the light of the day, and something infinite behind everything appeared, which talked with my expectation and moved my desire. The city seemed to stand in Eden, or to be built in heaven. The streets were mine, the temple was mine, the people were mine, their clothes and gold and silver were mine, as much as their sparkling eyes, fair skins and ruddy faces. The skies were mine, and so were the sun and moon and stars, and all the world was mine; and I the only spectator and enjoyer of it. I knew no churlish proprieties, [4] nor bounds, nor divisions: but all pro-

2. Shining.
3. This is the traditional, but incorrect plural; the Hebrew masculine plural, -im should give cherub, cherubim as the proper forms, but the solecism has become accepted.
4. Properties, possessions.

prieties and divisions were mine: all treasures and the possessors of them. So that with much ado I was corrupted, and made to learn the dirty devices of this world. Which now I unlearn, and become, as it were, a little child again that I may enter into the Kingdom of God.

7

The first light which shined in my infancy in its primitive and innocent clarity was totally eclipsed: insomuch that I was fain to learn all again. If you ask me how it was eclipsed? Truly by the customs and manners of men, which like contrary winds blew it out: by an innumerable company of other objects, rude, vulgar and worthless things, that like so many loads of earth and dung did overwhelm and bury it; by the impetuous torrent of wrong desires in all others whom I saw or knew that carried me away and alienated me from it: by a whole sea of other matters and concernments that covered and drowned it: finally by the evil influence of a bad education that did not foster and cherish it. All men's thoughts and words were about other matters. They all prized new things which I did not dream of. I was a stranger and unacquainted with them; I was little and reverenced their authority; I was weak, and easily guided by their example; ambitious also, and desirous to approve myself unto them. And finding no one syllable in any man's mouth of those things, by degrees they vanished, my thoughts (as indeed what is more fleeting than a thought?) were blotted out; and at last all the celestial, great, and stable treasures to which I was born, as wholly forgotten as if they had never been.

12

By this you may see who are the rude and barbarous Indians. For verily there is no savage nation under the cope of heaven, that is more absurdly barbarous than the Christian world. They that go naked and drink water and live upon roots are like Adam, or angels in comparison of us. But they indeed that call beads and glass buttons jewels, and dress themselves with feathers, and buy pieces of brass and broken hafts of knives of our merchants are somewhat like us. But we pass them in barbarous opinions and monstrous apprehensions, which we nickname civility and the mode, amongst us. I am sure those barbarous people that go naked come nearer Adam, God, and angels in the simplicity of their wealth, though not in knowledge.

from MS., pub. 1908

JOHN MILTON
1608–1674

The shape of a very great poetic career must always be discerned against a historical background even as the effects of powerful forming forces within it are being understood. The   intentions of Chaucer, Shakespeare, and Spenser to live a life of art, and their visions of the route along which they would move, must all be read from the inner biography of their poetry itself. In the case of Milton, both the historical determinants and the informing energies from within are documented for us, and in inner and outer biography together. From his university days on, he was possessed of a self-awareness as a poet that could still, without limitation or qualification, transcend self-consciousness in a way that became almost impossible in literary history after, and perhaps because of, him. He planned when young not only to become a poet but to become a major one, and lived a consecrated life; yet he did not shrink from responding to the demands of a historical moment, and at a crucial high point in his creative career was ready to abandon the service of his poetic imagination, to stand and wait, while his activities and errands were all in the service of the Commonwealth, the Just City of men in whose possibility his vision encouraged him to believe.

The Renaissance and Reformation which continued in England through the middle of the seventeenth century surrounded him in childhood. His father, John Milton senior, was the Protestant son of a recusant Catholic yeoman who had disinherited him; he came to London and became moderately wealthy as a moneylender and scrivener, or notary. Sacrifice and inconvenience tend to strengthen piety, and Milton's continuation of his family's devoted Protestantism remained no easy and habitual matter, but a commitment which flourished, rather than suffered, in the high winds of doctrinal controversy that buffeted his post-university years. His father was a musician of some competence as well; and his general culture may have aided an imaginative generosity about a son who decided to give himself a six-year postgraduate course at home, leading to no degree or to anything else save for possible distant laurels.

Milton's education formally began at St. Paul's School in London, under a scholarly and imaginative master, in late 1620 or early 1621; but he started soon after to extend his own education at home with voluminous and extensive reading, and shortly thereafter additional formal tutoring followed, in classics and modern languages as well. He was at Cambridge for the spring term of 1625, matriculating at Christ's College and taking his B.A. in the spring of 1629, despite some slight altercation with a tutor in 1626 that seems to have resulted in a suspension for a brief time. While at Cambridge, he produced an impressive body of Latin verse and prose, the latter being represented by a group of oratorical exercises, or *Prolusions*, which show more than a mechanical approach to rhetorical problems. Indeed, in such pieces as the first one, delivered in college and debating the claims of day and night to be more excellent, we see the beginnings of a kind of mythopoetic thinking which is more than a mere brilliant assemblage of classical texts, just as the problematic part of the exercise seems a far cry from the undergraduate scholastic jugglings of Donne (in his *Paradoxes and Problems*). The germ of the *L'Allegro—Il Penseroso* pairing may indeed lie in the ability of Milton's mind, evidenced by this early work, to generate energies from conflict. His Latin verses of the time were mostly elegiac, commendatory, funerary, or half-serious epistolary, but his longish, mock-heroic poem on the Gunpowder Plot, written for the annual university Guy Fawkes Day celebrations, was extremely ambitious and unusually powerful. After some talented but tentatively conventional exercises in Jacobean poetic in English—funeral elegy was an accessible mode, and from the experimental vigor of his fancy, no nearby death was safe—he produced, in December of 1629, an unquestionably major poem of its moment, his *On the Morning of Christ's Nativity*. Its handling of the harmonization of various modes of angelic and celestial harmony, in the presentation of the heavenly voices heard by the Bethlehem shepherds, is brilliant at one level; but its treatment of the main theme of the phasing-out of pagan mythology by the birth of a new truth is more than that. The poem's vision is so fine that it is unable to avoid even a feeling of pathetic generosity for the gentler among the displaced: "With flower-inwoven tresses torn / The Nymphs in twilight shade of tangled thickets mourn." It represents the first clear instance of the direction

Milton's poetic career is to take thenceforth, following neither the Tribe of Ben into the realms of gracefulness, nor the "strong lines" of Donne's school into the tense regions of wit, erotic or divine. "If the Athenians, as some say, made their small deeds great and renowned by their eloquent writers, England hath had her noble achievements made small by the unskillful handling of monks and mechanics," he would write in 1642 in *The Reason of Church Government*, in a spirited passage of self-defense in the midst of his pamphleteering. But the conviction behind this started to flower early on, while in continued residence at Cambridge for his Master of Arts degree, reading Italian and writing sonnets in it, and, in 1631, producing *L'Allegro* and *Il Penseroso*. After taking his M.A. in 1632, Milton moved back home to continue preparing himself for major eloquence; first in a suburb west of London, then, in about 1635, at the family's country estate at Horton, in Buckinghamshire, near Windsor.

It was at Horton that Milton's fierce period of reading and creative concentration began to focus on specific large goals. In 1634, through his friendship with the musician Henry Lawes, who was tutor to the children of the Earl of Bridgewater, he got a chance to write a public piece of some magnitude. *Comus* (or, *A Masque Presented at Ludlow Castle*, as the 1637 printed version calls it) enabled him not only to address himself to the exposition of a virtue that was far from being what he would call in *Areopagitica* "fugitive and cloistered," but also to import into the transitory conventions of court masque some of the Shakespearean and Spenserian language and modes of representation that lyric poetry had not allowed him, up till then, to attempt. Similarly with the great programmatic force of *Lycidas*, in 1637.

From the spring of 1638 until the middle of the summer of 1639, Milton was in Italy, traveling in Tuscany and to Rome and Naples; he went about some in society, met musicians and patrons and even, in Florence, Galileo. In general, Italy had come to stand, in its language and poetry, as a region of the creative imagination for him; he was fortunate, this being so, that his experience of the actuality was so pleasant. In 1640 he moved to London and set up as a private schoolmaster; his first pupils were his nephews, Edward and John Phillips. But his concerns began to move toward public conflict, for London was a center of the struggle between Parliament on the one hand, and king and bishops on the other. Milton was on the brink of moving into some of his grandest fields of accomplishment—"not to make verbal curiosities the end (that were a toilsome vanity), but to be an interpreter and relater of the best and sagest things among mine own citizens throughout this island in the mother dialect"— as he would put it two years later in *The Reason of Church Government*. But the crucial issues raging about him, and about the principles to which he felt so committed, would have betrayed any task in the realm of epic or major drama which he might have set himself. From 1641, when he published his first tract against the institution of bishops, until twenty years after, when those bishops had been reinstituted with the Restoration of the monarchy, Milton devoted himself to prose, to argument, to armed mental fight. Writing with what he referred to as his "left hand," he produced a major series of prose works in defense of various religious, political, and moral freedoms, moving with a majority Puritan consensus in his anti-episcopal writings and then finding that the Presbyterian cause could itself become the oppressive one. In the next phase of his life, during which he married Mary Powell in 1642 (she left him in a fit of incompatibility after three months, but returned in 1645 to live with him until her death in childbirth seven years later), Milton wrote tracts in favor of divorce on the grounds of disharmony rather than only for adultery, and a brilliant short essay, *Of Education*, which supported the reformation of the still pre-

dominantly scholastic educational systems which prevailed in Europe. Such a reformation had indeed been going on at Milton's own school, St. Paul's, whose more
"Platonic" tradition of humanist training had been established by Erasmus, John Colet,
and William Lily. Then, too, there were the influential educational theories of John
Amos Comenius (1592–1670), the Czech educator who likewise opposed the arbitrariness and wearisome stuffiness of older methods, but whose own methods and
curricula aimed at a more pragmatic and less imaginatively self-fulfilling kind of
literacy. Milton's argument for the centrality of humanist literary and philosophical
disciplines itself made use, in an almost Baconian way, of the very methods whose
inculcation it desired to foster. Thus, Milton urges that logic be employed to lead
toward a flowering of intellectual activity in the arts of rhetoric, but that poetry be
made an instrument in that process, "as being less subtle and fine, but more simple,
sensuous and passionate"; and thus, in setting out the very aims of education themselves, earlier in the treatise, he leaps to the heart of biblical example:

> The end then of learning is to repair the ruins of our first parents by re-
> gaining to know God aright, and out of that knowledge to love him, to imi-
> tate him, to be like him, as we may the nearest by possessing our souls of
> true virtue, which being united to the heavenly grace of faith makes up the
> highest perfection. But because our understanding cannot in this body found
> itself but on sensible things, nor arrive so clearly to the knowledge of God
> and things invisible as by orderly conning over the visible and inferior creature,
> the same method is necessarily to be followed in all discreet teaching. And
> seeing every nation affords not experience and tradition enough for all kind
> of learning, therefore we are chiefly taught the languages of those who have
> at any time been most industrious after wisdom; so that language is but the
> instrument conveying to us things useful to be known. And though a linguist
> should pride himself to have all the tongues that Babel cleft the world into,
> yet, if he have not studied the solid things in them as well as the words and
> lexicons, he were nothing so much to be esteemed a learned man as any
> yeoman or tradesman competently wise in his mother dialect only.

Of Education and Areopagitica appeared in 1644. The following year, amid more
pamphleteering, Milton published a volume of his verse, Poems of Mr. John Milton,
including the sonnets which he had been writing during the 1640's as his only
poetry. It would not be until after service to the Commonwealth as Secretary for
Foreign Tongues to the Council of State (from 1649 until 1655, three years after his
blindness had become total), and after a long series of prose works, that he was
able, under the most adverse of circumstances, to get on with his deferred epic task.
In 1649, The Tenure of Kings and Magistrates had argued, shortly after the execution
of Charles I, for the divine right of removing kings; later that year, he attacked in
Eikonoklastes the roots of a Royalist cult which was attempting to make the martyred
Charles into a kind of saint. His first and second Defences of the English People
apeared in 1651 and 1654; The Ready and Easy Way to Establish a Free Commonwealth
was published on the brink of the Restoration in 1660.

The return of a Stuart monarch to the throne brought with it more than disap-
pointment for Milton; he was in danger from royal prosecution, both as a propa-
gandist for the Commonwealth cause and as a formal member of its government. He
actually went into hiding in the summer of 1660 until the general pardon of August
of that year, in which he was finally included. For some reason he was arrested and
imprisoned briefly at the end of the year, probably in November, but by December he
was granted a full pardon and had no further fear that personal action would be
taken against him.

It was during these last years of his life that Milton was finally to fulfill himself. Despite his total blindness, which dated from 1651–52, he was able to dictate *Paradise Lost,* finish it by 1665, continue on to *Paradise Regained* and, if most critics are correct in their view of its date of composition, *Samson Agonistes,* all of which were published in these last fourteen years of Milton's life. He was blind, and poorer than he had been with a state salary to augment his inheritance; he had seen the Commonwealth for which he had labored submerged in what looked to be an irreversible current of reaction; and yet he was able to concentrate all of his visionary and creative energies for a poetic accomplishment which ranks with Virgil's and Dante's in its organization of the knowledge and the spirit of its age. Like them, too, he evolved from received materials a fable powerful enough to be able to insist that it was not merely a fable, but an image of evolving human consciousness itself. Milton's major poems are the crowning fulfillment, too, of a life of learning as well as of the exercise of mental and moral combat; William Hazlitt remarked that Milton's learning has "the effect of intuition," and certainly in *Paradise Lost* he was able to include all that he knew without a sense of intrusion. His precursors (Virgil, Dante, Spenser among them) were an unalloyed imaginative aid to him. He was able to take what he needed from them without moving into their shadows; Hazlitt could perceive in him "a mighty intellect that, the nearer it approaches to others, the more distinct it becomes from them." Milton's last years were spent in continuing work, including revisions of the 1667 *Paradise Lost,* the second edition of which appeared in the year of his death, 1674.

L'Allegro and Il Penseroso

L'Allegro and Il Penseroso are of an unprecedented form in English poetry, related only to what was called a *synkriseis,* or debating situation, in classical literature (of which Milton's own college exercise, a prose oration on "Whether Day or Night Is More Excellent," is an example), and to analogous treatments, in Renaissance paintings and prints, of pairs of allegorical figures, such as Nature and Grace—the first, nude and associated with Eve, the second robed, and associated with Mary. Milton's two spirits are his own, compounded by his myth-making from traditional figures, but transformed by their milieu and its details. *L'Allegro* is a picture of a kind not yet invented: imagine a film version of a series of paintings like Botticelli's *Primavera* (Spring), with different scenes, but connected by the presence of one figure. She is Euphrosyne, one of the three Graces, naked (like her sisters, considered to be aspects of Venus). *Il Penseroso,* dark-robed, derives from personified Melancholy; a somber muse, neither the self-creating and self-consuming obsession of Burton in his dark tower of books, nor the massive, brooding angel of Albrecht Dürer's great engraving. The introductory verses to Burton's *Anatomy of Melancholy* may have suggested the tetrameter couplets as a meter (their refrain rhymes "melancholy" alternately with "folly" and "jolly"), but the modulation of their rhythms in the two poems is most flexible. Each poem opens with a half-serious banishment of a parody version of the spirit in the other lyric; in the main portion of each, the complementary treatment of light and dark, sound and silence, society and solitude, is subtle and complex. (See Figs. 15–18).

L'Allegro

Hence, loathèd Melancholy,°
  Of Cerberus° and blackest Midnight born,
In Stygian cave forlorn
  'Mongst horrid shapes, and shrieks, and sights unholy,
Find out some uncouth° cell,
  Where brooding darkness spreads his jealous wings,
And the night-raven sings;
  There under ebon shades and low-browed rocks,
As ragged as thy locks
10   In dark Cimmerian° desert ever dwell.
But come, thou goddess fair and free,
In heaven yclept Euphrosyne,°
And by men heart-easing Mirth,
Whom lovely Venus at a birth°
With two sister Graces more
To ivy-crownèd Bacchus bore;
Or whether° (as some sager sing)
The frolic wind that breathes the spring,
Zephyr, with Aurora° playing,
20 As he met her once a-Maying,
There on beds of violets blue,
And fresh-blown roses washed in dew,
Filled her with thee, a daughter fair,
So buxom,° blithe, and debonair.°
Haste thee, Nymph, and bring with thee
Jest and youthful Jollity,
Quips and cranks,° and wanton wiles,
Nods and becks° and wreathèd smiles,
Such as hang on Hebe's° cheek,
30 And love to live in dimple sleek;
Sport that wrinkled Care derides,°
And Laughter holding both his sides.
Come, and trip it as ye go
On the light fantastic toe,
And in thy right hand lead with thee
The mountain nymph, sweet Liberty;

loathèd Melancholy See Headnote.
Cerberus three-headed watchdog of Hades, whose cave by the river Styx, Virgil says (*Aeneid* VI.418), is full of the shrieking souls of dead children
uncouth unknown
Cimmerian proverbially dark region, home of the cave of Morpheus, one of the three sons of sleep
yclept Euphrosyne called Euphrosyne, or "Mirth." She was one of the three Graces usually thought of as daughters of Zeus and Hera; her sisters were Aglaia ("Brightness") and Thalia ("Flowering") (see *The Faerie Queene* VI.x.21–24).

Venus at a birth other fables make the Graces daughters of Venus and Bacchus
Or whether In the tone of a commentator on mythology, Milton adduces yet another parentage, made up by him for this poem; in a sense, the new parentage redefines the meaning of the Grace.
Aurora goddess of the dawn
buxom compliant
debonair gracious
cranks word-play jokes
becks gestures of beckoning, or "come-on"
Hebe's the Olympian barmaid and youth goddess
derides "Care" is the object.

And if I give thee honour due,
Mirth, admit me of thy crew,
To live with her, and live with thee,
40 In unreprovèd pleasures free;
To hear the lark begin his flight,
And singing startle the dull night,
From his watch-tower in the skies,°
Till the dappled dawn doth rise;
Then to come in spite of sorrow
And at my window bid good-morrow,
Through the sweet-briar or the vine,
Or the twisted eglantine;
While the cock with lively din
50 Scatters the rear of darkness thin,
And to the stack or the barn door
Stoutly struts his dames before;
Oft listening how the hounds and horn
Cheerly rouse the slumbering morn,
From the side of some hoar° hill,
Through the high wood echoing shrill;
Sometime walking, not unseen,°
By hedgerow elms, on hillocks green,
Right against the eastern gate,
60 Where the great sun begins his state,°
Robed in flames and amber light,
The clouds in thousand liveries dight;°
While the ploughman near at hand
Whistles o'er the furrowed land,
And the milkmaid singeth blithe,
And the mower whets his scythe,
And every shepherd tells his tale°
Under the hawthorn in the dale.
Straight mine eye hath caught new pleasures,
70 Whilst the landscape round it measures:
Russet lawns and fallows gray,
Where the nibbling flocks do stray;
Mountains on whose barren breast
The labouring clouds° do often rest;
Meadows trim with daisies pied,°
Shallow brooks and rivers wide.
Towers and battlements it° sees

To hear . . . skies The poetic power of the skylark results from the intensity of his song, filling the sky which, because of the small size and great altitude of the singer, looks empty.
hoar not frosty, but gray from morning mist
Sometime . . . unseen Cf. *Il Penseroso,* l. 65.
state royal progress or tour
liveries dight gay costumes clad

tells his tale counts his tally (of sheep); perhaps "recounts his story"
labouring clouds unlike the barren hills, they will bring forth rain
daisies pied variegated daisies; like many other phrases in these poems, quoted from Shakespeare (the cuckoo's song from *Love's Labour's Lost* V.ii.882–85)
it "mine eye" (from l. 69)

Bosomed high in tufted trees,
Where perhaps some beauty lies,
80 The cynosure° of neighbouring eyes.
Hard by, a cottage chimney smokes
From betwixt two agèd oaks,
Where Corydon and Thyrsis met
Are at their savoury dinner set
Of herbs and other country messes,
Which the neat-handed Phillis dresses;
And then in haste her bower° she leaves,
With Thestylis to bind the sheaves;
Or if the earlier season lead,
90 To the tanned haycock in the mead.
Sometimes with secure° delight
The upland hamlets will invite,
When the merry bells ring round,
And the jocund rebecs° sound
To many a youth and many a maid
Dancing in the chequered shade;
And young and old come forth to play
On a sunshine holiday,
Till the livelong daylight fail:
100 Then to the spicy nut-brown ale,
With stories told of many a feat,
How fairy Mab the junkets eat;°
She was pinched and pulled, she said,
And he, by friar's lantern° led,
Tells how the drudging goblin sweat
To earn his cream-bowl duly set,
When in one night, ere glimpse of morn,
His shadowy flail hath threshed the corn
That ten day-labourers could not end;
110 Then lies him down the lubber fiend,°
And stretched out all the chimney's length,
Basks at the fire his hairy strength;
And crop-full out of doors he flings,
Ere the first cock his matin rings.
Thus done the tales, to bed they creep,
By whispering winds soon lulled asleep.
Towered cities please us then,°

---

cynosure the constellation Ursa Minor, containing Polaris; thus, a proverbial center of attention
bower cottage
secure carefree
rebecs primitive fiddles
eat ate. "Mab" is the fairy queen from Mercu-
tio's speech in *Romeo and Juliet* I.iv. 55–95.
friar's lantern the will-o'-the-wisp
lubber fiend spirit who is a lob, or household
drudge. Puck, in *Midsummer Night's Dream*

II.i.16 and 40, is called "lob of spirits" and
"Hobgoblin."
Towered . . . then Here comes the shift from
glad day to glad night, paralleled at almost
exactly the same point (l. 121) in *Il Penseroso*
by the dawning of sad day. The interpenetration
of the spirits of the poems is important:
L'Allegro's night is full of illuminations, comic
theater, songs, and festivals, while *Il Penseroso's*
day is shadowed and shrouded.

And the busy hum of men,
Where throngs of knights and barons bold
120 In weeds° of peace high triumphs hold,
With store of ladies, whose bright eyes
Rain influence,° and judge the prize
Of wit or arms, while both contend
To win her grace whom all commend.
There let Hymen° oft appear
In saffron robe, with taper clear,
And pomp, and feast, and revelry,
With masque and antique pageantry:
Such sights as youthful poets dream
130 On summer eves by haunted stream.
Then to the well-trod stage anon,
If Jonson's learnèd sock° be on,
Or sweetest Shakespeare, Fancy's child,°
Warble his native wood-notes wild;
And ever against eating° cares
Lap me in soft Lydian airs,°
Married to immortal verse,
Such as the meeting soul may pierce
In notes with many a winding bout°
140 Of linkèd sweetness long drawn out,
With wanton heed and giddy cunning,
The melting voice through mazes running,
Untwisting all the chains that tie
The hidden soul of harmony;
That Orpheus' self may heave his head
From golden slumber on a bed
Of heaped Elysian flowers, and hear
Such strains as would have won the ear
Of Pluto, to have quite set free
150 His half-regained Eurydice.
These delights if thou canst give,
Mirth, with thee I mean to live.°
1631–32?   1645

weeds costumes
Rain influence See *Astronomy . . . in* the Glossary.
The ladies are out of Petrarchan poetry—the conceit about the eyes of the beloved being stars is a cliché.
Hymen god of marriage, as a character in a masque
learnèd sock The sock, or low shoe, was emblematic of classical comedy; cf. *Il Penseroso*, l. 102.
sweetest . . . child In the earlier poem "On Shakespeare" Milton alluded to this spontaneous creativity; the juxtaposition of "learnèd" Jonson and "native" Shakespeare is a commonplace.
eating (adjectival)

soft Lydian airs melodies of a delightful and relaxing sort (the Lydian mode or key, in Greek tradition, was "lax," the Dorian "manly," the Phrygian "wild," etc., in the same way in which we think of minor as being "sad" and major "happy"; in addition, "airs" means breezes).
bout turn, or possibly, return. Milton may be thinking of the Italian aria, or solo air, with its turning ornamentations, and *ritornello*, or *da capo* repeat.
These delights . . . live yet one more response—here to the closing lines of Marlowe's "The Passionate Shepherd"

Il Penseroso

Hence, vain deluding Joys,°
  The brood of Folly without father bred,
How little you bestead,°
  Or fill the fixèd mind with all your toys;
Dwell in some idle brain,
  And fancies fond with gaudy shapes possess,
As thick and numberless
  As the gay motes that people the sunbeams,
Or likest hovering dreams,
10   The fickle pensioners of Morpheus' train.°
But hail, thou Goddess sage and holy,
Hail, divinest Melancholy,
Whose saintly visage is too bright
To hit the sense of human sight,
And therefore to our weaker view
O'erlaid with black, staid Wisdom's hue;
Black, but such as in esteem
Prince Memnon's sister° might beseem,
Or that starred Ethiop queen° that strove
20 To set her beauty's praise above
The sea-nymphs, and their powers offended.
Yet thou art higher far descended:
Thee bright-haired Vesta° long of yore
To solitary Saturn bore—
His daughter she (in Saturn's reign
Such mixture was not held a stain).
Oft in glimmering bowers and glades
He met her, and in secret shades
Of woody Ida's inmost grove,
30 While yet there was no fear of Jove.°
Come, pensive Nun, devout and pure,
Sober, steadfast, and demure,
All in a robe of darkest grain,°
Flowing with majestic train,
And sable stole of cypress lawn°
Over thy decent shoulders drawn.
Come, but keep thy wonted state,
With even step and musing gait,
And looks commercing with the skies,

---

deluding Joys See Headnote.
bestead help
pensioners . . . train attendants on Morpheus, god of dreams, son of Sleep
Memnon's sister Himera, an Ethiopian princess in Homer
Ethiop queen Cassiopeia who, in one version of her legend, was transformed into a constellation because she boasted so of her daughter Andromeda's beauty

Vesta usually virginal, Roman goddess of the hearth. Milton invents this myth of her incestuous parentage.
Jove Jupiter's childhood was spent on Mt. Ida on Crete; later, he overthrew Saturn, his father (or Zeus and his father Cronos, in Greek).
grain color
cypress lawn black, fine linen

40   Thy rapt soul sitting in thine eyes;
      There held in holy passion still,
      Forget thyself to marble, till
      With a sad° leaden downward cast
      Thou fix them on the earth as fast.
      And join with thee calm Peace and Quiet,
      Spare Fast, that oft with gods doth diet,
      And hears the Muses in a ring
      Aye round about Jove's altar sing;
      And add to these retired Leisure,°
50   That in trim gardens takes his pleasure;
      But first, and chiefest, with thee bring
      Him that yon soars on golden wing,
      Guiding the fiery-wheelèd throne,
      The Cherub Contemplatïon;°
      And the mute Silence hist° along,
      'Less Philomel will deign a song,
      In her sweetest, saddest plight,°
      Smoothing the rugged brow of Night,
      While Cynthia° checks her dragon yoke
60   Gently o'er th' accustomed oak.
      Sweet bird, that shunn'st the noise of folly,
      Most musical, most melancholy!
      Thee, chauntress, oft the woods among
      I woo to hear thy even-song;
      And missing thee, I walk unseen
      On the dry smooth-shaven green,
      To behold the wandering moon
      Riding near her highest noon,
      Like one that had been led astray
70   Through the heaven's wide pathless way;
      And oft, as if her head she bowed,
      Stooping through a fleecy cloud.
      Oft on a plat° of rising ground
      I hear the far-off curfew sound
      Over some wide-watered shore,
      Swinging slow with sullen° roar;
      Or if the air will not permit,
      Some still removèd place will fit,
      Where glowing embers through the room
80   Teach light to counterfeit a gloom,°

sad serious
Leisure See Marvell's "The Garden" for an instance of this theme of retirement.
Contemplatïon The diaeresis mark indicates that the diphthong is separated into two vowel sounds, here giving the word five syllables.
hist to whisper "hist!"—meaning "come along!"
'Less . . . plight the nightingale, changed form of Philomela whose brother-in-law raped her and tore out her tongue; her metamorphosis made her the bird of sad song
Cynthia the moon goddess; "dragon yoke" because a chariot drawn by dragons is Hecate's and Hecate is the antithetical form of the moon enchantress
plat plot
sullen solemn, religious
Teach . . . gloom This contrasts with the lighting of interiors at night in *L'Allegro*.

Far from all resort of mirth,
Save the cricket on the hearth,
Or the bellman's drowsy charm,°
To bless the doors from nightly harm:
Or let my lamp at midnight hour
Be seen in some high lonely tower,°
Where I may oft outwatch the Bear,°
With thrice great Hermes,° or unsphere
The spirit of Plato° to unfold
90   What worlds or what vast regions hold
The immortal mind that hath forsook
Her mansion in this fleshly nook;
And of those daemons that are found
In fire, air, flood, or under ground,
Whose power hath a true consent
With planet or with element.°
Sometime let gorgeous Tragedy
In sceptred pall come sweeping by,
Presenting Thebes, or Pelops' line,°
100   Or the tale of Troy divine,
Or what (though rare) of later age
Ennobled hath the buskined° stage.
But, O sad Virgin, that thy power
Might raise Musaeus° from his bower,
Or bid the soul of Orpheus sing
Such notes as, warbled to the string,
Drew iron tears down Pluto's cheek
And made hell grant what love did seek;°
Or call up him° that left half told
110   The story of Cambuscan bold,
Of Camball and of Algarsife,
And who had Canace to wife,
That owned the virtuous ring and glass,
And of the wondrous horse of brass,
On which the Tartar king did ride;
And if aught else great bards beside

bellman's . . . charm the chant of the night-watchman calling the hours
high lonely tower This is the central point of contemplative vision in the poem; it has been associated by critics with Isaiah's watchtower (Isaiah 21:8), and Plato's notion, in the *Republic* 560b, of a high place, or "acropolis" of the soul. The tower is ascended not like the major prophetic mountains, but, as here, to devote to the night skies the same attentive gaze as that which, in *L'Allegro*, follows the "live-long daylight."
outwatch the Bear Ursa Major, the Big Dipper, never sets; thus, to work all night.
thrice great Hermes Hermes Trismegistus, supposed author of neoplatonist writings, actually from Alexandria in the third and fourth centuries A.D. (See *Platonism* in the Glossary.)

unsphere . . . Plato to call Plato's ghost back from its home in the highest sphere of heaven
With planet . . . element Evil or marginal spirits were classified according to which of the four elements composed them, and with particular heavenly bodies.
Thebes, or Pelops' line the Oedipus cycle and the tales of the house of Atreus (Thyestes, Agamemnon, Orestes, etc.)
buskined booted with the emblematic footwear of tragedy; cf. *L'Allegro*, l. 132
Musaeus mythical Greek poet (fictionally associated by Marlowe with his actual, late 5th-century A.D. author in *Hero and Leander*)
what . . . seek Eurydice; cf. *L'Allegro*, ll. 145–50
him Chaucer; the half-told story, The Squire's Tale

In sage and solemn tunes have sung,
Of tourneys and of trophies hung,
Of forests and enchantments drear,
120 Where more is meant than meets the ear.°
Thus, Night, oft see me in thy pale career,°
Till civil-suited° Morn appear,
Not tricked and frounced° as she was wont
With the Attic boy° to hunt,
But kerchiefed in a comely cloud,
While rocking winds are piping loud,
Or ushered with a shower still,
When the gust hath blown his fill,
Ending on the rustling leaves,
130 With minute° drops from off the eaves.
And when the sun begins to fling
His flaring beams, me, Goddess, bring
To archèd walks of twilight groves,
And shadows brown° that Sylvan loves,
Of pine or monumental oak,
Where the rude axe with heavèd stroke
Was never heard the nymphs to daunt,
Or fright them from their hallowed haunt.
There in close covert by some brook,
140 Where no profaner eye may look,
Hide me from Day's garish eye,
While the bee with honied thigh,
That at her flowery work doth sing,
And the waters murmuring
With such consort° as they keep,
Entice the dewy-feathered Sleep;
And let some strange mysterious dream
Wave at his wings in airy stream
Of lively portraiture displayed,
150 Softly on my eyelids laid.
And as I wake, sweet music breathe
Above, about, or underneath,
Sent by some Spirit to mortals good,
Or the unseen Genius of the wood.
But let my due feet never fail
To walk the studious cloister's pale,°
And love the high embowèd° roof,

Where more . . . ear the corpus of allegorical
romance: particularly Spenser (see *Areopagitica*), but also Tasso and Ariosto
Thus, Night . . . career a deliberately placed
pentameter line, breaking the rhythm: it moves
away from the praise of dead poets, and is,
perhaps, a hidden defiance of Mirth
civil-suited simply dressed
frounced with hair curled

Attic boy Cephalus
minute falling once a minute (not "tiny")
brown standard term for "dark" in pastoral
diction
consort other polyphonic parts (sung by leaves,
sad birds, etc.)
pale enclosure
embowèd vaulted

With antique° pillars' massy proof,°
And storied windows richly dight,°
160   Casting a dim religious light.
There let the pealing organ blow
To the full-voiced quire below,
In service high and anthems clear,
As may with sweetness, through mine ear,
Dissolve me into ecstasies,
And bring all heaven before mine eyes.
And may at last my weary age
Find out the peaceful hermitage,
The hairy gown and mossy cell,
170   Where I may sit and rightly spell°
Of every star that heaven doth shew,
And every herb that sips the dew,
Till old experience do attain
To something like prophetic strain.
These pleasures, Melancholy, give,
And I with thee will choose to live.
1631–32?   1645

Sonnets

Milton started writing sonnets while still at Cambridge, but they were never of the traditionally Petrarchan sequence type (e.g. *Astrophel and Stella, Delia, Ideas Mirror*) that had gone out of fashion more than forty years earlier. His poems developed under the influence of the Italian sonnets of Giovanni della Casa and, in his later ones, of Tasso's *Sonnetti Eroici;* he learned particularly from their syntax, their placing of nouns and adjectives, and strong enjambments. Five of Milton's first six sonnets were in Italian; later on, he used the form in a more public, proclamatory, and even denunciatory manner—as a kind of ode in miniature. Based on the Italian sonnet form divided into octave-sestet sections (rather than the more logically schematic quatrain and couplet pattern used by Shakespeare), Milton's sonnets nevertheless grew to override that central division. They developed a flow of utterance building to a high (rather than to the kind of shutting-off that an epigrammatic or neat ending effects). Wordsworth likened their self-contained homogeneous character to that of a drop of dew. Their rhymes aside, these sonnets were a study for the eventual blank-verse paragraphs of *Paradise Lost*.

antique antic, grotesque
proof impenetrability
dight decorated (stained-glass)
spell decipher the meaning, read. At the end of the poem, Melancholy is left with a kind of resolute, scientific patience, a healthy introspection fulfilled in looking outward, not like Dürer's angel of the imagination whose abandoned scientific instruments lie around her.

Sonnet I°

O nightingale, that on yon bloomy spray
 Warblest at eve, when all the woods are still,
 Thou with fresh hope the lover's heart dost fill,
 While the jolly Hours° lead on propitious May;
Thy liquid notes that close the eye of day,°
 First heard before the shallow cuckoo's bill,
 Portend success in love; O if Jove's will
 Have linked that amorous power to thy soft lay,
Now timely sing, ere the rude bird of hate°
10 Foretell my hopeless doom in some grove nigh,
 As thou from year to year hast sung too late
For my relief, yet hadst no reason why:
 Whether the Muse or Love call thee his mate,°
 Both them I serve, and of their train am I.
 1629–30?   1645

Sonnet VII

How soon hath time, the subtle thief of youth,
 Stolen on his wing my three and twentieth year!°
 My hasting days fly on with full career,
 But my late spring no bud or blossom° showeth.
Perhaps my semblance° might deceive° the truth,
 That I to manhood am arrived so near,
 And inward ripeness doth much less appear,
 That some more timely-happy spirits° endueth.
Yet be it less or more, or soon or slow,
10 It shall be still° in strictest measure even
 To that same lot, however mean or high,
Toward which time leads me, and the will of heaven;
 All is, if I have grace to use it so,
 As ever° in my great task-master's eye.
 1631   1645

Sonnet I Milton's first sonnet in English, a response to the self-generated occasion of answering the song of the nightingale: he has never been in love, he has never written the kind of poetry he was going to demand of himself—what can the nightingale *mean*, then, as an emblem as well as by its song?
Hours daughters of Jupiter and Themis (see Spenser's *Epithalamium*, I. 98, 280)
eye of day the sun; a vestigial Petrarchanism
bird of hate the cuckoo. In medieval tradition, to hear him sing before the nightingale was a bad omen for a lover.
Whether . . . mate The sexes here are a bit confused, but "mate" merely implies mythological association: whether the nightingale is a myth of poetry (as in Ovid's story of the raped, mute Philomela, restored to her voice through change), or whether, as in popular tradition, the night-bird of love.

three and twentieth year thus, the poem written for his 24th birthday, a confrontation with his own inactivity and of his prolonged scholarly and imaginative apprenticeship
bud or blossom poetry (a 17th-century commonplace)
semblance appearance
deceive prove false
timely-happy spirits He is thinking of Cambridge friends, perhaps, who at his age seem more mature, fulfilled, and fashionable as poets; scholars have proposed his friend Charles Diodati, Thomas Randolph, Abraham Cowley, and even Spenser, as historical candidates.
still always
ever eternity. The last two lines probably mean "All time is, if I have grace to use it so, as eternity in the sight of God."

719

Sonnet VIII

When the Assault Was Intended to the City°

Captain or colonel,° or knight in arms,
    Whose chance on these defenseless doors may seize,
    If deed of honour did thee ever please,
    Guard them, and him within protect from harms;
He can requite thee, for he knows the charms
    That call fame on such gentle acts as these,
    And he can spread thy name o'er lands and seas,
    Whatever clime the sun's bright circle warms.
Lift not thy spear against the Muses' bower:
10   The great Emathian conqueror bid spare
    The house of Pindarus,° when temple and tower
Went to the ground; and the repeated air°
    Of sad Electra's poet had the power
    To save the Athenian walls from ruin bare.
    1642   1642

Sonnet XVII

When I consider how my light is spent,
    Ere half my days,° in this dark world and wide,
    And that one talent° which is death to hide
    Lodged with me useless, though my soul more bent
To serve therewith my maker, and present
    My true account, lest he, returning, chide.
    'Doth God exact day-labour, light denied?'
    I fondly ask; but Patience, to prevent°
That murmur, soon replies: 'God doth not need
10   Either man's work or his own gifts; who best
    Bear his mild yoke,° they serve him best; his state

When . . . City The assault was of Royalist troops on London, from which King Charles's army was turned back on November 13, 1642, at Turnham Green, and the poem is written as if to be posted on the author's door.
colonel here trisyllabic: cur-o-nel
Pindarus Alexander the Great reportedly spared Pindar's house when he burned Thebes; see E.K.'s gloss on the October Eclogue in Spenser's *Shepheards Calender.*
air song, here the first chorus of Euripides' *Electra,* recited ("repeated") by an Athenian officer in 404 B.C., so moving the victorious Spartans that they spared Athens
half my days Since there is some controversy over the dating of this sonnet, "half my days" does not necessarily mean 35, midpoint of the biblical life-span of "threescore years and ten," but perhaps half of Milton's mature life, or half the span of his father, who died at 84; some scholars would put it earlier, and have the

"spent" light indicate the onset of his blindness, which was gradually overcoming him between 1644 and 1652.
one talent Our modern word is derived from a word meaning a weight of gold, a sum of money equivalent to about $30,000 (if a silver talent, about $6,000), thus a possession or disposition. However, our modern use is shaped by the central allusion of this poem, the parable of the Kingdom of Heaven in Matthew 25: 14–30, in which a lord gives his servants various sums of money. The good ones use their talents to double the value by investment, but the "wicked and slothful servant" hides his in the ground and is rebuked when his master returns, asking for a true account. Milton's talent, for writing a great poem, seems to be burying itself in darkness against his will.
prevent forestall
Bear . . . yoke Milton is alluding to Matthew 11:29–30.

Is kingly—thousands° at his bidding speed
    And post o'er land and ocean without rest:
    They also serve who only stand and wait.'
1652?   1673

Sonnet XVIII

    On the Late Massacre in Piedmont°

Avenge, O Lord, thy slaughtered saints, whose bones
    Lie scattered on the Alpine mountains cold,
    Even them who kept thy truth so pure of old
    When all our fathers worshipped stocks and stones,°
Forget not; in thy book° record their groans
    Who were thy sheep, and in their ancient fold
    Slain by the bloody Piemontese that rolled
    Mother with infant down the rocks. Their moans
The vales redoubled to the hills, and they
    To heaven. Their martyred blood and ashes sow
    O'er all the Italian fields, where still doth sway
The triple tyrant,° that from these may grow
    A hundredfold,° who, having learnt thy way,
    Early may fly the Babylonian° woe.
1655   1673

Sonnet XIX

Methought I saw my late espousèd saint°
    Brought to me like Alcestis° from the grave,
    Whom Jove's great son to her glad husband gave,
    Rescued from death by force, though pale and faint.
Mine, as whom washed from spot of child-bed taint
    Purification in the old Law° did save,

---

thousands of angels
On . . . Piedmont The Vaudois, an early Protestant sect formed in the 12th century, lived in Alpine villages and were tolerated by the Dukes of Savoy, until the then Duke, Charles Emmanuel II, sent an army to remove them. On April 24, 1655, many were massacred, including prisoners.
stocks and stones gods of wood or stone
book the Book of Life in Revelation 5:1ff.
triple tyrant the triple-crowned pope
A hundredfold The army harvested by Cadmus from dragon's teeth he sowed combines with the seeds of the sower (Matthew 13:8) which "fell into good ground, and brought forth fruit, some an hundredfold."
Babylonian Just as the author of Revelation had encoded imperial Rome as Babylon, so did Puritan writers with the papal city.

saint a spirit in heaven, in this case, probably Katherine Woodcock, Milton's second wife, although some scholars, dating the sonnet earlier, apply it to Mary Powell, the first Mrs. Milton, who died in childbirth
Alcestis wife of Admetus who chose to die in his place and who, in Euripides' drama, was returned to him by Heracles, who wrestled with Death to win her back; Alcestis was veiled on her return, and Katherine also, in that Milton had never seen her face, being blind at their marriage
Law In Leviticus, the postpartum condition is deemed unclean for 66 days, and the woman must be purified; if this is literal, it might apply to Mary Powell; if figurative, to Katherine (from the Greek *kathara*, "pure"), who died the day after the feast of the Purification of the Virgin.

And such as yet once more I trust to have
Full sight of her in heaven without restraint,
Came vested all in white,° pure as her mind.
10 Her face was veiled, yet to my fancied sight
Love, sweetness, goodness in her person shined
So clear as in no face with more delight.
But O as to embrace me she inclined,
I waked, she fled, and day brought back my night.
1658   1673

Comus

The proper but less familiar title of *Comus* is "A Masque Presented at Ludlow
Castle, 1634," and it comes down to us in printed editions (an anonymous one of
1637 and, later, in the *Poems* of 1645) as well as in manuscripts which suggest what
the actual version was like. It was written as an entertainment for the household of
the Earl of Bridgewater, who had recently been made Lord President of Wales; Milton's
friend, the composer Henry Lawes, was employed there as tutor to the Earl's three
children, Alice, fifteen, and John and Thomas, eleven and nine. *Comus* is not strictly
a masque (see the Headnote to Ben Jonson's *Pleasure Reconciled to Virtue*), but it partakes of many elements of that major seventeenth-century form of symbolic entertainment, particularly in the relation of the masquing figures, or members of the courtly
audience who in fact participate in the emblematic dances, and those mythological
roles. In *Comus* the roles of the Lady, her younger brothers, and the Attendant Spirit
were played by the children and their tutor; the monsters attending Comus dance in
a version of the "antimasque" or grotesque prelude or interlude that in Ben Jonson's
masques provided different sorts of contrast to the main fiction. But the heart of
masque is dancing, and the heart of *Comus* is language; the mythological "action"
in it occurs through no staggering effects of stage machinery, in which one realm or
world "becomes" another, but in the great speeches of Comus and the Lady, and
in the recitations and songs of the Spirit and the goddess Sabrina. Milton's poetic
language is notably Shakespearean: his phrases echo *A Midsummer Night's Dream,*
The Tempest, The Winter's Tale, and other plays, and the syntax and the texture of
the blank verse throughout constantly remind us of the earlier poet. Word-forms
and archaisms are modeled on, but not actually borrowed from, Spenser.

Most critics today like to think of *Comus* as pastoral drama, objectifying platonistic
tradition and stemming from Tasso's *Aminta* (see Samuel Daniel's "A Pastoral" and
the analogous passage from Guarini's *Il Pastor Fido* adapted by Fanshawe). Here, the
allegory of chastity is embodied in the powers to resist deforming magic that a young
girl's virginity possesses. (It must be understood that lifelong virginity is not what
Milton, or Spenser, thought chastity to be, but that for a certain kind of symbolic
dramaturgy, that complex virtue seemed best represented by the power of virginity,
as a state, to preserve itself delicately and forcefully.) Chastity's antagonist is worthy
of her, making trial rather than crudely assaulting; he is Comus, a transformed version
of both the handsome young reveler from classical lore, and Ben Jonson's big-bellied

---

white With this word the rhymes shift from
those on the long ā sound to long ī; the last
line "waked . . . night" recapitulates this shift.

mockery of pleasure. Milton makes him the son of Circe, who, in the *Odyssey*, changed men who behaved like pigs into the swine they "really" were. Circe was the first satirist, in a sense, and the worse a person was, the more monstrous his transformed shape would be. But Comus is also a suave, learned seducer, master of the conventional *carpe diem* arguments which overran Caroline love poetry and which Milton augmented, presumably after more exposure to them, in his printed text.

The magic herb *haemony* which the "shepherd lad" (l. 619) produces is an example of Milton's kind of myth-making in his early poems; scholars are in doubt about its exact traditional source, but it is clearly modeled on the moly plant used against Circe in Homer, and may derive its name from Greek words for blood (thus associating it with the power of sacrificial blood, in both pagan and Christian story), or with the name of Thessaly, from which magic herbs came. In any event, it is a resonant name for a substance whose power, though limited, must be defined by the poem's own moral realm.

Comus

THE PERSONS

The Attendant Spirit, afterwards in the habit of Thyrsis
Comus with his crew
The Lady
First Brother
Second Brother
Sabrina the Nymph

The chief persons which presented were
The Lord Brackley
Mr. Thomas Egerton his Brother
The Lady Alice Egerton

> The first scene discovers a wild wood.
> [THE ATTENDANT SPIRIT *descends or enters*]

Before the starry threshold of Jove's court
My mansion is, where those immortal shapes
Of bright aërial Spirits live ensphered
In regions mild of calm and serene air,
Above the smoke and stir of this dim spot
Which men call Earth, and with low-thoughted care,
Confined and pestered° in this pinfold° here,
Strive to keep up a frail and feverish being,
Unmindful of the crown that Virtue gives,
10   After this mortal change,° to her true servants
Amongst the enthronèd gods on sainted seats.
Yet some there be that by due steps aspire
To lay their just hands on that golden key

---

pestered crowded together   **mortal change** death
pinfold pen for farm animals

That opes the palace of Eternity:
To such my errand is, and but for such
I would not soil these pure ambrosial weeds°
With the rank vapours of this sin-worn mould.°
   But to my task. Neptune, besides the sway
Of every salt flood and each ebbing stream,
20 Took in, by lot, 'twixt high and nether Jove°
Imperial rule of all the sea-girt isles
That like to rich and various gems inlay
The unadornèd bosom of the deep,
Which he, to grace his tributary gods,
By course° commits to several government,
And gives them leave to wear their sapphire crowns
And wield their little tridents;° but this isle,
The greatest and the best of all the main,
He quarters° to his blue-haired deities;
30 And all this tract° that fronts the falling sun
A noble peer° of mickle° trust and power
Has in his charge, with tempered awe° to guide
An old and haughty nation° proud in arms—
Where his fair offspring, nursed in princely lore,
Are coming to attend their father's state
And new-entrusted sceptre, but their way
Lies through the pérplexed° paths of this drear wood,°
The nodding horror of whose shady brows
Threats the forlorn and wandering passenger.
40 And here their tender age might suffer peril,
But that by quick command from sovereign Jove
I was dispatched for their defence and guard;
And listen why, for I will tell ye now
What never yet was heard in tale or song
From old or modern bard, in hall or bower.
   Bacchus, that first from out the purple grape
Crushed the sweet poison of misusèd wine,
After the Tuscan mariners transformed,°
Coasting the Tyrrhene shore, as the winds listed,
50 On Circe's° island fell (Who knows not Circe,
The daughter of the Sun? whose charmèd cup

---

ambrosial weeds heavenly garments
mould the earth, the body in which he in-
carnates
Neptune . . . Jove Zeus, high Jove, and Hades
or Pluto, nether Jove, ruled the realms of the
sky and the dead; over the third realm, the
sea, Neptune ruled.
By course duly
tridents Neptune's three-pronged spear
quarters deals out
this tract Wales, and Bridgewater's counties
in England
peer the Earl of Bridgewater
mickle great

awe awesomeness
nation the Welsh
pérplexed tangled
wood The dark wood at the opening of Dante's
Inferno and Book I of Spenser's *Faerie Queene*
represents the moral difficulties and obscurities
of life.
mariners transformed by Bacchus, whom they
had captured, into dolphins. The construction
is latinate *(post nautas mutatos)*, an early
instance of what was to become a dominant
feature of Milton's diction.
Circe's See Headnote.

Whoever tasted, lost his upright shape,
And downward fell into a groveling swine).
This nymph that gazed upon his clustering locks,
With ivy berries wreathed, and his blithe youth,
Had by him, ere he parted thence, a son
Much like his father, but his mother more,
Whom therefore she brought up and Comus° named;
Who, ripe and frolic° of his full-grown age,
60 Roving the Celtic and Iberian fields,
At last betakes him to this ominous wood,
And, in thick shelter of black shades embowered,
Excels his mother at her mighty art,
Offering to every weary traveller
His orient° liquor in a crystal glass,
To quench the drouth of Phoebus,° which as they taste
(For most do taste through fond intemperate thirst)
Soon as the potion works, their human countenance,
The express resemblance of the gods,° is changed
70 Into some brutish form of wolf, or bear,
Or ounce,° or tiger, hog, or bearded goat,
All other parts remaining as they were;°
And they, so perfect is their misery,
Not once perceive their foul disfigurement,
But boast themselves more comely than before
And all their friends, and native home forget
To roll with pleasure in a sensual sty.
Therefore when any favoured of high Jove
Chances to pass through this adventurous glade,
80 Swift as the sparkle of a glancing° star
I shoot from heaven to give him safe convoy,
As now I do—but first I must put off
These my sky-robes, spun out of Iris' woof,°
And take the weeds° and likeness of a swain
That to the service of this house belongs,
Who with his soft pipe and smooth-dittied song
Well knows to still the wild winds when they roar,
And hush the waving woods;° nor of less faith,°
And in this office of his mountain watch
90 Likeliest, and nearest to the present aid

Comus See Headnote.
frolic joyful
orient sparkling
drouth of Phoebus thirst caused by the sun
The express . . . gods "God created man in his
image" (Genesis 1:27)
ounce lynx
All . . . were Necessities of production (animal-
head masks are easier to manage than animal
suits) and emblematic meaning (the head,
the highest, most divine and least animal part

of man, is reduced to the bestial status of his
lower organs and limbs) here combine to
produce the monsters of Comus's retinue.
glancing shooting
Iris' woof rainbow fabric
weeds costume; cf. l. 16
That . . . woods Henry Lawes, a composer and
tutor, playing the part of the Spirit, is likened
to Orpheus, whose music was indeed so commanding.
nor of less faith no less loyal

Of this occasion. But I heard the tread
Of hateful steps; I must be viewless° now.

[COMUS *enters with a charming-rod in one hand, his glass in the other;
with him a rout of monsters headed like sundry sorts of wild beasts, but
otherwise like men and women, their apparel glistering. They come in
making a riotous and unruly noise, with torches in their hands.*]

COMUS   The star° that bids the shepherd fold°
Now the top of heaven doth hold,
And the gilded car° of day
His glowing axle doth allay°
In the steep Atlantic stream,
And the slope sun his upward beam
Shoots against the dusky pole,
100   Pacing toward the other goal
Of his chamber in the east.
Meanwhile welcome joy and feast,
Midnight shout and revelry,
Tipsy dance and jollity.
Braid your locks with rosy twine
Dropping odours, dropping wine.
Rigour now is gone to bed,
And Advice with scrupulous head,
Strict Age, and sour Severity,
110   With their grave saws° in slumber lie.
We that are of purer fire
Imitate the starry quire,
Who in their nightly watchful spheres
Lead in swift round the months and years.°
The sounds and seas with all their finny drove
Now to the moon in wavering morris° move,
And on the tawny sands and shelves
Trip the pert fairies and the dapper elves;
By dimpled brook and fountain brim
120   The wood-nymphs, decked with daisies trim,
Their merry wakes° and pastimes keep:
What hath night to do with sleep?
Night hath better sweets to prove,
Venus now wakes, and wakens Love.
Come, let us our rites begin;
'Tis only daylight that makes sin,
Which these dun shades will ne'er report.

viewless invisible
star Hesperus, the Evening Star
fold pen up the sheep
car chariot
allay cool
saws maxims
the starry . . . years The heavenly motions,

imaged as "the music of the spheres" in antiquity and later, were also thought of by Plato in *Timaeus* 40 as a great dance of the spheres (see *Astronomy*... in the Glossary).
morris morris dance (from "Moorish")
wakes night-long ceremonies

Hail, goddess of nocturnal sport,
Dark-veiled Cotytto,° to whom the secret flame
130 Of midnight torches burns; mysterious dame,
That ne'er art called but when the dragon womb
Of Stygian darkness spits her thickest gloom,
And makes one blot of all the air,
Stay thy cloudy ebon chair
Wherein thou rid'st with Hecat',° and befriend
Us thy vowed priests, till utmost end
Of all thy dues be done, and none left out
Ere the blabbing eastern scout,
The nice Morn° on the Indian steep,°
140 From her cabined loop-hole peep,
And to the tell-tale Sun descry°
Our concealed solemnity.°
Come, knit hands, and beat the ground,
In a light fantastic round.°

       [*The Measure*°]

Break off, break off, I feel the different pace
Of some chaste footing near about this ground.
Run to your shrouds° within these brakes and trees;
Our number may affright: some virgin sure
(For so I can distinguish by mine art)
150 Benighted in these woods. Now to my charms
And to my wily trains;° I shall ere long
Be well stocked with as fair a herd as grazed
About my mother Circe. Thus I hurl
My dazzling spells into the spongy air,
Of power to cheat the eye with blear° illusion,
And give it false presentments,° lest the place
And my quaint habits° breed astonishment,
And put the damsel to suspicious flight,
Which must not be, for that's against my course;
160 I, under fair pretence of friendly ends,
And well-placed words of glozing° courtesy
Baited with reasons not unplausible,
Wind me into the easy-hearted man,
And hug him into snares. When once her eye
Hath met the virtue° of this magic dust,

Cotytto Thracian goddess whose nocturnal rites were reputedly wildly lascivious
Hecat' Hecate, the witch goddess
nice Morn the overly fastidious goddess Aurora
Indian steep the Himalayas
descry reveal
solemnity celebration
round ring dance
Measure the antic dance of what would, in a traditional masque, have been the antimasque, or grotesque counterpart of the main dance and mythology
shrouds hiding places
trains allurements
blear deceiving
false presentments fake visions
quaint habits strange costume
glozing flattering
virtue power

I shall appear some harmless villager
Whom thrift keeps up about his country gear.
But here she comes; I fairly° step aside,
And hearken, if I may, her business here.

[THE LADY *enters*]

170   LADY   This way the noise was, if mine ear be true,
My best guide now. Methought it was the sound
Of riot and ill-managed merriment,
Such as the jocund flute or gamesome pipe
Stirs up among the loose unlettered hinds,°
When for their teeming° flocks, and granges° full,
In wanton dance they praise the bounteous Pan,°
And thank the gods amiss. I should be loth
To meet the rudeness and swilled insolence
Of such late wássailers;° yet O where else
180   Shall I inform my unacquainted feet
In the blind mazes of this tangled wood?
My brothers, when they saw me wearied out
With this long way, resolving here to lodge
Under the spreading favour of these pines,
Stepped as they said to the next thicket side
To bring me berries, or such cooling fruit
As the kind hospitable woods provide.
They left me then when the grey-hooded Even,
Like a sad votarist in palmer's weed,°
190   Rose from the hindmost wheels of Phoebus' wain.°
But where they are, and why they came not back,
Is now the labour of my thoughts; 'tis likeliest
They had engaged their wandering steps too far,
And envious darkness, ere they could return,
Had stole them from me—Else, O thievish Night,
Why shouldst thou, but for some felonious end,
In thy dark lantern thus close up the stars
That Nature hung in heaven, and filled their lamps
With everlasting oil, to give due light
200   To the misled and lonely traveller?
This is the place, as well as I may guess,
Whence even now the tumult of loud mirth
Was rife, and perfect in my listening ear,
Yet naught but single° darkness do I find.
What might this be? A thousand fantasies
Begin to throng into my memory

fairly silently
hinds farmhands
teeming both overflowing or abundant
granges barns
Pan god of woods and shepherds

wássailers revelers
votarist . . . weed pilgrim to the Holy Land
wain wagon
single absolute

Of calling shapes, and beckoning shadows dire,
And airy tongues that syllable men's names
On sands and shores and desert wildernesses.
210 These thoughts may startle well, but not astound
The virtuous mind, that ever walks attended
By a strong siding° champion, Consc̈ience.
O welcome, pure-eyed Faith, white-handed Hope,
Thou hovering angel girt with golden wings,
And thou unblemished form of Chastity,
I see ye visibly, and now believe
That He, the supreme Good, to whom all things ill
Are but as slavish officers of vengeance,
Would send a glistering guardian if need were
220 To keep my life and honour unassailed.
Was I deceived, or did a sable cloud
Turn forth her silver lining on the night?
I did not err, there does a sable cloud
Turn forth her silver lining on the night,°
And casts a gleam over this tufted grove.
I cannot hallo to my brothers, but
Such noise as I can make to be heard farthest
I'll venture, for my new-enlivened spirits
Prompt me; and they perhaps are not far off.

SONG°

230 *Sweet Echo, sweetest nymph that liv'st unseen*
    Within thy airy shell°
  By slow Maeander's margent° green,
And in the violet-embroidered vale
  Where the lovelorn nightingale
Nightly to thee her sad song mourneth well:
Canst thou not tell me of a gentle pair
  That likest thy Narcissus are?
    O if thou have
  Hid them in some flowery cave,
240   *Tell me but where,*
Sweet queen of parley,° daughter of the sphere;
So mayest thou be translated to the skies,
And give resounding grace° to all heaven's harmonies.

---

siding defending
Was I . . . night This exact repetition in answer
to a rhetorical question may seem almost ludi-
crous, but (1) these lines were not in the acting script; (2) they have a rhetorical source
in Ovid (*Fasti* V.549) for their use on the page;
and (3) they do serve to indicate the Lady's
calm self-possession.
Song The Lady's song to Echo is a prayer for
amplification (by natural acoustic means) of
her call, and also a song to her solitariness; unlike operatic "echo scenes" there is no audible
answer from hidden chorus or whatever, but the
effects on Comus are quite apparent.
shell personified echoes inhabit caverns; "shell"
has the sense both of "cell" or cave, and of the
higher "shell" of the arched sky
Maeander's margent the margin, or bank of a
(hence) "meandering" river in Asia Minor
parley discourse
resounding grace "grace" also in the musical
sense of embellishments like trills

Lawes's setting of this song uses in its last line Milton's earliest version of the text, which he later rewrote.

COMUS [*Aside*]   Can any mortal mixture of earth's mould
Breathe such divine enchanting ravishment?
Sure something holy lodges in that breast,
And with these raptures moves the vocal air
To testify° his hidden residence;
How sweetly did they float upon the wings
250   Of silence, through the empty-vaulted night,
At every fall° smoothing the raven down
Of darkness till it smiled. I have oft heard
My mother Circe with the Sirens three,°
Amidst the flowery-kirtled Naiades,°
Culling their potent herbs and baleful drugs,
Who as they sung would take the prisoned soul

testify attest to
fall musical cadence
Circe . . . three Milton means the sirens whose

song bewitched sailors; in Milton, they attend
Circe, but not in Homer.
flowery-kirtled Naiades fresh-water nymphs, perhaps dressed in pond lilies

And lap it in Elysium; Scylla° wept,
And chid her barking waves into attention,
And fell Charybdis murmured soft applause.
260   Yet they in pleasing slumber lulled the sense,
And in sweet madness robbed it of itself;
But such a sacred and home-felt° delight,
Such sober certainty of waking bliss,
I never heard till now. I'll speak to her,
And she shall be my queen. Hail, foreign wonder,
Whom certain these rough shades did never breed,
Unless° the goddess that in rural shrine
Dwellest here with Pan or Sylvan, by blest song
Forbidding every bleak unkindly fog
270   To touch the prosperous growth of this tall wood.
    LADY   Nay, gentle shepherd, ill is lost that praise
That is addressed to unattending ears;
Not any boast of skill, but éxtreme shift
How to regain my severed company
Compelled me to awake the courteous Echo
To give me answer from her mossy couch.
    COMUS   What chance, good lady, hath bereft you thus?
    LADY   Dim darkness and this leafy labyrinth.
    COMUS   Could that divide you from near-ushering guides?
280   LADY   They left me weary on a grassy turf.
    COMUS   By falsehood, or discourtesy, or why?
    LADY   To seek i' th' valley some cool friendly spring.
    COMUS   And left your fair side all unguarded, lady?
    LADY   They were but twain, and purposed quick return.
    COMUS   Perhaps forestalling night prevented them.
    LADY   How easy my misfortune is to hit!°
    COMUS   Imports their loss,° beside the present need?
    LADY   No less than if I should my brothers lose.
    COMUS   Were they of manly prime, or youthful bloom?
290   LADY   As smooth as Hebe's° their unrazored lips.
    COMUS   Two such I saw, what time the laboured ox
In his loose traces from the furrow came,°
And the swinked hedger° at his supper sat;
I saw them under a green mantling vine
That crawls along the side of yon small hill,
Plucking ripe clusters from the tender shoots;
Their port° was more than human, as they stood.
I took it for a faëry vision

Scylla . . . Charybdis The monster and, across
the straights of Messina from her, the whirlpool—all these Odyssean allusions are associated
with Circe.
home-felt deeply felt
Unless unless you are
Dim . . . labyrinth This line-for-line dialogue
imitates the stichomythia of Greek drama.

hit guess
Imports their loss does losing them matter
Hebe's the youth goddess and Olympian cup-
bearer
what time . . . came Unyoking the oxen is a
symbol of nightfall in Homer and Virgil.
swinked hedger tired hedge-cutter
port bearing

Of some gay creatures of the element,°
300 That in the colours of the rainbow live
And play i' th' plighted° clouds. I was awe-strook,
And as I passed, I worshipped; if those you seek,
It were a journey like the path to heaven
To help you find them.
    LADY   Gentle villager,°
What readiest way would bring me to that place?
    COMUS   Due west it rises from this shrubby point.
    LADY   To find out that, good shepherd, I suppose,
In such a scant allowance of star-light,
Would overtask the best land-pilot's art
310 Without the sure guess of well-practised feet.
    COMUS   I know each lane and every alley green,
Dingle° or bushy dell of this wild wood,
And every bosky bourn° from side to side
My daily walks and ancient neighbourhood,
And if your stray attendance° be yet lodged,
Or shroud° within these limits, I shall know
Ere morrow wake or the low-roosted lark
From her thatched pallet° rouse; if otherwise,
I can conduct you, lady, to a low
320 But loyal cottage, where you may be safe
Till further quest.
    LADY   Shepherd, I take thy word,
And trust thy honest-offered courtesy,
Which oft is sooner found in lowly sheds
With smoky rafters, than in tap'stry halls
And courts of princes, where it first was named,
And yet is most pretended. In a place
Less warranted than this, or less secure,
I cannot be, that I should fear to change it.
Eye me, blest Providence, and square my trial
330 To my proportioned strength. Shepherd, lead on.
       [*Exeunt*]

[*The two Brothers*]

    ELDER BROTHER   Unmuffle, ye faint stars, and thou, fair moon,
That wont'st to love the traveller's benison,
Stoop thy pale visage through an amber cloud,
And disinherit° Chaos, that reigns here
In double night of darkness and of shades;

element in this case, air
plighted folded
Gentle villager Comus is, of course, disguised
as a Shropshire countryman, to trap the Lady's
own "gentleness" which would assume no connection between rusticity or humble condition
and evil.

Dingle hollow
bosky bourn bushy brook
attendance attendants
shroud hide themselves
pallet straw bed
disinherit dispossess

Or if your influence be quite dammed up
With black usurping mists, some gentle taper
Though a rush-candle from the wicker hole
Of some clay habitation, visit us
340   With thy long levelled rule of streaming light,
And thou shalt be our star of Arcady,
Or Tyrian Cynosure.°
    SECOND BROTHER   Or if our eyes
Be barred that happiness, might we but hear
The folded flocks penned in their wattled cotes,°
Or sound of pastoral reed with oaten stops,°
Or whistle from the lodge, or village cock
Count the night-watches to his feathery dames,
'Twould be some solace yet, some little cheering,
In this close dungeon of innumerous° boughs.
350   But O that hapless virgin, our lost sister,
Where may she wander now, whither betake her
From the chill dew, amongst rude burrs and thistles?
Perhaps some cold bank is her bolster now,
Or 'gainst the rugged bark of some broad elm
Leans her unpillowed head fraught with sad fears.
What if in wild amazement and affright,
Or, while we speak, within the direful grasp
Of savage hunger or of savage heat?
    ELDER BROTHER   Peace, brother, be not over-exquisite°
360   To cast° the fashion of uncertain evils;
For grant they be so, while they rest unknown,
What need a man forestall his date of grief,
And run to meet what he would most avoid?
Or if they be but false alarms of fear,
How bitter is such self-delusïon?
I do not think my sister so to seek,°
Or so unprincipled in virtue's book,
And the sweet peace that goodness bosoms ever,
As that the single° want of light and noise
370   (Not being in danger, as I trust she is not)
Could stir the constant mood of her calm thoughts,
And put them into misbecoming plight.
Virtue could see to do what Virtue would
By her own radiant light, though sun and moon
Were in the flat sea sunk. And Wisdom's self
Oft seeks to sweet retired solitude,

---

star . . . Cynosure Ursa Major or Ursa Minor
(containing the pole star); Greek mariners
steered by the first, Phoenicians by the second
wattled cotes sheepfolds of interwoven branches
pastoral . . . stops The reed flute symbolized
pastoral poetry; cf. the "oaten pipe" of Colin
Clout in Spenser, *The Shepheards Calender,*
January Eclogue, l. 72, and the "oaten flute" in
Lycidas, l. 33.
innumerous numberless
over-exquisite too subtle
cast forecast
so to seek so lacking (here, virtue)
single mere

Where with her best nurse, Contemplatïon,
She plumes her feathers, and lets grow her wings,
That in the various bustle of resort
380 Were all to-ruffled,° and sometimes impaired.
He that has light within his own clear breast
May sit i' th'centre° and enjoy bright day,
But he that hides a dark soul and foul thoughts
Benighted walks under the mid-day sun;
Himself is his own dungeon.

SECOND BROTHER   'Tis most true
That musing meditation most affects
The pensive secrecy of desert cell,
Far from the cheerful haunt of men and herds,
And sits as safe as in a senate-house;
390 For who would rob a hermit of his weeds,
His few books, or his beads, or maple dish,
Or do his grey hairs any violence?
But beauty, like the fair Hesperian tree
Laden with blooming gold,° had need the guard
Of dragon-watch with unenchanted° eye
To save her blossoms and defend her fruit
From the rash hand of bold Incontinence.
You may as well spread out the unsunned heaps
Of miser's treasure by an outlaw's den,
400 And tell me it is safe, as bid me hope
Danger will wink on opportunity,
And let a single helpless maiden pass
Uninjured in this wild surrounding waste.
Of night or loneliness it recks me not;°
I fear the dread events that dog them both,
Lest some ill-greeting touch attempt the person
Of our unowned° sister.

ELDER BROTHER   I do not, brother,
Infer as if I thought my sister's state
Secure without all doubt or controversy;
410 Yet where an equal poise of hope and fear
Does arbitrate the event, my nature is
That I incline to hope rather than fear,
And gladly banish squint° suspicïon.
My sister is not so defenceless left
As you imagine; she has a hidden strength
Which you remember not.

SECOND BROTHER   What hidden strength,

---

to-ruffled ruffled up
centre of the earth
blooming gold the golden apples of the Hesperides
unenchanted unenchantable (Milton liked this
phrase so much that he reinserted it here after

having cut it from another place in the MS.;
cf. similar latinate use of participle in l. 215)
it recks me not I don't care
unowned unguarded
squint squinting

Unless the strength of heaven, if you mean that?
    ELDER BROTHER   I mean that too, but yet a hidden strength
Which, if heaven gave it, may be termed her own
420   —'Tis chastity, my brother, chastity:
She that has that is clad in cómplete steel,
And like a quivered° nymph with arrows keen
May trace huge forests and unharboured heaths,
Infamous hills and sandy perilous wilds,
Where, through the sacred rays of chastity,
No savage fierce, bandit, or mountaineer
Will dare to soil her virgin purity.
Yea, there where very desolation dwells,
By grots and caverns shagged with horrid shades,
430   She may pass on with unblenched° majesty,
Be it not done in pride or in presumption.
Some say no evil thing that walks by night
In fog or fire,° by lake or moorish fen,
Blue meagre hag, or stubborn unlaid° ghost
That breaks his magic chains at curfew time,
No goblin or swart fairy of the mine,
Hath hurtful power o'er true virginity.
Do ye believe me yet, or shall I call
Antiquity from the old schools° of Greece
440   To testify the arms of chastity?
Hence had the huntress Dian her dread bow,
Fair silver-shafted queen for ever chaste,
Wherewith she tamed the brinded° lioness
And spotted mountain pard,° but set at naught
The frivolous bolt of Cupid; gods and men
Feared her stern frown, and she was queen o' th' woods.
What was that snaky-headed Gorgon shield
That wise Minerva wore,° unconquered virgin,
Wherewith she freezed her foes to cóngealed stone,
450   But rigid looks of chaste austerity,
And noble grace that dashed brute violence
With sudden adoration and blank awe?
So dear to heaven is saintly chastity
That when a soul is found sincerely so,
A thousand liveried angels lackey° her,
Driving far off each thing of sin and guilt,
And in clear dream and solemn visïon
Tell her of things that no gross ear can hear,

---

quivered carrying a quiver of arrows; a nymph of Diana, the virgin goddess of the hunt
unblenched undismayed
fire *ignis fatuus:* will-o'-the-wisp or phosphorescent light
unlaid unexorcised
schools philosophical traditions

brinded tawny
pard panther
Minerva wore Athena (Minerva) had Medusa's petrifying head on her shield because, said a Renaissance mythographer, no one can turn his eyes against wisdom with impunity.
lackey attend

Till oft converse with heavenly habitants
460   Begin to cast a beam on the outward shape,
The unpolluted temple of the mind,
And turns it by degrees to the soul's essence,
Till all be made immortal. But when lust,
By unchaste looks, loose gestures, and foul talk,
But most by lewd and lavish act of sin,
Lets in defilement to the inward parts,
The soul grows clotted by contagion,°
Imbodies and imbrutes, till she quite lose
The divine property of her first being.
470   Such are those thick and gloomy shadows damp
Oft seen in charnel vaults and sepulchres
Lingering, and sitting by a new-made grave,
As loth to leave the body that it loved,
And linked itself by carnal sensuality
To a degenerate and degraded state.
    SECOND BROTHER   How charming is divine philosophy!
Not harsh and crabbèd, as dull fools suppose,
But musical as is Apollo's lute,
And a perpetual feast of nectared sweets,
Where no crude surfeit reigns.
480   ELDER BROTHER   List! list, I hear
Some far-off hallo break the silent air.
    SECOND BROTHER   Methought so too; what should it be?
    ELDER BROTHER   For certain,
Either some one like us night-foundered° here,
Or else some neighbour woodman, or at worst,
Some roving robber calling to his fellows.
    SECOND BROTHER   Heaven keep my sister! Again, again, and near!
Best draw, and stand upon our guard.
    ELDER BROTHER   I'll hallo;
If he be friendly, he comes well; if not,
Defense is a good cause, and Heaven be for us.

    [THE ATTENDANT SPIRIT, *habited like a shepherd*]

490   That hallo I should know; what are you? speak.
Come not too near, you fall on iron stakes° else.
    SPIRIT   What voice is that? my young lord? speak again.
    SECOND BROTHER   O brother, 'tis my father's shepherd, sure.
    ELDER BROTHER   Thyrsis,° whose artful strains have oft delayed
The huddling brook° to hear his madrigal,

The soul . . . contagion Plato's *Phaedo* 81 provides the doctrine for this explanation of why ghosts are always the souls of those who made of their bodies a prison while alive.
night-foundered sunk in night
iron stakes swords
Thyrsis name of a pastoral singer from Theo-critus and Virgil; it is the Attendant Spirit in disguise, or rather incarnated as a literary figure whose name Milton might have used to praise Henry Lawes, who is playing the part
huddling brook its waves crowd together to stop and listen

And sweetened every musk-rose of the dale,
How camest thou here, good swain? Hath any ram
Slipped from the fold, or young kid lost his dam,
Or straggling wether° the pent flock forsook?
500 How couldst thou find this dark sequestered nook?

    SPIRIT   O my loved master's heir, and his next° joy,
I came not here on such a trivial toy
As a strayed ewe, or to pursue the stealth
Of pilfering wolf; not all the fleecy wealth
That doth enrich these downs is worth a thought
To this my errand, and the care it brought.
But O my virgin lady, where is she?°
How chance she is not in your company?

    ELDER BROTHER   To tell thee sadly,° shepherd, without blame
510 Or our neglect, we lost her as we came.

    SPIRIT   Ay me unhappy, then my fears are true.

    ELDER BROTHER   What fears, good Thyrsis? Prithee briefly shew.

    SPIRIT   I'll tell ye. 'Tis not vain or fabulous°
(Though so esteemed by shallow ignorance)
What the sage poets, taught by the heavenly Muse,
Storied of old in high immortal verse
Of dire Chimeras and enchanted isles,
And rifted rocks whose entrance leads to hell—
For such there be, but unbelief is blind.
520   Within the navel° of this hideous wood,
Immured in cypress shades, a sorcerer dwells,
Of Bacchus and of Circe born, great Comus,
Deep skilled in all his mother's witcheries,
And here to every thirsty wanderer
By sly enticement gives his baneful cup,
With many murmurs° mixed, whose pleasing poison
The visage quite transforms of him that drinks,
And the inglorious likeness of a beast
Fixes instead, unmoulding reason's mintage
530 Charáctered° in the face; this have I learnt
Tending my flocks hard by i' th' hilly crofts°
That brow° this bottom glade, whence night by night
He and his monstrous rout are heard to howl
Like stabled wolves, or tigers at their prey,
Doing abhorrèd rites to Hecate
In their obscurèd haunts of inmost bowers.

wether castrated ram
next nearest and dearest
where is she? The Spirit clearly knows (see ll. 561–76) and the question is rhetorical in a way, drawing the audience's attention to the following long description.
sady seriously
fabulous mythical. The Spirit is here stating a basic position of Renaissance mythography,

namely, that not only did these old stories have ethical and psychological significance, but that they represented slightly misshapen versions of biblical truths.
navel center
murmurs incantations
Charactered imprinted
crofts small farms
brow overlook

Yet have they many baits and guileful spells
To inveigle and invite the unwary sense
Of them that pass unweeting° by the way.
540 This evening late, by then° the chewing flocks
Had ta'en their supper on the savoury herb
Of knot-grass dew-besprent, and were in fold,
I sat me down to watch upon a bank
With ivy canopied, and interwove
With flaunting honeysuckle, and began,
Wrapped in a pleasing fit of melancholy,
To meditate my rural minstrelsy,°
Till fancy had her fill. But ere a close°
The wonted roar was up amidst the woods,
550 And filled the air with barbarous dissonance,
At which I ceased, and listened them a while,
Till an unusual stop of sudden silence
Gave respite to the drowsy frighted steeds
That draw the litter of close-curtained Sleep.
At last a soft and solemn-breathing sound
Rose like a steam of rich distilled perfumes,
And stole upon the air, that even Silence
Was took ere she was ware, and wished she might
Deny her nature and be never more,
560 Still to be so displaced. I was all ear,
And took in strains that might create a soul
Under the ribs of Death, but O ere long
Too well I did perceive it was the voice
Of my most honoured lady, your dear sister.
Amazed I stood, harrowed with grief and fear,
And 'O poor hapless nightingale,' thought I,
'How sweet thou sing'st, how near the deadly snare!'
Then down the lawns I ran with headlong haste
Through paths and turnings often trod by day,
570 Till guided by mine ear I found the place
Where that damned wizard, hid in sly disguise
(For so by certain signs I knew), had met
Already, ere my best speed could prevent,
The aidless innocent lady, his wished prey,
Who gently asked if he had seen such two,
Supposing him some neighbour villager;
Longer I durst not stay, but soon I guessed
Ye were the two she meant; with that I sprung
Into swift flight, till I had found you here;
But further know I not.
580   SECOND BROTHER   O night and shades,

unweeting heedless   To meditate . . . minstrelsy to play a shep-
by then when   herd's pipe
                                      close musical cadence

How are ye joined with hell in triple knot
Against the unarmèd weakness of one virgin
Alone and helpless! Is this the confidence
You gave me, brother?

ELDER BROTHER   Yes, and keep it still,
Lean on it safely; not a period°
Shall be unsaid, for me—against the threats
Of malice or of sorcery, or that power
Which erring men call chance, this I hold firm:
Virtue may be assailed, but never hurt,
590   Surprised by unjust force, but not enthralled,
Yea, even that which mischief meant most harm
Shall in the happy trial prove most glory.
But evil on itself shall back recoil,
And mix no more with goodness, when at last,
Gathered like scum, and settled to itself,
It shall be in eternal restless change
Self-fed and self-consumèd;° if this fail,
The pillared firmament is rottenness,
And earth's base built on stubble. But come, let's on.
600   Against the opposing will and arm of heaven
May never this just sword be lifted up;
But for that damned magician, let him be girt
With all the grisly legïons that troop
Under the sooty flag of Acheron,°
Harpies° and Hydras,° or all the monstrous forms
'Twixt Africa and Ind, I'll find him out,
And force him to restore his purchase° back,
Or drag him by the curls to a foul death,
Cursed as his life.

SPIRIT   Alas, good venturous youth,
610   I love thy courage yet, and bold emprise,°
But here thy sword can do thee little stead;
For other arms and other weapons must
Be those that quell the might of hellish charms.
He with his bare wand can unthread thy joints,
And crumble all thy sinews.

ELDER BROTHER   Why, prithee, shepherd,
How durst thou then thyself approach so near
As to make this relation?

SPIRIT   Care and utmost shifts
How to secure the lady from surprisal
Brought to my mind a certain shepherd lad,
620   Of small regard to see to, yet well skilled

period sentence
But evil . . . self-consumed Cf. *Paradise Lost*
II.795–802.
Acheron one of the rivers of Hades; hell itself
Harpies horrible birds with women's faces

Hydras nine-headed monsters of the species
killed by Hercules
purchase prey
emprise enterprise

In every virtuous° plant and healing herb
That spreads her verdant leaf to the morning ray.
He loved me well, and oft would beg me sing;
Which when I did, he on the tender grass
Would sit, and hearken even to ecstasy,
And in requital ope his leathern scrip,°
And show me simples° of a thousand names,
Telling their strange and vigorous faculties;
Amongst the rest a small unsightly root,
630   But of divine effect, he culled me out;
The leaf was darkish, and had prickles on it,
But in another country, as he said,
Bore a bright golden flower, but not in this soil:
Unknown, and like esteemed, and the dull swain
Treads on it daily with his clouted shoon,°
And yet more med'cinal is it than that moly°
That Hermes once to wise Ulysses gave;
He called it haemony,° and gave it me,
And bade me keep it as of sovereign use
640   'Gainst all enchantments, mildew blast, or damp,
Or ghastly Furies' apparïtion;
I pursed it up, but little reckoning made,
Till now that this extremity compelled,
But now I find it true; for by this means
I knew the foul enchanter though disguised,
Entered the very lime-twigs° of his spells,
And yet came off. If you have this about you
(As I will give you when we go), you may
Boldly assault the necromancer's hall,
650   Where if he be, with dauntless hardihood
And brandished blade rush on him, break his glass,
And shed the luscious liquor on the ground,°
But seize his wand. Though he and his cursed crew
Fierce sign of battle make, and menace high,
Or like the sons of Vulcan vomit smoke,
Yet will they soon retire, if he but shrink.
    ELDER BROTHER   Thyrsis, lead on apace, I'll follow thee,
And some good angel bear a shield before us.

The scene changes to a stately palace, set out with all manner of deliciousness: soft music, tables spread with all dainties. COMUS *appears*

---

virtuous pharmacologically potent
scrip bag
simples medicinal herbs; called so because used uncompounded
clouted shoon hobnailed shoes
moly Hermes gave Odysseus this magic plant as an antidote to the transforming spells of Circe.
haemony See Headnote.

lime-twigs Twigs, smeared with lime, were used to trap birds.
And shed . . . ground one of many Spenserian reminiscences in this work; in the Bower of Bliss, Guyon breaks the cup of excess "And with the liquor stainèd all the lond" (*The Faërie Queene* II.xii.57); by this allusion, the overthrow of Comus is made to parallel Acrasia's in moral significance

with his rabble, and THE LADY *set in an enchanted chair, to whom he offers his glass, which she puts by, and goes about to rise.*

COMUS   Nay, lady, sit; if I but wave this wand,
660   Your nerves° are all chained up in alabaster,°
And you a statue, or as Daphne° was
Root-bound, that fled Apollo.
LADY   Fool, do not boast;
Thou canst not touch the freedom of my mind
With all thy charms, although this corporal rind
Thou hast immanacled,° while heaven sees good.
COMUS   Why are you vexed, lady? why do you frown?
Here dwell no frowns, nor anger; from these gates
Sorrow flies far: see, here be all the pleasures
That fancy can beget on youthful thoughts,.
670   When the fresh blood grows lively, and returns
Brisk as the April buds in primrose season.
And first behold this cordial julep here
That flames and dances in his crystal bounds
With spirits of balm and fragrant syrups mixed.
Not that nepenthes which the wife of Thone
In Egypt gave to Jove-born Helena°
Is of such power to stir up joy as this,
To life so friendly, or so cool to thirst.
Why should you be so cruel to yourself,
680   And to those dainty limbs which Nature lent
For gentle usage and soft delicacy?
But you invert the covenants of her trust,
And harshly deal like an ill borrower
With that which you received on other terms,
Scorning the unexempt conditïon
By which all mortal frailty must subsist,
Refreshment after toil, ease after pain,
That have been tired all day without repast,
And timely rest have wanted; but, fair virgin,
This will restore all soon.
690   LADY   'Twill not, false traitor,
'Twill not restore the truth and honesty
That thou hast banished from thy tongue with lies.
Was this the cottage and the safe abode
Thou told'st me of? What grim aspécts are these,
These ugly-headed monsters? Mercy guard me!
Hence with thy brewed enchantments, foul deceiver;
Hast thou betrayed my credulous innocence

---

nerves muscles
alabaster marble
Daphne Fleeing Apollo's desiring grasp, she turned into a laurel bush.
immanacled chained up

nepenthes . . . Helena In the *Odyssey* IV. 219–32 Helen gives her husband Menelaus an Egyptian drug of an opium-like sort to drive away his grief.

With vizored falsehood and base forgery,°
And wouldst thou seek again to trap me here
700 With lickerish° baits fit to ensnare a brute?
Were it a draught for Juno when she banquets,
I would not taste thy treasonous offer; none
But such as are good men can give good things,
And that which is not good is not delicious
To a well-governed and wise appetite.
      COMUS   O foolishness of men! that lend their ears
To those budge° doctors of the Stoic fur,°
And fetch their precepts from the Cynic tub,°
Praising the lean and sallow Abstinence.
710 Wherefore did Nature pour her bounties forth
With such a full and unwithdrawing hand,
Covering the earth with odours, fruits, and flocks
Thronging the seas with spawn innumerable,
But all to please and sate the curious taste?
And set to work millions of spinning worms,
That in their green shops weave the smooth-haired silk
To deck her sons, and that no corner might
Be vacant of her plenty, in her own loins
She hutched° the all-worshipped ore and precious gems
720 To store her children with. If all the world
Should in a pet of temperance feed on pulse,°
Drink the clear stream, and nothing wear but frieze,°
The All-giver would be unthanked, would be unpraised,
Not half his riches known, and yet despised;
And we should serve him as a grudging master,
As a penurious niggard of his wealth,
And live like Nature's bastards, not her sons,
Who would be quite surcharged with her own weight,
And strangled with her waste fertility;
730 The earth cumbered, and the winged air darked with plumes;
The herds would over-multitude their lords,
The sea o'erfraught would swell, and the unsought diamonds
Would so emblaze the forehead of the deep,°
And so bestud with stars, that they below
Would grow inured to light, and come at last
To gaze upon the sun with shameless brows.
List, lady, be not coy, and be not cozened°
With that same vaunted name 'Virginity':

forgery deception
lickerish pleasing to the taste, but also with a sense of "lecherous"
budge stiff, pompous (from the fur "budge" on academic gowns)
Stoic fur here, Stoic school or persuasion— Comus is sneering at philosophic asceticism
Cynic tub Diogenes the Cynic also scorned the things of this world; unlike the Stoics Epictetus and Seneca, his views were unsupported by theories of the relation of soul to body and he lived in a tub.
hutched laid away
pulse peas, beans, lentils, etc.
frieze coarse woolen cloth
deep the middle of the earth, specifically the outer layer where mining takes place, and where precious stones were thought to reproduce themselves like living organisms
cozened cheated

Beauty is Nature's coin, must not be hoarded,
740 But must be current, and the good thereof
Consists in mutual and partaken bliss,
Unsavoury in the enjoyment of itself.
If you let slip time, like a neglected rose
It withers on the stalk with languished head.
Beauty is Nature's brag,° and must be shown
In courts, at feasts, and high solemnities
Where most may wonder at the workmanship;
It is for homely features to keep home,
They had their name thence; coarse complexïons
750 And cheeks of sorry grain° will serve to ply
The sampler, and to tease° the housewife's wool.
What need a vermeil°-tinctured lip for that,
Love-darting eyes, or tresses like the morn?
There was another meaning in these gifts,
Think what, and be advised; you are but young yet.
    LADY   I had not thought to have unlocked my lips
In this unhallowed air, but that this juggler
Would think to charm my judgment, as mine eyes,
Obtruding false rules pranked° in reason's garb.
760 I hate when vice can bolt° her arguments,
And virtue has no tongue to check her pride.
Impostor, do not charge most innocent Nature,
As if she would her children should be riotous
With her abundance; she, good cateress,
Means her provision only to the good,
That live according to her sober laws
And holy dictate of spare Temperance.
If every just man that now pines with want
Had but a moderate and beseeming share
770 Of that which lewdly pampered luxury
Now heaps upon some few with vast excess,
Nature's full blessings would be well dispensed
In unsuperfluous even proportïon,
And she no whit encumbered with her store;
And then the Giver would be better thanked,
His praise due paid, for swinish gluttony
Ne'er looks to heaven amidst his gorgeous feast,
But with besotted base ingratitude
Crams, and blasphemes his Feeder. Shall I go on?
780 Or have I said enough? To him that dares
Arm his profane tongue with contemptuous words
Against the sun-clad power of Chastity,
Fain would I something say, yet to what end?

brag boast   vermeil vermilion
grain color   pranked decked out
tease comb   bolt sift; refine

Thou hast nor ear nor soul to apprehend
The sublime notion and high mystery°
That must be uttered to unfold the sage
And serious doctrine of Virginity,
And thou art worthy that thou shouldst not know
More happiness than this thy present lot.

790 Enjoy your dear wit and gay rhetoric
That hath so well been taught her dazzling fence;°
Thou art not fit to hear thyself convinced.°
Yet should I try, the uncontrollèd worth
Of this pure cause would kindle my rapt° spirits
To such a flame of sacred vehemence
That dumb things would be moved to sympathize,
And the brute Earth would lend her nerves, and shake,
Till all thy magic structures, reared so high,
Were shattered into heaps o'er thy false head.

800   COMUS   She fables not. I feel that I do fear
Her words set off by some superior power;
And though not mortal, yet a cold shuddering dew
Dips me all o'er, as when the wrath of Jove
Speaks thunder and the chains of Erebus°
To some of Saturn's crew.° I must dissemble,
And try her yet more strongly. Come, no more,
This is mere moral babble, and direct
Against the canon laws of our foundation;
I must not suffer this, yet 'tis but the lees°

810 And settlings of a melancholy blood;
But this will cure all straight; one sip of this
Will bathe the drooping spirits in delight
Beyond the bliss of dreams. Be wise, and taste.

[THE BROTHERS *rush in with swords drawn, wrest his glass out of his hand, and break it against the ground; his rout make sign of resistance, but are all driven in;* THE ATTENDANT SPIRIT *comes in*]

SPIRIT   What, have you let the false enchanter scape?
O ye mistook, ye should have snatched his wand
And bound him fast; without his rod reversed,°
And backward mutters of dissevering power,
We cannot free the lady that sits here

mystery Milton writes elsewhere, quoting I Corinthians 6:13, of "unfolding those chaste and high mysteries . . . that 'the body is for the Lord and the Lord for the body' " (*Apology for Smectymnuus,* Columbia Edition, Vol. 3, p. 306).
fence fencing, i.e. debating
convinced refuted
rapt transported
Erebus in Hesiod's account of creation, the son of Chaos, and the original darkness that existed before there was light

Saturn's crew Zeus (Jupiter) overthrew his ruling father Cronus, or Saturn, and imprisoned him in the underworld, Tartarus.
lees dregs of wine, here likened to the melancholy humor of blood
rod reversed In Ovid, *Metamorphoses* XIV.300, Circe's spells are undone by reversing the motion of the wand that cast them; the spells of Spenser's Busyrane are also revoked in this manner (*The Faerie Queene* III.xii.36).

In stony fetters fixed and motionless;
820 Yet stay, be not disturbed; now I bethink me,
Some other means I have which may be used,
Which once of Meliboeus° old I learnt,
The soothest shepherd that e'er piped on plains.
There is a gentle Nymph not far from hence,
That with moist curb sways the smooth Severn° stream;
Sabrina is her name, a virgin pure;
Whilom she was the daughter of Locrine,
That had the sceptre from his father Brute.°
She, guiltless damsel, flying the mad pursuit
830 Of her enragèd stepdame Guendolen,
Commended her fair innocence to the flood
That stayed her flight with his cross-flowing course;
The water-nymphs that in the bottom played
Held up their pearlèd wrists and took her in,
Bearing her straight to aged Nereus'° hall,
Who, piteous of her woes, reared her lank head,
And gave her to his daughters to imbathe
In nectared lavers° strewed with asphodel,°
And through the porch and inlet of each sense
840 Dropped in ambrosial oils, till she revived
And underwent a quick immortal change,
Made goddess of the river. Still she retains
Her maiden gentleness, and oft at eve
Visits the herds along the twilight meadows,
Helping all urchin blasts,° and ill-luck signs
That the shrewd meddling elf delights to make,
Which she with precious vialed liquors heals;
For which the shepherds at their festivals
Carol her goodness loud in rustic lays,
850 And throw sweet garland wreaths into her stream
Of pansies, pinks, and gaudy daffodils.
And, as the old swain° said, she can unlock
The clasping charm and thaw the numbing spell,
If she be right invoked in warbled song;
For maidenhood she loves, and will be swift
To aid a virgin such as was herself
In hard-besetting need: this will I try,
And add the power of some adjuring verse.

Meliboeus Milton's pastoral name for Spenser
Severn the river rising in Wales and flowing through Shropshire to the sea. Sabrina is her mythical personification, whose story Spenser tells in *The Faerie Queene* II.x.19; Milton transforms her into a local spirit for Ludlow Castle and makes her powers more complex and potent than those of a mere water nymph.
Brute in British mythology, Aeneas' great-grandson, who founded Britain
Nereus' father of the Nereids or sea nymphs
lavers basins
asphodel the undying flower growing in the Elysian fields (see Chapman's Homer)
urchin blasts boils or infections caused by the fairies
old swain Meliboeus

SONG

Sabrina fair,
860   Listen where thou art sitting
Under the glassy, cool, translucent wave,
    In twisted braids of lilies knitting
The loose train of thy amber-dropping hair;
    Listen for dear honour's sake,
    Goddess of the silver lake,
    Listen and save.

Listen and appear to us
In name of great Oceanus,°
By the earth-shaking Neptune's mace,°
870   And Tethys'° grave majestic pace,
By hoary Nereus'° wrinkled look,
And the Carpathian wizard's hook,°
By scaly Triton's° winding shell,
And old soothsaying Glaucus'° spell,
By Leucothea's° lovely hands,
And her son that rules the strands,
By Thetis'° tinsel-slippered feet,
And the songs of Sirens sweet,
By dead Parthenope's° dear tomb,
880   And fair Ligea's golden comb,°
Wherewith she sits on diamond rocks
Sleeking her soft alluring locks;
By all the nymphs that nightly dance
Upon thy streams with wily glance,
Rise, rise, and heave thy rosy head
From thy coral-paven bed,
And bridle in thy headlong wave,
Till thou our summons answered have.
                    Listen and save.

[Sabrina rises, attended by water-nymphs, and sings]

890   By the rushy-fringèd bank,
Where grows the willow and the osier dank,
    My sliding chariot stays,°

Oceanus god of the river of ocean which, in
Greek mythology, circled the earth
mace trident
Tethys' his wife
Nereus' See l. 835n.
Carpathian . . . hook the crook of Proteus,
shepherd of Poseidon's (Neptune's) seals
Triton's Triton was Neptune's trumpeter, who
played a conch; "winding" means "being blown
upon" as well as "twisting."
Glaucus' He became a sea god and prophet.
Leucothea's "bright goddess" who helps Odys-
seus in Odyssey V

Thetis' a Nereid, married to Peleus and mother
of Achilles
Parthenope's one of the sirens
Ligea's . . . comb another siren. Virgil mentions her hair, and Milton puts her in standard
mermaid position, sitting on the rocks, combing
her hair.
sliding chariot stays Her "chariot" is the water
itself, awaiting her in the sense that it is
always there, rushing by; the chariot of water
is the subject of l. 895.

Thick set with agate, and the azurn° sheen
Of turkis° blue, and emerald green,
   That in the channel strays.
Whilst from off the waters fleet
Thus I set my printless feet
O'er the cowslip's velvet head,
   That bends not as I tread.
900   *Gentle swain, at thy request*
      I am here.

SPIRIT Goddess dear,
We implore thy powerful hand
To undo the charmèd band
Of true virgin here distressed,
Through the force and through the wile
Of unblest enchanter vile.
    SABRINA Shepherd, 'tis my office best
To help ensnarèd chastity.
910 Brightest lady, look on me;
Thus I sprinkle on thy breast
Drops that from my fountain pure
I have kept of precious cure,
Thrice upon thy finger's tip,
Thrice upon thy rubied lip;
Next this marble venomed seat,
Smeared with gums of glutinous heat,
I touch with chaste palms moist and cold.
Now the spell hath lost his hold,
920 And I must haste ere morning hour
To wait in Amphitrite's° bower.

[SABRINA *descends, and* THE LADY *rises out of her seat*]

SPIRIT Virgin, daughter of Locrine,
Sprung of old Anchises' line,°
May thy brimmèd waves for this
Their full tribute never miss
From a thousand petty rills,
That tumble down the snowy hills;
Summer drouth or singèd air
Never scorch thy tresses fair,
930 Nor wet October's torrent flood
Thy molten crystal fill with mud,
May thy billows roll ashore
The beryl and the golden ore,
May thy lofty head be crowned

azurn azure
turkis turquoise
Amphitrite's Neptune's wife's
Virgin . . . line Sabrina is the daughter of

Locrine, who is the great-granddaughter of Aeneas, who is the son of Anchises; see l. 828n.

With many a tower and terrace round,
And here and there thy banks upon
With groves of myrrh and cinnamon.
   Come, lady, while heaven lends us grace,
Let us fly this cursèd place,
940 Lest the sorcerer us entice
With some other new device.
Not a waste or needless sound
Till we come to holier ground;
I shall be your faithful guide°
Through this gloomy covert wide,
And not many furlongs thence
Is your father's residence,
Where this night are met in state
Many a friend to gratulate
950 His wished presence, and beside
All the swains that there abide
We shall catch them at their sport,
With jigs and rural dance resort;
We shall catch them at their sport,
And our sudden coming there
Will double all their mirth and cheer.
Come let us haste, the stars grow high,
But Night sits monarch yet in the mid sky.

*The scene changes, presenting Ludlow Town and the President's Castle;
then come in Country Dancers, after them* THE ATTENDANT SPIRIT, *with
the* TWO BROTHERS *and* THE LADY.

SONG

SPIRIT   *Back, shepherds, back, enough your play*
Till next sunshine holiday;
960 *Here be without duck° or nod*
Other trippings to be trod
Of lighter toes, and such court guise
As Mercury did first devise
With the mincing Dryades°
On the lawns and on the leas.

[*This second song presents them to their father and mother*]

Noble Lord, and Lady bright,
I have brought ye new delight.

faithful guide Double meanings begin to emerge here as the Spirit, played by their tutor Henry Lawes, leads the Earl of Bridgewater's children (as the Brothers and the Lady) out of the dark wood in whose mythological realm the whole of the action has taken place, and into the transformed scene of "Ludlow Town" and the castle where the very masque is itself being given. What is underlined is how Lawes has indeed been their "guide" in their education, and the act of presenting them to their father occurs both within the fiction of the masque and outside it, as a kind of graduation ceremony.
duck bow or curtsy in country dancing
Dryades dryads, wood nymphs

Here behold so goodly grown
Three fair branches of your own;
970   *Heaven hath timely° tried their youth,*
Their faith, their patience, and their truth,
And sent them here through hard assays
With a crown of deathless praise,
    To triumph in victorious dance
O'er sensual folly and intemperance.

[*The dances ended,* THE SPIRIT *epiloguizes*]

    SPIRIT   To the ocean now I fly,°
And those happy climes that lie
Where day never shuts his eye,
Up in the broad fields of the sky.
980   There I suck the liquid air
All amidst the gardens fair
Of Hesperus, and his daughters three
That sing about the golden tree:°
Along the crispèd° shades and bowers
Revels the spruce and jocund Spring;
The Graces° and the rosy-bosomed Hours°
Thither all their bounties bring,
That there eternal summer dwells,
And west winds with musky wing
990   About the cedarn alleys fling
Nard and cassia's balmy smells.°
Iris° there with humid bow
Waters the odorous banks that blow°
Flowers of more mingled hue
Than her purfled° scarf can shew,
And drenches with Elysian dew
(List, mortals, if your ears be true)
Beds of hyacinth and roses,
Where young Adonis° oft reposes,
1000   Waxing well of his deep wound
In slumber soft, and on the ground

timely early
To . . . fly The ocean which surrounds the earth, and which contains such islands as those of the Hesperidean gardens, but this is also an ocean of heavenly sky, in which drift islands of light. This vision, like so many Renaissance earthly paradises, combines many elements from classical mythology: the Elysian fields and the Hesperides were often associated, and Milton has assimilated the vision of Venus and Adonis from Spenser's Garden of Adonis (in *The Faerie Queene* III.vi) as well. In the performance of the masque, the Spirit opened with a version of these lines, presenting his realm of origin in a more detailed way.
golden tree on which the golden apples grew
crispèd curled

Graces Euphrosyne, Aglaia, Thalia; see Spenser, *The Faerie Queene* VI.x
Hours goddesses of seasonal cycle and changing times, frequently associated with spring
Nard and cassia's balmy smells spikenard and a cinnamon-like bark
Iris the rainbow
blow cause to blossom
purfled with a decorated border
Adonis Here Venus and Adonis seem to be in a more transitional state than in Spenser, where they lie at the world's center of generation; here, Adonis is recovering from his wound, asleep, and Venus ("the Assyrian queen") sits "sadly" by; upon recovery, Adonis will presumably advance beyond this phase of representing wounded sexual love.

Sadly sits the Assyrian queen;
But far above in spangled sheen
Celestial Cupid,° her famed son, advanced,
Holds his dear Psyche sweet entranced
After her wandering labours long,
Till free consent the gods among
Make her his eternal bride,
And from her fair unspotted side
1010   Two blissful twins are to be born,
Youth and Joy; so Jove hath sworn.
    But now my task is smoothly done,
I can fly, or I can run
Quickly to the green earth's end,
Where the bowed welkin° slow doth bend,
And from thence can soar as soon
To the corners of the moon.
    Mortals that would follow me,
Love Virtue, she alone is free;
1020   She can teach ye how to climb
Higher than the sphery chime;°
Or if Virtue feeble were,
Heaven itself would stoop to her.
1634   1637

Lycidas

Lycidas is a pastoral elegy, but its relation to that tradition is most complex. Milton's college acquaintance Edward King was drowned in the Irish Sea in August 1637. *Lycidas* is Milton's response not so much to his death, which Dr. Johnson and many critics since have assumed, as to being asked to contribute a poem to a memorial volume, *Justa Edouardo King* (1638), of which the other contributions, such as John Cleveland's extravagant effusion, could easily lead one to believe that sincerity and eloquence frequently avoid each other's company. Milton's contribution is a very great poem about the death of The Poet by drowning; the consolation that all elegies must offer comes in this case from the unfolding realization that it is not Poetry which has died. Starting with his own feeling of unripeness for a major poetic task, the poem moves through a series of confrontations—with the chosen form of pastoral elegy and its symbolic devices; with the possible demands of epic poetry someday, perhaps, to be faced; and, finally, with a kind of floating processional of emblematic personages, each of whom is to disclaim responsibility for The Poet's death. This sequence is

Cupid Venus' son, he is "advanced" by being elevated to this higher realm; in the imagery of Christian Platonism, Cupid or Eros could be made to stand for heavenly love, and Apuleius' 2nd-century A.D. story of Cupid and Psyche came to be interpreted as Christ's love for the human soul. Spenser, following Apuleius, makes them the parents of Pleasure (*The Faerie Queene* III.vi.50); here, Milton gives them Youth and Joy.

bowed welkin the sky's curved vault
sphery chime the music of the spheres, supposedly produced by the movements of the crystalline heavenly spheres, each carrying one of the planets or all the fixed stars, as they moved through the ether (see *Music of the Spheres* in the Glossary). Above these would be heaven.

rather like a pageant or masque worked into a solo invocation (the model for this is Spenser's *Epithalamion,* made in "lieu of many ornaments" for Spenser's own wedding, and containing ceremony within an expanded kind of lyric poem). All the personages—classical, Christian, local, and made-up spirits—are relevant to the drowned *pastor*—which means "shepherd" (or poet, in pastoral symbolism) as well as "priest." Water nymphs and local deities are finally followed by the fisherman-priest, St. Peter, who denounces a corrupt clergy even more blatantly than Apollo had previously attacked easy, vulgar poetic successes.

The poem keeps shifting back to pastoral elegy from its digressions, and throughout there runs, like a stream of water itself, the myth of the Arcadian river god Alpheus (standing for pastoral poetry), reputedly ran underground and undersea to mix with his beloved Arethusa, a Sicilian fountain (Sicily, home of Theocritus, was the official home of pastoral). The rivers, lakes, and streams in *Lycidas* are all beneficent presences associated with poetic and religious traditions; the estranging salt water of tears and drowning sea is hostile. Central also is the myth of Orpheus floating down the Hebrus (see ll. 58 ff.) as a type of deliverance.

The verse is a brilliant adaptation of the Italian *canzone,* using ten- and six-syllabled lines for the Italian seven and eleven, irregular rhyming schemes, and occasional blank lines to build up its strophic paragraphs, moving at the end to two rhymed couplets just before a final stanza of *ottava rima.* This last replaces the *commiato* or usual formal address of the canzona to itself (as in Spenser's at the end of *Epithalamion*) with a stanza reminiscent of Renaissance epic narrative, distancing and framing the whole poem.

Lycidas

> In this monody the author bewails a learned friend, unfortunately drowned in his passage from Chester on the Irish Seas, 1637. And by occasion foretells the ruin of our corrupted clergy, then in their height.°

Yet once more, O ye laurels,° and once more,
Ye myrtles brown,° with ivy never sere,°
I come to pluck your berries harsh and crude,
And with forced fingers rude
Shatter your leaves before the mellowing year.
Bitter constraint, and sad occasion dear,°
Compels me to disturb your season due:
For Lycidas° is dead, dead ere his prime,
Young Lycidas, and hath not left his peer.

In this monody . . . height This note was added in an edition of 1645, after there was no danger from the church's censors. "By occasion" is a conventional one: Renaissance eclogues frequently used the bucolic mask for denouncing clerical abuses.
laurels sacred to Apollo, and the crown of poetic achievement. Myrtle is Venus', and ivy Bacchus', crown; the point is that poetry lives in the realm of all three of these deities, as Petrarch said in his Oration of 1341.

brown dark
ivy never sere All these plants are evergreen.
dear in both senses of "precious" and "dire"
Lycidas the name of a shepherd in Theocritus and Virgil, of a man who nearly drowned in Lucan's *Pharsalia,* and of the fisherman-swain in the first of Sannazaro's piscatory eclogues, which substituted Neapolitan marine life for a bucolic realm

10 Who would not sing for Lycidas? He knew
Himself to sing, and build the lofty rhyme.
He must not float upon his watery bier
Unwept, and welter° to the parching wind,
Without the meed of some melodious tear.°
Begin then, Sisters of the sacred well°
That from beneath the seat of Jove doth spring,
Begin, and somewhat loudly sweep the string.
Hence with denial vain, and coy° excuse,
So may some gentle Muse
20 With lucky words favour my destined urn,
And as he passes turn,
And bid fair peace be to my sable° shroud.
For we were nursed upon the self-same hill,
Fed the same flock, by fountain, shade, and rill.
Together both, ere the high lawns appeared
Under the opening eyelids of the morn,
We drove afield, and both together heard
What time the grey-fly winds° her sultry horn,
Battening° our flocks with the fresh dews of night,
30 Oft till the star that rose, at evening, bright
Toward heaven's descent had sloped his westering wheel.
Meanwhile the rural ditties were not mute,
Tempered to the oaten flute;°
Rough Satyrs danced, and Fauns with cloven heel
From the glad sound would not be absent long,
And old Damaetas° loved to hear our song.
But O the heavy change, now thou art gone,
Now thou art gone, and never must return!
Thee, Shepherd, thee the woods and desert caves,
40 With wild thyme and the gadding° vine o'ergrown,
And all their echoes mourn.
The willows and the hazel copses green
Shall now no more be seen
Fanning their joyous leaves to thy soft lays.
As killing as the canker° to the rose,
Or taint-worm to the weanling herds that graze,
Or frost to flowers, that their gay wardrobe wear,
When first the white-thorn blows;°
Such, Lycidas, thy loss to shepherd's ear.
50   Where were ye, Nymphs, when the remorseless deep
Closed o'er the head of your loved Lycidas?

welter be tossed about
the meed . . . tear the recompense of some
elegiac poem
Sisters . . . well the Muses; their well on Mt.
Helicon was Aganippe
coy reticent
sable black
winds blows

Battening fattening
oaten flute instrument symbolic of pastoral
poetry
Damaetas pastoral name, perhaps for some
Cambridge tutor
gadding wandering
canker a kind of worm
white-thorn blows hawthorn blossoms

For neither were ye playing on the steep°
Where your old bards, the famous Druids, lie,
Nor on the shaggy top of Mona° high,
Nor yet where Deva° spreads her wizard stream.
Ay me, I fondly° dream,
Had ye been there!—for what could that have done?
What could the Muse herself that Orpheus bore,°
The Muse herself, for her enchanting son
60   Whom universal nature did lament,
When by the rout that made the hideous roar
His gory visage down the stream was sent,
Down the swift Hebrus to the Lesbian shore?
  Alas! what boots° it with uncessant care
To tend the homely slighted shepherd's trade,
And strictly meditate the thankless Muse?
Were it not better done as others use,
To sport with Amaryllis° in the shade,
Or with° the tangles of Neaera's hair?
70   Fame is the spur that the clear spirit doth raise
(That last infirmity of noble mind)
To scorn delights, and live laborious days;
But the fair guerdon when we hope to find,
And think to burst out into sudden blaze,
Comes the blind Fury° with the abhorrèd shears,
And slits the thin-spun life. 'But not the praise,'
Phoebus replied, and touched my trembling ears:°
'Fame° is no plant that grows on mortal soil,
Nor in the glistering foil°
80   Set off to the world, nor in broad rumour lies,
But lives and spreads aloft by those pure eyes
And perfect witness of all-judging Jove;
As he pronounces lastly on each deed,
Of so much fame in heaven expect thy meed.'
  O fountain Arethuse,° and thou honoured flood,

---

steep mountain slope, perhaps on the island of Bardsey ("Bards' island")
Mona the island of Anglesey
Deva the river Dee, "wizard" because it was reputed to shift its channel
fondly foolishly
the Muse . . . bore Calliope. Orpheus was torn apart by Thracian Bacchantes and his head floated down the river Hebrus, and it was fabled that all of nature went into mourning for him.
boots profits
Amaryllis The poet-swain Tityrus in Virgil's First Eclogue writes poems that "teach the woods to echo" his girl's name, Amaryllis; she and Neaera, also known to Milton from classical tradition for her beautiful hair, stand for the objects of the fashionable erotic Caroline verse which it would be so much easier, and safer, to write than an ambitious work on the death of poets.

with Perhaps this is a form of the verb *"withe,"* "to twist."
blind Fury Atropos, nastiest of the Fates, cut the thread of life which her sisters had spun and measured; Milton calls her a "Fury" here as if to evoke a feeling of bungled retribution, of punishment for no crime.
touched . . . ears So Apollo tweaked Virgil's ear, warning him against over-ambition, Milton's allusion to whom being hardly modest, but contrasting heroic poetry with Pan's pastoral.
Fame Apollo properly defines it as immortal glory, whose acquisition cannot be arranged for
foil gold or silver leaf set under jewels before modern faceting could make them brilliant enough
Arethuse See Headnote; the juxtaposition with Mincius, a river of Lombardy associated with Virgil and his *Eclogues*, signals a return of the poem to a pastoral key, after the distant major ("that strain I heard") of Apollo's pronouncement.

Smooth-sliding Mincius, crowned with vocal reeds,
That strain I heard was of a higher mood.
But now my oat° proceeds,
And listens to the herald of the sea°
90   That came in Neptune's plea.
He asked the waves, and asked the felon winds,
What hard mishap hath doomed this gentle swain?
And questioned every gust of rugged wings
That blows from off each beakéd promontory—
They knew not of his story,
And sage Hippotades° their answer brings,
That not a blast was from his dungeon strayed;
The air was calm, and on the level brine
Sleek Panope° with her all sisters played.
100 It was that fatal and perfidious bark,
Built in the eclipse, and rigged with curses dark,
That sunk so low that sacred head of thine.

Next Camus,° reverend sire, went footing slow,
His mantle hairy, and his bonnet sedge,°
Inwrought with figures dim, and on the edge
Like to that sanguine flower° inscribed with woe.
'Ah, who hath reft,' quoth he, 'my dearest pledge?'°
Last came, and last did go,
The Pilot° of the Galilean lake;
110 Two massy keys he bore of metals twain
(The golden opes, the iron shuts amain°).
He shook his mitred locks, and stern bespake:
'How well could I have spared for thee, young swain,
Enow of such as for their bellies' sake
Creep and intrude and climb into the fold!
Of other care they little reckoning make
Than how to scramble at the shearers' feast,
And shove away the worthy bidden guest.
Blind mouths!° that scarce themselves know how to hold
120 A sheep-hook, or have learned aught else the least
That to the faithful herdman's art belongs!
What recks° it them? What need they? They are sped;°
And when they list,° their lean and flashy songs

oat See l. 33n.
herald of the sea Triton, blowing his shell
Hippotades Aeolus, wind god
Panope standing for all the Nereids, or sea nymphs
Camus the river Cam, standing for his university, Cambridge
sedge plants growing near water
sanguine flower the blood-colored hyacinth, which sprang up from the blood of the young man Apollo had accidentally killed, the streaks on its leaves reading like AI AI, Greek sounds of woe
pledge child
Pilot St. Peter, fisherman, the first bishop, to whom Jesus gave "the keys of the kingdom of heaven" (Matthew 16:19)
amain mightily
Blind mouths a startling and intense characterization of inauthentic bishops and corrupted clergy in general. John Ruskin's reading of it, in *Sesame and Lilies* I.22, remains the best: he points out that a *bishop* ("episcopus") is someone who oversees, and a pastor is someone who feeds, nurtures a flock. "The most unbishoply character a man can have is therefore to be blind. The most unpastoral is, instead of feeding, to want to be fed—to be a Mouth."
recks matters
are sped have more than enough
list want

Grate on their scrannel° pipes of wretched straw
The hungry sheep look up, and are not fed,
But swoln with wind, and the rank mist they draw,
Rot inwardly, and foul contagion spread,
Besides what the grim wolf° with privy paw
Daily devours apace, and nothing said;
130 But that two-handed engine° at the door
Stands ready to smite once, and smite no more.'
      Return, Alphéus,° the dread voice is past
That shrunk thy streams; return, Sicilian Muse,
And call the vales, and bid them hither cast
Their bells and flowerets of a thousand hues.
Ye valleys low where the mild whispers use°
Of shades and wanton winds and gushing brooks,
On whose fresh lap the swart star° sparely looks,
Throw hither all your quaint enamelled eyes,
140 That on the green turf suck the honied showers,
And purple all the ground with vernal flowers.
Bring the rathe° primrose that forsaken dies,
The tufted crowtoe, and pale jessamine,
The white pink, and the pansy freaked° with jet,
The glowing violet,
The musk-rose, and the well-attired woodbine,
With cowslips wan that hang the pensive° head,
And every flower that sad embroidery wears.
Bid amaranthus all his beauty shed,
150 And daffadillies fill their cups with tears,
To strew the laureate hearse where Lycid lies.
For so to interpose a little ease,
Let our frail thoughts dally with false surmise;
Ay me! whilst thee the shores and sounding seas
Wash far away, where'er thy bones are hurled,
Whether beyond the stormy Hebrides,
Where thou perhaps under the whelming° tide
Visit'st the bottom of the monstrous world;
Or whether thou, to our moist vows denied,
160 Sleep'st by the fable of Bellerus° old,

---

scrannel thin and squeaky-sounding
grim wolf the Roman Catholic Church, particularly in the person of the Jesuits, who can only devour (make converts) when the shepherd fails his flock
two-handed engine "Engine" usually means a device, and many scholars have suggested that Milton's visionary instrument of retribution is some kind of sword or axe, of symbolic nature in that it is identified in some scriptural or later text as such; others have suggested everything from two houses of Parliament to the two keys Peter holds. Some sort of sword seems most probable, and possibly one which combines the attributive significances of many of the single candidates proposed.

Alphéus See Headnote; the modulation is back to pastoral again, which the complexities of the poem's seriousness lead it to keep fleeing (where there is leisure for demonstrated grief, there is little room for the true fictions).
use are used to go
swart star Sirius
rathe early
freaked capriciously dressed
pensive The Latin words for "think" and "hang" are related, and Milton is reminding us of this.
whelming tossing
Bellerus mythical giant, perhaps invented by Milton, who would have given his name to Bellerium, the Roman designation of Land's End in Cornwall

Where the great Vision of the guarded mount°
Looks toward Namancos and Bayona's hold:°
Look homeward, Angel,° now, and melt with ruth;°
And, O ye dolphins,° waft the hapless youth.
   Weep no more, woeful shepherds, weep no more,
For Lycidas, your sorrow, is not dead,
Sunk though he be beneath the watery floor;
So sinks the day-star° in the ocean bed,
And yet anon repairs his drooping head,
170 And tricks his beams, and with new-spangled ore
Flames in the forehead of the morning sky:
So Lycidas sunk low, but mounted high,
Through the dear might of him that walked the waves,°
Where, other groves and other streams along,
With nectar pure his oozy locks he laves,
And hears the unexpressive nuptial song
In the blest kingdoms meek of joy and love.
There entertain him all the saints above,
In solemn troops and sweet societies
180 That sing, and singing in their glory move,
And wipe the tears for ever from his eyes.
Now, Lycidas, the shepherds weep no more;
Henceforth thou art the Genius° of the Shore,
In thy large recompense, and shalt be good
To all that wander in that perilous flood.
   Thus sang the uncouth° swain to the oaks and rills,
While the still morn went out with sandals grey;
He touched the tender stops of various quills,°
With eager thought warbling his Doric lay.°
190 And now the sun had stretched out all the hills,
And now was dropped into the western bay;
At last he rose, and twitched his mantle blue:
Tomorrow to fresh woods, and pastures new.
1637   1645

guarded mount St. Michael's Mount, off Cornwall
Namancos . . . hold the mountains of Namancos and the fortress of Bayona, on the coast of Spain
Angel the archangel Michael, patron of mariners, looking across the water from the top of St. Michael's Mount (as he is from the top of Mont St. Michel off Brittany)
ruth pity
dolphins The poet-musician Arion was carried to safety over the waves by a dolphin; also, Melicertes (see *Comus*, l. 876n) was carried to

shore by a dolphin and became the sea god Palaemon; dolphins are here invoked to carry the drowned poet over into myth.
day-star the sun
walked the waves Christ, of course (Matthew 14:25–26)
Genius in the sense of *genius loci*, the local spirit inhabiting and protecting a particular spot
uncouth awkward; also perhaps in the older sense of "unknown"
quills hollow stems of reeds in Pan's pipe
Doric lay rustic, pastoral song

Paradise Lost

Milton's blindness and the return of king and bishops combined to make of the 1660's an inner and outer darkness out of which, like a night bird and like a blind prophet, he could respond vocally to an inner light. The abandoned confrontation with epic was his first task. Early notes for a tragedy to be called *Adam Unparadised* proved more potent seeds than those of ideas specifically for heroic narrative—the Arthurian subject, for example, toward which English poetic vision has continued to gaze. Brought up for consideration in two of his early Latin poems (*Damon's Epitaph* and *Manso*), it is one of those alternatives to the poem's subject whose rejection is explained in IX.25–40. *Paradise Lost* was composed in the early 1660's, dictated in stretches of up to forty lines at once during days otherwise filled with walking, playing music, and being read to. It was published in 1667, originally in ten books which, considered in pairs, reflected the five-act structure of neoclassical drama. In 1674, the second edition reorganized the poem into an epic pattern of twelve books, but it required very little actual revision to do so.

Paradise Lost is a Renaissance, Protestant, English epic, confronting, containing, and reinterpreting the Homeric, Virgilian, Dantesque, and Spenserian poems which precede it. It enlists their aid in the poetic realization of a perfect state of man, and the fall from that perfection into a state of human reality. Whereas in Homeric epic the similes and other arts of language are employed to explain to an audience what a vanished heroic age was really like, Milton's analogous task was to describe Paradise in the kind of language that had developed in human history only since, and because of, the loss of it. The very form of his poem is an avowal of the nature of that task.

It begins with a literal "fall" to prefigure the metaphorical, but more general, Fall of Man—the dropping of Satan from heaven to the bottom of everything (save, as we soon see, the depths of his own thoughts) in hell. The once glorious leader of a rebellion against God evinces, in Book I, some of the virtues of the human heroic—energy, resolution, wit, power of command, what looks like imagination. It is only when we remember that these virtues—along with physical strength, competitiveness, craft, and enterprise, for example—are rather like spiritual crutches with which Fallen Man was supplied, that we can put into proper perspective the inverted heroics of Satan and the world of Pandemonium. Satan's perversion of activity brings about the primary (but, in the narrative, chronologically secondary) human one; this relation is like that of prophecy to fulfillment, if we read it correctly, of "shadowy type" (as Milton puts it in the terms used by biblical interpreters) to truth, or, an another way, of thought to action. The puzzle of the attractiveness and intensity of Books I and II, and the static, doctrinal quality of Book III (which directly treats of God and heaven) has been observed since William Blake's first perception of it ("Milton was of the Devil's party without knowing it") to represent the effects of unavowed forces in Milton's imagination. Critics since remain divided even about the proper language in which to describe the puzzle, let alone about how to solve it. Is Satan hero? Villain? Hero-villain from the Jacobean stage? Embodiment of energy or only of evil? Attractive because he speaks to our condition of vitality? Or only because we are fallen sinners who cannot respond without interest and pleasure to the embodiment of our worst fault?

The way in which Satan's fall introduces Adam's (and thereby, ours) is not only an act of obeisance to the classical epic tradition of starting *in medias res* ("in the midst of things"), rather than with true causal beginnings: rather is it at the heart of Milton's poetic method. Classical, biblical, and contemporary allusions, at the poem's beginning, to events which, in human time, are yet to occur, light up this world of events prior to all events. Classical myths in relation to their later interpretations are constantly and thematically present, and patristic biblical commentary, with its typological readings of earlier events in the light of later ones, provides both details and larger models. The complex relation *Satan—Adam—Christ,* for instance, is almost a typological triangle, and there are many interesting parallels to this. By alluding, for example, in the description of Satan's spear in Book I, to Ovid's Golden Age, Milton underlines Satan's destructive role: Renaissance mythographers associated Saturn, who ruled the Age of Gold in Hesiod and Ovid, and who taught men to farm and who was cast, by Zeus, out of the sky, with Adam. Momentary connections like this abound in *Paradise Lost,* where they have both local and general application.

Milton's language and style in the poem both reflect this too. His similes are always powerfully complex; they never merely compare the recounted to the familiar with respect to one quality or attribute (like Homeric similes), but always imply others, of a different sort or quality, as well. His references look forward and back, within and beyond the poem: the reader's knowledge of human history, Man's past, lies in the visionary future of the poem's events, and even the use of particular words shows an awareness of this. The unfallen world, the pre-historical dimension, has to be rendered in concepts themselves created by history. Milton compensates for this somewhat by associating the etymological meaning of a word with the unfallen domain, and the more common, ordinary sense of it with the world of biological-historical mankind. Other concepts—*crooked:straight, stand:rise:fall, up:down*—have this double role in the poem, an early use of a term in Paradise being "infected," as Christopher Ricks has called it, with the figurative moral meanings they would, in human vernaculars, come to have.

Milton's latinate syntax, attacked by T. S. Eliot and other associates in a modernist cause for its betrayal of the values of English speech, is by no means only latinate. His placing of adjectives (as in I. 18: "the upright heart and pure"), where the sequence *first adjective–noun–second adjective* is itself a miniature narrative or argument, is all Italian. Constructions like "Tree of Prohibition" (meaning "prohibited tree" primarily, but with complex overtones) are Hebrew. If Greek syntax were less like English, so that its use might set up new possibilities for enriching the forward movement of subject-predicate word order in English, there might have been more adaptations of it. The language of *Paradise Lost,* in fact, even echoes itself, time and again: phrases from earlier parts appear in later ones, and it is almost as if the story of Satan's fall were a minor epic lying in the background of the poem's central world —that of Books IV through IX: the region of Eden and the stories and lessons learned there.

Milton's poetic line is the blank verse of English stage tragedy, a counterpart of classical hexameters first used by Surrey for his *Aeneid* translation (but without, at the time, setting up a tradition). In a prose statement about the form of the poem, added to the second printing of the first edition purportedly because of complaints from readers that the poem was not in heroic couplets, Milton says something very revealing. "The sense variously drawn out from one verse to another," he declares, will do the work of orchestrating his line endings better than rhyme can. He refers to the enjambment (the way in which line-breaks cut into the syntactic flow, thus manipulating sense). We see this in the very first line of the poem, and throughout. In

IV.25 we are told of how conscience, in Satan, "wakes the bitter memory / Of what
he was, what is, and what must be"—and here the new line starts—"Worse"; the
very drama of discovery that the familiar liturgical *is–was–will be* phrasing is violated,
and that the verb "be" is auxiliary (predicating, and not identifying), is part of the
poetic action.

Milton's ambition in *Paradise Lost* was nothing short of the highest—as he does
not shrink from acknowledging. The poem's influence on subsequent English poetry
is only beginning to be fully understood today, and it remains perhaps the last poem
which could equal, if only as an intellectual achievement, any other accomplishment
—even Newton's *Principia*—of its century, or of our age.

Paradise Lost

From *Book I*

Of man's first disobedience, and the fruit°
Of that forbidden tree, whose mortal taste
Brought death into the world, and all our woe,
With loss of Eden, till one greater Man°
Restore us, and regain the blissful seat,
Sing, heavenly Muse,° that on the secret top
Of Oreb, or of Sinai,° didst inspire
That shepherd who first taught the chosen seed
In the beginning how the heavens and earth

10   Rose out of Chaos; or if Sion hill
Delight thee more, and Siloa's brook° that flowed
Fast by the oracle of God, I thence
Invoke thy aid to my adventurous song,
That with no middle flight° intends to soar
Above the Aonian mount,° while it pursues
Things unattempted yet in prose or rhyme.
And chiefly thou, O Spirit, that dost prefer
Before all temples the upright heart and pure,
Instruct me, for thou knowest; thou from the first

20   Wast present, and with mighty wings outspread
Dove-like sat'st brooding on the vast abyss
And mad'st it pregnant:° what in me is dark
Illumine, what is low raise and support;

Of . . . fruit The opening line's structure, with "disobedience," the commanding polysyllabic word framed by monosyllables, culminates in the "fruit" which, because of the enjambment, suggests both "results" and the fruit of "that forbidden tree," both the general and concrete meanings; notice also the end words of the first three lines, whose sequence "fruit–taste–woe" is the plot of the Fall.
one greater Man Christ, the "second Adam"
heavenly Muse invoking Urania, Muse of the most elevated vision, whom he will actually name only at the beginning of Book VII
Oreb . . . Sinai where Moses ("That shepherd") heard the word of God (Exodus 3:1) and received the law
Siloa's brook in Jerusalem, near the temple
Aonian mount Helicon, the hill of the Muses: Milton's epic will fly beyond antiquity
mad'st it pregnant The creation of the world as told in Genesis, the impregnation of Mary by the descending dove of the Holy Spirit, and the secondary creation of Milton's own great poem are here brought together.

That to the highth of this great argument
I may assert eternal providence,
And justify the ways of God to men.
   Say first, for heaven hides nothing from thy view,
Nor the deep tract of hell, say first what cause
Moved our grand° parents in that happy state,
30 Favoured of heaven so highly, to fall off
From their creator, and transgress his will
For one restraint, lords of the world besides?
Who first seduced them to that foul revolt?
The infernal serpent;° he it was whose guile,
Stirred up with envy and revenge, deceived
The mother of mankind, what time his pride
Had cast him out from heaven, with all his host
Of rebel angels, by whose aid aspiring°
To set himself in glory above his peers,
40 He trusted to have equalled the Most High,
If he opposed; and with ambitious aim
Against the throne and monarchy of God
Raised impious war in heaven and battle proud
With vain attempt. Him the Almighty Power
Hurled headlong flaming from the ethereal sky
With hideous ruin° and combustion down
To bottomless perdition, there to dwell
In adamantine° chains and penal fire,
Who° durst defy the omnipotent to arms.
50 Nine times the space that measures day and night
To mortal men, he with his horrid crew
Lay vanquished, rolling in the fiery gulf
Confounded though immortal. But his doom
Reserved him to more wrath; for now the thought
Both of lost happiness and lasting pain
Torments him; round he throws his baleful eyes,
That witnessed° huge affliction and dismay
Mixed with obdúrate pride and steadfast hate.
At once as far as angels' ken° he views
60 The dismal situation waste and wild:
A dungeon horrible, on all sides round
As one great furnace flamed, yet from those flames
No light, but rather darkness visible°

grand great, but also the parents of all the parents who would ever live
infernal serpent Only in the last book of the Bible, Revelation 12:9 and 20:2, is the wily serpent of Genesis associated with the rebel angel, Satan.
aspiring one of very few lines in *Paradise Lost* with a feminine, or unstressed, ending
ruin downfall
adamantine of the hardest substance imaginable; there is a hint of Prometheus, chained to his rock, too

Who he who
witnessed bore witness to
angels' ken their range of vision
darkness visible Light in all its forms—heavenly, created, the light of physical sight denied a blind man, symbolic light of reason, and divine creative power—is far too important in *Paradise Lost* to allow Milton to be careless with it: whatever makes things visible in hell, it is not light.

Served only to discover sights of woe,
Regions of sorrow, doleful shades, where peace
And rest can never dwell, hope never comes°
That comes to all; but torture without end
Still urges,° and a fiery deluge, fed
With ever-burning sulphur unconsumed:
70   Such place eternal justice had prepared
For those rebellious, here their prison ordained
In utter° darkness, and their portion set
As far removed from God and light of heaven
As from the centre thrice to the utmost pole.
O how unlike the place from whence they fell!
There the companions of his fall, o'erwhelmed
With floods and whirlwinds of tempestuous fire,
He soon discerns, and weltering° by his side
One next himself in power, and next in crime,
80   Long after known in Palestine, and named
Beelzebub.° To whom the arch-enemy,
And thence in heaven called Satan,° with bold words
Breaking the horrid silence thus began:
    'If thou beest he . . . but O how fallen! how changed
From him, who in the happy realms of light
Clothed with transcendent brightness didst outshine
Myriads though bright—if he whom mutual league,
United thoughts and counsels, equal hope
And hazard in the glorious enterprise,
90   Joined with me once, now misery hath joined
In equal ruin: into what pit thou seest
From what highth fallen, so much the stronger proved
He with his thunder, and till then who knew
The force of those dire arms? Yet not for those,
Nor what the potent victor in his rage
Can else inflict, do I repent or change,
Though changed in outward lustre that fixed mind
And high disdain, from sense of injured merit,°
That with the mightiest raised me to contend,
100   And to the fierce contention brought along
Innumerable force of spirits armed
That durst dislike his reign, and me preferring,
His utmost power with adverse power opposed
In dubious battle on the plains of heaven,
And shook his throne.° What though the field be lost?

hope never comes echoing Dante, over the entrance to whose hell is inscribed: "Abandon hope all ye enter here" (*Inferno* III.4–6)
urges presses
utter also in the sense of "outer"
weltering tossing
Beelzebub Hebrew for "lord of the flies"; Satan's lieutenant here
Satan The name in Hebrew means "enemy, opponent, adversary."

merit an important word: for Satan, it means "power," for Christ, goodness; cf.II.6 and 21
And shook his throne a lie—in the description of the war in heaven in Bk. VI, we learn that it was because of the chariot of the Son that "The steadfast Empyrean shook throughout." In this and subsequent speeches, one can view Satan as a crude liar or as a suffering, deposed leader, enthusiastically self-deceived.

All is not lost; the unconquerable will,
And study° of revenge, immortal hate,
And courage never to submit or yield:
And what is else not to be overcome?
That glory never shall his wrath or might
Extort from me. To bow and sue for grace
With suppliant knee, and deify his power—
Who° from the terror of this arm so late
Doubted° his empire—that were low indeed,
That were an ignominy° and shame beneath
This downfall; since by fate the strength of gods°
And this empyreal substance cannot fail,°
Since through experience of this great event,
In arms not worse, in foresight much advanced,
We may with more successful hope resolve
To wage by force or guile eternal war
Irreconcilable to our grand foe,
Who now triumphs, and in the excess of joy
Sole reigning holds the tyranny of heaven.'
So spake the apostate Angel, though in pain,
Vaunting aloud, but racked with deep despair;
And him thus answered soon his bold compeer:
'O Prince, O chief of many thronèd powers,°
That led the embattled seraphim to war
Under thy conduct, and in dreadful deeds
Fearless, endangered heaven's perpetual king,
And put to proof his high supremacy,
Whether upheld by strength, or chance, or fate;
Too well I see and rue the dire event,
That with sad overthrow and foul defeat
Hath lost us heaven, and all this mighty host
In horrible destruction laid thus low,
As far as gods and heavenly essences
Can perish: for the mind and spirit remains
Invincible, and vigour soon returns,
Though all our glory extinct,° and happy state
Here swallowed up in endless misery.
But what if he our conqueror (whom I now
Of force° believe almighty, since no less
Than such could have o'erpowered such force as ours)
Have left us this our spirit and strength entire
Strongly to suffer and support our pains,

110

120

130

140

study search for
Who I who
Doubted feared for
ignominy pronounced "ignomy"
gods As a relativist in theology and a Hobbesian in political theory, Satan thinks of God as being one of a collection of pagan deities; it is axiomatic that He is not.
substance cannot fail even the vanquished rebels are immortal (see l. 53, above)

thronèd powers Medieval angelology distinguished nine angelic orders: seraphim, cherubim, thrones, dominations, virtues, powers, principalities, angels, and archangels. Beelzebub obliquely invokes these now, but will trot out most of the list later, in his public rhetoric.
extinct extinguished
Of force perforce

That we may so suffice° his vengeful ire,
Or do him mightier service as his thralls
150   By right of war, whate'er his business be,
Here in the heart of hell to work in fire,
Or do his errands in the gloomy deep?
What can it then avail though yet we feel
Strength undiminished, or eternal being
To undergo eternal punishment?'
  Whereto with speedy words the arch-fiend replied:
'Fallen cherub, to be weak is miserable,
Doing or suffering: but of this be sure,
To do aught good never will be our task,
160   But ever to do ill our sole delight,
As being the contrary to his high will
Whom we resist. If then his providence
Out of our evil seek to bring forth good,
Our labour must be to pervert that end,
And out of good still to find means of evil;°
Which ofttimes may succeed, so as perhaps
Shall grieve him, if I fail not,° and disturb
His inmost counsels from their destined aim.
But see the angry victor hath recalled
170   His ministers of vengeance and pursuit
Back to the gates of heaven; the sulphurous hail
Shot after us in storm, o'erblown hath laid°
The fiery surge, that from the precipice
Of heaven received us falling, and the thunder,
Winged with red lightning and impetuous rage,
Perhaps hath spent his shafts, and ceases now
To bellow through the vast and boundless deep.
Let us not slip° the occasion, whether scorn
Or satiate fury yield it from our foe.
180   Seest thou yon dreary plain, forlorn and wild,
The seat of desolation, void of light,
Save what the glimmering of these livid flames
Casts pale and dreadful? Thither let us tend
From off the tossing of these fiery waves,
There rest, if any rest can harbour there,
And reassembling our afflicted° powers,
Consult how we may henceforth most offend°
Our enemy, our own loss how repair,
How overcome this dire calamity,
190   What reinforcement we may gain from hope;

suffice appease
If then . . . evil These lines frame the notion
of the *felix culpa*, or fortunate fall: out of their
evil God will bring forth human and divine
good; they also introduce Satan's dialectical
juggling of divine concepts and their opposites;
later on, it will get more tortured and desperate.
if I fail not unless I'm wrong
laid reduced
slip let go by
afflicted cast down
offend injure

If not, what resolution from despair.'
—Thus Satan talking to his nearest mate
With head uplift above the wave, and eyes
That sparkling blazed;° his other parts besides
Prone on the flood, extended long and large
Lay floating many a rood,° in bulk as huge
As whom the fables name of monstrous size,
Titanian° or Earth-born, that warred on Jove,
Briareos or Typhon, whom the den
200   By ancient Tarsus held, or that sea-beast
Leviathan,° which God of all his works
Created hugest that swim the ocean stream:
Him haply slumbering on the Norway foam,
The pilot of some small night-foundered° skiff,
Deeming some island, oft, as seamen tell,
With fixèd anchor in his scaly rind
Moors by his side under the lee, while night
Invests° the sea, and wishèd morn delays:
So stretched out huge in length the arch-fiend lay
210   Chained on the burning lake; nor ever thence
Had risen or heaved his head, but that the will
And high permission of all-ruling heaven
Left him at large to his own dark designs,
That with reiterated crimes he might
Heap on himself damnation, while he sought
Evil to others, and enraged might see
How all his malice served but to bring forth
Infinite goodness, grace and mercy shown
On man by him seduced, but on himself
220   Treble confusion, wrath and vengeance poured.
    Forthwith upright he rears from off the pool
His mighty stature; on each hand the flames
Driven backward slope their pointing spires, and rolled
In billows, leave i' th' midst a horrid ° vale.
Then with expanded wings he steers his flight
Aloft, incumbent° on the dusky air
That felt unusual weight, till on dry land
He lights, if it were land that ever burned
With solid, as the lake with liquid fire;
230   And such appeared in hue;° as when the force

With head . . . blazed There is a premonition of Satan's later—chosen—shape here, a touch of the sea serpent.
rood, rod, the unit of length: 5.5 yards
Titanian The Titans and the Giants both attacked the Olympian gods (Briareos represents the first, Typhon the second).
Leviathan the great sea beast of Scripture (Job 41, Isaiah 27:1, and elsewhere), thought of as a whale. The story about the whale's being mistaken for an island is from the

medieval bestiaries; every simile emphasizing Satan's magnitude or power in Books I and II of *Paradise Lost* will also show something false, illusory, or, as here, untrustworthy about it.
night-foundered sunk in night
Invests enfolds
horrid in the Latin sense, "bristling," with a touch of the modern sense
incumbent weighing down
hue surface color and texture

Of subterranean wind transports a hill
Torn from Pelorus,° or the shattered side
Of thundering Aetna, whose combustible
And fuelled entrails thence conceiving fire,
Sublimed° with mineral fury, aid the winds,
And leave a singèd bottom all involved°
With stench and smoke: such resting found the sole
Of unblest feet. Him followed his next° mate,
Both glorying to have scaped the Stygian flood°
240   As gods, and by their own recovered strength,
Not by the sufferance of supernal power.
    'Is this the region, this the soil, the clime,'
Said then the lost archangel, 'this the seat°
That we must change for heaven, this mournful gloom
For that celestial light? Be it so, since he
Who now is sovereign can dispose and bid
What shall be right: farthest from him is best,
Whom reason hath equalled, force hath made supreme
Above his equals. Farewell, happy fields,
250   Where joy for ever dwells: hail, horrors! hail,
Infernal world! and thou, profoundest hell,
Receive thy new possessor: one who brings
A mind not to be changed by place or time.
The mind is its own place, and in itself
Can make a heaven of hell, a hell of heaven.°
What matter where, if I be still the same,
And what I should be, all but less than he
Whom thunder hath made greater? Here at least
We shall be free; the Almighty hath not built
260   Here for his envy, will not drive us hence:
Here we may reign secure, and in my choice
To reign is worth ambition, though in hell:
Better to reign in hell than serve in heaven.°
But wherefore let we then our faithful friends,
The associates and co-partners of our loss,
Lie thus astonished on the oblivious pool,°
And call them not to share with us their part
In this unhappy mansion, or once more
With rallied arms to try what may be yet

Pelorus Cape Faro, near the volcano Aetna in Sicily
Sublimed vaporized; a term from alchemy meaning the refining of metals by fire
invòlved entwined
next closest
Stygian flood the "fiery gulf" of l. 52
seat proper place
The mind . . . heaven This sounds both like great self-reliance and courageous resolve, and like a bad mistake in denying the external, local existence of heaven and hell; the dramatic irony is that after twisting good and evil, rise and fall, up and down, heaven and hell into each other, Satan will complain, in his great speech on Mt. Niphates (IV.32–113), of the hell within him.
Better . . . heaven again, on the surface, a slogan asserting human dignity; but Satan is not human, heaven commands no "servitude," and what kind of kingdom hell is becomes clear
astonished . . . pool stupefied on the lake of forgetfulness

270   Regained in heaven, or what more lost in hell?'
      So Satan spake, and him Beelzebub
    Thus answered: 'Leader of those armies bright,
    Which but the omnipotent none could have foiled,
    If once they hear that voice, their liveliest pledge
    Of hope in fears and dangers, heard so oft
    In worst extremes, and on the perilous edge°
    Of battle when it raged, in all assaults
    Their surest signal, they will soon resume
    New courage and revive, though now they lie
280   Grovelling and prostrate on yon lake of fire,
    As we erewhile, astounded and amazed;
    No wonder, fallen such a pernicious highth!'
      He scarce had ceased when the superior fiend
    Was moving toward the shore; his ponderous shield,
    Ethereal temper,° massy, large, and round,
    Behind him cast; the broad circumference
    Hung on his shoulders like the moon,° whose orb
    Through optic glass the Tuscan artist° views
    At evening from the top of Fesole,
290   Or in Valdarno,° to descry new lands,
    Rivers or mountains in her spotty globe.
    His spear, to equal which the tallest pine
    Hewn on Norwegian hills, to be the mast
    Of some great ammiral,° were but a wand,
    He walked with to support uneasy steps
    Over the burning marl, not like those steps
    On heaven's azure; and the torrid clime
    Smote on him sore besides, vaulted with fire.
    Nathless° he so endured, till on the beach
300   Of that inflamèd sea, he stood and called
    His legions, angel forms, who lay entranced,
    Thick as° autumnal leaves that strow the brooks
    In Vallombrosa,° where the Etrurian shades
    High over-arched embower; or scattered sedge
    Afloat, when with fierce winds Orion armed°
    Hath vexed the Red Sea° coast, whose waves o'erthrew

perilous edge front line
Ethereal temper tempered by ethereal flame
like the moon In this sequence of similes, the grandeur of Satan's appearance and his authenticity are simultaneously developed; the moon, to which his shield is compared, looks startlingly huge through the artificial magnification of a telescope, and unlike the shield of Achilles in Homer (*Iliad* XIX) it does not have an emblem of human civilization upon it. **Tuscan artist** Galileo Galilei (1564–1642); Milton had actually visited him
Fesole . . . Valdarno Fiesole and the Arno valley, both near Florence
ammiral admiral's flagship. Like the shield, the comparison is to something technological, hence from fallen human life, and, in this case, quotes Ovid, *Metamorphoses* I (see Golding's translation of the Golden Age passage), to remind us that Satan will be doing the equivalent of wrenching the Golden Age into an Iron one, in which trees will become masts of ships. There is also a covert allusion to the blind Polyphemus, "of light bereft," in whose hand a pine tree guides and steadies his steps (Virgil, *Aeneid* III. 658–59.
Nathless nevertheless
Thick as also, dead as
Vallombrosa shady, wooded valley near Florence
Orion armed associated with seasonal storms
Red Sea in Hebrew, "sea of sedge"

Busiris° and his Memphian chivalry,
While with perfidious hatred they pursued
The sojourners of Goshen,° who beheld
310   From the safe shore their floating carcasses
And broken chariot wheels;° so thick bestrown,
Abject° and lost lay these, covering the flood,
Under amazement of° their hideous change.
He called so loud that all the hollow deeps
Of hell resounded: 'Princes, Potentates,
Warriors, the flower of heaven, once yours, now lost,
If such astonishment° as this can seize
Eternal Spirits; or have ye chosen this place
After the toil of battle to repose
320   Your wearied virtue,° for the ease you find
To slumber here, as in the vales of heaven?
Or in this abject posture have ye sworn
To adore the conqueror, who now beholds
Cherub and seraph rolling in the flood
With scattered arms and ensigns, till anon
His swift pursuers from heaven gates discern
The advantage, and descending tread us down
Thus drooping, or with linkèd thunderbolts
Transfix us to the bottom of this gulf?
330   Awake, arise, or be for ever fallen!'
    They heard, and were abashed, and up they sprung
Upon the wing, as when men wont to watch
On duty, sleeping found by whom they dread,
Rouse and bestir themselves ere well awake.
Nor did they not perceive the evil plight
In which they were, or the fierce pains not feel;
Yet to their general's voice they soon obeyed
Innumerable. As when the potent rod
Of Amram's son° in Egypt's evil day
340   Waved round the coast, up called a pitchy cloud
Of locusts, warping° on the eastern wind,
That o'er the realm of impious Pharaoh hung
Like night, and darkened all the land of Nile:
So numberless were those bad angels seen
Hovering on wing under the cope° of hell
'Twixt upper, nether, and surrounding fires;
Till, as a signal given, the uplifted spear

Busiris Pharaoh in Exodus
Goshen place of safety on the east of the Red Sea
chariot wheels again, a remarkable simile purporting to show how thick, numerous, and densely massed were Satan's troops, but reminding us of corpses and a defeated army that pursued Israel as Satan does Adam
abject cast down

amazement of stupefaction *of* and *at*
astonishment immobilization
virtue power, strength
Amram's son Moses
locusts, warping one of the ten plagues with which God smote the Egyptians (Exodus 10: 12–13); "warping" here means "swerving"
cope canopy

Of their great Sultan waving to direct
Their course, in even balance down they light
350   On the firm brimstone, and fill all the plain;
A multitude, like which the populous North
Poured never from her frozen loins, to pass
Rhene or the Danaw,° when her barbarous sons
Came like a deluge on the south, and spread
Beneath Gibraltar to the Libyan sands.
Forthwith from every squadron and each band
The heads and leaders thither haste where stood
Their great commander; godlike shapes and forms
Excelling human, princely dignities,
360   And powers that erst° in heaven sat on thrones;
Though of their names in heavenly records now
Be no memorial, blotted out and razed
By their rebellion from the books of life.°
Nor had they yet among the sons of Eve
Got them new names, till wandering o'er the earth,
Through God's high sufferance for the trial of man,
By falsities and lies the greatest part
Of mankind they corrupted to forsake
God their creator, and the invisible
370   Glory of him that made them to transform
Oft to the image of a brute, adorned
With gay religions° full of pomp and gold,
And devils to adore for deities:
Then were they known to men by various names,
And various idols through the heathen world.

[There follows a demonic parody of Homer's famous catalogue of ships in the
Iliad II, a list of all the Greek captains and princes allied against Troy. Milton's
list of demons includes names of devils from Hebraic and Christian folklore, as
well as a multitude of pagan gods, whose mythological ancestry, following
patristic tradition, Milton locates in fallen angels. In human history they
would (or, from this point on in the poem's time scheme, they *will*) come to
be false gods. This is Milton's visionary alternative to what might be a modern
anthropologist's observation that the gods of a conquered people may persist, in
changed form as demons or fairies or the like, under the imposed religion—or
to a psychologist's suggestion that vanquished, suppressed memories of trauma
return as the false gods of dream and hysterical symptom.

After Satan's troops are gathered, he urges them to pull themselves together,
to resolve to recover their lost glories; and, suggesting that God is going to
prepare a new garden world in which to "plant a generation," demands that
"War / Open or undeclared, must be resolved." The remainder of Book I tells
of the building of Pandemonium, capitol of Satan's realm.]

Rhene . . . Danaw Rhine and Danube. The
whole image compares Satan to a leader of
Asiatic barbarian raiders.
erst formerly

books of life God's ledgers, in which the Good
are enrolled
gay religions pagan ceremonies

670   There stood a hill not far whose grisly top
    Belched fire and rolling smoke; the rest entire
    Shone with a glossy scurf,° undoubted sign
    That in his womb was hid metallic ore,
    The work of sulphur.° Thither winged with speed
    A numerous brígade hastened: as when bands
    Of pioneers with spade and pickaxe armed
    Forerun the royal camp, to trench a field
    Or cast a rampart. Mammon° led them on,
    Mammon, the least erected° Spirit that fell
680   From heaven, for even in heaven his looks and thoughts
    Were always downward bent, admiring more
    The riches of heaven's pavement, trodden gold,
    Than aught divine or holy else enjoyed
    In vision beatific.° By him first
    Men also, and by his suggestion taught,
    Ransacked° the centre, and with impious hands
    Rifled the bowels of their mother earth
    For treasures better hid. Soon had his crew
    Opened into the hill a spacious wound
690   And digged out ribs of gold. Let none admire°
    That riches grow in hell; that soil may best
    Deserve the precious bane. And here let those
    Who boast in mortal things, and wondering tell
    Of Babel,° and the works of Memphian° kings,
    Learn how their greatest monuments of fame,
    And strength and art are easily outdone
    By spirits reprobate,° and in an hour
    What in an age they with incessant toil
    And hands innumerable scarce perform.
700   Nigh on the plain in many cells prepared,
    That underneath had veins of liquid fire
    Sluiced from the lake, a second multitude
    With wondrous art founded the massy ore,
    Severing each kind, and scummed the bullion dross.
    A third as soon had formed within the ground
    A various mould, and from the boiling cells
    By strange conveyance filled each hollow nook,
    As in an organ from one blast of wind

scurf scaly incrustation: gold ore is seen as a skin disease of hell's rocks
sulphur essential, in alchemy, to the production of metals
Mammon in Aramaic, "wealth," but in medieval tradition standing for the realm of this world. Milton's conception of him as a Pluto-like mining god is based on Spenser's Cave of Mammon (see *The Faerie Queene* II.vii); cf. Matthew 6:24.
erected uplifted
vision beatific the direct vision of God by the saints which constitutes paradise

Ransacked This word, and "Rifled" below, suggest the aggressive violence of mining, as opposed to the nurturing of agriculture; the truer, "vegetable" gold of the earth's fruits, rather than her guts, will be seen in Paradise (IV. 220).
admire wonder
Babel the tower of Babel (Genesis 11:1-9) and all of Babylon's famous structures, all emblems of pride and presumption
Memphian Egyptian
reprobate rejected

To many a row of pipes the sound-board breathes.
710 Anon out of the earth a fabric huge
Rose like an exhalation,° with the sound
Of dulcet symphonies and voices sweet,
Built like a temple, where pilasters round
Were set, and Doric pillars overlaid
With golden architrave; nor did there want
Cornice or frieze, with bossy° sculptures graven;
The roof was fretted° gold. Not Babylon,
Nor great Alcairo° such magnificence
Equalled in all their glories, to enshrine
720 Belus or Serapis° their gods, or seat
Their kings, when Egypt with Assyria strove
In wealth and luxury. The ascending pile
Stood fixed her stately highth, and straight the doors
Opening their brazen folds discover wide
Within, her ample spaces, o'er the smooth
And level pavement; from the archèd roof
Pendent by subtle magic many a row
Of starry lamps and blazing cressets° fed
With naphtha and asphaltus° yielded light
730 As from a sky. The hasty multitude
Admiring entered, and the work some praise,
And some the architect: his hand was known
In heaven by many a towered structure high,
Where sceptred angels held their residence,
And sat as princes, whom the súpreme king
Exalted to such power, and gave to rule,
Each in his hierarchy, the orders bright.
Nor was his name unheard or unadored
In ancient Greece, and in Ausonian land°
740 Men called him Mulciber;° and how he fell
From heaven, they fabled, thrown by angry Jove
Sheer o'er the crystal battlements: from morn
To noon he fell, from noon to dewy eve,
A summer's day; and with the setting sun
Dropped from the zenith like a falling star,
On Lemnos the Aégean isle. Thus they relate,
Erring; for he with this rebellious rout
Fell long before; nor aught availed him now

exhalation also, like a comet or meteor. This whole passage suggests a description of a masque transformation scene (see the Headnote to Ben Jonson's *Pleasure Reconciled to Virtue*)—rapid, illusory, dramatically impressive; the accompanying music hints at the power of Amphion raising the walls of Thebes to music, while the architectural details are those of massive, baroque architecture.
bossy in relief
fretted patterned, interlaced carving

Alcairo ancient Memphis
Belus or Serapis Baal or Osiris
cressets iron baskets
asphaltus pitch asphalt
Ausonian land Italy (its old Greek name)
Mulciber Hephaestus, Vulcan. Milton sums up the Homeric story (*Iliad* I.590–94) of his day-long, leisurely fall, almost as if a pleasant trip, then snaps in (l. 747) the corrective to what seems far too sweet a fable.

To have built in heaven high towers;° nor did he scape
750   By all his engines,° but was headlong sent
With his industrious crew to build in hell.
Meanwhile the wingèd heralds by command
Of sovereign power, with awful ceremony
And trumpet's sound, throughout the host proclaim
A solemn council forthwith to be held
At Pandemonium,° the high capitol
Of Satan and his peers; their summons called
From every band and squarèd regiment
By place or choice the worthiest; they anon
760   With hundreds and with thousands trooping came
Attended. All access was thronged, the gates
And porches wide, but chief the spacious hall
(Though like a covered field, where champions bold
Wont ride in armed, and at the Soldan's° chair
Defied the best of paynim° chivalry
To mortal combat or career with lance)
Thick swarmed, both on the ground and in the air,
Brushed with the hiss of rustling wings. As bees
In springtime, when the sun with Taurus° rides,
770   Pour forth their populous youth about the hive
In clusters; they among fresh dews and flowers
Fly to and fro, or on the smoothèd plank,
The suburb of their straw-built citadel,
New rubbed with balm, expatiate° and confer
Their state affairs: so thick the airy crowd
Swarmed° and were straitened; till the signal given,
Behold a wonder! they but now who seemed
In bigness to surpass earth's giant sons,
Now less than smallest dwarfs, in narrow room
780   Throng numberless, like that pygmean race
Beyond the Indian mount, or fairy elves,
Whose midnight revels by a forest side
Or fountain some belated peasant sees,
Or dreams he sees, while overhead the moon
Sits arbitress, and nearer to the earth
Wheels her pale course; they on their mirth and dance
Intent, with jocund music charm his ear;°

---

heaven high towers The reversed syntax reflects the climax-capping of adding height to heaven.
engines devices (machinery and machinations)
Pandemonium in Greek, "all demons"
Soldan's Sultan's
paynim pagan
Taurus the sun is in Taurus from mid-April to mid-May
expatiate amble about
so thick . . . Swarmed Again, the density, busy-ness, and multitude of the bees show us those qualities of Satan's legions, but the scale is reduced to a *tiny* model of human

industry and social organization (although a traditional one), and the "straw-built citadel" is both literal about straw beehives and figurative about vast structures (like Roman churches with hive-shaped domes) "built on straw."
fairy elves . . . ear (ll. 781–87) no longer reduced in size (bees, pygmies), but are now as illusory as spooks that the simple see. We are now in the English countryside for a moment, to give us a breath of pragmatic fresh air (as Chaucer does with his introduction of January in *The Franklin's Tale*); there are echoes of *A Midsummer Night's Dream*.

At once with joy and fear his heart rebounds.
Thus incorporeal spirits to smallest forms
790   Reduced their shapes immense, and were at large,°
Though without number still, amidst the hall
Of that infernal court. But far within,
And in their own dimensions like themselves,
The great seraphic lords and cherubim
In close° recess and secret conclave sat,
A thousand demi-gods and golden seats,
Frequent° and full. After short silence then
And summons read, the great consult° began.

    From *Book II*
High on a throne of royal state, which far
Outshone the wealth of Ormus° and of Ind,
Or where the gorgeous East with richest hand
Showers on her kings barbaric pearl and gold,
Satan exalted sat, by merit° raised
To that bad eminence; and from despair
Thus high uplifted beyond hope, aspires
Beyond thus high,° insatiate to pursue
Vain war with heaven, and by success° untaught,
10   His proud imaginations thus displayed:
    'Powers and dominions,° deities of heaven,
For since no deep within her gulf can hold
Immortal vigour, though oppressed and fallen,
I give not heaven for lost. From this descent
Celestial virtues° rising will appear
More glorious and more dread than from no fall,
And trust themselves to fear no second fate.
Me though just right and the fixed laws of heaven
Did first create your leader, next, free choice,
20   With what besides, in council or in fight,
Hath been achieved of merit, yet this loss,
Thus far at least recovered, hath much more
Established in a safe unenvied throne
Yielded with full consent. The happier state
In heaven, which follows dignity, might draw
Envy from each inferior; but who here
Will envy whom the highest place exposes
Foremost to stand against the thunderer's° aim
Your bulwark, and condemns to greatest share

---

at large The pun is quite deliberate.
close secret
Frequent crowded
consult debate
Ormus island city in the Persian gulf
merit power (see I.98n and II.21)
from despair . . . high again, the patterned
syntax reflects the overreaching of Satan's will

success the outcome, implying neither good nor
bad results; cf. II.123
Powers and dominions He still uses their angelic
titles (see I.128n).
virtues capabilities; also, the angelic order
the thunderer's Zeus, Jupiter; again, a false
reduction of God

30   Of endless pain? Where there is then no good
For which to strive, no strife can grow up there
From faction; for none sure will claim in hell
Precedence, none whose portion is so small
Of present pain that with ambitious mind
Will covet more. With this advantage then
To union, and firm faith, and firm accord,
More than can be in heaven, we now return
To claim our just inheritance of old,
Surer to prosper than prosperity
40   Could have assured us;° and by what best way,
Whether of open war or covert guile,
We now debate; who can advise, may speak.
He ceased, and next him Moloch,° sceptred king,
Stood up, the strongest and the fiercest Spirit
That fought in heaven, now fiercer by despair.
His trust was with the Eternal to be deemed
Equal in strength, and rather than be less
Cared not to be at all; with that care lost
Went all his fear: of God, or hell, or worse
50   He recked not, and these words thereafter spake:
'My sentence° is for open war. Of wiles,
More unexpert, I boast not: them let those
Contrive who need, or when they need, not now.
For while they sit contriving, shall the rest,
Millions that stand° in arms and longing wait
The signal to ascend, sit lingering here,
Heaven's fugitives, and for their dwelling-place
Accept this dark opprobrious den of shame,
The prison of his tyranny who reigns
60   By our delay? No, let us rather choose,
Armed with hell flames and fury, all at once
O'er heaven's high towers° to force resistless way,
Turning our tortures into horrid arms
Against the torturer; when to meet the noise
Of his almighty engine he shall hear
Infernal thunder, and for lightning see
Black fire and horror shot with equal rage
Among his angels, and his throne itself
Mixed with Tartarean° sulphur and strange fire,

Surer . . . assured us This shaping of words—
a b b a—called a "chiasmus," or "crossing,"
exemplifies Satan's use of rhetorical devices
common in the Renaissance.
Moloch One of the better known of Milton's
devils who later enter history as pagan gods;
he becomes a Canaanite idol to whom children
are sacrificed and is introduced in I.392–96
as the "horrid king besmeared with blood / Of
human sacrifice, and parents' tears / Though for
the noise of drums and timbrels loud / Their
children's cries unheard, that passed through
fire / To his grim idol."
sentence decision; cf. l. 291
stand metaphorically, as in "standing army,"
but notice the sequence of words in these
lines: "sit . . . stand . . . ascend . . . sit"
towers echoing I.749
Tartarean hellish. This is gunpowder, artillery
being an infernal parody of God's thunder and
an appropriate revenge.

70   His own invented torments. But perhaps
The way seems difficult and steep to scale
With upright wing against a higher foe?
Let such bethink them, if the sleepy drench
Of that forgetful lake benumb not still,
That in our proper motion we ascend
Up to our native seat; descent and fall
To us is adverse. Who but felt of late,
When the fierce foe hung on our broken rear
Insulting,° and pursued us through the deep,
80   With what compulsion and laborious flight
We sunk thus low? The ascent is easy then;
The event is feared; Should we again provoke
Our stronger, some worse way his wrath may find
To our destruction, if there be in hell
Fear to be worse destroyed: what can be worse
Than to dwell here, driven out from bliss, condemned
In this abhorrèd deep to utter woe;
Where pain of unextinguishable fire
Must exercise° us without hope of end
90   The vassals of his anger, when the scourge
Inexorably, and the torturing hour
Calls us to penance? More destroyed than thus
We should be quite abolished and expire.
What fear we then? What doubt we to incense
His utmost ire? Which to the highth enraged
Will either quite consume us, and reduce
To nothing this essential,° happier far
Than miserable to have eternal being;
Or if our substance be indeed divine,
100   And cannot cease to be, we are at worst
On this side nothing; and by proof we feel
Our power sufficient to disturb his heaven,
And with perpetual inroads to alarm,
Though inaccessible, his fatal° throne;
Which if not victory is yet revenge.'
        He ended frowning, and his look denounced°
Desperate revenge, and battle dangerous
To less than gods. On the other side up rose
Belial, in act more graceful and humane;
110   A fairer person lost not heaven; he seemed
For dignity composed and high exploit:
But all was false and hollow, though his tongue
Dropped manna,° and could make the worse appear

Insulting assaulting, as well as jeering
exercise torture
essential essence. Angelic substance is immaterial; cf. I.138.
fatal by fate; cf. I.116

denounced threatened
manna the heavenly food supplied to the
wandering Israelites (Exodus 16:14–16); this
is sarcastic, modeled on "dripping honey"

The better reason, to perplex and dash
Maturest counsels: for his thoughts were low;
To vice industrious, but to nobler deeds
Timorous and slothful: yet he pleased the ear,
And with persuasive accent thus began:
   'I should be much for open war, O Peers,
120 As not behind in hate, if what was urged
Main reason to persuade immediate war
Did not dissuade me most, and seem to cast
Ominous conjecture on the whole success:
When he who most excels in fact° of arms,
In what he counsels and in what excels
Mistrustful, grounds his courage on despair
And utter dissolution, as the scope
Of all his aim, after some dire revenge.
First, what revenge? The towers of heaven are filled
130 With armèd watch, that render all access
Impregnable; oft on the bordering deep
Encamp their legions, or with óbscure wing
Scout far and wide into the realm of Night,
Scorning surprise. Or could we break our way
By force, and at our heels all hell should rise
With blackest insurrection, to confound
Heaven's purest light, yet our great enemy
All incorruptible would on his throne
140 Sit unpolluted, and the ethereal mould
Incapable of stain would soon expel
Her mischief, and purge off the baser fire,°
Victorious. Thus repulsed, our final hope
Is flat despair; we must exasperate
The almighty victor to spend all his rage,
And that must end us, that must be our cure,
To be no more. Sad cure! for who would lose,
Though full of pain, this intellectual being,
Those thoughts that wander through eternity,°
To perish rather, swallowed up and lost
150 In the wide womb of uncreated Night,
Devoid of sense and motion? And who knows,
Let this be good, whether our angry foe
Can give it, or will ever? How he can
Is doubtful; that he never will is sure.
Will he, so wise, let loose at once his ire,
Belike° through impotence, or unaware,
To give his enemies their wish, and end

---

fact deed, feat
baser fire Heavenly light has been a refining
fire in this passage, burning off even the lower,
hellish sort.

for who . . . eternity An overtone of Hamlet's
"To be or not to be" soliloquy may be discerned
here.
Belike doubtless

Them in his anger, whom his anger saves
To punish endless? *Wherefore cease we then?*
160   Say they who counsel war; *We are decreed,*
Reserved, and destined to eternal woe;
Whatever doing, what can we suffer more,
What can we suffer worse?° Is this then worst,
Thus sitting, thus consulting, thus in arms?
What when we fled amain, pursued and strook
With heaven's afflicting thunder, and besought
The deep to shelter us? This hell then seemed
A refuge from those wounds—or when we lay
Chained on the burning lake?° That sure was worse.
170   What if the breath that kindled those grim fires
Awaked should blow them into sevenfold rage
And plunge us in the flames? or from above
Should intermitted vengeance arm again
His red right hand° to plague us? What if all
Her stores were opened and this firmament
Of hell should spout her cataracts of fire,
Impendent horrors, threatening hideous fall
One day upon our heads; while we perhaps
Designing or exhorting glorious war,
180   Caught in a fiery tempest shall be hurled
Each on his rock transfixed, the sport and prey
Of racking whirlwinds, or for ever sunk
Under yon boiling ocean, wrapped in chains;
There to converse with everlasting groans,
Unrespited, unpitied, unreprieved,
Ages of hopeless end? This would be worse.
War therefore, open or concealed, alike
My voice dissuades; for what can force or guile
With him, or who deceive his mind, whose eye
190   Views all things at one view? He from heaven's highth
All these our motions° vain, sees and derides;
Not more almighty to resist our might
Than wise to frustrate all our plots and wiles.
Shall we then live thus vile, the race of heaven
Thus trampled, thus expelled to suffer here
Chains and these torments? Better these than worse,
By my advice; since fate inevitable
Subdues us, and omnipotent decree,
The victor's will. To suffer, as to do,°

What . . . worse He will keep answering this rhetorical question in his own rhetorically brilliant speech.
burning lake an echo of I.52
red right hand quoted from Horace (*Odes* I.2), where it is used of civil war. This passage (to l. 186) also echoes classical accounts of Zeus' vanquishing the Titans.

motions plans
To suffer, as to do chimes against Satan's "Doing or suffering" (I.158) and the words of the Roman Mucius Scaevola, as he burned his right hand in the flames to show his captors his inner resources

200 Our strength is equal, nor the law unjust
That so ordains: this was at first resolved,
If we were wise, against so great a foe
Contending, and so doubtful what might fall.
I laugh when those who at the spear are bold
And venturous, if that fail them, shrink and fear
What yet they know must follow, to endure
Exile, or ignominy,° or bonds, or pain,
The sentence of their conqueror. This is now
Our doom; which if we can sustain and bear,
210 Our súpreme foe in time may much remit
His anger, and perhaps, thus far removed,
Not mind us not offending, satisfied
With what is punished; whence these raging fires
Will slacken, if his breath stir not their flames.
Our purer essence then will overcome
Their noxious vapour, or enured° not feel,
Or changed at length, and to the place conformed
In temper and in nature, will receive
Familiar the fierce heat, and void of pain;
220 This horror will grow mild, this darkness light,°
Besides what hope the never-ending flight
Of future days may bring, what chance, what change
Worth waiting, since our present lot appears
For happy° though but ill, for ill not worst,
If we procure not to ourselves more woe.'
    Thus Belial with words clothed in reason's garb,
Counselled ignoble ease, and peaceful sloth,
Not peace; and after him thus Mammon° spake—
    'Either to disenthrone the king of heaven
230 We war, if war be best, or to regain
Our own right lost: him to unthrone we then
May hope when everlasting fate shall yield
To fickle chance, and Chaos judge the strife:°
The former, vain to hope, argues as vain
The latter; for what place can be for us
Within heaven's bound, unless heaven's lord supreme
We overpower? Suppose he should relent
And publish grace to all, on promise made
Of new subjection; with what eyes could we
240 Stand in his presence humble, and receive
Strict laws imposed, to celebrate his throne
With warbled hymns, and to his Godhead sing
Forced halleluiahs; while he lordly sits
Our envied sovereign, and his altar breathes

---

ignominy See I.115n.
enured accustomed to
light not dark; not heavy

For happy as for happiness
Mammon See I.680.
strife between fate and chance

Ambrosial odours and ambrosial flowers,
Our servile offerings? This must be our task
In heaven, this our delight; how wearisome
Eternity so spent in worship paid
To whom we hate. Let us not then pursue
250 By force impossible, by leave obtained
Unácceptáble—though in heaven—our state
Of splendid vassalage, but rather seek
Our own good from ourselves, and from our own
Live to ourselves, though in this vast recess,
Free, and to none accountable, preferring
Hard liberty° before the easy yoke
Of servile pomp. Our greatness will appear
Then most conspicuous, when great things of small,
Useful of hurtful, prosperous of adverse
260 We can create, and in what place soe'er
Thrive under evil, and work ease out of pain
Through labour and endurance. This deep world
Of darkness do we dread? How oft amidst
Thick clouds and dark doth heaven's all-ruling sire
Choose to reside, his glory unobscured,
And with the majesty of darkness round
Covers his throne; from whence deep thunders roar,
Mustering their rage, and heaven resembles hell?
As he our darkness, cannot we his light
270 Imitate when we please? This desert soil
Wants not her hidden lustre, gems and gold;
Nor want we skill or art, from whence to raise
Magnificence; and what can heaven show more?
Our torments also may in length of time
Become our elements, these piercing fires
As soft as now severe, our temper changed
Into their temper; which must needs remove
The sensible° of pain. All things invite
To peaceful counsels, and the settled state
280 Of order, how in safety best we may
Compose° our present evils, with regard
Of what we are and where, dismissing quite
All thoughts of war. Ye have what I advise.'
   He scarce had finished, when such murmur filled
The assembly as when hollow rocks retain
The sound of blustering winds, which all night long
Had roused the sea, now with hoarse cadence lull

Hard liberty Mammon's declaration of independence cannot help but move the lover of human freedom, even one who appreciates the prophecy of the relation of individual liberty to the institution of wealth as acted out in the history of Western capitalism. In the context of the debate—Moloch's primitive, heroic violence and Belial's guileful parody of medieval quietism—Mammon's exhortation (ll. 269–73 below) to his fellows to produce light of their own follows as a version of what Max Weber called the Protestant ethic.
sensible felt part
Compose arrange

Seafaring men o'erwatched, whose bark by chance
Or pinnace anchors in a craggy bay
290 After the tempest. Such applause was heard
As Mammon ended, and his sentence° pleased,
Advising peace; for such another field
They dreaded worse than hell: so much the fear
Of thunder and the sword of Michaël°
Wrought still within them; and no less desire
To found this nether empire, which might rise
By policy,° and long procéss of time,
In emulation opposite to heaven.
Which when Beelzebub° perceived, than whom,
300 Satan except, none higher sat, with grave
Aspect he rose, and in his rising seemed
A pillar of state; deep on his front° engraven
Deliberation sat and public care;
And princely counsel in his face yet shone,
Majestic though in ruin: sage he stood,
With Atlantean° shoulders fit to bear
The weight of mightiest monarchies; his look
Drew audience and attention still as night
Or summer's noontide air, while thus he spake.

[Beelzebub's speech which follows dismisses the notion of merely trying to
make Hell a better place to live, and outlines his general Satan's plan to
attack the Kingdom of Heaven through its colony, a weak spot, "another
world, the happy seat / Of some new race called Man," the inhabitants of
which, currently "favoured more / Of him who rules above," might be corrupted, dispossessed, and added to their ranks. The assembly votes for this
plan, and Satan, with no volunteers for the dangerous mission of checking
the rumor and scouting the terrain, flies off himself. Meanwhile, the remaining demons occupy themselves in cultural pursuits: not only is the culture
of Pandemonium, as we might call it, a brilliantly prophetic version of that
of classical antiquity, but it shifts to Renaissance exploration, based on
mythical and actual accounts of journeys alike. Then we have Satan leaving
Hell to find earth, encountering the portress, a monster whom he does not
recognize, and another, impossible to describe in detail. This inset allegory
of Sin and Death is the narrative actualization of the imagery in James 1:15
which speaks of how lust, when it "hath conceived, it bringeth forth sin; and
sin, when it is finished, bringeth forth death."]

The Stygian council thus dissolved; and forth
In order came the grand infernal peers;
Midst came their mighty paramount,° and seemed

---

sentence opinion; cf. l. 51
Michaël archangel who commanded God's army
in Bk. VI
policy statecraft, with Machiavellian overtones

Beelzebub See I.81.
front forehead
Atlantean Atlas-like
paramount ruler

Alone the antagonist of heaven, nor less
510 Than hell's dread emperor, with pomp supreme
And god-like imitated state;° him round
A globe° of fiery seraphim enclosed
With bright emblazonry and horrent° arms.
Then of their session ended they bid cry
With trumpet's regal sound the great result.
Toward the four winds four speedy cherubim
Put to their mouths the sounding alchemy°
By herald's voice explained; the hollow abyss
Heard far and wide, and all the host of hell
520 With deafening shout returned them loud acclaim.
Thence more at ease their minds and somewhat raised°
By false presumptuous hope, the rangèd powers°
Disband, and wandering each his several way
Pursues, as inclination or sad choice
Leads him perplexed, where he may likeliest find
Truce to his restless thoughts, and entertain°
The irksome hours, till his great chief return.
Part on the plain, or in the air sublime°
Upon the wing, or in swift race contend,
530 As at the Olympian games or Pythian fields;°
Part curb their fiery steeds, or shun the goal
With rapid wheels, or fronted brígades form:
As when to warn proud cities war appears
Waged in the troubled sky, and armies rush
To battle in the clouds; before each van
Prick forth the airy knights, and couch their spears,
Till thickest legions close; with feats of arms
From either end of heaven the welkin° burns.
Others with vast Typhoean° rage more fell
540 Rend up both rocks and hills, and ride the air
In whirlwind; hell scarce holds the wild uproar;
As when Alcides° from Oechalia crowned
With conquest, felt the envenomed robe, and tore
Through pain up by the roots Thessalian pines,°
And Lichas from the top of Oeta threw
Into the Euboic sea. Others more mild,

---

state ceremonial royal trappings
globe phalanx
horrent bristling
alchemy metallic alloy
raised heartened
rangèd powers ranked armies
entertain pass away
sublime raise up
Olympian . . . fields This introduces the heroic
games.
welkin sky
Typhoean titanic (see I.199); also, through

"typhon" (influencing "typhoon" later on),
a whirlwind
Alcides Hercules, whose wife sent him a
poisoned robe, went mad with the pain and
hurled his friend Lichas, the mere bringer of
the gift, into the Euboean sea.
tore . . . pines Not only does the wrenched
syntax "imitate" the heroic action described
(mostly by separating "tore" and "up"), but
the whole of l. 544 itself is symmetrically
patterned, with a pun on "pain" and "pine"
(meaning "pain" as a noun, as well).

Retreated in a silent valley, sing°
With notes angelical to many a harp
Their own heroic deeds and hapless fall
550   By doom of battle; and complain that fate
Free virtue should enthrall to force or chance.
Their song was partial,° but the harmony
(What could it less when spirits immortal sing?)
Suspended° hell, and took with ravishment
The thronging audience. In discourse more sweet
(For eloquence the soul, song charms the sense)
Others apart sat on a hill retired,
In thoughts more elevate, and reasoned° high
Of providence, foreknowledge, will, and fate,
560   Fixed fate, free will, foreknowledge absolute,
And found no end, in wandering mazes lost.°
Of good and evil much they argued then,
Of happiness and final misery,
Passion and apathy, and glory and shame,
Vain wisdom all, and false philosophy—
Yet with a pleasing sorcery could charm
Pain for a while or anguish, and excite
Fallacious hope, or arm the obdurèd° breast
With stubborn patience as with triple steel.
570   Another part, in squadrons and gross° bands,
On bold adventure to discover wide
That dismal world, if any clime perhaps
Might yield them easier habitation, bend
Four ways their flying march, along the banks
Of four infernal rivers that disgorge
Into the burning lake their baleful streams:
Abhorrèd Styx,° the flood of deadly hate;
Sad Acheron of sorrow, black and deep;
Cocytus, named of lamentation loud
580   Heard on the rueful stream; fierce Phlegethon,
Whose waves of torrent fire inflame with rage.
Far off from these a slow and silent stream,
Lethe, the river of oblivion, rolls
Her watery labyrinth,° whereof who drinks
Forthwith his former state and being forgets,
Forgets both joy and grief, pleasure and pain.
Beyond this flood a frozen continent

---

sing epics, like their own versions of *Paradise
Lost* VI
partial one-sided; also, possibly "in parts," or
polyphonic musically
Suspended held rapt
reasoned a prophetic vision of fallen classical
philosophy, particularly of Stoicism
wandering mazes lost as in the syntax and the
twisting repetitions of abstract philosophical

concepts, their way to truth forever lost
obdurèd hardened
gross massive
Abhorrèd Styx Each of these four rivers of the
classical Hades has its name translated and
explained.
labyrinth ironically paralleling the labyrinthine
mazes of pagan thought, l. 561

Lies dark and wild, beat with perpetual storms
Of whirlwind and dire hail, which on firm land
590   Thaws not, but gathers heap, and ruin seems
Of ancient pile;° all else deep snow and ice,
A gulf profound as that Serbonian° bog
Betwixt Damiata and Mount Casius old,
Where armies whole have sunk; the parching air
Burns frore,° and cold performs the effect of fire.
Thither by harpy-footed Furies haled,
At certain revolutions all the damned
Are brought; and feel by turns the bitter change
Of fierce extremes, extremes by change more fierce,
600   From beds of raging fire to starve° in ice
Their soft ethereal warmth, and there to pine
Immovable, infixed, and frozen round,
Periods of time; thence hurried back to fire.
They ferry over this Lethean sound
Both to and fro, their sorrow to augment,
And wish and struggle, as they pass, to reach
The tempting stream, with one small drop to lose
In sweet forgetfulness all pain and woe,
All in one moment, and so near the brink;
610   But fate withstands, and to oppose the attempt
Medusa° with Gorgonian terror guards
The ford, and of itself the water flies
All taste of living wight, as once it fled
The lip of Tantalus.° Thus roving on
In cónfused march forlorn, the adventurous bands,
With shuddering horror pale, and eyes aghast,
Viewed first their lamentable lot, and found
No rest. Through many a dark and dreary vale
They passed, and many a region dolorous,
620   O'er many a frozen, many a fiery alp,°
Rocks, caves, lakes, fens, bogs, dens, and shades of death,°
A universe of death, which God by curse
Created evil, for evil only good,
Where all life dies, death lives, and Nature breeds,
Perverse, all monstrous, all prodigious things,
Abominable, inutterable, and worse
Than fables yet have feigned, or fear conceived,
Gorgons and Hydras, and Chimeras° dire.

---

pile building
Serbonian the quicksands which lay between
Lake Serbonis and Damiata, near the Nile
delta, renowned in antiquity for their danger
to armies
frore frozen
starve Only the syntax is misleading: "to starve
their warmth to death in ice."
Medusa one of the snaky-haired Gorgons whose
look turns men to stone
Tantalus In the *Odyssey*, Odysseus sees Tanta-

lus, desperately thirsty, standing in a pool that
always drops below his mouth when he tries to
drink from it; cf. *The Faerie Queene* I.v.35.
alp any mountain
Rocks . . . death again, a mimetic line, its list
of monosyllables tiring to get through, and
slow
Hydras, and Chimeras many-headed beasts, and
fire-breathing, triple-bodied (lion-serpent-goat)
monsters

Meanwhile the adversary of God and man,
630 Satan, with thoughts inflamed of highest design,
Puts on swift wings, and toward the gates of hell
Explores° his solitary flight; sometimes
He scours the right-hand coast, sometimes the left;
Now shaves with level wing the deep, then soars
Up to the fiery concave towering high:
As when far off at sea a fleet descried
Hangs in the clouds, by equinoctial winds
Close sailing from Bengala,° or the isles
Of Ternate and Tidore,° whence merchants bring
640 Their spicy drugs: they on the trading flood
Through the wide Ethiopian to the Cape°
Ply° stemming nightly toward the pole. So seemed
Far off the flying fiend. At last appear
Hell bounds high reaching to the horrid° roof,
And thrice threefold the gates; three folds were brass,
Three iron, three of adamantine rock,
Impenetrable, impaled° with circling fire,
Yet unconsumed. Before the gates there sat
On either side a formidable shape;
650 The one seemed woman to the waist, and fair,
But ended foul in many a scaly fold
Voluminous° and vast, a serpent armed
With mortal sting. About her middle round
A cry° of hell-hounds never ceasing barked
With wide Cerberean mouths full loud, and rung
A hideous peal; yet, when they list, would creep,
If aught disturbed their noise, into her womb,
And kennel there, yet there still barked and howled,
Within unseen. Far less abhorred than these
660 Vexed Scylla bathing in the sea that parts
Calabria from the hoarse Trinacrian° shore;
Nor uglier follow the Night-hag,° when called
In secret, riding through the air she comes,
Lured with the smell of infant blood, to dance
With Lapland witches, while the labouring° moon
Eclipses at their charms. The other shape—
If shape it might be called that shape had none°

Explores tests out
Bengala Bengal
Ternate and Tidore islands of the Moluccas,
or "spice islands"
Ethiopian to the Cape Indian Ocean to the
Cape of Good Hope
Ply beat to windward
horrid bristling
impaled not "spiked," but "enclosed"
Voluminous coiled
cry pack. Part of the description evokes Spenser's
Error (*The Faerie Queene* I.i.14–15).
Trinacrian Sicilian. In the *Odyssey*, the monster

Scylla and the whirlpool Charybdis control the
strait of Messina.
Night-hag Hecate
labouring undergoing eclipse
that shape had none Nobody can know what
death is like; only the dead, who cannot know
or tell, have seen it. Having Satan—and thus
the reader—encounter Sin and Death before
knowing who they are, is a higher kind of
allegorizing: were they both labeled with their
identities they would be more easily avoided.
Cf. *The Faerie Queene* VII.vii.46.

Distinguishable in member, joint, or limb,
Or substance might be called that shadow seemed,
670   For each seemed either—black it stood as Night,
Fierce as ten Furies, terrible as hell,
And shook a dreadful dart; what seemed his head
The likeness of a kingly crown had on.
Satan was now at hand, and from his seat
The monster moving onward came as fast
With horrid strides; hell trembled as he strode.
The undaunted fiend what this might be admired,
Admired, not feared; God and his Son except,
Created thing naught valued he nor shunned;
680   And with disdainful look thus first began:
    'Whence and what art thou, execrable shape,
That darest, though grim and terrible, advance
Thy miscreated front athwart my way
To yonder gates? Through them I mean to pass,
That be assured, without leave asked of thee.
Retire, or taste thy folly, and learn by proof,
Hell-born, not to contend with spirits of heaven.'
    To whom the goblin full of wrath replied:
'Art thou that traitor angel, art thou he,
690   Who first broke peace in heaven and faith, till then
Unbroken, and in proud rebellious arms
Drew after him the third part of heaven's sons
Conjured° against the highest, for which both thou
And they, outcast from God, are here condemned
To waste eternal days in woe and pain?
And reckonest thou thyself with spirits of heaven,
Hell-doomed, and breathest defiance here and scorn
Where I reign king, and to enrage thee more,
Thy king and lord? Back to thy punishment,
700   False fugitive, and to thy speed add wings,
Lest with a whip of scorpions I pursue
Thy lingering, or with one stroke of this dart
Strange horror seize thee, and pangs unfelt before.'
    So spake the grisly terror, and in shape,
So speaking and so threatening, grew tenfold
More dreadful and deform. On the other side,
Incensed with indignation Satan stood
Unterrified, and like a comet burned,
That fires the length of Ophiuchus° huge
710   In the arctic sky, and from his horrid hair°
Shakes pestilence and war. Each at the head

Conjured sworn together. The "third part of
the stars of heaven" were thrown to earth by
the dragon in Revelation 12:3–4.
Ophiuchus "serpent-bearer," a large and prominent constellation of the northern sky

horrid hair "Comet" means "long-haired" star,
and comets were portents of disaster; the Latin
horrere means "to bristle."

Levelled his deadly aim; their fatal hands
No second stroke intend; and such a frown
Each cast at the other, as when two black clouds
With heaven's artillery fraught, come rattling on
Over the Caspian, then stand front to front
Hovering a space, till winds the signal blow
To join their dark encounter in mid-air:°
So frowned the mighty combatants that hell
720 Grew darker at their frown, so matched they stood;
For never but once more was either like
To meet so great a foe.° And now great deeds
Had been achieved, whereof all hell had rung,
Had not the snaky sorceress that sat
Fast by hell gate, and kept the fatal key,
Risen, and with hideous outcry rushed between.

    'O father, what intends thy hand,' she cried,
'Against thy only son? What fury, O son,
Possesses thee to bend that mortal dart
730 Against thy father's head? And knowest for whom?
For him who sits above and laughs the while
At thee ordained his drudge, to execute
Whate'er his wrath, which he calls justice, bids,
His wrath which one day will destroy ye both.'

    She spake, and at her words the hellish pest
Forbore; then these to her Satan returned:

    'So strange thy outcry, and thy words so strange
Thou interposest, that my sudden hand
Prevented spares to tell thee yet by deeds
740 What it intends; till first I know of thee,
What thing thou art, thus double-formed, and why
In this infernal vale first met thou callest
Me father, and that phantasm callest my son.
I know thee not, nor ever saw till now
Sight more detestable than him and thee.'

    To whom thus the portress of hell gate replied:
'Hast thou forgot me then, and do I seem
Now in thine eye so foul? Once deemed so fair
In heaven, when at the assembly, and in sight
750 Of all the seraphim with thee combined
In bold conspiracy against heaven's king,
All on a sudden miserable pain
Surprised thee; dim thine eyes, and dizzy swum
In darkness, while thy head flames thick and fast
Threw forth, till on the left side opening wide,
Likest to thee in shape and countenance bright,

mid-air the middle region of atmospheric phenomena and air demons (as opposed to a more
visionary domain of sky)

so great a foe Christ, conquering them

Then shining heavenly fair, a goddess armed
Out of thy head I sprung.° Amazement seized
All the host of heaven; back they recoiled afraid
760   At first, and called me *Sin*, and for a sign
Portentous held me; but familiar grown,
I pleased, and with attractive graces won
The most averse, thee chiefly, who full oft
Thyself in me thy perfect image viewing
Becamest enamoured; and such joy thou tookest
With me in secret, that my womb conceived
A growing burden. Meanwhile war arose,
And fields were fought in heaven; wherein remained
(For what could else?) to our almighty foe
770   Clear victory, to our part loss and rout
Through all the empyrean: down they fell
Driven headlong from the pitch° of heaven, down
Into this deep, and in the general fall
I also; at which time this powerful key
Into my hand was given, with charge to keep
These gates for ever shut, which none can pass
Without my opening. Pensive here I sat
Alone, but long I sat not, till my womb,
Pregnant by thee, and now excessive grown,
780   Prodigious motion felt and rueful throes.
At last this odious offspring whom thou seest,
Thine own begotten, breaking violent way
Tore through my entrails, that with fear and pain
Distorted, all my nether shape thus grew
Transformed; but he my inbred enemy
Forth issued, brandishing his fatal dart
Made to destroy. I fled, and cried out *Death!*
Hell trembled at the hideous name, and sighed
From all her caves, and back resounded *Death!*
790   I fled, but he pursued (though more, it seems,
Inflamed with lust than rage) and swifter far,
Me overtook, his mother, all dismayed,
And in embraces forcible and foul
Engendering with me, of that rape begot
These yelling monsters that with ceaseless cry
Surround me, as thou sawest, hourly conceived
And hourly born, with sorrow infinite
To me; for when they list, into the womb
That bred them they return, and howl and gnaw
800   My bowels, their repast; then bursting forth

Out . . . sprung like Athena, Wisdom, from
the forehead of Zeus, to show the birth of
Mind. Similarly, Sin proceeds from Satan's
thought, not, for example, from his guts, or by
normal engendering; additionally, in the anti-
Trinity of Father, Daughter, and Unholy Monster, she is the second term.
pitch high point

Afresh, with conscious terrors vex me round,
That rest or intermission none I find.°
Before mine eyes in opposition sits
Grim Death my son and foe, who sets them on,
And me his parent would full soon devour
For want of other prey, but that he knows
His end with mine involved; and knows that I
Should prove a bitter morsel, and his bane,
Whenever that shall be; so fate pronounced.
810   But thou, O father, I forewarn thee, shun
His deadly arrow; neither vainly hope
To be invulnerable in those bright arms,
Though tempered heavenly, for that mortal dint,°
Save he who reigns above, none can resist.'
     She finished, and the subtle Fiend his lore
Soon learned, now milder, and thus answered smooth:
'Dear daughter, since thou claimest me for thy sire,
And my fair son here showest me, the dear pledge°
Of dalliance had with thee in heaven, and joys
820   Then sweet, now sad to mention, through dire change
Befallen us unforeseen, unthought of, know
I come no enemy, but to set free
From out this dark and dismal house° of pain
Both him and thee, and all the heavenly host
Of spirits that in our just pretences° armed
Fell with us from on high. From them I go
This uncouth errand sole, and one for all
Myself expose with lonely steps to tread
The unfounded° deep, and through the void immense
830   To search with wandering quest a place foretold
Should be, and, by concurring signs, ere now
Created vast and round, a place of bliss
In the purlieus° of heaven, and therein placed
A race of upstart creatures, to supply
Perhaps our vacant room, though more removed,
Lest heaven surcharged° with potent multitude
Might hap to move new broils. Be this or aught
Than this more secret now designed, I haste
To know, and this once known, shall soon return,
840   And bring ye to the place where thou and Death
Shall dwell at ease, and up and down unseen
Wing silently the buxom° air, embalmed
With odours; there ye shall be fed and filled

These yelling . . . find (ll. 795–802). Cf. *The Faerie Queene* I.i.15.
dint blow of a sword
pledge child
house hell, as in Job 30:23
pretences legal claims

unfounded bottomless
purlieus bordering region, but with an implication of a licentious neighborhood
surcharged overburdened
buxom unresisting

Immeasurably; all things shall be your prey.'
He ceased, for both seemed highly pleased, and Death
Grinned horrible a ghastly smile, to hear
His famine should be filled, and blessed his maw
Destined to that good hour. No less rejoiced
His mother bad, and thus bespake her sire:
850   'The key of this infernal pit by due°
And by command of heaven's all-powerful king
I keep, by him forbidden to unlock
These adamantine gates; against all force
Death ready stands to interpose his dart,
Fearless to be o'ermatched by living might.
But what owe I to his commands above
Who hates me, and hath hither thrust me down
Into this gloom of Tartarus profound,
To sit in hateful office here confined,
860   Inhabitant of heaven and heavenly-born,
Here in perpetual agony and pain,
With terrors and with clamours compassed round
Of mine own brood, that on my bowels feed?
Thou art my father, thou my author, thou
My being gavest me; whom should I obey
But thee, whom follow? Thou wilt bring me soon
To that new world of light and bliss, among
The gods who live at ease, where I shall reign
At thy right hand voluptuous,° as beseems
870   Thy daughter and thy darling, without end.'

· · ·

[Sin then unlocks the gate of hell. Satan flies out toward the world, moving
through atmosphere, tidal marshes, and a composite Chaos—part the classical
description (from Hesiod and Ovid) of warring unorganized elements, part an
allegorical picture of night and ethical and political disorder. Through these
and "O'er bog or steep, through strait, rough, dense, or rare, / With head,
hands, wings, or feet pursues his way, / And swims or sinks, or wades, or
creeps, or flies." The allegorized Chaos, lord of "Havoc and spoil and ruin,"
directs him toward regions by which hangs "in a golden chain / This pendant
world. . . . Thither full fraught with mischievous revenge / Accurst, and
in a cursèd hour he hies."]

From *Book III*

[The Muse is again invoked, here as light itself, which resulted from the
first act of creation (Genesis 1:3) but which also, in another aspect, coexisted
with its creator from the beginning. The original of all creative acts for
Milton is the lighting up of darkness—transforming a chaotic world by ex-

---

due right
At thy right hand voluptuous a parody of the
Nicene Creed: "who sittest on the right hand

of the Father" and "whose kingdom shall be
without end"

plaining it—and the physical reduction of general created light into the sun
and moon was the shaping of an attribute of this power. The present exordium
is a lyric spell spun to help the poet move from his description of hell, where
all the energies of heroic, epical poetry aided him, to scenes in heaven,
whose static and doctrinal character would pose a different sort of challenge.]

Hail, holy Light, offspring of heaven first-born,
Or of the eternal coeternal beam
May I express thee unblamed? since God is light,
And never but in unapproachèd light
Dwelt from eternity, dwelt then in thee,
Bright effluence of bright essence increate.
Or hearest thou rather° pure ethereal stream,°
Whose fountain who shall tell? Before the sun,
Before the heavens thou wert, and at the voice
10 Of God, as with a mantle didst invest
The rising world of waters dark and deep,
Won from the void and formless infinite.
Thee I revisit now with bolder wing,
Escaped the Stygian pool,° though long detained
In that obscure sojourn, while in my flight
Through utter° and through middle darkness° borne
With other notes° than to the Orphéan lyre
I sung of Chaos and eternal Night,
Taught by the heavenly Muse to venture down
20 The dark descent, and up to reascend,
Though hard and rare. Thee I revisit safe,
And feel thy sovereign vital lamp; but thou
Revisit'st not these eyes, that roll in vain
To find thy piercing ray, and find no dawn;
So thick a drop serene° hath quenched their orbs,
Or dim suffusion° veiled. Yet not the more
Cease I to wander where the Muses haunt
Clear spring, or shady grove, or sunny hill,
Smit with the love of sacred song; but chief
30 Thee, Sion,° and the flowery brooks beneath
That wash thy hallowed feet, and warbling flow,
Nightly I visit;° nor sometimes forget
Those other two equalled with me in fate,
So were I° equalled with them in renown,

hearest thou rather would you rather be
called?
stream like poetry in classical myth, an out-
break of expression
Stygian pool hell, the lower darkness
utter outer
middle darkness Chaos
other notes because he (his poetry) would
not merely make an Orphean visit to the underworld, nor would his Muse be lost to him
there

drop serene translates the Latin medical term for
his blindness, *gutta serena.*
suffusion cataract
Sion Hebrew poetry, rather than Helicon, or
Greek
Nightly I visit This theme of composing at
night, literally and figuratively, is taken up
again at VII. 29.
So were I would that I were

Blind Thamyris and blind Maeonides,°
And Tiresias and Phineus° prophets old:
Then feed on thoughts that voluntary move
Harmonious numbers,° as the wakeful bird
Sings darkling,° and in shadiest covert hid
40 Tunes her nocturnal note. Thus with the year
Seasons return; but not to me returns
Day, or the sweet approach of even or morn,
Or sight of vernal bloom, or summer's rose,
Or flocks, or herds, or human face divine;°
But cloud instead, and ever-during dark
Surrounds me, from the cheerful ways of men
Cut off, and for the book of knowledge° fair
Presented with a universal blank°
Of Nature's works to me expunged and razed,
50 And wisdom at one entrance° quite shut out.
So much the rather thou, celestial Light,
Shine inward, and the mind through all her powers
Irradiate, there plant eyes, all mist from thence
Purge and disperse, that I may see and tell
Of things invisible to mortal sight. . . .

[The world of Book III is unveiled with God enthroned in heaven, where all
the angels "stood thick as stars"; at his right hand is his Son, to whom he
points out the tiny image of distant Satan, about to alight, insect-like (as he
appears from heaven), on the outside of the world. Telling the Son of the
Satanic plan, God points out that Man will nevertheless be responsible for
the foreknown, but not foreordained Fall ("he had of me / All he could have:
I made him just and right, / Sufficient to have stood, though free to fall").
When the Father insists that justice must be done, the Son offers himself as a
sacrifice for human eternal life: "Behold me then, me for him, life for life / I
offer, on me let thine anger fall: / Account me man." God accepts, describing
the incarnation and passion, ordains "Be thou in Adam's room / The head of
all mankind, though Adam's son. / As in him perish all men, so in thee / As
from a second root shall be restored." An angelic choir celebrates this ordination. The action then cuts to Satan, alighting now vulture-like upon the world,
passing through a Limbo of Vanity where, blown by winds, types of folly
abound. He moves into the orb of the sun (descending, as he must, from the
outermost sphere of the Ptolemaic structure down toward the central earth),

Thamyris . . . Maeonides a mythical Thracian
bard, blinded for his presumption, and Homer
(from Maeonia)
Tiresias . . . Phineus Tiresias was the blind
seer of antiquity, Phineus a blinded Thracian
king who prophesied.
Harmonious numbers beautiful lines of verse
darkling in the dark. This bird is the nightingale, with whom is associated mute suffering
transformed into poetic song.
human face divine The word order makes the
adjectives play different roles, defining and at-

tributing, and in reading the phrase we progress
from low to high; Blake used this compound as a
model for a crucial phrase of his own: "human
form divine."
book of knowledge Nature, which, for the
hieroglyphic-minded, was a book to be read
and understood (see *Emblem* in the Glossary)
blank a blank page, a whiteness
one entrance too fragile a one: see Samson's
staggering eloquence on this matter in *Samson
Agonistes* ll. 90–96

encounters Uriel, "God's light," the guardian of that region, disguises himself
and is able by fraud to discover the whereabouts of Eden, and alights on
Mount Niphates.]

Book IV

O for that warning voice, which he who saw
The Apocalypse° heard cry in heaven aloud,
Then when the dragon, put to second rout,
Came furious down to be revenged on men,
'*Woe to the inhabitants on earth!*' that now,
While time was, our first parents had been warned
The coming of their secret foe, and scaped,
Haply so scaped, his mortal snare; for now
Satan, now first inflamed with rage, came down,
10   The tempter ere the accuser of mankind,
To wreak° on innocent frail man his loss
Of that first battle, and his flight to hell:
Yet not rejoicing in his speed, though bold,
Far off and fearless, nor with cause to boast,
Begins his dire attempt, which nigh the birth
Now rolling, boils in his tumultuous breast,
And like a devilish engine° back recoils
Upon himself; horror and doubt distract
His troubled thoughts, and from the bottom stir
20   The hell within him, for within him hell
He brings, and round about him, nor from hell°
One step no more than from himself can fly
By change of place. Now conscience wakes despair
That slumbered, wakes the bitter memory
Of what he was, what is, and what must be
Worse; of worse deeds worse sufferings must ensue.
Sometimes towards Eden which now in his view
Lay pleasant,° his grieved look he fixes sad,
Sometimes towards heaven and the full-blazing sun,
30   Which now sat high in his meridian tower.°
Then much revolving, thus in sighs began:
   'O thou° that with surpassing glory crowned
Look'st from thy sole dominion like the god

---

he . . . Apocalypse St. John, warning in Revelation 12:7–12 of another battle in heaven
between "the dragon" and Michael; would that
he could so prophetically warn, Milton pleads.
wreak avenge
devilish engine artillery, invented by Satan's
forces in the war; also, "engine" (in a sense
related to "ingenious") as a plan or scheme,
for which the word "recoils" is metaphoric,
suggesting the re-coiling or twisting of snaky
thought, of dialectic; cf. II.65
The hell within . . . hell This beautifully arranged line with its chiasmus (see II.39–40n)

mocks by its static order the churning of
Satan's inner state, an ironic fulfillment of his
statement in I.254–55 about the mind's being
"its own place"; cf. *Doctor Faustus* V.120–21.
pleasant In Hebrew, Eden means "delight."
meridian tower It is noon, and the Fall will
occur at noon with light at its height and
despite guarding enlightenment.
O thou the sun. According to Milton's nephew
Edward Phillips in his *Life of Milton*, these
lines were originally composed as the opening
lines of the tragedy about the Fall that *Paradise
Lost* was once to have been.

Of this new world; at whose sight all the stars
Hide their diminished heads; to thee I call,
But with no friendly voice, and add thy name,
O sun, to tell thee how I hate thy beams
That bring to my remembrance from what state
I fell, how glorious once above thy sphere;
40   Till pride and worse ambition threw me down
Warring in heaven against heaven's matchless king.
Ah wherefore? He deserved no such return
From me, whom he created what I was°
In that bright eminence,° and with his good
Upbraided none; nor was his service hard.
What could be less than to afford him praise,
The easiest recompense, and pay him thanks,
How due! Yet all his good proved ill in me,
And wrought but malice; lifted up so high
50   I sdained° subjection, and thought one step higher
Would set me highest, and in a moment quit°
The debt immense of endless gratitude,
So burdensome still paying, still° to owe;
Forgetful what from him I still received,
And understood not that a grateful mind
By owing owes not, but still pays, at once
Indebted and discharged; what burden then?
O had his powerful destiny ordained
Me some inferior angel, I had stood
60   Then happy; no unbounded hope had raised
Ambition. Yet why not? Some other power
As great might have aspired, and me though mean
Drawn to his part; but other powers as great
Fell not, but stand unshaken, from within
Or from without, to all temptations armed.
Hadst thou the same free will and power to stand?
Thou hadst. Whom hast thou then or what to accuse,
But heaven's free love dealt equally to all?
Be then his love accurst, since love or hate,
70   To me alike, it deals eternal woe.
Nay cursed be thou, since against his thy will
Chose freely what it now so justly rues.
Me miserable! which way shall I fly
Infinite wrath, and infinite despair?
Which way I fly is hell; myself am hell;°

---

whom he . . . was Satan admits this here, but denies it in his public, political oratory elsewhere.
that bright eminence Notice the echo of the reciprocal epithet in the narrator's lines in II.6.
sdained disdained
quit pay off

still continually
Which way . . . hell echoing IV.20, and Marlowe's *Doctor Faustus* III.76: "Why, this is hell, nor am I out of it" and, later on, V.120–121: "Hell hath no limits, nor is circumscribed / In one self place, but where we are is hell"; cf. also I.225 and IX.122–23

And in the lowest deep a lower deep
Still threatening to devour me opens wide,
To which the hell I suffer seems a heaven.°
O then at last relent: is there no place
80   Left for repentance, none for pardon left?
None left but by submission; and that word
Disdain forbids me, and my dread of shame
Among the spirits beneath, whom I seduced
With other promises and other vaunts
Than to submit, boasting I could subdue
The omnipotent.° Ay me, they little know
How dearly I abide that boast so vain,
Under what torments inwardly I groan;
While they adore me on the throne of hell,
90   With diadem and sceptre high advanced,
The lower still I fall, only supreme
In misery; such joy ambition finds.
But say I could repent and could obtain
By act of grace° my former state; how soon
Would highth recall high thoughts, how soon unsay
What feigned submission swore: ease would recant
Vows made in pain, as violent and void.
For never can true reconcilement grow
Where sounds of deadly hate have pierced so deep;
100 Which would but lead me to a worse relapse
And heavier fall: so should I purchase dear
Short intermission bought with double smart.
This knows my punisher; therefore as far
From granting he, as I from begging peace.
All hope excluded thus, behold instead
Of us outcast, exiled, his new delight,
Mankind created, and for him this world.
So farewell hope, and with hope farewell fear,
Farewell remorse! All good to me is lost;
110 Evil, be thou my good;° by thee at least
Divided empire with heaven's king I hold
By thee, and more than half perhaps will govern;
As man ere long, and this new world shall know.'
    Thus while he spake, each passion dimmed his face
Thrice changed with° pale, ire, envy, and despair,
Which marred his borrowed visage,° and betrayed
Him counterfeit, if any eye beheld.

---

the hell . . . heaven Local and general, concrete and abstract, literal ad figurative uses of words have become all mixed up in Satan's tangled thought.
None left . . . omnipotent (ll. 81–86) Cf. ll. 388–92 below.
act of grace formal pardon, not an admission of right

Evil . . . good Again, the dramatic irony here is crushing: at IX.121–23 he realizes, almost with disgust, that his command has been obeyed; cf. I.165.
changed with changed to
borrowed visage explained in III.636 to be that of a "stripling cherub"

For heavenly minds from such distempers foul
Are ever clear. Whereof he soon aware,
120 Each perturbation smoothed with outward calm,
Artificer of fraud; and was the first
That practised falsehood under saintly show,
Deep malice to conceal, couched with revenge:
Yet not enough had practised to deceive
Uriel° once warned, whose eye pursued him down
The way he went, and on the Assyrian mount°
Saw him disfigured, more than could befall
Spirit of happy sort: his gestures fierce
He marked and mad demeanour, then alone,
130 As he supposed, all unobserved, unseen.
So on he fares, and to the border comes
Of Eden, where delicious Paradise,
Now nearer, crowns with her enclosure green
As with a rural mound the champaign head°
Of a steep wilderness, whose hairy sides
With thicket overgrown, grotesque° and wild,
Access denied; and overhead up grew
Insuperable highth of loftiest shade,
Cedar, and pine, and fir, and branching palm,
140 A sylvan scene, and as the ranks ascend
Shade above shade, a woody theatre
Of stateliest view. Yet higher than their tops
The verdurous wall of Paradise up sprung;
Which to our general sire° gave prospect large°
Into his nether empire neighbouring round.
And higher than that wall a circling row
Of goodliest trees loaden with fairest fruit,
Blossoms and fruits at once° of golden hue,
Appeared, with gay enamelled colours mixed;
150 On which the sun more glad impressed his beams
Than in fair evening cloud, or humid bow,
When God hath showered the earth; so lovely seemed
That landscape. And of pure now purer air
Meets his approach, and to the heart inspires
Vernal delight and joy, able to drive
All sadness but despair; now gentle gales
Fanning their odoriferous wings dispense

Uriel In III.623 ff. this archangel is deceived
by Satan's disguise.
Assyrian mount Mount Niphates, on which this
soliloquy occurs, and which Milton makes the
scene of Christ's temptation in *Paradise Regained*
champaign head a treeless plateau. The imagery
of the human body persists in the following
lines.
grotesque grotto-like
general sire Adam
large broad

Blossoms and fruits at once This description
assembles images of pastoral perfection from
such myths as the Hesperides (cf. *Comus* ll.
980–81), the Elysian fields, the Golden Age,
and Spenser's Garden of Adonis (*The Faerie
Queene* III.vi); in Eden, the spring of beauty
and promise, the fall of ripeness and fulfillment,
coexist with no intervening extreme seasons,
which will come into being with the Fall, and
the origin of biological "nature."

Native perfumes, and whisper whence they stole
Those balmy spoils. As when to them who sail
160 Beyond the Cape of Hope,° and now are past
Mozambic,° off at sea north-east winds blow
Sabaean° odours from the spicy shore
Of Araby the Blest, with such delay
Well pleased they slack their course, and many a league
Cheered with the grateful smell old ocean smiles;
So entertained those odorous sweets the fiend
Who came their bane, though with them better pleased
Than Asmodëus° with the fishy fume,
That drove him, though enamoured, from the spouse
170 Of Tobit's son, and with a vengeance sent
From Media post to Egypt, there fast bound.
    Now to the ascent of that steep savage° hill
Satan had journeyed on, pensive and slow;
But further way found none, so thick entwined,
As one continued brake, the undergrowth
Of shrubs and tangling bushes had perplexed
All path of man or beast that passed that way.
One gate there only was, and that looked east
On the other side; which when the arch-felon saw,
Due entrance he disdained, and in contempt
180 At one slight bound high overleaped all bound
Of hill or highest wall, and sheer within
Lights on his feet. As when a prowling wolf,
Whom hunger drives to seek new haunt for prey,
Watching where shepherds pen their flocks at eve
In hurdled cotes° amid the field secure,
Leaps o'er the fence with ease into the fold;
Or as a thief bent to unhoard the cash
Of some rich burgher, whose substantial doors,
190 Cross-barred and bolted fast, fear no assault,
In at the window climbs, or o'er the tiles:
So clomb° this first grand thief into God's fold;
So since into his church lewd° hirelings climb.
Thence up he flew, and on the Tree of Life,
The middle tree and highest there that grew,
Sat like a cormorant;° yet not true life
Thereby regained, but sat devising death°
To them who lived; nor on the virtue thought

Hope Good Hope
Mozambic Mozambique
Sabaean Sheban, from modern Yemen
Asmodëus a nasty demon, driven off by Tobias, Tobit's son, on Raphael's advice, by means of a stink-bomb (Tobit 7:6)
savage wooded
hurdled cotes crowded folds
clomb climbed

lewd ignorant and uneducated, as well as vile. Milton is attacking, in the same ecclesiastical pastoral imagery as in *Lycidas,* "hirelings," or salaried clergy.
cormorant literally "sea-crow"; emblem of greed
death both "death in general" and, reading on across the enjambment, the deaths of Adam and Eve

Of that life-giving plant, but only used
200 For prospect, what well used had been the pledge
Of immortality. So little knows
Any, but God alone, to value right
The good before him, but perverts best things
To worst abuse, or to their meanest use.

    Beneath him with new wonder now he views
To all delight of human sense exposed
In narrow room Nature's whole wealth,° yea more,
A heaven on earth, for blissful Paradise
Of God the garden was, by him in the east
210 Of Eden planted; Eden stretched her line
From Auran° eastward to the royal towers
Of great Seleucia,° built by Grecian kings,
Or where the sons of Eden long before
Dwelt in Telassar.° In this pleasant soil
His far more pleasant garden God ordained;
Out of the fertile ground he caused to grow
All trees of noblest kind for sight, smell, taste;
And all amid them stood the Tree of Life,
High eminent, blooming ambrosial fruit
220 Of vegetable gold,° and next to life
Our death,° the Tree of Knowledge, grew fast by,
Knowledge of good bought dear by knowing ill.°
Southward through Eden went a river large,
Nor changed his course, but through the shaggy hill
Passed underneath engulfed, for God had thrown
That mountain as his garden mould, high raised
Upon the rapid current, which through veins
Of porous earth with kindly thirst up drawn,
Rose a fresh fountain, and with many a rill
230 Watered the garden; thence united fell
Down the steep glade, and met the nether flood,
Which from his darksome passage now appears,
And now divided into four main streams
Runs diverse, wandering° many a famous realm
And country whereof here needs no account;
But rather to tell how, if art could tell,
How from that sapphire fount the crispèd brooks,
Rolling on orient pearl and sands of gold,

Nature's whole wealth all the fruitfulness that was ever to be was there (see *The Faerie Queene* III.vi.30)
Auran a town in northwestern Mesopotamia; see Genesis 11:31
Seleucia built as a capital city by Alexander the Great's viceroy for Syria, Seleucus
Telassar a city in Mesopotamia, mentioned in II Kings 19:12 as a land ruined by war
vegetable gold the figurative "gold" of grain and natural fruitfulness; also in the sense of "vegetative" (cf. I.685–87)
life . . . death perhaps the most startling enjambment in the poem. Reading along, we expect something like *"and next to life / the brightest gift* . . . etc., and then realize, with a shock, that the juxtaposition of the two Trees in Paradise, reinforced by "Our," means a good deal more.
Knowledge . . . ill Cf. *Areopagitica*, note 28.
wandering wandering through

With mazy error° under pendant shades
240 Ran nectar, visiting each plant, and fed
Flowers worthy of Paradise, which not nice art
In beds and curious knots,° but Nature boon°
Poured forth profuse on hill and dale and plain,
Both where the morning sun first warmly smote
The open field, and where the unpierced shade
Embrowned° the noontide bowers. Thus was this place,
A happy rural seat of various view;
Groves whose rich trees wept odorous gums and balm,
Others whose fruit burnished with golden rind
250 Hung amiable, Hesperian fables true,°
If true, here only, and of delicious taste.
Betwixt them lawns, or level downs, and flocks
Grazing the tender herb, were interposed,
Or palmy hillock, or the flowery lap
Of some irriguous° valley spread her store,
Flowers of all hue, and without thorn the rose.°
Another side, umbrageous° grots and caves
Of cool recess, o'er which the mantling vine
Lays forth her purple grape, and gently creeps
260 Luxuriant; meanwhile murmuring waters fall
Down the slope hills, dispersed, or in a lake,
That to the fringèd bank with myrtle° crowned
Her crystal mirror holds, unite their streams.
The birds their quire apply; airs, vernal airs,°
Breathing the smell of field and grove, attune
The trembling leaves, while universal Pan,°
Knit with the Graces and the Hours in dance,
Led on the eternal spring. Not that fair field
Of Enna, where Prosérpine° gathering flowers,
270 Herself a fairer flower by gloomy Dis
Was gathered, which cost Ceres all that pain

---

mazy error "Error" in Latin means "wandering," with no negative moral sense; this is an unfallen usage (see Headnote) as well as the first instance of unfallen, beautiful twisting, turning, and curling imagery, later to be corrupted.
curious knots labyrinthine patterns in which flowerbeds were frequently laid out; is Milton remembering the beneficent "curious knots" of Pleasure and Virtue in Jonson's masque? See *Pleasure Reconciled to Virtue*.
boon bountiful
Embrowned darkened
Hesperian fables true as if the golden apples of the Hesperides were a fiction mistakenly based on the truth of Paradise's "vegetable gold"
irriguous irrigated
the rose a traditional interpretation; in Genesis 3:18 part of Adam's curse involves the origins of thorns and thistles
umbrageous shadowy
myrtly sacred to Venus. The mirror is also her

emblem, and they both partake of the unfallen, pre-erotic sensual joy of this bower.
airs songs, melodies. Notice the whole musical sequence of waters, birds, and leaves; cf. its perverted version in Spenser's *Bower of Bliss*, an artfully faked Eden (*The Faerie Queene* II. xii).
Pan In Greek, his name means "all, everything"; the classical figures here are metaphorical for the forces of unfallen nature.
Prosérpine Persephone (Proserpine), daughter of Demeter (Ceres), the harvest goddess, carried to the underworld by Dis (Pluto) to be his queen. Ceres sought her throughout the world, which in sympathy became barren. When she was finally restored, it was only for half the year (hence, spring and summer), because while Queen of the Underworld, she had eaten seven pomegranate seeds. Renaissance mythographers seized on the obvious parallels to Eve, who, in Bk. IX, will be "gathered" by Satan while "gathering flowers."

To seek her through the world; nor that sweet grove
Of Daphne° by Orontes, and the inspired
Castalian spring, might with this Paradise
Of Eden strive; nor that Nyseian isle°
Girt with the river Triton, where old Cham,
Whom Gentiles Ammon call and Libyan Jove,
Hid Amalthea and her florid son
Young Bacchus from his stepdame Rhea's eye;
280   Nor where Abassin kings their issue guard,
Mount Amara,° though this by some supposed
True Paradise, under the Ethiop line°
By Nilus' head, enclosed with shining rock,
A whole day's journey high, but wide remote
From this Assyrian garden, where the fiend
Saw undelighted all delight, all kind
Of living creatures new to sight and strange.
    Two of far nobler shape erect and tall,
God-like erect, with native honour° clad
290   In naked majesty seemed lords of all,
And worthy seemed, for in their looks divine
The image of their glorious maker shone,
Truth, wisdom, sanctitude severe and pure,
Severe but in true filial freedom placed;
Whence true authority in men; though both
Not equal, as their sex not equal seemed;
For contemplation he and valour formed,
For softness she and sweet attractive grace;
He for God only, she for God in him.
300   His fair large front° and eye sublime° declared
Absolute rule; and hyacinthine locks°
Round from his parted forelock manly hung
Clustering, but not beneath his shoulders broad:
She as a veil down to the slender waist
Her unadornèd golden tresses wore
Dishevelled, but in wanton° ringlets waved
As the vine curls her tendrils, which implied
Subjection, but required with gentle sway,°

Daphne a grove near the river Orontes, famous for its oracle
Nyseian isle Nysa in Tunisia, where Ammon (Jupiter) hid the infant Dionysus (Bacchus) from his wife, Rhea (Ops)
Amara where Abyssinian princes were brought up
Ethiop line the equator
native honour The natural dignity of being complete in their skin; the very concepts "nakedness" and "nudity" would be as meaningless if applied to them here as to a lion or a human fetus; see l. 314. Milton suggests that the "honour" as used in fallen human society, whether of women or of "gentlemen," is as inferior to this original honor as fallen is to

"original Justice." Fallen "honour," the "honour dishonourable" against which Milton rages in l.314, is a show, or mask of virtue, more like "reputation."
front forehead
sublime upward-looking
hyacinthine locks probably not referring to color, but to curliness, and invoking the doomed beauty of Hyacinth, Apollo's beloved. The curling hair in this passage is an emblem of luxuriant sensuality and uncorrupted complexity (like the "curious knots," l. 242), as well as "Subjection."
wanton unrestrained
sway influence

And by her yielded, by him best received,
310   Yielded with coy° submission, modest pride,
And sweet reluctant amorous delay.
Nor those mysterious parts were then concealed;
Then was not guilty shame; dishonest shame
Of Nature's works, honour dishonourable,°
Sin-bred, how have ye troubled all mankind
With shows instead, mere shows of seeming pure,
And banished from man's life his happiest life,
Simplicity and spotless innocence!
So passed they naked on, nor shunned the sight
320   Of God or angel, for they thought no ill;
So hand in hand° they passed, the loveliest pair
That ever since in love's embraces met,
Adam the goodliest man of men since born
His sons, the fairest of her daughters Eve.
Under a tuft of shade that on a green
Stood whispering soft, by a fresh fountain side
They sat them down; and after no more toil
Of their sweet gardening labour than sufficed
To recommend cool Zephyr, and made ease
330   More easy,° wholesome thirst and appetite
More grateful, to their supper fruits they fell,
Nectarine fruits which the compliant boughs
Yielded them, sidelong as they sat recline°
On the soft downy bank damasked° with flowers.
The savoury pulp they chew, and in the rind
Still as they thirsted scoop the brimming stream;
Nor gentle purpose,° nor endearing smiles
Wanted,° nor youthful dalliance, as beseems
Fair couple linked in happy nuptial league,
340   Alone as they. About them frisking played
All beasts of the earth, since wild, and of all chase°
In wood or wilderness, forest or den;
Sporting the lion ramped, and in his paw
Dandled the kid; bears, tigers, ounces, pards,°
Gambolled before them; the unwieldy elephant
To make them mirth used all his might, and wreathed
His lithe proboscis; close° the serpent sly

coy reticent
honour dishonourable In this context, even the
thought of sexual shame, of guilt about bodies,
of covering up genitalia, disgusts Milton, and his
meditation gives way to indignation.
hand in hand Clasped hands appear in emblem
books in pictures of Faith, Concord, and Married
Love; but see also *Paradise Lost* XII.648,
and intervening glimpses of the pair at 488,
689, and 739 of Bk. IV, VIII.510, IX.385 and
1037.
easy comfortable
recline recumbent

damasked patterned
gentle purpose polite discourse
Wanted were lacking
of all chase of every habitat, part of "Nature's
whole wealth" (l. 207)
ounces, pards lynxes, leopards
close Close by (in the garden and in the line
of verse) the serpent's "curious knot" of
motion, uninfected yet by Satan's possession of
it, is a sort of emblem requiring prophecy, or
a fallen reader, correctly to understand (thus,
"proof unheeded").

Insinuating,° wove with Gordian twine
His braided train, and of his fatal guile
350 Gave proof unheeded; others on the grass
Couched, and now filled with pasture gazing sat,
Or bedward ruminating; for the sun
Declined was hasting now with prone career
To the ocean isles,° and in the ascending scale°
Of heaven the stars that usher evening rose:
When Satan still in gaze, as first he stood,
Scarce thus at length failed speech recovered sad:
     'O hell! what do mine eyes with grief behold!
Into our room° of bliss thus high advanced
360 Creatures of other mould, earth-born perhaps,
Not spirits, yet to heavenly spirits bright
Little inferior; whom my thoughts pursue
With wonder, and could love, so lively shines
In them divine resemblance, and such grace
The hand that formed them on their shape hath poured.
Ah gentle pair, ye little think how nigh
Your change approaches, when all these delights
Will vanish and deliver ye to woe,
More woe, the more your taste is now of joy;
370 Happy, but for so happy ill secured
Long to continue, and this high seat your heaven
Ill fenced, for heaven, to keep out such a foe
As now is entered; yet no purposed foe
To you whom I could pity thus forlorn,
Though I unpitied. League with you I seek,
And mutual amity so strait,° so close,
That I with you must dwell, or you with me
Henceforth; my dwelling haply may not please,
Like this fair Paradise, your sense, yet such
380 Accept your maker's work; he gave it me,
Which I as freely give;° hell shall unfold,°
To entertain you two, her widest gates,
And send forth all her kings; there will be room,
Not like these narrow limits, to receive
Your numerous offspring; if no better place,
Thank him who puts me loth to this revenge
On you who wrong me not, for him who wronged.
And should I at your harmless innocence
Melt, as I do, yet public reason just,
390 Honour and empire with revenge enlarged

Insinuating winding
ocean isles the Azores; see l. 592
scale both Libra, now rising, and the heavens'
balance of light and darkness in the then
eternal equinox
room region, space
strait intimate

freely give not only half-sarcastic, but echoing
Matthew 10:8
hell shall unfold At Isaiah 14:9 the destruction
of Babylon is envisaged in these terms, but
Satan is offering Adam and Eve part of his
kingdom, as Dis had given Proserpine his.

By conquering this new world, compels me now
To do what else though damned I should abhor.'
    So spake the fiend, and with necessity—
The tyrant's plea—excused his devilish deeds.
Then from his lofty stand on that high tree
Down he alights among the sportful herd
Of those four-footed kinds, himself now one,
Now other, as their shape served best his end
Nearer to view his prey, and unespied
400   To mark what of their state he more might learn
By word or action marked. About them round
A lion now he stalks with fiery glare;
Then as a tiger, who by chance hath spied
In some purlieu° two gentle fawns at play,
Straight° couches close, then rising, changes oft
His couchant watch, as one who chose his ground
Whence rushing he might surest seize them both
Gripped in each paw; when Adam first of men
To first of women Eve thus moving speech,
410   Turned him° all ear to hear new utterance flow—
    'Sole partner and sole part° of all these joys,
Dearer thyself than all, needs must the power
That made us, and for us this ample world,
Be infinitely good, and of his good
As liberal and free as infinite,
That raised us from the dust and placed us here
In all this happiness, who at his hand
Have nothing merited, nor can perform
Aught whereof he hath need; he who requires
420   From us no other service than to keep
This one, this easy charge, of all the trees
In Paradise that bear delicious fruit
So various, not to taste° that only Tree
Of Knowledge, planted by the Tree of Life,
So near grows death to life,° whate'er death is,
Some dreadful thing no doubt; for well thou knowest
God hath pronounced it death to taste that Tree,
The only sign of our obedience left
Among so many signs of power and rule
430   Conferred upon us,° and dominion given
Over all other creatures that possess
Earth, air, and sea. Then let us not think hard
One easy prohibition, who enjoy
Free leave so large to all things else, and choice

purlieu borders of a forest
Straight immediately; also, "tightly" (punning
on "strait")
him Satan
Sole partner and sole part only partner and

principal part
not to taste the commandment at Genesis
2:16–17
death to life See ll. 220–21.
Conferred upon us at Genesis 1:28

Unlimited of manifold delights;
But let us ever praise him, and extol
His bounty, following our delightful task
To prune these growing plants, and tend these flowers,
Which were it toilsome, yet with thee were sweet.'

440   To whom thus Eve replied, 'O thou for whom
And from whom I was formed flesh of thy flesh,
And without whom am to no end, my guide
And head,° what thou hast said is just and right.
For we to him indeed all praises owe,
And daily thanks, I chiefly who enjoy
So far the happier lot, enjoying thee
Pre-eminent by so much odds,° while thou
Like consort to thyself canst nowhere find.
That day I oft remember, when from sleep
450   I first awaked, and found myself reposed
Under a shade of flowers, much wondering where
And what I was, whence thither brought, and how.
Not distant far from thence a murmuring sound
Of waters issued from a cave and spread
Into a liquid plain,° then stood unmoved
Pure as the expanse of heaven; I thither went
With unexperienced thought, and laid me down
On the green bank, to look into the clear
Smooth lake, that to me seemed another sky.°
460   As I bent down to look, just opposite
A shape within the watery gleam appeared
Bending to look on me: I started back,
It started back, but pleased I soon returned,
Pleased it returned as soon with answering looks
Of sympathy and love; there I had fixed
Mine eyes till now, and pined with vain desire,
Had not a voice thus warned me:° *What thou seest,*
What there thou seest, fair creature, is thyself,
With thee it came and goes; but follow me,
470   *And I will bring thee where no shadow stays°*
Thy coming, and thy soft embraces, he
Whose image thou art, him thou shalt enjoy
Inseparably thine; to him shalt bear

---

head echoing I Corinthians 11:3: "The head
of every man is Christ; and the head of the
woman is the man . . . ," but also combining
the two in a kind of single human body, an
image suggested for the garden itself, ll. 134 ff.
by so much odds by so much
liquid plain The first mirror forms when "murmuring" water stops and reflects.
another sky There is only the subtlest hint here
("another sky": "another heaven") of the idolatry implicit in the use of mirrors; in the fallen
world, mirrors are emblems of Venus and of

the other nude figure, personified Vanitas,
"vanity."
warned me Narcissus, Eve's prototype here who
fell in love with his own image (like Eve, not
knowing it was himself), died when he discovered the truth—the only warning had been
from the blind seer Tiresias, in the boy's childhood, that he would die when he knew himself;
Eve is not abandoned to his fate, at least at
this point.
no shadow stays no illusory image awaits

Multitudes like thyself, and thence be called
Mother of human race." What could I do
But follow straight, invisibly thus led?
Till I espied thee, fair indeed and tall,
Under a platane;° yet methought less fair,
Less winning soft, less amiably mild,
480   Than that smooth watery image; back I turned,
Thou following cried'st aloud, "Return, fair Eve,
Whom fli'st thou? Whom thou fli'st, of him thou art,
His flesh, his bone;° to give thee being I lent
Out of my side to thee, nearest my heart,
Substantial life, to have thee by my side
Henceforth an individual° solace dear.
Part of my soul° I seek thee, and thee claim
My other half." With that thy gentle hand
Seized mine, I yielded, and from that time see°
490   How beauty is excelled by manly grace
And wisdom, which alone is truly fair.'
    So spake our general mother, and with eyes
Of conjugal attraction unreproved,
And meek surrender, half embracing leaned
On our first father; half her swelling breast
Naked met his under the flowing gold
Of her loose tresses hid. He in delight
Both of her beauty and submissive charms
Smiled with superior love, as Jupiter
500   On Juno smiles, when he impregns° the clouds
That shed May flowers; and pressed her matron lip
With kisses pure. Aside the devil turned
For envy,° yet with jealous leer malign
Eyed them askance, and to himself thus plained:
    'Sight hateful, sight tormenting! thus these two
Imparadised in one another's arms,
The happier Eden,° shall enjoy their fill
Of bliss on bliss, while I to hell am thrust,
Where neither joy nor love, but fierce desire,
510   Among our other torments not the least,
Still unfulfilled with pain of longing pines;°
Yet let me not forget what I have gained
From their own mouths. All is not theirs, it seems;

platane plane tree
His flesh, his bone Here, and at l. 441, the
reference is to Genesis 2:23.
individual undividable
Part of my soul a musical and rhetorical resonance, if not a pun, from l. 411
see Again, the enjambment brings a surprise—
"see / How," or "know," "understand"; Eve
never really totally *"sees"* wisdom as fairer
than beauty.
impregns impregnates

envy Part of the torment of Hell is sexual dep-
rivation, a practice common to various sorts
of imprisonment in most Christian societies.
Imparadised . . . Eden Satan is almost at his
most pitiable at this poignant moment, for it
is only after the Fall that human love will be
able (and be forced) to "imparadise" the lovers.
Here, at this unfallen moment, when the two are
in Paradise, literally, he sees them as they will
be in Bk. XII (see ll. 614–19).
pines tortures

One fatal tree there stands, of Knowledge called,
Forbidden them to taste. Knowledge forbidden?
Suspicious, reasonless. Why should their lord
Envy them that? Can it be sin to know?
Can it be death? And do they only stand
By ignorance, is that their happy state,
520   The proof of their obedience and their faith?
O fair foundation laid whereon to build
Their ruin!° Hence I will excite their minds
With more desire to know, and to reject
Envious commands, invented with design
To keep them low whom knowledge might exalt
Equal with gods. Aspiring to be such,
They taste and die: what likelier can ensue?
But first with narrow search I must walk round
This garden, and no corner leave unspied;
530   A chance but chance may lead where I may meet
Some wandering Spirit of heaven, by fountain side,
Or in thick shade retired, from him to draw
What further would be learnt. Live while ye may,
Yet happy pair; enjoy, till I return,
Short pleasures, for long woes are to succeed.'
     So saying, his proud step he scornful turned,
But with sly circumspection, and began
Through wood, through waste, o'er hill, o'er dale, his roam.°
Meanwhile in utmost longitude, where heaven
540   With earth and ocean meets, the setting sun
Slowly descended, and with right aspéct
Against the eastern gate of Paradise
Levelled his evening rays. It was a rock
Of alabaster, piled up to the clouds,
Conspicuous far, winding with one ascent
Accessible from earth, one entrance high;
The rest was craggy cliff, that overhung
Still as it rose, impossible to climb.
Betwixt these rocky pillars Gabriel° sat,
550   Chief of the angelic guards, awaiting night;
About him exercised° heroic games
The unarmèd youth of heaven, but nigh at hand
Celestial armoury, shields, helms, and spears,
Hung high, with diamond flaming and with gold.
Thither came Uriel, gliding through the even
On a sunbeam, swift as a shooting star
In autumn thwarts the night, when vapours fired
Impress the air, and shows the mariner

---

ruin both "destruction" and the wreckage, or
remnants, of that destruction ("ruins")
roam walk

Gabriel one of the four archangels in apocryphal
tradition assigned to Paradise as guards .
exercised played

From what point of his compass to beware
560   Impetuous winds. He thus began in haste:
'Gabriel, to thee thy course by lot hath given
Charge and strict watch that to this happy place
No evil thing approach or enter in;
This day at highth of noon came to my sphere
A Spirit, zealous, as he seemed, to know
More of the Almighty's works, and chiefly man,
God's latest image.° I described° his way
Bent all on speed, and marked his airy gait;
But in the mount that lies from Eden north,
570   Where he first lighted, soon discerned his looks
Alien from heaven, with passions foul obscured.
Mine eye pursued him still, but under shade
Lost sight of him; one of the banished crew,
I fear, hath ventured from the deep, to raise
New troubles; him thy care must be to find.'
To whom the wingèd warrior thus returned:
'Uriel, no wonder if thy perfect sight,
Amid the sun's bright circle where thou sit'st,
See far and wide. In at this gate none pass
580   The vigilance° here placed, but such as come
Well known from heaven; and since meridian hour
No creature thence. If spirit of other sort,
So minded, have o'erleaped these earthy bounds°
On purpose, hard thou knowest it to exclude
Spiritual substance with corporeal bar.
But if within the circuit of these walks,
In whatsoever shape he lurk, of whom
Thou tell'st, by morrow dawning I shall know.'
So promised he, and Uriel to his charge
590   Returned on that bright beam, whose point now raised
Bore him slope downward to the sun now fallen
Beneath the Azores—whether the prime orb,°
Incredible how swift, had thither rolled
Diurnal, or this less volúble° earth
By shorter flight to the east, had left him there
Arraying with reflected purple and gold
The clouds that on his western throne attend.
Now came still evening on, and twilight grey
Had in her sober livery all things clad;
600   Silence accompanied,° for beast and bird,
They to their grassy couch, these to their nests
Were slunk, all but the wakeful nightingale—

---

latest image The first image was Christ, the Son.
described perceived
The vigilance Gabriel
o'erleaped . . . bounds reminding us of the
easy joke back at l. 181
prime orb the sun, in the Ptolemaic system.

Milton allows for both accounts, as if either
might be a distorting reduction of an actual
Edenic sunset.
volúble rapidly revolving; see ll. 661–64
Silence accompanied in both a musical and a
general sense

She all night long her amorous descant° sung:
Silence was pleased.° Now glowed the firmament
With living sapphires; Hesperus° that led
The starry host, rode brightest, till the moon
Rising in clouded majesty, at length
Apparent queen° unveiled her peerless light,
And o'er the dark her silver mantle threw;
610   When Adam thus to Eve: 'Fair consort, the hour
Of night, and all things now retired to rest
Mind us of like repose, since God hath set
Labour and rest, as day and night to men
Successive, and the timely dew of sleep
Now falling with soft slumbrous weight inclines
Our eyelids; other creatures all day long
Rove idle, unemployed, and less need rest;
Man hath his daily work° of body or mind
Appointed, which declares his dignity,
620   And the regard of heaven on all his ways;
While other animals unactive range,
And of their doings God takes no account.
Tomorrow ere fresh morning streak the east
With first approach of light, we must be risen,
And at our pleasant labour, to reform
Yon flowery arbours, yonder alleys green,
Our walk at noon, with branches overgrown,
That mock our scant manuring,° and require
More hands than ours to lop their wanton° growth.
630   Those blossoms also, and those dropping gums,
That lie bestrown unsightly and unsmooth,
Ask riddance, if we mean to tread with ease;
Meanwhile, as nature wills, night bids us rest.'
    To whom thus Eve with perfect beauty adorned:
'My author and disposer,° what thou bid'st
Unargued I obey; so God ordains.
God is thy law, thou mine; to know no more
Is woman's happiest knowledge and her praise.
With thee conversing I forget all time,
640   All seasons° and their change, all please alike.
Sweet is the breath of morn, her rising sweet,
With charm° of earliest birds; pleasant the sun
When first on this delightful land he spreads
His orient beams, on herb, tree, fruit, and flower,

---

descant highest free contrapuntal part
Silence was pleased at her pupil?
Hesperus the Evening Star
Apparent queen manifestly the queen (of the sky, now that she has risen), who rules this whole part of Bk. IV, from the opening Virgilian night-piece just concluded (see the selection from the Earl of Surrey's *Aeneid* translation) to the love scene which follows
daily work Even in Paradise there is gardening

to do, not to be confused with agriculture, done "with the sweat of thy brow."
manuring cultivating
wanton luxuriant (like Eve's hair at l. 306)
My . . . disposer In Books IX through XII these formal titles of address are not used.
seasons times of day (it is always spring and fall at once in Eden)
charm song

Glistering with dew; fragrant the fertile earth
After soft showers; and sweet the coming on
Of grateful evening mild, then silent night
With this her solemn bird° and this fair moon,
And these the gems of heaven, her starry train:
650   But neither breath of morn when she ascends
With charm of earliest birds, nor rising sun
On this delightful land, nor herb, fruit, flower,
Glistering with dew, nor fragrance after showers,
Nor grateful evening mild, nor silent night
With this her solemn bird, nor walk by moon
Or glittering starlight without thee is sweet.
But wherefore all night long° shine these, for whom
This glorious sight, when sleep hath shut all eyes?'
    To whom our general ancestor replied:
660   'Daughter of God and man, accomplished° Eve,
Those have their course to finish, round the earth,
By morrow evening, and from land to land
In order, though to nations yet unborn,
Ministering light prepared, they set and rise;
Lest total darkness should by night regain
Her old possession,° and extinguish life
In nature and all things; which these soft fires
Not only enlighten, but with kindly° heat
Of various influence° foment and warm,
670   Temper or nourish, or in part shed down
Their stellar virtue on all kinds that grow
On earth, made hereby apter to receive
Perfection from the sun's more potent ray.
These then, though unbeheld in deep of night,
Shine not in vain, nor think, though men were none,
That heaven would want spectators, God want praise;
Millions of spiritual creatures walk the earth
Unseen, both when we wake, and when we sleep:
All these with ceaseless praise his works behold
680   Both day and night—how often from the steep
Of echoing hill or thicket have we heard
Celestial voices to the midnight air,
Sole, or responsive each to other's note,°
Singing their great creator; oft in bands
While they keep watch, or nightly rounding walk,
With heavenly touch of instrumental sounds
In full harmonic number joined, their songs

---

solemn bird the nightingale
wherefore all night long Eve's question is
innocent, straightforward, reasonable, personal,
and anticlimactically deadly to the cadence of
the ode she has just recited.
accomplished Cf. *Samson Agonistes*, l. 230.

Her old possession Chaos originally reigned
in darkness; creation of light meant a dispossession of her rule.
kindly natural
influence See *Astronomy . . .* in the Glossary.
responsive . . . note in antiphonal choirs

Divide° the night, and lift our thoughts to heaven.'
   Thus talking, hand in hand alone they passed
690 On to their blissful bower;° it was a place
Chosen by the sovereign planter, when he framed
All things to man's delightful use; the roof
Of thickest covert was inwoven shade,
Laurel and myrtle,° and what higher grew
Of firm and fragrant leaf; on either side
Acanthus, and each odorous bushy shrub
Fenced up the verdant wall; each beauteous flower,
Iris all hues, roses, and jessamine
Reared high their flourished° heads between, and wrought
700 Mosaic; under foot the violet,
Crocus, and hyacinth with rich inlay
Broidered the ground, more coloured than with stone
Of costliest emblem. Other creature here,
Beast, bird, insect, or worm durst enter none;
Such was their awe of man. In shadier bower
More sacred and sequestered, though but feigned,°
Pan or Silvanus never slept, nor nymph
Nor Faunus haunted. Here in close recess
With flowers, garlands, and sweet-smelling herbs
710 Espousèd Eve decked first her nuptial bed,
And heavenly quires the hymenean sung,
What day the genial angel° to our sire
Brought her in naked beauty more adorned,
More lovely than Pandora,° whom the gods
Endowed with all their gifts, and O too like
In sad event, when to the unwiser son
Of Japhet° brought by Hermes, she ensnared
Mankind with her fair looks, to be avenged
On him who had stole Jove's authentic° fire.
720   Thus at their shady lodge arrived, both stood,
Both turned, and under open sky adored
The God that made both sky, air, earth, and heaven
Which they beheld, the moon's resplendent globe
And starry pole: 'Thou also mad'st the night,

Divide by marking off the watches of the night, and also by playing "divisions" or melodic improvisations
blissful bower not the artificial Bower of Bliss (*The Faerie Queene* II.xii), but a brilliant reversal of Spenser's construct of false love, where art imitates nature deceptively. In the following lines, natural beauties triumph over artificiality by anticipating it.
Laurel and myrtle Apollo's plant and Venus' entwined together, making an emblem of married attributes such as male-female, wisdom-beauty
flourished flowered
feigned fictionalized; see Sidney's discussion of

"the feigned image of poesie" in *The Defence of Poetry*
genial angel nuptial, generative spirit, parallel to Old Genius at the boundary of the Garden of Adonis, *The Faerie Queene* III.vi
Pandora another Greek Eve-parallel. Her name means "all gifts," and she was given to the Titan Epimetheus ("after-knowledge"), brother of Prometheus ("fore-knowledge") who stole fire from Olympus for mankind; she opened a box she was forbidden to and loosed evils and miseries on the world.
Japhet Iapetus, father of the two Titans above
authentic original

Maker omnipotent, and thou the day,
Which we in our appointed work employed
Have finished happy in our mutual help
And mutual love, the crown of all our bliss
Ordained by thee, and this delicious place
730   For us too large, where thy abundance wants
Partakers, and uncropped falls to the ground.
But thou hast promised from us two a race
To fill the earth, who shall with us extol
Thy goodness infinite, both when we wake,
And when we seek, as now, thy gift of sleep.'
  This said unanimous, and other rites
Observing none, but adoration pure
Which God likes best, into their inmost bower
Handed° they went; and eased the putting off
740   These troublesome disguises which we wear,
Straight side by side were laid, nor turned, I ween,
Adam from his fair spouse, nor Eve the rites
Mysterious° of connubial love refused;
Whatever hypocrites austerely talk
Of purity and place and innocence,
Defaming as impure what God declares
Pure, and commands to some, leaves free to all.
Our Maker bids increase; who bids abstain
But our destroyer, foe to God and man?
750   Hail, wedded Love, mysterious law, true source
Of human offspring, sole propriety°
In Paradise of all things common else.
By thee adulterous lust was driven from men
Among the bestial herds to range; by thee
Founded in reason, loyal, just, and pure,
Relations dear, and all the charities°
Of father, son, and brother first were known.
Far be it that I should write thee sin or blame,
Or think thee unbefitting holiest place,
760   Perpetual fountain of domestic sweets,
Whose bed is undefiled and chaste pronounced,
Present or past, as saints and patriarchs used.
Here Love his golden shafts° employs, here lights
His constant lamp, and waves his purple wings,
Reigns here and revels; not in the bought smile
Of harlots, loveless, joyless, unendeared,
Casual fruition; nor in court amours,
Mixed dance, or wanton masque, or midnight ball,

Handed hand in hand (see l. 321n)
Mysterious The representation of unfallen sex
is indeed tinged with mystery, and Milton
will be able only to insist, as he does below,
that it transcends fallen eroticism, and that its

mysteries are re-created in human marriage.
propriety domain of belonging, of possessing
charities loves
golden shafts Cupid had golden arrows of desire and leaden ones of disaffection.

Or serenate,° which the starved lover° sings
770 To his proud fair, best quitted with disdain.
These lulled by nightingales, embracing slept,
And on their naked limbs the flowery roof
Showered roses, which the morn repaired. Sleep on,
Blest pair; and O yet happiest if ye seek
No happier state, and know° to know no more.
        Now had night measured with her shadowy cone
Half way up hill this vast sublunar vault,
And from their ivory port° the cherubim
Forth issuing at the accustomed hour stood armed
780 To their night-watches in warlike parade,
When Gabriel to his next in power thus spake:
        'Uzziel, half these draw off, and coast the south
With strictest watch; these other wheel the north;
Our circuit meets full west.' As flame they part,
Half wheeling to the shield, half to the spear.°
From these, two strong and subtle spirits he called
That near him stood, and gave them thus in charge:
        'Ithuriel and Zephon, with winged speed
Search through this garden; leave unsearched no nook,
790 But chiefly where those two fair creatures lodge,
Now laid perhaps asleep secure of harm.
This evening from the sun's decline arrived
Who° tells of some infernal spirit seen
Hitherward bent (who could have thought?) escaped
The bars of hell, on errand bad no doubt:
Such where ye find, seize fast, and hither bring.'
        So saying, on he led his radiant files,
Dazzling the moon; these to the bower direct
In search of whom they sought. Him there they found
800 Squat like a toad, close at the ear of Eve,
Assaying by his devilish art to reach
The organs of her fancy, and with them forge
Illusions as he list, phantasms and dreams,
Or if, inspiring venom, he might taint
The animal spirits° that from pure blood arise
Like gentle breaths from rivers pure, thence raise
At least distempered, discontented thoughts,
Vain hopes, vain aims, inordinate desires
Blown up with high conceits° engendering pride.
810 Him thus intent Ithuriel with his spear

serenate serenade
starved lover Milton's point is that fallen Eros, here imaged in Ovidian, courtly, and Cavalier love, flourishes in a world of sexual denial, of loss.
know know enough
ivory port through the gates of ivory came false dreams, through gates of horn, true ones;

the Cherubim will interfere with the Satanically induced false dream
Half . . . spear to left and right
Who one who
animal spirits See *Renaissance Psychology* in the Glossary.
conceits ideas

Touched lightly; for no falsehood can endure
Touch of celestial temper, but returns
Of force to its own likeness. Up he starts
Discovered and surprised. As when a spark
Lights on a heap of nitrous powder,° laid
Fit for the tun° some magazine to store
Against a rumoured war, the smutty grain
With sudden blaze diffused, inflames the air:
So started up in his own shape the fiend.
820 Back stepped those two fair angels half amazed
So sudden to behold the grisly king,
Yet thus, unmoved with fear, accost him soon:
    'Which of those rebel spirits adjudged to hell
Com'st thou, escaped thy prison; and transformed,
Why sat'st thou like an enemy in wait
Here watching at the head of these that sleep?'
    'Know ye not then,' said Satan, filled with scorn,
'Know ye not me? Ye knew me once no mate
For you, there sitting where ye durst not soar;
830 Not to know me argues yourselves unknown,
The lowest of your throng; or if ye know,
Why ask ye, and superfluous begin
Your message, like to end as much in vain?'
To whom thus Zephon, answering scorn with scorn:
'Think not, revolted Spirit, thy shape the same,
Or undiminished brightness, to be known
As when thou stood'st in heaven upright and pure;
That glory then, when thou no more wast good,
Departed from thee, and thou resemblest now
840 Thy sin and place of doom obscure° and foul.
But come, for thou, be sure, shalt give account
To him who sent us, whose charge is to keep
This place inviolable, and these° from harm.'
    So spake the cherub, and his grave rebuke,
Severe in youthful beauty, added grace
Invincible. Abashed the devil stood,
And felt how awful° goodness is, and saw
Virtue in her shape how lovely; saw, and pined
His loss; but chiefly to find here observed
850 His lustre visibly impaired; yet seemed
Undaunted. 'If I must contend,' said he,
'Best with the best, the sender not the sent;
Or all at once; more glory will be won,
Or less be lost.' 'Thy fear,' said Zephon bold,

---

nitrous powder gunpowder
tun keg
obscure dark (whereas "dark," as in I Corinthians 13:12, and Spenser's phrase "dark

conceit," means "obscure" in the modern sense
of "hard to make out")
these Adam and Eve, asleep
awful awe-engendering

'Will save us trial what the least can do
Single against thee wicked, and thence weak.'
    The fiend replied not, overcome with rage;
But like a proud steed reined, went haughty on,
Champing his iron curb. To strive or fly
He held it vain; awe from above had quelled   860
His heart, not else dismayed. Now drew they nigh
The western point, where those half-rounding guards
Just met, and closing stood in squadron joined
Awaiting next command. To whom their chief
Gabriel from the front thus called aloud:
    'O friends, I hear the tread of nimble feet
Hasting this way, and now by glimpse discern
Ithuriel and Zephon through the shade,
And with them comes a third, of regal port,
But faded splendour wan, who by his gait   870
And fierce demeanour seems the prince of hell,
Not likely to part hence without contést;
Stand firm, for in his look defiance lours.'
    He scarce had ended, when those two approached
And brief related whom they brought, where found,
How busied, in what form and posture couched.
    To whom with stern regard thus Gabriel spake:
'Why hast thou, Satan, broke the bounds prescribed
To thy transgressions, and disturbed the charge
Of others,° who approve not to transgress   880
By thy example, but have power and right
To question thy bold entrance on this place;
Employed it seems to violate sleep, and those
Whose dwelling God hath planted here in bliss?'
    To whom thus Satan, with contemptuous brow:
'Gabriel, thou hadst in heaven the esteem of wise,
And such I held thee; but this question asked
Puts me in doubt. Lives there who loves his pain?
Who would not, finding way, break loose from hell,
Though thither doomed? Thou wouldst thyself, no doubt,   890
And boldly venture to whatever place
Farthest from pain, where thou mightst hope to change
Torment with ease, and soonest recompense
Dole° with delight, which in this place I sought;
To thee no reason, who knowest only good,
But evil hast not tried. And wilt object°
His will who bound us? Let him surer bar
His iron gates, if he intends our stay
In that dark durance°—thus much what was asked.

charge Of others their responsibility (Adam   object make legal objection about
and Eve)   durance confinement
Dole distress

900 The rest is true, they found me where they say;
But that implies not violence or harm.'
　　Thus he in scorn. The warlike angel moved,
Disdainfully half smiling thus replied:
'O loss of one in heaven to judge of wise,°
Since Satan fell, whom folly overthrew,
And now returns him from his prison scaped,°
Gravely in doubt whether to hold them wise
Or not, who ask what boldness brought him hither
Unlicensed from his bounds in hell prescribed;
910 So wise he judges it to fly from pain
However,° and to scape his punishment.
So judge thou still, presumptuous, till the wrath,
Which thou incurrest by flying, meet thy flight
Sevenfold, and scourge that wisdom back to hell,
Which taught thee yet no better, that no pain
Can equal anger infinite provoked.
But wherefore thou alone? Wherefore with thee
Came not all hell broke loose? Is pain to them
Less pain, less to be fled, or thou than they
920 Less hardy to endure? Courageous chief,
The first in flight from pain, hadst thou alleged
To thy deserted host this cause of flight,
Thou surely hadst not come sole fugitive.'
　　To which the fiend thus answered frowning stern:
'Not that I less endure, or shrink from pain,
Insulting angel, well thou knowest I stood°
Thy fiercest, when in battle to thy aid
The blasting volleyed thunder made all speed
And seconded thy else not dreaded spear.
930 But still thy words at random, as before,
Argue thy inexperience what behoves,
From hard assays° and ill successes past,
A faithful leader, not to hazard all
Through ways of danger by himself untried.
I therefore, I alone first undertook
To wing the desolate abyss, and spy
This new-created world, whereof in hell
Fame° is not silent, here in hope to find
Better abode, and my afflicted° powers
940 To settle here on earth, or in mid-air;
Though for possession put to try once more
What thou and thy gay legions dare against,
Whose easier business were to serve their Lord

O loss . . . wise What a loss . . . wisdom!　　　stood withstood
returns . . . scaped returns himself from his　　assays attempts
escape　　　　　　　　　　　　　　　　　　　　Fame rumor
However whichever way　　　　　　　　　　　　afflicted outcast

High up in heaven, with songs to hymn his throne,
And practiced distances to cringe, not fight.'
    To whom the warrior angel soon replied:
'To say and straight unsay, pretending first
Wise to fly pain, professing next the spy,
Argues no leader but a liar traced,°
950 Satan, and couldst thou "faithful" add? O name,
O sacred name of faithfulness profaned!
Faithful to whom? To thy rebellious crew?
Army of fiends, fit body to fit head;
Was this your discipline and faith engaged,
Your military obedience, to dissolve
Allegiance to the acknowledged power supreme?
And thou sly hypocrite, who now wouldst seem
Patron of liberty, who more than thou
Once fawned, and cringed, and servilely adored
960 Heaven's awful monarch? Wherefore but in hope
To dispossess him, and thyself to reign?
But mark what I areed° thee now: Avaunt!
Fly thither whence thou fled'st. If from this hour
Within these hallowed limits thou appear,
Back to the infernal pit I drag thee chained,
And seal thee so, as henceforth not to scorn
The facile° gates of hell too slightly barred.'
    So threatened he, but Satan to no threats
Gave heed, but waxing more in rage replied:
970 'Then when I am thy captive talk of chains,
Proud limitary° cherub, but ere then
Far heavier load thyself expect to feel
From my prevailing arm, though heaven's king
Ride on thy wings, and thou with thy compeers,
Used to the yoke, drawest his triumphant wheels
In progress through the road of heaven star-paved.'
    While thus he spake, the angelic squadron bright
Turned, fiery red, sharpening in mooned horns°
Their phalanx, and began to hem him round
980 With ported spears, as thick as when a field
Of Ceres° ripe for harvest waving bends
Her bearded grove of ears, which way the wind
Sways them; the careful° ploughman doubting stands
Lest on the threshing-floor his hopeful sheaves
Prove chaff. On the other side Satan alarmed°
Collecting all his might dilated° stood,

traced disclosed
areed advise
facile easily opened
limitary frontier-guard (with a bit of a snarl)
mooned horns crescent-shaped
Ceres here, the goddess standing for the grain
itself

careful anxious, even as God, the thresher and
winnower, might be for the outcome of this
renewed combat. This image is reinforced
shortly by that of God as weigher.
alarmed aroused
dilated into more ethereal condition by Ithuriel's spear

Like Teneriffe or Atlas unremoved:°
His stature reached the sky, and on his crest
Sat Horror plumed; nor wanted in his grasp
990   What seemed both spear and shield. Now dreadful deeds
Might have ensued, nor only Paradise
In this commotion, but the starry cope°
Of heaven perhaps, or all the elements
At least had gone to wrack, disturbed and torn
With violence of this conflict, had not soon
The Eternal to prevent such horrid fray
Hung forth in heaven his golden scales,° yet seen
Betwixt Astraea° and the Scorpion sign,
Wherein all things created first he weighed,
1000   The pendulous round earth with balanced air
In counterpoise, now ponders° all events,
Battles and realms. In these he put two weights,
The sequel° each of parting and of fight;
The latter quick up flew, and kicked the beam;
Which Gabriel spying, thus bespake the fiend:
    'Satan, I know thy strength, and thou knowest mine,
Neither our own but given; what folly then
To boast what arms can do, since thine no more
Than heaven permits, nor mine, though doubled now
1010   To trample thee as mire. For proof look up,
And read thy lot in yon celestial sign
Where thou art weighed,° and shown how light, how weak,
If thou resist.' The fiend looked up and knew
His mounted scale aloft: nor more; but fled
Murmuring, and with him fled the shades of night.

From *Book V*

Now Morn her rosy steps in the eastern clime
Advancing, sowed the earth with orient pearl,
When Adam waked, so customed—for his sleep
Was airy light, from pure digestion bred,
And temperate vapours° bland, which the only° sound
Of leaves and fuming rills, Aurora's fan,°
Lightly dispersed, and the shrill matin song
Of birds on every bough—so much the more

Teneriffe . . . unremoved peak in the Canary islands, and the Atlas range in Morocco, both unremovable
cope canopy
golden scales the constellation Libra now, at midnight, at the zenith; also reminiscent of the Homeric golden scales in which Zeus weighed the destinies of Greek and Trojans, Achilles and Hector, and, in Virgil, Aeneas and Turnus
Astraea the constellation Virgo was formed when Astraea, or Justice, left the world at the end of the Golden Age

ponders weighs, with an overtone of "considers"
sequel consequence
thou art weighed "—in the balance, and art found wanting," the warning to Belshazzar in the Book of Daniel 5:27
vapours a medical term referring to the exhalations of digestion
only mere
Aurora's fan the leaves

His wonder was to find unwakened Eve
10 With tresses discomposed, and glowing cheek,
As through unquiet rest. He on his side
Leaning half-raised, with looks of cordial love
Hung over her enamoured, and beheld
Beauty, which whether waking or asleep
Shot forth peculiar graces;° then with voice
Mild, as when Zephyrus on Flora breathes,
Her hand soft touching, whispered thus: 'Awake,
My fairest,° my espoused, my latest found,
Heaven's last best gift, my ever new delight,
20 Awake, the morning shines, and the fresh field
Calls us; we lose the prime,° to mark how spring
Our tended plants, how blows° the citron grove,
What drops the myrrh, and what the balmy° reed,
How Nature paints her colours, how the bee
Sits on the bloom extracting liquid sweet.'
　　Such whispering waked her, but with startled eye
On Adam, whom embracing, thus she spake:
　　'O sole in whom my thoughts find all repose,
My glory, my perfection, glad I see
30 Thy face, and morn returned, for I this night—
Such night till this I never passed—have dreamed,
If dreamed, not as I oft am wont, of thee,
Works of day past, or morrow's next design,
But of offence and trouble, which my mind
Knew never till this irksome night. Methought
Close at mine ear one called me forth to walk
With gentle voice; I thought it thine. It said:
"Why sleep'st thou, Eve? Now is the pleasant time,
The cool, the silent, save where silence yields
40 *To the night-warbling bird, that now awake*
Tunes sweetest his° love-laboured song; now reigns
Full-orbed the moon, and with more pleasing light
Shadowy sets off the face of things;° in vain,
If none regard; heaven wakes with all his eyes,°
Whom to behold but thee, Nature's desire,
In whose sight all things joy, with ravishment
Attracted by thy beauty still to gaze?"
I rose as at thy call, but found thee not;
To find thee I directed then my walk;
50 And on, methought, alone I passed through ways
That brought me on a sudden to the tree

---

peculiar graces graces peculiar to her
Awake, My fairest echoes the morning song
in the Song of Songs 2:10.
prime early morning hours
blows blooms
balmy yielding aromatic resin
his The nightingale is, normally, "she" (because

the transformed Philomela), but here is masculine by association with Satan.
Shadowy . . . things This serenade (evening
song), the opposite of Adam's aubade (morning
song), praises moonlight's qualities of ambi-
guity, soft vagueness, and outline-blurring.
all his eyes the stars

Of interdicted° knowledge. Fair it seemed,
Much fairer to my fancy than by day;
And as I wondering looked, beside it stood
One shaped and winged like one of those from heaven
By us oft seen; his dewy locks distilled
Ambrosia; on that tree he also gazed;
And *"O fair plant,"* said he, *"with fruit surcharged,*
Deigns none to ease thy load and taste thy sweet,
60   *Nor god,° nor man; is knowledge so despised?*
Or envy, or what reserve forbids to taste?
Forbid who will, none shall from me withhold
Longer thy offered good, why else set here?"
This said he paused not, but with venturous arm
He plucked, he tasted; me damp horror chilled
At such bold words vouched with a deed so bold.
But he thus, overjoyed: *"O fruit divine,°*
Sweet of thyself, but much more sweet thus cropped,
Forbidden here, it seems, as only fit
70   *For gods, yet able to make gods of men;*
And why not gods of men, since good, the more
Communicated, more abundant grows,
The author not impaired, but honoured more?
Here, happy creature, fair angelic Eve,
Partake thou also; happy though thou art,
Happier thou may'st be, worthier canst not be;
Taste this, and be henceforth among the gods
Thyself a goddess, not to earth confined,
But sometimes in the air, as we; sometimes
80   *Ascend to heaven, by merit thine, and see*
What life the gods live there, and such live thou."
So saying, he drew nigh, and to me held,
Even to my mouth of that same fruit held part
Which he had plucked; the pleasant savoury smell
So quickened appetite that I, methought,
Could not but taste. Forthwith up to the clouds
With him I flew, and underneath beheld
The earth outstretched immense, a prospect wide
And various. Wondering at my flight and change
90   To this high exaltation, suddenly
My guide was gone, and I, methought, sunk down,
And fell asleep; but O how glad I waked
To find this but a dream!'° Thus Eve her night
Related, and thus Adam answered sad:°

---

interdicted forbidden
god spirit, as at l. 117, below
O fruit divine Satan's voice mistakenly over-emphasizes the power of the fruit itself which, "well used" (IV.200), would have remained uneaten.
but a dream as Eve recounts it, a prophetic one, having its fulfillment in Bk. IX, when details of the temptation of Eve will echo those of her narration here. This non-biblical dream raises interesting interpretive questions: if a "true dream," is Eve already lost? if a false one (see IV.778n.), then a necessary educational experience?
sad serious

'Best image of myself and dearer half,
The trouble of thy thoughts this night in sleep
Affects me equally; nor can I like
This uncouth° dream, of evil sprung, I fear;
Yet evil whence? In thee can harbour none,
100   Created pure. But know that in the soul
Are many lesser faculties° that serve
Reason as chief; among these fancy next
Her office holds; of all external things,
Which the five watchful senses represent,°
She forms imaginations,° airy shapes,
Which reason joining or disjoining frames
All what we affirm or what deny, and call
Our knowledge or opinion; then retires
Into her private cell when nature rests.
110   Oft in her absence mimic fancy wakes
To imitate her; but misjoining shapes,
Wild work produces oft, and most in dreams,
Ill matching words and deeds long past or late.
Some such resemblances methinks I find
Of our last evening's talk in this thy dream,
But with addition strange; yet be not sad.
Evil into the mind of god or man
May come and go, so unapproved, and leave
No spot or blame behind; which gives me hope
120   That what in sleep thou didst abhor to dream,
Waking thou never wilt consent to do.
Be not disheartened then, nor cloud those looks
That wont to be more cheerful and serene
Than when fair morning first smiles on the world,
And let us to our fresh employments rise
Among the groves, the fountains, and the flowers
That open now their choicest bosomed smells
Reserved from night, and kept for thee in store.'

.   .   .

[Eve's anxiety allayed, they proceed to the first day's activities, starting with a morning hymn followed by the unfallen work of gardening. God instructs the archangel Raphael to descend to Paradise and visit Adam and Eve in the garden in order to teach them who they are and what their relation to the world is, and, most particularly, "to render man inexcusable" by telling them who their enemy is. This entails a sub-epic, Raphael's narration of all that has gone before, modeled on the flashback narration in Homer and Virgil by which we

---

uncouth unpleasant
lesser faculties In a brilliant parody of the story of the Fall, Chaucer's Pertelote explains to her husband Chaunteclere that his prophetic dream must have been something he ate. Here, Adam gives Eve a lecture on the psychology of the faculties, notably about fancy, or imagination (they were usually not distinguished). See

Renaissance Psychology in the Glossary, the passage on fancy from Burton's *Anatomy of Melancholy*, and the allegory of Phantastes in *The Faerie Queene* II.ix.49–58.
represent show
imaginations visions; the objects, rather than the faculty itself

learn of all of Odysseus' adventures between Troy and Calypso's island, for example, only when he narrates them at the court of Alcinous. *Paradise Lost,* too, has started *in medias res,* and now we learn of the total time sequence stretching back behind the Fall of Satan. The promotion of the Son by God, the jealousy and scheming of Satan, and the beginning of the revolution in heaven are all unfolded.]

Book VI

[Raphael's narration continues. It describes the three days' battle in heaven in a grim and animated fashion, including the invention of "devilish engines," the first artillery, and other war matériel, "which in the second day's fight put Michael and his angels to some disorder," as Milton puts it in his prose *argument* to Book VI. The third day's victory is given not to Michael, the general, but the Son, whose thundering chariot ride routs Satan's legions; as they retreat in disarray, the wall of heaven opens, and "they leap down with horror and confusion into the place of punishment prepared for them in the deep." The Son returns to his Father in triumph.]

From Book VII

[Here, in the proem to Book VII, Milton finally names his "heavenly Muse." His invocation calls on her for help in making a difficult imaginative transition from the almost mock-heroic liveliness of the war in heaven in Book VI to the monumental task of revealing, through Raphael's narration, the story of creation. His poem is "descending" to earth from heavenly subjects, but his efforts and craft must rise to this harder task. This is also the midpoint of the poem, and from here the action is all downhill; there are no more scenes taking place in heaven. As always, too, there is Milton's anxiety, as a poet, about falling.]

Descend from heaven, Urania,° by that name
If rightly thou art called, whose voice divine
Following, about the Olympian hill I soar,
Above the flight of Pegasean wing.°
The meaning, not the name° I call; for thou
Nor of the Muses nine, nor on the top
Of old Olympus dwell'st, but heavenly born,
Before the hills appeared or fountain flowed,
Thou with eternal wisdom didst converse,
10   Wisdom thy sister, and with her didst play
In presence of the almighty father, pleased
With thy celestial song. Up led by thee
Into the heaven of heavens I have presumed,

Urania See I.6n.
Pegasean wing Pegasus, the winged horse ridden by Bellerophon when he killed the Chimera (see II.628n), thus committing an act of truth. The flying horse was symbolic of poetry itself (1) because he struck Mt. Helicon with his hoof to produce the Muses' spring and (2) from his flights above even the fountains which stood for poetic expression, for breaking out and flowing.
meaning, not the name not Urania only as one of the nine (Muse of astronomy, who will preside over the discussion of the cosmos in Bk. VII), but as a kind of Christian Muse of religious poetry

An earthly guest, and drawn empyreal air,
Thy tempering; with like safety guided down,
Return me to my native element,°
Lest from this flying steed unreined (as once
Bellerophon, though from a lower clime)
Dismounted, on the Aleian field° I fall,
20   Erroneous° there to wander and forlorn.
Half yet remains unsung,° but narrower bound
Within the visible diurnal° sphere;
Standing on earth, not rapt° above the pole,
More safe I sing with mortal voice, unchanged
To hoarse or mute, though fallen on evil days,°
On evil days, though fallen, and evil tongues;
In darkness,° and with dangers compassed round,
And solitude; yet not alone, while thou
Visit'st my slumbers nightly,° or when morn
30   Purples the east. Still govern thou my song,
Urania, and fit audience find, though few.
But drive far off the barbarous dissonance
Of Bacchus and his revellers, the race
Of that wild rout that tore the Thracian bard°
In Rhodope,° where woods and rocks had ears
To rapture, till the savage clamour drowned°
Both harp and voice; nor could the Muse defend
Her son. So fail not thou who thee implores;
For thou art heavenly, she° an empty dream.

[Book VII tells the story of Creation. Raphael tells of God's desire to create
another world and "out of one man a race / Innumerable" in further despite of
Satan's decimation of heaven's ranks, "there to dwell, / Not here, till by degrees
of merit raised" they will become as angels (a promise Satan makes to Eve)
"And Earth be changed to heaven, and heaven to earth." The Son, as the
Word of God, then creates the world in six days, starting out with a pair of
compasses which draw circles and boundaries of limitation, then creating light,
and so on through the processes of the text in Genesis. The work culminates in
the creation, among the animals, of the vertical animal, man; the Word re-
ascends to heaven, and angelic rejoicing celebrates the completion of the act.
    Book VIII continues the education of man, following his two heroic narra-
tions of warfare and of creation and founding of living places with a brief

native element earth
Aleian field Bellerophon finally tried to reach
heaven on Pegasus, and Zeus threw him off onto
the plain of Aleia (in Greek: "error").
Erroneous Latin *error* means "wandering," and
Milton plays here, as so often, on both the
original and derived meanings of words.
Half . . . unsung See Headnote to Bk. VII.
diurnal rotating daily
rapt entranced, "caught up" (into heaven?)
evil days the Restoration, which commenced
with an anti-Puritan reaction during which
Milton felt in great danger; also, evil in that

the decade of political writing and work during
which he had gone blind had come to nothing
darkness his blindness; this echoes part of the
meditation on light (III. 145)
nightly See III.31 and IX.21–24.
Thracian bard Orpheus, torn apart by the
Bacchantes (see *Comus*, l. 550, and *Lycidas*,
ll. 57–63)
Rhodope a mountain in Thrace
drowned Given the fate of the dismembered
Orpheus, harp and head floating down the
Hebrus, this word is doubly powerful.
she Orpheus' muse

response to Adam's questions about the relation of Paradise to the celestial phenomena apparent from it: he asks about sun, moon, and stars, and what accounts for their motions through the visible sky (an original and fruitful question for fallen man's science). Raphael instructs him to forget such pseudo-problems, implying that in Paradise the phenomena are the reality, and presenting a satiric picture of the search "through wandering mazes lost" (like the philosophy of the demons in Book II) for knowledge of reality in fallen human history. He particularly ridicules the way in which theories, or models, succeed each other in the history of science, how astronomers "build, unbuild, contrive / To save appearances, how gird the sphere / With centric and eccentric scribbled o'er, / Cycle and epicycle, orb in orb"—the picture of a Ptolemaic chart scribbled over with constant revisions. His account finished, Adam responds with one of his own, of his memories of everything since the dawn of his own consciousness, on awaking from his creation, his first sight of Eve, and so forth. Raphael, "after admonitions repeated" to Adam about not letting his feelings for Eve overcome his higher reason, departs.]

> *Book IX*
> No more of talk where God or angel guest
> With man, as with his friend, familiar used
> To sit indulgent, and with him partake
> Rural repast, permitting him the while
> Venial° discourse unblamed. I now must change
> Those notes to tragic; foul distrust, and breach
> Disloyal on the part of man, revolt,
> And disobedience; on the part of heaven
> Now alienated, distance° and distaste,°
> 10   Anger and just rebuke, and judgment given,
> That brought into this world a world of woe,°
> Sin and her shadow Death, and misery,
> Death's harbinger. Sad task, yet argument
> Not less but more heroic than the wrath°
> Of stern Achilles on his foe pursued
> Thrice fugitive about Troy wall; or rage
> Of Turnus for Lavinia disespoused;°
> Or Neptune's ire or Juno's, that so long
> Perplexed the Greek° and Cytherea's son;°
> 20   If answerable style I can obtain
> Of my celestial patroness,° who deigns
> Her nightly visitation° unimplored,

venial allowable
distance may also have the sense "discord" or "quarrel."
distaste completes the list of hissing *"dis-"* 's starting at l. 6 with what will be the operative word in the plot now, "taste" (see I.2).
world . . . woe The two "world"'s are local and general, literal and figurative; "woe," soon after "taste," echoes I.3.
wrath the first word of the *Iliad*. Milton shifts from describing his modulating tone to the subject of epic and what its subject should be.
Turnus . . . disespoused Turnus is Aeneas'

major antagonist in the latter portion of Virgil's epic; to Turnus he loses Italy, his beloved, and his life.
the Greek Odysseus
Cytherea's son Aeneas
celestial patroness Urania (see the invocations to Bks. I, III, VII)
nightly visitation Milton dictated *Paradise Lost* in the mornings from inspiration in the previous night; at any rate this is the poem's own myth of its composition, of having been sung out of darkness.

And dictates to me slumbering, or inspires
Easy my unpremeditated verse,
Since first this subject for heroic song
Pleased me long choosing, and beginning late;
Not sedulous by nature to indite
Wars, hitherto the only argument
Heroic deemed, chief maistry° to dissect
30   With long and tedious havoc fabled knights
In battles feigned (the better fortitude
Of patience and heroic martyrdom
Unsung), or to describe races and games,
Or tilting° furniture, emblazoned shields,
Impresses° quaint, caparisons and steeds,
Bases and tinsel trappings,° gorgeous knights
At joust and tournament; then marshalled feast
Served up in hall with sewers and seneschals;°
The skill of artifice or office mean,
40   Not that which justly gives heroic name
To person or to poem. Me of these
Nor skilled nor studious, higher argument
Remains, sufficient of itself to raise
That name,° unless an age too late, or cold
Climate,° or years damp my intended wing
Depressed, and much they may, if all be mine,
Not hers who brings it nightly to my ear.
        The sun was sunk,° and after him the star
Of Hesperus, whose office is to bring
50   Twilight upon the earth, short arbiter
'Twixt day and night, and now from end to end
Night's hemisphere had veiled the horizon round,
When Satan, who late fled before the threats
Of Gabriel out of Eden, now improved°
In meditated fraud and malice, bent
On man's destruction, maugre° what might hap
Of heavier on himself, fearless returned.°
By night he fled, and at midnight returned
From compassing the earth, cautious of day,
60   Since Uriel, regent of the sun, descried
His entrance, and forewarned the Cherubim
That kept their watch; thence full of anguish driven,
The space of seven continued nights he rode

---

maistry mastery, skill. The word has an archaic flavor, and introduces the terms associated with Renaissance epic and its world of medieval romance (Tasso, Ariosto, and Spenser).
tilting jousting
Impresses emblems or devices on shields
Bases . . . trappings draperies, caparisons, and trimmings for horses
sewers and seneschals waiters and stewards
That name epic poetry ("heroic name")
an age . . . Climate the burden of an epic

tradition, even mastered, is very great. These phrases refer to a moment of Western history, Restoration England, as well as to the northern climate and the winter weather, during which, we are told, he wrote.
sun was sunk The transition to narrative is from the echoing "nightly."
improved intensified
maugre despite
returned to where the narrative left him at the end of Bk. IV

With darkness, thrice the equinoctial line
He circled, four times crossed the car° of Night
From pole to pole, traversing each colure;°
On the eighth returned, and on the coast averse°
From entrance or Cherubic watch, by stealth
Found unsuspected way. There was a place—
70   Now not, though sin, not time, first wrought the change—
Where Tigris at the foot of Paradise
Into a gulf shot under ground, till part
Rose up a fountain by the Tree of Life;
In with the river sunk, and with it rose
Satan, involved in rising mist, then sought
Where to lie hid; sea he had searched and land
From Eden over Pontus,° and the pool
Maeotis,° up beyond the river Ob;°
Downward as far antarctic; and in length
80   West from Orontes° to the ocean barred
At Darien,° thence to the land where flows
Ganges and Indus. Thus the orb he roamed
With narrow search, and with inspection deep
Considered every creature, which of all
Most opportune might serve his wiles, and found
The serpent subtlest beast of all the field.
Him after long debate, irresolute°
Of thoughts revolved,° his final sentence° chose
Fit vessel, fittest imp° of fraud, in whom
90   To enter, and his dark suggestions hide
From sharpest sight; for in the wily snake,
Whatever sleights none would suspicious mark,
As from his wit and native subtlety
Proceeding, which, in other beasts observed,
Doubt° might beget of diabolic power
Active within beyond the sense of brute.
Thus he resolved, but first from inward grief
His bursting passion into plaints thus poured:
        'O earth, how like to heaven, if not preferred
100   More justly, seat worthier of gods, as built
With second thoughts, reforming what was old!°
For what God after better worse would build?

---

car chariot
colure one of two longitudinal circles drawn
from the celestial poles, cutting the ecliptic at
solstice and equinox
averse opposite
Pontus the Black Sea
Maeotis the Sea of Azov
river Ob in Siberia
Orontes Syrian river
Darien Isthmus of Panama
irresolute unresolved
thoughts revolved turned and twisted, like a

serpent's motion
sentence decision
imp offshoot
Doubt suspicion
With . . . old Satan's address to the earth,
paralleling his invocation of the sun in IV.32,
begins here with a fallen reading of an unfallen
event: wise men learn by experience, and a
second version, in a technological context, improves on the first; this is not true of Creation,
nor necessarily of poems.

Terrestrial heaven, danced round by other heavens
That shine, yet bear their bright officious° lamps,
Light above light, for thee alone, as seems,
In thee concentring all their precious beams
Of sacred influence! As God in heaven
Is centre, yet extends to all, so thou
Centring receivest from all those orbs; in thee,
110   Not in themselves, all their known virtue appears
    Productive in herb, plant, and nobler birth
Of creatures animate with gradual° life
Of growth, sense, reason,° all summed up in man.
With what delight could I have walked thee round,
If I could joy in aught, sweet interchange
Of hill and valley, rivers, woods, and plains,
Now land, now sea, and shores with forest crowned,
Rocks, dens, and caves; but I in none of these
Find place or refuge; and the more I see
120   Pleasures about me, so much more I feel
Torment within me, as from the hateful siege°
Of contraries; all good to me becomes
Bane,° and in heaven much worse would be my state.
But neither here seek I, no nor in heaven
To dwell, unless by mastering heaven's Supreme;
Nor hope to be myself less miserable
By what I seek, but others to make such
As I, though thereby worse to me redound.
For only in destroying I find ease
130   To my relentless thoughts; and him destroyed,
Or won to what may work his utter loss,
For whom all this was made, all this will soon
Follow, as to him linked in weal or woe;
In woe then, that destruction wide may range.
To me shall be the glory sole among
The infernal powers, in one day to have marred
What he, almighty styled, six nights and days
Continued making, and who knows how long
Before had been contriving? Though perhaps
140   Not longer than since I in one night freed
From servitude inglorious well-nigh half
The angelic name, and thinner left the throng
Of his adorers. He to be avenged,
And to repair his numbers thus impaired,
Whether such virtue spent of old now failed

---

officious serviceable
gradual on a scale of nature
growth, sense, reason functions of the vegetable, animal, and rational souls in man; see *Renaissance Psychology* in the Glossary
siege The contraries Satan has manipulated in his dialectic are now besieging him, with the final and appropriate irony that "siege" can also mean "seat" or "throne," his internal state in which these contraries are enshrined. **all good . . . Bane** "bane": "evil"; can he remember saying "Evil, be thou my good" (IV.110)? Cf. IV.32–113 and IX.467–70.

More angels to create, if they at least
Are his created, or to spite us more,
Determined to advance into our room°
A creature formed of earth, and him endow,
150 Exalted from so base original,
With heavenly spoils, our spoils. What he decreed
He effected; man he made, and for him built
Magnificent this world, and earth his seat,
Him lord pronounced, and, O indignity!
Subjected to his service angel wings,
And flaming ministers to watch and tend
Their earthy charge. Of these the vigilance
I dread, and to elude, thus wrapped in mist
Of midnight vapour glide obscure, and pry
160 In every bush and brake, where hap° may find
The serpent sleeping, in whose mazy folds
To hide me, and the dark intent I bring.
O foul descent!° that I who erst contended
With Gods to sit the highest, am now constrained
Into a beast, and mixed with bestial slime,
This essence to incarnate and imbrute,
That to the height of deity aspired;
But what will not ambition and revenge
Descend to? Who aspires must down as low
170 As high he soared, obnoxious° first or last
To basest things. Revenge, at first though sweet,
Bitter ere long back on itself recoils;
Let it; I reck not, so it light well aimed,
Since higher I fall short, on him who next
Provokes my envy, this new favourite
Of heaven, this man of clay, son of despite,
Whom us the more to spite his maker raised
From dust: spite then with spite is best repaid.'
    So saying, through each thicket dank or dry,
180 Like a black mist low creeping, he held on
His midnight search, where soonest he might find
The serpent: him fast sleeping soon he found
In labyrinth of many a round self-rolled,
His head the midst, well stored with subtle wiles:
Not yet in horrid° shade or dismal den,
Nor nocent° yet, but on the grassy herb
Fearless, unfeared, he slept. In at his mouth
The devil entered, and his brutal sense,
In heart or head, possessing soon inspired

room place
hap chance
O foul descent! and a hideous parody of the
other Incarnation, the other Descent (of the
Holy Ghost to incarnate in Mary)

obnoxious exposed
horrid bristling
nocent harmful (snakes become poisonous only
after the Fall); also, perhaps, "guilty"

190 With act intelligential, but his sleep
Disturbed not, waiting close° the approach of morn.
Now whenas sacred light began to dawn
In Eden on the humid flowers, that breathed
Their morning incense, when all things that breathe
From the earth's great altar send up silent praise
To the Creator, and his nostrils fill
With grateful smell, forth came the human pair
And joined their vocal worship to the quire
Of creatures wanting° voice; that done, partake
200 The season, prime for sweetest scents and airs;°
Then cómmune how that day they best may ply
Their growing work; for much their work outgrew
The hands' dispatch of two gardening so wide.
And Eve first to her husband thus began:
'Adam, well may we labour still to dress
This garden, still to tend plant, herb, and flower,
Our pleasant task enjoined, but till more hands
Aid us, the work under our labour grows,
Luxurious by restraint; what we by day
210 Lop overgrown, or prune, or prop, or bind,
One night or two with wanton growth derides,
Tending to wild. Thou therefore now advise
Or hear what to my mind first thoughts present:
Let us divide our labours, thou where choice
Leads thee, or where most needs, whether to wind
The woodbine° round this arbour, or direct
The clasping ivy where to climb, while I
In yonder spring° of roses intermixed
With myrtle, find what to redress° till noon.
220 For while so near each other thus all day
Our task we choose, what wonder if so near
Looks intervene and smiles, or object new
Casual discourse draw on, which intermits
Our day's work, brought to little, though begun
Early, and the hour of supper comes unearned.'
To whom mild answer Adam thus returned:
'Sole Eve,° associate sole, to me beyond
Compare above all living creatures dear,
Well hast thou motioned,° well thy thoughts employed
230 How we might best fulfill the work which here
God hath assigned us, nor of me shalt pass
Unpraised; for nothing lovelier can be found

---

close hidden
wanting lacking
airs also in a musical sense: "tunes"
wind The woodbine She leaves to Adam the
intertwining plants.
spring grove of young trees or bushes
redress prop up again. The trouble with all

these immensely practical suggestions is that
it will leave her unpropped (ll. 432–33) by
Adam.
Eve as by her epithet, "Mother of all life"
(Genesis 3:2)
motioned proposed

In woman, than to study household good,
And good works in her husband to promote.
Yet not so strictly hath our Lord imposed
Labour, as to debar us when we need
Refreshment, whether food, or talk between,
Food of the mind, or this sweet intercourse
Of looks and smiles, for smiles from reason flow,
To brute denied, and are of love the food,
Love not the lowest end of human life.
For not to irksome toil, but to delight
He made us, and delight to reason joined.
These paths and bowers doubt not but our joint hands
Will keep from wilderness with ease, as wide
As we need walk, till younger hands ere long
Assist us. But if much convérse perhaps
Thee satiate, to short absence I could yield.
For solitude sometimes is best society,
And short retirement urges sweet return.
But other doubt possesses me, lest harm
Befall thee severed from me; for thou knowest
What hath been warned us, what malicious foe,
Envying our happiness, and of his own
Despairing, seeks to work us woe and shame
By sly assault; and somewhere nigh at hand
Watches, no doubt, with greedy hope to find
His wish and best advantage, us asunder,
Hopeless to circumvent us joined, where each
To other speedy aid might lend at need;
Whether his first design be to withdraw
Our fealty° from God, or to disturb
Conjugal love, than which perhaps no bliss
Enjoyed by us excites his envy more;
Or this,° or worse, leave not the faithful side
That gave thee being, still shades thee and protects.
The wife, where danger or dishonour lurks,
Safest and seemliest by her husband stays,
Who guards her, or with her the worst endures.'
    To whom the virgin° majesty of Eve,
As one who loves, and some unkindness meets,
With sweet austere composure thus replied:
    'Offspring of heaven and earth, and all earth's lord,
That such an enemy we have, who seeks
Our ruin, both by thee informed I learn,
And from the parting angel overheard
As in a shady nook I stood behind,
Just then returned at shut° of evening flowers.

240

250

260

270

---

fealty fidelity
Or this whether (his plan) is this
virgin innocent; but literally too: she is not

a virgin, but her majesty is so far unruptured
shut folding-up time

But that thou shouldst my firmness therefore doubt
280 To God or thee, because we have a foe
May tempt it, I expected not to hear.
His violence thou fear'st not, being such
As we, not capable of death or pain,
Can either not receive, or can repel.
His fraud is then thy fear, which plain infers
Thy equal fear that my firm faith and love
Can by his fraud be shaken or seduced;
Thoughts, which how found they harbour in thy breast,
Adam, misthought of her to thee so dear?'
290   To whom with healing words Adam replied:
'Daughter of God and man, immortal Eve,
For such thou art, from sin and blame entire;°
Not diffident of thee do I dissuade
Thy absence from my sight, but to avoid
The attempt itself, intended by our foe.
For he who tempts, though in vain, at least asperses°
The tempted with dishonour foul, supposed
Not incorruptible of faith, not proof
Against temptation. Thou thyself with scorn
300 And anger wouldst resent the offered wrong,
Though ineffectual found. Misdeem not then,
If such affront I labour to avert
From thee alone, which on us both at once
The enemy, though bold, will hardly dare,
Or daring, first on me the assault shall light.
Nor thou his malice and false guile contemn;
Subtle he needs must be, who could seduce
Angels, nor think superfluous others' aid.
I from the influence° of thy looks receive
310 Access° in every virtue, in thy sight
More wise, more watchful, stronger, if need were
Of outward strength; while shame, thou looking on,
Shame to be overcome or overreached,
Would utmost vigour raise, and raised unite.
Why shouldst not thou like sense within thee feel
When I am present, and thy trial choose
With me, best witness of thy virtue tried?'
    So spake domestic Adam in his care
And matrimonial love; but Eve, who thought
320 Less° attribúted to her faith sincere,
Thus her reply with accent sweet renewed:
    'If this be our condition, thus to dwell
In narrow circuit straitened° by a foe,

---

entire integral, untarnished
asperses sprays about
influence the beams of stars. Adam has fallen
into Petrarchan poetry.

Access increase
Less too little
straitened constricted

Subtle or violent, we not endued
Single with like defence, wherever met,
How are we happy, still in fear of harm?
But harm precedes not sin: only our foe
Tempting affronts us with his foul esteem
Of our integrity; his foul esteem
330   Sticks no dishonour on our front,° but turns
Foul on himself; then wherefore shunned or feared
By us? Who rather double honour gain
From his surmise proved false, find peace within,
Favour from heaven, our witness, from the event.
And what is faith, love, virtue, unassayed
Alone, without exterior help sustained?
Let us not then suspect our happy state
Left so imperfect by the maker wise
As not secure to single or combined.
340   Frail is our happiness, if this be so,
And Eden were no Eden° thus exposed.'
    To whom thus Adam fervently replied:
'O woman, best are all things as the will
Of God ordained them; his creating hand
Nothing imperfect or deficient left
Of all that he created, much less man,
Or aught that might his happy state secure,
Secure from outward force: within himself
The danger lies, yet lies within his power;
350   Against his will he can receive no harm.
But God left free the will, for what obeys
Reason is free, and reason he made right,°
But bid her well beware, and still erect,°
Lest by some fair appearing good surprised
She dictate false, and misinform the will
To do what God expressly hath forbid.
Not then mistrust, but tender love enjoins,
That I should mind° thee oft, and mind° thou me.
Firm we subsist, yet possible to swerve,°
360   Since reason not impossibly may meet
Some specious object by the foe suborned,
And fall into deception unaware,
Not keeping strictest watch, as she was warned.
Seek not temptation then, which to avoid
Were better, and most likely if from me
Thou sever not; trial will come unsought.

---

front brow, forehead
Eden in its Hebrew meaning of "pleasure"
right right reason, as distinguished from capable wit
erect attentive

mind remind admonishingly; but when repeated, "pay heed to"
Firm . . . swerve a subtly modulated echo of the central doctrinal statement of God: "I made him just and right, / Sufficient to have stood, though free to fall" (III.98–99)

Wouldst thou approve thy constancy, approve°
First thy obedience; the other who can know,
Not seeing thee attempted, who attest?
370 But if thou think trial unsought may find
Us both securer° than thus warned thou seem'st,
Go; for thy stay, not free, absents thee more;
Go in thy native innocence, rely
On what thou hast of virtue, summon all,
For God towards thee hath done his part, do thine.'
    So spake the patriarch of mankind, but Eve
Persisted; yet submiss,° though last, replied:
'With thy permission then, and thus forewarned,
Chiefly by what thy own last reasoning words
380 Touched only, that our trial, when least sought,
May find us both perhaps far less prepared,
The willinger I go, nor much expect
A foe so proud will first the weaker seek;
So bent, the more shall shame him his repulse.'
    Thus saying, from her husband's hand her hand
Soft she withdrew,° and like a wood-nymph light,
Oread or Dryad, or of Delia's° train,
Betook her to the groves, but Delia's self
In gait surpassed and goddess-like deport,°
390 Though not as she with bow and quiver armed,
But with such gardening tools as art yet rude
—Guiltless of fire°—had formed, or angels brought.
To Pales,° or Pomona,° thus adorned,
Likest she seemed, Pomona when she fled
Vertumnus,° or to Ceres in her prime,
Yet virgin of Proserpina° from Jove.
Her long with ardent look his eye pursued
Delighted, but desiring more her stay.
Oft he to her his charge of quick return
400 Repeated, she to him as oft engaged
To be returned by noon amid the bower,
And all things in best order to invite
Noontide repast, or afternoon's repose.
O much deceived, much failing, hapless Eve,
Of thy presumed return! event perverse!
Thou never from that hour in Paradise
Found'st either sweet repast or sound repose;

---

approve prove
Us both securer surer of ourselves (and thus,
more careless)
submiss submissively
her hand . . . withdrew Casual as this detail
may seem, it makes a picture of an emblem
being broken (see IV.321n.).
Oread . . . Delia's mountain or tree nymph of
Diana's

deport bearing
fire The fire Prometheus stole stands for all
technology.
Pales Roman goddess of pastures
Pomona goddess of fruit trees
Vertumnus god of seasons, her lover
Proserpina See IV.269n.

Such ambush hid, among sweet flowers and shades
Waited with hellish rancour imminent
410   To intercept thy way, or send thee back
Despoiled of innocence, of faith, of bliss.
For now, and since first break of dawn the fiend,
Mere serpent° in appearance, forth was come,
And on his quest, where likeliest he might find
The only two of mankind, but in them
The whole included race, his purposed prey.
In bower and field he sought, where any tuft
Of grove or garden-plot more pleasant lay,
Their tendance° or plantation for delight;
420   By fountain or by shady rivulet
He sought them both, but wished his hap might find
Eve separate; he wished, but not with hope
Of what so seldom chanced, when to his wish,
Beyond his hope, Eve separate he spies,
Veiled in a cloud of fragrance, where she stood,
Half spied, so thick the roses bushing round
About her glowed, oft stooping to support
Each flower of slender stalk, whose head though gay
Carnation, purple, azure, or specked with gold,
430   Hung drooping unsustained; them she upstays
Gently with myrtle band, mindless° the while,
Herself, though fairest unsupported flower,
From her best prop° so far, and storm so nigh.
Nearer he drew, and many a walk traversed
Of stateliest covert, cedar, pine, or palm,
Then voluble° and bold, now hid, now seen
Among thick-woven arborets° and flowers
Embordered on each bank, the hand of Eve:
Spot more delicious than those gardens feigned°
440   Or of revived Adonis, or renowned
Alcinous, host of old Laertes' son,°
Or that, not mystic, where the sapient king°
Held dalliance with his fair Egyptian spouse.
Much he the place admired, the person more.
As one who long in populous city pent,
Where houses thick and sewers annoy the air,
Forth issuing on a summer's morn to breathe
Among the pleasant villages and farms
Adjoined, from each thing met conceives delight,

Mere serpent He did not look like Northern Renaissance pictures of the temptation of Eve, in which the serpent has a human head.
tendance something to be tended
mindless heedless
her best prop Cf. ll. 210 and 219n.
voluble coiling; perhaps now in the sense of "glib" as well

arborets shrubs
feigned imagined; see *The Faerie Queene* III.vi, and Chapman's translation of the corresponding passage from Homer
Laertes' son Ulysses
not mystic . . . king Solomon's garden, real, historical biblical, hence not mythical like the garden of Adonis ("mystic")

450 The smell of grain, or tedded° grass, or kine,°
     Or dairy, each rural sight, each rural sound;
     If chance with nymph-like step fair virgin pass,
     What pleasing seemed, for her now pleases more,
     She most, and in her look sums all delight:
     Such pleasure took the Serpent to behold
     This flowery plat,° the sweet recess of Eve
     Thus early, thus alone; her heavenly form
     Angelic, but more soft and feminine,
     Her graceful innocence, her every air
460 Of gesture or least action overawed
     His malice, and with rapine sweet bereaved
     His fierceness of the fierce intent it brought.
     That space the evil one abstracted stood
     From his own evil, and for the time remained
     Stupidly° good, of enmity disarmed,
     Of guile, of hate, of envy, of revenge;
     But the hot hell that always in him burns,
     Though in mid-heaven, soon ended his delight,
     And tortures him now more, the more he sees
470 Of pleasure not for him ordained; then soon
     Fierce hate he recollects, and all his thoughts
     Of mischief, gratulating,° thus excites:
         'Thoughts, whither have ye led me, with what sweet
     Compulsion thus transported to forget
     What hither brought us? Hate, not love, nor hope
     Of Paradise for hell, hope here to taste
     Of pleasure, but all pleasure to destroy,
     Save what is in destroying; other joy
     To me is lost. Then let me not let pass
480 Occasion which now smiles: behold alone
     The woman, opportune° to all attempts,
     Her husband, for I view far round, not nigh,
     Whose higher intellectual° more I shun,
     And strength, of courage haughty, and of limb
     Heroic built, though of terrestrial mould,°
     Foe not informidable, exempt from wound,
     I not; so much hath hell debased, and pain
     Enfeebled me, to what I was in heaven.
     She fair, divinely fair, fit love for gods,
490 Not terrible, though terror be in love
     And beauty, not° approached by stronger hate,
     Hate stronger, under show of love well feigned,

---

tedded spread out for haymaking
kine cattle
plat plot of ground
Stupidly stupefied (and thus incapable, for the moment, of evil)

gratulating expressing pleasure
opportune opportunely placed
intellectual mind
terrestrial mould formed of earth
not if not

The way which to her ruin now I tend.'
  So spake the Enemy of mankind, enclosed
In serpent, inmate bad, and toward Eve
Addressed his way, not with indented wave,
Prone on the ground, as since, but on his rear,
Circular base of rising folds, that towered
Fold above fold a surging maze; his head
500 Crested aloft, and carbuncle his eyes;
With burnished neck of verdant gold, erect
Amidst his circling spires,° that on the grass
Floated redundant.° Pleasing was his shape,
And lovely, never since of serpent kind
Lovelier; not those that in Illyria changed
Hermione and Cadmus,° or the god
In Epidaurus;° nor to which transformed
Ammonian Jove,° or Capitoline° was seen,
He with Olympias, this with her who bore
510 Scipio, the highth of Rome. With tract° oblique
At first, as one who sought accéss, but feared
To interrupt, sidelong he works his way.
As when a ship by skilful steersman wrought
Nigh river's mouth or foreland, where the wind
Veers oft, as oft so steers, and shifts her sail,
So varied he, and of his tortuous train
Curled many a wanton wreath in sight of Eve,
To lure her eye; she busied heard the sound
Of rustling leaves, but minded not, as used
520 To such disport before her through the field
From every beast, more duteous at her call
Than at Circean call the herd disguised.°
He bolder now, uncalled before her stood,
But as in gaze admiring. Oft he bowed
His turret crest, and sleek enamelled neck,
Fawning, and licked the ground whereon she trod.
His gentle dumb expression turned at length
The eye of Eve to mark his play; he glad
Of her attention gained, with serpent tongue
530 Organic,° or impulse of vocal air,
His fraudulent temptation thus began:
    'Wonder not, sovereign mistress, if perhaps
Thou canst, who art sole wonder, much less arm
Thy looks, the heaven of mildness, with disdain,

---

spires spirals
redundant excessively flowing, wave-like
Hermione and Cadmus Hermione (Harmonia) and her king were changed into serpents.
god In Epidaurus Aesculapius' statue in Epidaurus represented the god of healing as an erect serpent.
Ammonian Jove Jupiter took Olympias, Alex-
ander the Great's mother, in the form of a snake; Capitoline Jupiter, similarly, the father of the Roman general Scipio Africanus.
tract path
herd disguised Ulysses' men turned by Circe into pigs
Organic instrumental

Displeased that I approach thee thus, and gaze
Insatiate, I thus single, nor have feared
Thy awful brow, more awful thus retired.
Fairest resemblance of thy maker fair,
Thee all things living gaze on, all things thine
540   By gift, and thy celestial beauty adore,
With ravishment beheld, there best beheld
Where universally admired; but here
In this enclosure wild, these beasts among,
Beholders rude, and shallow to discern
Half what in thee is fair, one man except,
Who sees thee? (and what is one?) who shouldst be seen
A goddess among gods, adored and served
By angels numberless, thy daily train.'
     So glozed° the Tempter, and his proem tuned;
550   Into the heart of Eve his words made way,
Though at the voice much marvelling; at length
Not unamazed she thus in answer spake:
     'What may this mean? Language of man pronounced
By tongue of brute, and human sense expressed?
The first at least of these I thought denied
To beasts, whom God on their creation-day
Created mute to all articulate sound;
The latter I demur,° for in their looks
Much reason, and in their actions oft appears.
560   Thee, Serpent, subtlest beast of all the field
I knew, but not with human voice endued;
Redouble then this miracle, and say,
How cam'st thou speakable of mute,° and how
To me so friendly grown above the rest
Of brutal kind, that daily are in sight?
Say, for such wonder claims attention due.'
     To whom the guileful tempter thus replied:
'Empress of this fair world, resplendent Eve,
Easy to me it is to tell thee all
570   What thou command'st, and right thou shouldst be obeyed.
I was at first as other beasts that graze
The trodden herb, of abject° thoughts and low,
As was my food, nor aught but food discerned
Or sex, and apprehended nothing high:
Till on a day roving the field, I chanced
A goodly tree far distant to behold,
Loaden with fruit of fairest colours mixed,
Ruddy and gold. I nearer drew to gaze;

---

glozed flattered
The latter I demur I have doubts about
"human sense expressed"—obviously, animals
communicate, but don't have language

speakable of mute capable of speech, from
being mute
abject cast down

When from the boughs a savoury odour blown,
580 Grateful to appetite, more pleased my sense
Than smell of sweetest fennel or the teats
Of ewe or goat dropping with milk at even,
Unsucked of lamb or kid, that tend their play.
To satisfy the sharp desire I had
Of tasting those fair apples,° I resolved
Not to defer;° hunger and thirst at once,
Powerful persuaders, quickened at the scent
Of that alluring fruit, urged me so keen.
About the mossy trunk I wound me soon,
590 For high from ground the branches would require
Thy utmost reach or Adam's: round the tree
All other beasts that saw, with like desire
Longing and envying stood, but could not reach.
Amid the tree now got, where plenty hung
Tempting so nigh, to pluck and eat my fill
I spared not, for such pleasure till that hour
At feed or fountain never had I found.
Sated at length, ere long I might perceive
Strange alteration in me, to degree°
600 Of reason in my inward powers, and speech
Wanted not long, though to this shape retained.
Thenceforth to speculations high or deep
I turned my thoughts, and with capacious mind
Considered all things visible in heaven,
Or earth, or middle,° all things fair and good;
But all that fair and good in thy divine
Semblance, and in thy beauty's heavenly ray
United I beheld; no fair to thine
Equivalent or second, which compelled
610 Me thus, though importune perhaps, to come
And gaze, and worship thee of right declared
Sovereign of creatures, universal dame.'°
    So talked the spirited° sly snake; and Eve
Yet more amazed unwary thus replied:
    'Serpent, thy overpraising leaves in doubt
The virtue° of that fruit, in thee first proved.
But say, where grows the tree, from hence how far?
For many are the trees of God that grow
In Paradise, and various, yet unknown
620 To us; in such abundance lies our choice
As leaves a greater store of fruit untouched,
Still hanging incorruptible, till men

apples The identification of the fruit with the
apple is folkloristic, not biblical.
defer delay
to degree to an extent

middle the air
dame mistress
spirited animated
virtue power

Grow up to their provision, and more hands
Help to disburden Nature of her birth.'
   To whom the wily adder, blithe and glad:
'Empress, the way is ready, and not long,
Beyond a row of myrtles, on a flat,
Fast by a fountain, one small thicket past
Of blowing° myrrh and balm; if thou accept
630 My conduct,° I can bring thee thither soon.'
   'Lead then,' said Eve. He leading swiftly rolled
In tangles, and made intricate seem straight,°
To mischief swift. Hope elevates, and joy
Brightens his crest, as when a wandering fire,
Compact° of unctuous vapour, which the night
Condenses, and the cold environs round,
Kindled through agitation to a flame,
Which oft, they say, some evil spirit attends,°
Hovering and blazing with delusive light,
640 Misleads the amazed night-wanderer from his way
To bogs and mires, and oft through pond or pool,
There swallowed up and lost, from succour far.
So glistered the dire Snake, and into fraud
Led Eve our credulous mother, to the tree
Of prohibition,° root of all our woe;
Which when she saw, thus to her guide she spake:
   'Serpent, we might have spared our coming hither,
Fruitless to me, though fruit be here to excess,
The credit of whose virtue rest with thee,
650 Wondrous indeed, if cause of such effects.
But of this tree we may not taste nor touch;
God so commanded, and left that command
Sole daughter of his voice;° the rest, we live
Law to ourselves, our reason is our law.'
   To whom the Tempter guilefully replied:
'Indeed? Hath God then said that of the fruit
Of all these garden trees ye shall not eat,
Yet lords declared of all in earth or air?'
   To whom thus Eve yet sinless: 'Of the fruit
660 Of each tree in the garden we may eat,
But of the fruit of this fair tree amidst
The garden, God hath said, "Ye shall not eat
Thereof, nor shall ye touch it, lest ye die."'

---

blowing blooming
conduct lead (the moral sense is there, un-avowed)
intricate seem straight again, his shaky motion and his moral direction. From this moment on in human history, "crooked" and "straight" will have moral connotations.
Compact composed
evil spirit attends the *ignis fatuus,* or will-o'-the-wisp, often associated with self-delusion
tree Of prohibition prohibited tree. The impact of "root," following immediately in the meta-phorical sense, and "fruitless" three lines further on, is strengthened by the literalness of "tree."
daughter of his voice the only commandment He enjoined on us

She scarce had said, though brief, when now more bold
The tempter, but with show of zeal and love
To man, and indignation at his wrong,
New part puts on, and as to passion moved,
Fluctuates° disturbed, yet comely, and in act
Raised, as of some great matter to begin.
670   As when of old some orator renowned
In Athens or free Rome, where eloquence
Flourished, since mute, to some great cause addressed,
Stood in himself collected, while each part,
Motion, each act won audience° ere the tongue,
Sometimes in highth° began, as no delay
Of preface brooking through his zeal of right:
So standing, moving, or to highth upgrown,
The tempter all impassioned thus began:
    'O sacred, wise, and wisdom-giving plant,
680   Mother of science,° now I feel thy power
Within me clear, not only to discern
Things in their causes, but to trace the ways
Of highest agents, deemed however wise.
Queen of this universe, do not believe
Those rigid threats of death; ye shall not die:
How should ye? By the fruit? It gives you life
To° knowledge; by the threatener? Look on me,
Me who have touched and tasted, yet both live,
And life more perfect have attained than fate
690   Meant me, by venturing higher than my lot.
Shall that be shut to man, which to the beast
Is open? Or will God incense his ire
For such a petty trespass, and not praise
Rather your dauntless virtue, whom the pain
Of death denounced,° whatever thing death be,
Deterred not from achieving what might lead
To happier life, knowledge of good and evil?
Of good, how just? Of evil, if what is evil
Be real, why not known, since easier shunned?
700   God therefore cannot hurt ye, and be just;
Not just, not God; not feared then, nor obeyed:
Your fear itself of death removes the fear.
Why then was this forbid? Why but to awe,
Why but to keep ye low and ignorant,
His worshippers? He knows that in the day
Ye eat thereof, your eyes that seem so clear,
Yet are but dim, shall perfectly be then
Opened and cleared, and ye shall be as gods,

Fluctuates changes appearance   science knowledge
audience attention   To as well as
highth height of feeling   denounced proclaimed

Knowing both good and evil as they know.
710 That ye should be as gods, since I as man,
Internal man,° is but proportion meet,
I of brute human, ye of human gods.
So ye shall die perhaps, by putting off
Human, to put on gods,° death to be wished,
Though threatened, which no worse than this can bring.
And what are gods that man may not become
As they, participating° godlike food?
The gods are first, and that advantage use
On our belief, that all from them proceeds;
720 I question it, for this fair earth I see,
Warmed by the sun, producing every kind,
Them nothing. If they° all things, who enclosed
Knowledge of good and evil in this tree,
That whoso eats thereof, forthwith attains
Wisdom without their leave? And wherein lies
The offence, that man should thus attain to know?
What can your knowledge hurt him, or this tree
Impart against his will, if all be his?
Or is it envy, and can envy dwell
730 In heavenly breasts? These, these and many more
Causes import° your need of this fair fruit.
Goddess humane,° reach then, and freely taste!'
    He ended, and his words replete with guile
Into her heart too easy entrance won.
Fixed on the fruit she gazed, which to behold
Might tempt alone, and in her ears the sound
Yet rung of his persuasive words, impregned
With reason, to her seeming, and with truth;
Meanwhile the hour of noon° drew on, and waked
740 An eager appetite, raised by the smell
So savoury of that fruit, which with desire,
Inclinable now grown to touch or taste,
Solicited her longing eye; yet first
Pausing a while, thus to herself she mused:
    'Great are thy virtues, doubtless, best of fruits,
Though kept from man, and worthy to be admired,
Whose taste, too long forborne, at first assay
Gave elocution° to the mute, and taught

Internal man See above, l. 600, where Satan
claims that his inner state has become human
through the agency of the fruit.
put on gods Satan brilliantly and nastily adapts
the language of Colossians 3:9–10 to his perverse construction of spiritual regeneration:
"Lie not one to another, seeing that ye have put
off the old man with his deeds; And have put
on the new man, which is renewed in knowledge after the image of him that created him."
participating sharing

they they produced
import indicate
Goddess humane "Human," the first reading,
concludes Satan's rhetoric with a blatant
oxymoron; the second sense, "gentle," is only
to mellow it in afterthought.
noon The tasting and falling must occur at
noon, less light be denied, and reason be
cheated.
elocution eloquence

The tongue not made for speech to speak thy praise.
750   Thy praise he also who forbids thy use
Conceals not from us, naming thee the Tree
Of Knowledge, knowledge both of good and evil;
Forbids us then to taste, but his forbidding
Commends thee more, while it infers the good
By thee communicated, and our want;
For good unknown sure is not had, or had
And yet unknown, is as not had at all.
In plain° then, what forbids he but to know,
Forbids us good, forbids us to be wise?
760   Such prohibitions bind not. But if Death
Bind us with after-bands, what profits then
Our inward freedom? In the day we eat
Of this fair fruit, our doom is, we shall die.
How dies the serpent? He hath eaten and lives,
And knows, and speaks, and reasons, and discerns,
Irrational till then. For us alone
Was death invented? Or to us denied
This intellectual food, for beasts reserved?
For beasts it seems—yet that one beast which first
770   Hath tasted, envies not, but brings with joy
The good befallen him, author unsuspect,°
Friendly to man, far from deceit or guile.
What fear I then, rather what know to fear
Under this ignorance of good and evil,
Of God or death, of law or penalty?
Here grows the cure° of all, this fruit divine,
Fair to the eye, inviting to the taste,
Of virtue° to make wise; what hinders then
To reach, and feed at once both body and mind?'
780   So saying, her rash hand in evil hour°
Forth reaching to the fruit, she plucked, she eat.°
Earth felt the wound, and Nature from her seat
Sighing through all her works gave signs of woe,
That all was lost.° Back to the thicket slunk
The guilty Serpent, and well might, for Eve
Intent now wholly on her taste, naught else
Regarded; such delight till then, as seemed,
In fruit she never tasted, whether true
Or fancied so, through expectation high
790   Of knowledge, nor was godhead from her thought.
Greedily she engorged without restraint,

In plain put simply
author unsuspect unsuspected authority
cure The secondary sense is "charge, responsibility."
Of virtue able

evil hour Our sense that "evil" puns on "Eve" is confirmed at l. 1067.
eat ate
Nature . . . lost Nature only sighs in pain here, but see ll. 1000–1004.

And knew not eating death.° Satiate at length,
And heightened as with wine, jocund and boon,°
Thus to herself she pleasingly began;
    'O sovereign, virtuous, precious of all trees
In Paradise, of operation° blest
To sapience, hitherto obscured, infamed,
And thy fair fruit let hang, as to no end
Created; but henceforth my early care,

800 Not without song, each morning, and due praise,
Shall tend thee, and the fertile burden ease
Of thy full branches offered free to all;
Till dieted by thee I grow mature
In knowledge, as the gods° who all things know;
Though others envy what they cannot give;
For had the gift been theirs, it had not here
Thus grown. Experience, next to thee I owe,
Best guide; not following thee, I had remained
In ignorance; thou open'st wisdom's way,

810 And giv'st accéss, though secret she retire.
And I perhaps am secret;° heaven is high,
High and remote to see from thence distinct
Each thing on earth; and other care perhaps
May have diverted from continual watch
Our Great Forbidder, safe° with all his spies
About him. But to Adam in what sort
Shall I appear? Shall I to him make known
As yet my change, and give him to partake
Full happiness with me, or rather not,

820 But keep the odds of knowledge in my power
Without copartner? So to add what wants
In female sex, the more to draw his love,
And render me more equal, and perhaps—
A thing not undesirable—sometime
Superior; for inferior who is free?°
This may be well. But what if God have seen,
And death ensue? Then I shall be no more,
And Adam wedded to another Eve
Shall live with her enjoying, I extinct;

830 A death to think.° Confirmed then I resolve,
Adam shall share with me in bliss or woe.
So dear I love him, that with him all deaths
I could endure, without him live no life.'

---

knew not eating death knew not that she was
eating death
boon jolly
operation effectiveness
gods Echoes Satan's equivocal use of the plural
in ll. 712, 718, and I.116.
secret hidden, secreted

safe of no danger
for inferior who is free? The rhetorical questioning and the political theory are both recognizably Satan's.
A death to think Having literalized death by her
act, Eve's using the word figuratively is in
odious taste.

So saying, from the tree her step she turned,
But first low reverence done,° as to the power
That dwelt within, whose presence had infused
Into the plant sciential° sap, derived
From nectar, drink of gods.° Adam the while
Waiting desirous her return, had wove
840   Of choicest flowers a garland to adorn
Her tresses, and her rural labours crown,
As reapers oft are wont their harvest queen.
Great joy he promised to his thoughts, and new
Solace in her return, so long delayed;
Yet oft his heart, divine° of something ill,
Misgave him; he the faltering measure° felt;
And forth to meet her went, the way she took
That morn when first they parted. By the Tree
Of Knowledge he must pass; there he her met,
850   Scarce from the tree returning; in her hand
A bough of fairest fruit that downy smiled,
New gathered, and ambrosial smell diffused.
To him she hasted; in her face excuse
Came prologue, and apology to prompt,°
Which with bland words at will she thus addressed:
    'Hast thou not wondered, Adam, at my stay?
Thee I have missed, and thought it long, deprived
Thy presence, agony of love till now
Not felt, nor shall be twice, for never more
860   Mean I to try what rash untried I sought,
The pain of absence from thy sight. But strange
Hath been the cause, and wonderful to hear:
This tree is not as we are told, a tree
Of danger° tasted, nor to evil unknown
Opening the way, but of divine effect
To open eyes, and make them gods who taste;
And hath been tasted° such. The serpent wise,
Or° not restrained as we, or not obeying,
Hath eaten of the fruit, and is become
870   Not dead, as we are threatened, but thenceforth
Endued with human voice and human sense,
Reasoning to admiration, and with me
Persuasively hath so prevailed, that I
Have also tasted, and have also found

---

low reverence done a bow, the first act of
idolatry, and the first myth. Eve is worshiping
a Dryad of some sort by treating the power
in the fruit in this way.
sciential knowledge-giving
nectar, drink of gods Her personal religion
implies a whole pagan pantheon.

divine prophet
faltering measure irregular heartbeat
prologue . . . prompt These are theatrical terms:
Eve's facial expression is visible before she
speaks, like a prologue to a play; cf. IX.670–76.
Of danger of danger if
tasted tested
Or either

The effects to correspond, opener° mine eyes,
Dim erst, dilated spirits, ampler heart,
And growing up to godhead; which for thee
Chiefly I sought, without thee can despise.
For bliss, as thou hast part, to me is bliss;
880   Tedious, unshared with thee, and odious soon.
Thou therefore also taste, that equal lot
May join us, equal joy, as equal love;
Lest thou not tasting, different degree
Disjoin us, and I then too late renounce
Deity for thee, when fate will not permit.'
    Thus Eve with countenance blithe her story told;
But in her cheek distemper° flushing glowed.
On the other side, Adam, soon as he heard
The fatal trespass done by Eve, amazed,
890   Astonied° stood and blank, while horror chill
Ran through his veins, and all his joints relaxed;
From his slack hand the garland wreathed for Eve
Down dropped, and all the faded roses° shed.
Speechless he stood and pale, till thus at length
First to himself he inward silence broke:
    'O fairest of creation, last and best
Of all God's works, creature in whom excelled
Whatever can to sight or thought be formed,
Holy, divine, good, amiable,° or sweet!
900   How art thou lost, how on a sudden lost,
Defaced, deflowered,° and now to death devote!°
Rather how hast thou yielded to transgress
The strict forbiddance, how to violate
The sacred fruit forbidden! Some cursèd fraud
Of enemy hath beguiled thee, yet unknown,
And me with thee hath ruined, for with thee
Certain my resolution is to die;
How can I live without thee, how forgo
Thy sweet converse and love so dearly joined,
910   To live again in these wild woods forlorn?°
Should God create another Eve, and I
Another rib afford, yet loss of thee
Would never from my heart; no, no! I feel
The link of nature draw me: flesh of flesh,
Bone of my bone thou art,° and from thy state

---

opener The insistence on this word arises from Genesis 3:7, "And the eyes of them both were opened" (this is shortly to occur), but its force comes from our ironic realization that her act has closed off everything.
distemper intoxication, disorder of temperament
Astonied petrified, paralyzed
faded roses the first instance of natural cycle, of withering flowers
amiable lovely

deflowered in a host of senses, given the association of Eve with flowers throughout
devote cursed
To live . . . forlorn To see Adam think of Eden as "wild woods" is touching; to see, through the ambiguous syntax, that "forlorn" can mean the woods, Eden, as well as the speaker, is tragic.
flesh . . . art echoing IV.483

Mine never shall be parted, bliss or woe.'
   So having said, as one from sad dismay
Recomforted, and after thoughts disturbed
Submitting to what seemed remédiless,
920   Thus in calm mood his words to Eve he turned:
   'Bold deed thou hast presumed, adventurous Eve,
And peril great provoked, who thus hast dared
Had it been only coveting to eye
That sacred fruit, sacred to abstinence,
Much more to taste it under ban to touch.
But past who can recall, or done undo?
Not God omnipotent, nor fate. Yet so
Perhaps thou shalt not die; perhaps the fact°
Is not so heinous now, foretasted fruit,
930   Profaned first by the Serpent, by him first
Made common and unhallowed ere our taste,
Nor yet on him found deadly; he yet lives,
Lives, as thou saidst, and gains to live as man
Higher degree of life, inducement strong
To us, as likely tasting to attain
Proportional ascent, which cannot be
But to be gods, or angels, demi-gods.
Nor can I think that God, Creator wise,
Though threatening, will in earnest so destroy
940   Us his prime creatures, dignified so high,
Set over all his works, which in our fall,
For us created, needs with us must fail,
Dependent made; so God shall uncreate,
Be frustrate, do, undo, and labour lose,°
Not well conceived of God, who though his power
Creation could repeat, yet would be loth
Us to abolish, lest the adversary
Triumph and say,° *"Fickle their state whom God
Most favours, who can please him long? Me first*
950   *He ruined, now mankind; whom will he next?"*
Matter of scorn not to be given the foe;
However, I with thee have fixed my lot,
Certain° to undergo like doom: if death
Consort with thee, death is to me as life;
So forcible within my heart I feel
The bond of nature draw me to my own,
My own in thee, for what thou art is mine;
Our state cannot be severed; we are one,
One flesh; to lose thee were to lose myself.'

fact deed, crime
lose or perhaps, "loose," in the sense of "undo"
say Even before tasting the fruit himself, Adam

has become sensitive to Satanic rhetoric: he parodies the adversary too well.
Certain resolved

960   So Adam, and thus Eve to him replied:
'O glorious trial of exceeding love,
Illustrious evidence, example high!
Engaging me to emulate, but short
Of thy perfection, how shall I attain,
Adam, from whose dear side I boast me sprung,
And gladly of our union hear thee speak,
One heart, one soul in both; whereof good proof
This day affords, declaring thee resolved,
Rather than death or aught than death more dread
970   Shall separate us, linked in love so dear,
To undergo with me one guilt, one crime,
If any be, of tasting this fair fruit,
Whose virtue (for of good still good proceeds,
Direct, or by occasion) hath presented
This happy trial of thy love, which else
So eminently never had been known.
Were it I thought death menaced would ensue
This my attempt, I would sustain alone
The worst, and not persuade thee, rather die
980   Deserted, than oblige° thee with a fact
Pernicious to thy peace, chiefly assured°
Remarkably so late of thy so true,
So faithful love unequalled; but I feel
Far otherwise the event,° not death, but life
Augmented, opened eyes, new hopes, new joys,
Taste so divine, that what of sweet before
Hath touched my sense, flat seems to this and harsh.
On my experience, Adam, freely taste,
And fear of death deliver to the winds.'
990   So saying, she embraced him, and for joy
Tenderly wept, much won that he his love
Had so ennobled, as of choice to incur
Divine displeasure for her sake, or death.
In recompense (for such compliance bad
Such recompense best merits) from the bough
She gave him of that fair enticing fruit
With liberal hand. He scrupled not to eat
Against his better knowledge, not deceived,
But fondly overcome with female charm.
1000   Earth trembled from her entrails, as again
In pangs, and Nature gave a second groan;
Sky loured and, muttering thunder,° some sad drops

oblige involve in guilt
chiefly assured especially with the assurance
event result
muttering thunder the first thunderstorm, imprinting on all subsequent storms, particularly
in myth (Shakespearean tempests, etc.), traces
of this original rupture between man and his
garden, this birth of the natural environment.
From the point of view of a 16th-century usage,
Nature, cracking, is decaying into "nature"—
physical and biological dispositions (see Fulke
Greville, "O Wearisome Condition of Humanity").

Wept at completing of the mortal sin
Original;° while Adam took no thought,
Eating his fill, nor Eve to iterate
Her former trespass feared, the more to soothe
Him with her loved society, that now
As with new wine intoxicated both
They swim in mirth, and fancy that they feel
1010   Divinity within them breeding wings°
Wherewith to scorn the earth. But that false fruit
Far other operation first displayed,
Carnal desire inflaming: he on Eve
Began to cast lascivious eyes, she him
As wantonly repaid; in lust they burn,
Till Adam thus 'gan Eve to dalliance move:
    'Eve, now I see thou art exact of taste,°
And elegant, of sapience no small part;
Since to each meaning savour we apply,
1020   And palate call judicious; I the praise
Yield thee, so well this day thou hast purveyed.°
Much pleasure we have lost, while we abstained
From this delightful fruit, nor known till now
True relish, tasting; if such pleasure be
In things to us forbidden, it might be wished
For this one tree had been forbidden ten.°
But come, so well refreshed, now let us play,
As meet is, after such delicious fare;
For never did thy beauty since the day
1030   I saw thee first and wedded thee, adorned
With all perfections, so inflame my sense
With ardour to enjoy thee, fairer now
Than ever, bounty of this virtuous tree.'
    So said he, and forbore not glance or toy
Of amorous intent, well understood
Of Eve, whose eye darted contagious fire.
Her hand he seized,° and to a shady bank,
Thick overhead with verdant roof embowered,
He led her nothing loth; flowers were the couch,
1040   Pansies, and violets, and asphodel,
And hyacinth, earth's freshest softest lap.
There they their fill of love and love's disport

---

sin Original that one, first, comprehensive
disobedience, containing a host of others "which
our first parents, and in them all their posterity,
committed," as Milton says in the *Christian
Doctrine*
breeding wings This is an expansion of Eve's
first intoxication, at l. 793, and an ironic
fulfillment of the trip in her dream (V.86–90).
exact of taste having "good taste" (discern-
ment, moral and esthetic wisdom). Like so many
fundamental dramatic ironies affecting the institution of human death, this word-play, unwitting on Adam's part, perhaps, is in the
worst taste imaginable.
purveyed provided
ten ten times over. Now that they are mortal,
number games seem appealing; now that there
will never be world enough and time, the
counting starts.
seized The word has all the strength of
"grabbed."

Took largely,° of their mutual guilt the seal,
The solace of their sin, till dewy sleep
Oppressed them, wearied with their amorous play.°
Soon as the force of that fallacious fruit,
That with exhilarating vapour bland
About their spirits had played, and inmost powers
Made err, was now exhaled, and grosser sleep°
1050 Bred of unkindly° fumes, with conscious dreams
Encumbered, now had left them, up they rose
As from unrest, and each the other viewing,
Soon found their eyes how opened, and their minds
How darkened; innocence, that as a veil
Had shadowed them° from knowing ill, was gone;
Just confidence, and native righteousness,
And honour from about them, naked left
To guilty shame; he covered, but his robe
Uncovered more. So rose the Danite strong,
1060 Herculean Samson, from the harlot-lap
Of Philistéan Dálilah, and waked
Shorn of his strength, they destitute and bare
Of all their virtue. Silent, and in face
Confounded, long they sat, as strucken mute,
Till Adam, though not less than Eve abashed,
At length gave utterance to these words constrained:
   'O Eve, in evil hour° thou didst give ear
To that false worm, of whomsoever taught
To counterfeit man's voice, true in our fall,
1070 False in our promised rising; since our eyes
Opened we find indeed, and find we know
Both good and evil, good lost and evil got,
Bad fruit of knowledge, if this be to know,
Which leaves us naked thus, of honour void,
Of innocence, of faith, of purity,
Our wonted ornaments now soiled and stained,
And in our faces evident the signs
Of foul concupiscence; whence evil store,
Even shame, the last° of evils; of the first
1080 Be sure then. How shall I behold the face
Henceforth of God or angel, erst with joy
And rapture so oft beheld? Those heavenly shapes

---

their fill . . . largely Milton quotes Proverbs
7:18, where a prostitute uses these phrases.
amorous play This is the first act of fallen sex,
casual and desperate in its needed effects of
consolation, "of their mutual guilt the seal"—
and guilt for the disobedience of eating the
fruit. The horror of "honour dishonourable" is
that they will now feel guilt about the sex,
certainly the one thing for which they should
not. In their shame (ll. 1092–93) they wish not
to cover the mouths that ate, but the innocent

parts of love. This is the horror of the Fall, and
the means by which sin infects life around it.
grosser sleep as opposed to the "airy light"
sleep at V.4
unkindly unnatural
shadowed them The figurative, inner moral
shade being removed, Adam and Eve will
begin to feel the pain of light (ll. 1080–90).
Eve . . . hour The pun is now Adam's.
last least

Will dazzle now this earthly,° with their blaze
Insufferably bright. O might I here
In solitude live savage, in some glade
Obscured, where highest woods impenetrable
To star or sunlight, spread their umbrage° broad
And brown as evening! Cover me, ye pines,
Ye cedars, with innumerable boughs
1090   Hide me, where I may never see them° more.
But let us now, as in bad plight, devise
What best may for the present serve to hide
The parts of each from other that seem most
To shame obnoxious,° and unseemliest seen,
Some tree whose broad smooth leaves together sewed,
And girded on our loins, may cover round
Those middle parts, that this newcomer, shame,
There sit not, and reproach us as unclean.'
    So counselled he, and both together went
1100   Into the thickest wood; there soon they chose
The fig-tree,° not that kind for fruit renowned,
But such as at this day to Indians known
In Malabar or Deccan° spreads her arms
Branching so broad and long, that in the ground
The bended twigs take root, and daughters grow
About the mother tree, a pillared shade
High overarched, and echoing walks between;
There oft the Indian herdsman shunning heat
Shelters in cool, and tends his pasturing herds
1110   At loop-holes cut through thickest shade. Those leaves
They gathered, broad as Amazonian targe,
And with what skill they had, together sewed,
To gird their waist, vain covering if to hide
Their guilt and dreaded shame, O how unlike
To that first naked glory! Such of late
Columbus found the American so girt
With feathered cincture, naked else and wild
Among the trees on isles and woody shores.
Thus fenced, and as they thought, their shame in part
1120   Covered, but not at rest or ease of mind,
They sat them down to weep; nor only tears
Rained at their eyes, but high winds worse within°
Began to rise, high passions, anger, hate,

earthly earthly shape
umbrage shade
them the "heavenly shapes" of l. 1082
obnoxious exposed
fig-tree The elaborate, encyclopedic digression occurs here to reinforce the enormity of the institution of clothing; by the description of the Indian banyan tree, and by the allusion to Caribbean savages (ll. 1116–18), we now see Adam and Eve as having suddenly become not Primal man but merely Primitive man. "And

with what skill they had" (l. 1112) betokens the touching but inadequate technology of paleolithic people.
Malabar or Deccan on the southwest Indian coast, or the southern peninsula of the subcontinent
Rained . . . within The first thunderstorm has been internalized, the Renaissance microcosmic view of man now becoming an adequate model for comprehending the relation of man and nature.

Mistrust, suspicion, discord, and shook sore
Their inward state of mind, calm region once
And full of peace, now tossed and turbulent;
For understanding ruled not, and the will
Heard not her lore, both in subjection now
To sensual appetite, who from beneath
1130 Usurping over sovereign reason claimed
Superior sway.° From thus distempered breast,
Adam, estranged° in look and altered style,
Speech intermitted thus to Eve renewed:
    'Would thou hadst hearkened to my words, and stayed
With me, as I besought thee, when that strange
Desire of wandering this unhappy morn,
I know not whence possessed thee; we had then
Remained still happy, not as now, despoiled
Of all our good, shamed, naked, miserable.°
1140 Let none henceforth seek needless cause to approve°
The faith they owe;° when earnestly they seek
Such proof, conclude they then begin to fail.'
    To whom, soon moved with touch of blame, thus Eve:
'What words have passed thy lips, Adam severe!
Imput'st thou that to my default, or will
Of wandering, as thou callest it, which who knows
But might as ill have happened thou being by,
Or to thyself perhaps? Hadst thou been there,
Or here the attempt, thou couldst not have discerned
1150 Fraud in the serpent, speaking as he spake;
No ground of enmity between us known
Why he should mean me ill, or seek to harm.
Was I to have never parted from thy side?
As good have grown there still a lifeless rib.
Being as I am, why didst not thou, the head,°
Command me absolutely not to go,
Going into such danger as thou saidst?
Too facile then, thou didst not much gainsay,
Nay didst permit, approve, and fair dismiss.
1160 Hadst thou been firm and fixed in thy dissent,
Neither had I transgressed, nor thou with me.'
    To whom then first incensed Adam replied:
'Is this the love, is this the recompense
Of mine to thee, ingrateful Eve, expressed°
Immutable when thou wert lost, not I,
Who might have lived and joyed° immortal bliss,

Superior sway greater power. The imagery in
ll. 1125–31 has moved from storm to political
discord.
estranged changed
shamed, naked, miserable See Hobbes's characterization of the life of man in the state of
nature: "Solitary, poor, nasty, brutish and

short" (*Leviathan*, 1651).
approve prove
owe own
head See IV.433n.
expressed revealed
joyed enjoyed

Yet willingly chose rather death with thee?
And am I now upbraided, as the cause
Of thy transgressing? Not enough severe,
1170   It seems, in thy restraint. What could I more?
I warned thee, I admonished thee, foretold
The danger, and the lurking enemy
That lay in wait; beyond this had been force,
And force upon free will hath here no place.
But confidence then bore thee on, secure
Either to meet no danger, or to find
Matter of glorious trial; and perhaps
I also erred in overmuch admiring
What seemed in thee so perfect, that I thought
1180   No evil durst attempt thee, but I rue
That error now, which is become my crime,
And thou the accuser. Thus it shall befall
Him who to worth in women overtrusting
Lets her will rule; restraint she will not brook,
And left to herself, if evil thence ensue,
She first his weak indulge will accuse.'
　　Thus they in mutual accusation spent
The fruitless° hours, but neither self-condemning,
And of their vain contést appeared no end.

From *Book X*

[Man fallen, the guardian angels informed that it was not through their failure
that the Fall occurred. Satan in triumph, Sin and Death depart from their
locale at the gate of hell and enter the world. They build a broad causeway,
over the realm of Chaos, connecting hell and the world, the prototype of all
easy, populous routes. Satan decends to Pandemonium, where he delivers an
address of victory, concluding with the exhortation, "What remains ye Gods,
/ But up and enter now into full bliss." As if in rhyme, applauding with a hiss,
the demons (they are now serpents whose only song is hissing) they fall to
a meal on the fruit of a multitude of replicas of the Forbidden Tree, but
instead of fruit, they find themselves chewing "bitter ashes." Sin and Death
now loose in the world, the latter to feed henceforth on all living things in
order to surround man with continual emblems of his own end, God predicts
the apocalypse and final revision of the created world. The details of the birth
of fallen, biological nature are unfolded, and the introduction of inimical
natural forces is followed by a long lament of self-recrimination from Adam
which culminates in rhetoric reminiscent of Satan's: "O conscience, into what
abyss of fears / And horrors hast thou driven me; out of which / I find no
way, from deep to deeper plunged!"]

　　Thus Adam to himself lamented loud
Through the still night, not now, as ere man fell,

fruitless with the pun still working from the
opening line of the poem

Wholesome and cool and mild, but with black air
Accompanied, with damps and dreadful gloom,
Which to his evil conscience represented
850   All things with double terror. On the ground
Outstretched he lay, on the cold ground, and oft
Cursed his creation, death as oft accused
Of tardy execution, since denounced°
The day of his offence. 'Why comes not death,'
Said he, 'with one thrice-ácceptáble stroke
To end me? Shall truth fail to keep her word,
Justice divine not hasten to be just?
But death comes not at call, justice divine
Mends not her slowest pace for prayers or cries.
860   O woods, O fountains, hillocks, dales, and bowers,
With other echo late I taught your shades
To answer, and resound far other song.'
Whom thus afflicted when sad Eve beheld,
Desolate where she sat, approaching nigh,
Soft words to his fierce passion she assayed:°
But her with stern regard he thus repelled:
    'Out of my sight, thou serpent!° that name best
Befits thee with him leagued, thyself as false
And hateful; nothing wants, but that thy shape,
870   Like his, and colour serpentine, may show
Thy inward fraud, to warn all creatures from thee
Henceforth; lest that too heavenly form, pretended°
To hellish falsehood, snare them. But for thee
I had persisted happy, had not thy pride
And wandering vanity, when least was safe,
Rejected my forewarning, and disdained
Not be trusted, longing to be seen
Though by the devil himself, him overweening
To overreach, but with the serpent meeting
880   Fooled and beguiled, by him thou, I by thee.
To trust thee from my side, imagined wise,
Constant, mature, proof against all assaults,
And understood not all was but a show
Rather than solid virtue, all but a rib
Crooked by nature, bent, as now appears,
More to the part siníster° from me drawn;
Well if thrown out, as supernumerary
To my just° number found. O why did God,

denounced announced (on)
assayed tried out
serpent An interpretive false etymology could
connect "Eve" with a word for "serpent."
pretended held out in order to screen or
disguise
sinister left side, but also "evil." It is Adam,
not Milton (through Raphael, in his account of

the Creation in Bk. VII), who comes up with
the traditional anti-feminist rhetoric and imagery here, in his self-loathing; according to
some traditions, Eve came from Adam's left
side where there was an extra ("supernumerary")
rib.
just exact

Creator wise, that peopled highest heaven
890   With spirits masculine, create at last
This novelty on earth, this fair defect
Of Nature, and not fill the world at once
With men as angels without feminine,
Or find some other way to generate
Mankind? This mischief had not then befallen,
And more that shall befall, innumerable
Disturbances on earth through female snares,
And strait° conjunction with this sex. For either
He never shall find out fit mate, but such
900   As some misfortune brings him, or mistake,
Or whom he wishes most shall seldom gain,
Through her perverseness, but shall see her gained
By a far worse, or if she love, withheld
By parents, or his happiest choice too late
Shall meet, already linked and wedlock-bound
To a fell adversary, his hate or shame;
Which infinite calamity shall cause
To human life, and household peace confound.'
   He added not, and from her turned, but Eve,
910   Not so repulsed, with tears that ceased not flowing,
And tresses all disordered, at his feet
Fell humble, and embracing them, besought
His peace, and thus proceeded in her plaint:
   'Forsake me not thus, Adam, witness heaven
What love sincere and reverence in my heart
I bear thee, and unweeting° have offended,
Unhappily deceived; thy suppliant
I beg, and clasp thy knees; bereave me not
Whereon I live, thy gentle looks, thy aid,
920   Thy counsel in this uttermost distress,
My only strength and stay. Forlorn of thee,
Whither shall I betake me, where subsist?
While yet we live, scarce one short hour perhaps,
Between us two let there be peace, both joining,
As joined in injuries, one enmity
Against a foe by doom express assigned us,
That cruel serpent. On me exercise not
Thy hatred for this misery befallen,
On me already lost, me than thyself
930   More miserable. Both have sinned, but thou
Against God only, I against God and thee,
And to the place of judgment will return,
There with my cries importune heaven, that all
The sentence from thy head removed may light

strait intimate   unweeting unwitting

On me, sole cause to thee of all this woe,
Me, me only, just object of his ire.'
　　She ended weeping, and her lowly plight,
Immovable° till peace obtained from fault
Acknowledged and deplored, in Adam wrought
940　Commiseration; soon his heart relented
Towards her, his life so late and sole delight,
Now at his feet submissive in distress,
Creature so fair his reconcilement seeking,
His counsel whom she had displeased, his aid;
As one disarmed, his anger all he lost,
And thus with peaceful words upraised her soon:
　　'Unwary, and too desirous, as before
So now, of what thou know'st not, who desir'st
The punishment all on thyself; alas,
950　Bear thine own first, ill able to sustain
His full wrath whose thou feel'st as yet least part,
And my displeasure bear'st so ill. If prayers
Could alter high decrees, I to that place
Would speed before thee, and be louder heard,
That on my head all might be visited,
Thy frailty and infirmer sex forgiven,
To me committed and by me exposed.
But rise, let us no more contend, nor blame
Each other, blamed enough elsewhere,° but strive
960　In offices of love, how we may lighten
Each other's burden in our share of woe;
Since this day's death denounced,° if aught I see,
Will prove no sudden, but a slow-paced evil,
A long day's dying to augment our pain,
And to our seed (O hapless seed!) derived.'°
　　To whom thus Eve, recovering heart, replied:
'Adam, by sad experiment I know
How little weight my words with thee can find,
Found so erroneous, thence by just event
970　Found so unfortunate; nevertheless,
Restored by thee, vile as I am, to place
Of new acceptance, hopeful to regain
Thy love, the sole contentment of my heart
Living or dying, from thee I will not hide
What thoughts in my unquiet breast are risen,
Tending to some relief of our extremes,
Or end, though sharp and sad, yet tolerable,
As in our evils, and of easier choice.

Immovable Modifies both "plight" and "Adam."
elsewhere in heaven?

death denounced here, as at l. 853, an echo
of that telling phrase in IX.695
derived descended

If care of our descent° perplex us most,
980   Which must be born to certain woe, devoured
By death at last (and miserable it is
To be to others cause of misery,
Our own begotten, and of our loins to bring
Into this cursèd world a woeful race,
That after wretched life must be at last
Food for so foul a monster), in thy power
It lies, yet ere conception, to prevent°
The race unblest, to being yet unbegot.
Childless thou art, childless remain; so death
990   Shall be deceived his glut, and with us two
Be forced to satisfy his ravenous maw.
But if thou judge it hard and difficult,
Conversing, looking, loving, to abstain
From love's due rites, nuptial embraces sweet,
And with desire to languish without hope,
Before the present object° languishing
With like desire—which would be misery
And torment less than none of what we dread
—Then both ourselves and seed at once to free
1000   From what we fear for both, let us make short,
Let us seek death, or he not found, supply
With our own hands his office on ourselves;
Why stand we longer shivering under fears
That show no end but death, and have the power,
Of many ways to die the shortest choosing,
Destruction with destruction to destroy?'°
       She ended here, or vehement despair
Broke off the rest; so much of death her thoughts
Had entertained as dyed her cheeks with pale.
1010   But Adam with such counsel nothing swayed,
To better hopes his more attentive mind
Labouring had raised, and thus to Eve replied:
       'Eve, thy contempt of life and pleasure seems
To argue in thee something more sublime°
And excellent than what thy mind contemns;
But self-destruction therefore sought refutes
That excellence thought in thee, and implies,
Not thy contempt, but anguish and regret
For loss of life and pleasure overloved.
1020   Or if thou covet death, as utmost end
Of misery, so thinking to evade

---

descent descendants
prevent preclude
object Eve
Destruction . . . destroy This ordinarily easy
paradox is more than rhetorical here, acknowl-

edging the difficulty (". . . with destruction
. . .").
Eve thy . . . sublime In this scene we have
had Adam's ranting and Eve's genuine desperation; now, we have a clerical, moralizing tone
from Adam at the opening of this speech.

The penalty pronounced, doubt not but God
Hath wiselier armed his vengeful ire than so
To be forestalled; much more I fear lest death
So snatched will not exempt us from the pain
We are by doom° to pay; rather such acts
Of contumácy will prove the Highest
To make death in us live. Then let us seek
Some safer resolution, which methinks
1030   I have in view, calling to mind with heed
Part of our sentence, that thy seed shall bruise
The serpent's head;° piteous amends, unless
Be meant, whom I conjecture, our grand foe
Satan, who in the serpent hath contrived
Against us this deceit. To crush his head
Would be revenge indeed; which will be lost
By death brought on ourselves, or childless days
Resolved, as thou proposest; so our foe
Shall scape his punishment ordained, and we
1040   Instead shall double ours upon our heads.
No more be mentioned then of violence
Against ourselves, and wilful barrenness,
That cuts us off from hope, and savours only
Rancor and pride, impatience and despite,
Reluctance° against God and his just yoke
Laid on our necks. Remember with what mild
And gracious temper he both heard and judged,
Without wrath or reviling; we expected
Immediate dissolution, which we thought
1050   Was meant by death that day, when lo, to thee
Pains only in child-bearing were foretold,
And bringing forth, soon recompensed with joy,
Fruit of thy womb; on me the curse aslope
Glanced on the ground: with labour I must earn
My bread; what harm? Idleness° had been worse;
My labour will sustain me; and lest cold
Or heat should injure us, his timely care
Hath unbesought provided, and his hands
Clothed us unworthy, pitying while he judged;
1060   How much more, if we pray him, will his ear
Be open, and his heart to pity incline,
And teach us further by what means to shun
The inclement seasons, rain, ice, hail, and snow,
Which now the sky with various face begins

---

doom judgment
bruise The serpent's head This prophecy from
Genesis 3:15 is another glimpse of Eve's compensatory fulfillment promised at X.179, outlined in detail in Bk. XII.
Reluctance struggle
Idleness Notice that with the fall from per-

fection into biological nature, comes not only
the institution of labor, but of its complement,
idleness. Both idleness and its inner state,
boredom, are generally regarded as faults in
most contrived Utopias; in Paradise, they are
not even conceivable.

To show us in this mountain, while the winds
Blow moist and keen, shattering the graceful locks
Of these fair spreading trees; which bids us seek
Some better shroud,° some better warmth to cherish
Our limbs benumbed, ere this diurnal star°
1070 Leave cold the night, how we his gathered beams
Reflected, may with matter sere° foment,
Or by collision of two bodies grind
The air attrite° to fire, as late the clouds,
Justling° or pushed with winds rude in their shock,
Tine° the slant lightning, whose thwart° flame driven down
Kindles the gummy bark of fir or pine,
And sends a comfortable heat from far,
Which might supply° the sun. Such fire to use,
And what may else be remedy or cure
1080 To evils which our own misdeeds have wrought,
He will instruct us praying,° and of grace
Beseeching him, so as we need not fear
To pass commodiously this life, sustained
By him with many comforts, till we end
In dust, our final rest and native home.
What better can we do, than to the place
Repairing where he judged us, prostrate fall
Before him reverent, and there confess
Humbly our faults, and pardon beg, with tears
1090 Watering the ground, and with our sighs the air
Frequenting,° sent from hearts contrite, in sign
Of sorrow unfeigned, and humiliation meek?
Undoubtedly he will relent and turn
From his displeasure; in whose look serene,
When angry most he seemed and most severe,
What else but favour, grace, and mercy shone?'
   So spake our father penitent, nor Eve
Felt less remorse. They forthwith to the place
Repairing where he judged them, prostrate fell
1100 Before him reverent, and both confessed
Humbly their faults, and pardon begged, with tears
Watering the ground, and with their sighs the air
Frequenting, sent from hearts contrite, in sign
Of sorrow unfeigned, and humiliation meek.

Book XI
[Books XI and XII form a reciprocal pair to the historical accounts recited
by Raphael to Adam and Eve in Books VI and VII; they are revealed, not

shroud shelter	**Tine** kindle (hence, "tinder")
diurnal star the sun	**thwart** transverse
sere dry	**supply** substitute for
attrite ground down	**praying** if we pray
Justling jostling	**Frequenting** crowding

narrated, and they are a vision of the future, not of the past, being selected glimpses of human history leading away from the Fall and toward the redemption and fulfillment of fallen man. Michael, commissioned by God to lead Adam and Eve out of Paradise forever, takes Adam to the top of a high hill, where he sees in vision the extent of the world and a pastoral scene which ends in the first human death, in the concrete sense: Cain's murder of Abel. "Death hast thou seen / In his first shape on man," says Michael, reminding us that the original of all deaths was a murder. Other episodes from biblical history are shown, leading up to the Flood.]

From *Book XII*

[Book XII resumes the vision of the human future, starting at a point "Betwixt the world destroyed and world restored," both in the broadest sense of history as an intermediate area between loss and reconstitution, and, in particular, as applying to the Flood and subsequent history. This leads to the promise of analogous redemptive fulfillment for Eve, in that the Son will manifest himself on earth in normal human form, born of woman; the Incarnation, Death, Resurrection, and Ascension of Christ are shown, and the history of his church on earth is mapped out until the Second Coming; the final overcoming of Satan is foretold, and a promise that "then the earth / Shall be all Paradise, far happier place / Than this of Eden, and far happier days."]

So spake the Archangel Michaël, then paused,
As at the world's great period; and our sire
Replete with joy and wonder thus replied:
    'O goodness infinite, goodness immense!
470 That all this good of evil shall produce,
And evil turn to good;° more wonderful
Than that which by creation first brought forth
Light out of darkness! Full of doubt I stand,
Whether I should repent me now of sin
By me done and occasioned, or rejoice
Much more, that much more good thereof shall spring,
To God more glory, more good will to men
From God, and over wrath grace shall abound.°
But say, if our Deliverer up to heaven
480 Must reascend, what will betide the few
His faithful, left among the unfaithful herd,
The enemies of truth; who then shall guide
His people, who defend? Will they not deal
Worse with his followers than with him they dealt?'

---

evil turn to good This whole speech is an expression of the theme of the Fortunate Fall (from the hymn *O Felix Culpa:* "O lucky sin!"), completing the reversal of, and triumph over, Satan's plan "out of good still to find means of evil" (I.165). The Fortunate Fall paradox praises the first sin on the grounds that, without it, there would have been no need for a Redeemer; it is appropriate that Adam responds to Michael's prophecy of Christ's victory over Satan by invoking the paradox.

grace shall abound an important echo: "where sin abounded, grace did much more abound" (Romans 5:20); cf. Bunyan, *Grace Abounding to the Chief of Sinners* (1666)

'Be sure they will,' said the Angel; 'but from heaven
He to his own a Comforter° will send,
The promise of the Father, who shall dwell,
His Spirit, within them, and the law of faith
Working through love, upon their hearts shall write,
490   To guide them in all truth, and also arm
With spiritual armour,° able to resist
Satan's assaults, and quench his fiery darts,
What man can do against them, not afraid,
Though to the death, against such cruelties
With inward consolations recompensed,
And oft supported so as shall amaze
Their proudest persecutors. For the Spirit
Poured first on his apostles, whom he sends
To evangelize the nations, then on all
500   Baptized, shall them with wondrous gifts endue
To speak all tongues, and do all miracles,
As did their Lord before them.° Thus they win
Great numbers of each nation to receive
With joy the tidings brought from heaven: at length
Their ministry performed, and race well run,
Their doctrine and their story written left,
They die; but in their room, as they forewarn,
Wolves° shall succeed for teachers, grievous wolves,
Who all the sacred mysteries of heaven
510   To their own vile advantages shall turn
Of lucre and ambition, and the truth
With superstitions and traditions taint,
Left only in those written records pure,
Though not but by the Spirit understood.
Then shall they seek to avail themselves of names,
Places and titles, and with these to join
Secular power, though feigning still to act
By spiritual, to themselves appropriating
The Spirit of God, promised alike and given
520   To all believers; and from that pretence,
Spiritual laws by carnal power shall force
On every conscience; laws which none shall find
Left them enrolled, or what the Spirit within
Shall on the heart engrave. What will they then
But force the Spirit of Grace itself, and bind

Comforter the Holy Spirit (sent, according to Milton, "by the Son, from the Father," and thus an emanation of his power; cf. John 15:26)
spiritual armour from Ephesians 6:11–17, the same armor the Red Cross Knight wears in Bk. I of *The Faerie Queene*. All of Michael's discourse is full of scriptural allusions and echoes, some of which will be identified.

For the Spirit . . . them (ll. 497–502) from Acts 2
Wolves from Acts 20:29, also as used in *Lycidas*, l. 128. This whole passage foresees the decline of the institutional church, first Roman, then Anglican, contrasting this with the forever uncorrupted internalized authority of conscience.

His consort Liberty,° what but unbuild
His living temples,° built by faith to stand,
Their own faith, not another's; for on earth
Who against faith and conscience can be heard
530 Infallible? Yet many will presume:
Whence heavy persecution shall arise
On all who in the worship persevere
Of spirit and truth; the rest, far greater part,
Will deem in outward rites and specious forms
Religion satisfied; Truth shall retire
Bestuck with slanderous darts, and works of faith
Rarely be found. So shall the world go on,
To good malignant, to bad men benign,
Under her own weight groaning,° till the day
540 Appear of respiration° to the just,
And vengeance to the wicked, at return
Of him so lately promised to thy aid,
The woman's seed, obscurely then foretold,
Now amplier known thy saviour and thy Lord,
Last in the clouds from heaven to be revealed
In glory of the Father, to dissolve
Satan with his perverted world; then raise
From the conflagrant mass, purged and refined,
New heavens, new earth,° ages of endless date
550 Founded in righteousness and peace and love,
To bring forth fruits,° joy and eternal bliss.'
    He ended; and thus Adam last replied:
'How soon hath thy prediction, seer blest,
Measured this transient world, the race of time,
Till time stand fixed: beyond is all abyss,
Eternity, whose end no eye can reach.
Greatly instructed I shall hence depart,
Greatly in peace of thought, and have my fill
Of knowledge, what this vessel can contain;
560 Beyond which was my folly to aspire.
Henceforth I learn that to obey is best,
And love with fear the only God, to walk
As in his presence, ever to observe
His providence, and on him sole depend,
Merciful over all his works, with good
Still overcoming evil,° and by small
Accomplishing great things, by things deemed weak
Subverting worldly strong, and worldly wise

---

consort Liberty II Corinthians 3:17
temples I Corinthians 3:17 and 6:19
groaning Romans 8:22, perhaps also a continuation of Nature's groans (IX.783, 1001) as Eve and Adam fall
respiration refreshment, rest
new earth The final apocalypse as envisioned

here culminates in an allusion to Revelation 21:1: "And I saw a new heaven and a new earth."
fruits not the fruit of I.1, followed by "taste" and "woe," but appositively here by "joy and eternal bliss"
good . . . evil Romans 12:21

By simply meek; that suffering for truth's sake
570   Is fortitude to highest victory,
And to the faithful death the gate of life;
Taught this by his example whom I now
Acknowledge my redeemer ever blest.'
    To whom thus also the Angel last replied:
'This having learnt, thou hast attained the sum
Of wisdom; hope no higher, though all the stars
Thou knew'st by name, and all the ethereal powers,
All secrets of the deep, all Nature's works,
Or works of God in heaven, air, earth, or sea,
580   And all the richest of this world enjoy'dst,
And all the rule, one empire; only add
Deeds to thy knowledge answerable, add faith,
Add virtue, patience, temperance, add love,
By name to come called charity,° the soul
Of all the rest: then wilt thou not be loth
To leave this Paradise, but shalt possess
A paradise within thee, happier far.°
Let us descend now therefore from this top
Of speculation;° for the hour precise
590   Exacts our parting hence; and see the guards,
By me encamped on yonder hill, expect°
Their motion, at whose front a flaming sword,
In signal of remove, waves fiercely round;
We may no longer stay: go, waken Eve;
Her also I with gentle dreams have calmed,
Portending good, and all her spirits composed
To meek submission: thou at season fit
Let her with thee partake what thou hast heard,
Chiefly what may concern her faith to know,
600   The great deliverance by her seed to come
(For by the woman's seed) on all mankind:
That ye may live, which will be many days,°
Both in one faith unanimous though sad,
With cause for° evils past, yet much more cheered
With meditation on the happy end.'
    He ended, and they both descend the hill;
Descended, Adam to the bower where Eve
Lay sleeping ran before, but found her waked;
And thus with words not sad she him received:
610   'Whence thou return'st, and whither went'st, I know;

charity literally "love," from the Latin *caritas*, translating Greek *agapē*, as at I Corinthians 13, especially 13:13 (see section on The English Bible, above)
A paradise . . . far This final internalization of a lost exterior place also contrasts finally with Satan's "the mind is its own place" and the hell within him (IV.20); the rhythms of this authentic transfer continue into Eve's final words below.
top Of speculation mount of vision; see *Paradise Regained* IV.236n
expect await
many days 930 years, according to Genesis 5:5
With cause for in view of

For God is also in sleep, and dreams advise,
Which he hath sent propitious, some great good
Presaging, since with sorrow and heart's distress
Wearied I fell asleep. But now lead on;
In me is no delay; with thee to go,
Is to stay here;° without thee here to stay,
Is to go hence unwilling; thou to me
Art all things under heaven, all places thou,
Who for my wilful crime art banished hence.
620   This further consolation yet secure
I carry hence; though all by me is lost,
Such favour I unworthy am vouchsafed,
By me the promised seed shall all restore.'
    So spake our mother Eve, and Adam heard
Well pleased, but answered not; for now too nigh
The archangel stood, and from the other hill
To their fixed station, all in bright array
The Cherubim descended; on the ground
Gliding metéorous,° as evening mist
630   Risen from a river o'er the marish° glides,
And gathers ground fast at the labourer's heel
Homeward returning. High in front advanced,
The brandished sword of God before them blazed
Fierce as a comet; which with torrid heat,
And vapour as the Libyan air adust,°
Began to parch that temperate clime; whereat
In either hand the hastening Angel caught
Our lingering parents, and to the eastern gate
Led them direct, and down the cliff as fast
640   To the subjected° plain; then disappeared.
They, looking back, all the eastern side beheld
Of Paradise, so late their happy seat,
Waved over by that flaming brand, the gate
With dreadful faces thronged and fiery arms.
Some natural tears they dropped, but wiped them soon;
The world was all before them, where to choose
Their place of rest, and Providence their guide:
They hand in hand,° with wandering steps and slow,
Through Eden took their solitary° way.
1658?–1665?   1667

---

with thee . . . here not merely an echo of the
Hebrew matriarch Ruth to her mother-in-law
Naomi, "Whither thou goest, I will go, . . ."
(Ruth 1:16), but an avowal of the loss the seed
of compensation, and the ultimate arbitrariness
of place, of location on the planet, in subsequent
human history
metéorous in mid-air
marish marsh
adust parched

subjected lying below; but also subject to
hand in hand catching up the emblematic
meaning present at the first appearance of the
two, hand in hand (IV.321), but moving
beyond hieroglyphic somehow to a larger human
meaning; "wandering" and "slow" perhaps with
overtones of error and hesitancy, but only with
overtones
solitary They are together, which is to say,
Man is alone.

Paradise Regained

Written between the publication of *Paradise Lost* (1667) and 1670, *Paradise Regained* was published with *Samson Agonistes* in 1671. It is of the genre "brief epic," of which the ultimate model was the Book of Job. Milton takes the account of the temptation in the wilderness from Luke 4:1–13, and treats it as a victory over sin which prefigures the later victory over death at the Crucifixion. He also follows a tradition of the exegetes whereby this is a *total* temptation; they built on St. Luke's words, "all the temptation" in v.13. The scheme Milton follows is almost exactly that of Marvell's *Dialogue Between the Resolved Soul and Created Pleasure,* though there are other parallels; for example, as the second Adam, Jesus rejects the temptations (gluttony, ambition, avarice) which the first accepted. Christian heroic virtue resides in "humiliation and strong sufferance" and not, like pagan heroism, in action. Consequently Jesus does nothing except decline what is offered, and finally, when swept up to the pinnacle of the temple, he simply stands still. This is his initiation into the new and higher heroism, a point which Milton enforces by frequent favorable comparisons with pagan heroes.

He first rejects the sensual banquet arranged by Satan; he prefers a celestial banquet, and gets one at the end of the poem. Then he turns down earthly honor, favoring heavenly honor, which does not depend on what fallible and foolish men say about one, but on the testimony of God. The military power of Persia he rejects "unmoved," and also the more significant power of Rome. He turns down the earthly in favor of the heavenly city. The final temptation, before the crisis at the temple, is that of knowledge. Satan, having failed with "the kingdoms of this world," tries instead, in the great encomium of Athens, the temptations of intellect. But Jesus rejects learning for the same reason he turned down the others; he already has a superior version of what the tempter offers, namely, heavenly learning. That such learning made all other kinds redundant was a common enough position in the seventeenth century and earlier; it is surprising only because we know of Milton's love of classical poetry and philosophy, which he cannot quite keep out of this very denunciation of them. But it was necessary to take a diagrammatic position here; and the hidden conflict between the needs of the work and the temper of his mind makes this the finest thing in Milton's brief epic.

From *Book IV*

Therefore let pass, as they are transitory,
The kingdoms of this world; I shall no more
Advise thee; gain them as thou canst, or not.
And thou thyself seem'st otherwise inclined
Than to a worldly crown, addicted more
To contemplation and profound dispute,
As by that early action may be judged,
When slipping from thy mother's eye thou went'st
Alone into the temple; there wast found
Among the gravest rabbis disputant
On points and questions fitting Moses' chair,
Teaching, not taught; the childhood shows the man,

As morning shows the day. Be famous then
By wisdom; as thy empire must extend,
So let extend thy mind o'er all the world,
In knowledge, all things in it comprehend.
All knowledge is not couched in Moses' Law,
The Pentateuch° or what the Prophets wrote;
The Gentiles also know, and write, and teach
To admiration,° led by nature's light;
And with the Gentiles much thou must converse,
230 Ruling them by persuasion as thou mean'st;
Without their learning, how wilt thou with them,
Or they with thee hold conversation meet?
How wilt thou reason with them, how refute
Their idolisms,° traditions, paradoxes?
Error by his own arms is best evinced.°
Look once more, ere we leave this specular mount,°
Westward, much nearer'by southwest; behold
Where on the Aegean shore a city stands
Built nobly, pure the air, and light the soil,
240 Athens, the eye° of Greece, mother of arts
And eloquence, native to famous wits
Or hospitable, in her sweet recess,
City or suburban, studious walks and shades;
See there the olive grove of Academe,°
Plato's retirement, where the Attic bird°
Trills her thick-warbled notes the summer long;
There flowery hill Hymettus° with the sound
Of bees' industrious murmur oft invites
To studious musing; there Ilissus° rolls
250 His whispering stream..Within the walls then view
The schools of ancient sages: his° who bred
Great Alexander to subdue the world,
Lyceum° there, and painted Stoa° next.
There thou shalt hear and learn the secret power°
Of harmony in tones and numbers hit
By voice or hand, and various-measured verse,
Aeolian charms° and Dorian lyric odes,°
And his who gave them breath, but higher sung,

Pentateuch the first five books of the Old
Testament
To admiration admirably
idolisms idolatries
evinced defeated
specular mount lookout hill (Latin *specula*,
watchtower)
eye highest faculty, chief city
Academe Plato's Academy, a park planted with
olives, just outside Athens
Attic bird nightingale
Hymettus the hills, famous for honey, in which
the Ilissus rises
Ilissus stream near Athens

his Aristotle's: he was Alexander's tutor
Lyceum the park where Aristotle ran his
Peripatetic School of Philosophy, so called
because he and his pupils walked around as
they talked
painted Stoa porch, painted with frescoes,
where Zeno taught Stoicism
secret power The Greeks attributed therapeutic
and other powers to music.
Aeolian charms songs in the Aeolian dialect
used by Sappho
Dorian lyric odes Pindar's odes in the Dorian
dialect

Blind Melesigenes,° thence° Homer called,
260 Whose poem Phoebus challenged for his own.°
Thence what the lofty grave tragedians taught
In chorus or iambic,° teachers best
Of moral prudence, with delight received
In brief sententious precepts, while they treat
Of fate, and chance, and change in human life,
High actions and high passions best describing.
Thence to the famous orators repair,
Those ancient, whose resistless eloquence
Wielded at will that fierce democraty,°
270 Shook the Arsenal° and fulmined° over Greece,
To Macedon, and Artaxerxes' throne;°
To sage philosophy next lend thine ear,
From heaven descended to the low-roofed house
Of Socrates°—see there his tenement—
Whom well inspired the oracle° pronounced
Wisest of men; from whose mouth issued forth
Mellifluous streams that watered all the schools
Of Academics old and new,° with those
Surnamed Peripatetics,° and the sect
280 Epicurean,° and the Stoic severe;°
These here revolve, or, as thou lik'st, at home,
Till time mature thee to a kingdom's weight;
These rules will render thee a king complete
Within thyself, much more with empire joined.'
     To whom our Saviour sagely° thus replied:
'Think not but that I know these things, or think
I know them not; not therefore am I short
Of knowing what I ought. He who receives
Light from above, from the fountain of light,
290 No other doctrine needs, though granted true;°
But these are false, or little else but dreams,
Conjectures, fancies, built on nothing firm.
The first and wisest of them all professed

Melesigenes Homer, after his reputed birth-place near the river Meles; Milton invented this **thence** because he was blind; from the doubtful Greek word *homeros*, blind
poem . . . own An epigram in the Greek Anthology makes Apollo say "It was I who sang, but divine Homer wrote it down."
chorus or iambic Greek tragedy had choral odes, and dialogue in iambics.
democraty democracy
Arsenal naval dockyard at Piraeus near Athens, here used as military threat
fulmined hurled forth thunder and lightning
Artaxerxes' throne Artaxerxes was king of Persia, allied to Sparta.
From heaven . . . Socrates Cicero said that Socrates brought philosophy down from the heavens and made it deal with morality.

oracle The Delphic oracle said that there was no one wiser than Socrates (Plato's *Apology*).
Academics . . . new successive schools of Platonism
Peripatetics See l. 253n.
Epicurean Epicurus, 341–270 B.C. taught that happiness arose from the senses, and that virtuous pleasure was the end of life; the Stoics attacked him for debauchery.
Stoic severe Stoics thought of the soul as imprisoned in the body, and that the ideal man was totally immune to passion.
sagely Milton gives Jesus the adverb appropriate to the temptation here, as elsewhere.
He . . . true the heart of Jesus' reply; none of this knowledge is necessary, or even desirable, to those who have revealed truth

To know this only, that he nothing knew;°
The next to fabling fell and smooth conceits;°
A third sort doubted all things, though plain sense;°
Others in virtue placed felicity,°
But virtue joined with riches and long life;
In corporal pleasure he,° and careless ease;
300   The Stoic last in philosophic pride,
By him called virtue; and his virtuous man,
Wise, perfect in himself, and all possessing
Equal to God, oft shames not to prefer,
As fearing God nor man, contemning all
Wealth, pleasure, pain or torment, death and life,
Which when he lists, he leaves, or boasts he can;
For all his tedious talk is but vain boast,
Or subtle shifts conviction to evade.°
Alas what can they teach, and not mislead,
310   Ignorant of themselves, of God much more,
And how the world began, and how man fell
Degraded by himself, on grace depending?
Much of the soul they talk, but all awry,
And in themselves seek virtue, and to themselves
All glory arrogate, to God give none;°
Rather accuse him under usual names,
Fortune and fate, as one regardless quite
Of mortal things. Who therefore seeks in these
True wisdom, finds her not, or by delusion
320   Far worse, her false resemblance only meets,
An empty cloud.° However, many books,
Wise men have said, are wearisome;° who reads
Incessantly, and to his reading brings not
A spirit and judgment equal or superior
(And what he brings, what needs he elsewhere seek?),
Uncertain and unsettled still remains,
Deep versed in books and shallow in himself,
Crude° or intoxicate, collecting toys
And trifles for choice matters, worth a sponge,°
330   As children gathering pebbles on the shore.
Or if I would delight my private hours
With music or with poem, where so soon

professed . . . knew Socrates in the *Apology*
said that his superiority consisted only in that
he knew nothing.
To fabling . . . conceits Plato made myths in
his philosophy.
doubted . . . sense the Skeptics, who did not
believe that the human mind could know anything truly, and thought that a state of suspended judgment was the best
in virtue . . . felicity the Peripatetics
he Epicurus
The Stoic . . . evade The Stoics believed that
the virtuous man was equal to the gods, and
indifferent to pain and pleasure; he could
commit suicide if he so decided.
All . . . none Cicero said that praiseworthy
virtue must be a man's own, not a lucky
gift of fortune.
cloud recalling the cloud embraced by Ixion
in mistake for Juno
books . . . wearisome Ecclesiastes 12:12
Crude surfeited
worth a sponge worthy to be erased

As in our native language can I find
That solace? All our law and story° strewed
With hymns, our Psalms with artful terms° inscribed,
Our Hebrew songs and harps in Babylon,°
That pleased so well our victors' ear, declare
That rather Greece from us these arts derived;°
Ill imitated, while they loudest sing
340   The vices of their deities, and their own,
In fable, hymn, or song, so personating
Their gods ridiculous, and themselves past shame.
Remove their swelling epithets° thick laid
As varnish on a harlot's cheek, the rest,
Thin sown with aught of profit or delight,°
Will far be found unworthy to compare
With Sion's songs, to all true tastes excelling,°
Where God is praised aright, and godlike men,
The Holiest of Holies, and his saints;
350   Such are from God inspired, not such from thee;
Unless° where moral virtue is expressed
By light of nature not in all quite lost.
Their orators thou then extoll'st, as those
The top of eloquence, statists° indeed,
And lovers of their country, as may seem;
But herein to our Prophets far beneath,
As men divinely taught, and better teaching
The solid rules of civil government
In their majestic unaffected style
360   Than all the oratory of Greece and Rome.
In them is plainest taught, and easiest learnt,
What makes a nation happy, and keeps it so,
What ruins kingdoms, and lays cities flat;
These only with our Law best form a king.'

. . .

[Satan, remarking that Jesus is equally unconcerned about the active and the
contemplative virtues, asks "What dost thou in this world?" and leaves him
for what turns into a stormy night. Next morning he bears him by force to
the highest pinnacle of the temple, telling him scornfully either to stand or
to cast himself down for angels to save him. Jesus simply says "Tempt not
the Lord thy God," and stands. Satan falls. Jesus, who has throughout been
without divine powers or aid—like Guyon in the Cave of Mammon—is
provided by angels with "a table of celestial food." Finally "he unobserved /
Home to his mother's house private returned," and so the epic ends.]

story history
artful terms The Psalms were thought to orig-
inate all the arts of poetry and rhetoric.
Babylon Psalms 137:1
derived A common Renaissance opinion was
that all Greek learning and poetry derived
from Hebrew.
swelling epithets for example, in the odes of
Pindar

profit or delight That poetry should provide both
was the traditional view derived from Horace,
Ars Poetica.
Sion's . . . excelling Sion was in this way
regularly preferred to Parnassus as a source of
poetry; see Sidney's *Defence of Poesie,* where
the best poets are said to be biblical writers
like David and Solomon.
Unless refers to "unworthy," above.
statists statesmen

Samson Agonistes

The date of *Samson Agonistes* is disputed; the argument for an early date is most fully stated in W. R. Parker's *John Milton: A Biography* (1968). The most important points are, first, there is no evidence that it was a late work except its late publication, and Milton had little time between the publication of *Paradise Lost* and that of *Paradise Regained* and *Samson Agonistes* to write more than *Paradise Regained*. Nobody ever treated it as late until Upton in 1746 said that it represented Milton after the Restoration, and Thomas Newton, on similar grounds, called it in his edition (1749) Milton's last work. Second, *Samson Agonistes* has a good deal of rhyme, which Milton rejected in a paragraph on "The Verse" affixed to *Paradise Lost*. Parker, now followed by other scholars, chooses an early date, about 1647–53, and supports it on various stylistic and autobiographical grounds. Another view, supported by the notes for tragedies surviving in Milton's Commonplace Book, is that he sketched it early and finished it late.

It does not seem impossible that Milton could have fitted the play in between 1667 and 1670; *Paradise Regained* is not so long a work. As for the rhyme, there was current a theory, as it happens erroneous, that Hebrew verse used rhymes and half-rhymes, and Milton, using a Hebrew subject and perhaps fresh from the commendation to the Psalms in *Paradise Regained* iv.334–38, could have thought it proper to use rhyme in the same irregular way; what he complains of in his note on verse is the "modern bondage of rhyming," calling it "the invention of a barbarous age"; but Hebrew rhyme was neither barbarous, nor modern, nor a bondage, since it rhymed at will and not by compulsion. Furthermore it is hard to believe (despite the tenuous parallels adduced in Milton's Latin ode *Ad Rousium,* written in 1647) that his prosodic experiments in *Samson Agonistes* should have preceded the long works in blank verse; having explored the range of effects to be had from irregular strophes —the impact of short choric lines, and the effect of such transitions as that from 79 to 80—it is highly improbable that he would return to regular blank verse without such variation. We need not give up the view that *Samson Agonistes* is a triumphant tragic conclusion to Milton's work.

Milton had explored heroism in *Paradise Lost* and *Paradise Regained*. His tragic hero is an Old Testament type of Christian heroism, though in its active mode, Christ's in *Paradise Regained* being passive. (Much of the irony turns on the apparent passivity of Samson, "vigorous most when most unactive deemed.") His subject is accordingly Hebraic. The appropriate form for tragedy is, however, Greek. Milton knew Aeschylus, Sophocles, and Euripides, and built his drama out of that knowledge. It is generally agreed that Sophocles, perhaps especially in his *Oedipus at Colonus,* affected Milton most strongly, and that the persistent ironies of the work are Sophoclean in that they depend on the ignorance of the characters as to what is to ensue. Milton Christianizes this; it is the inaccessibility of God's design to human questioning that makes everybody go wrong about the true state of affairs, at all stages up to the entry of the messenger. The plight of Samson is considered in the light of partial human explanations, some of which Milton borrowed from the exegetical tradition: Samson as a warning against pride or uxoriousness; Samson as a subject for casuistry on the subject of suicide; Samson as a case history of despair. He had formerly referred to the story (in *The Reason of Church Government,* 1641) as an allegory of the enfeebling of the king by the bishops, and there is certainly nothing implausible in the supposition that in the 1660's he was thinking of Samson's apparent eclipse and eventual triumph as an allegory of the condition, under the Restoration, of the Good Old Cause of the Puritan Commonwealth (Harapha almost certainly reflects some satirical intention). Samson proves a highly adaptable theme for exegesis and allegory.

Milton, however much he might use such interpretations as material for irony and topical comment, was primarily concerned with the relations between his hero, the elected one, and the God who seemed to have deserted him. If this is remembered, the narrative structure of the work will seem simple enough. Samson is accustomed to visitations from the spirit of God, and to "intimate impulse." In the case of the woman of Timna this impulse led him into a marriage that would ordinarily have been forbidden; the marriage was a disaster, but it furthered the ends of God. His desire for Dalila seemed to him to proceed from an exactly analogous impulse. It was another disaster, and resulted in his captivity and blindness. Therefore, he supposes, and the Israelites suppose, that he has made a mistake, for which he is now punished and abandoned. Of course this is wrong; the analogy between the two marriages is exact, but the action is not yet complete, so that God's plan cannot be seen. The completion of the action stems from a third intimate impulse, occurring between the departure and return of the Philistine Public Officer. That impulse vindicates not only itself, but also the unclean marriage to Dalila, in the destruction of the temple.

Throughout most of the work discussion of Samson's powers is erroneous simply because it is assumed that they are now forever out of use, and this accounts for the mistake of the Chorus in its comments (ll. 1268 ff.) on the heroic virtue of God's champions; they think Samson's heroism can no longer be active, and that he must now exhibit the heroism of patience. The clarification of these errors, and the motivation of the intimate impulse by God, constitute the main action of the poem. Samson begins in total suffering, lamenting the contrast with the past, blaming himself for acts which would indeed be blameworthy if God did not provide a dispensation for them as part of his plan. The important question of the marriages is brought up by Manoa, who cannot see their relation to the signs given him at Samson's birth; the Dalila marriage is agreed to have resulted from intemperance. Dalila herself continues to be the instrument of God in angering Samson, beginning the process of rousing him from his apathy which the contemptible Harapha completes. The dramatic crisis occurs at line 1382; Samson is again authorized to break the Law, take part in a heathen festival; what impels him is a force he recognizes from the past. His humility before the officer is a *conscious* irony.

There is a persistent critical charge, first made by Dr. Johnson, that whereas *Samson Agonistes* has a beginning and an end it lacks a middle, "since nothing passes between the first act and the last, that either hastens or delays the death of Samson." The criticism, which has many variants, is invalidated by such considerations as those of the preceding paragraph. Perhaps the Dalila and Harapha episodes are too long, but that is virtually the extent of the case against Milton's structure. Milton had rethought the heroic poem, and the brief heroic poem; here he rethinks tragedy. The humanist enterprise which involved the Christianizing and modernizing of the great ancient modes was at last, though at a very late date, accomplished.

Samson Agonistes [1]

A Dramatic Poem

Of That Sort of Dramatic Poem Which Is Called Tragedy

Tragedy, as it was anciently composed, hath been ever held the gravest, moralest, and most profitable of all other poems: therefore said by Aristotle to be of power, by raising pity and fear, or terror, to purge the mind of those and suchlike passions, that is, to temper and reduce them to just measure with a kind of delight, stirred up by reading or seeing those passions well imitated.[2] Nor is Nature wanting in her own effects to make good his assertion; for so in physic, things of melancholic hue and quality are used against melancholy, sour against sour, salt to remove salt humours. Hence philosophers and other gravest writers, as Cicero, Plutarch, and others, frequently cite out of tragic poets, both to adorn and illustrate their discourse. The Apostle Paul himself thought it not unworthy to insert a verse of Euripides into the text of Holy Scripture, I Cor. 15, 33,[3] and Pareus,[4] commenting on the Revelation, divides the whole book as a tragedy, into acts distinguished each by a chorus of heavenly harpings and song between. Heretofore men in highest dignity have laboured not a little to be thought able to compose a tragedy. Of that honour Dionysius the elder was no less ambitious than before of his attaining to the tyranny.[5] Augustus Caesar also had begun his *Ajax*, but, unable to please his own judgment with what he had begun, left it unfinished.[6] Seneca the philosopher is by some thought the author of those tragedies (at least the best of them) that go under that name.[7] Gregory Nazianzen, a Father of the Church, thought it not unbeseeming the sanctity of his person to write a tragedy, which he entitled *Christ Suffering*.[8] This is mentioned to vindicate tragedy from the small esteem, or rather infamy, which in the account of many it undergoes at this day with other common interludes; happening through the poet's error of intermixing comic stuff with tragic sadness and gravity, or introducing trivial and vulgar persons, which by all judicious hath been counted absurd, and brought in without discretion, corruptly to gratify the people.[9] And though

1. Samson the performer or contestant, Samson at the Games.
2. Aristotle, *Poetics* VI: "Tragedy is the imitation of a serious action, effecting through pity and terror the *catharsis* of such passions." The dispute as to what *catharsis* means here has continued since the 16th century, but Milton partly follows Italian interpretations, partly provides his own. He thinks that small doses of pity and terror in an imitated action will drive out the real and dangerous passions, not only pity and terror but others ("those and suchlike"). The purgation depends on *delight* in the imitation; the medicine is pleasant.
3. See note on Sidney's *Defence* (n.54); of St. Paul's several references to poets Milton is thinking of "Evil communications corrupt good manners" (I Corinthians 15:33), which is from Menander.
4. David Paraeus (1548–1622) in his work *On the Divine Apocalypse* (1618).
5. Tyrant of Syracuse (431–367 B.C.), who sought fame as poet and playwright.
6. According to Suetonius, *Lives of the Caesars* II.85, Augustus erased what he had written of this tragedy.
7. Lucius Annaeus Seneca (3 B.C.–65 A.D.). The Renaissance distinction between Seneca the philosopher and Seneca the dramatist has since disappeared.
8. St. Gregory of Nazianzus, fourth-century bishop of Constantinople who wrote *Christus Patiens*.
9. This condemnation was made by Sidney in the *Defence*.

ancient tragedy use no prologue,[10] yet using sometimes, in case of self-defence, or explanation, that which Martial calls an epistle;[11] in behalf of this tragedy, coming forth after the ancient manner, much different from what among us passes for best, thus much beforehand may be epistled: that chorus is here introduced after the Greek manner, not ancient only but modern, and still in use among the Italians.[12] In the modelling therefore of this poem, with good reason, the ancients and Italians are rather followed, as of much more authority and fame. The measure of verse used in the chorus is of all sorts, called by the Greeks *monostrophic*, or rather *apolelymenon*,[13] without regard had to strophe, antistrophe, or epode, which were a kind of stanzas framed only for the music, then used with the chorus that sung; not essential to the poem, and therefore not material; or, being divided into stanzas or pauses, they may be called *alloeostropha*.[14] Division into act and scene, referring chiefly to the stage (to which this work never was intended), is here omitted.

It suffices if the whole drama be found not produced beyond the fifth act. Of the style and uniformity, and that commonly called the plot, whether intricate or explicit [15]—which is nothing indeed but such economy, or disposition of the fable, as may stand best with verisimilitude and decorum [16]—they only will best judge who are not unacquainted with Aeschylus, Sophocles, and Euripides, the three tragic poets unequalled yet by any, and the best rule to all who endeavour to write tragedy. The circumscription of time wherein the whole drama begins and ends is, according to ancient rule and best example, within the space of twenty-four hours.[17]

The Argument

Samson, made captive, blind, and now in the prison at Gaza, there to labour as in a common workhouse, on a festival day, in the general cessation from labour, comes forth into the open air, to a place nigh, somewhat retired, there to sit a while and bemoan his condition. Where he happens at length to be visited by certain friends and equals of his tribe, which make the chorus, who seek to comfort him what they can; then by his old father, Manoa, who endeavours the like, and withal tells him his purpose to procure his liberty by ransom; lastly, that this feast was proclaimed by the Philistines as a day of thanksgiving for their deliverance from the hands of Samson, which yet more troubles him. Manoa then departs to prosecute his endeavour with the Philistian

10. Preliminary address to the audience, not the part of the tragedy which precedes the first entrance of the chorus, the sense in which it is used in Greek tragedy.

11. Martial's "Letter to the Reader" introducing his epigrams is the model.

12. Milton uses the chorus in the manner adapted by modern Italians from the Greek (in drama and opera) rather than in the original Greek way.

13. "Freed"—from the limits of a regular stanzaic pattern. In Greek drama the chorus sang the strophe as they moved or danced one way, the antistrophe as they reversed the movement, and the epode, standing still.

14. Insofar as the verse does seem to divide into stanzas, these should be regarded as "irregular strophes."

15. Referring to Aristotle's distinction between "simple" and "complex" plots (*Poetics* VI).

16. Two important aims of neoclasic thought; see *Rhetoric* in the Glossary.

17. Aristotle's words in *Poetics* V were not prescriptive, and became so only when the Unities were evolved in 16th-century Italian criticism.

lords for Samson's redemption; who in the meanwhile is visited by other persons; and lastly by a public officer to require his coming to the feast before the lords and people, to play or show his strength in their presence. He at first refuses, dismissing the public officer with absolute denial to come; at length persuaded inwardly that this was from God, he yields to go along with him, who came now the second time with great threatenings to fetch him. The chorus yet remaining on the place, Manoa returns full of joyful hope to procure ere long his son's deliverance; in the midst of which discourse an Hebrew comes in haste, confusedly at first, and afterward more distinctly, relating the catastrophe, what Samson had done to the Philistines, and by accident to himself; wherewith the tragedy ends.

THE PERSONS

SAMSON	PUBLIC OFFICER
MANOA, *the father of Samson*	MESSENGER
DALILA, *his wife*	CHORUS OF DANITES
HARAPHA OF GATH	

The Scene, before the Prison in Gaza

SAMSON   A little onward lend thy guiding hand
To these dark steps,° a little further on,
For yonder bank hath choice of sun or shade;
There I am wont to sit, when any chance
Relieves me from my task of servile toil,
Daily in the common prison else enjoined me,
Where I, a prisoner chained, scarce freely draw
The air imprisoned also, close and damp,
Unwholesome draught. But here I feel amends,
10   The breath of heaven fresh-blowing, pure and sweet,
With day-spring° born; here leave me to respire.°
This day a solemn feast the people hold
To Dagon° their sea-idol, and forbid
Laborious works; unwillingly this rest
Their superstition yields me; hence with leave
Retiring from the popular noise, I seek
This unfrequented place to find some ease,
Ease to the body some, none to the mind
From restless thoughts, that like a deadly swarm
20   Of hornets armed, no sooner found alone,
But rush upon me thronging, and present
Times past, what once I was, and what am now.
O wherefore was my birth from heaven foretold
Twice by an angel, who at last in sight

---

dark steps The very phrase echoes the language of Greek tragedy, particularly the "blind feet" of Tiresias guided by his daughter, who will be "eyes" to them, in Euripides' *Phoenissae;* one is also to think of the opening of Sophocles' *Oedipus at Colonus.*
day-spring daybreak
respire breathe
Dagon Philistine fish god, worshiped at Gaza

Of both my parents all in flames ascended
From off the altar, where an offering burned,
As in a fiery column charioting
His godlike presence, and from some great act
Or benefit revealed to Abraham's race?
30 Why was my breeding ordered and prescribed
As of a person separate to God,
Designed for great exploits, if I must die
Betrayed, captived, and both my eyes put out,
Made of my enemies the scorn and gaze;°
To grind in brazen fetters under task
With this heaven-gifted strength? O glorious strength,
Put to the labour of a beast, debased
Lower than bondslave! Promise was° that I
Should Israel from Philistian yoke deliver;
40 Ask for this great deliverer now, and find him
Eyeless in Gaza at the mill with slaves,
Himself in bonds under Philistian yoke;
Yet stay, let me not rashly call in doubt
Divine prediction; what if all foretold
Had been fulfilled but through mine own default?
Whom have I to complain of but myself?
Who this high gift of strength committed to me,
In what part lodged, how easily bereft me,
Under the seal of silence could not keep,
50 But weakly to a woman must reveal it,
O'ercome with importunity and tears.
O impotence of mind, in body strong!°
But what is strength without a double share
Of wisdom? Vast, unwieldy, burdensome,
Proudly secure,° yet liable to fall
By weakest subtleties; not made to rule,
But to subserve where wisdom bears command.
God, when he gave me strength, to show withal
How slight the gift was, hung it in my hair.
60 But peace! I must not quarrel with the will
Of highest dispensation, which herein
Haply had ends above my reach to know:
Suffices that to me strength is my bane,
And proves the source of all my miseries,
So many, and so huge, that each apart
Would ask a life to wail; but chief of all,
O loss of sight, of thee I most complain!

---

gaze object of jeering gazes (did Milton pronounce "Gaza" this way?)
Promise was at Judges 13:5, that he should
"begin to deliver Israel out of the hands of the
Philistines"

O impotence . . . strong And towering strength,
like any fortress when it tumbles in, imprisons
its inhabitant; see the continuation of this image
in that of burial in self, ll. 101–5 and 155–56.
secure careless of danger

Blind among enemies, O worse than chains,
Dungeon, or beggary, or decrepit age!
70   Light, the prime work of God, to me is extinct,
And all her various objects of delight
Annulled, which might in part my grief have eased,
Inferior to the vilest now become
Of man or worm; the vilest here excel me,
They creep, yet see; I, dark in light exposed
To daily fraud, contempt, abuse and wrong,
Within doors, or without, still as a fool,
In power of others, never in my own;
Scarce half I seem to live, dead more than half.
80   O dark, dark, dark,° amid the blaze of noon,
Irrecoverably dark, total eclipse
Without all hope of day!
O first-created beam, and thou great Word,
'Let there be light, and light was over all';
Why am I thus bereaved thy prime decree?
The sun to me is dark
And silent° as the moon,
When she deserts the night,
Hid in her vacant° interlunar cave.
90   Since light so necessary is to life,
And almost life itself, if it be true
That light is in the soul,
She all in every part,° why was the sight
To such a tender ball as the eye confined?
So obvious° and so easy to be quenched,
And not, as feeling, through all parts diffused,
That she might look at will through every pore?
Then had I not been thus exiled from light,
As in the land of darkness, yet in light,
100   To live a life half dead, a living death,
And buried; but O yet more miserable!
Myself my sepulchre, a moving grave,
Buried, not yet exempt
By privilege of death and burial
From worst of other evils, pains and wrongs,
But made hereby obnoxious° more
To all the miseries of life,
Life in captivity

O dark, dark, dark Here Milton abandons the blank verse of the dialogue for one of the many unrhymed lyrical passages in Samson's speeches.
silent meaning the dark of the moon, but significant here in its transfer of location from the visual domain to the aural one
vacant idle, resting in her fabled cave between visible phases

all in every part The soul, in Augustinian tradition and thereafter, was not thought to be localized in any part of the body, but rather suffusing it all like warmth, until Milton's contemporary, René Descartes, decided that it was in the surgically inaccessible pineal gland.
obvious evident, thus vulnerable
obnoxious exposed to

Among inhuman foes,
110   But who are these? For with joint pace I hear
The tread of many feet steering this way;
Perhaps my enemies who come to stare
At my affliction, and perhaps to insult,
Their daily practice to afflict me more.
    CHORUS   This, this is he; softly a while;
Let us not break in upon him.
O change beyond report, thought, or belief!
See how he lies at random, carelessly diffused,°
With languished head unpropped,
120   As one past hope, abandoned,
And by himself given over;
In slavish habit, ill-fitted weeds°
O'erworn and soiled;
Or do my eyes misrepresent? Can this be he,
That heroic, that renowned,
Irresistible Samson? Whom unarmed
No strength of man, or fiercest wild beast could withstand;
Who tore the lion, as the lion tears the kid,°
Ran on embattled armies clad in iron,
130   And, weaponless himself,
Made arms ridiculous, useless the forgery°
Of brazen shield and spear, the hammered cuirass,
Chalýbean°-tempered steel, and frock of mail
Adamantean° proof;
But safe he who stood aloof,
When insupportably° his foot advanced,
In scorn of their proud arms and warlike tools,
Spurned them to death by troops. The bold Ascalonite°
Fled from his lion ramp,° old warriors turned
140   Their plated° backs under his heel;
Or grovelling soiled their crested helmets in the dust.
Then with what trivial weapon came to hand,
The jaw of a dead ass, his sword of bone,
A thousand foreskins° fell, the flower of Palestine,
In Ramath-lechi, famous to this day;
Then by main force pulled up, and on his shoulders bore
The gates of Azza,° post and massy bar,
Up to the hill by Hebron, seat of giants old,
No journey of a Sabbath day,° and loaded so;

---

diffused spread out
weeds clothing
Who tore . . . kid See Judges 14:6.
forgery making; faking
Chalybean made by fabled metalworkers
Adamantean diamond-hard; steely
insupportably irresistibly
Ascalonite Ascalon: one of the five principal
Philistine cities

lion ramp leonine, rampant posture
plated armor-clad
foreskins synecdoche for uncircumcised Philistines
Azza Gaza
No journey . . . day Jewish law permits no labor or travel on the Sabbath.

150 Like whom the Gentiles feign° to bear up heaven.
Which shall I first bewail,
Thy bondage or lost sight,
Prison within prison
Inseparably dark?
Thou art become (O worst imprisonment!)
The dungeon of thyself; thy soul
(Which men enjoying sight oft without cause complain)
Imprisoned now indeed,
In real darkness of the body dwells,
160 Shut up from outward light
To incorporate with gloomy night;
For inward light, alas,
Puts forth no visual beam.
O mirror of our fickle state,
Since man on earth unparalleled!
The rarer thy example stands,
By how much from the top of wondrous glory,
Strongest of mortal men,
To lowest pitch of abject fortune thou art fallen.
170 For him I reckon not in high estate
Whom long descent of birth
Or the sphere° of fortune raises;
But thee whose strength, while virtue was her mate,
Might have subdued the earth,
Universally crowned with highest praises.
    SAMSON   I hear the sound of words, their sense the air
Dissolves unjointed ere it reach my ear.
    CHORUS   He speaks, let us draw nigh. Matchless in might,
The glory late of Israel, now the grief,
180 We come thy friends and neighbours not unknown
From Eshtaol and Zora's fruitful vale°
To visit or bewail thee, or if better,
Counsel or consolation we may bring,
Salve to thy sores; apt words have power to 'suage
The tumours° of a troubled mind,
And are as balm to festered wounds.
    SAMSON   Your coming, friends, revives me, for I learn
Now of my own experience, not by talk,
How counterfeit a coin they are who friends
190 Bear in their superscription° (of the most
I would be understood); in prosperous days
They swarm, but in adverse withdraw their head,

---

feign From a Hebraic viewpoint, classical myths, like those of Atlas holding up the world, were uninterestingly fictitious.
sphere Fortune's emblematic wheel frequently became a ball, sometimes the globe, in Renaissance pictures.

Eshtaol . . . vale Samson was born at Zora; Eshtaol was near by.
tumours swellings, disturbances
superscription the legend on a coin

Not to be found, though sought. Ye see, O friends,
How many evils have enclosed me round;
Yet that which was the worst now least afflicts me,
Blindness, for had I sight, confused with shame,
How could I once look up, or heave the head,
Who like a foolish pilot have shipwrecked
My vessel trusted to me from above,
200   Gloriously rigged; and for a word, a tear,
Fool, have divulged the secret gift of God
To a deceitful woman: tell me, friends,
Am I not sung and proverbed° for a fool
In every street, do they not say, how well
Are come upon him his deserts? yet why?
Immeasurable strength they might behold
In me, of wisdom nothing more than mean;°
This with the other should, at least, have paired,
These two proportioned ill drove me transverse.°
210   CHORUS   Tax not divine disposal, wisest men
Have erred, and by bad women been deceived;
And shall again, pretend they ne'er so wise.
Deject not then so overmuch thyself,
Who hast of sorrow thy full load besides;
Yet truth to say, I oft have heard men wonder
Why thou shouldst wed Philistian women rather
Than of thine own tribe fairer, or as fair,
At least of thine own nation, and as noble.
SAMSON   The first I saw at Timna, and she pleased
220   Me, not my parents, that I sought to wed
The daughter of an infidel;° they knew not
That what I motioned was of God; I knew
From intimate impulse, and therefore urged
The marriage on; that by occasion hence
I might begin Israel's deliverance,
The work to which I was divinely called;
She proving false, the next I took to wife
(O that I never had! fond wish too late)
Was in the vale of Sorec, Dálila,°
230   That specious° monster, my accomplished snare.°
I thought it lawful from my former act,

---

proverbed made a byword
mean average
transverse astray; a nautical term, meaning "off-course"
The first . . . infidel In Judges 14:3–4 Samson's parents complain of his choice, though he insists: "she pleaseth me well." But his father and mother "knew not that it was of the Lord, that he sought an occasion [see l. 237] against the Philisitines." He marries the woman, but then propounds to the Philistines the riddle of the honey which came from the lion's carcass,

which they get right by making his wife pester him for the answer; whereupon Samson slays thirty Philistines, takes their clothes and pays his wager (thirty changes of garments). He breaks with his wife.
Dálila "He loved a woman in the valley of Sorek, whose name was Delilah" (Judges 16:4)
specious superficially beautiful
accomplished snare snare that has now fulfilled its task; both Dalila's accomplished charms and her accomplishment of Samson's ruin

And the same end;° still watching to oppress
Israel's oppressors: of what now I suffer
She was not the prime cause, but I myself,
Who vanquished with a peal of words° (O weakness!)
Gave up my fort of silence to a woman.

CHORUS   In seeking just occasion to provoke
The Philistine, thy country's enemy,
Thou never wast remiss, I bear thee witness:
240   Yet Israel still serves with all his sons.

SAMSON   That fault I take not on me, but transfer
On Israel's governors, and heads of tribes,
Who seeing those great acts which God had done
Singly by me against their conquerors,
Acknowledged not, or not at all considered
Deliverance offered: I on the other side
Used no ambition° to commend my deeds;
The deeds themselves, though mute, spoke loud the doer;
But they persisted deaf, and would not seem
250   To count them things worth notice, till at length
Their lords the Philistines with gathered powers
Entered Judea seeking me, who then
Safe to the rock of Etham° was retired,
Not flying, but forecasting in what place
To set upon them, what advantaged best;
Meanwhile the men of Judah, to prevent
The harass of their land, beset me round;
I willingly on some conditions° came
Into their hands, and they as gladly yield me
260   To the uncircumcised a welcome prey,
Bound with two cords; but cords to me were threads
Touched with the flame: on their whole host I flew
Unarmed, and with a trivial weapon° felled
Their choicest youth; they only lived who fled.
Had Judah that day joined, or one whole tribe,
They had by this° possessed the towers of Gath,°

I thought . . . end This is a very important source of the main ironies that animate the drama. Samson is saying that his first marriage, though a failure, was right because it was ordered by God as part of His plans, a fact he knew "by intimate impulse." But in undertaking the second, with Dalila, he now supposes that he argued wrongly from analogy; the circumstances were similar but this was *not* part of God's plan, merely an indication of his own weakness. Hence his present situation, blind, disgraced, and with no future. But the irony is that the marriage with Dalila was as much part of God's plan as that with the women of Timna. The consequences of it are not yet worked out; everybody thinks the action is over, but it is not. The provision of "just occasion to provoke / The Philistine,"

and of course what follows justify Samson's confidence in the inspired nature of his second marriage.
peal of words as it were, surrendering to the mere noise of the attacker's weapons
ambition canvasing (from original Latin meaning "walking around")
Etham Judges 15
conditions Samson gave himself up to the men of Judah, who wanted to hand him over to the Philistines, on a promise that they would not "fall on him." They bound him, but he burst the cords and seized the jawbone of an ass, with which he slew a thousand men (Judges 15).
trivial weapon the jawbone, casually acquired
this this time
Gath Philistian city

And lorded over them whom now they serve;
But what more oft in nations grown corrupt,
And by their vices brought to servitude,
270   Than to love bondage more than liberty,
Bondage with ease than strenuous liberty;
And to despise, or envy, or suspect
Whom God hath of his special favour raised
As their deliverer; if he aught begin,
How frequent° to desert him, and at last
To heap ingratitude on worthiest deeds?
    CHORUS   Thy words to my remembrance bring
How Succoth and the fort of Penuel
Their great deliverer contemned,
280   The matchless Gideon in pursuit
Of Madian and her vanquished kings:°
And how ingrateful Ephraim
Had dealt with Jephtha, who by argument,
Not worse than by his shield and spear,
Defended Israel from the Ammonite,
Had not his prowess quelled their pride
In that sore battle when so many died
Without reprieve adjudged to death,
For want of well pronouncing *Shibboleth.*°
290   SAMSON   Of such examples add me to the roll;
Me easily indeed mine° may neglect,
But God's proposed deliverance not so.
    CHORUS   Just are the ways of God,
And justifiable to men;
Unless there be who think not God at all:
If any be, they walk obscure;
For of such doctrine never was there school,
But the heart of the fool,°
And no man therein doctor but himself.
300   Yet more there be who doubt his ways not just,
As to his own edicts, found contradicting,
Then give the reins to wandering thought,
Regardless of his glory's diminution;
Till by their own perplexities involved
They ravel° more, still less resolved,
But never find self-satisfying solution.
    As if they would confine the interminable,
And tie him to his own prescript,

frequent accustomed
How Succoth . . . kings Gideon in pursuit of the enemy asked bread from Succoth and Penuel and was refused (Judges 8).
And how . . . Shibboleth The Ephraimites refused help to Jephtha, who nevertheless defeated the Ammonites. Then a quarrel grew up between the Ephraimites and Jephtha's Gile-adites, and Jephtha's men used as a test the Hebrew *shibboleth,* which the Ephraimites could not pronounce; so infiltrators were detected and slain.
mine my people
heart . . . fool "The fool hath said in his heart, there is no God" (Psalms 14:1)
ravel become entangled

Who made our laws to bind us, not himself,
310 And hath full right to exempt
Whomso it pleases him by choice
From national obstriction,° without taint
Of sin, or legal debt;
For with his own laws he can best dispense.
He would not else, who never wanted means,
Nor in respect of the enemy just cause,
To set his people free,
Have prompted this heroic Nazarite,°
Against his vow of strictest purity,
320 To seek in marriage that fallacious° bride,
Unclean, unchaste.°
Down, reason, then, at least vain reasonings down,
Though reason here aver
That moral verdict quits her of unclean:
Unchaste was subsequent; her stain, not his.
But see, here comes thy reverend sire
With careful° step, locks white as down,
Old Mánoa: advise
Forthwith how thou ought'st to receive him.
330 SAMSON Ay me, another inward grief awaked
With mention of that name renews the assault.
MANOA Brethren and men of Dan, for such ye seem,
Though in this uncouth° place; if old respect,
As I suppose, towards your once gloried friend,
My son now captive, hither hath informed°
Your younger feet, while mine cast back with age
Came lagging after; say if he be here.
CHORUS As signal° now in low dejected state,
As erst° in highest, behold him where he lies.
340 MANOA O miserable change! is this the man,
That invincible Samson, far renowned,
The dread of Israel's foes, who with a strength
Equivalent to angels' walked their streets,
None offering fight;° who single combatant
Duelled their armies ranked in proud array,°
Himself an army, now unequal match
To save himself against a coward armed

obstriction obligation (the law against marriage with Gentiles)
Nazarite member of ascetic religious sect (the broken vow is not of celibacy but of impure marriage)
fallacious treacherous (referring of course to the woman of Timna)
Unclean, unchaste As the Chorus goes on to say, she was not morally unclean, only ceremonially so, as a Gentile; she was not unchaste until after the marriage and the episode of the riddle. In short, God can dispense with His own law and make any arrangements He likes without regard to such considerations; but here, as it happens, He did not make Samson marry uncleanly and unchastely.
careful full of care
uncouth unfamiliar
informed directed
signal distinguished
erst formerly
The dread . . . fight presumably after his visit to the harlot of Gaza, when he went home with the town gates
Duelled . . . array in the jawbone fight

At one spear's length? O ever-failing trust
In mortal strength! and oh what not in man
350   Deceivable and vain! Nay, what thing good
Prayed for, but often proves our woe, our bane?
I prayed for children, and thought barrenness
In wedlock a reproach; I gained a son,
And such a son as all men hailed me happy:
Who would be now a father in my stead?
O wherefore did God grant me my request,
And as a blessing with such pomp adorned?
Why are his gifts desirable, to tempt
Our earnest prayers, then given with solemn hand
360   As graces,° draw a scorpion's tail behind?
For this did the angel twice descend?° For this
Ordained thy nurture holy, as of a plant;
Select and sacred, glorious for a while,
The miracle of men; then in an hour
Ensnared, assaulted, overcome, led bound,
Thy foes' derision, captive, poor, and blind,
Into a dungeon thrust, to work with slaves?
Alas, methinks whom God hath chosen once
To worthiest deeds, if he through frailty err,
370   He should not so o'erwhelm, and as a thrall
Subject him to so foul indignities,
Be it but for honour's sake of former deeds.°
    SAMSON   Appoint° not heavenly disposition, father.
Nothing of all these evils hath befallen me
But justly; I myself have brought them on,
Sole author I, sole cause: if aught seem vile,
As vile hath been my folly, who have profaned
The mystery of God given me under pledge
Of vow, and have betrayed it to a woman,
380   A Canaanite,° my faithless enemy.
This well I knew, nor was at all surprised,
But warned by oft experience: did not she
Of Timna first betray me, and reveal
The secret wrested from me in her highth
Of nuptial love professed, carrying it straight
To them who had corrupted her, my spies,
And rivals? In this other was there found
More faith? Who also in her prime of love,
Spousal embraces, vitiated with gold,

---

graces favors
twice descend He does so in Judges 13, describing the signs and admonitions accompanying the conception and prescribing the education of Samson.
former deeds Manoa thinks the story is over,
and so wonders at God's desertion of his

former champion; he does not understand
that this apparent desertion is part of the
arrangement for Samson's last exploit, still
to come.
Appoint arraign, charge
Canaanite Philistine

390 Though offered only, by the scent conceived°
  Her spurious first-born, treason against me.
  Thrice she assayed with flattering prayer and sighs
  And amorous reproaches to win from me
  My capital° secret, in what part my strength
  Lay stored, in what part summed, that she might know:
  Thrice I deluded her, and turned to sport
  Her importunity, each time perceiving
  How openly, and with what impudence,
  She purposed to betray me, and (which was worse
400 Than undissembled hate) with what contempt
  She sought to make me traitor to myself;
  Yet the fourth time, when mustering all her wiles,
  With blandished parleys, feminine assaults,
  Tongue-batteries, she surceased not day nor night
  To storm me over-watched,° and wearied out,
  At times when men seek most repose and rest,
  I yielded, and unlocked her all my heart,
  Who with a grain of manhood well resolved
  Might easily have shook off all her snares;
410 But foul effeminacy held me yoked
  Her bondslave; O indignity, O blot
  To honour and religion! servile mind
  Rewarded well with servile punishment!
  The base degree to which I now am fallen,
  These rags, this grinding,° is not yet so base
  As was my former servitude, ignoble,
  Unmanly, ignominious, infamous,
  True slavery, and that blindness worse than this,
  That saw not how degenerately I served.
420 MANOA   I cannot praise thy marriage choices, son,
  Rather approved them not; but thou didst plead
  Divine impulsion prompting how thou might'st
  Find some occasion to infest° our foes.
  I state not that; this I am sure, our foes
  Found soon occasion thereby to make thee
  Their captive, and their triumph; thou the sooner
  Temptation found'st, or over-potent charms,
  To violate the sacred trust of silence
  Deposited within thee; which to have kept
430 Tacit was in thy power; true; and thou bear'st
  Enough, and more, the burden of that fault;
  Bitterly hast thou paid, and still art paying,
  That rigid score.° A worse thing yet remains:

---

by . . . conceived conceived, not a child from the spousal embraces, but treason from the mere promise of reward (Judges 16:5)
capital relating to the head—Samson's uncut hair; most important

over-watched too long awake. The whole story of Dalila's temptation is in Judges 16.
grinding working at the flour mill
infest harass
score account of a debt

This day the Philistines a popular feast
Here celebrate in Gaza, and proclaim
Great pomp, and sacrifice, and praises loud
To Dagon, as their god who hath delivered
Thee, Samson, bound and blind into their hands,
Them out of thine,° who slew'st them many a slain.
440   So Dagon shall be magnified, and God,
Besides whom is no god, compared with idols,
Disglorified, blasphemed, and had in scorn
By the idolatrous rout amidst their wine;
Which to have come to pass by means of thee,
Samson, of all thy sufferings think the heaviest,
Of all reproach the most with shame that ever
Could have befallen thee and thy father's house.
     SAMSON   Father, I do acknowledge and confess
That I this honour, I this pomp have brought
450   To Dagon, and advanced his praises high
Among the heathen round; to God have brought
Dishonour, obloquy, and oped the mouths
Of idolists° and atheists; have brought scandal
To Israel, diffidence of° God, and doubt
In feeble hearts, propense° enough before
To waver, or fall off and join with idols:
Which is my chief affliction, shame and sorrow,
The anguish of my soul, that suffers not
Mine eye to harbour sleep, or thoughts to rest.
460   This only hope° relieves me, that the strife
With me hath end; all the contést is now
'Twixt God and Dagon; Dagon hath presumed,
Me overthrown, to enter lists with God,
His deity comparing and preferring
Before the God of Abraham. He, be sure,
Will not connive,° or linger, thus provoked,
But will arise and his great name assert:
Dagon must stoop, and shall ere long receive
Such a discomfit,° as shall quite despoil him
470   Of all these boasted trophies won on me,
And with confusion blank° his worshippers.
     MANOA   With cause this hope relieves thee, and these words
I as a prophecy receive; for God,
Nothing more certain, will not long defer
To vindicate the glory of his name
Against all competition, nor will long
Endure it doubtful whether God be Lord,

Them . . . thine and delivered them out of
your hands
idolists idolaters
diffidence of lack of faith in
propense disposed

only hope hope alone
connive acquiesce
discomfit defeat
blank confound

Or Dagon. But for thee what shall be done?
Thou must not in the meanwhile, here forgot,
480 Lie in this miserable loathsome plight
Neglected. I already have made way
To some Philistian lords, with whom to treat
About thy ransom:° well they may by this
Have satisfied their utmost of revenge
By pains and slaveries, worse than death, inflicted
On thee, who now no more canst do them harm.
    SAMSON   Spare that proposal, father, spare the trouble
Of that solicitation; let me here,
As I deserve, pay on my punishment;
490 And expiate, if possible, my crime,
Shameful garrulity. To have revealed
Secrets of men, the secrets of a friend,
How heinous had the fact° been, how deserving
Contempt, and scorn of all, to be excluded
All friendship, and avoided as a blab,
The mark of fool set on his front!° But I
God's counsel have not kept, his holy secret
Presumptuously have published, impiously,
Weakly at least, and shamefully: a sin
500 That Gentiles in their parables condemn
To their abyss and horrid pains confined.°
    MANOA   Be penitent and for thy fault contrite,
But act not in thy own affliction, son;
Repent the sin, but if the punishment
Thou canst avoid, self-preservation bids;
Or the execution leave to high disposal,°
And let another hand, not thine, exact
Thy penal forfeit from thyself; perhaps
God will relent, and quit thee all his debt;
510 Who ever more approves and more accepts
(Best pleased with humble and filial submission)
Him who imploring mercy sues for life,
Than who self-rigorous chooses death as due;
Which argues over-just, and self-displeased
For self-offence, more than for God offended.°
Reject not then what offered means who knows
But God hath set before us, to return thee
Home to thy country and his sacred house,
Where thou mayst bring thy offerings, to avert
520 His further ire, with prayers and vows renewed.

ransom This is an incident Milton added to the
biblical account.
fact deed
front forehead
a sin . . . confined the myth of Tantalus, who
was tormented in hell for having revealed the
secrets of the gods (see Spenser, *The Faerie
Queene* II.vii and notes)
the execution . . . disposal leave the carrying
out of the punishment to God
Which . . . offended an argument against self-
punishment, including suicide, used by Milton
in his *Christian Doctrine*

SAMSON   His pardon I implore; but as for life,
To what end should I seek it? When in strength
All mortals I excelled, and great in hopes
With youthful courage and magnanimous thoughts
Of birth from heaven foretold and high exploits,
Full of divine instinct, after some proof
Of acts indeed heroic, far beyond
The sons of Anak,° famous now and blazed,
Fearless of danger, like a petty god
530   I walked about admired of all and dreaded
On hostile ground, none daring my affront.
Then swollen with pride into the snare I fell
Of fair fallacious looks, venereal trains,°
Softened with pleasure and voluptuous life;
At length to lay my head and hallowed pledge
Of all my strength in the lascivious lap
Of a deceitful concubine who shore me
Like a tame wether, all my precious fleece,
Then turned me out ridiculous, despoiled,
540   Shaven, and disarmed among my enemies.
    CHORUS   Desire of wine and all delicious drinks,
Which many a famous warrior overturns,
Thou couldst repress,° nor did the dancing ruby
Sparkling outpoured, the flavour, or the smell,
Or taste that cheers the heart of gods and men,
Allure thee from the cool crystálline stream.
    SAMSON   Wherever fountain or fresh current flowed
Against° the eastern ray, translucent, pure
With touch ethereal of heaven's fiery rod,°
550   I drank, from the clear milky juice allaying
Thirst, and refreshed; nor envied them the grape
Whose heads that turbulent liquor fills with fumes.
    CHORUS   O madness, to think use of strongest wines
And strongest drinks our chief support of health,
When God with these forbidden made choice to rear
His mighty champion, strong above compare,
Whose drink was only from the liquid brook.
    SAMSON   But what availed this temperance, not complete
Against another object more enticing?
560   What boots it° at one gate to make defence,
And at another to let in the foe,
Effeminately vanquished? By which means,
Now blind, disheartened, shamed, dishonoured, quelled,
To what can I be useful, wherein serve

sons of Anak giants; see Numbers 13:33
venereal trains amorous snares
Desire . . . repress The Nazarites abstained
from wine.

Against in the direction of (east-flowing water
was thought purer)
fiery rod sun ray
What boots it what use is it?

My nation, and the work from heaven imposed,
But to sit idle on the household hearth,
A burdenous drone? To visitants a gaze,°
Or pitied object; these redundant° locks,
Robustious° to no purpose, clustering down,
570   Vain monument of strength; till length of years
And sedentary numbness craze° my limbs
To a contemptible old age obscure.
Here rather let me drudge and earn my bread,
Till vermin or the draff° of servile food
Consume me, and oft-invocated death
Hasten the welcome end of all my pains.
    MANOA   Wilt thou then serve the Philistines with that gift
Which was expressly given thee to annoy° them?
Better at home lie bed-rid, not only idle,
580   Inglorious, unemployed, with age outworn.
But God, who caused a fountain at thy prayer
From the dry ground to spring,° thy thirst to allay
After the brunt of battle, can as easy
Cause light again within thy eyes to spring,
Wherewith to serve him better than thou hast;
And I persuade me so; why else this strength
Miraculous yet remaining in those locks?
His might continues in thee not for naught,
Nor shall his wondrous gifts be frustrate° thus.
590   SAMSON   All otherwise to me my thoughts portend,
That these dark orbs no more shall treat with light,
Nor the other light of life continue long,
But yield to double darkness nigh at hand:
So much I feel my genial spirits° droop,
My hopes all flat; nature within me seems
In all her functions weary of herself;
My race of glory run, and race of shame,
And I shall shortly be with them that rest.
    MANOA   Believe not these suggestions,° which proceed
600   From anguish of the mind and humours black,°
That mingle with thy fancy. I however
Must not omit a father's timely care
To prosecute the means of thy deliverance
By ransom or how else: meanwhile be calm,
And healing words from these thy friends admit.
    SAMSON   O that torment should not be confined
To the body's wounds and sores,

---

a gaze something to be stared at
redundant flowing; serving no purpose
Robustious robust, flourishing
craze enfeeble
draff refuse, garbage
annoy molest

But God . . . spring Judges 15:18–19
frustrate rendered vain
genial spirits vital and generative powers
suggestions modern sense, plus "temptations"
humours black Melancholy was the black humor.

With maladies innumerable
In heart, head, breast, and reins;°
610 But must secret passage find
To the inmost mind,
There exercise all his fierce accidents,°
And on her purest spirits prey,
As on entrails, joints, and limbs,
With answerable° pains, but more intense,
Though void of corporal sense.
   My griefs not only pain me
As a lingering disease,
But finding no redress, ferment and rage,
620 Nor less than wounds immedicable
Rankle, and fester, and gangrene,
To black mortification.°
Thoughts, my tormentors, armed with deadly stings
Mangle my apprehensive° tenderest parts,
Exasperate, exulcerate, and raise
Dire inflammation which no cooling herb
Or med'cinal liquor can assuage,
Nor breath of vernal air from snowy alp.
Sleep hath forsook and given me o'er
630 To death's benumbing opium as my only cure.
Thence faintings, swoonings of despair,
And sense of heaven's desertion.
   I was his nursling once and choice delight,
His destined from the womb,
Promised by heavenly message twice descending.°
Under his special eye
Abstemious I grew up and thrived amain;
He led me on to mightiest deeds
Above the nerve° of mortal arm
640 Against the uncircumcised, our enemies.
But now hath cast me off as never known,
And to those cruel enemies,
Whom I by his appointment had provoked,
Left me all helpless with the irreparable loss
Of sight, reserved alive to be repeated°
The subject of their cruelty or scorn.
Nor am I in the list of them that hope;
Hopeless are all my evils, all remediless;
This one prayer yet remains, might I be heard,
650 No long petition—speedy death,
The close of all my miseries, and the balm.

---

reins kidneys
accidents symptoms
answerable corresponding
mortification gangrene

apprehensive sensitive
twice descending See l. 361n.
nerve sinew; strength
repeated talked of as

CHORUS   Many are the sayings of the wise
In ancient and in modern books enrolled,
Extolling patience as the truest fortitude;
And to the bearing well of all calamities,
All chances incident to man's frail life,
Consolatories° writ
With studied argument, and much persuasion sought,
Lenient° of grief and anxious thought;
660 But with the afflicted in his pangs their sound
Little prevails, or rather seems a tune
Harsh, and of dissonant mood° from his complaint,
Unless he feel within
Some source of consolation from above,
Secret refreshings that repair his strength,
And fainting spirits uphold.
    God of our fathers, what is man!°
That thou towards him with hand so various—
Or might I say contrarious?—
670 Temper'st thy providence through his short course,
Not evenly, as thou rul'st
The angelic orders and inferior creatures mute,
Irrational and brute.°
Nor do I name of men the common rout,
That wandering loose about
Grow up and perish, as the summer fly,
Heads without name no more remembered;
But such as thou hast solemnly elected,
With gifts and graces eminently adorned
680 To some great work, thy glory,
And people's safety, which in part they effect;
Yet toward these thus dignified, thou oft
Amidst their highth of noon
Changest thy countenance and thy hand, with no regard
Of highest favours past
From thee on them, or them to thee of service.
    Nor only dost degrade them, or remit
To life obscured, which were a fair dismission,°
But throw'st them lower than thou didst exalt them high,
690 Unseemly falls in human eye,
Too grievous for the trespass or omission;
Oft leav'st them to the hostile sword

Consolatories writings intended to console in distress
Lenient soothing
mood a pun on a term both musical and spiritual
what is man "What is man, that thou art mindful of him?" (Psalms 8:4)
That thou . . . brute (ll. 667–73) Here the uncomprehending complaint against God for maltreating his champions takes the form of the old complaint that in the orders of angel and beast, between which men stand, there is no similar problem; the angels understand intuitively their duties, and the beasts, lacking reason, are spared both moral choices and God's election.
dismission dismissal

Of heathen and profane, their carcasses
To dogs and fowls a prey, or else captíved,
Or to the unjust tribunals, under change of times,
And condemnation of the ingrateful multitude.°
If these they scape, perhaps in poverty
With sickness and disease thou bow'st them down,
Painful diseases and deformed,
In crude° old age;
Though not disordinate, yet causeless suffering
The punishment of dissolute days;° in fine,
Just or unjust, alike seem miserable,
For oft alike, both come to evil end.
    So deal not with this once thy glorious champion,
The image of thy strength, and mighty minister.
What do I beg? How hast thou dealt already?
Behold him in this state calamitous, and turn
His labours, for thou canst, to peaceful end.
    But who is this, what thing of sea or land?
Female of sex it seems,
That so bedecked, ornate, and gay,
Comes this way sailing
Like a stately ship
Of Tarsus,° bound for the isles
Of Javan or Gadire,°
With all her bravery on, and tackle trim,
Sails filled, and streamers waving,
Courted by all the winds that hold them play,
An amber scent of odorous perfume
Her harbinger,° a damsel train behind;
Some rich Philistian matron she may seem,
And now at nearer view, no other certain
Than Dálila thy wife.
    SAMSON My wife, my traitress, let her not come near me.
    CHORUS Yet on she moves, now stands and eyes thee fixed,
About to have spoke; but now, with head declined
Like a fair flower surcharged with dew, she weeps,
And words addressed seem into tears dissolved,
Wetting the borders of her silken veil;
But now again she makes address° to speak.
    DALILA With doubtful° feet and wavering resolution

700

710

720

730

Oft leav'st . . . multitude It is often remarked
(by those who take *Samson Agonistes* to be a
late work) that Milton must have had in mind
the sufferings of the Commonwealth leaders
after the Restoration—including his own, which
included diseases of the kind mentioned immediately afterward.
crude premature
Though . . . days not themselves intemperate,
they nevertheless suffer diseases thought to be
the penalty of dissolute living (such as Milton's
gout)
Tarsus Tarshish (Isaiah 23:1), a Spanish port
(Tarsus, birthplace of St. Paul, was a port in
Turkey)
Javan or Gadire the Ionian isles of Greece, and
Cadiz
An amber . . . harbinger scent of ambergris,
which precedes her like a herald
makes address prepares
doubtful doubting

I came, still dreading thy displeasure, Samson,
Which to have merited, without excuse,
I cannot but acknowledge; yet if tears
May expiate (though the fact° more evil drew
In the perverse event° than I foresaw),
My penance° hath not slackened, though my pardon°
No way assured. But conjugal affection,
740   Prevailing over fear and timorous doubt,
Hath led me on, desirous to behold
Once more thy face, and know of thy estate;°
If aught in my ability may serve
To lighten what thou suffer'st, and appease
Thy mind with what amends is in my power,
Though late, yet in some part to recompense
My rash but more unfortunate misdeed.
        SAMSON   Out, out, hyena!° These are thy wonted arts,
And arts of every woman false like thee,
750   To break all faith, all vows, deceive, betray;
Then as repentant to submit, beseech,
And reconcilement move° with feigned remorse,
Confess, and promise wonders in her change,
Not truly penitent, but chief to try
Her husband, how far urged his patience bears,
His virtue or weakness which way to assail;
Then with more cautious and instructed skill
Again transgresses, and again submits;
That wisest and best men, full oft beguiled,
760   With goodness principled not to reject
The penitent, but ever to forgive,
Are drawn to wear out miserable days,
Entangled with a poisonous bosom snake,°
If not by quick destruction soon cut off,
As I by thee, to ages an example.
        DALILA   Yet hear me, Samson; not that I endeavour
To lessen or extenuate my offense,
But that on the other side if it be weighed
By itself, with aggravations° not surcharged,
770   Or else with just allowance counterpoised,
I may, if possible, thy pardon find
The easier towards me, or thy hatred less.
First granting, as I do, it was a weakness
In me, but incident to all our sex,
Curiosity, inquisitive, importúne

---

fact deed
perverse event unhappy outcome
penance penitence
pardon "Be" is understood in this latinate
construction.
estate condition

hyena The hyena was thought to imitate the
human voice and so lure men to destruction.
move propose
bosom snake "nourish a viper in one's bosom"
(proverb)
aggravations exaggerations

Of° secrets, then with like infirmity
To publish them, both common female faults;
Was it not weakness also to make known
For importunity, that is for naught,
780   Wherein consisted all thy strength and safety?
To what I did thou show'dst me first the way.
But I to enemies revealed, and should not?
Nor shouldst thou have trusted that to woman's frailty:
Ere I to thee, thou to thyself wast cruel.
Let weakness then with weakness come to parle,°
So near related, or the same of kind;°
Thine forgive mine, that men may censure thine
The gentler, if severely thou exact not
More strength from me than in thyself was found.
790   And what if love, which thou interpret'st hate,
The jealousy of love, powerful of sway
In human hearts, nor less in mine towards thee,
Caused what I did? I saw thee mutable
Of fancy,° feared lest one day thou wouldst leave me
As her at Timna, sought by all means therefore
How to endear, and hold thee to me firmest:
No better way I saw than by impórtuning
To learn thy secrets, get into my power
Thy key of strength and safety. Thou wilt say,
800   'Why then revealed?' I was assured by those
Who tempted me that nothing was designed
Against thee but safe custody and hold:
That made for me;° I knew that liberty
Would draw thee forth to perilous enterprises,
While I at home sat full of cares and fears,
Wailing thy absence in my widowed bed;
Here I should still enjoy thee day and night,
Mine and love's prisoner, not the Philistines',
Whole to myself, unhazarded abroad,
810   Fearless at home of partners in my love.
These reasons in love's law have passed for good,
Though fond° and reasonless to some perhaps;
And love hath oft, well meaning, wrought much woe,
Yet always pity or pardon hath obtained.
Be not unlike all others, not austere
As thou art strong, inflexible as steel.
If thou in strength all mortals dost exceed,
In uncompassionate anger do not so.
    SAMSON   How cunningly the sorceress displays
820   Her own transgressions, to upbraid me mine!

importune Of persistent in inquiry concerning   fancy affection
parle parley   made for me was to my advantage
kind nature   fond foolish

That malice, not repentance, brought thee hither,
By this appears: I gave, thou say'st, the example,
I led the way—bitter reproach, but true;
I to myself was false ere thou to me;
Such pardon therefore as I give my folly,
Take to thy wicked deed; which° when thou seest
Impartial, self-severe, inexorable,
Thou wilt renounce thy seeking, and much rather
Confess it feigned. Weakness is thy excuse,
830 And I believe it, weakness to resist
Philistian gold; if weakness may excuse,
What murtherer, what traitor, parricide,
Incestuous, sacrilegious, but may plead it?
All wickedness is weakness: that plea therefore
With God or man will gain thee no remission.
But love constrained thee? Call it furious rage
To satisfy thy lust: love seeks to have love;
My love how couldst thou hope, who took'st the way
To raise in me inexpiable hate,
840 Knowing, as needs I must, by thee betrayed?°
In vain thou striv'st to cover shame with shame,
Or by evasions thy crime uncover'st more.
      DALILA   Since thou determin'st weakness for no plea
In man or woman, though to thy own condemning,
Hear what assaults I had, what snares besides,
What sieges girt me round, ere I consented;
Which might have awed the best-resolved of men,
The constantest, to have yielded without blame.
It was not gold, as to my charge thou lay'st,
850 That wrought with me: thou know'st the magistrates
And princes of my country came in person,
Solicited, commanded, threatened, urged,
Adjured by all the bonds of civil duty
And of religion, pressed how just it was,
How honourable, how glorious to entrap
A common enemy, who had destroyed
Such numbers of our nation: and the priest°
Was not behind, but ever at my ear,
Preaching how meritorious with the gods
860 It would be to ensnare an irreligious
Dishonourer of Dagon. What had I
To oppose against such powerful arguments?
Only my love of thee held long debate;
And combated in silence all these reasons
With hard contést. At length that grounded° maxim,

which Refers to "pardon" in l. 825.   priest an addition to the biblical story
Knowing . . . betrayed knowing myself to   grounded well-established
have beeen betrayed by you

So rife and celebrated in the mouths
Of wisest men, that to the public good
Private respects° must yield, with grave authority
Took full possession of me and prevailed;
870   Virtue, as I thought, truth, duty, so enjoining.
      SAMSON   I thought where all thy circling wiles would end,
In feigned religion, smooth hypocrisy.
But had thy love, still odiously pretended,
Been, as it ought, sincere, it would have taught thee
Far other reasonings, brought forth other deeds.
I before all the daughters of my tribe
And of my nation chose thee from among
My enemies, loved thee, as too well thou knewest,
Too well; unbosomed all my secrets to thee,
880   Not out of levity, but overpowered
By thy request, who could deny thee nothing;
Yet now am judged an enemy. Why then
Didst thou at first receive me for thy husband,
Then, as since then, thy country's foe professed?
Being once a wife, for me thou wast to leave
Parents and country; nor was I their subject,
Nor under their protection, but my own;
Thou mine, not theirs. If aught against my life
Thy country sought of thee, it sought unjustly,
890   Against the law of nature, law of nations;
No more thy country, but an impious crew
Of men conspiring to uphold their state
By worse than hostile deeds, violating the ends
For which our country is a name so dear;
Not therefore to be obeyed. But zeal moved thee;
To please thy gods thou didst it; gods unable
To acquit themselves° and prosecute their foes
But by ungodly deeds, the contradiction
Of their own deity, gods cannot be:
900   Less therefore to be pleased, obeyed, or feared.
These false pretexts and varnished colours° failing,
Bare in thy guilt how foul must thou appear!
      DALILA   In argument with men a woman ever
Goes by the worse,° whatever be her cause.
      SAMSON   For want of words, no doubt, or lack of breath;
Witness when I was worried with thy peals.
      DALILA   I was a fool, too rash, and quite mistaken
In what I thought would have succeeded best.
Let me obtain forgiveness of thee, Samson;
910   Afford me place to show what recompense
Towards thee I intend for what I have misdone,

respects interests	**varnished colours** false arguments
acquit themselves maintain their positions	**Goes by the worse** gets the worst of it

Misguided; only what remains past cure
Bear not too sensibly,° nor still insist
To afflict thyself in vain. Though sight be lost,
Life yet hath many solaces, enjoyed
Where other senses want not their delights
At home in leisure and domestic ease,
Exempt from many a care and chance to which
Eyesight exposes daily men abroad.
920   I to the lords will intercede, not doubting
Their favourable ear, that I may fetch thee
From forth this loathsome prison-house, to abide
With me, where my redoubled love and care
With nursing diligence, to me glad office,
May ever tend about thee to old age
With all things grateful° cheered, and so supplied,
That what by me thou hast lost thou least shall miss.
     SAMSON   No, no, of my condition take no care;
It fits not; thou and I long since are twain;
930   Nor think me so unwary or accurst
To bring my feet again into the snare
Where once I have been caught; I know thy trains,°
Though dearly to my cost, thy gins,° and toils;
Thy fair enchanted cup and warbling charms°
No more on me have power, their force is nulled;°
So much of adder's wisdom° I have learnt
To fence my ear against thy sorceries.
If in my flower of youth and strength, when all men
Loved, honoured, feared me, thou alone could hate me,
940   Thy husband, slight me, sell me, and forgo me,
How wouldst thou use me now, blind, and thereby
Deceivable, in most things as a child
Helpless, thence easily contemned, and scorned,
And last neglected? How wouldst thou insult
When I must live uxorious to thy will
In perfect thraldom, how again betray me,
Bearing my words and doings to the lords
To gloss° upon, and censuring, frown or smile?
This jail I count the house of liberty
950   To° thine whose doors my feet shall never enter.
     DALILA   Let me approach at least, and touch thy hand.
     SAMSON   Not for thy life, lest fierce remembrance wake
My sudden rage to tear thee joint by joint.
At distance I forgive thee, go with that;

---

sensibly feelingly, sensitively
grateful pleasing
trains tricks
gins traps
fair . . . charms attributing to Dalila the instruments of Circe (see *Comus*, ll. 51–53, and
Spenser, *The Faerie Queene* II.xii)

nulled nullified, extinguished
adder's wisdom ". . . they are like the deaf
adder that stoppeth her ear; Which will not
hearken to the voice of charmers" (Psalms 58:
4f.)
gloss comment
To compared with

Bewail thy falsehood, and the pious works
It hath brought forth to make thee memorable
Among illustrious women, faithful wives;
Cherish thy hastened widowhood with the gold
Of matrimonial treason: so farewell.
960   DALILA   I see thou art implacable, more deaf
To prayers than winds and seas; yet winds to seas
Are reconciled at length, and sea to shore:
Thy anger, unappeasable, still rages,
Eternal tempest never to be calmed.
Why do I humble thus myself, and suing
For peace, reap nothing but repulse and hate?
Bid go with evil omen° and the brand
Of infamy upon my name denounced?
To mix with thy concernments I desist
970   Henceforth, nor too much disapprove my own.
Fame, if not double-faced, is double-mouthed,
And with contráry blast proclaims most deeds;
On both his wings, one black, the other white,
Bears greatest names in his wild airy flight.°
My name perhaps among the circumcised
In Dan,° in Judah, and the bordering tribes,
To all posterity may stand defamed,
With malediction mentioned, and the blot
Of falsehood most unconjugal traduced.
980   But in my country where I most desire,
In Ekron, Gaza, Asdod, and in Gath,°
I shall be named among the famousest
Of women, sung at solemn festivals,
Living and dead recorded, who, to save
Her country from a fierce destroyer, chose
Above the faith of wedlock bands, my tomb
With odours° visited and annual flowers:
Not less renowned than in Mount Ephraim
Jael, who with inhospitable guile
990   Smote Sisera sleeping, through the temples nailed.°
Nor shall I count it heinous to enjoy
The public marks of honour and reward
Conferred upon me for the piety°
Which to my country I was judged to have shown.
At this whoever envies or repines,
I leave him to his lot, and like my own.
CHORUS   She's gone, a manifest serpent by her sting

---

evil omen predictions of bad luck
Fame . . . flight This allegory of Fame differs
in some ways from the conventional, and Milton
must have invented it.
Dan Samson's own tribe
Ekron . . . Gath principal cities of the Philistines

odours spices
Jael . . . nailed Jael allowed Sisera, a Philistine general, to hide in her tent. While he
was sleeping she knocked a nail into his head;
the story is in Deborah's song, Judges 5.
piety from the Latin pietas, meaning devotion
to one's country

Discovered in the end, till now concealed.

SAMSON   So let her go; God sent her to debase me,

1000 And aggravate my folly who committed

To such a viper his most sacred trust

Of secrecy, my safety, and my life.

CHORUS   Yet beauty, though injurious, hath strange power,

After offence returning, to regain

Love once possessed, nor can be easily

Repulsed, without much inward passion° felt

And secret sting of amorous remorse.

SAMSON   Love-quarrels oft in pleasing concord end,

Not wedlock-treachery endangering life.

1010 CHORUS   It is not virtue, wisdom, valour, wit,

Strength, comeliness of shape, or amplest merit

That woman's love can win or long inherit;°

But what it is, hard is to say,

Harder to hit,

(Which way soever men refer it),

Much like thy riddle,° Samson, in one day

Or seven, though one should musing sit;

If any of these, or all, the Timnian bride

Had not so soon preferred

1020 Thy paranymph,° worthless to thee compared,

Successor in thy bed,

Nor both° so loosely disallied

Their nuptials, nor this last so treacherously

Had shorn the fatal harvest of thy head.

Is it for that° such outward ornament

Was lavished on their sex, that inward gifts

Were left for haste unfinished, judgment scant,

Capacity not raised to apprehend

Or value what is best

1030 In choice, but oftest to affect° the wrong?

Or was too much of self-love mixed,

Of constancy no root infixed,

That either they love nothing, or not long?

Whate'er it be, to wisest men and best

Seeming at first all heavenly under virgin veil,

Soft, modest, meek, demure,

Once joined, the contrary she proves, a thorn

Intestine,° far within defensive arms

A cleaving° mischief, in his way to virtue

1040 Adverse and turbulent; or by her charms

passion suffering
inherit possess
riddle the riddle of the lion and the honey-comb, which caused the breakup of Samson's first marriage (Judges 14)
paranymph groomsman, companion of the bride-

groom, to whom Samson's wife turned (Judges 14:20) for consolation
both both wives
for that because
affect desire
Intestine domestic
cleaving closely fitting, enwrapping, hindering

Draws him awry enslaved
With dotage, and his sense depraved
To folly and shameful deeds which ruin ends.
What pilot so expert but needs must wreck,
Embarked with such a steers-mate at the helm?
   Favoured of heaven who finds
One virtuous, rarely found,
That in domestic good combines:
Happy that house! his way to peace is smooth;
1050 But virtue which breaks through all opposition,
And all temptation can remove,
Most shines and most is ácceptáble above.
   Therefore God's universal law
Gave to the man despotic power
Over his female in due awe,
Nor from that right to part an hour,
Smile she or lour:°
So shall he least confusion draw
On his whole life, not swayed
1060 By female usurpation, nor dismayed.°
   But had we best retire? I see a storm.
   SAMSON   Fair days have oft contracted wind and rain.
   CHORUS   But this another kind of tempest brings.
   SAMSON   Be less abstruse, my riddling days are past.
   CHORUS   Look now for no enchanting voice, nor fear
The bait of honied words; a rougher tongue
Draws hitherward; I know him by his stride,
The giant Hárapha° of Gath, his look
Haughty as is his pile° high-built and proud.
1070 Comes he in peace? What wind hath blown him hither
I less conjecture than when first I saw
The sumptuous Dálila floating this way;
His habit carries peace, his brow defiance.
   SAMSON   Or peace or not, alike to me he comes.
   CHORUS   His fraught° we soon shall know, he now arrives.
   HARAPHA   I come not, Samson, to condole thy chance,
As these perhaps, yet wish it had not been,
Though for no friendly intent. I am of Gath;
Men call me Hárapha, of stock renowned

---

lour frown
Is it . . . dismayed In this "misogynist" chorus (ll. 1025–60) Milton both repeats some traditional antifeminist positions and echoes his own complaints in the pamphlets on divorce. In 1046 ff. he remembers Proverbs 31 on virtuous wives ("The heart of her husband doth safely trust in her . . . she will do him good and not evil all the days of her life," etc.). Samson was used as a negative example in discussions about good marriages. Milton, despite his own disappointments, took a more exalted view of marriage than many contemporaries, and perhaps lets the Chorus state the argument against wives as gloomily as possible for dramatic reasons: they are again showing no understanding of the reality of Samson's position, nor of the reason that he married Dalila. **Harapha** not in the biblical story; Milton made him up from the Hebrew for giant and the exploits of Goliath.
pile building, here probably meaning Gath
fraught freight, message

1080   As Og or Anak and the Emims old
    That Kiriathaim held;° thou knowest me now,
    If thou at all art known.° Much I have heard
    Of thy prodigious might and feats performed
    Incredible to me, in this displeased,
    That I was never present on the place
    Of those encounters where we might have tried
    Each other's force in camp° or listed field:°
    And now am come to see of whom such noise
    Hath walked° about, and each limb to survey,
1090   If thy appearance answer loud report.
        SAMSON   The way to know were not to see but taste.
        HARAPHA   Dost thou already single° me? I thought
    Gyves° and the mill had tamed thee. O that fortune
    Had brought me to the field where thou art famed
    To have wrought such wonders with an ass's jaw;
    I should have forced thee soon wish other arms,
    Or left thy carcass where the ass lay thrown:
    So had the glory of prowess been recovered
    To Palestine, won by a Philistine
1100   From the unforeskinned race, of whom thou bear'st
    The highest name for valiant acts; that honour,
    Certain to have won by mortal duel from thee.
    I lose, prevented by thy eyes put out.
        SAMSON   Boast not of what thou wouldst have done, but do
    What then thou wouldst; thou seest it in thy hand.
        HARAPHA   To combat with a blind man I disdain,
    And thou hast need much washing to be touched.
        SAMSON   Such usage as your honourable lords
    Afford me, assassinated° and betrayed;
1110   Who durst not with their whole united powers
    In fight withstand me single and unarmed,
    Nor in the house with chamber ambushes
    Close-banded° durst attack me, no, not sleeping,
    Till they had hired a woman with their gold,
    Breaking her marriage faith to circumvent me.
    Therefore without feigned shifts° let be assigned
    Some narrow place enclosed, where sight may give thee,
    Or rather flight, no great advantage on me;
    Then put on all thy gorgeous arms, thy helmet
1120   And brigandine° of brass, thy broad habergeon,°

Og . . . held "Only Og king of Bashan remained of the . . . giants" (Deuteronomy 3:11); "the giants, the sons of Anak" (Numbers 13:33); "The Emims . . . were accounted giants" (Deuteronomy 2:10–11); "the Emims in Shaveh Kiriathaim" (Genesis 14:5)
If . . . known if you know anything at all
camp field
listed field equipped with lists for jousting

walked gone
single pick me out (as opponent)
Gyves fetters
assassinated treacherously attacked
Close-banded secretly associated
shifts tricks
brigandine ringed body-armor
habergeon coat of mail

Vant-brace° and greaves,° and gauntlet; add thy spear,
A weaver's beam,° and seven-times-folded shield;°
I only with an oaken staff will meet thee,
And raise such outcries on thy clattered iron,
Which long shall not withhold me from thy head,
That in a little time while breath remains thee,
Thou oft shalt wish thyself at Gath to boast
Again in safety what thou wouldst have done
To Samson, but shalt never see Gath more.

1130   HARAPHA   Thou durst not thus disparage glorious arms
Which greatest heroes have in battle worn,
Their ornament and safety, had not spells
And black enchantments, some magician's art,
Armed thee or charmed thee strong, which thou from heaven
Feign'dst at thy birth was given thee in thy hair,
Where strength can least abide, though all thy hairs
Were bristles ranged like those that ridge the back
Of chafed° wild boars, or ruffled porcupines.

      SAMSON   I know no spells, use no forbidden arts;°
1140 My trust is in the living God who gave me
At my nativity this strength, diffused
No less through all my sinews, joints and bones,
Than thine, while I preserved these locks unshorn,
The pledge of my unviolated vow.
For proof hereof, if Dagon be thy god,
Go to his temple, invocate his aid
With solemnest devotion, spread before him
How highly it concerns his glory now
To frustrate and dissolve these magic spells,
1150 Which I to be the power of Israel's God
Avow, and challenge Dagon to the test,
Offering to combat thee, his champion bold,
With the utmost of his godhead seconded:
Then thou shalt see, or rather to thy sorrow
Soon feel, whose God is strongest, thine or mine.

      HARAPHA   Presume not on thy God, whate'er he be;
Thee he regards not, owns not, hath cut off
Quite from his people, and delivered up
Into thy enemies' hand; permitted them
1160 To put out both thine eyes and fettered send thee
Into the common prison, there to grind
Among the slaves and asses, thy comrádes,
As good for nothing else, no better service
With those thy boisterous° locks; no worthy match

Vant-brace armor for forearm
greaves thigh-armor
weaver's beam wooden roller in loom (the armor comes from the description of Goliath in I Samuel 17)

shield recalling that of Ajax in Homer
chafed angry
forbidden arts Duelists were required to swear that they would use no magic.
boisterous thick-growing

For valour to assail, nor by the sword
Of noble warrior, so to stain his honour,°
But by the barber's razor best subdued.
    SAMSON   All these indignities, for such they are
From thine,° these evils I deserve and more,
1170   Acknowledge them from God inflicted on me
Justly, yet despair not of his final pardon
Whose ear is ever open, and his eye
Gracious to readmit the suppliant;
In confidence whereof I once again
Defy° thee to the trial of mortal fight,
By combat to decide whose god is God,
Thine or whom I with Israel's sons adore.
    HARAPHA   Fair honour that thou dost thy God, in trusting
He will accept thee to defend his cause,
1180   A murderer, a revolter, and a robber.
    SAMSON   Tongue-doughty° giant, how dost thou prove me these?
    HARAPHA   Is not thy nation subject to our lords?
Their magistrates confessed it, when they took thee
As a league-breaker and delivered bound
Into our hands:° for hadst thou not committed
Notorious murder on those thirty men
At Ascalon, who never did thee harm,
Then like a robber stripp'dst them of their robes?°
The Philistines, when thou hadst broke the league,
1190   Went up with armèd powers thee only seeking,
To others did no violence nor spoil.
    SAMSON   Among the daughters of the Philistines
I chose a wife, which argued me no foe,
And in your city held my nuptial feast;
But your ill-meaning politician° lords,
Under pretence of bridal friends and guests,
Appointed to await me thirty spies,
Who threatening cruel death constrained the bride
To wring from me and tell to them my secret,
1200   That solved the riddle which I had proposed.
When I perceived all set on enmity,
As on my enemies, wherever chanced,
I used hostility, and took their spoil
To pay my underminers in their coin.
My nation was subjected to your lords.
It was the force of conquest; force with force
Is well ejected when the conquered can.
But I a private person, whom my country

honour Milton gives Harapha some of the punctilio of the kind of courtier he hated.
thine your people
Defy challenge to combat, as in the medieval tradition of trying justice by means of a joust

Tongue-doughty brave in speech
delivered . . . hands See l. 258n.
stripp'dst . . . robes See l. 221n.
politician Machiavellian

As a league-breaker gave up bound, presumed
1210   Single rebellion and did hostile acts.
I was no private but a person raised
With strength sufficient and command from heaven
To free my country; if their servile minds
Me their deliverer sent would not receive,
But to their masters gave me up for naught,
The unworthier they; whence to this day they serve.
I was to do my part from heaven assigned,
And had performed it if my known offence
Had not disabled me, not all your force.
1220   These shifts° refuted, answer thy appellant,°
Though by his blindness maimed for high attempts,
Who now defies thee thrice to single fight,
As a petty enterprise of small enforce.°

HARAPHA   With thee, a man condemned, a slave enrolled,
Due by the law to capital punishment?
To fight with thee no man of arms will deign.

SAMSON   Cam'st thou for this, vain boaster, to survey me,
To descant° on my strength, and give thy verdict?
Come nearer, part not hence so slight informed;
1230   But take good heed my hand survey not thee.

HARAPHA   O Baal-zebub!° can my ears unused°
Hear these dishonours, and not render death?

SAMSON   No man withholds thee, nothing from thy hand
Fear I incurable; bring up thy van;°
My heels are fettered, but my fist is free.

HARAPHA   This insolence other kind of answer fits.

SAMSON   Go, baffled coward, lest I run upon thee,
Though in these chains, bulk without spirit vast,
And with one buffet lay thy structure low,
1240   Or swing thee in the air, then dash thee down
To the hazard of thy brains and shattered sides.

HARAPHA   By Astaroth,° ere long thou shalt lament
These braveries° in irons loaden on thee.

CHORUS   His giantship is gone somewhat crestfallen,
Stalking with less unconscionable° strides,
And lower looks, but in a sultry chafe.°

SAMSON   I dread him not, nor all his giant brood,
Though fame divulge him father of five sons,
All of gigantic size, Goliah chief.°
1250   CHORUS   He will directly to the lords, I fear,

shifts dishonest arguments
appellant challenger
enforce effort
descant play variations on
Baal-zebub (probably) Beelzebub, lord of the
flies, a Philistine idol
unused unaccustomed
van vanguard

Astaroth Philistine moon goddess
braveries boasts
unconscionable excessive
sultry chafe sullen temper
father . . . chief II Samuel 21.16 ff. describes
four Philistine giants killed by David, but of
course makes no mention of Harapha.

And with malicious counsel stir them up
Some way or other yet further to afflict thee.
    SAMSON   He must allege some cause, and offered fight
Will not dare mention, lest a question rise
Whether he durst accept the offer or not,
And that he durst not plain enough appeared.
Much more affliction than already felt
They cannot well impose, nor I sustain,
If they intend advantage of my labours,
1260 The work of many hands, which earns my keeping
With no small profit daily to my owners.
But come what will, my deadliest foe will prove
My speediest friend, by death to rid me hence,
The worst that he can give, to me the best.
Yet so it may fall out, because their end
Is hate, not help to me, it may with mine
Draw their own ruin who attempt the deed.°
    CHORUS   Oh how comely it is and how reviving
To the spirits of just men long oppressed,
1270 When God into the hands of their deliverer
Puts invincible might
To quell the mighty of the earth, the oppressor,
The brute and boisterous force of violent men,
Hardy and industrious to support
Tyrannic power, but raging to pursue
The righteous and all such as honour truth!
He all their ammunition°
And feats of war defeats
With plain heroic magnitude of mind
1280 And celestial vigour armed;
Their armories and magazines contemns,
Renders them useless, while
With wingèd expedition
Swift as the lightning glance he executes
His errand on the wicked, who surprised
Lose their defence, distracted and amazed.
    But patience is more oft the exercise
Of saints, the trial of their fortitude,°
Making them each his own deliverer,
1290 And victor over all
That tyranny or fortune can inflict;
Either of these is in thy lot,
Samson, with might endued
Above the sons of men; but sight bereaved

---

yet so . . . deed Samson has a premonition
of the sequel; the Chorus comments, but soon
abandons the idea that this kind of heroic act
is still open to Samson.

ammunition military stores
patience . . . fortitude Of the two heroisms,
passive and active, the Chorus wrongly opts for
the first.

May chance to number thee with those
Whom patience finally must crown.
    This idol's day° hath been to thee no day of rest,
Labouring thy mind
More than the working day thy hands;
1300 And yet perhaps more trouble is behind.
For I descry this way
Some other tending; in his hand
A sceptre or quaint° staff he bears,
Comes on amain, speed in his look.
By his habit I discern him now
A public officer, and now at hand.
His message will be short and voluble.°
     OFFICER   Hebrews, the prisoner Samson here I seek.
     CHORUS   His manacles remark° him; there he sits.
1310   OFFICER   Samson, to thee our lords thus bid me say:
This day to Dagon is a solemn feast,
With sacrifices, triumph, pomp, and games;
Thy strength they know surpassing human rate,
And now some public proof thereof require
To honour this great feast, and great assembly;
Rise therefore with all speed and come along,
Where I will see thee heartened and fresh clad
To appear as fits before the illustrious lords.
     SAMSON   Thou knowest I am an Hebrew, therefore tell them
1320 Our law forbids at their religious rites
My presence; for that cause I cannot come.
     OFFICER   This answer, be assured, will not content them.
     SAMSON   Have they not sword-players, and every sort
Of gymnic artists, wrestlers, riders, runners,
Jugglers and dancers, antics,° mummers,° mimics,
But they must pick me out with shackles tired,
And over-laboured at their public mill,
To make them sport with blind activity?
Do they not seek occasion of new quarrels,
1330 On my refusal, to distress me more,
Or make a game of my calamities?
Return the way thou cam'st; I will not come.
     OFFICER   Regard thyself;° this will offend them highly.
     SAMSON   Myself? My conscience and internal peace.
Can they think me so broken, so debased
With corporal servitude, that my mind ever
Will condescend to such absurd commands?
Although their drudge, to be their fool or jester,
And in my midst of sorrow and heart-grief

---

idol's day on the analogy of holy-day, holiday   antics clowns
quaint elaborately carved   mummers actors
voluble rapid   Regard thyself look to your own interests
remark indicate

¹³⁴⁰ To show them feats and play before their god,
The worst of all indignities, yet on me
Joined° with extreme contempt? I will not come.
 OFFICER My message was imposed on me with speed,
Brooks no delay; is this thy resolution?
  SAMSON So take it with what speed thy message needs.
  OFFICER I am sorry what this stoutness° will produce.
  SAMSON Perhaps thou shalt have cause to sorrow indeed.
  CHORUS Consider, Samson; matters now are strained
Up to the highth, whether to hold or break;
¹³⁵⁰ He's gone, and who knows how he may report
Thy words by adding fuel to the flame?
Expect another message more imperious,
More lordly thundering than thou well wilt bear.
  SAMSON Shall I abuse this consecrated gift
Of strength, again returning with my hair
After my great transgression, so requite
Favour renewed, and add a greater sin
By prostituting holy things to idols;
A Nazarite in place abominable
¹³⁶⁰ Vaunting my strength in honour to their Dagon?
Besides, how vile, contemptible, ridiculous,
What act more execrably unclean, profane?
  CHORUS Yet with this strength thou serv'st the Philistines,
Idolatrous, uncircumcised, unclean.
  SAMSON Not in their idol-worship, but by labour
Honest and lawful to deserve my food
Of those who have me in their civil power.
  CHORUS Where the heart joins not, outward acts defile not.
  SAMSON Where outward force constrains, the sentence° holds;
¹³⁷⁰ But who constrains me to the temple of Dagon,
Not dragging? The Philistian lords command.
Commands are no constraints. If I obey them,
I do it freely, venturing to displease
God for the fear of man, and man prefer,
Set God behind; which in his jealousy
Shall never, unrepented, find forgiveness.
Yet that he may dispense with° me or thee,
Present in temples at idolatrous rites
For some important cause, thou need'st not doubt.
¹³⁸⁰   CHORUS How thou wilt here come off surmounts my reach.
  SAMSON Be of good courage; I begin to feel
Some rousing motions° in me which dispose
To something extraordinary my thoughts.

Joined enjoined, commanded
stoutness stubbornness
sentence saying, maxim
dispense with grant a dispensation to; Samson
is beginning to form a different plan
rousing motions He is recognizing an "intimate

impulse" like those which caused his marriages;
it, too, will send him among the Philistines and
put him in a position in which he seems to be
breaking Hebrew law; and of course the end—
the killing of Philistines—is the same, and
part of God's concealed plan for his champion.

I with this messenger will go along,
Nothing to do, be sure, that may dishonour
Our law, or stain my vow of Nazarite.
If there be aught of presage in the mind,
This day will be remarkable in my life
By some great act, or of my days the last.°
1390   CHORUS   In time thou hast resolved; the man returns.
        OFFICER   Samson, this second message from our lords
To thee I am bid say: art thou our slave,
Our captive, at the public mill our drudge,
And dar'st thou at our sending and command
Dispute thy coming? Come without delay;
Or we shall find such engines to assail
And hamper thee, as thou shalt come of° force,
Though thou wert firmlier fastened than a rock.
        SAMSON   I could be well content to try their art,
1400   Which to no few of them would prove pernicious.
Yet knowing their advantages too many,
Because° they shall not trail me through their streets
Like a wild beast, I am content to go.
Masters' commands come with a power resistless
To such as owe them absolute subjection;
And for a life who will not change his purpose?
(So mutable are all the ways of men.)°
Yet this be sure, in nothing to comply
Scandalous or forbidden in our law.
1410   OFFICER   I praise thy resolution;° doff° these links.
By this compliance thou wilt win the lords
To favour, and perhaps to set thee free.
        SAMSON   Brethren, farewell; your company along
I will not wish, lest it perhaps offend them
To see me girt with friends; and how the sight
Of me as of a common enemy,
So dreaded once, may now exasperate them,
I know not. Lords are lordliest in their wine;
And the well-feasted priest then soonest fired
1420   With zeal, if aught° religion seem concerned;
No less the people on their holy-days
Impetuous, insolent, unquenchable;
Happen what may, of me expect to hear
Nothing dishonourable, impure, unworthy
Our God, our law, my nation, or myself;
The last of me or no I cannot warrant.
        CHORUS   Go, and the Holy One

some . . . last Samson says either-or; it turns   Masters' . . . men all ironical
out to be both.   resolution decision
of by   doff take off
Because so that   aught to any degree

Of Israel be thy guide
To what may serve his glory best, and spread his name
1430 Great among the heathen round;
Send thee the angel of thy birth, to stand
Fast by thy side, who from thy father's field
Rode up in flames after his message told
Of thy conception,° and be now a shield
Of fire; that spirit that first rushed on thee
In the camp of Dan,°
Be efficacious in thee now at need.
For never was from heaven imparted
Measure of strength so great to mortal seed,
1440 As in thy wondrous actions hath been seen.
But wherefore comes old Mánoa in such haste
With youthful steps? Much livelier than erewhile
He seems: supposing here to find his son,
Or of him bringing to us some glad news?
    MANOA   Peace with you, brethren; my inducement hither
Was not at present here to find my son,
By order of the lords new parted hence
To come and play before them at their feast.
I heard all as I came, the city rings,
1450 And numbers thither flock; I had no will,
Lest I should see him forced to things unseemly.
But that which moved my coming now was chiefly
To give ye part° with me what hope I have
With good success° to work his liberty.
    CHORUS   That hope would much rejoice us to partake
With thee; say, reverend sire; we thirst to hear.
    MANOA   I have attempted° one by one the lords,
Either at home, or through the high street passing,
With supplication prone and father's tears
1460 To accept of ransom for my son their prisoner.
Some much averse I found and wondrous harsh,
Contemptuous, proud, set on revenge and spite;
That part most reverenced Dagon and his priests;
Others more moderate seeming, but their aim
Private reward, for which both God and State
They easily would set to sale; a third
More generous far and civil, who confessed
They had enough revenged, having reduced
Their foe to misery beneath their fears;
1470 The rest was magnanimity to remit,
If some convenient ransom were proposed.

Rode . . . conception Judges 13:10
that spirit . . . Dan Judges 13:25. At other
times the angel, or "the Spirit of the Lord,"
attended Samson at need.

give ye part share
success outcome
attempted appealed to

What noise or shout was that? It tore the sky.

CHORUS   Doubtless the people shouting to behold
Their once great dread, captive and blind before them,
Or at some proof of strength before them shown.

MANOA   His ransom, if my whole inheritance
May compass it, shall willingly be paid
And numbered down; much rather I shall choose
To live the poorest in my tribe, than richest,
1480   And he in that calamitous prison left.°
No, I am fixed not to part hence without him.
For his redemption all my patrimony,
If need be, I am ready to forgo
And quit; not wanting him, I shall want nothing.

CHORUS   Fathers are wont to lay up for their sons,
Thou for thy son art bent to lay out all;
Sons wont° to nurse their parents in old age,
Thou in old age car'st how to nurse thy son,
Made older than thy age through eyesight lost.
1490   MANOA   It shall be my delight to tend his eyes,
And view him sitting in the house, ennobled
With all those high exploits by him achieved,
And on his shoulders waving down those locks
That of a nation armed the strength contained.
And I persuade me God had not permitted
His strength again to grow up with his hair
Garrisoned round about him like a camp
Of faithful soldiery, were not his purpose
To use him further yet in some great service,
1500   Not to sit idle with so great a gift
Useless, and thence ridiculous, about him.
And since his strength with eyesight was not lost,
God will restore him eyesight to° his strength.

CHORUS   Thy hopes are not ill-founded nor seem vain
Of his delivery, and thy joy thereon
Conceived, agreeable to a father's love;
In both which we, as next,° participate.°

MANOA   I know your friendly minds and—O what noise!
Mercy of heaven, what hideous noise was that!
1510   Horribly loud, unlike the former shout.

CHORUS   Noise call you it, or universal groan,
As if the whole inhabitation° perished?
Blood, death, and dreadful deeds are in that noise,
Ruin, destruction at the utmost point.

And he . . . left while he . . . is left
wont "Are" is understood.
to to match
next nearest; kinsmen, fellow tribesman
fathers . . . participate This conversation between Manoa and the Chorus (ll. 1485–1507)
develops the ironical little plot of Manoa's
attempts to find a human plan for the comfort
of Samson despite his professed belief that
God's plan is still operative. It comes to a
head, and accordingly seems, like most human
stratagems, ridiculous, at exactly the moment
when God declares himself, and uses Samson,
as before, in an actively heroic role.
inhabitation population

MANOA   Of ruin indeed methought I heard the noise.
Oh it continues, they have slain my son.
　　CHORUS   Thy son is rather slaying them; that outcry
From slaughter of one foe could not ascend.
　　MANOA   Some dismal accident it needs must be;
1520　What shall we do, stay here or run and see?
　　CHORUS   Best keep together here, lest running thither
We unawares run into danger's mouth.
This evil on the Philistines is fallen;
From whom could else a general cry be heard?
The sufferers then will scarce molest us here;
From other hands we need not much to fear.
What if his eyesight (for to Israel's God
Nothing is hard) by miracle restored,
He now be dealing dole° among his foes,
1530　And over heaps of slaughtered walk his way?
　　MANOA   That were a joy presumptuous to be thought.
　　CHORUS   Yet God hath wrought things as incredible
For his people of old; what hinders now?
　　MANOA   He can I know, but doubt to think he will;
Yet hope would fain subscribe, and tempts belief.
A little stay will bring some notice hither.
　　CHORUS   Of good or bad so great, of bad the sooner;
For evil news rides post, while good news baits.°
And to our wish I see one hither speeding,
1540　A Hebrew, as I guess, and of our tribe.
　　MESSENGER°   O whither shall I run, or which way fly
The sight of this so horrid spectacle
Which erst° my eyes beheld and yet behold;
For dire imagination still pursues me.
But providence or instinct of nature seems,
Or reason though disturbed, and scarce consulted
To have guided me aright, I know not how,
To thee first reverend Manoa, and to these
My countrymen, whom here I knew remaining,
1550　As at some distance from the place of horror,
So in the sad event too much concerned.°
　　MANOA   The accident was loud, and here before thee
With rueful cry, yet what it was we hear not,
No preface needs, thou seest we long to know.
　　MESSENGER   It would burst forth, but I recover breath,
And sense distract,° to know well what I utter.
　　MANOA   Tell us the sum, the circumstance defer.°

---

dole a pun on "that which is dealt (or doled) out" and "grief, or pain"
baits pauses for refreshment on the way
Messenger Since violent incidents were forbidden by the rules of classical tragedy, the Messenger or Nuntius is a regular feature of tragedies at this point.

erst a little while ago
As . . . concerned both removed from the scene of the occurrence and deeply concerned in it
distract distracted
Tell . . . defer give us the gist of it, leave the detail till later

MESSENGER   Gaza yet stands, but all her sons are fallen,
All in a moment overwhelmed and fallen.
1560   MANOA   Sad, but thou know'st to Israelites not saddest
The desolation of a hostile city.
    MESSENGER   Feed on that first, there may in grief be surfeit.°
    MANOA   Relate by whom.
    MESSENGER   By Samson.
    MANOA   That still lessens
The sorrow, and converts it nigh to joy.
    MESSENGER   Ah Manoa I refrain, too suddenly
To utter what will come at last too soon;
Lest evil tidings with too rude irruption
Hitting thy agèd ear should pierce too deep.
    MANOA   Suspense in news is torture, speak them out.
1570   MESSENGER   Then take the worst in brief, Samson is dead.
    MANOA   The worst indeed, O all my hope's defeated
To free him hence! but death who sets all free
Hath paid his ransom now and full discharge.
What windy joy this day had I conceived°
Hopeful of his delivery, which now proves
Abortive as the first-born bloom of spring
Nipped with the lagging rear of winter's frost.
Yet ere I give the reins to grief, say first,
How died he? death to life is crown or shame.
1580   All by him fell thou say'st, by whom fell he,
What glorious hand gave Samson his death's wound?
    MESSENGER   Unwounded of his enemies he fell.
    MANOA   Wearied with slaughter then or how? explain.
    MESSENGER   By his own hands.
    MANOA   Self-violence? what cause
Brought him so soon at variance with himself
Among his foes?
    MESSENGER   Inevitable cause
At once both to destroy and be destroyed;
The edifice where all were met to see him
Upon their heads and on his own he pulled.
1590   MANOA   O lastly over-strong against thyself!
A dreadful way thou took'st to thy revenge.
More than enough we know; but while things yet
Are in confusion, give us if thou canst,
Eye-witness of what first or last was done,
Relation more particular and distinct.
    MESSENGER   Occasions drew me early to this city,
And as the gates I entered with sunrise,
The morning trumpets festival proclaimed

Feed . . . surfeit digest that news first; what
follows may make you sick with grief

What . . . conceived what seemed to be a
pregnancy turns out to be mere flatulence

Through each high street. Little I had despatched°
1600 When all abroad was rumoured that this day
Samson should be brought forth to show the people
Proof of his mighty strength in feats and games;
I sorrowed at his captive state, but minded°
Not to be absent at that spectacle.

The building was a spacious theatre,
Half round on two main pillars vaulted high,
With seats where all the lords, and each degree
Of sort, might sit in order to behold;
The other side was open, where the throng
1610 On banks° and scaffolds under sky might stand;
I among these aloof obscurely stood.

The feast and noon grew high, and sacrifice
Had filled their hearts with mirth, high cheer, and wine,
When to their sports they turned. Immediately
Was Samson as a public servant brought,
In their state livery clad; before him pipes
And timbrels; on each side went armèd guards,
Both horse and foot before him and behind
Archers, and slingers, cataphracts° and spears.
1620 At sight of him the people with a shout
Rifted the air, clamouring their god with praise,
Who had made their dreadful enemy their thrall.
He, patient but undaunted, where they led him,
Came to the place; and what was set before him,
Which without help of eye might be assayed,
To heave, pull, draw, or break, he still performed,
All with incredible, stupendious° force,
None daring to appear antagonist.
At length for intermission sake they led him
1630 Between the pillars; he his guide requested
(For so from such as nearer stood we heard),
As over-tired, to let him lean a while
With both his arms on those two massy pillars
That to the archèd roof gave main support.
He unsuspicious led him; which when Samson
Felt in his arms, with head a while inclined,
And eyes fast fixed he stood, as one who prayed,
Or some great matter in his mind revolved.°
At last with head erect thus cried aloud:
1640 'Hitherto, lords, what your commands imposed
I have performed, as reason was, obeying,
Not without wonder or delight beheld.

despatched done in the way of business
minded resolved
banks benches
cataphracts armored men on armored mounts
stupendious stupendous

in his mind revolved In Judges 16:30, Samson
prays to be allowed to die with his enemies;
Milton substitutes an inner resolution and an
outer declaration to absolve Samson of suicide,
a Christian sin.

Now of my own accord such other trial
I mean to show you of my strength, yet greater,
As with amaze° shall strike all who behold.'
This uttered, straining all his nerves he bowed;
As with the force of winds and waters pent
When mountains tremble, those two massy pillars
With horrible convulsion to and fro
1650 He tugged, he shook, till down they came and drew
The whole roof after them, with burst of thunder
Upon the heads of all who sat beneath,
Lords, ladies, captains, counsellors, or priests,
Their choice nobility and flower, not only
Of this but each Philistian city round,
Met from all parts to solemnize this feast.
Samson, with these inmixed, inevitably
Pulled down the same destruction on himself;
The vulgar only scaped who stood without.
1660   CHORUS   O dearly bought revenge, yet glorious!
Living or dying thou hast fulfilled
The work for which thou wast foretold
To Israel, and now li'st victorious
Among thy slain self-killed,
Not willingly, but tangled in the fold
Of dire necessity, whose law in death conjoined
Thee with thy slaughtered foes, in number more
Than all thy life had slain before.
    SEMICHORUS   While their hearts were jocund and sublime,°
1670 Drunk with idolatry, drunk with wine,
And fat regorged of bulls and goats,
Chanting their idol, and preferring
Before our living dread who dwells
In Silo,° his bright sanctuary,
Among them he a spirit of frenzy sent,
Who hurt their minds,
And urged them on with mad desire
To call in haste for their destroyer;
They only set on sport and play
1680 Unweetingly° importuned
Their own destruction to come speedy upon them.
So fond are mortal men
Fallen into wrath divine,
As their own ruin on themselves to invite,
Insensate left, or to sense reprobate,
And with blindness internal struck.
    SEMICHORUS   But he, though blind of sight,

amaze confusion; cf. l. 1286
sublime elated

Silo Shiloh, where the Ark of the Covenant
was set up
Unweetingly unwittingly

Despised and thought extinguished quite,
With inward eyes illuminated,
His fiery virtue roused
From under ashes into sudden flame,
And as an evening dragon° came,
Assailant on the perchèd roosts
And nests in order ranged
Of tame villatic° fowl; but as an eagle
His cloudless thunder bolted on their heads.
So virtue, given for lost,
Depressed, and overthrown, as seemed,
Like that self-begotten bird°
In the Arabian woods embost,°
That no second knows nor third,°
And lay erewhile a holocaust,°
From out her ashy womb now teemed,°
Revives, reflourishes, then vigorous most
When most unactive deemed,
And though her body die, her fame survives,
A secular° bird, ages of lives.
    MANOA   Come, come, no time from lamentation now,
Nor much more cause; Samson hath quit himself
Like Samson, and heroicly hath finished
A life heroic, on his enemies
Fully revenged; hath left them years of mourning,
And lamentation to the sons of Caphtor°
Through all Philistian bounds. To Israel
Honour hath left, and freedom: let but them
Find courage to lay hold on this occasion;
To himself and father's house eternal fame;
And, which is best and happiest yet, all this
With God not parted from him, as was feared,
But favouring and assisting to the end.
Nothing is here for tears, nothing to wail
Or knock the breast, no weakness, no contempt,
Dispraise, or blame, nothing but well and fair,
And what may quiet us in a death so noble.
Let us go find the body where it lies
Soaked in his enemies' blood, and from the stream
With lavers° pure and cleansing herbs wash off
The clotted gore. I with what speed° the while

1690
1700
1710
1720

---

dragon serpent
villatic barnyard; the Italian meaning of *villa* is farmhouse
self-begotten bird the phoenix, not used literally as an emblem of resurrection, but of fame and glory and, perhaps, some kind of spiritual regeneration; an image of Christian heroic virtue and God's use of it
embost "embosked"—hidden in woods like a hunted animal

That . . . third Only one phoenix is alive at a time.
holocaust a sacrificial animal burned entire
teemed delivered in birth
secular age-enduring
Caphtor original home of the Philistines
lavers basins
with what speed with whatever speed I can

(Gaza is not in plight° to say us nay)
1730 Will send for all my kindred, all my friends,
To fetch him hence and solemnly attend
With silent obsequy and funeral train
Home to his father's house: there will I build him
A monument, and plant it round with shade
Of laurel ever green, and branching palm,
With all his trophies hung, and acts enrolled
In copious legend, or sweet lyric song.
Thither shall all the valiant youth resort,
And from his memory inflame their breasts
1740 To matchless valour and adventures high;
The virgins also shall on feastful days
Visit his tomb with flowers, only bewailing
His lot unfortunate in nuptial choice,
From whence captivity and loss of eyes.
    CHORUS   All is best, though we oft doubt,
What the unsearchable dispose
Of highest wisdom brings about,
And ever best found in the close.
Oft he seems to hide his face,
1750 But unexpectedly returns
And to his faithful champion hath in place°
Bore witness gloriously; whence Gaza mourns,
And all that band them to resist
His uncontrollable intent:
His servants he, with new acquist°
Of true experience from this great event,
With peace and consolation hath dismissed,
And calm of mind, all passion spent.
1647–70?   1671

Areopagitica

If *Areopagitica* is Milton's most resonant prose work, it may be because, first, its specific polemical purpose was one which still moves us today, and whose importance has not diminished, and, second, because its author evolved during the course of his argument a powerful vision of the moral life as embodied in the world of the intellect, and, particularly for Milton, in the representation of truth in terms of major fictions. Milton's essay is an address to Parliament on the subject of licensing—not censorship, to which he was by no means totally opposed, but the prior censorship imposed by requiring books to be approved before publication. Such approval had been entrusted in 1637, by Star Chamber decision, to a small group of churchmen; and a predominantly Presbyterian Parliament, in the ordinance of 1643 to which Milton is objecting, was in effect continuing the oppressive measure, which had

in plight in condition   **acquist** acquisition
in place at hand

given great personal licensing power to Archbishop Laud before. *Areopagitica,* like Milton's divorce tracts of the previous year, itself appeared without license. Its title derives from a famous address of the Greek orator Isocrates, to the Areopagus, or high court, which held session on the Athenian hill of Ares (Mars); like Milton's, that address was not written for oral delivery.

From Areopagitica

A Speech for the Liberty of Unlicensed Printing, to the Parliament of England

> This is true liberty, when free-born men,
> Having to advise the public, may speak free,
> Which he who can and will, deserves high praise;
> Who neither can nor will, may hold his peace;
> What can be juster in a State than this?
> EURIPIDES, *The Suppliants*

They who to states [1] and governors of the Commonwealth direct their speech, High Court of Parliament, or, wanting [2] such access in a private condition, write that which they foresee may advance the public good, I suppose them, as at the beginning of no mean endeavour, not a little altered [3] and moved inwardly in their minds: some with doubt of what will be the success,[4] others with fear of what will be the censure; [5] some with hope, others with confidence of what they have to speak. And me perhaps each of these dispositions, as the subject was whereon I entered, may have at other times variously affected; and likely might in these foremost expressions now also disclose which of them swayed most, but that the very attempt of this address thus made, and the thought of whom it hath recourse to, hath got the power within me to a passion far more welcome than incidental to a preface. Which though I stay not to confess ere any ask I shall be blameless, if it be no other than the joy and gratulation which it brings to all who wish and promote their country's liberty; whereof this whole discourse proposed will be a certain testimony, if not a trophy.[6] For this is not the liberty which we can hope, that no grievance ever should arise in the Commonwealth—that let no man in this world expect; but when complaints are freely heard, deeply considered, and speedily reformed, then is the utmost bound of civil liberty attained that wise men look for. . . .

I deny not, but that it is of greatest concernment in the Church and Commonwealth, to have a vigilant eye how books demean themselves as well as men; and thereafter to confine, imprison, and do sharpest justice on them as malefactors. For books are not absolutely dead things, but do contain a potency

1. The three estates of lords, clergy, and commons forming the parliaments of England and France.
2. Lacking.
3. Worried.
4. Result.
5. Decision; a neutral term.
6. Of victory in his argument.

of life in them to be as active as that soul was whose progeny they are; nay, they do preserve as in a vial the purest efficacy and extraction of that living intellect that bred them. I know they are as lively, and as vigorously productive, as those fabulous dragon's teeth,[7] and being sown up and down, may chance to spring up armed men. And yet, on the other hand, unless wariness be used, as good almost kill a man as kill a good book: who kills a man kills a reasonable creature, God's image; but he who destroys a good book, kills reason itself, kills the image of God, as it were in the eye.[8] Many a man lives a burden to the earth; but a good book is the precious life-blood of a master spirit, embalmed and treasured up on purpose to a life beyond life. 'Tis true, no age can restore a life, whereof perhaps there is no great loss; and revolutions of ages do not oft recover the loss of a rejected truth, for the want of which whole nations fare the worse. We should be wary therefore what persecution we raise against the living labours of public men, how we spill that seasoned life of man, preserved and stored up in books; since we see a kind of homicide may be thus committed, sometimes a martyrdom, and if it extend to the whole impression, a kind of massacre, whereof the execution ends not in the slaying of an elemental life, but strikes at that ethereal and fifth essence,[9] the breath of reason itself, slays an immortality rather than a life. But lest I should be condemned of introducing license, while I oppose licensing, I refuse not the pains to be so much historical as will serve to show what hath been done by ancient and famous commonwealths, against this disorder, till the very time that this project of licensing crept out of the Inquisition,[10] was catched up by our prelates, and hath caught some of our presbyters. [Milton now goes on to summarize the history of censorship, in Greece, Rome, and in the early days of the church, concluding with the introduction of prohibitions against reading heretical books in the 15th century, and the activities of the Spanish Inquisition and the Council of Trent (1545–63). A witty passage attacking ecclesiastical approval follows.]

Nor did they stay in matters heretical, but any subject that was not to their palate they either condemned in a Prohibition or had it straight into the new Purgatory of an Index. To fill up the measure of encroachment, their last invention was to ordain that no book, pamphlet, or paper should be printed (as if St. Peter had bequeathed them the keys of the press also out of Paradise) unless it were approved and licensed under the hands of two or three glutton friars. For example:

'Let the Chancellor Cini be pleased to see if in this present work be contained aught that may withstand the printing.

Vincent Rabbatta, Vicar of Florence.'

'I have seen this present work, and find nothing athwart the Catholic

---

7. Cadmus and Jason both slew dragons and sowed their teeth, from which sprang up a crop of soldiers (Ovid, *Metamorphoses* III.95 ff. and VII.121 ff.).

8. In the reader's eye.

9. Beyond the four elements lay a fifth entity, ether, the heavenly essence (see Donne, "A Nocturnal upon S. Lucy's Day," l. 15n).

10. The church's inquisitorial institution rooted out heresy and heterodoxy; its powers, Milton insists, were inherited by Rome's Anglican opponents ("prelates") and, in turn, by the latter's Presbyterian antagonists ("New Presbyter is but old Priest writ large" Milton would write two years later).

faith and good manners: in witness whereof I have given, etc.

Nicolo Cini, Chancellor of Florence.'

'Attending the precedent relation, it is allowed that this present work of Davanzati may be printed.

Vincent Rabbatta, etc.'

'It may be printed, July 15.
Friar Simon Mompei d'Amelia,
Chancellor of the holy office in Florence.'

Sure they have a conceit, if he of the bottomless pit had not long since broke prison, that this quadruple exorcism would bar him down. I fear their next design will be to get into their custody the licensing of that which they say Claudius intended,[11] but went not through with. Vouchsafe to see another of their forms, the Roman stamp:

'Imprimatur,[12] If it seem good to the reverend master of the holy Palace, Belcastro, Vicegerent.'

'Imprimatur, Friar Nicolo Rodolphi, Master of the holy Palace.'

Sometimes five Imprimaturs are seen together dialogue-wise in the piazza of one title-page, complimenting and ducking each to other with their shaven reverences, whether the author who stands by in perplexity at the foot of his epistle shall to the press or to the sponge.[13] These are the pretty responsories,[14] these are the dear antiphonies,[15] that so bewitched of late our prelates and their chaplains with the goodly echo they made; and besotted us to the gay imitation of a lordly Imprimatur, one from Lambeth House,[16] another from the west end of Paul's; [17] so apishly romanizing that the word of command still was set down in Latin; as if the learned grammatical pen that wrote it would cast no ink without Latin; or perhaps, as they thought, because no vulgar tongue was worthy to express the pure conceit [18] of an Imprimatur; but rather, as I hope, for that our English, the language of men ever famous and foremost in the achievements of liberty, will not easily find servile letters enow to spell such a dictatory presumption English.[19] And thus ye have the inventors and the original of book-licensing ripped up [20] and drawn as lineally as any pedigree. We have it not, that can be heard of, from any ancient state, or polity, or church, nor by any statute left us by our ancestors elder or later; nor from the

---

11. A license allowing one to fart at table: Milton's marginal note quotes Suetonius' *Life of Claudius* to this effect.

12. "Let it be printed"—the phrase giving official ecclesiastical permission for publication of manuscripts.

13. "To the sponge," meaning to have the contents wiped off, was an expression applied to manuscripts unworthy of publication.

14. Sections of the Psalms sung between other biblical readings in the mass.

15. Hymns or anthems sung in responsive parts by two choirs.

16. Lambeth Palace, residence of the Archbishop of Canterbury when in London.

17. This may refer either to the Bishop of London (at St. Paul's), or to the home of the Stationers' Company, who urged the enforcement of the licensing order.

18. Idea.

19. In English.

20. Revealed.

modern custom of any reformed city or church abroad; but from the most anti-christian council and the most tyrannous inquisition that ever inquired. Till then books were ever as freely admitted into the world as any other birth; the issue of the brain was no more stifled than the issue of the womb: no envious Juno sat cross-legged [21] over the nativity of any man's intellectual offspring; but if it proved a monster, who denies but that it was justly burnt, or sunk into the sea. But that a book, in worse condition than a peccant soul, should be to stand before a jury ere it be born to the world, and undergo yet in darkness the judgment of Radamanth and his colleagues,[22] ere it can pass the ferry backward into light, was never heard before, till that mysterious iniquity, provoked and troubled at the first entrance of Reformation, sought out new limbos and new hells wherein they might include our books also within the number of their damned. And this was the rare morsel so officiously snatched up, and so ill-favouredly imitated by our inquisiturient [23] bishops, and the attendant minorites [24] their chaplains. That ye like not now these most certain authors of this licensing order, and that all sinister intention was far distant from your thoughts, when ye were importuned the passing it, all men who know the integrity of your actions, and how ye honour truth, will clear ye readily. [Milton then attacks the notion that there is any good in licensing itself aside from its proponents' vices, and adducing a remark of John Selden, the legal scholar (1584–1654), that "all opinions, yea errors, known, read and collated, are of main service and assistance toward the speedy attainment of what is truest," moves to the imaginative center of his argument.]

I conceive, therefore, that when God did enlarge the universal diet of man's body, saving ever the rules of temperance, he then also, as before, left arbitrary the dieting and repasting of our minds; as wherein every mature man might have to exercise his own leading capacity. How great a virtue is temperance, how much of moment through the whole life of man! Yet God commits the managing so great a trust, without particular law or prescription, wholly to the demeanour [25] of every grown man. And therefore when he himself tabled the Jews from heaven, that omer,[26] which was every man's daily portion of manna, is computed to have been more than might have well sufficed for the heartiest feeder thrice as many meals. For those actions which enter into a man, rather than issue out of him, and therefore defile not, God uses not to captivate under a perpetual childhood of prescription, but trusts him with the gift of reason to be his own chooser; there were but little work left for preaching if law and compulsion should grow so fast upon those things which heretofore were governed only by exhortation. Solomon informs us that much reading is a weariness to the flesh; but neither he nor other inspired author tells us that such or such reading is unlawful; yet certainly had God thought good to limit us herein, it had been much more expedient to have told us what was unlawful than what

---

21. She tried, with charms and spells, to prevent the birth of Hercules, whose mother was in labor with him for seven days.

22. Rhadamanthus, Minos, and Aeacus, the three judges of Hades.

23. Would-be inquisitors.

24. The Franciscans called themselves "minorites," alluding to their humility, with which Milton here remains unimpressed.

25. Management.

26. A biblical measure, here, of manna (Exodus 16:16 ff.), the daily ration Moses was commanded to distribute.

was wearisome. As for the burning of those Ephesian books by St. Paul's converts, 'tis replied the books were magic, the Syriac so renders them. It was a private act, a voluntary act, and leaves us to a voluntary imitation: the men in remorse burnt those books which were their own; the magistrate by this example is not appointed: these men practised the books, another might perhaps have read them in some sort usefully. Good and evil we know in the field of this world grow up together almost inseparably; and the knowledge of good is so involved and interwoven with the knowledge of evil, and in so many cunning resemblances hardly to be discerned, that those confused seeds which were imposed upon Psyche as an incessant labour to cull out, and sort asunder, were not more intermixed.[27] It was from out the rind of one apple tasted, that the knowledge of good and evil, as two twins cleaving together, leaped forth into the world. And perhaps this is that doom which Adam fell into of knowing good and evil, that is to say of knowing good by evil.[28] As therefore the state of man is, what wisdom can there be to choose, what continence to forbear, without the knowledge of evil? He that can apprehend and consider vice with all her baits and seeming pleasures, and yet abstain, and yet distinguish, and yet prefer that which is truly better, he is the true warfaring [29] Christian. I cannot praise a fugitive and cloistered virtue, unexercised and unbreathed, that never sallies out and sees her adversary, but slinks out of the race, where that immortal garland [30] is to be run for, not without dust and heat. Assuredly we bring not innocence into the world, we bring impurity much rather; that which purifies us is trial, and trial is by what is contrary. That virtue therefore which is but a youngling in the contemplation of evil, and knows not the utmost that vice promises to her followers, and rejects it, is but a blank virtue, not a pure; her whiteness is but an excremental [31] whiteness; which was the reason why our sage and serious poet Spenser, whom I dare be known to think a better teacher than Scotus or Aquinas,[32] describing true temperance under the person of Guyon, brings him in with his palmer through the cave of Mammon, and the bower of earthly bliss,[33] that he might see and know, and yet abstain. Since therefore the knowledge and survey of vice is in this world so necessary to the constituting of human virtue, and the scanning of error to the confirmation of truth, how can we more safely and with less danger scout into the regions of sin and falsity than by reading all manner of tractates and hearing all manner of reason? And this is the benefit which may be had of books promiscuously read.

. . .

27. In Apuleius' *The Golden Ass,* Venus set Psyche the task of sorting out a heap of mixed seeds, in anger at Cupid's love for her.
28. "Knowledge of good bought dear by knowing ill" (*Paradise Lost* IV.222); in his great poem, Milton expands and elaborates this theme.
29. *Wayfaring* in the first edition, but there is strong evidence for the present reading.
30. The garland is the crown of virtue; being good is likened both to medieval knight-errantry and to Greek and Roman games.
31. Superficial.
32. Duns Scotus and Thomas Aquinas, two great 13th-century logicians (the second, the master-theologian of scholasticism); they represent abstract philosophy here, as opposed to the concreteness of poetic myth.
33. See *The Faerie Queene* II. vii and xii. The Palmer does *not* accompany Guyon into the Cave of Mammon, however; Milton's memory failed him here.

Seeing, therefore, that those books, and those in great abundance which are likeliest to taint both life and doctrine, cannot be suppressed without the fall of learning, and of all ability in disputation, and that these books of either sort are most and soonest catching to the learned, from whom to the common people whatever is heretical or dissolute may quickly be conveyed, and that evil manners are as perfectly learnt without books a thousand other ways which cannot be stopped, and evil doctrine not with books can propagate, except a teacher guide, which he might also do without writing, and so beyond prohibiting, I am not unable to unfold how this cautelous [34] enterprise of licensing can be exempted from the number of vain and impossible attempts. And he who were pleasantly disposed could not well avoid to liken it to the exploit of that gallant man who thought to pound up the crows by shutting his park gate. Besides another inconvenience, if learned men be the first receivers out of books and dispreaders both of vice and error, how shall the licensers themselves be confided in, unless we can confer upon them, or they assume to themselves above all others in the land, the grace of infallibility and uncorruptedness? And again if it be true, that a wise man, like a good refiner, can gather gold out of the drossiest volume, and that a fool will be a fool with the best book, yea, or without book; there is no reason that we should deprive a wise man of any advantage to his wisdom, while we seek to restrain from a fool that which being restrained will be no hindrance to his folly. For if there should be so much exactness always used to keep that from him which is unfit for his reading, we should in the judgment of Aristotle [35] not only, but of Solomon [36] and of our Saviour,[37] not vouchsafe him good precepts, and by consequence not willingly admit him to good books; as being certain that a wise man will make better use of an idle pamphlet than a fool will do of sacred Scripture.

. . .

For if we be sure we are in the right, and do not hold the truth guiltily, which becomes not, if we ourselves condemn not our own weak and frivolous teaching, and the people for an untaught and irreligious gadding rout, what can be more fair than when a man judicious, learned, and of a conscience, for aught we know as good as theirs that taught us what we know, shall not privily from house to house, which is more dangerous, but openly by writing publish to the world what his opinion is, what his reasons, and wherefore that which is now thought cannot be sound? Christ urged it as wherewith to justify himself that he preached in public; [38] yet writing is more public than preaching; and more easy to refutation, if need be, there being so many whose business and profession merely it is to be the champions of Truth; which if they neglect, what can be imputed but their sloth, or inability?

Thus much we are hindered and disenured [39] by this course of licensing toward the true knowledge of what we seem to know. For how much it hurts

34. Tricky, liable to backfire.
35. At the end of the *Nicomachean Ethics,* rejecting the possibility that philosophy can influence ordinary men, instead of guiding the best of them.
36. Throughout the Book of Proverbs, as for example 17:24 and 26:5.
37. ". . . Neither cast ye your pearls before swine" (Matthew 7:6).
38. John 18:19–20.
39. Grown unaccustomed.

and hinders the licensers themselves in the calling of their ministry, more than any secular employment, if they will discharge that office as they ought, so that of necessity they must neglect either the one duty or the other, I insist not, because it is a particular,[40] but leave it to their own conscience, how they will decide it there.

There is yet behind of what I purposed to lay open, the incredible loss and detriment that this plot of licensing puts us to, more than if some enemy at sea should stop up all our havens and ports and creeks, it hinders and retards the importation of our richest merchandise, Truth: nay, it was first established and put in practice by anti-christian malice and mystery [41] on set purpose to extinguish, if it were possible, the light of Reformation, and to settle falsehood; little differing from that policy wherewith the Turk upholds his Alcoran, by the prohibition of Printing. 'Tis not denied, but gladly confessed, we are to send our thanks and vows to Heaven, louder than most of nations for that great measure of truth which we enjoy, especially in those main points between us and the Pope, with his appurtenances the Prelates: but he who thinks we are to pitch our tent here, and have attained the utmost prospect of reformation, that the mortal glass [42] wherein we contemplate can show us, till we come to beatific vision, that man by this very opinion declares that he is yet far short of truth.

Truth indeed came once into the world with her divine Master, and was a perfect shape most glorious to look on: but when he ascended, and his Apostles after him were laid asleep, then straight arose a wicked race of deceivers, who (as that story goes of the Egyptian Typhon with his conspirators, how they dealt with the good Osiris) [43] took the virgin Truth, hewed her lovely form into a thousand pieces, and scattered them to the four winds. From that time ever since, the sad friends of Truth, such as durst appear, imitating the careful [44] search that Isis made for the mangled body of Osiris, went up and down gathering up limb by limb still as they could find them. We have not yet found them all, Lords and Commons, nor ever shall do, till her Master's second coming; he shall bring together every joint and member, and shall mould them into an immortal feature of loveliness and perfection. Suffer not these licensing prohibitions to stand at every place of opportunity forbidding and disturbing them that continue seeking, that continue to do our obsequies to the torn body of our martyred saint. We boast our light; but if we look not wisely on the sun itself, it smites us into darkness. Who can discern those planets that are oft combust,[45] and those stars of brightest magnitude that rise and set with the sun, until the opposite motion of their orbs bring them to such a place in the firmament where they may be seen evening or morning. The light which we have gained was given us, not to be ever staring on, but by it to discover

40. Matter of particular concern.

41. Mystification.

42. Mirror (see I Corinthians 13:12, and comment on it in The English Bible section).

43. Typhon, Osiris' brother, murdered and dismembered him; the body floated down the Nile and was reassembled by his wife, Isis, and Horus, their son. As early as Plutarch, this was read as a myth of the mangling and scattering of Truth, and its reconstitution, both eternal processes (compare Bacon's essay, "Of Truth").

44. Full of cares.

45. "Burnt up," figuratively, by closely approaching the sun; an astrological term.

onward things more remote from our knowledge. It is not the unfrocking of
a priest, the unmitring of a bishop, and the removing him from off the Presbyterian shoulders that will make us a happy nation, no, if other things as great
in the church, and in the rule of life both economical [46] and political be not
looked into and reformed. We have looked so long upon the blaze that Zwing-
lius and Calvin [47] hath beaconed up to us that we are stark blind. There be
who perpetually complain of schisms and sects, and make it such a calamity
that any man dissents from their maxims. 'Tis their own pride and ignorance
which causes the disturbing, who neither will hear with meekness, nor can
convince, yet all must be suppressed which is not found in their syntagma.[48]
They are the troublers, they are the dividers of unity, who neglect and permit
not others to unite those dissevered pieces which are yet wanting to the body of
Truth. To be still searching what we know not by what we know, still closing
up truth to truth as we find it (for all her body is homogeneal,[49] and proportional),[50] this is the golden rule in theology as well as in arithmetic, and
makes up the best harmony in a church; not the forced and outward union of
cold and neutral and inwardly divided minds.

There have been not a few since the beginning of this Parliament,[51] both
of the Presbytery and others, who by their unlicensed books to the contempt
of an Imprimatur first broke that triple ice [52] clung about our hearts, and taught
the people to see day. I hope that none of those were the persuaders to renew
upon us this bondage which they themselves have wrought so much good by
contemning. But if neither the check that Moses gave to young Joshua, nor
the countermand which our Saviour gave to young John, who was so ready to
prohibit those whom he thought unlicensed, be not enough to admonish our
elders how unacceptable to God their testy mood of prohibiting is, if neither
their own remembrance what evil hath abounded in the Church by this let [53]
of licensing, and what good they themselves have begun by transgressing it,
be not enough, but that they will persuade, and execute the most Dominican
part of the Inquisition over us, and are already with one foot in the stirrup so
active at suppressing, it would be no unequal distribution in the first place to
suppress the suppressors themselves: whom the change of their condition hath
puffed up, more than their late experience of harder times hath made wise.

And as for regulating the Press, let no man think to have the honour of
advising ye better than yourselves have done in that order published next
before this,[54] *that no book be printed, unless the printer's and the author's*

46. Concerning household management, thus, here, private affairs.
47. Ulrich Zwingli (1484–1531), of Zurich; John Calvin (1509–64), of Geneva—the
two Swiss reformers.
48. System of doctrine.
49. All of a piece throughout.
50. Harmoniously composed in relations of parts to whole.
51. The Long Parliament, which first assembled November 3, 1640.
52. Punning on, and nevertheless seriously alluding to, the *aes triplex* ("triple bronze"),
needed, says Horace (*Odes* I.3), to gird the heart of a man setting out, for the first time,
to sea.
53. Hindrance.
54. An order previous to the one (of June 14, 1643) which Milton is disputing.

name, or at least the printer's be registered.' Those which otherwise come
forth, if they be found mischievous and libellous, the fire and the executioner
will be the timeliest and the most effectual remedy that man's prevention can
use. For this authentic [55] Spanish policy of licensing books, if I have said aught,
will prove the most unlicensed book itself within a short while; and was the
immediate image of a Star Chamber decree to that purpose made in those very
times when that Court did the rest of those her pious works, for which she is
now fallen from the stars with Lucifer. Whereby ye may guess what kind of
state prudence, what love of the people, what care of Religion or good manners
there was at the contriving, although with singular hypocrisy it pretended to
bind books to their good behaviour. And how it got the upper hand of your
precedent Order so well constituted before, if we may believe those men whose
profession gives them cause to inquire most, it may be doubted there was in
it the fraud of some old patentees and monopolizers in the trade of bookselling;
who under pretence of the poor in their Company not to be defrauded, and the
just retaining of each man his several copy, which God forbid should be gain-
said, brought divers glozing [56] colours to the House, which were indeed but
colours, and serving to no end except it be to exercise a superiority over their
neighbours, men who do not therefore labour in an honest profession to which
learning is indebted, that they should be made other men's vassals. Another end
is thought was aimed at by some of them in procuring by petition this Order,
that having power in their hands, malignant books might the easier scape
abroad, as the event shows. But of these sophisms and elenchs [57] of merchandise
I skill not. This I know, that errors in a good government and in a bad are
equally almost incident; for what Magistrate may not be misinformed, and
much the sooner, if liberty of Printing be reduced into the power of a few?
But to redress willingly and speedily what hath been erred, and in highest
authority to esteem a plain advertisement [58] more than others have done a
sumptuous bribe, is a virtue (honoured Lords and Commons) answerable to
your highest actions, and whereof none can participate but greatest and wisest
men.

1644   1644

The Development of Prose

JOHN LYLY
1554?–1606

Lyly came of a family much involved in scholarly humanism and was himself a
master at St. Paul's choir school, though his job was mostly to produce the boys' plays.
His court comedies, written for boys, are his most distinguished work, but earlier he
had made himself famous with *Euphues: The Anatomy of Wit* (1578) and *Euphues
and His England* (1580), works which combine an appearance of moral rectitude with

---

55. Peculiarly.
56. Flattering.
57. Fallacious points.
58. Notification.

a prose style of great though rhetorically repetitive elaboration. They achieved great success, and continued to be read even after Lyly's reputation was dimmed in the late 1580's by that of Sidney, whose "Arcadianism"—still ornate, but less rigid—replaced "Euphuism" as a favored rhetorical style.

The story of *Euphues* is unimportant, being no more than a "trellis," as C. S. Lewis called it, for the flowers of rhetoric and the festoons of similes to grow on. Euphues is a noble young Greek (his name means "gentleman") who ignores advice and goes from Athens (the university) to Naples (the city, specifically London), where he makes a friend of Philautus, betrays him, is reconciled, lectures him in moral philosophy, and so on. *Euphues and His England* has more story, and concludes with a long passage in praise of England, London, the court, and, most of all, the Queen. In the present extract Philautus' girl has entertained him and Euphues (whom she received rather coldly) at supper; and Euphues is afterwards required to discourse concerning love or learning. He chooses to speak on whether beauty or wit in women move men most to love; but in fact he speaks against the fickleness and cruelty of women. When he breaks off and leaves, Lucilla soliloquizes, exhibiting most of the characteristics of Euphuism in the process.

Lyly did not invent this kind of "wit"; he took certain tendencies already existing in prose, and even in the fashionable Oxford lectures of his undergraduate days and brought them to a new pitch. The forced balances and antitheses, "terms and contrarieties," can be given various rhetorical names, and exist elsewhere. The extended similes (drawn from what has been called "unnatural natural history") and the copious use of proverbs are part of the common stock, but nowhere else occur in this concentration. As Lewis rightly says, "What constitutes euphuism is neither the structural devices nor the 'unnatural history' but the unremitting use of both." It was a "camp" style; Sidney complained of it and Shakespeare parodied it in a famous passage in I *Henry IV*—but the parody doesn't sound much different from parts of the original: compare Shakespeare's lines (II.iv.440 ff.) with "Though the camomile the more it is trodden and pressed down the more it spreadeth," which is genuine Lyly. Most of *Euphues* is in the same manner, and a small sample suffices.

From Euphues: The Anatomy of Wit

. . . Lucilla, who now began to fry in the flames of love, all the company being departed to their lodgings, entered into these terms and contrarieties: [1]—

'Ah, wretched wench Lucilla, how art thou perplexed! What a doubtful fight dost thou feel betwixt faith and fancy, hope and fear, conscience and concupiscence! O my Euphues, little dost thou know the sudden sorrow that I sustain for thy sweet sake, whose wit hath bewitched me, whose rare qualities have deprived me of mine old quality, whose courteous behaviour without curiosity, whose comely feature without fault, whose filed [2] speech without fraud hath wrapped me in this misfortune. And canst thou, Lucilla, be so light of love in forsaking Philautus to fly to Euphues? Canst thou prefer a stranger

1. Opposing considerations.
2. Polished.

before thy countryman; a starter [3] before thy companion? Why, Euphues doth perhaps desire my love, but Philautus hath deserved it. Why, Euphues' feature is worthy as good as I, but Philautus his faith is worthy a better. Aye, but the latter love is most fervent; aye, but the first ought to be most faithful. Aye, but Euphues hath greater perfection; aye, but Philautus hath deeper affection.

'Ah fond wench, dost thou think Euphues will deem thee constant to him, when thou hast been unconstant to his friend? Weenest thou [4] that he will have no mistrust of thy faithfulness, when he hath had trial [5] of thy fickleness? Will he have no doubt of thine honour, when thou thyself callest thine honesty [6] in question? Yes, yes, Lucilla, well doth he know, that the glass once crazed [7] will with the least clap be cracked, [8] that the cloth which staineth with milk will soon lose his colour with vinegar, that the eagle's wing [9] will waste the feather as well of the phœnix as of the pheasant, that she that hath been faithless to one will never be faithful to any.

'But can Euphues convince [10] me of fleeting, seeing for his sake I break my fidelity? Can he condemn me of disloyalty, when he is the only cause of my disliking? May he justly condemn me of treachery, who hath this testimony as trial [11] of my good will? Doth he not remember that the broken bone once set together is stronger than ever it was? That the greatest blot is taken off with the pumice? [12] That though the spider poison the fly, she cannot infect the bee? That although I have been light to Philautus, yet I may be lovely to Euphues? It is not my desire but his deserts that moveth my mind to this choice, neither the want of the like good will in Philautus but the lack of the like good qualities that removeth my fancy from the one to the other.

'For as the bee that gathereth honey out of the weed when she espieth the fair flower flieth to the sweetest; or as the kind [13] spaniel though he hunt after birds yet forsakes them to retrive the partridge; or as we commonly feed on beef hungerly at the first, yet seeing the quail more dainty change our diet; so I although I loved Philautus for his good properties, yet seeing Euphues to excel him I ought by nature to like him better. By so much the more, therefore, my change is to be excused, by how much the more my choice is excellent; and by so much the less I am to be condemned, by how much the more Euphues is to be commended. Is not the diamond of more value than the ruby because he is of more virtue? [14] Is not the emerald preferred before the sapphire for his wonderful property? Is not Euphues more praiseworthy than Philautus being more witty?

3. Newcomer.
4. Do you suppose.
5. Experience.
6. Meaning much the same as honor.
7. Cracked.
8. Broken.
9. Referring to the belief that the eagle's feathers, after death, will corrode or destroy those of other birds, so maintaining his superiority in life.
10. Convict.
11. Evidence.
12. Used in the 16th century to absorb ink.
13. Acting according to his nature.
14. Power.

'But fie, Lucilla, why dost thou flatter thyself in thine own folly! Canst thou feign Euphues thy friend, whom by thine own words thou hast made thy foe? Didst not thou accuse women of inconstancy? Didst not thou account them easy to be won? Didst not thou condemn them of weakness? What sounder argument can he have against thee than thine own answer; what better proof than thine own speech; what greater trial than thine own talk? If thou hast belied women, he will judge thee unkind; [15] if thou have revealed the troth,[16] he must needs think thee unconstant; if he perceive thee to be won with a nut, he will imagine that thou wilt be lost with an apple; [17] if he find thee wanton before thou be wooed, he will guess thou wilt be wavering when thou art wedded.'

1578

RICHARD HOOKER
1554–1600

Hooker was the greatest of Elizabethan prose writers. He transformed controversy into philosophy, making the dispute between the middle-of-the-way churchmen and the Puritan extremists an occasion for a great meditation on natural, human, and divine law. In 1585 Hooker was preferred over the Puritan Walter Travers for the post of Master of the Temple, a London law school. Travers held that Scripture was the sole source of truth and authority in the church, so that ceremonies without scriptural warrant, and the elaborate hierarchical organization of the clergy, were wrong. Hooker deplored the contentious zeal of the Puritans as a disturber of the church's peace, and also refused to admit an absolutely sharp distinction between different kinds of law and learning, human and divine. He valued tradition without giving it the force attributed to it by Catholics; and he defended ceremony in terms of natural common sense. Out of the controversy with Travers grew the eight books *Of The Laws of Ecclesiastical Polity*, of which four were published in 1593. Book I speaks of laws generally, the laws of nature and societies; Books II and III treat of Scripture and its authority; Book IV is in defense of ceremony. Hooker proceeds with a calm stateliness to the defeat of the enemy position; as C. S. Lewis observes, "Long before the close fighting in Book III begins, the puritan position has been rendered desperate by the great flanking movements in Book I and II."

The first selection below comes from the discussion in Book I of the law of nature, the obedience of natural things to laws of which they cannot consciously have knowledge. Their performance, though in consequence of the fall of man not perfect, is nonetheless so regular as to allow us to suppose nature to have a faithful relationship with the divinity; we should therefore not exclude knowledge achieved by the light of nature.

The second selection makes the point that total dependence on Scripture for necessary knowledge is in fact impossible. Scripture tells us whatever is necessary to salvation that we could not otherwise know; but this cannot mean that all other knowledge, natural or otherwise, is superfluous, since it is by reason of it that we

15. Unnatural (also with modern sense).
16. Truth.
17. Proverbial for the inconstant mind.

know, for example, that the Scriptures are the "oracles of God." This is an indirect assault on the central Puritan position.

The third selection justifies ceremony, not as part of an inviolable tradition, but as a means of making the word and the sacraments of God more solemn and memorable. Like all Hooker's work, it is an appeal to reason in the midst of fierce and dangerous controversies. He is always ready to consider usefulness to human beings as an important recommendation, and to avoid dogmatism. In hoping that although "nature hath need of grace" (I Corinthians 2:14)he was not opposing St. Paul when he added, "grace hath use of nature" (III.viii.6), Hooker was proposing for the Church of England a reasonable alternative to a Puritanism which accepted the first but denied the second proposition—just as by giving ceremony a natural human use he avoided the extreme formulations imposed on the Roman church at the Council of Trent.

Of the Laws of Ecclesiastical Polity

From Book I, Chapter 3

. . . Now if nature should intermit [1] her course, and leave altogether though it were but for a while the observation of her own laws; if those principal and mother elements of the world, whereof all things in this lower world are made, should lose the qualities which now they have; if the frame of that heavenly arch erected over our heads should loosen and dissolve itself; if celestial spheres should forget their wonted motions, and by irregular volubility turn themselves any way as it might happen; if the prince of the lights of heaven, which now as a giant doth run his unwearied course,[2] should as it were through a languishing faintness begin to stand and to rest himself; if the moon should wander from her beaten way, the times and seasons of the year blend themselves by disordered and confused mixture, the winds breathe out their last gasp, the clouds yield no rain, the earth be defeated of heavenly influence, the fruits of the earth pine away as children at the withered breasts of their mother no longer able to yield them relief: what would become of man himself, whom these things now do all serve? See we not plainly that obedience of creatures unto the law of nature is the stay of the whole world? Notwithstanding with nature it cometh sometimes to pass as with art. Let Phidias [3] have rude and obstinate stuff to carve, though his art do that it should, his work will lack that beauty which otherwise in fitter matter it might have had. He that striketh an instrument with skill may cause notwithstanding a very unpleasant sound, if the string whereon he striketh chance to be uncapable of harmony. In the matter whereof things natural consist, that of Theophrastus [4] taketh place, 'Much of it is oftentimes such as will by no means yield to receive that impression which were best and most perfect.' Which defect in the matter of things natural, they who gave themselves unto the contemplation of nature amongst

1. Interrupt.
2. Psalms 19:5.
3. Greek sculptor, architect, and painter of 4th century B.C., for the Parthenon frieze responsibly.
4. C. 371–c. 287 B.C.; pupil of Aristotle and prolific writer, best known for his *Characters*, outlines of personality types, which were imitated, e.g. by Earle and Overbury (see below).

the heathen observed often: but the true original cause thereof, divine male-diction, laid for the sin of man upon these creatures which God had made for the use of man,[5] this being an article of that saving truth which God hath revealed unto his Church, was above the reach of their merely natural capacity and understanding. But howsoever these swervings are now and then incident into the course of nature, nevertheless so constantly the laws of nature are by natural agents observed, that no man denieth but those things which nature worketh are wrought, either always or for the most part, after one and the same manner.

If here it be demanded what that is which keepeth nature in obedience to her own law, we must have recourse to that higher law whereof we have already spoken, and because all other laws do thereon depend, from thence we must borrow so much as shall need for brief resolution in this point. Although we are not of opinion therefore, as some are, that nature in working hath before her certain exemplary draughts or patterns, which subsisting in the bosom of the Highest, and being thence discovered, she fixeth her eye upon them, as travellers by sea upon the pole-star of the world, and that according thereunto she guideth her hand to work by imitation: although we rather embrace the oracle of Hippocrates,[6] that 'each thing both in small and in great fulfilleth the task which destiny hath set down'; and concerning the manner of executing and fulfilling the same, 'what they do they know not, yet is it in show and appear-ance as though they did know what they do; and the truth is they do not discern the things which they look on': nevertheless, forasmuch as the works of nature are no less exact, than if she did both behold and study how to express some absolute shape or mirror always present before her; yea, such her dexterity and skill appeareth, that no intellectual creature in the world were able by capacity to do that which nature doth without capacity and knowledge; it cannot be but nature hath some director of infinite knowledge to guide her in all her ways. Who the guide of nature, but only the God of nature? 'In Him we live, move, and are.'[7] Those things which nature is said to do, are by divine art performed, using nature as an instrument; nor is there any such art or knowl-edge divine in nature herself working, but in the Guide of nature's work.

From Book I, Chapter 14

Although the scripture of God therefore be stored with infinite variety of matter in all kinds, although it abound with all sorts of laws, yet the principal intent of scripture is to deliver the laws of duties supernatural.[1] Oftentimes it hath been in very solemn manner disputed whether all things necessary unto salvation be necessarily set down in the holy scriptures or no. If we define that necessary unto salvation whereby the way to salvation is in any sort made more plain, apparent and easy to be known, then is there no part of true philosophy, no art of accompt,[2] no kind of science rightly so called, but the scripture must

5. The doctrine that the fall of Adam entailed that of nature.
6. Great 5th-century b.c. Greek physician, here quoted from Aristotle's *Rhetoric* I.39.
7. Acts 17:28.

1. The distinction is between natural law, of which Hooker speaks elsewhere, and super-natural or "positive" law, which we should not know if it were not revealed in Scripture.
2. Account (meaning here history, narration).

contain it. If only those things be necessary, as surely none else are, without the knowledge and practice whereof it is not the will and pleasure of God to make any ordinary grant of salvation, it may be, notwithstanding, and oftentimes hath been, demanded, how the books of holy scripture contain in them all necessary things, when of things necessary the very chiefest is to know what books we are bound to esteem holy, which point is confessed impossible for the scripture itself to teach. Whereunto we may answer with truth that there is not in the world any art or science, which proposing unto itself an end, as every one doth some end or other, hath been therefore thought defective if it have not delivered simply whatsoever is needful to the same end; but all kinds of knowledge have their certain bounds and limits: each of them presupposeth many necessary things learned in other sciences and known beforehand. He that should take upon him to teach men how to be eloquent in pleading causes must needs deliver unto them whatsoever precepts are requisite unto that end; otherwise he doth not the thing which he taketh upon him. Seeing then no man can plead eloquently unless he be able first to speak, it followeth that ability of speech is in this case a thing most necessary. Notwithstanding every man would think it ridiculous that he which undertaketh by writing to instruct an orator should therefore deliver all the precepts of grammar, because his profession is to deliver precepts necessary unto eloquent speech, yet so that they which are to receive them be taught beforehand so much of that [3] which is thereunto necessary as comprehendeth the skill of speaking. In like sort, albeit scripture do profess to contain in it all things which are necessary unto salvation, yet the meaning cannot be simply of all things that are necessary, but all things that are necessary in some certain kind or form, as: all things that are necessary and either could not at all or could not easily be known by the light of natural discourse; all things which are necessary to be known that we may be saved, but known with presupposal of knowledge concerning certain principles whereof it receiveth us already persuaded and then instructeth us in all the residue that are necessary. In the number of these principles one is the sacred authority of scripture. Being therefore persuaded by other means that these scriptures are the oracles of God, themselves do then teach us the rest and lay before us all the duties which God requireth at our hands as necessary unto salvation. . . .

From *Book IV, Chapter 1*
Book IV. Ch. i. 1, 2. [Ceremony] [1]

I. Such was the ancient simplicity and softness of spirit which sometimes [2] prevailed in the world, that they whose words were even as oracles amongst

---

3. Grammar.

1. This characteristically moderate defense of ceremonies, regardless of their origin, as not as of the essence of religion but as making an important contribution to it not only answers Puritan objections (ceremonies are not derived from the Word) but also illustrates the contemporary understanding of the relation between outward and visible signs and inward meanings. In particular compare Chapman, *Hero and Leander*, and in general the ceremonial of masque and pageant, and the use of emblems and devices. It is also worth recalling that rhetorical speaking was accompanied by standardized gestures, so that ear was reinforced by eye.

2. Long ago.

men, seemed evermore loth to give sentence [3] against any thing publicly received in the Church of God, except it were wonderful apparently [4] evil; for that they did not so much incline to that severity which delighteth to reprove the least things it seeth amiss, as to that charity which is unwilling to behold any thing that duty bindeth it to reprove. The state of this present age, wherein zeal hath drowned charity, and skill meekness, will not now suffer any man to marvel, whatsoever he shall hear reproved by whomsoever. Those rites and ceremonies of the Church therefore, which are the selfsame now that they were when holy and virtuous men maintained them against profane and deriding adversaries, her own children [5] have at this day in derision. Whether justly or no, it shall then appear, when all things are heard which they have to allege against the outward received orders of this church. Which inasmuch as themselves do compare unto 'mint and cummin,' [6] granting them to be no part of those things which in the matter of polity are weightier, we hope that for small things their strife will neither be earnest nor long. . . .

. . . we are to note, that in every grand or main public duty which God requireth at the hands of his Church, there is, besides that matter and form wherein the essence thereof consisteth, a certain outward fashion whereby the same is in decent sort administered. The substance of all religious actions is delivered from God himself in few words. For example's sake in the sacraments. 'Unto the element let the word be added, and they both do make a sacrament,' saith St. Augustine. Baptism is given by the element of water, and that prescript [7] form of words which the Church of Christ doth use; the sacrament of the body and blood of Christ is administered in the elements of bread and wine, if those mystical words be added thereunto. But the due and decent form of administering those holy sacraments doth require a great deal more.

The end which is aimed at in setting down the outward form of all religious actions is the edification of the Church. Now men are edified, when either their understanding is taught somewhat [8] whereof in such actions it behoveth all men to consider, or when their hearts are moved with any affection suitable thereunto; when their minds are in any sort [9] stirred up unto that reverence, devotion, attention, and due regard, which in those cases seemeth requisite. Because therefore unto this purpose not only speech but sundry sensible means besides have always been thought necessary, and especially those means which being object to the eye, the liveliest and the most apprehensive sense of all other, have in that respect seemed the fittest to make a deep and a strong impression: from hence have risen not only a number of prayers, readings, questionings, exhortings, but even of visible signs also; which being used in performance of holy actions, are undoubtedly most effectual to open such matter, as men when they know and remember carefully, must needs be a great deal the better informed

3. Speak against.
4. Very obviously.
5. The Puritans.
6. "Woe unto you, scribes and Pharisees, hypocrites! for ye pay tithe of mint and anise and cummin, and have omitted the weightier matters of the law . . ." (Matthew 23:23). Cummin is a seed used for flavoring.
7. Prescribed.
8. Something.
9. Way.

to what effect such duties serve. We must not think but that there is some ground of reason even in nature,[10] whereby it cometh to pass that no nation under heaven either doth or ever did suffer public actions which are of weight, whether they be civil and temporal or else spiritual and sacred, to pass without some visible solemnity: the very strangeness whereof and difference from that which is common, doth cause popular eyes to observe and to mark the same. Words, both because they are common, and do not so strongly move the fancy of man, are for the most part but slightly heard: and therefore with singular wisdom it hath been provided, that the deeds of men which are made in the presence of witnesses should pass not only with words, but also with certain sensible actions, the memory whereof is far more easy and durable than the memory of speech can be.

The things which so long experience of all ages hath confirmed and made profitable, let not us presume to condemn as follies and toys, because we sometimes know not the cause and reason of them. A wit disposed to scorn whatsoever it doth not conceive, might ask wherefore Abraham should say to his servant, 'Put thy hand under my thigh and swear' [11]: was it not sufficient for his servant to show the religion of an oath by naming the Lord God of heaven and earth, unless that strange ceremony were added? In contracts, bargains, and conveyances, a man's word is a token sufficient to express his will. Yet 'this was the ancient manner in Israel concerning redeeming and exchanging, to establish all things; a man did pluck off his shoe and gave it his neighbour; and this was a sure witness in Israel.' [12] Amongst the Romans in their making of a bondman free, was it not wondered wherefore so great ado should be made? The master to present his slave in some court, to take him by the hand, and not only to say in the hearing of the public magistrate, 'I will that this man become free,' but after these solemn words uttered, to strike him on the cheek, to turn him round, the hair of his head to be shaved off, the magistrate to touch him thrice with a rod, in the end a cap and a white garment to be given him. To what purpose all this circumstance? Amongst the Hebrews how strange and in outward appearance almost against reason, that he which was minded to make himself a perpetual servant, should not only testify so much in the presence of the judge, but for a visible token thereof have also his ear bored through with an awl.[13] It were an infinite labour to prosecute these things so far as they might be exemplified both in civil and religious actions. For in both they have their necessary use and force. 'The sensible things which religion hath hallowed, are resemblances framed according to things spiritually understood, whereunto they serve as a hand to lead, and a way to direct.' [14]

1593

10. Hooker's constant appeal is to nature thus conceived.
11. Genesis 24:2.
12. Ruth 4:7.
13. Exodus 21:6.
14. From the *Ecclesiastical Hierarchies* of Dionysius the Areopagite.

LANCELOT ANDREWES
1555–1626

Chaplain to Queen Elizabeth, bishop of Winchester, important figure at the court of
James I, Andrewes was one of the translators of the Authorized Version of the
Bible (King James Bible). This sermon was one of a long series preached before the
King at Christmas. James was a theologian, and Andrewes gave learned sermons
which would have been unsuitable for large popular congregations. His terse Senecan
style, extracting every possible meaning from the text, is aimed at intellectuals, but
he was regarded as *stella predicantium*, the star among the preachers of his time.
The style became obsolete before the century was out, but Andrewes has retained some
appeal, and was venerated by T. S. Eliot, who compares him with Donne to Donne's
discredit. "Intellect and sensibility were in harmony; and hence arise the particular
qualities of his style."

The present sermon examines—or as some might say, torments—its text in characteristic fashion. It opens by setting up two topics, the persons arriving, and their
errand. This second topic he enlarges. First he shows that the text, though on the
face of it more appropriate to the feast of the Epiphany, suits Christmas Day; and
the whole sermon is shaped by this.

From A Sermon Preached Before the King's Majesty

at Whitehall, on Wednesday, the Twenty-fifth of December, A.D. MDCXXII., Being Christmas-Day

Behold there came wise men from the East to Jerusalem,
Saying, Where is the King of the Jews that is born? For we have
seen His star in the East, and are come to worship Him.

Ecce magi ab oriente venerunt Jerosolymam,
Dicentes, ubi est qui natus est Rex Judæorum? vidimus enim
stellam ejus in oriente, et venimus adorare eum. (Latin Vulgate)
MATTHEW ii. 1, 2.

Their errand we may best learn from themselves out of their *dicentes,*[1] etc.
Which, in a word, is to worship Him. Their errand our errand, and the errand
of this day.

This text may seem to come a little too soon, before the time; and should
have stayed till the day it was spoken on,[2] rather than on this day. But if you
mark them well, there are in the verse four words that be *verba diei hujus,*
'proper and peculiar to this very day.' 1. For first, *natus est*[3] is most proper to
this day of all days, the day of His Nativity. 2. Secondly, *vidimus stellam;*[4] for
on this day it was first seen, appeared first. 3. Thirdly, *venimus;*[5] for this day

---

1. "Saying" (refers to the Latin text).
2. The feast of the Epiphany, twelve days after Christmas.
3. "(He) is born" (referring to the Latin text).
4. "We have seen the star."
5. "We have come."

they set forth, began their journey. 4. And last, *adorare eum*,[6] for 'when He brought His only-begotten Son into the world, He gave in charge, Let all the angels of God worship Him.'[7] And when the angels to do it, no time more proper for us to do it as then. So these four appropriate it to this day, and none but this.

The main heads of their errand are 1. *Vidimus stellam*, the occasion; 2. and *Venimus adorare*, the end[8] of their coming. But for the better conceiving it I will take another course, to set forth these points to be handled.

I. Their faith first: faith—in that they never ask 'Whether He be,' but 'Where He is born'; for that born He is, that they steadfastly believe.

II. Then 'the work or service'[9] of this faith, as St. Paul calleth it; 'the touch or trial,' 'δοχίμιον,'[10] as St. Peter; the *ostende mihi*, as St. James.[11]. . .

[He develops these divisions, and further subdivisions, until, at this point, he explains the significance of the fact that the wise men knew this was *His* (Christ's) star.]

Vidimus stellam—we can well conceive that; any that will but look up, may see a star. But how could they see the *ejus* of it, that it was His? Either that it belonged to any, or that He it was it belonged to. This passeth all perspective;[12] no astronomy could show them this. What by course of nature the stars can produce, that they by course of art or observation may discover. But this birth was above nature. No trigon, triplicity, exaltation could bring it forth. They are but idle that set figures for it. The star should not have been His, but He the star's, if it had gone that way. Some other light then, they saw this *ejus* by.

Now with us in Divinity there be but two in all; 1. *Vespertina*,[13] and 2. *Matutina lux*.[14] *Vespertina*, 'the owl-light' of our reason or skill, is too dim to see it by. No remedy then but it must be as Esay[15] calls it, *matutina lux*, 'the morning-light,' the light of God's law must certify them of the *ejus* of it. There, or not at all, to be had whom this star did portend.

[After extracting more doctrine from the star, he finds a text to authorize a switch to another subject, namely *venimus*, we came, and meditates on this journey in a passage made famous by Eliot's *Journey of the Magi*, which begins "A cold coming we had of it."]

It is not commended to stand 'gazing up into heaven'[16] too long; not on Christ Himself ascending, much less on His star. For they sat not still gazing on the star. Their *vidimus* begat *venimus*; their seeing made them come, come a great journey. *Venimus* is soon said, but a short word; but many a wide and weary step they made before they could come to say *Venimus*, Lo, here 'we are

6. To adore Him.
7. Hebrews 1:6.
8. Purpose.
9. Philippians 2:17.
10. I Peter 1:7.
11. James 2:18.
12. Telescope.
13. "Evening twilight."
14. "Morning twilight."
15. Isaiah 58:8.
16. Acts 1:11.

come'; come, and at our journey's end. To look a little on it. In this their coming we consider, 1. First, the distance of the place they came from. It was not hard by as the shepherds—but a step to Bethlehem over the fields; this was riding many a hundred miles, and cost them many a day's journey. 2. Secondly, we consider the way that they came, if it be pleasant, or plain and easy; for if it be, it is so much the better. 1. This was nothing pleasant, for through deserts, all the way waste and desolate. 2. Nor secondly, easy either; for over the rocks and crags of both Arabias, specially Petræa,[17] their journey lay. 3. Yet if safe—but it was not, but exceeding dangerous, as lying through the midst of the 'black tents of Kedar,'[18] a nation of thieves and cut-throats; to pass over the hills of robbers, infamous then, and infamous to this day. No passing without great troop or convoy. 4. Last we consider the time of their coming, the season of the year. It was no summer progress. A cold coming they had of it at this time of the year, just the worst time of the year to take a journey, and specially a long journey in. The ways deep, the weather sharp, the days short, the sun farthest off, *in solstitio brumali*,[19] 'the very dead of winter.' *Venimus*, 'we are come,' if that be one, *venimus*, 'we are now come,' come at this time, that sure is another.

And these difficulties they overcame, of a wearisome, irksome, troublesome, dangerous, unseasonable journey; and for all this they came. And came it cheerfully and quickly, as appeareth by the speed they made. It was but *vidimus, venimus*, with them; 'they saw,' and 'they came'; no sooner saw, but they set out presently. So as upon the first appearing of the star, as it might be last night, they knew it was Balaam's star;[20] it called them away, they made ready straight to begin their journey this morning. A sign they were highly conceited of [21] His birth, believed some great matter of it, that they took all these pains, made all this haste that they might be there to worship Him with all the possible speed they could. Sorry for nothing so much as that they could not be there soon enough, with the very first, to do it even this day, the day of His birth. All considered, there is more in *venimus* than shows at the first sight.[22] It was not for nothing it was said in the first verse, *ecce venerunt;* their coming hath an *ecce* [23] on it, it well deserves it.

And we, what should we have done? Sure these men of the East shall rise in judgment against the men of the West,[24] that is us, and their faith against ours in this point. With them it was but *vidimus, venimus;* with us it would have been but *veniemus* [25] at most. Our fashion is to see and see again before we stir a foot, specially if it be to the worship of Christ. Come such a journey at such a time? No; but fairly have put it off to the spring of the year, till the days

---

17. Arabia was divided into three parts by ancient geographers: *Arabia felix* (fertile Arabia), *Arabia deserta, Arabia petraea* (stony Arabia).
18. Song of Songs 1:5.
19. "In the winter solstice."
20. Balaam's trance: "I shall behold him, but not nigh: there shall come a Star out of Jacob, and a sceptre shall rise out of Israel . . ." (Numbers 24:17).
21. Had a strong notion of.
22. This sentence expresses the method of Andrewes and his contemporaries in unfolding the full significance of their sermon texts.
23. "Behold." He means that there was something remarkable in their speedy action.
24. Matthew 8:11.
25. "We shall come."

longer, and the ways fairer, and the weather warmer, till better travelling to Christ. Our Epiphany would sure have fallen in Easter-week at the soonest.

But then for the distance, desolateness, tediousness, and the rest, any of them were enough to mar our *venimus* quite. It must be no great way, first, we must come; we love not that. Well fare the shepherds, yet they came but hard by; rather like them than the Magi. Nay, not like them neither. For with us the nearer, lightly the farther off; our proverb is, you know, 'The nearer the Church, the farther from God.'

Nor it must not be through no desert, over no Petræa. If rugged or uneven the way, if the weather ill-disposed, if any never so little danger, it is enough to stay us. To Christ we cannot travel, but weather and way and all must be fair. If not, no journey, but sit still and see farther. As indeed, all our religion is rather *vidimus*, a contemplation, than *venimus*, a motion, or stirring to do aught.

But when we do it, we must be allowed leisure. Ever *veniemus*, never *venimus*; ever coming, never come. We love to make no very great haste. To other things perhaps; not to *adorare*, the place of the worship of God. Why should we? Christ is no wild-cat.[26] What talk ye of twelve days?[27] And if it be forty days hence, ye shall be sure to find His Mother and Him; she cannot be churched[28] till then. What needs such haste? The truth is, we conceit Him and His birth but slenderly, and our haste is even thereafter. But if we be at that point, we must be out of this *venimus;* they like enough to leave us behind. Best get us a new Christmas in September; we are not like to come to Christ at this feast. Enough for *venimus*.

[From *venimus* he passes to the purpose of the journey, *invenimus*, we find. The wise men found, and fell down before Christ, and made offerings to him. We should do likewise.]

We cannot say *vidimus stellam;* the star is gone long since, not now to be seen. Yet I hope for all that, that *venimus adorare*, 'we be come thither to worship.' It will be the more acceptable, if not seeing it we worship though. It is enough we read of it in the text; we see it there. And indeed as I said, it skills[29] not for the star in the firmament, if the same day-star be risen in our hearts that was in theirs, and the same beams of it to be seen, all five. For then we have our part in it no less, nay full out as much as they. And it will bring us whither it brought them, to Christ. Who at His second appearing in glory shall call forth these wise men and all that have ensued[30] the steps of their faith, and that upon the reason specified in the text; for I have seen their star shining and showing forth itself by the like beams; and as they came to worship Me, so am I come to do them worship. A *venite*[31] then, for a *venimus*

26. A sentence admired but not explained by T. S. Eliot. The sense requires it to mean that there is no hurry to get to Christ, as if a wildcat were something shown as a public sensation, like a dead Indian. Or it may mean that he will not attack us for being late.

27. The twelve days between Christmas and the Epiphany.

28. Churching is the service of thanksgiving for women after childbirth.

29. Matters.

30. Followed.

31. "Come!"—imperative form of *venire*, "to come," and the short title of a canticle in the Prayer Book, *Venite omnia opera* ("Come All Ye Works of the Lord"). This playing on the moods and tenses of the verb from the text is characteristic of the preaching method of the period, though Andrewes does it more tersely than, say, Donne.

now. Their star I have seen, and give them a place above among the stars. They fell down: I will lift them up, and exalt them. And as they offered to Me, so am I come to bestow on them, and to reward them with the endless joy and bliss on My heavenly kingdom.

1622   1629

FRANCIS BACON
1561–1626

At the beginning of the seventeenth century, the word "science" still meant both "knowledge," acquired by a systematic acquaintance with the assertions of authority from Aristotle down through his scholastic interpreters, and general truths, made evident by the controlling fictions of art or literature. The phrase "natural philosophy" could still include anything from the dying stages of alchemy and astrology to the exciting and frightening new revisions of the age's sense of the universe. These revisions were being brought about by a century of global exploration and revolutionary astronomical thought, but they would soon extend into other areas of knowledge. "And new philosophy calls all in doubt," lamented John Donne in his "An Anatomy of the World," and it was not only the old maps of that world—the Ptolemaic cosmology, the macro-microcosmic relationships, the hierarchies of being and condition in animal, vegetable, and mineral kingdoms, as well as in those of nations and churches—whose loss he bemoaned. It was also a whole attitude toward certainty, a condition of comfort taken in demonstrations logically deduced from propositions of unquestioned authoritativeness. The new empirical attitudes toward truths about nature threatened some of that deductive security, that sense of protection which closure affords. To the active humanist intellect, compensation could lie in the energies of reason at work, in the spreading of reason's light which some radical reformers could feel was focusing (and which many of the orthodox feared was threatening to supplant) divine illumination.

Although the name of Francis Bacon is associated with the most systematic early vision of the generation and distribution of that empirical light, he was no true natural philosopher himself. At best he was an amateur experimentalist, innocent of mathematics, for the most part—a lawyer, a major legal theorist, an administrator and judge, and above all, a literary intellect whose thought seldom strayed far from the gardens of imagery and symbol in which they flourished. Bacon's great idea for a reconstruction of the institutions by which truths are discovered, recorded, and maintained could in no way be said to constitute one of the major advances of seventeenth-century science. That Great Reconstruction (the *Instauratio Magna,* his uncompleted general work) remains in many ways more like a poem than a theory, more like a fiction than a model.

Bacon's private program for the reform of knowledge was so much a public plan that it is odd to find such inconsistencies between his private and public lives. His career was marked by the difficulties which beset a world of public service governed by the caprices of courts rather than by the machinery of self-perpetuating bureaucracies. Bacon was well-connected, the younger son of the Lord Keeper of the Great Seal, Sir Nicholas Bacon. At Cambridge (he went to Trinity in 1573 but left two years later without a degree) and at Gray's Inn, where he read law, he trained for the kind of government post which would allow him either leisure to philosophize about the world or power to control it; yet even his relation to Lord Burghley and his friendship with the favorite, Essex, were of no help to him in Elizabeth's court. He was, indeed, finally put in the position of having to help prepare the prosecution of the Earl of Essex for treason; and only in the Jacobean court, with its scholarly airs and its penchant for rapid promotions, did Bacon prosper. But he did so rapidly, after receiving the knighthood in 1603 and a succession of honors thereafter—Solicitor General, Attorney General, Lord Keeper, Lord Chancellor—and became Baron Verulam in 1618 and Viscount St. Albans three years after. But at the height of his career he was indicted, by a Parliament hostile to James's court and its conduct, for accepting bribes while on the bench. His plea of guilty to the charge, coupled with the insistence that he had never let bribes (so common as to be almost customary) influence any of his judgments, left his accusers unimpressed; there were few among them who could have grasped the truth of this, as there were even fewer who might have said, as Bacon did about himself, "I was the justest judge that was in England these fifty years, but it was the justest censure in Parliament these two hundred years." Bacon lived on for about five years after a token imprisonment, and died of pneumonia resulting from overexposure to snow in which he was attempting experimentally to preserve food.

Bacon's *Essays*, for which he remained most famous, first appeared in 1597; an expanded edition of thirty-eight essays was published in 1612, and in 1625 the complete series of fifty-eight. Memorable for their crisp, "pointed" style, the *Essays or Counsels, Civil and Moral* eschewed abstract theorizing as they fled the lengthy balance of Ciceronian prose. They provide excellent evidence of Bacon's early seriousness about his belief, elaborated in *The Advancement of Learning*, that many of the miseries of truth could be traced to diseases of language. Aphoristic, flexible, far less bound in their structure to the quoted words of other men than even Montaigne's *Essais*, they have remained celebrated and widely quoted. The great project of the Instauration was launched only in pieces. In 1605, *The Advancement of Learning* outlined the problems with which the whole plan was to deal. The second part, the Latin *Novum Organum* (a "new instrument" to replace, presumably, the logical treatises or *Organon* of the Aristotelian canon against which his scholastic experiences at Cambridge had turned him early in youth) appeared in 1620. *Sylva Sylvarum*, his collection of observations on, and designs for experiments in, natural history, was published in 1626–27; likewise, the unfinished utopia called *The New Atlantis*. Throughout all of these runs an ultimately cheerful intellectual energy, a sense of manifest human destiny over nature. That state of nature sketched by Hobbes, wherein man is stripped down to his common bestiality, contrasts strongly with the Baconian one, wherein man is freed from the conceptual and institutional shadows of societies and theories, to walk about bathed in the light of his own reason.

From Essays or Counsels, Civil and Moral

Of Truth

What is Truth? said jesting Pilate, and would not stay for an answer. Certainly there be that delight in giddiness,[1] and count it a bondage to fix a belief, affecting [2] free will in thinking, as well as in acting. And though the sects of philosophers [3] of that kind be gone, yet there remain certain discoursing wits [4] which are of the same veins, though there be not so much blood in them as was in those of the ancients. But it is not only the difficulty and labour which men take in finding out of truth, nor again that when it is found it imposeth upon [5] men's thoughts, that doth bring lies in favour, but a natural though corrupt love of the lie itself. One of the later school of the Grecians examineth the matter, and is at a stand to think what should be in it, that men should love lies, where neither they make for pleasure, as with poets, nor for advantage, as with the merchant, but for the lie's sake. But I cannot tell: this same truth is a naked and open daylight, that doth not show the masks and mummeries and triumphs of the world, half so stately and daintily [6] as candlelights. Truth may perhaps come to the price of a pearl, that showeth best by day; but it will not rise to the price of a diamond or carbuncle, that showeth best in varied lights. A mixture of a lie doth ever add pleasure. Doth any man doubt, that if there were taken out of men's minds vain opinions, flattering hopes, false valuations, imaginations as one would, and the like, but it would leave the minds of a number of men poor shrunken things, full of melancholy and indisposition, and unpleasing to themselves? One of the Fathers, in great severity, called poesy *vinum dæmonum,*[7] because it filleth the imagination, and yet it is but with the shadow of a lie. But it is not the lie that passeth through the mind, but the lie that sinketh in and settleth in it, that doth the hurt; such as we spake of before. But howsoever these things are thus in men's depraved judgments and affections, yet truth, which only doth judge itself, teacheth that the inquiry of truth, which is the love-making or wooing of it, the knowledge of truth, which is the presence of it, and the belief of truth, which is the enjoying of it, is the sovereign good of human nature. The first creature of God, in the works of the days, was the light of the sense, the last was the light of reason; and his sabbath work ever since is the illumination of His Spirit. First He breathed light upon the face of the matter or chaos; then He breathed light into the face of man; and still He breatheth and inspireth light into the face of his chosen. The poet [8] that beautified the sect that was otherwise inferior to the rest saith yet excellently well: *It is a pleasure to stand upon the shore, and to see ships tossed upon the sea; a pleasure to stand in the window of a castle, and to see a battle and the ad-*

---

1. Intellectual fickleness.
2. Trying for.
3. The Skeptical school, probably; they simply denied the possibility of certainty.
4. Rambling or talkative minds.
5. Influences.
6. Elegantly.
7. "The wine of devils" (possibly quoted from St. Augustine, *Confessions* I.xvi).
8. Lucretius; Bacon is paraphrasing the opening of Bk. II of his *De Rerum Natura* (Of the Nature of Things).

ventures [9] *thereof below; but no pleasure is comparable to the standing upon the vantage ground of Truth* (a hill not to be commanded,[10] and where the air is always clear and serene), *and to see the errors, and wanderings, and mists, and tempests, in the vale below;* so [11] always that this prospect be with pity and not with swelling or pride. Certainly it is heaven upon earth to have a man's mind move in charity, rest in providence, and turn upon the poles of truth.

To pass from theological and philosophical truth to the truth of civil business, it will be acknowledged even by those that practise it not that clear and round [12] dealing is the honour of man's nature; and that mixture of false-hood is like allay [13] in coin of gold and silver, which may make the metal work the better, but it embaseth [14] it. For these winding and crooked courses are the goings of the serpent, which goeth basely upon the belly and not upon the feet. There is no vice that doth so cover a man with shame as to be found false and perfidious. And therefore Montaigne saith prettily, when he inquired the reason, why the word of the lie should be such a disgrace and such an odious charge? Saith he, *If it be well weighed, to say that a man lieth, is as much to say, as that he is brave towards God and a coward towards men.*[15] For a lie faces God and shrinks from man. Surely the wickedness of falsehood and breach of faith cannot possibly be so highly expressed, as in that it shall be the last peal to call the judgments of God upon the generations of men, it being foretold that when Christ cometh, *he shall not find faith upon the earth.*[16]

1625

Of Death

Men fear Death, as children fear to go in the dark; and as that natural fear in children is increased with tales, so is the other. Certainly the contemplation of death, as the wages of sin [1] and passage to another world, is holy and religious, but the fear of it, as a tribute due unto nature, is weak. Yet in religious meditations there is sometimes mixture of vanity and of superstition. You shall read in some of the friars' books of mortification, that a man should think with himself what the pain is if he have but his finger's end pressed or tortured, and thereby imagine what the pains of death are, when the whole body is corrupted and dissolved; when many times death passeth with less pain than the torture of a limb, for the most vital parts are not the quickest of sense. And by him that spake only as a philosopher and natural man, it was well said, *Pompa mortis magis terret, quam mors ipsa.*[2] Groans and convulsions, and a discoloured face, and friends weeping, and blacks, and ob-

9. What chances to happen.
10. Taken.
11. So long as.
12. Honest.
13. Alloy.
14. Debases.
15. From his *Essays* II.18.
16. Luke 18:8.

1. Romans 6:23.
2. "The circumstances surrounding death are more frightening than death itself" (possibly from Seneca, *Epistles* XXIV.14.)

sequies, and the like show death terrible. It is worthy the observing that there is no passion in the mind of man so weak, but it mates [3] and masters the fear of death; and therefore death is no such terrible enemy when a man hath so many attendants about him that can win the combat of him. Revenge triumphs over death; Love slights it; Honour aspireth to it; Grief flieth to it; Fear preoccupateth [4] it; nay we read, after Otho the emperor [5] had slain himself, Pity (which is the tenderest of affections) provoked many to die out of mere compassion to their sovereign, and as the truest sort of followers. Nay Seneca adds niceness [6] and satiety: *Cogita quamdiu eadem feceris; mori velle, non tantum fortis, aut miser, sed etiam fastidiosus potest*.[7] A man would die, though he were neither valiant nor miserable, only upon a weariness to do the same thing so oft over and over. It is no less worthy to observe how little alteration in good spirits the approaches of death make, for they appear to be the same men till the last instant. Augustus Cæsar died in a compliment: *Livia, conjugii nostri memor, vive et vale;* [8] Tiberius in dissimulation, as Tacitus saith of him: *Jam Tiberium vires et corpus, non dissimulatio, deserebant;* [9] Vespasian in a jest, sitting upon the stool: *Ut puto Deus fio;* [10] Galba with a sentence: *Feri, si ex re sit populi Romani,*[11] holding forth his neck; Septimius Severus in despatch: *Adeste si quid mihi restat agendum.*[12] And the like. Certainly the Stoics bestowed too much cost upon death, and by their great preparations made it appear more fearful. Better saith he, *qui finem vitæ extremum inter munera ponat naturæ.*[13] It is as natural to die as to be born; and to a little infant, perhaps, the one is as painful as the other. He that dies in an earnest pursuit is like one that is wounded in hot blood, who, for the time, scarce feels the hurt; and therefore a mind fixed and bent upon somewhat that is good doth avert the dolours [14] of death. But above all, believe it, the sweetest canticle is, *Nunc dimittis;* [15] when a man hath obtained worthy ends and expectations. Death hath this also, that it openeth the gate to good fame, and extinguisheth envy. *Extinctus amabitur idem.*[16]

1625

Of Love

The stage is more beholding [1] to love than the life of man. For as to the stage, love is ever matter of comedies, and now and then of tragedies, but in

---

3. Overcomes.
4. Anticipates (by causing suicide).
5. The Roman emperor who died by his own hand when his army was defeated, 69 A.D.
6. Fastidiousness.
7. Again from *Epistles* LXXVII.6, paraphrased, as frequently, in the next lines.
8. "Live, remembering our marriage, Livia, and farewell."
9. "Tiberius' strength was leaving him, but not his power to fake."
10. "I guess I'm becoming a god" ("stool": toilet).
11. "Strike, if it's for the people of Rome."
12. "Hurry, if there's anything left for me to do."
13. "Who thinks the end of life one of nature's blessings" (Juvenal, *Satires* X.358).
14. Pains.
15. "Now lettest thou thy servant depart in peace" (Luke 2:29).
16. "(Envied when alive) the same man, dead, will be loved" (Horace, *Epistles* II.i.14).

1. Beholden, indebted.

life it doth much mischief, sometimes like a siren, sometimes like a fury. You may observe that among all great and worthy persons (whereof the memory remaineth, either ancient or recent) there is not one that hath been transported to the mad degree of love, which shows that great spirits and great business do keep out this weak passion. You must except nevertheless Marcus Antonius, the half partner of the empire of Rome, and Appius Claudius,[2] the decemvir and lawgiver; whereof the former was indeed a voluptuous man, and inordinate, but the latter was an austere and wise man; and therefore it seems (though rarely) that love can find entrance not only into an open heart, but also into a heart well fortified, if watch be not well kept. It is a poor saying of Epicurus, *Satis magnum alter alteri theatrum sumus,*[3] as if man, made for the contemplation of heaven and all noble objects, should do nothing but kneel before a little idol, and make himself a subject, though not of the mouth (as beasts are), yet of the eye, which was given him for higher purposes. It is a strange thing to note the excess of this passion, and how it braves [4] the nature and value of things, by this: that the speaking in a perpetual hyperbole is comely in nothing but in love. Neither is it merely in the phrase, for whereas it hath been well said that the arch-flatterer, with whom all the petty flatterers have intelligence,[5] is a man's self, certainly the lover is more. For there was never proud man thought so absurdly well of himself as the lover doth of the person loved; and therefore it was well said, *That it is impossible to love and to be wise.* Neither doth this weakness appear to others only, and not to the party loved, but to the loved most of all, except the love be reciproque.[6] For it is a true rule that love is ever rewarded either with the reciproque or with an inward and secret contempt. By how much the more men ought to beware of this passion, which loseth not only other things but itself. As for the other losses, the poet's relation doth well figure them: that he [7] that preferred Helena quitted the gifts of Juno and Pallas. For whosoever esteemeth too much of amorous affection quitteth both riches and wisdom. This passion hath his floods in the very times of weakness, which are great prosperity and great adversity, though this latter hath been less observed, both which times kindle love, and make it more fervent, and therefore show it to be the child of folly. They do best who, if they cannot but admit love, yet make it keep quarter [8] and sever it wholly from their serious affairs and actions of life, for if it check [9] once with business, it troubleth men's fortunes, and maketh men that they can no ways be true to their own ends. I know not how, but martial men are given to love; I think it is but as they are given to wine, for perils commonly ask to be paid in pleasures. There is in man's

2. Appius Claudius (not the lawgiver; Bacon confused the two) desired Virginia, and her father, Virginius, killed him in order to spare her (449 B.C.). Told by Livy, the story was a popular tragic subject, from Chaucer's day through Bacon's.
3. "Each of us is a big enough theater to one another."
4. Insults.
5. Are confederates.
6. Reciprocal.
7. Paris; asked to award a golden apple (Discord, it was) to the most beautiful of three goddesses, he took Venus' bribe (Helen, wife of Menelaus), rejecting Minerva's offer of wisdom, and Juno's, of power.
8. Proper place.
9. Interfere.

nature a secret inclination and motion towards love of others, which if it be not spent upon some one or a few, doth naturally spread itself towards many, and maketh men become humane and charitable, as it is seen sometime in friars. Nuptial love maketh mankind; friendly love perfecteth it; but wanton love corrupteth and embaseth it.

1625

Of Innovations [1]

As the births of living creatures at first are ill-shapen, so are all Innovations, which are the births of time. Yet notwithstanding, as those that first bring honour into their family are commonly more worthy than most that succeed, so the first precedent (if it be good) is seldom attained by imitation. For Ill, to man's nature as it stands perverted, hath a natural motion, strongest in continuance, but Good, as a forced motion, strongest at first. Surely every medicine is an innovation; and he that will not apply new remedies must expect new evils, for time is the greatest innovator, and if time of course [2] alter things to the worse, and wisdom and counsel shall not alter them to the better, what shall be the end? It is true that what is settled by custom, though it be not good, yet at least it is fit; and those things which have long gone together are as it were confederate within themselves; whereas new things piece not so well, but though they help by their utility, yet they trouble by their inconformity. Besides, they are like strangers, more admired and less favoured. All this is true, if time stood still, which contrariwise moveth so round [3] that a froward retention of custom is as turbulent a thing as an innovation; and they that reverence too much old times are but a scorn to the new. It were good therefore that men in their innovations would follow the example of time itself, which indeed innovateth greatly, but quietly and by degrees scarce to be perceived. For otherwise, whatsoever is new is unlooked for, and ever it mends some, and pairs [4] other; and he that is holpen [5] takes it for a fortune, and thanks the time; and he that is hurt, for a wrong, and imputeth it to the author. It is good also not to try experiments in states, except the necessity be urgent, or the utility evident, and well to beware that it be the reformation that draweth on the change, and not the desire of change that pretendeth the reformation. And lastly, that the novelty, though it be not rejected, yet be held for a suspect,[6] and, as the Scripture saith, *that we make a stand upon the ancient way, and then look about us, and discover what is the straight and right way, and so to walk in it.*[7]

1625

1. Bacon will give the word a double sense of "renewal," and "rebellion against" old things.
2. As a matter of course.
3. Swiftly.
4. Impairs.
5. Helped, cured, mended.
6. Suspicion.
7. Paraphrase of Jeremiah 6:16.

Of Prophecies

I mean not to speak of divine prophecies, nor of heathen oracles, nor of natural predictions, but only of prophecies that have been of certain memory and from hidden causes. Saith the Pythonissa [1] to Saul, *Tomorrow thou and thy son shall be with me.* Homer hath these verses:

> *At domus Æneæ cunctis dominabitur oris,*
> *Et nati natorum, et qui nascentur ab illis.* [2]

A prophecy, as it seems, of the Roman empire. Seneca the tragedian hath these verses:

> *Venient annis*
> *Sæcula seris, quibus Oceanus*
> *Vincula rerum laxet, et ingens*
> *Pateat Tellus, Tiphysque novos*
> *Detegat orbes; nec sit terris*
> *Ultima Thule.* [3]

a prophecy of the discovery of America. The daughter of Polycrates [4] dreamed that Jupiter bathed her father, and Apollo anointed him, and it came to pass that he was crucified in an open place, where the sun made his body run with sweat, and the rain washed it. Philip of Macedon dreamed he sealed up his wife's belly, whereby he did expound it, that his wife should be barren, but Aristander [5] the soothsayer told him his wife was with child, because men do not use to seal vessels that are empty. A phantasm that appeared to M. Brutus in his tent said to him, *Philippis iterum me videbis.* [6] Tiberius said to Galba, *Tu quoque, Galba, degustabis imperium.* [7] In Vespasian's time there went a prophecy in the East, that those that should come forth of Judea should reign over the world, which though it may be was meant of our Saviour, yet Tacitus expounds it of Vespasian. Domitian dreamed, the night before he was slain, that a golden head was growing out of the nape of his neck, and indeed the succession that followed him for many years made golden times. Henry the Sixth of England said of Henry the Seventh, when he was a lad, and gave him water, *This is the lad that shall enjoy the crown for which we strive.* When I was in France, I heard from one Dr. Pena that the Queen Mother, who was given to curious arts, caused the King [8] her husband's

1. The Pythonissa was the priestess of the oracle at Delphi (because of Apollo's epithet of Pythian, who had killed a python); here, she is identified with the Witch of Endor (in I Samuel 28).

2. "The house of Aeneas will reign in all lands, and his children's children, and their descendants" (Virgil, *Aeneid* III.97–98).

3. "In years to come, Oceanus will unloose the chains that bind things, revealing the vast earth, Tiphys will discover new lands, and Thule will not be the limit of the world" (Seneca, *Medea* II.374–8). Tiphys was the *Argo's* pilot, *Ultima Thule* the northmost land.

4. A tyrant of Samos; the story is from Herodotus.

5. A favorite soothsayer of Alexander the Great, Philip's son.

6. "You will see me again at Philippi."

7. "You too, Galba, will taste of empire."

8. King Henry II of France; the tournament in which he was accidentally killed took place in 1559.

nativity to be calculated under a false name; and the astrologer gave a judgment, that he should be killed in a duel, at which the Queen laughed, thinking her husband to be above challenges and duels, but he was slain upon a course at tilt, the splinters of the staff of Montgomery going in at his beaver.[9] The trivial [10] prophecy which I heard when I was a child and Queen Elizabeth was in the flower of her years, was,

> When hempe is sponne
> England's done:

whereby it was generally conceived that after the princes had reigned which had the principial [11] letters of that word *hempe* (which were Henry, Edward, Mary, Philip, and Elizabeth), England should come to utter confusion, which, thanks be to God, is verified only in the change of the name, for that the King's style is now no more of England but of Britain.[12] There was also another prophecy before the year of eighty-eight, which I do not well understand:

> There shall be seen upon a day,
> Between the Baugh and the May,
> The black fleet of Norway.
> When that that is come and gone,
> England build houses of lime and stone,
> For after wars shall you have none.

It was generally conceived to be meant of the Spanish fleet that came in eighty-eight, for that the king of Spain's surname, as they say, is Norway. The prediction of Regiomontanus,

> *Octogesimus octavus mirabilis annus,*[13]

was thought likewise accomplished in the sending of that great fleet, being the greatest in strength, though not in number, of all that ever swam upon the sea. As for Cleon's dream, I think is was a jest. It was that he was devoured of a long dragon; and it was expounded of [14] a maker of sausages, that troubled him exceedingly. There are numbers of the like kind, especially if you include dreams and predictions of astrology. But I have set down these few only of certain credit for example. My judgment is that they ought all to be despised, and ought to serve but for winter talk by the fireside. Though when I say *despised,* I mean it as for belief, for otherwise, the spreading or publishing of them is in no sort to be despised. For they have done much mischief, and I see many severe laws made to suppress them. That that hath given them grace and some credit consisteth in three things. First, that men mark when

9. Movable part of the tilting helmet.
10. Common.
11. Initial.
12. Because James I, formerly King of Scotland, ruled over a new "Great Britain" in which the nations were joined.
13. "Eighty-eight, a year most great," Regiomontanus (Johannes Müller, a 15th-century German mathematician and astrologer).
14. By.

they hit, and never mark when they miss, as they do generally also of dreams. The second is that probable conjectures or obscure traditions many times turn themselves into prophecies, while the nature of man, which coveteth divination, thinks it no peril to foretell that which indeed they do but collect. As that of Seneca's verse. For so much was then subject to demonstration that the globe of the earth had great parts beyond the Atlantic, which mought [15] be probably conceived not to be all sea, and adding thereto the tradition in Plato's Timæus and his Atlanticus,[16] it mought encourage one to turn it to a prediction. The third and last (which is the great one) is that almost all of them, being infinite in number, have been impostures, and by idle and crafty brains merely contrived and feigned after the event past.

1625

Of Studies

Studies serve for delight, for ornament, and for ability. Their chief use for delight is in privateness and retiring; [1] for ornament, is in discourse; and for ability, is in the judgment and disposition of business. For expert [2] men can execute and perhaps judge of particulars, one by one, but the general counsels and the plots and marshalling of affairs come best from those that are learned. To spend too much time in studies is sloth; to use them too much for ornament is affectation; to make judgment wholly by their rules is the humour of a scholar. They perfect nature, and are perfected by experience, for natural abilities are like natural plants, that need proyning [3] by study; and studies themselves do give forth directions too much at large, except they be bounded in by experience. Crafty men contemn studies; simple men admire them; and wise men use them, for they teach not their own use, but that is a wisdom without them and above them, won by observation. Read not to contradict and confute, nor to believe and take for granted, nor to find talk and discourse, but to weigh and consider. Some books are to be tasted, others to be swallowed, and some few to be chewed and digested; that is, some books are to be read only in parts; others to be read, but not curiously; [4] and some few to be read wholly and with diligence and attention. Some books also may be read by deputy, and extracts made of them by others, but that would [5] be only in the less important arguments and the meaner sort of books; else distilled books are like common distilled waters, flashy things. Reading maketh a full man, conference a ready man, and writing an exact man. And therefore, if a man write little, he had need have a great memory; if he confer little, he had need have a present wit; and if he read little, he had need have much cunning, to seem to know that he doth not. Histories make men wise, poets witty, the mathematics subtile, natural philosophy deep, moral grave,

---

15. Might.
16. This dialogue, relating the myth of Atlantis, is called the *Critias*.
1. Privacy and retirement.
2. Experienced (rather than learned).
3. Pruning.
4. Carefully.
5. Should.

logic and rhetoric able to contend. *Abeunt studia in mores.*[6] Nay there is no stond [7] or impediment in the wit but may be wrought out by fit studies, like as diseases of the body may have appropriate exercises. Bowling is good for the stone and reins; [8] shooting for the lungs and breast; gentle walking for the stomach; riding for the head; and the like. So if a man's wit be wandering, let him study the mathematics, for in demonstrations, if his wit be called away never so little, he must begin again. If his wit be not apt to distinguish or find differences, let him study the schoolmen, for they are *cymini sectores.*[9] If he be not apt to beat over [10] matters, and to call up one thing to prove and illustrate another, let him study the lawyers' cases. So every defect of the mind may have a special receipt.

1625

Aphorisms

The Aphorisms of the *Novum Organum* were written in Latin, but like Bacon's English prose, they generate their pith through a stalk of metaphor. Bacon remarks in another context that just as hieroglyphics preceded alphabets, so parables (by which he means what we would call myths) preceded argument, or logical exposition. His own style remains close to parable, as in the famous image of the four classes of Idols or false images which interfere with the perception of truth. The English translation used here is the standard one of Ellis and Spedding.

1

Man, being the servant and interpreter of Nature, can do and understand so much and so much only as he has observed in fact or in thought of the course of nature; beyond this he neither knows anything nor can do anything.

2

Neither the naked hand nor the understanding left to itself can effect much. It is by instruments and helps that the work is done, which are as much wanted for the understanding as for the hand. And as the instruments of the hand either give motion or guide it, so the instruments of the mind supply either suggestions for the understanding or cautions.

3

Human knowledge and human power meet in one, for where the cause is not known the effect cannot be produced. Nature to be commanded must be obeyed, and that which in contemplation is as the cause, is in operation as the rule.

6. "Studies become ways of life" (Ovid, *Heroides* XV. 83).
7. Block.
8. Gallstone and kidneys.
9. "Hair-splitters."
10. Work over, conceptually.

19

There are and can be only two ways of searching into and discovering truth. The one flies from the senses and particulars to the most general axioms,[1] and from these principles, the truth of which it takes for settled and immovable, proceeds to judgment and to the discovery of middle axioms. And this way is now in fashion. The other derives axioms from the senses and particulars, rising by a gradual and unbroken ascent, so that it arrives at the most general axioms last of all. This is the true way, but as yet untried.

38

The idols and false notions which are now in possession of the human understanding, and have taken deep root therein, not only so beset men's minds that truth can hardly find entrance, but even after entrance obtained, they will again in the very instauration[2] of the sciences meet and trouble us, unless men being forewarned of the danger fortify themselves as far as may be against their assaults.

39

There are four classes of Idols[3] which beset men's minds. To these for distinction's sake I have assigned names, calling the first class *Idols of the Tribe*; the second, *Idols of the Cave*; the third, *Idols of the Marketplace*; the fourth, *Idols of the Theatre*.

40

The formation of ideas and axioms by true induction is no doubt the proper remedy to be applied for the keeping off and clearing away of idols. To point them out, however, is of great use, for the doctrine of Idols is to the Interpretation of Nature what the doctrine of the refutation of sophisms[4] is to common logic.

41

The Idols of the Tribe have their foundation in human nature itself and in the tribe or race of men. For it is a false assertion that the sense of man is the measure of things.[5] On the contrary, all perceptions as well of the sense

1. Bacon means true assertions, not logical or mathematical postulates. The first of these "ways" is deduction, essential in closed systems like logic and mathematics, crippling in the investigation of nature. Thus: "All swans are white; here is what looks like a black swan." The deductive way forces us to conclude "It cannot be a true swan." The "untried" way Bacon is advocating would lead us to say: "Since this is swan-like in every way save for its color, then it must *be* a swan, and the original generalization about swan-whiteness must be revised to include, at least, black swans."
2. Reconstruction.
3. From Greek *eidōlon*, image; Bacon means by these not false gods, as in the Bible, but specters and phantasms, entities which appear to exist in nature, but which are only part of our describing or interpreting apparatus.
4. Fallacies.
5. A remark attributed to Protagoras, discussed by Plato in the *Theaetetus*, and in Aristotle's *Metaphysics*.

as of the mind are according to the measure of the individual and not according to the measure of the universe. And the human understanding is like a false mirror, which, receiving rays irregularly, distorts and discolours the nature of things by mingling its own nature with it.

42

The Idols of the Cave are the idols of the individual man. For every one (besides the errors common to human nature in general) has a cave or den of his own, which refracts and discolours the light of nature, owing either to his own proper and peculiar nature, or to his education and conversation with others, or to the reading of books, and the authority of those whom he esteems and admires, or to the differences of impressions, accordingly as they take place in a mind preoccupied and predisposed or in a mind indifferent and settled, or the like. So that the spirit of man (according as it is meted out to different individuals) is in fact a thing variable and full of perturbation, and governed as it were by chance. Whence it was well observed by Heraclitus [6] that men look for sciences in their own lesser worlds and not in the greater or common world.

43

There are also Idols formed by the intercourse and association of men with each other, which I call Idols of the Marketplace on account of the commerce and consort of men there. For it is by discourse that men associate, and words are imposed according to the apprehension of the vulgar.[7] And therefore the ill and unfit choice of words wonderfully obstructs the understanding. Nor do the definitions or explanations wherewith in some things learned men are wont to guard and defend themselves, by any means set the matter right. But words plainly force and overrule the understanding, and throw all into confusion, and lead men away into numberless empty controversies and idle fancies.

44

Lastly, there are Idols which have immigrated into men's minds from the various dogmas of philosophies and also from wrong laws of demonstration. These I call Idols of the Theatre, because in my judgment all the received systems are but so many stage plays, representing worlds of their own creation after an unreal and scenic fashion. Nor is it only of the systems now in vogue or only of the ancient sects and philosophies that I speak, for many more plays of the same kind may yet be composed and in like artificial manner set forth, seeing that errors the most widely different have nevertheless causes for the most part alike. Neither again do I mean this only of entire systems, but also of many principles and axioms in science, which by tradition, credulity, and negligence have come to be received.

But of these several kinds of Idols I must speak more largely and exactly, that the understanding may be duly cautioned.

6. Important pre-Socratic Greek philosopher (540–475 B.C.).
7. The common understanding.

45

The human understanding is of its own nature prone to suppose the existence of more order and regularity in the world than it finds. And though there be many things in nature which are singular and unmatched, yet it devises for them parallels and conjugates and relatives which do not exist. Hence the fiction that all celestial bodies move in perfect cicles, spirals and dragons[8] being (except in name) utterly rejected. Hence too the element of fire with its orb[9] is brought in, to make up the square with the other three which the sense perceives. Hence also the ratio of density of the so-called elements is arbitrarily fixed at ten to one.[10] And so on of other dreams. And these fancies affect not dogmas only, but simple notions also.

46

The human understanding when it has once adopted an opinion (either as being the received opinion or as being agreeable to itself) draws all things else to support and agree with it. And though there be a greater number and weight of instances to be found on the other side, yet these it either neglects and despises, or else by some distinction sets aside and rejects; in order that by this great and pernicious predetermination the authority of its former conclusions may remain inviolate. And therefore it was a good answer that was made by one who when they showed him hanging in a temple a picture of those who had paid their vows as having escaped shipwreck, and would have him say whether he did not now acknowledge the power of the gods. 'Aye,' asked he again, 'but where are they painted that were drowned after their vows?' And such is the way of all superstition, whether in astrology, dreams, omens, divine judgments, or the like wherein men, having a delight in such vanities, mark the events where they are fulfilled, but where they fail, though this happen much oftener, neglect and pass them by. But with far more subtlety does this mischief insinuate itself into philosophy and the sciences, in which the first conclusion colours and brings into conformity with itself all that come after, though far sounder and better. Besides, independently of that delight and vanity which I have described it is the peculiar and perpetual error of the human intellect to be more moved and excited by affirmatives than by negatives, whereas it ought properly to hold itself indifferently disposed towards both alike. Indeed in the establishment of any true axiom, the negative instance is the more forcible of the two.

8. Probably helical movements, possibly the ones traced by the epicycles moving about the main orb (see *Astronomy* in the Glossary). Bacon is attacking the disposition of astronomers to believe that the orbits of the planets must be circular, circles being the shape of perfection, etc. He was correct in fact, as well as in principle: Kepler's revision of Copernicus showed that the orbits were elliptical, with the sun at one of the foci.

9. In the older Ptolemaic model of the universe, Earth was surrounded by the elemental spheres of water, air, and fire, just inside the first celestial sphere of the moon.

10. Bacon may be alluding to Aristotle (*On Generation and Corruption*) or to some contemporary alchemical writer; in either case, the prior dogmatism of the notion displeased him.

49

The human understanding is no dry light, but receives an infusion from the will and affections; whence proceed sciences which may be called 'sciences as one would.' For what a man had rather were true he more readily believes. Therefore he rejects difficult things from impatience of research; sober things because they narrow hope; the deeper things of nature from superstition; the light of experience for arrogance and pride, lest his mind should seem to be occupied with things mean and transitory; things not commonly believed, out of deference to the opinion of the vulgar. Numberless, in short, are the ways, and sometimes imperceptible, in which the affections [11] colour and infect the understanding.

50

But by far the greatest hindrance and aberration of the human understanding proceeds from the dulness, incompetency, and deceptions of the senses; in that things which strike the sense outweigh things which do not immediately strike it, though they be more important. Hence it is that speculation commonly ceases where sight ceases; insomuch that of things invisible there is little or no observation. Hence all the working of the spirits [12] inclosed in tangible bodies lies hid and unobserved of men. So also all the more subtle changes of form in the parts of coarser substances (which they commonly call alteration, though it is in truth local motion through exceedingly small spaces) is in like manner unobserved. And yet, unless these two things just mentioned be searched out and brought to light, nothing great can be achieved in nature as far as the production of works is concerned. So again, the essential nature of our common air and of all bodies less dense than air (which are very many) is almost unknown. For the sense by itself is a thing infirm and erring; neither can instruments for enlarging or sharpening the senses do much; but all the truer kind of interpretation of nature is effected by instances and experiments fit and apposite, wherein the sense decides touching the experiment only, and the experiment touching the point in nature and the thing itself.

51

The human understanding is of its own nature prone to abstractions and gives a substance and reality to things which are fleeting. But to resolve nature into abstractions is less to our purpose than to dissect her into parts, as did the school of Democritus,[13] which went further into nature than the rest. Matter rather than forms [14] should be the object of our attention, its configurations

---

11. Emotions.
12. The "spirits" or "subtle vapors," diffused throughout the substance of bodily tissues were of three types, natural, vital, and animal. See Burton's section on "The Division of the Body," from *The Anatomy of Melancholy,* and also *Renaissance Psychology* in the Glossary.
13. The Greek atomist, who held that all phenomena were the product of random assemblages of ultimate particles of matter ("a fortuitous concourse of atoms" is the tag phrase).
14. Aristotle's concept of those non-material entities which constitute the essence, the "whatness" or particularity of any substance or object; Bacon views these mental fictions with disfavor.

and changes of configuration, and simple action, and law of action or motion, for forms are figments of the human mind, unless you will call those laws of action forms.

52

Such then are the idols which I call Idols of the Tribe, and which take their rise either from the homogeneity of the substance of the human spirit, or from its preoccupation, or from its narrowness, or from its restless motion, or from an infusion of the affections, or from the incompetency of the senses, or from the mode of impression.

53

The Idols of the Cave take their rise in the peculiar constitution, mental or bodily, of each individual, and also in education, habit, and accident. Of this kind there is a great number and variety, but I will instance those the pointing out of which contains the most important caution, and which have most effect in disturbing the clearness of the understanding.

54

Men become attached to certain particular sciences and speculations, either because they fancy themselves the authors and inventors thereof, or because they have bestowed the greatest pains upon them and become most habituated to them. But men of this kind, if they betake themselves to philosophy and contemplations of a general character, distort and colour them in obedience to their former fancies, a thing especially to be noticed in Aristotle, who made his natural philosophy a mere bondservant to his logic, thereby rendering it contentious and well nigh useless. The race of chemists [15] again out of a few experiments of the furnace have built up a fantastic philosophy, framed with reference to a few things, and Gilbert [16] also, after he had employed himself most laboriously in the study and observation of the loadstone, proceeded at once to construct an entire system in accordance with his favourite subject.

55

There is one principal and as it were radical distinction between different minds, in respect of philosophy and the sciences, which is this: that some minds are stronger and apter to mark the differences of things, others to mark their resemblances. The steady and acute mind can fix its contemplations and dwell and fasten on the subtlest distinctions, the lofty and discursive mind recognizes and puts together the finest and most general resemblances. Both kinds however easily err in excess, by catching the one at gradations, the other at shadows.

15. The alchemists.
16. William Gilbert (1540–1603), Queen Elizabeth's physician. In 1600 his *De Magnete* appeared, describing magnetic phenomena and those of static electricity (the latter word being his coinage), but attempting, wrongly, to attribute both gravity and electricity to magnetic force.

56

There are found some minds given to an extreme admiration of antiquity, others to an extreme love and appetite for novelty; but few so duly tempered that they can hold the mean, neither carping at what has been well laid down by the ancients, nor despising what is well introduced by the moderns. This however turns to the great injury of the sciences and philosophy: since these affectations of antiquity and novelty are the humours of partisans rather than judgments; and truth is to be sought for not in the felicity of any age, which is an unstable thing, but in the light of nature and experience, which is eternal. These factions therefore must be abjured, and care must be taken that the intellect be not hurried by them into assent.

57

Contemplations of nature and of bodies in their simple form break up and distract the understanding, while contemplations of nature and bodies in their composition and configuration overpower and dissolve the understanding—a distinction well seen in the school of Leucippus and Democritus as compared with the other philosophies. For that school is so busied with the particles that it hardly attends to the structure, while the others are so lost in admiration of the structure that they do not penetrate to the simplicity of nature. These kinds of contemplation should therefore be alternated and taken by turns, that so the understanding may be rendered at once penetrating and comprehensive, and the inconveniences above mentioned, with the idols which proceed from them, may be avoided.

58

Let such then be our provision and contemplative prudence for keeping off and dislodging the Idols of the Cave, which grow for the most part either out of the predominance of a favourite subject, or out of an excessive tendency to compare or to distinguish, or out of partiality for particular ages, or out of the largeness or minuteness of the objects contemplated. And generally let every student of nature take this as a rule, that whatever his mind seizes and dwells upon with peculiar satisfaction is to be held in suspicion, and that so much the more care is to be taken in dealing with such questions to keep the understanding even and clear.

59

But the Idols of the Marketplace are the most troublesome of all—idols which have crept into the understanding through the alliances of words and names. For men believe that their reason governs words, but it is also true that words react on the understanding, and this it is that has rendered philosophy and the sciences sophistical and inactive. Now words, being commonly framed and applied according to the capacity of the vulgar, follow those lines of division which are most obvious to the vulgar understanding. And whenever an understanding of greater acuteness or a more diligent observation would alter those lines to suit the true divisions of nature, words stand in the way and resist the change. Whence it comes to pass that the high and formal discussions of learned men end oftentimes in disputes about words and names, with which (according to the use[17] and wisdom of the mathematicians) it would be more prudent to begin, and so by means of definitions reduce them to order. Yet even definitions cannot cure this evil in dealing with natural and material things; since the definitions themselves consist of words, and those words beget others, so that it is necessary to recur to individual instances, and those in due series and order, as I shall say presently when I come to the method and scheme for the formation of notions and axioms.

60

The idols imposed by words on the understanding are of two kinds. They are either names of things which do not exist (for as there are things left unnamed through lack of observation, so likewise are there names which result from fantastic suppositions and to which nothing in reality corresponds), or they are names of things which exist, but yet confused and ill defined and hastily and irregularly derived from realities. Of the former kind are Fortune, the Prime Mover,[18] Planetary Orbits,[19] Element of Fire, and like fictions which owe their origin to false and idle theories. And this class of idols is more easily expelled, because to get rid of them it is only necessary that all theories should be steadily rejected and dismissed as obsolete.

But the other class, which springs out of a faulty and unskilful abstraction, is intricate and deeply rooted. Let us take for example such a word as *humid,* and see how far the several things which the word is used to signify agree with each other; and we shall find the word *humid* to be nothing else than a mark loosely and confusedly applied to denote a variety of actions which will not bear to be reduced to any constant meaning. For it both signifies that which easily spreads itself round any other body; and that which in itself is indeterminate and cannot solidise; and that which readily yields in every direction; and that which easily divides and scatters itself; and that which easily unites and collects itself; and that which readily flows and is put in motion; and that which readily clings to another body and wets it; and that which is easily reduced to a liquid, or being solid easily melts. Accordingly when you come to apply the word, if you take it in one sense, flame is humid; if in another, air is not humid; if in another, fine dust is humid; if in another, glass is humid. So that it is easy to see that the notion is taken by abstraction only from water and common and ordinary liquids without any due verification.

There are however in words certain degrees of distortion and error. One of the least faulty kinds is that of names of substances, especially of lowest species and well deduced (for the notion of *chalk* and of *mud* is good, of *earth* bad); a more faulty kind is that of actions, as *to generate, to corrupt, to alter;* the most faulty is of qualities (except such as are the immediate objects of

17. Practice.
18. The "prime mover," or outermost celestial sphere, which imparted motion through the ether to the others (think of a kind of fluid transmission system) in the Ptolemaic system (see *Astronomy* in the Glossary).
19. Bacon means the concrete *orbs* or spheres of the old system, not the abstract *orbits,* or paths, of the new.

the sense) as *heavy, light, rare, dense,* and the like. Yet in all these cases some notions are of necessity a little better than others, in proportion to the greater variety of subjects that fall within the range of the human sense.

61

But the Idols of the Theatre are not innate, nor do they steal into the understanding secretly, but are plainly impressed and received into the mind from the playbooks[20] of philosophical systems and the perverted rules of demonstration. To attempt refutations in this case would be merely inconsistent with what I have already said, for since we agree neither upon principles nor upon demonstrations there is no place for argument. And this is so far well, inasmuch as it leaves the honour of the ancients untouched. For they are no wise disparaged, the question between them and me being only as to the way. For as the saying is, the lame man who keeps the right road outstrips the runner who takes a wrong one. Nay, it is obvious that when a man runs the wrong way, the more active and swift he is, the further he will go astray.

But the course I propose for the discovery of sciences is such as leaves but little to the acuteness and strength of wits, but places all wits and understandings nearly on a level. For as in the drawing of a straight line or a perfect circle much depends on the steadiness and practice of the hand, if it be done by aim of hand only, but if with the aid of rule or compass, little or nothing; so is it exactly with my plan. But though particular confutations would be of no avail, yet touching the sects and general divisions of such systems I must say something; something also touching the external signs which show that they are unsound; and finally something touching the causes of such great infelicity and of such lasting and general agreement in error: that so the access to truth may be made less difficult, and the human understanding may the more willingly submit to its purgation and dismiss its idols.

62

Idols of the Theatre, or of Systems, are many, and there can be and perhaps will be yet many more. For were it not that now for many ages men's minds have been busied with religion and theology; and were it not that civil governments, especially monarchies, have been averse to such novelties, even in matters speculative; so that men labour therein to the peril and harming of their fortunes,—not only unrewarded, but exposed also to contempt and envy: doubtless there would have arisen many other philosophical sects like to those which in great variety flourished once among the Greeks. For as on the phenomena of the heavens many hypotheses may be constructed, so likewise (and more also) many various dogmas may be set up and established on the phenomena of philosophy.[21] And in the plays of this philosophical theatre you may observe the same thing which is found in the theatre of the poets, that stories invented for the stage are more compact and elegant, and more as one would wish them to be, than true stories out of history.

20. Collections of plays (with reference to the Idols of the Theater).
21. "Philosophy" means science here, as it usually does in this discussion; the word "science" still retains its Latin general meaning of "knowledge."

In general however there is taken for the material of philosophy either a great deal out of a few things, or a very little out of many things; so that on both sides philosophy is based on too narrow a foundation of experiment and natural history, and decides on the authority of too few cases. For the rational school of philosophers snatches from experience a variety of common instances, neither duly ascertained nor diligently examined and weighed, and leaves all the rest to meditation and agitation of wit.

There is also another class of philosophers, who having bestowed much diligent and careful labour on a few experiments, have thence made bold to educe and construct systems; wresting all other facts in a strange fashion to conformity therewith.

And there is yet a third class, consisting of those who out of faith and veneration mix their philosophy with theology and traditions; among whom the vanity of some has gone so far aside as to seek the origin of science among spirits and genii. So that this parent stock of errors—this false philosophy—is of three kinds; the sophistical, the empirical, and the superstitious.

The Wisdom of the Ancients

In 1609 Bacon published a strange little collection in Latin of mythographic essays on certain classical stories, by way of recreation, as he confessed in the Preface. *De Sapientia Veterum* (or *The Wisdom of the Ancients* in its 1619 English version) belongs to a tradition of Renaissance interpretation we have seen before (see The Renaissance Ovid); and although Bacon's readings would sometimes be very strange indeed, they influenced subsequent commentators like George Sandys and Sir Thomas Browne. Bacon himself expanded some of these essays in his later remarks on mytho-poetic poetry ("parabolical poesy," he calls it) in the 1623 *De Dignitate et Augmentis Scientarium*. Pan means Nature, conventionally enough; but in Bacon's reading, the nature he represents becomes the object of scientific knowledge. Even his horns are allegorized as a kind of project-director's flow-chart: "Horns are attributed to the Universe, broad at the base and pointed at the top. For all nature rises to a point like a pyramid. Individuals, which lie at the base of nature, are infinite in number; these are collected into Species, which are themselves manifold; the Species rise again into Genera . . . so that at last nature seems to end as it were in unity, as is signi-fied by the pyramidal form of the horns of Pan." Sometimes, as in making Proteus (the sea god who kept changing his form) a myth of matter (maintaining itself through change of phase), Bacon is interpretively tactful. The section below will seem less allegorically strained if it is remembered that even Lucretius, at the beginning of his great scientific poem *De Rerum Natura* (Of the Nature of Things), makes Venus and Mars, Love and War, into Creation and De-creation, the two phases of eternal process.

From The Wisdom of the Ancients

Cupid Or the Atom [1]

The accounts given by the poets of Cupid, or Love, are not properly applicable to the same person; yet the discrepancy is such that one may see where the confusion is and where the similitude, and reject the one and receive the other.

They say then that Love was the most ancient of all the gods; the most ancient therefore of all things whatever, except Chaos, which is said to have been coeval with him; and Chaos is never distinguished by the ancients with divine honour or the name of a god. This Love is introduced without any parent at all; only, that some say he was an egg of Night. And himself out of Chaos begot all things, the gods included. The attributes which are assigned to him are in number four: he is always an infant; he is blind; [2] he is naked; he is an archer. There was also another Love, the youngest of all the gods, son of Venus, to whom the attributes of the elder are transferred, and whom in a way they suit.

The fable relates to the cradle and infancy of nature, and pierces deep. This Love I understand to be the appetite or instinct of primal matter; or to speak more plainly, *the natural motion of the atom*; which is indeed the original and unique force that constitutes and fashions all things out of matter. Now this is entirely without parent; that is, without cause. For the cause is as it were parent of the effect; and of this virtue there can be no cause in nature (God always excepted): there being nothing before it, therefore no efficient; nor anything more original in nature, therefore neither kind nor form. Whatever it be therefore, it is a thing positive and inexplicable. And even if it were possible to know the method and process of it, yet to know it by way of cause is not possible; it being, next to God, the cause of causes—itself without cause. That the method even of its operation should ever be brought within the range and comprehension of human inquiry, is hardly perhaps to be hoped; with good reason therefore it is represented as an egg hatched by night. Such certainly is the judgment of the sacred philosopher,[3] when he says, *He hath made all things beautiful according to their seasons; also he hath submitted the world to man's inquiry, yet so that man cannot find out the work which God worketh from the beginning to the end*. For the summary law of nature, that impulse of desire impressed by God upon the primary particles of matter which makes them come together, and which by repetition and multiplication produces all the variety of nature, is a thing which mortal thought may glance at, but can hardly take in.

Now the philosophy of the Greeks, which in investigating the material principles of things is careful and acute, in inquiring the principles of motion,

---

1. This essay is in the 1619 English translation of Sir Arthur Gorges; Bacon later expanded his interpretation of Cupid at great length in another Latin work, *De Dignitate et Augmentis Scientiarum*.
2. For the blindness of Cupid and its interest for the Renaissance, see Marlowe, *Hero and Leander* I.48n (as well as the elaborate studies by Erwin Panofsky, in *Studies in Iconology*, and Edgar Wind, *Pagan Mysteries in the Renaissance*, 2nd ed.) See also the extract from Sir Thomas Browne's *Miscellanies*, below.
3. Ecclesiastes 3:11.

wherein lies all vigour of operation, is negligent and languid; and on the point now in question seems to be altogether blind babbling; for that opinion of the Peripatetics[4] which refers the original impulse of matter to privation, is little more than words—a name for the thing rather than a description of it. And those who refer it to God, though they are quite right in that, yet they ascend by a leap and not by steps. For beyond all doubt there is a single and summary law in which nature centres and which is subject and subordinate to God; the same in fact which in the text just quoted is meant by the words: *the work which God worketh from the beginning to the end.* Democritus considered the matter more deeply; and having first given the atom some dimension and shape, attributed to it a single desire or primary motion simply and absolutely, and a second by comparison. For he thought that all things move by their proper nature towards the centre of the world; but that that which has more matter, moving thither faster, strikes aside that which has less, and forces it to go the other way. This however was but a narrow theory, and framed with reference to too few particulars: for it does not appear that either the motion of the heavenly bodies in circle, or the phenomena of contraction and expansion, can be reduced to this principle, or reconciled with it. As for Epicurus's opinion of the declination and fortuitous agitation of the atom, it is a relapse to trifling and ignorance. So it is but too plain that the parentage of this Cupid is wrapped in night.

Let us now consider his attributes. He is described with great elegance as a little child, and a child for ever; for things compounded are larger and are affected by age; whereas the primary seeds of things, or atoms, are minute and remain in perpetual infancy.

Most truly also is he represented as naked: for all compounds (to one that considers them rightly) are masked and clothed; and there is nothing properly naked, except the primary particles of things.

The blindness likewise of Cupid has an allegorical meaning full of wisdom. For it seems that this Cupid, whatever he be, has very little providence; but directs his course, like a blind man groping, by whatever he finds nearest; which makes the supreme divine Providence all the more to be admired, as that which contrives out of subjects peculiarly empty and destitute of providence, and as it were blind, to educe[5] by a fatal and necessary law all the order and beauty of the universe.

His last attribute is archery: meaning that this virtue is such as acts at a distance: for all operation at a distance is like shooting an arrow. Now whoever maintains the theory of the atom and the vacuum (even though he suppose the vacuum not to be collected by itself but intermingled through space), necessarily implies the action of the virtue of the atom at a distance: for without this no motion could be originated, by reason of the vacuum interposed; but all things would remain fixed and immovable.

As for that younger Cupid, it is with reason that he is reported to be the youngest of the gods; since until the species were constituted he could have no operation. In the description of him the allegory changes its aim and passes

4. The school of Aristotle.
5. Elicit, develop.

to morals. And yet there remains a certain conformity between him and the elder Cupid. For Venus excites the general appetite of conjunction and procreation; Cupid, her son, applies the appetite to an individual object. From Venus therefore comes the general disposition, from Cupid the more exact sympathy. Now the general disposition depends upon causes near at hand, the particular sympathy upon principles more deep and fatal, and as if derived from that ancient Cupid, who is the source of all exquisite sympathy.

1619

The New Atlantis

Bacon's utopia, The New Atlantis (1627), grew out of an impulse to provide, in the words of his secretary quoted in a preface, "a model or description of a college instituted for the interpreting of nature and the producing of great and marvellous works for the benefit of men, under the name of Salomon's House." On the imaginary island of Bensalem in the south, Bacon places a community whose social and legal system is developed in brief detail, sometimes avowedly differing from More's Utopia. But Bacon's greatest concern lay in a society which might support the life of the mind as he conceived it, embodied in a project-director's vision of an institute for the pursuit of knowledge. Salomon's House is that ideal institution, here described to the narrator at the end of The New Atlantis by its venerable director.

From The New Atlantis

[Salomon's House]

'God bless thee, my son; I will give thee the greatest jewel I have. For I will impart unto thee, for the love of God and men, a relation of the true state of Salomon's House. Son, to make you know the true state of Salomon's House, I will keep this order. First, I will set forth unto you the end of our foundation. Secondly, the preparations and instruments we have for our works. Thirdly, the several employments and functions whereto our fellows are assigned. And fourthly, the ordinances and rites which we observe.

'The End of our Foundation is the knowledge of Causes and secret motions of things, and the enlarging of the bounds of Human Empire,[1] to the effecting of all things possible.

'The Preparations and Instruments are these. We have large and deep caves of several depths; the deepest are sunk six hundred fathom, and some of them are digged and made under great hills and mountains, so that if you reckon together the depth of the hill and the depth of the cave, they are (some of them) above three miles deep. For we find that the depth of a hill and the depth of a cave from the flat is the same thing, both remote alike from the sun and heaven's beams and from the open air. These caves we call the Lower Region. And we use them for all coagulations, indurations,[2] refrigerations,

1. Empire over Nature.
2. Preservations by hardening.

and conservations of bodies. We use them likewise for the imitation of natural mines and the producing also of new artificial metals by compositions and materials which we use, and lay there for many years. We use them also sometimes (which may seem strange) for curing of some diseases and for prolongation of life in some hermits that choose to live there, well accommodated of [3] all things necessary; and indeed live very long, by whom also we learn many things.

'We have burials in several earths, where we put divers cements, as the Chineses do their porcelain. But we have them in greater variety, and some of them more fine. We have also great variety of composts and soils for the making of the earth fruitful.

'We have high towers, the highest about half a mile in height, and some of them likewise set upon high mountains, so that the vantage of the hill with the tower is in the highest of them three miles at least. And these places we call the Upper Region, accounting the air between the high places and the low as a Middle Region. We use these towers, according to their several heights and situations, for insolation, refrigeration, conservation, and for the view of divers meteors,[4] as winds, rain, snow, hail, and some of the fiery meteors also. And upon them, in some places, are dwellings of hermits, whom we visit sometimes, and instruct what to observe.

'We have great lakes both salt and fresh, whereof we have use for the fish and fowl. We use them also for burials of some natural bodies, for we find a difference in things buried in earth or in air below the earth and things buried in water. We have also pools, of which some do strain fresh water out of salt, and others by art do turn fresh water into salt. We have also some rocks in the midst of the sea, and some bays upon the shore, for some works wherein is required the air and vapour of the sea. We have likewise violent streams and cataracts, which serve us for many motions, and likewise engines for multiplying and enforcing[5] of winds, to set also on going divers motions.

'We have also a number of artificial wells and fountains, made in imitation of the natural sources and baths, as tincted upon[6] vitriol, sulphur, steel, brass, lead, nitre, and other minerals. And again we have little wells for infusions of many things, where the waters take the virtue[7] quicker and better than in vessels or basins. And amongst them we have a water which we call Water of Paradise, being, by what we do to it, made very sovereign for health and prolongation of life.

'We have also great and spacious houses, where we imitate and demonstrate meteors, as snow, hail, rain, some artificial rains of bodies and not of water, thunders, lightnings, also generations of bodies in air, as frogs, flies, and divers others.

'We have also fair and large baths of several mixtures for the cure of diseases and the restoring of man's body from arefaction,[8] and others for the confirming

---

3. Supplied with.
4. The word means meteorological phenomena of all sorts; "fiery meteors" are comets, what we would call meteors, and other astral appearances.
5. Intensifying.
6. Tinctured with.
7. Absorb the properties of the thing dissolved.
8. Drying up.

of it in strength of sinews, vital parts, and the very juice and substance of the body.

'We have also large and various orchards and gardens, wherein we do not so much respect beauty as variety of ground and soil, proper for divers trees and herbs, and some very spacious, where trees and berries are set whereof we make divers kinds of drinks, besides the vineyards. In these we practise likewise all conclusions[9] of grafting and inoculating, as well of wild trees as fruit trees, which produceth many effects. And we make (by art) in the same orchards and gardens trees and flowers to come earlier or later than their seasons, and to come up and bear more speedily than by their natural course they do. We make them also by art greater much than their nature, and their fruit greater and sweeter and of differing taste, smell, colour, and figure, from their nature. And many of them we so order as they become of medicinal use.

'We have also means to make divers plants rise by mixtures of earths without seeds, and likewise to make divers new plants differing from the vulgar,[10] and to make one tree or plant turn into another.

'We have also parks and inclosures of all sorts of beasts and birds, which we use not only for view or rareness but likewise for dissections and trials, that thereby we may take light[11] what may be wrought upon the body of man. Wherein we find many strange effects: as continuing life in them, though divers parts, which you account vital, be perished and taken forth; resuscitating of some that seem dead in appearance; and the like. We try also all poisons and other medicines upon them, as well of chirurgery[12] as physic. By art likewise we make them greater or taller than their kind is, and contrariwise dwarf them, and stay their growth; we make them more fruitful and bearing than their kind is, and contrariwise barren and not generative. Also we make them differ in colour, shape, activity, many ways. We find means to make commixtures and copulations of different kinds, which have produced many new kinds, and them not barren, as the general opinion is. We make a number of kinds of serpents, worms, flies, fishes, of putrefaction, whereof some are advanced (in effect) to be perfect creatures, like beasts or birds, and have sexes, and do propagate. Neither do we this by chance, but we know beforehand of what matter and commixture what kind of those creatures will arise.

'We have also particular pools, where we make trials upon fishes, as we have said before of beasts and birds.

'We have also places for breed and generation of those kinds of worms and flies which are of special use, such as are with you your silkworms and bees.

'I will not hold you long with recounting of our brew-houses, bakehouses, and kitchens, where are made divers drinks, breads, and meats, rare and of special effects. Wines we have of grapes, and drinks of other juice of fruits,

---

9. Procedures.
10. Ordinary.
11. Gain knowledge; this metaphor of light, "enlightenment," "illumination," now virtually a cliché in our language, is crucial in Bacon; elsewhere, he distinguishes between experiments of *fruit* and of *light,* between those which are directed toward a potential technological result, and those simply exploratory (a version of a later distinction between "pure" and "applied" science which has lately been re-examined by critics such as P. B. Medawar).
12. Surgery.

of grains, and of roots, and of mixtures with honey, sugar, manna, and fruits dried and decocted. Also of the tears or woundings of trees and of the pulp of canes. And these drinks are of several ages, some to the age or last[13] of forty years. We have drinks also brewed with several herbs and roots and spices, yea with several fleshes and white meats,[14] whereof some of the drinks are such as they are in effect meat and drink both, so that divers, especially in age, do desire to live with[15] them, with little or no meat or bread. And above all, we strive to have drinks of extreme thin parts to insinuate into the body, and yet without all biting, sharpness, or fretting, insomuch as some of them put upon the back of your hand will, with a little stay, pass through to the palm, and yet taste mild to the mouth. We have also waters which we ripen in that fashion, as they become nourishing, so that they are indeed excellent drink, and many will use no other. Breads we have of several grains, roots, and kernels; yea and some of flesh and fish dried, with divers kinds of leavenings and seasonings, so that some do extremely move appetites; some do nourish so, as divers do live of them without any other meat, who live very long. So for meats: we have some of them so beaten and made tender and mortified,[16] yet without all corrupting, as a weak heat of the stomach will turn them into good chylus,[17] as well as a strong heat would meat otherwise prepared. We have some meats also and breads and drinks, which taken by men enable them to fast long after, and some other that, used, make the very flesh of men's bodies sensibly more hard and tough, and their strength far greater than otherwise it would be.

'We have dispensatories, or shops of medicines. Wherein you may easily think, if we have such variety of plants and living creatures more than you have in Europe (for we know what you have), the simples,[18] drugs, and ingredients of medicines must likewise be in so much the greater variety. We have them likewise of divers ages and long fermentations. And for their preparations, we have not only all manner of exquisite distillations and separations, and especially by gentle heats and percolations through divers strainers, yea and substances, but also exact forms of composition,[19] whereby they incorporate almost, as they were natural simples.

'We have also divers mechanical arts, which you have not, and stuffs made by them, as papers, linen, silks, tissues, dainty works of feathers of wonderful lustre, excellent dyes, and many others; and shops likewise as well for such as are not brought into vulgar use amongst us as for those that are. For you must know that of the things before recited, many of them are grown into use throughout the kingdom, but yet if they did flow from our invention, we have of them also for patterns and principals.[20]

'We have also furnaces of great diversities and that keep great diversity

13. Duration.
14. Foods.
15. On.
16. Aged to the point of tenderness.
17. Chyle, the macerated, half-digested contents of the stomach.
18. Medicinal herbs, called so because they were used uncompounded.
19. Compound.
20. Models.

of heats: fierce and quick; strong and constant; soft and mild; blown, quiet; dry, moist; and the like. But above all, we have heats in imitation of the sun's and heavenly bodies' heats, that pass divers inequalities and (as it were) orbs, progresses, and returns,[21] whereby we produce admirable effects. Besides, we have heats of dungs, and of bellies and maws of living creatures, and of their bloods and bodies, and of hays and herbs laid up moist, of lime unquenched,[22] and such like. Instruments also which generate heat only by motion. And farther, places for strong insolations; [23] and again, places under the earth, which by nature or art yield heat. These divers heats we use, as the nature of the operation which we intend requireth.

'We have also perspective-houses,[24] where we make demonstrations of all lights and radiations, and of all colours; and out of things uncoloured and transparent we can represent unto you all several colours, not in rainbows, as it is in gems and prisms, but of themselves single. We represent also all multiplications of light, which we carry to great distance, and make so sharp as to discern small points and lines; also all colourations of light, all delusions and deceits of the sight in figures, magnitudes, motions, colours, all demonstrations of shadows. We find also divers means, yet unknown to you, of producing of light originally from divers bodies. We procure means of seeing objects afar off, as in the heaven and remote places, and represent things near as afar off and things afar off as near, making feigned distances. We have also helps for the sight, far above spectacles and glasses in use. We have also glasses and means to see small and minute bodies perfectly and distinctly, as the shapes and colours of small flies and worms, grains and flaws in gems, which cannot otherwise be seen, observations in urine and blood, not otherwise to be seen. We make artificial rainbows, haloes, and circles about light. We represent also all manner of reflexions, refractions, and multiplications of visual beams of objects.

'We have also precious stones of all kinds, many of them of great beauty and to you unknown; crystals likewise; and glasses of divers kinds; and amongst them some of metals vitrificated,[25] and other materials besides those of which you make glass. Also a number of fossils and imperfect minerals,[26] which you have not. Likewise loadstones of prodigious virtue [27] and other rare stones, both natural and artificial.

'We have also sound-houses, where we practise and demonstrate all sounds and their generation. We have harmonies, which you have not, of quarter-sounds and lesser slides of sounds.[28] Divers instruments of music likewise to you unknown, some sweeter than any you have, together with bells and rings that are dainty and sweet. We represent small sounds as great and deep, likewise great sounds extenuate [29] and sharp; we make divers tremblings and

21. Planetary motions.
22. Unslaked.
23. Sunbaking.
24. Laboratories for the study of optics.
25. Turned into glass.
26. Mineral ores.
27. Power.
28. Quarter-tones and other microtones.
29. Thin; the following clause refers to inventions that decompose single natural sounds into harmonic groups.

warblings of sound, which in their original are entire. We represent and imitate all articulate sounds and letters, and the voices and notes of beasts and birds. We have certain helps which set to the ear do further the hearing greatly. We have also divers strange and artificial echoes, reflecting the voice many times, and as it were tossing it, and some that give back the voice louder than it came, some shriller and some deeper; yea, some rendering the voice differing in the letters or articulate sound from that they receive. We have also means to convey sounds in trunks [30] and pipes, in strange lines and distances.

'We have also perfume-houses, wherewith we join also practices of taste. We multiply smells, which may seem strange. We imitate smells, making all smells to breathe out of other mixtures than those that give them. We make divers imitations of taste likewise, so that they will deceive any man's taste. And in this house we contain also a confiture-house, where we make all sweetmeats, dry and moist, and divers pleasant wines, milks, broths, and sallets,[31] far in greater variety than you have.

'We have also engine-houses, where are prepared engines and instruments for all sorts of motions. There we imitate and practise to make swifter motions than any you have, either out of your muskets or any engine that you have; and to make them and multiply them more easily and with small force by wheels and other means, and to make them stronger and more violent than yours are, exceeding your greatest cannons and basilisks.[32] We represent also ordnance and instruments of war, and engines of all kinds, and likewise new mixtures and compositions of gunpowder, wildfires burning in water and unquenchable. Also fireworks of all variety both for pleasure and use. We imitate also flights of birds; we have some degrees of flying in the air; we have ships and boats for going under water, and brooking of seas, also swimming-girdles and supporters. We have divers curious clocks and other like motions of return [33] and some perpetual motions. We imitate also motions of living creatures by images of men, beasts, birds, fishes, and serpents. We have also a great number of other various motions, strange for equality, fineness, and subtilty.

'We have also a mathematical house, where are represented all instruments, as well of geometry as astronomy, exquisitely made.

'We have also houses of deceits of the senses, where we represent all manner of feats of juggling, false apparitions, impostures, and illusions, and their fallacies. And surely you will easily believe that we that have so many things truly natural which include admiration [34] could in a world of particulars deceive the senses, if we would disguise those things and labour to make them seem more miraculous. But we do hate all impostures and lies; insomuch as we have severely forbidden it to all our fellows, under pain of ignominy and fines, that they do not show any natural work or thing adorned or swelling, but only pure as it is, and without all affectation of strangeness.

'These are, my son, the riches of Salomon's House.

30. Tubes.
31. Salads.
32. Kind of artillery, named for the mythical serpent whose eye turns one to stone.
33. Pendulum mechanisms.
34. Visual atention.

'For the several employments and offices of our fellows, we have twelve that sail into foreign countries, under the names of other nations (for our own we conceal), who bring us the books and abstracts and patterns of experiments of all other parts. These we call Merchants of Light.

'We have three that collect the experiments which are in all books. These we call Depredators.

'We have three that collect the experiments of all mechanical arts, and also of liberal sciences, and also of practices which are not brought into arts. These we call Mystery Men.

'We have three that try new experiments, such as themselves think good. These we call Pioneers or Miners.

'We have three that draw the experiments of the former four into titles and tables, to give the better light for the drawing of observations and axioms out of them. These we call Compilers.

'We have three that bend [35] themselves, looking into the experiments of their fellows, and cast about how to draw out of them things of use and practice for man's life, and knowledge as well for works as for plain demonstration of causes, means of natural divinations, and the easy and clear discovery of the virtues and parts of bodies. Those we call Dowry Men or Benefactors.

'Then, after divers meetings and consults of our whole number to consider of the former labours and collections, we have three that take care, out of them, to direct new experiments of a higher light, more penetrating into nature than the former. These we call Lamps.

'We have three others that do execute the experiments so directed, and report them. These we call Inoculators.

'Lastly, we have three that raise the former discoveries by experiments into greater observations, axioms, and aphorisms. These we call Interpreters of Nature.

'We have also, as you must think, novices and apprentices, that the succession of the former employed men do not fail, besides a great number of servants and attendants, men and women. And this we do also: we have consultations, which of the inventions and experiences which we have discovered shall be published, and which not; and take all an oath of secrecy for the concealing of those which we think fit to keep secret, though some of those we do reveal sometimes to the state, and some not.[36]

'For our ordinances and rites, we have two very long and fair galleries: in one of these we place patterns and samples of all manner of the more rare and excellent inventions, in the other we place the statues of all principal inventors. There we have the statue of your Columbus, that discovered the West Indies; also the inventor of ships; your monk [37] that was the inventor of ordnance and of gunpowder; the inventor of music; the inventor of letters; the inventor of printing; the inventor of observations of astronomy; the inventor of works in metal; the inventor of glass; the inventor of silk of the worm; the inventor of wine; the inventor of corn and bread; the inventor of

---

35. Apply.
36. Bacon had, by experience, developed enough distrust of government to anticipate modern problems here; Salomon's House can be fragile.
37. Roger Bacon, 13th-century Franciscan philosopher and alchemist.

sugars; and all these by more certain tradition than you have. Then have we divers inventors of our own, of excellent works, which since you have not seen, it were too long to make descriptions of them; and besides, in the right understanding of those descriptions you might easily err. For upon every invention of value we erect a statua [38] to the inventor, and give him a liberal and honourable reward. These statuas are some of brass, some of marble and touchstone,[39] some of cedar and other special woods gilt and adorned, some of iron, some of silver, some of gold.

'We have certain hymns and services, which we say daily, of laud and thanks to God for his marvellous works, and forms of prayers imploring his aid and blessing for the illumination of our labours and the turning of them into good and holy uses.

'Lastly, we have circuits or visits of divers principal cities of the kingdom, where, as it cometh to pass, we do publish such new profitable inventions as we think good. And we do also declare natural divinations [40] of diseases, plagues, swarms of hurtful creatures, scarcity, tempests, earthquakes, great inundations, comets, temperature of the year, and divers other things; and we give counsel thereupon what the people shall do for the prevention and remedy of them.'

And when he had said this, he stood up, and I, as I had been taught, kneeled down, and he laid his right hand upon my head, and said, 'God bless thee, my son, and God bless this relation which I have made. I give thee leave to publish it for the good of other nations, for we here are in God's bosom, a land unknown.' And so he left me, having assigned a value of about two thousand ducats for a bounty to me and my fellows. For they give great largesses where they come upon all occasions.

[THE REST WAS NOT PERFECTED]

1626

ROBERT BURTON
1577–1640

The life of this remarkable figure is so nearly co-extensive with his one great work that its mere chronology yields little of interest: he was born in Leicestershire, came to Oxford (to Brasenose College) in 1593, and in 1599 was elected Student of Christ Church, "the most flourishing college of Europe." He took his B.A. in 1602 there, and his M.A. in 1605, and lived at the college for the rest of his life. In 1616 he became vicar of St. Thomas's church in Oxford and held, toward the end of his life, two absentee livings; but his time was mainly spent in reading and in composing his *Anatomy*, that vast systematic work which started out as a compendium of medical and moral knowledge and ended up, constantly revised in five editions before its author's death, as a study of the morbidity of its own studiousness. From its first appearance in 1621 Burton kept augmenting his compilation of learned opinion, allusion, and eloquence, adding new light as it came into his dark tower of self-

38. Statue.
39. A kind of jasper, used for the testing of alloys.
40. Make predictions.

consciousness through the windows of countless books. If *The Anatomy of Melancholy* is about the human psyche's entire range of states—manic, depressed, light, dark, high, and low, and the ways in which they lead to each other—it is also about the very condition of being learned.

Burton's systematic structure embraces physiology, medicine, moral philosophy, and literary history; it moves from detailed exposition of received pre-scientific doctrine to long, wide-ranging essays on such questions as the woes and miseries of scholars, or the effects of literary eroticism (Burton calls it "heroic love") on psychic stability.

Burton's melancholy is not only the totality of the types he classifies so exhaustively. A cult of melancholia was fashionable in early Jacobean England, particularly around the Inns of Court, the theaters, and the haunts of young men down from the universities. This melancholy was associated with the intellectual life which—through lack of preferment at court and insufficient civil service posts to absorb the over-educated and under-inherited—could not fulfill itself. Such diverse Shakespearean figures as Hamlet and Malvolio reflect this condition, which for Burton is almost identical with the human one. His own private melancholy is, ultimately, that of the book itself, a strange mixture of inner enterprise and practical idleness, as far removed from the healthy, somber joy of Milton's *Il Penseroso* as from the massive brooding figure of intellect abandoned in Dürer's *Melancolia*. The introduction to Burton's work, explaining why he adopts the pseudonym of Democritus Jr., is a masterpiece of self-revelation through disguise, moving at times beyond even the candor and wisdom of Montaigne, discussing its own prose style as if it were an inner life; apologizing for the intrusions of its own English into its mosaic of Latin quotations (the interior dialogue of the whole work is between scholar and books, English and Latin); gloomily propounding a scholarly utopia based upon the certain conviction of human imperfectibility; and refurbishing its mythical progenitor, the laughing Greek atomist Democritus, into an ancestor of the self-contemplating lyricist of the late eighteenth century—that poet of the crucial modern mode, the therapeutic work, whose internal sanity is its author's only hedge against madness. (See Figs. 15–18 in the illustrations for this volume.)

From The Anatomy of Melancholy

Democritus Junior to the Reader

Gentle Reader, I presume thou wilt be very inquisitive to know what antic or personate actor this is, that so insolently intrudes upon this common theatre to the world's view, arrogating another man's name; whence he is, why he doth it, and what he hath to say. Although, as he said,[1] *Primum si noluero, non respondebo, quis coacturus est?* I am a free man born, and may choose whether I will tell; who can compel me? if I be urged, I will as readily reply as that Egyptian in Plutarch, when a curious fellow would needs know what he had in his basket, *Quum vides velatam, quid inquiris in rem absconditam?* It was therefore covered, because he should not know what was in it. Seek not after that which is hid; if the contents please thee, 'and be for thy use, suppose the

1. Seneca, the Roman tragedian and philosopher.

Man in the Moon, or whom thou wilt, to be the author'; [2] I would not willingly be known. Yet in some sort to give thee satisfaction, which is more than I need, I will show a reason, both of this usurped name, title, and subject. And first of the name of Democritus; lest any man by reason of it should be deceived, expecting a pasquil,[3] a satire, some ridiculous treatise (as I myself should have done), some prodigious tenet, or paradox of the earth's motion, of infinite worlds, *in infinito vacuo, ex fortuita atomorum collisione*, in an infinite waste, so caused by an accidental collision of motes in the sun, all which Democritus held, Epicurus and their master Leucippus of old maintained, and are lately revived by Copernicus, Brunus, and some others.[4] . . .

Democritus, as he is described by Hippocrates[5] and Laertius,[6] was a little wearish old man, very melancholy by nature, averse from company in his latter days, and much given to solitariness, a famous philosopher in his age, *coævus*[7] with Socrates, wholly addicted to his studies at the last, and to a private life: writ many excellent works, a great divine, according to the divinity of those times, an expert physician, a politician, an excellent mathematician, as *Diacosmus*[8] and the rest of his works do witness. He was much delighted with the studies of husbandry, saith Columella,[9] and often I find him cited by Constantinus[10] and others treating of that subject. He knew the natures, differences of all beasts, plants, fishes, birds; and, as some say, could understand the tunes and voices of them. In a word, he was *omnifariam doctus*, a general scholar, a great student; and to the intent he might better contemplate, I find it related by some, that he put out his eyes, and was in his old age voluntarily blind, yet saw more than all Greece besides, and writ of every subject, *Nihil in toto opificio naturæ, de quo non scripsit.*[11] A man of an excellent wit, profound conceit; and to attain knowledge the better in his younger years he travelled to Egypt and Athens, to confer with learned men, 'admired of some, despised of others.' After a wandering life, he settled at Abdera, a town in Thrace, and was sent for thither to be their law-maker, recorder, or town clerk as some will; or as others, he was there bred and born. Howsoever it was, there he lived at last in a garden in the suburbs, wholly betaking himself to his studies and a private life, 'saving that sometimes he would walk down to the haven, and laugh heartily at such variety of ridiculous objects, which there he saw.'[12] Such a one was Democritus.

But in the meantime, how doth this concern me, or upon what reference do I usurp his habit? I confess, indeed, that to compare myself unto him for

2. Burton is quoting J. J. Wecker, a 16th-century Swiss physician and author.
3. A burlesque.
4. A good deal of physical and astronomical theory is lumped together here; the most spectacular formulation of the notion that there are infinite worlds besides our own was by Giordano Bruno (1548–1600), who was burned by the Inquisition for his views.
5. The great Greek physician (c. 460–c. 360 B.C.).
6. Diogenes Laertius (2nd century A.D.), author of *Lives of the Philosophers*.
7. Contemporary with.
8. Democritus' great cosmological work (literally, "orderly pattern of the cosmos").
9. Augustan Roman author of *De Re Rustica* (On Agriculture).
10. Supposed author of a 6th- or 7th-century book on agriculture.
11. "There was nothing in Nature about which he did not write."
12. Partly quoted from Juvenal's Tenth Satire.

aught I have yet said, were both impudency and arrogancy. I do not presume to make any parallel, *antistat mihi millibus trecentis,*[13] *parvus sum, nullus sum, altum nec spiro, nec spero.*[14] Yet thus much I will say of myself, and that I hope without all suspicion of pride, or self-conceit, I have lived a silent, sedentary, solitary, private life, *mihi et musis*[15] in the university, as long almost as Xenocrates in Athens, *ad senectam fere*[16] to learn wisdom as he did, penned up most part in my study. For I have been brought up a student in the most flourishing college of Europe, *augustissimo collegio,*[17] and can brag with Jovius, almost, *in ea luce domicilii Vaticani, totius orbis celeberrimi, per 37 annos multa opportunaque didici;*[18] for thirty years I have continued (having the use of as good libraries as ever he had) a scholar, and would be therefore loath, either by living as a drone to be an unprofitable or unworthy member of so learned and noble a society, or to write that which should be anyway dishonourable to such a royal and ample foundation. Something I have done, though by my profession a divine, yet *turbine raptus ingenii,* as he[19] said, out of a running wit, an unconstant, unsettled mind, I had a great desire (not able to attain to a superficial skill in any) to have some smattering in all, to be *aliquis in omnibus, nullus in singulis,*[20] which Plato commends, out of him Lipsius approves and furthers, 'as fit to be imprinted in all curious wits, not to be a slave of one science, or dwell altogether in one subject, as most do, but to rove abroad, *centum puer artium,*[21] to have an oar in every man's boat, to taste of every dish, and sip of every cup, which, saith Montaigne, was well performed by Aristotle and his learned countryman Adrian Turnebus. This roving humour (though not with like success) I have ever had, and like a ranging spaniel, that barks at every bird he sees, leaving his game, I have followed all, saving that which I should, and may justly complain, and truly, *qui ubique est, nusquam est,*[22] which Gesner[23] did in modesty, that I have read many books, but to little purpose, for want of good method, I have confusedly tumbled over divers authors in our libraries, with small profit for want of art, order, memory, judgment. I never travelled but in map or card,[24] in which my unconfined thoughts have freely expatiated, as having ever been especially delighted with the study of cosmography. Saturn was lord of my geniture, culminating, etc., and Mars principal significator of manners, in partile conjunction with mine ascendant; both fortunate in their houses, etc.[25] I am not poor, I am not rich; *nihil est, nihil deest,* I have little, I want nothing: all my treasure

13. "He is far ahead of me."
14. "I'm nobody; I'm nothing; with neither hopes nor prospects."
15. "For my work and myself."
16. "Almost to old age."
17. Christ Church, Oxford, whose students still think of it as such.
18. "In that splendid, world-famous Vatican library, I've made the best of my opportunities for 37 years"; Jovius is Paolo Giovio (1483–1552), biographer, historian, and Latin stylist.
19. Julius Caesar Scaliger (1484–1558), Italian scholar and physician.
20. "Knowing something about everything, nothing about any one thing."
21. "Child of a hundred skills."
22. "He who is everywhere is nowhere."
23. Konrad von Gesner (1516–65), Swiss naturalist.
24. Chart, nautical map.
25. These all constitute astrological signs governing a melancholy temperament.

is in Minerva's tower. Greater preferment as I could never get, so am I not in debt for it, I have a competency (*laus Deo*[26]) from my noble and munificent patrons, though I live still a collegiate student, as Democritus in his garden, and lead a monastic life, *ipse mihi theatrum*,[27] sequestered from those tumults and troubles of the world, *et tanquam in specula positus* (as he said [28]), in some high place above you all, like *Stoicus sapiens, omnia sæcula, præterita præsentiaque videns, uno velut intuitu*,[29] I hear and see what is done abroad, how others run, ride, turmoil, and macerate themselves in court and country, far from those wrangling lawsuits, *aulæ vanitatem, fori ambitionem, ridere mecum soleo*,[30] I laugh at all; 'only secure lest my suit go amiss, my ships perish,' corn and cattle miscarry, trade decay, 'I have no wife nor children good or bad to provide for.' [31] A mere spectator of other men's fortunes and adventures, and how they act their parts, which methinks are diversely presented unto me, as from a common theatre or scene. I hear new news every day, and those ordinary rumours of war, plagues, fires, inundations, thefts, murders, massacres, meteors, comets, spectrums, prodigies apparitions, of towns taken, cities besieged in France, Germany, Turkey, Persia, Poland, etc., daily musters and preparations, and such-like, which these tempestuous times afford, battles fought, so many men slain, monomachies,[32] shipwrecks, piracies, and sea-fights, peace, leagues, stratagems and fresh alarums. A vast confusion of vows, wishes, actions, edicts, petitions, lawsuits, pleas, laws, proclamations, complaints, grievances are daily brought to our ears. New books every day, pamphlets, currantoes,[33] stories, whole catalogues of volumes of all sorts, new paradoxes, opinions, schisms, heresies, controversies in philosophy, religion, etc. Now come tidings of weddings, maskings, mummeries, entertainments, jubilees, embassies, tilts and tournaments, trophies, triumphs, revels, sports, plays: then again, as in a new shifted scene, treasons, cheating tricks, robberies, enormous villainies in all kinds, funerals, burials, deaths of princes, new discoveries, expeditions: now comical, then tragical matters. Today we hear of new lords and officers created, tomorrow of some great men deposed, and then again of fresh honours conferred; one is let loose, another imprisoned; one purchaseth, another breaketh; he thrives, his neighbour turns bankrupt; now plenty, then again death and famine; one runs, another rides, wrangles, laughs, weeps, etc. Thus I daily hear, and such-like, both private and public news; amidst the gallantry and misery of the world—jollity, pride, perplexities and cares, simplicity and villainy; subtlety, knavery, candour and integrity, mutually mixed and offering themselves—I rub on *privus privatus;* [34] as I have still lived, so I now continue, *statu quo prius,* left to a solitary life and mine own domestic discontents: saving that sometimes, *ne quid mentiar*,[35] as Diogenes went into the city and Democ-

---

26. "Praise God."
27. "Entertainment enough for myself."
28. Daniel Heinsius (1580–1655), Dutch scholar and poet.
29. "The Stoic philosopher, seeing in one glance all ages down to the present one."
30. "I laugh to myself at the court's vanities, the competitiveness of the Forum."
31. Quoted from St. Cyprian (*c*. 200–258), early Church Father.
32. Hand-to-hand fights.
33. Newspapers, just coming into existence.
34. "In total privacy."
35. "To be absolutely candid."

ritus to the haven to see fashions, I did for my recreation now and then walk abroad, look into the world, and could not choose but make some little observation, *non tam sagax observator, ac simplex recitator,*[36] not as they did, to scoff or laugh at all, but with a mixed passion.

> *Bilem sæpe, jocum vestri movere tumultus.*[37]

I did sometime laugh and scoff with Lucian,[38] and satirically tax with Menippus,[39] lament with Heraclitus,[40] sometimes again I was *petulanti splene cachinno,*[41] and then again, *urere bilis jecur,*[42] I was much moved to see that abuse which I could not mend. In which passion howsoever I may sympathize with him or them, 'tis for no such respect I shroud myself under his name; but either in an unknown habit to assume a little more liberty and freedom of speech, or if you will needs know, for that reason and only respect which Hippocrates relates at large in his Epistle to Damagetus, wherein he doth express, how coming to visit him one day, he found Democritus in his garden at Abdera, in the suburbs, under a shady bower, with a book on his knees, busy at his study, sometimes writing, sometimes walking. The subject of his book was melancholy and madness; about him lay the carcasses of many several beasts, newly by him cut up and anatomized; not that he did contemn God's creatures, as he told Hippocrates, but to find out the seat of this *atra bilis,* or melancholy, whence it proceeds, and how it was engendered in men's bodies, to the intent he might better cure it in himself, and by his writings and observations teach others how to prevent and avoid it. Which good intent of his, Hippocrates highly commended: Democritus Junior is therefore bold to imitate, and because he left it unperfect, and it is now lost, *quasi succenturiator Democriti,*[43] to revive again, prosecute, and finish in this treatise.

You have had a reason of the name. If the title and inscription offend your gravity, were it a sufficient justification to accuse others, I could produce many sober treatises, even sermons themselves, which in their fronts carry more phantastical names. Howsoever, it is a kind of policy in these days, to prefix a phantastical title to a book which is to be sold; for, as larks come down to a day-net, many vain readers will tarry and stand gazing like silly passengers at an antic picture in a painter's shop, that will not look at a judicious piece. . . .

One or two things yet I was desirous to have amended if I could, concerning the manner of handling this my subject, for which I must apologize, *deprecari,* and upon better advice give the friendly reader notice. It was not mine intent to prostitute my muse in English, or to divulge *secreta Minervæ,*[44] but to have

---

36. "Not as clever observer, but as simple reporter."
37. "Your passions have often produced my mirth and spleen" (Horace, *Epistles* I.20).
38. The famous and influential Greek satirist, 2nd century A.D.
39. Greek Cynic philosopher, 3rd century B.C., author of essays (now lost) part in prose, part in verse.
40. Ephesian philosopher (540–575 B.C.) known as "The Weeping Philosopher" (whereas Democritus was proverbially the "laughing" one).
41. "Move by mockery to laughter."
42. "My liver burns with gall" (misquoted from Horace, *Sermones* I.ix.66).
43. "As a substitute Democritus."
44. "The secrets of Minerva."

exposed this more contract in Latin, if I could have got it printed. Any scurrile pamphlet is welcome to our mercenary stationers in English; they print all,

> *cuduntque libellos*
> *In quorum foliis vix simia nuda cacaret;* [45]

but in Latin they will not deal; which is one of the reasons Nicholas Car,[46] in his oration of the paucity of English writers, gives, that so many flourishing wits are smothered in oblivion, lie dead and buried in this our nation. Another main fault is, that I have not revised the copy, and amended the style, which now flows remissly, as it was first conceived; but my leisure would not permit; *Feci nec quod potui, nec quod volui,* I confess it is neither as I would, nor as it should be.

> *Cum relego scripsisse pudet, quia plurima cerno*
> *Me quoque quæ fuerant judice digna lini.*[47]

> When I peruse this tract which I have writ,
> I am abashed, and much I hold unfit.

Et quod gravissimum [48] in the matter itself, many things I disallow at this present, which when I writ, *Non eadem est ætas, non mens;* [49] I would willingly retract much, etc., but 'tis too late, I can only crave pardon now for what is amiss.

I might indeed (had I wisely done), observed that precept of the poet, *Nonumque prematur in annum,*[50] and have taken more care: or, as Alexander the physician would have done by lapis lazuli, fifty times washed before it be used, I should have revised, corrected, and amended this tract; but I had not (as I said) that happy leisure, no amanuenses or assistants. Pancrates in Lucian, wanting a servant as he went from Memphis to Coptus in Egypt, took a door-bar, and after some superstitious words pronounced (Eucrates the relater was then present) made it stand up like a serving-man, fetch him water, turn the spit, serve in supper, and what work he would besides; and when he had done that service he desired, turned his man to a stick again. I have no such skill to make new men at my pleasure, or means to hire them; no whistle to call like the master of a ship, and bid them run, etc. I have no such authority, no such benefactors, as that noble Ambrosius was to Origen,[51] allowing him six or seven amanuenses to write out his dictates; I must for that cause do my business myself, and was therefore enforced, as a bear doth her whelps, to bring forth this confused lump; I had not time to lick it into form, as she doth her young ones, but even so to publish it as it was first written, *quicquid in buccam venit,*[52] in an extemporean style, as I do commonly all other exercises, *effudi quicquid dictavit genius meus,*[53] out of a confused company of notes, and writ with as

---

45. "They run off books on whose pages a naked ape would scarcely deign to shit."
46. 1524–68; professor of Greek at Cambridge, later a physician.
47. Ovid, *Letters from Pontus* I.5.
48. "And what is most serious."
49. "I was younger and sillier" (Horace, *Epistles* I.14).
50. "Don't publish for nine years."
51. Origen (185–254), prolific theologian, early Church Father martyred under Decius.
52. "Whatever came out first."
53. "I poured out whatever came into my mind."

small deliberation as I do ordinarily speak, without all affectation of big words, fustian phrases, jingling terms, tropes, strong lines, that like Acestes' arrows caught fire as they flew,[54] strains of wit, brave heats, elogies, hyperbolical exornations,[55] elegancies, etc., which many so much affect. I am *aquæ potor*,[56] drink no wine at all, which so much improves our modern wits, a loose, plain, rude writer, *ficum voco ficum et ligonem ligonem*,[57] and as free, as loose, *idem calamo quod in mente*,[58] I call a spade a spade, *animis hæc scribo, non auribus*,[59] I respect matter, not words; remembering that of Cardan, *verba propter res, non res propter verba*,[60] and seeking with Seneca, *quid scribam, non quemadmodum*, rather what than how to write: for as Philo thinks, 'He that is conversant about matter neglects words, and those that excel in this art of speaking have no profound learning.'

> *Verba nitent phaleris, at nullas verba medullas*
> *Intus habent.*[61]

Besides, it was the observation of that wise Seneca, 'When you see a fellow careful about his words, and neat in his speech, know this for a certainty, that man's mind is busied about toys, there's no solidity in him.' *Non est ornamentum virile concinnitas:* [62] as he said of a nightingale, *Vox es, præterea nihil*,[63] etc. I am therefore in this point a professed disciple of Apollonius, a scholar of Socrates, I neglect phrases, and labour wholly to inform my reader's understanding, not to please his ear; 'tis not my study or intent to compose neatly, which an orator requires, but to express myself readily and plainly as it happens. So that as a river runs sometimes precipitate and swift, then dull and slow; now direct, then *per ambages;* [64] now deep, then shallow; now muddy, then clear; now broad, then narrow; doth my style flow: now serious, then light; now comical, then satirical; now more elaborate, then remiss, as the present subject required, or as at that time I was affected. And if thou vouchsafe to read this treatise, it shall seem no otherwise to thee than the way to an ordinary traveller, sometimes fair, sometimes foul; here champaign, there enclosed; barren in one place, better soil in another: by woods, groves, hills, dales, plains, etc. I shall lead thee *per ardua montium, et lubrica vallium, et roscida cespitum, et glebosa camporum*,[65] through variety of objects, that which thou shalt like and surely dislike. . . .

54. A king in Virgil's *Aeneid* V.
55. Rhetorical extravagancies.
56. "A drinker of water."
57. "I call a fig a fig and a spade a spade."
58. "My pen writes what's in my mind."
59. "I write for the mind, not the ear."
60. "Language for the subject, not vice versa."
61. "Words may sound well, but hollow with no meaning."
62. "Prettiness is no masculine ornament."
63. "You are nothing but a voice."
64. "Winding"; this whole passage compares stylistic flow, the movement of fluent language, to that of a stream. (See the selection from Denham's *Cooper's Hill*.)
65. "I shall lead thee among steep mountains, slippery valleys, wet meadows, and rough fields."

From *Part I. Section I*

Subsection II. Division of the Body, Humours, Spirits

Of the parts of the body there may be many divisions: the most approved is that of Laurentius,[1] out of Hippocrates: which is, into parts contained, or containing. Contained, are either humours or spirits.

A humour is a liquid or fluent part of the body, comprehended in it, for the preservation of it; and is either innate or born with us, or adventitious and acquisite. The radical or innate is daily supplied by nourishment, which some call cambium, and make those secondary humours of ros and gluten [2] to maintain it: or acquisite, to maintain these four first primary humours, coming and proceeding from the first concoction in the liver, by which means chylus is excluded. Some divide them into profitable and excrementitious. But Crato,[3] out of Hippocrates, will have all four to be juice, and not excrements, without which no living creature can be sustained: which four, though they be comprehended in the mass of blood, yet they have their several affections, by which they are distinguished from one another, and from those adventitious, peccant, or diseased humours, as Melancthon calls [4] them.

Blood is a hot, sweet, temperate, red humour, prepared in the meseraic [5] veins, and made of the most temperate parts of the chylus in the liver, whose office is to nourish the whole body, to give it strength and colour, being dispersed by the veins through every part of it. And from it spirits are first begotten in the heart, which afterwards by the arteries are communicated to the other parts.

Pituita, or phlegm, is a cold and moist humour, begotten of the colder part of the chylus (or white juice coming out of the meat digested in the stomach), in the liver; his office is to nourish and moisten the members of the body which, as the tongue, are moved, that they be not over-dry.

Choler is hot and dry, bitter, begotten of the hotter parts of the chylus, and gathered to the gall: it helps the natural heat and senses, and serves to the expelling of excrements.

Melancholy, cold and dry, thick, black, and sour, begotten of the more feculent part of nourishment, and purged from the spleen, is a bridle to the other two hot humours, blood and choler, preserving them in the blood, and nourishing the bones. These four humours have some analogy with the four elements,[6] and to the four ages in man.

To these humours you may add serum, which is the matter of urine, and those excrementitious humours of the third concoction, sweat and tears.

Spirit is a most subtle vapour, which is expressed from the blood, and the instrument of the soul, to perform all his actions; a common tie or medium

1. Andrew Lawrence, a 17th-century British physician (?); at any rate, the author of a treatise on melancholy.
2. "Gluten" is fibrin; "ros" (Latin for "dew"), some other blood component.
3. Johannes Craton von Kraftheim, 16th-century German medical writer.
4. Philip Schwartzerd (German: "black earth," thus Hellenized; 1497–1560), scholar, church reformer, and follower of Luther.
5. Mesenteric: blood vessels supplying the mesenterum, or membrane holding the intestines to the abdominal wall.
6. See *Renaissance Psychology* in the Glossary.

between the body and the soul, as some will have it; or as Paracelsus,[7] a fourth soul of itself. Melancthon holds the fountain of these spirits to be the heart, begotten there; and afterward conveyed to the brain, they take another nature to them. Of these spirits there be three kinds, according to the three principal parts, brain, heart, liver; natural, vital, animal. The natural are begotten in the liver, and thence dispersed through the veins, to perform those natural actions. The vital spirits are made in the heart of the natural, which by the arteries are transported to all the other parts: if the spirits cease, then life ceaseth, as in a syncope or swooning. The animal spirits, formed of the vital, brought up to the brain, and diffused by the nerves to the subordinate members, give sense and motion to them all.

.   .   .

Subsection VII. Of the Inward Senses

Inner senses are three in number, so called because they be within the brain-pan, as common sense, phantasy, memory. Their objects are not only things present, but they perceive the sensible species of things to come, past, absent, such as were before in the sense. This common sense is the judge or moderator of the rest, by whom we discern all differences of objects; for by mine eye I do not know that I see, or by mine ear that I hear, but by my common sense, who judgeth of sounds and colours: they are but the organs to bring the species to be censured; so that all their objects are his, and all their offices are his. The fore-part of the brain is his organ or seat.

Phantasy, or imagination, which some call estimative, or cogitative (confirmed, saith Fernelius,[1] by frequent meditation), is an inner sense which doth more fully examine the species perceived by common sense, of things present or absent, and keeps them longer, recalling them to mind again, or making new of his own. In time of sleep this faculty is free, and many times conceives, strange, stupend,[2] absurd shapes, as in sick men we commonly observe. His organ is the middle cell of the brain; his objects all the species communicated to him by the common sense, by comparison of which he feigns infinite other unto himself. In melancholy men this faculty is most powerful and strong, and often hurts, producing many monstrous and prodigious things, especially if it be stirred up by some terrible object, presented to it from common sense or memory. In poets and painters imagination forcibly works, as appears by their several fictions, antics, images: as Ovid's house of Sleep,[3] Psyche's palace in Apuleius,[4] etc. In men it is subject and governed by reason, or at least should be; but in brutes it hath no superior, and is *ratio brutorum*, all the reason they have.

Memory lays up all the species which the senses have brought in, and records them as a good register, that they may be forthcoming when they are called for by phantasy and reason. His object is the same with phantasy, his seat and organ the back part of the brain.

7. Theophrastus Bombastus von Hohenheim (1493?–1541), alchemist and physician.

1. Jean François Fernel (1497–1558), French physician.
2. Astonishing.
3. In *Metamorphoses XI*.
4. In *The Golden Ass*.

The affections of these senses are sleep and waking, common to all sensible creatures. "Sleep is a rest or binding of the outward senses, and of the common sense, for the preservation of body and soul' (as Scaliger [5] defines it); for when the common sense resteth, the outward senses rest also. The phantasy alone is free, and his commander, reason: as appears by those imaginary dreams, which are of divers kinds, natural, divine, demoniacal, etc., which vary according to humours, diet, actions, objects, etc., of which Artemidorus,[6] Cardanus,[7] and Sambucus,[8] with their several interpretators, have written great volumes. This ligation of senses proceeds from an inhibition of spirits, the way being stopped by which they should come; this stopping is caused of vapours arising out of the stomach, filling the nerves, by which the spirits should be conveyed. When these vapours are spent, the passage is open, and the spirits perform their accustomed duties: so that 'waking is the action and motion of the senses, which the spirits dispersed over all parts cause.'

1621–51

SIR THOMAS BROWNE
1605–1682

Browne, who loved paradoxes and found in them a kind of reassurance in an age torn by religious and political dogmatisms, embodied some milder paradoxes in his own life. A physician, natural scientist, and Baconian bringer of light, he had before he was forty acquired an international reputation for a religious work; a Royalist and Anglican, he spent more than half his life in the Puritan and Parliamentarian East Anglian city of Norwich, where he was liked and admired; a naturalist whose notebooks and larger works are full of detailed observations; a killer of the chimerical dragons of superstition in his work usually known as *Vulgar Errors*,[1] he delighted in mysteries and puzzles, and delighted most to read all of nature as one vast hieroglyphic which would reflect, on close inspection, the mind that read and understood it. There is little wonder that Ralph Waldo Emerson was so devoted to his writings. Browne was born in London, studied at Winchester School and Pembroke College, Oxford, studied medicine at Montpellier, Padua, and Leyden (from which he took a degree probably in 1633, being granted the M.D. by Oxford in 1637). He moved to Norwich, then the second largest city in England, where he practised medicine, botanized along the shore, and wrote. He had a good many children (accounts differ between ten and twelve) and was knighted in 1671, on a royal visit to Norwich.

The *Religio Medici* (Faith of a Physician) was written in 1634–35 as an attempt to come to terms with the doctrinal winds that were blowing up into the storms of the English revolution, and which had plunged the Continent into the Thirty Years War.

5. Julius Caesar Scaliger (1484–1558), Italian scholar and physician.
6. Artemidorus of Daldianus (2nd century A.D.), author of *Oneirokritika*, a treatise on dreams.
7. Girolamo Cardano (1501–76), Italian mathematician and natural philosopher.
8. Johann Zsámboky (1554–84), Hungarian scholar and emblematist.

1. *Pseudodoxia Epidemica: or Enquiries into Very Many Received Tenets and Commonly Presumed Truths* (1646). Two works published posthumously were *A Letter to a Friend* (1690) and *Christian Morals* (1716).

Published first in two pirated editions in 1642, it was followed the next year by an authorized text and, in 1644, a Latin translation. It is less remarkable for its opening sections' sophisticated Anglican compromise (between ritualistic orthodoxy and reformed independence of Rome) than for its exposition of both a world view and a sense of self within that view. What C. S. Lewis called "the discarded image"—that model of the structure of the cosmos and all its component parts, concentric, hierarchical, attentive to natural phenomena but with no method for going behind them to anything but Providence—shows up beautifully in Browne's informal exploration of self. Ultimately, the faith revealed by the two parts of the long chain of meditations is in that model, and in the way in which it allows all of nature, both the horrific and the benign, to be read as evidence of ultimate human dignity. Browne's mode of thinking in images, rather more Baconian in many ways than his style would warrant, allows him to contain the doubts of a Hobbes or a Descartes, the probings and anatomies which would ultimately collapse the old model of the universe.

Religio Medici

From *Part I*

1.

For my religion, though there be several circumstances that might persuade the world I have none at all, as the general scandal of my profession, the natural course of my studies, the indifferency of my behaviour and discourse in matters of religion, neither violently defending one, nor with that common ardour and contention opposing another; yet, in despite hereof, I dare without usurpation [1] assume the honourable style of a Christian. Not that I merely owe this title to the font, my education, or the clime wherein I was born, as being bred up either to confirm those principles my parents instilled into my unwary understanding, or by a general consent proceed in the religion of my country. But having in my riper years and confirmed judgement seen and examined all, I find myself obliged by the principles of grace, and the law of mine own reason, to embrace no other name but this. Neither doth herein my zeal so far make me forget the general charity I owe unto humanity, as rather to hate than pity Turks, Infidels, and (what is worse) Jews; rather contenting myself to enjoy that happy style, than maligning those who refuse so glorious a title.

2.

But, because the name of a Christian is become too general to express our faith, there being a geography of religions as well as lands, and every clime distinguished not only by their laws and limits, but circumscribed by their doctrines and rules of faith; to be particular, I am of that reformed new-cast religion, wherein I dislike nothing but the name; of the same belief our Saviour taught, the Apostles disseminated, the Fathers authorised, and the Martyrs confirmed; but by the sinister ends of princes, the ambition and avarice of

1. Wrongly so doing.

prelates, and the fatal corruption of times, so decayed, impaired, and fallen from its native beauty, that it required the careful and charitable hands of these times to restore it to its primitive integrity. Now the accidental occasion whereupon, the slender means whereby, the low and abject condition of the person by whom so good a work was set on foot, which in our adversaries beget contempt and scorn, fills me with wonder, and is the very same objection the insolent pagans first cast at Christ and his disciples.

．．．

3.

Yet I have not so shaken hands with those desperate resolutions [2] who had rather venture at large their decayed bottom, than bring her in to be new trimmed in the dock; who had rather promiscuously retain all, than abridge any, and obstinately be what they are, than what they have been, as to stand in diameter [3] and sword's point with them. We have reformed from them, not against them; for, omitting those improperations [4] and terms of scurrility betwixt us which only difference our affections and not our cause, there is between us one common name and appellation, one faith and necessary body of principles common to us both; and therefore I am not scrupulous to converse or live with them, to enter their churches in defect of ours, and either pray with them, or for them. I am, I confess, naturally inclined to that which misguided zeal terms superstition. My common conversation I do acknowledge austere, my behaviour full of rigour, sometimes not without morosity; yet at my devotion I love to use the civility of my knee, my hat, and hand,[5] with all those outward and sensible motions which may express or promote my invisible devotion. I should violate my own arm rather than a church; nor willingly deface the name of saint or martyr. At the sight of a cross or crucifix I can dispense with my hat, but scarce with the thought or memory of my Saviour. I cannot laugh at, but rather pity, the fruitless journeys of pilgrims, or contemn the miserable condition of friars; for, though misplaced in circumstances, there is something in it of devotion. I could never hear the Ave-Mary Bell [6] without an elevation; or think it a sufficient warrant, because they erred in one circumstance, for me to err in all, that is, in silence and dumb contempt. Whilst, therefore, they directed their devotions to her, I offered mine to God, and rectified the errors of their prayers by rightly ordering mine own. At a solemn procession I have wept abundantly while my consorts, blind with opposition and prejudice, have fallen into an excess of scorn and laughter. There are, questionless,[7] both in Greek, Roman and African churches solemnities and ceremonies whereof the wiser zeals do make a Christian use, and stand condemned by us, not as evil in themselves, but as allurements and baits of superstition to those vulgar heads that look asquint on the face of truth, and those unstable judgements that

2. Roman Catholics; Browne is putting the Anglican case for accommodation of orthodoxy without the necessity of submitting to the papacy.
3. Opposed to.
4. Reproaches.
5. That is, genuflecting, uncovering his head, crossing himself.
6. The Angelus, rung at six, twelve, and six o'clock as a summons to prayer, usually to the Virgin: a specifically Roman Catholic custom.
7. Unquestionably.

cannot consist in the narrow point and centre of virtue without a reel or stagger to the circumference.

.   .   .

6.

I could never divide myself from any man upon the difference of an opinion, or be angry with his judgement for not agreeing with me in that from which perhaps within a few days I should dissent myself. I have no genius to disputes in religion, and have often thought it wisdom to decline them, especially upon a disadvantage, or when the cause of truth might suffer in the weakness of my patronage. Where we desire to be informed, 'tis good to contest with me above ourselves; but to confirm and establish our opinions, 'tis best to argue with judgements below our own, that the frequent spoils and victories over their reasons may settle in ourselves an esteem and confirmed opinion of our own. Every man is not a proper champion for truth, nor fit to take up the gauntlet in the cause of verity: many, from the ignorance of these maxims, and an inconsiderate zeal unto truth, have too rashly charged the troops of error, and remain as trophies unto the enemies of truth. A man may be in as just possession of truth as of a city, and yet be forced to surrender; 'tis therefore far better to enjoy her with peace, than to hazard her on a battle. If, therefore, there rise any doubts in my way, I do forget them, or at least defer them till my better settled judgement and more manly reason be able to resolve them; for I perceive every man's own reason is his best Œdipus,[8] and will, upon a reasonable truce, find a way to loose those bonds wherewith the subtleties of error have enchained our more flexible and tender judgements. In philosophy, where truth seems double-faced, there is no man more paradoxical than myself: but in divinity I love to keep the road; and, though not in an implicit, yet an humble faith, follow the great wheel of the church, by which I move, not reserving any proper poles or motion from the epicycle [9] of my own brain. By this means I leave no gap for heresies, schisms, or errors, of which at present I hope I shall not injure truth to say I have no taint or tincture. . . . I must confess my greener studies have been polluted with two or three—not any begotten in the latter centuries, but old and obsolete—such as could never have been revived but by such extravagant and irregular heads as mine; for indeed, heresies perish not with their authors, but like the river *Arethusa*,[10] though they lose their currents in one place, they rise up again in another. One general council is not able to extirpate one single heresy, it may be cancelled for the present, but revolution of time and the like aspects of heaven will restore it, when it will flourish till it be condemned again. For as though there were a *metempsychosis*,[11] and the soul of one man passed into another, opinions do find, after certain revolutions, men and minds like those that first begat them. To see ourselves again we need not look for Plato's year; [12] every man is not only

8. As problem-solver (Oedipus answered the Sphinx's riddle).
9. The circle-on-the-circle of the orbits in the old astronomy (see *Astronomy* in the Glossary).
10. "That loseth itself in Greece and riseth again in Sicily" (Browne's note); see also Headnote to Milton's *Lycidas*.
11. Transmigration of souls; reincarnation.
12. The *magnus annus* or great year of Plato; "a revolution of several thousand years when all things should return to their former estate and he teaching again in his school as when he delivered this opinion" (Browne's note).

himself—there have been many Diogenes and as many Timons, though but few of that name. Men are lived over again; the world is now as it were in ages past; there was none then but there hath been some one since that parallels him, and is, as it were, his revived self.

      · · ·

9.

As for those wingy mysteries in divinity, and airy subtleties in religion, which have unhinged the brains of better heads, they never stretched the *pia mater* [13] of mine. Methinks there be not impossibilities enough in religion for an active faith; the deepest mysteries ours contains have not only been illustrated, but maintained by syllogism and the rule of reason. I love to lose myself in a mystery, to pursue my reason to an *O altitudo!* [14] 'Tis my solitary recreation to pose my apprehension with those involved enigmas and riddles of the Trinity, with incarnation, and resurrection. I can answer all the objections of Satan and my rebellious reason with that odd resolution I learned of Tertullian, *Certum est, quia impossibile est.*[15] I desire to exercise my faith in the difficultest point; for to credit ordinary and visible objects is not faith, but persuasion. Some believe the better for seeing Christ's sepulchre; and, when they have seen the Red Sea, doubt not of the miracle. Now, contrarily, I bless myself and am thankful that I lived not in the days of miracles, that I never saw Christ nor his disciples. I would not have been one of those Israelites that passed the Red Sea, nor one of Christ's patients on whom he wrought his wonders, then had my faith been thrust upon me; nor should I enjoy that greater blessing pronounced to all that believe and saw not. 'Tis an easy and necessary belief, to credit what our eye and sense hath examined. I believe he was dead, and buried, and rose again; and desire to see him in his glory, rather than to contemplate him in his cenotaph or sepulchre. Nor is this much to believe; as we have reason, we owe this faith unto history: they only had the advantage of a bold and noble faith who lived before his coming, who upon obscure prophecies and mystical types [16] could raise a belief, and expect apparent impossibilities.

      · · ·

15.

Natura nihil agit frustra [17] is the only indisputed axiom in philosophy. There are no grotesques in nature; not anything framed to fill up empty cantons,[18] and unnecessary spaces. In the most imperfect creatures, and such as were not preserved in the ark, but, having their seeds and principles in the womb of nature, are everywhere, where the power of the sun is, in these is the wisdom of

13. The vascular membrane covering the brain.
14. Bacon, in *The Advancement of Learning* II.xxv.13, says that "In divinity many things must be left abrupt, and concluded with this: 'O altitudo sapientiae et scientiae Dei! quam incomprehensibilia sunt judicia ejus, et non investigabiles viae ejus!'" (O the depth of the riches both of the wisdom and knowledge of God! how unsearchable are his judgments, and his ways past finding out!—Romans 11:33).
15. "It is certain just because it is impossible"—a famous paradox of faith posed by Tertullian (160–230 A.D.), theologian and polemicist.
16. The foreshadowing figures of biblical interpretation.
17. "Nature does nothing in vain" (a basic principle of Aristotelian scientific tradition).
18. Regions, divisions.

his hand discovered. Out of this rank Solomon chose the object of his admiration.[19] Indeed, what reason may not go to school to the wisdom of bees, ants, and spiders? what wise hand teacheth them to do what reason cannot teach us? Ruder heads stand amazed at those prodigious pieces of nature, whales, elephants, dromedaries and camels; these, I confess, are the colossus and majestic piece of her hand: but in these narrow engines there is more curious mathematics; and the civility of these little citizens more neatly sets forth the wisdom of their Maker. Who admires not Regiomontanus [20] his fly beyond his eagle, or wonders not more at the operation of two souls in those little bodies, than but one in the trunk of a cedar? I could never content my contemplation with those general pieces of wonder, the flux and reflux of the sea,[21] the increase of Nile, the conversion of the needle [22] to the north; and have studied to match and parallel those in the more obvious and neglected pieces of nature, which without further travel I can do in the cosmography of myself. We carry with us the wonders we seek without us: there is all Africa and her prodigies in us; we are that bold and adventurous piece of nature, which he that studies wisely learns in a compendium what others labour at in a divided piece and endless volume.

16.

Thus there are two books from whence I collect my divinity; besides that written one of God, another of his servant nature, that universal and public manuscript that lies expansed [23] unto the eyes of all: those that never saw him in the one, have discovered him in the other. This was the scripture and theology of the heathens: the natural motion of the sun made them more admire him than its supernatural station did the children of Israel; the ordinary effects of nature wrought more admiration in them than in the other all his miracles. Surely the heathens knew better how to join and read these mystical letters than we Christians, who cast a more careless eye on these common hieroglyphics, and disdain to suck divinity from the flowers of nature. Nor do I so forget God as to adore the name of nature; which I define not, with the schools, to be the principle of motion and rest, but that straight and regular line, that settled and constant course the wisdom of God hath ordained the actions of his creatures, according to their several kinds. To make a revolution every day is the nature of the sun, because of that necessary course which God hath ordained it, from which it cannot swerve but by a faculty from that voice which first did give it motion. Now this course of nature God seldom alters or perverts, but like an excellent artist, hath so contrived his work, that with the selfsame instrument, without a new creation, he may effect his obscurest designs. Thus he sweeteneth the water with a wood, preserveth the creatures in the ark, which the blast of his mouth might have as easily created; for God is like a skillful geometrician, who, when more easily and with one stroke of his compass

19. The ant ("Go to the ant, thou sluggard; consider her ways, and be wise"—Proverbs 6:6).

20. Johann Müller (1436–75) was supposed to have built an iron fly and a wooden eagle, both of which flew.

21. The tides.

22. The compass needle.

23. Open.

he might describe or divide a right line, had yet rather do this in a circle or longer way, according to the constituted and fore-laid principles of his art. Yet this rule of his he doth sometimes pervert, to acquaint the world with his prerogative, lest the arrogancy of our reason should question his power, and conclude he could not. And thus I call the effects of nature the works of God, whose hand and instrument she only is; and therefore to ascribe his actions unto her, is to devolve [24] the honour of the principal agent upon the instrument; which if with reason we may do, then let our hammers rise up and boast they built our houses, and our pens receive the honour of our writings. I hold there is a general beauty in the works of God, and therefore no deformity in any kind or species of creature whatsoever. I cannot tell by what logic we call a toad, a bear, or an elephant ugly; they being created in those outward shapes and figures which best express the actions of their inward forms, and having passed that general visitation of God, who saw that all that he had made was good, that is, conformable to his will, which abhors deformity, and is the rule of order and beauty. There is no deformity but in monstrosity; wherein, notwithstanding, there is a kind of beauty, nature so ingeniously contriving the irregular parts, as they become sometimes more remarkable than the principal fabric. To speak yet more narrowly, there was never anything ugly or misshapen, but the chaos; wherein, notwithstanding, to speak strictly, there was no deformity, because no form; nor was it yet impregnant by the voice of God. Now nature is not at variance with art, nor art with nature, they being both servants of his providence. Art is the perfection of nature. Were the world now as it was the sixth day, there were yet a chaos. Nature hath made one world, and art another. In brief, all things are artificial; for nature is the art of God.

. . .

27.

That miracles are ceased, I can neither prove, nor absolutely deny, much less define the time and period of their cessation. That they survived Christ is manifest upon the record of Scripture; that they outlived the Apostles also, and were revived at the conversion of nations many years after, we cannot deny, if we shall not question those writers whose testimonies we do not controvert in points that make for our own opinions. Therefore that may have some truth in it that is reported by the Jesuits of their miracles in the Indies; I could wish it were true, or had any other testimony than their own pens. They may easily believe those miracles abroad, who daily conceive a greater at home, the transmutation of those visible elements into the body and blood of our Saviour.[25] For the conversion of water into wine, which he wrought in Cana,[26] or, what the Devil would have had him done in the wilderness, of stones into bread,[27] compared to this, will scarce deserve the name of a miracle: though indeed, to speak properly, there is not one miracle greater than another, they being the extraordinary effects of the hand of God, to which all things are of an equal facility; and to create the world, as easy as one single creature. For this is also a miracle,

24. Transfer.
25. Browne refers to the mystery of the Eucharist, with apparent total acceptance of the transubstantiation of Christ's body and blood.
26. John 2:3–9.
27. Luke 4:1–4.

not only to produce effects against or above nature, but before nature; and to create nature, as great a miracle as to contradict or transcend her. We do too narrowly define the power of God, restraining it to our capacities. I hold that God can do all things; how he should work contradictions, I do not understand, yet dare not therefore deny. I cannot see why the angel of God should question Esdras [28] to recall the time past, if it were beyond his own power; or that God should pose [29] mortality in that which he was not able to perform himself. I will not say God cannot, but he will not, perform many things, which we plainly affirm he cannot. This, I am sure, is the mannerliest [30] proposition, wherein, notwithstanding, I hold no paradox; for, strictly, his power is the same with his will, and they both, with all the rest, do make but one God.

28.

Therefore that miracles have been, I do believe; that they may yet be wrought by the living, I do not deny; but have no confidence in those which are fathered on the dead. And this hath ever made me suspect the efficacy of relics, to examine the bones, question the habits and appurtenances of saints, and even of Christ himself. I cannot conceive why the cross that Helena found, and whereon Christ himself died, should have power to restore others unto life. I excuse not Constantine from a fall off his horse, or a mischief from his enemies, upon the wearing those nails on his bridle which our Saviour bore upon the cross in his hands. I compute among your *piæ fraudes*,[31] nor many degrees before consecrated swords and roses, that which Baldwin, King of Jerusalem, returned the Genovese for their cost and pains in his war, to wit, the ashes of John the Baptist. Those that hold the sanctity of their souls doth leave behind a tincture [32] and sacred faculty on their bodies, speak naturally of miracles, and do not salve the doubt. Now one reason I tender so little devotion unto relics, is, I think, the slender and doubtful respect I have always held unto antiquities. For that indeed which I admire, is far before antiquity, that is, eternity; and that is, God himself; who, though he be styled *the Ancient of Days,* cannot receive the adjunct of antiquity; who was before the world, and shall be after it, yet is not older than it; for in his years there is no climacter; [33] his duration is eternity, and far more venerable than antiquity.

. . .

39.

Some divines count Adam thirty years old at his creation, because they suppose him created in the perfect age and stature of man. And surely we are all out of the computation of our age, and every man is some months elder than he bethinks him; for we live, move, have a being,[34] and are subject to the actions

---

28. "Then he said unto me, Go to, weigh me a weight of fire, or measure me a measure of wind, or call me again the day that is past" (II Esdras 4:5).

29. Perplex.

30. Most sophisticated.

31. "Pious frauds"; Browne is discussing the claims made for famous relics.

32. Tint; here, of holiness.

33. Climacteric: a crucial point of change in human life.

34. Echoing St. Paul in Acts 17:28.

of the elements, and the malice of diseases, in that other world, the truest microcosm, the womb of our mother. For besides that general and common existence we are conceived to hold in our chaos, and whilst we sleep within the bosom of our causes, we enjoy a being and life in three distinct worlds, wherein we receive most manifest graduations. In that obscure world and womb of our mother, our time is short, computed by the moon, yet longer than the days of many creatures that behold the sun; ourselves being not yet without life, sense, and reason; though for the manifestation of its actions, it awaits the opportunity of objects, and seems to live there but in its root and soul of vegetation. Entering afterwards upon the scene of the world, we arise up and become another creature, performing the reasonable actions of man, and obscurely manifesting that part of divinity in us; but not in complement and perfection, till we have once more cast our secondine, that is, this slough of flesh, and are delivered into the last world, that is, that ineffable place of Paul, that proper *ubi* [35] of spirits. The smattering I have of the philosopher's stone [36] (which is something more than the perfect exaltation of gold) hath taught me a great deal of divinity, and instructed my belief, how that immortal spirit and incorruptible substance of my soul may lie obscure, and sleep a while within this house of flesh. Those strange and mystical transmigrations that I have observed in silk-worms, turned my philosophy into divinity. There is in these works of nature, which seem to puzzle reason, something divine, and hath more in it than the eye of a common spectator doth discover.

From *Part II*

9.

I was never yet once,[1] and commend their resolutions who never marry twice: not that I disallow of second marriage; as neither, in all cases, of polygamy, which, considering some times, and the unequal number of both sexes, may be also necessary. The whole world was made for man, but the twelfth part of man for woman: man is the whole world, and the breadth of God, woman the rib and crooked piece [2] of man. I could be content that we might procreate like trees, without conjunction, or that there were any way to perpetuate the world without this trivial and vulgar way of union: it is the foolishest act a wise man commits in all his life: nor is there anything that will more deject his cooled imagination, when he shall consider what an odd and unworthy piece of folly he hath committed. I speak not in prejudice, nor am averse from that sweet sex, but naturally amorous of all that is beautiful. I can look a whole day with delight upon a handsome picture, though it be but of an horse. It is my temper, and I like it the better, to affect all harmony; and sure there is music even in the beauty and the silent note which Cupid strikes, far sweeter than the

35. "Where."
36. The philosopher's stone was the object of the alchemical quest, and, with it, transmutation of metals could be effected; but it came, in time, to develop more allegorical meaning (see *Alchemy* in the Glossary).

1. Browne did in fact marry (in 1641).
2. Alluding to the old misogynistic fable that the rib from which Eve was created was a crooked one.

sound of an instrument. For there is a music wherever there is a harmony, order, or proportion: and thus far we may maintain the music of the spheres; [3] for those well-ordered motions, and regular paces, though they give no sound unto the ear, yet to the understanding they strike a note most full of harmony. Whosoever is harmonically composed delights in harmony, which makes me much distrust the symmetry of those heads which declaim against all church-music. For myself, not only from my obedience, but my particular genius,[4] I do embrace it: for even that vulgar and tavern-music which makes one man merry, another mad, strikes in me a deep fit of devotion, and a profound contemplation of the First Composer. There is something in it of divinity more than the ear discovers: it is an hieroglyphical and shadowed [5] lesson of the whole world, and creatures of God; such a melody to the ear, as the whole world, well understood, would afford the understanding. In brief, it is a sensible [6] fit of that harmony which intellectually sounds in the ears of God. I will not say, with Plato, the soul is an harmony, but harmonical, and hath its nearest sympathy unto music: thus some, whose temper of body agrees, and humours the constitution of their souls, are born poets, though indeed all are naturally inclined unto rhythm. This made Tacitus, in the very first line of his story,[7] fall upon a verse; and Cicero, the worst of poets but declaiming for a poet, fall in the very first sentence upon a perfect hexameter.[8] I feel not in me those sordid and unchristian desires of my profession; I do not secretly implore and wish for plagues, rejoice at famines, revolve ephemerides [9] and almanacs in expectation of malignant aspects, fatal conjunctions, and eclipses. I rejoice not at unwholesome springs, nor unseasonable winters: my prayer goes with the husbandman's; I desire everything in its proper season, that neither men nor the times be put out of temper. Let me be sick myself, if sometimes the malady of my patient be not a disease unto me. I desire rather to cure his infirmities than my own necessities. Where I do him no good, methinks it is scarce honest gain; though I confess 'tis but the worthy salary of our well-intended endeavours. I am not only ashamed, but heartily sorry, that, besides death, there are diseases incurable: yet not for my own sake, or that they be beyond my art, but for the general cause and sake of humanity, whose common cause I apprehend as mine own. . . .

10.

For my conversation,[10] it is like the sun's, with all men, and with a friendly aspect to good and bad. Methinks there is no man bad, and the worst, best; that is, while they are kept within the circle of those qualities wherein they are good: there is no man's mind of such discordant and jarring a temper, to which a tuneable disposition may not strike a harmony. *Magnæ virtutes, nec*

3. See *Music of the Spheres* in the Glossary.
4. Cast of mind.
5. Figurative.
6. Audible.
7. The first line of his *Annals* seems to scan.
8. A well-known bit of lore, involving his *Pro Archia*.
9. Astronomical charts.
10. Conduct.

minora vitia; [11] it is the posy of the best natures, and may be inverted on the worst; there are in the most depraved and venomous dispositions, certain pieces that remain untouched, which by an *antiperistasis* [12] become more excellent, or by the excellency of their antipathies are able to preserve themselves from the contagion of their enemy vices, and persist entire beyond the general corruption. For it is also thus in nature: the greatest balsams [13] do lie enveloped in the bodies of most powerful corrosives. I say, moreover, and I ground upon experience, that poisons contain within themselves their own antidote, and that which preserves them from the venom of themselves, without which they were not deleterious to others only, but to themselves also. But it is the corruption that I fear within me, not the contagion of commerce without me. 'Tis that unruly regiment within me, that will destroy me; 'tis I that do infect myself; the man without a navel [14] yet lives in me; I feel that original canker corrode and devour me; and therefore *Defenda me Dios de me,* Lord deliver me from myself, is a part of my litany, and the first voice of my retired imaginations. There is no man alone, because every man is a microcosm, [15] and carries the whole world about him. *Nunquam minus solus quam cum solus,* [16] though it be the apothegm of a wise man, is yet true in the mouth of a fool. Indeed, though in a wilderness, a man is never alone, not only because he is with himself and his own thoughts, but because he is with the Devil, who ever consorts with our solitude, and is that unruly rebel that musters up those disordered motions which accompany our sequestered imaginations. And to speak more narrowly, there is no such thing as solitude, nor anything that can be said to be alone and by itself, but God, who is his own circle, and can subsist by himself; all others, besides their dissimilar and heterogeneous parts, which in a manner multiply their natures, cannot subsist without the concourse of God, and the society of that hand which doth uphold their natures. In brief, there can be nothing truly alone and by itself, which is not truly one; and such is only God: all others do transcend an unity, and so by consequence are many.

11.

Now for my life, it is a miracle of thirty years, which to relate were not a history, but a piece of poetry, and would sound to common ears like a fable. For the world, I count it not an inn, but an hospital; and a place not to live, but to die in. The world that I regard is myself; it is the microcosm of my own frame that I cast mine eye on; for the other, I use it but like my globe, and turn it round sometimes for my recreation. Men that look upon my outside, perusing only my condition and fortunes, do err in my altitude; for I am above Atlas [17] his shoulders. The earth is a point not only in respect of the heavens

11. "Great virtues and no lesser vices" (Plato quoted by Plutarch).
12. An intensification of contraries, by virtue of their very opposition.
13. Healing salves; "balms" in the most general sense.
14. Adam, who had no navel, presumably because he was not born of woman; theologically, the old Adam within man, the unexpunged sinful element in his nature (see I Corinthians 15:45).
15. For an extremely detailed treatment of this, see the extract from Ralegh's *History of the World.*
16. "Never less lonely than when alone" (Cicero, *De Officiis* III.1).
17. The mythical giant Atlas bore the globe on his shoulders.

above us, but of that heavenly and celestial part within us; that mass of flesh that circumscribes me, limits not my mind. That surface that tells the heavens it hath an end, cannot persuade me I have any: I take my circle to be above three hundred and sixty; [18] though the number of the arc do measure my body, it comprehendeth not my mind: whilst I study to find how I am a microcosm, or little world, I find myself something more than the great. There is surely a piece of divinity in us, something that was before the elements, and owes no homage unto the sun. Nature tells me I am the image of God, as well as Scripture: he that understands not thus much, hath not his introduction or first lesson, and is yet to begin the alphabet of man. Let me not injure the felicity of others, if I say I am as happy as any: *Ruat cœlum, fiat voluntas tua*,[19] salveth all; so that whatsoever happens, it is but what our daily prayers desire. In brief, I am content; and what should Providence add more? Surely this is it we call happiness, and this do I enjoy; with this I am happy in a dream, and as content to enjoy a happiness in a fancy, as others in a more apparent truth and realty. There is surely a nearer apprehension of anything that delights us in our dreams, than in our waked senses: without this I were unhappy; for my awaked judgement discontents me, ever whispering unto me, that I am from my friend; but my friendly dreams in the night requite me, and make me think I am within his arms. I thank God for my happy dreams, as I do for my good rest; for there is a satisfaction in them unto reasonable desires, and as such can be content with a fit of happiness: and surely it is not a melancholy conceit [20] to think we are all asleep in this world, and that the conceits of this life are as mere dreams to those of the next, as the phantasms of the night to the conceits of the day. There is an equal delusion in both, and the one doth but seem to be the emblem or picture of the other: we are somewhat more than ourselves in our sleeps, and the slumber of the body seems to be but the waking of the soul. It is the ligation [21] of sense, but the liberty of reason; and our waking conceptions do not match the fancies of our sleeps. At my nativity my ascendant [22] was the watery sign of Scorpius; I was born in the planetary hour of Saturn, and I think I have a piece of that leaden planet in me. I am no way facetious, not disposed for the mirth and galliardize [23] of company; yet in one dream I can compose a whole comedy, behold the action, apprehend the jests, and laugh myself awake at the conceits thereof. Were my memory as faithful as my reason is then fruitful, I would never study but in my dreams; and this time also would I choose for my devotions: but our grosser memories have then so little hold of our abstracted understandings, that they forget the story, and can only relate to our awaked souls a confused and broken tale of that that hath passed. Aristotle, who hath written a singular tract Of Sleep, hath not, methinks, thoroughly defined it; nor yet Galen,[24] though he seem to have corrected it; for those *noctambuloes* [25] and night-

18. That is, if the self is likened to a circle, it is one of more than 360 degrees.
19. "Though heaven fall, thy will be done."
20. Notion.
21. Binding, constricting.
22. Rising zodiacal sign, with astrological implications.
23. Merriment; from "galliard," a dance in three-quarter time.
24. Claudius Galenus (130–200 A.D.), Greek writer on medicine.
25. Somnambulists.

walkers, though in their sleep, do yet enjoy the action of their senses. We must therefore say that there is something in us that is not in the jurisdiction of Morpheus; and that those abstracted and ecstatic souls do walk about in their own corpse as spirits with the bodies they assume, wherein they seem to hear, see, and feel, though indeed the organs are destitute of sense, and their natures of those faculties that should inform them. Thus it is observed, that men sometimes, upon the hour of their departure, do speak and reason above themselves; for then the soul, beginning to be freed from the ligaments of the body, begins to reason like herself, and to discourse in a strain above mortality.

12.

We term sleep a death; and yet it is waking that kills us, and destroys those spirits that are the house of life. 'Tis indeed a part of life that best expresseth death; for every man truly lives, so long as he acts his nature, or some way makes good the faculties of himself. Themistocles, therefore, that slew his soldier in his sleep, was a merciful executioner: 'tis a kind of punishment the mildness of no laws hath invented: I wonder the fancy of Lucan and Seneca did not discover it. It is that death by which we may be literally said to die daily; a death which Adam died before his mortality; a death whereby we live a middle and moderating point between life and death: in fine, so like death, I dare not trust it without my prayers, and an half adieu unto the world, and take my farewell in a colloquy with God. . . .

1634–35   1642

Hydriotaphia

Hydriotaphia, Urn-Burial (published 1658) is a long meditation on death, time, and memory, occasioned by antiquarian researches. Some burial urns, discovered in a field in Norfolk, led Browne to consider their provenance (he mistakenly thought them to be Roman), and from there to meditate upon burial customs, cremations, tombs, and monuments among as many cultures as he could. But like any emblem or sonnet of the sixteenth century, the consideration of the object led to the *significatio* or interpretation; in his great last chapter, worthy of Montaigne at his best (of whom Browne claimed never to have read more than a few pages), the vanity of all the false technologies of immortality is relentlessly, but not cruelly, disclosed.

From Hydriotaphia

Chapter V

Now since these dead bones have already outlasted the living ones of Methuselah,[1] and in a yard under ground, and thin walls of clay, out-worn all the strong and spacious buildings above it, and quietly rested under the

---

1. Who lived 969 years, according to Genesis 5:27.

drums and tramplings of three conquests: what prince can promise such diuturnity [2] unto his relics, or might not gladly say,

Sic ego componi versus in ossa velim? [3]

Time, which antiquates antiquities, and hath an art to make dust of all things, hath yet spared these minor monuments.

In vain we hope to be known by open and visible conservatories, when to be unknown was the means of their continuation, and obscurity their protection. If they died by violent hands, and were thrust into their urns, these bones become considerable, and some old philosophers would honour them, whose souls they conceived most pure, which were thus snatched from their bodies, and to retain a stronger propension unto [4] them; whereas they weariedly left a languishing corpse, and with faint desires of reunion. If they fell by long and aged decay, yet wrapt up in the bundle of time, they fall into indistinction,[5] and make but one blot with infants. If we begin to die when we live, and long life be but a prolongation of death, our life is a sad composition; we live with death, and die not in a moment. How many pulses made up the life of Methuselah, were work for Archimedes: common counters sum up the life of Moses his man.[6] Our days become considerable, like petty sums, by minute accumulations; where numerous fractions make up but small round numbers; and our days of a span long, make not one little finger.[7]

If the nearness of our last necessity brought a nearer conformity into it, there were a happiness in hoary hairs, and no calamity in half-senses.[8] But the long habit of living indisposeth us for dying; when avarice makes us the sport of death, when even David grew politicly cruel, and Solomon could hardly be said to be the wisest of men. But many are too early old, and before the date of age. Adversity stretcheth our days, misery makes Alcmena's nights,[9] and time hath no wings unto it. But the most tedious being is that which can unwish itself, content to be nothing, or never to have been, which was beyond the malcontent of Job, who cursed not the day of his life, but his nativity; [10] content to have so far been, as to have a title to future being, although he had lived here but in an hidden state of life, and as it were an abortion.

What song the Sirens sang, or what name Achilles assumed when he hid himself among women, though puzzling questions, are not beyond all conjecture.[11] What time the persons of these ossuaries entered the famous nations of the dead, and slept with princes and counselors, might admit a wide [12]

2. Long life; the three conquests of Celtic Britain were by the Romans, Saxons, and Normans.
3. "Thus I, when turned to bones, should wish to rest" (Tibullus).
4. Inclination for.
5. Indistinctness.
6. Moses' man is the canonical man of Psalm 90 (traditionally and mistakenly said to be by Moses), the days of whose years are threescore and ten.
7. "According to the ancient arithmetic of the hand, wherein the little finger of the right hand contracted signified an hundred" (Browne's note).
8. Deterioration of sight, hearing, and other senses.
9. Jupiter so liked his night of love with Alcmena that he prevented the sun from rising, thus producing three adjacent nights; Hercules was born of this union.
10. "Let the day perish wherein I was born" (Job 3:3–12).
11. Famous pointless questions of antiquity (like Donne's "Who cleft the devil's foot?").
12. Tentative or approximate.

solution. But who were the proprietaries of these bones, or what bodies these ashes made up, were a question above antiquarism; not to be resolved by man, nor easily perhaps by spirits, except we consult the provincial guardians, or tutelary observators. Had they made as good provision for their names, as they have done for their relics, they had not so grossly erred in the art of perpetuation. But to subsist in bones, and be but pyramidally [13] extant, is a fallacy in duration. Vain ashes which in the oblivion of names, persons, times, and sexes, have found unto themselves a fruitless continuation, and only arise unto late posterity, as emblems of mortal vanities, antidotes against pride, vainglory, and madding vices. Pagan vainglories which thought the world might last for ever, had encouragement for ambition; and, finding no Atropos [14] unto the immortality of their names, were never damped with the necessity of oblivion. Even old ambitions had the advantage of ours, in the attempts of their vainglories, who acting early, and before the probable meridian [15] of time, have by this time found great accomplishment of their designs, whereby the ancient heroes have already outlasted their monuments and mechanical preservations. But in this latter scene of time, we cannot expect such mummies unto our memories, when ambition may fear the prophecy of Elias,[16] and Charles the Fifth can never hope to live within two Methuselahs of Hector.[17]

And therefore, restless unquiet for the diuturnity [18] of our memories unto present considerations seems a vanity almost out of date, and superannuated piece of folly. We cannot hope to live so long in our names, as some have done in their persons. One face of Janus [19] holds no proportion unto the other. 'Tis too late to be ambitious. The great mutations of the world are acted, or time may be too short for our designs. To extend our memories by monuments whose death we daily pray for, and whose duration we cannot hope without injury to our expectations in the advent of the last day, were a contradiction to our beliefs. We whose generations are ordained in this setting part of time, are providentially taken off from such imaginations; and, being necessitated to eye the remaining particle of futurity, are naturally constituted unto thoughts of the next world, and cannot excusably decline the consideration of that duration which maketh pyramids pillars of snow, and all that's past a moment.

Circles and right lines limit and close all bodies, and the mortal right-lined circle [20] must conclude and shut up all. There is no antidote against the opium of time, which temporally considereth all things: our fathers find their

13. Like the dead Egyptians (in the days before hieroglyphics could be read), who were unknown, though their pyramids were themselves emblems of fame.

14. Third and most terrifying of the three Fates (with Clotho and Lachesis); they spun and measured the thread of life, Atropos cut it.

15. Noon, or midpoint.

16. "That the world will last but six thousand years" (Browne's note).

17. The Emperor Charles V lived from 1500 to 1588; two Methuselahs would put Hector back in the Athens of Socrates, so that if any historical Hector can be surmised, he surely antedates this.

18. Long life.

19. Two-faced (away from each other) Roman god, presiding over commencements and openings (hence, January).

20. The Greek letter theta, θ; Browne calls it "the character of death" because it is the initial letter of *thanatos* (death).

graves in our short memories, and sadly tell us how we may be buried in our survivors. Gravestones tell truth scarce forty years.[21] Generations pass while some trees stand, and old families last not three oaks. To be read by bare inscriptions like many in Gruter,[22] to hope for eternity by enigmatical epithets or first letters of our names, to be studied by antiquaries, who we were, and have new names given us like many of the mummies, are cold consolations unto the students of perpetuity, even by everlasting languages.

To be content that times to come should only know there was such a man, not caring whether they knew more of him, was a frigid ambition in Cardan,[23] disparaging his horoscopical inclination and judgement of himself. Who cares to subsist like Hippocrates' patients, or Achilles' horses in Homer, under naked nominations, without deserts and noble acts, which are the balsam of our memories, the *entelechia* [24] and soul of our subsistences? To be nameless in worthy deeds, exceeds [25] an infamous history. The Canaanitish woman [26] lives more happily without a name, than Herodias [27] with one. And who had not rather have been the good thief than Pilate?

But the iniquity of oblivion blindly scattereth her poppy, and deals with the memory of men without distinction to merit of perpetuity. Who can but pity the founder of the pyramids? Herostratus [28] lives that burnt the temple of Diana, he is almost lost that built it. Time hath spared the epitaph of Adrian's [29] horse, confounded that of himself. In vain we compute our felicities by the advantage of our good names, since bad have equal durations, and Thersites [30] is like to live as long as Agamemnon. Who knows whether the best of men be known, or whether there be not more remarkable persons forgot, than any that stand remembered in the known account of time? Without the favour of the everlasting register, the first man had been as unknown as the last, and Methuselah's long life had been his only chronicle.

Oblivion is not to be hired. The greater part must be content to be as though they had not been, to be found in the register of God, not in the record of man. Twenty-seven names make up the first story,[31] and the recorded names ever since contain not one living century. The number of the dead long exceedeth all that shall live. The night of time far surpasseth the day, and who knows when was the equinox? Every hour adds unto that current [32] arithmetic, which scarce stands one moment. And since death must be the *Lucina* [33] of

---

21. "Old ones being taken up, and other bodies laid under them" (Browne's note); see also Donne, "The Relic."
22. Jan Gruter (1560–1627), Dutch Latinist.
23. Girolamo Cardano, Italian mathematician (1501–76).
24. Essential life force or principle.
25. Outdoes.
26. Matthew 15:22–28; she is known only as "a woman of Canaan."
27. Mark 6:17; Herodias forced her daughter Salome to ask for the head of John the Baptist.
28. He burned the Ephesian temple in order to be remembered.
29. The Emperor Hadrian's, for whom he composed an epitaph.
30. Homer's nasty cynic, in the *Iliad*.
31. In Genesis 5, the genealogy from Adam to Noah contains 27 names; there have not been 100 (a century of) generations of recorded names since the Deluge.
32. Continual.
33. Roman goddess of childbirth.

life, and even Pagans could doubt, whether thus to live were to die; since our longest sun sets at right descensions, and makes but winter arches, and therefore it cannot be long before we lie down in darkness, and have our light in ashes; [34] since the brother of death [35] daily haunts us with dying mementos, and time that grows old in itself, bids us hope no long duration;—diuturnity is a dream and folly of expectation.

Darkness and light divide the course of time, and oblivion shares with memory a great part even of our living beings; we slightly remember our felicities, and the smartest strokes of affliction leave but short smart upon us. Sense endureth no extremities, and sorrows destroy us or themselves. To weep into stones [36] are fables. Afflictions induce callosities; [37] miseries are slippery, or fall like snow upon us, which notwithstanding is no unhappy stupidity. To be ignorant of evils to come, and forgetful of evils past, is a merciful provision in nature, whereby we digest the mixture of our few and evil days, and, our delivered senses not relapsing into cutting rememberances, our sorrows are not kept raw by the edge of repetitions. A great part of antiquity contented their hopes of subsistency with a transmigration of their souls,—a good way to continue their memories, while having the advantage of plural successions, they could not but act something remarkable in such variety of beings, and enjoying the fame of their passed selves, make accumulation of glory unto their last durations. Others, rather than be lost in the uncomfortable night of nothing, were content to recede into the common being, and make one particle of the public soul of all things, which was no more than to return into their unknown and divine original again. Egyptian ingenuity was more unsatisfied, contriving their bodies in sweet consistencies, to attend the return of their souls. But all was vanity, feeding the wind, and folly. The Egyptian mummies which Cambyses [38] or time hath spared, avarice now consumeth. Mummy [39] is become merchandise, Mizraim [40] cures wounds, and Pharaoh is sold for balsams.

In vain do individuals hope for immortality, or any patent from oblivion, in preservations below the moon; [41] men have been deceived even in their flatteries above the sun, and studied conceits to perpetuate their names in heaven. The various cosmography of that part hath already varied the names of contrived constellations. Nimrod is lost in Orion, and Osiris in the Dog-star.[42] While we look for incorruption in the heavens, we find they are but like the earth;—durable in their main bodies, alterable in their parts; whereof, beside comets and new stars, perspectives [43] begin to tell tales, and the

---

34. "According to the custom of the Jews, who place a lighted wax candle in a pot of ashes by the corpse" (Browne's note, added to later editions).
35. Sleep.
36. To turn, like the weeping Niobe of myth, into stone.
37. Hardenings, insensitivities.
38. The Persian conqueror of Egypt.
39. Powdered mummies, sold as a pharmaceutical.
40. In Hebrew, "Egypt"; also, one of the sons of Ham, Noah's son.
41. Hope of continued existence in any sublunary (actual) mode.
42. Now called Sirius.
43. Telescopes.

spots that wander about the sun, with Phaeton's favour,[44] would make clear conviction.

There is nothing strictly immortal but immortality. Whatever hath no beginning may be confident of no end (all others have a dependent being and within the reach of destruction); which is the peculiar [45] of that necessary Essence that cannot destroy itself; and the highest strain of omnipotency, to be so powerfully constituted as not to suffer even from the power of itself. But the sufficiency of Christian immortality frustrates all earthly glory, and the quality of either state after death, makes a folly of posthumous memory. God who can only [46] destroy our souls, and hath assured our resurrection, either of our bodies or names, hath directly promised no duration. Wherein there is so much of chance that the boldest expectants [47] have found unhappy frustration; and to hold long subsistence seems but a scape in [48] oblivion. But man is a noble animal, splendid in ashes, and pompous [49] in the grave, solemnizing nativities and deaths with equal lustre, nor omitting ceremonies of bravery in the infamy of his nature.

Life is a pure flame, and we live by an invisible sun within us. A small fire sufficeth for life, great flames seemed too little after death, while men vainly affected precious pyres, and to burn like Sardanapalus; [50] but the wisdom of funeral laws found the folly of prodigal blazes, and reduced undoing fires unto the rule of sober obsequies, wherein few could be so mean as not to provide wood, pitch, a mourner, and an urn.

Five languages secured not the epitaph of Gordianus.[51] The man of God lives longer without a tomb, than any by one, invisibly interred by angels,[52] and adjudged to obscurity, though not without some marks directing human discovery. Enoch and Elias,[53] without either tomb or burial, in an anomalous state of being, are the great examples of perpetuity, in their long and living memory, in strict account being still on this side death, and having a late part yet to act upon this stage of earth. If in the decretory term [54] of the world, we shall not all die but be changed, according to received translation, the last day will make but few graves; at least quick resurrections will anticipate lasting sepultures. Some graves will be opened before they be quite closed, and Lazarus [55] be no wonder. When many that feared to die, shall groan that they can die but once, the dismal state is the second and living death, when life puts despair on the damned, when men shall wish the coverings of mountains, not of monuments, and annihilations shall be courted.

44. Phaëthon, who drove his father's chariot of the sun in a reckless course (burning the deserts and freezing out the poles), was also for Browne a wandering spot (sunspots had recently been observed by Galileo).
45. Peculiarity.
46. Alone.
47. Those who wait and watch for something.
48. Cheat for.
49. Stately.
50. An Assyrian king who had an entire palace and its inhabitants burned as his funeral pyre.
51. Roman emperor (238–244); all his five epitaphs were obliterated.
52. Moses (Deuteronomy 34:6).
53. Elijah and Enoch were both so good that they were transported directly to heaven.
54. The decreed end, at the Last Judgment.
55. Raised from the dead by Christ (John 11:1–45).

While some have studied monuments, others have studiously declined them, and some have been so vainly boisterous, that they durst not acknowledge their graves; wherein Alaricus [56] seems most subtle, who had a river turned to hide his bones at the bottom. Even Sylla,[57] that thought himself safe in his urn, could not prevent revenging tongues, and stones thrown at his monument. Happy are they whom privacy makes innocent, who deal so with men in this world, that they are not afraid to meet them in the next; who, when they die, make no commotion among the dead, and are not touched with that poetical taunt of Isaiah.[58]

Pyramids, arches, obelisks, were but the irregularities of vainglory, and wild enormities of ancient magnanimity. But the most magnanimous resolution rests in the Christian religion, which trampleth upon pride, and sits on the neck of ambition, humbly pursuing that infallible perpetuity, unto which all others must diminish their diameters, and be poorly seen in angles of contingency.[59]

Pious spirits who passed their days in raptures of futurity, made little more of this world than the world that was before it, while they lay obscure in the chaos of preordination, and night of their forebeings. And if any have been so happy as truly to understand Christian annihilation, ecstasies, exolution,[60] liquefaction, transformation, the kiss of the spouse, gustation of God, and ingression into the divine shadow, they have already had an handsome anticipation of heaven; the glory of the world is surely over, and the earth in ashes unto them.

To subsist in lasting monuments, to live in their productions, to exist in their names and predicament of chimeras,[61] was large satisfaction unto old expectations, and made one part of their Elysiums. But all this is nothing in the metaphysics of true belief. To live indeed, is to be again ourselves, which being not only an hope, but an evidence in noble believers, 'tis all one to lie in St. Innocents' [62] church-yard, as in the sands of Egypt. Ready to be any thing, in the ecstasy of being ever, and as content with six foot as the *moles* of Adrianus.[63]

> —*tabesne cadavera solvat,*
> An *rogus, haud refert.*[64]—Lucan

1658

56. Alaric the Goth had himself interred beneath a river-bed.
57. Roman general.
58. "Is this the man that made the earth to tremble, that did shake kingdoms?"—asked of those about to be cast into Hell (Isaiah 14:16).
59. "*Angulus contingentiae*, the least of angles" (Browne's note); the smallest possible angle, thus the narrowest view and the most contingent in the ordinary sense.
60. The escape of soul from the body's confines.
61. Fictive monsters.
62. "In Paris, where bodies soon consume" (Browne's note).
63. "A stately mausoleum or sepulchural pile, built by Adrianus in Rome, where now stands the castle of St. Angelo" (Browne's note).
64. "Whether funeral pyre or grave swallows the corpses matters little" (*Pharsalia* VII. 809).

The Garden of Cyrus

A strange and, to us, obsessive little work, one that nevertheless manages to combine Browne's scientific and hieroglyphical interests even more elegantly than the *Hydriotaphia, Urn Burial,* is *The Garden of Cyrus.* It begins with a discussion of the quincunx, or "decussated" pattern of planting employed in the Persian emperor's fabled gardens, but quickly dissolves into a meditation on the hieroglyphical and emblematic significances of the quincunxial figure

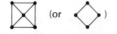

Rectangles, rhombs, cones, and pyramids, figures denoting five and ten, men and trees inverted into one another—all of these fancies are intermingled with piercing botanical and zoological questions. Readers interested in the mathematics of biological patterns will want to look at the great *Growth and Form* by Darcy Wentworth Thompson, a modern work curiously analogous to Browne's in some ways.

From The Garden of Cyrus

Chapter IV

The cylindrical figure of trees is virtually contained and latent in this order: a cylinder or long round being made by the conversion or turning of a parallelogram, and most handsomely by a long square, which makes an equal, strong, and lasting figure in trees, agreeable unto the body and motive part of animals, the greatest number of plants, and almost all roots, though their stalk be angular, and of many corners, which seem not to follow the figure of their seeds (since many angular seeds send forth round stalks, and spherical seeds arise from angular spindles, and many rather conform unto their roots, as the round stalks of bulbous roots and in tuberous roots stems of like figure). But why, since the largest number of plants maintain a circular figure, there are so few with teretous or long round leaves? Why coniferous trees are tenuifolious or narrow-leafed? Why plants of few or no joints have commonly round stalks? Why the greatest number of hollow stalks are round stalks; or why in this variety of angular stalks the quadrangular most exceedeth, were too long a speculation? Meanwhile obvious experience may find, that in plants of divided leaves above, nature often beginneth circularly in the two first leaves below, while in the singular plant of ivy she exerciseth a contrary geometry, and beginning with angular leaves below, rounds them in the upper branches.

. . . .

Beside, in this kind of aspect the sight being not diffused, but circumscribed between long parallels and the ἐπισκιασμὸς [1] and adumbration [2] from the branches, it frameth a penthouse over the eye, and maketh a quiet vision:— and therefore in diffused and open aspects, men hollow their hand above their

1. Episkiasmos, a shading or covering.
2. The same in Latinate English.

eye, and make an artificial brow, whereby they direct the dispersed rays of sight, and by this shade preserve a moderate light in the chamber of the eye; keeping the pupilla plump and fair, and not contracted or shrunk, as in light and vagrant vision.

And therefore Providence hath arched and paved the great house of the world, with colours of mediocrity, that is, blue and green, above and below the sight, moderately terminating the *acies* [3] of the eye. For most plants, though green above ground, maintain their original white below it, according to the candour of their seminal pulp: and the rudimental leaves do first appear in that colour, observable in seeds sprouting in water upon their first foliation. Green seeming to be the first supervenient,[4] or above ground complexion of vegetables, separable in many upon ligature or inhumation, as succory, endive, artichokes, and which is also lost upon fading in the autumn.

. . .

Nor are only dark and green colours, but shades and shadows contrived through the great volume of nature, and trees ordained not only to protect and shadow others, but by their shades and shadowing parts, to preserve and cherish themselves: the whole radiation or branchings shadowing the stock and the root;—the leaves, the branches and fruit, too much exposed to the winds and scorching sun. The calicular [5] leaves enclose the tender flowers, and the flowers themselves lie wrapt about the seeds, in their rudiment and first formations, which being advanced, the flowers fall away; and are therefore contrived in variety of figures, best satisfying the intention; handsomely observable in hooded and gaping flowers, and the butterfly blooms of leguminous plants, the lower leaf closely involving the rudimental cod, and the alary or wingy divisions embracing or hanging over it.

But seeds themselves do lie in perpetual shades, either under the leaf, or shut up in coverings; and such as lie barest, have their husks, skins, and pulps about them, wherein the nib and generative particle lieth moist and secured from the injury of air and sun. Darkness and light hold interchangeable dominions, and alternately rule the seminal state of things. Light unto Pluto is darkness unto Jupiter. Legions of seminal ideas lie in their second chaos and Orcus [6] of Hippocrates; till putting on the habits of their forms, they show themselves upon the stage of the world, and open dominion of Jove. They that held the stars of heaven were but rays and flashing glimpses of the empyreal light, through holes and perforations of the upper heaven, took off the natural shadows of stars; while according to better discovery the poor inhabitants of the moon have but a polary life, and must pass half their days in the shadow of that luminary.

Light that makes things seen, makes some things invisible; were it not for darkness and the shadow of the earth, the noblest part of the creation had remained unseen, and the stars in heaven as invisible as on the fourth day, when they were created above the horizon with the sun, or there was not an eye to behold them. The greatest mystery of religion is expressed by adumbra-

3. Range of vision.
4. Suddenly appearing.
5. Of the calyx.
6. The original Roman god of the Underworld, later assimilated with the Greek Hades.

tion, and in the noblest part of Jewish types,[7] we find the cherubims shadowing the mercy-seat. Life itself is but the shadow of death, and souls departed but the shadows of the living. All things fall under this name. The sun itself is but the dark *simulachrum*,[8] and light but the shadow of God. . . .

Chapter V

To enlarge this contemplation unto all the mysteries and secrets accommodable unto this number, were inexcusable Pythagorism,[9] yet cannot omit the ancient conceit of five surnamed the number of justice; as justly dividing between the digits, and hanging in the centre of nine, described by square numeration, which angularly divided will make the decussated [10] number; and so agreeable unto the quincuncial ordination, and rows divided by equality, and just decorum, in the whole com-plantation; and might be the original of that common game among us, wherein the fifth place is sovereign, and carrieth the chief intention—the ancients wisely instructing youth, even in their recreations unto virtue, that is, early to drive at the middle point and central seat of justice.

Nor can we omit how agreeable unto this number an handsome division is made in trees and plants, since Plutarch, and the ancients have named it the divisive number, justly dividing the entities of the world, many remarkable things in it, and also comprehending the general division of vegetables.[11] And he that considers how most blossoms of trees, and greatest number of flowers, consist of five leaves, and therein doth rest the settled rule of nature— so that in those which exceed, there is often found, or easily made, a variety— may readily discover how nature rests in this number, which is indeed the first rest and pause of numeration in the fingers, the natural organs thereof. Nor in the division of the feet of perfect animals doth nature exceed this account. And even in the joints of feet, which in birds are most multiplied, surpasseth not this number; so progressionally making them out in many,[12] that from five in the fore-claw she descendeth unto two in the hindmost; and so in four feet makes up the number of joints, in the five fingers or toes of man.

Not to omit the quintuple section of a cone,[13] of handsome practice in ornamental garden-plots, and in same way discoverable in so many works of nature, in the leaves, fruits, and seeds of vegetables, and scales of some fishes; so much considerable in glasses, and the optic doctrine; wherein the learned may consider the crystalline humour of the eye in the cuttle-fish and loligo.

He that forgets not how antiquity named this the conjugal or wedding number, and made it the emblem of the most remarkable conjunction, will

---

7. Prefigurations in the Old Testament of events in the New.
8. Likeness.
9. But Browne is, in pursuing this discussion of 5-ness, being wildly Pythagorean.
10. Literally, criss-crossed like an X, that being the Roman numeral denoting ten. The decussated pattern, or quincunx, is the central hieroglyphic of this meditation. See Headnote.
11. Browne lists *arbor, frutex, suffrutex, herba,* and a fifth category including *fungi* and *tubera.*
12. "As herons, bitterns and long-clawed fowls" (Browne's note).
13. Browne lists as the conic sections: ellipse, parabola, hyperbola, circle, and triangle.

conceive it duly appliable unto this handsome economy, and vegetable combination: and may hence apprehend the allegorical sense of that obscure expression of Hesiod,[14] and afford no improbable reason why Plato admitted his nuptial guests by fives, in the kindred of the married couple.[15]

And though a sharper mystery might be implied in the number of the five wise and foolish virgins, which were to meet the bridegroom, yet was the same agreeable unto the conjugal number, which ancient numerists made out by two and three, the first parity and imparity, the active and passive digits, the material and formal principles in generative societies. And not discordant even from the customs of the Romans, who admitted but five torches in their nuptial solemnities. Whether there were any mystery or not, implied, the most generative animals were created on this day, and had accordingly the largest benediction. And under a quintuple consideration, wanton antiquity considered the circumstances of generation, while by this number of five they naturally divided the nectar of the fifth planet.

. . .

If any shall question the rationality of that magic, in the cure of the blind man by Serapis,[16] commanded to place five fingers on his altar, and then his hand on his eyes? Why, since the whole comedy is primarily and naturally comprised in four parts,[17] and antiquity permitted not so many persons to speak in one scene, yet would not comprehend the same in more or less than five acts? Why amongst sea-stars nature chiefly delighteth in five points? And since there are found some of no fewer than twelve, and some of seven, and nine, there are few or none discovered of six or eight? If any shall enquire why the flowers of rue properly consist of four leaves, the first and third flower have five? Why, since many flowers have one leaf or none, as Scaliger will have it, divers three, and the greatest number consist of five divided from their bottoms, there are yet so few of two? or why nature generally beginning or setting out with two opposite leaves at the root, doth so seldom conclude with that order and number at the flower? He shall not pass his hours in vulgar speculations.

If any shall further query why magnetical philosophy excludeth decussations, and needles transversely placed do naturally distract their verticities? Why geomancers [18] do imitate the quintuple figure, in their mother characters of acquisition and amission,[19] &c., somewhat answering the figures in the lady or speckled beetle? With what equity chiromantical [20] conjecturers decry these decussations in the lines and mounts of the hand? What that decussated figure intendeth in the medal of Alexander the Great? Why the goddesses sit commonly cross-legged in ancient draughts, since Juno is described in the same as a beneficial posture to hinder the birth of Hercules? If any shall doubt why at

14. To the effect that it was a marriage number (*Works and Days*, l. 802).
15. In the *Laws*.
16. Osiris in his role as ruler of the Underworld.
17. Browne lists: *protasis* (introduction); *epitasis* (onset of action); *katastasis* (development); and *katastrophe* (turnabout).
18. Earth magicians.
19. Loss.
20. Chiromancy is palmistry.

the amphidromical feasts,[21] on the fifth day after the child was born, presents were sent from friends, of polypuses and cuttle-fishes? Why five must be only left in that symbolical mutiny among the men of Cadmus? [22] Why Proteus in Homer, the symbol of the first matter, before he settled himself in the midst of his sea-monsters, doth place them out by fives? Why the fifth year's ox was acceptable sacrifice unto Jupiter? Or why the noble Antoninus [23] in some sense doth call the soul itself a rhombus? He shall not fall on trite or trivial disquisitions. And these we invent and propose unto acuter enquirers, nauseating crambe verities and questions over-queried. Flat and flexible truths are beat out by every hammer; but Vulcan and his whole forge sweat to work out Achilles his armour. A large field is yet left unto sharper discerners to enlarge upon this order, to search out the *quaternios* [24] and figured draughts of this nature, and (moderating the study of names, and mere nomenclature of plants), to erect generalities, disclose unobserved proprieties, not only in the vegetable shop, but the whole volume of nature; affording delightful truths, confirmable by sense and ocular observation, which seems to me the surest path to trace the labyrinth of truth. For though discursive enquiry and rational conjecture may leave handsome gashes and flesh-wounds; yet without conjunction of this, expect no mortal or dispatching blows unto error.

But the quincunx [25] of heaven runs low, and 'tis time to close the five ports of knowledge. We are unwilling to spin out our awaking thoughts into the phantasms of sleep, which often continueth precogitations, making cables of cobwebs, and wildernesses of handsome groves. Beside Hippocrates [26] hath spoke so little, and the oneirocritical [27] masters have left such frigid interpretations from plants, that there is little encouragement to dream of Paradise itself. Nor will the sweetest delight of gardens afford much comfort in sleep; wherein the dulness of that sense shakes hands with delectable odours; and though in the bed of Cleopatra,[28] can hardly with any delight raise up the ghost of a rose.

Night, which Pagan theology could make the daughter of Chaos, affords no advantage to the description of order; although no lower than that mass can we derive its genealogy. All things began in order, so shall they end, and so shall they begin again; according to the ordainer of order and mystical mathematics of the city of heaven.

Though Somnus in Homer be sent to rouse up Agamemnon, I find no such effects in these drowsy approaches of sleep. To keep our eyes open longer, were but to act our Antipodes.[29] The huntsmen are up in America, and they are already past their first sleep in Persia. But who can be drowsy at that hour

21. Athenian festival of consecration of the newborn.
22. Cadmus sowed a crop of dragon's teeth and reaped an army whose combatants fought each other to death, except for five survivors.
23. Marcus Aurelius, in his *Meditations*.
24. Quadruples.
25. "The Hyades, near the horizon about midnight at that time" (Browne's note).
26. The great Greek physician.
27. Pertaining to the theory of dreams.
28. "Strewed with roses" (Browne's note).
29. "To act out the roles of our diametrical counterparts at the bottom of the globe" (Browne's note).

which freed us from everlasting sleep? or have slumbering thoughts at that time, when sleep itself must end, and as some conjecture all shall awake again. . . .

1658

From Miscellanies

[On the Blindness of Cupid]

Cupid is seen to be blind;[1] affection should not be too sharp-sighted, and love not to be made by magnifying glasses: if things were seen as they are, the beauty of bodies would be much abridged, and therefore the wisdom of God hath drawn the pictures and outsides of things softly and amiably unto the natural edge of our eyes, not to be able to discover those unlevel asperities which make oystershells in good faces, and hedgehogs even in Venus' moles.

From The Notebooks

[On Dreams]

Half our days we pass in the shadow of the earth; and the brother of death exacteth a third part of our lives. A good part of our sleep is peered out with visions and fantastical objects, wherein we are confessedly deceived. The day supplieth us with truths; the night with fictions and falsehoods, which uncomfortably divide the natural account of our beings. And, therefore, having passed the day in sober labours and rational enquiries of truth, we are fain to betake ourselves unto such a state of being, wherein the soberest heads have acted all the monstrosities of melancholy, and which unto open eyes are no better than folly and madness.

Happy are they that go to bed with grand music, like Pythagoras, or have ways to compose the fantastical spirit, whose unruly wanderings take off inward sleep, filling our heads with St. Anthony's visions, and the dreams of Lipara[1] in the sober chambers of rest.

Virtuous thoughts of the day lay up good treasures for the night; whereby the impressions of imaginary forms arise into sober similitudes, acceptable unto our slumbering selves and preparatory unto divine impressions. Hereby Solomon's sleep was happy. Thus prepared, Jacob might well dream of angels upon a pillow of stone. And the best sleep of Adam might be the best of any after.[2]

1. See Bacon's account of this in "Cupid, or the Atom," and Marlowe's *Hero and Leander* I.48n. Also see Jonathan Swift's "A Digression Concerning Madness" for a brilliant and sharp use of Browne's providential biology to bait, and entrap, the optimistic reader.

1. St. Anthony of Egypt was tempted by and plagued by monstrous visions; the Lipari were the Aeolian Islands off Sicily, and the site of the fabled workshop of Vulcan, where all the automata of antiquity were made.

2. The sleep of Adam's unfallen first night, calmer than ours.

That there should be divine dreams seems unreasonably doubted by Aristotle. That there are demoniacal dreams we have little reason to doubt. Why may there not be angelical? If there be guardian spirits, they may not be inactively about us in sleep; but may sometimes order our dreams: and many strange hints, instigations, or discourses, which are so amazing unto us, may arise from such foundations.

. . .

There is an art to make dreams, as well as their interpretations, and physicians will tell us that some food makes turbulent, some gives quiet, dreams. Cato,[3] who doted upon cabbage, might find the crude effects thereof in his sleep; wherein the Egyptians might find some advantage by their superstitious abstinence from onions. Pythagoras might have calmer sleeps, if he totally abstained from beans. Even Daniel, the great interpreter of dreams, in his leguminous diet, seems to have chosen no advantageous food for quiet sleeps, according to Grecian physic.[4]

To add unto the delusion of dreams, the fantastical objects seem greater than they are; and being beheld in the vaporous state of sleep, enlarge their diameters unto us; whereby it may prove more easy to dream of giants than pigmies. Democritus[5] might seldom dream of atoms, who so often thought of them. He almost might dream himself a bubble extending unto the eighth sphere. A little water makes a sea; a small puff of wind a tempest. A grain of sulphur kindled in the blood may make a flame like Ætna;[6] and a small spark in the bowels of Olympias a lightning over all the chamber.

But, beside these innocent delusions, there is a sinful state of dreams. Death alone, not sleep, is able to put an end unto sin; and there may be a night-book of our iniquities; for beside the transgressions of the day, casuists will tell us of mortal sins in dreams, arising from evil precogitations; meanwhile human law regards not noctambulos; and if a night-walker should break his neck, or kill a man, takes no notice of it.

Dionysius was absurdly tyrannical to kill a man for dreaming that he had killed him; and really to take away his life, who had but fantastically taken away his. Lamia[7] was ridiculously unjust to sue a young man for a reward, who had confessed that pleasure from her in a dream which she had denied unto his awaking senses: conceiving that she had merited somewhat from his fantastical fruition and shadow of herself. If there be such debts, we owe deeply unto sympathies; but the common spirit of the world must be ready in such arrearages.

If some have swooned, they may have also died in dreams, since death is but a confirmed swooning. Whether Plato died in a dream, as some deliver,[8] he must rise again to inform us. That some have never dreamed, is as improbable as that some have never laughed. That children dream not the first

---

3. Marcus Porcius Cato ("The Censor"), Roman leader (234–149 B.C.).
4. Medical science.
5. The Greek atomist; see above, Burton's *Anatomy of Melancholy*.
6. The great Sicilian volcano.
7. One of the monsters with women's heads and breasts and serpents' bodies; they drank the blood of fair young men and children.
8. Report.

half-year; that men dream not in some countries, with many more, are unto me sick men's dreams—dreams out of the ivory gate,[9] and visions before midnight.

THOMAS HOBBES
1588–1679

Hobbes, who worked for Bacon as his secretary, began his own philosophical career late, as a Royalist exile in Paris (1640–51). His major work, *Leviathan*, came out in the year of his return, when he made his peace with the Cromwellian regime. The writing of the book, and that of the *Answer to Davenant's Preface Before "Gondibert,"* belongs to his time in Paris, where Davenant was also in exile. After the Restoration he wrote many more works of all kinds—translations, histories, geometrical studies, controversies with Descartes and others. Aubrey, his close friend, left an amusing account of the philosopher: he grew healthy after forty, was bald, good-natured, and witty, got drunk one hundred times in his long life, played tennis at seventy-five, was timid by nature, and liked to shut himself up and sing for the good of his health.

As a thinker, however, he attracted fierce opposition; his thought was too ruthlessly materialistic to escape censure from many different opponents. "The universe is corporeal; all that is real is material, and what is not material is not real" (*Leviathan* 46). Although Hobbes was at least nominally a Christian, this kind of philosophy pleased neither orthodox Christians nor others who accepted a supernatural element in the workings of the world. He had a particular contempt for the Aristotelianism of the scholastic philosophers, and this endeared him to proponents of the new science, so that his name was associated with that of Bacon in the minds of those who formed the Royal Society for the study by observation and experiment of problems in natural philosophy.

Hobbes attempted a return to first principles, to a few axioms of the kind he admired in Euclid, and banished from his philosophy the kind of abstraction favored by the scholastics, which seemed to him to signify nothing. The soul and its operations had to be reduced to materiality to mean anything. Our perceptions of the world are really of the pressures materially exerted on us by external "motions."

Rejecting the soul, he rejected free will as well; the passions are influenced by external "motions," which, if they please, cause in us an appetite and seem good, and, if they displease, cause aversion and seem evil. Men are therefore complicated automata, and their involuntary appetites would cause them to destroy one another if there were no arrangements whereby their common life could be regulated by authority and force. So Hobbes defended absolute sovereignty; men must "confer all their power and strength upon one man, or upon one assembly of men. . . ." This is his Commonwealth, in which all men conjoin their power in one, the great Leviathan.

In the chapter "Of Imagination" we see Hobbes providing a materialist explanation of that power of the soul which was usually thought to have least dependence on

9. There were two fabled gates to the regions of sleep: through the ivory gates, false dreams emerged into the world; through the more ordinary gates of horn, the true dreams.

outward impulses: the imagination, or fantasy, surely, operated independently of the senses in lunatics, lovers, poets, and dreamers. Not for Hobbes; it is merely decayed memory. A proper understanding of this would abolish superstition and fit men better for "civil obedience." The importance of all this emerges both in his account of man's natural lust for power (Chapter XI) and in the famous Chapter XIII, on the natural state of man without the order and restraint of the state: a life "solitary, poor, nasty, brutish, and short."

In the *Answer to Davenant's Preface* we find Hobbes in a more urbane mood, but his aesthetic is consistent with the rest of his philosophy. From Memory derive both Judgment and Fancy (Imagination); the first handles the design, the second the ornaments of the poem. Thus "wit," which earlier meant the full power of the mind, was now, without losing its distinctive characteristics of speed and "farfetchedness," given a subordinate role and distinguished from judgment.

On the divisions of poetry Hobbes is again consistent; nature imposes externally three styles of life, in country, city, and court, and men arrange their poetry accordingly. And the manners of men are the true subject of poetry, not the gods, ghosts, and fictive beings of the old epic. It is worth remembering, finally, that Hobbes's philosophy did not impel him to dismiss poetry altogether, despite his materialism. He can, indeed, be defended as a pioneer of the new aesthetic theories required to support poetry in an age of rationalism which might have rejected it.

Leviathan

From *Chapter II: Of Imagination*

That when a thing lies still, unless somewhat else stir it, it will lie still for ever, is a truth that no man doubts of. But that when a thing is in motion, it will eternally be in motion, unless somewhat else stay it, though the reason be the same, namely, that nothing can change itself, is not so easily assented to. For men measure, not only other men, but all other things, by themselves; and because they find themselves subject, after motion, to pain and lassitude, think everything else grows weary of motion, and seeks repose of its own accord; little considering whether it be not some other motion, wherein that desire of rest they find in themselves consisteth. From hence it is that the schools [1] say, heavy bodies fall downwards out of an appetite to rest, and to conserve their nature in that place which is most proper for them; ascribing appetite, and knowledge of what is good for their conservation, which is more than man has,[2] to things inanimate, absurdly.

When a body is once in motion, it moveth, unless something else hinder it, eternally; and whatsoever hindereth it cannot in an instant, but in time and by degrees, quite extinguish it; and as we see in the water, though the wind cease, the waves give not over rolling for a long time after: so also it happeneth in that motion which is made in the internal parts of a man, then,

---

1. Scholastic philosophers.
2. It is an essential condition of Hobbes's thought that man does not naturally possess the means of self-preservation.

when he sees, dreams, etc. For after the object is removed, or the eye shut, we still retain an image of the thing seen, though more obscure than when we see it. And this is it, the Latins call *imagination,* from the image made in seeing; and apply the same, though improperly, to all the other senses. But the Greeks call it *fancy;* which signifies appearance, and is as proper to one sense, as to another. Imagination therefore is nothing but *decaying sense;* and is found in men, and many other living creatures, as well sleeping as waking.

The decay of sense in men waking, is not the decay of the motion made in sense; but an obscuring of it, in such manner as the light of the sun obscureth the light of the stars; which stars do no less exercise their virtue, by which they are visible, in the day than in the night. But because amongst many strokes which our eyes, ears, and other organs receive from external bodies, the predominant only is sensible; therefore, the light of the sun being predominant, we are not affected with the action of the stars. And any object being removed from our eyes, though the impression it made in us remain, yet other objects more present succeeding and working on us, the imagination of the past is obscured and made weak, as the voice of a man is in the noise of the day. From whence it followeth that the longer the time is, after the sight or sense of any object, the weaker is the imagination. For the continual change of man's body destroys in time the parts which in sense were moved; so that distance of time, and of place, hath one and the same effect in us. For as at a great distance of place, that which we look at appears dim, and without distinction of the smaller parts; and as voices grow weak, and inarticulate; so also, after great distance of time, our imagination of the past is weak; and we lose, for example, of cities we have seen, many particular streets, and of actions, many particular circumstances. This decaying sense, when we would express the thing itself, I mean fancy itself, we call *imagination,* as I said before; but when we would express the decay, and signify that the sense is fading, old, and past, it is called *memory.* So that imagination and memory are but one thing,[3] which for divers considerations hath divers names.

Much memory, or memory of many things, is called *experience.* Again, imagination being only of those things which have been formerly perceived by sense, either all at once or by parts at several times; the former, which is the imagining the whole object as it was presented to the sense, is *simple* imagination, as when one imagineth a man, or horse, which he hath seen before. The other is *compounded;* as when, from the sight of a man at one time and of a horse at another, we conceive in our mind a centaur. So when a man compoundeth the image of his own person with the image of the actions of another man, as when a man imagines himself a Hercules or an Alexander, which happeneth often to them that are much taken with reading of romances, it is a compound imagination, and properly but a fiction of the mind. There be also other imaginations that rise in men, though waking, from the great impression made in sense: as from gazing upon the sun, the impression leaves an image of the sun before our eyes a long time after; and from being long and vehemently attent upon geometrical figures, a man shall in the dark, though awake, have

---

3. This is slightly different from the formulation used in the *Answer to Davenant's Preface* (below), but both are consistent with Hobbes's materialism.

the images of lines and angles before his eyes; which kind of fancy hath no particular name, as being a thing that doth not commonly fall into men's discourse.

The imaginations of them that sleep are those we call *dreams*. And these also, as all other imaginations, have been before, either totally or by parcels, in the sense. And because in sense, the brain and nerves, which are the necessary organs of sense, are so benumbed in sleep, as not easily to be moved by the action of external objects, there can happen in sleep no imagination, and therefore no dream, but what proceeds from the agitation of the inward parts of man's body; which inward parts, for the connexion they have with the brain and other organs when they be distempered, do keep the same in motion; whereby the imaginations there formerly made, appear as if a man were waking; saving that the organs of sense being now benumbed, so as there is no new object which can master and obscure them with a more vigorous impression, a dream must needs be more clear, in this silence of sense, than our waking thoughts. And hence it cometh to pass that it is a hard matter, and by many thought impossible, to distinguish exactly between sense and dreaming. For my part, when I consider that in dreams I do not often constantly think of the same persons, places, objects, and actions, that I do waking; nor remember so long a train of coherent thoughts, dreaming, as at other times; and because waking I often observe the absurdity of dreams, but never dream of the absurdities of my waking thoughts; I am well satisfied that, being awake, I know I dream not, though when I dream I think myself awake.

And seeing dreams are caused by the distemper of some of the inward parts of the body, divers distempers must needs cause different dreams. And hence it is that lying cold breedeth dreams of fear, and raiseth the thought and image of some fearful object, the motion from the brain to the inner parts and from the inner parts to the brain being reciprocal; and that as anger causeth heat in some parts of the body when we are awake, so when we sleep the over-heating of the same parts causeth anger, and raiseth up in the brain the imagination of an enemy. In the same manner, as natural kindness,[4] when we are awake, causeth desire, and desire maketh heat in certain other parts of the body; so also too much heat in those parts, while we sleep, raiseth in the brain the imagination of some kindness [5] shown. In sum, our dreams are the reverse of our waking imaginations; the motion when we are awake beginning at one end, and when we dream at another.

The most difficult discerning of a man's dream from his waking thoughts is, then, when by some accident we observe not that we have slept: which is easy to happen to a man full of fearful thoughts, and whose conscience is much troubled; and that sleepeth, without the circumstances of going to bed or putting off his clothes, as one that noddeth in a chair. For he that taketh pains, and industriously lays himself to sleep, in case any uncouth and exorbitant fancy come unto him, cannot easily think it other than a dream. We read of Marcus Brutus (one that had his life given him by Julius Caesar, and was

---

4. Sexual attraction.
5. This usage well illustrates the range of meanings the word has in talk about love.

also his favourite, and notwithstanding murdered him), how at Philippi, the night before he gave battle to Augustus Caesar, he saw a fearful apparition, which is commonly related by historians as a vision; but considering the circumstances, one may easily judge to have been but a short dream. For sitting in his tent, pensive and troubled with the horror of his rash act, it was not hard for him, slumbering in the cold, to dream of that which most affrighted him; which fear, as by degrees it made him wake, so also it must needs make the apparition by degrees to vanish; and having no assurance that he slept, he could have no cause to think it a dream, or anything but a vision. And this is no very rare accident; for even they that be perfectly awake, if they be timorous and superstitious, possessed with fearful tales, and alone in the dark, are subject to the like fancies, and believe they see spirits and dead men's ghosts walking in churchyards; whereas it is either their fancy only, or else the knavery of such persons as make use of such superstitious fear, to pass disguised in the night to places they would not be known to haunt.

From this ignorance of how to distinguish dreams, and other strong fancies, from vision and sense, did arise the greatest part of the religion of the Gentiles in time past, that worshipped satyrs, fawns, nymphs, and the like; and nowadays the opinion that rude people have of fairies, ghosts, and goblins, and of the power of witches. For, as for witches, I think not that their witchcraft is any real power; but yet that they are justly punished, for the false belief they have that they can do such mischief, joined with their purpose to do it if they can; their trade being nearer to a new religion than to a craft or science. And for fairies, and walking ghosts, the opinion of them has, I think, been on purpose either taught or not confuted, to keep in credit the use of exorcism, of crosses, of holy water, and other such inventions of ghostly men. Nevertheless, there is no doubt but God can make unnatural apparitions; but that He does it so often as men need to fear such things more than they fear the stay or change of the course of nature, which He also can stay and change, is no point of Christian faith. But evil men, under pretext that God can do anything, are so bold as to say anything when it serves their turn, though they think it untrue; it is the part of a wise man, to believe them no farther than right reason makes that which they say appear credible. If this superstitious fear of spirits were taken away, and with it, prognostics from dreams, false prophecies, and many other things depending thereon, by which crafty ambitious persons abuse the simple people, men would be much more fitted than they are for civil obedience.

And this ought to be the work of the schools; but they rather nourish such doctrine. For, not knowing what imagination or the senses are, what they receive, they teach: some saying that imaginations rise of themselves, and have no cause; others, that they rise most commonly from the will; and that good thoughts are blown (inspired) into a man by God, and evil thoughts by the Devil; or that good thoughts are poured (infused) into a man by God, and evil ones by the Devil. Some say the senses receive the species of things, and deliver them to the common sense; and the common sense delivers them over to the fancy, and the fancy to the memory, and the memory to the judgement, like handling of things from one to another with many words making nothing understood.

The imagination that is raised in man, or any other creature indued with the faculty of imagining, by words, or other voluntary signs, is that we generally call *understanding;* and is common to man and beast. For a dog by custom will understand the call, or the rating of his master; and so will many other beasts. That understanding which is peculiar to man, is the understanding not only his will, but his conceptions and thoughts, by the sequel and contexture of the names of things into affirmation, negations, and other forms of speech. . . .

From *Chapter IV: Of Speech*

The invention of *printing,* though ingenious, compared with the invention of *letters* is no great matter. But who was the first that found the use of letters, is not known. He that first brought them into Greece, men say was Cadmus, the son of Agenor, king of Phoenicia. A profitable invention for continuing the memory of time past, and the conjunction of mankind dispersed into so many and distant regions of the earth; and withal difficult, as proceeding from a watchful observation of the divers motions of the tongue, palate, lips, and other organs of speech; whereby to make as many differences of characters, to remember them. But the most noble and profitable invention of all other, was that of *speech,* consisting of *names* or *appellations,* and their connexion; whereby men register their thoughts, recall them when they are past, and also declare them one to another for mutual utility and conversation; without which there had been amongst men neither commonwealth, nor society, nor contract, nor peace, no more than amongst lions, bears, and wolves. . . .

The general use of speech is to transfer our mental discourse into verbal, or the train of our thoughts into a train of words; and that for two commodities, whereof one is the registering of the consequences of our thoughts; which, being apt to slip out of our memory and put us to a new labour, may again be recalled by such words as they were marked by. So that the first use of names is to serve for *marks,* or *notes* of remembrance. Another is, when many use the same words, to signify, by their connexion and order, one to another, what they conceive, or think of each matter; and also what they desire, fear, or have any other passion for. And for this use they are called *signs.* Special uses of speech are these: first, to register what by cogitation we find to be the cause of anything, present or past, and what we find things present or past may produce or effect; which, in sum, is acquiring of arts. Secondly, to show to others that knowledge which we have attained; which is, to counsel and teach one another. Thirdly, to make known to others our wills and purposes, that we may have the mutual help of one another. Fourthly, to please and delight ourselves and others, by playing with our words, for pleasure or ornament, innocently.

To these uses, there are also four 'correspondent abuses. First, when men register their thoughts wrong, by the inconstancy of the signification of their words; by which they register for their conception, that which they never conceived, and so deceive themselves. Secondly, when they use words metaphorically; that is, in other sense than that they are ordained for; and thereby deceive others. Thirdly, by words, when they declare that to be their will which is not. Fourthly, when they use them to grieve one another; for seeing nature hath armed living creatures, some with teeth, some with horns, and some with hands, to grieve an enemy, it is but an abuse of speech, to grieve him with the tongue, unless it be one whom we are obliged to govern; and then it is not to grieve, but to correct and amend.

Seeing then that truth consisteth in the right ordering of names in our affirmations, a man that seeketh precise truth had need to remember what every name he uses stands for, and to place it accordingly, or else he will find himself entangled in words, as a bird in lime twigs, the more he struggles the more belimed. And therefore in geometry, which is the only science that it hath pleased God hitherto to bestow on mankind, men begin at settling the significations of their words; which settling of significations they call *definitions*, and place them in the beginning of their reckoning. . . .

From *Chapter XI: Of the Difference of Manners*

By *manners*, I mean not here, decency of behaviour; as how one should salute another, or how a man should wash his mouth, or pick his teeth before company, and such other points of the *small morals;* but those qualities of mankind, that concern their living together in peace, and unity. To which end we are to consider, that the felicity of this life, consisteth not in the repose of a mind satisfied. For there is no such *finis ultimus*, utmost aim, nor *summum bonum*, greatest good, as is spoken of in the books of the old moral philosophers. Nor can a man any more live, whose desires are at an end, than he, whose senses and imaginations are at a stand. Felicity is a continual progress of the desire, from one object to another; the attaining of the former, being still but the way to the latter. The cause whereof is, that the object of man's desire, is not to enjoy once only, and for one instant of time; but to assure for ever, the way of his future desire. And therefore the voluntary actions, and inclinations of all men, tend, not only to the procuring, but also to the assuring of a contented life; and differ only in the way: which ariseth partly from the diversity of passions, in divers men; and partly from the difference of the knowledge, or opinion each one has of the causes, which produce the effect desired.

So that in the first place, I put for a general inclination of all mankind, a perpetual and restless desire of power after power, that ceaseth only in death. And the cause of this, is not always that a man hopes for a more intensive delight, than he has already attained to; or that he cannot be content with a moderate power: but because he cannot assure the power and means to live well, which he hath present, without the acquisition of more. . . .

From *Chapter XIII: Of the Natural Condition of Mankind as Concerning Their Felicity and Misery*

. . . In the nature of man, we find three principal causes of quarrel. First, competition; second, diffidence; thirdly, glory.

The first maketh men invade for gain; the second, for safety; and the third, for reputation. The first use violence to make themselves masters of other men's persons, wives, children, and cattle; the second, to defend them; the third, for trifles, as a word, a smile, a different opinion, and any other sign of undervalue, either direct in their persons, or by reflection in their kindred, their friends, their nation, their profession, or their name.

Hereby it is manifest that during the time men live without a common power to keep them all in awe, they are in that condition which is called war; and such a war as is of every man against every man. For *war* consisteth not in battle only, or the act of fighting, but in a tract of time wherein the will to contend by battle is sufficiently known, and therefore the notion of *time* is to be considered in the nature of war, as it is in the nature of weather. For as the nature of foul weather lieth not in a shower or two of rain, but in an inclination thereto of many days together; so the nature of war consisteth not in actual fighting, but in the known disposition thereto, during all the time there is no assurance to the contrary. All other time is *peace*.

Whatsoever therefore is consequent to a time of war, where every man is enemy to every man; the same is consequent to the time wherein men live without other security than what their own strength and their own invention shall furnish them withal. In such condition there is no place for industry, because the fruit thereof is uncertain: and consequently no culture of the earth; no navigation, nor use of the commodities that may be imported by sea; no commodious building; no instruments of moving, and removing, such things as require much force; no knowledge of the face of the earth; no account of time; no arts; no letters; no society; and which is worst of all, continual fear, and danger of violent death; and the life of man, solitary, poor, nasty, brutish, and short.

It may seem strange to some man that has not well weighed these things, that nature should thus dissociate, and render men apt to invade and destroy one another; and he may therefore, not trusting to this inference, made from the passions, desire perhaps to have the same confirmed by experience. Let him therefore consider with himself, when taking a journey, he arms himself and seeks to go well accompanied; when going to sleep, he locks his doors; when even in his house he locks his chests; and this when he knows there be laws, and public officers, armed, to revenge all injuries shall be done him: what opinion he has of his fellow-subjects, when he rides armed; of his fellow-citizens, when he locks his doors; and of his children, and servants, when he locks his chests. Does he not there as much accuse mankind by his actions, as I do by my words? But neither of us accuse man's nature in it. The desires, and other passions of man, are in themselves no sin. No more are the actions that proceed from those passions, till they know a law that forbids them: which till laws be made they cannot know; nor can any law be made, till they have agreed upon the person that shall make it.

It may peradventure be thought, there was never such a time nor condition of war as this; and I believe it was never generally so, over all the world: but there are many places where they live so now. For the savage people in many places of America, except the government of small families, the concord whereof dependeth on natural lust, have no government at all; and live at this day in that brutish manner, as I said before. Howsoever, it may be perceived what manner of life there would be, where there were no common power to fear; by the manner of life which men that have formerly lived under a peaceful government, use to degenerate into in a civil war.

But though there had never been any time wherein particular men were in a condition of war one against another; yet in all times, kings, and persons of sovereign authority, because of their independency, are in continual jealousies, and in the state and posture of gladiators; having their weapons pointing, and their eyes fixed on one another; that is, their forts, garrisons, and guns upon the frontiers of their kingdoms; and continual spies upon their neighbours; which is a posture of war. But because they uphold thereby the industry of their subjects, there does not follow from it that misery which accompanies the liberty of particular men.

To this war of every man against every man, this also is consequent: *that nothing can be unjust.* The notions of right and wrong, justice and injustice, have there no place. Where there is no common power, there is no law; where no law, no injustice. Force and fraud are in war the two cardinal virtues. Justice and injustice are none of the faculties neither of the body nor mind. If they were, they might be in a man that were alone in the world, as well as his senses and passions. They are qualities that relate to men in society, not insolitude. It is consequent also to the same condition, that there be no propriety, no dominion, no *mine* and *thine* distinct; but only that to be every man's, that he can get; and for so long as he can keep it. And thus much for the ill condition which man by mere nature is actually placed in; though with a possibility to come out of it, consisting partly in the passions, partly in his reason.

The passions that incline men to peace are fear of death, desire of such things as are necessary to commodious living, and a hope by their industry to obtain them. And reason suggesteth convenient articles of peace, upon which men may be drawn to agreement. . . .

1651

The Answer to Davenant's Preface Before *Gondibert*

SIR,

If to commend your poem, I should only say (in general terms) that in the choice of your argument, the disposition of the parts, the maintenance of the characters of your persons, the dignity and vigour of your expression you have performed all the parts of various experience, ready memory, clear judgment, swift and well governed fancy, though it were enough for the truth, it were too little for the weight and credit of my testimony. For I lie open to two exceptions, one of an incompetent, the other of a corrupted witness. Incompetent, because I am not a poet; [1] and corrupted with the honour done me by your preface.[2] The former obliges me to say something (by the way) of the nature and differences of poesy.

As philosophers have divided the universe (their subject) into three regions, celestial, aerial, and terrestrial; so the poets (whose work it is by imitating human life, in delightful and measured lines, to avert men from vice, and incline them to virtuous and honourable actions) have lodged themselves in the three regions of mankind, court, city, and country correspondent in some proportion, to those three regions of the world. For there is in princes and men of con-

---

1. In fact Hobbes wrote a good deal of poetry, nearly all in Latin.
2. Davenant's long and critically important *Preface* was dedicated "to his much honoured friend, Mr. Hobbes."

spicuous power (anciently called heroes) a lustre and influence upon the rest of men, resembling that of the heavens; and an insincereness, inconstancy, and troublesome humour of those that dwell in populous cities, like the mobility, blustering, and impurity of the air; and a plainness, and (though dull) yet a nutritive faculty in rural people, that endures a comparison with the earth they labour.

From hence have proceeded three sorts of poesy, heroic, scommatic,[3] and pastoral. Every one of these is distinguished again in the manner of representation, which sometimes is narrative, wherein the poet himself relateth, and sometimes dramatic, as when the persons are every one adorned and brought upon the theatre, to speak and act their own parts. There is therefore neither more nor less than six sorts of poesy. For the heroic poem narrative (such as is yours) is called an epic poem; the heroic poem dramatic, is tragedy. The scommatic narrative, is satire; dramatic is comedy. The pastoral narrative, is called simply pastoral (anciently bucolic) the same dramatic, pastoral comedy. The figure therefore of an epic poem, and of a tragedy, ought to be the same, for they differ no more but in that they are pronounced by one, or many persons. Which I insert to justify the figure of yours, consisting of five books divided into songs or cantos, as five acts divided into scenes has ever been the approved figure of a tragedy.[4]

They that take for poesy whatsoever is writ in verse, will think this division imperfect, and call in sonnets, epigrams, eclogues, and the like pieces (which are but essays, and parts of an entire poem) and reckon Empedocles and Lucretius (natural philosophers) for poets, and the moral precepts of Phocylides, Theognis, and the quatrains of Pybrach, and the history of Lucan,[5] and others of that kind amongst poems; bestowing on such writers for honour the name of poets, rather then of historians or philosophers. But the subject of a poem is the manners of men, not natural causes; manners presented, not dictated; and manners feigned (as the name of poesy imports), not found in men. They that give entrance to fictions writ in prose, err not so much, but they err.[6] For poesy requireth delightfulness, not only of fiction, but of style; in which if prose contend with verse, it is with disadvantage (as it were) on foot, against the strength and wings of Pegasus.

For verse amongst the Greeks was appropriated anciently to the service of their gods, and was the holy style; the style of the oracles; the style of the laws; and the style of men that publicly recommended to their gods, the vows and thanks of the people; which was done in their holy songs called hymns, and the composers of them were called prophets and priests before the name of poet was known. When afterwards the majesty of that style was observed, the poets chose it as best becoming their high invention. And for the antiquity

3. Satirical.
4. Davenant, following a minor tradition of heroic poetry which Sidney also knew, planned his poem in five long sections or acts.
5. Phocylides, 6th-century B.C. Greek author of moralistic poems; Theognis, elagiac and moralizing poet of the same period; Gui de Faur, seigneur de Pibrac, wrote moralizing quatrains in French, published 1574 and later translated into English by Joshua Sylvester; Lucan (39–65 A.D.) wrote *Pharsalia*, an epic about the war between Julius Caesar and Pompey.
6. Sidney in the *Defence* is therefore said to err.

of verse it is greater than the antiquity of letters. For it is certain Cadmus was the first that (from Phœnicia, a country that neighboureth Judea) brought the use of letters into Greece.[7] But the service of the Gods, and the laws (which by measured sounds were easily committed to the memory) had been long time in use, before the arrival of Cadmus there.

There is besides the grace of style, another cause why the ancient poets chose to write in measured language, which is this. Their poems were made at first with intention to have them sung, as well epic as dramatic (which custom hath been long time laid aside, but began to be revived in part, of late years in Italy) [8] and could not be made commensurable to the voice or instruments, in prose; the ways and motions whereof are so uncertain and undistinguished (like the way and motion of a ship in the sea) as not only to discompose the best composers, but also to disappoint sometimes the most attentive reader, and put him to hunt counter for the sense. It was therefore necessary for poets in those times, to write in verse.

. . .

Time and education begets experience; experience begets memory; memory begets judgment and fancy: judgment begets the strength and structure, and fancy begets the ornaments of a poem. The ancients therefore fabled not absurdly, in making memory the mother of the muses.[9] For memory is the world (though not really, yet so as in a looking glass) in which the judgment (the severer sister) busieth herself in a grave and rigid examination of all the parts of nature, and in registering by letters, their order, causes, uses, differences and resemblances; whereby the fancy, when any work of art is to be performed, findeth her materials at hand and prepared for use, and needs no more than a swift motion over them, that what she wants, and is there to be had, may not lie too long unespied. So that when she seemeth to fly from one Indies to the other, and from heaven to earth, and to penetrate into the hardest matter, and obscurest places, into the future, and into herself, and all this in a point of time; the voyage is not very great, herself being all she seeks; and her wonderful celerity consisteth not so much in motion as in copious imagery discreetly ordered, and perfectly registered in the memory; which most men under the name of philosophy have a glimpse of, and is pretended to by many that grossly mistaking her embrace contention in her place. But so far forth as the fancy of man has traced the ways of true philosophy, so far it hath produced very marvellous effects to the benefit of mankind. All that is beautiful or defensible [10] in building; or marvellous in engines [11] and instruments of motion; whatsoever commodity men receive from the observation of the heavens, from the description of the earth, from the account of time, from walking on the seas; and whatsoever distinguisheth the civility of Europe, from the barbarity of the American savages, is the workmanship of fancy, but guided by the precepts of true

7. The myth of Cadmus reflects the historical fact that the Greek alphabet derived from Phoenician script.
8. Refers to the origin of Italian opera, at first supposed to re-create the conditions of ancient tragedy.
9. Mnemosyne, goddess of Memory; that she should be called mother of the Muses suits Hobbes; later Blake rejected the idea with disgust.
10. Suited to defensive operations.
11. Machines, mechanical devices.

philosophy. But where these precepts fail, as they have hitherto failed in the doctrine of moral virtue, there the architect (fancy) must take the philosophers part, upon herself. He therefore that undertakes an heroic poem (which is to exhibit a venerable and amiable image of heroic virtue) must not only be the poet, to place and connect, but also the philosopher, to furnish and square his matter, that is, to make both body and soul, colour and shadow of his poem out of his own store: which how well you have performed I am now considering.

. . .

There are some that are not pleased with fiction, unless it be bold not only to exceed the work, but also the possibility of nature; they would have impenetrable armours, enchanted castles, invulnerable bodies, iron men, flying horses, and a thousand other such things which are easily feigned by them that dare. Against such I defend you (without assenting to those that condemn either Homer or Virgil by dissenting only from those that think the beauty of a poem consisteth in the exorbitancy of the fiction). For as truth is the bound of historical, so the resemblance of truth is the utmost limit of poetical liberty. In old time amongst the heathens, such strange fictions and metamorphoses were not so remote from the articles of their faith, as they are now from ours, and therefore were not so unpleasant. Beyond the actual works of nature a poet may now go; but beyond the conceived possibility of nature, never. I can allow a geographer to make in the sea, a fish or a ship, which by the scale of his map would be two or three hundred miles long, and think it done for ornament, because it is done without the precincts of his undertaking; but when he paints an elephant so, I presently apprehend it as ignorance, and a plain confession of terra incognita.[12] . . .

. . .

That which giveth a poem the true and natural colour, consisteth in two things, which are, to know well; that is, to have images of nature in the memory distinct and clear; and to know much. A sign of the first is perspicuity, property, and decency, which delight all sorts of men, either by instructing the ignorant or soothing the learned in their knowledge: A sign of the latter is novelty of expression, and pleaseth by excitation of the mind; for novelty causeth admiration; and admiration, curiosity; which is a delightful appetite of knowledge.

There be so many words in use at this day in the English tongue, that, though of magnific sound, yet (like the windy blisters of a troubled water) have no sense at all; and so many others that lose their meaning by being ill coupled, that it is a hard matter to avoid them; for having been obtruded upon youth in the Schools (by such as make it, I think, their business there, as 'tis expressed by the best poet)

With terms to charm the weak and pose the wise,[13]

they grow up with them, and gaining reputation with the ignorant, are not easily shaken off.

To this palpable darkness, I may also add the ambitious obscurity of expressing more than is perfectly conceived; or perfect conception in fewer words

12. "Unknown territory" (an expression sometimes used on maps of that period).
13. From *Gondibert* I.5.

than it requires. Which expressions, though they have had the honour to be called strong lines, are indeed no better than riddles, and not only to the reader, but also (after a little time) to the writer himself, dark and troublesome. To the property of expression, I refer that clearness of memory, by which a poet when he hath once introduced any person whatsoever, speaking in his poem, maintaineth in him, to the end, the same character he gave to him in the beginning. The variation whereof, is a change of pace that argues the poet tired.

. . .

From knowing much, proceedeth the admirable variety and novelty of metaphors and similitudes, which are not possibly to be lighted on in the compass of a narrow knowledge. And the want whereof compelleth a writer to expressions that are either defaced by time or sullied with vulgar or long use. For the phrases of poesy, as the airs of music, with often hearing become insipid; the reader having no more sense of their force, than our flesh is sensible of the bones that sustain it. As the sense we have of bodies, consisteth in change and variety of impression, so also does the sense of language in the variety and changeable use of words. I mean not in the affectation of words newly brought home from travel, but in new (and withal, significant) translation to our purposes, of those that be already received, and in far fetched (but withal, apt, instructive, and comely) similitudes.[14] . . .

1650

IZAAK WALTON
1593–1683

Walton did well in business and became the friend of literary men; he was a parishioner of Donne's. His most famous work is The Compleat Angler (1653), a meditative essay on fishing, but he is also important as a biographer. His Lives, written at various stages of his own life, include those of Hooker, Wotton, Sanderson, Herbert, and Donne. He took care over detail, but occasionally interpreted evidence, especially from poems, in too literal a fashion; and it is clear that he imposed upon Donne a pattern of repentance which, though it may in general correspond to the facts, is heightened in the presentation. This is true of the speeches he attributes to the dying Dean. He wanted his books to be exemplary as well as informative. The manner of Walton's prose—simple, lucid, unambiguously pious—is represented in these extracts, first in what is his most elaborate set piece, the death of Donne, and secondly in his simple account of the religious community at Little Gidding.

14. Reflecting the new doctrine of wit, and indicating that the element of the new and surprising ("farfetched") is not abolished but modified; it is now set on the course which leads to Pope's "What oft was thought but ne'er so well expressed," but still has a long way to go.

From The Life of Dr. John Donne

The latter part of his life may be said to be a continued study; for as he usually preached once a week, if not oftener, so after his sermon he never gave his eyes rest till he had chosen out a new text, and that night cast his sermon into form and his text into divisions; and the next day betook himself to consult the fathers, and so commit his meditations to his memory, which was excellent. But upon Saturday he usually gave himself and his mind a rest from the weary burden of his week's meditations and usually spent that day in visitation of friends or some other diversions of his thoughts and would say, 'that he gave both his body and mind that refreshment that he might be enabled to do the work of the day following, not faintly, but with courage and cheerfulness.'

Nor was his age only so industrious, but in the most unsettled days of his youth his bed was not able to detain him beyond the hour of four in a morning; and it was no common business that drew him out of his chamber till past ten. All which time was employed in study; though he took great liberty after it; and if this seem strange, it may gain a belief by the visible fruits of his labours, some of which remain as testimonies of what is here written, for he left the resultance [1] of 1400 authors most of them abridged and analysed with his own hand; he left also six-score of his sermons, all written with his own hand, also an exact and laborious treatise concerning self-murder, called *Biathanatos*, wherein all the laws violated by that act are diligently surveyed and judiciously censured, a treatise written in his younger days which alone might declare him then not only perfect in the civil and canon law but in many other such studies and arguments as enter not into the consideration of many that labour to be thought great clerks and pretend to know all things.

Nor were these only found in his study, but all businesses that passed of any public consequence, either in this or any of our neighbour nations, he abbreviated either in Latin or in the language of that nation and kept them by him for useful memorials. So did he the copies of divers letters and cases of conscience that had concerned his friends, with his observations and solutions of them, and divers other businesses of importance, all particularly and methodically digested by himself.

He did prepare to leave the world before life left him, making his will when no faculty of his soul was damped or made defective by pain or sickness or he surprised by a sudden apprehension of death; but it was made with mature deliberation, expressing himself an impartial father by making his children's portions equal, and a lover of his friends, whom he remembered with legacies fitly and discreetly chosen and bequeathed. I cannot forbear a nomination of some of them; for methinks they be persons that seem to challenge a recordation in this place; as namely, to his brother-in-law, Sir Thomas Grimes, he gave that striking clock which he had long worn in his pocket. To his dear friend and executor, Dr. King, late Bishop of Chichester, that model of gold of the synod of Dort with which the States presented him at his last being at The Hague, and the two pictures of Padre Paulo and Fulgentio, men of his acquaintance when he travelled Italy and of great note in that nation for their remarkable learning. To his ancient friend, Dr. Brooke, that married him, Master

1. Summaries.

of Trinity College in Cambridge, he gave the picture of the blessed Virgin and Joseph. To Dr. Winniff, who succeeded him in the deanery he gave a picture called the Skeleton. To the succeeding dean, who was not then known, he gave many necessaries of worth and useful for his house, and also several pictures and ornaments for the chapel, with a desire that they might be registered, and remain as a legacy to his successors. To the Earls of Dorset and Carlisle, he gave several pictures. And so he did to many other friends—legacies given rather to express his affection than to make any addition to their estates. But unto the poor he was full of charity, and unto many others who by his constant and long continued bounty might entitle themselves to be his alms-people, for all these he made provision; and so largely as having then six children living might to some appear more than proportionable to his estate. I forbear to mention any more lest the reader may think I trespass upon his patience. But I will beg his favour to present him with the beginning and end of his will:

'In the name of the blessed and glorious Trinity, Amen. I, John Donne, by the mercy of Jesus Christ and by the calling of the Church of England priest, being at this time in good health and perfect understanding (praised be God therefore) do hereby make my last will and testament in manner and form following:

'First, I give my gracious God an entire sacrifice of body and soul, with my most humble thanks for that assurance which his blessed Spirit imprints in me now of the salvation of the one and the resurrection of the other; and for that constant and cheerful resolution which the same Spirit hath established in me to live and die in the religion now professed in the Church of England. In expectation of that resurrection, I desire my body may be buried, in the most private manner that may be, in that place of St. Paul's Church, London, that the now residenciaries have at my request designed for that purpose, &c.———. And this my last will and testament, made in the fear of God, whose mercy I humbly beg and constantly rely upon in Jesus Christ, and in perfect love and charity with all the world, whose pardon I ask from the lowest of my servants to the highest of my superiors. Written all with my own hand and my name subscribed to every page, of which there are five in number.'

Sealed Decemb. 13, 1630

Nor was this blessed sacrifice of charity expressed only at his death but in his life also by a cheerful and frequent visitation of any friend whose mind was dejected or his fortune necessitous. He was inquisitive after the wants of prisoners and redeemed many from thence that lay for their fees or small debts; he was a continual giver to poor scholars, both of this and foreign nations. Besides what he gave with his own hand, he usually sent a servant or a discreet and trusty friend to distribute his charity to all the prisons in London at all the festival times of the year, especially at the birth and resurrection of our Saviour. He gave an hundred pounds at one time to an old friend whom he had known live plentifully and by a too liberal heart and carelessness become decayed in his estate. And when the receiving of it was denied by the gentleman saying, 'He wanted not'; for the reader may note that as there be some spirits so generous as to labour to conceal and endure a sad poverty rather than expose themselves to those blushes that attend the confession of it so there be others to whom nature and grace have afforded such sweet and compassionate souls as to pity and prevent the distresses of mankind; which I have mentioned because of Mr. Donne's reply, whose answer was, 'I know you want not what will sustain nature, for a little will do that; but my desire is that you who in the days of your plenty have cheered and raised the hearts of so many of your dejected friends would now receive this from me and use it as a cordial for the cheering of your own.' And upon these terms it was received. He was an happy reconciler of many differences in the families of his friends and kindred—which he never undertook faintly, for such undertakings have usually faint effects—and they had such a faith in his judgment and impartiality that he never advised them to anything in vain. He was even to her death a most dutiful son to his mother, careful to provide for her supportation, of which she had been destitute but that God raised him up to prevent her necessities; who having sucked in the religion of the Roman Church with her mother's milk spent her estate in foreign countries to enjoy a liberty in it and died in his house but three months before him.

And to the end it may appear how just a steward he was of his Lord and Master's revenue I have thought fit to let the reader know that after his entrance into his deanery, as he numbered his years, he—at the foot of a private account to which God and his angels were only witnesses with him—computed first his revenue, then what was given to the poor and other pious uses, and lastly what rested for him and his; and having done that, he then blest each year's poor remainder with a thankful prayer. . . .

But I return from my long digression. We left the author sick in Essex, where he was forced to spend much of that winter by reason of his disability to remove from that place. And having never for almost twenty years omitted his personal attendance on his Majesty in that month in which he was to attend and preach to him nor having ever been left out of the roll and number of Lent preachers, and there being then (in January, 1630) a report brought to London or raised there that Dr. Donne was dead, that report gave him occasion to write this following letter to a dear friend:

SIR,

This advantage you and my other friends have by my frequent fevers, that I am so much the oftener at the gates of heaven, and this advantage by the solitude and close imprisonment that they reduce me to after, that I am so much the oftener at my prayers, in which I shall never leave out your happiness; and I doubt not among his other blessings, God will add some one to you for my prayers. A man would almost be content to die (if there were no other benefit in death) to hear of so much sorrow and so much good testimony from good men as I (God be blessed for it) did upon the report of my death; yet I perceive it went not through all; for one writ to me that some (and he said of my friends) conceived I was not so ill as I pretended but withdrew myself to live at ease, discharged of preaching. It is an unfriendly and, God knows, an ill-grounded interpretation; for I have always been sorrier when I could not preach than any could be they could not hear me. It hath been my desire, and God may be pleased to grant it, that I might die in the pulpit; if not that, yet that I might take my death in the pulpit, that is, die the sooner by occasion of those labours. Sir, I hope to see you presently after Candlemass, about which time will fall my Lent sermon at court, except my Lord Chamberlain believe me to be dead and so leave me out of the roll; but as long as I live and am not speechless, I would not willingly decline that service, I have better leisure to write than you to read; yet I would not willingly oppress you with too much letter. God so bless you and your son as I wish to

Your poor friend and servant in Christ Jesus,

J. DONNE

Before that month [2] ended, he was appointed to preach upon his old constant day, the first Friday in Lent; he had notice of it and had in his sickness so prepared for that employment that as he had long thirsted for it so he resolved his weakness should not hinder his journey; he came therefore to London some few days before his appointed day of preaching. At his coming thither many of his friends—who with sorrow saw his sickness had left him but so much flesh as did only cover his bones—doubted his strength to perform that task and did therefore dissuade him from undertaking it, assuring him, however, it was like to shorten his life; but he passionately denied their requests, saying, 'he would not doubt that that God who in so many weaknesses had assisted him with an unexpected strength would now withdraw it in his last employment,' professing an holy ambition to perform that sacred work. And when to the amazement of some beholders he appeared in the pulpit, many of them thought he presented himself not to preach mortification by a living voice but mortality by a decayed body and a dying face. And doubtless many did secretly ask that question in Ezekiel; 'Do these bones live? [3] or can that soul organize that tongue to speak so long time as the sand in that glass will move towards its centre [4] and measure out an hour of this dying man's unspent life? Doubtless it cannot'; and yet, after some faint pauses in his zealous prayer, his strong desires enabled his weak body to discharge his memory of his preconceived meditations, which were of dying, the text being, 'To God the Lord belong the issues from death.' Many that then saw his tears and heard his faint and hollow voice professing they thought the text prophetically chosen and that Dr. Donne 'had preached his own funeral sermon.'

Being full of joy that God had enabled him to perform this desired duty, he hastened to his house; out of which he never moved till, like St. Stephen, he was carried by devout men to his grave.

The next day after his sermon, his strength being much wasted and his spirits so spent as indisposed him to business or to talk, a friend that had often been a witness of his free and facetious discourse asked him, 'Why are you sad?' To whom he replied with a countenance so full of cheerful gravity as gave testimony of an inward tranquillity of mind and of a soul willing to take a farewell of this world and said:

2. January 1631.
3. Ezekiel 37:3.
4. Sink; the preacher preached for an hour by the glass.

'I am not sad, but most of the night past I have entertained myself with many thoughts of several friends that have left me here and are gone to that place from which they shall not return, and that within a few days I also shall go hence and be no more seen. And my preparation for this change is become my nightly meditation upon my bed, which my infirmities have now made restless to me. But, at this present time, I was in a serious contemplation of the providence and goodness of God to me, to me who am less than the least of his mercies; and looking back upon my life past, I now plainly see it was his hand that prevented me from all temporal employment and that it was his will I should never settle nor thrive till I entered into the ministry; in which I have now lived almost twenty years (I hope to his glory) and by which, I most humbly thank him, I have been enabled to requite most of those friends which showed me kindness when my fortune was very low, as God knows it was; and as it hath occasioned the expression of my gratitude, I thank God most of them stood in need of my requital. I have lived to be useful and comfortable to my good father-in-law, Sir George More, whose patience God hath been pleased to exercise with many temporal crosses; I have maintained my own mother, whom it hath pleased God after a plentiful fortune in her younger days to bring to a great decay in her very old age. I have quieted the consciences of many that have groaned under the burthen of a wounded spirit, whose prayers I hope are available for me. I cannot plead innocency of life, especially of my youth. But I am to be judged by a merciful God who is not willing to see what I have done amiss. And, though of myself I have nothing to present to him but sins and misery, yet I know he looks not upon me now as I am of myself but as I am in my Saviour and hath given me even at this present time some testimonies by his holy Spirit that I am of the number of his elect. I am therefore full of inexpressible joy and shall die in peace.'

I must here look so far back as to tell the reader that at his first return out of Essex to preach his last sermon, his old friend and physician, Dr. Fox, a man of great worth, came to him to consult his health and that after a sight of him and some queries concerning his distempers he told him, 'That by cordials and drinking milk twenty days together there was a probability of his restoration to health'; but he passionately denied to drink it. Nevertheless, Dr. Fox, who loved him most entirely, wearied him with solicitations till he yielded to take it for ten days; at the end of which time he told Dr. Fox, 'He had drunk it more to satisfy him than to recover his health and that he would not drink it ten days longer upon the best moral assurance of having twenty years added to his life, for he loved it not, and was so far from fearing death, which to others is the king of terrors, that he longed for the day of his dissolution.'

It is observed that a desire of glory or commendation is rooted in the very nature of man and that those of the severest and most mortified lives, though they may become so humble as to banish self-flattery and such weeds as naturally grow there, yet they have not been able to kill this desire of glory, but that, like our radical heat, it will both live and die with us; and many think it should be so; and we want not sacred examples to justify the desire of having our memory to outlive our lives. Which I mention, because Dr. Donne, by the persuasion of Dr. Fox, easily yielded at this very time to have a monument made for him; but Dr. Fox undertook not to persuade him how or what monument it should be; that was left to Dr. Donne himself.

A monument being resolved upon, Dr. Donne sent for a carver to make for him in wood the figure of an urn, giving him directions for the compass and height of it, and to bring with it a board of the just height of his body. These being got, then without delay a choice painter was got to be in a readiness to draw his picture, which was taken as followeth: Several charcoal fires being first made in his large study, he brought with him into that place his winding-sheet in his hand and, having put off all his clothes, had this sheet put on him and so tied with knots at his head and feet and his hands so placed as dead bodies are usually fitted to be shrouded and put into their coffin or grave. Upon this urn he thus stood with his eyes shut and with so much of the sheet turned aside as might show his lean, pale, and death-like face, which was purposely turned toward the East, from whence he expected the second coming of his and our Saviour, Jesus. In this posture he was drawn at his just height; and when the picture was fully finished, he caused it to be set by his bed-side, where it continued and became his hourly object till his death and was then given to his dearest friend and executor, Doctor Henry King, then chief residenciary of St. Paul's, who caused him to be thus carved in one entire piece of white marble, as it now stands in that church; and by Doctor Donne's own appointment these words were to be affixed to it as his epitaph:

JOHANNES DONNE
Sac. Theol. Profess.

Post varia studia quibus ab annis tenerrimis
fideliter, nec infeliciter incubuit,
instinctu et impulsu Sp. Sancti, monitu
et hortatu

REGIS JACOBI, ordines sacros
amplexus, anno sui Jesu, 1614, et suæ ætatis 42,
dęcanatu hujus ecclesiæ indutus 27,
Novembris, 1621,

exutus morte ultimo die Martii, 1631,
hic licet in occiduo cinere aspicit eum
cujus nomen est Oriens.[5]

And now, having brought him through the many labyrinths and perplexities of a various life, even to the gates of death and the grave, my desire is he may rest till I have told my reader that I have seen many pictures of him in several habits and at several ages and in several postures. And I now mention this because I have seen one picture of him, drawn by a curious hand at his age of eighteen, with his sword and what other adornments might then suit with the present fashions of youth and the giddy gaieties of that age; and his motto then was,

5. "John Donne, Doctor of Divinity, after various studies, pursued by him from his earliest years with assiduity, and not without success, entered into holy orders under the influence and impulse of the Holy Ghost and by the advice and exhortation of King James, in the year of our Lord 1614, when he was 42. Having been invested with the Deanery of this church on November 27, 1621, he was stripped of it by death on the last day of March 1631: and here, though himself set in dust, he beholdeth Him whose name is the Rising Sun."

> How much shall I be changed
> Before I am changed!

And if that young and his now dying picture were at this time set together, every beholder might say, 'Lord! how much is Dr. Donne already changed, before he is changed!' And the view of them might give my reader occasion to ask himself with some amazement, 'Lord! how much may I also that am now in health be changed, before I am changed! before this vile, this changeable body shall put off mortality!' and therefore to prepare for it.——But this is not writ so much for my reader's *memento* [6] as to tell him that Dr. Donne would often in his private discourses and often publicly in his sermons mention the many changes both of his body and mind, especially of his mind from a vertiginous giddiness, and would as often say his great and most blessed change was from a temporal to a spiritual employment. In which he was so happy that he accounted the former part of his life to be lost and the beginning of it to be from his first entering into sacred orders and serving his most merciful God at his altar.

Upon Monday after the drawing of this picture he took his last leave of his beloved study, and being sensible of his hourly decay, retired himself to his bed-chamber; and that week sent at several times for many of his most considerable friends, with whom he took a solemn and deliberate farewell, commending to their considerations some sentences useful for the regulation of their lives, and then dismissed them, as good Jacob did his sons, with a spiritual benediction. The Sunday following he appointed his servants, that if there were any business yet undone that concerned him or themselves, it should be prepared against Saturday next; for after that day he would not mix his thoughts with anything that concerned this world; nor ever did, but, as Job,[7] so he waited for the appointed day of his dissolution.

And now he was so happy as to have nothing to do but to die; to do which he stood in need of no longer time, for he had studied it long and to so happy a perfection that in a former sickness [8] he called God to witness, 'He was that minute ready to deliver his soul into his hands if that minute God would determine his dissolution.' In that sickness he begged of God the constancy to be preserved in that estate forever; and his patient expectation to have his immortal soul disrobed from her garment of mortality makes me confident he now had a modest assurance that his prayers were then heard and his petition granted. He lay fifteen days earnestly expecting his hourly change; and in the last hour of his last day, as his body melted away and vapoured into spirit, his soul having, I verily believe, some revelation of the beatifical vision, he said, 'I were miserable if I might not die'; and after those words, closed many periods of his faint breath by saying often, 'Thy kingdom come, thy will be done.' His speech, which had long been his ready and faithful servant, left him not till the last minute of his life, and then forsook him not to serve another master (for who speaks like him!) but died before him for that it was then become useless to him that now conversed with God on earth as angels

6. *Memento mori,* a reminder of mortality.
7. Job 30:23.
8. The serious illness of 1623, when Donne wrote his *Devotions.*

are said to do in heaven, only by thoughts and looks. Being speechless and seeing heaven by that illumination by which he saw it, he did, as St. Stephen, look steadfastly into it, till he saw the Son of Man, standing at the right hand of God, his Father; and being satisfied with this blessed sight, as his soul ascended and his last breath departed from him, he closed his own eyes; and then disposed his hands and body into such a posture as required not the least alteration by those that came to shroud him.

Thus variable, thus virtuous was the life; thus excellent, thus exemplary was the death of this memorable man.

. . .

He was of stature moderately tall, of a straight and equally-proportioned body, to which all his words and actions gave an inexpressible addition of comeliness.

The melancholy and pleasant humour were in him so contempered that each gave advantage to the other and made his company one of the delights of mankind.

His fancy was inimitably high, equalled only by his great wit; both being made useful by a commanding judgment.

His aspect was cheerful and such as gave a silent testimony of a clear-knowing soul and of a conscience at peace with itself.

His melting eye showed that he had a soft heart, full of noble compassion, of too brave a soul to offer injuries and too much a Christian not to pardon them in others.

He did much contemplate—especially after he entered into his sacred calling—the mercies of Almighty God, the immortality of the soul, and the joys of heaven, and would often say, in a kind of sacred ecstasy, 'Blessed be God that he is God only and divinely like himself.'

He was by nature highly passionate but more apt to reluct at [9] the excesses of it. A great lover of the offices of humanity and of so merciful a spirit that he never beheld the miseries of mankind without pity and relief.

He was earnest and unwearied in the search of knowledge; with which his vigorous soul is now satisfied and employed in a continual praise of that God that first breathed it into his active body, that body which once was a temple of the Holy Ghost and is now become a small quantity of Christian dust.

But I shall see it reanimated.

1640

From The Life of Mr. George Herbert
[On Nicholas Ferrar]

Mr. Nicholas Ferrar (who got the reputation of being called St. Nicholas at the age of six years) was born in London, and doubtless had good education in his youth, but certainly was at an early age made Fellow of Clare Hall in Cambridge, where he continued to be eminent for his piety, temperance and learning. About the twenty-sixth year of his age he betook himself to travel, in which he added to his Latin and Greek a perfect knowledge of all the

9. Resist.

languages spoken in the western parts of our Christian world, and understood well the principles of their religion and of their manner, and the reasons of their worship. In this his travel he met with many persuasions to come into a communion with that Church which calls itself Catholic; but he returned from his travels as he went, eminent for his obedience to his mother, the Church of England. In his absence from England Mr. Ferrar's father (who was a merchant) allowed him a liberal maintenance, and, not long after his return into England, Mr. Ferrar had, by the death of his father or an elder brother, or both, an estate left him, that enabled him to purchase land to the value of four or five hundred pounds a year, the greatest part of which land was at Little Gidden [1] four or six miles from Huntingdon, and about eighteen from Cambridge; which place he chose for the privacy of it, and for the Hall, which had the parish church or chapel belonging and adjoining near to it; for Mr. Ferrar having seen the manners and vanities of the world, and found them to be, as Mr. Herbert says, a nothing between two dishes, did so contemn it, that he resolved to spend the remainder of his life in mortifications, and in devotion and charity, and to be always prepared for death; and his life was spent thus:

He and his family, which were like a little college, and about thirty in number, did most of them keep Lent and all Ember-weeks strictly, both in fasting and using all those mortifications and prayers that the Church hath appointed to be then used; and he and they did the like constantly on Fridays, and on the Vigils or Eves appointed to be fasted before the Saints' days; and this frugality and abstinence turned to the relief of the poor; but this was but a part of his charity, none but God and he knew the rest.

This family, which I have said to be in number about thirty, were a part of them his kindred; and the rest chosen to be of a temper fit to be moulded into a devout life; and all of them were for their dispositions serviceable and quiet and humble, and free from scandal. Having thus fitted himself for his family, he did, about the year 1630, betake himself to a constant and methodical service of God, and it was in this manner:—He, being accompanied with most of his family, did himself use to read the common prayers (for he was a deacon) every day at the appointed hours of ten and four, in the parish church, which was very near his house, and which he had both repaired and adorned; for it was fallen into a great ruin, by reason of a depopulation of the village, before Mr. Ferrar bought the manor; and he did also constantly read the matins every morning at the hour of six, either in the church, or in an oratory which was within his own house; and many of the family did there continue with him after the prayers were ended, and there they spent some hours in singing hymns or anthems, sometimes in the church, and often to an organ in the oratory. And there they sometimes betook themselves to meditate, or to pray privately, or to read a part of the New Testament to themselves, or to continue their praying or reading the Psalms; and, in case the Psalms were not always read in the day, then Mr. Ferrar and others of the congregation did at night, at the ring of a watch-bell, repair to the church or oratory, and

---

1. Little Gidding, the religious community where Herbert, Crashaw, and perhaps Charles I visited, and which is celebrated in Eliot's poem of the same title (1942). It was a unique example of Anglican piety, in a country which of course no longer had monasteries.

there betake themselves to prayers and lauding God, and reading the Psalms that had not been read in the day; and when these or any part of the congregation grew weary or faint, the watch-bell was rung, sometimes before and sometimes after midnight, and then another part of the family rose, and maintained the watch, sometimes by praying or singing lauds to God or reading the Psalms; and when after some hours they also grew weary and faint, then they rung the watch-bell, and were also relieved by some of the former, or by a new part of the society which continued their devotions (as hath been mentioned) until morning. And it is to be noted, that in this continued serving of God, the Psalter, or whole Book of Psalms, was in every four-and-twenty hours sung or read over, from the first to the last verse; and this was done as constantly as the sun runs his circle every day about the world, and then begins again the same instant that it ended.

Thus did Mr. Ferrar and his happy family serve God day and night—thus did they always behave themselves as in his presence. And they did always eat and drink by the strictest rules of temperance; eat and drink so as to be ready to rise at midnight, or at the call of a watch-bell, and perform their devotions to God. And it is fit to tell the reader, that many of the clergy that were more inclined to practical piety and devotion than to doubtful and needless disputations, did often come to Gidden Hall, and make themselves a part of that happy society, and stay a week or more, and then join with Mr. Ferrar and the family in these devotions, and assist and ease him or them in the watch by night. And these various devotions had never less than two of the domestic family in the night; and the watch was always kept in the church or oratory, unless in extreme cold winter nights, and then it was maintained in a parlour which had a fire in it, and the parlour was fitted for that purpose. And this course of piety, and great liberality to his poor neighbours, Mr. Ferrar maintained till his death, which was in the year 1639. . . .

1670

CHARACTERS

We think of the word "character" as referring either to a person's moral nature or else, in a more limited usage, to a written or printed letter or ideograph. What connects these two totally separate senses of the word is its original meaning in Greek, a sharp tool for inscribing or engraving and thus, by extension, the inscription so made, thought of as an "impression" or "mark." In addition, a kind of verbal sketch, a short prose description of a type of vice, originated by the Athenian writer Theophrastus (372–287 B.C.) was called a "character," and eventually the name came to stand for the contents of the sketch, rather than the form itself. Informally speaking, the written character abounds in literature: the passage on the nature of the Magnanimous Man in Aristotle's *Nichomachean Ethics* might be considered one, for example; and some of Chaucer's descriptions of people in the General Prologue to the *Canterbury Tales* move toward the representation of type. The actual Theophrastan character in the Renaissance dates from the first Latin translation of Theophrastus, in 1592; in English, Joseph Hall's *Characters of Virtues and Vices* appeared in 1608. Numerous characters by various hands (the dramatists John Webster and Thomas Dekker, and others) were published in 1614 to accompany the posthumous appearance of Sir Thomas Overbury's poem, A Wife. Overbury, who had been murdered by a former associate and his wife (whose marriage he had opposed), was a famous figure, and even though few of the characters in the collection were by him, the term "Overburian character" to represent the deft, tight, single long paragraph of characterization of a type of actual person, rather than a virtue or vice embodied, is still used. The character figured significantly in the development of expository writing in the seventeenth century, particularly in the early move away from long, Ciceronian, periodic sentences toward a more "pointed," brisk manner.

SIR THOMAS OVERBURY
1581–1613

From Sir Thomas Overbury His Wife: New News and Divers More Characters

What a Character Is

If I must speak the schoolmaster's language, I will confess that character comes from this infinite mood χαράξω,[1] that signifieth to engrave, or make a deep impression. And for that cause, a letter (as A.B.) is called a character.

Those elements which we learn first, leaving a strong seal in our memories.

Character is also taken from an Egyptian hieroglyphic, for an impress, or short emblem; in little comprehending much.

To square out a character by our English level, it is a picture (real or personal) quaintly drawn, in various colours, all of them heightened by one shadowing.

It is a quick and soft touch[2] of many strings, all shutting up in one musical close; it is wit's descant on any plain song.

A Puritan

Is a diseased piece of Apocrypha;[1] bind him to the Bible, and he corrupts the whole text, ignorance and fat feed are his founders, his nurses, railing, rabies, and round breeches; his life is but a borrowed blast of wind, for between two religions, as between two doors, he is ever whistling. Truly whose child he is is yet unknown, for willingly his faith allows no father; only thus far his pedigree is found, Bragger and he flourished about a time first, his fiery zeal keeps him continually costive, which withers him into his own translation, and till he eat a schoolman, he is hide-bound; he ever prays against non residents, but is himself the greatest discontinuer, for he never keeps near his text; anything that the law allows, but marriage, and March beer,[2] he

1. Actually, *charactēr* in Greek means both the engraving tool and, sometimes, the engraver (see Headnote).
2. A musical phrase; also, a "close" is a cadence; a "descant on a plain song" has nothing to do with Gregorian chant, but more simply, an improvised part over a stated theme.

1. Biblical material ruled out of the canon and therefore considered spurious.
2. Thin, light spring beer, on the weak side.

murmurs at; what it disallows and holds dangerous, makes him a discipline; where the gate stands open, he is ever seeking a stile; [3] and where his learning ought to climb, he creeps through; give him advice, you run into traditions, and urge a modest course, he cries out councils. His greatest care is to condemn obedience, his last care to serve God handsomely and cleanly. He is now become so cross a kind of teaching, that should the Church enjoin clean shirts, he were lousy; more sense than single prayers is not his, nor more in those, than still the same Petitions; from which he either fears a learned faith, or doubts God understands not at first hearing. Show him a ring, he runs back like a bear, and hates square dealing as allied to caps; a pair of organs blow him out o' the parish, and are the only clyster-pipes [4] to cool him. Where the meat is best there he confutes most, for his arguing is but the effacacy of his eating; good bits he holds breed good positions, and the Pope he best concludes against, in plum-broth. He is often drunk, but not as we are, temporally, nor can his sleep then cure him, for the fumes of his ambition make his very soul reel, and the small beer that should allay him (silence) keeps him more surfeited, and makes his heat break out in private houses; women and lawyers are his best disciples, the one next fruit, longs for forbidden doctrine, the other to maintain forbidden titles, both which he sows amongst them. Honest he dare not be, for that loves order; yet if he can be brought to ceremony, and made but master of it, he is converted.

An Amorist

Is a man blasted or planet-strooken, and is the dog that leads blind Cupid; when he is at the best his fashion exceeds the worth of his weight. He is never without verses and musk confects,[1] and sighs to the hazard of his buttons. His eyes are all white, either to wear the livery of his mistress' complexion or to keep Cupid from hitting the black. He fights with passion, and loseth much of his blood by his weapon; dreams, thence his paleness. His arms are carelessly used, as if their best use was nothing but embracements. He is untrussed, unbuttoned, and ungartered, not out of carelessness, but care; his farthest end being but going to bed. Sometimes he wraps his petition in neatness, but he goeth not alone; for then he makes some other quality moralize his affection, and his trimness is the grace of that grace. Her favour lifts him up as the sun moisture; when he disfavours, unable to hold that happiness, it falls down in tears. His fingers are his orators, and he expresseth much of himself upon some instrument. He answers not, or not to the purpose, and no marvel, for he is not at home. He scotcheth time with dancing with his mistress, taking up of her glove, and wearing her feather, he is confined to her colour, and dares not pass out of the circuit of her memory. His imagination is a fool, and it goeth in a pied coat of red and white. Shortly he is translated out of a man into folly; his imagination is the glass [2] of lust, and himself the traitor to his own discretion.

3. Ladder-like arrangement for getting over fences.
4. Enemas.

1. Perfumed sachets.
2. Mirror.

A Chambermaid

She is her mistress's she-secretary, and keeps the box of her teeth, her hair, and her painting very private. Her industry is upstairs and downstairs like a drawer: and by her dry hand you may know she is a sore starcher. If she lie at her master's bed's feet, she is quit of the green sickness forever; for she hath terrible dreams when she's awake, as if she were troubled with the nightmare. She hath a good liking to dwell in the country, but she holds London the goodliest forest in England to shelter a great belly. She reads Greene's [1] works over and over, but is so carried away with the Mirror of Knighthood [2] she is many times resolved to run out of herself, and become a lady-errant. If she catch a clap,[3] she divides it so equally between the master and the serving-man as if she had cut out the getting of it by a thread; only the knave sumner makes her bowl booty,[4] and overreach the master. The pedant of the house, though he promise her marriage, cannot grow further inward with her; she hath paid for her credulity often, and now grows wary. She likes the form of our marriage very well, in that a woman is not tied to answer any articles concerning questions of virginity; her mind, her body, and clothes are parcels loosely packed together, and for want of good utterance, she perpetually laughs out her meaning. Her mistress and she help to make away time, to the idlest purpose that can be, either for love or money. In brief, these chambermaids are like lotteries: you may draw twenty ere one worth anything.

1614

JOHN EARLE
1600?–1665

From Microcosmography

Or A Piece of the World Discovered in Essays and Characters

A Child

Is a man in a small letter, yet the best copy of Adam before he tasted of Eve or the apple; and he is happy whose small practice in the world can only write his character. He is nature's fresh picture newly drawn in oil, which time, and much handling, dims and defaces. His soul is yet a white paper [1] unscribbled with observations of the world, wherewith, at length, it becomes a blurred note-book. He is purely happy, because he knows no evil, nor hath made means by sin to be acquainted with misery. He arrives not at the

---

1. Robert Greene (1560–92), author of romances, plays, and pamphlets.
2. A chivalric romance, mentioned in Cervantes' Don Quixote.
3. Then, as now, gonorrhea.
4. The "knave sumner" is the serving man, who arranges with her to sleep with their master in order to get an edge on him ("bowl booty": to have a secret confederate in a game).

1. This anticipates John Locke's concept of the tabula rasa, the infant mind as a blank slate upon which experience will write its impressions.

mischief of being wise, nor endures evils to come, by foreseeing them. He kisses and loves all, and, when the smart of the rod is past, smiles on his beater. Nature and his parents alike dandle him, and tice [2] him on with a bait of sugar to a draught of wormwood. He plays yet, like a young 'prentice the first day, and is not come to his task of melancholy. All the language he speaks yet is tears, and they serve him well enough to express his necessity. His hardest labour is his tongue, as if he were loth to use so deceitful an organ; and he is best company with it when he can but prattle. We laugh at his foolish sports, but his game is our earnest; and his drums, rattles, and hobby-horses, but the emblems and mocking of man's business. His father hath writ him as his own little story, wherein he reads those days of his life that he cannot remember, and sighs to see what innocence he has out-lived. The older he grows, he is a stair lower from God; and, like his first father, much worse in his breeches.[3] He is the Christian's example, and the old man's relapse; the one imitates his pureness, and the other falls into his simplicity. Could he put off his body with his little coat, he had got eternity without a burden, and exchanged but one heaven for another.

1633

JOSEPH HALL
1574–1656

From Characters of Virtues and Vices

The Slothful [1]

He is a religious man, and wears the time in his cloister, and, as the cloak of his doing nothing, pleads contemplation; yet he is no whit the leaner for his thoughts, no whit learneder. He takes no less care how to spend time than others how to gain by the expense, and, when business importunes him, is more troubled to forethink what he must do than another to affect it. Summer is out of his favour for nothing but long days, that make no haste to their even. He loves still to have the sun witness of his rising, and lies long, more for lothness to dress him than will to sleep; and, after some stretching and yawning calls for dinner unwashed; which having digested with a sleep in his chair, he walks forth to the bench in the market-place and looks for companions; whomsoever he meets he stays with idle questions and lingering discourse; how the days are lengthened, how kindly the weather is, how false the clock, how forward the spring, and ends ever with 'What shall we do?' It pleases him no less to hinder others, than not to work himself.

2. Entice.

3. Punning on "breach," or sin, and the original figleaf in Genesis 3:7; in the Geneva Bible, called for this reason the "Breeches Bible," Adam and Eve are said to have "made themselves breeches."

1. The deadly sin of *accidie* or sloth was not, in orthodox Christian ethics, a matter of physical laziness, but of a want of spiritual and intellectual energy, a moral fault rather than a more trivial physical one. Hall's vice lies somewhere between the sin and the garden variety of laziness.

When all the people are gone from Church, he is left sleeping in his seat alone. He enters bonds, and forfeits them by forgetting the day; and asks his neighbour, when his own field was fallowed, whether the next piece of ground belong not to himself. His care is either none or too late; when winter is come, after some sharp visitations, he looks on his pile of wood, and asks how much was cropped the last spring. Necessity drives him to every action, and what he cannot avoid, he will yet defer. Every change troubles him, although to the better; and his dullness counterfeits a kind of contentment. When he is warned on a jury, he would rather pay the mulct [1] than appear. All but that which nature will not permit, he doth by a deputy; and counts it troublesome to do nothing, but to do any thing yet more. He is witty in nothing but framing excuses to sit still, which, if the occasion yield not, he coineth with ease. There is no work that is not either dangerous or thankless, and whereof he foresees not the inconvenience and gainlessness before he enters; which if it be verified in event, his next idleness hath found a reason to patronize it. He would rather freeze than fetch wood; and choses rather to steal than work, to beg than take pains to steal, and in many things to want than beg. He is so loth to leave his neighbour's fire, that he is fain to walk home in the dark, and, if he be not looked to, wears out the night in the chimney-corner, or if not that, lies down in his clothes to save two labours. He eats and prays himself asleep, and dreams of no other torment but work. This man is a standing pool, and cannot chose but gather corruption; he is descried amongst a thousand neighbours by a dry and nasty hand that still savours of the sheet, a beard uncut, uncombed, an eye and ear yellow with their excretions, a coat, shaken on, ragged, unbrushed, by linen and face striving whether shall excel in uncleanliness. For body, he hath a swollen leg, a dusky and swinish eye, a blown cheek, a drawling tongue, a heavy foot, and is nothing but a colder earth moulded with standing water; to conclude, is a man in nothing, but in speech and shape.

1608

NICHOLAS BRETON
1555?–1626?

From The Good and the Bad

Or Descriptions of the Worthies and Unworthies of This Age

An Effeminate [1] Fool

An Effeminate Fool is the figure of a baby. He loves nothing but to be gay, to look in a glass, to keep among wenches, and to play with trifles; to feed on sweet-meats and to be danced in laps, to be embraced in arms, and to be kissed on the cheek; to talk idly, to look demurely, to go nicely, and to laugh

1. Fine.

1. Here the word has no reference to homosexuality, but rather to a foppish lack of other characteristics of stylish manliness.

continually; to be his mistress' servant, and her maid's master, his father's love and his mother's none-child; to play on a fiddle and sing a love-song, to wear sweet gloves[2] and look on fine things; to make purposes and write verses, devise riddles and tell lies; to follow plays and study dances, to hear news and buy trifles; to sigh for love and weep for kindness and mourn for company, and be sick for fashion; to ride in a coach and gallop a hackney, to watch all night and sleep out the morning; to lie on a bed and take tobacco and to send his page of an idle message to his mistress; to go upon gigs,[3] to have his ruffs set in print,[4] to pick his teeth, and to play with a puppet. In sum, he is a man-child and a woman's man, a gaze[5] of folly and wisdom's grief.

1616

OWEN FELLTHAM
1602?–1668

From Resolves, Divine, Moral, and Political

Of Women [1]

Some are so uncharitable as to think all women bad; and others are so credulous as they believe they all are good. Sure, though every man speaks as he finds, there is reason to direct our opinion, without experience of the whole sex; which, in a strict examination, makes more for their honour than most men have acknowledged. At first, she was created his equal; only the difference was in the sex; otherwise they both were man. If we argue from the text that male and female made man, so the man being put first was worthier, I answer, so the evening and morning was the first day,[2] yet few will think the night the better. That man is made her governor, and so above her, I believe rather the punishment of her sin, than the prerogative of his worth. Had they both stood, it may be thought, she had never been in that subjection; for then had it been no curse, but a continuance of her former estate, which had nothing but blessedness in it. Peter Martyr, indeed, is of opinion that man before the Fall had priority; but Chrysostom, he says, does doubt it. All will grant her body more admirable, more beautiful than man's; fuller of curiosities and noble Nature's wonders; both for conception, and fostering the producted birth. And can we think God would put a worser soul into a better body? When man was created, 'tis said, God made man; but when woman, 'tis said, God builded her; as if he had then been about a frame of rarer rooms, and more exact com-

2. Perfumed gloves.
3. To spend time with flighty girls; possibly to be flighty oneself (like "whirligigs").
4. His ruffs starched to an excessive stiffness.
5. Object of regard.

1. Felltham's essay is a kind of expanded character, in the fashionable "Senecan" or sharp, choppy, lively prose style of the Jacobean and Caroline periods. It is far from being like a rambling section of Burton's disquisition, or even a Baconian essay; it also has the air of a "Problem" about it—he is arguing what is, alas, a heterodox view against an official, or at least a received, misogyny.
2. In Genesis 1:5 (as, in subsequent Hebraic tradition, each day starts with the previous sundown).

position. And, without doubt, in her body she is much more wonderful, and by this we may think so in her mind. Philosophy tells us though the soul be not caused by the body, yet in the general it follows the temperament of it; so the comeliest outsides are naturally (for the most part) more virtuous within. If place can be any privilege, we shall find her built in Paradise, when man was made without it. 'Tis certain they are by constitution colder than the boiling man; so by this more temperate; 'tis heat that transports man to immoderation and fury; 'tis that which hurries him to a savage and libidinous violence. Women are naturally the more modest; and modesty is the seat and dwelling place of virtue. Whence proceed the most abhorred villainies, but from a masculine unblushing impudence? What a deal of sweetness do we find in a mild disposition! When a woman grows bold and daring, we dislike her, and say, she is too like a man; yet in ourselves we magnify what we condemn in her. Is not this injustice? Every man is so much the better by how much he comes nearer to God. Man in nothing is more like him than in being merciful. Yet woman is far more merciful than man; it being a sex wherein pity and compassion have dispersed far brighter rays. God is said to be love; and I am sure everywhere woman is spoken of for transcending in that quality. It was never found but in two men only,[3] that their love exceeded that of the feminine sex; and if you observe them you shall find they were both of melting dispositions. I know when they prove bad, they are a sort of the vilest creatures, yet still the same reason gives it; for, *optima corrupta pessima*, the best things corrupted become the worst. They are things whose souls are of a more deductible temper than the harder metal of man; so may be made both better and worse. The representations of Sophocles and Euripides may be both true; and for the tongue-vice, talkativeness, I see not but at meetings men may very well vie words with them. 'Tis true, they are not of so tumultuous a spirit, so not so fit for great actions. Natural heat does more actuate the stirring genius of man. Their easy natures make them somewhat more unresolute; whereby men have argued them of fear and inconstancy. But men have always held the parliament, and have enacted their own wills, without ever hearing them speak; and then, how easy is it to conclude them guilty! Besides, education makes more difference between men and them than Nature; and all their aspersions are less noble for that they are only from their enemies, men. Diogenes snarled bitterly when, walking with another, he spied two women talking, and said, 'See, the viper and the asp are changing poison.' The poet was conceited that said, after they were made ill, that God made them fearful, that man might rule them; otherwise they had been past dealing with. Catullus his conclusion[4] was too general, to collect a deceit in all women, because he was not confident of his own.

> *Nulli se dicit mulier mea nubere malle*
> *Quam mihi; non si se Jupiter ipse petat.*
> *Dicit: sed mulier Cupido quod dicit amanti,*
> *In vento et rapida scribere oportet aqua.*

> My mistress swears, she'd leave all men for me:
> Yea, though that Jove himself should suitor be.

3. The biblical David and Jonathan (I Samuel 18–20).
4. In his Ode given below.

She says it: but what women swear to kind
Loves, may be writ in rapid streams and wind.

I am resolved to honour virtue, in what sex soever I find it. And I think, in
the general, I shall find it more in women than men, though weaker and more
infirmly guarded. I believe they are better, and may be wrought to be worse.
Neither shall the faults of many make me uncharitable to all; nor the goodness
of some make me credulous of the rest. Though hitherto, I confess, I have not
found more sweet and constant goodness in man than I have found in woman;
and yet of these, I have not found a number.

1620–28

THOMAS FULLER
1608–1661

A voluminous writer of devotional manuals, religious verse, didactic character books
(*The Holy State*, published in 1642), and historical works, Fuller is perhaps best
remembered for his two large and comprehensive surveys of his native land, chronologically in *The Church History of Britain* (1655) and topographically (a prose and
prosaic version both, of the format of Michael Drayton's *Poly-Olbion*) in his posthumous *The History of the Worthies of England* (1662), organized county by county.
Fuller, whose degree was from Queen's College, Cambridge, was a moderate Anglican
churchman, his posts temporary and various until he became curate of a chapel in
London and, briefly, chaplain to the infant royal princess. He did not go into exile,
survived the Puritan regime, and was reinstated at the Restoration. The biographical
sketches given below are from the book usually known as "Fuller's *Worthies*"; their
superficial organization is more finished than are Aubrey's random notes, but the
approach to history and character no more systematic. Still, the shared antiquarian
gusto and the general good humor of these little accounts easily explain their popularity.

From The History of the Worthies of England

Warwickshire: William Shakespeare

William Shakespeare was born at Stratford-on-Avon in this country; in whom
three eminent poets may seem in some sort to be compounded. 1. *Martial*, in
the warlike sound of his surname (whence some may conjecture him of military
extraction) *Hasti-vibrans*, or Shake-speare. 2. *Ovid*, the most natural and witty
of all poets; and hence it was that Queen Elizabeth, coming into a grammar
school, made this extemporary phrase,

Persius a crab-staff, bawdy Martial, Ovid a fine wag.

3. *Plautus*, who was an exact comedian, yet never any scholar, as our Shakespeare (if alive) would confess himself. Add to all these, that though his genius
generally was jocular, and inclining him to festivity, yet he could (when so
disposed) be solemn and serious, as appears by his tragedies; so that Heraclitus [1]

1. The Greek philosopher, taken as a type of gloominess.

himself (I mean if secret and unseen) might afford to smile at his comedies, they were so merry; and Democritus [2] scarce forbear to sigh at his tragedies, they were so mournful.

He was an eminent instance of the truth of that rule, 'Poeta non fit sed nascitur' (one is not made but born a poet). Indeed his learning was very little; so that, as Cornish diamonds are not polished by any lapidary, but are pointed and smooth even as they are taken out of the earth, so nature itself was all the art which was used upon him.

Many were the wit-combats betwixt him and Ben Jonson; which two I behold like a Spanish great galleon and an English man-of-war; Master Jonson (like the former) was built far higher in learning; solid, but slow, in his performances. Shakespeare, with the English man-of-war, lesser in bulk, but lighter in sailing, could turn with all tides, tack about, and take advantage of all winds, by the quickness of his wit and invention. He died *anno Domini* 1616, and was buried at Stratford-upon-Avon, the town of his nativity.

Westminster: Benjamin Jonson

Benjamin Jonson was born in this city. Though I cannot, with all my industrious inquiry, find him in his cradle, I can fetch him from his long coats. When a little child, he lived in Harts-horn-lane near Charingcross, where his mother married a bricklayer for her second husband.

He was first bred in a private school in Saint Martin's Church; then in Westminster School; witness his own epigram; [1]

> Camden, most reverend head, to whom I owe
> All that I am in arts, all that I know;
> How nothing's that to whom my country owes
> The great renown and name wherewith she goes, etc.

He was statutably admitted into Saint John's College in Cambridge (as many years after incorporated an honourary member of Christ Church in Oxford), where he continued but few weeks for want of further maintenance, being fain to return to the trade of his father-in-law. And let them blush not that have, but those who have not, a lawful calling. He helped in the new structure of Lincoln's Inn, when, having a trowel in his hand, he had a book in his pocket.

Some gentlemen, pitying that his parts should be buried under the rubbish of so mean a calling, did by their bounty manumise [2] him freely to follow his own ingenious inclinations. Indeed his parts were not so ready to run of themselves as able to answer the spur; so that it may be truly said of him, that he had an elaborate wit wrought out in his own industry. He would sit silent in a learned company, and suck in (besides wine) their several humours into his observation. What was one in others, he was able to refine to himself.

He was paramount in the dramatic part of poetry, and taught the stage an exact conformity to the laws of comedians. His comedies were above the *volge* [3]

2. Another, as a type of laughter (but see Robert Burton, *The Anatomy of Melancholy*).

1. Epigram XIV (to William Camden, the antiquarian, his headmaster).
2. Set him free (economically).
3. Crowd.

(which are only tickled with downright obscenity), and took not so well at the first stroke as at the rebound, when beheld the second time; yea, they will endure reading, and that with due commendation, so long as either ingenuity or learning are fashionable in our nation. If his later be not so spriteful and vigorous as his first pieces, all that are old will, and all that desire to be old should, excuse him therein.

He was not very happy in his children, and most happy in those which died first, though none lived to survive him. This he bestowed as part of an epitaph on his eldest son, dying in infancy:

> Rest in soft peace; and, asked, say here doth lie,
> Ben Jonson his best piece of poetry.[4]

He died *anno Domini* 1638; and was buried about the belfry, in the abbey church at Westminster.

1662

Cornwall: King Arthur

King Arthur, son of Uther Pendragon, was born in Tintagel castle in this county; and proved afterwards monarch of Great Britain. He may fitly be termed the British Hercules in three respects:

1. For his illegitimate birth, both being bastards, begotten on other men's the other by art magic of Merlin, in others personating their husbands. wives,[1] and yet their mothers honest women; deluded, the one by a miracle,

2. Painful life; one famous for his twelve labours, the other for his twelve victories against the Saxons; and both of them had been greater, had they been made less, and the reports of them reduced within the compass of probability.

3. Violent and woeful death; our Arthur's being as lamentable, and more honourable; not caused by feminine jealousy, but masculine treachery, being murdered by Modred, near the place where he was born:

> As though no other place on Britain's spacious earth
> Were worthy of his end, but where he had his birth.[2]

As for his Round Table, with his knights about it, the tale whereof hath trundled so smoothly along for many ages, it never met with much belief amongst the judicious. He died about the year 542.

And now to speak of the Cornish in general. They ever have been beheld men of valour. It seemeth in the reign of the aforesaid King Arthur they ever made up his vanguard, if I can rightly understand the barbarous verses of a Cornish poet: [3]

> *Nobilis Arcturus nos primos Cornubienses*
> *Bellum facturus vocat (ut puta Cæsaris enses).*
> *Nobis (non aliis reliquis) dat primitus ictum.*

4. Epigram XLV; see above.

1. "Alcmena, wife to Amphytrion, and Igern, wife to Gorloise, prince of Cornwall" (Fuller's note).
2. Michael Drayton's *Poly-Olbion* (First Song, ll. 189–90).
3. "Michael Cornubiensis" (Fuller's note).

> Brave Arthur, when he meant a field to fight,
> Us Cornish men did first of all invite.
> Only to Cornish (count them Cæsar's swords)
> He the first blow in battle still affords.

But afterwards, in the time of King Canutus, the Cornish were appointed to make up the rear of our armies. Say not they were much degraded by this transposition from head to foot, seeing the judicious, in marshalling of an army, count the strength (and therefore the credit) to consist in the rear thereof.

But it must be pitied that this people, misguided by their leaders, have so often abused their valour in rebellions, and particularly in the reign of King Henry the Seventh, at Blackheath, where they did the greatest execution with their arrows, reported to be the length of a tailor's yard, the last of that proportion which ever were seen in England. However, the Cornish have since plentifully repaired their credit, by their exemplary valour and loyalty in our late civil wars.

London: Edmund Spenser

Edmund Spenser, born in this city, was brought up in Pembroke Hall in Cambridge, where he became an excellent scholar; but especially most happy in English poetry, as his works do declare; in which the many Chaucerisms used (for I will not say affected by him) are thought by the ignorant to be blemishes, known by the learned to be beauties, to his book, which notwithstanding had been more saleable, if more conformed to our modern language.

There passeth a story commonly told and believed, that Spenser presenting his poems to Queen Elizabeth, she, highly affected therewith, commanded the Lord Cecil, her treasurer, to give him a hundred pounds; and when the treasurer (a good steward of the Queen's money) alleged that the sum was too much, 'Then give him,' quoth the queen, 'what is reason'; to which the lord consented. But was so busied, belike, about matters of high concernment that Spenser received no reward; whereupon he presented this petition in a small piece of paper to the queen in her progress:

> I was promised on a time,
> To have reason for my rhyme;
> From that time unto this season,
> I received nor rhyme nor reason.

Hereupon the queen gave strict order (not without some check to her treasurer) for the present payment of the hundred pounds she first intended unto him.

He afterwards went over into Ireland, secretary to the Lord Gray, Lord Deputy thereof; and though that his office under his lord was lucrative, yet got he no estate; but, saith my author,[1] *'peculiari poetis fato, semper cum paupertate conflictatus est.'* So that it fared little better with him than with William Xilander the German (a most excellent linguist, antiquary, philosopher, and mathematician), who was so poor that (as Thuanus saith) he was thought, *'fami non fame scribere.'* [2]

1. "Camden's *Elizabeth*, *in anno 1598*" (Fuller's note).
2. "To write because famished, not for want of fame."

Returning into England, he was robbed by the rebels of that little he had; and dying for grief in great want, *anno* 1598, was honourably buried nigh Chaucer in Westminster, where this distich concluded his epitaph on his monument:

> *Anglica te vivo vixit plausitque poesis,*
> *Nunc moritura timet te moriente mori.*

> Whilst thou didst live, lived English poetry,
> Which fears, now thou art dead, that she shall die.[3]

Nor must we forget, that the expense of his funeral and monument was defrayed at the sole charge of Robert, first of that name, Earl of Essex.

1662

JOHN AUBREY
1627?–1697

Born in Wiltshire, educated at home and, for a time, at Trinity College, Oxford, Aubrey returned to his home in the late 1640's, inherited, eventually, a good-sized estate from his father—and subsequently lost most of it—and, in 1654, began "to enter into pocket memorandum books, philosophical and antiquarian remarks," as he put it. He endeavored, in a devoted and unsystematic fashion, to write of natural science and regional antiquities; and years later, after having assisted the Oxford historian Anthony à Wood in the compilation of his biographical *Athenae Oxonienses,* began to keep the records for his *Brief Lives.* They remained unpublished, and even unfinished, at his death. Sprawling, tentative, gossipy, Aubrey's notebooks have nevertheless come to be admired for the shading and coloring they can give to the more reliable historical biographies of their subjects, even when that shading may blur the true outlines. He was a close friend of Hobbes (whose biography is the longest and most elaborate in the collection), of Sir Christopher Wren, and others; and Aubrey's talents were those of the anecdotalist and, even with his human subjects, the amateur archaeologist. Hearsay was more intimate for him than recorded fact, and plays an even greater part in his repertory of sources. His style is often pithy and sly, sometimes unconsciously poignant or half-intentionally comical. Aubrey was wistfully realistic about his own role. Reporting seeing a bust of the once famous beauty Lady Venetia Digby, pilfered from her tomb and now on sale in a shop, he remarked: "How these curiosities would be quite forgot, did not such idle fellows as I am put them down."

3. Only this English inscription survives: "The Prince of Poets in his time, whose Divine Spirit needs no other witness than the Works which he left behind him."

From Brief Lives

Andrew Marvell (1621–1678)

He was of middling stature, pretty strong set, roundish faced, cherry cheeked, hazel eye, brown hair. He was in his conversation very modest, and of very few words; and though he loved wine, he would never drink hard in company, and was wont to say that he would not play the good-fellow in any man's company in whose hands he would not trust his life. He had not a general acquaintance.

In the time of Oliver the Protector he was Latin Secretary. He was a great master of the Latin tongue; an excellent poet in Latin or English: for Latin verses there was no man could come into competition with him.

I remember I have heard him say that the Earl of Rochester was the only man in England who had the true vein of satire.

His native town of Hull loved him so well that they elected him for their representative in Parliament, and gave him an honourable pension to maintain him.

He kept bottles of wine at his lodging, and many times he would drink liberally by himself to refresh his spirits and exalt his muse. (I remember I have been told that the learned Goclenius [1] (an High-German) was wont to keep bottles of good Rhenish wine in his study and, when his spirits wasted, he would drink a good rummer of it.)

Obiit Londini,[2] Aug. 18, 1678, and is buried in St. Giles Church-in-the-Fields about the middle of the south aisle. Some suspect that he was poisoned by the Jesuits, but I cannot be positive.

from MS. 1898

Sir Walter Ralegh (1552–1618)

Sir Walter Ralegh was of Oriel College. Mr. Child's father of Worcestershire was his chamberfellow and lent him a gown, which he could never get, nor satisfaction for it.—From Mr. Child.

He was a tall, handsome and bold man; but his naeve [1] was that he was damnable proud. . . .

He had a most remarkable aspect, an exceeding high forehead, long-faced and sour eye-lidded, a kind of pig's eye. His beard turned up naturally.

In the great parlour at Downton, at Mr. Ralegh's, is a good piece [2] (an original) of Sir W. in a white satin doublet, all embroidered with rich pearls, and a mighty rich chain of great pearls about his neck, and the old servants have told me that the pearls were near as big as the painted ones.

Old Sir Thomas Malette, one of the Justices of the King's Bench *tempore Caroli I et II* [3] knew Sir Walter; and I have heard him say that notwithstanding his so great mastership in style and his conversation with the learnedest and

---

1. Rudolph Goeckel (1547–1628), German logician.
2. "Died in London."

1. Blemish.
2. Painting.
3. "In the days of Charles I and II."

polite persons, yet he spake broad Devonshire to his dying day. His voice yet was small, as likewise were my schoolfellows his grand-nephews.

Durham House was a noble palace; after he came to his greatness he lived there or in some apartment of it. I well remember his study, which was a little turret that looked into and over the Thames, and had the prospect which is pleasant perhaps as any in the world, and which not only refreshed the eyesight and cheers the spirits and (to speak my mind) I believe enlarges an ingenious man's thoughts.

Sherburne Castle, -Park, -Manor, etc. did belong (and still ought to belong) to the Church of Sarum.[4] Sir W.R. begged it as a Bon from Queen Elizabeth; where he built a delicate lodge in the park, of brick, not big, but very convenient for the bigness, a place to retire from the court in summertime, and to contemplate, etc. Upon his attainder it was begged by the favourite, Carr, Earl of Somerset, who forfeited it (I think) about the poisoning of Sir John Overbury.[5] Then John, Earl of Bristowe,[6] had it given him for his good service to the ambassade in Spain, and added two wings to Sir Walter Ralegh's lodge. In short and indeed, 'tis a most sweet and pleasant place and site as any in the West [7]— perhaps none like it.

He was the first that brought tobacco into England and into fashion.—In our part of North Wilts, e.g. Malmesbury hundred, it came first into fashion by Sir Walter Long.

I have heard my grandfather Lyte say that one pipe was handed from man to man round about the table. They had first silver pipes; the ordinary sort made use of a walnut shell and a straw.

It was sold then for its weight in silver. I have heard some of our old yeomen neighbours say that when they went to Malmesbury or Chippenham market, they culled out their biggest shillings to lay in the scales against the tobacco.

Sir W.R., standing in a stand at Sir Robert Poyntz's part at Acton, took a pipe of tobacco, which made the ladies quit till he had done.

Within these 35 years 'twas scandalous for a divine to take tobacco.

Now the customs of it are the greatest his Majesty hath—Rider's Almanac (1682, *scilicet*) [8]—Since tobacco brought into England by Sir Walter Ralegh, 99 years, the custom whereof is now the greatest of all others and amounts to ——yearly.[9]

Sir Walter Ralegh was a great chemist; and amongst some MSS. receipts I have seen some secrets from him. He studied most in his sea voyages, where he carried always a trunk of books along with him, and had nothing to divert him.

4. Salisbury Cathedral; "a Bon" is a boon, a favor.
5. Aubrey makes an almost unbelievable slip here: the Sir *Thomas* Overbury poisoning case was one of the scandals of the age, and Aubrey probably wrote "John" for "Thomas" because of the Earl of Bristol's name following.
6. Bristol (as pronounced there).
7. The West Country.
8. "Namely."
9. As a matter of fact, the then staggering sum of £400,000 per annum in Aubrey's day. In Ralegh's, the price of a *pipeful* of tobacco was one-fourth of a laborer's daily wage.

A person so much immersed in action all along and in fabrication of his own fortunes, till his confinement in the Tower, could have but little time to study but what he could spare in the morning. He was no slug; without doubt had a wonderful waking spirit and great judgement to guide it.

An attorney's father (that did my business in Herefordshire before I sold it [10]) married Dr. Burhill's widow. She said that he [Burhill] was a great favourite of Sir Walter Ralegh's and, I think, had been his chaplain; but all the greatest part of the drudgery of his book [11] for criticisms, chronology, and reading of Greek and Hebrew authors was performed by him for Sir Walter Ralegh, whose picture my friend has as part of the Doctor's goods.

I have heard old Major Cosh say that Sir W. Ralegh did not care to go on the Thames in a wherry boat; he would rather go round about over London Bridge.

He loved a wench well; and one time getting up one of the Maids of Honour up against a tree in a wood ('twas his first Lady) who seemed at first boarding to be somewhat fearful of her honour and modest, she cried: 'Sweet Sir Walter, what do you me ask? Will you undo me? Nay, sweet Sir Walter! Sweet Sir Walter! Sir Walter!' At last, as the danger and the pleasure at the same time grew higher, she cried in the extasy, 'Swisser Swatter Swisser Swatter.' She proved with child, and I doubt not but that this hero took care of them both, as also that the product was more than an ordinary mortal.

My old friend James Harrington, Esq. was well acquainted with Sir Benjamin Rudyerd, who was an acquaintance of Sir Walter Ralegh's. He told Mr. J.H. that Sir Walter Ralegh, being invited to dinner with some great person where his son was to go with him, he said to his son, 'Thou art such a quarrelsome, affronting creature that I am ashamed to have such a bear in my company.' Mr. Walt humbled himself to his father, and promised he would behave himself mightily mannerly. So away they went, and Sir Benjamin, I think, with them. He sat next to his father and was very demure at least half dinner time. Then said he: 'I this morning, not having the fear of God before my eyes but by the instigation of the Devil, went to a whore. I was very eager of her, kissed and embraced her, and went to enjoy her, but she thrust me from her and vowed I should not, "For your father lay with me but an hour ago." ' Sir Walt, being so strangely surprised and put out of his countenance at so great a tale, gives his son a damned blow over the face. His son, as rude as he was, would not strike his father, but strikes over the face of the gentleman that sat next to him and said, 'Box about, 'twill come to my father anon.' 'Tis now a common-used proverb.

At the end of his *History of the World,* he laments the death of the most noble and hopeful Prince Henry, whose great favourite he was, and who, had he survived his father, would quickly have enlarged him with rewards of honour. . . .

His book sold very slowly at first, and the bookseller complained of it, and told him that he should be a loser by it, which put Sir W. into a passion, and said that since the world did not understand it, they should not have his second part, which he took and threw into the fire, and burned before his face.

---

10. Aubrey's own estate.
11. *The History of the World.*

He was prisoner in the Tower . . . (*quære*) years; [12] *quære* where his lodgings were. He there, besides his compiling his *History of the World*, studied chemistry. The Earl of Northumberland was a prisoner at the same time, who was the patron to Mr. . . .[13] Hariot and Mr. Warner, two of the best mathematicians then in the world, as also Mr. Hues, [author of] *De Globis*. Serjeant Hoskins, the poet, was a prisoner there too. I heard my cousin Whitney say that he saw him [Sir Walter] in the Tower. He had a velvet cap laced and a rich gown and trunk hose.

He was scandalized with atheism, but he was a bold man, and would venture at discourse which was unpleasant to the churchmen. I remember my Lord Scudamour said 'twas basely said of Sir W.R. to talk of the anagram of Dog.[14] In his speech on the scaffold, I have heard my cousin Whitney say (and I think 'tis printed) that he spake not one word of Christ, but of the great and incomprehensible God, with much zeal and adoration, so that he concluded that he was an a-Christ, not an atheist.

He took a pipe of tobacco a little before he went to the scaffold, which some formal persons were scandalized at, but I think 'twas well and properly done, to settle his spirits.

> *Even such is time, which takes in trust*
> *Our youth, our joys, and all we have*
> *And pays us but with age and dust.*
> *Within the dark and silent grave,*
> *When we have wandered all our ways,*
> *Shuts up the story of our days.*
> *But from which grave and earth and dust*
> *The Lord will raise me up I trust.*

These lines Sir Walter Ralegh wrote in his Bible the night before he was beheaded and desired his relations with these words, viz. 'Beg my dead body which living is denied you; and bury it either in Sherburne or Exeter Church.'

from MS. 1898

[As the conclusion to the very brief account of one Nicholas Towes, a friend of the father of the ill-fated Duke of Buckingham who appeared to him as a ghost saying "I am dead, but cannot rest in peace for the wickedness and abomination of my son George at Court," Aubrey adds the following paragraph, concerning a ghost:]

Anno 1670, not far from Cirencester, was an apparition. Being demanded whether a good spirit or bad, returned no answer, but disappeared with a curious perfume and most melodious twang. Mr. W. Lilly believes it was a fairy.

from MS. 1898

12. Thirteen years, in fact; the "quaere" (a modern scholar would write "?") indicates that Aubrey intended to check up on these facts later.
13. Thomas Hariot.
14. The only anagram of "Dog" is "God."

EDWARD HYDE, EARL OF CLARENDON
1608–1674

Lawyer, Parliamentarian, moderate Royalist, and Anglican, counselor to Charles I and, later, to Charles II, victim of court intrigue and unwilling exile, finally, by another turn of fate, father and grandfather of three English queens (Anne, wife of James II, and the reigning queens Mary and Anne), Clarendon is best known today as a historian of his times. Many chroniclers, from the Athenian Thucydides on, have written of their own times and homes from exile. So with Clarendon; while in the Scilly Isles, in retreat from Parliamentary forces with Prince Charles, the future king, he started in 1646 a *History of the Rebellion,* which he was finally to complete in a second exile—from the court of Charles II at the end of his life—in France. In his early days Clarendon had been associated, through Lucius Cary, Viscount Falkland, with the Ben Jonson circle (see Jonson's Cary and Morison ode). As a Royalist, he urged legality and flexibility, and it was perhaps unfortunate for the king that he chose to follow other advice. The two excerpts from *The History of the Rebellion* (first published 1702–4) represent in retrospect the blend of firm conviction and just reasonableness which must have marked him as an adviser. The first selection is from the material covering 1649, the year of Charles's death; the second, 1658, that of Cromwell's. For another view of one of these figures from the opposition—complex rather than balanced—see Marvell's *Horatian Ode.*

From The History of the Rebellion

[The Character of Charles I]

His kingly virtues had some mixture and allay[1] that hindered them from shining in full lustre, and from producing those fruits they should have been attended with. He was not in his nature bountiful, though he gave very much: which appeared more after the duke of Buckingham's[2] death, after which those showers fell very rarely; and he paused too long in giving, which made those to whom he gave less sensible of the benefit. He kept state[3] to the full, which made his Court very orderly; no man presuming to be seen in a place where he had no pretence to be. He saw and observed men long before he received any about his person, and did not love strangers, nor very confident men. He was a patient hearer of causes, which he frequently accustomed himself to, at the Council board; and judged very well, and was dexterous in the mediating part: so that he often put an end to causes by persuasion, which the stubbornness of men's humours made dilatory in courts of justice.

He was very fearless in his person, but not enterprising; and had an excellent understanding, but was not confident enough of it; which made him oftentimes change his own opinion for a worse, and follow the advice of a man that did not judge so well as himself. And this made him more irresolute than the conjec-

---

1. Alloy.
2. George Villiers (1592–1626), first Duke of Buckingham; friend and playmate of James I, who made him vastly rich; thereafter adviser to Charles I; finally assassinated.
3. Elaborate, formal courtly pomp.

ture of his affairs would admit. If he had been of a rougher and more imperious nature, he would have found more respect and duty; and his not applying some severe cures to approaching evils proceeded from the lenity of his nature and the tenderness of his conscience, which in all cases of blood made him choose the softer way, and not hearken to severe counsels, how reasonably soever urged. This only restrained him from pursuing his advantage in the first Scots' expedition,[4] when, humanly speaking, he might have reduced that nation to the most slavish obedience that could have been wished. But no man can say he had then many who advised him to it, but the contrary, by a wonderful indisposition all his Council had to fighting or any other fatigue. He was always an immoderate lover of the Scottish nation, having not only been born there, but educated by that people, and besieged by them always, having few English about him until he was king; and the major number of his servants being still of those, who he thought could never fail him; and then no man had such an ascendant over him, by the lowest and humblest insinuations, as duke Hambleton [5] had.

As he excelled in all other virtues, so in temperance he was so strict, that he abhorred all deboshry [6] to that degree, that, at a great festival solemnity, where he once was, when very many of the nobility of the English and Scots were entertained, being told by one who withdrew from thence, what vast draughts of wine they drank, and that there was one earl who had drank most of the rest down and was not himself moved or altered, the King said that he deserved to be hanged; and that earl coming shortly into the room where his majesty was, in some gaiety, to show how unhurt he was from that battle, the King sent one to bid him withdraw from his majesty's presence; nor did he in some days after appear before the King.

There were so many miraculous circumstances contributed to his ruin, that men might well think that heaven and earth conspired it, and that the stars designed it. Though he was, from the first declension [7] of his power, so much betrayed by his own servants, that there were very few who remained faithful to him, yet that treachery proceeded not from any treasonable purpose to do him any harm, but from particular and personal animosities against other men. And afterwards, the terror all men were under of the Parliament, and the guilt they were conscious of themselves, made them watch all opportunities to make themselves gracious to those who could do them good; and so they became spies upon their master, and from one piece of knavery were hardened and confirmed to undertake another, till at last they had no hope of preservation but by the destruction of their master. And after all this, when a man might reasonably believe that less than a universal defection of three nations could not have reduced a great king to so ugly a fate, it is most certain that in that very hour when he was this wickedly murdered in the sight of the sun he had as great a share in the hearts and affections of his subjects in general, was as much beloved, esteemed, and longed for by the people in general of the three nations as any

4. In 1639, Charles made an ill-fated attempt to subdue Scottish Presbyterian forces that had refused to accept Archibishop Laud's reorganization of their church.
5. James, first Duke of Hamilton (1606–49), led a Royalist Scottish army into England and was defeated by Cromwell and beheaded.
6. Debauchery.
7. Decline.

of his predecessors had ever been. To conclude: he was the worthiest gentleman, the best master, the best friend, the best husband, the best father, and the best Christian that the age in which he lived produced. And if he was not the greatest king, if he was without some parts and qualities which have made some kings great and happy, no other prince was ever unhappy who was possessed of half his virtues and endowments, and so much without any kind of vice.

[The Character of Cromwell]

He was one of those men, *quos vituperare ne inimici quidem possunt nisi ut simul laudent;*[1] for he could never have done half that mischief without great parts of courage and industry and judgement. And he must have had a wonderful understanding in the natures and humours of men and as great a dexterity in the applying them; who, from a private and obscure birth—though of a good family—without interest of[2] estate, alliance or friendship, could raise himself to such a height and compound and knead such opposite and contradictory tempers, humours, and interests into a consistence that contributed to his designs, and to their own destruction; whilst himself grew insensibly powerful enough to cut off those by whom he had climbed in the instant that they projected to demolish their own building. What Velleius Paterculus said of Cinna may very justly be said of him, *ausum eum quœ nemo auderet bonus perfecisse, quœ a nullo, nisi fortissimo, perfici possent.*[3] Without doubt, no man with more wickedness ever attempted anything or brought to pass what he desired more wickedly, more in the face and contempt of religion and moral honesty; yet wickedness as great as his could never have accomplished those designs without the assistance of a great spirit, an admirable circumspection and sagacity, and a most magnanimous resolution.

When he appeared first in the Parliament, he seemed to have a person in no degree gracious, no ornament of discourse, none of those talents which use[4] to reconcile the affections of the standers by: yet as he grew into place and authority, his parts seemed to be renewed, as if he had concealed faculties till he had occasion to use them; and when he was to act the part of a great man, he did it without any indecency through the want of custom.

After he was confirmed and invested Protector by *The humble Petition and Advice,*[5] he consulted with very few upon any action of importance, nor communicated any enterprise he resolved upon with more than those who were to have principal parts in the execution of it; nor to them sooner than was absolutely necessary. What he once resolved in which he was not rash, he would not be dissuaded from, nor endure any contradiction of his power and authority, but extorted obedience from them who were not willing to yield it.

When he had laid some very extraordinary tax upon the city, one Cony, an

---

1. "Whom even his enemies could not denigrate without at the same time praising."
2. Vested interest in.
3. "He attempted what no good man ought to have tried, and succeeded where only a great man could" (from Velleius Paterculus' *Res Gestae Divi Augusti,* a history of the age of Augustus Caesar).
4. Act.
5. In 1657, a new draft constitution was presented to Parliament by which, among other things, Cromwell was to be given the title of king, a privilege he refused.

eminent fanatic, and one who had heretofore served him very notably, positively refused to pay his part, and loudly dissuaded others from submitting to it, as an imposition notoriously against the law and the propriety of the subject, which all honest men were bound to defend. Cromwell sent for him, and cajoled him with the memory of the old kindness and friendship that had been between them, and that of all men he did not expect this opposition from him, in a matter that was so necessary for the good of the commonwealth. But it was always his fortune to meet with the most rude and obstinate behaviour from those who had formerly been absolutely governed by him, and they commonly put him in mind of some expressions and saying of his own in cases of the like nature; so this man remembered him how great an enemy he had expressed himself to such grievances, and declared that all who submitted to them and paid illegal taxes were more to blame, and greater enemies to their country, than they who imposed them, and that the tyranny of princes could never be grievous but by the tameness and stupidity of the people. When Cromwell saw that he could not convert him, he told him that he had a will as stubborn as his, and he would try which of them two should be master; and thereupon, with some terms of reproach and contempt, he committed the man to prison; whose courage was nothing abated by it; but as soon as the term came, he brought his *habeas corpus* [6] in the King's Bench, which they then called the Upper Bench. Maynard, who was of counsel with the prisoner, demanded his liberty with great confidence, both upon the illegality of the commitment, and the illegality of the imposition, as being laid without any lawful authority. The judges could not maintain or defend either, but enough declared what their sentence would be; and therefore the Protector's Attorney required a farther day to answer what had been urged. Before that day, Maynard was committed to the Tower, for presuming to question or make doubt of his authority; and the judges were sent for, and severely reprehended for suffering that license; and when they with all humility mentioned the law and *Magna Charta,* Cromwell told them, their *magna farta* should not control his actions, which he knew were for the safety of the commonwealth. He asked them who made them judges; whether they had any authority to sit there but what he gave them; and that if his authority were at an end, they knew well enough what would become of themselves; and therefore advised them to be more tender of that which could only preserve them; and so dismissed them with caution, that they should not suffer the lawyers to prate what it would not become them to hear.

Thus he subdued a spirit that had been often troublesome to the most sovereign power, and made Westminster Hall [7] as obedient and subservient to his commands as any of the rest of his quarters. In all other matters which did not concern the life of his jurisdiction, he seemed to have great reverence for the law, and rarely interposed between party and party. And as he proceeded with this kind of indignation and haughtiness with those who were refractory and dared to contend with his greatness, so toward those who complied with his good pleasure, and courted his protection, he used [8] a wonderful civility, generosity, and bounty. . . .

6. His writ of *habeas corpus.*
7. The Presbyterian assembly, which had met there.
8. Practiced.

To reduce three nations, which perfectly hated him, to an entire obedience to all his dictates, to awe and govern those nations by an army that was indevoted to him and wished his ruin, was an instance of a very prodigious address. But his greatness at home was but a shadow of the glory he had abroad. It was hard to discover which feared him most, France, Spain, or the Low Countries, where his friendship was current at the value he put upon it. And as they did all sacrifice their honour and their interest to his pleasure, so there is nothing he could have demanded that either of them would have denied him. . . .

He was not a man of blood, and totally declined Machiavel's method,[9] which prescribes, upon any alteration of a government, as a thing absolutely necessary, to cut off all the heads of those, and extirpate their families, who are friends to the old one. And it was confidently reported that in the council of officers it was more than once proposed, that there might be a general massacre of all the royal party as the only expedient to secure the government, but Cromwell would never consent to it; it may be, out of too much contempt of his enemies. In a word, as he had all the wickednesses against which damnation is denounced and for which hellfire is prepared, so he had some virtues which have caused the memory of some men in all ages to be celebrated; and he will be looked upon by posterity as a brave, bad man.

1702–1704

JEREMY TAYLOR
1613–1667

The author of *Holy Living* and *Holy Dying* was more highly regarded in the early nineteenth century than Sir Thomas Browne (except by Ralph Waldo Emerson, whose response to seventeenth-century poetry and prose anticipated modern taste); and although it is easy to select haunting and resonant passages from his devotional books and from his sermons, it was not for these that he was so admired. It is instructive to realize that Coleridge liked tremendously the Samuel Daniel of *The Civil Wars,* discursive rather than lyrical; similarly, Taylor's extended meditative seriousness, unmarred by the brilliant leaps and twists and turns of a style like that of Donne, stood for all that was most elegantly solemn in an expository style still untouched by the criteria that the Enlightenment would exact of prose argument. Taylor's style strikes a balance, too, between the slightly archaic and the less mannered, more modern syntax; and, for his age, he is under-, rather than over-allusive.

Taylor was born in Cambridgeshire, educated at Cambridge, took holy orders in 1633, preached in London, became a fellow of All Souls' at Oxford (a college consisting solely of fellows, with no undergraduates), and for a while was attached to the royal household. He spent a good many years at Golden House, the estate in Wales of the Earl of Carbey; while there, he preached some and wrote extensively, including an unusually ecumenical treatise, *A Discourse on the Liberty of Prophesying* (1647),

---

9. Any and all harsh *Realpolitik* could be blamed, in Elizabethan England and thereafter, on a stock figure of Italianate evil, called Machiavel, having not much to do with the major political thought of the Florentine Niccolò Machiavelli (1469–1527). Clarendon's knowledge of both *The Prince* and the more important *Discourses on Livy*, however, was profound.

and his two most famous works, *The Rule and Exercise of Holy Living* (1650) and *Holy Dying* (1651). After the Restoration he lived in London, and before his death was made Bishop of Down and Connor in Ireland.

Holy Dying

Chapter I

A General Preparation Towards a Holy and Blessed Death, by Way of Consideration

From Section I: Consideration of the Vanity and Shortness of Man's Life

A man is a bubble, said the Greek proverb; which Lucian [1] represents with advantages and its proper circumstances, to this purpose; saying, that all the world is a storm, and men rise up in their several generations, like bubbles descending *a Jove pluvio*, from God and the dew of heaven, from a tear and drop of man, from nature and providence: and some of these instantly sink into the deluge of their first parent, and are hidden in a sheet of water, having had no other business in the world but to be born that they might be able to die: others float up and down two or three turns, and suddenly disappear, and give their place to others: and they that live longest upon the face of the waters, are in perpetual motion, restless and uneasy; and, being crushed with the great drop of a cloud, sink into flatness and a froth; the change not being great, it being hardly possible it should be more a nothing than it was before. So is every man: he is born in vanity and sin; he comes into the world like morning mushrooms, soon thrusting up their heads into the air, and conversing with their kindred of the same production, and as soon they turn into dust and forgetfulness: some of them without any other interest in the affairs of the world but that they made their parents a little glad, and very sorrowful: others ride longer in the storm; it may be until seven years of vanity be expired, and then peradventure the sun shines hot upon their heads, and they fall into the shades below, into the cover of death and darkness of the grave to hide them. But if the bubble stands the shock of a bigger drop, and outlives the chances of a child, of a careless nurse, of drowning in a pail of water, of being overlaid by a sleepy servant, or such little accidents, then the young man dances like a bubble, empty and gay, and shines like a dove's neck, or the image of a rainbow, which hath no substance, and whose very imagery and colours are fantastical; and he dances out the gaiety of his youth, and is all the while in a storm, and endures only because he is not shocked on the head by a drop of bigger rain, or crushed by the pressure of a load of indigested meat, or quenched by the disorder of an ill-placed humour: and to preserve a man alive in the midst of so many chances and hostilities, is as great a miracle as to create him; to preserve him from rushing into nothing, and at first to draw him up from nothing, were equally the issues of an almighty power. And

1. Lucian, the satirist, in his dialogue *Charon*.

therefore the wise men of the world have contended who shall best fit man's condition with words signifying his vanity and short abode. Homer[2] calls a man 'a leaf,' the smallest, the weakest piece of a short-lived, unsteady plant: Pindar[3] calls him 'the dream of a shadow': another, 'the dream of the shadow of smoke': but St. James spake by a more excellent spirit, saying, 'our life is but a vapour' (James 4:14, ἀτμὶς, viz., drawn from the earth by a celestial influence; made of smoke, or the lighter parts of water, tossed with every wind, moved by the motion of a superior body, without virtue in itself, lifted up on high or left below, according as it pleases the sun its foster-father. But it is lighter yet; it is but 'appearing' (φαινομένη); a fantastic vapour, an apparition, nothing real: it is not so much as a mist, not the matter of a shower, nor substantial enough to make a cloud; but it is like Cassiopeia's chair, or Pelops' shoulder, or the circles of heaven, φαινόμενα, than which you cannot have a word that can signify a verier nothing. And yet the expression is one degree more made diminutive: a 'vapour,' and 'fantastical,' or a 'mere appearance,' and this but for a little while neither (πρὸς ὀλίγον); the very dream, the phantasm disappears in a small time, 'like the shadow that departeth'; or 'like a tale that is told'; or 'as a dream when one awaketh.' A man is so vain, so unfixed, so perishing a creature, that he cannot long last in the scene of fancy: a man goes off, and is forgotten, like the dream of a distracted person. The sum of all is this: that thou art a man, than whom there is not in the world any greater instance of heights and declensions,[4] of lights and shadows, of misery and folly, of laughter and tears, of groans and death.

. . .

Thus nature calls us to meditate of death by those things which are the instruments of acting it: and God by all the variety of his providence makes us see death everywhere, in all variety of circumstances, and dressed up for all the fancies and the expectation of every single person. Nature hath given us one harvest every year, but death hath two, and the spring and the autumn send throngs of men and women to charnel-houses; and all the summer long men are recovering from their evils of the spring, till the dog-days come, and then the Sirian star[5] makes the summer deadly; and the fruits of autumn are laid up for all the year's provision, and the man that gathers them eats and surfeits, and dies and needs them not, and himself is laid up for eternity; and he that escapes till winter only stays for another opportunity which the distempers of that quarter minister to him with great variety. Thus death reigns in all the portions of our time; the autumn with its fruits provides disorders for us, and the winter's cold turns them into sharp diseases, and the spring brings flowers to strew our hearse, and the summer gives green turf and brambles to bind upon our graves. Calentures[6] and surfeit, cold and agues, are the four

2. In the Iliad VI.146.
3. In the eighth Pythian Ode, l. 135.
4. Declinings.
5. Sirius, the Dog Star. The "dog days" in August are so-called because the constellation Orion, followed by Sirius, rises near dawn, and Sirius, the brightest star in the skies, was thought to add its heat to that of the sun.
6. Heat spells.

quarters of the year, and all minister to death; and you can go no whither [7] but you tread upon a dead man's bones.

Section IV   Consideration of the Miseries of Man's Life

As our life is very short, so it is very miserable; and therefore it is well it is short. God, in pity to mankind, lest his burden should be insupportable and his nature an intolerable load, hath reduced our state of misery to an abbreviature; and the greater our misery is, the less while it is like to last; the sorrows of a man's spirit being like ponderous weights, which by the greatness of their burden make a swifter motion, and descend into the grave to rest and ease our wearied limbs; for then only we shall sleep quietly, when those fetters are knocked off, which not only bound our souls in prison, but also ate the flesh till the very bones opened the secret garments of their cartilages, discovering their nakedness and sorrow.

1. Here is no place to sit down in, but you must rise as soon as you are set, for we have gnats in our chambers, and worms in our gardens, and spiders and flies in the palaces of the greatest kings. How few men in the world are prosperous! What an infinite number of slaves and beggars, of persecuted and oppressed people, fill all corners of the earth with groans, and heaven itself with weeping prayers and sad remembrances! How many provinces and kingdoms are afflicted by a violent war, or made desolate by popular diseases! Some whole countries are remarked with fatal evils, or periodical sicknesses. Grand Cairo in Egypt feels the plague every three years returning like a quartan ague, and destroying many thousands of persons. All the inhabitants of Arabia the desert [8] are in continual fear of being buried in huge heaps of sand, and therefore dwell in tents and ambulatory houses, or retire to unfruitful mountains, to prolong an uneasy and wilder life. And all the countries round about the Adriatic Sea feel such violent convulsions by tempests and intolerable earthquakes, that sometimes whole cities find a tomb, and every man sinks with his own house made ready to become his monument, and his bed is crushed into the disorders of a grave. Was not all the world drowned at one deluge and breach of the divine anger; and shall not all the world again be destroyed by fire? Are there not many thousands that die every night, and that groan and weep sadly every day? But what shall we think of that great evil which for the sins of men God hath suffered to possess the greatest part of mankind? Most of the men that are now alive, or that have been living for many ages, are Jews, Heathens, or Turks; and God was pleased to suffer a base epileptic person,[9] a villain and a vicious, to set up a religion which hath filled all the nearer parts of Asia, and much of Africa, and some part of Europe; so that the greatest number of men and women born in so many kingdoms and provinces are infallibly made Mahometans, strangers and enemies to Christ by whom alone we can be saved: this consideration is extremely sad, when we remember how universal and how great an evil it is that so many millions of sons and daughters are born to enter into the possession of devils to eternal

7. Nowhere.
8. "Arabia deserta": the Arabian peninsula.
9. Mahommed.

ages. These evils are miseries of great parts of mankind, and we cannot easily consider more particularly the evils which happen to us, being the inseparable affections or incidents to the whole nature of man.

2. We find that all the women in the world are either born for barrenness, or the pains of childbirth, and yet this is one of our greatest blessings; but such indeed are the blessings of this world, we cannot be well with nor without many things. Perfumes make our heads ache, roses prick our fingers, and in our very blood, where our life dwells, is the scene under which nature acts many sharp fevers and heavy sicknesses. It were too sad if I should tell how many persons are afflicted with evil spirits, with spectres and illusions of the night; and that huge multitudes of men and women live upon man's flesh; nay, worse yet, upon the sins of men, upon the sins of their sons and of their daughters, and they pay their souls down for the bread they eat, buying this day's meal with the price of the last night's sin.

1651

From Sermons

[*Children*]

When we see a child strike a servant rudely, or jeer a silly person, or wittily cheat his play-fellow, or talk words light as the skirt of a summer garment, we laugh and are delighted with the wit and confidence of the boy; and encourage such hopeful beginnings; and in the meantime we consider not that from these beginnings he shall grow up till he become a tyrant, an oppressor, a goat and a traitor. *Nemo simul malus fit & malus esse cernitur; sicut nec scorpiis tum innascuntur stimuli cum pungunt.*[1] No man is discerned to be vicious so soon as he is so, and vices have their infancy and their childhood and it cannot be expected that in a child's age should be the vice of a man; that were monstrous as if he wore a beard in his cradle; and we do not believe that a serpent's sting does just then grow when he strikes us in a vital part. The venom and the little spear was there, when it first began to creep from his little shell. And little boldnesses and looser words and wranglings for nuts, and lying for trifles, are of the same proportion to the malice of a child, as impudence and duels and injurious law-suits, and false witness in judgement and perjuries are in men.

1651

[*Children*]

No man can tell but he that loves his children, how many delicious accents make a man's heart dance in the pretty conversation of those dear pledges; their childishness, their stammering, their little angers, their innocence, their imperfections, their necessities are so many little emanations of joy and comfort to him that delights in their persons and society; but he that loves not his wife and children, feeds a Lioness at home, and broods a nest of sorrows.

1653

1. Quoted from Plutarch.

Glossary

A Commentary on Selected Literary and Historical Terms

Airs (1) Songs, or tunes in general. (2) The songs for solo voice with lute accompaniment, as opposed to the polyphonic madrigals (*q.v.*) of the late 16th and early 17th centuries. Airs were strophic, and the successive strophes, or stanzas, of a poem were set to the same melody.

Alchemy The predecessor of chemistry, based upon classical and medieval mythological notions of the structure of matter; it was a study that nevertheless produced a great deal of practical chemical knowledge. Believing in the ancient notion of the relative nobility of metals—for example, from gold down to "baser" substances like lead—alchemists sought to discover a mysterious *philosopher's* (i.e. "scientist's") *stone* enabling them to perform transmutations of baser metals into gold. Since it thus constituted reversing a natural order, it could be thought of as theologically subversive. Alchemists themselves were by way of being practitioners of a hermetic (*q.v.*) religion, and transmuting metals was by no means their sole aim. Alchemical theory employed what would be today regarded as poetic concepts: e.g. sexual combination for chemical compounding, where today one might think of valence or charge. During the 17th century, when chemistry evolved as a science, alchemical lore and language, alluded to in poetry, became part of the body of myth, like Ptolemaic astronomy and the astrological theory it supported.

Allegory Literally, "other reading"; originally a way of interpreting a narrative or other text in order to extract a more general, or a less literal, meaning from it, e.g. reading Homer's *Odyssey* as the universal voyage of human life— with Odysseus standing for all men—which must be made toward a final goal. In the Middle Ages allegory came to be associated with ways of reading the Bible, particularly the Old Testament in relation to the New. In addition, stories came to be written with the intention of being interpreted symbolically; thus e.g. the *Psychomachia* or "battle for the soul" of Prudentius (b. 348 A.D.) figured the virtues and vices as contending soldiers in a battle (see *Personification*). There is allegorical lyric poetry and allegorical drama as well as allegorical narrative. In works such as Spenser's *The Faerie Queene* and Bunyan's *Pilgrim's Progress* allegory becomes a dominant literary form. See also *Dream Vision; Figure; type.*

Alliteration   A repeated initial consonant in successive words. In Old English verse, any vowel alliterates with any other, and alliteration is not an unusual or expressive phenomenon but a regularly recurring structural feature of the verse, occurring on the first and third, and often on the first, second, and third, primary-stressed syllables of the four-stressed line. Thus, from "The Seafarer":

> hréran mid hóndum hrímcælde sǽ
> ("to stir with his hand the rime-cold sea")

In later English verse tradition, alliteration becomes expressive in a variety of ways. Spenser uses it decoratively, or to link adjective and noun, verb and object, as in the line: "Much daunted with that dint, her sense was dazed." In the 18th and 19th centuries it becomes even less systematic and more "musical."

Amplificatio, Amplifying   The rhetorical enlargement of a statement or dilation of an argument, especially used in tragedy or epic (*q.v.*) poetry or in mock-heroic (*q.v.*). Language and stylistic ornament are deployed so as to increase the importance of a subject or to raise the level of its treatment.

Assonance   A repeated vowel sound, a part-rhyme, which has great expressive effect when used internally (within lines), e.g. "An old, mad, blind, despised and dying king,—" (Shelley, "Sonnet: England in 1819").

Astronomy and Astrology   Astrology may be regarded as an earlier phase or state of the science of astronomy—with an added normative provision in the notion that the *apparent* positions of the heavenly bodies, when viewed from a central earth about which all were thought to move, determined the shape of human life. (See *Zodiac.*) The geocentric astronomy of Ptolemy, wrong as it was about the relation between what was seen by an observer on earth and what caused him to see what he saw, nevertheless enabled men to predict with some accuracy events such as eclipses. In the microcosmic-macrocosmic world-view of the Middle Ages and the Renaissance, in which perspective the microcosm, or little world of man, constituted a miniature version of the whole cosmos, the relations between patterns discernible in the heavens and those of the four elements (*q.v.*), or the humors of the human constitution (*q.v.*), came to have great meaning. Specifically, the stars (meaning sun, moon, planets, fixed stars) were thought to radiate non-material substances called influences (literally, "in flowings") that beamed down to earth and affected human lives. Although the new astronomy of Copernicus, Kepler, and Galileo helped to destroy the conceptual basis for the belief in stellar influence, it is improper to think of a 16th- or 17th-century intellectual (and far less, a medieval man of letters and learning) as being superstitious in his use of astrological lore that was losing its centrality only with acceptance of the new ideas.

Aubade   The French form of the Provençal *alba* ("dawn"), the morning song complementary to the evening *serenade;* it took its name from the word *alba* in the refrain (e.g. that of a famous anonymous poem, *L'alba, l'alba, oc l'alba, tan tost ve* ("the dawn, the dawn, o the dawn, it comes too soon"). In English such a song as Shakespeare's "Hark, hark, the lark / At heaven's gate sings" (from *Cymbeline*) exemplifies this tradition.

Aureate Literally, "golden"; used of the poetic and sometimes the prose language of 14th- and 15th-century England and Scotland; an idiom highly wrought and specializing in vernacular coinages from Latin.

Baroque (1) Originally (and still), an oddly shaped rather than a spherical pearl, and hence something twisted, contorted, involuted. (2) By a complicated analogy, a term designating stylistic periods in art, music, and literature during the 16th and 17th centuries in Europe. The analogies among the arts are frequently strained, and the stylistic periods by no means completely coincide. But the relation between the poetry of Richard Crashaw in English and Latin, and the sculpture and architecture of Gianlorenzo Bernini (1598–1680), is frequently taken to typify the spirit of the baroque. (See Wylie Sypher, *Four Stages of Renaissance Style*, 1955.)

Balade, Ballade The dominant lyric form in French poetry of the 14th and 15th centuries; a strict form consisting of three stanzas of eight lines each, with an *envoi* (*q.v.*), or four-line conclusion, addressing either a person of importance or a personification. Each stanza, including the *envoi*, ends in a refrain.

Ballad Meter Or *common meter;* four-lined stanzas, rhyming *abab,* the first and third lines in iambic tetrameter (four beats), and the second and fourth lines in iambic trimeter (three beats). See *Meter.*

Blazon, Blason (*Fr.*) A poetic genre cataloguing the parts or attributes of an object in order to praise it (or, in its satirical form, to condemn it). The first type, most influential chiefly on English Renaissance poetry, had its origin in a poem by Clément Marot in 1536 in praise of a beautiful breast. The English verb, *to blazon,* thus came to mean to catalogue poetically.

Bob and Wheel The bob (usually consisting of a two-syllable line) and the wheel (a brief set of short lines) are used either singly or together as a kind of *envoi* (*q.v.*) or comment on the action of the stanza preceding them. See *Sir Gawain and the Green Knight* for a prime example.

Calvin, Calvinist John Calvin (1509–64), French organizer of the strict religious discipline of Geneva (Switzerland), and author of its *Institutes* (1st ed., 1536). Calvin's teachings include among other things, the doctrine of Scripture as the sole rule of faith, the denial of free will in fallen man, and God's absolute predestination of every man, before his creation, to salvation or to damnation. There are Calvinist elements in the Thirty-Nine Articles (1563) of the Church of England, but the English (as opposed to the Scottish) tradition modified the rigor of the doctrine; Milton passed through a phase of strict Calvinism into greater independence and a rejection of absolute predestination.

Carol, Carole Originally (apparently) a song sung to an accompaniment of dance, and often set out in ballad meter and uniform stanzas of which the leader probably sang the verse and the dancers a refrain; later, generally, a song of religious joy, usually rapid in pace.

Carpe Diem Literally, "seize the day"; from Horace's Ode I.xi, which ends, *Dum loquimur, fugerit invida / aetas: carpe diem, quam minimum credula postero* ("Even while we're talking, envious Time runs by: seize the day, putting a minimum of trust in tomorrow"). This became a standard theme of Ren-

aissance erotic verse, as in Robert Herrick's "Gather ye rosebuds while ye
may."

Cavalier Designating the supporters of Charles I and of the Anglican church
establishment, in opposition to the Puritans, or Roundheads, during the
English Civil War. In a literary context, the lyric poetry of some of these
so-named soldier-lover-poets (e.g. Thomas Carew, Richard Lovelace) is
implied with its elegant wit (*q.v.*) and grace. (See *Civil War*.)

Chanson d'aventure A French poetic form describing a conversation about love
or between lovers, and represented as overheard by the poet.

Civil War The struggle between Charles I and his Parliament came to a head in
1641, when the King tried forcibly to arrest five dissident members of Parliament. He failed, and in April 1642 raised his standard at Northampton,
intending to advance on London. For some time there was a military dead-
lock, but in January 1644 the Parliamentary forces, allied with the Scots,
defeated the King at Marston Moor. The Parliament men now controlled the
North, but not until they instituted major military reforms did they overcome
the King decisively at Naseby in June 1645. Charles became the captive of
Parliament in January 1647 and was executed two years later. In 1653 Oliver
Cromwell expelled the "Rump" of the Long Parliament (*q.v.*), which had
survived since 1640, and became Lord Protector.

The terms "Cavalier" and "Roundhead," implying respectively aristocratic
dash and middle-class puritanism, are not wholly misleading as descriptive
of the Royalist and Parliamentary sides in the war; but the fact of new money
and religious fervor on the winning side was not the whole story. The split
between "Presbyterian" and "Independent" in the Parliament faction was
partly religious, partly a division between the affluent and the enthusiastic;
and with the victory of the "monied" interest the Revolution itself became
conservative. But the execution of the King was an event that for a century
or more resonated throughout the course of English history, and, as Marvell
understood (see his "Horation Ode"), ended a whole phase of civilization.

Complaint Short poetic monologue, expressing the poet's sorrow at unrequited
love or other pains and ending with a request for relief from them.

Complexion See *Temperaments*.

Conceit From the Italian *concetto*, "concept" or "idea"; used in Renaissance poetry
to mean a precise and detailed comparison of something more remote or abstract with something more present or concrete, and often detailed through
a chain of metaphors or similes (see *Rhetoric*). In Petrarchan (*q.v.*) poetry,
certain conceits became conventionalized and were used again and again in
various versions. The connection between the Lady's eyes and the Sun, so
typical of these, was based on the proportion *her gaze : love's life and day ::
sun's shining: world's life and daylight.* Conceits were closely linked to emblems (*q.v.*), to the degree that the verbal connection between the emblem
picture and its *significatio,* or meaning, was detailed in an interpretive conceit. See also *Personification*.

Contemptus Mundi Contempt for the world, i.e. rejection of temporal and transitory pleasures and values in favor of the spiritual and eternal.

Contraries See *Qualities*.

Courtly Love Modern scholarship has coined this name for a set of conventions around which medieval love-poetry was written. It was essentially chivalric and a product of 12th-century France, especially of the troubadours. This poetry involves an idealization of the beloved woman, whose love, like all love, refines and ennobles the lover so that the union of their minds and/or bodies—a union that ought not to be apparent to others—allows them to attain excellence of character.

Dance of Death Poem accompanied by illustrations on the inevitability and universality of death, which is shown seizing men and women of all ranks and occupations, one after the other.

Decorum Propriety of discourse; what is becoming in action, character, and style; the avoidance of impossibilities and incongruities in action, style, and character: "the good grace of everything after his kind" and the "great masterpiece to observe." More formally, a neoclassical doctrine maintaining that literary style—grand, or high, middle, and low—be appropriate to the subject, occasion, and genre. Thus Milton, in *Paradise Lost* (I.13–14), invokes his "adventurous song, / That with no middle flight intends to soar. . . ." See also *Rhetoric*.

Digressio Interpolated story or description in a poem or oration, introduced for ornamentation or some structural purpose.

Dissenters In England, members of Protestant churches and sects that do not conform to the doctrines of the established Church of England; from the 16th century on, this would include Baptists, Puritans of various sorts within the Anglican Church, Presbyterians, Congregationalists, and (in the 18th century) Methodists. Another term, more current in the 19th century, is *Nonconformist*.

Dream Vision, Dream Allegory A popular medieval poetic form. Its fictional time is usually Spring; as the poet falls alseep in some pleasant place—a wood or garden—to the music of a stream and the song of birds, he dreams of "real" people or personified abstractions, who illuminate for him the nature of some aspect of knowledge, mode of behavior, or social or political question. See also *Allegory*.

Elegy Originally, in Greek and Latin poetry, a poem composed not in the hexameter lines of epic (*q.v.*) and, later, of pastoral, but in the elegiac couplets consisting of one hexameter line followed by a pentameter. Elegiac poetry was amatory, epigrammatic. By the end of the 16th century, English poets were using heroic couplets (*q.v.*), to stand for both hexameters and elegiacs; and an elegiac poem was any serious meditative piece. Perhaps because of the tradition of the pastoral elegy (*q.v.*), the general term "elegy" came to be reserved, in modern terminology, for an elaborate and formal lament, longer than a *dirge* or *threnody*, for a dead person. By extension, "elegiac" has come to mean, in general speech, broodingly sad.

Elements In ancient and medieval science, the four basic substances of which all matter was composed: earth, water, air, fire—in order of density and heaviness. They are often pictured in that order in diagrams of the universe. All four elements, being material, are below the sphere of the moon (above, there is a fifth: the quintessence). The elements are formed of combinations of the

Qualities (*q.v.*) or Contraries: the union of hot and dry makes fire; of hot and moist, air; of cold and moist, water; of cold and dry, earth.

Emblem   A simple allegorical picture, or *impresa*, labeled with a motto to show its significance, and usually accompanied by a poetic description that connects the picture or "device" with the meaning, frequently by means of elaborate conceits (*q.v.*), sometimes with more obvious moralizing. Many Renaissance paintings are emblems, without the text. The first Renaissance emblem book was that of the Venetian lawyer Andrea Alciati, in 1531; for the next century and one-half, the pictures and verses were copied, translated, expanded upon, added to, and adapted in French, Dutch, Spanish, German, and Italian as well as his original Latin. Famous English books of emblems were those of Geoffrey Whitney (1586), Henry Peacham (*Minerva Brittana, or A Garden of Heroical Devices,* 1612), George Wither (1635), and Francis Quarles (1635). Based originally on classical mythography, an interest in ancient coins and statuary, as well as "hieroglyphics" in all ancient art, emblem traditions generally divided, in the 17th century, into "Jesuitical" types (involving precise and intense images such as tears, wings, hearts, and classical Cupids signifying not *amor*, but *caritas*), and more pragmatic Protestant emblems (particularly in the Dutch tradition), which tend toward genre scenes of everyday life illustrating proverbs in the text. In the Renaissance, pictures were to be *read* and understood, like texts; and this kind of reading of hieroglyphics extends, in a writer like Sir Thomas Browne, to all of creation:

> The world's a book in folio, printed all
> With God's great works in letters capital:
> Each creature is a page, and each effect
> A fair character, void of all defect.

These lines of Joshua Sylvester are a commonplace. See also *Conceit; Symbolism;* and Figs. 16–21 in illustrations for the Renaissance section of this Anthology.

Enjambment   The "straddling" of a clause or sentence across two lines of verse, as opposed to closed, or end-stopped, lines. Thus, in the opening lines of Shakespeare's *Twelfth Night:*

> If music be the food of love, play on!
> Give me excess of it, that, surfeiting
> The appetite may sicken and so die . . .

the first line is stopped, the second enjambed. When enjambment becomes strong or violent, it may have an ironic or comic effect.

The Enlightenment   A term used very generally, to refer to the late 17th and the 18th century in Europe, a period characterized by a programmatic rationalism—i.e. a belief in the ability of human reason to understand the world and thereby to transform whatever in it needed transforming; an age in which ideas of science and progress accompanied the rise of new philosophies of the relation of man to the state, an age which saw many of its hopes for human betterment fulfilled in the French Revolution.

Envoi, Envoy   Short concluding stanza found in certain French poetic forms and their English imitations, e.g. the *ballade* (*q.v.*). It serves as a dedicatory postscript, and a summing up of the poem of which it repeats the refrain.

Epic Or, *heroic poetry;* originally, oral narrative delivered in a style different from that of normal discourse by reason of verse, music, and heightened diction, and concerning the great deeds of a central heroic figure, or group of figures, usually having to do with a crisis in the history of a race or culture. Its setting lies in this earlier "heroic" period, and it will often have been written down only after a long period of oral transmission. The Greek *Iliad* and *Odyssey* and the Old English *Beowulf* are examples of this, in their narration mixing details from both the heroic period described and the actual time of their own composition and narration. What is called *secondary* or *literary* epic is a long, ambitious poem, composed by a single poet on the model of the older, primary forms, and of necessity being more allusive and figurative than its predecessors. Homer's poems lead to Virgil's *Aeneid,* which leads to Milton's *Paradise Lost,* in a chain of literary dependency. Spenser's *Faerie Queene* might be called *romantic epic* of the secondary sort, and Dante's *Divine Comedy* might also be assimilated to post-Virgilian epic tradition.

Epic Simile An extended comparison, in Homeric and subsequently in Virgilian and later epic poetry, between an event in the story (the *fable*) and something in the experience of the epic audience, to the effect of making the fabulous comprehensible in terms of the familiar. From the Renaissance on, additional complications have emerged from the fact that what is the familiar for the classical audience becomes, because of historical change, itself fabled (usually, pastoral) for the modern audience. Epic similes compare the fabled with the familiar usually with respect to one property or element; thus, in the *Odyssey,* when the stalwart forward motion of a ship in high winds is described, the simile goes:

> And as amids a fair field four brave horse
> Before a chariot, stung into their course
> With fervent lashes of the smarting scourge
> That all their fire blows high, and makes them rise
> To utmost speed the measure of their ground:
> So bore the ship aloft her fiery bound
> About whom rushed the billows, black and vast
> In which the sea-roars burst . . .
> (*Chapman translation*)

Notice the formal order of presentation: "even as . . .": *the familiar event, often described in detail;* "just so . . .": *the fabled one.*

Epicureanism A system of philosophy founded by the Greek Epicurus (342–270 B.C.), who taught that the five senses are the sole source of ideas and sole criterion of truth, and that the goal of human life is pleasure (i.e. hedonism), though this can be achieved only by practicing moderation. Later the term came to connote bestial self-indulgence, which Epicurus had clearly rejected.

Exclamatio Rhetorical figure representing a cry of admiration or grief.

Exemplum A short narrative used to illustrate a moral point in didactic literature (especially sermons) or in historical writing. Its function is to recommend or dissuade from a particular course of conduct.

Fabliau A short story in verse, comic in character, its subject matter often indecent, and the joke hinging on sex or excretion. The plot usually involves a witty turn or practical joke, the motive of which is love or revenge. See The Miller's Tale of Chaucer.

Fathers of the Church The earliest Christian theologians and ecclesiastical writers (also referred to as "patristic"), flourishing from the late 1st century through the 8th, composing severally in Greek or Latin. Well-known "Fathers" are St. Augustine, St. Jerome, Tertullian.

Feudal System The system of land tenure and political allegiance characteristic of Europe during the Middle Ages. The king, as owner of all land, gives portions of it to his vassals, by whom it can be passed on to heirs, in return for their pledge of loyalty and of specified military service. These nobles divide their land among their followers, the subdivision continuing until it reaches the serfs, who cultivate the land but must hand over most of their produce to the lord.

Figurative Language In a general sense, any shift away from a literal meaning of words, brought about by the use of tropes (*q.v.*) or other rhetorical devices. See *Rhetoric*.

Figure As defined by Erich Auerbach in his essay "Figura," a mode of interpretation establishing a connection between two events or persons, the first of which signifies both itself and the second, while the second encompasses or fulfills the first—e.g. the Eucharist, which is the "figure" of Christ. See *Allegory*.

Free Verse, Vers Libre Generally, any English verse form whose lines are measured neither by the number of 1) stressed syllables (see *Meter* §3, accentual verse), 2) alternations of stressed and unstressed syllables (§4, accentual-syllabic verse), nor syllables alone (§2, syllabic verse). The earliest English free verse —that of Christopher Smart in *Jubilate Agno* (18th century)—imitates the prosody of Hebrew poetry (reflected also in the translation of the English Bible), in maintaining unmeasured units marked by syntactic parallelism. While many free-verse traditions (e.g. that of Walt Whitman) remain close to the impulses of this biblical poetry, yet others, in the 20th century, have developed new *ad hoc* patternings of their own. *Vers libre* usually refers to the experimental, frequently very short unmeasured lines favored by poets of the World War I period, although the term, rather than the form, was adopted from French poetry of the 19th century.

Gothic Term (originally pejorative, as alluding to the Teutonic barbarians) designating the architectural style of the Middle Ages. The revival of interest in medieval architecture in the later 18th century produced not only pseudo-Gothic castles like Horace Walpole's "Strawberry Hill", and more modest artificial ruins on modern estates, but also a vogue for atmospheric prose romances set in medieval surroundings and involving improbable terrors, and known as Gothic novels. The taste for the Gothic, arising during the Age of Sensibility (*q.v.*), is another reflection of a reaction against earlier 18th-century neoclassicism (*q.v*).

Hermetic, Hermeticism, Hermetist Terms referring to a synthesis of Neoplatonic and other occult philosophies, founded on a collection of writings attributed to Hermes Trismegistus ("Thrice-greatest Hermes"—a name given the Egyptian god Thoth), but which in fact date from the 2nd and 3rd centuries A.D. An important doctrine was that of correspondences between earthly and heavenly things. By studying these correspondences, a man might "walk to the sky" (in the words of Henry Vaughan) in his lifetime. Hermetic tradition favored *esoteric* or forbidden knowledge, over what could be more publicly avowed.

Heroic Couplet In English prosody, a pair of rhyming, iambic pentameter lines, used at first for closure—as at the end of the Shakespearean sonnet (*q.v.*)—or to terminate a scene in blank-verse drama; later adapted to correspond in English poetry to the elegiac couplet of classical verse as well as to the heroic, unrhymed, Greek and Latin hexameter. Octosyllabic couplets, with four stresses (eight syllables) to the line, are a minor, shorter, jumpier form, used satirically unless in implicit allusion to the form of Milton's "Il Penseroso," in which they develop great lyrical power. (See *Meter.*)

Humors The combinations, in men and women (the *microcosm*) of the qualities (*q.v.*), or contraries. In primitive physiology, the four principal bodily fluids in their combinations produce the temperaments (*q.v.*) or "complexions" These "humors," with their properties and effects—at least in the Middle Ages—are, respectively: Blood (hot and moist)—cheerfulness, warmth of feeling; Choler (hot and dry)—a quick, angry temper; Phlegm (cold and moist)—dull sluggishness; Melancholy (cold and dry)—fretful depression. The Renaissance introduced the concept of "artificial" humors—e.g. scholars' and artists' melancholy, creative brooding. The humors, the temperaments, and the four elements (*q.v.*) of the macrocosm, or universe, were all looked upon as interrelated. See *Renaissance Psychology.*

Irony Generally, a mode of saying one thing to mean another. *Sarcasm*, in which one means exactly the opposite of what one says, is the easiest and cheapest form; thus, .e.g. "Yeah, it's a *nice day!*" when one means that it's a miserable one. But serious literature produces ironies of a much more complex and revealing sort. *Dramatic irony* occurs when a character in a play or story asserts something whose meaning the audience or reader knows will change in time. Thus, in Genesis when Abraham assures his son Isaac (whom he is about to sacrifice) that "God will provide his own lamb," the statement is lighted with dramatic irony when a sacrificial ram is actually provided at the last minute to save Isaac. Or, in the case of Sophocles' *Oedipus*, when almost everything the protagonist says about the predicament of his city is hideously ironic in view of the fact (which he does not know) that he is responsible therefor. The ironies generated by the acknowledged use of non-literal language (see *Rhetoric*) and fictions in drama, song, and narrative are at the core of imaginative literature.

Judgment In Catholic doctrine, God's retributive judgment, which decides the fate of rational creatures according to their merits and faults. Particular judgment is the decision about the eternal destiny of each soul made immediately after death; General (Last) Judgment is at the Second Coming of Christ as God and Man, when all men will be judged again in the sight of all the world. See Fig. 50 in illustrations for the Medieval section of this anthology.

Kenning An Old Norse form designating, strictly, a condensed simile or metaphor of the kind frequently used in Old Germanic poetry; a figurative circumlocution for a thing not actually named—e.g. "swan's path" for sea; "world-candle" or "sky-candle" for sun. More loosely, often used to mean also a metaphorical compound word or phrase such as "ring-necked" or "foamy-necked" for a ship, these being descriptive rather than figurative in character.

Lancastrians See *Wars of the Roses*.

Locus Amoenus Literally, "pleasant place"; a garden, either Paradise, the most perfect of all gardens, or its pagan equivalent, or the later literary garden that was a figure (*q.v.*) of Paradise. See *Topos*.

Long Parliament The Parliament summoned by Charles I on November 3, 1640; the last remnant, not dissolved until 1660, opposed the King and brought about his downfall and execution. See *Civil War*.

Macaronic Verse in which two languages are mingled, usually for burlesque purposes.

Machiavelli, Niccolò Italian diplomat, historian, and political theorist (1469–1527), whose chief work, *Il Principe* (*The Prince*, 1513), based in part on the career of Cesare Borgia, outlines a pragmatic rule of conduct for a ruler; thus, politics should have nothing to do with morality; the prince should be an exponent of ruthless power in behalf of his people. In England his theories were put into practice by Thomas Cromwell in the reign of Henry VIII; his writings, however, were not translated until the 17th century, and his image in England, based on rumor and the reports of his adversaries, fostered a myth of the evil "Machiavel" as he appears in Marlowe (*Titus Andronicus*) and Shakespeare (*Richard III*).

Madrigal Polyphonic setting of a poem, in the 16th and 17th centuries, for several voice parts, unaccompanied or with instruments. Because of the contrapuntal texture, the words were frequently obscured for a listener, though not for the performers.

Meter Verse may be made to differ from prose and from ordinary speech in a number of ways, and in various languages these ways may be very different. Broadly speaking, lines of verse may be marked out by the following regularities of pattern:

1. *Quantitative Verse*, used in ancient Greek poetry and adopted by the Romans, used a fixed number of what were almost musical measures, called *feet;* they were built up of long and short syllables (like half- and quarter-notes in music), which depended on the vowel and consonants in them. *Stress accent* (the *word* stress which, when accompanied by vowel reduction, distinguishes the English noun "content" from the adjective "content") did not exist in ancient Greek, and played no part in the rhythm of the poetic line. Thus, the first line of the *Odyssey: Andra moi ennepe mousa, polytropon hos mala polla* ("Sing me, O muse, of that man of many resources who, after great hardship . . .") is composed in *dactyls* of one long syllable followed by two shorts (but, as in musical rhythm, replaceable by two longs, a *spondee*).

With six dactyls to a line, the resulting meter is called *dactylic hexameter* (*hexameter*, for short), the standard form for epic poetry. Other kinds of foot or measure were: the *anapest* ($\cup \cup -$); the *iamb* ($\cup -$); the *trochee* ($- \cup$); and a host of complex patterns used in lyric poetry. Because of substitutions, however, the number of syllables in a classical line was not fixed, only the number of measures.

2. *Syllabic Verse*, used in French, Japanese, and many other languages, and in English poetry of the mid-20th century, measures only the *number* of syllables per line with no regard to considerations of *quantity* or *stress*. Because of the prominence of stress in the English language, two lines of the same purely syllabic length may not necessarily sound at all as though they were in the same meter, e.g.:

> These two incommensurably sounding
> Lines are both written with ten syllables.

3. *Accentual Verse*, used in early Germanic poetry, and thus in Old English poetry, depended upon the number of strong *stress accents* per line. These accents were four in number, with no fixed number of unstressed. Folk poetry and nursery rhymes often preserve this accentual verse, e.g.:

> Sing, sing, what shall I sing?
> The cat's run away with the pudding-bag string

The first line has six syllables, the second, eleven, but they sound more alike (and not merely by reason of their rhyme) than the two syllabic lines quoted above.

4. *Accentual-Syllabic Verse*, the traditional meter of English poetry from Chaucer on, depends upon both numbered *stresses* and numbered *syllables*, a standard form consisting of ten syllables alternately stressed and unstressed, and having five stresses; thus it may be said to consist of five syllable pairs.

For complex historical reasons, accentual-syllabic groups of stressed and unstressed syllables came to be known by the names used for Greek and Latin feet—which can be very confusing. The analogy was made between *long* syllables in the classical languages, and *stressed* syllables in English. Thus, the pair of syllables in the adjective "*content*" is called an *iamb*, and in the noun "*content*," a *trochee*; the word "classical" is a *dactyll*, and the phrase "of the best," an *anapest*. When English poetry is being discussed, these terms are always used in their adapted, accentual-syllabic meanings, and hence the ten-syllable line mentioned earlier is called "iambic pentameter" in English. The phrase "high-tide" would be a *spondee* (as would, in general, two monosyllables comprising a proper name, e.g. "John Smith"); whereas compound nouns like "highway" would be *trochaic*. In this adaptation of classical nomenclature, the terms *dimeter, trimeter, tetrameter, pentameter, hexameter* refer not to the number of quantitative feet but to the number of syllable-groups (pairs or triplets, from one to six) composing the line. Iambic pentameter and tetrameter lines are frequently also called *decasyllabic* and *octosyllabic* respectively.

5. *Versification*. In verse, lines may be arranged in patterns called *stichic*

or *strophic*, that is, the same linear form (say, iambic pentameter) repeated without grouping by rhyme or interlarded lines of another form, or varied in just such a way into *stanzas* or *strophes* ("turns"). Unrhymed iambic pentameter, called *blank verse*, is the English stichic form that Milton thought most similar to classic hexameter or *heroic* verse. But in the Augustan period iambic pentameter rhymed pairs, called heroic couplets (*q.v.*), came to stand for this ancient form as well as for the classical elegiac verse (*q.v.*). Taking couplets as the simplest strophic unit, we may proceed to *tercets* (groups of three lines) and to *quatrains* (groups of four), rhymed *abab* or *abcb*, and with equal or unequal line lengths. Other stanzaic forms: *ottava rima*, an eight-line, iambic pentameter stanza, rhyming *abababcc*; *Spenserian stanza*, rhyming *ababbcbcc*, all pentameter save for the last line, an iambic hexameter, or *alexandrine*. There have been adaptations in English (by Shelley, notably, and without rhyme by T. S. Eliot) of the Italian *terza rima* used by Dante in *The Divine Comedy*, interlocking tercets rhyming *aba bcb cdc ded*, etc. More elaborate stanza forms developed in the texts of some Elizabethan songs and in connection with the ode (*q.v.*).

Microcosm Literally, "the small world"—man. For fuller explanation see selections of Walter Ralegh and Thomas Browne on this theme. See also *Astronomy, Astrology; Humors; Qualities.*

Mirror for Princes A treatise setting out the education necessary to make a ruler and the modes of mental, moral, and physical activity that befitted him.

Mock-heroic, Mock-epic The literary mode resulting when low or trivial subjects are treated in the high, artificial literary language of classical epic (*q.v.*) poetry. The point of the joke is usually to expose not the inadequacies of the style but those of the subject, although occasionally the style may be caricatured, and the joke made about decorum (*q.v.*) itself. Alexander Pope's *The Rape of the Lock* is a famous example.

Music of the Spheres The ancient fiction held that the celestial spheres made musical sounds, either by rubbing against the ether, or because an angel—the Christian replacement for the Intelligence which in Plato's *Timaeus* guided each one—sang while riding on his charge. The inaudibility of this music was ascribed by later Platonism (*q.v.*) to the imprisonment of the soul in the body, and by Christian writers, to man's fallen state. Frequent attempts were made to preserve some meaning for this beautiful idea: thus, Aristotle's conclusion that the continuous presence of such sounds would make them inaudible to habituated ears (a sophisticated prefiguration of the modern notion of background noise). And thus the belief of the Ptolemaic astronomy that at a certain point the ratios of the diameters of the spheres of the various heavenly bodies were "harmonious" in that they would generate the overtone series. Even Kepler, who demonstrated that the planetary orbits, let alone non-existent spheres, could not be circular, suggested that the ratios of the angular velocities of the planets would generate a series of melodies; he then proceeded to put them together contrapuntally. See *Astronomy and Astrology.*

Myth A primitive story explaining the origins of certain phenomena in the world and in human life, and usually embodying gods or other supernatural forces, heroes (men who are either part human and part divine, or are placed between an ordinary mortal and a divine being), men, and animals. Literature continues to incorporate myths long after the mythology (the system of stories containing them) ceases to be a matter of actual belief. Moreover, discarded beliefs of all sorts tend to become myths when they are remembered but no longer literally clung to, and are used in literature in a similar way. The classical mythology of the Greeks and Romans was apprehended in this literary, or interpreted, way, even in ancient times. The gods and heroes and their deeds came to be read as allegory (*q.v.*). During the Renaissance, *mythography*—the interpretation of myths in order to make them reveal a moral or historical significance (rather than merely remaining entertaining but insignificant stories)—was extremely important, both for literature and for painting and sculpture. In modern criticism, mythical or *archetypal* situations and personages have been interpreted as being central objects of the work of the imagination.

Neoclassicism   (1) In general the term refers to Renaissance and post-Renaissance attempts to model enterprises in the various arts on Roman and Greek originals—or as much as was known of them. Thus, in the late Renaissance, the architectural innovations of Andrea Palladio may be called "neoclassic," as may Ben Jonson's relation, and Alexander Pope's as well, to the Roman poet Horace. The whole Augustan period in English literary history (1660–1740) was a deliberately neoclassical one.

(2) More specifically, neoclassicism refers to that period in the history of all European art spanning the very late 18th and early 19th century, which period may be seen as accompanying the fulfillment, and the termination, of the Enlightenment (*q.v.*). In England such neoclassic artists as Henry Fuseli, John Flaxman, George Romney, and even, in some measure, William Blake, are close to the origins of pictorial and literary Romanticism itself.

Neoplatonism   See *Platonism.*

Nonconformist   See *Dissenters.*

Octosyllabic Couplet   See *Heroic Couplet; Meter.*

Ode   A basic poetic form, originating in Greek antiquity. The *choral ode* was a public event, sung and danced, at a large ceremony, or as part of the tragic and comic drama. Often called *Pindaric ode,* after a great Greek poet, the form consisted of *triads* (groups of three sections each). These were units of song and dance, and had the form *aab*—that is, a *strophe* (or "turn"), an *antistrophe* (or "counter-turn"), and an *epode* (or "stand"), the first two being identical musically and metrically, the third different. In English poetry, the Pindaric ode form, only in its metrical aspects, became in the 17th century a mode for almost essayistic poetic comment, and was often used also as a kind of cantata libretto, in praise of music and poetry (the so-called *musical ode*). By the 18th century the ode became the form for a certain kind of personal, visionary poem, and it is this form that Wordsworth and Coleridge transmitted to Romantic tradition. A second English form, known as *Horatian ode,* was based on the lyric (not choral) poems of Horace, and is written in *aabb* quatrains, with the last two lines shorter than the first two by a pair of syllables or more.

Oral Formula A conventional, fossilized phrase common in poetry composed as it was recited, or composed to be recited, and repeated frequently in a single poem. It serves as either a means of slowing or even stopping the action momentarily, or of filling out a verse: e.g. "Beowulf, son of Ecgtheow," or "go or ride"—i.e. "whatever you do."

Paradox In logic, a self-contradictory statement, hence meaningless (or a situation producing one), with an indication that something is wrong with the language in which such a situation can occur, e.g. the famous paradox of Epimenedes the Cretan, who held that all Cretans are liars (and thus could be lying if— and only if—he wasn't), or that of Zeno, of the arrow in flight: since at any instant of time the point of the arrow can always be said to be at one precise point, therefore it is continually at rest at a continuous sequence of such points, and therefore never moves. In literature, however, particularly in the language of lyric poetry, paradox plays another role. From the beginnings of lyric poetry, paradox has been deemed necessary to express feelings and other aspects of human inner states, e.g. Sappho's invention of the Greek word *glykypikron* ("bittersweet") to describe love, or her assertion that she was freezing and burning at the same time. So too the Latin poet Catullus, in his famous couplet

> I'm in hate and I'm in love; why do I? you may ask.
> Well, I don't know, but I feel it, and I'm in agony.

may be declaring thereby that true love poetry must be illogical.

In Elizabethan poetry, paradoxes were frequently baldly laid out in the rhetorical form called *oxymoron* (see *Rhetoric*), as in "the victor-victim," or across a fairly mechanical sentence structure, as in "My feast of joy is but a dish of pain." In the highest poetic art, however, the seeming self-contradiction is removed when one realizes that either, or both, of the conflicting terms is to be taken figuratively, rather than literally. The apparent absurdity, or strangeness, thus gives rhetorical power to the utterance. Elaborate and sophisticated paradoxes, insisting on their own absurdity, typify the poetic idiom of the tradition of John Donne.

Pastoral A literary mode in which the lives of simple country people are celebrated, described, and used allegorically by sophisticated urban poets and writers. The *idylls* of Sicilian poet Theocritus (3rd century B.C.) were imitated and made more symbolic in Virgil's *eclogues;* shepherds in an Arcadian landscape stood for literary and political personages, and the Renaissance adapted these narrative and lyric pieces for moral and aesthetic discussion. Spenser's *Shepheardes Calendar* is an experimental collection of eclogues involving an array of forms and subjects. In subsequent literary tradition, the pastoral imagery of both Old and New Testaments (Psalms, Song of Songs, priest as *pastor* or shepherd of his flock, and so on) joins with the classical mode. Modern critics, William Empson in particular, have seen the continuation of pastoral tradition in other versions of the country-city confrontation, such as child-adult and criminal-businessman. See *Pastoral Elegy*.

Pastoral Elegy A form of lament for the death of a poet, originating in Greek bucolic tradition (Bion's lament for Adonis, a lament for Bion by a fellow poet, Theocritus' first idyll, Virgil's tenth eclogue) and continued in use by Renaissance poets as a public mode for the presentation of private, inner, and even coterie matters affecting poets and their lives, while conventionally treating questions of general human importance. At a death one is moved to ask, "Why this death? Why now?" and funeral elegy must always confront these questions, avoiding easy resignation as an answer. Pastoral elegy handled these questions with formal mythological apparatus, such as the Muses, who should have protected their dead poet, local spirits, and other presences appropriate to the circumstances of the life and death, and perhaps figures of more general mythological power. The end of such poems is the eternalization of the dead poet in a monument of myth, stronger than stone or bronze: Spenser's *Astrophel*, a lament for Sir Philip Sidney, concludes with an Ovidian change—the dead poet's harp, like Orpheus' lyre, becomes the constellation Lyra. Milton's *Lycidas* both exemplifies and transforms the convention. Later examples include Shelley's *Adonais* (for Keats), Arnold's *Thyrsis* (for Clough), and Swinburne's *Ave Atque Vale* (for Baudelaire).

Penance In Catholic doctrine, the moral virtue by which a sinner is disposed to hate his sin as an offense against God; and the sacrament, of which the outward signs are the acknowledgment of sin, self-presentation of the sinner to priest to confess his sins, the absolution pronounced by the priest, and the satisfaction (penance) imposed on the sinner by the priest and to be performed before the sinner is delivered from his guilt. See Figs. 32 and 52 in illustrations for the Medieval section of this Anthology.

Peroration Final part of an oration, reviewing and summarizing the argument, often in an impassioned form. (See also *Rhetoric*.)

Personification Treating a thing or, more properly, an abstract quality, as though it were a person. Thus, "Surely *goodness* and *mercy* shall follow me all the days of my life" tends to personify the italicized terms by reason of the metaphoric use of "follow me." On the other hand, a conventional, complete personification, like *Justice* (whom we recognize by her *attributes*—she is blindfolded, she has scales and a sword) might also be called an *allegorical figure* in her own right, and her attributes *symbols* (blindness = impartiality; scales = justly deciding; sword = power to mete out what is deserved). Often the term "personification" applies to momentary, or *ad hoc*, humanizations.

Petrarch, Petrarchan Francesco Petrarca (1304–74), the Italian founder of humanistic studies, with their revival of Greek and Latin literature, was influential in Renaissance England chiefly for his *Rime sparse*, the collection of love sonnets in praise of his muse, Laura. These poems, translated and adapted in England from the 1530's on, provided not only the sonnet (*q.v.*) form but also many devices of imagery widely used by English poets of the 16th and 17th centuries.

Physiognomics The "art to read the mind's complexion in the face." From ancient times to the Renaissance, it was believed possible to gauge a person's character precisely from his outward appearance and physical characteristics.

Platonism The legacy of Plato (429–347 B.C.) is virtually the history of philosophy. His *Timaeus* was an important source of later cosmology; his doctrine of ideas is central to Platonic tradition. His doctrine of love (especially in the *Symposium*) had enormous influence in the Renaissance, at which time its applicability was shifted to heterosexual love specifically. The *Republic* and the *Laws* underlie a vast amount of political thought, and the *Republic* contains also a philosophical attack on poetry (fiction) which defenders of the arts have always had to answer. Neoplatonism—a synthesis of Platonism, Pythagoreanism, and Aristotelianism—was dominant in the 3rd century A.D.; and the whole tradition was revived in the 15th and 16th centuries. The medieval Plato was Latinized, largely at second-hand; the revival of Greek learning in the 15th century led to another Neoplatonism: a synthesis of Platonism, the medieval Christian Aristotle, and Christian doctrine. Out of this came the doctrines of love we associate with some Renaissance poetry; a sophisticated version of older systems of allegory and symbol; and notions of the relation of spirit and matter reflected in Marvell and many other poets.

Prayer Book   The Book of Common Prayer, containing the order of services in the Church of England. Based on translations from medieval service books, it first appeared in 1549, under the direction of Thomas Cranmer (1489–1556), Archbishop of Canterbury. It was much revised, partly to meet Puritan complaints, but in 1662 achieved the form it has since kept, with only slight alteration.

Purgatory   According to Catholic doctrine, a place or condition of temporal punishment for those who die in the grace of God, but without having made full satisfaction for their transgressions. In Purgatory they are purified so as to be fit to come into God's presence.

Quadrivium   The second division of the seven liberal arts, which together with the trivium (*q.v.*) comprised the full course of a medieval education and fitted a man to study theology, the crown of the arts and sciences. The quadrivium consisted of music, arithmetic, geometry, and astronomy.

Qualities Or **contraries;** the properties of all material things, the various combinations of which were held to determine their nature. They were four in number, in two contrasting pairs: hot and cold; moist and dry. See *Elements; Humors; Temperaments.*

Recusant   Literally, "refuser"; in the Elizabethan period, anyone who refused to join the Church of England—although now the term is commonly used to allude to "popish recusants," i.e. Roman Catholics, and "recusancy," to English writings of certain Catholics during the late 16th century.

Renaissance Psychology   Poetic language, particularly that of lyric poetry, is always implicitly raising assumptions about inner states of people who have feelings and who wish to express them. In the Renaissance, several informal ways coexisted of talking about the relation which we now see as one of mind and body. From Aristotelian tradition the concept of three orders of soul was maintained: in ascending order these were the *vegetable* (the "life," immobile and inactive, of plants), the *animal* (accounting for the behavior of beasts), and the *rational* (the power of reason, often associated with language as well as thought, in men). On the other hand, *wit* (*q.v.*) meant intellect, and in Elizabethan language, the conflict of *wit* and *will* correspond roughly, but not precisely, to a modern opposition of reason and emotion. Physical, as well as psychological, human diversity was explained by the theory of the humors and temperaments (*qq.v.*). On the other hand, there were mysterious entities called *spirits* (associated with the Latin root, meaning "breath," and its application to alcoholic fluids: waters that "breathe" and "burn"). Spirits were fine vapors mediating between the body and the soul, and patching up a connection which scientific psychology is still trying to make. *Natural spirits* came from the liver and circulated through the veins. *Vital spirits* came from the heart and circulated arterially. *Animal spirits* were distilled from the vital spirits (which can be associated with blood) and went to the brain through the nerves, which were thought to be conducting vessels. (See the selection from Burton's *Anatomy of Melancholy*.) Other faculties of the soul included the power of *fancy* or *fantasy* (the word "imagination" most often referred to something imagined, rather than to a faculty).

Reverdie Old French dance poem imitated in other languages, usually consisting of five or six stanzas without refrain, in joyful celebration of the coming of Spring.

Rhetoric In classical times, rhetoric was the art of persuading through the use of language. The major treatises on style and structure of discourse—Aristotle's *Rhetoric*, Quintilian's *Institutes of Oratory*, the *Rhetorica ad Herrenium* ascribed for centuries to Cicero—were concerned with the "arts" of language in the older sense of "skills." In the Middle Ages the *trivium* (*q.v.*), or program that led to the degree of Bachelor of Arts, consisted of grammar, logic, and rhetoric, but it was an abstract study, based on the Roman tradition. In the Renaissance, classical rhetorical study became a matter of the first importance, and it led to the study of literary stylistics and the application of principles and concepts of the production and structure of eloquence to the higher eloquence of poetry.

Rhetoricians distinguished three stages in the production of discourse: *inventio* (finding or discovery), *dispositio* (arranging), and *elocutio* (style). Since the classical discipline aimed always at practical oratory (e.g. winning a case in court, or making a point effectively in council), *memoria* (memory) and *pronuntiatio* (delivery) were added. For the Renaissance, however, rhetoric became the art of writing. Under the heading of *elocutio*, style became stratified into three levels, *elevated* or high, *elegant* or middle, and *plain* or low. The proper fitting of these styles to the subject of discourse comprised the subject of decorum (*q.v.*).

Another area of rhetorical theory was concerned with classification of devices of language into *schemes*, *tropes*, and *figures*. A basic but somewhat confused distinction between figures of speech and figures of thought need not concern us here, but we may roughly distinguish between schemes (or patterns) of words, and tropes as manipulations of meanings, and of making words non-literal.

Common Schemes

anadiplosis repeating the terminal word in a clause as the start of the next one: "Pleasure might cause her read; reading might cause her know; / Knowledge might pity win, and pity grace obtain" (Sidney, *Astrophel and Stella*).

anaphora the repetition of a word or phrase at the openings of successive clauses, e.g. "The Lord sitteth above the water floods. The Lord remaineth King forever. The Lord shall give strength unto his people. The Lord shall give his people the blessing of peace."

chiasmus a pattern of criss-crossing a syntactic structure, whether of noun and adjective, e.g. "Empty his bottle, and his girlfriend gone," or of a reversal of normal syntax with similar effect, e.g. "A fop her passion, and her prize, a sot," reinforced by assonance (*q.v.*). Chiasmus may even extend to assonance, as in Coleridge's line "In Xanadu did Kubla Khan."

Common Tropes

metaphor and simile both involve comparison of one thing to another, the difference being that the *simile* will actually compare, using the words "like" or "as," while the metaphor identifies one with the other, thus producing a non-literal use of a word or attribution. Thus, Robert Burns's "O, my love is like a red, red rose / That's newly sprung in June" is a simile; had Burns written, "My love, thou art a red, red rose . . .", it would have been a metaphor—and indeed, it would not mean that the lady had acquired petals. In modern critical theory, *metaphor* has come to stand for various non-expository kinds of evocative signification. I. A. Richards, the modern critic most interested in a general theory of metaphor in this sense, has contributed the terms *tenor* (as in the case above, the girl) and *vehicle* (the rose) to designate the components. See also *Epic Simile*.

metonymy a trope in which the vehicle is closely and conventionally associated with the tenor, e.g. "crown" and "king," "pen" and "writing," "pencil" and "drawing," "sword" and "warfare."

synecdoche a trope in which the part stands for the whole, e.g. "sail" for "ship."

hyperbole intensifying exaggeration, e.g. the combined synecdoche and hyperbole in which Christopher Marlowe's Faustus asks of Helen of Troy "Is this the face that launched a thousand ships / And burned the topless towers of Ilium?"

oxymoron literally, sharp-dull; a figure of speech involving a witty paradox, e.g. "sweet harm"; "darkness visible" (Milton, *Paradise Lost* I.63).

Rhyme Royal See *Troilus stanza*.

Right Reason A natural faculty of intelligence in man, his capability of choosing between moral alternatives. In the humanism of the Renaissance, Aristotle's term, *orthos logos*, associated with the Latin word *ratio*, was thought of as having preceded the fallen knowledge acquired in Paradise by Adam and Eve's first sin.

Romance (1) A medieval tale of chivalric or amorous adventure, in prose or verse, with the specification that the material be fictional. Later on, there developed cycles of stories, such as those involving Arthurian material or the legends of Charlemagne. Many of these, particularly the Arthurian, came to involve the theme of courtly love (*q.v.*)

(2) In the Renaissance, romance becomes more complex and literary, involving some degree of consciousness on the part of the author that he was reworking medieval materials (Spenser's *Faerie Queene*, of Arthurian legends; Ariosto's *Orlando Furioso*, of Charlemagne's heroic knight; Tasso's *Gerusalemme Liberata*, of stories of the Crusades).

(3) Prose romance, the 19th-century outgrowth of earlier essays into the

Gothic (*q.v.*) tale, represents a poetic kind of narrative to be clearly distinguished (in England if not in America) from the mode of the novel (e.g. Mary Shelley's *Frankenstein* and Hawthorne's *The Scarlet Letter* are both prose romance).

Rondeau, Roundel   A strict French poetic form, thirteen lines of eight to ten syllables, divided into stanzas of five, three, and five lines, using two rhymes only and repeating the first word or first few words of line one after the second and third stanzas. The two terms are used interchangeably in the Middle Ages.

Satire   A literary mode painting a distorted verbal picture of part of the world in order to show its true moral, as opposed merely to its physical, nature. In this sense, Circe, the enchantress in Homer's *Odyssey* who changed Odysseus' men into pigs (because they made pigs of themselves while eating) and would have changed Odysseus into a fox (for he was indeed foxy), was the first satirist. Originally the Latin word *satura* meant a kind of literary grab bag, or medley, and a satire was a fanciful kind of tale in mixed prose and verse; but later a false etymology connected the word with *satyr* and thus with the grotesque. Satire may be in verse or in prose; in the 16th and 17th centuries, the Roman poets Horace and Juvenal were imitated and expanded upon by writers of satiric moral verse, the tone of the verse being wise, smooth, skeptical, and urbane, that of the prose, sharp, harsh, and sometimes nasty. A tradition of English verse satire runs through Donne, Jonson, Dryden, Pope, and Samuel Johnson; of prose satire, Addison, Swift, and Fielding.

Scholasticism, Schoolmen   Scholasticism is the term used for the philosophy and theology of the Middle Ages. This consisted of rational inquiry into revealed truth; for it was important to understand what one believed. This technique of disposition was developed by the Schoolmen over a long period, reaching its perfection in Peter Abelard (1079–1142). In the 13th century it absorbed the newly discovered Aristotelian philosophy and method. In this phase its greatest exponent was St. Thomas Aquinas (*c.* 1225–74), who became the chief medieval philosopher and theologian; his authority, challenged in the 16th century, was more seriously contested in the 17th century by the adherents of the "new science."

Seneca   Lucius Annaeus Seneca (4 B.C.–65 A.D.) was an important source of Renaissance stoicism (*q.v.*), a model for the "closet" drama of the period, and an exemplar for the kind of prose that shunned the Ciceronian loquacity of early humanism and cultivated terseness. He was Nero's tutor; in 62 A.D. he retired from public life, and in 65 was compelled to commit suicide for taking part in a political conspiracy. He produced writings on ethics and physics, as well as ten tragedies often imitated in the Renaissance.

Sensibility   (1) In the mid-18th century, the term came to be used in a literary context to refer to a susceptibility to fine or tender feelings, particularly involving the feelings and sorrows of others. This became a quality to be cultivated in despite of stoical rejections of unreasonable emotion which the neoclassicism (*q.v.*) of the earlier Augustan age had prized. The meaning of the word blended easily into "sentimentality"; but the literary period in England characterized by the work of writers such as Sterne, Goldsmith, Gray, Collins, and Cowper is often called the Age of Sensibility.

(2) A meaning more important for modern literature is that of a special kind of total awareness, an ability to make the finest discriminations in its perception of the world, and yet at the same time not lacking in a kind of force by the very virtue of its own receptive power. The varieties of awareness celebrated in French literature from Baudelaire through Marcel Proust have been adapted by modernist English critics, notably T. S. Eliot, for a fuller extension of the meaning of *sensibility*. By the term "dissociation of sensibility," Eliot implied the split between the sensuous and the intellectual faculties which he thought characterized English poetry after the Restoration (1660).

Sententia   A wise, fruitful saying, functioning as a guide to morally correct thought or action.

Sestina   Originally a Provençal lyric form supposedly invented by Arnaut Daniel in the 12th century, and one of the most complex of those structures. It has six stanzas of six lines each, followed by an *envoi* (*q.v.*) or *tornada* of three lines. Instead of rhyming, the end-words of the lines of the first stanza are all repeated in the following stanzas, but in a constant set of permutations. The *envoi* contains all six words, three in the middle of each line. D. G. Rossetti, Swinburne, Pound, Auden, and other modern poets have used the form, and Sir Philip Sidney composed a magnificent double-sestina, "Ye Goat-herd Gods."

Skepticism   A philosophy that denies the possibility of certain knowledge, and, although opposed to Stoicism and Epicureanism (*q.v.*), advocated *ataraxy*, imperturbability of mind. Skepticism originated with Pyrrhon (*c.* 360–270 B.C.), and its chief transmitter was Sextus Empiricus (*c.* 200 B.C.). In the Renaissance, skepticism had importance as questioning the power of the human mind to know truly (for a classic exposition see Donne's *Second Anniversary*, ll. 254–300), and became a powerful influence in morals and religion through the advocacy of Montaigne.

Sonnet   A basic lyric form, consisting of fourteen lines of iambic pentameter rhymed in various patterns. The *Italian* or *Petrarchan* sonnet is divided clearly into *octave* and *sestet*, the first rhyming *abba abba* and the second in a pattern such as *cdc dcd*. The *Shakespearean* sonnet consists of three quatrains followed by a couplet: *abab cdcd efef gg*. In the late 16th century in England, sonnets were written either independently as short epigrammatic forms, or grouped in sonnet sequences, i.e. collections of upwards of a hundred poems, in imitation of Petrarch, purportedly addressed to one central figure or muse—a lady usually with a symbolic name like "Stella" or "Idea." Milton made a new kind of use of the Petrarchan form, and the Romantic poets continued in the Miltonic tradition. Several variations have been devised, including the addition of "tails" or extra lines, or the recasting into sixteen lines, instead of fourteen.

Stoicism, Stoics   Philosophy founded by Zeno (335–263 B.C.), and opposing the hedonistic tendencies of Epicureanism (*q.v.*). The Stoics' world-view was pantheistic: God was the energy that formed and maintained the world, and wisdom lay in obedience to this law of nature as revealed by the conscience. Moreover, every man is free because the life according to nature and conscience is available to all; so too is suicide—a natural right. Certain Stoics saw the end of the world as caused by fire. In the Renaissance, Latin Stoicism, especially that of Seneca (*q.v.*), had a revival of influence and was Christianized in various ways.

Strong Lines The term used in the 17th century to refer to the tough, tense conceit (*q.v.*)-laden verse of Donne and his followers.

Style See *Decorum*.

Sublime "Lofty"; as a literary idea, originally the basic concept of a Greek treatise (by the so-called "Longinus") on style. In the 18th century, however, the *sublime* came to mean a loftiness perceivable in nature, and sometimes in art—a loftiness different from the composed vision of landscape known as the *picturesque*, because of the element of wildness, power, and even terror. The *beautiful*, the picturesque, and the sublime became three modes for the perception of nature.

Symbolism (1) Broadly, the process by which one phenomenon, in literature, stands for another, or group of others, and usually of a different sort. Clearcut cases of this in medieval and Renaissance literature are *emblems* or *attributes* (see *Personification; Allegory*). Sometimes conventional symbols may be used in more than one way, e.g. a mirror betokening both truth and vanity. See also *Figure; Emblem*.

(2) In a specific sense (and often given in its French form, *symbolisme*), an important esthetic concept for modern literature, formulated by French poets and critics of the later 19th century following Baudelaire. In this view, the literary symbol becomes something closer to a kind of commanding, central metaphor, taking precedence over any more discursive linguistic mode for poetic communication. The effects of this concept on literature in English have been immense; and some version of the concept survives in modern notions of the poetic *image*, or *fiction*.

Temperaments The balance of combinations of humors (*q.v.*) which in the medieval and Renaissance periods was believed to determine the psychosomatic make-up or "complexion" of a man or a woman. See *Renaissance Psychology*.

Topographical Poem A descriptive poem popular in the 17th and 18th centuries and devoted to a specific scene or landscape with the addition (in the words of Samuel Johnson in 1799) of "historical retrospection or incidental meditation." Sir John Denham's "Cooper's Hill" (1642) is an influential example of the tradition (which includes also Pope's "Windsor Forest") and sometimes blends with the genre of a poem in praise of a particular house or garden.

Topos Greek for "place," commonplace; in rhetoric (*q.v.*), either a general argument, description, or observation that could serve for various occasions; or a method of inventing arguments on a statement or contention. It is often used now to mean a basic literary topic (either a proposition such as the superiority of a life of action to that of contemplation, or vice versa; of old age vs. youth; or a description, such as that of the *locus amoenus* (*q.v.*), the pleasant garden place, Paradise, which allows many variations of thought and language.

Trivium The course of study in the first three of the seven liberal arts—grammar, rhetoric, and logic (or dialectic): the basis of the medieval educational program in school and university. See also *Quadrivium.*

Troilus stanza Or *rhyme royal;* iambic pentameters in stanzas of seven lines, rhyming *ababbcc,* popularized by Chaucer in his poem *Troilus and Criseyde* and called *rhyme royal* supposedly on account of its use by James I of Scotland, king and poet.

Trope (1) See *Rhetoric.* (2) In the liturgy of the Catholic Church, a phrase, sentence, or verse with its musical setting, introduced to amplify or embellish some part of the text of the mass or the office (i.e. the prayers and Scripture readings recited daily by priests, religious, and even laymen) when chanted in choir. Tropes of this second kind were discontinued in 1570 by the authority of Pope Pius V. Troping new material into older or conventional patterns seems to have been, in a general way, a basic device of medieval literature, and was the genesis of modern drama.

Type, Typology (1) Strictly, in medieval biblical interpretation, the prefiguration of the persons and events of the New Testament by persons and events of the Old, the Old Testament being fulfilled in, but not entirely superseded by, the New. Thus, the Temptation and Fall of Man were held to prefigure the first Temptation of Christ, pride in each case being the root of the temptation, and a warning against gluttony the moral lesson to be drawn from both. The Brazen Serpent raised up by Moses was held to prefigure the crucifixion of Christ; Isaac, as a sacrificial victim ("God will provide his own Lamb," says Abraham to him) is a *type* of Christ. The forty days and nights of the Deluge, the forty years of Israel's wandering in the desert, Moses' forty days in the desert are all typologically related.

(2) In a looser sense, a person or event seen as a model or paradigm. See also *Figure.*

Ubi Sunt . . . A motif introducing a lament for the passing of all mortal and material things: e.g. *"Ubi sunt qui ante nos in mundo fuere?"* (Where are they who went before us in this world?), or "Where are the snows of yesteryear?" (Swinburne's translation from the French of Villon's *ballade*).

Virelay A French poetic form, a dance song; short, with two or three rhymes, and two lines of the first stanza as a refrain.

Wars of the Roses Series of encounters between the house of Lancaster (whose emblem was the red rose) and the house of York (whose emblem was the white), which took place between 1455 and 1485 to decide the right of possession of the English throne. At the Battle of Bosworth Field in 1485 the Lancastrian Henry Tudor defeated the Yorkist Richard III and was proclaimed king as Henry VII. He married Elizabeth of York, daughter of King Edward IV.

Worthies, Nine Nine exemplary heroes, three from the Bible (Joshua, David, Judas Maccabaeus); three from pagan antiquity (Hector of Troy, Alexander the Great, Julius Caesar), and three from "Christian" romance (King Arthur, the Emperor Charlemagne, and Godfrey of Bouillon, a leader of the First Crusade and King of Jerusalem). They were favorite figures for tapestries (see Fig. 46 in illustrations for the Medieval section of this Anthology) and pageants.

Wit (1) Originally, "intellect," "intelligence"; later, "creative intelligence," or poetical rather than merely mechanical intellectual power. Thus, during the age of Dryden and Pope, a poet might be called a wit without any compromising sense, In the 19th century, "wit" came to mean verbal agility or cleverness, as opposed to the more creative powers of the mind. (2) More specifically, in literary history, as characterizing the poetic style of John Donne and his 17th-century followers. The Augustan age would contrast this with the "true wit" of *neoclassical* (*q.v*) poetry.

Yorkists See *Wars of the Roses.*

Zodiac In astrology, a belt of the celestial sphere, about eight or nine degrees to either side of the ecliptic (the apparent orbit of the sun), within which the apparent motions of the sun, moon, and planets take place. It is divided into twelve equal parts, the signs, through each of which the sun passes in a month. Each division once coincided with one of the constellations after which the signs are named: Aries (Ram)—in Chaucer's time the sun entered this sign on 12 March; Taurus (Bull); Gemini (Twins); Cancer (Crab); Leo (Lion); Virgo (Virgin); Libra (Scales); Scorpio; Sagittarius (Archer); Capricornus (Goat); Aquarius (Water-Carrier); Pisces (Fishes). Each zodiacal sign was believed to govern a part of the human body. See *Astronomy and Astrology.*

Suggestions for Further Reading

General Historical Works J. Burckhardt, *The Civilization of the Renaissance in Italy* (1860), tr. S. G. C. Middleman, two vols., 1958. J. D. Mackie, *The Early Tudors*, 1952. J. B. Black, *The Reign of Elizabeth*, 2nd ed., 1959. A. L. Rowse, *The England of Elizabeth*, 1950. Garrett Mattingly, *The Armada*, 1959. R. H. Tawney, *Religion and the Rise of Capitalism*, 1926, *Shakespeare's England*, 1916. William Haller, *The Rise of Puritanism*, 1938. Louis B. Wright, *Middle-Class Culture in Elizabethan England*, 1935. Godfrey Davies, *The Early Stuarts*, rev. ed., 1959. Carl J. Friedrich, *The Age of the Baroque*, 1952. G. M. Trevelyan, *England under the Stuarts*, 21st ed., 1949. Christopher Hill, *Puritanism and Revolution*, 1958, *A Century of Revolution*, 1961, *Intellectual Origins of the English Revolution*, 1965, and *God's Englishman* 1970, a study of Cromwell: all brilliant and Marxist. Different approaches are represented by C. V. Wedgwood's *The Great Rebellion: The King's Peace* (1955), and *The King's War* (1958); and by Perez Zagorin's *The Court and the Country*, 1970.

Intellectual and Cultural History Arthur O. Lovejoy, *The Great Chain of Being*, 1936. E. M. W. Tillyard, *The Elizabethan World Picture*, rev. ed., 1956. C. S. Lewis, *The Discarded Image*, 1964. E. A. Burtt, *Metaphysical Foundations of Modern Science*, rev. ed., 1932. Sir Herbert Butterfield, *The Origins of Modern Science*, 1957. Donald S. Westfall, *Science and Religion in Seventeenth-Century England*, 1958. Thomas S. Kuhn, *The Copernican Revolution*, 1959. Charles Singer, *A Short History of Scientific Ideas to 1900*, 1959. Basil Willey, *The Seventeenth Century Background*, 1934. H. H. Rhys ed., *XVII Century Science and the Arts*, 1961. Norman Davy ed., *British Scientific Literature in the XVIIth Century*, 1953. Wilbur S. Howell, *Logic and Rhetoric in England*, 1956. Kitty Scoular, *Natural Magic*, 1965. J. A. Mazzeo, *Renaissance and Revolution*, 1965. John R. Mulder, *The Temple of the Mind*, 1969.

Literary History C. S. Lewis, *English Literature in the Sixteenth Century, excluding Drama*, 1954. Douglas Bush, *English Literature in the Earlier Seventeenth Century*, (2nd rev. ed., 1962. Hallett Smith, *Elizabethan Poetry*, 1952. Frank Kermode, *English Pastoral Poetry from the Beginnings to Marvell*, 1952. F. P. Wilson, *Elizabethan and Jacobean*, 1945. J. W. Lever, *The Elizabethan Love Sonnet*, 1956. Wylie Sypher, *Four Stages of Renaissance Style*, 1955.

Critical Studies (Early) *Elizabethan Critical Essays*, ed. G. G. Smith, two vols.,

1904; and *Critical Essays of the Seventeenth Century*, three vols., 1908–1909, are important collections of texts. (**Modern**) Helpful anthologies are *Elizabethan Poetry: Modern Essays in Criticism*, ed. Paul J. Alpers, 1967; *Seventeenth-Century English Poetry: Modern Essays in Criticism*, ed. William R. Keast, rev. ed., 1971; *Seventeenth Century Prose: Modern Essays in Criticism*, ed. Stanley Fish, 1971; *The Metaphysical Poets*, ed. Frank Kermode, 1969. *Literary English Since Shakespeare*, ed. George Watson, 1970, is a useful guide. Works of one author include Mario Praz, *Studies in Seventeenth-Century Imagery*, 1939 (2nd ed., 1964); Rosamond Tuve, *Elizabethan and Metaphysical Imagery*, 1947; Austin Warren, *Rage for Order*, 1948; Ruth C. Wallerstein, *Studies in Seventeenth Century Poetic*, 1950; Odette de Mourgues, *Metaphysical, Baroque and Précieux Poetry*, 1953; M. M. Mahood, *Poetry and Humanism*, 1950; Marjorie Hope Nicolson, *The Breaking of the Circle*, 1960; Don Cameron Allen, *Image and Meaning*, 1960; A. Alvarez, *The School of Donne*, 1961; J. A. Mazzeo ed., *Reason and Imagination*, 1962; John Hollander, *The Untuning of the Sky*, 1961; Stanley Stewart, *The Enclosed Garden*, 1966.

On Prose Writing   Donald A. Stauffer, *English Biography before 1700*, 1930; George Williamson, *Seventeenth-Century Contexts*, 1960; F. P. Wilson, *Seventeenth-Century Prose: Five Lectures*, 1960; Joan Webber, *The Eloquent I*, 1968.

On Mythology   Douglas Bush, *Mythology and the Renaissance Tradition in English Poetry*, 1932 (rev. ed., 1936). Jean Seznec, *The Survival of the Pagan Gods*, 1953. Harry Levin, *The Myth of the Golden Age in the Renaissance*, 1969. John Armstrong, *The Paradise Myth*, 1969. Don Cameron Allen, *Mysteriously Meant*, 1970.

On Pictures and Images   Rosemary Freeman, *English Emblem Books*, 1967, is, along with Mario Praz (see above), the best introduction to what is becoming an important study. Geoffrey Whitney's *A Choice of Emblems*, 1586, Henry Peacham's *Minerva Brittana*, 1610, and George Wither's *A Collection of Emblems*, 1635, are all available in facsimile. E. H. Gombrich's *Symbolic Images*, 1972, provides theoretical backgrounds.

The Visual Arts in England   Ellis Waterhouse, *Painting in Britain 1530–1790*, 1953. John Summerson, *Architecture in Britain 1530–1830*, 4th ed., 1963; and *Inigo Jones*, 1966. Jean H. Hagstrum, *The Sister Arts*, 1958, and Mario Praz, *Mnemosyne*, 1970, are both good introductions to the relation of art and poetry. John Shearman's *Mannerism*, 1967, is a good corrective to some of the uneasy generalities of Wylie Sypher's *Four Stages of Renaissance Style* mentioned above. Edward Hyams, *The English Garden*, 1964, provides background material for a major poetic theme. Roy Strong, *The English Icon*, 1969, and his catalogue of *Tudor and Jacobean Portraits*, 1969, are both excellent, as is Marcia R. Poynton's *Milton and English Art*, 1970.

The English Bible   V. F. Storr, *The English Bible*, 1938. E. E. Willoughby, *The Making of the English Bible*, 1956. G. S. Paine, *The Learned Men*, 1959. F. F. Bruce, *The English Bible: A History of Translations . . .* , rev. ed. 1970.

THE ENGLISH HUMANISTS

There is no single work that is adequate on the Humanists, but C. S. Lewis, *English Literature in the Sixteenth Century, excluding Drama*, 1954, in the Oxford History of English Literature, has a characteristically vigorous survey. On sixteenth-century preoccupation with the English language, see Richard Foster Jones, *The Triumph of the English Language: A Survey of Opinions . . . from the Introduction of Printing to the Restoration*, 1953.

Sir Thomas More   The standard modern edition of More's works is far from complete, four volumes having been published so far, including the splendid text of *History of Richard III*, ed. R. S. Sylvester, 1963, with excellent introduction and commentary; and the very thorough *Utopia*, ed. Edward Surtz, S.J., and J. H. Hexter, 1965. Both these volumes in the Yale edition supply Latin and English texts, and the Yale *Utopia* translation is available in paperback, without commentary. As a translation it is less satisfactory than Paul Turner's version (1965) with its economical, first-rate commentary. Ralph Robinson's translation, available in Everyman's Library (n.d.) without annotation, is printed, along with the Latin text, in J. H. Lupton's edition of *Utopia*, 1895. More's translation of *The Life of John Picus, Earl of Mirandula* was edited by J. M. Rigg, 1890. An excellent introduction to More is provided by his letters, of which a selection, in translation, has been edited by Elizabeth Frances Rogers (1961) —including the letter from which an extract is given in the account of More's death in William Roper's *Life*. The standard edition of this *Life* by More's son-in-law was edited by E. V. Hitchcock (1935), with full commentary. There is a modernized version in R. S. Sylvester and Davis P. Harding eds., *Two Early Tudor Lives*, 1962.

Still the best general account of More is R. W. Chambers, *Thomas More*, 1935; but the most useful accounts of *Utopia* are to be found in J. H. Hexter, *More's Utopia: The Biography of an Idea*, 1952, and in the essays in William Nelson ed., *Twentieth-Century Interpretations of Utopia*, 1968.

Sir Thomas Elyot   The edition of *The Book Named the Governor*, ed. H. H. S. Croft, two vols., 1880, in old spelling with copious commentary, has not been superseded. A modernized version, without notes, is edited by Stanford E. Lehmberg in Everyman's Library (1962).

The best study of the "courtesy" literature, including Elyot, Castiglione, and Hoby, is Ruth Kelso, *The Doctrine of the English Gentleman in the Sixteenth Century*, 1929; and the best book-length study of Elyot is by John M. Major, *Sir Thomas Elyot and Renaissance Humanism*, 1964.

Baldassare Castiglione and Sir Thomas Hoby   The standard edition of Castiglione's Italian is *Il Libro del Cortegiano*, ed. V. Cian, 4th ed., 1949. Hoby's translation was edited by Sir Walter Ralegh, as *The Book of the Courtier*, in the Tudor Translations series, 1900 (old spelling, no notes). It was also reprinted in Everyman's Library (n.d.). Two good modern translations of Castiglione, with introductions, are by Charles S. Singleton (1959) and George Bull (1967), both entitled *The Book of the Courtier*. An interesting essay on Hoby's translation is in F. O. Matthiessen, *Translation, an Elizabethan Art*, 1931, which is also relevant to the topic of sixteenth-century prose in general.

Roger Ascham   The only complete edition is by J. A. Giles, *The Whole Works*, four vols., 1864–65, in modern spelling, with some notes. *The English Works*, ed. W. A. Wright, 1904, uses old spelling, without annotation. The standard edition of *The Schoolmaster* is by J. E. B. Mayor, 1863, with fine annotation; and there is a useful annotated edition by R. J. Schoeck, 1966. A thorough, book-length study is Lawrence V. Ryan, *Roger Ascham*, 1963.

ELIZABETHAN SONG

Aside from modern editions of many of the anthologies and miscellanies by Hyder E. Rollins and other scholars, the main repository of texts set by the madrigal and lutenist composers is E. H. Fellowes, *English Madrigal Verse, 1588–1632*, 3rd ed., revised and enlarged by F. W. Sternfeld and D. Greer, 1967; but a vastly superior scholarly and critical edition, albeit of the solo songs alone, is Edward Doughtie, *Lyrics from English Airs*, 1970. Important studies dealing with relations between text and music are Bruce Pattison, *Music and Poetry of the English Renaissance*, 1948; and Catherine Ing, *Elizabethan Lyrics*, 1951. E. H. Fellowes, *The English Madrigal* (1926), and Peter Warlock, *The English Ayre* (1927), are older, more musicological studies; a good modern one is John Kerman, *The Elizabethan Madrigal*, 1962. John Stevens, *Music and Poetry in the Early Tudor Court*, 1961, is an important work. M. C. Boyd, *Elizabethan Music and Musical Criticism*, 1940, remains a good, but rambling, introductory treatment. Douglas L. Peterson's *The English Lyric from Wyatt to Donne*, 1967, is concerned purely with texts.

SIR THOMAS WYATT

The best edition is *Poems*, ed. Kenneth Muir, 1949, with additional poems in H. A. Mason's *Humanism and Poetry in the Early Tudor Court*, 1959. John Stevens's *Music and Poetry in the Early Tudor Court*, 1961, Kenneth Muir's *Life and Letters of Sir Thomas Wyatt*, 1963, Raymond Southall's *The Courtly Maker*, 1964, and Patricia Thomson's *Sir Thomas Wyatt and His Background*, 1965, all provide valuable historical and cultural materials. Also see Douglas L. Peterson's *The English Lyric from Wyatt to Donne*, 1967.

HENRY HOWARD, EARL OF SURREY

The best edition of the *Poems* is that of Emrys Jones, 1964, replacing F. M. Padelford's earlier *Poems*, rev. ed., 1928. Hyder Rollins edited Tottel's Miscellany, rev. ed., 1965. Gerald Bullett, *Silver Poets of the Sixteenth Century*, 1947, reproduces all but the Virgil translation. See also John L. Thompson, *The Founding of English Metre*, 1961. A biography is *Henry Howard, Earl of Surrey*, by E. Casaday, 1938.

SIR PHILIP SIDNEY

Editions *The Complete Works* were edited in four volumes by Albert Feuillerat (1912–16), but the standard text of the poems is that of William A. Ringler (1962). *An Apology for Poetry* was edited by Geoffrey Shepherd (1965), and the recently discovered Norwich MS. of the *Apology* was edited by Mary R. Mahl (1969). The translation of the Psalms, with the Countess of Pembroke, was edited by J. C. Rathmell (1963).

Critical Studies Kenneth O. Myrick, *Sir Philip Sidney as a Literary Craftsman*, 1935. John Buxton, *Sir Philip Sidney and the English Renaissance*, 1954. Walter Davis and Richard A. Lanham, *Sidney's Arcadia*, 1965. David Kalstone, *Sidney's Poetry*, 1965. Neil Rudenstine, *Sidney's Poetic Development*, 1967. Mark Rose, *Heroic Love*, 1968.

Biography Fulke Greville's *Life of Sidney* was edited by Nowell Smith in 1907, and there are modern biographies by M. W. Wallace, *Life of Sir Philip Sidney*, 1915 (repr. 1967), and Mona Wilson, *Sir Philip Sidney*, 1931. The definitive life is that of James Osborn, *Young Philip Sidney*, 1972.

FULKE GREVILLE, LORD BROOKE

G. Bullough edited *Poems and Dramas*, two vols., 1939. *Caelica* has been edited by Una Ellis-Fermor, 1936. There is a *Selected Poems* with a splendid essay by Thom Gunn (1965). A good study is Morris W. Croll's *The Works of Fulke Greville*, 1903; and Joan Rees published her *Fulke Greville . . . A Critical Biography* in 1971.

EDMUND SPENSER

Editions *The Poetical Works*, ed. J. C. Smith and E. de Selincourt, three vols., 1909–10; and in one vol., 1912. *Variorum Edition*, ten vols., 1932–49. *Selections . . .* (with commentary), edited by F. Kermode, 1965.

Critical Studies W. L. Renwick, *Edmund Spenser*, 1925. E. Greenlaw, *Spenser's Historical Allegory*, 1932. C. B. Millican, *Spenser and the Table Round*, 1934. I. E. Rathborne, *The Meaning of Spenser's Fairyland*, 1937. C. S. Lewis, *The Allegory of Love*, 1936, and later editions; see also his *English Literature in the Sixteenth Century, excluding Drama* (Vol. III of the Oxford History of English Literature), 1954, and the posthumous *Spenser's Images of Life*, 1967. J. W. Bennett, *The Evolution of the Faerie Queene*, 1942. V. K. Whitaker, *The Religious Basis of Spenser's Thought*, 1950. A. K. Hieatt, *Short Time's Endless Monument*, 1960. A. C. Hamilton, *Structure of Allegory in Faerie Queene*, 1961. G. Hough, *A Preface to The Faerie Queene*, 1962. R. Ellrodt, *Neoplatonism in the Poetry of Spenser*, 1960. D. S. Cheney, *Spenser's Image of Nature*, 1966. William Nelson, *The Poetry of Edmund Spenser* (dealing with all the poetry), 1963. A. Fowler, *Spenser and the Numbers of Time*, 1964. R. Tuve, *Allegorical Imagery*, 1966. P. Alpers, *The Poetry of the Faerie Queene*, 1967. H. Tonkin, *Spenser's Courteous Pastoral*, 1972. Angus Fletcher, *The Prophetic Moment*, 1972. F. Kermode, *Shakespeare, Spenser, Donne*, 1971. An article of high interest is F. Yates's "Queen Elizabeth as Astraea," in *Journal of the Warburg and Courtauld Institutes*, X (1947), 27–82. See also Roy C. Strong, *Portraits of Queen Elizabeth*, 1963.

SIR WALTER RALEGH

There is a *Complete Works* in eight volumes, 1829, and a selection from the *History of the World* by C. A. Patrides, 1972. Agnes M. C. Latham's edition of the poems is standard (rev. ed., 1951). E. A. Strathmann's *Ralegh: A Study in Elizabethan Skepticism*, 1951, remains unexcelled. Recent biographies are *Sir Walter Raleigh* by Willard M. Wallace, 1959, and W. F. Oakeshott's *The Queen and the Poet*, 1960.

CHRISTOPHER MARLOWE

Editions The writings have been edited by R. H. Case and others in six volumes, (1930–33). W. W. Greg's parallel text of *Dr. Faustus*, 1950, is standard, and his smaller conjectural reconstruction of the original (1950) is the other text from which all others now derive, though the validity of his textural arguments has now been contested by Fredson Bowers. See also the edition of J. D. Jump (1968), as well as the *Complete Poems and Translations*, ed. Stephen Orgel, 1971.

Critical Studies   F. S. Boas, *Christopher Marlowe*, 1940. P. H. Kochner, *Christopher Marlowe*, 1946. J. Bakeless, *The Tragical History of Christopher Marlowe*, 1942. H. Levin, *The Overreacher*, 1953. D. Cole, *Suffering and Evil in the Plays of Christopher Marlowe*, 1962. J. B. Steane, *Marlowe*, 1964.

Biography   Major discoveries about Marlowe's life have been reported in L. Hotson's *The Death of Christopher Marlowe*, 1925.

SAMUEL DANIEL

The only complete edition is by A. B. Grosart, *The Complete Works in Verse and Prose*, five vols., 1885–96 (repr. 1963). The *Poems, and A Defence of Ryme* was edited by A. C. Sprague in 1930. See also, G. G. Smith, *Elizabethan Critical Essays*, 1904, and studies by Ernest W. Talbert, *Problem of Order*, 1962, and Cecil Seronsy, *Samuel Daniel*, in the English Authors series, 1967.

MICHAEL DRAYTON

There is a standard edition of the *Works*, ed. J. W. Hebel, five vols., 1931–41. Oliver Elton's *Introduction to Michael Drayton*, 1895, and his later *Michael Drayton: A Critical Study*, 1905 (repr. 1966), have been reissued. A biographical study is B. H. Newdigate, *Michael Drayton and His Circle*, 1941. See also L. Zocca, *Elizabethan Narrative Poetry*, 1950.

WILLIAM SHAKESPEARE

Editions   Standard editions, one volume per play, are the Arden, the Yale, the Pelican, and the Signet, all annotated. The best one-volume text is the Houghton Mifflin Shakespeare, scheduled for 1973, to which the six-volume *Concordance* of Marvin Spevack, 1970, is keyed.

Critical Studies   Two very different critical approaches (out of very many) to the sonnets are G. Wilson Knight's *The Mutual Flame*, 1955, and Stephen Booth's *An Essay on Shakespeare's Sonnets*, 1969. Knight deals also with *The Phoenix and Turtle*, on which see also F. Kermode, *Shakespeare, Spenser, Donne*, 1971. Kermode discusses *The Tempest* in the Arden edition (1954, and later revisions), and in *Shakespeare, Spenser, Donne*. See also N. Frye, *A Natural Perspective*, 1965, and A. D. Nuttall, *Two Concepts of Allegory*, 1967; and, on the songs, Peter Seng, *The Vocal Songs in the Plays of Shakespeare*, 1967.

Biographies   While the major work in Shakespearean biography is Samuel Schoenbaum, *Shakespeare's Lives*, 1970, the most useful brief work on Shakespeare's life is G. E. Bentley, *Shakespeare: A Biographical Handbook*, 1961.

THOMAS CAMPION

The standard text is that of Percival Vivian, *Campion's Works*, 1909; but a new one, ed. Walter R. Davis, *Works* . . . *with a Selection of the Latin Verse*, 1967, is more sophisticated in its annotations. There is a selection with essays by W. H. Auden and John Hollander (1972). Campion's musical settings are transcribed from lute tablature and edited by E. H. Fellowes in *The English School of Lutenist Song-Writers*, First and Second Series, 1920–66. Miles W. Kastendieck's *England's Musical Poet*, 1938, is the first study, a more recent one being by Edward Lowbury and others, *Thomas Campion, Poet, Composer, Physician*, 1970.

JOHN DONNE

Editions H. J. C. Grierson's 1912 edition of the *Poems* is supplemented rather than superseded by the editions of H. Gardner, *Divine Poems*, 1952, and *Elegies and the Songs and Sonnets*, 1965; and of W. Milgate, *Satires, Epigrams, and Verse Letters*, 1967. There is a separate edition of *Anniversaries* by F. Manley, 1963; of *Sermons*, in ten volumes, by G. R. Potter and E. Simpson, 1953–62; of the *Devotions*, by J. Sparrow, 1923. The best selection, with complete verse and selected prose, was prepared by J. Hayward, 1929. Among other collections are *Complete Poetry*, ed. J. T. Shawcross, 1967; *Selected Prose*, chosen by E. Simpson and edited by H. Gardner and T. Healy, 1967; and *Poems*, ed. with commentary by A. J. Smith, 1970.

Critical Studies For the history of Donne criticism see J. E. Duncan, *The Revival of Metaphysical Poetry*, 1959, as well as the selections in F. Kermode ed., *Discussions of John Donne*, 1962. For specialized commentary, see P. Legouis, *Donne the Craftsman*, 1928; R. Tuve, *Elizabethan and Metaphysical Imagery*, 1947; J. B. Leishman, *The Monarch of Wit*, 1951 (1962); L. Unger, *The Man in the Name*, 1956. G. Williamson, *The Donne Tradition*, 1930, supports the orthodoxy founded on Eliot's essays, shaken by Tuve and others. Among shorter introductions are K. W. Gransden's *John Donne*, 1954; F. Kermode's *John Donne*, 1957; and also his *Shakespeare, Spenser, Donne*, 1971. The Twentieth Century Views collection of critiques was edited by Helen Gardner, 1962. On prose, see E. Simpson, *A Study of the Prose Works of John Donne*, 1948; and Joan Webber, *Contrary Music*, 1963. *Bibliography* by Geoffrey Keynes, 1914, 1932, 1958.

Biography Standard biography is *John Donne: A Life*, by R. C. Bald, 1970.

BEN JONSON

Editions The standard edition is that of C. H. Herford and P. and E. Simpson, eleven volumes, 1925–51; but in some instances, the modernized texts of the Yale Ben Jonson (1962–71) provide better readings. A good text of the poems is William B. Hunter ed., *The Complete Poetry of Ben Jonson*, 1963; that of the *Complete Masques* by Stephen Orgel, 1969, is masterful.

Critical Studies Important works include A. C. Swinburne's early *Study of Ben Jonson*, 1889; C. F. Wheeler's *Classical Mythology in the Plays, Masques and Poems of Ben Jonson*, 1938; L. C. Knights's *Drama and Society in the Age of Jonson*, 1937;

Jonas A. Barish's *Ben Jonson and the Language of Prose Comedy*, 1960; and Wesley Trimpi's *Ben Jonson's Poems: A Study in the Plain Style*, 1962. Stephen Orgel's *The Jonsonian Masque* may lead the reader to H. A. Evans, *English Masques*, 1897. Further works include Enid Welsford, *The Court Masque*, 1927; Allardyce Nicoll, *Stuart Masques and the Renaissance Stage*, 1937; D. J. Gordon, "Poet and Architect: The Intellectual Setting of the Quarrel Between Ben Jonson and Inigo Jones," *Journal of the Warburg and Courtauld Institutes*, XII (1949), 152–78; and Andrew J. Sabol, *Songs and Dances for the Stuart Masque*, 1959.

SEVENTEENTH-CENTURY LYRIC MODES

Wilfred Mellers, *Harmonious Meeting*, 1965, is particularly interesting in its treatment of music, poem, and stage spectacle. A standard series of texts on lyric traditions would include: F. R. Leavis, "The Line of Wit," in *Revaluation*, 1936; Geoffrey Walton, *Metaphysical to Augustan*, 1955; A. Alvarez, *The School of Donne*, 1961; Louis L. Martz, *The Poetry of Meditation*, rev. ed., 1962; Lowry Nelson, Jr., *Baroque Lyric Poetry*, 1961; Frank J. Warnke, *European Metaphysical Poetry*, 1961, an anthology with comment; H. M. Richmond, *The School of Love*, 1964; Earl C. Miner, *The Metaphysical Mode from Donne to Cowley*, 1969; Jerome Mazzaro, *Transformations in the English Renaissance Lyric*, 1970. R. K. Ruthven, *The Conceit*, 1969, is an excellent handbook.

ROBERT HERRICK

The standard edition is L. C. Martin's *The Poetical Works* . . . (1956); also useful is the edition of J. Max Patrick, *The Complete Poetry* . . . 1963. There is a biographical and critical study by F. W. Moorman (1910). See also Sidney Musgrove, *The Universe of Herrick*, 1950; and John Press, *Robert Herrick*, 1961.

THOMAS CAREW

The standard edition is *Poems*, ed. Rhodes Dunlap, 1949. Edward I Selig's *The Flourishing Wreath*, 1958, is a modern study. Louis L. Martz's *The Wit of Love*, 1970, deals in good part with Carew, and with his masque *Coelum Britannicum*; but for an authoritative treatment of Carew's masque see the Stephen Orgel–Roy C. Strong edition of the drawings of Inigo Jones, 1973.

RICHARD LOVELACE

The standard text is C. H. Wilkinson ed., *Poems*, 1930. Cyril H. Hartmann, *The Cavalier Spirit and Its Influence on the Life and Work of Richard Lovelace*, 1925, is a primary study; but essays on "The Grasshopper" by D. C. Allen in *Image and Meaning*, 1960, and on "La Bona Bella Roba" by Marius Bewley in *Masks and Mirrors; Essays in Criticism*, 1970, give far more penetrating readings while representing radically different critical approaches. Also see H. M. Richmond, *The School of Love*, 1964.

EDMUND WALLER

The modern edition of the poems is by G. Thorn-Drury in two volumes (1893). Two recent studies are Alexander W. Allison, *Toward an Augustan Poetic: Edmund*

Waller's "Reform" of English Poetry, 1962, and Warren L. Chernaik, *Poetry of Limitation*, 1968.

ABRAHAM COWLEY

The most complete modern edition is that of A. R. Waller, *English Writings*, two volumes, 1905–1906; but probably more accessible is *Poetry and Prose* . . . with introduction and notes by L. C. Martin (1949). The standard biography is *Abraham Cowley: The Muse's Hannibal*, by A. H. Nethercot, 1931; a good critical study is Robert B. Hinman, *Abraham Cowley's World of Order*, 1960. Samuel Johnson's famous assay on Cowley in the *Lives of the Poets*(1779) defined the "metaphysical" tradition from a somewhat hostile, neoclassical viewpoint.

ANDREW MARVELL

Editions   The standard edition of Marvell's writings by M. H. Margoliouth (1927; repr. 1952) was revised by P. Legouis and E. E. Duncan Jones (1971). There is a *Selected Poetry* with notes edited by F. Kermode (1967).

Critical studies   P. Legouis, *Andrew Marvell*, 1928. M. C. Bradbrook and M. G. Lloyd Thomas, *Andrew Marvell*, 1962. Rosalie Colie, *My Ecchoing Song: Andrew Marvell's Poetry of Criticism*, 1969. J. M. Wallace, *Destiny His Choice*, 1968. Donald M. Friedman, *Marvell's Pastoral Art*, 1970. The best essay remains that of T. S. Eliot in *Selected Essays*, 1932.

GEORGE HERBERT

The standard edition is of the works of F. E. Hutchinson (rev. ed., 1945), but an excellent text of the English poems was edited by Joseph H. Summers (1967); the Latin Poems were translated by Mark McCloskey and Paul R. Murphy (1965). The principal critical studies are: Rosamond Tuve, *A Reading of George Herbert*, 1952 (which is at its best in dealing with biblical allusions), and *Studies in Spenser, Herbert, and Milton*, 1970; Joseph H. Summers, *George Herbert: His Religion and Art*, 1954; Mary Ellen Rickey, *Utmost Art*, 1966; Arnold Stein, *George Herbert's Lyrics*, 1968; and Coburn Freer, *Music for a King*, 1971. Helen Vendler's critical work is in preparation. See also Louis L. Martz, *The Poetry of Meditation*, rev. ed., 1962.

RICHARD CRASHAW

The Poems, English, Latin and Greek, ed. L. C. Martin, 2nd ed., 1957, is the standard text. Important critical studies are those of Ruth C. Wallerstein, *Richard Crashaw: A Study in Style and Development*, 1959; and Austin Warren, *Richard Crashaw: A Study in Baroque Sensibility*, 1937; Mario Praz, *The Flaming Heart*, 1958; Mary Ellen Rickey, *Rhyme and Meaning in Richard Crashaw*, 1961; George W. Williams, *Image and Symbol in the Sacred Poetry of Richard Crashaw*, 1963. Robert T. Petersson, *Art of Ecstasy: Teresa, Bernini, and Crashaw*, 1970, examines in detail a famous set of correspondences in baroque art. See also John Hollander, *The Untuning of the Sky* (1961), Chap. IV.

HENRY VAUGHAN

The standard edition is *Poetry and Selected Prose*, ed. L. C. Martin, 1914 (repr. 1957); and there is French Fogle's *Complete Poetry*, 1965. E. Holmes, *Henry Vaughan and the Hermetic Philosophy*, 1932, initiated a new line of research. Of works on Vaughan the most useful are E. C. Pettet's *Of Paradise and Light*, 1960, and R. A. Durr's *On the Mystical Poetry of Henry Vaughan*, 1962. See also Louis L. Martz, *The Paradise Within*, 1964. F. E. Hutchinson's *Life*, 1932, supplies the personal background.

THOMAS TRAHERNE

Editions The editions are those of H. M. Margoliouth, *Centuries, Poems, and Thanksgivings*, two vols., 2nd ed., 1958; and of Anne Ridler, *Poems, Centuries, and Three Thanksgivings*, 1966. *Christian Ethicks* is edited by C. L. Marks and G. R. Guffey, 1968.

Critical Studies Gladys I. Wade, *Thomas Traherne: A Critical Bibliography*, 1944. K. W. Salter, *Thomas Traherne: Mystic and Poet*, 1965. Louis L. Martz, *The Paradise Within*, 1964, contains some interesting discussion of Traherne in a tradition of poetic meditation previously explored by the author. More recent works are A. J. Sherrington, *Mystical Symbolism in the Poetry of Thomas Traherne*, 1969; A. L. Clements, *Mystical Poetry of Thomas Traherne*, 1969; and Stanley Steward, *Expanded Voice*, 1970.

JOHN MILTON

The Columbia Milton (eighteen vols., 1931–38) is still the standard edition of the complete verse and prose, although it is being replaced, for the prose, by the Yale Edition, currently in process of publication. Helen Darbishire's text of the *Poems*, 1952–55 (rev. ed., 1958), is somewhat eccentric. The students will find most helpful the texts edited by Merritt Y. Hughes in *Complete Poems and Major Prose*, 1957, and by John Carey and Alistair Fowler, *Poems*, 1968. Douglas Bush has done a *Complete Poetical Works*, 1965, but it is less heavily annotated than either of the above. A. W. Verity's 1910 text of *Paradise Lost* in separate volumes is unusually helpful. Perhaps the most exciting new edition of Milton will be the *Cambridge Milton for Schools and Colleges*, under the general editorship of J. B. Broadbent, appearing in separate volumes (1972–). Good selections of prose appear in Hughes's edition and in *Prose of John Milton*, by J. Max Patrick, 1965.

Critical Studies The volume of critical literature since 1950 alone is overwhelming, but excellent selections have been made by Frank Kermode in *The Living Milton*, 1960; by Arthur Barker, in *John Milton: Modern Essays in Criticism*, 1965; by C. A. Patrides, in *Milton's Epic Poetry*, 1967, and *Approaches to Paradise Lost*, 1968; and by B. Rajan, *Paradise Lost: A Tercentenary Tribute*, 1969. Central major studies are C. S. Lewis, *A Preface to Paradise Lost*, 1942; William Empson, *Milton's God*, 1961; A. J. A. Waldock, *Paradise Lost and Its Critics*, 1947; Isabel G. MacCaffrey, *Paradise Lost as "Myth,"* 1959; J. B. Broadbent, *Some Graver Subject*, 1967; Christopher Ricks, *Milton's Grand Style*, 1963; and Northrop Frye, *The Return of Eden*,

1965. On Milton's prose work, and intellectual background in general, see Arthur Barker, *Milton and the Puritan Dilemma*, 1942, and Michael J. Fixler, *Milton and the Kingdoms of God*, 1964. On *Paradise Regained*: Barbara K. Lewalski, *Milton's Brief Epic*, 1966. On *Samson Agonistes*: the edition of F. T. Prince (1957) and Arnold Stein, *Heroic Knowledge*, 1957. On *Comus*: John Arthos, *On A Masque Presented at Ludlow-Castle*, 1954, and Angus Fletcher, *The Transcendental Masque*, 1972. Other studies of the minor poems: F. T. Prince, *The Italian Element in Milton's Verse*, 1954; D. C. Allen, *The Harmonious Vision*, 1954; Rosamund Tuve, *Images and Themes in Five Poems by Milton*, 1957; C. A. Patrides ed., *Lycidas: The Tradition and the Poem*, 1961; and J. H. Summers ed., *The Lyric and Dramatic Milton*, 1965; E. A. Honigmann ed., *Milton's Sonnets*, 1966.

Biography   The standard life is now that of William Riley Parker, *Milton: A Biography*, two vols., 1968, superseding the older work by David Masson, *Life of John Milton: Narrated in Connection with . . . the History of His Time*, rev. ed., eight vols., 1881–96.

JOHN LYLY

Complete Works was edited by R. W. Bond, three vols., 1902. The *Euphues* books were edited together by M. W. Cross and H. Clemons, 1916. Critical studies include V. M. Jeffery, *John Lyly and the Italian Renaissance*, 1928, and most notably G. K. Hunter, *John Lyly*, 1962. A recent study of the plays is Peter Saccio's *Court Comedies of John Lyly*, 1969.

RICHARD HOOKER

The modern edition of *Of the Laws of Ecclesiastical Polity* by J. Keble, 1836, was revised in 1888 and again for the Everyman Edition. The *Life* by Izaac Walton is much changed by the discoveries recorded in C. J. Sisson's *The Judicious Marriage of Mr. Hooker*, 1940. See also P. Munz, *The Place of Hooker in the History of Thought*, 1953.

LANCELOT ANDREWES

The complete writings appear in the Library of Anglo-Catholic Theology, eleven volumes, 1841–54. The standard biography is by P. A. Welsby (1955; repr. 1958). The most valuable study of Andrewes as a preacher is W. Fraser Mitchell's *English Pulpit Oratory from Andrewes to Tillotson*, 1932. T. S. Eliot's *For Lancelot Andrewes*, 1928, and *Bishop Lancelot Andrewes* by M. F. Reidy, S.J., may also be consulted.

FRANCIS BACON

Editions   The principal edition is that of James Spedding, R. L. Ellis, and D. D. Heath (seven vols., 1857–59), supplemented by Spedding's *The Letters and the Life* (seven vols., 1861–74); and there are several modern reprintings. Generous selections are given in editions by J. M. Robertson (1905), Richard Foster Jones (1937), and Hugh G. Dick (1955).

Critical Studies   Larger works include Richard Foster Jones, *Ancients and Moderns*, 2nd. ed., 1961; Loren C. Eiseley, *Francis Bacon and the Modern Dilemma*, 1962;

Virgil K. Whitaker, *Francis Bacon's Intellectual Milieu*, 1962; Benjamin Farrington, *The Philosophy of Francis Bacon*, 1964; Paolo Rossi, *Francis Bacon: From Magic to Science*, trans. S. Rabinovitch, 1968. George Williamson, *The Senecan Amble*, 1951; and Brian Vickers, *Bacon and Renaissance Prose*, 1968, deal with stylistic matters. Vickers has also edited the bibliographical *Essential Articles for the Study of Bacon*, 1969. J. Max Patrick has a small introductory study in the Writers and Their Work series, 1961.

Biography   Among the lives are those of David Mallet (1740); Charles Williams, *Bacon*, 1933; and Catherine Drinker Bowen, *Francis Bacon: Temper of a Man*, 1963.

ROBERT BURTON

The modern edition by Floyd Dell and Paul Jordan-Smith of *The Anatomy of Melancholy*, 1941, translates all the Latin; there is also an edition in three volumes by A. R. Shilleto (1903); and Holbrook Jackson's modernized but splendid three-volume edition (1932) is still in print in the Everyman edition. Paul Jordan-Smith's *Bibliographia Burtoniana*, 1931, deals with Burton's reading. Bergen Evans, *The Psychiatry of Robert Burton*, 1944, and Lawrence Babb, *Sanity in Bedlam*, 1959, are both useful studies, and Babb has edited a good selection from the *Anatomy*, 1965. See also William R. Mueller's *The Anatomy of Robert Burton's England*, 1952.

SIR THOMAS BROWNE

Editions   The *Complete Works*, edited by Geoffrey Keynes, six vols., 1928–31 (rev., four vols., 1964) remains the complete edition; however, there are excellent selections, including the same editor's *Selected Writings*, 1969. L. C. Martin's selection, *Religio Medici and Other Works*, 1964, is wonderfully annotated, as is that of Norman Endicott, entitled *The Prose of Sir Thomas Browne*, 1968, Keynes's *Bibliography of Sir Thomas Browne*, 2nd ed., 1968, is of course useful.

Critical Studies   There are also studies by Egon S. Merton, *Science and Imagination in Thomas Browne*, 1949; Frank L. Huntley, *Sir Thomas Browne: A Biographical and Critical Study*, 1962; Joan Bennett, *Sir Thomas Browne*, 1962; Robert Cawley and George Yost, *Studies in Sir Thomas Browne*, 1965; and Leonard Nathanson, *Strategy of Truth*, 1967.

THOMAS HOBBES

The standard edition of the *English Works* is that of Sir William Molesworth, eleven vols., 1839–45. The best modern edition of *Leviathan* is by M. Oakeshott (1946, 1957). There is a good introductory account in B. Willey's *The Seventeenth Century Background*, 1934; D. Krook's *Three Traditions of Moral Thought*, 1959; and T. E. Jessop's *Thomas Hobbes*, 1960. Samuel Mintz, *The Hunting of Leviathan*, 1962, studies contemporary reactions to its publication. *Hobbes*, by Richard Peters, 1968, is an excellent general treatment from the viewpoint of technical philosophy.

IZAAK WALTON

There is no standard edition, but Geoffrey Keynes edited *The Compleat Angler* and the *Lives*, 1929. The complicated bibliographical history of the *Lives* is studied most fully in D. Novarr, *The Making of Walton's Lives*, 1958. An introductory study by Margaret Bottral, *Izaak Walton*, 1968, is good.

CHARACTERS

There is a Loeb Library edition, in Greek and English, of Theophrastus (1946). Standard works are Benjamin Boyce's *The Theophrastan Character in England to 1642*, 1947, and *The Polemic Character, 1640–1661*, 1955. Collections have been edited by Gwendolyn Murphy, *A Cabinet of Characters*, 1925, and Richard Aldington, *A Book of Characters*, 1924. Sir Thomas Overbury's *Miscellaneous Works in Prose and Verse* was edited by E. F. Rimbault, in 1856, and W. J. Paylor's *The Overburian Characters*, in 1936. John Earle's *Microcosmography* was edited by Gwendolyn Murphy (1928), by Harold Osborn (1933), and by A. S. West (1951). Joseph Hall's *Characters of Virtues and Vices* was edited by Rudolf Kirk in 1948.

THOMAS FULLER

The History of the Worthies of England was edited by A. Nuttall (1840); John Freeman's version of 1952 is an abridgment and modernization. *The Holy State and the Profane State*, ed. M. C. Walten, 1938, is a facsimile of the first edition of 1642, with introduction and notes in a second volume. Studies include Walter E. Houghton, Jr., *The Formation of Thomas Fuller's Holy and Profane States*, 1938, and William Addison, *Worthy Dr. Fuller*, 1951.

JOHN AUBREY

The basic text of the *Brief Lives* is still that of Andrew Clark (two vols., 1898); there is a good selection of 134 lives with a long introduction in an edition by Oliver Lawson Dick, 1957 (3rd ed., 1960). The novelist Anthony Powell made a collection of *Brief Lives and Other Selected Writings* in 1948, and published a biography entitled *John Aubrey and His Friends*, rev. ed., 1963.

EDWARD HYDE, EARL OF CLARENDON

The *History*, in twelve volumes, was edited by W. Dunn Macray in 1888. A good biography is *Life of Clarendon* by Sir Henry Craik, two vols., 1911. Critical studies include L. C. Knights, "Reflections on Clarendon's History of the Rebellion," in *Scrutiny*, XV (1948), 105–16; and Brian Wormald, *Clarendon: Politics, Historiography and Religion, 1640–1660*, 1951.

JEREMY TAYLOR

The standard edition of the *Works* is by Reginald Heber, as revised by the Rev. C. P. Eden, in ten volumes (1847–54). Selections have been edited by Margaret Gest, *The House of Understanding*, 1954, and Thomas S. Kepler, *Rule and Exercises of Holy Living*, 1956. Critical studies include W. J. Brown, *Jeremy Taylor*, 1925; H. Trevor Hughes, *The Piety of Jeremy Taylor*, 1960; and Frank L. Huntley, *Jeremy Taylor and the Great Rebellion*, 1970.

Author and Title Index

First-Line Index

1089